Name and Type of Organization as Focus Illustration of Each Chapter

Chapter Title	Focus Company	Type of Organization	Managerial Focus	Contrast Companies
8. Reporting and Interpreting Property, Plant and Equipment; Natural Resources; and Intangibles	Delta Air Lines	Major international air carrier	Planning productive capacity	Singapore Airlines (Singapore) Exxon Corp. Sony International Paper
9. Reporting and Interpreting Liabilities	General Mills	Manufacturer of popular food items	Capital structure	Eastman Kodak Southwest Airlines Toys "R" Us
10. Reporting and Interpreting Bonds	Showboat, Inc.	Operator of gambling casinos and hotels	Long-term debt financing	Sears, Roebuck Eastman Kodak Hilliburton
11. Reporting and Interpreting Owners' Equity	Wal-Mart	Retail industry	Corporate ownership	May Dept. Store Chrysler Alcoa
12. Reporting and Interpreting Investments in Other Corporations	General Electric	Global consumer products holding company	Strategic investment in other companies	Chiquita Brands Lands' End Mattel Nike
13. Statement of Cash flows	Boston Beer	Beer brewing company	Management of cash	Pete's Brewing Foster's Brewing (of Australia) US Airways
14. Analyzing Financial Statements	Home Depot	Home improvement retailers	Financial statement analysis	Lowe's Hechinger Grossman's

Financial Accounting

SECOND EDITION

Robert Libby
Cornell University

Patricia A. Libby
Ithaca College

Daniel G. Short
Miami University

Irwin
McGraw-Hill

**Boston   Burr Ridge, IL   Dubuque, IA   Madison, WI   New York   San Francisco   St. Louis
Bangkok   Bogotá   Caracas   Lisbon   London   Madrid
Mexico City   Milan   New Delhi   Seoul   Singapore   Sydney   Taipei   Toronto**

Irwin/McGraw-Hill

A Division of The **McGraw·Hill** Companies

FINANCIAL ACCOUNTING

Copyright © 1998 by The McGraw-Hill Companies, Inc. All rights reserved. Previous edition ©1996 by Richard D. Irwin, a Times Mirror Higher Education Group, Inc. company. Printed in the United States of America. Except as permitted under the United States Copyright Act of 1976, no part of this publication may be reproduced or distributed in any form or by any means, or stored in a data base or retrieval system, without the prior written permission of the publisher.

This book is printed on acid-free paper.

1 2 3 4 5 6 7 8 9 0 VNH/VNH 9 0 9 8 7   (US edition)
1 2 3 4 5 6 7 8 9 0 VNH/VNH 9 0 9 8 7   (International edition)

ISBN 0-256-24568-1 (regular edition)
ISBN 0-07-289773-2 (*Business Week* edition)

Vice president and editorial director: *Michael W. Junior*
Publisher: *Jeffrey J. Shelstad*
Sponsoring editor: *George Werthman*
Developmental editor: *Tracey Klein Douglas*
Senior marketing manager: *Heather L. Woods*
Senior project manager: *Beth Cigler*
Senior production supervisor: *Madelyn Underwood*
Senior photo research coordinator: *Keri Johnson*
Photo research: *Corrine Johns*
Senior designer: *Laurie J. Entringer*
Compositor: GAC *Shepard Poorman Communications*
Typeface: *8.5/13.5 Leawood Book*
Printer: *Von Hoffmann Press, Inc.*

Library of Congress Cataloging-in-Publication Data

Libby, Robert.
    Financial accounting / Robert Libby, Patricia A. Libby, Daniel G.
Short.—2nd ed.
      p. cm.
    Includes bibliographical references and indexes.
    ISBN 0-256-24568-1 (acid-free paper).—
ISBN 0-07-289773-2 (Business Week ed.)
    1. Accounting. 2. Corporations—Accounting. 3. Financial
statements.   I. Libby, Patricia A.   II. Short, Daniel G.
III. Title.
HF5635.L684   1998
657—dc21   97-38002
                                                        CIP

INTERNATIONAL EDITION
Copyright © 1998. Exclusive rights by The McGraw-Hill Companies, Inc. for manufacture and export. This book cannot be re-exported from the country to which it is consigned by McGraw-Hill.

The International edition is not available in North America.

When ordering the title, use ISBN 0-07-115385-3.

http://www.mhhe.com

About the Authors

Robert Libby

Robert Libby is the David A. Thomas Professor of Management at the Johnson Graduate School of Management at Cornell University. Bob teaches the introductory financial accounting course. He previously taught at the University of Illinois, Pennsylvania State University, the University of Texas, the University of Chicago, and the University of Michigan. He received his B.S. from Pennsylvania State University and his M.A.S. and Ph.D. from the University of Illinois; he is also a CPA. Bob is a widely published author specializing in behavioral accounting. His prior text, *Accounting and Human Information Processing* (Prentice Hall, 1981), was awarded the AICPA/AAA Notable Contributions to the Accounting Literature Award. He received this award again in 1996 for a paper. He has published numerous articles in the *Journal of Accounting Research; Accounting, Organizations, and Society;* and other accounting journals. He is an active member of the American Accounting Association and the American Institute of CPAs, and is a member of the editorial boards of the *Journal of Accounting Research; Accounting, Organizations, and Society; Journal of Accounting Literature;* and *Journal of Behavioral Decision Making.*

Patricia Libby

Patricia Libby is Associate Professor of Accounting at Ithaca College where she teaches the undergraduate financial accounting course. She previously taught graduate and undergraduate financial accounting at Eastern Michigan University and the University of Texas. Before entering academe, she was an auditor with Price Waterhouse and a financial administrator at the University of Chicago. She received her B.S. from Pennsylvania State University, M.B.A. from DePaul University, and Ph.D. from the University of Michigan; she is also a CPA. Pat conducts research on how to use cases in the introductory course and in other parts of the accounting curriculum. She has published articles in *The Accounting Review, Issues in Accounting Education,* and *The Michigan CPA.* She also conducts seminars nationally on active learning strategies, including cooperative learning methods, and is the chair of the Collaborative Learning at Ithaca College faculty support group.

Daniel G. Short

Dan Short is Dean of the Richard T. Farmer School of Business at Miami University. Previously, Dan was dean of the College of Business at Kansas State University and before that associate dean at the University of Texas at Austin, where he taught the undergraduate and graduate financial accounting courses. He also taught at the University of Chicago. He received his undergraduate degree from Boston University and his M.B.A. and Ph.D. from the University of Michigan. Dan has won numerous awards for his outstanding teaching abilities and has published articles in *The Accounting Review,* the *Journal of Accounting Research, The Wall Street Journal,* and other business journals. He has worked with a large number of Fortune 500 companies, commercial banks, and investment banks to develop and teach executive education courses on the effective use of accounting information. Dan has also served on the board of directors of several companies, including manufacturing, commercial banking, and medical services. He is currently chair of the audit committee of a large manufacturing company.

Instructor Summary

We wrote the first edition in the belief that the subject of financial accounting is inherently interesting but that financial accounting textbooks often are not. Furthermore, the typical texts do not demonstrate that accounting is an exciting major field or important to future careers in marketing, finance, and other areas of management. We approached the writing of the second edition as we did the first: with **career relevance** as our guide to selection of material, and the need to **engage the student** as our guide to style, pedagogy, and design. During the preparation of the second edition, we remained very attentive to the feedback that instructors and students using the first edition provided us. In every aspect of writing and designing this edition, we have been mindful of the challenge to capture students' interest. Based on what our reviewers and the students and instructors who have used our text have told us, we've succeeded.

We have met this challenge by

1. *Integrating real-world business and accounting practices by building each chapter around the operations and financial statements of its own "focus company" (e.g., Callaway Golf in Chapter 5, Harley-Davidson in Chapter 7, Boston Beer in Chapter 13) through which the key concepts in the chapter material are examined.* Learning accounting and financial reporting in real business contexts naturally creates interest for students, demonstrates career relevance, and illustrates management and external uses of financial statements. This can't be accomplished effectively by inserting disjointed vignettes or colorful short features into a traditional preparer-oriented text. We wrote our chapters from scratch around our realistic focus companies, and our financial analysis, international, ethics, cash flow, and financial ratio features are integrated into the chapters.

2. *Choosing material for its managerial significance, relevance to using real financial statements, and student interest.* Actual company practices and decisions made by our focus companies and "contrast companies" illustrate the variety in real-world situations. More importantly, they make our choice of material more interesting and relevant to users of financial statements in finance, marketing, and management, as well as to future accountants. Chapter 5, which illustrates the complete financial reporting process in the information environment of modern financial markets, is unique.

3. *Choosing examples and explaining material in a manner appropriate for the introductory student.* To ensure accessibility of the material, we employ a building block approach; we carefully cover the basics before we address more complex issues. As students' sophistication develops throughout the term, so does the sophistication of the focus company and contrasting company illustrations. Smaller, single industry companies with simple operations, capital structures,

and disclosures are used for the early chapters. The examples increase in sophistication as a student's knowledge grows, both within chapters (e.g., Chapter 7's coverage of LIFO) and between chapters (e.g., Chapter 1 versus Chapter 5 versus Chapter 14).

4. *Including active-learning features that engage the student, provide interactive feedback, and promote critical thinking skills.* Our unique Self-Study Quizzes reinforce key concepts and provide important feedback before students move to the next part of each chapter. Many of the quizzes and end-of-chapter materials rely on real statements and require students to make judgments, search for additional information, and think backward from outputs to inputs, thereby giving students exposure to and practice in managerial thinking.

Preface

We wrote the first edition in the belief that the subject of financial accounting is inherently interesting but that financial accounting textbooks often are not. Furthermore, the typical texts do not demonstrate that accounting is an exciting major field or important to future careers in marketing, finance, and other areas of management. We approached the writing of the second edition as we did the first: with **career relevance** as our guide to selection of material, and the need to **engage the student** as our guide to style, pedagogy, and design. During the preparation of the second edition, we remained very attentive to the feedback that the instructors and students using the first edition have provided us. In every aspect of writing and designing this edition, we have been mindful of the challenge to capture the students' interest; based on what our reviewers and the students who have used our text have told us, we've succeeded. However, in the final analysis it is you and your students who will determine the true worth of our efforts.

This text is aimed at students with career interests in marketing, finance, banking, manufacturing, and human resources, as well as accounting, but with no prior exposure to accounting and financial statements, and often little exposure to the business world. We have carefully designed the scope and depth of the text so that most or all of it can be covered in a single term.

Goals of the Second Edition

To truly engage and stimulate students' interest in the subject matter is an obvious, yet often overlooked, goal of a textbook. Only you can tell us if we've succeeded in motivating the reader and increasing concept retention where so many others haven't. Again, our adopters, reviewers, and students using the first edition think so, and if you and your classes are at all like them, investing the time to read a chapter, we believe, will ultimately make a big difference to you and your students! Other key goals we had in mind when writing the text were

- To convey to students the importance of financial accounting and financial statements to managers.
- To help students learn how investing, financing, and operating decisions of different **real** merchandising, manufacturing, and service businesses are reflected in their **financial statements.**
- To help students understand how these statements are used in **real business decisions.**
- To encourage and develop students' critical thinking by incorporating a strong decision-making orientation.

Besides meeting our overall objective of stimulating an interest in the subject matter to improve learning, these goals are in accordance with the recommendations of the Accounting Education Change Commission **to teach students more effectively the relevance and use of accounting information.**

Development Story of the Second Edition

Meeting the ever-changing needs of instructors and students, many of which are driven by continuous change in the accounting profession and the dynamic business environment of the 1990s, requires input from many people. We have received tremendous feedback from instructors and students around the country who represent both users and nonusers of the first edition. This extensive development process was instrumental in making this text and package truly market-driven. In virtually every instance where preferences were at stake, we deferred to the suggestions of our colleagues and their students. In the second edition, we paid particular attention to student recommendations concerning pedagogy and design. In our acknowledgments we will attempt to thank everyone involved, but first we wanted to provide a brief overview of the market-driven process that guided the development of the second edition.

In the fall of 1995, we conducted the Libby Challenge that asked students and instructors to compare a chapter of our book with the corresponding chapter in the text they were currently using and then provide us with their comments. In 1996, we conducted extensive market research, including instructor and student reviews, surveys, seminars, and class testing. We used this feedback to craft the first draft of the second edition. Then, in the spring of 1997, we had the first draft of the second edition reviewed, chapter-by-chapter, by over 25 instructors around the country. We used the feedback from these individuals to fine-tune our presentation and ensure clarity and accuracy. In addition, we solicited and incorporated suggestions from over 200 students around the country.

The tremendous feedback provided by this process helped us develop and enhance the numerous differences and advantages we believe distinguish our text and allow us to meet our goals. The five features listed below are ones that you have told us are the most important.

What's Different and Why: Key Features

1. *Integration of real-world business and accounting practices into the material by building each chapter around the operations and financial statements of an interesting "focus company" (e.g., Timberland; see Exhibit A).*

    The major topics of each chapter are *integrated around a single focus company*, its operations, and its financial statements and related disclosures. Focus companies were selected from Forbes' Best Small Companies in America as well as the Fortune 1,000. They include well-known and exciting companies such as Timberland, Harley-Davidson, Callaway Golf, Sbarro, Inc., Boston Beer, and General Electric. Each accounting and reporting issue raised is discussed in the context of the focus company and its financial statements and other disclosures. In addition, each chapter emphasizes a different aspect of management, including marketing strategy, human resources, financing strategy, manufacturing, corporate communication, and mergers and acquisitions. (See the inside front cover for a listing of our focus and contrast companies by chapter.) This directly demonstrates the relevance of the material to a variety of future careers.

EXHIBIT A

THE TIMBERLAND COMPANY

CONSOLIDATED BALANCE SHEETS

As of December 31, 1995 and 1994

(Dollars in Thousands, Except Per Share Data)	1995	1994
Assets		
Current assets		
Cash and equivalents	$ 38,389	$ 6,381
Accounts receivable, net of allowance for doubtful accounts of $2,658 in 1995 and $2,704 in 1994	95,786	128,435
Inventories	180,636	218,219

THE TIMBERLAND COMPANY

CONSOLIDATED STATEMENTS OF OPERATIONS

For the Years Ended December 31, 1995, 1994 and 1993

(Amounts in Thousands Except Per Share Data)	1995	1994	1993
Revenues	$655,138	$638,097	$420,062
Cost of goods sold	451,741	428,702	266,211
Gross profit	203,397	209,395	153,851

Integration as opposed to add-on, disjointed vignettes distinguishes our approach from that of other texts; it is also the key to demonstrating career relevance and conveying the excitement of real accounting and reporting problems. For example, in Chapters 2 through 4 typical transactions from Sbarro, Inc., a family-style Italian restaurant chain, are shown to demonstrate this firm's investing, financing, and operating decisions.

We also regularly integrate "contrast company" examples where appropriate to illustrate the variety in real-world practices, and the effect of a company's particular circumstances on its accounting and reporting practices. Our selection of focus and contrast companies provides the proper balance of merchandising, manufacturing, and service companies.

For example, Harley-Davidson is the focus company for Chapter 7, "Reporting and Interpreting Cost of Goods Sold and Inventory." We first examine the inventory accounting issues faced by Harley's motorcycle and Motorclothes™ product lines to demonstrate the effects of its growing operations where Harley faces rising costs. We then compare it to three contrast companies that face very different inventory accounting issues: Deere & Co., which is a shrinking manufacturer; Compaq Computer, which is a declining-cost manufacturer; and the housing division of Asahi Chemicals (of Japan), which produces valuable, distinguishable inventory items.

By the time students complete the semester, they have examined a wide variety of company situations and real financial disclosures. Just as important, these examples are appropriate for the introductory student. For example, in Chapter 5, where we discuss the communication of accounting information using Callaway Golf as the focus company, we take time to define acronyms such as CEO and CFO and terms like *institutional investor* to be sure that the introductory student has an understanding of common business terminology. The reviewers of our text have unanimously endorsed our superior use of real company examples and believe as we do that they will maintain students' interest in the material. In the first edition and in this edition, we have made every effort to select focus companies that students are familiar with and find interesting. The student feedback from the first edition has been overwhelmingly positive in this regard. Acting on student suggestions, we have substituted General Electric for American Brands as the focus company in Chapter 12 and Boston Beer Company for Home Shopping Network as the focus company in Chapter 13.

2. *Material selected for its managerial significance and its relevance to understanding and using real company financial statements—a true user orientation.*

The material included in this text was selected for its relevance to understanding real companies, financial statements, and real management decisions. Unrealistic topics and practices have been eliminated. For example, LIFO applied on a perpetual basis was eliminated because it is rarely used in practice. Further, in keeping with the financial statement focus of the text, pure recordkeeping functions have been included in appendixes or reserved for future coursework. We replace these topics with often omitted material that is fundamental to understanding financial statements. By eliminating the recordkeeping emphasis, we can use basic transaction analysis, journal entries, and T-accounts to provide the structure for understanding the interplay between management decisions and financial statements and the analysis of financial statements. We demonstrate how this structure is as important to future financial statement users as it is to accountants.

An equal part of this feature is the integration of discussions of the decisions made by management and financial statement users in our focus and contrasting companies. Our financial analysis features, shown on the next page, along with the international, ethics, cash flow, and financial ratio features, relate directly to the decisions faced by managers and financial statement users at our focus and contrasting companies. For example, the focus company in Chapter 5, "The Communication of Accounting Information," is Callaway Golf. Here we trace the decisions of Ely Callaway (chairman and CEO), Carol Kerley (CFO) and her accounting staff, as well as the auditors at Price Waterhouse, bankers at First Interstate Bank of California, investment bankers at Merrill Lynch, and the managers at Sumitomo Corporation (which exports and sells Callaway's golf clubs in Japan), as Callaway develops the necessary financial statements and related reports needed to obtain both private and public financing for the growing company.

This decision-making focus encourages and develops critical thinking. At the same time, we cover the highly technical requirements for financial reporting format and content within a context that literally makes some of the most technical accounting material come alive. As a consequence, students will better remember the technical material and better understand its importance.

3. *Earlier introduction to ratio analysis and cash flow analysis.*

During the development process for the first edition and again during the development of this edition, many instructors have mentioned that they would like to introduce students to ratio analysis and cash flow analysis earlier in the course but they can't because most financial accounting textbooks wait until the last few chapters to cover this material. Many instructors feel like they give these two extremely important topics short shrift because it is difficult to cover them thoroughly in a one-semester or one-quarter course. In the second edition, we

Increased Profitability Due to an Accounting Adjustment? Reading the Footnotes

Financial analysts are particularly interested in changes in accounting estimates because they can have a large impact on a company's before-tax operating income. In Delta's case, the changes added $34.3 million because of reduced depreciation expense and add a similar amount each year over the remaining life of the aircraft. Analysts pay close attention to this number because it represents increased profitability due to an accounting adjustment.

As another example, in May 1996, "Japan Airlines, the country's largest carrier, reported its first operating profit since 1991. The company attributed the improvement in the 12 months to March to its extensive restructuring and strong demand in growing Asian markets. But a change in its method of accounting for depreciation also improved JAL's results." The company changed from the declining-balance method (higher depreciation expense) to the straight-line method (lower depreciation expense), and reported an increase in recurring profit compared with last year of ¥10.9 billion. "Although the move suggested the company would have recorded a large recurring loss for the year under the old principles, JAL said the change was a fairer reflection of the costs and benefits of the big outlays on new airports and other facilities recently made by JAL."

SOURCE: Gerard Baker, *Financial Times*, May 30, 1996.

have satisfied their desire to introduce these topics earlier by integrating ratio analysis and cash flow analysis throughout the text.

Although ratios were sporadically incorporated throughout the first edition, we have made a conscious effort to introduce relevant ratios in each chapter of the second edition. Most ratios are introduced in the context of the Financial Analysis sections found in each chapter throughout the text. We agree with our reviewers that an earlier introduction to ratio analysis will prove beneficial to students, especially in situations where, because of time constraints, ratio analysis and financial statement analysis are not covered in any degree of detail. Here is an example from Chapter 3:

Analyzing Your Return on Investment

A very common ratio that investors and financial analysts use is return on investment (ROI). It measures the profitability of a company for investors who expect to earn a certain rate on their investment. ROI is computed as follows:

$$\text{Return on investment} = \frac{\text{Net income}}{\text{Average stockholders' equity}}$$

Average stockholders' equity is computed as the sum of the beginning and ending balances of stockholders' equity divided by 2. Sbarro's 1995 ROI was 11.7 percent [$21,300 ÷ ([$185,600 + 179,500] ÷ 2)]. To analyze this return, we need to compare it to the ratio for other companies in the industry for the same year:

Outback Steakhouse	25.1%
McDonald's Corporation	19.4%
Wendy's International, Inc.	14.5%

Sbarro appears to be providing a comparable return to its investors.

Beginning in Chapter 1 and continuing through Chapter 12, we have incorporated a discussion and analysis of changes in the cash flow of the focus company being discussed and the decisions that caused the changes in cash flow. The earlier introduction of cash flows is sure to encourage students to think more critically about the decisions they will be faced with as managers and the impact those decisions will have on the company's cash flow. Here's an example from Chapter 4:

FOCUS ON CASH FLOWS

A common misconception is that positive net income is equivalent to an increase in cash. Because net income is calculated on the accrual basis, however, revenues may be recognized although the cash has not yet been received, and cash may have been paid before expenses are recognized. The Sbarro illustration in this chapter is a clear example of this. The net income for the month was determined to be a positive $4,975,000, yet we see in the statement of cash flows that cash actually declined for the period by $3,820,000 and cash flows from operations resulted in a negative $4,530,000.

We must be careful in drawing any conclusions from this observation because the time period is only one month. However, over the long run, companies must have positive cash flows from operations to remain viable. In fact, Sbarro has generated approximately $54,000 in positive cash flows from operations each year since 1994.

4. *Exposing students to the variety of accounting methods used around the world and the ethical dilemmas that arise in certain situations involving accounting.*

We feel it is important to expose students to the variety of reporting practices used throughout the world. Today's students will become tomorrow's global executives, and as a result, they need to understand and appreciate the implications of different accounting practices. International accounting sections are incorporated in each chapter and in the homework material.

Taking a Different Strategy to Success

Singapore Airlines, formed in 1972, has recognized continued profitability as one of the world's largest operators of the most technologically advanced "jumbo jets," the Boeing 747-400. Unlike the rest of the airline industry with an average fleet age of more than 12 years, Singapore Airlines uses its aircraft for an average of just under six years. This strategy for managing the company's operational productivity has a dual effect. Depreciation expense is significantly higher due to the shorter estimated useful life, thus reducing net income. Singapore Airlines sells its used aircraft, however, an activity that has resulted in gains (entitled "Surplus on Sale of Aircraft and Spares") reported on the income statement. Both depreciation computations (through the use of estimates) and asset sales (through differences in the timing of the sales) provide management with the flexibility to manage earnings.

On October 28, 1996, *The Straits Times* (page 48) reported that Singapore Airlines' six-month earnings were up 7.2% compared to the same period in the prior year. However, the surplus on sales of aircraft was up 734.7%. "Without the surplus in the six months ended Sept. 30, the national carrier's net earnings would have declined for the first time since 1994."

In every business, decision makers are occasionally confronted with ethical dilemmas that require them to make choices that will impact various groups of people differently. We integrate accounting ethics in each chapter of the text to convey to students the importance of acting responsibly in business practice.

Fierce Pressure to Report Smooth, Ever Higher Earnings

Corporate executives have been under intense pressure over the past decade to keep earnings rising smoothly to meet the consensus expectations of analysts. As the expectations have become more explicit, so too have the mechanisms executives use to manage earnings and hit their targets. Long-lived assets can play a significant role in the ability of companies to meet or beat the estimates, as indicated in the financial press:

. . .

How the pros do it

Plan ahead: Time store openings or asset sales to keep earnings rising smoothly. In most cases, this is earnings management at its least controversial. The master of it is General Electric.

. . .

Capitalize it: Usually it's pretty clear which costs you capitalize and which you expense. But there are gray areas—software R & D is one—and you can get creative about the length of time an asset should be depreciated. America Online was, until it stopped in October, a noted aggressive capitalizer.

Write it off: Take a "big bath" and charge a few hundred million in restructuring costs, and meeting future earnings targets will be easier. Among the biggest restructurers in the 1990s: IBM.

. . .

QUESTION OF ETHICS

REAL WORLD EXCERPT

"Learn to Play the Earnings Game (and Wall Street will love you)"

5. *Choosing examples and explaining material in a manner appropriate for the introductory student.*

The pace, depth of coverage, and level of difficulty of the material and examples are carefully matched to the needs and abilities of introductory students. To ensure accessibility of the material, we employ a building block approach; we carefully cover the basics before we address more complex issues. As the students' sophistication develops throughout the term, so does the sophistication of the focus company and contrasting company illustrations. Smaller, single industry companies with simple operations, capital structures, and disclosures are used in the early chapters. The examples increase in sophistication as a student's knowledge grows both within chapters (e.g., Chapter 7's coverage of LIFO) and between chapters (e.g., Chapter 1 versus Chapter 5 versus Chapter 14).

The technical material is conveyed with clear step-by-step presentations within the realistic examples. For example, Chapters 2, 3, and 4 follow Sbarro, Inc. (a chain of Italian fast-food restaurants) through each step of the basic accounting process, ensuring that students are prepared for the later material. The emphasis on contrasting company practices is conveyed through side-by-side illustrations that punctuate the effects of differences in financial statement presentations and accounting methods. Numerous exhibits and other visual aids are included to enhance comprehension and learning (see Exhibit B). To further increase comprehension, we define unfamiliar terminology (including terms that develop general business knowledge rather than strictly accounting terminology) within the text material, in marginal definitions, and in a glossary of key terms at the end of the book. We also list key terms with page references at the end of each chapter.

EXHIBIT B

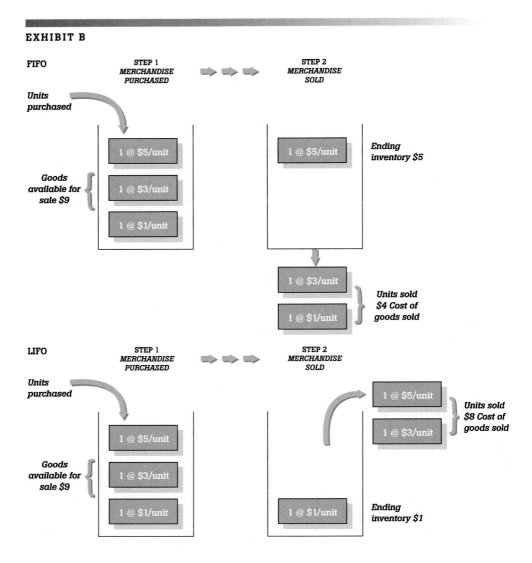

6. *Active-learning features engage the student, provide interactive feedback, and promote critical thinking skills.*

   Active learning creates attention and promotes retention. The integration of technical material in the real-world context produces major advantages here. A unique feature, Self-Study Quizzes (see Exhibit C), stops the student at strategic points throughout each chapter to make sure that key points are well understood. These quizzes help students avoid reading the text in the same fashion as they do a novel; to understand accounting, students must be able to work with the numbers. Students who used the first edition commented that in anticipation of a quiz, they think about what they are reading, which improves learning. The quizzes often require that students prepare or use financial statement disclosures based on actual companies to reinforce the usefulness of what they are learning. For example, in Chapter 5 students actually determine whether Callaway's senior management had earned their bonuses. The quizzes are part of our integrative approach. These are followed by Demonstration Cases presented at the end of the chapter. Students who have carefully worked with these two types of learning aids are ready to work the end-of-chapter homework assignments.

EXHIBIT C

SELF-STUDY QUIZ

Callaway executives receive maximum bonuses if pretax earnings growth meets or exceeds the target of 30 percent. Use Exhibit 5.5 to see whether Callaway executives earned their maximum bonuses in the most recent year.

COMPUTATIONS

_____

_____

Discuss why Callaway might choose to pay executives based on performance and why they use the same accounting numbers used in reports to shareholders to measure the executives' performance.

_____

_____

Now check your answers to those in the footnote at the bottom of the page.[*]

The material within chapters is followed by an extensive selection of end-of-chapter questions, exercises, problems, cases, and projects that examine single concepts or integrate multiple concepts presented in the chapter. To maintain the real-world flavor of the chapter material, they are often based on other real domestic and international companies, and require analysis, conceptual thought, calculation, and written communication. Assignments suitable for individual or group written projects and oral presentations are included in strategic locations. In addition, we have included a considerable number of assignments that require students to use the Internet. In this edition, we have included a new section at the end of the homework material called Projects. These projects can be used as group or individual assignments, and they ask students to analyze and compare financial statements, consider ethical dilemmas, perform financial analysis using ratios, and use the Internet to locate information.

Treatment of Difficult Topics

Among the myriad topics that are covered in an introductory financial accounting course, a number were identified by our reviewers as difficult for students to comprehend. A listing of some of these follows along with a brief discussion of some strengths of our approach to these areas.

Bonds. Our primary coverage of bonds (in Chapter 10) begins with a strong discussion of the uses and nature of bonds, presented in context with the Showboat, Inc., focus company example. This allows students to understand the relevance of this material better. At one point in the chapter, KC Southern's amortization policy is contrasted with Showboat's to point out a financial analyst's potential interpretation of the two policies.

---

[*]Pretax earnings growth % = (195,595 − 158,401) ÷ 158,401 = 23.5% versus 30% target.

They did not earn their maximum bonuses. (In reality, they received 64.2 percent of their maximum bonuses.) The company believes that higher pretax earnings growth will result in higher prices for Callaway stock. Paying Callaway executives a bonus for increasing earnings growth thus helps align the interests of the executives with those of the shareholders. In addition, companies often pay shareholders bonuses based on the numbers in the annual report because they have been independently verified by the auditors.

Time Value of Money. Our reviewers clearly feel that a key strength of our discussion of the time value of money (Chapter 9) is a practical illustration of its applications to accounting through short cases with General Mills, Inc., as the focus company.

Inventory. We clearly took a user-oriented approach to the discussion of this material in Chapter 7 with a goal of providing an understanding of what accountants do with inventory and why. Throughout the entire chapter the focus is on the key concepts of inventory valuation and their effects on financial statements without placing undue emphasis on recordkeeping.

Adjusting Entries. Again, we start with the premise that students will better understand the *how* behind this concept if we first illustrate through a real-company example *why* adjusting entries are necessary. To an introductory student, the process of adjusting entries is often not intuitive, and so our reviewers unanimously endorsed our walk-through of the Sbarro, Inc., analysis as an effective tool for presenting this hard-to-grasp concept.

Changes in the Second Edition

Body of Chapter

- All financial statements have been updated to reflect 1995 and 1996 annual reports.
- A new section focusing on cash flows entitled "Focus on Cash Flows" has been incorporated into each chapter, beginning in Chapter 2 and ending in Chapter 12.
- Financial ratios are introduced in each chapter where appropriate and a summary of key ratios is presented at the end of each chapter.

Homework

- We have incorporated a new Projects section in the end-of-chapter material. These projects require students to work either in groups or individually. Students will need to use the Internet, ratio analysis, and cash flow analysis, consider ethical dilemmas, and much more. They are located at the end of the Cases section.
- We have added a Team Project at the end of each chapter's critical writing homework. A semester-long team project can be created by assigning each chapter's Team Project. This allows students a more in-depth review of financial statements and uses by company and industry. This type of project also may be created from the Toys "R" Us Cases at the end of each chapter.
- We have incorporated twice the amount of real world companies used in the assignment material of the previous edition. Companies such as Mercury Finance, Fruit of the Loom, Apple, and Federal Express are utilized in the assignment material to reinforce the real world company focus of the text.
- We have increased the emphasis on using accounting information as opposed to preparing financial statements by increasing the number of homework assignments that require students to analyze financial data and interpret the economic impact of management decisions.
- We have incorporated more information- and technology-related assignments to reflect the ever-increasing use and value of such systems in the business world. These assignments require students to utilize the Internet among other sources.

Key Features in Each Chapter and Changes in the Second Edition

Chapter 1: Financial Statements and Business Decisions (Maxidrive)

- Students are introduced immediately to an overview of the four basic financial statements through an interesting company example based on an exciting case. At the same time, inter-industry differences in financial reporting are illustrated to begin building critical thinking skills for the student.
- Financial Analysis discussions are introduced throughout this chapter (and then carried through all chapters) to show students how useful accounting knowledge can be in making economic decisions.

Changes in the Second Edition

- The price/earnings ratio is introduced in the context of the introduction to financial statement analysis. Ratio analysis and related homework assignments are incorporated in each chapter leading up to Chapter 14, "Analyzing Financial Statements," which integrates the earlier discussion.
- New project assignments, which require students to access information sources from outside the textbook and to work on team-based financial analysis tasks, are located in each chapter of the book, starting in Chapter 1.

Chapter 2: Investing and Financing Decisions and the Balance Sheet (Sbarro)

- Exhibit 2.1 illustrates a unique presentation of the conceptual framework that becomes the building block for the transaction analysis approach to follow.
- Balance sheet concepts are examined and reinforced before the income statement concepts are presented in Chapter 3.
- As an active learning feature for better comprehension, students must complete the transaction analysis illustration following the process discussed in the chapter.
- Debit–credit and T-account concepts are presented clearly and are shown in addition to transaction analysis. Students thus see the relevance and use of these often confusing procedural topics.
- Financial Analysis discussions emphasize financing and investing decisions.

Changes in the Second Edition

- The debt-to-equity ratio is introduced in the context of the Sbarro, Inc., focus company case for analyzing the financing strategies that companies employ. It is then reinforced in related homework assignments.
- The effects of transactions on the accounting equations are emphasized in context with the ongoing Sbarro, Inc., focus company case.
- The new Focus on Cash Flows discussion with related homework assignments is continued and then carried through each chapter, culminating in Chapter 13, where the complete statement is reviewed.

Chapter 3: Operating Decisions and the Income Statement (Sbarro)

- Income statement concepts and their relationships to balance sheet concepts are examined and reinforced in their own separate chapter.
- The transaction analysis model as illustrated through the Sbarro, Inc., example is continued to allow students to build upon concepts presented in Chapter 2.
- Financial Analysis discussions emphasize operating decisions.

- Strong development of the principles related to revenue recognition and the matching concepts are introduced in this chapter, including a conceptual discussion of accruals and deferrals. Timelines are presented as useful analytical tools for providing visual representations of transactions or series of transactions.

Changes in the Second Edition

- Chapters 3 and 4 have been thoroughly revised to improve clarity of presentation.
- We have increased the use of visuals to help explain the flow of events when accounting for transactions.
- The transaction analysis presentation has been streamlined to increase efficacy, and the presentation of adjustments has also been streamlined for greater clarity.
- The return on investment ratio is introduced as a common measure utilized by investors and financial analysts. It is computed for Sbarro and its competitor to provide a framework for analysis.
- The Focus on Cash Flows discussion illustrates the difference between net income and cash from operations.

Chapter 4: The Adjustment Process and Financial Statements (Sbarro)

- After first showing students the *why* behind adjusting entries, we show them the *how* through a consistent three-step process that can be applied to analyze any situation requiring an adjusting journal entry. The focus is on understanding versus rote memorization.
- The discussion of the statement of cash flows, its importance, and its origin is continued here so that students can keep cash effects in mind through later chapters without being overburdened with technical details.
- Formal recordkeeping formats and reversing entries can be found in Appendix C of the text.

Changes in the Second Edition

- Earnings per share is introduced as a required disclosure item.
- The adjusting entries have been simplified to focus on the effects of adjustments.
- The chapter supplements found at the end of Chapter 4 are now located in Appendix C at the end of the book.
- The closing process has been streamlined for greater clarity and to focus on the effects of closing the records.

Chapter 5: The Communication of Accounting Information (Callaway Golf)

- This unique chapter clearly and concisely presents how financial statements are disseminated and used, emphasizing not just the output but the people and process involved. Exhibits 5.1 and 5.2 are truly innovative (Exhibit 5.2 is shown on the next page.)
- Through a presentation of financial information sources, electronic information services, and actual reports used by companies, we help students redefine the uses behind the process presented in the previous three chapters. We have expanded the discussion of electronic information services and the benefits of such services now and in the future.
- An often overlooked item, notes to financial statements, which were first presented in Chapter 1, are discussed in greater detail here with actual corporate examples used to illustrate these important components of the reporting process.

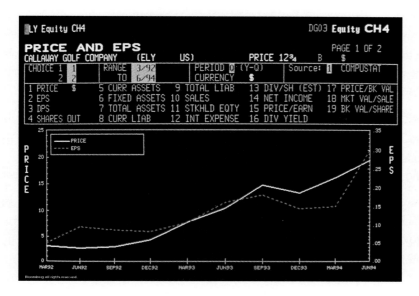

Changes in the Second Edition

- We have dramatically expanded the discussion of effective uses of the Internet as a tool for distributing and researching financial data with examples that the students can immediately use. This presentation is coupled with an overall increase in Internet awareness across chapters and across homework assignments.
- New standards on EPS and comprehensive income are incorporated.

Chapter 6: Reporting and Interpreting Sales Revenue, Receivables, and Cash (Timberland)

- To improve student understanding, receivable issues are linked with revenue recognition.
- Issues related to discounts, returns, and bad debts are presented as part of marketing strategy and financial management at Timberland not as pure record-keeping functions.
- The concept of bad debt expense is presented clearly with an emphasis on analyzing the effects of this expense on actual financial statements; students work with actual statements and footnotes.
- Recognizing revenue in unusual circumstances is covered at a level appropriate for the introductory student.

Changes in the Second Edition

- The end-of-chapter supplement on bank reconciliations has been incorporated into the chapter.
- The petty cash supplement has been eliminated.
- The section on special circumstances of the application of the revenue principle has been removed from the chapter and placed in a chapter supplement.

Chapter 7: Reporting and Interpreting Cost of Goods Sold and Inventory (Harley-Davidson)

- The influence of choice of inventory method on financial statement information is presented through examples of choices facing Harley-Davidson, Inc., a company with which most students can readily identify.

- Harley-Davidson's inventory method choices are compared to those of other companies in different circumstances.
- In the discussion of periodic versus perpetual inventory systems, the focus is on the usefulness of perpetual inventory systems for managerial decisions rather than heavy coverage of recordkeeping.

Changes in the Second Edition

- The discussion of the periodic inventory system has been abbreviated and the discussion of the perpetual inventory system has been expanded.
- The discussion of LIFO liquidations has been placed in a chapter supplement.

Chapter 8: Reporting and Interpreting Property, Plant, and Equipment; Natural Resources; and Intangibles (Delta Air Lines)

- The depreciation methods are presented in a decision-making framework that minimizes procedure and emphasizes how methods are chosen.
- The discussion of residual value and estimated useful life is strengthened by the continued use of examples from Delta Air Lines, Inc.
- The chapter develops student interest in a potentially dry topic by showing how planning productive capacity is an essential management responsibility.

Changes in the Second Edition

- The discussion of the use of property, plant, and equipment has been moved to precede the discussion of depreciation methods for property, plant, and equipment to make the topical presentation more logical to students.
- The sum of the year's digits depreciation method has been eliminated since it is not often used in practice.
- The impairment of assets is discussed along with its effects on financial analysis.
- The fixed asset turnover ratio is illustrated for Delta Air Lines and its competitors to provide a framework for analysis.
- The discussion of trade-ins has been eliminated.

Chapter 9: Reporting and Interpreting Liabilities (General Mills)

- As in other chapters, ratios (e.g., current ratio) are discussed as the accounts used in computations are covered, allowing students to more clearly see the linkages and understand the importance of ratio analysis.
- Topics were selected based on a review of hundreds of financial statements. To provide relevance, students are exposed to liabilities that they will see on most statements. Complex issues are introduced without excessive details.

Changes in the Second Edition

- A brief discussion of leases has been added to the chapter.

Chapter 10: Reporting and Interpreting Bonds (Showboat)

- Student interest is maintained by following an actual bond issuance for Showboat, Inc., from the prospectus stage through sale, concluding with a vote by bondholders to amend bond covenants.
- Based on reviewer feedback, material was added on bond investments held to maturity, which briefly illustrates why certain companies choose this as an investment strategy and how they report it in their financial statements. By combining bond liabilities and bond investments, students develop a better understanding of these instruments.

Changes in the Second Edition

- A discussion of variable interest rate debt has been added.

Chapter 11: Reporting and Interpreting Owners' Equity (Wal-Mart)

- Through the primary use of examples from Wal-Mart, which represents a corporate success story that all students can appreciate and understand, the focus is on comprehending the relationships among dividends, cash, and retained earnings. Students are shown real-world examples such as notice of an annual meeting, a vote to amend a corporate charter, a dividend declaration, and a stock repurchase.
- Material on initial public offerings (IPOs) is presented here, with a discussion of the reasons why a company might want to go public and examples of formerly small start-up operations that are now corporate giants (e.g., Dell Computers and Microsoft, Inc.).

Changes in the Second Edition

- A new discussion of stock options has been included.

Chapter 12: Reporting and Interpreting Investments in Other Corporations (General Electric)

- By illustrating actual examples from General Electric, Chiquita Brands, Lands' End, Nike, and others, the student is shown the strategies behind a company's decision to invest in other companies.
- As in other chapters, the approach focuses on presenting the business environment that drives transactions and then on developing the accounting treatments necessary to capture and present properly the information in financial statements.
- The chapter discussion uses a modular approach that permits the instructor to cover as much or as little of intercorporate investments as is deemed appropriate.

Changes in the Second Edition

- General Electric has replaced American Brands as the focus company.
- We have increased the use of T-accounts to help explain various transaction and accounting methods.
- Consolidated statements for the pooling of interest method have been eliminated.
- A new discussion of why consolidated financial statements are prepared and used is incorporated into the chapter.

Chapter 13: Statement of Cash Flows (Boston Beer Company)

- Financial Analysis sections, a feature that appears in all chapters, are inserted frequently here to show the use and importance of cash flows so that students are able to view the statement of cash flows as an analytical tool to help convey new information about a company.
- The Focus on Cash Flows sections found in Chapters 2 through 12 culminate in the presentation of the statement of cash flows found in this chapter.
- The indirect method, which is most commonly used in actual practice, is presented first and with greater emphasis.
- Boston Beer Company is the focus company of the chapter and is compared to contrast companies, which include Pete's Brewing and U•S Airways, to illustrate the various impacts that different decisions can have on the statement of cash flows of companies in the same and different industries.

Changes in the Second Edition

- Chapter 13 has been completely rewritten to emphasize the uses and analysis of the statement of cash flows that include its role in ratio analysis as opposed to its preparation.
- Boston Beer Company and its easy-to-understand operations has replaced Home Shopping Network as the focus company.
- The section describing the adjustments for gains and losses has been moved to a chapter supplement.
- The spreadsheet approach to the statement of cash flows has been moved to a chapter supplement.

Chapter 14: Analyzing Financial Statements (Home Depot)

- Financial ratios are used to compare Home Depot with leading competitors Hechinger and Lowe's to illustrate the uses and potential shortcomings of ratio analysis.
- To increase understanding of actual practices, students are briefly introduced to how information is used in an efficient market.
- Financial analysis is integrated with Home Depot's business strategy and operating decisions to allow students to see the types of strategic and other decisions facing business managers.

Changes in the Second Edition

- Several new ratios have been introduced, including the times interest earned ratio, the cash coverage ratio, the quality of income ratio, the fixed ratio, and the cash ratio.

End-of-Chapter Material

For success in the business world overall and especially in accounting, students must possess strong written and oral communication skills and be able to deal with ambiguity, solve unstructured problems, gather information from human and electronic sources, use critical thinking skills to make good judgments, and work effectively in groups. The AECC and the Big 6 firms stress a broad liberal arts foundation with an understanding of business and organizations as being more important than specific accounting or auditing knowledge. We have responded to these needs by framing each chapter in a business setting so as to enhance students' understanding of accounting in the context of various businesses. Although the material within the chapters provides varied resources for students to use in developing the necessary skills, we have also included numerous end-of-chapter items that (1) incorporate a writing component, (2) drill students on key concepts, (3) require students to search for information by contacting companies, searching libraries, and utilizing computerized services (see especially Chapter 5), (4) require students to make judgments without having access to additional information, often necessitating thinking backward from outputs to inputs, and (5) can be structured by the instructor as group learning experiences.

The end-of-chapter material consists of five types of items: questions, exercises, problems, cases, and projects. The questions and exercises usually cover single topics and require less time and effort to complete than the problems, cases, and projects, which typically integrate more than one concept and require more analytical and criti-

EXHIBIT D

C5–14 **Project: Performing Comparative Analysis of Gross Profit Percentages**

Using your web-browser, contact the websites of Microsoft, the leading computer *software* company (http://www.microsoft.com/msft/), and Compaq Computer, the leading manufacturer of personal computer *hardware* (http:// www.compaq.com). On the basis of information provided in their latest annual reports, determine their gross profit percentages. Write a short memo comparing the companies' ratios. Indicate what differences in their businesses might account for any difference in the ratios.

C13–6 **Project: Competitive Analysis of Differences in Quality of Earnings Ratio**

Boston Beer's competitors in the craft brewing industry include Redhook, Pete's, Big Rock, Minnesota Brewing, and others. Obtain the cash flow statement for Boston Beer and two of its competitors. (Library files, the SEC EDGAR service at www.sec.gov, Compustat, or the companies themselves are good sources.) Write a short memo comparing the companies' quality of earnings ratios. Based on the reconciliation of net income to cash flow from operations, indicate what caused the differences in their ratios.

Microsoft
Compaq Computer

cal thinking skills. Examples of projects that are new to this edition are illustrated in Exhibit D. The material follows the topical coverage as outlined in the chapter, includes multiple items on each topic, and moves from easy to more challenging, with very challenging items noted. We carry through the user orientation in the end-of-chapter material by including examples from small business settings, problems that deal with real financial statement excerpts, international company examples, and ethical issues examples. To allow maximum instructor flexibility and ample student practice, each of the key topics is covered by at least two items (i.e., questions, exercises, problems, cases, and projects).

Unique, Real-World Offering

Financial Accounting, *The Business Week Edition* (ISBN 0-07-289773-2). The price of this version of the text includes a 10-week subscription to *Business Week,* the best-selling business magazine in the world.

Supplements for the Instructor

Instructor's Resource Manual (ISBN 0-256-25441-9). Authored by Betty McMechen of Mesa State College, all supplements, including the Test Bank, Videos, Study Guide, and PowerPoint Presentation, are topically cross-referenced in the IRM to help instructors systematically direct students to various ancillaries to reinforce key concepts. For example, an instructor interested in teaching transaction analysis will be able to look in the IRM and see which videos to use, which study guide and test bank questions focus on transaction analysis, and which PowerPoint and overhead transparencies are appropriate. Also included are detailed chapter outlines that present alternate methods of covering the material should the instructor wish to de-emphasize procedural detail or omit certain topics.

Solutions Manual (ISBN 0-256-25436-2), prepared by the textbook authors and carefully reviewed for accuracy by outside sources, contains solutions to all assignment material.

Solutions Transparencies (ISBN 0-256-25446-X) are set in large, boldface type to maximize their effectiveness in large classrooms.

Electronic Solutions Manual (ISBN 0-256-25439-7) is an electronic version of the Solutions Manual.

Ready Shows (ISBN 0-256-25440-0) **and Ready Slides** (ISBN 0-256-25446-X) are teaching enhancement packages prepared by Jon A. Booker, Charles W. Caldwell, Susan C. Galbreath, and Richard S. Rand, all of Tennessee Technological University.

Ready Shows. This is a package of multimedia lecture enhancement aids that uses PowerPoint software to illustrate chapter concepts.

Ready Slides. These selected four-color teaching transparencies are printed from the PowerPoint Ready Shows. (See also "Ready Notes" under Student Supplements.)

Test Bank (ISBN 0-256-25437-0) by Betty McMechen of Mesa State College contains multiple-choice, true/false, matching and completion questions, and short problems requiring analysis and written answers. The testing material is coded by type of question and level of difficulty.

Computest is a computerized version of the manual test bank for more efficient use, available in Macintosh and Windows versions. The extensive features of this test generator program include random question selection based on the user's specification of learning objectives, type of question, and level of difficulty.

Windows Version (ISBN 0-256-25443-5)

MAC Version (ISBN 0-256-25442-7)

Teletest allows users to call a toll-free number, specify the content of desired exams, and have a laser-printed copy of the exams mailed to them.

Lecture Enhancement Video Series and Video Guide are short, action-oriented videos that provide the impetus for lively classroom discussion. The *Financial Accounting Video Library* includes videos from the Financial Accounting Standards Board, Ben & Jerry's, and a video with Art Wyatt discussing the impact of the International Accounting Standards Committee.

Web Page. Visit this site at *http://www.mhhe.com/business/accounting/libby*.

The Web site was created to satisfy the needs of students and instructors alike. Instructor features will include

- Online Discussion Group for instructors to swap ideas about teaching accounting.
- Active Learning/Technology Integration suggestions from instructors on how to effectively integrate these items into your course.
- Related links to focus companies with additional exercises.
- Related readings featuring recent news items related to accounting topics.
- And much more . . .

Presentation Manager. This integrated CD-ROM allows you to maneuver from PowerPoint slides to solutions to test bank questions and much more. You no longer need to worry about the various disk supplements that come with Libby/Libby/Short. Now you can get them on one convenient CD-ROM. Ideal for using in class.

Check Figures (ISBN 0-256-25438-9). Provide answers to select problems and cases. These figures are available for distribution to students.

SPATS—Instructor (ISBN 0-07-292415-2). Spreadsheet Applications Template Software allows students to develop important spreadsheet skills by using Excel templates to solve selected assignments from various introductory accounting texts.

Supplements for the Student

Study Guide (ISBN 0-256-25433-8) by Jeannie Folk of College of DuPage contains a number of useful references for the student. Each chapter includes Overview of Chapter, Restatement of Learning Objectives, Chapter Outline, Questions and Exercises (multiple-choice, true/false, matching, short answer, and group exercises), and a word search puzzle of key terms to build critical thinking skills.

Active Learning Workbook: Student Learning Tools (ISBN 0-256-25577-6) by Barbara Chiappetta of Nassau Community College contains material for students' use in an active learning environment. It is designed to facilitate a concept approach with a user emphasis and the development of interpersonal skills. Functional aspects of learning teams are explained, and forms for team usage are provided. The material is divided into three sections: class activities, team presentation assignments, and writing assignments. For instructors who address procedural issues, accounting forms (journal paper, two- and three-column paper, and T-accounts) are provided for reproduction.

Ready Notes (ISBN 0-256-25435-4) is a booklet of Ready Show screen printouts that enables students to take notes during Ready Show or Ready Slide presentations.

Web Page. Visit this site at *http://www.mhhe.com/business/accounting/libby*.

The Web site was created to satisfy the needs of students and instructors alike. Student features will include

- How To Get an "A" in Accounting, which reviews techniques and strategies for studying accounting.
- Related links to focus companies with additional exercises.
- Related readings featuring recent news items related to accounting topics.
- And much more . . .

Interactive Financial Accounting Lab, Version 2.0 (ISBN 0-07-847293-8). Created and programmed by Ralph Smith and Rick Birney, both of Arizona State University. This powerful software provides an innovative, multimedia environment for students to learn the fundamentals of the accounting process. Available in a new "take home" package.

Essentials of Accounting: A Multimedia Approach (ISBN 0-256-27003-1). This CD-ROM offers students a multimedia overview of the accounting cycle transaction process and utilizes audio, interactive animation, and actual video footage.

Windows97 Tutorial Software (ISBN 0-07-292414-4). Leland Mansuetti and Keith Weidkamp, both of Sierra College, present this Windows-based tutorial, which provides multiple-choice, true/false, journal entry review, and glossary review questions that can be randomly accessed by students. Explanations of right and wrong answers are provided and scores are tallied. Instructors may request a free master template for students to use or copy, or students may purchase shrinkwrapped versions for a nominal fee.

Real-World Accounting Series contains financial analysis projects from Timothy Louwers and William Pasewark, both of the University of Houston, that offer students hands-on experience in analyzing and understanding corporate annual reports. They are intended to show the big picture at the end of the accounting process, thereby emphasizing interpretation and analysis rather than preparation of financial statements.

Understanding Corporate Annual Reports (ISBN 0-07-290132-2). This financial analysis project contains instructions for obtaining an annual report from a publicly traded corporation and performing analysis on that report.

Shoe Business, Inc. (ISBN 0-256-19077-1) This humorous yet serious financial analysis project focuses on the frequent overemphasis of bottom-line net income by investors. The student is led through extensive analysis of footnote disclosures, financial ratios, and bankruptcy prediction models.

Athletronics, Inc. (ISBN 0-256-18872-6) This financial analysis project emphasizes the effect of generally accepted accounting principles on decisions based on accounting data. The student is required to perform financial analysis on the data contained in the manual.

GLAS (ISBN 0-07-292412-8). Irwin/McGraw-Hill's popular General Ledger Applications Software is a revised package containing most of the features of commercial accounting software, yet it can be easily used by students with little or no computer background. A large number of problem assignments are preloaded on the package, and it can also be used to solve any problem that calls for journal entries.

SPATS—Student Version (ISBN 0-07-292413-6). Spreadsheet Applications Template Software allows students to develop important spreadsheet skills by using Excel templates to solve selected assignments from various introductory accounting texts. "What if" questions are added to show the power of spreadsheets and a simple tutorial is included. Instructors may request a free master template for students to use or copy, or students may purchase shrinkwrapped versions for a nominal fee.

"You Name It" Company Practice Set (ISBN 0-07-007492-5): From Donald Saftner of University of Toledo and Rosalind Cranor of Virginia Polytechnic Institute, the "You Name It" Company practice set is a Windows-based practice set designed to take you through the accounting process from journalizing to statement preparation and statement analysis. Each month introduces new concepts and procedures and integrates them with the concepts and procedures presented in previous months—leading to a better understanding of the accounting process.

Practice Sets, Computerized and Manual. Leland Mansuetti and Keith Weidkamp, both of Sierra College, have created both a DOS and a new Windows version of their dynamic educational practice sets.

Room Zoom: The CPA Source Disc (ISBN 0-256-21568-5) is a multimedia, interactive CD-ROM that provides an exciting guide to a CPA career. Students will be able to experience a day in the life of a CPA, review salary statistics, learn about scholarships and internships, understand the technology inherent in the profession, learn about the CPA exam, and much more. Available to students for a nominal charge when purchased with *Financial Accounting* from Irwin/McGraw-Hill, this innovative technology component would also be perfect for the first day of class.

Working Papers (ISBN 0-256-25434-6) selected and prepared by the authors contain all the forms necessary for completing the end-of-chapter materials.

IEM: Iowa Electronics Market is the first ever Introductory Accounting product offered via the Internet, by Joyce Berg, Robert Forsythe, and Tom Rietz (all of the University of Iowa). This fully interactive, real-time experience allows students to explore accounting issues beyond just the numbers. Contact your Irwin/McGraw-Hill sales representative for more information on this innovative offering.

Acknowledgments

Writing a successful text requires a team effort, and we have enjoyed working with excellent teammates. Throughout the process of writing this text, many people stepped forward with tremendous efforts that allowed us to accomplish our stated goals. We would like to recognize the sincere and devoted efforts of the many people who added their input to the process of developing this text. As stated in the Development Story section, we received invaluable advice and suggestions during the manuscript development and revision process.

For this assistance, we thank the following colleagues:

First Edition Reviewers

D'Arcy Becker, *University of New Mexico*
Linda Bell, *William Jewell College*
Wayne Boutell, *University of California at Berkeley*
Patricia Doherty, *Boston University*
Allan Drebin, *Northwestern University*
Marie Dubke, *University of Memphis*
Gary Fish, *Illinois State University*
Paul Frishkoff, *University of Oregon*
Flora Guidry, *University of New Hampshire*
Marcia Halvorsen, *University of Cincinnati*
Leon Hanouille, *Syracuse University*
Peggy Hite, *Indiana University*
David Hoffman, *University of North Carolina at Chapel Hill*
Kathy Horton, *University of Illinois at Chicago*
Sharon Jackson, *Auburn University at Montgomery*
Naida Kaen, *University of New Hampshire*
Sue Kattelus, *Eastern Michigan University*
Jim Kurtenbach, *Iowa State University*
David Lavin, *Florida International University*
Joan Luft, *Michigan State University*
Betty McMechen, *Mesa State College*
Greg Merrill, *California State University at Fullerton*
Brian Nagle, *Duquesne University*
Ron Pawliczek, *Boston College*
Don Putnam, *California State University Polytechnic at Pomona*
Michael Ruble, *Western Washington University*
Mary Alice Seville, *Oregon State University*
Wayne Shaw, *Southern Methodist University*
Ken Smith, *Idaho State University*
Ralph Spanswick, *California State University at Los Angeles*
Kevin Stocks, *Brigham Young University*
Kathryn Sullivan, *George Washington University*
Michael Welker, *Drexel University*
T. Sterling Wetzel, *Oklahoma State University*
William Zorr, *University of Wisconsin—Oshkosh*

Second Edition Reviewers

Dawn Addington, *University of New Mexico*
Holly Ashbaugh, *University of Northern Iowa*
Ken Boze, *University of Alaska—Anchorage*
Anne Clem, *Iowa State University*
Carol Dicino, *University of Southern Colorado*
Jim Emig, *Villanova University*
Alan Falcon, *Loyola Marymount University*
Arthur Goldman, *University of Kentucky*
Tim Griffin, *University of Missouri—KC*
Donna Hetzel, *Western Michigan University*
Ken Hiltebeitel, *Villanova University*
Marge Hubbert, *Cornell University*
Frank Korman, *Mountain View College*
Jim Kurtenbach, *Iowa State University*
Larry Logan, *University of Massachusetts—Dartmouth*
Ron Mannino, *University of Massachusetts—Amherst*
Noel McKeon, *Florida Community College*
Betty McMechen, *Mesa State College*
Paul Mihalek, *University of Hartford*
Brian Nagle, *Duquesne University*
John Osborn, *California State University—Fresno*
Mawdudur Rahman, *Suffolk University*
Jane Reimers, *Florida State University*
Keith Richardson, *Indiana State University*
Bruce Samuelson, *Pepperdine University*
Gene Sauls, *California State University—Sacramento*
Wayne Shaw, *Southern Methodist University*
Blair Terry, *Fresno City College*
Laverne Thompson, *St. Louis Community College at Meramec*
Steven Wong, *San Jose City College*

In addition, we are deeply indebted to the following individuals who helped develop, critique, and shape the extensive ancillary package: Betty McMechen, Mesa State College; Jeannie Folk, College of DuPage; Jon Booker, Tennessee Technological University; Charles Caldwell, Tennessee Technological University; Susan Galbreath, Tennessee Technological University; Leland Mansuetti, Sierra College; Richard Rand, Tennessee Technological University; Barbara Schnathorst, The Write Solution, Inc.; Jack Terry, ComSource, Inc.; and Keith Weidkamp, Sierra College.

We also received invaluable input and support from numerous colleagues and associates, in particular William Wright, University of California at Irvine; Marge Hubbard, Kristina Szafara, Steve Gallucci, and Carol Marquardt, all of Cornell University; and Susan Dahl, Kansas State University. Furthermore, we appreciate the additional comments, suggestions, and support of our students and our colleagues at Cornell University, Ithaca College, and Miami University.

Finally, the extraordinary efforts of a talented group of individuals at Irwin/McGraw-Hill made all of this come together. We would especially like to thank our sponsoring editor, George Werthman, for championing this project through the revision process; Jeff Shelstad for encouraging us to write the first edition and providing input and support during the writing of the second edition; creative marketing ideas and support from our marketing manager, Heather Woods; Laurie Entringer, for outstanding design work; Beth Cigler, our tireless project manager; our production supervisor, Madelyn Underwood; and Tracey Douglas, for outstanding editorial development and feedback.

Robert Libby
Patricia A. Libby
Daniel G. Short

Contents in Brief

Contents

CHAPTER TWO
Investing and Financing Decisions and the Balance Sheet 52

CHAPTER THREE
Operating Decisions and the Income Statement 108

CHAPTER FOUR
The Adjustment Process and Financial Statements 170

CHAPTER FIVE

The Communication of Accounting Information 234

CHAPTER SIX
Reporting and Interpreting Sales Revenue, Receivables, and Cash 296

CHAPTER SEVEN
Reporting and Interpreting Cost of Goods Sold and Inventory 354

CHAPTER EIGHT
Reporting and Interpreting Property, Plant, and Equipment; Natural Resources; and Intangibles 414

CHAPTER NINE
Reporting and Interpreting Liabilities 470

CHAPTER ELEVEN
Reporting and Interpreting Owners' Equity 562

CHAPTER TWELVE
Reporting and Interpreting Investments in Other Corporations 612

CHAPTER THIRTEEN
Statement of Cash Flows 652

BOSTON BEER COMPANY 653

CHAPTER 14
Analyzing Financial Statements 700

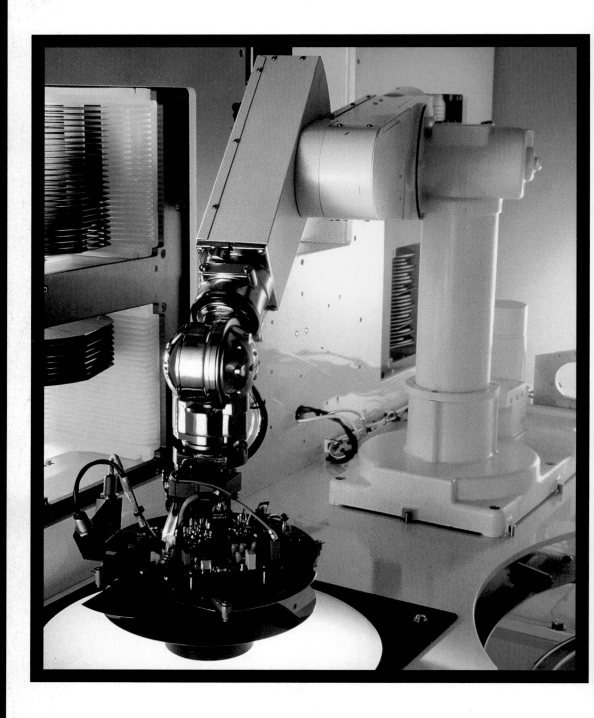

CHAPTER ONE

Financial Statements and Business Decisions

Maxidrive Corporation
AN ACQUISITION GONE WRONG*

I n January, Exeter Investors purchased Maxidrive Corp., a fast-growing

manufacturer of personal computer disk drives, for $32 million. The price

Exeter paid was decided by considering the value of the economic resources

owned by Maxidrive, its debts to others, its ability to sell goods for more than

the cost to produce them, and its ability to generate the cash necessary to pay

its current bills. Much of this assessment was based on financial information

provided by Maxidrive to Exeter. This financial information was presented in

the form of financial statements. By July, Exeter discovered a variety of prob-

lems both in the operations of Maxidrive and in the financial statements that

Maxidrive had provided. It then appeared that Maxidrive was worth only

about half of what Exeter had paid. Further, Maxidrive did not have enough

cash to pay its debt to American Bank. In response, Exeter filed a lawsuit

---

*The Maxidrive case is a realistic representation of an actual case of fraud. No names in the case are real.
 The actual fraud is discussed in the epilogue to the chapter.

LEARNING OBJECTIVES
After studying this chapter, you
should be able to:
1. Recognize the information conveyed in the four basic financial
   statements and the way that it is
   used by different decision makers
   (investors, creditors, and managers). 6
2. Identify the role of generally
   accepted accounting principles
   (GAAP) in determining the content
   of financial statements. 22
3. Distinguish the roles of managers
   and auditors in the accounting
   communication process. 26
4. Appreciate the importance of
   ethics, reputation, and legal liability in accounting. 27

**against the previous owners and others responsible for Maxidrive's
financial statements to recover the overpayment.**

■ ■ ■

The Objectives of *Financial Accounting*

Determining the price that Exeter was willing to pay for Maxidrive is typical of the
economic decisions that are made based on financial statements. Businesses use
financial statements as the primary means to communicate financial information to
parties outside the organization. The purpose of this text is to help you develop the
ability to read and interpret financial statements of business organizations and understand the system that produces those statements. This book is aimed at two groups
of readers: *future managers,* who will need to interpret and use financial statement
information in business decisions, and *future accountants*, who will prepare financial
statements for those managers. The book provides future managers with a firm basis
for using financial statement information in their careers in marketing, finance,
banking, manufacturing, human resources, sales, information systems, or other areas
of management. It also provides future accountants with a solid foundation for further
professional study.

Both managers and accountants must understand *financial statements* (what the
statements tell you and what they do not tell you about a business enterprise), *business
operations*, and *the use of financial statements in decision making* to perform their duties
successfully. As a consequence, we integrate actual business practice in our discussions starting with Chapter 1. We examine the fundamentals of financial accounting in
a variety of business contexts relevant to your future careers. Each chapter's material is
integrated around a *focus company* (in this chapter, Maxidrive). The focus companies
are drawn from 12 different industries, providing you with a broad range of experience
with realistic business and financial accounting practices. When appropriate, the focus
company's operations and financial statements are then compared to those of the *contrast companies*. When you complete this book, you will be able to read and understand
financial statements of real companies.

The way that seasoned managers use financial statements in modern businesses
has guided our selection of learning objectives and content. At the same time, our
teaching approach recognizes that students using this book have no previous exposure
to accounting and financial statements and often little exposure to the business world.
The book also is aimed at helping you learn how to learn by teaching efficient and
effective approaches for learning the material.

We begin this process with a brief but comprehensive overview of the four basic
financial statements and the people and organizations involved in their preparation
and use. This overview provides you with a context in which you can learn the more
detailed material that is presented in the following chapters. We begin our discussion
by returning to the Maxidrive acquisition. In particular, we focus on how two primary
users of the statements, investors (owners) and creditors (lenders), relied on each of
Maxidrive's four basic financial statements in their ill-fated decisions to buy and lend
money to Maxidrive. Later in the chapter, we begin to discuss a broader range of uses
of financial statement data in marketing, management, human resources, and other
business contexts.

Business Background

Understanding the Players

Maxidrive was founded by two engineers who had formerly worked for General Data, then a manufacturer of large computers. Predicting the rise in demand for personal computers with a hard disk drive, they started a company specializing in the manufacture of this important computer component (now called Maxidrive Corp.). To start the enterprise, the founders invested a major portion of their savings, becoming the sole owners of Maxidrive. As is common in new businesses, the founders also functioned as the managers of the business (they were *owner-managers*).

The founders soon discovered that they needed additional money to develop the business. Based on the recommendation of a close friend, they turned to American Bank to borrow money. Maxidrive has borrowed from others over the years, but American Bank continued to lend to Maxidrive as the need arose, becoming its largest lender, or *creditor*. Early last year, one of the founders of the business became gravely ill. This event, plus the stresses of operating in their highly competitive industry, led the founders to search for a buyer for their company. In January of this year, they struck a deal for the sale of the company to the company's *new owners*, Exeter Investors, a small group of wealthy private investors. Both founders retired and a new manager was hired to run Maxidrive for the new owners. The new *manager* had formerly worked for another company owned by Exeter but was not an owner of the company.

Owners (often called *investors* or *stockholders*)—whether they are groups such as Exeter who recently bought all of Maxidrive Corp. or individuals who buy small percentages of large corporations—make their purchases hoping to gain in two ways. They hope to sell them in the future at a higher price than they paid and/or receive a portion of what the company earns in the form of cash payments called *dividends*. As the Maxidrive case suggests, not all companies increase in value or have sufficient cash to pay dividends. *Creditors*—whether they are individuals, business organizations, or financial institutions such as banks—lend money to a company for a specific length of time. They hope to gain by charging interest on the money they lend. As American Bank, Maxidrive's major creditor, has learned, some borrowers are not able to repay their debts.

Understanding the Business Operations

To understand any company's financial statements, you must first understand its operations. As noted above, Maxidrive designs and manufactures hard disk drives for personal computers. The major parts that go into the drive include the disks on which information is stored, the motors that spin the disks, the heads that read and write to the disks, and the computer chips that control the operations of the drive. Maxidrive purchases the disks and motors from other companies, referred to as *suppliers*. It designs and manufactures the heads and chips and then assembles the drives. Maxidrive does not sell disk drives directly to the public. Instead, its *customers* are computer manufacturers such as IBM and Apple Computer, which install the drives in machines they sell to retailers (businesses that sell to consumers) such as Computerland. Thus, Maxidrive is a supplier to IBM and Apple.

The hard disk drive business is very competitive. Maxidrive competes with much larger drive companies by investing a great deal of money in developing new and improved drives. It uses robots in its factory to keep labor costs low and ensure product

Accounting is a system that collects and processes (analyzes, measures, and records) financial information about an organization and reports that information to decision makers.

quality. Among the employees working for Maxidrive are 36 engineers and technical staff who work in research and development to develop new disk drives.

Like all businesses, Maxidrive has an **accounting** system that collects and processes (analyzes, measures, and records) financial information about an organization and reports that information to decision makers. Maxidrive's managers (often called *internal decision makers*) and parties outside the firm such as investors like the managers at Exeter Investors and the loan officer at American Bank (often called *external decision makers*) use reports produced by this system. Exhibit 1.1 outlines the two parts of the accounting system. Internal managers typically require continuous detailed information because they must plan and manage the day-to-day operations of the organization. Developing accounting information for internal decision makers is called *managerial* or *management accounting* and is the subject of a separate accounting course. The focus of this text is accounting for external decision makers, called *financial accounting*, and the four basic financial statements and related disclosures that are the output of that system.

To determine the type of information reported in each statement, we now examine the financial statements that Maxidrive's former owner-managers presented to Exeter. Then we test what you have learned by trying to correct the errors in each of the statements and discuss the implications of the errors for Maxidrive's value. Finally, we discuss the ethical and legal responsibilities of various parties for those errors.

Reflecting Business Operations in Financial Statements

LEARNING OBJECTIVE 1
Recognize the information conveyed in the four basic financial statements and the way that it is used by different decision makers (investors, creditors, and managers).

Both Exeter Investors (Maxidrive's new owner) and American Bank (Maxidrive's largest creditor) used Maxidrive's financial statements to learn more about the company before making their purchase and lending decisions. In doing so, Exeter and American Bank assumed that the statements accurately represented Maxidrive's financial condition. As they soon learned and now have claimed in their lawsuits, however, the statements were in error. Maxidrive had (1) on its *balance sheet* overstated the economic resources it owned and understated its obligations to others, (2) on its *income statement* overstated its ability to sell goods for more than the costs to produce and sell them, and (3) on its *cash flow statement* overstated its ability to generate from those

---

EXHIBIT 1.1
The Accounting System and Decision Makers

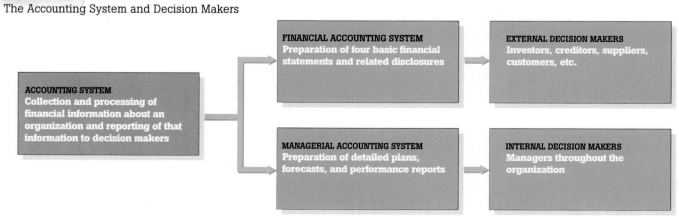

sales the cash necessary to meet its current debts. These three financial statements and the *retained earnings statement* are the four basic statements normally prepared by profit-making organizations for external reporting to owners, potential investors, creditors, and other decision makers.

The four basic statements summarize the financial activities of the business. They can be prepared at any point in time (such as the end of the year, quarter, or month) and can apply to any time span (such as one year, one quarter, or one month). Like most companies, Maxidrive prepares financial statements for investors and creditors at the end of each quarter (known as *quarterly reports*) and at the end of the year (known as *annual reports*).

To understand the way that Exeter Investors used financial statements in its decision and the way it was misled, we must first understand what specific information is presented in the four basic financial statements for a company such as Maxidrive. Essential to this process is an emphasis on learning the *definitions* of key business and accounting terms that we rely on throughout the book and the key *relationships* among the terms used in financial statements. As is common with other professions, the terminology of accounting is technical because precision is necessary. In this chapter, we provide general definitions of these key terms; for certain key accounting terms, we add more detail to the definitions in later chapters.

Overview

We present many new business and financial statement terms in this next section. Since so many terms will be new to you, the material that follows may seem overwhelming at first. This will be particularly true if you try to memorize the definitions of every term used in this chapter. Remember that the purpose of this overview is to provide a general context for the more detailed discussions that follow. Try to focus your attention on learning the general structure and content of the statements. Specifically, you should focus on these questions:

1. What categories of items (often called *elements*) are reported on each of the four statements? This will tell you what types of information the statements convey and where you as a statement reader can find each type.
2. How are the elements within a statement related? These relationships usually are described by an equation that tells you how the elements fit together.
3. Why are each of the elements important to an owner's or creditor's decisions? This will provide you with a general idea of how important financial statement information is to decision makers.

To provide feedback, we will test your ability to answer these questions in the *Self-Study Quizzes*, which occur throughout the chapter. After you complete the quizzes, you may check your answers against the solution provided in a footnote. If you are still unclear about any of the answers, you should refer back to the chapter material preceding the quiz before moving on.

The terms that are critical to understanding the answers to these questions are highlighted in bold print and repeated in the margins. You should pay special attention to the definitions of these terms. To be sure that you understand each definition, we repeat these key terms at the end of the chapter. If you are unsure of the definitions of other terms, please refer to the glossary at the back of the book. Also remember that since this chapter is an overview, each concept discussed here will be discussed again in chapters 2 through 5.

The Balance Sheet

We can learn a great deal about what the balance sheet reports just by reading the statement from the top. The balance sheet of Maxidrive Corp., presented by its former owners to Exeter Investors, is presented in Exhibit 1.2. Notice that the *heading* specifically identifies four significant items related to the statement:

1.	*the name of the entity*	**Maxidrive Corp.**

> An **accounting entity** is the organization for which financial data are to be collected.

Accounting requires a precise definition of the specific organization for which financial data are to be collected. When the organization is defined, it is called an **accounting entity.** For measurement purposes, the resources, debts, and activities of the entity are kept separate from those of the owners and other entities. This focus is called the *separate-entity assumption.*[1] The business entity itself, not the business owners, is viewed as owning the economic resources it uses and as owing its debts.

2.	*the title of the statement*	**Balance Sheet**

> A **balance sheet (statement of financial position)** reports the financial position (assets, liabilities, and stockholders' equity) of an accounting entity at a point in time.

The purpose of the **balance sheet** is to report the financial position (assets, liabilities, and stockholders' equity) of an accounting entity at a point in time. Therefore, the balance sheet is sometimes called the **statement of financial position.** The meaning of financial position will become more evident when we read the body of the statement.

3.	*the specific date of the statement*	**At December 31, 19A**

The heading of each statement indicates the *time dimension* of the report. The balance sheet is like a financial snapshot indicating the entity's financial position *at a specific point in time*—in this case, December 31, 19A—which is stated clearly on the balance sheet. Note that this book often uses the convention "19A" for the first year, "19B" for the second, and so forth. Thus, the sequence of years 19A, 19B, and 19C can be thought of as equivalent to any three-year sequence such as 1997, 1998, and 1999.

4.	*unit of measure*	**(in thousands of dollars)**

Companies normally prepare reports denominated in the major currency of the country in which they are located, in this case U.S. dollars. Similarly, Canadian companies report in Canadian dollars and Mexican companies in pesos. Medium-sized companies such as Maxidrive and much larger companies such as Wal-Mart often report in thousands of dollars; that is, the last three digits are rounded to the nearest thousand. As a result, the listing of Cash $4,895 actually means $4,895,000. After the statement heading, the three elements reported on a balance sheet are listed—assets, liabilities, and stockholders' equity.

Assets

Maxidrive lists five items under the category Assets:

Cash	$4,895	*the amount of cash in the company's bank accounts*
Accounts receivable	5,714	*amounts owed by customers from prior sales*
Inventories	8,517	*parts and completed but unsold disk drives*
Plant and equipment	7,154	*factories and production machinery*
Land	981	*land on which the factories are built*

---

[1] The separate-entity assumption is used for all types of business entities (corporations as well as sole proprietorships and partnerships, which we discuss later in the chapter).

EXHIBIT 1.2
Balance Sheet

MAXIDRIVE CORP.			
Balance Sheet			*name of the entity*
At December 31, 19A			*title of the statement*
(in thousands of dollars)			*specific date of the statement*
			unit of measure
ASSETS			
Cash		$ 4,895	*the amount of cash in the company's bank accounts*
Accounts receivable		5,714	*amounts owed by customers from prior sales*
Inventories		8,517	*parts and completed but unsold disk drives*
Plant and equipment		7,154	*factories and production machinery*
Land		981	*land on which the factories are built*
Total assets		$27,261	
LIABILITIES			
Accounts payable	$7,156		*amounts owed to suppliers for prior purchases*
Notes payable	9,000		*amounts owed on written debt contracts*
Total liabilities		$16,156	
STOCKHOLDERS' EQUITY			
Contributed capital	$2,000		*amounts invested in the business by stockholders*
Retained earnings	9,105		*past earnings not distributed to stockholders*
Total stockholders' equity		11,105	
Total liabilities and stockholders' equity		$27,261	

The notes are an integral part of these financial statements.

These items called *assets* are the probable (expected) future economic benefits owned by the entity as a result of past transactions. The exact items listed as assets on a company's balance sheet depend on the nature of its operations. The five items listed by Maxidrive are the economic resources needed to manufacture and sell disk drives to companies such as IBM. Each of these economic resources is expected to provide

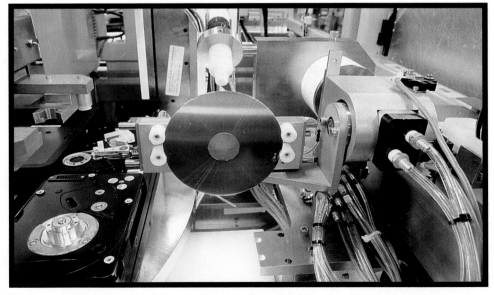

Maxidrive owns equipment necessary for the production of its disk drives. Which financial statement reports equipment?

future benefits to the firm. To prepare to manufacture the drives, Maxidrive first needed *cash* to purchase *land* on which to build factories and install production machinery (*plant and equipment*). Maxidrive then began purchasing parts and producing disk drives, which led to the balance assigned to *inventories*. When Maxidrive sells its disk drives to IBM and others, it sells them on credit and receives promises to pay called *accounts receivable*, which are collected in cash later. Maxidrive lists as cash the amount of cash in its bank accounts on the balance sheet date, which it will use to pay its own bills.

Every asset is initially measured on the balance sheet by the total cost incurred to acquire it. For example, the balance sheet for Maxidrive reports Land, $981; this is the amount paid (in thousands) for the land when it was acquired. Even if the market value of the land increases, the balance sheet reports the land at its *original acquisition cost* (this is called the *cost principle*). Balance sheets *do not purport to show the current market value* of the assets listed. If Maxidrive attempted to sell the land, it might receive more or less than the amount listed.

Financial
ANALYSIS

Interpreting Assets on the Balance Sheet

Assessment of Maxidrive's assets was important to its creditor, American Bank, and to its prospective investor, Exeter, because assets provide a basis for judging whether sufficient resources are available to operate the company. Assets also are important because they could be sold for cash in the event that Maxidrive goes out of business. As indicated, however, if the assets were sold, there is no assurance that the amount listed on the balance sheet would be the amount received from the sale. Some unsophisticated users of financial statements do not understand this point and can easily misinterpret the financial position of a business.

Liabilities and Stockholders' Equity

Maxidrive's balance sheet next lists its liabilities and stockholders' equity. They are the sources of financing or claims against the company's economic resources. Financing provided by creditors creates a liability. Financing provided by owners creates owners' equity. Since Maxidrive is a corporation, its owners' equity is designated as *stockholders' equity*.[2] Since the acquisition of each asset must have a source of financing, a company's assets must, by definition, always be equal to the company's liabilities and stockholders' equity. This **basic accounting equation**, often called the **balance sheet equation**, is restated here:

Basic accounting equation (balance sheet equation): Assets = Liabilities + Stockholders' Equity.

Assets	=	Liabilities + Stockholders' Equity
Economic Resources (e. g., cash, inventory)		Sources of financing for the economic resources Liabilities: From creditors Stockholders' Equity: From stockholders

---

[2] A corporation is a business that is incorporated under the laws of a particular state. The owners are called *stockholders* or *shareholders*. Ownership is represented by shares of capital stock that usually can be bought and sold freely. The corporation operates as a separate legal entity, separate and apart from its owners. The stockholders enjoy limited liability; they are liable for the debts of the corporation only to the extent of their investments. Chapter Supplement A discusses forms of ownership in more detail.

The basic accounting equation shows what we mean when we refer to the company's *financial position*, the economic resources that the company owns and the sources of financing for those resources.

Under the category Liabilities, Maxidrive lists two items:

Accounts payable	$7,156	*amounts owed to suppliers for prior purchases*
Notes payable	9,000	*amounts owed on written debt contracts*

Liabilities are probable (expected) debts or obligations of the entity that result from past transactions and will be paid with assets or services in the future. They arise primarily from the *purchase of goods or services* on credit and through *cash borrowings* to finance the business.

Many businesses purchase goods and services from their suppliers on credit without a formal written contract (a note). For example, for the disk drives it produces, Maxidrive purchases electric motors from Magnalite, Inc. This transaction creates a liability known as *accounts payable*. Since there is no formal written contract, such purchases are often described as being on *open account*. The amount of accounts payable listed by Maxidrive includes all of its debts to suppliers on open account.

Business entities often borrow money, primarily from lending institutions such as banks, by entering into a formal written debt contract. In this case, a liability called *notes payable* is created. A note payable specifies an amount to be repaid, a definite maturity or payment date, and the rate of interest charged by the lender. The amount listed as Maxidrive's notes payable ($9,000,000) is owed to American Bank, is due in five years, and also requires a yearly (annual) interest payment of 5 percent of the debt every December 31 (5% × $9,000,000 = $450,000).

Interpreting Liabilities on the Balance Sheet

Maxidrive's existing debts were relevant to American Bank's decision to lend it money because these existing creditors share American Bank's claim against Maxidrive's assets. If a business does not pay its creditors, the law may give the creditors the right to force the sale of assets sufficient to meet their claims. If Maxidrive does not find another source of funds to pay its debts, American Bank and its other creditors will likely take this action. Exeter Investors also was interested in information concerning Maxidrive's debts because of its concern for whether the company had sufficient sources of cash to pay its debts.

Stockholders' equity indicates the amount of financing provided by owners of the business and operations. Stockholders' equity comes from two sources: (1) *contributed capital*, the investment of cash and other assets in the business by the owners, and (2) *retained earnings*, the amount of accumulated earnings kept in the business and thus not distributed to owners in the form of dividends.

In Exhibit 1.2, the Stockholders' Equity section reports the following:

Contributed capital	$2,000	*amounts invested in the business by stockholders*
Retained earnings	9,105	*past earnings not distributed to stockholders*

The two founding stockholders of Maxidrive invested a total of $2,000,000 in the business. Each stockholder received 10,000 shares of capital stock (20,000 shares in total). They invested an average price of $100 per share ($2,000,000 ÷ 20,000 shares). It should be noted that the amounts in contributed capital on Maxidrive's balance sheet did not change when the two founding stockholders sold their shares to Exeter Investors since the transaction did not involve an additional contribution of cash or other assets to Maxidrive. This transaction, which took place between Maxidrive's original owners and Exeter, occurred outside of the accounting entity Maxidrive and thus was not recorded by its accounting system.

The accumulated amount of earnings (or losses incurred) less all dividends paid to the stockholders since formation of the corporation is reported as *retained earnings*. Thus, retained earnings includes the portion of earnings not distributed to owners. The computation is reported on the retained earnings statement discussed later. Total stockholders' equity of $11,105,000 equals the sum of the original owners' investment ($2,000,000) plus the retained earnings ($9,105,000).

Interpreting Shareholders' Equity on the Balance Sheet

The basic accounting equation (Assets = Liabilities + Stockholders' Equity) shows that stockholders' equity is equal to total assets minus total liabilities of the business. Stockholders' equity sometimes is called *net worth*. The amount of total stockholders' equity or net worth of Maxidrive is important to American Bank because creditors' claims legally come before those of owners. This is important if Maxidrive goes out of business and its assets are sold. In those circumstances, the proceeds of that sale must be used to pay back creditors such as American Bank before the owners receive any money. Thus, stockholders' equity is considered a "cushion" that protects creditors should the entity go out of business. When Exeter Investors was considering buying Maxidrive, it also looked at stockholders' equity. Recall, however, that the amount recorded on the balance sheet for assets (called the *book value*) could be more or less than the current prices for those assets (called *market value*). As a consequence, Exeter knew that the amount of stockholders' equity did not represent the market value of the company as a whole to its owners.

A Note on Format

A few additional formatting conventions are worth noting here. Assets are listed on the balance sheet by ease of conversion to cash. Liabilities are listed by their maturity (due date). Most financial statements include the monetary unit sign (in the United States, the $) beside the first dollar amount in a group of items (e.g., the cash amount in the assets). Also, it is common to place a single underline below the last item in a group (e.g., land). A dollar sign is also placed beside group totals (e.g., total assets) and a double underline below. The same conventions are followed in all four basic financial statements. We will discuss alternative balance sheet formats in more detail in Chapter 5.

SELF-STUDY QUIZ

1. Maxidrive's *assets* are listed in one section and *liabilities* and *stockholders' equity* in another. Notice that the two sections balance in conformity with the basic accounting equation. In the following chapters, you will learn that the basic accounting equation is the basic building block for the entire accounting process. Your task here is to verify that the stockholders' equity of $11,105,000 is correct using the numbers for assets and liabilities presented in Exhibit 1.2 and the basic accounting equation in the form

$$\text{Assets} - \text{Liabilities} = \text{Stockholders' Equity}$$

2. Learning which items belong in each of the balance sheet categories is an important first step in understanding their meaning. Mark each balance sheet item in the following list as an asset (A), liability (L), or stockholders' equity (SE), without referring to Exhibit 1.2.

_____	Accounts payable	_____	Inventories
_____	Accounts receivable	_____	Land
_____	Cash	_____	Notes payable
_____	Contributed capital	_____	Retained earnings
_____	Plant and equipment		

After you have completed your answers, check them with the solutions presented at the bottom of this page.*

The Income Statement

A quick reading of Maxidrive's income statement also indicates a great deal about its purpose and content. The income statement of Maxidrive Corp. is presented in Exhibit 1.3. The heading of the income statement again specifically identifies the name of the entity, the title of the report, and unit of measure used in the statement. Unlike the balance sheet, however, which reports as of a certain date, the income statement reports for a *specified period of time* (for the year ended December 31, 19A). The time period covered by the financial statements (one year in this case) is called an **accounting period**.

The **income statement (statement of income, statement of earnings, or statement of operations)** reports the accountant's primary measure of performance of a business, the revenues less the expenses of the accounting period. The term *profit* is used widely in our language for this measure of performance, but accountants prefer to use the

The **accounting period** is the time period covered by the financial statements.
The **income statement (statement of income, statement of earnings, or statement of operations)** reports the revenues less the expenses of the accounting period.

EXHIBIT 1.3
Income Statement

MAXIDRIVE CORP.
Income Statement
For the Year Ended December 31, 19A
(in thousands of dollars)

Revenues			
Sales revenue	$37,436		*revenue earned from sale of disk drives*
Total revenues		$37,436	
Expenses			
Cost of goods sold expense	26,980		*cost to produce disk drives sold*
Selling, general, and administrative expense	3,624		*operating expenses not directly related to production*
Research and development expense	1,982		*expenses incurred to develop new products*
Interest expense	450		*cost of using borrowed funds*
Total expenses		33,036	
Pretax income		4,400	
Income tax expense		1,100	*income taxes on period's pretax income*
Net income		$ 3,300	

The notes are an integral part of these financial statements.

* 1. Assets ($27,261,000) – Liabilities ($16,156,000) = Stockholders' Equity ($11,105,000).
  2. L, A, A, SE, A, A, A, L, SE.

technical terms *net income* or *net earnings*. Maxidrive's net income measures its success in selling disk drives for more than it cost to generate those sales.

Notice that Maxidrive's income statement has three major captions: *revenues*, *expenses*, and *net income*.[3] The income statement equation that describes their relationships is

$$\text{Net Income} = \text{Revenues} - \text{Expenses}$$

Revenues

Revenues are earned from the sale of goods or services to customers (in Maxidrive's case, its sale of disk drives). They are defined as inflows of assets or reductions of liabilities from ongoing operations (sales to customers). Revenues normally are reported on the income statement when the goods or services are sold to the customer who has either paid for them or promised to pay in the future. When a business sells goods or renders services, it may receive cash immediately. This is a rare occurrence, however, with the exception of retail stores such as Wal-Mart or McDonald's. Goods or services are normally sold on credit. When Maxidrive sells its disk drives to IBM and Apple Computer, it receives a promise of future payment called an *account receivable*, which later is collected in cash. In either case, the business recognizes total sales (cash and credit) as revenue for the period. *Revenue is normally reported in the period in which goods and services are sold. This may be different from the period in which cash is received since customers sometimes pay before or after the sale.* Revenue is measured in dollars as the cash-equivalent price agreed on by the two parties to the transaction. Various terms are used in financial statements to describe different sources of revenue (e.g., provision of services, sale of goods, rental of property). Maxidrive lists only one, *sales revenue*, for disk drives delivered to customers.

Expenses

Maxidrive lists five items as expenses on its income statement. *Expenses* represent the dollar amount of resources the entity used up to earn revenues during a period of time. Expenses are defined as the outflows of assets or increases in liabilities from ongoing operations. *Cost of goods sold expense* is the total cost to Maxidrive to produce the disk drives delivered to customers during the year. These include the costs of parts used in production, wages paid to the factory workers, and even a portion of the cost of the factories and equipment used to produce the goods that were sold (called *depreciation*). *Selling, general, and administrative expense* (also called *operating expenses*) includes a wide variety of expenses, such as the salaries of management, the sales staff, the internal company accountants and other general costs of operating the company not directly related to production.

Maxidrive is a high-technology company and must constantly spend money developing new products to keep ahead of competitors. These costs are listed as *research and development expense*. Maxidrive also reported *interest expense* for one year on the $9,000,000, 5 percent note payable to American Bank ($9,000,000 × 5% = $450,000), which was outstanding for all of 19A. Finally, as a corporation, Maxidrive must pay income tax at a 25 percent rate on pretax income.[4] Therefore, Maxidrive incurred *income tax expense* of $1,100,000 (pretax income of $4,400,000 × 25%).

---

[3] Other less commonly occurring elements of the income statement are discussed in later chapters.

[4] Federal tax rates for corporations actually ranged from 15 percent to 35 percent at the time this book was written. State and local governments may levy additional taxes on corporate income, resulting in a higher total income tax rate.

Expenses may require the immediate payment of cash, a payment of cash in a later period, or the use of some other resource such as an inventory item, which may have been paid for in a previous period. For accounting purposes, *the period in which an expense is reported on the income statement is the period in which goods and services are used to earn revenues. This is not necessarily the period in which cash is paid for the expense item.* The expense reported in one accounting period may be paid for in another accounting period.

Net Income

Net income or net earnings (often called *profit* or *the bottom line* by nonaccountants) is the excess of total revenues over total expenses. If the total expenses exceed the total revenues, a net loss is reported. (Net losses are normally noted by parentheses around the income figure.) When revenues and expenses are equal for the period, the business has operated at breakeven. Alternative formats for the income statement are discussed in Chapter 5.

We noted earlier that revenues are not necessarily the same as collections from customers and expenses are not necessarily the same as payments to suppliers. As a result, net income is normally not equal to the net cash generated by operations. This latter amount is reported on the cash flow statement discussed later in the chapter.

Analyzing the Income Statement: Beyond the Bottom Line

Financial
ANALYSIS

Investors such as Exeter and creditors such as American Bank closely monitor a firm's net income because it indicates the ability to sell goods and services for more than they cost to produce and deliver. The details of the statement also are important. For example, Maxidrive had to sell more than $37 million worth of disk drives to make just over $3 million. The disk drive industry is very competitive. If Maxidrive is forced to match a competitor that lowers prices just 10 percent or if Maxidrive needs to triple research and development to catch up to a competitor's innovative new product, its net income could easily turn into a net loss.

SELF-STUDY QUIZ

1. Learning which items belong in each of the income statement categories is an important first step in understanding their meaning. Mark each income statement item in the following list as a revenue (R) or an expense (E) without referring to Exhibit 1.3.

    _____ Cost of goods sold   _____ Sales
    _____ Research and development   _____ Selling, general, and administrative

2. During the period 19A, Maxidrive delivered disk drives to customers for which the customers paid or promised to pay in the future amounts totaling $37,436,000. During the same period, it collected $33,563,000 in cash from its customers. Without referring to Exhibit 1.3, indicate which of the two numbers will be shown on Maxidrive's income statement as *sales revenue* for 19A. Why did you select your answer? _____

    _____

3. During the period 19A, Maxidrive *produced* disk drives with a total cost of production of $27,130,000. During the same period, it *delivered* to customers disk drives that had cost a total of $26,980,000 to produce. Without referring to Exhibit 1.3, indicate which of the two numbers will be shown on Maxidrive's income statement as *cost of goods sold expense* for 19A. Why did you select your answer?

_____

_____

After you have completed your answers, check them with the solutions presented at the bottom of this page.*

Statement of Retained Earnings

The **statement of retained earnings** reports the way that net income and the distribution of dividends affected the financial position of the company during the accounting period. As we discussed in our look at the balance sheet, two major factors cause changes in retained earnings. The earning of net income during the year increases the balance of retained earnings, showing the relationship of the income statement to the balance sheet. The declaration of dividends to the stockholders decreases retained earnings.[5] The retained earnings equation that describes these relationships is

Ending Retained Earnings = Beginning Retained Earnings + Net Income – Dividends

Maxidrive prepares a separate statement of retained earnings, shown in Exhibit 1.4, which explains changes to the retained earnings balance that occurred during the year. Other corporations report these changes at the end of the income statement or in a more general statement of stockholders' equity, which we discuss in Chapter 4. Like the income statement, the statement of retained earnings reports for a specified period of time (the accounting period), which in this case is one year. It begins with Maxidrive's beginning-of-the-year *retained earnings*. The current year's *net income* reported on the income statement is added and the current year's *dividends* are subtracted from this amount.

During 19A, Maxidrive earned $3,300,000, as shown on the income statement (Exhibit 1.3). This amount was added to the beginning-of-the-year retained earnings in computing end-of-the-year retained earnings. A cash *dividend* pays an equal amount for each share of stock outstanding. During 19A, Maxidrive declared and paid a total of $1,000,000 in dividends to its two original stockholders. This amount was subtracted in computing end-of-the-year retained earnings on the balance sheet. The ending retained earnings amount is the same as that reported in Exhibit 1.2 on the Maxidrive balance sheet. Thus, the retained earnings statement indicates the relationship of the income statement to the balance sheet.

---

*1. E, E, R, E. 2. Sales revenue in the amount of $37,436,000 is recognized because sales revenue is normally reported on the income statement when the goods or services have been delivered to the customer who has either paid or promised to pay for them in the future. 3. Cost of goods sold expense is $26,980,000 because expenses are the dollar amount of resources used up to earn revenues during the period. Only those disk drives delivered to customers are used up. Those disk drives still on hand are part of the asset inventory.

[5] Net losses are subtracted. The complete process of declaring and paying dividends is discussed in a later chapter.

EXHIBIT 1.4
Statement of Retained Earnings

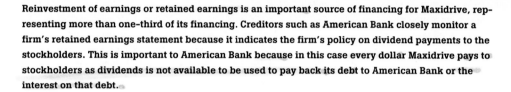

MAXIDRIVE CORP. Statement of Retained Earnings For the Year Ended December 31, 19A (in thousands of dollars)		*name of the entity* *title of the statement* *accounting period* *unit of measure*
Retained earnings, January 1, 19A	$6,805	*last period's ending retained earnings*
Net income for 19A	3,300	*net income reported on the income statement*
Dividends for 19A	(1,000)	*dividends declared during the period*
Retained earnings, December 31, 19A	$9,105	*ending retained earnings on the balance sheet*

The notes are an integral part of these financial statements.

Interpreting Retained Earnings

Financial
ANALYSIS

Reinvestment of earnings or retained earnings is an important source of financing for Maxidrive, representing more than one-third of its financing. Creditors such as American Bank closely monitor a firm's retained earnings statement because it indicates the firm's policy on dividend payments to the stockholders. This is important to American Bank because in this case every dollar Maxidrive pays to stockholders as dividends is not available to be used to pay back its debt to American Bank or the interest on that debt.

Statement of Cash Flows

Maxidrive's statement of cash flows is presented in Exhibit 1.5. As discussed earlier in this chapter, reported revenues do not always equal cash collected from customers because some sales may be on credit. Also, expenses reported on the income statement may not be equal to the cash paid out during the period because expenses may be incurred in one period and paid for in another. As a result, net income (revenues minus expenses) is usually *not* the amount of cash received minus the amount paid out during the period. In fact, many successful companies may earn large amounts of income and still have to borrow more money from the bank because they do not have

Maxidrive overstated the amount of cash that was generated by the sales of hard drives and other products. Think about how this affects the statement of cash flows.

EXHIBIT 1.5
Statement of Cash Flows

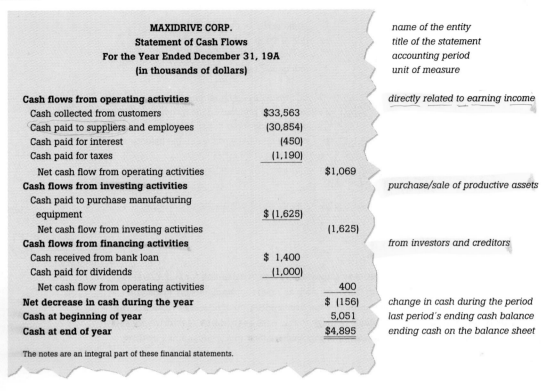

MAXIDRIVE CORP. Statement of Cash Flows For the Year Ended December 31, 19A (in thousands of dollars)			
Cash flows from operating activities			*directly related to earning income*
Cash collected from customers	$33,563		
Cash paid to suppliers and employees	(30,854)		
Cash paid for interest	(450)		
Cash paid for taxes	(1,190)		
Net cash flow from operating activities		$1,069	
Cash flows from investing activities			*purchase/sale of productive assets*
Cash paid to purchase manufacturing equipment	$ (1,625)		
Net cash flow from investing activities		(1,625)	
Cash flows from financing activities			*from investors and creditors*
Cash received from bank loan	$ 1,400		
Cash paid for dividends	(1,000)		
Net cash flow from operating activities		400	
Net decrease in cash during the year		$ (156)	*change in cash during the period*
Cash at beginning of year		5,051	*last period's ending cash balance*
Cash at end of year		$4,895	*ending cash on the balance sheet*

name of the entity
title of the statement
accounting period
unit of measure

The notes are an integral part of these financial statements.

The **statement of cash flows** reports inflows and outflows of cash during the accounting period in the categories of operations, investing, and financing.

sufficient cash to meet their other obligations. Because the income statement does not provide any information concerning cash flows, accountants prepare the **statement of cash flows** to report inflows and outflows of cash in the categories of operations, investing, and financing. Like the income statement, the cash flow statement reports for a specified period of time (the accounting period), which in this case is one year. Many bankers consider this the most important statement they use to estimate whether companies can afford to pay their debts.

The statement divides Maxidrive's cash inflows and outflows (receipts and payments) into the three primary categories of cash flows in a typical business. *Cash flows from operating activities* are cash flows directly related to earning income (normal business activity including *interest paid* and *income taxes paid*). For example, when IBM, Apple Computer, and other *customers* pay Maxidrive for disk drives that have previously been delivered, the amounts collected are listed as cash collected from customers. When Maxidrive pays salaries to its 36 *employees* involved in research and development or pays bills received from its parts *suppliers*, the amounts are included in cash paid to suppliers and employees. Alternative ways to present cash flows from operations are discussed in Chapter 5.

Cash flows from investing activities include cash flows related to the acquisition or sale of productive assets used by the company. This year, Maxidrive had only one cash outflow from investing activities, the *purchase of additional manufacturing equipment* to meet growing demand for its products. *Cash flows from financing activities* are directly related to the financing of the enterprise itself. They involve receipt or payment of money to investors and creditors (except for suppliers). This year, Maxidrive *borrowed* an additional $1,400,000 from the bank to purchase most of the new manufacturing equipment. It also paid out $1,000,000 in *dividends* to the founding stockholders before the company was sold.

The cash flow statement equation describes the causes of the change in cash reported on the balance sheet from the end of last period to the end of the current period:

> Change in Cash = Cash Flows from Operating Activities
> + Cash Flows from Investing Activities
> + Cash Flows from Financing Activities

Note that each of the three cash flow sources can be positive or negative.

Interpreting the Cash Flow Statement

Many analysts believe that the statement of cash flows is particularly useful for predicting future cash flows that may be available for payment of debt to creditors and dividends to investors. Each section provides analysts with important information. Bankers often consider the operating activities section most important because it indicates the company's ability to generate cash from sales to meet current cash needs. Any amount left can be used to pay back the bank debt or expand the company.

Stockholders will invest in a company only if they believe that it will eventually generate more cash from operations than it uses because only this cash is available to pay dividends in the long run. The investing section tells us that Maxidrive is making heavy investments in new manufacturing capacity to meet the increasing demand for its products. This is a good sign if demand continues to increase. As the financing section indicates, however, if Maxidrive is not able to sell more drives, it may have trouble meeting the payments that the new bank debt will require.

FOCUS ON CASH FLOWS

SELF-STUDY QUIZ

1. During the period 19A, Maxidrive delivered disk drives to customers that paid or promised to pay in the future amounts totaling $37,436,000. During the same period, it collected $33,563,000 in cash from its customers. Without referring to Exhibit 1.5, indicate which of the two numbers will be shown on Maxidrive's cash flow statement for 19A. _____

2. Learning which items belong in each cash flow statement category is an important first step in understanding their meaning. Mark each item in the following list as a cash flow from operating activities (O), investing activities (I), or financing activities (F), without referring to Exhibit 1.5. Also place parentheses around the letter only if it is a cash *outflow*.

    _____ Cash paid for dividends
    _____ Cash paid for interest
    _____ Cash received from bank loan
    _____ Cash paid for taxes
    _____ Cash paid to purchase manufacturing equipment
    _____ Cash paid to suppliers and employees
    _____ Cash collected from customers

After you have completed your answers, check them with the solutions presented at the bottom of this page.*

---

* 1. $33,563,000 is recognized on the cash flow statement because this number represents the actual cash collected from customers related to current and prior years' sales. 2. (F), (O), F, (O), (I), (O), O.

Notes

At the bottom of each of Maxidrive's four basic financial statements is this statement: *"The notes are an integral part of these financial statements."* This is the accounting equivalent of the Surgeon General's warning on a package of cigarettes. It warns users that failure to read the **notes** (or **footnotes**) to these financial statements will result in an incomplete picture of the company's financial health. Footnotes provide supplemental information about the financial condition of a company, without which the financial statements cannot be fully understood.

There are three basic types of notes. The first type provides descriptions of the accounting rules applied in the company's statements. The second presents additional detail about a line on the financial statements. For example, Maxidrive's inventory note indicates the amount of parts, drives under construction, and finished disk drives included in its total inventory amount listed on the balance sheet. The third type of note presents additional financial disclosures about items not listed on the statements themselves. For example, Maxidrive leases one of its production facilities; terms of the lease are disclosed in a note. We will discuss many note disclosures throughout the book because understanding their content is critical to understanding the company.

Notes (footnotes) provide supplemental information about the financial condition of a company, without which the financial statements cannot be fully understood.

Management Uses of Financial Statements

In our discussion of financial analysis thus far, we have focused on the perspectives of *investors* and *creditors*. In addition, managers within the firm often make direct use of financial statements. For example, Maxidrive's *marketing managers* and *credit managers* use customers' financial statements to decide whether to extend them credit for their purchases of disk drives. Maxidrive's *purchasing managers* analyze parts suppliers' financial statements. This allows them to judge whether the suppliers have the resources necessary to meet Maxidrive's current demand for parts and to invest in the development of new parts in the future. Both the *employees' union* and Maxidrive's *human resource managers* use Maxidrive's financial statements as a basis for contract negotiations in determining what pay rates the company can afford. The net income figure even serves as a basis to pay *bonuses* not only to management but also to all employees through the profit-sharing plan. Regardless of the functional area of management in which you are employed, you will *use* financial statement data. You also will be *evaluated* based on the impact of your decisions on your company's financial statement data. Learning financial accounting now will benefit you in the future.

The Fraud

Correcting the Errors

We next look at the errors that Exeter Investors later found in Maxidrive's statements to see whether we have learned enough to make the necessary corrections. Then we discuss the responsibilities of various parties in the financial reporting process for the information in these financial statements. The article that began the chapter continues as follows:

Maxidrive Corp.

Among Exeter's claims are that:

1. Disk drives available for sale (part of inventories) included $1 million of obsolete drives that could not be sold and must be scrapped.

2. **Reported sales to customers (and accounts receivable) for last year included $700,000 of overstatements. Maxidrive had cut the price of a certain type of disk drive by 40 percent. But Maxidrive personnel had created fake customer bills (called *invoices*) with the old higher prices to support these sales amounts.**
3. **Maxidrive had included in the amounts collectible from customers for last year's sales (accounts receivable) $500,000 owed by now bankrupt companies.**

These three items together significantly overstate on the balance sheet the economic resources owned by Maxidrive (its assets) and overstate on the income statement Maxidrive's ability to sell goods for more than the cost of production (its net income).

For purposes of our discussion, we focus on these effects on the income statement because they were most relevant to Exeter Investors' evaluation of Maxidrive. The simplest way to determine the effects of these three errors on the income statement is to use the income statement equation we have just examined in this chapter. As we indicated earlier, one of the keys to understanding financial statements is to learn the elements of each of the basic financial statements and their relationships, which are represented in the basic equations. The top line in Exhibit 1.6 presents the income statement equation, followed by the amounts reported in Maxidrive's 19A income statement. Following them is each of the three errors that were subsequently discovered and the correction necessary to eliminate the effect of each error.

Correcting the three errors, in total, reduces pretax income to $2,200,000. After we subtract 25 percent for income tax expense, we are left with a corrected net income equal to $1,650,000, just *half* of the amount Maxidrive initially reported.

Determining the Purchase Price for Maxidrive

Even at this early stage of your study of accounting, we can provide some examples of the process Exeter Investors went through to determine the price it was willing to pay for Maxidrive Corp. This is a particularly interesting case for analysis because Exeter Investors has claimed that the financial statements it used to estimate the value of Maxidrive were in error. The price Exeter paid was decided by considering a variety of factors including the value of the economic resources owned by Maxidrive, its debts to

EXHIBIT 1.6
Correction of the Income Statement Amounts (in thousands of dollars)

	Revenues	−	Expenses	=	Pretax Income
As presented on Maxidrive's 19A income statement	$37,436		$33,036		$4,400
Record expense for scrapping obsolete inventory			1,000		(1,000)
Reduce sales revenue by amount of overstatement	(700)				(700)
Record expense for uncollectible amounts			500		(500)
After correction of errors	$36,736		$34,536		$2,200

Item 1: Since the obsolete inventory items are held for sale, but now have no value, their cost should be added to this year's expenses. Accordingly, expenses should decrease by $1,000,000.

Item 2: This involved recording the sales price of a certain type of disk drive at an amount too high, and, thus, total sales revenue is too high. Its correction requires a reduction of $700,000 of revenues.

Item 3: The $500,000 of accounts receivable that will not be paid (bad debts) is no longer an asset or economic resource of Maxidrive. Like the first item, this is an added expense of $500,000.

others, its ability to sell goods for more than their production cost, and its ability to generate the cash necessary to pay its current bills. As we have now learned, these factors are the subject matter of financial statements: balance sheet, income statement, and cash flow statement.

Maxidrive's current and prior years' income statements played a particularly important part in Exeter's evaluation. Prior years' income statements (which were not presented to you) indicated that the company had earned income every year since its founding, except for the first year of operations. Many new companies do not become profitable this quickly. Further, both sales revenue and net income had been rising rapidly every year. One method for estimating the value of a company is with a *price/earnings ratio* (or *multiplier*).[6]

$$\text{Price/Earnings} = \frac{\text{Market Price}}{\text{Net Earnings}}$$

A key to Exeter's decision was the fact that other companies in the same industry with similar performance and growth were selling for 12 times their current year's earnings. Accordingly, the opportunity to buy Maxidrive for 10 times its current earnings seemed to be an excellent one, particularly since economic forecasts suggested that the next five years would see continuing growth and profitability for disk drive manufacturers. The key calculation that determined the price Exeter paid was

$$\text{Purchase Price} = 10 \times \text{Net Income}$$
$$\$33,000,000 = 10 \times \$3,300,000$$

The number 10 in the formula is called the *price/earnings multiplier*. Using the same formula, the corrected net income figure suggests a much lower price for Maxidrive.

$$\$16,500,000 = 10 \times \$1,650,000$$

A difficult part of this analysis is deciding what price/earnings multiplier is appropriate for this situation. Exeter carefully considered this issue, and its analysis involved more than this simple formula. However, it provides a very real first approximation of Exeter's loss—a $16.5 million overpayment. This is the amount that Exeter hopes to recover from those responsible for the fraudulent financial statements it relied on in its analysis.

Responsibilities for the Accounting Communication Process

LEARNING OBJECTIVE 2
Identify the role of generally accepted accounting principles (GAAP) in determining the content of financial statements.

Effective communication means that the recipient understands what the sender intends to convey. Communication involves problems in understanding the words, symbols, and sounds used by the parties involved. Accounting uses words and symbols to communicate financial information that is relevant to decision makers. For the decision makers at Exeter to use the information in Maxidrive's financial statements effectively, they had to understand what information each of the statements conveys. This is the reason that we began our discussion with the content of the four basic financial statements, yet the fraud suggests that this understanding is not sufficient.

---

[6] Note that this ratio can be computed on a per share basis with the same number resulting:

$$\text{Price/Earnings} = \frac{\text{Market Price per Share}}{\text{Net Earnings per Share}}$$

Decision makers also needed to understand the *measurement rules* applied in computing the numbers on the statements, and they needed to know that the numbers in the statements represented what was claimed. The first point is a simple one in concept: a swim coach would never try to evaluate a swimmer's time in the 100 freestyle without first asking if the time was for a race in meters or in yards. Likewise, a decision maker should never attempt to use accounting information without first understanding the measurement rules that were used to develop the information. These measurement rules are called **generally accepted accounting principles**, or **GAAP**. The second point is equally important in concept: numbers that do not represent what they claim to are meaningless. For example, if the balance sheet lists $2,000,000 for a factory that does not exist, that part of the statement does not convey useful information. Actually developing a system of measurement rules for complex business transactions (GAAP) and a system for ensuring that statements fairly represent what they claim (called *auditing*) is much more complicated, however, as the Maxidrive fraud suggests.

Generally accepted accounting principles (GAAP) are the measurement rules used to develop the information in financial statements.

Generally Accepted Accounting Principles

How Are Generally Accepted Accounting Principles Determined?

As the preceeding discussion suggests, we must understand the measurement rules used to develop the information in the statements to understand the numbers in them. The accounting system that we use today has a long history. Its foundations are normally traced back to the works of an Italian monk and mathematician, Fr. Luca Pacioli. In 1494, he described an approach developed by Italian merchants to account for their activities as owner-managers of business ventures. Although many others wrote works on accounting after Pacioli, prior to 1933, financial reporting practices were largely determined by each company's management. Thus, little uniformity in practice existed among companies.

The Securities Act of 1933 and The Securities Exchange Act of 1934 were passed into law by the U.S. Congress in response to the dramatic stock market decline of 1929. Part of these securities acts created the **Securities and Exchange Commission (SEC)** and gave it broad powers to determine the measurement rules for financial statements that companies must provide to stockholders. Contrary to popular belief, these rules are different from those that companies follow when filing their income tax returns. We discuss these differences further in later chapters.

The Securities and Exchange Commission (SEC) is the U.S. government agency that determines the financial statements that public companies must provide to stockholders and the measurement rules that they must use in producing those statements.

Since its establishment, the SEC has worked with organizations of professional accountants to establish groups that are given the primary responsibilities to work out the detailed rules that become generally accepted accounting principles. The name of the current group that has this responsibility is the **Financial Accounting Standards Board (FASB)**. The Board has seven full-time voting members and a permanent staff who consider the appropriate financial reporting responses to ever-changing business practices. As of the date of publication of this book, the official pronouncements of the FASB (*Financial Accounting Standards*) and its predecessors total more than 2,500 pages of very fine print. Such detail is made necessary by the enormous diversity and complexity of current business practices.

The Financial Accounting Standards Board (FASB) is the private sector body given the primary responsibility to work out the detailed rules that become generally accepted accounting principles.

Stock of *privately held* corporations such as Maxidrive is owned by small groups of individuals and is not available for sale to the public at large. Like all prospective purchasers of shares of privately held companies, Exeter had to negotiate directly with the current owners to arrange the purchase. The stock of some corporations such as Maxidrive's largest customers, Apple Computer and IBM, and other well-known companies such as General Motors, Wal-Mart, and McDonald's is *publicly traded*. This means that it can be bought and sold by investors on established stock exchanges (organized markets for stocks) such as the New York Stock Exchange. The SEC sets additional financial reporting requirements that only publicly traded companies must follow. We introduce some of these additional requirements later in the book.

Most managers do not need to learn all of the details included in these standards. Our approach is to focus on those details that have the *greatest impact on the numbers presented in financial statements* and are appropriate for a course at this level.

Why Do Managers, Accountants, and Users Care What Is Generally Accepted?

You can be sure that what is included in generally accepted accounting principles (GAAP) is of great interest to the companies that must prepare the statements, to auditors, and to the readers of the statements. *Companies and their managers and owners are most directly affected by the information presented in the statements and for that reason express the most interest.* Companies incur the cost of preparing the statements and bear the major economic consequences of their publication. These economic consequences include, among others, *potential*

1. Effects on the selling price of a company's stock.
2. Effects on the amount of bonuses received by management and employees.
3. Loss of competitive advantage over other companies.

Recall that the amount that Exeter was willing to pay to purchase Maxidrive was determined in part by net income computed under GAAP. This presents the possibility that changes in GAAP can affect the price buyers are willing to pay for companies, either to the benefit or the detriment of the current owners. The business press often suggests this possibility. Regardless of the validity of these claims, the owners and managers (who are obligated to make money for owners) are concerned by these occurrences.

Managers and other employees often receive part of their pay based on reaching stated targets for net income. As a result, they are directly concerned with any changes in how net income is computed under GAAP. For example, *USA Today* cited the fact that the chairman of Ford Motor Company did not receive his annual bonus one year because of a slump in auto sales.

Managers and owners also often are concerned that publishing more information in financial statements will disclose the details of their successes and failures, which will help similar companies compete with them. Claims are even made that more detailed U.S. accounting requirements make it more difficult for U.S. companies to compete with international competitors that operate in countries with less revealing accounting rules.

As a consequence of these and other concerns, changes in GAAP are actively debated, and the use of political muscle and lobbying often takes place. For example, owners and managers who were concerned about a proposed change in accounting for management pay let their elected representatives in government know about their concerns. In response, numerous senators and the Secretary of the Treasury sent letters to the FASB opposing this proposed change in GAAP. The result was a modification of the proposal which was reported in the following *Accounting Today* headline:

REAL WORLD EXCERPT

Accounting Today

POLITICS KILLS FASB STOCK OPTIONS PLAN

Norwalk, Conn.—Ending a decade of study and more than two years of increasingly acrimonious opposition, the Financial Accounting Standards Board has dropped its plan forcing companies to charge executive stock options against earnings.

SOURCE: *Accounting Today*, January 2–15, 1995, p. 1.

Are Generally Accepted Accounting Principles Similar in Other Countries?

While business people compete in a single global economy, different sets of generally accepted accounting principles have developed within particular countries. Differences in political, cultural, and economic histories have produced a great number of cross-national differences in practice. These differences can have dramatic effects on the numbers presented in the financial statements. For example, Daimler-Benz, the manufacturer of Mercedes Benz automobiles, recently began preparing two sets of financial statements for the same accounting period, one using German standards and one using U.S. standards. *The Wall Street Journal* reported the following:

REAL WORLD EXCERPT

The Wall Street Journal

DAIMLER-BENZ REPORTS FIRST EVER LOSS, REFLECTING NEW ACCOUNTING . . .

Stuttgart, Germany—Daimler-Benz AG, bound by a new set of strict U.S. disclosure rules, was forced to report its first loss since World War II.

The loss wouldn't have appeared in the German auto concern's six-month profit and loss account without the stringent standards imposed by the U.S. Securities and Exchange Commission, Daimler officials said. . . . Daimler swung to a 949 million mark ($592 million) group net loss under the U.S. system in the first half. . . . Under Germany's less transparent rules, the company showed a small profit. . . .

Source: *The Wall Street Journal*, September 20, 1993, p. A10.

The International Accounting Standards Board and others are attempting to eliminate these differences. But for now, managers and users of financial statements who cross national borders must be aware of the specific nature of these reporting differences to interpret financial statements successfully. Although our primary focus is on U.S. GAAP, we briefly discuss practice in other countries when appropriate.

International companies must accommodate differences in GAAP. Visit this text's home page at http://www.mhhe.com/business/ accounting/libby to view the Daimler-Benz financial statement.

Management Responsibility and the Demand for Auditing

LEARNING OBJECTIVE 3
Distinguish the roles of managers and auditors in the accounting communication process.

Exeter's owners and managers were well aware of the details of U.S. GAAP, but they were still misled. Although the measurement rules that Maxidrive had used to produce its financial statements were consistent with GAAP, the underlying figures in the accounting system were fictitious; that is, they did not fairly represent reality. Any measurement system applied to underlying facts that do not match reality will produce unrepresentative measures. Who is responsible for the accuracy of the numbers in Maxidrive's financial statements? Two documents taken from Maxidrive's annual report provide us with much of the answer to this question.

The **report of management** indicates management's primary responsibility for financial statement information and the steps to ensure the accuracy of the company's records.

The **report of management,** shown in Exhibit 1.7, makes two points clear. First, primary responsibility for the information in the financial statements lies with management, as represented by the highest officer of the company and the highest officer involved with the financial side of the company. Second, the managers take three important steps to ensure the accuracy of the company's records: (1) they maintain a system of controls over both the records and assets of the company, (2) they hire outside independent auditors to verify the fairness of the statement presentations, and (3) they have a committee of the board of directors whose job it is to review these other two safeguards. These safeguards failed in the case of Maxidrive, and those primarily responsible, whether directly involved or not, are listed in the report of management.

The **report of independent accountants (audit report)** describes the auditors' opinion of the fairness of the financial statement presentations and the evidence gathered to support that opinion.

The role of the independent auditor is described in more detail in the second report (Exhibit 1.8), the **report of independent accountants** or **audit report,** which describes the auditor's opinion of the fairness of the financial statement presentations and the evidence gathered to support that opinion. An accountant may be licensed as a *certified public accountant*, or *CPA*. This designation is granted only on completion of

EXHIBIT 1.7
Report of Management

Report of Management

The management of Maxidrive is responsible for preparing the financial statements and other information contained in this annual report. Management believes that the financial statements fairly reflect, in all material respects, the form and substance of events and transactions and that the financial statements present the Company's financial position and results of operations in conformity with generally accepted accounting principles. Management has included in the Company's financial statements amounts that are based on informed judgments and estimates, which it believes are reasonable under the circumstances.

Maxidrive maintains a system of internal accounting policies, procedures and controls intended to provide reasonable assurance, at appropriate cost, that transactions are processed in accordance with Company authorization and are properly recorded and reported in the financial statements, and that assets are adequately safeguarded.

Smith and Walker, CPAs, the Company's independent auditing firm, audits the Company's financial statements in accordance with generally accepted auditing standards, which provide the basis of its report on the financial statements.

The Board of Directors of the Company has an Audit Committee composed of nonmanagement directors. The Committee meets with financial management and the independent auditors to review internal accounting controls and accounting, auditing, and financial reporting matters. In addition, Smith and Walker, CPAs, has full and free access to the Audit Committee, without management present, to discuss the results of its audits, the adequacy of the company's internal accounting controls, and the quality of its financial reporting.

Harold T. West

Harold T. West
President and Chairman of the Board

Robert P. Malony

Robert P. Malony
Chief Financial Officer

requirements specified by each state. Other accountants can offer various accounting services to the public, but only a licensed CPA can issue an audit report. In this role, accountants are known as *independent CPAs* (or *independent accountants*) because they have certain responsibilities that extend to the general public in addition to those to the specific business that pays for the services. Independent CPAs, although paid by their clients, are not employees of their clients.

An **audit** involves the examination of the financial reports (prepared by the management of the entity) to ensure that they represent what they claim and conform with generally accepted accounting principles (GAAP). In performing an audit, the independent CPA examines the underlying transactions, including the collection, classification, and assembly of the financial data incorporated in the financial reports. To appreciate the magnitude of these responsibilities, consider the enormous number of transactions involving a major enterprise such as General Motors that total billions of dollars each year. The CPA does not examine each of these transactions, however; rather, professional approaches are used to ascertain beyond reasonable doubt that transactions were measured and reported properly. Many unintentional and, as we have learned in the Maxidrive case, intentional opportunities exist to prepare misleading financial reports. The audit function performed by an independent CPA is the best protection available to the public. When that protection fails, however, the independent CPA is often found liable for losses incurred by those who rely on the statements.

An **audit** is an examination of the financial reports to ensure that they represent what they claim and conform with generally accepted accounting principles.

Ethics, Reputation, and Legal Liability

If financial statements are to be of any value to decision makers, users must have confidence in the fairness of the information. These users will have greater confidence in the information if they know that the people who were associated with auditing the financial statements were required to meet professional standards of ethics and competence.

LEARNING OBJECTIVE 4
Appreciate the importance of ethics, reputation, and legal liability in accounting.

EXHIBIT 1.8
Report of Independent Accountants

Report of Independent Accountants
To the Stockholders and Board of Directors of Maxidrive Corp.

We have audited the accompanying balance sheet of Maxidrive Corp. as of December 31, 19A, and the related statements of income, retained earnings and cash flows for the period ended December 31, 19A. These financial statements are the responsibility of the Company's management. Our responsibility is to express an opinion on these financial statements based on our audits.

We conducted our audits in accordance with generally accepted auditing standards. Those standards require that we plan and perform the audit to obtain reasonable assurance about whether the financial statements are free of material misstatement. An audit includes examining, on a test basis, evidence supporting the amounts and disclosures in the financial statements. An audit also includes assessing the accounting principles used and significant estimates made by management, as well as evaluating the overall financial statement presentation. We believe that our audits provide a reasonable basis for our opinion.

In our opinion, the financial statements referred to above present fairly, in all material respects, the financial position of Maxidrive Corp. at December 31, 19A, and the results of its operations and its cash flows for the period ended December 31, 19A, in conformity with generally accepted accounting principles.

Smith and Walker
Smith and Walker, CPAs

The American Institute of Certified Public Accountants (AICPA) requires all of its members to adhere to a professional code of ethics. These broad principles are supported by specific rules that govern the performance of audits by members of the AICPA. Failure to comply with the rules of conduct can result in serious professional penalties. The potential economic effects of damage to reputation and malpractice liability, however, provide even stronger incentives to abide by professional standards.

CPAs' reputations for honesty and competence are their most important assets. If the Smith and Walker firm is found to be either negligent or dishonest in the audit of Maxidrive, American Bank and other lenders will refuse to lend money based on statements that firm has audited, and the firm's other clients will quickly choose new auditors. Financial statement fraud is a fairly rare event, due in part to the diligent efforts of practicing CPAs. In fact, many such frauds are first identified in the course of the annual audit. Even the most diligent audit, however, may not immediately uncover the results of fraud involving collusion of the top officers of a corporation, such as occurred with Maxidrive.

In case of malpractice in the audit function, the independent CPA is subject to potential liability that may extend to all parties (whether known to the CPA or not) who have suffered loss because they relied on financial statements examined by the CPA. Even if Smith and Walker was unaware that Exeter was using the statements as input to its decision to buy Maxidrive, if the CPAs' failure to detect the errors in the statements was a result of their malpractice, they could be liable for Exeter's loss.

As a result of the fraud, Maxidrive filed for bankruptcy and will likely be sold in an attempt to pay off creditors. Exeter Investors and American Bank claimed losses of $16.5 million and $9 million, respectively, in a civil lawsuit. It claimed that the officers of Maxidrive had "perpetrated a massive fraud" and the auditors had "overlooked the errors" in the audit.[7] Exeter and American Bank also have asked for punitive damages for gross negligence. The president and the chief financial officer of Maxidrive are under indictment by a federal grand jury for three counts of criminal securities fraud for which they face possible fines and prison terms.

Epilogue

Although financial statement fraud is a fairly rare event, the misrepresentations in Maxidrive's statements aptly illustrate the importance of fairly presented financial statements to investors and creditors. It also depicts the crucial importance of the public accounting profession in ensuring the integrity of the financial reporting system. As noted at the beginning of the chapter, Maxidrive is not a real company but is based on a real company that perpetrated a similar fraud.[8] The focus companies and contrasting examples in the remaining chapters are *real* companies except when indicated.

Maxidrive is loosely based on the infamous MiniScribe fraud. The size of the real fraud, however, was more than *10 times* as great as that in the fictional case, as were the losses incurred and the amounts in the lawsuits that followed. (Many of the numbers in the financial statements are simply one-tenth the amounts presented in MiniScribe's fraudulent statements.) The nature of the fraud also was quite similar. At

---

[7] Even some accountants are confused about the auditor's responsibility to detect fraud. *Statement on Auditing Standards No. 82*, "Consideration of Fraud in a Financial Statement Audit" (and the earlier rules in *SAS No. 53*), requires that auditors design tests to ensure detection of fraud that materially affects financial statements. The statement notes, however, that no audit can guarantee the discovery of sophisticated collusive fraud.

[8] None of the names of individuals in the case are real.

MiniScribe, sales revenue was overstated by transferring nonexistent inventory between two of MiniScribe's own facilities and creating phony documents to make it look as though the inventory were transferred to customers. MiniScribe even packaged *bricks* as finished products, shipped them to distributors, and counted them as sold. Cost of goods sold was understated by activities such as counting scrap parts and damaged drives as usable inventory. Further, members of management even broke into the auditors' locked trunks to change numbers on their audit papers. As a consequence, MiniScribe reported net income of $31 million, which was subsequently shown to be $9 million. Prior years' statements contained similar errors. MiniScribe's investors and creditors filed lawsuits asking for more than $1 billion in damages. Actual damages in the hundreds of millions were paid. Both the chairman and the chief financial officer of MiniScribe were convicted of federal securities and wire fraud charges and sentenced to jail. Although most managers and owners act in an honest and responsible fashion, this incident is a stark reminder of the economic consequences of lack of fair presentation in financial reports. Sales revenue and inventory frauds to this day are the most frequently occurring financial statement frauds.[9]

Demonstration Case

At the end of most chapters, one or more demonstration cases are presented. These cases provide an overview of the primary issues discussed in the chapter. Each demonstration case is followed by a recommended solution. You should read the case carefully and then prepare your own solution before you study the recommended solution. This self-evaluation is highly recommended.

The introductory case presented here helps you to start thinking in financial statement terms of some of the resource inflows and outflows of a business.

ABC Service Corporation was organized by Able, Baker, and Cain on January 1, 19A. On that date, the investors exchanged $36,000 cash for all of the stock of the company. On the same day, the corporation borrowed $10,000 from a local bank and signed a three-year, 15 percent note payable. The interest is payable each December 31. On January 1, 19A, the corporation purchased service supplies for $20,000 cash. Operations started immediately.

At the end of 19A, the corporation had completed the following additional business transactions (summarized):
(a) Performed services and billed customers for $100,500, of which $94,500 was collected in cash by year-end.
(b) Used up $5,000 of service supplies while rendering services.
(c) Paid $54,000 cash for other service expenses.
(d) Paid $1,500 in annual interest expense on the note payable.
(e) Paid all income taxes in cash to the Internal Revenue Service (IRS). (The income tax rate was 20 percent.)

Required:
Complete the following two 19A financial statements by entering the correct amounts. The suggested solution follows the blank statements.

---

[9] *Fraud Survey Results 1993*, KPMG Peat Marwick, 1993.

ABC SERVICE CORPORATION
Income Statement
_____ (date)
(in dollars)

		Computation
Revenues		
Service revenue	$ 100 500	
Expenses		
Service expenses	$ 59000	54 + 5
Interest expense	1500	
Total expenses	60 500	
Pretax income	40 000	
Income tax expense	8000	
Net income	$ 32000	

ABC SERVICE CORPORATION
Balance Sheet
_____ (date)
(in dollars)

		Computation
ASSETS		
Cash	$ 57000 ·	+36 +10 −20 + 94.5
		−54 − 1.5 − 8
Accounts receivable	6000	100,500 − 94,500
Service supplies	15000	20 − 5
Total assets	$ 78000	
LIABILITIES		
Note payable (15%)	$ 10000	
Total liabilities	$ 10000	
STOCKHOLDERS' EQUITY		
Contributed capital	$ 36000	
Retained earnings	32000.	
Total stockholders' equity	68 000	
Total liabilities and stockholders' equity	$ 78000	

Suggested Solution

ABC SERVICE CORPORATION
Income Statement
For the Year Ended December 31, 19A
(in dollars)

			Computation
Revenues			
Service revenue		$100,500	Given (cash & on open account)
Expenses			
Service expenses	$59,000		$54,000 cash + $5,000 supplies
Interest expense	1,500		$10,000 × 15%
Total expenses		60,500	
Pretax income		40,000	
Income tax expense		8,000	$40,000 × 20%
Net income		$ 32,000	

ABC SERVICE CORPORATION
Balance Sheet
at December 31, 19A
(in dollars)

			Computation
ASSETS			
Cash		$57,000	$36,000 + $10,000 + $94,500 −
			$54,000 − $1,500 − $8,000 − $20,000
Accounts receivable		6,000	$100,500 − $94,500
Service supplies		15,000	$20,000 − $5,000
Total assets		$78,000	
LIABILITIES			
Note payable (15%)	$10,000		Given, bank loan
Total liabilities		$10,000	
STOCKHOLDERS' EQUITY			
Contributed capital	$36,000		Given
Retained earnings	32,000		From income statement
Total stockholders' equity		68,000	
Total liabilities and stockholders' equity		$78,000	

Summary

The four basic financial statements are the balance sheet, the income statement, the statement of retained earnings, and the statement of cash flows.

The *balance sheet* is a statement of financial position that reports dollar amounts for the assets, liabilities, and stockholders' equity at a specific point in time.

The *income statement* is a statement of operations that reports revenues, expenses, and net income for a stated period of time.

The *statement of retained earnings* explains changes to the retained earnings balance that occurred during the reporting period.

The *statement of cash flows* reports inflows and outflows of cash for a specific period of time.

The financial statements and the parties to the accounting communication process were illustrated in the context of the purchase of a disk drive company that published fraudulent financial statements. In the next four chapters, we look more closely at financial statements, specifically, the process of preparing them and their use in business decision making. You will learn to analyze business transactions using the basic accounting equations to determine exactly how the results of your future business decisions will be reflected in financial statements. You also will begin learning how to examine other companies' financial statements to draw inferences about the quality of the decisions their managers made. This is the heart of financial statement analysis. The accounting equation for the balance sheet, *Assets = Liabilities + Stockholders' Equity,* is the foundation for the entire accounting process and the understanding of financial statements.

   In this chapter, we studied the basic financial statements that communicate financial information to external users. Chapters 2, 3, and 4 will provide a more detailed look at financial statements and examine how to translate data about business transactions into these statements. Learning how to translate back and forth between business transactions and financial statements is the key to using financial statements in planning and decision making. Chapter 2 will begin our discussion of the way that the accounting function collects data about business transactions and processes the data to provide periodic financial statements, with emphasis on the balance sheet. To accomplish this purpose, Chapter 2 will discuss key accounting concepts, the accounting model, transaction analysis, and analytical tools. We will examine typical business activities of an actual service-oriented company to demonstrate the concepts in Chapters 2, 3, and 4.

Chapter Supplement A

TYPES OF BUSINESS ENTITIES

This textbook emphasizes *accounting for profit-making business entities*. The three main types of business entities are sole proprietorship, partnership, and corporation. A *sole proprietorship* is an unincorporated business owned by one person; it usually is small in size and is common in the service, retailing, and farming industries. Often the owner is the manager. Legally, the business and the owner are not separate entities. Accounting views the business as a separate entity, however, that must be accounted for separately from its owner.

A *partnership* is an unincorporated business owned by two or more persons known as *partners*. Some partnerships are large in size (e.g., international public accounting firms and law firms). The agreements between the owners are specified in a partnership contract. This contract deals with matters such as division of income each reporting period and distribution of resources of the business on termination of its operations. A partnership is not legally separate from its owners. Legally, each partner in a general partnership is responsible for the debts of the business (each general partner has *unlimited liability*). The partnership, however, is a separate business entity to be accounted for separately from its several owners.

A *corporation* is a business incorporated under the laws of a particular state. The owners are called *stockholders* or *shareholders*. Ownership is represented by shares of capital stock that usually can be bought and sold freely. When an approved application for incorporation is filed by the organizers, the state issues a charter. This charter gives the corporation the right to operate as a separate legal entity, separate and apart from its owners. The stockholders enjoy *limited liability*. Stockholders are liable for the corporation's debts only to the extent of their investments. The corporate charter specifies the types and amounts of capital stock that can be issued. Most states require a minimum of two or three stockholders and a minimum amount of resources to be contributed at the time of organization. The stockholders elect a governing board of directors, which in turn employs managers and exercises general supervision of the corporation. Accounting also views the corporation as a separate business entity that must be accounted for separately from its owners.

In terms of economic importance, the corporation is the dominant form of business organization in the United States. This dominance is caused by the many advantages of the corporate form: (1) limited liability for the stockholders, (2) continuity of life, (3) ease in transferring ownership (stock), and (4) opportunities to raise large amounts of money by selling shares to a large number of people. The primary disadvantage of a corporation is that its income may be subject to double taxation (it is taxed when it is earned and again when it is distributed to stockholders as dividends). In this textbook, we emphasize the corporate form of business. Nevertheless, the accounting concepts and procedures that we discuss also apply to other types of businesses.

Chapter Supplement B

EMPLOYMENT IN THE ACCOUNTING PROFESSION TODAY

Since 1900, accounting has attained the stature of professions such as law, medicine, engineering, and architecture. As with all recognized professions, accounting is subject to professional competence requirements, is dedicated to service to the public, requires a high level of academic study, and rests on a common body of knowledge. An accountant may be licensed as a certified public accountant, or CPA. This designation is granted only on completion of requirements specified by the state that issues the license. Although CPA requirements vary among states, they include a college degree with a specified number of accounting courses, good character, one to five years of professional experience, and successful completion of a professional examination. The CPA examination, scheduled in each state simultaneously on a semiannual basis, is prepared by the American Institute of Certified Public Accountants.

Accountants (including CPAs) commonly are engaged in professional practice or are employed by businesses, government entities, nonprofit organizations, and so on. Accountants employed in these activities may take and pass a professional examination to become a certified management accountant, or CMA (the CMA examination is administered by the Institute of Management Accountants), or a certified internal auditor, or CIA (the CIA examination is administered by the Institute of Internal Auditors).

Practice of Public Accounting

Although an individual may practice public accounting, usually two or more individuals organize an accounting firm in the form of a partnership (in many cases, a limited liability partnership or LLP). Accounting firms vary in size from a one-person office, to regional firms, to the Big Six firms (Arthur Andersen & Co., Coopers and Lybrand, Deloitte & Touche, Ernst & Young, KPMG Peat Marwick, and Price Waterhouse), which have hundreds of offices located worldwide. Accounting firms usually render three types of services: auditing, management consulting services, and tax services.

Auditing

The most important service performed by the CPA in public practice is *auditing*, the attest function. The purpose of an audit is to lend credibility to the financial reports, that is, to ensure that they fairly represent what they claim. An audit involves an examination of the financial reports (prepared by the management of the entity) to ensure that they conform with generally accepted accounting principles (GAAP).

Management Consulting Services

Many independent CPA firms offer *management consulting services*. These services usually are accounting based and encompass such activities as the design and installation of accounting, data processing, and profit-planning and control (budget) systems; financial advice; forecasting; inventory controls; cost-effectiveness studies; and operational analysis. This facet of public CPA practice is growing rapidly.

Tax Services

CPAs in public practice usually provide income tax services to their clients. These services include both tax planning as a part of the decision-making process and the determination of the income tax liability (reported on the annual income tax return). Because of the increasing complexity of state and federal tax laws, a high level of competence is required, which CPAs specializing in taxation can provide. The CPA's involvement in tax planning often is quite significant. Most major business decisions have significant tax impacts; in fact, tax-planning considerations often govern certain business decisions.

Employment by Organizations

Many accountants, including CPAs, CMAs, and CIAs, are employed by profit-making and nonprofit organizations. An organization, depending on its size and complexity, may employ from a few to hundreds of accountants. In a business enterprise, the chief financial officer (usually a vice president or controller) is a member of the management team. This responsibility usually entails a wide range of management, financial, and accounting duties.

In a business entity, accountants typically are engaged in a wide variety of activities, such as general management, general accounting, cost accounting, profit planning and control (budgeting), internal auditing, and computerized data processing. A primary function of the accountants in organizations is to provide data that are useful for internal managerial decision making and for controlling operations. The functions of external reporting, tax planning, control of assets, and a host of related responsibilities normally are also performed by accountants in industry.

Employment in the Public and Not-for-Profit Sector

The vast and complex operations of governmental units, from the local to the international level, create a need for accountants. The same holds true for other not-for-profit organizations such as hospitals and universities. Accountants employed in the public and not-for-profit sector perform functions similar to those performed by their counterparts in private organizations. The General Accounting Office (GAO) and the regulatory agencies, such as the Securities and Exchange Commission (SEC) and Federal Communications Commission (FCC), also use the services of accountants in carrying out their regulatory duties.

Key Ratios

Price/earnings ratio (price/earnings multiplier) measures the relationship between current market price of a company and its net earnings and is a measure of expected company growth. It is computed as follows (p. 22):

$$\text{Price/Earnings} = \frac{\text{Market Price}}{\text{Net Earnings}}$$

Key Terms

Accounting A system that collects and processes (analyzes, measures, and records) financial information about an organization and reports that information to decision makers. *6*

Accounting Entity The organization for which financial data are to be collected (separate and distinct from its owners). *8*

Accounting Period The time period covered by the financial statements. *13*

Audit An examination of the financial reports to ensure that they represent what they claim and conform with generally accepted accounting principles. *27*

Balance Sheet (Statement of Financial Position) A statement that reports the financial position (assets, liabilities, and stockholders' equity) of an accounting entity at a point in time. *8*

Basic Accounting Equation (Balance Sheet Equation) Assets = Liabilities + Stockholders' Equity. *10*

Financial Accounting Standards Board (FASB) The private sector body given the primary responsibility to work out the detailed rules that become generally accepted accounting principles. *23*

Generally Accepted Accounting Principles (GAAP) The measurement rules used to develop the information in financial statements. *23*

Income Statement (Statement of Income, Statement of Earnings, or Statement of Operations) A statement that reports the revenues less the expenses of the accounting period. *13*

Notes (Footnotes) Supplemental information about the financial condition of a company, without which the financial statements cannot be fully understood. *20*

Report of Independent Accountants (Audit Report) A report that describes the auditors' opinion of the fairness of the financial statement presentations and the evidence gathered to support that opinion. *26*

Report of Management A report that indicates management's primary responsibility for financial statement information and the steps taken to ensure the accuracy of the company's records. *26*

Securities and Exchange Commission (SEC) The U.S. government agency that deter-

mines the financial statements that public companies must provide to stockholders and the measurement rules that they must use in producing those statements. *23*

Statement of Cash Flows A statement that reports inflows and outflows of cash during the accounting period in the categories of operations, investing, and financing. *18*

Statement of Retained Earnings A statement that reports the way that net income and the distribution of dividends affected the financial position of the company during the accounting period. *16*

Questions

1. Define *accounting*.
2. Briefly distinguish financial accounting from managerial accounting.
3. The accounting process generates financial reports for both internal and external users. Identify some of the groups of users.
4. Briefly distinguish investors from creditors.
5. What is an accounting entity? Why is a business treated as a separate entity for accounting purposes?
6. Briefly explain the importance of assets and liabilities to the decisions of investors and creditors.
7. Financial statements are the end products of the accounting process. Explain.
8. Define *communication*.
9. Complete the following:

	Name of Statement		Alternative Title
a.	Income statement	a.	_____
b.	Balance sheet	b.	_____
c.	Audit report	c.	_____

10. What information should be included in the heading of each of the four primary financial statements?
11. Explain why the income statement and the statement of cash flows are dated "For the Year Ended December 31, 19X," whereas the balance sheet is dated "At December 31, 19X."
12. Briefly define the following: *net income, net loss,* and *breakeven*.
13. What are the purposes of (*a*) the income statement, (*b*) the balance sheet, (*c*) the statement of cash flows, and (*d*) the statement of retained earnings?
14. Explain the accounting equation for the income statement. What are the three major items reported on the income statement?
15. Explain the accounting equation for the balance sheet. Define the three major components reported on the balance sheet.
16. Explain the accounting equation for the statement of cash flows. Explain the three major components reported on the statement.
17. Explain the accounting equation for the statement of retained earnings. Explain the four major items reported on the statement of retained earnings.

18. What are the two primary sources of stockholders' equity in a business?
19. Financial statements discussed in this chapter are aimed at *external* users. Briefly explain how a company's *internal* managers in different functional areas (e.g., marketing, purchasing, human resources) might use financial statement information.
20. Briefly describe the way that accounting measurement rules (generally accepted accounting principles) are determined in the United States.
21. Briefly describe why managers and owners care what measurement methods are generally accepted.
22. Briefly explain the responsibility of company management and the independent auditors in the accounting communication process.
23. (Supplement A) Briefly differentiate between a sole proprietorship, a partnership, and a corporation.
24. (Supplement B) List and briefly explain the three primary services that CPAs in public practice provide.

Exercises

E1–1 Identifying Important Accounting Abbreviations

The following is a list of important abbreviations used in the chapter. These abbreviations also are used widely in business. For each abbreviation give the full designation. The first one is an example.

ABBREVIATION		FULL DESIGNATION
_____	(1) CPA	certified public accountant
_____	(2) GAAP	
_____	(3) CMA	
_____	(4) AICPA	
_____	(5) SEC	
_____	(6) FASB	

E1–2 Matching Definitions with Terms or Abbreviations

Match each definition with its related term or abbreviation by entering the appropriate letter in the space provided.

TERM OR ABBREVIATION		DEFINITION
K	1. SEC	A. A system that collects and processes financial information about an organization and reports that information to decision makers.
G	2. Audit	B. Measurement of information about an entity in the monetary unit—dollars or other national currency.
I	3. Sole proprietorship	C. An unincorporated business owned by two or more persons.
E	4. Corporation	D. The organization for which financial data are to be collected (separate and distinct from its owners).
A	5. Accounting	E. An incorporated entity that issues shares of stock as evidence of ownership.
D	6. Separate entity	F. Initial recording of financial statement elements at acquisition cost.
J	7. Audit report	G. An examination of the financial reports to ensure that they represent what they claim and conform with generally accepted accounting principles.
F	8. Cost principle	
C	9. Partnership	

(These lists continue on the next page.)

_O_ 10. AICPA

_L_ 11. FASB

_H_ 12. CPA

_B_ 13. Unit of measure

_N_ 14. GAAP

_M_ 15. Publicly traded

H. Certified public accountant.

I. An unincorporated business owned by one person.

J. A report that describes the auditors' opinion of the fairness of the financial statement presentations and the evidence gathered to support that opinion.

K. Securities and Exchange Commission.

L. Financial Accounting Standards Board.

M. Company that can be bought and sold by investors on established stock exchanges.

N. Generally accepted accounting principles.

O. American Institute of Certified Public Accountants.

E1–3 Assigning Financial Statement Items to Financial Statement Categories

Procter & Gamble

According to its annual report, "Procter & Gamble markets a broad range of laundry, cleaning, paper, beauty care, health care, food and beverage products in more than 140 countries around the world, with leading brands including Tide, Ariel, Crest, Crisco, Vicks and Max Factor." The following are items taken from its recent balance sheet and income statement. Note that different companies use slightly different titles for the same item. Mark each item in the following list as an asset (A), liability (L), or stockholders' equity (SE) that would appear on the balance sheet or a revenue (R) or expense (E) that would appear on the income statement.

_____ Accounts payable

_____ Accounts receivable

_____ Cash and cash equivalents

_____ Cost of products sold

_____ Property, plant, and equipment

_____ Income taxes

_____ Interest expense

_____ Inventories

_____ Land

_____ Marketing, administrative, and other operating expenses

_____ Long-term debt

_____ Net sales

_____ Notes payable

_____ Retained earnings

_____ Taxes payable

E1–4 Assigning Financial Statement Items to Financial Statement Categories

Tootsie Roll

Tootsie Roll Industries is engaged in the manufacture and sale of candy. Major products include Tootsie Roll, Tootsie Roll Pops, Tootsie Pop Drops, Tootsie Flavor Rolls, Charms, and Blow-Pop lollipops. The following items were listed on Tootsie Roll's recent income statement and balance sheet. Mark each item from the balance sheet as an asset (A), liability (L), or shareholders' equity (SE) and each item from the income statement as a revenue (R) or expense (E).

_____ Accounts payable

_____ Accounts receivable

_____ Cost of goods sold

_____ Distribution and warehousing

_____ Dividends payable

_____ General and administrative

_____ Income taxes payable

_____ Inventories

_____ Investments

_____ Buildings

_____ Cash and cash equivalents

_____ Land

_____ Machinery and equipment

_____ Marketing, selling, and advertising

_____ Net sales

_____ Notes payable to banks

_____ Provision for income taxes*

_____ Retained earnings

*In the United States, "provision for income taxes" is most often used as a synonym for "income tax expense."

E1–5 Using the Income Statement and Balance Sheet Equations

Review the chapter explanations of the income statement and the balance sheet equations. Apply these equations in each independent case following to compute the two missing amounts for each case. Assume that it is the end of 19A, the first full year of operations for the company. (*Hint:* Organize the listed items as they are presented in the equations before computing the amounts.)

Independent Cases	Total Revenues	Total Assets	Total Expenses	Total Liabilities	Net Income (Loss)	Stockholders' Equity
A	$100,000	$150,000	$82,000	$70,000	$	$
B		112,000	80,000		12,000	60,000
C	80,000	104,000	86,000	26,000		
D	50,000			22,000	13,000	77,000
E			81,000	73,000	(6,000)	28,000

E1–6 Analyzing an Income Statement and Price/Earnings Ratio

Pest Away Corporation was organized by three individuals on January 1, 19A, to provide insect extermination services. At the end of 19A, the following income statement was prepared:

PEST AWAY CORPORATION
Income Statement
For the Year Ended December 31, 19A

Revenues		
Service revenue (cash)	$192,000	
Service revenue (credit)	24,000	
Total revenues		$216,000
Expenses		
Salaries expense	$ 76,000	
Rent expense	21,000	
Utilities expense	12,000	
Advertising expense	14,000	
Supplies expense	25,000	
Interest expense	8,000	
Total expenses		156,000
Pretax income		$ 60,000
Income tax expense		21,000
Net income		$ 39,000

Required:
1. What was the average monthly revenue amount?
2. What was the monthly rent amount?
3. Explain why supplies are reported as an expense.
4. Explain why interest is reported as an expense.
5. What was the average income tax rate for Pest Away Corporation?
6. Can you determine how much cash the company had on December 31, 19A? Explain.
7. If the company had a market value of $468,000, what is its price/earnings ratio?

E1–7 Preparing an Income Statement

Assume that you are the owner of The Collegiate Shop, which specializes in items that interest students. At the end of January 19A, you find (for January only) this information:
- (a) Sales, per the cash register tapes, of $120,000, plus one sale on credit (a special situation) of $1,000.

(b) With the help of a friend (who majored in accounting), you determined that all of the goods sold during January had cost $40,000 to purchase.

(c) During the month, according to the checkbook, you paid $38,000 for salaries, rent, supplies, advertising, and other expenses; however, you have not yet paid the $600 monthly utilities for January on the store and fixtures.

Required:

On the basis of the data given, what was the amount of income for January (disregard income taxes)? Show computations. (*Hint*: A convenient form to use has the following major side captions: Revenue from Sales, Expenses, and the difference—Net Income.)

E1–8 Focus on Cash Flows: Matching Cash Flow Statement Items to Categories

Compaq Computer is a leading designer and manufacturer of personal computers. The following items were taken from its recent cash flow statement. Note that different companies use slightly different titles for the same item. Without referring to Exhibit 1.5, mark each item in the list as a cash flow from operating activities (O), investing activities (I), or financing activities (F). Also place parentheses around the letter only if it is a cash outflow.

Compaq Computer

_____ Cash paid to suppliers and employees

_____ Cash received from customers

_____ Income taxes paid

_____ Interest and dividends received

_____ Interest paid

_____ Proceeds from sale of investment in Conner Peripherals, Inc.

_____ Purchases of property, plant, and equipment

_____ Repayment of borrowings

E1–9 Focus on Cash Flows: Analyzing Cash Flows from Operations

Paul's Painters, a service organization, prepared the following special report for the month of January 19A:

Service Revenue, Expenses, and Income		
Service revenue		
Cash services (per cash register tape)	$105,000	
Credit services (per charge bills; not yet		
collected by end of January)	30,500	
		$135,500
Expenses		
Salaries and wages expense (paid by check)	$ 50,000	
Salary for January not yet paid	3,000	
Supplies used (taken from stock, purchased		
for cash during December)	2,000	
Estimated cost of using company-owned		
truck for the month (depreciation)	500	
Other expenses (paid by check)	26,000	81,500
Pretax income		$ 54,000
Income tax expense (not yet paid)		13,500
Income for January		$ 40,500

Required:

1. The owner (who knows little about the financial part of the business) asked you to compute the amount by which cash had increased in January 19A from the operations of the company. You decided to prepare a detailed report for the owner with the following major side captions: Cash Inflows (collections), Cash Outflows (payments), and the difference—Net Increase (or decrease) in Cash.
2. What was the average income tax rate?
3. See if you can reconcile the difference—net increase (or decrease) in cash—you computed in requirement (1) with the income for January 19A.

Wal-Mart

E1–10   Preparing an Income Statement

Wal-Mart Stores, Inc., is the largest retail chain in the United States, operating more than 2,000 stores. Its recent quarterly income statement contained the following items (in thousands). Solve for the missing amounts and prepare a condensed income statement for the quarter ended October 31, 19A.

Cost of sales	$16,200,873
Interest costs	184,190
Net income	?
Net sales	20,417,717
Operating, selling, and general and administrative expenses	3,340,263
Provision for income taxes*	339,422
Rental and other income	235,116
Total costs and expenses	?
Total revenues	?
Pretax income	?

*In the United States, "provision for income taxes" is a common synonym for "income tax expense."

Honda Motor Co.

E1–11   Preparing a Condensed Balance Sheet

Established less than 50 years ago, Honda Motor Co., Ltd. of Japan is a leading international manufacturer of automobiles and the largest manufacturer of motorcycles in the world. As a Japanese company, it follows Japanese GAAP and reports its financial statements in millions of yen (the sign for yen is ¥). Its recent condensed balance sheet contained the following items (in millions). Prepare a condensed balance sheet as of March 31, 19A, solving for the missing amount.

✓Cash and cash equivalents	¥ 150,554
✓Contributed capital	281,208
✓Accounts payable and other current liabilities	1,308,748
✓Inventories	606,689
✓Investments	212,294
✓Long-term debt	569,479
✓Net property, plant, and equipment	1,008,196
✓Other assets	213,845
✓Other liabilities	94,485
Retained earnings	755,419
✓Total assets	3,009,339
Total liabilities and stockholders' equity	?
✓Trade accounts, notes, and other receivables	817,761

E1–12   Preparing an Income Statement and Balance Sheet

Clay Corporation was organized by five individuals on January 1, 19A. At the end of January 19A, the following monthly financial data are available:

Total revenues	$130,000 ✓
Total expenses (excluding income taxes)	80,000 ✓
Cash balance, January 31, 19A	30,000 ✓
Receivables from customers (all considered collectible)	15,000 ✓
Merchandise inventory (by inventory count at cost)	42,000 ✓
Payables to suppliers for merchandise purchased from them (will be paid during February 19A)	11,000 ✓
Contributed capital (2,600 shares)	26,000
No dividends were declared or paid during 19A.	

Assume a 30 percent tax on the income of this corporation is income tax expense (30% × Pretax income); the income taxes will be paid during the first quarter of 19B so they must also be listed as a liability (30% × Pretax income).

Required:

Complete the following two statements:

CLAY CORPORATION
Income Statement
For the Month of January 19A

Total revenues	$ 130,000
Less: Total expenses (excluding income tax)	80
Pretax income	50
Less: Income tax expense (30% × Pretax income)	15
Net income	$ 35

CLAY CORPORATION
Balance Sheet
At January 31, 19A

ASSETS

Cash	$ 30
Receivables from customers	15
Merchandise inventory	42
Total assets	$ 87

LIABILITIES

Payables to suppliers	$ 11
Income taxes payable	15
Total liabilities	26

STOCKHOLDERS' EQUITY

Contributed capital	$ 26
Retained earnings	35
Total liabilities and stockholders' equity	(61)
	$ 87

E1–13 Completing a Balance Sheet

Read More Store was organized as a corporation by Terry Lloyd and Joan Lopez; each contributed $50,000 cash to start the business and received 4,000 shares of common stock. The store completed its first year of operations on December 31, 19A. On that date, the following financial items for the year were determined: December 31, 19A, cash on hand and in the bank, $48,900; December 31, 19A, amounts due from customers from sales of books, $26,000; unused portion of store and office equipment, $48,000; December 31, 19A, amounts owed to publishers for books purchased, $8,000; and a 12%, one-year note payable, dated July 1, 19A, to a local bank for $2,000. No dividends were declared or paid to the stockholders during the year.

Required:
1. Complete the following balance sheet as of the end of 19A.
2. What was the amount of net income for the year?
3. Show how the $120 liability for interest payable was computed. Why is it shown as a liability on this date?

_____

_____

_____

ASSETS		LIABILITIES	
Cash	$ ____	Accounts payable	$ ____
Accounts receivable	____	Note payable	____
Store and office equipment	____	Interest payable	120
		Total liabilities	$ ____
		STOCKHOLDERS' EQUITY	
		Contributed capital	$ ____
		Retained earnings	12,780
		Total stockholders' equity	____
Total assets	$ ____	Total liabilities and stockholders' equity	$ ____

E1–14 Focus on Cash Flows: Preparing a Statement of Cash Flows

NITSU Manufacturing Corporation is preparing the annual financial statements for the stockholders. A statement of cash flows must be prepared. The following data on cash flows were developed for the entire year ended December 31, 19D: cash inflow from operating revenues, $270,000; cash expended for operating expenses, $180,000; sale of unissued NITSU stock for cash, $30,000; cash dividends declared and paid to stockholders during the year, $22,000; and payments on long-term notes payable, $80,000. During the year, a tract of land was sold for $15,000 cash (which was the same price that NITSU had paid for the land in 19C), and $38,000 cash was expended for two new machines. The machines were used in the factory. The beginning-of-the-year cash balance was $63,000.

Required:
Prepare the statement of cash flows for 19D. Follow the format illustrated in the chapter.

E1–15 Completing an Income Statement

Home Realty, Incorporated, has been operating for three years and is owned by three investors. J. Doe owns 60 percent of the total outstanding stock of 9,000 shares and is the managing executive in charge. On December 31, 19C, the following financial items for the entire year were determined: commissions earned and collected in cash, $150,000, plus $16,000 uncollected; rental service fees earned and collected, $20,000; salaries expense paid, $62,000; commissions expense paid, $35,000; payroll taxes paid, $2,500; rent paid, $2,200 (not including December rent yet to be paid); utilities expense paid, $1,000; promotion and advertising paid, $8,000; and miscellaneous expenses paid, $500. There were no other unpaid expenses at December 31. Home Realty rents its office space but owns the furniture in it. The furniture cost $6,000 when acquired. The portion used this period (called *depreciation*) was $600. The average income tax rate for this corporation is 25 percent. Also during the year, the company paid the owners "out-of-profit" cash dividends amounting to $12,000. Complete the following income statement:

_____

_____

_____

Revenues		
Commissions earned	$ _____	
Rental service fees	_____	
Total revenues		$ _____
Expenses		
Salaries expense	$ _____	
Commission expense	_____	
Payroll tax expense	_____	
Rent expense	_____	
Utilities expense	_____	
Promotion and advertising expense	_____	
Miscellaneous expenses	_____	
Depreciation expense	_____	
Total expenses (excluding income taxes)		_____
Pretax income		$ _____
Income tax expense		_____
Net income		$55,500

E1–16 Applying the Balance Sheet Equation

On June 1, 19F, Bland Corporation prepared a balance sheet just prior to going out of business. The balance sheet totals showed the following:

Assets (no cash)	$90,000
Liabilities	50,000
Stockholders' equity	40,000

Shortly thereafter, all of the assets were sold for cash.

Required:

1. How would the balance sheet appear immediately after the sale of the assets for cash for each of the following cases? Use the format given below.

		BALANCES IMMEDIATELY AFTER SALES			
	Cash Received for the Assets	Assets	± Liabilities	=	Stockholders' Equity
Case A	$ 90,000	$ _____	$ _____		$ _____
Case B	80,000	$ _____	$ _____		$ _____
Case C	100,000	$ _____	$ _____		$ _____

2. How should the cash be distributed in each separate case? (_Hint:_ Creditors must be paid in full before owners receive any payment.) Use the following format.

	To Creditors	To Stockholders	Total
Case A	$ _____	$ _____	$ _____
Case B	$ _____	$ _____	$ _____
Case C	$ _____	$ _____	$ _____

Problems

P1–1 Analyzing Data to Support a Loan Application

On January 1, 19A, three individuals organized West Company as a corporation. Each individual invested $10,000 cash in the business. On December 31, 19A, they prepared a list of resources owned (assets) and a list of the debts (liabilities) to support a company loan request for $70,000 submitted to a local bank. None of the three investors had studied accounting. The two lists prepared were as follows:

Company resources	
Cash	$ 12,000
Service supplies inventory (on hand)	7,000
Service trucks (four practically new)	68,000
Personal residences of organizers (three houses)	190,000
Service equipment used in the business (practically new)	30,000
Bills due from customers (for services already completed)	15,000
Total	$322,000

Company obligations	
Unpaid wages to employees	$ 19,000
Unpaid taxes	8,000
Owed to suppliers	10,000
Owed on service trucks and equipment (to a finance company)	50,000
Loan from organizer	10,000
Total	$ 97,000

Required:

1. If you were advising the local bank about the two lists, what issues would you raise? Explain the basis for each question and include any recommendations that you have (consider the fact that the company is considered to be separate from the owners).
2. In view of your response to (1), what do you think the amount of *net resources* (i.e., assets minus liabilities) of the company would be? Show your computations.

P1–2 Comparing Income with Cash Flow

New Delivery Company was organized on January 1, 19A. At the end of the first quarter (three months) of operations, the owner prepared a summary of its operations as shown in the first row of the following tabulation:

Summary of Transactions	Computation of	
	Income	Cash
(a) Services performed for customers, $66,000, of which one-sixth remained uncollected at the end of the quarter.	+$66,000	+$55,000
(b) Cash borrowed from the local bank, $30,000 (one-year note).		
(c) Small service truck purchased for use in the business: cost, $9,000; paid 30% down, balance on credit.		
(d) Expenses, $36,000, of which one-sixth remained unpaid at the end of the quarter.		
(e) Service supplies purchased for use in the business, $3,000, of which one-fourth remained unpaid (on credit) at the end of the quarter. Also, one-fifth of these supplies were unused (still on hand) at the end of the quarter.		
(f) Wages earned by employees, $21,000, of which one-half remained unpaid at the end of the quarter.		
Based only on these transactions, compute the following for the quarter: Income (or loss) Cash inflow (or outflow)		

Required:
1. For each of the six transactions given in this tabulation, enter what you consider the correct amounts. Enter a zero when appropriate. The first transaction is illustrated.
2. For each transaction, explain the basis for your dollar responses.

P1–3 Preparing an Income Statement and Balance Sheet

Assume that you are the president of Nuclear Company. At the end of the first year (December 31, 19A) of operations, the following financial data for the company are available:

Cash	$ 25,000
Receivables from customers (all considered collectible)	12,000
Inventory of merchandise (based on physical count and priced at cost)	90,000
Equipment owned, at cost less used portion	45,000
Accounts payable owed to suppliers	47,370
Salary payable for 19A (on December 31, 19A, this was owed to an employee who was away because of an emergency; will return around January 10, 19B, at which time the payment will be made)	2,000
Total sales revenue	140,000
Expenses, including the cost of the merchandise sold (excluding income taxes)	89,100
Income taxes expense at 30% × pretax income; all paid during 19A	?
Contributed capital, 7,000 shares outstanding	87,000
No dividends were declared or paid during 19A.	

Required (show computations):
1. Prepare a summarized income statement for the year 19A.
2. Prepare a balance sheet at December 31, 19A.

P1–4 Analyzing a Student's Business and Preparing an Income Statement

During the summer between her junior and senior years, Susan Irwin needed to earn sufficient money for the coming academic year. Unable to obtain a job with a reasonable salary, she decided to try the lawn care business for three months. After a survey of the market potential, Susan bought a used pickup truck on June 1 for $1,500. On each door she painted "Susan's Lawn Service, Phone 471-4487." She also spent $900 for mowers, trimmers, and tools. To acquire these items, she borrowed $2,500 cash on a note at 12 percent interest per annum, payable at the end of the three months (ending August 31).

At the end of the summer, Susan realized that she had done a lot of work, and her bank account looked good. This fact prompted her to become concerned about how much profit the business had earned.

A review of the check stubs showed the following: Bank deposits of collections from customers totaled $12,600. The following checks were written: gas, oil, and lubrication, $920; pickup repairs, $210; mower repair, $75; miscellaneous supplies used, $80; helpers, $4,500; payroll taxes, $175; payment for assistance in preparing payroll tax forms, $25; insurance, $125; telephone, $110; and $2,575 to pay off the note including interest (on August 31). A notebook kept in the pickup, plus some unpaid bills, reflected that customers still owed her $800 for lawn services rendered and that she owed $200 for gas and oil (credit card charges). She estimated that the depreciation for use of the truck and the other equipment for three months amounted to $500.

Required:
1. Prepare a quarterly income statement for Susan's Lawn Service for the months June, July, and August 19A. Use the following main captions: Revenues from Services,

Expenses, and Net Income. Because this is a sole proprietorship, the company will not be subject to income tax.

2. Do you see a need for one or more additional financial reports for this company for 19A and thereafter? Explain.

P1–5 Analyzing a Student's Business and Preparing an Income Statement

Upon graduation from high school, John Abel immediately accepted a job as an electrician's assistant for a large local electrical repair company. After three years of hard work, John received an electrician's license and decided to start his own business. He had saved $12,000, which he invested in the business. First, he transferred this amount from his savings account to a business bank account for Abel Electric Repair Company, Incorporated. His lawyer had advised him to start as a corporation. He then purchased a used panel truck for $9,000 cash and secondhand tools for $1,500; rented space in a small building; inserted an ad in the local paper; and opened the doors on October 1, 19A. Immediately, John was very busy; after one month, he employed an assistant.

Although John knew practically nothing about the financial side of the business, he realized that a number of reports were required and that costs and collections had to be controlled carefully. At the end of the year, prompted in part by concern about his income tax situation (previously he had to report only salary), John recognized the need for financial statements. His wife Jane developed some financial statements for the business. On December 31, 19A, with the help of a friend, she gathered the following data for the three months just ended. Bank account deposits of collections for electric repair services totaled $32,000. The following checks were written: electrician's assistant, $8,500; payroll taxes, $175; supplies purchased and used on jobs, $9,500; oil, gas, and maintenance on truck, $1,200; insurance, $700; rent, $500; utilities and telephone, $825; and miscellaneous expenses (including advertising), $600. Also, uncollected bills to customers for electric repair services amounted to $3,000. The $200 rent for December had not been paid. The average income tax rate is 30 percent. John estimated that the depreciation on the truck and tools due to use during the three months to be $1,200.

Required:

1. Prepare a quarterly income statement for Abel Electric Repair for the three months October through December 19A. Use the following main captions: Revenue from Services, Expenses, Pretax Income, and Net Income.
2. Do you think that John may have a need for one or more additional financial reports for 19A and thereafter? Explain.

Cases and Projects

C1–1 Analyzing the Assets and Liabilities of a Business

Elizabeth Watkins owns and operates Liz's Boutique (a sole proprietorship). An employee prepares a financial report for the business at each year-end. This report lists all of the resources (assets) owned by Watkins, including such personal items as the home she owns and occupies. It also lists all of the debts of the business, but not her personal debts.

Required:

1. From the accounting point of view, in what ways do you disagree with what is being included in and excluded from the report of business assets and liabilities?
2. Upon questioning, Watkins responded, "Don't worry about it; we use it only to support a loan from the bank." How would you respond to this comment?

C1-2 Deciding about a Proposed Audit

You are one of three partners who own and operate Mary's Maid Service. The company has been operating for seven years. One of the other partners has always prepared the company's annual financial statements. Recently you proposed that the statements be audited each year because it would benefit the partners and preclude possible disagreements about the division of profits. The partner who prepares the statements proposed that his Uncle Ray, who has a lot of financial experience, can do the job and at little cost. Your other partner remained silent.

Required:
1. What position would you take on the proposal? Justify your response.
2. What would you strongly recommend? Give the basis for your recommendation.

C1-3 Identifying and Correcting Deficiencies in an Income Statement and Balance Sheet

Performance Corporation was organized on January 1, 19A. At the end of 19A, the company had not yet employed an accountant; however, an employee who was "good with numbers" prepared the following statements at that date:

PERFORMANCE CORPORATION
December 31, 19A

Income from sales of merchandise	$175,000
Total amount paid for goods sold during 19A	(90,000)
Selling costs	(25,000)
Depreciation (on service vehicles used)	(10,000)
Income from services rendered	52,000
Salaries and wages paid	(62,000)

PERFORMANCE CORPORATION
December 31, 19A

Resources		
Cash		$ 32,000
Merchandise inventory (held for resale)		42,000
Service vehicles		50,000
Retained earnings (profit earned in 19A)		30,000
Grand total		$154,000
Debts		
Payables to suppliers		$ 22,000
Note owed to bank		25,000
Due from customers		13,000
Total		$ 60,000
Supplies on hand (to be used in rendering services)	$15,000	
Accumulated depreciation* (on service vehicles)	10,000	
Contributed capital, 6,500 shares	65,000	
Total		90,000
Grand total		$150,000

* Accumulated depreciation represents the used portion of the asset and should be subtracted from the asset balance.

Required:
1. List all the deficiencies that you can identify in these statements. Give a brief explanation of each one.
2. Prepare a proper income statement (correct net income is $30,000) and balance sheet (correct total assets are $142,000).

C1–4 Ethics Case: Ethics and Auditor Responsibilities

A key factor that an auditor provides is independence. The *AICPA Code of Professional Conduct* states that "a member in public practice should be independent in fact and appearance when providing auditing and other attestation service."

Required:

Do you consider the following circumstances to suggest a lack of independence? Justify your position. (Use your imagination. Specific answers are not provided in the chapter.)

1. Jack Jones is a partner with a large audit firm and is assigned to the Ford audit. Jack owns 10 shares of Ford.
2. Jane Winkler has invested in a mutual fund company that owns 500,000 shares of Sears stock. She is the auditor of Sears.
3. Bob Franklin is a clerk/typist who works on the audit of AT&T. He has just inherited 50,000 shares of AT&T stock. (Bob enjoys his work and plans to continue despite his new wealth.)
4. Nancy Sodoma worked on weekends as the controller for a small business that a friend started. Nancy quit the job in midyear and now has no association with the company. She works full time for a large CPA firm and has been assigned to do the audit of her friend's business.
5. Mark Jacobs borrowed $100,000 for a home mortgage from First City National Bank. The mortgage was granted on normal credit terms. Mark is the partner in charge of the First City audit.

Toys "R" Us

C1–5 Financial Statement Analysis

Refer to the financial statements of Toys "R" Us in Appendix B at the end of this book.

Required:

1. What is the amount of net income for the current year?
2. What amount of revenue was earned in the current year?
3. How much long-term debt does the company have at the end of the current year?
4. By what amount did cash and cash equivalents* change during the year?
5. Who is auditor for the company?

*Cash equivalents are short-term investments readily convertible to cash whose value is unlikely to change.

Toys "R" Us

C1–6 Financial Statement Analysis

Refer to the financial statements of Toys "R" Us in Appendix B at the end of this book.

Required:

Read the annual report. Look at the income statement, balance sheet, and cash flow statement closely and attempt to infer what kinds of information they report. Then answer the following questions based on the report.

1. What types of products does it sell?
2. Did the chief executive officer (CEO) believe that the company had a good year?
3. On what day of the year does its fiscal year end?
4. For how many years does it present complete
   a. Balance sheets?
   b. Income statements?
   c. Cash flow statements?
5. Are its financial statements audited by independent CPAs? How do you know?

6. Did its total assets increase or decrease over the last year?

7. What was the ending balance of inventories?

8. Write out its basic accounting (balance sheet) equation in dollars at year-end.

C1–7   Project: Examining an Annual Report

Acquire the annual report of a public company you find interesting. We suggest you pick a company of local interest or a company whose products or services you often purchase. (Library files, the SEC EDGAR service at www.sec.gov, Compustat CD, or the company itself are good sources.)

Required:

Read the annual report. Look at the income statement, balance sheet, and cash flow statement closely and attempt to infer what kinds of information they report. Then answer the following questions based on the report.

1. What types of products or services does it sell?

2. Did the chief executive officer (CEO) believe that the company had a good year?

3. On what day of the year does its fiscal year end?

4. For how many years does it present complete

    a.   Balance sheets?

    b.   Income statements?

    c.   Cash flow statements?

5. Are its financial statements audited by independent CPAs? How do you know?

6. Did its total assets increase or decrease over the last year?

7. What was the ending balance of inventories?

8. Write out its basic accounting (balance sheet) equation in dollars at year-end.

C1–8   Project: Finding Information in an Annual Report

Acquire the annual report of a public company you find interesting. We suggest you pick a company of local interest or a company whose products or services you often purchase. (Library files, the SEC EDGAR service at www.sec.gov, Compustat CD, or the company itself are good sources.)

Required:

1. What is the amount of net income for the current year?

2. What amount of revenue was earned in the current year?

3. How much long-term debt does the company have at the end of the current year?

4. By what amount did cash and cash equivalents* change during the year?

5. Who is auditor for the company?

Cash equivalents are short-term investments readily convertible to cash whose value is unlikely to change.

**C1–9   Project: Analysis of the Price/Earnings Ratio for Disk-Drive Companies
from *The Wall Street Journal***

Three of the largest producers of disk drives are Seagate Technology, Inc., Quantum Corporation, and Western Digital Corporation. All are public companies: Seagate and Western Digital are traded on the New York Stock Exchange and Quantum on the NASDAQ National Market. Obtain a recent copy of *The Wall Street Journal* from your library or a newsstand. Section C, "Money & Investing," lists a variety of facts about each of these companies. The column headings of the stock listing identify each of the listed facts. A box normally printed at the bottom of one of the early pages in the section "Explanatory Notes" explains the information provided.

Required:

Find the listing for one of the three disk drive companies. Then answer the following questions (refer to the "Explanatory Notes" box as necessary):

1. What was the closing price for one share of the stock?
2. What was the Price/Earnings (PE) ratio? (If the symbol "**cc**" or "**dd**" was reported, what does that mean?)

C1–10 **Project: Analysis of the Price/Earnings Ratio from *The Wall Street Journal***

Choose a company from the list of focus companies printed on the inside cover of this book. We suggest you pick a company of local interest or a company whose products or services you often purchase. All of the focus companies (other than Maxidrive) are public companies traded on the New York Stock Exchange, the American Stock Exchange, or the NASDAQ National Market. Obtain a recent copy of *The Wall Street Journal* from your library or a newsstand. Section C, "Money & Investing," lists a variety of facts about these companies. The column headings of the stock listing identify each of the listed facts. A box normally printed at the bottom of one of the early pages in the section "Explanatory Notes" explains the information provided.

Required:

Find the listing for your selected company. Then answer the following questions (refer to the "Explanatory Notes" box as necessary):

1. What was the closing price for one share of the stock?
2. What was the Price/Earnings (PE) ratio? (If the symbol "**cc**" or "**dd**" was reported, what does that mean?)

C1–11 **Project: Focus on Cash Flows**

Acquire the annual report of a company you find interesting. We suggest you pick a company of local interest or a company whose products or services you often purchase. (Library files, the SEC EDGAR service at www.sec.gov, Compustat CD, or the company itself are good sources.)

Required:

Look at the cash flow statement closely. Then answer the following questions based on the report.

1. Was cash flow from operating activities equal to net income? What causes the difference? (*Hint:* Consider the difference between cash inflows and outflows and revenues and expenses.)
2. List and explain two items listed under Cash Flows from Investing Activities and Cash Flows from Financing Activities.

Toys "R" Us **C1–12** **Project: Financial Analysis Update**

Acquire the most recent year's annual report for Toys "R" Us. (Library files, the SEC EDGAR service at www.sec.gov, Compustat, or the company itself are good sources.) Write a short memo comparing the company's total assets and net income for the most current year to that ended in January 1997. Indicate what reasons the letter from the chief executive officer gives for the increase or decrease in earnings.

C1–13 Ethics Project: Analysis of an Accounting Irregularity

Obtain a recent news story outlining an accounting irregularity. (Library files, *Wall Street Journal Index, Dow Jones News/Retrieval,* and *Bloomberg Business News* are good sources. Search for the term *accouting irregularities.*) Write a short memo outlining the effect of the irregularity on reported net income, the impact of the announcement of the irregularity on the company's stock price, and any fines or civil penalties against the company and its officers.

C1–14 Team Project: Examining an Annual Report

As a group, select an industry to analyze. Each group member should acquire the annual report or 10-K for one publicly traded company in the industry, with each member selecting a different company. (Library files, the SEC EDGAR service at www.sec.gov, Compustat CD, or the company itself are good sources.) On an individual basis, each group member should write a short report answering the following questions about their selected company.

1. What types of products or services does it sell?
2. On what day of the year does its fiscal year end?
3. For how many years does it present complete
   a. Balance sheets?
   b. Income statements?
   c. Cash flow statements?
4. Are its financial statements audited by independent CPAs? If so, by whom?
5. Did its total assets increase or decrease over the last year?
6. Did its net income increase or decrease over the last year?

Discuss any patterns that you as a group observe. Then, as a group, write a short report comparing and contrasting your companies using the attributes listed above.

CHAPTER TWO

Investing and Financing Decisions and the Balance Sheet

Sbarro, Inc.

TOPS IN THE ITALIAN FAST-FOOD SECTOR

Americans appear to love Italian food, and the Sbarro family, headed by brothers Mario Sbarro (chairman of the board) and Anthony Sbarro (president and chief operating officer), seems to have carved out its own niche in the highly competitive restaurant business. Sbarro remains one of only 13 companies that appear on both the 1989 and 1994 Forbes' 200 Best Small Companies in America lists.*

Incorporated in 1977, Sbarro develops and operates or franchises a national chain of family-style Italian restaurants located mostly in shopping malls.† The restaurants feature popular freshly prepared Italian foods including pizza, pasta, and hot and cold Italian entrees, salads, and desserts. Most of the more than 816 restaurants serve the food cafeteria style. Sbarro has restaurants in 48 states, the District of Columbia, Puerto Rico, Canada, Great Britain, Australia, Belgium, Kuwait, Qatar, Saudi Arabia, Chile, and the

Philippines, with plans for continued rapid expansion. Approximately three-fourths of the restaurants are company owned, and one-fourth are franchises (owned by others who pay fees to Sbarro for various services Sbarro provides to them).

Sbarro has experienced continuing growth as indicated in its balance sheets presented for two recent years (in thousands of dollars[‡]):

	Assets	=	Liabilities	+	Stockholders' Equity
1/1/95	$232,000	=	$52,500	+	$179,500
12/31/95	$242,700	=	$57,100	+	$185,600
Change	+$ 10,700	=	+$ 4,600	+	+$ 6,100

* See *Forbes,* November 7, 1994.

† For stock price information, Sbarro is listed on the New York Stock Exchange under the symbol SBA.

‡ These totals are rounded amounts from the actual financial statements for the respective years. Amounts used in illustrations throughout Chapters 2, 3, and 4 are realistic estimates of actual monthly amounts, which are not publicly available.

Business Background

To understand the meaning of these amounts for Sbarro, we must answer the following questions:

1. What business activities cause changes in balance sheet amounts from one period to the next?
2. How do specific activities affect each of the balances?
3. How do companies keep track of these balance sheet amounts?

Once we have answered these questions, we will be able to perform two key analytical tasks. First, we will be able to analyze and predict the effects of our business decisions on our firm's financial statements. Second, we will be able to use financial statements of other companies to identify and evaluate activities that other managers engaged in during a past period. These latter inferences are a key to *financial statement analysis*.

In this chapter, we focus on typical asset acquisition activities (often called *investing activities*) that Sbarro engages in, along with the related *financing activities* such as borrowing funds from creditors and receiving funds from investors to acquire the assets. We examine activities affecting only balance sheet amounts; we discuss operating activities affecting both income statement and balance sheet amounts in Chapters 3 and 4. This simplification is to aid your understanding. Let us begin our answers to the three questions by returning to the basic concepts introduced in Chapter 1.

Overview of the Conceptual Framework

LEARNING OBJECTIVE 1

Define the objective of financial reporting, the elements of the balance sheet, and the related key accounting assumptions and principles.

We defined many key accounting terms and concepts in Chapter 1. These are part of a framework of accounting theory developed over many years and synthesized by the Financial Accounting Standards Board (FASB) in a series of publications called *FASB Statements of Financial Accounting Concepts*. These Statements make up the conceptual framework of accounting outlined in Exhibit 2.1 and will be discussed in each of the next four chapters. In the exhibit in each chapter, terms and concepts emphasized in the current chapter are indicated in bold white print. Terms and concepts from prior chapters are indicated in bold black print. This pyramid will be used to organize the concepts and terms. An understanding of the accounting concepts will be helpful as you study. It is much easier to learn and remember how the accounting process works if you know why it works a certain way. A clear understanding will also help you in future chapters as we examine more complex business activities.

Concepts Emphasized in Chapter 2

Objective of Financial Reporting

The top of the pyramid in Exhibit 2.1 indicates the **primary objective of external financial reporting,** which guides the remaining sections of the conceptual framework. The primary objective of financial accounting is to provide useful economic information about a business to help external parties, primarily investors and creditors, make sound financial decisions. The users of accounting information are identified as *decision makers*. These decision makers are defined in the conceptual framework as average, prudent investors, creditors, and experts who provide financial advice. They are expected to have a reasonable understanding of accounting concepts and procedures (this may be one of the reasons you are studying accounting). Of course, as we discussed in Chapter 1, many other groups, such as suppliers and customers, also use external financial statements. Users usually are interested in information to assist them in projecting a business's future cash inflows and outflows.

The **primary objective of external financial reporting** is to provide useful economic information about a business to help external parties make sound financial decisions.

Underlying Assumptions of Accounting

The assumptions of accounting are primarily based on the business environment in which accounting operates. They reflect the scope of accounting and the expectations that set certain limits on the way accounting information is reported. Three of these assumptions were discussed in Chapter 1. Under the **separate-entity assumption,** each business must be accounted for as an individual organization, separate and apart from its owners, all other persons, and other entities. Under the **unit-of-measure assumption,** each business entity accounts for and reports its financial results primarily in terms of the national monetary unit (dollars in the United States, yen in Japan, francs in France, etc.).

For accounting purposes, a business is normally assumed to continue operating long enough to meet contractual commitments and plans. This **continuity assumption** is sometimes called the *going-concern assumption* because we expect a business to continue to operate into the foreseeable future. Violation of this assumption means that assets and liabilities can be valued and reported on the balance sheet as if the company were to be liquidated (that is, discontinued with all assets sold and all debts paid). In all future chapters, unless indicated otherwise, we assume that businesses meet the continuity assumption.

The **separate-entity assumption** requires business transactions to be separate from the transactions of the owners.

The **unit-of-measure assumption** requires accounting information to be measured and reported in the national monetary unit.

Under the **continuity assumption** (going-concern assumption), businesses are assumed to continue to operate into the foreseeable future.

Elements of the Balance Sheet

As discussed in Chapter 1, assets, liabilities, and shareholders' equity are the key elements of the balance sheet. Let's review the definitions.

Assets are probable future economic benefits owned or controlled by the entity as a result of past transactions. For illustration purposes, the balance sheet of Sbarro, Inc., has been simplified in Exhibit 2.2, with amounts rounded to the nearest hundred thousand dollars. Notice that Sbarro's year ends on the Sunday closest to December 31, which in 1994 was January 1 and in 1995 was December 31. The choice of year-ends will be discussed in the next chapter. As indicated in Sbarro's simplified balance sheet

Assets are probable future economic benefits owned by the entity as a result of past transactions.

EXHIBIT 2.1
Financial Accounting and Reporting Conceptual Framework

PRIMARY OBJECTIVE OF EXTERNAL FINANCIAL REPORTING
To provide useful economic information to external users for decision making (for assessing future cash flows) [Ch. 2]

QUALITATIVE CHARACTERISTICS OF INFORMATION
[Ch. 5]
Primary:
Relevance Information influences decisions; it is timely and has predictive and/or feedback value.
Reliability Information is accurate, unbiased, and verifiable.
Secondary:
Comparability Information can be compared to that of other businesses.
Consistency Information can be compared across time.

ELEMENTS OF FINANCIAL STATEMENTS
Assets Probable future economic benefits owned by the entity from past transactions. [Ch. 2]
Liabilities Probable debts or obligations from past transactions to be paid with assets or services. [Ch. 2]
Stockholders' Equity Financing provided by owners and operations. [Ch. 2]
Revenues Increases in assets or settlements of liabilities from ongoing operations. [Ch. 3]
Expenses Decreases in assets or increases in liabilities from ongoing operations. [Ch. 3]
Gains Increases in assets or decreases in liabilities from peripheral transactions. [Ch. 3]
Losses Decreases in assets or increases in liabilities from peripheral transactions. [Ch. 3]

ASSUMPTIONS
1. Separate-entity Transactions of the business are separate from transactions of the owners. [Ch. 2]
2. Unit-of-measure Accounting measurements will be in the national monetary unit. [Ch. 2]
3. Continuity The entity will not go out of business in the near future. [Ch. 2]
4. *Time-period* The long life of a company can be reported over a series of shorter time periods. [Ch. 3]

PRINCIPLES
1. Cost The historical cash-equivalent cost given up is the basis for initial recording of elements. [Ch. 2 and 3]
2. *Revenue* Record revenues when earned and measurable (an exchange has taken place, the earnings process is nearly complete, and collection is probable). [Ch. 3]
3. *Matching* Record expenses when incurred in earning revenue. [Ch. 3]
4. *Full-disclosure* Disclose relevant economic information. [Ch. 5]

CONSTRAINTS
[Ch. 5]
1. *Materiality* Relatively small amounts not likely to influence decisions are to be recorded in the most cost-beneficial way.
2. *Cost-benefit* Benefits of recording and reporting information should outweigh costs.
3. *Conservatism* Exercise care not to overstate assets and revenues or understate liabilities and expenses.
4. *Industry peculiarities* Differences in accounting and reporting for certain items are permitted if there is a clear precedent in the industry.

in Exhibit 2.2, its assets include cash and cash equivalents (very short-term investments), marketable securities (stocks and bonds Sbarro purchased as investments of excess cash), receivables (due from franchisees[1] and others on account), inventories (of food, beverages, and paper supplies), prepaid expenses (such as rent Sbarro paid

---

[1] Franchises are contracts in which a franchisor provides rights to franchisees to sell or distribute a specific line of products or provide a particular service. The franchisees in return usually pay initial fees to obtain the franchise and make annual payments to receive ongoing services from the franchisor (such as accounting, advertising, and training). When franchisees owe the annual payments, the franchisor records the receivable. Examples of franchises include Holiday Inn, McDonald's, Dairy Queen, and National Football League teams.

Identify the Sbarro assets in this photograph.

EXHIBIT 2.2
Balance Sheet

SBARRO, INC. AND SUBSIDIARIES*
Balance Sheets
at December 31, 1995, and January 1, 1995
(in thousands of dollars)

	December 31, 1995	January 1, 1995
ASSETS		
Cash and cash equivalents	$ 93,500	$ 42,400
Marketable securities	10,000	38,600
Receivables (franchise fees and other)	2,600	2,700
Inventories	2,800	2,800
Prepaid expenses	1,700	1,500
Property and equipment	126,800	140,700
Other assets	5,300	3,300
Total assets	**$242,700**	**$232,000**
LIABILITIES		
Accounts payable	$ 7,400	$ 6,400
Accrued expenses payable (rent, payroll, and other)	27,000	18,700
Dividend payable	3,900	3,200
Income taxes payable	4,700	4,900
Deferred income taxes	14,100	19,300
Total liabilities	**$ 57,100**	**$ 52,500**
STOCKHOLDERS' EQUITY		
Contributed capital	$ 30,500	$ 30,200
Retained earnings	155,100	149,300
Total stockholders' equity	185,600	179,500
Total liabilities and stockholders' equity	**$242,700**	**$232,000**

*A subsidiary is a company owned by another company that controls more than 50 percent of the voting stock of the subsidiary.

in advance of the use of mall space), and property and equipment. The other assets category includes a number of assets with smaller balances that total the amount presented. Assets are usually listed on the balance sheet *in order of liquidity* (how soon an asset can be used or turned into cash) with the most liquid listed first.

Unrecorded but Valuable Assets

Managers and analysts use the balance sheet as a basis for managing the firm's assets and for valuing the firm. At the same time, they recognize that often a firm's most valuable assets are not even listed on the balance sheet (they have no "book value").* One such asset is a firm's trademark or brand name. For example, *Financial World* estimated that the Budweiser brand name is worth $10 billion to its owner, Anheuser-Busch. Its book value is zero, however, because it was developed internally over time (created through research, development, and advertising); there was no identifiable exchange transaction (it was not purchased). Many valuable intangible assets, such as trademarks, patents, and copyrights that are developed inside the firm, have no book value.

This same asset recognition rule (that assets are recorded at cost based on an exchange with an external party) suggests the circumstances in which trademarks and brand names are reported on the balance sheet. As with the Budweiser example, General Electric's balance sheet reveals no listing for the GE trademark. Again, this trademark was developed internally. GE recently sold its television business, however, to a French company, Thomson SA, which is the world's largest producer of televisions. Since the Thomson brand name has no value in the United States, it also purchased the right to use GE's trademark for 10 years at a cost of 250 million French francs (approximately $50 million). Thomson's balance sheet lists GE's trademark, which was initially recorded at its acquisition cost of 250 million francs.

* *Book value* is the amount reported on the balance sheet that is usually an asset's original acquisition cost minus amounts used in past operations.

Liabilities are probable debts or obligations of the entity as a result of past transactions, which will be paid with assets or services.

Liabilities are an entity's probable debts or obligations as a result of its past transactions, which will be paid with assets or services. Those entities that a company owes money to are called *creditors*. Creditors usually receive payment of the amount owed and sometimes interest on those amounts. Sbarro's balance sheet includes five liabilities: accounts payable, accrued expenses payable, dividends payable, income taxes payable, and deferred income taxes. Accrued expenses payable is actually a summary of several liabilities related to payroll, rent, and other obligations. Dividends payable is the amount due to stockholders as a distribution of company earnings based on the board of directors' authorization. They become a liability until paid. These and other liabilities will be discussed in subsequent chapters. Liabilities are listed on the balance sheet *in order of maturity* (how soon a liability is to be paid).

QUESTION OF ETHICS

Environmental Liabilities

Due to changing legal requirements and concerns for social responsibility, companies are facing significant pressure to disclose environmental liabilities, such as the cleanup of hazardous waste sites. In a recent survey of 523 companies, however, 62 percent indicated that "they have known environmental exposures that haven't been recorded in their financial statements."* By definition, liabilities are recorded when they are probable; they also need to be reasonably estimable. Determining the amounts and likelihood of environmental obligations can be very difficult. Given the growing magnitude of these issues, the accounting profession, led by the Financial Accounting Standards Board, will need to address the challenge.

*L. Berten, "SEC Rule Forces More Disclosure," *The Wall Street Journal*, December 13, 1993, p. B1.

Stockholders' equity (owners' equity or **shareholders' equity)** is the financing provided by the owners and the operations of business.

Stockholders' equity (owners' equity or **shareholders' equity)** is the financing provided by the owners and the operations of the business. **Contributed capital** results from owners providing cash (and sometimes other assets) to the business. When this occurs, we often say that owners invest in the business, or the company sells or issues its stock to owners. The investors in Sbarro, Inc., are the members of the Sbarro family, who own approximately 38 percent of the company, and corporate employees and the general public, who together own the rest of the company. Owners invest (or buy stock) in a company in the hope of receiving two types of cash flows: dividends, which are a distribution of a company's earnings (a return on the shareholders' investment), and gains from selling their stock in the company for more than they paid (known as *capital gains*). Earnings that are not distributed to the owners and are reinvested in the business by management are called **retained earnings**.[2] A look at Sbarro's balance sheet (Exhibit 2.2) indicates that its growth has been predominantly financed by the substantial reinvestment of earnings in the business; 84 percent of Sbarro's stockholders' equity is retained earnings ($155,100 retained earnings ÷ $185,600 total stockholders' equity).

Contributed capital results from owners providing cash (and sometimes other assets) to the business.

Retained earnings are the cumulative earnings of a company that are not distributed to the owners and are reinvested in the business.

Financial
ANALYSIS

Financing Strategies

Sbarro's approach to financing involves relatively little borrowing and a great deal of stockholders' equity with heavy reinvestment of earnings. In fact, Sbarro's total debt compared to stockholders' equity at December 31, 1995, is 31 percent.

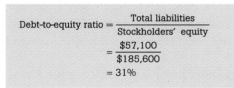

$$\text{Debt-to-equity ratio} = \frac{\text{Total liabilities}}{\text{Stockholders' equity}}$$
$$= \frac{\$57,100}{\$185,600}$$
$$= 31\%$$

This debt-to-equity ratio is a common measure of a company's risk level. Debt financing (also called *leverage*) is considered riskier than financing with stockholders' equity because the interest payments on debt must be made every period (they are legal obligations), whereas dividends on stock can be postponed if Sbarro has a bad year. We include additional discussion of this ratio in Chapter 14.

Robert Morris Associates Annual Statement Studies for 1995 indicates that the average fast-food restaurant chain is financed 79 percent with debt. This suggests that Sbarro is following a less risky (more conservative) financing strategy than are other companies in its industry. A low ratio makes sense given that Sbarro typically rents mall space instead of constructing new buildings financed by borrowings as do some other fast-food companies. When comparing companies to an industry average, differences in business strategy such as this should be considered. A significantly different value for one company may or may not suggest that the company is being overly risky or conservative in its financing.

Basic Accounting Principle

The **cost principle** states that the cash-equivalent cost needed to acquire the asset (the historical cost) should be used for initially recognizing (recording) all financial statement elements. Under the cost principle, cost is measured on the date of the transaction as the cash paid plus the current dollar value of all noncash considerations (any assets, privileges, or rights) also given in the exchange. For example, if you trade your computer plus cash for a new car, the cost of the new car is equal to the cash paid plus the market value of the computer. Thus, in most cases, cost is relatively easy to determine and can be verified. A disadvantage is that, subsequent to the date of acquisition, the continued use of historical cost on the balance sheet does not reflect any changes in market value.

The **cost principle** requires assets to be recorded at the historical cash-equivalent cost, which on the date of the transaction is cash paid plus the current dollar value of all noncash considerations also given in the exchange.

---

[2] Retained earnings can increase only from profitable operations. In addition, as we will learn in Chapter 3, a company's annual income from operations is usually not equal to the net cash flows for the year.

Now that we have reviewed several of the basic accounting concepts and terms, we need to understand the economic activities of a business that result in changes in amounts reported in financial statements and the process used in generating the financial statements.

What Business Activities Cause Changes in Financial Statement Amounts?

Nature of Business Transactions

Accounting focuses on certain events, though not all events, that have an economic impact on the entity. Those events that are recorded as a part of the accounting process are called **transactions**. The first step in translating the results of business events to financial statement numbers is determining which events are and are not reflected in the statements. Note that the definitions of *assets* and *liabilities* indicate that only economic resources and debts *resulting from past transactions* are recorded on the balance sheet. A broad definition includes two types of transactions:

1. *External events:* These are *exchanges* of assets and liabilities between the business and one or more other parties. Examples include the purchase of a machine, the sale of merchandise, the borrowing of cash, and the investment in the business by the owners. These types of transactions will be discussed in this chapter as they affect the balance sheet elements and in Chapter 3 as they affect income statement elements.
2. *Internal events:* These are certain events that are not exchanges between the business and other parties but have a direct and measurable effect on the accounting entity. Examples include losses due to fire or other natural disasters and *adjustments* such as those to record the use of property, plant, and equipment in operations and interest expense on money that was borrowed. Adjustments will be discussed in Chapter 4.

Throughout this textbook, the word *transaction* will be used in the broad sense to include both types of events.

At the same time, some important events that have an economic impact on the company are not reflected in Sbarro's statements. In most cases, signing a contract, which involves no cash, goods, services, or property changing hands, is not considered to be a transaction because it involves only the exchange of promises, not of assets or liabilities. For example, if Sbarro hires a new district manager and signs an employment contract, no transaction occurs from an accounting perspective because no exchange of assets or liabilities has occurred. Each party to the contract has made promises (the manager agrees to work; Sbarro agrees to pay in exchange for the manager's work). For each day the new manager works, however, the exchange of services by the employee results in a transaction that Sbarro must record (as an obligation to pay the manager's salary).

Accounts

An **account** is a standardized format that organizations use to accumulate the dollar effects of transactions on each financial statement item. The resulting balances are kept separate for financial statement purposes. Each company must establish a chart of accounts to facilitate recording transactions. A chart of accounts is the list of all the account names, usually organized by financial statement element. That is, asset accounts are listed first (such as Cash, Inventory, Accounts Receivable, Equipment, and Land) followed by liability accounts (such as Accounts Payable, Notes Payable, and Taxes Payable), stockholders' equity accounts (Contributed Capital and Retained Earnings), revenue accounts (such as Sales Revenue), and expense accounts (such as Payroll Expense). The account names listed here are quite common and are used by most companies.

The chart of accounts also lists a unique number for each account that is used when entering data into the accounting system. For example, 1-111 could be the account number for Cash, 1-146 for Supplies Inventory, 2-221 for Long-Term Notes Payable, 3-111 for Contributed Capital, 4-235 for Rent Revenue, and 5-138 for Salaries Expense. In formal recordkeeping systems, using appropriate account numbers is important.

The accounts you see in the financial statements are actually summations (or aggregations) of a number of more detailed accounts in a company's accounting system. For example, Sbarro keeps separate inventory accounts for paper supplies, food, and beverages, but combines them as Inventories on the balance sheet. Since our aim is to understand financial statements, we focus on aggregated accounts as presented in the statements.

Every company has a different chart of accounts, depending on the nature of its business activities. For example, a small lawn care service may have an asset account called Lawn Mowing Equipment, but it is unlikely that General Motors would need such an account. These differences will become more apparent as we examine the balance sheets of many various companies.

Understanding the Meaning of Account Titles in Foreign Financial Statements

The News Corporation Limited

Chapter 1 states that differences in the political, cultural, and economic environment of other countries have produced significant variations in accounting and reporting rules. Foreign companies' account titles often use different words with the same meanings as U.S. companies commonly use. Some use additional accounts for financial statement items not normally reported under U.S. accounting rules. For example, the Australian company, The News Corporation Limited, headed by K. Rupert Murdoch, follows A-GAAP (Australian generally accepted accounting principles). The principal activities of the group of corporations making up The News Corporation Limited include printing and publishing newspapers and magazines, television broadcasting, film production and distribution, motion picture studio operations, and book publishing. U.S. corporations included in the news group include Fox Broadcasting Company and Twentieth Century Fox Film Corporation. The titles of asset accounts in a recent financial report are similar to those used by U.S. companies, but the liabilities and stockholders' equity account titles are different:

Australian Accounts	U.S. Equivalents
Liabilities:	
Borrowings	Similar to Notes and Bonds Payable
Creditors	Relates to what is owed to suppliers and others, similar to Accounts Payable
Provision	A summary of payables for income tax, dividends, payroll, and other liabilities
Shareholders' Equity:	
Share Capital	Similar to Contributed Capital
Retained Profits	Similar to Retained Earnings

Because each company has a different chart of accounts, you should not try to memorize a typical chart of accounts. When you prepare homework problems, either you will be given the account names the company uses or you should select appropriate descriptive names. Once a name is selected for an account, the exact name must be used in all transactions that affect the account.

SELF-STUDY QUIZ

1. The following is a list of accounts from a recent Wendy's International, Inc. balance sheet. Indicate on the line provided whether each of the following is an asset (A), liability (L), or stockholders' equity account (SE).

Salaries and Wages Payable	_____	Long-Term Capital Lease Obligations	_____
Buildings	_____	Restaurant Equipment	_____
Notes Receivable	_____	Retained Earnings	_____
Accounts and Drafts Payable	_____	Short-Term Investments	_____

2. Wendy's had the following balances (in thousands):

   assets—$996,486; liabilities—$395,691; stockholders' equity—$600,795

   Compute Wendy's debt-to-equity ratio: _____

   _____

   What does this tell you about Wendy's financing strategy?

   _____

   _____

   _____

   After you have completed the schedules, check your solutions with the answers in the footnote at the bottom of the page.*

How Do Transactions Affect Accounts?

LEARNING OBJECTIVE 4
Apply transaction analysis to analyze simple business transactions in terms of the accounting model: Assets = Liabilities + Stockholders' Equity.

Managers make business decisions that often result in transactions affecting financial statements. Typical decisions are to expand the number of stores, advertise a new product, change employee benefit packages, and invest excess cash. Keeping a historical record (like a diary of important events) allows managers to evaluate the effects of past decisions and plan future business activities. In planning, managers are interested in how the implementation of their plans (their decisions) will be reflected on the financial statements. For example, the decision to purchase additional inventory for cash in anticipation of a major sales initiative increases the inventory and decreases cash. If the demand for the inventory does not occur, a lower cash balance reduces the company's flexibility and ability to pay other obligations. Business decisions often

---

*1. Column 1: L; A; A; L. Column 2: L; A; SE; A.
   2. $395,691 ÷ $600,795 = 65.9%. Wendy's is following a slightly less risky financing strategy than other companies in the industry. The ratio is lower than the industry average, although it is higher than Sbarro's. This appears reasonable in that Wendy's builds and leases facilities, but Sbarro typically leases mall space.

involve an element of risk that should be assessed. Therefore, it is necessary for business managers to understand how transactions impact the accounts on the financial statements. The process for determining the effects of transactions is called *transaction analysis* and is discussed next.

Transaction Analysis

Transaction analysis is the process of studying a transaction to determine its economic effect on the entity in terms of the accounting equation (also known as the *accounting model*). We will outline the process in this section of the chapter and create a visual tool representing the process (the transaction analysis model). The basic accounting equation and two principles are the foundation for the transaction analysis model. You will recall from Chapter 1 that the basic accounting equation for a business organized as a corporation is as follows:

> **Transaction analysis** is the process of studying a transaction to determine its economic effect on the business in terms of the accounting equation.

$$\text{Assets (A)} = \text{Liabilities (L)} + \text{Stockholders' Equity (SE)}$$

The two principles underlying the transaction analysis process follow:

1. Every transaction affects at least two accounts (duality of effects); it is critical to identify correctly the accounts affected and the direction of the effect (increase or decrease).
2. The accounting equation must remain in balance after each transaction.

Success in performing transaction analysis depends on your clear understanding of how the transaction analysis model is constructed based on these concepts. Study this material well. You should not move on to a new concept until you understand and can apply all prior concepts. Now let's create the transaction analysis model from these basic principles.

Duality of Effects

The first concept is that every transaction has *at least two effects* on the basic accounting equation. This is known as the *duality of effects*. (From this duality concept we have developed what is known as the *double-entry system* of recordkeeping.) Most transactions with external parties involve an *exchange* by which the business entity both gives up something and receives something in return. For example, suppose that Sbarro purchased some paper napkins inventory for cash.

Which accounts could be affected in the purchase of equipment for a new restaurant?

Transaction (1)	Sbarro Received	Sbarro Gave Up
Purchased paper napkins for cash	Inventory	Cash

In analyzing this transaction, we determined that the appropriate accounts affected were Inventory and Cash. Identifying the appropriate accounts affected and the direction of the effect on each are critical in transaction analysis. In the exchange, Sbarro received inventory (an increase in an asset) and gave up cash in return (a decrease in an asset).

As we discussed in Chapter 1, however, most inventory is purchased on credit (money is owed to suppliers). In this case, Sbarro engages in *two* transactions: (1) a purchase of an asset on credit and (2) an eventual payment. In the first, it receives inventory (an increase in an asset) and in return gives a promise to pay later called *accounts payable* (an increase in a liability). In the second, Sbarro eliminates (receives back) its promise to pay, accounts payable (a decrease in a liability), and gives up cash (a decrease in an asset).

Transactions (2)	Sbarro Received (eliminated)	Sbarro Gave Up
Purchased paper napkins on credit	Inventory	Accounts payable
Paid accounts payable	Accounts payable	Cash

As noted earlier, not all important business activities result in a transaction that affects the financial statements. Most important, signing a contract involving the exchange of two promises to perform does not result in an accounting transaction that is recorded. For example, consider the case in which Sbarro and Xerox sign an agreement with Xerox promising to provide repair service on Sbarro's copy machines at a price of $50 for each visit during the next year and Sbarro promising to pay for the service when Xerox provides it. No accounting transaction has taken place here because Sbarro and Xerox have exchanged only promises. Any time Xerox provides service, however, a transaction occurs since service has been exchanged for a promise to pay.

Similarly, if Sbarro sent an order to its paper supplier for more napkins and the supplier accepted the order, which will be filled next week, no transaction has taken place for accounting purposes. Only two promises have been exchanged. From the supplier's perspective, the same holds true. No transaction has taken place, so the supplier's financial statements are unaffected. As soon as the goods are shipped to Sbarro, however, the supplier has given up inventory in exchange for a promise from Sbarro to pay for them, and Sbarro has exchanged its promise to pay for the goods that it received as ordered. Now *one promise* has been exchanged for *goods*, so a transaction has taken place, and both Sbarro's and the supplier's statements will be affected.

Balancing the Accounting Equation

The accounting equation must remain in balance after each transaction. Total assets must equal total liabilities and stockholders' equity. If all of the correct accounts have been identified, and the appropriate direction of the effect on each account has been determined, the equation should remain in balance. Therefore, in performing the transaction analysis process, you should complete the following steps in this order:

1. *Accounts and effects*
   - **Identify the accounts affected**, making sure that the duality principle is met (at least two accounts change).
   - **Classify each account** as an asset (A), liability (L), or stockholders' equity (SE).

- Determine the **direction of the effect** (amount of increase [+] or decrease [–] on each A, L, and/or SE).

2. *Balancing*

- **Determine that the accounting equation (A = L + SE) remains in balance.**

Let us consider typical transactions of Sbarro, Inc., and most other businesses, as examples to illustrate the use of this process. As we stated earlier, only transactions affecting balance sheet accounts are presented in this chapter. Assume that Sbarro has the following transactions during January 1996 (the month following the balance sheet in Exhibit 2.2). The month will end on the Sunday closest to January 31, which will be February 2. The chart of accounts to be used here and in Chapters 3 and 4 is provided in Exhibit 2.3. Remember that all amounts are in thousands of dollars:

(*a*) **Sbarro issues $200 of additional common stock to new investors for cash.**

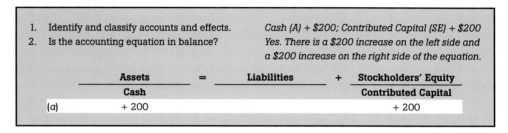

| | 1. Identify and classify accounts and effects. | *Cash (A) + $200; Contributed Capital (SE) + $200* |
| | 2. Is the accounting equation in balance? | *Yes. There is a $200 increase on the left side and a $200 increase on the right side of the equation.* |

	Assets	=	Liabilities	+	Stockholders' Equity
	Cash				Contributed Capital
(*a*)	+ 200				+ 200

EXHIBIT 2.3
Chart of Accounts

CHART OF ACCOUNTS (to be used in our Sbarro example)	To account for:
ASSETS (A)	
Cash	– Cash on hand
Inventory	– Food and paper products supplies on hand
Notes Receivable	– Funds lent to others (e.g., affiliates, employees)
Prepaid Expenses	– Benefits or rights to be received in the future (e.g., insurance coverage, advertising, rent)
Equipment	– The cost of equipment to be used in operations in the future
LIABILITIES (L)	
Accounts Payable	– Amount owed to suppliers (e.g., for food deliveries, for utility usage)
Notes Payable	– Borrowings, usually from a financial institution, to be paid
Dividends Payable	– Dividend authorization by the board of directors to be paid in cash in the future
Income Taxes Payable	– Amount owed to the federal, state, local, and foreign governments
Unearned Revenue	– Amount of future service owed by Sbarro to customers
STOCKHOLDERS' EQUITY (SE)	
Contributed Capital	– Amount investors paid for the company's stock
Retained Earnings	– Accumulated net income not distributed to shareholders as dividends
REVENUES AND GAINS (R)	
Restaurant Sales Revenue	– Sales of food service to customers
Franchise Related Income	– Funds earned from franchisees through the franchise agreement
EXPENSES AND LOSSES (E)	
Cost of Food and Paper Products	– Amount of food and paper products used to generate revenues
Wages Expense	– Amount earned by employees for work performed to generate revenues
Repairs Expense	– Amount incurred to maintain buildings and equipment in good operating condition
Utilities Expense	– Amount of electricity, gas, telephone, etc., used to generate revenues

(b) The company borrows $1,000 from its local bank, signing a promissory note to be paid in one year.

1.	Identify and classify accounts and effects.		*Cash (A) + $1,000; Notes Payable (L) + $1,000*
	Notes Payable is the name of the account that represents a signed promise to pay.		
2.	Is the accounting equation in balance?		*Yes. There is a $1,000 increase on the left and a $1,000 increase on the right.*

	Assets	=	Liabilities	+	Stockholders' Equity
	Cash		Notes Payable		Contributed Capital
(a)	+ 200				+ 200
(b)	+ 1,000		+ 1,000		
Balances	+ 1,200		+ 1,000		+ 200
Cumulative effect	**+1,200**	**= +1,200**			

Transactions (a) and (b) are financing transactions. Companies that need cash, for example, to buy or build additional facilities as part of their plans for growth, often seek funds by selling stock to investors, as in Transaction (a) or borrowing from creditors, usually banks, as in Transaction (b). Operating transactions also affect cash available to the business; this type of transaction will be discussed in Chapter 3.

(c) Sbarro acquires $70 in paper supplies, paying cash to its suppliers.

1.	Identify and classify accounts and effects.		*Inventory (A) + $70; Cash (A) – $70.*
2.	Is the accounting equation in balance?		*Yes. The equation balances remain the same because assets increase and decrease by the same amount.*

	Assets		=	Liabilities	+	Stockholders' Equity
	Cash	Inventory		Notes Payable		Contributed Capital
(a)	+ 200					+ 200
(b)	+ 1,000			+ 1,000		
(c)	– 70	+ 70				
Balances	+ 1,130	+ 70		+ 1,000		+ 200
Cumulative effect		**+1,200**	**= +1,200**			

(d) Sbarro opens a new restaurant and purchases $600 in equipment (primarily ovens and refrigeration equipment), paying $100 in cash with the rest due in six months on a promissory note to the equipment manufacturer.

1.	Identify and classify accounts and effects.		*Equipment (A) + $600; Cash (A) – $100; Notes Payable (L) + $500.*
	This transaction is more complex. The equipment is acquired by giving up an asset and also promising to pay.		
2.	Is the equation in balance?		*Yes. There is a $500 net increase on the left (+ $600 – $100) and a $500 increase on the right.*

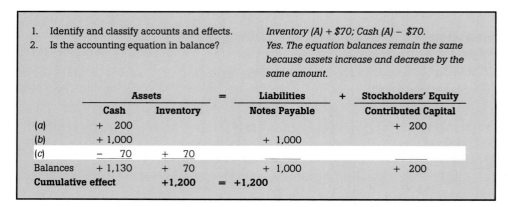

	Assets			=	Liabilities	+	Stockholders' Equity
	Cash	Inventory	Equipment		Notes Payable		Contributed Capital
(a)	+ 200						+ 200
(b)	+ 1,000				+ 1,000		
(c)	– 70	+ 70					
(d)	– 100		+ 600		+ 500		
Balances	+ 1,030	+ 70	+ 600		+ 1,500		+ 200
Cumulative effect			**+1,700**	**= +1,700**			

(e) Sbarro acquires $300 in food and beverage supplies on credit.

1. Identify and classify accounts and effects.	*Inventory (A) + $300; Accounts Payable (L) + $300.*	
2. Is the accounting equation in balance?	*Yes. There is a $300 increase on the left and a $300 increase on the right.*	

	Assets			=	Liabilities		+	Stockholders' Equity
	Cash	Inventory	Equipment		Accounts Payable	Notes Payable		Contributed Capital
(a)	+ 200							+ 200
(b)	+ 1,000					+ 1,000		
(c)	– 70	+ 70						
(d)	– 100		+ 600			+ 500		
(e)		+ 300			+ 300			
Balances	+ 1,030	+ 370	+ 600		+ 300	+ 1,500		+ 200
Cumulative effect		+2,000		=	+2,000			

The analysis of Transactions (f) through (h) follows. The effects are listed in the chart at the end of the Self-Study Quiz. For Transactions (i) and (j), space is left on the chart for your answers to the quiz that follows Transaction (h).

(f) Sbarro lends $40 to a franchisee who signed a note agreeing to repay the loan in one month.

1. Identify and classify accounts and effects.	*Notes Receivable (A) + $40; Cash (A) – $40.*
2. Is the accounting equation in balance?	*Yes. The equation remains the same because assets increase and decrease by the same amount.*

(g) Sbarro pays $200 cash on its accounts payable to suppliers.

1. Identify and classify accounts and effects.	*Accounts Payable (L) – $200; Cash (A) – $200.*
2. Is the accounting equation in balance?	*Yes. There is a $200 decrease on the left and a $200 decrease on the right.*

(h) Sbarro collects $40 cash on the note receivable from the franchisee.

1. Identify and classify accounts and effects.	*Cash (A) + $40; Notes Receivable (A) – $40.*
2. Is the accounting equation in balance?	*Yes. The equation remains the same because assets increase and decrease by the same amount.*

SELF-STUDY QUIZ

The most effective way to develop your transaction analysis skills is to practice with many transactions. Therefore, beginning with the balances generated in (a) through (h), complete the transaction analysis steps and following chart for Transactions (i) and (j). The key is repeating the steps until they become a natural part of your thought process.

(i) Sbarro paid $300 on the promissory note with the local bank.

1. Identify and classify accounts and effects.
2. Is the accounting equation in balance?

(j)   Sbarro purchased $250 of new tables and chairs (equipment), paying $90 in cash and the rest on account (owed to the furniture manufacturer in 60 days).

> 1.   Identify and classify accounts and effects.
> 2.   Is the accounting equation in balance?

Complete the following chart.

	Assets				=	Liabilities		+	Stockholders' Equity
	Cash	Notes Receivable	Inventory	Equipment	=	Accounts Payable	Notes Payable		Contributed Capital
(a) to (e)	+ 1,030	+ 0	+ 370	+ 600	=	+ 300	+ 1,500		+ 200
(f)	− 40	+ 40							
(g)	− 200					− 200			
(h)	+ 40	− 40							
(i)									
(j)									
Balances					=				
Cumulative effect					=				

After you have completed the schedule, check your solution with the answers in the footnote at the bottom of the page.*

How Do Companies Keep Track of Account Balances?

Because companies have significantly more transactions every day than those illustrated, recording transaction effects and keeping track of account balances in the manner used in the preceding illustration is impractical for most organizations. We will now expand the transaction analysis model and develop two very important tools that aid in reflecting the results of transaction analysis and performing other financial analysis tasks: journal entries and T-accounts.

LEARNING OBJECTIVE 5
Determine the impact of transaction analysis using two basic tools: (1) journal entries and (2) T-accounts.

These analytical tools are more efficient mechanisms for reflecting the effects of transactions and for determining account balances for financial statement preparation. These efficiencies are important from the standpoint of accounting systems design. As future business managers, you should develop your understanding and use of these tools in financial analysis. For those studying accounting, this knowledge is the foundation for understanding the accounting system and future course work. After we learn to perform transaction analysis using these tools, we will illustrate their use in financial analysis.

---

*(i) Notes Payable – $300; Cash – $300.
(j) Equipment + $250; Cash – $90; Accounts Payable + $160.
    Assets ($1,660) = Liabilities ($1,460) + Stockholders' Equity ($200)
If your answers did not agree with ours, we recommend that you go back to each transaction to make sure that you have completed each of the steps for each transaction.

The Direction of Transaction Effects

As discussed earlier, assets, liabilities, and stockholders' equity account balances increase and decrease from the effects of transactions. To learn how to reflect the effects efficiently, the transaction analysis model first needs to be structured in a manner that shows the *direction* of the effects. This direction rule is critical for constructing the model as a tool for transaction analysis. As you can see in the following model, *the word* increase *is written on the left when we are on the left side of the accounting equation and on the right when we are on the right side of the accounting equation.* The transaction analysis model is as follows:

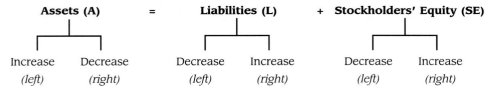

As we illustrated earlier for Transactions (*a*) through (*j*), each account (such as Cash and Accounts Payable) in each of these categories can be increased (+) or decreased (–) by transactions, and each account has a balance.

The Debit–Credit Framework

The concepts of *debit* and *credit* are now added to the model. **Debit** means the left side of an account, and **credit** means the right. For each element of the model, we substitute the term *debit* for left and the term *credit* for right. The transaction analysis model now is as follows:

Debit means the left side of an account; **credit** means the right side of an account.

From this model, we can also observe the following:
- Asset accounts have debit balances (their positive, or increase, side).
- Liabilities and stockholders' equity accounts have credit balances (their positive, or increase, side).

As you are learning to perform transaction analysis, you should refer to this model often until you can construct it on your own without assistance. We build on this model in Chapter 3 when we add transactions affecting operations.

    Many students have trouble with accounting because they forget that the only meaning for *debit* is the left side of an account and the only meaning for *credit* is the right side of an account. Perhaps someone once told you that you were a credit to your school or your family. As a result, you may think that there is "goodness" attached to credits and perhaps a "badness" attached to debits. Such is not the case. Just remember that *debit means left* and *credit means right*.

    It also should be easy to remember which accounts debits increase and which accounts credits increase. A debit (left) increases asset accounts because assets are on the left side of the accounting equation (A = L + SE). A credit (right) increases liability and stockholders' equity accounts because they are on the right side of the accounting equation.

If the correct accounts and effects have been identified through transaction analysis, the accounting equation will remain in balance. What will also be true is that *the total dollar value of all debits equals the total dollar value of all credits* in a transaction. Therefore, this equality check (debits = credits) should be added to the transaction analysis process.

Analytical Tool: The Journal Entry

A **journal entry** is an accounting method for expressing the effects of a transaction on accounts in a debits-equal-credits format.

In a bookkeeping system, transactions are initially recorded in chronological order in a *journal*. After analyzing the business documents that describe a transaction, the accountant prepares the formal entry in the journal. Using debits and credits, a journal entry is written for each transaction. The **journal entry** is an accounting method for expressing the effects of a transaction on accounts in a debits-equal-credits format.[3] The journal entry for Transaction (*d*) in the Sbarro illustration is as follows:

(date or reference)	Equipment (A)	600	
	Cash (A)		100
	Notes payable (L)		500

Notice the following:

- Including a date or some form of reference for each transaction is useful.
- The debits are written first (on top); the credits are written below all of the debits.
- The credits are indented (both words and amounts) a few spaces to the right below the debits.
- Total debits ($600) equal total credits ($100 + $500).
- Any journal entry that affects more than two accounts is called a *compound entry*. Three accounts are affected by this transaction. Although this and Transaction (*j*) are the only transactions in the preceding illustration that require a compound entry, many transactions in future chapters will require recording a compound journal entry.

While you are learning to perform transaction analysis, use the symbols A, L, and SE next to each account title, as is done in the preceding journal entry, including all homework problems. Specifically identifying accounts as assets (A), liabilities (L), or stockholders' equity (SE) makes using the transaction analysis model clearer and journal entries easier.

We have found that many students try to memorize journal entries without understanding or using the transaction analysis model. The task becomes increasingly more difficult as new detailed transactions are presented in subsequent chapters. However, *memorizing, understanding, and using the transaction analysis model* presented and *following the steps in the transaction analysis process* will work for any transaction, including those in future chapters.

Analytical Tool: The T–Account

After the journal entries have been recorded, the bookkeeper posts (transfers) the dollar amounts to each account that was affected by the transaction to determine account balances. In most computerized accounting systems, this happens automatically upon recording the journal entry. As a group, the accounts are called a *ledger*. In a manual

---

[3] Exhibit C.1 in Appendix C illustrates a page from a formal journal.

EXHIBIT 2.4
T-Accounts Illustrated

	Cash (A)					Accounts Payable (L)		
Increase (debit)		**Decrease (credit)**				**Decrease (debit)**	**Increase (credit)**	
Beginning							Beginning	
balance	93,500						balance	7,400
(a)	200	(c)	70		−200 { (g)	200	(e)	300 } +460
+1,240 { (b)	1,000	(d)	100				(j)	160
(h)	40	(f)	40	} −800				
		(g)	200					
		(i)	300					
		(j)	90					
Ending							Ending	
balance	93,940						balance	7,660

accounting system used by some small organizations, the ledger is often a three-ring binder with a separate page for each account. In a computerized system, accounts are stored on a disk.

Journal entries by themselves do not provide balances in accounts. One very useful tool for summarizing transaction effects and determining balances for individual accounts is called a **T-account,** which is a simplified representation of a ledger account. The T-accounts for the Cash and Accounts Payable accounts for Sbarro, Inc., based on Transactions (a) through (j) are presented in Exhibit 2.4. Notice that, for Cash, which is classified as an asset, increases are on the left and decreases are on the right side of the T-account. For Accounts Payable, however, increases are on the right and decreases are on the left since the account is a liability.

> The **T-account** is a tool for summarizing transaction effects for each account, determining balances, and drawing inferences about a company's activities.

T-accounts can be written as equations that yield balances for financial statement purposes:

		Cash	Accounts Payable
	Beginning Balance	93,500	7,400
+	All effects on the increase side	+ 1,240	+ 460
−	All effects on the decrease side	− 800	− 200
+	Ending Balance	93,940	7,660

Handwritten or manually maintained accounts in the T-account format shown here may be used in small businesses. Computerized systems retain the concept of the account but not the T-account format.

The words *debit* and *credit* are used as verbs, nouns, and adjectives. For example, we can say that (1) Sbarro's Cash account was debited (verb) when stock was issued to investors; (2) to credit (verb) an account means to put the amount on the right side of the T-account; (3) a debit (noun) is the left side of an account; and (4) Notes Payable is a credit account (adjective). These terms will be used instead of *left* and *right* throughout the rest of the textbook. The next section illustrates the steps you should follow in using the model to analyze the effects of transactions, record the effects in journal entries, and determine account balances by using T-accounts.

Transaction Analysis Illustrated

The typical monthly transactions of Sbarro, Inc., presented earlier will be used to demonstrate transaction analysis and the use of journal entries and T-accounts. We analyze each transaction, checking that the accounting equation remains in balance and debits equal credits. In the T-accounts, located together at the end of the illustration, the amounts from Sbarro's December 31, 1995, balance sheet have been inserted as the beginning balances in each account. After reviewing or preparing each journal entry, trace the effects to the appropriate T-accounts using the transaction letters as a reference. The first transaction has been highlighted for you.

You should study this illustration carefully (including the explanations of transaction analysis). Careful study of the illustration is *essential* to the understanding of (1) the accounting model, (2) transaction analysis, (3) recording the dual effects of each transaction, and (4) the dual-balancing system. The most effective way to learn these critical concepts that affect material throughout the rest of the text is to practice, practice, practice.

(a) Sbarro sells $200 in additional stock to new investors.

Transaction Analysis					Journal Entry		
Assets	=	Liabilities	+	Stockholders' Equity	Cash (A)	200	
Cash +200				Contributed Capital +200	Contributed capital (SE)		200

The accounting equation is in balance. Debits $200 = Credits $200.

These effects were posted to the appropriate T-accounts at the end of the illustration. To post, transfer or copy the debit or credit amount on each line to the appropriate T-account indicated to accumulate balances for each account. For example, the $200 debit is listed in the Debit column of the Cash T-account.

(b) The company borrows $1,000 from its local bank, signing a promissory note to be paid in one year.

Transaction Analysis					Journal Entry		
Assets	=	Liabilities	+	Stockholders' Equity	Cash (A)	1,000	
Cash +1,000		Notes Payable +1,000			Notes payable (L)		1,000

The accounting equation is in balance. Debits $1,000 = Credits $1,000.

(c) Sbarro acquires $70 in paper supplies, paying cash to its suppliers.

Transaction Analysis					Journal Entry		
Assets	=	Liabilities	+	Stockholders' Equity	Inventory (A)	70	
Inventory +70					Cash (A)		70
Cash −70							

The accounting equation is in balance. Debits $70 = Credits $70.

(d) Sbarro opens a new restaurant and purchases $600 in equipment (primarily ovens and refrigeration equipment), paying $100 in cash with the rest due in six months on a promissory note to the equipment manufacturer.

Transaction Analysis					Journal Entry		
Assets	=	Liabilities	+	Stockholders' Equity	Equipment (A)	600	
Equipment +600		Notes Payable +500			Cash (A)		100
Cash −100					Notes payable (L)		500

The accounting equation is in balance. Debits $600 = Credits $600.

(e) Sbarro acquires $300 in food and beverage supplies on credit owed to its suppliers.

Transaction Analysis				Journal Entry		
Assets	=	Liabilities	+	Stockholders' Equity	Inventory (A)	300
Inventory +300		Accounts Payable +300			Accounts payable (L)	300
The accounting equation is in balance. Debits $300 = Credits $300.						

(f) Sbarro lends $40 to a franchisee who signed a note agreeing to repay the loan in one month.

Transaction Analysis				Journal Entry		
Assets	=	Liabilities	+	Stockholders' Equity	Notes receivable (A)	40
Cash −40					Cash (A)	40
Notes Receivable +40						
The accounting equation is in balance. Debits $40 = Credits $40.						

(g) Sbarro pays $200 cash on its accounts payable to suppliers.

Transaction Analysis				Journal Entry		
Assets	=	Liabilities	+	Stockholders' Equity	Accounts payable (A)	200
Cash −200		Accounts Payable −200			Cash (A)	200
The accounting equation is in balance. Debits $200 = Credits $200.						

(h) Sbarro collects on the note receivable from the franchisee.

Transaction Analysis				Journal Entry		
Assets	=	Liabilities	+	Stockholders' Equity	Cash (A)	40
Cash +40					Notes receivable (A)	40
Notes Receivable −40						
The accounting equation is in balance. Debits $40 = Credits $40.						

SELF-STUDY QUIZ

For Transactions (i) through (j), fill in the missing information, including postings to T-accounts. You can check your answers with the solution at the end of the illustration:

(i) Sbarro pays $300 on the promissory note with the local bank.

Transaction Analysis				Journal Entry
Assets	=	Liabilities	+	Stockholders' Equity	
Cash −300		Notes Payable −300			
The accounting equation is in balance. Debits $300 = Credits $300.				

(*j*) Sbarro purchases $250 of new tables and chairs (equipment), paying $90 in cash and the rest on credit.

Transaction Analysis			Journal Entry
Assets	=	Liabilities + Stockholders' Equity	
Cash −90 Equipment +250		Accounts Payable +160	
The accounting equation is in balance. Debits $_____ = Credits $_____.			

The following are the T-accounts that changed during the period because of these transactions. The balances of all other accounts remained the same. The December 31, 1995, balances from Sbarro's balance sheet have been included as the beginning balances:

Cash (A)

Debit (Inc.)		Credit (Dec.)	
Beg. Bal.	93,500	(c)	70
(a)	200	(d)	100
(b)	1,000	(f)	40
(h)	40	(g)	200
		(i)	
		(j)	
End. Bal.	93,940		

Receivables (Notes and other) (A)

Debit (Inc.)		Credit (Dec.)	
Beg. Bal.	2,600		
(f)	40	(h)	40
End. Bal.	2,600		

Inventory (A)

Debit (Inc.)		Credit (Dec.)
Beg. Bal.	2,800	
(c)	70	
(e)	300	
End. Bal.	3,170	

Equipment (A)

Debit (Inc.)		Credit (Dec.)
Beg. Bal.	126,800	
(d)	600	
(j)		
End. Bal.	127,650	

Accounts Payable (L)

Debit (Dec.)		Credit (Inc.)	
		Beg. Bal.	7,400
(g)	200	(e)	300
		(j)	
		End. Bal.	7,660

Notes Payable (L)

Debit (Dec.)		Credit (Inc.)	
		Beg. Bal.	0
(i)		(b)	1,000
		(d)	500
		End. Bal.	1,200

Contributed Capital (SE)

Debit (Dec.)	Credit (Inc.)	
	Beg. Bal.	30,500
	(a)	200
	End. Bal.	30,700

You can verify that you posted the entries properly by adding the increase side and subtracting the decrease side and then comparing your answer to the ending balance given in each of the T-accounts. You can check your answers with the solutions at the bottom of this page.*

---

* (i) Journal entry: Notes payable (L)   300
                              Cash (A)   300
  (j) Journal entry: Equipment (A)   250
                              Accounts payable (L)   160
                              Cash (A)   90
  Debits $250 = Credits $250. This is a compound entry with three accounts affected by the transaction.

Inferring Business Activities from T-Accounts

T-accounts are useful primarily for instructional purposes and as a financial analysis tool. In many cases we will use the T-account tool to determine what transactions a company engaged in during a period. For example, the primary transactions affecting accounts payable for a period are purchases of assets on account and cash payments to suppliers. If we know the beginning and ending balances of accounts payable and all of the amounts that were purchased on credit during a period, we can determine the amount of cash paid. The T-account will include the following:

Accounts Payable (L)			
Debit (Dec.)		**Credit (Inc.)**	
		Beginning balance	600
Cash payments	?	Purchases on account	1,500
		Ending Balance	300

SOLUTION

Beg. balance + Purchases – Cash payments = Ending balance
$600 + $1,500 – Cash payments = $300
$2,100 – Cash payments = $300
Cash payments = $1,800

Balance Sheet Preparation

It is possible to prepare a balance sheet at any point in time from the balances in the accounts. The date February 2, 1996, is the Sunday closest to the end of the month. Using the new balances shown in the T-accounts in the preceding Sbarro illustration plus the original balances in the accounts that did not change, the balance sheet in Exhibit 2.5 compares the account balances at February 2, 1996, with those at December 31, 1995. Notice that when multiple periods are presented, the most recent balance sheet amounts are usually listed on the left, although this may vary.

At the beginning of the chapter, we presented the changes in Sbarro's balance sheets from the beginning of the year (January 1, 1995) to the end of the year (December 31, 1995). We questioned what made the accounts change and what the process was for reflecting the changes. Now we can see that the accounts have changed again in one month:

LEARNING OBJECTIVE 6
Prepare and analyze a simple balance sheet.

	Total Assets	=	Total Liabilities	+	Stockholders' Equity
12/31/95	$242,700	=	$57,100	+	$185,600
2/2/96	244,360	=	58,560	+	185,800
Change	+ $ 1,660	=	+ $ 1,460	+	+ $ 200

Comparing Companies in the Same Industry

One of the important uses of balance sheet information is to compare companies' financing and investing strategies (other analyses will be discussed in future chapters). For example, let's compare Sbarro, Inc., to another company in the same industry ("retail eating places," Standard Industrial Classification 5812).

Sbarro was incorporated in 1977 and Sizzler in 1968. Sbarro owns (versus franchises) 74 percent of its restaurants and Sizzler owns 41 percent. They are in the same industry classification yet have very different investing and financing strategies. The following chart reflects the differences:

		Sbarro, Inc.	Sizzler International, Inc.
Investing	Property, plant, and equipment as a percentage of total assets	52%	80%
Financing	Debt-to-equity ratio	31%	56%

One of the most dramatic differences is in the amount of property and equipment. For 1995, Sbarro had 52 percent of its total assets in property and equipment ($126,700 property and equipment ÷ $242,700 total assets), whereas Sizzler had 80 percent of its total assets in property and equipment. This appears reasonable because, unlike Sbarro, which primarily leases space in shopping malls across the country, Sizzler often constructs its own buildings.

Such an investment strategy often requires a different financing strategy, usually involving increased borrowing. More of the financing for Sizzler's heavier investment in land, buildings, and equipment comes from borrowing through long-term liabilities (debt financing) than issuing stock to investors (equity financing). Sbarro, on the other hand, does not have any long-term debt, relying on equity financing to a greater degree.

EXHIBIT 2.5
Balance Sheet

SBARRO INC. AND SUBSIDIARIES
Balance Sheets
at February 2, 1996 and December 31, 1995
(in thousands of dollars)

	February 2, 1996	December 31, 1995
ASSETS		
Cash and cash equivalents	$ 93,940	$ 93,500
Marketable securities	10,000	10,000
Receivables (franchise fees and other)	2,600	2,600
Inventories	3,170	2,800
Prepaid expenses	1,700	1,700
Property and equipment	127,650	126,800
Other assets	5,300	5,300
Total assets	**$244,360**	**$242,700**
LIABILITIES		
Notes payable	$ 1,200	$ 0
Accounts payable	7,660	7,400
Accrued expenses payable (rent, payroll, and other)	27,000	27,000
Dividend payable	3,900	3,900
Income taxes payable	4,700	4,700
Deferred income taxes	14,100	14,100
Total liabilities	$ 58,560	$ 57,100
STOCKHOLDERS' EQUITY		
Contributed capital	$ 30,700	$ 30,500
Retained earnings	155,100	155,100
Total stockholders' equity	185,800	185,600
Total liabilities and stockholders' equity	**$244,360**	**$242,700**

Recall from Chapter 1 that companies report on cash inflows and outflows for a period in their Statement of Cash Flows. This statement divides all transactions that affect cash into three categories: operating, investing, and financing activities. Let's examine the $440 cash increase in our Sbarro example to determine the sources and uses of cash.

We stated at the beginning of the chapter that we would focus on investing and financing activities in this chapter and operating activities in Chapter 3. Investing activities include buying and selling productive assets and investments. In our example, the following transactions are categorized as investing activities:

FOCUS ON CASH FLOWS

	Transaction	Type of Activity	Effect on Cash
(d)	Sbarro purchases $600 in equipment, paying $100 in cash with the rest due in six months on a note to the manufacturer.	Purchasing a productive asset is an investing activity.	– $100
(f)	Sbarro lends $40 to a franchisee who agrees to repay the loan in one month.	Lending is an investing activity.	– 40
(j)	Sbarro purchases $250 of new equipment, paying $90 in cash and the rest on account.	Purchasing a productive asset is an investing activity.	– 90
(h)	Sbarro collects on the note receivable from the franchisee.	Receiving payment on a loan is an investing activity.	+ 40
	Net effect on cash from investing activities		– $190

Financing activities include borrowing and repaying funds, usually on notes to banks, selling stock to investors for cash, and paying dividends. In our example, the following transactions are categorized as financing activities:

	Transaction	Type of Activity	Effect on Cash
(a)	Sbarro sells $200 in additional stock to investors.	Selling stock for cash is a financing activity.	+$ 200
(b)	The company borrows $1,000 from its local bank, signing a note to be paid in one year.	Borrowing from banks is a financing activity.	+ 1,000
(i)	Sbarro pays $300 on the note with the local bank.	Repaying notes is a financing activity.	– 300
	Net effect on cash from financing activities		+$ 900

In this chapter, you may have noticed that no transactions resulted in revenues or expenses for Sbarro (e.g., selling food, paying employees). Several transactions must have affected cash from operations, however, because the net effect on cash from investing and financing activities was +$710 (+$900 financing – $190 investing), not the $440 change that occurred. In Chapter 3, we will analyze transactions with an operating emphasis and add them to the analysis.

SELF-STUDY QUIZ

Lance, Inc., manufactures and sells snack products. From a recent annual statement of cash flows, indicate whether the transaction affected cash flow as an investing (I) activity or a financing (F) activity and indicate the direction of the effect on cash (+ = increases cash; – = decreases cash):

Transaction	Type of Activity (I or F)	Effect on Cash Flows (+ or -)
1. Paid dividends.		
2. Sold property.		
3. Sold marketable securities.		
4. Purchased vending machines.		
5. Purchased its own common stock.*		

*Companies often repurchase stock from investors, reducing the company's contributed capital.

After you have completed the schedule, check your solution with the answers in the footnote at the bottom of the page.*

Some Misconceptions

Some people confuse bookkeeping with accounting. In effect, they confuse a part of accounting with the whole. Bookkeeping involves the routine, clerical part of accounting and requires only minimal knowledge of accounting. A bookkeeper may record the repetitive and uncomplicated transactions in most businesses and may maintain the simple records of a small business. In contrast, the accountant is a highly trained professional, competent in the design of information systems, analysis of complex transactions, interpretation of financial data, financial reporting, auditing, taxation, and management consulting.

Another prevalent misconception is that all transactions are subject to precise and objective measurement and that the accounting results reported in the financial statements are exactly what happened that period. In reality, accounting numbers are influenced by estimates, as subsequent chapters will illustrate. Some people believe that financial statements report the entity's market value (including its assets), but they do not. To understand and interpret financial statements, the user must be aware of their limitations as well as their usefulness. One should understand what the financial statements do and do not try to accomplish.

Finally, financial statements are often thought to be inflexible because of their quantitative nature. As you study accounting, you will learn that it requires considerable *professional judgment* on the part of the accountant to capture the economic essence of complex transactions. Accounting is stimulating intellectually; it is not a cut-and-dried subject. It calls on your intelligence, analytical ability, creativity, and judgment. Accounting is a communication process involving an audience (users) with

*1. F –
 2. I +
 3. I +
 4. I –
 5. F –

a wide diversity of knowledge, interest, and capabilities; therefore, it will call on your ability as a communicator. The language of accounting uses concisely written phrases and symbols to convey information about the resource flows measured for specific organizations.

To understand financial statements, you must have a certain level of knowledge of the concepts and the measurement procedures used in the accounting process. You should learn what accounting is really like and appreciate the reasons for using certain procedures. This level of knowledge cannot be gained by reading a list of the concepts and a list of the misconceptions. Neither can a generalized discussion of the subject matter suffice. A certain amount of involvement, primarily problem solving (similar to the requirement in mathematics courses), is essential in the study of accounting focused on the needs of the user. Therefore, we provide problems aimed at the desirable knowledge level for the user as well as the preparer of financial statements.

Demonstration Case

On April 1, 1998, three ambitious college students started the Terrific Lawn Maintenance Corporation. Completed transactions (summarized) through April 30, 1998, for Terrific Lawn Maintenance Corporation follow:

(a) Issued $9,000 of common stock in total to the three investors in exchange for cash. Each investor received 500 shares of stock (totaling 1,500 issued shares).

(b) Acquired rakes and other hand tools (equipment) with a list price of $690 for $600; paid $200 cash and the balance on account with the hardware store.

(c) Ordered three lawn mowers and two edgers from XYZ Lawn Supply, Inc., for $4,000.

(d) Purchased 4 acres of land as a future building site of a storage garage. Paid cash, $5,000.

(e) Received the mowers and edgers that had been ordered, agreeing to pay XYZ Lawn Supply in full in 30 days.

(f) Sold one acre of land to the city for a park. The city signed a note to pay Terrific Lawn Maintenance Corp. $1,250 by the end of the month.

(g) Paid $700 owed on account to suppliers (XYZ and the hardware store).

(h) Collected cash on note owed by the city.

(i) One of the owners borrowed $3,000 from a local bank for personal use.

Required:

1. Set up T-accounts for Cash, Notes Receivable (from the city), Lawn Equipment (for hand tools and mowing equipment), Land, Accounts Payable (to suppliers), and Contributed Capital. Beginning balances are $0; indicate these beginning balances in the T-accounts. Analyze each transaction using the process outlined in the chapter. Prepare journal entries in chronological order. Enter the effects of the transactions on the accounting model in the appropriate T-accounts. Identify each amount with its letter in the preceding list.

2. Use the amounts in the T-accounts developed in requirement (1) to prepare a balance sheet for Terrific Lawn Maintenance Corporation at April 30, 1998. The April 30, 1998, balance sheet requires use of the account balances for all assets, liabilities, and stockholders' equity. The transaction analysis model is presented for your use:

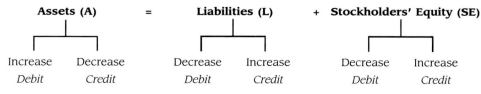

3. Identify investing and financing transactions affecting cash.

Now you can check your answers with the solution to these requirements in the following section.

Suggested Solution

1. Transaction analysis, journal entries, and T-accounts:

	Transaction Analysis	Journal Entry
(a)	**Assets** = **Liabilities** + **Stockholders' Equity** Cash + 9,000 .... Contributed Capital + 9,000	Cash (A) 9,000 Contributed capital (SE) 9,000

(b)	**Assets** = **Liabilities** + **Stockholders' Equity**
	Cash − 200 Accounts Payable + 400
	Equipment + 600
	The **cost principle** states that assets should be recorded at the amount paid on the date of the transaction. This is $600, not the $690 list price.
		Equipment (A) 600
		    Cash (A) 200
		    Accounts payable (L) 400

(c)	No accounts are affected. **This is not an accounting transaction; no exchange takes place.**	
(d)	**Assets** = **Liabilities** + **Stockholders' Equity** Cash − 5,000 Land + 5,000	Land (A) 5,000 Cash (A) 5,000
(e)	**Assets** = **Liabilities** + **Stockholders' Equity** Equipment + 4,000 Accounts Payable + 4,000	Equipment (A) 4,000 Accounts payable (L) 4,000
(f)	**Assets** = **Liabilities** + **Stockholders' Equity** Notes Receivable + 1,250 Land − 1,250	Notes receivable (A) 1,250 Land (A) 1,250
(g)	**Assets** = **Liabilities** + **Stockholders' Equity** Cash − 700 Accounts Payable − 700	Accounts payable (L) 700 Cash (A) 700
(h)	**Assets** = **Liabilities** + **Stockholders' Equity** Cash +1,250 Notes Receivable −1,250	Cash (A) 1,250 Notes receivable (A) 1,250
(i)	There is no transaction for the company, The **separate-entity assumption** states that transactions of the owners are separate from transactions of the business.	

Cash (A)				Notes Receivable (A)				Equipment (A)		
Debit (Inc.)		**Credit (Dec.)**		**Debit (Inc.)**		**Credit (Dec.)**		**Debit (Inc.)**		**Credit (Dec.)**
Beg. bal.	0			Beg. bal.	0			Beg. bal.	0	
(a)	9,000	(b)	200	(f)	1,250	(h)	1,250	(b)	600	
(h)	1,250	(d)	5,000					(e)	4,000	
		(g)	700							
End. bal.	4,350			End. bal.	0			End. bal.	4,600	

Land (A)				Accounts Payable (L)				Contributed Capital (SE)		
Debit (Inc.)		**Credit (Dec.)**		**Debit (Dec.)**		**Credit (Inc.)**		**Debit (Dec.)**		**Credit (Inc.)**
Beg. bal.	0					Beg. bal.	0			Beg. bal.	0
(d)	5,000	(f)	1,250	(g)	700	(b)	400			(a)	9,000
						(e)	4,000				
End. bal.	3,750					End. bal.	3,700			End. bal.	9,000

2. Balance sheet:

TERRIFIC LAWN MAINTENANCE CORPORATION
Balance Sheet
At April 30, 1998

Assets		Liabilities	
Cash	$4,350	Accounts payable	$ 3,700
Equipment	4,600		
Land	3,750	**Stockholders' Equity**	
		Contributed capital	9,000
Total assets	$12,700	Total liabilities and stockholders' equity	$12,700

Notice that balance sheets presented earlier in the text listed assets on the top and liabilities and stockholders' equity on the bottom. This is called the **report form**. Preparing a balance sheet with assets on the left side and liabilities and stockholders' equity on the right side, such as the preceding one, is called the **account form**. Both are used in practice.

Two balance sheet forms: **Report form** lists assets on top, liabilities and stockholders' equity on the bottom.

Account form lists assets on the left, liabilities and stockholders' equity on the right.

3. Investing and financing effects on cash:

Transaction	Type of Activity	Effect on Cash
(a) Issued $9,000 in stock to three investors for cash.	Issuing stock is a financing activity.	+ $9,000
(b) Acquired $600 equipment; paid $200 cash, the rest on account.	Purchasing a productive asset is an investing activity.	– 200
(d) Purchased 4 acres of land for $5,000 cash .	Purchasing a productive asset is an investing activity.	– 5,000
(h) Collected cash on note owed by the city.	Receiving payment on a note is an investing activity.	+ 1,250

Summary

This chapter reviewed the parts of the conceptual framework relevant to the balance sheet (the objective of external financial reporting, definitions of balance sheet elements, and the cost principle). This chapter then discussed the accounting model and illustrated its application in the accounting system for a business. For accounting purposes, transactions were defined as (1) exchanges of assets and liabilities between the business and other individuals and organizations and (2) certain events that do not occur between the business and other parties but exert a direct effect on the entity (such as recording adjustments to reflect the use of equipment in operations).

Application of the accounting model—Assets = Liabilities + Stockholders' Equity—was illustrated for Sbarro, Inc. The application involved (1) transaction analysis, (2) journal entries, and (3) the accounts (T-account format). Each transaction causes at least two different accounts to be affected in terms of the accounting model. The model often is referred to as a *double-entry system* because each transaction has a dual effect. The process used in transaction analysis involves (1) identifying and classifying the accounts and effects and (2) determining that the accounting equation remains in balance.

The transaction analysis model (built on the accounting equation) and the mechanics of the debit–credit concept in T-account format can be summarized as follows:

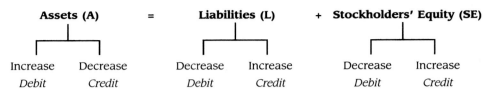

TRANSACTION ANALYSIS MODEL

Assets (A)	=	Liabilities (L)	+	Stockholders' Equity (SE)

Increase	Decrease		Decrease	Increase		Decrease	Increase
Debit	*Credit*		*Debit*	*Credit*		*Debit*	*Credit*

T-ACCOUNT FORMAT

Assets		Liabilities		Stockholder' Equity	
Increase *Debit*	**Decrease *Credit***	**Decrease *Debit***	**Increase *Credit***	**Decrease *Debit***	**Increase *Credit***
Beg. bal.			Beg. bal.		Beg. bal.
End. bal.			End. bal.		End. bal.

In this chapter, we discussed the fundamental accounting model and transaction analysis. Journal entries and T-accounts were used to record the results of transaction analysis for investing and financing decisions that affect balance sheet accounts. In Chapter 3, we continue our detailed look at financial statements, in particular the income statement. The purpose of Chapter 3 is to build on your knowledge by discussing concepts for the measurement of revenues and expenses and by illustrating transaction analysis for operating decisions.

Key Ratios

Debt-to-equity ratio is a measure of the proportion of debt to owners' equity. It reflects a company's equity position and the level of risk a company assumes by financing the business through debt. It is computed as follows (p. 000):

$$\text{Debt to equity} = \frac{\text{Total liabilities}}{\text{Stockholders' equity}}$$

Key Terms

Account A standardized format that organizations use to accumulate the dollar effects of transactions on each financial statement item. *60*

Assets Probable future economic benefits owned by the entity as a result of past transactions. *55*

Continuity Assumption (Going-Concern) The belief that businesses are assumed to continue to operate into the foreseeable future. *55*

Contributed Capital Cash (and sometimes other assets) provided to the business by owners. *59*

Cost Principle An accounting rule that requires assets to be recorded at the historical cash-equivalent cost, which on the date of the transaction is cash paid plus the current dollar value of all noncash considerations also given in the exchange. *59*

Debits and Credits *Debit* is the name for the left side of an account. Debits represent increases in assets and decreases in liabilities and stockholders' equity. *Credit* is the name for the right side of an account. Credits represent decreases in assets and increases in liabilities and stockholders' equity. *69*

Journal Entry An accounting method for expressing the effects of a transaction on accounts in a debits-equal-credits format. *70*

Liabilities Probable debts or obligations of the entity as a result of past transactions, which will be paid with assets or services. *58*

Primary Objective of External Financial **Reporting** Providing useful economic information about a business to help external parties make sound financial decisions. *55*

Retained Earnings Cumulative earnings of a company that are not distributed to the owners and are reinvested in the business. *59*

Report and Account Forms Two common balance sheet preparation forms. The report form lists assets on the top and liabilities and stockholders' equity on the bottom. The account form lists assets on the left side and liabilities and stockholders' equity accounts on the right side. *81*

Separate-Entity Assumption The concept that business transactions are separate from the transactions of the owners. *55*

Stockholders' Equity (Owners' Equity or Shareholders' Equity) The financing provided by the owners and the operations of the business. *58*

T-accounts An analytical tool for summarizing transaction effects for each account, determining balances for financial statement preparation, and drawing inferences about a company's activities. *71*

Transaction (1) An exchange between a business and one or more external parties, such as borrowing money from a bank or (2) a measurable event internal to a business, such as adjustments for the use of assets in operations. *60*

Transaction Analysis The process of studying a transaction to determine its economic effect on the business in terms of the accounting equation: Assets = Liabilities + Stockholders' Equity. *63*

Unit-of-Measure Assumption Accounting information is measured and reported in the national monetary unit. *55*

Questions

1. What is the primary objective of financial reporting for external users?
2. Give the accounting model and define each category.
3. Define a business transaction in the broad sense and give an example of the two different kinds of transactions.
4. Explain what the separate-entity assumption means in accounting.
5. Explain what the unit-of-measure assumption means in accounting.
6. Explain what the continuity assumption means in accounting.
7. Explain what the cost principle means in accounting.
8. Why are accounting assumptions necessary?
9. What are the owners of a business organized as a corporation called? What is the basis for this name?
10. At December 31, 19A (end of year 1), the accounting model for THIS Company showed the following: stockholders' equity, $90,000; and liabilities, $30,000.
    a. Show how THIS Company stands in terms of the accounting model.
    b. Show the summarized balance sheet.

11. For accounting purposes, what is an account? Explain why accounts are used in an accounting system.
12. Explain what *debit* and *credit* mean.
13. What two equalities in accounting must be maintained in transaction analysis?
14. Briefly explain what is meant by transaction analysis. What are the two steps in transaction analysis?
15. Complete the following table by entering either the word *debit* or *credit* in each column.

Item	Increase	Decrease
Assets		
Liabilities		
Stockholders' equity		

16. Complete the following table by entering either the word *increases* or *decreases* in each column.

Item	Debit	Credit
Assets		
Liabilities		
Stockholders' equity		

17. What is a T-account? What is its purpose?
18. What is a journal entry?
19. Assume that you and a friend started a new business called Dos Amigos Corporation. Each of you invested $5,000 in cash for equal shares of stock. Give the effect of this transaction on the company in terms of
    a. The accounting model.
    b. A journal entry.
    c. The T-accounts.

Exercises

E2–1 Matching Definitions with Terms

Match each definition with its related term by entering the appropriate letter in the space provided.

TERM	DEFINITION
____ (1) Separate-entity assumption	A. = Liabilities + Stockholders' Equity.
____ (2) Cost principle	B. Reports assets, liabilities, and stockholders' equity.
____ (3) Credits	C. Accounts for a business separate from its owners.
____ (4) Assets	D. Increase assets; decrease liabilities and stockholders' equity.
____ (5) Transaction	E. An exchange between an entity and other parties.
____ (6) Continuity assumption	F. The concept that businesses will operate into the foreseeable future.
____ (7) T-account	G. Decrease assets; increase liabilities and stockholders' equity.
____ (8) Balance sheet	H. The concept that assets should be recorded at cash-equivalent cost.
____ (9) Debits	I. A standardized format used to accumulate data about each item reported on financial statements.

E2–2 Identifying Asset Accounts

Assets are probable future economic benefits owned by an entity as a result of past transactions (cash, goods, or services must be exchanged). Following the cost principle, the initial valuation of assets is the cash-equivalent cost (the amount of cash and other assets needed to acquire the asset).

Required:

Using the preceding definition and valuation rule, indicate whether or not the following events would result in recording an asset on the balance sheet. If an asset would be recorded, indicate an appropriate account title and amount. Then indicate other accounts affected. Use the following headings:

Event	Does an Asset Result?	Asset Account Title	Amount	Title of Other Account(s) Affected

1. A company orders and receives 10 personal computers for office use for which it promises to pay $25,000 within three months.
2. A company purchases a new delivery truck that has a list, or sticker, price of $24,000 for $21,000 cash.
3. A women's clothing retailer orders 1,000 fall blouses for $18 each for future delivery. The terms require payment within 30 days of delivery. Answer from the standpoint of the retailer.
4. The manufacturer of women's blouses receives the written order described in requirement (3). Answer from the standpoint of the manufacturer.
5. A manufacturing company signs a contract for the construction of a new warehouse for $500,000. At the signing, the company writes a check for $50,000 as a deposit on the future construction.
6. A publishing firm purchases the copyright (an intangible asset) to a manuscript for an introductory accounting text from the author for $40,000.
7. A manufacturing firm pays an advertising agency $100,000 to produce an advertising campaign for a new product.
8. A company purchases 100 shares of Apple Computer common stock for $5,000 cash.

E2–3 Identifying Asset Accounts

Assets are probable future economic benefits owned by an entity as a result of past transactions (cash, goods, or services must be exchanged). Following the cost principle, the initial valuation of assets is the cash-equivalent cost (the amount of cash and other assets needed to acquire the asset).

Required:

Using the preceding definition and valuation rule, indicate whether or not the following events would result in recording an asset on the balance sheet. If an asset would be recorded, indicate an appropriate account title and amount. Then indicate other accounts affected. Use the following headings:

Event	Does an Asset Result?	Asset Account Title	Amount	Title of Other Account(s) Affected

1. A company purchases a piece of land for $50,000 cash. An appraiser for the buyer valued the land at $52,500.
2. A new company is formed and sells 100 shares of stock for $12 per share to investors.

3. A manufacturing company purchases the patent on a new digital satellite system for television reception for $500,000 cash and a $400,000 note payable due in one year at 10 percent annual interest.

4. The accountant for a well-known snowboard manufacturing company believes that the company has accumulated $800,000 in goodwill over the 10 years it has been in business. The company has never been sold in the marketplace.

5. A local construction company receives a delivery of $5,000 of lumber. Terms indicate that payment will be due within 60 days of delivery.

6. An insurance company receives $1,200 from a customer for coverage for next year. Answer from the insurance company's point of view.

7. Answer requirement (6) from the customer's point of view.

8. A local company is a sole proprietorship (one owner); its owner buys a car for $10,000 for personal use. Answer from the company's point of view.

E2–4 Identifying Liability Accounts

Liabilities are probable debts or obligations of an entity as a result of past transactions (the receipt of cash, goods, or services) that will be paid with assets or services. The general rule for initial valuation is the cash-equivalent cost (what you could pay it off for today in cash, goods, or services).

Required:

Using the preceding definition and valuation rule, indicate whether or not the following events would result in recording a liability on the balance sheet. If a liability would be recorded, indicate an appropriate account title and amount. Then indicate other accounts affected. Use the following headings:

Event	Does a Liability Result?	Liability Account Title	Amount	Title of Other Account(s) Affected

1. A company orders and receives 10 personal computers for office use for which it promises to pay $25,000 within three months.

2. A company signs a note and receives a $10,000 loan from the bank, which it agrees to pay back in one year with 10 percent interest.

3. A women's clothing retailer orders 1,000 fall blouses for $18 each for future delivery. The terms require payment within 30 days of delivery. Answer from the standpoint of the retailer.

4. The manufacturer of women's blouses receives the written order described in requirement (3). Answer from the standpoint of the manufacturer.

5. A manufacturing company signs a contract for the construction of a new warehouse for $500,000. At the signing, the company writes a check for $50,000 as a deposit on the future construction.

6. Answer requirement (5) from the standpoint of the construction company.

7. A publishing firm uses $1,000 worth of electricity and natural gas for which it has not yet been billed (the other account affected is Utilities Expense).

8. Apple Computer issues 100 shares of its common stock for $5,000 cash.

E2–5 Identifying Liability Accounts

Liabilities are probable debts or obligations of an entity as a result of past transactions (the receipt of cash, goods, or services) that will be paid with assets or services. The general rule for initial valuation is the cash-equivalent cost (what you could pay it off for today in cash, goods, or services).

Required:

Using the preceding definition and valuation rule, indicate whether or not the following events would result in recording a liability on the balance sheet. If a liability would be recorded, indicate an appropriate account title and amount. Then indicate other accounts affected. Use the following headings:

Event	Does a Liability Result?	Liability Account Title	Amount	Title of Other Account(s) Affected

1. A local construction company places a $5,000 order for lumber to be received next week. The terms indicate that payment is due within 60 days of delivery.
2. The company in requirement (1) receives the lumber today.
3. A company signs a six-month note for a $1,000 loan on 6/30/19A to be paid back on 12/31/19A with 10 percent annual interest. Answer for the 6/30/19A date.
4. A company pays $1,500 on its accounts payable.
5. A retail company orders and receives $1,000 of merchandise inventory on accounts payable.
6. A landlord receives $12,000 from the local bookstore for rent for the next 12 months. Answer from the landlord's point of view.
7. A local business receives its telephone bill for $200 for the past month. The bill is not yet due, nor has it been paid (the other account affected is Utilities Expense).
8. An airline receives $800 from you for a ticket purchased in advance to go to Honolulu next month. Answer from the airline's point of view.

E2–6 Identifying Accounts and Their Usual Balances

As described in a recent annual report, Polaroid Corporation designs, manufactures, and markets worldwide a variety of products primarily in instant image recording fields, including instant photographic cameras and films, electronic imaging recording devices, conventional films, and light polarizing filters and lenses. For each of the following accounts from Polaroid's recent balance sheet, complete the chart below by indicating whether the account is categorized as an asset (A), liability (L), or stockholders' equity (SE), and whether the account usually has a debit or credit balance.

Polaroid Corporation

	Account	Balance Sheet Categorization	Debit or Credit
a.	Land		
b.	Retained earnings		
c.	Notes payable		
d.	Prepaid expenses		
e.	Investments		
f.	Contributed capital		
g.	Machinery and equipment		
h.	Accounts payable		
i.	Short-term investments		
j.	Federal, state, and foreign taxes payable		

E2–7 Applying Transaction Analysis

Complete the following tabulation by indicating the amount and direction of the effect of each transaction (+ or –):

Transaction		Assets	Liabilities	Stockholders' Equity
(a)	Investment of cash by organizers, $20,000			
(b)	Borrowed cash from a bank, $6,000			
(c)	Purchased $12,000 in inventory on account			
(d)	Loaned $300 to an employee			
(e)	Paid bank $6,000 (amount borrowed in (b))			
(f)	Purchased $8,000 equipment, paying $1,000 in cash and the rest on account			
Ending balances				

Nike, Inc.

E2–8 Applying Transaction Analysis

Nike, Inc., with headquarters in Beaverton, Oregon, is one of the world's leading manufacturers of athletic shoes and sports apparel.

Required:

1. Using the transaction analysis process outlined in the text ([1] identify and classify accounts and amounts affected and [2] determine that the accounting equation remains in balance), perform transaction analysis on each of the following transactions for Nike, Inc., based on information in a recent annual financial report. The amounts are rounded to millions of dollars. A sample transaction is provided.

Transaction	Assets	=	Liabilities	+	Stockholders' Equity
Sample: Nike borrowed $47.9 in notes payable during the year.	Cash + 47.9		Notes Payable + 47.9		

   (a) Paid $4,981.9 on accounts payable.

   (b) Purchased $216.3 in property, plant, and equipment; paid $5 in long-term debt and the rest in cash.

   (c) Issued $21.1 in additional stock for cash.

   (d) Customers paid $6,470.6 on account.

   (e) Declared $100 in dividends; paid $78.8 during the year with the rest due in the following year.

   (f) Several Nike investors sold their own stock on the stock exchange for $21.

2. Explain your response to Transaction *f*.

E2–9 Applying Transaction Analysis

Reilly Service Company, Inc., was organized by Bridget Reilly and five other investors.

Required:

1. Using the transaction analysis process outlined in the text ([1] identify and classify accounts and amounts affected and [2] determine that the accounting equation remains in balance), perform transaction analysis on each of the following transactions for Reilly Service Company. A sample transaction is provided.

Transaction	Assets	=	Liabilities	+	Stockholders' Equity
Sample: The investors paid in $60,000 cash to start the business. Each one was issued 1,000 shares of capital stock.	Cash + 60,000				Contributed Capital + 60,000

   (a) Purchased equipment for use in the business at a cost of $12,000; one-fourth was paid in cash, and the balance is due in six months.

    (b) Signed an agreement with a cleaning service to pay it $120 per week for cleaning the corporate offices.

    (c) Purchased $2,000 of office supplies on account.

    (d) Collected $4,000 in cash from customers in advance for services to be performed by Reilly Service Company (an unearned revenue).

    (e) Paid cash, $2,000, on accounts payable.

    (f) Bridget Reilly borrowed $10,000 for personal use from a local bank and signed a one-year, 10 percent note for that amount.

  2. Explain your response to Transactions b and f.

E2–10 Matching Definitions with Terms

Match each definition with its related term by entering the appropriate letter in the space provided.

TERM	DEFINITION
_____ (1) Journal entry	A. Accounting model.
_____ (2) Note payable	B. Four periodic financial statements.
_____ (3) Assets = Liabilities + Stockholders' Equity	C. The two equalities in accounting that aid in providing accuracy.
_____ (4) Assets	D. The results of transaction analysis in accounting format.
_____ (5) Duality	E. The account that is credited when money is borrowed from a bank.
_____ (6) A = L + SE, and Debits = Credits	F. Probable future economic benefits owned by an entity.
_____ (7) Income statement, balance sheet, statement of retained earnings, andstatement of cash flows	G. Cumulative earnings of a company that are not distributed to the owners.
_____ (8) Liabilities	H. Every transaction has at least two effects.
_____ (9) Retained earnings	I. Probable debts or obligations to be paid with assets or services.

E2–11 Understanding Effects of Transactions on Balance Sheet Accounts and Analyzing the Debt-to-Equity Ratio

During its first week of operations, January 1–7, Fitch Furniture Company completed eight transactions with the dollar effects indicated in the following schedule:

Accounts									Ending Balance
	DOLLAR EFFECT OF EACH OF THE EIGHT TRANSACTIONS								Ending Balance
	1	2	3	4	5	6	7	8	
Cash	$12,000	$50,000	$(4,000)	$(3,000)	$(7,000)	$(8,000)	$(9,000)	$2,000	$33,000
Note receivable				3,000				(2,000)	1,000
Inventory						59,000			59,000
Store fixtures					7,000				7,000
Land			12,000						12,000
Accounts payable						51,000	(9,000)		42,000
Note payable		50,000	8,000						58,000
Contributed capital	12,000								12,000

Required:

  1. Write a brief explanation of Transactions 1 through 8. The effects of each transaction are shown above. Explain any assumptions that you made.

  2. Complete the following tabulation after the eight transactions:

Balance Sheet Summary

Total assets	_____
Total liabilities	_____
Total stockholders' equity	_____

3. What is Fitch Furniture's debt-to-equity ratio? Explain what this ratio means.

E2–12 **Understanding Effects of Transactions on Balance Sheet Accounts and Analyzing the Debt-to-Equity Ratio**

During its first month of operations, Scoones Sports, Inc., completed seven transactions with the dollar effects indicated in the following schedule:

Accounts	DOLLAR EFFECT OF EACH OF THE SEVEN TRANSACTIONS							Ending Balance
	1	2	3	4	5	6	7	
Cash	$50,000	$(2,000)	$(500)		$(2,000)	$(450)	$200	$45,250
Note receivable			500				(200)	300
Inventory				$2,000				2,000
Truck		10,000						10,000
Accounts payable				2,000	(2,000)			0
Note payable		8,000				(450)		7,550
Contributed capital	50,000							50,000

Required:

1. Give the journal entry for Transactions 1 through 7, and give a brief explanation for each. Explain any assumptions that you made.
2. Complete the following tabulation after the seven transactions:

Balance Sheet Summary

Total assets	_____
Total liabilities	_____
Total stockholders' equity	_____

3. Compute the debt-to-equity ratio for Scoones Sports. What does this mean?

E2–13 **Analyzing Transaction Effects on Balance Sheet Accounts**

For each of the following, complete the amount and direction of the effect for the missing data and write a description of a possible transaction that would cause the effects (+ = increase, – = decrease, NE = no effect).

	Assets	Liabilities	Stockholders' Equity	Possible Transaction
(a)	+ 10,000		NE	
(b)	+ 4,000 – 1,000		NE	
(c)		– 2,500	NE	
(d)	NE	+ 3,000		
(e)	– 1,200	NE	NE	
(f)		NE	+ 5,000	

E2–14 **Applying Transaction Analysis and Preparing Journal Entries**

The following transactions occurred for Coppola Company during the first month of operations.

Required:

1. Complete the following tabulation by indicating the amount and direction (+ or –) of the effect of each transaction:

	Transaction	Assets	Liabilities	Stockholders' Equity
(a)	Investment of cash by organizers, $55,000.			
(b)	Purchased $13,500 in inventory on account.			
(c)	Loaned $300 to an employee.			
(d)	Purchased a truck; paid $1,000 cash and signed a note for $9,000.			
(e)	Paid $2,000 on account from (b).			
(f)	Received $500 from a customer for services to be rendered next month.			
	Ending balances			

2. Prepare journal entries for these transactions.

E2–15 Applying Transaction Analysis and Preparing Journal Entries

The following transactions occurred for Cohen & Collins Company during its first month of operations.

Required:

1. Complete the following tabulation by indicating the amount and direction of the effect of each transaction (+ or –):

	Transaction	Assets	Liabilities	Stockholders' Equity
(a)	Investment of cash by organizers, $80,000.			
(b)	Borrowed $25,000 from the bank and signed a note payable due in one year with 10% annual interest.			
(c)	Purchased $12,000 in inventory for $5,000 cash and the remainder on account.			
(d)	Received $200 from a customer for services to be rendered next month.			
(e)	Prepaid next month's rent of $2,000.			
(f)	Paid the balance due on account from Transaction (c).			
	Ending balances			

2. Prepare journal entries for these transactions.

E2–16 Preparing Simple Journal Entries

Perform transaction analysis for each of the following transactions. Based on your analysis, prepare journal entries for each (be sure to categorize each account as an asset [A], liability [L], or stockholders' equity [SE]).

(a) Example: Three investors who own Boyce Corporation each invested $20,000 additional cash.

> Cash (A) ($20,000 × 3)   60,000
>   Contributed capital (SE)   60,000

(b) Borrowed $6,000 cash and signed a 12% note.

(c) Purchased $10,000 in equipment, paying $8,000 in cash and the rest on account.

(d) Ordered $16,000 in inventory.

(e) Paid off $2,000 on accounts payable.

(f) Collected $1,000 on accounts receivable.

(g) Received the inventory ordered in Transaction (d); it will be paid next month.

Philippine Long Distance Telephone Company

E2–17 Preparing Simple Journal Entries

In its recent annual report, Philippine Long Distance Telephone Company describes itself as "the largest of 63 entities furnishing telephone services in the Philippines. It has a network of 145 central office exchanges serving the Metro Manila area and 146 other cities and municipalities throughout the country." The stock is traded on the New York Stock Exchange and Pacific Stock Exchange. The monetary unit is the Philippine peso.

Perform transaction analysis for each of the following transactions using information adapted from the annual report. Based on your analysis, prepare journal entries for each (be sure to categorize each account as an asset [A], liability [L], or stockholders' equity [SE]). The amounts are in millions of pesos.

Example: The Company declared and paid P1,115.8 in dividends.

Retained earnings (SE)	1,115.8	
Dividends payable (L)		1,115.8

(a) Prepaid P261.2 in insurance.

(b) Ordered P450 in materials and supplies.

(c) Paid P1,115.8 in dividends previously declared (in the preceding example).

(d) Issued additional stock for P6,127.1 in cash.

(e) Collected P23,549.9 on customers' accounts.

(f) Received P320.7 in materials and supplies on account that were ordered in Transaction b.

(g) Purchased temporary investments for P745.6.

(h) Paid P4,642.6 in long-term debt.

E2–18 Using T-Accounts; Summarizing the Results; Analyzing the Debt-to-Equity Ratio

Vogel Company has been operating one year (19A). At the start of 19B, its T-account balances were as follows:

ASSETS

Cash		Accounts Receivable		Land	
5,000		2,000		4,000	

LIABILITIES

Accounts Payable		Note Payable		Income Taxes Payable	
	300		400		200

STOCKHOLDERS' EQUITY

Contributed Capital	
	10,100

Required:

1. Using the data from these T-accounts, amounts for the following on January 1, 19B, were

   Assets $ _____ = Liabilities $ _____ + Stockholders' Equity $ _____.

2. Enter the following 19B transactions in the T-accounts:
    (a)   Paid the income tax.
    (b)   Collected the accounts receivable.
    (c)   Paid the accounts payable.
    (d)   Sold one-fourth of the land for $1,000 in cash.
    (e)   Borrowed $1,600 at 6% from the bank (signing a note).

3. Using the data from the preceding T-accounts, amounts for the following on December 31, 19B, were:

    Assets $_____ = Liabilities $_____ + Stockholders' Equity $_____.

4. Calculate and compare the debt-to-equity ratio at January 1, 19B, and at December 31, 19B. What accounted for the change in the ratio?

E2–19 Constructing the Balance Sheet

From the ending balances in the T-accounts in E2–18, prepare a balance sheet for December 31, 19B, in good form.

E2–20 Using T-Accounts; Summarizing the Results

Vialago Delivery Company, Inc., was organized and issued 10,000 shares of its capital stock for $40,000 cash. The following transactions occurred during year 19E:

(a)   Received the cash from the organizers, $40,000.
(b)   Collected $20,000 cash in advance for future services (an unearned income account).
(c)   Purchased supplies for $2,000 on account.
(d)   Bought two used delivery trucks for operating purposes at the start of the year at a cost of $10,000 each; paid $3,000 cash and signed a promissory note due in three years for the rest.
(e)   Paid $3,000 cash to a truck repair shop for a new motor for one of the trucks. (*Hint:* Increase the account you used to record the purchase of the trucks.)
(f)   Traded the other truck and $6,000 cash for a new one.
(g)   Stockholder Kristine Vialago paid $22,000 cash for a vacant lot (land) for her personal use.

Required:

Set up appropriate T-accounts with beginning balances of $0 for Cash, Supplies, Equipment, Accounts Payable, Notes Payable, Unearned Service Fees, and Contributed Capital. Record in them the dual effects on the accounting model of each of these transactions that should be recorded by Vialago Delivery Company. Identify the amounts with the letters starting with *a*.

E2–21 Constructing the Balance Sheet

Use the balances of the completed T-accounts in E2–20 to prepare a balance sheet in good form.

E2–22 Constructing the Balance Sheet; Analyzing the Debt-to-Equity Ratio

Boston Chicken, Inc.

From its recent annual report, "Boston Chicken, Inc. franchises and operates food service stores that specialize in complete meals featuring home-style entrees, hot, hand-carved sandwiches, fresh vegetables, salads and other side dishes." The company operates under the name Boston Market with nearly 900 stores and has an interest in Einstein Bros. Bagels, Inc., with nearly 120 stores nationwide. The following accounts, not necessarily in good order, are adapted from the company's annual report (amounts are in millions of dollars):

Contributed capital	$ 676.2	Deferred franchise revenue	$	11.0
Accounts payable	12.3	Retained earnings		40.6
Long-term debt	324.6	Prepaid expenses		1.5
Cash and cash equivalents	310.4	Accrued expenses		9.1
Other assets	24.3	Net property and equipment		258.5
Accounts and notes receivable	479.1			

Required:

1. Construct a balance sheet for Boston Chicken, Inc., in good form (assume that the year ends on December 31, 19A).
2. Compute the company's debt-to-equity ratio.
3. In comparison to the ratio for other companies in the fast-food industry (as indicated in the chapter), how do you interpret this ratio for Boston Chicken?

E2–23 Identifying Typical Activities in Accounts

The following T-accounts indicate the effects of normal business transactions:

Equipment			Accounts Receivable			Income Taxes Payable		
1/1	300		1/1	75			1/1	130
	250	?		?	290	?		170
12/31	450		12/31	50			12/31	180

Required:

1. For each T-account, compute the missing amounts.
2. For each T-account, describe the typical transactions that affect each account.

Woolworth Corporation

E2–24 Focus on Cash Flows: Identifying Investing and Financing Cash Flows

Woolworth Corporation is a large global retailer with stores and related support facilities. It operates the athletic and specialty footwear companies (Foot Locker family of businesses and Kinney shoe stores), specialty nonfootwear chains (After Thoughts, Accessory Lady, The San Francisco Music Box Company, and The Best of Times specialty stores), and clothing stores (Northern Reflections, Northern Elements, and Northern Getaway). The following are several of Woolworth's investing and financing activities that were reflected in a recent annual statement of cash flows.

1. Reduction of long-term debt.
2. Purchase of investments.
3. Issuance of common stock.
4. Capital expenditures (for property, plant, and equipment).
5. Issuance of long-term debt.
6. Proceeds from sales of assets and investments.
7. Dividends paid.

Required:

For each of these, indicate whether the activity is investing (I) or financing (F) and the direction of the effect on cash flows (+ = increases cash; – = decreases cash).

Hilton Hotels E2–25 Focus on Cash Flows: Analyzing Investing and Financing Transactions

Hilton Hotels Corporation constructs, operates, and franchises domestic and international hotel and hotel-casino properties. Information from the company's recent annual statement of cash flows indicates the following investing and financing activities during that year (simplified):

Investing Activities		In Millions
(a)	Purchase and renovation of properties	$274.5
(b)	Purchase of investments	282.2
(c)	Receipt of notes receivable	5.4
(d)	Sale of property (assume sold at cost)	4.7
Financing Activities		
(e)	Additional borrowings from banks	438.5
(f)	Payment of debt	32.2
(g)	Issuance of stock	2.9

Required:

1. For each activity, (*a*) through (*g*), identify the accounts that were affected and the direction of the effect (increase +, or decrease –).
2. Calculate the net inflow or outflow of cash as a result of the financing and investing activities, respectively.

E2–26 Focus on Cash Flows: Analyzing Transactions and Preparing Journal Entries

Walt Disney Company owns and operates theme parks and destination resorts, produces live-action and animated films, and licenses the Walt Disney name and characters for consumer products. Information from the company's recent annual statement of cash flows indicates the following investing and financing activities during that year (simplified):

Walt Disney

Investing Activities		In Millions
(a)	Expansion of theme parks and resort properties	$ 794.7
(b)	Investment in films	1,264.6
(c)	Advance to Euro Disney	140.1
(d)	Other investments (net)	461.3
Financing Activities		
(e)	Borrowings	1,256.0
(f)	Reduction of borrowings	1,119.2
(g)	Repurchase of capital stock	31.6
(h)	Payment of cash dividends	128.6
(i)	Other loans	136.1

Required:

1. Prepare journal entries for each activity. State the effect (increase +, or decrease –) on each account balance after the account name in your journal entry.
2. Calculate the net inflow or outflow of cash as a result of the financing and investing activities, respectively.

E2–27 Understanding the Effects of Transactions on Balance Sheet Accounts

Post and Fitzsimmons Furniture Repair Service, a company with two stockholders, began operations on June 1, 19A. The T-accounts on the following page indicate the activities for the month of June.

Required:

Explain Transactions (*a*) through (*g*), which gave rise to the entries in the T-accounts.

Cash (A)			
(a)	17,000	(b)	10,000
(f)	500	(d)	1,500
(g)	800	(e)	1,000

Notes Receivable (A)			
(d)	1,500	(f)	500

Parts Inventory	
(c)	2,200

Tools and Equipment			
(a)	3,000	(g)	800

Building	
(b)	50,000

Accounts Payable			
		(e)	1,000	(c)	2,200

Notes Payable	
(b)	40,000

Contributed Capital	
(a)	20,000

Ben & Jerry's **E2–28** **Constructing the Balance Sheet; Analyzing the Debt-to-Equity Ratio**

Ben & Jerry's Homemade, Inc., based in Vermont, produces Ben & Jerry's superpremium ice cream, lowfat frozen yogurt, and ice cream novelties. These products are marketed through supermarkets, grocery stores, convenience stores, and restaurants. The company also franchises Ben & Jerry's ice cream scoop shops. The following lists the accounts and balances from the company's recent annual report. The accounts, although not necessarily listed in good order, have normal debit and credit balances. Some of the information has been simplified.

Investments	$25,200,000	Prepaid expenses	$ 208,996
Bonds and leases payable	3,269,080	Accounts receivable	8,849,326
Retained earnings	18,579,709	Property, plant, and equipment	26,737,425
Inventories	17,089,857	Net deferred income tax (an asset)*	411,000
Cash and cash equivalents	7,356,133	Accounts payable and accrued	
Contributed capital	48,180,107	expenses	16,858,919
Income taxes receivable	306,193	Other assets	728,885

*Represents future lower taxes due to differences between tax accounting rules and financial accounting rules.

Required:

1. Prepare a balance sheet in good form for Ben & Jerry's (assume the year-end is December 31, 19A).
2. Compute the debt-to-equity ratio for Ben & Jerry's.
3. What does this ratio indicate?

Walt Disney **E2–29** **Constructing the Balance Sheet; Analyzing the Debt-to-Equity Ratio**

Walt Disney Company's balance sheet accounts from a recent annual report follow. The accounts have normal debit and credit balances; however, the accounts are not listed in good order. Some of the information has been simplified for this exercise. The amounts are stated in millions.

A Short-term investment	$1,888.5	L Accounts payable	$2,530.1
L Income taxes payable	291.0	A Cash	363.0
A Attractions, buildings, and		L Borrowings	2,385.8
equipment	5,133.9	SE Retained earnings	4,869.8
L Unearned royalties	840.7	L Deferred taxes payable	673.0
A Receivables	1,390.3	A Merchandise inventory	608.9
A Land	94.3	A Films in progress (an asset)	1,360.9
SE Contributed capital	160.7	A Other assets	911.3

Required:

1. Prepare a balance sheet in good form for Walt Disney Company (assume that the fiscal year ends on September 30, 19A).
2. Calculate the debt-to-equity ratio for Walt Disney. What does this mean?

Problems

P2–1 Analyzing Transactions and Recording Transaction Effects

Nee's Home Healthcare Services was organized on January 1, 19A, by four friends. Each organizer invested $10,000 in the company and, in turn, was issued 8,000 shares of stock. To date, they are the only stockholders. During the first month (January 19A), the company completed the following six transactions:

(a) Collected a total of $40,000 from the organizers and, in turn, issued the shares of stock.

(b) Purchased a building for $65,000, equipment for $16,000, and three acres of land for $12,000; paid $13,000 in cash, with the balance due in 15 years on a 10 percent mortgage payable to the local bank. (*Hint:* Five different accounts are affected.)

(c) One stockholder reported to the company that 500 shares of his Nee stock had been sold and transferred to another stockholder for a cash consideration of $5,000.

(d) Purchased supplies for $3,000 on account.

(e) Sold one acre of land for $4,000 in cash.

(f) Loaned one of the shareholders $5,000 for moving costs, receiving a signed note due in one year from the shareholder.

Required:

1. Was Nee's Home Healthcare Services organized as a sole proprietorship, a partnership, or a corporation? Explain the basis for your answer.

2. During the first month, the records of the company were inadequate. You were asked to prepare the summary of the preceding transactions. To develop a quick assessment of their economic effects on Nee's Home Healthcare Services, you have decided to complete the tabulation that follows and to use plus (+) for increases and minus (–) for decreases for each account. The first transaction is used as an example.

Accounts	(a)	(b)	(c)	(d)	(e)	(f)	Ending Balance
Cash	+$40,000	$-13,000	$	$	$+4000	$-5000	$26000
Note receivable						+5000	5000
Inventory				+300			300
Land		+12,000			-4000		8000
Building		+65,000					65000
Equipment		+16,000					16000
Accounts payable				+300			300
Mortgage payable							
Contributed capital	+$40,000						

(handwritten left margin labels: Assets, Liabilities, SE)

(handwritten right margin: 123,000 ✓   − 83000 ✓   40,000 ✓)

3. Did you include the transaction between the two stockholders in the tabulation? Why?

4. Based only on the completed tabulation, provide the following amounts (show computations):

   a. Total assets at the end of the month.

   b. Total liabilities at the end of the month.

   c. Total shareholders' equity at the end of the month.

   d. Cash balance at the end of the month.

   e. Debt-to-equity ratio.

Chevron Corporation

P2–2 Classifying Accounts as Assets, Liabilities, and Stockholders' Equity and Their Normal Balances (Debit versus Credit)

Chevron Corporation explores, produces, refines, markets, and supplies crude oil, natural gas, and petroleum products in the United States and 24 other countries. The following are several of the accounts from a recent balance sheet of Chevron Corporation:

a. Cash and cash equivalents.
b. Accounts and notes receivable.
c. Contributed capital.
d. Long-term debt.
e. Prepaid expenses.
f. Patents (an intangible asset).
g. Federal and other taxes payable.
h. Materials, supplies and other inventories.
i. Accounts payable.
j. Marketable securities.
k. Capital lease obligations.
l. Retained earnings.
m. Crude oil and petroleum products inventories.
n. Investments (long-term).
o. Property, plant, and equipment.

Complete a tabulation similar to the following. Enter two checkmarks for each account listed, one for the type of account and one for its usual balance. Account *a* is used as an example.

	TYPE OF ACCOUNT			USUAL BALANCE	
Account	Asset	Liability	Stockholders' Equity	Debit	Credit
a.	✓			✓	

P2–3 Classifying Accounts as Assets, Liabilities, and Stockholders' Equity and Their Normal Balances (Debit versus Credit)

The following are several of the accounts of Hunt Company:

a. Cash.
b. Accounts payable.
c. Retained earnings.
d. Goodwill.*
e. Prepaid rent.
f. Investments.
g. Notes payable.
h. Notes receivable.
i. Petty cash.
j. Wages payable.
k. Buildings.
l. Land (store parking lot).
m. Merchandise inventory.
n. Supplies inventory (unused).
o. Utilities payable.
p. Accounts receivable.
q. Income taxes payable.
r. Contributed capital.

* An intangible asset resulting from purchasing another company.

Complete a tabulation similar to the following. Enter two checkmarks for each account listed, one for the type of account and one for its usual balance. Account *a* is used as an example.

	TYPE OF ACCOUNT			USUAL BALANCE	
Account	Asset	Liability	Stockholders' Equity	Debit	Credit
a.	✓			✓	

P2–4 Focus on Cash Flows: Analyzing and Recording Transactions, Summarizing Transaction Effects, and Identifying Cash Flow Effects

Kline Plastics Company has been operating for three years. At the end of 19C, the accounting records reflected assets of $320,000 and liabilities of $120,000. During the year 19D, the following summarized transactions were completed:

(a) Purchased equipment that cost $30,000; paid $10,000 cash; the balance is due next year.
(b) Issued an additional 2,000 shares of capital stock for $20,000 cash.
(c) Collected $12,000 on accounts receivable.
(d) Purchased $15,000 in investments.
(e) Paid $15,000 on accounts payable.

(f) Borrowed $20,000 cash on a 10 percent interest-bearing note from a local bank (on December 31, 19D), payable June 30, 19E.

(g) Purchased a patent (an intangible asset) for $6,000.

(h) Built an addition to the factory for $42,000 in cash.

(i) Hired a new president at the end of the year. The contract was for $85,000 per year plus options to purchase company stock at a set price based on company performance.

(j) Returned defective supplies to the manufacturer, receiving a cash refund of $2,000.

Required:

1. Enter each of these transactions in the following schedule. The first transaction is used as an example.

Transaction	ASSETS		LIABILITIES		STOCKHOLDERS' EQUITY	
	Debit	*Credit*	*Debit*	*Credit*	*Debit*	*Credit*
Balances, January 1, 19D	$320,000			$120,000		$200,000
(a) Equipment purchase	30,000	10,000		20,000		
(b)						
Etc.						

2. Respond to the following:

   a. Why were two credits entered in this schedule for Transaction (a)?

   b. Complete the following at the end of 19D:

BALANCE SHEET	
Assets	$ _____
Liabilities	$ _____
Stockholders' equity	$ _____

3. Explain your response to Transaction (i).

4. For transactions (a) through (j), indicate which transactions are investing activities or financing activities. Then indicate the direction and amount of the effect on cash.

P2–5 Analyzing and Recording Transactions; Summarizing Transaction Effects

Russeck Incorporated is a small manufacturing company that makes model trains to sell to toy stores. It has a small service department that repairs customers' trains for a fee. The company has been in business for five years. At the end of the most recent year, 19E, the accounting records reflected total assets of $500,000 and total liabilities of $200,000. During the current year, 19F, the following summarized transactions were completed:

(a) Issued an additional 10,000 shares of capital stock for $100,000 cash.

(b) Borrowed $120,000 cash from the bank and signed a note with terms of 12 percent annual interest with principal and interest due in a lump sum in two years.

(c) Built an addition on the factory for $200,000 and paid cash to the contractor.

(d) Purchased equipment for the new addition for $30,000 cash.

(e) Received $85,000 on accounts receivable.

(f) Returned a $3,000 piece of equipment, from (d), because it proved to be defective.

(g) Paid $48,000 on accounts payable.

(h) Purchased a delivery truck for $10,000; paid $5,000 cash and the remainder on a note payable.

(i) Loaned the company president, Kal Russeck, $2,000 cash. Mr. Russeck signed a note with terms showing the principal plus 10 percent annual interest due in one year.

(j) A stockholder sold $5,000 of his capital stock in Russeck Incorporated to his neighbor.

(k) Received $250 cash from a customer, Mr. Dittman, for services to be provided at the beginning of 19G.

Required:

1. Enter each of these transactions in the following schedule. The first transaction is used as an example.

| | ASSETS | | LIABILITIES | | STOCKHOLDERS' EQUITY | |
Transaction	Debit	Credit	Debit	Credit	Debit	Credit
Balances, January 1, 19F	$500,000			$200,000		$300,000
(a) Issued Stock	100,000					100,000
(b)						
Etc.						

2. Complete the following at the end of 19F:

BALANCE SHEET

Assets	$ _____
Liabilities	$ _____
Stockholders' equity	$ _____

3. Explain your response to Transaction (*j*).

Foster's Brewing

P2–6 Analyzing Transactions; Preparing Journal Entries, T-Accounts, and the Balance Sheet; Analyzing the Debt-to-Equity Ratio—A Challenging Problem

Foster's Brewing Group Limited is an Australian corporation that brews beer, including the popular Foster's and Molson brands, and markets its products around the world. The following is Foster's balance sheet from a recent year.

FOSTER'S BREWING GROUP LIMITED AND CONTROLLED ENTITIES
Balance Sheet at 30 June 19A
(in millions of Australian dollars)

ASSETS	
Cash	$ 106.6
Receivables	1,129.8
Inventories	227.1
Investments	1,198.2
Property, plant, and equipment	2,030.3
Intangibles	717.8
Other assets	893.9
Total assets	6,303.7

LIABILITIES	
Creditors	928.9
Borrowings	1,958.9
Provisions*	596.6
Total liabilities	3,484.4
Net assets	$2,819.3

SHAREHOLDERS' EQUITY	
Share capital	3,267.4
Reserves	882.6
Accumulated losses	(1,362.8)
Outside equity interest in controlled entities†	32.1
Total shareholders' equity	$2,819.3

*Includes dividends payable, taxes payable, amounts owed to employees for wages earned and pension plans.

†100% of the assets and liabilities of controlled entities are included; however, not all controlled entities are owned at 100% (say 80% ownership). This account represents the minority ownership of outside parties (the amount not owned by Foster's).

Assume that the following transactions occurred in July 19A:

(a) Received $822.3 on receivables owed by customers.

(b) Paid $134.1 in dividends owed to shareholders.

(c) Paid $59.7 cash for income taxes owed.

(d) Paid suppliers $657.7 cash on account.

(e) Purchased inventories of $443.1 on account.

(f) Issued additional shares of stock for $850.3 in cash.

(g) Repaid $150.0 of borrowings to banks.

(h) Purchased property, plant, and equipment; paid $161.1 in cash and $479.4 with additional bank loans.

(i) Acquired additional investments; paid $48.3 in cash.

(j) Sold additional shares of stock for $352.8 in cash.

Required:

1. Analyze each transaction by identifying the accounts affected, the direction of the effects, and the impact on the accounting equation.

2. Prepare a journal entry for each transaction.

3. Create T-accounts for each balance sheet account and include the June 30, 19A, balances. Post each journal entry to the appropriate T-accounts.

4. Prepare a balance sheet from the T-account ending balances for Foster's at July 31, 19A, based on these transactions.

5. Explain the meaning of "Accumulated losses."

6. Compute Foster's debt-to-equity ratio. What does this indicate?

P2–7 Analyzing Transactions and Preparing Journal Entries, T-Accounts, and the Balance Sheet

Lance, Inc.

Lance, Inc., is a manufacturer and distributor of snacks. The following is adapted from a recent annual financial report.

LANCE, INC.
Balance Sheet
at December 31, 19A
(in thousands of dollars)

ASSETS	
Cash and cash equivalents	$ 12,585
Marketable securities	31,905
Accounts receivable	29,429
Inventories	32,521
Property	126,656
Other assets	23,364
Total assets	$256,460

LIABILITIES	
Accounts payable	$ 6,202
Accrued expenses payable	25,744
Other liabilities	27,971
Total liabilities	59,917

SHAREHOLDERS' EQUITY	
Contributed capital	25,579
Retained earnings	170,964
Total liabilities and shareholders' equity	$256,640

Assume that the following transactions occurred in the first quarter of 19B:

(a) Received $16,310 on receivables owed by customers.

(b) Paid $12,340 in accrued expenses payable owed to employees and others.

(c) Paid $3,400 cash for income taxes owed (in other liabilities).

(d) Paid suppliers $4,020 cash on account.

(e) Purchased inventories of $22,980 on account.

(f) Issued additional shares of stock for $1,020 in cash.

(g) Purchased property, plant, and equipment; paid $1,830 in cash and $9,400 with additional bank loans (other liabilities).

(h) Acquired additional investments in marketable securities; paid $6,310 in cash.

Required:

1. Analyze each transaction by identifying the accounts affected, the direction of the effects, and the impact on the accounting equation.

2. Prepare a journal entry for each transaction.

3. Create T-accounts for each balance sheet account and include the December 31, 19A, balances. Post each journal entry to the appropriate T-accounts.

4. Prepare a balance sheet from the T-account ending balances for Lance, Inc., at March 31, 19B, based on the preceding transactions.

5. Calculate the debt-to-equity ratio for Lance at March 31, 19B. Explain its meaning.

Cases and Projects

C2–1 Evaluating the Reliability of a Balance Sheet

A. Smith asked a local bank for a $50,000 loan to expand his small company. The bank asked Smith to submit a financial statement of the business to supplement the loan application. Smith prepared the following balance sheet.

Balance Sheet
June 30, 19F

Assets	
Cash and CDs (investments)...	$ 9,000
Inventory	30,000
Equipment	46,000
Personal residence (monthly payments, $2,800)	300,000
Remaining assets..	20,000
Total assets	$405,000
Liabilities	
Short-term debt to suppliers	$ 62,000
Long-term debt on equipment	38,000
Total debt...	100,000
Stockholders' equity, A. Smith	305,000
Total liabilities and stockholders' equity.............................	$405,000

Required:

The balance sheet has several flaws; however, there is at least one major deficiency. Identify it and explain its significance.

C2–2 Analytical Case

Your best friend from home writes you a letter about an investment opportunity that has come her way. A company is raising money by issuing shares of stock and wants your friend to invest $20,000 (her recent inheritance from her great-aunt's estate). Your friend has never invested in a company before and, knowing that you are taking an accounting class, asks that you look over the balance sheet and send her some advice. An *unaudited* balance sheet, in only moderately good form, is enclosed with the letter:

DEWEY, CHEETUM, AND HOWE, INC.
Balance Sheet
For the Year Ending December 31, 199A

Accounts receivable	$ 8,000
Cash	1,000
Inventory	8,000
Furniture and fixtures	52,000
Delivery truck (net)	12,000
Buildings (estimated market value)	98,000
Total assets	$179,000
Accounts payable	$ 16,000
Payroll taxes payable	13,000
Notes payable	15,000
Mortgage payable	50,000
Total liabilities	$ 94,000
Contributed capital	$ 80,000
Retained earnings	5,000
Total stockholders' equity	$ 85,000

There is only one footnote, and it states that the building was purchased for $65,000, has been depreciated by $5,000 on the books, and still carries a mortgage (shown in the liability section). The footnote further states that, in the opinion of the company president, the building is "easily worth $98,000."

Required:
1. Draft a new balance sheet for your friend, correcting any errors you note. (If any of the account balances need to be corrected, you may need to adjust the retained earnings balance correspondingly.) If no errors or omissions exist, state so.
2. Write a letter to your friend explaining the changes you made to the balance sheet, if any, and offer your comments on the company's apparent financial condition. Suggest other information your friend might want to review before coming to a final decision on whether to invest.

C2–3 Ethical Considerations

Leslie Fay

In 1993, Leslie Fay Companies, manufacturer of women's apparel, filed for Chapter 11 bankruptcy protection shortly after a scandal erupted over fraudulent accounting information. As reported in *The Wall Street Journal* (March 28, 1995, p. B1, B16), the company's audit committee report sharply criticized top management, suggesting that "it would have been difficult for senior management not to spot the extensive inventory and sales fraud." There were numerous ways in which Leslie Fay committed the fraud, according to the report: To boost sales and lower costs, mid-level company officials forged inventory tags, ignored expected inventory shrinkage, multiplied the value of items in inventory, improperly inflated sales, and made up phantom inventory. These officials also constantly altered records to meet sales targets. In March 1995, Leslie Fay's independent auditors, BDO Seidman, filed charges against Leslie Fay management, suggesting a cause of the fraudulent activity was due to senior management's adoption of unrealistic budgets: "senior management created an environment which encouraged and rewarded the cooking of Leslie Fay's books and records" (*The Wall Street Journal*, March 29, 1995).

Required:

1. Describe the parties who were harmed or helped in this fraud.
2. Explain how adopting unrealistic budgets may have contributed to the fraud.
3. Why do you think the independent auditor filed charges against its former client?

Marvel Comics

C2–4 Financial Statement Analysis

Refer to the balance sheet of Marvel Entertainment Group (producer of Marvel Comics) on the next page and answer the following questions:

Required:

1. Is Marvel Entertainment Group a corporation, sole proprietorship, or partnership? Explain the basis of your answer.
2. Use the company's balance sheet to determine the amounts in the accounting equation (A = L + SE).
3. Calculate the company's ratio of debt-to-equity. Interpret the ratio you calculated. What other information would make your interpretation more useful?
4. Give the journal entry the company will make when it pays its accounts payable.
5. Does the company appear to have been profitable over its years in business? On what account are you basing your answer? If impossible to determine without an income statement, state so.

Toys "R" Us

C2–5 Financial Statement Analysis

Refer to the financial statements of Toys "R" Us given in Appendix B at the end of the book.

Required:

1. If the company repaid in cash all of its short-term notes payable to the bank at the end of the current year, what journal entry would be prepared?
2. Is the company a corporation, a partnership, or a proprietorship?
3. Use the company's balance sheet to determine the amounts in the accounting equation (A = L + SE).
4. The company shows on the balance sheet that merchandise inventories are worth $2,214.6 million. Does this amount represent the expected selling price?
5. Give an example of an account from the company's balance sheet.
6. Compute the company's debt-to-equity ratio and explain its meaning.
7. How much cash did the company spend on purchasing property, plant, and equipment each year (capital expenditures)?

C2–6 Project: Comparing Balance Sheets within Industries

Acquire the balance sheets from the annual reports or 10-Ks of three companies within an industry. (Library files, the SEC EDGAR service at www.sec.gov, Compustat CD, or the companies themselves are good sources.) Write a short report indicating any differences, if any, in the accounts used by the three companies and their location on the balance sheet.

C2–7 Project: Comparing Balance Sheets between Industries

Acquire the balance sheets from the annual reports or 10-Ks of three companies from different industries. (Library files, the SEC EDGAR service at www.sec.gov, Compustat CD, or the companies themselves are good sources.) Write a short report indicating any differences, if any, in the accounts used by the three companies and their location on the balance sheet.

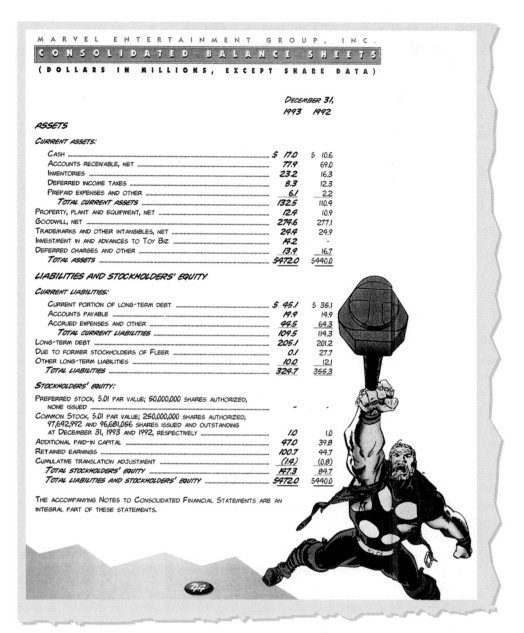

MARVEL ENTERTAINMENT GROUP, INC.
CONSOLIDATED BALANCE SHEETS
(DOLLARS IN MILLIONS, EXCEPT SHARE DATA)

	December 31, 1993	1992
ASSETS		
CURRENT ASSETS:		
CASH	$ 17.0	$ 10.6
ACCOUNTS RECEIVABLE, NET	77.9	69.0
INVENTORIES	23.2	16.3
DEFERRED INCOME TAXES	8.3	12.3
PREPAID EXPENSES AND OTHER	6.1	2.2
TOTAL CURRENT ASSETS	132.5	110.4
PROPERTY, PLANT AND EQUIPMENT, NET	12.4	10.9
GOODWILL, NET	274.6	277.1
TRADEMARKS AND OTHER INTANGIBLES, NET	24.4	24.9
INVESTMENT IN AND ADVANCES TO TOY BIZ	14.2	-
DEFERRED CHARGES AND OTHER	13.9	16.7
TOTAL ASSETS	$472.0	$440.0
LIABILITIES AND STOCKHOLDERS' EQUITY		
CURRENT LIABILITIES:		
CURRENT PORTION OF LONG-TERM DEBT	$ 45.1	$ 35.1
ACCOUNTS PAYABLE	19.9	14.9
ACCRUED EXPENSES AND OTHER	44.5	64.3
TOTAL CURRENT LIABILITIES	109.5	114.3
LONG-TERM DEBT	205.1	201.2
DUE TO FORMER STOCKHOLDERS OF FLEER	0.1	27.7
OTHER LONG-TERM LIABILITIES	10.0	12.1
TOTAL LIABILITIES	324.7	355.3
STOCKHOLDERS' EQUITY:		
PREFERRED STOCK, $.01 PAR VALUE; 50,000,000 SHARES AUTHORIZED, NONE ISSUED	-	-
COMMON STOCK, $.01 PAR VALUE; 250,000,000 SHARES AUTHORIZED, 97,642,992 AND 96,681,056 SHARES ISSUED AND OUTSTANDING AT DECEMBER 31, 1993 AND 1992, RESPECTIVELY	1.0	1.0
ADDITIONAL PAID-IN CAPITAL	47.0	39.8
RETAINED EARNINGS	100.7	44.7
CUMULATIVE TRANSLATION ADJUSTMENT	(1.4)	(0.8)
TOTAL STOCKHOLDERS' EQUITY	147.3	84.7
TOTAL LIABILITIES AND STOCKHOLDERS' EQUITY	$472.0	$440.0

THE ACCOMPANYING NOTES TO CONSOLIDATED FINANCIAL STATEMENTS ARE AN INTEGRAL PART OF THESE STATEMENTS.

C2–8 Project: Analyzing Differences in Debt-to-Equity Ratios among Competitors

Sbarro's competitors in the restaurant business include Outback Steakhouse, Boston Chicken, Cheesecake Factory, Au Bon Pain, and Uno's Pizzeria. Obtain the recent balance sheet for Sbarro and two of its competitors. (Library files, the SEC EDGAR service at www.sec.gov, Compustat CD, or the companies themselves are good sources. All of these companies are included under the SIC [Standard Industrial Classification] code 5812 for retail eating places.) Write a short memo comparing the companies' debt-to-equity ratios. Indicate what differences in their businesses might account for any differences in the ratio.

C2–9   Project: Analyzing Changes in Debt-to-Equity Ratios

Acquire the three most recent years' financial statements for a single company. (Library files, the SEC EDGAR service at www.sec.gov, Compustat CD, or the company itself are good sources.) Write a short memo comparing the company's debt-to-equity ratio over the three years. Indicate what differences in financing and investing activities might account for any difference in the ratio.

C2–10   Project: Focus on Cash Flows

Acquire the three most recent years' financial statements for a single company. (Library files, the SEC EDGAR service at www.sec.gov, Compustat CD, or the company itself are good sources.) Write a short memo describing each of the major investing and financing activities for each year presented.

C2–11   Project: Financial Analysis Update

Acquire the most recent year's annual report and Form 10-K for Sbarro. (Library files, the SEC EDGAR service at www.sec.gov, Compustat CD, or the company itself are good sources.) Write a short memo comparing the company's recent debt-to-equity ratio to the Sbarro ratio presented in the chapter. Indicate what differences in financing and investing activities might account for any difference in the ratio.

C2–12   Ethics Project: Analyzing Deficiencies in Reporting Environmental Liabilities

Obtain a recent news story concerning a company reporting or failing to report an environmental liability. (Library files, the SEC EDGAR service at www.sec.gov, Compustat CD, or other busines news services are good sources.) Write a short memo outlining the nature of the environmental incident and how it was or was not disclosed in the financial statements.

C2–13   Team Project: Analysis of Balance Sheets and Ratios

As a group, select an industry to analyze. Each group member should acquire the annual report or 10-K for one publicly traded company in the industry, with each member selecting a different company. (Library files, the SEC EDGAR service at www.sec.gov, Compustat CD, or the companies themselves are good sources.) On an individual basis, each group member should write a short report that lists the following information.

1. The date of the balance sheet.
2. The asset accounts.
3. The major investing and financing activities for the most recent period.
4. The debt-to-equity ratio for the most recent period.

Then, as a group, write a short report comparing and contrasting your companies using the preceding attributes. Discuss any patterns across the companies that you as a group observe, and provide potential explanations for any differences discovered.

CHAPTER THREE

Operating Decisions and the Income Statement

Sbarro, Inc.
PEOPLE ARE A KEY TO PROFITS

As stated in a recent annual report:

THE MISSION OF SBARRO, INC. is to deliver high quality, affordably priced Italian food products to a wide range of consumers.

We will serve our guests in attractive, distinctively designed, strategically located restaurants, wherever the demand for our products exists.

We are committed to excellent service, dedicated to achieving Company objectives and maintaining profitability through the pride and commitment to excellence by our people.

We create new guests through entrepreneurial-minded people who operate their restaurants with the Sbarro passion for guest satisfaction and maximum profit.

Based on this mission, Sbarro has opened restaurants across the United States in shopping malls and airports and more recently in foreign countries and

nontraditional sites such as universities, hospitals, toll road service plazas, convention centers, and sports arenas ("wherever the demand for our products exists"). Sbarro relies on its people, mentioned twice in the mission statement, to accomplish its goals, including profit maximization. A primary goal during the past decade has been to realize systemwide sales of $500 million by the mid-1990s from franchised and company-owned restaurants. Recently, however, Sbarro ignored its stated tie between its people and profitability.

Forbes reported that Sbarro added a new organizational level of regional and district managers to manage its growth.* Instead of promoting qualified people from within the company, the Sbarro family decided to recruit managers from larger fast-food chains who would add broader industry and managerial experience to their talent pool. How will Sbarro and investors know whether this strategy of hiring outside managers is working?

■   ■   ■

---

*R. La Franco, "Promote from within," Forbes, February 28, 1994, pp. 86–87.

Business Background

To reach its long-range sales target, Sbarro must develop goals, plans (expectations), strategies, and measurable indicators of progress toward its goals. Companies such as Sbarro plan their companywide operations in terms of the elements of the income statement (specific revenues and expenses). Financial analysts also develop their own set of expectations about Sbarro's future performance. The published income statement provides the primary basis for comparing these plans or projections to actual results of operations. We discuss these comparisons and the stock market's reactions to Sbarro's results throughout this chapter as we learn about income measurement. To understand how business plans and the results of operations are reflected on the income statement, we need to answer the following questions:

1. What business activities affect the income statement?
2. How is each of these activities measured?
3. How are these activities reported on the income statement?

In this chapter, we focus on Sbarro's operating activities that involve the sale of food to the public and the sale of goods and services to the owners of franchised restaurants. The results of these activities are reported on its income statement. First we discuss relevant accounting terms and concepts related to income measurement and reporting. Then we expand the transaction analysis model outlined in Chapter 2 to incorporate operating activities. Finally, we create an income statement from the operating activities. We also create a statement of stockholders' equity that links the income statement to the balance sheet.

Return to the Conceptual Framework

The accounting conceptual framework initially outlined in Chapter 2 is presented again in Exhibit 3.1. The concepts relevant to the income statement will be reviewed as they apply to Sbarro, Inc. Concepts and terms in Exhibit 3.1 that are emphasized in this chapter are indicated in bold white print and concepts emphasized in previous chapters are indicated in bold black print.

LEARNING OBJECTIVE 1

Understand the time period assumption and the elements of the income statement.

EXHIBIT 3.1
Financial Accounting and Reporting Conceptual Framework

PRIMARY OBJECTIVE OF EXTERNAL FINANCIAL REPORTING
To provide useful economic information to external users for decision making (for assessing future cash flows) [Ch. 2]

QUALITATIVE CHARACTERISTICS OF INFORMATION
[Ch. 5]
Primary:
  Relevance Information influences decisions; it is timely and has predictive and/or feedback value.
  Reliability Information is accurate, unbiased, and verifiable.
Secondary:
  Comparability Information can be compared to that of other businesses.
  Consistency Information can be compared across time.

ELEMENTS OF FINANCIAL STATEMENTS
Assets Probable future economic benefits owned by the entity from past transactions. [Ch. 2]
Liabilities Probable debts or obligations from past transactions to be paid with assets or services. [Ch. 2]
Stockholders' Equity Financing provided by owners and operations. [Ch. 2]
Revenues Increases in assets or settlements of liabilities from ongoing operations. [Ch. 3]
Expenses Decreases in assets or increases in liabilities from ongoing operations. [Ch. 3]
Gains Increases in assets or decreases in liabilities from peripheral transactions. [Ch. 3]
Losses Decreases in assets or increases in liabilities from peripheral transactions. [Ch. 3]

ASSUMPTIONS
1. **Separate-entity** Transactions of the business are separate from transactions of the owners. [Ch. 2]
2. **Unit-of-measure** Accounting measurements will be in the national monetary unit. [Ch. 2]
3. **Continuity** The entity will not going out of business in the near future. [Ch. 2]
4. **Time period** The long life of a company can be reported over a series of shorter time periods. [Ch. 3]

PRINCIPLES
1. **Cost** The historical cash-equivalent cost given up is the basis for initial recording of elements. [Ch. 2 and 3]
2. **Revenue** Record revenues when earned and measurable (an exchange has taken place, the earnings process is nearly complete, and collection is probable). [Ch. 3]
3. **Matching** Record expenses when incurred in earning revenue. [Ch. 3]
4. *Full-disclosure* Disclose relevant economic information. [Ch. 5]

CONSTRAINTS
[Ch. 5]
1. *Materiality* Relatively small amounts not likely to influence decisions are to be recorded in the most cost-beneficial way.
2. *Cost-benefit* Benefits of recording and reporting information should outweigh costs.
3. *Conservatism* Exercise care not to overstate assets and revenues or understate liabilities and expenses.
4. *Industry peculiarities* Differences in accounting and reporting for certain items are permitted if there is a clear precedent in the industry.

Concepts Emphasized in Chapter 3

Underlying Assumption of Accounting

In Chapter 2, we defined the separate-entity, unit-of-measure, and continuity assumptions. The remaining accounting assumption, the **time period assumption,** is directly relevant to the income statement. It recognizes that decision makers require periodic information about the financial condition and performance of a business. Most businesses exist for several years, decades, and even centuries. To meet decision makers' needs for periodic information, we assume that the long life of a company can be reported in shorter time periods, usually months, quarters, and years. In addition to the audited annual statements, most businesses prepare quarterly financial statements (also known as *interim reports* covering a three-month period) for external users. The Securities and Exchange Commission requires publicly traded companies to do so.

The annual accounting period does not have to conform to the calendar year. In a recent survey of 600 companies, 235 (39 percent) did not use a December 31 year-end.[1] In addition, 133 companies (22 percent) chose a fiscal year-end defined, for example, as "the last Saturday of the month" or "the Saturday closest to the end of the month," which results in financial information in some years covering 52 weeks and in other years 53 weeks. Sbarro, Inc., defines its fiscal year-end as the Sunday nearest December 31. For example, Sbarro's 1994 year ended on Sunday, January 1, 1995; the 1995 year ended on Sunday, December 31, 1995; and the 1996 year ended on Sunday, December 29, 1996.

Furthermore, many companies use a natural business year-end, which occurs at the lowest point in their annual business cycle. Retail stores, for example, tend to experience much seasonal fluctuation in business activity. The holiday shopping period in November and December and merchandise returns in January are usually the months of highest activity followed immediately by several months of lowest activity. They often use a January 31 year-end. The following is a sample of well-known companies and their year-end dates:

Company	Industry	Year-End
Campbell Soup Company	Foods	Sunday nearest July 31
U·S Airways	Airline	December 31
Federal Express	Delivery	May 31
Honda Motor Co., Ltd.	Automobile	March 31
Wendy's International, Inc.	Fast food	Sunday nearest December 31
McDonald's Corporation	Fast food	December 31
Kmart Corporation	Retail	Last Wednesday in January
Dayton Hudson Corp.	Retail	Sunday nearest January 31
Woolworth Corporation	Retail	Last Saturday in January except European and Mexican operations, which end December 31

Although the time period assumption may appear to be of little consequence at first glance, many of the most difficult accounting problems we examine in this book involve issues in assigning business activities to time periods.

Elements of the Income Statement

A recent income statement for Sbarro, Inc., is presented in Exhibit 3.2. For purposes of this chapter, the income statement has been simplified by rounding the dollar amounts.[2] In addition, only one year's income statement is presented here. Publicly

---

[1] *Accounting Trends & Techniques,* 50th ed. (New York: AICPA, 1996), p. 27.

[2] As another simplification, the Other Income account is listed in Exhibit 3.2 under revenues, but Sbarro actually reports the account as a negative amount at the end of the Costs and Expenses section.

traded companies such as Sbarro are required to present income information for three years to help users assess trends over time.

Revenues result from selling goods or services as part of a company's normal ongoing operations (that is, what they are in business to do). When revenues occur, assets (usually cash or receivables) increase or liabilities (usually deferred or unearned revenue) decrease when the obligation is settled. We can say then that revenues are increases in assets or settlements of liabilities from ongoing operations.

Sbarro's income statement in Exhibit 3.2 indicates that Restaurant Sales is Sbarro's largest revenue account. These revenues are recognized when Sbarro's company-owned restaurants provide food service for which they usually receive cash immediately. Sbarro also has contractual arrangements with its franchisees (owners of franchised restaurants) from which Sbarro earns two kinds of revenues: (1) initial franchise fees for opening each new franchised restaurant and (2) royalties based on a percentage of revenues earned by each franchised restaurant. These two revenues are combined in the account Franchise Related Income. Interest income represents the amount of interest earned on investments (marketable securities owned by Sbarro). The last revenue listed on the income statement, Other Income, is a summary of several small income sources, including gains (defined later).

Expenses are necessary to generate revenues. Sbarro hires employees to make and serve food, uses electricity to operate equipment and light facilities, and uses food and paper supplies. Without incurring these costs, Sbarro could not generate revenues. When an expense occurs, assets (such as supplies inventory and cash) decrease or are used up or liabilities (such as salaries payable or utilities payable) increase. We can say then that expenses are decreases in assets or increases in liabilities from ongoing operations. The following are Sbarro's three largest expenses:

> **Revenues** are increases in assets or settlements of liabilities from ongoing operations.

> **Expenses** are decreases in assets or increases in liabilities from ongoing operations.

EXHIBIT 3.2
Income Statement

SBARRO, INC., AND SUBSIDIARIES
Statement of Income
For the Year Ended December 31, 1995
(In thousands of dollars, except for per share data)

Revenues:		
Restaurant sales		$310,100
Franchise related income		5,900
Interest income		3,100
Other income		1,400
Total revenues		$320,500
Costs and expenses:		
Cost of food and paper products		67,400
Restaurant operating expenses:		
Payroll and other employee benefits	$78,300	
Occupancy and other expenses	84,400	162,700
Depreciation and amortization		23,600
General and administrative		16,100
Other		16,400
Total costs and expenses		$286,200
Income before income taxes		34,300
Income taxes		13,000
Net income		$ 21,300
Earnings per share		$1.05

How will these transactions be reflected on Sbarro's income statement?

1. The cost of food and paper products from using inventories of these items.
2. Payroll and other employee benefits, a restaurant operating expense primarily paid directly in cash to employees.
3. Occupancy and other expenses, primarily rent paid to shopping mall owners.

Depreciation and amortization expense is the portion of the cost of long-lived assets (property, equipment, and intangibles) used in the period to generate revenue. The general and administrative expense category includes the business expenses not directly related to serving food to customers. This category includes the salary of the president and other officers, advertising costs, office supplies, and insurance. We noted in Chapter 2 that Sbarro is not financed with short- or long-term debt. If Sbarro had debt, interest expense also would be reported separately on the income statement.

Income taxes is the last expense listed. All profit-making corporations are required to compute income taxes owed to federal, state, and foreign governments. Although we will add detail in Chapter 9, income tax expense is calculated as a percentage of the difference between revenues and expenses determined by applying IRS tax rates. Using the information in Sbarro's income statement in Exhibit 3.2, we can determine its effective income tax rate for taxes owed to federal, state, and foreign governments as follows:

$$\text{Effective tax rate} = \frac{\$13{,}000 \text{ income taxes}}{\$34{,}300 \text{ income before income taxes}}$$
$$= 37.9\%$$

This rate indicates that for every dollar of profit that Sbarro makes, the company pays almost $.38 to taxing authorities.

Gains are increases in assets or decreases in liabilities from peripheral transactions.

Gains, like revenues, result in increases in assets or decreases in liabilities. The activities resulting in the net inflow are not related, however, to the central operations of the business. We say then that gains are increases in assets or decreases in liabilities from peripheral transactions. If, for example, Sbarro sells an oven (equipment) at a price of $2,500, but the equipment is recorded in Sbarro's accounts at $2,000 (its book value), a gain (not a revenue) of $500 results. Sbarro is not in the business of selling its equipment, although buying and selling equipment occurs occasionally. The equipment sale is a peripheral transaction (an investing, not an operating, activity).

Losses are decreases in assets or increases in liabilities from peripheral transactions.

Losses are decreases in assets or increases in liabilities from peripheral transactions. If equipment with a recorded book value of $2,800 is sold for $2,500, Sbarro recognizes a loss of $300 on the sale. In Sbarro's income statement in Exhibit 3.2, no gains or losses are reported separately. As noted earlier, most companies, including Sbarro, combine small gains and losses in the Other Income category on the income statement. We will present the transaction analysis for gains and losses in future chapters dealing with the valuation and disposition of specific assets and liabilities.

Basic Accounting Principles Affecting Income Determination

The basic principles of accounting are important because they provide the conceptual guidelines for measuring, recording, and reporting business transactions. Three of the principles apply to income determination:

1. The revenue principle.
2. The matching principle.
3. The cost principle.

These principles need to be understood clearly. We discuss and illustrate them in the next section of the chapter.

Income Measurement

To understand how to apply the three principles just listed, you must first understand the operating cycle (also called the *cash-to-cash cycle* or *earnings process*) for a typical business.

The Operating Cycle

Exhibit 3.3 presents a typical operating cycle in the form of a timeline. In simple terms, the long-term objective for any business is *to turn cash into more cash*. The **operating cycle** (cash-to-cash cycle or earnings process) is the *time* it takes for a company to purchase goods or services from suppliers, sell those goods or services to customers, and collect cash from customers. A merchandiser or manufacturer (1) purchases or manufactures and stocks the inventory, (2) pays cash to suppliers, (3) sells the product on credit (hopefully at a price exceeding costs), and (4) finally receives cash from the

LEARNING OBJECTIVE 2
Understand a typical business operating cycle and the phases in the accounting cycle.
The **operating cycle** (cash-to-cash cycle; earnings process) is the time it takes for a company to purchase goods or services from suppliers, sell those goods and services to customers, and collect cash from customers.

EXHIBIT 3.3
A Typical Business Operating Cycle (or Cash-to-Cash Cycle)

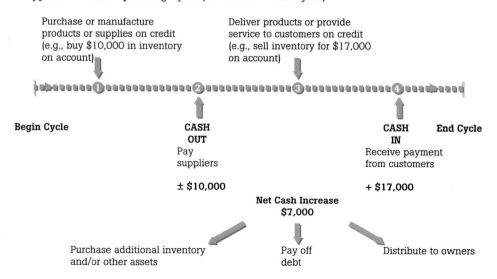

customer. Thus, cash is turned into more cash. For ongoing businesses, additional inventory is purchased or produced, and the cycle is repeated.

For service companies, the operating cycle is similar. Although spending cash on a product is not necessary, other relevant costs are incurred in providing the service, such as rent, the use of necessary supplies and equipment, and employee wages. Then the service is provided on credit at a price exceeding costs. Finally, the cash is received from the customer.

In the example in Exhibit 3.3, $10,000 was expended and $17,000 was received for a net increase of $7,000 in cash. The net increase can be used to buy additional assets (resources for the business), pay off debt, and/or be distributed to owners. Although the $7,000 cash increase is the result of completing the operating cycle, we will learn in this chapter and Chapter 4 that different portions of the $7,000 may be reported in different time periods (e.g., $3,000 this year and $4,000 next year) because the company's accounting period ends at a point other than the end of the operating cycle.

The length of time for a company's operating cycle depends on the nature of its business. Sbarro's cycle should be shorter than that for a company producing consumer products such as refrigerators or clothing. Shortening the operating cycle by creating incentives to encourage customers to buy sooner and/or pay faster reduces costs and improves the company's financial position.

Although Exhibit 3.3 presents a typical operating cycle, it is important to note that in many instances cash is received (point 4) or paid (point 2) at other times. For example, companies that sell magazine subscriptions receive cash from customers well *before* they deliver any product. Insurance premiums also are usually paid *before* companies are covered for risk of loss, but utility bills usually are received for payment *after* the company has used the utilities. Sbarro receives cash from customers at the point of sale (point 3).

Short-Term Debt Financing and the Operating Cycle

From the timing of the cash outflows and inflows in Exhibit 3.3, we can see that most businesses often need short-term borrowing to pay suppliers and employees until they receive cash from customers. That is, a cash outflow occurs before a cash inflow, causing companies to seek short-term financing. Then when the companies receive cash from customers, they pay the liability off. In addition, if a company plans to grow, say to sell twice as many goods as in the prior period, it may not have collected enough cash from the prior period's customers to purchase the amount of inventory needed in the next period. Sources of financing include suppliers through accounts payable and financial institutions (banks and commercial credit companies) through notes payable. Short- and long-term debt financing are discussed in Chapters 9 and 10.

Notice in Exhibit 3.3 that the typical earnings process involves four basic activities or transactions that take place in sequence over time. Timelines similar to the one in Exhibit 3.3 that list activities, dates, and amounts are useful tools to illustrate the income recognition issues discussed next. Timelines can help you focus on the two primary questions for income measurement:

1. *When* should revenues and expenses be recognized (recorded)? [Timing issues]
2. *What amounts* should be recognized? [Measurement issues]

We answer these as we discuss the principles relating to the accrual basis of accounting.

Accrual Basis of Accounting

Cash versus Accrual Basis

Most of you determine your personal financial position by the cash balance in your bank account. Your financial performance is measured as the difference between your cash balance at the beginning of the period and the balance at the end of the period (that is, whether you end up with more or less cash). If you have a higher cash balance, cash receipts exceeded cash disbursements for the period. Measuring income in this manner is called **cash basis accounting.** Using this system, revenues are recorded when cash is received, and expenses are recorded when cash is paid, regardless of when the revenues are earned and expenses are incurred.

> Revenues (when cash is received)
> − Expenses (when cash is paid)
> Net Income on the cash basis

Many small retailers, medical offices, and other small businesses use the cash basis of accounting. This basis is often quite adequate for these organizations that usually do not have to report to external users. For publicly traded corporations, however, the cash basis is not considered appropriate for two main reasons. First, except for transactions involving cash, no assets or liabilities are recorded; therefore, a complete financial position is not available for analysis. In addition, cash basis net income, which is the difference between cash receipts and disbursements, can be manipulated. For example, a company using the cash basis can report higher net income simply by postponing certain payments until the next period. Since financial statements created under the cash basis of accounting normally postpone or accelerate recognition of revenues and expenses long before or after goods and services are produced and delivered, these statements can be misleading and are less relevant to external decision makers.

Generally accepted accounting principles require **accrual basis accounting** for financial reporting purposes. This means that assets, liabilities, revenues, and expenses should be recognized when the transaction that causes them occurs, not necessarily when cash is received or paid. Revenues are recognized when earned and expenses when incurred. Thus, the accrual basis is less subject to manipulation.

> Revenues (when earned)
> − Expenses (when incurred)
> Net Income on the accrual basis

Even though the accrual basis of accounting is followed, cash flow information is important for estimating whether companies can afford to pay their debts. In fact, this information is reported on a separate statement, the statement of cash flows, which is very important in financial statement analysis and will be discussed in Chapters 4 and 5 and in greater detail in Chapter 13. The two basic accounting principles that determine when revenues and expenses are to be recorded under the accrual basis of accounting are the *revenue principle* and the *matching principle.*

Timing of Revenues: The Revenue Principle

Under the **revenue principle,** three conditions normally must be met for revenue to be recognized. If *any* of the following conditions is *not* met, revenue normally is *not* considered recognized and cannot be recorded.

LEARNING OBJECTIVE 3
Explain the accrual basis of accounting.

Cash basis accounting records revenues when cash is received and expenses when cash is paid.

Accrual basis accounting requires recording revenues when earned and expenses when incurred, regardless of the timing of cash receipts or payments.

LEARNING OBJECTIVE 4
Apply the revenue and matching principles to determine the timing and amount of revenue and expense recognition.

The **revenue principle** states that revenues are recognized when the earnings process is complete or nearly complete, an exchange has taken place, and collection is probable.

1. *The earnings process is complete or nearly complete.* This means that the company has performed or substantially performed the promised acts (provided goods or services).
2. *An exchange transaction takes place.* In exchange for the company's performance, the customer provides cash or a promise to pay cash (a receivable).
3. *Collection is reasonably assured.* As discussed in more depth in Chapter 6, companies establish credit policies to reduce the risk of extending credit to customers who fail to pay. On the date of a sale on credit, assuming that the credit policies have been followed, collection is usually considered reasonably probable. We will learn in Chapter 6 that, even with strong credit policies, companies need to evaluate the likelihood that some accounts will not be collected. Probable bad debts will need to be estimated.

In practice, these conditions are met for most businesses at the point of delivery of goods or services. In Exhibit 3.3, revenue is usually recorded on the date of delivery (point 3). For sales of magazine subscriptions, even though cash is received, revenue is not recorded until the magazines are delivered. Instead, since the earnings process is not complete, the initial cash transaction results in a liability until delivery. The deferred or unearned revenue account represents the amount of goods or services owed to the customers or a refund due if they cancel their orders. As stated before, revenue is recorded according to the revenue principle when the three conditions are met, *regardless of when cash is received.*

As is typical in the fast-food industry, Sbarro receives nearly 98 percent of its revenues in cash at the time of sale of food products to customers. Thus, points 3 and 4 in the operating cycle occur on the same day. Sbarro also sells franchises from which it receives cash from new franchisees *before* it provides start-up services to them. Later, when Sbarro provides the services, it earns and records revenues. Typical liabilities (recorded when cash is received before revenue is earned) that become revenues when earned are the following:

Liability (cash received before being earned)	Becomes	Revenue (earned when good or service is provided)
Rent collected in advance	→	Rent revenue
Unearned air traffic revenue	→	Air traffic revenue
Deferred subscription revenue	→	Subscription revenue

As time passes, the liability accounts (also known as *deferrals* because revenue recognition is deferred until earned in the future) should be adjusted to reflect the correct amounts earned and unearned. These accounts usually are adjusted at the end of a period. We will discuss the amounts and timing of adjustments in Chapter 4.

Franchisees must also pay royalties to Sbarro based on a percentage of their sales revenues. Sbarro receives cash *after* it earns royalty revenue. Typical assets reflecting revenues earned but not yet received in cash are as follows:

Asset (resource)	Resulting from	Revenue (earned before cash is received)
Interest receivable	→	Interest revenue
Rent receivable	→	Rent revenue
Royalties receivable	→	Royalty revenue

These asset accounts (known as *accruals*) typically are recorded at the end of a period because revenue has been earned but has not been recorded because cash will be received in the future. These adjustments ensure that revenues are recognized in the proper period.

Companies usually disclose their revenue recognition practices in a footnote to the financial statements. The following excerpt from Sbarro's Footnote 1 describes how it recognizes these two forms of franchise related income:

> **Notes To Consolidated Financial Statements**
> **Sbarro, Inc. and Subsidiaries**
> 1. Summary of Significant Accounting Policies
> . . .
> Franchise related income
> Initial franchise fees are recorded as income as restaurants are opened by the franchisees and all services have been substantially performed by the Company. . . . Royalties and other fees from franchisees are accrued as earned. . . .

REAL WORLD EXCERPT
SBARRO, INC.
Annual Report

These practices follow the conditions of the revenue principle discussed earlier. In Chapter 6 we will discuss special generally accepted practices applied in certain circumstances when one of the conditions is not met (such as accounting for revenue under long-term construction contracts before the projects are completed).

Determining the Amount of Revenue

In Chapter 2, we defined the *cost principle* as the requirement that financial statement elements be recorded at the cash-equivalent price on the date of the transaction (historical cost). We apply this same principle to revenue recognition. By definition, revenues are increases in assets or decreases in liabilities. Since assets are recorded on the balance sheet at the cash or cash-equivalent price, revenues are measured at the cash or cash-equivalent value of the assets to be received from customers.

In determining how much revenue to record in a particular period, a **timeline** like the one in Exhibit 3.3 often is helpful in providing a visual representation of a transaction or series of transactions. Timelines indicate relevant activities, dates, and amounts.

A **timeline** is a visual representation of a series of business activities, listing dates and amounts over time.

To illustrate, consider a transaction in which a company provides a service to a customer on May 23 who pays for the service on June 16. On the date the service is provided, the earnings process is complete, an exchange transaction of service for a promise to pay has taken place, and the cash collection is reasonably assured. Therefore, as indicated on the timeline, $300 is recognized as revenue in May, not in June when the cash is collected from the customer. The name of the revenue account is Service Revenue.

Activities:		Company provided service to customer		Cash ($300) collected from customer	
Dates:	4/30	5/23	5/31	6/16	6/30
Amounts:		$300 Revenue earned in May			

SELF-STUDY QUIZ

This self-study quiz allows you to practice applying the revenue principle under accrual accounting. We recommend that you refer back to the three revenue recognition criteria presented earlier as you answer each question. It is important to complete this quiz now to make sure you can apply these principles.

The following transactions are samples of typical monthly operating activities of Sbarro, Inc. Indicate whether or not a revenue would be recognized in **January.** If so, indicate an appropriate account title and amount. You should refer to the Sbarro income statement presented in Exhibit 3.2 for examples of account titles. Then indicate other accounts affected on the date of the transaction. A formatted timeline is provided for your use.

December	January	February	Does a Revenue Result for Sbarro in January?	Revenue Account Title	Amount of Revenue Sbarro Recognizes in January	Title of Other Account(s) Affected
1. In January, Sbarro's company-owned restaurants sold food to customers for $25,800 in cash.						
2. Sbarro is entitled to royalties from franchisees based on a percentage of their gross revenues. At the end of January, franchisees report that, based on January's gross revenues, they owe Sbarro $500, which they will pay in February.						
3. A mall department store paid Sbarro a $30 deposit in January in exchange for Sbarro's promise to provide food for an employee party in February.						
4. Sbarro received $700 in cash for royalties from franchisees in January based on the franchisees' December revenues.						

After you have completed the quiz, check your solution with the answers in the footnote at the bottom of this page.*

Management's Incentives to Violate the Revenue Principle

In two recent articles, *The Wall Street Journal* reported the following:

TECH CONCERNS FUDGE FIGURES TO BUY STOCKS

More small technology companies are pumping up their sales and earnings through aggressive and sometimes questionable accounting to help inflate their stock prices, accountants say.

SOURCE: L. Berton, *The Wall Street Journal,* May 19, 1994, p. B1.

THREE KURZWEIL OFFICIALS QUIT, FOURTH FIRED AFTER SALES INQUIRY; STOCK PLUNGES

Kurzweil Applied Intelligence Inc. said three top managers resigned and a fourth was fired following the discovery that "a number of significant" sales had been booked as revenues before actually being completed. The company's stock price plunged nearly 40%.

SOURCE: S. Stecklow, *The Wall Street Journal,* May 24, 1994, p. B6.

*					
1.	Yes	Restaurant Sales Revenue (R)	$25,800	Cash (A)	
2.	Yes	Franchise Related Income (R)	$500	Receivables (A)	
3.	No	—		Cash (A) and Unearned Revenue (L)	
4.	No	—		Cash (A) and Receivables (A)	

These headlines refer to companies in the very competitive computer industry. They suggest that when companies experience financial difficulty, some managers attempt to improve the picture painted in the financial statements by violating revenue recognition rules. The hope is to fool investors so that much-needed funds can be raised through the stock market.

Mentioned in the first article is Kendall Square Research Corp., maker of supercomputers, which "has acknowledged that it counted as sales numerous computers that customers apparently couldn't pay for." This violates the condition that collection should be reasonably assured. The second article indicates that Kurzweil, a software manufacturer, recorded revenues before the earnings process was complete, thus violating the first condition. The importance of revenue recognition and earnings to the value of a company's stock is emphasized by the dramatic drop in share price often experienced when the discovery of such improprieties is announced.

The following is an epilogue to the Kurzweil case:

TWO FORMER OFFICERS AT KURZWEIL FOUND GUILTY IN FRAUD SCHEME

Two former executives of Kurzweil Applied Technologies Inc. were convicted of securities fraud for their part in cooking the books before the company went public in 1993. . . . To improve the bottom line's appearance, the defendants padded the top line by prematurely booking sales, according to testimony at the trial, federal regulators said. . . . The defendants, who are scheduled for sentencing Sept. 11, each face up to $1 million in fines and 10 years in prison.

Source: Staff Reporter, *The Wall Street Journal,* May 16, 1996, p. A4.

Timing of Expenses: The Matching Principle

Resources that are used to earn revenues are called *expenses*. The **matching principle** requires that when the period's revenues are properly recognized according to the revenue principle, all of the resources consumed in earning those revenues should be recorded in that same period, *regardless of when cash is paid.* Thus, expenses are "matched" with revenue in the period incurred. When Sbarro records total restaurant sales revenue for the period, all of the related expenses (such as the cost of food and paper products from inventories, payroll expense, and occupancy expense) used to generate the revenues also should be recorded. The expense should be matched with revenues for the same period.

The **matching principle** requires that expenses be recorded when incurred in earning revenue.

As in the case of revenues and cash receipts, expenses and cash outlays are not necessarily recorded on the same date. For example, the acquisition of, and sometimes the cash outlay for, food and paper product supplies occurs *prior* to their use. They are recorded as inventory, an asset, however, when purchased and are not expensed as the cost of food and paper products until they are used. Similarly, companies usually pay for rent in *advance* of using the property and record the cash outlay in an asset account, Prepaid Expense, that represents future benefits to the company. The asset is allocated over time to occupancy expense as it is used. In addition, a part of the cost of long-lived assets, such as equipment used in operations, needs to be matched with the revenues generated by their use in a period. The used portion of the assets is allocated to depreciation expense. Typical assets and their related expense accounts are as follows:

Asset (resource)	Becomes	Expense (when resource is used)
Supplies inventory	→	Supplies expense (or cost of supplies used)
Prepaid expense	→	Insurance expense (or rent expense, etc.)
Buildings and equipment	→	Depreciation expense

As time passes, the asset accounts (also known as *deferrals* because expense recognition is deferred until matched with the earning of revenue in the future) should be

Identify the related expenses to be matched with the sales revenue.

adjusted to reflect the correct amounts used for the period or with remaining future benefits. These accounts usually are adjusted at the end of a period. We discuss the amounts and timing of adjustments in Chapter 4.

In other cases, resources are used to generate revenues prior to the cash outlay. For Sbarro, payroll expense represents the amount earned by managers and employees who prepare and serve the food and is an expense of that period. Cash is usually paid to employees *after* the point when they provide their services. Expense should be recorded, however, when the service is provided. Typical liabilities and their related expense accounts are as follows:

Liability	Resulting from	Expense (incurred before cash is paid)
Salaries payable	→	Salaries expense
Interest payable	→	Interest expense
Property taxes payable	→	Property taxes expense

These liability accounts (known as *accruals*) result from incurring expenses before cash is paid. Expense accruals typically are recorded at the end of a period as adjustments to ensure that expenses are recognized in the proper period.

Determining the Amount of Expense

Expenses are the decreases in (or using up of) assets or increases in liabilities from ongoing operations. Similar to the practice with revenues, expenses are measured as the proportion of the historical cost of the assets expended or to be expended. Again, a timeline is a tool to use to determine the amount of the expense incurred in each period.

SELF-STUDY QUIZ

This self-study quiz allows you to practice applying the matching principle under accrual accounting. We recommend that you refer back to the description of the matching principle presented earlier as you answer each question. It is important to complete this quiz now to make sure you can apply these principles.

The following transactions are samples of typical monthly operating activities of Sbarro, Inc. Indicate whether or not an expense would be recognized in **January.** If so, indicate an appropriate account title and amount. Then indicate other accounts affected in January. A formatted timeline is provided for your use.

December	January	February	Does an Expense Result for Sbarro in January?	Expense Account Title	Amount of Expense Sbarro Recognizes in January	Title of Other Account(s) Affected
1. An oven in a company-owned restaurant was repaired in January. Sbarro received and paid the bill for $50 in January.						
2. Sbarro received bills for $60 in February from electric and gas companies for utility usage by its company-owned restaurants in January.						
3. In December, Sbarro paid $18,600 to mall owners to rent mall space in January, February, and March.						
4. In January, Sbarro received and paid suppliers $120 cash for paper products that will be used in February.						

After you have completed the quiz, check your solution with the answers in the footnote at the bottom of this page.*

The Accounting Cycle

Measuring a company's financial performance and financial position requires establishing a distinct accounting period—usually a month, quarter, or year. We know from Exhibit 3.3 that the operating cycle involves both cash inflows and outflows and a series of revenues and expenses that are recognized according to the revenue recognition and matching principles of accrual accounting. *Often revenue and expense recognition dates do not coincide with cash flow dates. Further, one accounting period may include several operating cycles, or the operating cycle may extend over more than one accounting period.* The length of a company's operating cycle depends on the nature of its business operations and can differ for every company; the length of a company's accounting cycle is similar to that of every other company (a period of one month, quarter, or year). To understand the impact of these timing issues, let's return to our definitions of the two types of business transactions discussed in Chapter 2 and examine when and how these transactions are accounted for in typical accounting systems.

Transactions of the first type are exchanges of assets and liabilities between the business and one or more other parties. The second type of transaction includes certain events that do not result in an actual exchange between the business and other parties but do have a direct and measurable effect on the accounting entity, particularly

*					
1.	Yes	Repair Expense (E)	$50	Cash (A)
2.	Yes	Utilities Expense (E)	$60	Accounts Payable (L)
3.	Yes	Occupancy (Rent) Expense (E)	$6,200	Prepaid (Rent) Expense (A)
4.	No	—	—	Supplies Inventory (A), Cash (A)

for revenue and expense recognition. This second type of transaction is based on one of the following:

1. Past business activities for which the passage of time causes revenues to be earned or expenses to be incurred. Examples include recognition of interest revenue on a note receivable and depreciation expense on the equipment used during the period.

2. Reasonable estimates. An example is an estimate of the amount of utilities used during the period.

These transactions that normally are recorded at the end of the accounting period are called *adjusting entries*. They are adjustments of accrual and deferral accounts.

Phases in the Accounting Cycle

The **accounting cycle** is the recordkeeping process used during and at the end of the accounting period that results in financial statements.

The recordkeeping process used during and at the end of the accounting period that results in the preparation of financial statements is often referred to as the **accounting cycle**. Exhibit 3.4 highlights the fundamental steps in the accounting cycle. (A more detailed description of the formal recordkeeping process is provided in Appendix C at the end of the textbook.) The exhibit indicates two separate phases. Phase 1 includes the analysis and recording of the first type of transactions, those based on exchanges with external parties *during* the accounting period. Sbarro's investing and financing transactions that we presented in Chapter 2 occurred in Phase 1. Sbarro's operating activities to be discussed in this chapter also occur during Phase 1.

EXHIBIT 3.4
Fundamental Steps in the Accounting Cycle

START OF ACCOUNTING PERIOD

Phase 1:
During the Accounting Period
(discussed in Chapters 2 and 3)

Perform **transaction analysis** based on a review of source documents from each transaction

Record **journal entries** for each transaction (in chronological order in the general journal)

Post amounts to the general ledger (pages are similar to **T-accounts**)

Phase 2:
At the End of the Accounting Period
(discussed in Chapter 4)

Prepare a **trial balance** (a list of accounts and balances to date) to verify the equality of debits and credits

Analyze adjustments (to update all accounts for proper revenue recognition and expense matching)

Prepare and distribute **financial statements** (from adjusted balances)

Record and post **adjusting and closing entries** (to create zero balances in temporary accounts for use in the next period)*

*Temporary accounts are those that accumulate balances for the period. They are revenue and expense accounts.

END OF ACCOUNTING PERIOD

We will learn to recognize which of the Phase 1 transactions require adjusting entries in Phase 2.

The second phase includes all of the activities at the *end* of the accounting period to update account balances for proper revenue and expense recognition (the adjustment process), to prepare financial statements, and to prepare the records for the beginning of the next period of activity. These steps are discussed in Chapter 4. We briefly note in Exhibit 3.4 that organizations maintain two basic types of accounting records (or books): a General Journal, which is a formal list of each journal entry in chronological order, and a General Ledger, in which each page resembles a more detailed T-account. Although some small businesses maintain manual records, computer technology has become so inexpensive and easy to use that most companies have computerized accounting systems; however, even sophisticated computerized accounting systems still produce records similar in form to the basic General Journal and General Ledger. The accounting concepts employed remain the same whether a manual or computerized recordkeeping system is used.

Many students confuse the accounting cycle and the business operating cycle. Remember that the timing of the operating cycle is determined by the nature of the business. It may be short or long and represents the time it takes a company to turn cash into more cash. The accounting cycle coincides with the accounting period, usually a month, quarter, or year, which is similar across all companies.

LEARNING OBJECTIVE 5
Apply transaction analysis to examine and record the effects of operating activities on the financial statements.

Completion of the Transaction Analysis Model

Now that we have indicated what business activities affect the income statement and how they are measured, we need to complete the transaction analysis model to show how these business activities are recorded in the accounting system and reflected in the financial statements. Only investing and financing activities affecting assets, liabilities, and contributed capital were presented in Chapter 2. We now expand the transaction analysis model to include transactions involving revenues and expenses (from operating activities), gains and losses (from investing and financing activities), and the distribution of earnings to investors known as *dividends* (an additional financing activity). The model as we left it in Chapter 2 follows:

Assets (A)	=	Liabilities (L)	+	Stockholders' Equity (SE)
Increase　　Decrease		Decrease　　Increase		Decrease　　Increase
Debit　　　*Credit*		*Debit*　　　*Credit*		*Debit*　　　*Credit*

To begin, we need to add detail to the stockholders' equity element of the equation. Recall from Chapter 1 that stockholders' equity consists of contributed capital and retained earnings. The Retained Earnings account is the accumulation of all past revenues and expenses minus any income distributed as dividends to stockholders (earnings not retained in the business). By adding these concepts, the transaction analysis model becomes

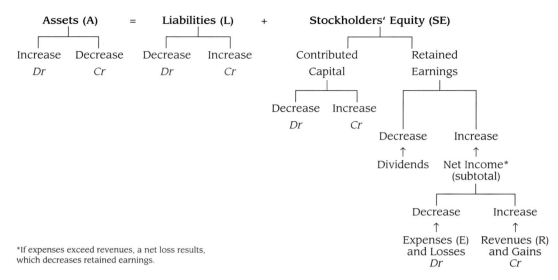

*If expenses exceed revenues, a net loss results, which decreases retained earnings.

In constructing this complete model, we maintained the direction rule and debit–credit framework described in Chapter 2:

■ For direction, the word *Increase* is written on the left when we are on the left side of the equation, and the word *Increase* is written on the right when we are on the right side of the equation at each level.

■ Debits are written on the left side of each element and credits are written on the right; however, we have used abbreviations. *Debit* becomes *Dr.,* and credit becomes *Cr.* These abbreviations often are used when writing journal entries.

Retained Earnings increases by the net income of the period when income is positive and decreases when a net loss is reported. Net income is not an account name but is a subtotal of all of the revenues, expenses, gains, and losses. Retained Earnings also decreases when dividends are declared as a distribution of the earnings to shareholders. (Instead of reducing Retained Earnings directly when dividends are declared, companies may use the account Dividends Declared. It has a debit balance.)

Before we illustrate the use of the transaction analysis model for these new elements, it is important to emphasize the following. The word *increase* is written above revenues because these accounts increase retained earnings. The word *decrease* is written above expenses because these accounts decrease retained earnings. Since retained earnings is on the right side of the equation, to increase an expense and thus decrease net income, however, the expense account needs to be debited. Therefore, *revenues normally have credit balances, and expenses normally have debit balances.* A company that has revenues exceeding expenses reports positive net income. If expenses exceed revenues, however, the company reports a net loss.

ANALYSIS

The Feedback Value of Accounting Information

A net loss does not have to occur for a company to recognize that it is experiencing difficulty. Any unexpected variance in actual performance from the operating plan, such as lower than expected quarterly earnings, should trigger an investigation into the cause. Recall from the management decision

setting at the beginning of the chapter that Sbarro, Inc., made the decision to hire outside managers to fill the new regional and district manager positions; many of these outsiders soon tried to change the Sbarro corporate culture. Morale among the restaurant managers sagged, and company earnings began to fall below expectations. Sbarro was not meeting its stated mission of "maintaining profitability through the pride and commitment to excellence by our people."

Stock market analysts and investors use accounting information to make investment decisions. These buy-and-sell decisions affect the price of a company's stock. In Sbarro's case, the stock price reached a high of $50 per share by the end of 1991. During the first quarter of 1992, however, as reports in the press suggested problems at Sbarro restaurants due primarily to the hiring decision, the stock price began to fall to $38 per share by early May. When Sbarro's actual first quarter earnings were announced on May 12, the stock price fell 11 points to $27 per share in one day. Analysts, investors, and Sbarro's management noticed the marked decline in earnings from expectations. *Forbes* reported that "in the first quarter of 1992 the company's earnings came in 33 percent below analysts' expectations."*

This is a clear example of how corporate decisions affect financial data and how internal and external users use the information. Accounting information has a pervasive effect on all forms of corporate decision making, as well as on the economic decisions that investors and creditors make.

* R. La Franco, "Promote from within," *Forbes*, February 28, 1994, pp. 86–87.

Transaction Analysis Rules

As discussed in Chapter 2, (1) every transaction affects at least two accounts (the duality rule), and (2) the accounting equation must remain in balance after each transaction (the equality rule). Since revenues are defined as inflows of net assets, then by definition to increase a revenue (a credit), an asset is usually increased or a liability is usually decreased (debited). In like manner, when increasing an expense (a debit), an asset is usually decreased or a liability is usually increased (credited). Revenues and expenses normally are not recorded in the same journal entry.

Transaction Analysis Illustrated

We follow the same process used in Chapter 2 to examine the effects of typical simplified income-related transactions of Sbarro, Inc. Recall that transaction analysis requires identifying and classifying two or more accounts and determining the way that they are affected while maintaining the accounting model's equality. Based on the analysis, a journal entry can be prepared (verifying that debits equal credits), and amounts can be posted to the appropriate T-accounts. In this illustration, we also identify entries (deferrals) or business activities (accruals) that require an adjusting entry at the end of the period.

As we emphasized in Chapter 2, refer to the transaction analysis model until you can construct it on your own without assistance. You also should study this illustration carefully to make sure that you understand the impact of operating activities on the balance sheet and income statement. We begin with Sbarro's February 2, 1996, balance sheet constructed at the end of Chapter 2, which included the effects of the transactions illustrated in that chapter. We use the account titles listed in that balance sheet and those shown on the income statement in Exhibit 3.2 as we analyze operating activities and additional financing and investing activities. A list is also provided in Exhibit 2.3 (chart of accounts). All amounts are in thousands of dollars.

(a) During January, Sbarro's company-owned restaurants sold food to customers for $25,800 in cash.

Transaction Analysis				Journal Entry		
Assets	=	Liabilities	+	Stockholders' Equity	Cash (A)	25,800
Cash +25,800				Restaurant sales revenue +25,800	Restaurant sales revenue (R)	25,800

The accounting equation is in balance. Debits $25,800 = Credits $25,800. Here and in all following revenue transactions, revenues increase retained earnings, which is part of stockholders' equity. Revenues have credit balances.

Cash is received at the same time a revenue is earned (not an accrual or deferral).

(b) Several ovens in company-owned restaurants were repaired in January. Sbarro received and paid bills for $50 in January.

Transaction Analysis				Journal Entry		
Assets	=	Liabilities	+	Stockholders' Equity	Repairs expense (E)	50
Cash −50				Repairs expense −50	Cash (A)	50

The accounting equation is in balance. Debits $50 = Credits $50. Here and in all following expense transactions, expenses decrease retained earnings, which is part of stockholders' equity. Expenses have debit balances.

Cash is paid at the same time an expense is incurred (not an accrual or deferral).

(c) At the beginning of January, Sbarro paid $18,600 to mall owners to rent mall space in January, February, and March.

Transaction Analysis				Journal Entry		
Assets	=	Liabilities	+	Stockholders' Equity	Prepaid expenses (A)	18,600
Cash −18,600					Cash (A)	18,600
Prepaid expenses +18,600						

The accounting equation is in balance. Debits $18,600 = Credits $18,600.

An asset (prepaid rent) with future benefits is acquired. This is a deferral (cash paid *before* incurring the expense) that must be adjusted at the end of the period to reflect the amount of the asset that has been used.

(d) In January, Sbarro purchased $120 of paper products from suppliers, paying $80 in cash and the rest on account.

Transaction Analysis				Journal Entry		
Assets	=	Liabilities	+	Stockholders' Equity	Inventory (A)	120
Cash −80		Accounts payable +40			Accounts payable (L)	40
Inventory +120					Cash (A)	80

The accounting equation is in balance. Debits $120 = Credits $120.

An asset (supplies inventory) with future benefits is acquired. This is a deferral (cash paid *before* incurring the expense) that must be adjusted at the end of the period to reflect the amount of the asset that has been used.

(e) In January, Sbarro's board of directors declared a $2,000 cash dividend to be paid to stockholders in March. Dividends are a return of assets to owners (a share in profits). Often, as in this example, a delay occurs between the decision to pay dividends to owners and the actual writing of the checks. Therefore, this entry decreases Retained Earnings (the accumulated profits) and increases the liability Dividends Payable.

Transaction Analysis				Journal Entry		
Assets	=	Liabilities	+	Stockholders' Equity	Retained earnings (SE)	2,000
		Dividends payable +$2,000		Retained earnings −2,000	Dividends payable (L)	2,000

The accounting equation is in balance. Debits $2,000 = Credits $2,000.

This is a financing activity that will not result in an accrual or deferral.

(*f*) Sbarro's company-owned restaurants received $2,100 in fresh fruits and vegetables from local grocers who bill Sbarro for the delivered goods. These food products are used immediately.

Transaction Analysis					Journal Entry		
Assets	=	Liabilities	+	Stockholders' Equity	Cost of food and		
		Accounts payable +2,100		Cost of food and	paper products (E)	2,100	
				paper products −$2,100	Accounts payable (L)		2,100
The accounting equation is in balance. Debits $2,100 = Credits $2,100.							
The purchase of the food and paper products (assets) coincides with their use (an expense) (not an accrual or deferral).							

(*g*) In January, Sbarro paid the $4,700 income taxes due to federal, state, and foreign governments as reported on the December 31, 1995, balance sheet.

Transaction Analysis					Journal Entry		
Assets	=	Liabilities	+	Stockholders' Equity	Income taxes payable (L)	4,700	
Cash −4,700		Income taxes payable −4,700			Cash (A)		4,700
The accounting equation is in balance. Debits $4,700 = Credits $4,700.							
This transaction is paying a liability for income tax expense incurred (and accrued) in the prior period.							

(*h*) Bills totaling $190 were received in late January from electric and gas companies for utility usage by Sbarro company-owned restaurants for January; it paid $60 in cash in January and will pay the rest in February.

Transaction Analysis					Journal Entry		
Assets	=	Liabilities	+	Stockholders' Equity	Utilities expense (E)	190	
Cash −60		Accounts payable +130		Utilities expense −190	Accounts payable (L)		130
					Cash (A)		60
The accounting equation is in balance. Debits $190 = Credits $190.							
The $130 in unpaid bills is an accrued expense for January that will be paid *after* being incurred.							

SELF-STUDY QUIZ

For transactions (*i*) through (*l*), fill in the missing information. Be sure to post journal entries to the T-accounts at the end of the illustration. When completed, you can check your answers with the solution at the end of the illustration:

(*i*) A mall department store paid Sbarro a $30 deposit in January in exchange for Sbarro's promise to provide food for an employee party in February.

Transaction Analysis					Journal Entry		
Assets	=	Liabilities	+	Stockholders' Equity	Cash (A)	30	
					Unearned revenue (L)		30
The accounting equation is in balance. Debits $30 = Credits $30.							
An obligation exists to provide service in the future. This is a deferral because cash is received *before* revenue is earned. (Companies also call this account *Deferred Income*.) The account is adjusted when earned.							

(*j*) Sbarro paid $6,000 in wages to employees for working the first three weeks of the month.

Transaction Analysis			Journal Entry
Assets = Liabilities + Stockholders' Equity			
Cash −6,000 Wages expense −6,000			
The accounting equation is in balance. Debits $6,000 = Credits $6,000.			
An expense is incurred when employees work. Therefore, this is an expense in January.			

(*k*) Near the end of January, Sbarro purchased insurance for $600 cash to cover potential property loss in February through July (the next six months).

Transaction Analysis		Journal Entry	
Assets = Liabilities + Stockholders' Equity		Prepaid expenses (A) 600	
		Cash (A) 600	
The accounting equation is in balance. Debits $600 = Credits $600.			
An asset (prepaid insurance) with future benefits is acquired. This is a deferral (cash paid *before* incurring the expense) that must be adjusted at the end of each period to reflect the amount of the asset that has been used.			

(*l*) Sbarro is entitled to royalties from franchisees based on a percentage of their weekly revenues. Near the end of January, franchisees reported that they owe Sbarro $500 based on the first three weeks of January's revenues. They will pay the royalties in early February.

Transaction Analysis			Journal Entry
Assets = Liabilities + Stockholders' Equity			
Receivables +500 Franchise related income +500			
The accounting equation is in balance. Debits $500 = Credits $500.			
The $500 is an accrued revenue in January that will be collected in February *after* being earned.			

You may check your answers with the solutions at the bottom of the page. The T-accounts are on pages 132 and 133.*

Preparation of the Income Statement and Statement of Stockholders' Equity

LEARNING OBJECTIVE 6

Construct a simple income statement and statement of stockholders' equity.

Based on the January transactions that have been posted in the T-accounts, we can prepare an income statement reflecting operating activities in January. The statement is called *unadjusted,* however, because no adjusting entries for accruals or deferrals have been recorded. Therefore, the revenue and expense accounts and related assets

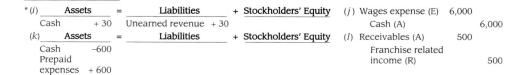

* (*i*) Assets = Liabilities + Stockholders' Equity				(*j*) Wages expense (E) 6,000	
Cash + 30 Unearned revenue + 30				Cash (A) 6,000	
(*k*) Assets = Liabilities + Stockholders' Equity				(*l*) Receivables (A) 500	
Cash −600				Franchise related	
Prepaid				income (R) 500	
expenses + 600					

and liabilities are not up-to-date. For example, many large expenses are not yet included, especially the cost of food and paper products used in January and depreciation on equipment used during the month. Also notice that we have not calculated income taxes. Because this statement is unadjusted, the amount of taxes due is not yet determinable. These statements do not at this point reflect generally accepted accounting principles based on accrual accounting. We will adjust the accounts and prepare complete statements in Chapter 4.

SBARRO, INC. AND SUBSIDIARIES
Statement of Income (unadjusted)
For the Period Ended February 2, 1996
(in thousands of dollars)

Revenues		
Restaurant sales	$25,800	
Franchise related income	500	
Total revenues		$26,300
Costs and expenses		
Cost of food and paper products	2,100	
Restaurant operating expenses:		
Payroll and other employee benefits (wages)	$6,000	
Occupancy and other expenses (utilities and repairs)	240	6,240
Total costs and expenses		8,340
Net income		$17,960

Reporting Financial Information by Geographic Segments

International PERSPECTIVE

Many companies, especially very large ones, operate in multiple geographic segments. These companies are often called *multinationals.* The simple income statement just presented based on aggregated data may not prove as useful to investors seeking to assess possible risks and returns from companies operating in foreign markets. Therefore, additional summary information about geographic segments is provided in footnotes to the financial statements. For example, an excerpt from the 1995 annual report of General Motors Corporation follows:

REAL WORLD EXCERPT

GENERAL MOTORS
CORPORATION
Annual Report

NOTE 21. Segment Reporting
Geographic Segments

Net Sales and Revenues (Dollars in millions)	United States	Other North America	Europe	Latin America	All Other	Total
1995	$119,813.4	$8,320.9	$32,036.2	$6,464.1	$2,194.0	$168,828.6
1994	110,910.3	9,335.4	27,227.2	5,716.6	1,761.7	154,951.2
1993	99,573.2	8,203.5	24,140.1	4,838.8	1,463.9	138,219.5

In addition, General Motors reports net income, total assets, net assets, and the average number of employees for the same segments. For companies operating in multiple industries, summary financial information also is provided by major industrial segment. For General Motors, the major segments are automotive products, financing and insurance operations, and other products.

T-Accounts

Each T-account begins with a summary balance of the effects of the transactions in Chapter 2. The transactions in January from this chapter are referenced (a) through (l).

Debit +	ASSETS	Credit –

Cash

Ch. 2 Bal.	93,940		
(a)	25,800	(b)	50
(i)		(c)	18,600
		(d)	80
		(g)	4,700
		(h)	60
		(j)	
		(k)	
End. Bal.	89,680		

Marketable Securities

Ch. 2 Bal.	10,000	
End. Bal.	10,000	

Receivables

Ch. 2 Bal.	2,600	
(l)		
End. Bal.	3,100	

Inventory

Ch. 2 Bal.	3,170	
(d)	120	
End. Bal.	3,290	

Prepaid Expenses

Ch. 2 Bal.	1,700	
(c)	18,600	
(k)		
End. Bal.	20,900	

Property and Equipment

Ch. 2 Bal.	127,650	
End. Bal.	127,650	

Other Assets

Ch. 2 Bal.	5,300	
End. Bal.	5,300	

Debit –	LIABILITIES	Credit +

Notes Payable

		Ch. 2 Bal.	1,200
		End. Bal.	1,200

Accounts Payable

		Ch. 2 Bal.	7,660
		(d)	40
		(f)	2,100
		(h)	130
		End. Bal.	9,930

Accrued Expenses Payable

		Ch. 2 Bal.	27,000
		End. Bal.	27,000

Dividends Payable

		Ch. 2 Bal.	3,900
		(e)	2,000
		End. Bal.	5,900

Income Taxes Payable

		Ch. 2 Bal.	4,700
(g)	4,700		
		End. Bal.	0

Unearned Revenue

		Ch. 2 Bal.	0
		(i)	
		End. Bal.	30

Deferred Income Taxes

		Ch. 2 Bal.	14,100
		End. Bal.	14,100

Debit −	STOCKHOLDERS' EQUITY		Credit +

Contributed Capital

		Ch. 2 Bal.	30,700
		End. Bal.	30,700

Retained Earnings

		Ch. 2	155,100
(e)	2,000		
		End. Bal.	153,100

EXPENSES	**REVENUES**
(Increase on the debit side, but an increase in an expense decreases SE)	(Increase on the credit side, and an increase in a revenue increases SE)

Cost of Food and Paper Products

Ch. 2 Bal.	0	
(f)	2,100	
End. Bal.	2,100	

Restaurant Sales Revenue

	Ch. 2 Bal.	0
	(a)	25,800
	End. Bal.	25,800

Wages Expense

Ch. 2 Bal.	0	
(j)		
End. Bal.	6,000	

Franchise Related Income

	Ch. 2 Bal.	0
	(l)	
	End. Bal.	500

Utilities Expense

Ch. 2 Bal.	0	
(h)	190	
End. Bal.	190	

Repair Expense

Ch. 2 Bal.	0	
(b)	50	
End. Bal.	50	

Returning to our Sbarro illustration, we also can prepare a statement of stockholders' equity that ties the information on the income statement to the balance sheet. Any transactions affecting Contributed Capital (issuing additional stock or repurchasing stock from shareholders) and Retained Earnings (generating net income and declaring dividends) are summarized in the statement.

SBARRO, INC. AND SUBSIDIARIES
Statement of Stockholders' Equity (unadjusted)
For the Period Ended February 2, 1996
(in thousands of dollars)

	Contributed Capital	Retained Earnings	Total Stockholders' Equity
Balance, December 31, 1995	$30,500	$155,100	$185,600
Additional common stock issuance (Ch.2)	200		200
Net income		17,960	17,960
Dividends declared		(2,000)	(2,000)
Balance, February 2, 1996	$30,700	$171,060	$201,760

Now we can revise the balance sheet from Chapter 2 to reflect the effects of the operating activities discussed in this chapter. Again, the balance sheet reflects all investing, financing, and operating transactions as of February 2 (Sbarro's month-end). It is called *unadjusted,* however, because no adjusting entries have been recorded. Notice that the balance in Retained Earnings is now the sum of its beginning balance ($155,100) plus the partial net income ($17,960) minus dividends that were declared ($2,000). Revenue, expense, and dividend amounts are not included on the balance sheet directly but are summarized in Retained Earnings. We explore the relationships among each of the financial statements again in the next chapter.

SBARRO, INC. AND SUBSIDIARIES
Balance Sheet (unadjusted)
at February 2, 1996
(in thousands of dollars)

ASSETS

Cash and cash equivalents	$ 89,680
Marketable securities	10,000
Receivables (franchise fees and other)	3,100
Inventory	3,290
Prepaid expenses	20,900
Property and equipment	127,650
Other assets	5,300
Total assets	**$259,920**

LIABILITIES

Notes payable	$ 1,200
Accounts payable	9,930
Accrued expenses payable (rent, payroll, and other)	27,000
Dividends payable	5,900
Income taxes payable	0
Unearned revenue	30
Deferred income taxes	14,100
Total liabilities	$ 58,160

STOCKHOLDERS' EQUITY

Contributed capital	$ 30,700
Retained earnings	171,060
Total stockholders' equity	$ 201,760
Total liabilities and stockholders' equity	**$259,920**

FOCUS ON CASH FLOWS

It is interesting that Sbarro has *positive* unadjusted net income of $17,960,000 based on the January transactions in this chapter. The balance in the Cash account *decreased* (see the T-account), however. This is a very clear example of the effect of the accrual basis of accounting as compared to the cash basis. *Net income on an accrual basis is not equivalent to the change in cash.* Yet a company's ability to generate cash flows from operations in the future is a critical element in evaluating its strength. Users want to know the sources and uses of cash; they also want to understand the company's operating, financing, and investing strategies. As we examined in Chapter 2, companies report on cash inflows and outflows for a period in their statement of cash flows.

The focus on cash flows in Chapter 2 illustrated Sbarro's investing and financing activities. Investing activities include buying and selling productive assets and investments. Financing activities include borrowing and paying back on notes to banks, selling stock to investors for cash, and paying dividends. Now we want to add to the list the operating activities from both chapters. Chapter 3 has no additional cash investing or financing activities. The following transactions are categorized as operating activities:

Chapter and Transaction		Effect on Cash	
Cash Inflows from Operations			
3a	Received cash from selling food to customers	$25,800	
3i	Received cash deposit from customers	30	$25,830
Cash Outflows from Operations			
2c	Paid suppliers for paper products	$ 70	
2g	Paid suppliers on accounts payable	200	
3b	Paid suppliers for oven repairs	50	
3c	Paid mall owners rent	18,600	
3d	Paid suppliers for additional paper products	80	
3g	Paid income taxes	4,700	
3h	Paid utility bills	60	
3j	Paid employees	6,000	
3k	Paid insurance company	600	(30,360)
	Net effect on cash from operating activities		(**$ 4,530**)
Other			
3e	Declared dividends, but not yet paid		No effect on cash
3f	Receipt of food supplies, but not yet paid		No effect on cash

In Chapter 4 we will combine the operating, investing, and financing activities into a statement of cash flows.

SELF-STUDY QUIZ

AST Research, Inc.

AST Research, Inc., manufactures computer hardware. From a recent annual statement of cash flows, indicate whether the transaction affected cash flow as an operating (O) activity, investing (I) activity, or a financing (F) activity, and indicate the direction of the effect on cash (+ = increases cash; – = decreases cash):

Transaction	Type of Activity (O, I, or F)	Effect on Cash Flows (+ or −)
(a) Cash paid to suppliers and employees.		
(b) Proceeds from issuance of common stock.		
(c) Interest received.		
(d) Purchases of capital equipment.		
(e) Cash received from customers.		
(f) Repayments of long-term debt.		
(g) Income taxes paid.		

After you have completed the schedule, check your solution with the answers in the footnote at the bottom of the page.*

*(a) O −   (b) F +   (c) O +   (d) I −   (e) O +   (f) F −   (g) O −

Analyzing Your Return on Investment

A very common ratio that investors and financial analysts use is return on investment (ROI). It measures the profitability of a company for investors who expect to earn a certain rate on their investment. ROI is computed as follows:

$$\text{Return on investment} = \frac{\text{Net income}}{\text{Average stockholders' equity}}$$

Average stockholders' equity is computed as the sum of the beginning and ending balances of stockholders' equity divided by 2. Sbarro's 1995 ROI was 11.7 percent [\$21,300 ÷ ([\$185,600 + 179,500] ÷ 2)]. To analyze this return, we need to compare it to the ratio for other companies in the industry for the same year:

Outback Steakhouse	25.1%
McDonald's Corporation	19.4%
Wendy's International, Inc.	14.5%

Sbarro appears to be providing a comparable return to its investors.

Epilogue

We noted earlier that Sbarro saw dramatic drops in earnings compared to expectations after hiring outside managers. According to *Forbes,* "Fortunately, the brothers had seen and corrected their mistake before it could do irreparable damage."[3] In the spring of 1992, they fired 14 of the 20 new managers and promoted—to the regional and district managerial positions—long-term Sbarro employees who knew the products and had the entrepreneurial talent to "operate their restaurants with the Sbarro passion for guest satisfaction and maximum profit" (from the mission statement). Within six months, sales and earnings were again meeting growth expectations, and the stock price rose to more normal levels.

Company Wins Workers' Loyalty by Opening Its Books

We saw throughout the chapter that Sbarro came to realize the tremendous value of a loyal workforce in reaching corporate goals. An increasing number of companies are developing innovative programs to build employee loyalty and improve their financial performance. One such pioneering human resource development effort is occurring at Springfield ReManufacturing Corporation (SRC), an engine rebuilder in Missouri.

Until 1983, the company, then a division of International Harvester, was considered poorly managed with deep worker distrust. Thirteen managers, who recognized that employees were a key to improved plant operations, purchased the division. They immediately instituted several employee incentives, including an employee stock ownership plan and expanded bonus program. Even more radical was the decision to distribute on a weekly basis all company financial information to the employees and to help them learn how to evaluate the information. As noted in *The Wall Street Journal,* "SRC employees, who also own 31 percent of the company, clearly have responded positively to this strategy, known as 'open-book management.'" In part due to this disclosure policy, SRC escaped ruin and is reporting record growth. According to company officials, "The more [employees] learned, the more they could do. We matched up higher levels of thinking with higher levels of perfor-

---

[3] R. LaFranco, "Promote from within," *Forbes,* February 28, 1994, pp. 86–87.

mance." In addition, "every employee knows that if the value of the company increases, so does the value of their shares." Loyalty among the employees to the company is markedly strong. *The Wall Street Journal* reported that, "while SRC workers obviously value their big stock holding, they maintain that *it's even more important to understand the company's numbers*" (emphasis added).

SOURCE: T. L. O'Brien, *The Wall Street Journal*, December 20, 1993, pp. B1–2.

Demonstration Case

This case is a continuation of the Terrific Lawn Maintenance Corporation introduced in Chapter 2. The company was established with supplies, property, and equipment purchased ready for business. The balance sheet at April 30, 1998, based on investing and financing activities is as follows:

TERRIFIC LAWN MAINTENANCE CORPORATION
Balance Sheet
At April 30, 1998

Assets		Liabilities	
Cash	$ 4,350	Accounts payable	$ 3,700
Equipment	4,600	Total liabilities	3,700
Land	3,750		
		Stockholders' Equity	
		Contributed capital	9,000
		Total liabilities and stockholders'	
Total assets	$12,700	equity	$12,700

The following completed activities occurred during April 1998:

(a) Purchased gasoline for mowers and edgers for $90 in cash at a local gas station. Terrific Lawn also established an account with the gas station owner to purchase gas in the future on account to be billed and paid monthly. Gasoline is used very quickly.

(b) In early April, the city paid Terrific Lawn $1,600 cash in advance for lawn maintenance service for April through July, $400 each month.

(c) Mowed lawns for residential customers who are billed every two weeks. A total of $5,200 of service was billed in April.

(d) Residential customers paid $3,500 on their accounts.

(e) Paid the balance due of $3,700 on account to XYZ Lawn Supply, Inc., and the hardware store.

(f) Paid wages every two weeks. Total cash paid in April was $3,900.

(g) Purchased and used additional gasoline of $320 on account in April.

(h) In early April, purchased insurance costing $300 covering six months, April through September.

(i) Declared a $100 dividend for each of the three owners to be paid in May ($100 × 3 = $300).

Required:

1. *a.* On a separate sheet of paper, set up T-accounts for Cash, Accounts Receivable, Lawn Equipment, Land, Prepaid Expenses, Accounts Payable, Dividends Payable, Unearned Revenue (same as deferred revenue), Contributed Capital, Retained Earnings, Mowing Service Revenue, Fuel Expense, and Wages Expense. Beginning balances for balance sheet accounts should be taken from the preceding balance sheet. Beginning balances for operating accounts are $0. Indicate these balances on the T-accounts.

   b. Analyze each transaction using the steps outlined in Chapter 2 and indicate whether an accrual or deferral results that needs to be adjusted. Please refer to the complete transaction analysis model presented in this chapter.

    c. On a separate sheet of paper, prepare journal entries in chronological order.

    d. Enter the effects on the accounting model in the appropriate T-accounts. Identify each amount with its letter in the list of activities.

    e. Compute balances in each of the T-accounts.

2. Use the amounts in the T-accounts developed in requirement 1 in Chapters 2 and 3 to prepare an unadjusted income statement, unadjusted statement of stockholders' equity, and unadjusted balance sheet for Terrific Lawn Maintenance Corporation at April 30, 1998. Adjustments will be recorded in Chapter 4.

3. Identify operating transactions affecting cash (amount and direction of the effect).

Now you can check your answers to these requirements with the following solution.

1. Transaction analysis, journal entries, and T-accounts:

(a)

Transaction Analysis				Journal Entry		
Assets	=	**Liabilities**	+	**Stockholders' Equity**	Fuel expense (E)	90
Cash −90				Fuel expense −90	Cash (A)	90

The accounting equation is in balance. Debits $90 = Credits $90. Cash is paid at almost the same time as an expense is incurred (not an accrual or deferral).

(b)

Assets	=	**Liabilities**	+	**Stockholders' Equity**	Cash (A)	1,600
Cash +1,600		Unearned revenue +1,600			Unearned revenue (L)	1,600

The accounting equation is in balance. Debits $1,600 = Credits $1,600. Cash is received before a revenue is earned. This is a deferral (cash received before revenue is earned) that needs to be adjusted at the end of the period to reflect the amount of revenue that has been earned and the amount that remains unearned.

(c)

Assets	=	**Liabilities**	+	**Stockholders' Equity**	Accounts receivable (A)	5,200
Accounts				Mowing service	Mowing service revenue (R)	5,200
receivable +5,200				revenue +5,200		

The accounting equation is in balance. Debits $5,200 = Credits $5,200. Service has been provided, so revenue has been earned. The earnings process is nearly complete (not an accrual or deferral).

(d)

Assets	=	**Liabilities**	+	**Stockholders' Equity**	Cash (A)	3,500
Cash +3,500					Accounts receivable (A)	3,500
Accounts						
receivable −3,500						

The accounting equation is in balance. Debits $3,500 = Credits $3,500. Revenue was recorded earlier when earned. The receipt of cash is the completion of the operating cycle.

(e)

Assets	=	**Liabilities**	+	**Stockholders' Equity**	Accounts payable (L)	3,700
Cash − 3,700		Accounts payable −3,700			Cash (A)	3,700

The accounting equation is in balance. Debits $3,700 = Credits $3,700. Cash is paid on a liability (not an accrual or deferral).

(f)

Assets	=	**Liabilities**	+	**Stockholders' Equity**	Wages expense (E)	3,900
Cash −3,900				Wages expense −3,900	Cash (A)	3,900

The accounting equation is in balance. Debits $3,900 = Credits $3,900. Cash is paid at the same time as the expense is incurred (not an accrual or deferral).

(g)

Assets	=	**Liabilities**	+	**Stockholders' Equity**	Fuel expense (E)	320
		Accounts payable +320		Fuel expense −320	Accounts payable (L)	320

The accounting equation is in balance. Debits $320 = Credits $320. Fuel is used and is recognized as an expense at the same time, even though cash will be paid in the future (not an accrual or deferral).

(h)

Transaction Analysis					Journal Entry		
Assets	=	**Liabilities**	+	**Stockholders' Equity**	Prepaid expenses (A)	300	
Cash −300					Cash (A)		300
Prepaid expenses +300							

The accounting equation is in balance. Debits $300 = Credits $300. Cash is paid before an expense is incurred. This is a deferral (cash paid *before* expense is incurred) that needs to be adjusted at the end of the period to reflect the amount of expense that has been incurred (used) and the amount that remains as future benefits.

(i)

Assets	=	Liabilities	+	Stockholders' Equity	Retained earnings (SE)	300	
		Dividends payable +300		Retained earnings −300	Dividends payable (L)		300

The accounting equation is in balance. Debits $300 = Credits $300. The declaration of dividends is a financing activity, not a deferral or accrual.

+ ASSETS −			− LIABILITIES +			− STOCKHOLDERS' EQUITY +		
Cash			**Accounts Payable**			**Contributed Capital**		
Ch. 2 Bal	4,350	(a) 90	(e) 3,700	Ch. 2 Bal.	3,700		Ch. 2 Bal.	9,000
(b)	1,600	(e) 3,700		(g)	320		End. Bal.	9,000
(d)	3,500	(f) 3,900		End. Bal.	320			
		(h) 300				**Retained Earnings**		
End. Bal.	1,460		**Unearned Revenue**			(i) 300	Ch. 2 Bal.	0
				Ch. 2 Bal.	0		End Bal.	?
Accounts Receivable				(b)	1,600			
Ch. 2 Bal.	0	(d) 3,500		End. Bal.	1,600	**Mowing Service Revenue**		
(c)	5,200						Ch. 2 Bal.	0
End. Bal.	1,700		**Dividends Payable**				(c)	5,200
				Ch. 2 Bal.	0		End. Bal.	5,200
Prepaid Expenses				(i)	300			
Ch. 2 Bal.	0			End. Bal.	300	**Fuel Expense**		
(h)	300					Ch. 2 Bal.	0	
End. Bal.	300					(a)	90	
						(g)	320	
Equipment						End. Bal.	410	
Ch. 2 Bal.	4,600							
End. Bal.	4,600					**Wages Expense**		
						Ch. 2 Bal.	0	
Land						(f)	3,900	
Ch. 2 Bal.	3,750					End. Bal.	3,900	
End. Bal.	3,750							

2. Income statement, statement of stockholders' equity, and balance sheet:

TERRIFIC LAWN MAINTENANCE CORPORATION
Income Statement (unadjusted)
For the Period Ended April 30, 1998

Revenues		
Mowing service revenue		$5,200
Expenses		
Fuel expense	410	
Wages expense	3,900	
Total expenses		4,310
Net income		$ 890

TERRIFIC LAWN MAINTENANCE CORPORATION
Statement of Stockholders' Equity (unadjusted)
For the Period Ended April 30, 1998

	Contributed Capital	Retained Earnings	Stockholders' Equity
Balance, April 1, 1998	$ 0	$ 0	$ 0
Issuance of stock	9,000		9,000
Unadjusted net income		890	890
Dividends declared		(300)	(300)
Balance, April 30, 1998	$9,000	$590	$9,590

TERRIFIC LAWN MAINTENANCE CORPORATION
Balance Sheet (unadjusted)
At April 30, 1998

Assets		Liabilities	
Cash	$ 1,460	Accounts payable	$ 320
Accounts receivable	1,700	Dividends payable	300
Prepaid expenses	300	Unearned revenue	1,600
Lawn equipment	4,600	Total liabilities	$ 2,220
Land	3,750		
		Stockholders' Equity	
		Contributed capital	$ 9,000
		Retained earnings	590
		Total stockholders' equity	$ 9,590
		Total liabilities and	
Total assets	$11,810	stockholders' equity	$11,810

3. Operating effects on cash:

Transaction	Effect on Cash
(a) Paid suppliers for gasoline for mowers and edgers.	– $ 90
(b) Received cash from city for service to be performed.	+ 1,600
(d) Received cash from residential customers.	+ 3,500
(e) Paid suppliers.	– 3,700
(f) Paid wages to employees.	– 3,900
(h) Paid insurance company for future coverage.	– 300

Transactions (c), (g), and (i) did not involve cash.

Summary

This chapter discussed the accounting concepts relevant to income determination: the time period assumption, definitions for the income statement elements (revenues, expenses, gains, and losses), the revenue principle, the matching principle, and the cost principle. These accounting principles are defined in accordance with the accrual basis of accounting, which requires revenues to be recorded when earned and expenses to be recorded when incurred in generating revenues during the period.

The operating and accounting cycles were discussed as they apply to income measurement. The operating cycle is the span of time it takes a company to acquire goods or services, sell them to customers, and receive cash from customers. The cycle varies by company. The accounting cycle is the recordkeeping process used during the accounting period (usually a month, quarter, or year) that results in financial statements.

The transaction model introduced in Chapter 2 was completed by adding revenues (gains) and expenses (losses). Application of the income recognition rules combined with the complete transaction analysis model was illustrated for Sbarro, Inc., continuing the illustration from Chapter 2. In addition to using the transaction analysis steps discussed in Chapter 2, the need for an adjusting entry based on the transaction was determined. Transactions in which cash is received before the revenue is earned or paid before the expense is incurred often result in adjusting entries at the end of the period to record income in the proper period. Transactions in which revenues have been earned or expenses have been incurred but are not yet recorded by the end of the accounting period also require an adjusting entry.

Based on the balances in the T-accounts in the illustration, an unadjusted income statement, unadjusted statement of stockholders' equity, and unadjusted balance sheet were prepared. These statements will be used in the next chapter, which presents the second phase of the accounting process that takes place at the end of the accounting period.

This chapter and Chapter 2 introduced you to the fundamental accounting model and transaction analysis. The two chapters also discussed the use of journal entries and T-accounts to reflect the results of transaction analysis for operating, investing, and financing activities during the accounting period. In Chapter 4, we will build on your knowledge and discuss the activities at the end of the accounting period: the adjustment process, the preparation of financial statements, and the closing process. For those who want information on formal recordkeeping procedures in the accounting cycle, Appendix C to the text is included.

Key Ratios

Return on investment (ROI) is a common measure of profitability. It is computed as follows (p. 136):

$$\text{Return on investment} = \frac{\text{Net income}}{\text{Average stockholders' equity*}}$$

*Average stockholders' equity is the sum of the beginning and ending balances of stockholders' equity divided by 2.

Key Terms

Accounting Cycle The recordkeeping process used during and at the end of the accounting period that results in the preparation of financial statements. *124*

Accrual Basis Accounting Revenues are recorded when earned and expenses when incurred, regardless of when the related cash is received or paid. *117*

Cash Basis Accounting Revenues are recorded when cash is received and expenses are recorded when cash is paid, regardless of when the revenues are earned or expenses are incurred. *117*

Expenses Expenses are decreases in assets or increases in liabilities from ongoing operations. *113*

Gains Gains are increases in assets or decreases in liabilities from peripheral transactions. *114*

Losses Losses are decreases in assets or increases in liabilities from peripheral transactions. *114*

Matching Principle Expenses are recognized (recorded) when incurred in earning revenue. *121*

Operating Cycle The time it takes for a company to purchase goods or services from suppliers, sell those goods or services to customers, and collect cash from customers. It is also known as the *cash-to-cash cycle* or the *earnings process*. *115*

Revenues Revenues are increases in assets or settlements of liabilities from ongoing operations. *113*

Revenue Principle Revenues are recognized (recorded) when the earnings process is complete or nearly complete, an exchange has taken place, and collection is probable. *118*

Time Period Assumption The long life of a company can be reported in shorter time periods, usually months, quarters, and years. *112*

Timeline A visual representation of a series of business activities, listing dates and amounts over time. *119*

Questions

1. Explain what the time period assumption means in accounting.
2. Indicate the income statement equation and define each element.
3. Explain the difference between
   a. Revenues and gains.
   b. Expenses and losses.
4. Assume that your personal finances currently consist of assets, $40,000, and debts, $15,000. You borrow $12,000 to buy a car and receive $120 in interest on your savings account for the year. Show how your personal financial condition will change in terms of the accounting model.
5. Big Company paid principal and interest on a note to the bank. Show how this transaction affects the accounting equation (use + for increase, – for decrease, and NE for no effect).
6. Explain a typical business operating cycle.
7. Define *accrual accounting.* Contrast it with cash basis accounting.
8. What three conditions normally must be met for revenue to be recognized under the accrual basis of accounting?
9. Explain the matching principle.
10. Describe the accounting cycle. List the sequence of activities in each phase of the cycle.
11. Explain why stockholders' equity is increased by revenues and decreased by expenses.
12. Explain why revenues are recorded as credits and expenses as debits.
13. Demonstrate the dual effect on the accounting equation of (a) a cash sale of services for $2,000 and (b) a cash payment of $700 for office rent for the business.
14. Create a transaction for each of the following situations:
    a. Revenue is recognized before cash is received during the accounting cycle.
    b. Expense is recognized after cash is paid.
    c. Revenue is recognized before cash is received in the next accounting cycle.
    d. Expense is recognized before cash is paid.
    e. Revenue is recognized after cash is received.
15. Complete the following matrix by entering either *debit* or *credit* in each cell:

Item	Increase	Decrease
Revenues		
Losses		
Gains		
Expenses		

16. Complete the following matrix by entering either *increase* or *decrease* in each cell:

Item	Debit	Credit
Revenues		
Losses		
Gains		
Expenses		

17. Complete the following tabulation, indicating the amount and effect (+ for increase and – for decrease) of each transaction. (Remember that A = L + SE, R – E = NI, and NI affects SE)

Transaction	Assets	Liabilities	Stockholders' Equity	Revenues	Expenses	Net Income
(a) Received investment of cash from organizers, $20,000						
(b) Borrowed cash, $6,000						
(c) Performed legal services for cash, $12,000						
(d) Paid expenses, $3,000 cash						
(e) Purchased equipment, $8,000 cash						
Ending balances						

18. For each of the following transactions, indicate whether an adjusting entry is needed at the end of the accounting period and why or why not:

Transaction	Need an Adjusting Entry?	Why or Why Not?
(a) Received a utility bill covering utility usage for the first three weeks of the month.		
(b) Paid off a six-month bank loan (principal and interest).		
(c) Sold merchandise to customers for cash.		
(d) Purchased a large machine at the beginning of the year, paying half with cash and borrowing the other half from a bank to be paid back in five years.		
(e) Received cash in advance from a company renting an office in your building; the rent covers the next six months.		

Exercises

E3–1 Matching Definitions with Terms

Match each definition with its related term by entering the appropriate letter in the space provided.

TERM	DEFINITION
_C_ (1) Losses	A. Decreases in assets or increases in liabilities from ongoing operations.
_F_ (2) Matching principle	B. The cash-equivalent (historical) cost given up is the basis for initially recording assets, liabilities, revenues and expenses.
_E_ (3) Revenues	C. Decreases in assets or increases in liabilities from peripheral transactions.
_G_ (4) Time period assumption	D. Record revenues when earned and measurable (an exchange takes place, the earnings process is complete or nearly complete, and collection is probable).
_B_ (5) Cost principle	E. Increases in assets or decreases in liabilities from ongoing operations.
_A_ (6) Expenses	F. Record expenses when incurred in earning revenue.
_H_ (7) Gains	G. Reports the long life of a company in shorter time periods.
_D_ (8) Revenue principle	H. Increases in assets or decreases in liabilities from peripheral transactions.

E3–2 Identifying Revenue Accounts

Revenues are normally recognized when the earnings process is complete or nearly complete, a transaction has taken place, and collection is reasonably assured. The amount recorded is the cash-equivalent sales price.

Required:

Using the preceding definition and valuation rules, indicate whether or not each of the following events results in recognizing a revenue for the month indicated. If a revenue is recorded, indicate an appropriate account title and amount. Then indicate other accounts affected. Use the following headings:

Event	Does a Revenue Result?	Revenue Account Title	Amount	Title of Other Accounts(s) Affected

1. In February, a customer orders and receives 10 personal computers from Gateway 2000; the customer promises to pay $25,000 within three months. Answer from Gateway's standpoint.
2. In March, Sam Shell Dodge sells a delivery truck with a list, or "sticker," price of $24,000 for $21,000 cash.
3. In April, Hudson's Department Store orders 1,000 men's shirts from Arrow Shirt Company for $18 each for future delivery. The terms require payment in full within 30 days of delivery. Answer from the manufacturer's standpoint.
4. In May, Arrow Shirt Company completes production of the shirts described in (3). Answer from the manufacturer's standpoint.
5. In May, Arrow Shirt Company delivers the order described in (3). Answer from the manufacturer's standpoint.
6. In June, Arrow receives payment from Hudson's for the order described in (3). Answer from the manufacturer's standpoint.
7. In December, a customer purchases a ticket from American Airlines for $500 cash to travel the following January. Answer from American Airlines' standpoint.
8. In October, General Motors issues $26 million in new common stock.
9. In May, Penn State University receives $20,000,000 cash for 80,000 five-game season football tickets.
10. In September, the first game referred to in (9) is played.
11. In November, Turner Construction Company signs a contract with a customer for the construction of a new $500,000 warehouse. At the signing, Turner receives a check for $50,000 as a deposit on the future construction. Answer from Turner's standpoint.

E3–3 Identifying Revenue Accounts

Revenues are normally recognized when the earnings process is complete or nearly complete, a transaction has taken place, and collection is reasonably assured. The amount recorded is the cash-equivalent sales price.

Required:

Using the preceding definition and valuation rules, indicate whether each of the following events results in recognizing a revenue for the month indicated. If a revenue is recorded, indicate an appropriate account title and amount. Then indicate other accounts affected. Use the following headings:

Event	Does a Revenue Result?	Revenue Account Title	Amount	Title of Other Accounts(s) Affected

1. Staples, an office supply store, sells a computer desk with a list price of $700 for $425 cash.

2. A local car dealer sells a used car for $5,000 cash. The salesperson receives a $500 ~~not rev~~ commission for the sale. Answer from the car dealer's standpoint.

3. Answer 3, 4, 5, and 6 from the Roth Company point of view. Ford Motor Company orders 3 tons of aluminum from the Roth Company. Ford is quoted a price of $2,000 per ton.

4. Roth Company produces 3 tons of aluminum to be shipped next week to Ford Motor Company.

5. The Roth Company delivers 3 tons of aluminum to Ford. Payment is due within 45 days after delivery.

6. Thirty-five days after delivery, Ford pays Roth in full for the shipment.

7. Nationwide Insurance Company receives a $1,200 check for a fire insurance policy. The policy covers the current month as well as the next 11 months.

8. On July 1, 19A, a bank lends $1,000 to a company. The loan carries a 12 percent annual interest rate, and the principal and interest are due in a lump sum on June 30, 19B. Today is December 31, 19A; the bank is preparing its year-end financial reports. Answer from the bank's standpoint.

9. Sears, a retail store, sells a $100 lamp to a customer who charges the sale on his store credit card. Answer from the standpoint of Sears.

10. A popular ski magazine company receives a total of $1,800 today from subscribers. The subscriptions begin in the next fiscal year. Answer from the magazine company's standpoint.

E3–4 Identifying Expense Accounts

Revenues are normally recognized when goods or services have been provided and payment or promise of payment has been received. Expense recognition is guided by an attempt to match the costs associated with the generation of those revenues to the same time period.

Required:

Using the preceding expense recognition rule, indicate whether each of the following events (continued on the next page) results in recognizing an expense for the month of February. If an expense is recorded, indicate an appropriate account title and amount. Then indicate other accounts affected. Use the following headings:

Event	Does a Expense Result?	Expense Account Title	Amount	Title of Other Accounts(s) Affected

1. On February 8, Gateway 2000 pays its computer service technicians $90,000 in salary for the two weeks ended February 7. Answer from Gateway's standpoint.

2. On January 2, Turner Construction Company pays $4,500 in worker's compensation insurance for the first three months of the year.

3. During February, McGraw-Hill Publishing Company uses $1,000 worth of electricity and natural gas in its headquarters building for which it has not yet been billed.

4. On February 9, Arrow Shirt Company completes production of 1,000 men's shirts ordered by Hudson's Department Store at a cost of $9 each. Answer from the manufacturer's standpoint.

5. On February 14, Arrow Shirt Company delivers the order described in (4). Answer from the manufacturer's standpoint.

6. On February 28, Arrow receives payment in cash for the order described in (4). Answer from the manufacturer's standpoint.

7. On February 2, Sam Shell Dodge pays its salespersons $3,500 in commissions related to January automobile sales. Answer from Sam Shell Dodge's standpoint.

8. On February 28, Sam Shell Dodge determines that it will pay its salespersons $4,200 in commissions related to February sales. The payment will be made on March 3. Answer from Sam Shell Dodge's standpoint.

9. On February 28, a new grill is installed at a McDonald's restaurant. On the same day, payment of $12,000 is made in cash.

10. On February 15, the University of Florida orders 60,000 season football tickets from its printer and pays $6,000 in advance for the custom printing. The first game will be played in September. Answer from the university's standpoint.

11. On February 1, Pyramid Mall had janitorial supplies costing $1,000 in storage. An additional $600 worth of supplies was purchased during February. At the end of February, $900 worth of janitorial supplies remained in storage.

E3–5 Identifying Expense Accounts

Revenues are normally recognized when goods or services have been provided and payment or promise of payment has been received. Expense recognition is guided by an attempt to match the costs associated with the generation of revenues in the period in which the earning process occurs.

Required:

Using the preceding expense recognition rule, indicate whether each of the following events results in recognizing an expense for the month indicated. If an expense is recorded, indicate an appropriate account title and amount. Then indicate other accounts affected. Use the following headings:

Event	Does a Expense Result?	Expense Account Title	Amount	Title of Other Accounts(s) Affected

1. On January 1, the campus bookstore orders 500 accounting texts for the spring semester. The store is quoted a cost of $50 per book.

2. On January 10, the campus bookstore receives 500 accounting texts at a cost of $50 each. The terms indicate that payment is due within 30 days of delivery.

3. During the last week of January, 450 accounting texts are sold to students at a sales price of $60 each.

4. A Colorado State University employee works eight hours, at $15 per hour, on June 30. The university's fiscal year ends on June 30; however, payday is not until July 3. Answer from the university's point of view.

5. On January 2, 19B, Amber Incorporated purchased a delivery van for $12,000 cash. The van will be used for five years and is expected to have a $2,000 residual value. Answer for the year 19B.

6. Wang Company paid $3,600 for a fire insurance policy in August. The policy covers the current month and the next 11 months. Answer from Wang's point of view.

7. Amber Incorporated has its delivery van repaired in March for $280 and charges the amount on account.

8. Rob & Company had a supply inventory of $500 on April 1, purchased $250 of supplies with cash during April, and had a supply inventory on April 30 of $400.

9. Ziegler Company, a farm equipment company, receives its phone bill for $230 in December. The bill has not been paid to date.

10. Spina Company receives and pays in June a $1,500 invoice from a consulting firm for services received in June.
11. In January, Falkowski's Taxi Company pays a $600 invoice from a consulting firm for services received and recorded in the prior fiscal year.

E3–6 Matching Definitions with Terms

Match each definition with its related term by entering the appropriate letter in the space provided.

	TERM		DEFINITION
F	(1) Cash basis accounting	A.	A liability account used to record cash received before revenues have been earned; the account may need to be adjusted at the end of the accounting cycle to reflect the amount of revenues earned during the period.
A	(2) Deferred revenue		
D	(3) Operating cycle		
H	(4) Ending retained earnings = Beginning retained earnings + Net income – Dividends declared	B.	The recordkeeping process used during and at the end of the accounting period that results in financial statements.
		C.	Record revenues when earned and expenses when incurred.
B	(5) Accounting cycle	D.	The time it takes to purchase goods or services from suppliers, sell goods or services to customers, and collect cash from customers.
C	(6) Accrual basis accounting	E.	Total assets minus total liabilities.
E	(7) Net assets	F.	Record revenues when received and expenses when paid.
G	(8) Revenue – Expenses = Net income	G.	The income statement equation.
		H.	The retained earnings equation.

E3–7 Performing Transaction Analysis: Nonquantitative

For each of the following transactions, indicate the effect on assets, liabilities, and stockholders' equity by entering a plus for increase and a minus for decrease. A sample is provided.

		EFFECT ON		
	Transactions	Assets	Liabilities	Stockholders' Equity
(a)	Issued stock to organizers for cash (example).	+		+
(b)	Borrowed cash from local bank.			
(c)	Purchased equipment on credit.			
(d)	Earned revenue, collected cash.			
(e)	Incurred expenses, on credit.			
(f)	Earned revenue, on credit.			
(g)	Paid cash on account.			
(h)	Incurred expenses, paid cash.			
(i)	Earned revenue, collected three-fourths in cash, balance on credit.			
(j)	Experienced theft of $100 cash.			
(k)	Declared and paid cash dividends.			
(l)	Collected cash from customers on account.			
(m)	Incurred expenses, paid four-fifths in cash, balance on credit.			
(n)	Paid income tax expense for the period.			

Wolverine World Wide, Inc.

E3–8 Performing Transaction Analysis: Nonquantitative

Wolverine World Wide, Inc., manufactures military, work, sport, and casual footwear and leather accessories under a variety of brand names, such as Hush Puppies, Wolverine, and Bates, to a global market. The following transactions are inferred from a recent annual report:

- (a) Issued $48,869,000 in common stock to investors.
- (b) Purchased $299,794,000 of additional inventory of raw materials on account.
- (c) Borrowed $58,181,000 on long-term notes.
- (d) Sold $413,957,000 of products to customers on account; cost of the products sold was $290,469.
- (e) Paid cash dividends of $2,347,000.
- (f) Purchased $18,645,000 in additional property, plant, and equipment.
- (g) Incurred $85,993,000 in selling expenses with two-thirds paid in cash and the rest on account.
- (h) Earned $1,039,000 interest on investments, received 90 percent in cash.
- (i) Incurred $4,717,000 in interest expense.

Required:

For each of these transactions, enter in the table the effect of the transaction on the elements of the financial statements. Use + for increases and – for decreases. Transaction (a) is used as an example.

	TRANSACTION								
	(a)	(b)	(c)	(d)	(e)	(f)	(g)	(h)	(i)
Assets	+								
Liabilities									
Contributed capital	+								
Retained earnings									
Revenues									
Expenses									

E3–9 Using the Accounting Model—Personal Financial Transactions

You finished college and began working for Murphy Services Company. At the start of the first month, your financial situation was as shown in the following schedule. You are to complete the schedule by recording your transactions for the first month, summarized in the first column, and indicating your ending financial position on the last line.

Transaction	Assets	Liabilities	Owner's Equity
(a) Beginning financial position (personal items, including your rather used auto).	$4,000	$800	$3,200
(b) Borrowed $1,500 to get through the first month.			
(c) Paid rent on apartment, $700.			
(d) Paid utility deposits, $250.			
(e) Personal expenses: food, cleaning, etc., $800.			
(f) Auto payment, $450 (including $35 interest).			
(g) Trip to visit a special person, $400.			
(h) Received a gift from your family, $200 cash.			
(i) You gave your date a special present, $100.			
(j) You received your first paycheck (net of deductions), $2,100.			
Your ending financial position			

E3–10 Performing Transaction Analysis

Sysco

Sysco, formed in 1969, is America's largest marketer and distributor of food service products, serving nearly a quarter million restaurants, hotels, schools, hospitals, and other institutions. The following summarized transactions are typical of those that occurred in a recent year.

(a) Borrowed $80 million from a bank, signing a short-term note.

(b) Provided $10.02 billion in service to customers during the year, with $9.5 billion on account and the rest received in cash.

(c) Purchased plant and equipment for $127.9 million in cash.

(d) Purchased $8.268 billion inventory on account.

(e) Paid payroll, $1.02 billion during the year.

(f) Received $410 million on account paid by customers.

(g) Purchased and used fuel of $400 million in delivery vehicles during the year (paid for in cash).

(h) Declared and paid $48.8 million in dividends for the year.

(i) Paid $8.2 billion cash on accounts payable.

(j) Incurred $20 million in utility usage during the year; paid $15 million in cash and the rest on account.

Required:

For each of the transactions:

1. Perform transaction analysis as outlined in the chapter and prepare journal entries.
2. Determine whether the accounting equation remains in balance and debits equal credits.
3. Determine whether an adjusting entry will be needed at the end of the accounting cycle.

E3–11 Performing Transaction Analysis

Greek Peak

Greek Peak Incorporated is a ski resort in upstate New York. The company sells lift tickets, ski lessons, and ski equipment. It operates several restaurants and rents townhouses to vacationing skiers. The following hypothetical December transactions are typical of those that occur at the resort.

(a) Borrowed $500,000 from the bank on December 1 with a six-month note at 12 percent annual interest to finance the beginning of the new season. The principal and interest are due on the maturity date.

(b) Purchased a new snow plow for $20,000 cash on December 1. The plow is estimated to have a five-year life and a $5,000 residual value.

(c) Purchased and received $10,000 of ski equipment on account to sell in the ski shop.

(d) Incurred $22,000 in routine maintenance expenses for the chair lifts; paid cash.

(e) Sold $72,000 of season passes and received cash.

(f) Sold daily lift passes for a total of $76,000 in cash.

(g) Sold a pair of skis for $350 on account. (The cost of the pair was $250.)

(h) Received a $320 deposit on a townhouse to be rented for five days in January.

(i) Paid half the charges incurred on account in (c).

(j) Received $200 on account from the customer in (g).

(k) Paid $108,000 in wages to employees for the month of December.

Required:

1. Prepare journal entries for each transaction. (Remember to check that debits equal credits and that the accounting equation is in balance after each transaction.)
2. Assume that Greek Peak had a $1,200 balance in Accounts Receivable at the beginning of the year. Determine the ending balance in the Accounts Receivable account. Show your work in T-account format.

E3–12 Analyzing the Effect of Transactions on Financial Statement Elements

For each of the following transactions, indicate the effect on assets, liabilities, stockholders' equity, revenues, expenses, and net income by entering a plus (+) for increase, a minus (–) for decrease, and NE for no effect. An example is provided.

Transactions	Assets	Liabilities	Stockholders' Equity	Revenues	Expenses	Net Income
Provided services to customers on account.	+	NE	+	+	NE	+
(a) Incurred expenses on credit.						
(b) Declared and paid cash dividends.						
(c) Collected cash on account.						
(d) Incurred expenses, paid part cash and part on credit.						
(e) Borrowed cash from bank.						
(f) Purchased equipment on credit.						
(g) Paid cash on account.						
(h) Issued additional stock.						

E3–13 Analyzing the Effect of Transactions on Financial Statement Elements

For each of the following transactions, indicate the effect on assets, liabilities, stockholders' equity, revenues, expenses, and net income by entering a plus (+) for increase, a minus (–) for decrease, and NE for no effect. An example is provided.

Transactions	Assets	Liabilities	Stockholders' Equity	Revenues	Expenses	Net Income
Received the property tax bill. It has not yet been paid.	NE	+	–	NE	+	–
(a) Purchased equipment on account.						
(b) Sold services on account.						
(c) Issued additional stock for cash.						
(d) Paid the property tax bill shown in the example.						
(e) Declared and paid cash dividends.						
(f) Received cash from a customer on an account receivable.						
(g) Recognized the depreciation on equipment.						
(h) Paid next year's rent in advance.						

Wendy's International, Inc.

E3–14 Analyzing the Effect of Transactions on Financial Statement Elements

According to its annual report, Wendy's serves "the best hamburgers in the business" and other fresh food including salads, chicken sandwiches, and baked potatoes in more than 4,000 restaurants worldwide. The following activities were inferred from a recent annual report.

For each of the following transactions, indicate the effect on assets, liabilities, stockholders' equity, revenues, expenses, and net income by entering a plus (+) for increase, a minus (−) for decrease, and NE for no effect.

	Transactions	Assets	Liabilities	Stockholders' Equity	Revenues	Expenses	Net Income
(a)	Purchased additional investments.						
(b)	Served food to customers for cash.						
(c)	Paid cash dividends.						
(d)	Incurred restaurant operating costs in company-owned facilities; paid part in cash and the rest on account.						
(e)	Sold franchises, receiving part in cash and the rest in notes due from franchisees.						
(f)	Paid interest on debt.						
(g)	Purchased food and paper products; paid part in cash and the rest on account.						
(h)	Used food and paper products.						

E3–15 Analyzing Transactions and Preparing Journal Entries

Lustig-Liebman Air Transport Service has been in operation for three years. Perform transaction analysis for each of the following transactions during the first week in February and prepare journal entries for each. Be sure to categorize each account as an asset (A), liability (L), stockholders' equity (SE), revenue (R), or expense (E).

Example:

February 1   Cargo was flown from Chicago to Denver. The customer was billed $1,600.

2/1	Assets	=	Liabilities	+	Stockholders' Equity	
	Accounts receivable	+1,600			Transport revenue	+1,600

Accounts receivable (A)	1,600	
Transport revenue (R)		1,600

February 1   Lustig-Liebman paid $200 for rent of hangar space in February.

February 2   Fuel costing $450 was purchased on account for the next flight to Dallas.

February 2   A customer paid Lustig-Liebman $800 to ship several items to Philadelphia next month.

February 3   Cargo was flown from Denver to Dallas; the customer paid $900 for the air transport.

February 4   The pilot was paid $1,200 in wages for flying in January.

February 4   Lustig-Liebman paid $60 for an advertisement in the local paper to run on February 7.

February 5   Cargo for two customers was flown from Dallas to Albuquerque for $1,700; one customer paid $500 cash and the other asked to be billed.

February 6   Lustig-Liebman purchased spare parts for the planes costing $1,350 on account.

February 7   Lustig-Liebman declared a $200 cash dividend to be paid in March.

E3–16 **Analyzing Transactions and Preparing Journal Entries**

Scott Newman organized a new company, CollegeCaps. The company operates a small store in an area mall and specializes in baseball-type caps with logos printed on them. Scott, who is never without a cap, believes that his target market is college students. You have been hired to record the transactions occurring in the first two weeks of operation.

Required:

Perform transaction analysis for each of the following transactions that occurred during March and prepare journal entries for each transaction. Be sure to categorize each account as an asset (A), liability (L), stockholders' equity (SE), revenue (R), or expense (E).

Example:

March 1   One thousand shares of capital stock were issued for $30 per share.

3/1	Assets		=	Liabilities	+	Stockholders' Equity	
	Cash	+30,000				Contributed capital	+30,000

Cash (A) 30,000
    Contributed capital (SE)   30,000

March 1	Borrowed $50,000 from the bank to provide additional working capital to begin operations. The interest rate is 14 percent annually; principal and interest are due in 24 months.
March 1	Paid $1,200 for the current month's rent and another $1,200 for next month's rent.
March 1	Paid $2,400 for a one-year fire insurance policy.
March 3	Purchased furniture and fixtures for the store for $15,000 on account. The amount is due within 30 days.
March 4	Purchased a supply of University of Iowa and Iowa State University baseball caps for the store for $1,800 cash.
March 5	Placed advertisements in local college newspapers for a total of $250 cash.
March 9	Total sales of caps amounted to $400, half of which was charged on account. The cost of the caps sold was $150.
March 10	Full payment was made for the furniture and fixtures purchased on account on March 3.
March 14	Received $50 from a customer on account.

E3–17 **Analyzing Transactions and Preparing Journal Entries**

Rhonda Bennett is the president of ServicePro, Inc., a company that provides temporary employees for not-for-profit companies. ServicePro has been operating for five years; its revenues are increasing with each passing year. You have been hired to help Rhonda in analyzing transactions for ServicePro.

Required:

Perform transaction analysis for each of the following transactions during September. Based on your analysis, prepare journal entries for each transaction. Be sure to categorize each account as an asset (A), liability (L), stockholders' equity (SE), revenue (R), or expense (E).

Example:

April 2   Purchased office supplies for $500 on account.

4/2 An asset (Office Supplies Inventory) increased by $500; debit the account. A liability (Accounts Payable) increased; credit the account.

Office supplies inventory (A)	500	
Accounts payable (L)		500

April 2	Purchased office supplies for $500 on account.
April 3	Received the telephone bill for $245.
April 5	Billed United Way $1,950 for temporary services provided.
April 8	Paid $250 for supplies purchased and recorded on account last period.
April 8	Placed an advertisement in the local paper for $400 cash.
April 9	Purchased a new computer for the office costing $2,300 cash.
April 10	Paid employee wages of $1,200. Of this amount, $200 had been earned and recorded in the prior period.
April 11	Received $1,000 on account from United Way.
April 12	Purchased land as the site of a future office for $10,000. Paid $2,000 down and signed a note payable for the balance. The note is due in five years and has an annual interest rate of 10 percent.
April 13	Issued 2,000 additional shares of capital stock for $40 per share in anticipation of building a new office.
April 14	Billed Family & Children's Service $2,000 for services rendered.

E3–18 Using T-Accounts

Fitzsimmons' Piano Rebuilding Company has been operating for one year (19A). At the start of 19B, its income statement accounts had zero balances and its balance sheet account balances were as follows:

Cash	$ 6,000	Accounts payable	8,000
Accounts receivable	25,000	Deferred revenue (deposits)	3,200
Supplies	1,200	Note payable (due in three years with	
Equipment	8,000	12% annual interest due annually)	40,000
Land	6,000	Contributed capital	8,000
Building	22,000	Retained earnings	9,000

Required:

1. Create T-accounts for the balance sheet accounts and for these additional accounts: Rebuilding Fees Revenue, Rent Revenue, Wages Expense, and Utilities Expense. Enter the beginning balances.
2. Enter the following January 19B transactions in the T-accounts, using the letter of each transaction as the reference:
   (a) Received a $500 deposit from a customer who wanted her piano rebuilt.
   (b) Rented a part of the building to a bicycle repair shop; received $300 for rent in January.
   (c) Delivered 10 rebuilt pianos to customers who paid $14,500 in cash.
   (d) Received $6,000 from customers as payment on their accounts.
   (e) Received an electric and gas utility bill for $350 to be paid in February.
   (f) Ordered $800 in supplies.
   (g) Paid $1,700 on account in January.
   (h) Ms. Fitzsimmons, the major shareholder, brought a $600 tool (equipment) from home to use in the business.
   (i) Paid $10,000 in wages to employees in January.
   (j) Declared and paid a $3,000 dividend.
   (k) Received and paid for the supplies in (f) in cash.

(continued on next page)

3. Using the data from the T-accounts, amounts for the following on January 31, 19B, were

Revenues, $_____ – Expenses, $_____ = Net Income, $_____
Assets, $_____ = Liabilities, $_____ + Stockholders' Equity, $_____

4. What is net income if Fitzsimmons used the cash basis of accounting?

E3–19 Preparing an Income Statement, Statement of Stockholders' Equity, and Balance Sheet

Use the ending balances in the T-accounts in E3–18 to complete the following.
1. Prepare an unadjusted income statement for January 19B in good form.
2. Prepare an unadjusted statement of stockholders' equity for January 19B.
3. Prepare an unadjusted balance sheet as of January 31, 19B, in good form.

E3–20 Using T-Accounts to Summarize Transactions

Vivianne Macedo and Stephanie Meltzer had been operating a catering business, Traveling Gourmet, for several years. In March 19C, the partners were planning to expand by opening a retail sales shop and decided to form the business as a corporation called Traveling Gourmet, Inc. The following transactions occurred in March 19C:

(a) Each of the two shareholders contributed $10,000 to form the corporation, along with $2,000 in accounts receivable, $5,300 in equipment, a van (equipment) appraised at a fair market value of $13,000, and $1,200 in supplies.

(b) Vivianne and Stephanie found a vacant store for sale in a good location. In March, the business purchased the building for $60,000 with a $9,000 cash down payment and a mortgage from a local bank for the rest.

(c) The company borrowed $25,000 from the local bank on a 10 percent, one-year note and immediately purchased $15,000 of equipment (refrigerated display cases, cabinets, tables, and chairs) and renovated and decorated the new store for $10,000 (added to the cost of the building).

(d) Food and paper supplies costing $8,830 were purchased for cash and used in March.

(e) Vivianne and Stephanie made and sold food at the retail store for $10,900 in cash.

(f) Traveling Gourmet catered four parties in March for $3,200; $1,500 was billed and the rest was received in cash.

(g) A $320 telephone bill for March was received in March but not paid.

(h) Traveling Gourmet paid $63 in gas for the van in March.

(i) The company paid $5,080 in wages to employees in March.

(j) Each of the owners received a $300 dividend from the corporation.

Required:
1. Set up appropriate T-accounts for Cash, Accounts Receivable, Supplies, Equipment, Building, Accounts Payable, Note Payable, Mortgage Payable, Contributed Capital, Retained Earnings, Food Sales Revenue, Catering Sales Revenue, Cost of Food and Paper Products, Utilities Expense, Wages Expense, and Gasoline Expense.
2. Record in the T-accounts the effects of each transaction for Traveling Gourmet, Inc., in March. Identify the amounts with the letters starting with (a).
3. Indicate which of the transactions will require adjusting entries at the end of the month.

E3–21 Preparing an Income Statement, Statement of Stockholders' Equity, and a Balance Sheet

Use the balances in the completed T-accounts in E3–20 to respond to the following:

1. Prepare an unadjusted income statement in good form for the month of March 19C.
2. Prepare an unadjusted statement of stockholders' equity for the month of March 19C.
3. Prepare an unadjusted balance sheet in good form as of March 19C.
4. What do you think about the success of this company based on the results of the first month of operation?

E3–22 Focus on Cash Flows

Analyze each of the transactions in E3-20 and indicate the direction and amount of the effect of the transaction on cash for the month of March. Categorize the effects as operating, investing, or financing. Use the following headings. A sample is provided.

	EFFECT ON CASH			
Transaction	Operating	Investing	Financing	No Effect on Cash
(a)			+ 20,000	

E3–23 Using T-Accounts to Summarize Transactions

Tracey Malloy, a connoisseur of fine chocolate, opened Tracey's Treats in Collegetown on February 1, 19A. The shop specializes in a selection of gourmet chocolate candies and a line of gourmet ice cream. You have been hired to maintain the store's financial records. The following transactions occurred in February 19A, the first month of operations.

(a) Four shareholders contributed a total of $16,000 to form the corporation.
(b) Paid three months' store rent at $800 per month (for February, March, and April).
(c) Purchased supplies for $300 cash.
(d) Purchased and received candy for $5,000, on account, due in 60 days.
(e) Negotiated a $10,000 loan at the bank, at 12 percent annual interest. The principal and interest are due in a lump sum in two years.
(f) Used the money from (e) to purchase a computer for $2,500 (for recordkeeping and inventory tracking) and the balance for furniture and fixtures for the store.
(g) Placed a grand opening advertisement in the local paper for $425 cash.
(h) Sales on Valentine's Day totaled $1,800; $1,525 was in cash and the rest on accounts receivable. The cost of the candy sold was $1,000.
(i) Made a $500 payment on accounts payable.
(j) Incurred and paid employee wages of $420.
(k) Collected accounts receivable of $50 from customers.
(l) Made a repair on one of the display cases for $118 cash.
(m) Made cash sales of $2,000 during the rest of the month. The cost of the goods sold was $1,100.

Required:

1. Set up appropriate T-accounts for Cash, Accounts Receivable, Supplies, Merchandise Inventory, Prepaid Rent, Equipment, Furniture and Fixtures, Accounts Payable, Notes Payable, Contributed Capital, Sales Revenue, Cost of Goods Sold (Expense), Advertising Expense, Wage Expense, and Repair Expense.

2. Record in the T-accounts the effects of each transaction for Tracey's Treats in February. Identify the transactions in the accounts with letters beginning with (a).
3. Show the unadjusted ending balances in the T-accounts.
4. Indicate which of the transactions will require adjusting entries at the end of the month (for simplicity, do not record the entries).

E3–24 Preparing an Income Statement, Statement of Stockholders' Equity, and Balance Sheet

Use the balances in the completed T-accounts in E3–23 to respond to the following:

1. Prepare an unadjusted income statement in good form for the month of February 19A.
2. Prepare an unadjusted statement of stockholders' equity for the month of February 19A.
3. Prepare an unadjusted balance sheet in good form as of the end of February 19A.
4. Write a short memo to Tracey offering your opinion on the results of operations during the first month of business.

E3–25 Focus on Cash Flows

Analyze each of the transactions in E3–23 and indicate the direction and amount of the effect of the transaction on cash for the month of February. Categorize the effects as operating, investing, or financing. Use the following headings. A sample is provided.

Transaction	EFFECT ON CASH			No Effect on Cash
	Operating	Investing	Financing	
(a)			+ 16,000	

Snapple Beverage Corp.

E3–26 Preparing an Income Statement

In June 1993, Snapple Beverage Corporation purchased Mr. Natural, Inc., Snapple's distributor for New York City and Westchester County, New York. Included in Snapple's 1993 annual report is the December 31, 1993, statement of operations for Mr. Natural for the six months since the acquisition. The following is a list of the accounts and balances from the annual report for Mr. Natural. The accounts are not necessarily listed in good order and have normal debit and credit balances:

Interest expense	$ 643,423	Income tax expense	$1,555,619
Goodwill amortization expense*	305,700	Promotion and marketing expense	261,947
Advertising expense	832,489	Professional fees expense	342,075
Net revenues	36,481,638	Other income	133,744
Interest income	35,674	Payroll expense	1,410,642
Other expenses	867,284	Repairs and maintenance expense	243,149
Cost of sales (products sold)	28,605,529	Depreciation and amortization expense*	156,132

*Goodwill (an intangible) results from purchasing another company at a price higher than its book value. The amount is recorded as an asset, and the cost is allocated over several years. The allocated amount of an intangible asset is called *amortization expense*.

Required:

Prepare a statement of operations (income statement) in good form for Mr. Natural, Inc., for the six months ended December 31, 1993.

Epilogue: In 1994, Quaker Oats acquired Snapple Beverage Corporation for more than $1 billion. In 1997, Quaker Oats sold Snapple Beverage for approximately $300 million.

Problems

P3–1 Analyzing Transactions

The following list includes a series of accounts for Dinjian Corporation, which has been operating for three years. These accounts are listed and numbered for identification. Following the accounts is a series of transactions. For each transaction, indicate the account(s) that should be debited and credited by entering the appropriate account number(s) to the right of each transaction. If no journal entry is needed, write *none* after the transaction. The first transaction is used as an example.

Account No.	Account Title	Account No.	Account Title
1	Cash	9	Wages payable
2	Accounts receivable	10	Income taxes payable
3	Supplies inventory on hand	11	Contributed capital
4	Prepaid expense	12	Retained earnings
5	Equipment	13	Service revenue
6	Patents	14	Operating expenses
7	Accounts payable	15	Income tax expense
8	Note payable	16	None of the above

	Transactions	Debit	Credit
(a)	Example: Purchased equipment for use in the business; paid one-third cash and gave a note payable for the balance.	5	1, 8
(b)	Issued stock to new investors.		
(c)	Paid cash for salaries and wages.		
(d)	Collected cash for services performed this period.		
(e)	Collected cash for services performed last period.		
(f)	Performed services this period on credit.		
(g)	Paid operating expenses incurred this period.		
(h)	Paid cash for operating expenses incurred last period.		
(i)	Incurred operating expenses this period to be paid next period.		
(j)	Purchased supplies for inventory to be used later; paid cash.		
(k)	Used some of the supplies from inventory for operations.		
(l)	Purchased a patent (an intangible); paid cash.		
(m)	Made a payment on the equipment note in (a); the payment was part principal and part interest expense.		
(n)	Collected cash on accounts receivable for services previously performed.		
(o)	Paid cash on accounts payable for expenses previously incurred.		
(p)	Paid three-fourths of the income tax expense for the year, the balance to be paid next period.		
(q)	On the last day of current period, paid cash for an insurance policy covering the next two years.		

P3–2 Analyzing Transactions

The following is a series of accounts for Ortiz & Ortiz, Incorporated, which has been operating for two years. The accounts are listed and numbered for identification. Following the accounts is a series of transactions. For each transaction, indicate the account(s) that should be debited and credited by entering the appropriate account number(s) to the right of each transaction. If no journal entry is needed, write *none* after the transaction. The first transaction is given as an example.

Account No.	Account Title	Account No.	Account Title
1	Cash	9	Wages payable
2	Accounts receivable	10	Income taxes payable
3	Supplies inventory	11	Contributed capital
4	Prepaid expense	12	Retained earnings
5	Buildings	13	Service revenue
6	Land	14	Operating expenses
7	Accounts payable	15	Income tax expense
8	Mortgage payable		

	Transactions	Debit	Credit
(a)	Example: Issued stock to new investors.	1	11
(b)	Performed services this period on credit.		
(c)	Purchased (but did not use) supplies this period on credit.		
(d)	Prepaid a fire insurance policy this period to cover the next 12 months.		
(e)	Purchased a building this period with a 20 percent cash down payment and a mortgage loan for the balance.		
(f)	Collected cash this year for services rendered and recorded in the prior year.		
(g)	Paid cash this period for wages earned and recorded last period.		
(h)	Paid cash for operating expenses charged on accounts payable in the prior period.		
(i)	Paid cash for operating expenses charged on accounts payable in the current period.		
(j)	Incurred and recorded operating expenses on credit to be paid next period.		
(k)	Collected cash at the point of sale for services rendered.		
(l)	Used supplies from inventory to clean the offices.		
(m)	Recorded income taxes for this period to be paid at the beginning of the next period.		
(n)	Declared and paid a cash dividend this period.		
(o)	Made a payment on the building, which was part principal repayment and part interest.		
(p)	This period a shareholder sold some shares of her stock to another person for an amount above the original issuance price.		

Cedar Fair

P3–3 Performing Transaction Analysis, Preparing Journal Entries, and Posting to T-Accounts

Cedar Fair, L. P. (Limited Partnership), owns and operates four seasonal amusement parks: Cedar Point in Ohio, Valleyfair near Minneapolis/St. Paul, Dorney Park and Wildwater Kingdom near Allentown, Pennsylvania, and Worlds of Fun/Oceans of Fun in Kansas City. The following are summarized transactions similar to those that occurred in a recent year (19A):

(a) Guests at the parks paid $89,664,000 cash in admissions.

(b) The primary operating expenses (such as employee wages, utilities, and repairs and maintenance) for the year 19A were $66,347,000 with $60,200,000 paid in cash and the rest on account.

(c) Interest paid on long-term debt was $6,601,000.

(d) The parks sell food and merchandise and operate games. The cash received in 19A for these combined activities was $77,934,000.

(e) The cost of products sold for cash during the year was $19,525,000.

(f)   Cedar Fair purchased and built additional buildings, rides, and equipment during 19A, paying $23,813,000 in cash.

(g)   The most significant assets for the company are land, buildings, rides, and equipment. Therefore, a large expense for Cedar Fair is depreciation expense. In 19A, the amount was $14,473,000 (credit Accumulated Depreciation, which will reduce the asset account).

(h)   Guests may stay at accommodations owned by the company at the parks. In 19A, Accommodations Revenue was $11,345,000; $11,010,000 was paid by the guests in cash and the rest was on account.

(i)   Cedar Fair paid $2,900,000 on notes payable.

(j)   The company purchased $19,100,000 in food and merchandise inventory for the year, paying $18,000,000 in cash and the rest on account.

(k)   The selling, general, and administrative expenses (those not classified as operating expenses, such as the president's salary and advertising for the parks) for 19A were $21,118,000; $19,500,000 was paid in cash and the rest was on account.

(l)   Cedar Fair paid $8,600,000 on accounts payable during the year.

Required:

1. For each of these transactions, perform transaction analysis following the illustration in the chapter and prepare journal entries.

2. Create T-accounts for the income statement accounts only and post the income statement effects of each of the transactions. Determine ending balances.

P3–4   Preparing an Income Statement

Use the balances of the completed T-accounts in P3–3 to prepare in good form an unadjusted income statement for Cedar Fair at December 31, 19A.

P3–5   Performing Transaction Analysis, Preparing Journal Entries, and Posting to T-Accounts

Green Stables, Inc., is a Philadelphia company that provides stables, care for animals, and grounds for riding and showing horses. You have been hired to assist Jennifer Dembeck, the chief financial officer, with analysis. The following transactions for April 19C are provided for your review.

(a)   The company provided animal care services, all on credit, for $5,260. The company rented stables to customers who cared for their animals and was paid cash of $3,200. Use one revenue account.

(b)   The company collected $1,100 on a note receivable from a customer who previously purchased riding equipment. Of the amount collected, $100 was interest.

(c)   Straw (a supply inventory) was purchased on account for $3,210. (This was added to the $1,400 of straw already on hand in the barn.)

(d)   Utilities for the month totaled $845 and were paid in cash as incurred.

(e)   A customer paid $1,500 to board her horse in April, May, and June.

(f)   A small barn was built for $42,000. The company paid half the amount in cash and signed a three-year note payable for the balance on April 1, 19C. The note carries an annual interest rate of 12 percent; the principal is due on the maturity date and an interest payment is due at the end of each month.

(g)   Paid $3,210 on accounts payable for a previous purchase of straw.

(h)   Received $50,000 from customers on accounts receivable.

(i) Wages expense of $2,600 was incurred and paid.

(j) Dividends of $5,000 were declared and paid.

(k) Paid $3,600 for property insurance. The policy runs from April 1, 19C to March 31, 19D.

(l) An interest payment of $210 was made for the note in (f) for April.

(m) An inventory count indicated that $925 of straw remained unused at the end of the month.

(n) The company incurred $480 in income taxes for the month to be paid at the end of the next quarter.

Required:

1. For each of these transactions, perform transaction analysis as illustrated in the chapter and prepare journal entries. If a transaction does not require a journal entry, state so.

2. Create T-accounts for the income statement accounts only and post the income statement effects of each transaction. Determine and label the ending balances.

P3–6 Preparing an Income Statement and Computing Effective Tax Rate

Use the balances of the completed T-accounts in P3–5 to answer the following.

Required:

1. Prepare an unadjusted income statement in good form for Green Stables, Inc., for the month ending April 30, 19C.

2. Determine the effective tax rate for Green Stables, Inc.

Federal Express

P3–7 Preparing T-Accounts; Constructing Financial Statements; Analyzing Return on Investment and Cash Flow Effects

The following are several May 31 account balances (in thousands of dollars) from a recent annual report of Federal Express Corporation, followed by several typical transactions. The business is described in the annual report as follows:

Federal Express Corporation offers a wide range of express services for the time-definite transportation of goods and documents throughout the world using an extensive fleet of aircraft and vehicles and leading-edge information technologies.

Account	Balance	Account	Balance
Flight and ground equipment	$3,476,268	Contributed capital	$ 701,866
Retained earnings	969,515	Receivables	922,727
Accounts payable	554,111	Other assets	1,010,953
Prepaid expenses	63,573	Cash	155,456
Accrued expenses payable	761,357	Spare parts, supplies, and fuel	164,087
Notes payable	2,016,076	Deferred income taxes (credit)	72,479
Other liabilities	717,660		

These accounts are not necessarily in good order and have normal debit or credit balances.

Transactions (June)

(a) Provided delivery service to customers, receiving $600,000 in accounts receivable and $50,000 in cash.

(b) Purchased new equipment costing $68,000 on account.

(c) Paid $62,000 cash to rent equipment and aircraft, with $54,000 for June rental and the rest for rent in July and August.

(d) Spent $33,000 cash to maintain and repair facilities and equipment in June.

(e) Collected $302,000 from customers on account.

(f) Borrowed $75,000 by signing a note.

(g) Issued additional stock for $20,000.

(h) Paid employees $317,000 in June.

(i) Purchased for cash and used $41,000 in fuel for the aircraft and equipment.

(j) Paid $32,000 on accounts payable.

(k) Ordered $6,000 in spare parts and supplies.

Required:

1. Prepare T-accounts for May 31 from the preceding list; enter the respective balances. You will need additional T-accounts for income statement accounts; enter $0 balances.

2. For each transaction, record the effects in the T-accounts. Label each using the letter of the transaction.

3. Prepare an unadjusted income statement, unadjusted statement of stockholders' equity, and unadjusted balance sheet in good form.

4. Based on the unadjusted amounts, compute the company's return on investment. What does it mean?

5. Analyze each of the transactions and indicate the direction and amount of the effect of the transaction on cash for the month of June. Categorize the effects as operating, investing, or financing. Use the following headings. A sample is provided.

| Transaction | EFFECT ON CASH | | | No Effect on Cash |
	Operating	Investing	Financing	
(a)	+$50,000			

P3–8 Preparing T-Accounts; Constructing Financial Statements; Analyzing Return on Investment and Cash Flow Effects

Exxon Corp.

The following are the summary account balances from a recent balance sheet of Exxon Corporation. The accounts are followed by a list of hypothetical transactions for the month of January. The following accounts are shown in millions of dollars.

Cash	$ 1,157	Marketable securities	$ 618
Notes payable	3,858	Accounts payable	13,391
Accounts receivable	8,073	Income tax payable	2,244
Inventories	5,541	Prepaid expenses	1,071
Other debt	30,954	Investments	5,394
Property & equipment, net	63,425	Intangibles, net	2,583
Shareholders' equity*	37,415		

*This account is a combination of Contributed Capital and Retained Earnings.

The accounts have normal debit or credit balances, but they are not necessarily listed in good order.

Transactions (January)

(a) Purchased new equipment costing $150 million on account.

(b) Received $500 million on accounts receivable.

(c) Received and paid the telephone bills for $1 million.

(d) Earned $5 million in sales to customers on account; cost of sales was $1 million.

(e) Paid employees $1 million for wages earned in January.

(f) Paid half of the income taxes payable.

(g) Purchased supplies inventory for $23 million on account.

(h) Prepaid rent for February for a warehouse for $12 million.

(i) Paid $10 million of other debt and $1 million in interest on the debt.

(j) Purchased a patent (an intangible asset) for $8 million cash.

Required:

1. Prepare T-accounts for January 31, 19D, from the preceding account balances. Make additional T-accounts for the revenues and expenses, and enter $0 for the beginning balances.

2. For each transaction, record the effects in the T-accounts. Label each using the letter of the transaction.

3. Prepare an unadjusted income statement, statement of stockholders' equity, and unadjusted balance sheet in good form.

4. Based on the unadjusted amounts, compute the company's return on investment. What does it mean?

5. Analyze each transaction and indicate the direction and amount of its effect on cash for the month of June. Categorize the effects as operating, investing, or financing. Use the following headings. A sample is provided.

	EFFECT ON CASH			
Transaction	Operating	Investing	Financing	No Effect on Cash
(a)				No effect

Cases and Projects

C3–1 Analyzing and Restating an Income Statement that Has Major Deficiencies: A Challenging Case

Tom Martinez started and operated a small service company during 19A. At the end of the year, he prepared the following statement based on information stored in a large filing cabinet:

MARTINEZ COMPANY

Profit for 19A

Service fees income collected during 19A		$75,000
Cash dividends received		10,000
Total		$85,000
Expense for operations paid during 19A	$52,000	
Cash stolen	500	
Supplies purchased for use on service jobs (cash paid)	1,200	
Total		53,700
Profit		$31,300

The following is a summary of completed transactions:

(a) Service fees earned during 19A, $87,000.

(b) The cash dividends received were on shares of ABC Industrial stock purchased by Tom Martinez six years earlier.

(c) Expenses incurred during 19A, $61,000.

(d) Supplies on hand (unused) at the end of 19A, $700.

Required:

1. Did Martinez prepare the statement on a cash basis or an accrual basis? Explain how you can tell. Which basis should be used? Explain why.

2. Revise the statement to make it consistent with proper accounting and reporting. Explain (using footnotes) the reason for each change that you make.

C3–2 Challenging Analytical Case Related to Application of the Accounting Model

Wilsey Painting Service Company was organized during January 19A by three individuals. On January 20, 19A, the company issued 5,000 shares of stock to each of its organizers. The following is a schedule of the cumulative account balances immediately after each of the first 10 transactions.

Accounts	CUMULATIVE BALANCES									
	(a)	(b)	(c)	(d)	(e)	(f)	(g)	(h)	(i)	(j)
Cash	$75,000	$70,000	$85,000	$71,000	$61,000	$61,000	$57,000	$46,000	$41,000	$57,000
Accounts receivable			12,000	12,000	12,000	26,000	26,000	26,000	26,000	10,000
Office fixtures		20,000	20,000	20,000	20,000	20,000	20,000	20,000	20,000	20,000
Land				18,000	18,000	18,000	18,000	18,000	18,000	18,000
Accounts payable					3,000	3,000	3,000	10,000	5,000	5,000
Note payable		15,000	15,000	19,000	19,000	19,000	19,000	19,000	19,000	19,000
Contributed capital	75,000	75,000	75,000	75,000	75,000	75,000	75,000	75,000	75,000	75,000
Retained earnings							(4,000)	(4,000)	(4,000)	(4,000)
Paint revenue			27,000	27,000	27,000	41,000	41,000	41,000	41,000	41,000
Supplies expense					5,000	5,000	5,000	8,000	8,000	8,000
Wages expense					8,000	8,000	8,000	23,000	23,000	23,000

Required:

1. Analyze the changes in this schedule for each transaction; then explain the transaction. Transactions (*a*) and (*b*) are examples:

   (*a*) Cash increased $75,000, and Contributed Capital (stockholders' equity) increased $75,000. Therefore, transaction (*a*) was an issuance of the capital stock of the corporation for $75,000 cash.

   (*b*) Cash decreased $5,000, office fixtures (an asset) increased $20,000, and note payable (a liability) increased $15,000. Therefore, transaction (*b*) was a purchase of office fixtures that cost $20,000. Payment was made as follows: cash, $5,000; note payable, $15,000.

2. Based only on the preceding schedule—disregarding your response to requirement 1— respond to the following after transaction (*j*):

   Income statement
   Revenues $_____
   Expenses $_____
   Net income $_____
   Balance sheet $_____
   Assets $_____
   Liabilities $_____
   Stockholders' equity $_____

C3–3 An Ethical Dilemma

Ray Ramsay is the manager of an upstate New York regional office for an insurance company. As the regional manager, his compensation package comprises a base salary, commissions, and a bonus when the region sells new policies in excess of its quota. Ray has been under enormous pressure lately, stemming largely from two factors. First, he is experiencing a mounting personal debt due to a family member's illness. Second, compounding his worries, the region's sales of new policies have dipped below the normal quota for the first time in years.

You have been working for Ray for two years, and like everyone else in the office, you consider yourself lucky to work for such a supportive boss. You also feel great sympathy for his personal problems over the last few months. In your position as accountant for the regional office, you are only too aware of the drop in new policy sales and the impact this will have on the manager's bonus. While you are working late at year-end, Ray stops by your office.

Ray asks you to change the manner in which you have accounted for a new property insurance policy for a large local business. A check for the premium, substantial in amount, came in the mail on December 31, the last day of the reporting year. The premium covers a period beginning on January 5. You deposited the check and correctly debited cash and credited a *revenue collected in advance* account. Ray says, "Hey, we have the money this year, so why not count the revenue this year? I never did understand why you accountants are so picky about these things anyway. I'd like you to change the way you have recorded the transaction. I want you to credit a *revenue* account. And anyway, I've done favors for you in the past, and I am asking for such a small thing in return." With that, he leaves for the day.

Required:

How should you handle this situation? What are the ethical implications of Ray's request? Who are the parties who would be helped or harmed if you complied with the request? If you fail to comply with his request, how will you explain your position to him in the morning?

Volkswagen

C3–4 International Financial Statements: A Challenging Case

Your cousin, an engineering major, has inherited some money and wants to invest in an auto company. She has never taken an accounting course and has asked you to help her compare a U.S. automaker's financial statements to those of a German automaker. Your cousin has given you the income statement, asset section of the balance sheet, and audit opinion for Volkswagen for 1992.

Required:

Review the following excerpts of Volkswagen's financial statements. Write a letter to your cousin explaining the similarities and the dissimilarities you would expect to find if you compared Volkswagen's statements to a company in the United States. Offer your opinion on whether you would expect the underlying accounting principles of the two countries to be similar or dissimilar. On what are you basing your opinion?

AUDIT CERTIFICATE

The consolidated financial statements, which we have audited in accordance with professional standards, comply with the German legal provisions. With due regard to the generally accepted accounting principles, the consolidated financial statements give a true and fair view of the Group's assets, liabilities, financial position and profit or loss. The Group management report is consistent with the consolidated financial statements.

Hanover, February 24, 1993

C&L TREUARBEIT

DEUTSCHE REVISION

Aktiengesellschaft

**Statement of Earnings of the Volkswagen Group for the Fiscal Year
Ended December 31, 1992—DM million—**

	Note	1992	1991
Sales	(13)	85,403	76,315
Cost of sales		79,155	69,472
Gross profit		+ 6,248	+ 6,843
Selling and distribution expenses		5,661	5,414
General administration expenses		2,316	2,185
Other operating income	(14)	4,246	4,406
Other operating expenses	(15)	2,634	3,104
Results from participations	(16)	+ 55	+ 97
Interest results	(17)	+ 739	+ 1,228
Write-down of financial assets and securities classified as current assets		75	86
Results from ordinary business activities		+ 602	+ 1,785
Taxes on income		455	671
Net earnings	(18)	147	1,114

Balance Sheet of the Volkswagen Group, December 31, 1992—DM million—

Assets	Note	Dec. 31, 1992	Dec. 31, 1991
Fixed assets	(1)		
Intangible assets		631	372
Tangible assets		24,050	21,126
Financial assets		2,747	2,655
Leasing and rental assets		7,393	6,293
		34,821	30,446
Current assets			
Inventories	(2)	9,736	9,049
Receivables and other assets	(3)	21,065	18,675
Securities	(4)	1,497	2,329
Cash on hand, deposits at German Federal Bank and postal giro balances, cash in banks		7,836	9,255
		40,134	39,308
Prepaid and deferred charges	(5)	329	336
Balance sheet total		75,284	70,090

C3–5 Analyzing International Financial Statements and Ratio Analysis

Daimler-Benz AG

Daimler-Benz is "an integrated technology group with extensive competence in the field of transportation and traffic systems." Based in Stuttgart, Germany, the company is most recognizable as the manufacturer of Mercedes-Benz cars and trucks but also is involved with microelectronics, rail systems, energy systems technology, and aerospace technologies. The following is a recent income statement (adapted) and a partial footnote on geographic segments:

Consolidated Statement of Income	DM in Millions
Revenues	99,494
Other Operating Income	7,370
Costs of Materials	(51,076)
Personnel Expenses including Pension Provisions	(33,790)
Amortization of Intangible Assets, Depreciation of Property, Plant and Equipment and Leased Equipment	(8,059)
Other Operating Expenses	(15,281)
Income from Affiliated, Associated and Related Companies	103
Interest Income (net of interest expense)	456
Other Losses	(300)
Income from Ordinary Business Activities	(1,083)
Extraordinary Income and Other Expenses	2,213
Income Taxes	(515)
Net Income	615

Segment Report
By Geographical Region:
(in Millions of DM)

Total Revenues	Germany	Other European Countries	North America	Latin-America	Other Countries	Consolidated
19B	55,525	17,263	14,760	4,544	5,645	97,737
19A	60,659	17,225	12,314	3,573	4,778	98,549

Total assets were DM 90,926 million, total liabilities were DM 72,781 million, and stockholders' equity was DM 18,145 million. In the prior year, the stockholders' equity was DM 19,719 million.

Required:
1. Compute Daimler-Benz's debt-to-equity ratio. What does this suggest?
2. Compute the company's return on investment. How does it compare to that of other companies in the automotive industry? (Chrysler's ROI = 34%; Ford's ROI = 16%; Honda's ROI = 3.7%)
3. For the year 19B, compute each region's revenues as a percentage of consolidated revenue. For example, for Germany, the ratio is 56.8 percent (DM 55,525 ÷ DM 97,737). Then compute the same percentages for the most recent year reported by General Motors (in the chapter). Compare the percentages for the two companies. Based only on these percentages, what are the similarities and differences between the two companies in operating in various segments?

Toys "R" Us   **C3–6 Financial Statement Analysis**

Refer to the February 1, 1997 financial statements of Toys "R" Us given in Appendix B at the end of the book.

Required:
1. State the amount of the largest expense on the 1997 income statement and describe the transaction represented by the expense.
2. Give the journal entry for interest expense for the year ended February 1, 1997 (for this question, assume that the amount has not yet been paid).

3. Assuming that all net sales are on credit, how much cash did Toys "R" Us collect from customers? (*Hint:* Use a T-account of accounts receivable to infer collection.)

4. A shareholder has complained that "more dividends should be paid because the company had net earnings of $427.4 million. Since this amount is all cash, more of it should go to the owners." Explain why the shareholder's assumption that earnings equal net cash inflow is valid. If you believe that the assumption is not valid, state so and support your position concisely.

5. Describe and contrast the purpose of an income statement versus a balance sheet.

6. Compute the company's return on investment for 1997. Explain its meaning.

C3–7 Project: Comparing Income Statements within Industries

Acquire the income statements from the annual reports or 10-Ks of three companies within an industry. (Library files, the SEC EDGAR service at www.sec.gov, Compustat CD, or the companies themselves are good sources.) Write a short report indicating any differences, if any, in the accounts used by the three companies and their location on the income statement.

C3–8 Project: Comparing Income Statements among Industries

Acquire the income statements from the annual reports or 10-Ks of three companies from different industries. (Library files, the SEC EDGAR service at www.sec.gov, Compustat CD, or the companies themselves are good sources.) Write a short report indicating any differences, if any, in the accounts used by the three companies and their location on the income statement.

C3–9 Project: Analyzing Differences in Return on Investment among Competitors

Sbarro's competitors in the restaurant business include Outback Steakhouse, Boston Chicken, Cheesecake Factory, Au Bon Pain, and Uno's Pizzeria. Obtain the recent balance sheet and income statement for Sbarro and two of its competitors. (Library files, the SEC EDGAR service at www.sec.gov, Compustat CD, or the companies themselves are good sources. All of these companies are included under the SIC [Standard Industrial Classification] code 5812 for retail eating places.) Write a short memo comparing the companies' return on investment ratios. Indicate what differences in their businesses might account for any differences in the ratio.

C3–10 Project: Analyzing Changes in Effective Tax Rate and Return on Investment

Acquire the three most recent years' income statements and balance sheet for a single company. (Library files, the SEC EDGAR service at www.sec.gov, Compustat CD, or the company itself are good sources.) Write a short memo comparing the company's effective tax rate and return on investment over the three years. Indicate what differences in activities might account for any difference in the ratios.

C3–11 Project: Focus on Cash Flows

Acquire the three most recent years' statement of cash flows for a single company. (Library files, the SEC EDGAR service at www.sec.gov, Compustat CD, or the company itself are good sources.) Compute the percentage of cash from operating activities to total change in cash for each year. Write a short memo comparing the three percentages. Indicate what differences might account for any difference in the percentages.

C3–12 Project: Financial Analysis Update

Acquire the most recent year's annual report and Form 10-K for Sbarro. (Library files, the SEC EDGAR service at www.sec.gov, Compustat CD, or the company itself are good sources.) Write a short memo comparing the company's return on investment to its ROI presented in the chapter. Indicate what differences in operating, financing, and investing activities might account for any difference in the ratio.

C3–13 Ethics Project: Analyzing Revenue Recognition Policy

Obtain a recent news story concerning the way that Boston Chicken records revenues and expenses related to franchises. (Library files, the SEC EDGAR service at www.sec.gov, Compustat CD, or other business news retrieval services are good sources.) Write a short memo outlining the nature of the revenue or expense recognition issue, how it compares to the revenue or matching principle, and who is hurt or helped by the recognition policy. Indicate your opinion on whether there is a question of ethics in this case.

C3–14 Team Project: Analysis of Income Statements and Ratios

As a group, select an industry to analyze. Each group member should acquire the annual report or 10-K for one publicly traded company in the industry, with each member selecting a different company. (Library files, the SEC EDGAR service at www.sec.gov, Compustat CD, or the company itself are good sources.) On an individual basis, each group member should write a report listing the following:

1. The major revenue and expense accounts on the most recent income statement.
2. The percentage of net income to cash from operating activities (on the statement of cash flows).
3. The return on investment ratio.
4. The percentage of domestic sales to total sales for the most recent year (in the note to the financial statements on geographic segments, if provided).

Then, as a group, write a short report comparing and contrasting your companies using these attributes. Discuss any patterns across the companies that you as a group observe. Provide potential explanations for any differences discovered.

CHAPTER FOUR

The Adjustment Process and Financial Statements

Sbarro, Inc.
THE BUSIEST TIME OF THE FISCAL YEAR

As indicated in a recent annual report, "the Company's business is subject to seasonal fluctuations, the effects of weather and economic conditions. Earnings have been highest in its fourth fiscal quarter due primarily to increased [sales] volume in shopping malls during the holiday shopping season. . . ." These differences in volume are borne out by the accompanying graph of quarterly sales. For Sbarro, the fourth and first quarters are the busiest from an operating standpoint.

LEARNING OBJECTIVES

After studying this chapter, you should be able to:

1. Explain the purpose of a trial balance. 173
2. Analyze the adjustments necessary at the end of the period to update balance sheet and income statements accounts. 176
3. Present a complete set of financial statements: Income statement, statement of stockholders' equity, balance sheet, and statement of cash flows. 189
4. Explain the closing process. 195

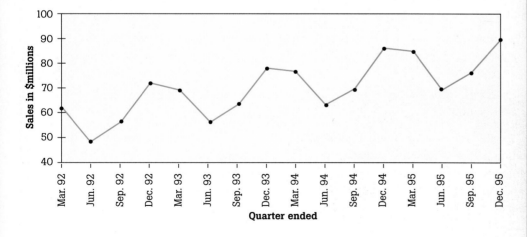

The end of the fourth quarter and beginning of the first quarter also mark the busiest and most critical times from an accounting standpoint—the time accounts are adjusted, financial statements are prepared, and the books are closed. It is also the point at which the external auditor completes audit work and issues an opinion on the fairness of the financial statements and the company makes the statements available to external users. For Sbarro, even though 1995 operations ended on December 31, 1995, the company's auditor, Arthur Andersen, LLP, performed the audit and signed the opinion on February 9, 1996 (six weeks later).

■ ■ ■

Business Background

In Chapter 3 we noted that Sbarro, like all well-managed companies, organizes its accounting system with recordkeeping efficiency in mind. As a consequence, it usually records external transactions when it processes the business documents supporting those transactions. For example, the sale of food is recorded at the end of each day based on the daily cash register total. When the end of the accounting period falls at a point other than the end of the operating cycle, the asset, liability, revenue, and expense accounts may not be fully up-to-date following accrual accounting principles. That is, some revenues and expenses and the related changes in assets and liabilities may not be properly recorded in the correct accounting period. As a consequence, adjustments or corrections are necessary.

This problem is particularly acute in the case of internal activities that do not result in an actual exchange between the business and other parties but have a direct and measurable effect on the business entity. These internal transactions, introduced in Chapter 3, include the following:

Accruals are revenues that have been earned and expenses that have been incurred by the end of the accounting period but will not be collected or paid until a future accounting period.

Deferrals are previously recorded assets, liabilities, revenues, or expenses that need to be adjusted at the end of the period to reflect earned revenues or incurred expenses.

■ **Accruals.** Revenues that have been earned or expenses that have been incurred by the end of the period but have not been recorded and *no cash has been received or paid.*

■ **Deferrals.** *Cash received or paid in advance* of the related revenue or expense recognition.

Exhibit 4.1 presents the fundamental steps in the accounting cycle. Phase 1 of the accounting cycle involves analyzing and recording transactions that occur during the accounting period. In this chapter, we examine the end-of-period steps in Phase 2 that focus primarily on adjustments relating to accruals and deferrals. We need to understand the steps in the second phase of the accounting cycle because balance sheet valuation and income measurement are incomplete without updating accounts to ensure proper revenue recognition and expense matching for the period (the adjustment process).

Unlike the fairly routine entries based on supporting documentation during the accounting period, *knowledge* and *judgment* are primary inputs in determining end-of-period adjustments to revenues and expenses. As such, the accounts most subject to year-end adjustment are of considerable interest to external users of the financial statements. Analysts recognize that management's judgment plays the greatest role in determining year-end adjustments and that these judgments may provide important

EXHIBIT 4.1
Fundamental Steps in the Accounting Cycle

START OF ACCOUNTING PERIOD

Phase 1:
During the Accounting Period
(discussed in Chapters 2 and 3)

> Perform **transaction analysis** based on a review of source documents from each transaction.
>
> Record **journal entries** for each transaction (in chronological order in the general journal).
>
> Post amounts to the general ledger (pages are similar to **T-accounts**).

Phase 2:
At the End of the Accounting Period
(discussed in Chapter 4)

> Prepare a **trial balance** (a list of accounts and balances to date) to verify the equality of debits and credits.
>
> **Analyze adjustments** (to update all accounts for proper revenue recognition and expense matching).
>
> Prepare and distribute **financial statements** (from adjusted balances).
>
> Record and post **adjusting and closing entries** (to create zero balances in temporary accounts for use in the next period).*

*Temporary accounts are those that accumulate balances for the period. They are revenue and expense accounts.

END OF ACCOUNTING PERIOD

signals of management's expectations for the future. At the same time, analysts recognize that these adjustments are therefore most subject to error and manipulation. As a result, auditors also scrutinize adjustments. You must understand the mechanics of the adjustment process before you can understand the information that adjustments contain and the errors that can occur.

After these adjustments are determined, financial statements can be prepared. (Many businesses use accounting worksheets, described in Appendix C to the text, to speed up the production of financial statements.) In addition, certain accounts, such as revenues and expenses, need to be prepared for the beginning of the next accounting period. This step is called the *closing process*.

You must understand these steps before you can fully understand the process of communicating accounting information to users, which we discuss in Chapter 5. In this chapter, we emphasize the use of the same analytical tools employed in Chapters 2 and 3 (T-accounts, journal entries, and timelines) to understand how adjustments are analyzed and recorded.

The Trial Balance

The first step normally taken at the end of the accounting period is to create a trial balance, also known as an *unadjusted trial balance.* A **trial balance** is a list of individual accounts, usually in financial statement order, with their ending debit or credit balances. In a two-column format, debit balances are indicated in the left column and

LEARNING OBJECTIVE 1
Explain the purpose of a trial balance.
A trial balance is a list of all accounts with their balances to provide a check on the equality of the debits and credits.

credit balances are indicated in the right column. Then the two columns are totaled to provide a check on the equality of the debits and credits. In fact, that is all that the trial balance reflects. Many types of errors may still have been made even though debits equal credits:

- Wrong accounts may have been used in journal entries.
- Wrong but equal amounts may have been used in journal entries.
- Wrong accounts may have been posted from correct journal entries.
- Wrong but equal amounts may have been posted from correct journal entries.

The trial balance does not indicate a problem due to these errors. If the two columns are not equal, however, errors have occurred in one or more of the following:

- In preparing journal entries when debits do not equal credits.
- In posting the correct dollar effects of transactions from the journal entry to the ledger.
- In computing ending balances in accounts.
- In copying ending balances in the ledger to the trial balance.

These errors can be traced and should be corrected before moving to the next step. Even though computerized accounting systems should reduce some of these potential errors, the use of improper accounts or equal but incorrect amounts in transaction analysis may still occur.

We ended Chapter 3 with incomplete, unadjusted financial statements for Sbarro, Inc., because several internal transactions relating to revenue and expense items had not been recorded in the proper period. The unadjusted balances in the Chapter 3 T-accounts are listed in the trial balance in Exhibit 4.2. A trial balance is a schedule prepared for internal purposes and is not considered a financial statement for external users. The schedule should be clearly labeled, however, for future reference as in Exhibit 4.2.

You will notice that the Equipment account is stated at original cost of $235,300 in the trial balance but was stated at $127,650 (original cost minus the portion allocated to past operations) in the T-accounts in previous chapters. For long-lived assets such as equipment used in operations, individual account balances remain at original cost to preserve the historical information. To reflect the used-up portion of the assets' cost, a **contra**-asset, or offset, **account** is created. *Any contra-account is directly related to another account but has the opposite balance.* For equipment, the contra-asset is called Accumulated Depreciation—Equipment. It has a credit balance of $107,650. We will discuss many contra-accounts in other chapters and will designate contra-accounts with an X in front of the type of account to which it is related (e.g., Accumulated Depreciation [XA] for contra-asset).

The difference between an asset's acquisition cost and accumulated depreciation is called **book value (net book value** or **carrying value).** The book value does *not* represent the current market value of the asset because accounting for depreciation is a cost allocation process rather than a market valuation process (discussed later in the chapter). As do many other companies, Sbarro subtracts the balance in Accumulated Depreciation from the cost in the Equipment account, reporting the net amount on the balance sheet. The balance of each individual account is disclosed in a footnote to the financial statements. The note disclosure from a recent Sbarro annual report appears at the bottom of the opposite page.

A **contra-account** is an account that is an offset to, or reduction of, the primary account.

Book value (net book value, carrying value) of an asset is the difference between its acquisition cost and accumulated depreciation, its related contra-account.

EXHIBIT 4.2
Trial Balance for Sbarro, Inc.

REAL WORLD EXCERPT

SBARRO, INC.
Annual Report

SBARRO, INC. AND SUBSIDIARIES
Unadjusted Trial Balance
At February 2, 1996

	Debit	Credit
Cash	89,680	
Marketable securities	10,000	
Receivables (from franchisees and others)	3,100	
Inventory (supplies of food and paper products)	3,290	
Prepaid expenses	20,900	
Property and equipment	235,300	
Accumulated depreciation—equipment		107,650
Other assets	5,300	
Notes payable		1,200
Accounts payable		9,930
Accrued expenses payable (rent, payroll, and other)		27,000
Dividends payable		5,900
Income taxes payable		0
Unearned revenue		30
Deferred income taxes		14,100
Contributed capital		30,700
Retained earnings		153,100
Restaurant sales revenue		25,800
Franchise related income		500
Cost of food and paper products	2,100	
Wages expense	6,000	
Utilities expense	190	
Repairs expense	50	
Totals	375,910	375,910

Notes to Consolidated Financial Statements

3. PROPERTY AND EQUIPMENT

	(In thousands)	
	December 31, 1995	January 1, 1995
Leasehold improvements	$142,341	$142,264
Furniture, fixtures and equipment	83,679	83,773
Construction-in-progress (*)	9,278	9,102
	235,298	235,139
Less accumulated depreciation and amortization	108,541	94,430
	$126,757	$140,709

(*) Includes $6,351 in 1995 and $5,350 in 1994 related to the improvement and acquisition of the new corporate headquarters.

[1]*Note: Leasehold improvements* are modifications to leased property (property that is being rented), such as installing new plumbing or flooring or replacing an existing elevator or roof. These expenditures are assets because they have use beyond the current accounting period. *Construction-in-progress* refers to the accumulated costs to date for the construction of buildings and equipment that are not yet ready for use. In addition, the total amounts in the footnote do not exactly match with the property and equipment amounts indicated on Sbarro's balance sheets in Exhibit 2.2 because the amounts in the exhibit were rounded for simplification.

Adjusting Entries

We learned in the last chapter that under accrual accounting, revenues are recorded when earned and expenses are matched with the related revenues in the same period. Operating income for a period of time, therefore, is determined by measuring *all* revenues and expenses of that period. Often **adjusting entries** are necessary at the end of the accounting period to meet this objective. We also learned in the last chapter to identify when an account may need to be adjusted at the end of the accounting period. In reality, nearly all asset and liability accounts need to be analyzed and adjusted at year-end to measure income properly, correct errors, and provide for adequate valuation of accounts on the balance sheet. We introduce the adjustment process in this chapter for common adjusting entries. You will learn about additional adjustments in future chapters, most of which relate to the valuation of specific accounts such as accounts receivable and the corrections of errors.

You will recall that the two types of internal transactions requiring adjustment are deferrals and accruals:

1. *Deferrals.* Previously recorded assets, liabilities, revenues, or expenses that need to be adjusted at the end of the period to reflect revenues earned or expenses incurred in the current period. The following are examples:
   a. Insurance premium paid in advance of coverage:
      Prepaid Insurance (A)—*a deferred (or prepaid) expense*
   b. Rent collected in advance of occupancy by tenant:
      Unearned Rent Revenue (L)—*a deferred (or unearned) revenue*
2. *Accruals.* Revenues that have been earned and expenses that have been incurred by the end of the current accounting period but that will be collected or paid in a future accounting period. Examples follow:
   a. Interest earned but not yet collected on a loan made to an affiliate:
      Accrued Interest Receivable (A) (or simply Interest Receivable)—*an accrued revenue*
   b. Wages earned by employees but not yet paid:
      Accrued Wages and Salaries Payable (L) (or simply Wages and Salaries Payable)—*an accrued expense*

The process for determining the proper adjusting entry in each case is slightly more complex for deferrals than accruals. The three primary tools used in the process are T–accounts, timelines, and journal entries. We begin with deferrals.

Deferrals

Let's assume that the fiscal year for a dental office ends on December 31. The dentist maintains her accounting records on an accrual basis. At the end of the year, she identifies two items that require adjustment: (1) professional liability insurance paid in the past that provides for insurance coverage in the future and (2) unearned dental fees she received in advance from local businesses to provide dental care to their employees in the future. Insurance coverage and dental services are assumed to occur evenly over time unless otherwise indicated.

On November 15, she paid $1,800 for six months of insurance coverage (from November 15 to May 15 of next year). This results in $300 coverage each full month. By December 31 (the end of the fiscal period), the dentist will have received one and one-half months of coverage ($450). Therefore, for the current year, Insurance

Expense (E) should be $450 with $1,350 in the Prepaid Insurance (A) account on the balance sheet.

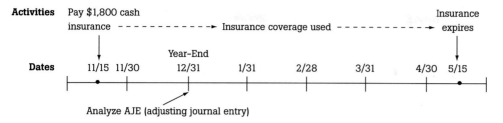

Amounts $1,800 for 6 months = $300 per month. By December 31, insurance for one and one-half months has been used; $450 should be the ending balance in insurance expense. The remaining $1,350 ($1,800 − $450) represents four and one-half months of future insurance coverage (an asset) on December 31.

Performing this level of analysis each time an entry is made, however, is cumbersome. It is easier for organizations to make a simple journal entry when cash is paid *without* anticipating the year-end balances and then adjust accounts at the end of the period. Therefore on November 15, the following entry is made:

Original entry on November 15:

Prepaid insurance expense (A)	1,800	
Cash (A)		1,800

On November 15, the amount paid represents future benefits (insurance coverage) to the dental office. This is the definition of an asset. As time passes while the dental office is insured, however, an adjustment is necessary to reflect that a portion of the asset has been used during the period. The used-up portion is an expense. The remaining unused portion provides future benefits into next year.

The process to determine the necessary adjustment at the end of the period utilizes the T-account:

Step 1. Create two T-accounts, one for the noncash balance sheet account and one for its related income statement account.

Fill in the unadjusted amount of the balance sheet account from the original entry (❶ in the following T-accounts).

Step 2. Determine the amounts needed as ending balances in each of the accounts. Consider using a timeline as created in the preceding analysis.

Fill in the desired ending balances in the T-accounts (❷ in the following T-accounts).

Step 3. The amounts needed to convert from the original entry to the appropriate ending balances create the adjusting journal entry (AJE) (❸ in the following T-accounts).

Prepaid Insurance Expense (A)		Insurance Expense (E)	
❶ 1,800			0
	AJE ❸ 450	AJE ❸ 450	
❷ 1,350		❷ 450	

Adjusting entry at the end of the period:

Insurance expense (E)	450	
Prepaid insurance expense (A)		450

Now we consider the second situation when, on December 1, the dental office accepted a $2,400 payment from local businesses to provide dental care to their employees over the next three months. The initial entry on December 1 was as follows:

Original entry on December 1:
Cash (A) 2,400
   Unearned dental fees (L) 2,400

The amount of cash received on December 1 represents what the dental office owes to clients in the future. This is a liability since either the cash received must be returned or the services must be delivered.

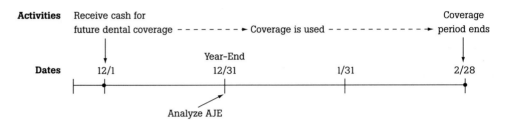

Activities Receive cash for future dental coverage - - - - - - - - ► Coverage is used - - - - - - - - - - - ► Coverage period ends

Dates 12/1   Year-End 12/31   1/31   2/28

Analyze AJE

Amounts $2,400 for 3 months = $800 per month. From December 1 to December 31, one month of dental service has been provided; $800 × 1 month = $800 dental fee revenue. The remainder of $1,600 ($2,400 − $800) represents future dental service owed to businesses (a liability).

The same 3-step adjustment process used in the preceding illustration is now followed:

Step 1. Create two T-accounts, one for the noncash balance sheet account and one for its related income statement account.

Fill in the unadjusted amount of the balance sheet account from the original entry (❶ in the following T-accounts).

Step 2. Determine the amounts needed as ending balances in each of the accounts. Consider using a timeline as created in the preceding analysis.

Fill in the desired ending balances in the T-accounts (❷ in the following T-accounts).

Step 3. The amounts needed to convert from the original entry to the appropriate ending balances create the adjusting journal entry (AJE) (❸ in the following T-accounts).

Unearned Dental Fees (L)		Dental Fees Revenue (R)	
	❶ 2,400		0
AJE ❸ 800		AJE ❸ 800	
	❷ 1,600	❷	800

Adjusting entry at the end of the period:
Unearned dental fees (L) 800
   Dental fees revenue (R) 800

Financial
ANALYSIS

An Optional Recordkeeping Efficiency

In the preceding examples, cash received or paid prior to revenue or expense recognition was recorded in a balance sheet account. This approach is consistent with accrual accounting since, on the cash exchange date, either an asset or liability exists. Payments or receipts are often recorded, however, as expenses or revenues on the cash transaction date. This is done to simplify recordkeeping since revenues or expenses are frequently earned or incurred by the end of the accounting period. When the full amount is not completely incurred or earned, an adjustment is necessary in these cases also.

For example, for the December 1 illustration, the original entry could have been recorded as follows:

Optional original entry on December 1:

Cash (A) 2,400

Dental fees revenue (R) 2,400

To determine the necessary adjustment, use the same process to create T-accounts and calculate the appropriate ending balances. The adjusting entry is the differences in the T-accounts.

Unearned Dental Fees (L)		Dental Fees Revenue (R)	
	0	❶	2,400
	AJE ❸ 1,600	AJE ❸ 1,600	
	❷ 1,600		❷ 800

Adjusting entry at the end of the period:

Dental fees revenue (R) 1,600

Unearned dental fees (L) 1,600

Regardless of how the original entry is recorded, the same correct ending balances in the Unearned Dental Fees and Dental Fees Revenue accounts result after the adjustment. The adjusting entry is different, however, in each case.

Accruals

Accruals occur when no cash has been received or paid, but the company has undertaken activities that result in earning revenues or incurring expenses. Unlike deferrals, no original entry has been recorded. Therefore, the process for adjusting the accounts is simpler. Here we compute the amount to be recorded directly.

Let us continue our example of the adjustment process for the dental office. Two activities that normally require an accrued expense and an accrued revenue adjustment are wages to employees and interest on a loan to an employee.

Assume that all employees are paid $3,000 biweekly. Payment for 10 working days is made on the second Friday. The last payment for the year was on Friday, December 27. The employees continued to work through December 31, the end of the accounting period, but they will not be paid until January 10.

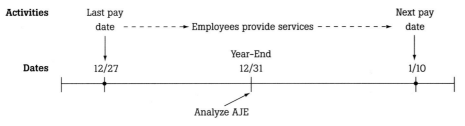

Activities	Last pay date	- - - - - - - ► Employees provide services - - - - - - - - ►	Next pay date
		Year-End	
Dates	12/27	12/31	1/10

Analyze AJE

Amounts $3,000 for 10 working days = $300 per working day. Assume that there are two weekend days and two working days from December 28 through December 31; $300 × 2 working days = $600 to be recorded as wages expense in the current period.

The adjusting journal entry is as follows:

Wages expense (E)	600
Wages payable (L)	600

Since no entry related to the $600 expense had been recorded in the past, the adjusting entry increases an expense and increases a payable by the computed amount. Then, on the January 10 payday in the next period, the entry is as follows:

Wages expense (E)	2,400
Wages payable (L)	600
Cash	3,000

The $3,000 is paid, but only $2,400 relates to the expense incurred in the second period. The $600 was properly recorded as an expense in the prior period and is now paid (the liability is reduced).

As a second example, the dental office loaned $2,000 to an employee on September 1 for which the employee signed a note. The note principal along with interest at a 12 percent annual rate is to be repaid in six months. Interest is the cost of borrowing money. As each day passes, more interest is owed. By the end of the year, four months have passed, so the dental office has earned four months of interest revenue for which it will not be paid until March 1.

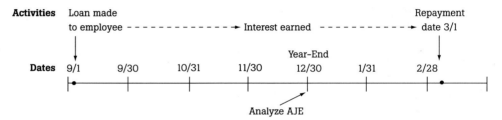

Amounts   Interest is calculated by the following formula:

Principal	×	Annual interest rate	×	Time period (part of year)	=	Interest for the period
$2,000	×	.12	×	4/12	=	$80

The adjusting journal entry is as follows:

Interest receivable (A)	80
Interest revenue (R)	80

Since the accrued revenue has not yet been recorded until the end of the period, the adjusting entry increases a receivable and increases a revenue by the computed amount. When the employee pays the interest and principal on March 1 of the next period, the entry is as follows:

Cash (A)	2,120
Note receivable (A)	2,000
Interest receivable (A)	80
Interest revenue (R)	40

The $2,120 received in cash on March 1 includes $2,000 in principal repayment and $120 for interest. Four months of interest were recognized in the preceding year as interest revenue and the other two months of interest ($40) will be recognized in the next period.

In summary, since no previous entry has been made, expense accruals *increase* an expense and a payable and revenue accruals *increase* a revenue and a receivable. As a consequence, we directly compute the amount of the needed adjustment. Deferred accounts already exist, however, at the end of the accounting period from a previous entry. Either a revenue, expense, asset, or liability is overstated and must be *decreased;* its related account is understated and must be *increased.* Here we compute the cor-

Sbarro considers its flagship product, the Sbarro pizza, its "Best Pie Chart."

rected ending balance in the account and adjust the balances to that number. In each case, T-accounts and timelines can be quite useful.

When adjustments are completed, the adjusted balances are used to prepare financial statements, which is the next step of the accounting cycle. Before we illustrate a complete set of financial statements, we need to adjust the accounts of Sbarro, Inc., at the end of the month. Recall from Chapter 3 that Sbarro's policy for fiscal year-end is the Sunday closest to the end of the month. Therefore, we adjust the accounts on February 2, the Sunday closest to month-end.[1] Companies can choose fiscal periods other than actual month-ends, and financial statements can cover different accounting periods (month, quarter, or year).

Accruals and Deferrals: The Keys to Financial Reporting Strategy

Most of the deferrals and accruals discussed in this chapter, such as the allocation of prepaid insurance or the determination of accrued interest revenue, involve direct calculations and little judgment on the part of the company's accountants. In later chapters, we will discuss many other adjustments that involve difficult and complex estimates about the future. These include, for example, estimates of customers' ability to make payments to the company for purchases on account, the useful lives of new machines, and future amounts that a company may owe on warranties of products sold in the past. Each of these estimates and many others can have significant effects on the stream of net earnings that companies report over time.

When analysts attempt to value firms based on their balance sheet and income statement data, they also evaluate the estimates that form the basis for accruals and deferrals. Those firms that make relatively pessimistic estimates that reduce current income are judged to follow conservative financial reporting strategies, and their reports of performance are given more credence by experienced analysts. The earnings numbers reported by these companies are often said to be of "higher quality" because they are less influenced by management's natural optimism. Firms that consistently make optimistic estimates that result in reporting higher net income, however, are judged to be aggressive. Analysts judge these companies' operating performance to be of lower quality.

---

[1] Adjusting entries may be prepared monthly, quarterly, and/or annually to ensure that proper amounts are included on the financial reports presented to external users.

Adjusting Entries Illustrated

We illustrate common adjusting entries by updating the accounts of Sbarro, Inc., based on the account balances and transactions in Chapters 2 and 3. As we review Sbarro's trial balance in Exhibit 4.2, we can identify several deferral accounts that will need to be analyzed and may need to be adjusted:

Inventory	A portion of each has been used during the month.
Prepaid Expenses (e.g., rent and insurance)	All or a portion may have been used by month-end.
Property and Equipment	A portion has been used during the month.
Unearned Revenue	All or a portion may have been earned by month-end; however, the entire balance represents services due to customers in February. No adjustment will be necessary.

In addition, we can see that several accruals need to be recorded for activities that have generated unrecorded revenues or expenses:

Marketable Securities	An investment in stocks and bonds usually produces investment income (dividends on stocks and interest on bonds).
Receivables	Franchisees may owe additional royalties to Sbarro that should be recognized as revenue by February 2.
Notes Payable	Sbarro would normally owe interest on any borrowed funds that should be recognized as an expense and interest payable.
Accrued Expenses Payable	Any rent due to mall owners, wages due to employees, and amounts due for utilities not yet due by or billed to Sbarro need to be recorded as expenses.
Income Taxes Payable	Income tax expense needs to be recorded for the period.

We use the three steps outlined earlier for deferrals and the simpler process for accruals. You should study the following illustration carefully to understand the steps in the adjustment process, paying close attention to the computation of the amounts in the adjustment and the effects on the account balances. First, we adjust the deferrals and then the accruals.

Adjusting Deferral Accounts

We adjust the following deferral accounts as identified: *Prepaid Expenses* for rent and insurance, *Inventory* of food and paper product supplies, *Property and Equipment* used during the month, and *Unearned Revenue*. In each adjusting transaction for deferrals, we (1) create T-accounts for the balance sheet account and its related income statement account, (2) determine the appropriate ending balances, and (3) identify the adjustment that is necessary.

Adjustment (a) On January 30, the managers of the company-owned restaurants counted $2,670 (❷ in the following T-accounts) in food and paper products supplies inventory on hand. The rest was used during January.

Inventory used during the period is an expense account, "Cost of Food and Paper Products." This account has a balance of $2,100 (❶ in the following T-accounts) from the transactions during the month (illustrated in Chapters 2 and 3). The unadjusted balance in the Inventory account is $3,290 (also ❶). The adjustment for the used portion is $620 (❸).

Inventory (A)		Cost of Food and Paper Products (E)	
❶ 3,290	AJE ❸ 620	❶ 2,100	
		AJE ❸ 620	
❷ 2,670		❷ 2,720	

Cost of food and paper products (E) 620
    Inventory (A) 620

The effect on the accounting equation is as follows:

Assets	=	Liabilities	+	Stockholders' Equity
Inventory – 620				Cost of Food and Paper Products – 620

Adjustment (b) Prepaid Expenses of $20,900 (❶ in the following T-accounts) includes an $18,600 payment made in early January for the rental of mall space at several malls for the three-month period from January through March. (The remaining $2,300 in Prepaid Expenses pertains to insurance and other items that were not used in January and therefore do not need to be adjusted at the end of the month.)

Rent expense is $18,600 for 3 months or $6,200 per month. At the end of January, one month has passed and two months remain. The Prepaid Expenses ending balance = $20,900 – 6,200 = $14,700 (❷). The adjustment is for the used portion (Rent Expense) of $6,200 (❸).

Prepaid Expenses (A)		Rent Expense (occupancy and other) (E)	
❶ 20,900	AJE ❸ 6,200	❶ 0	
		AJE ❸ 6,200	
❷ 14,700		❷ 6,200	

Rent expense—occupancy and other (E) 6,200
    Prepaid expenses (A) 6,200

The words *occupancy and other* added after Rent Expense represent the categorization of rent expense on Sbarro's income statement. Many accounts of similar nature are often aggregated or combined in the financial statements. In this case, rent expense that Sbarro categorizes as Occupancy and Other Expenses relates to operating the company-owned restaurants. We need to know this categorization when we prepare the financial statements. We will see in the next analysis that expenses for operations often are separated from expenses not directly related to operations, such as rent for administrative offices and salaries of the employees working in the offices.

The effect on the accounting equation is as follows:

Assets	=	Liabilities	+	Stockholders' Equity
Prepaid Expenses – 6,200				Rent Expense – 6,200

> **Adjustment (c)** Property and Equipment with a historical cost of $235,300 and Accumulated Depreciation of $107,650 (❶ in the following T-accounts) has an estimated useful life of eight years (or 96 months = 8 years × 12 months per year) and an estimated residual (salvage) value of $4,900.

When long-lived assets are used over time, accountants say that they are *depreciated* (for tangible assets such as plant and equipment) or *amortized* (for intangible assets such as patents on inventions). The accounting process of depreciation and amortization involves the systematic and rational allocation of the cost of an operational asset over its useful life to the periods in which the asset is used to generate revenues.

A common misconception held by students and others unfamiliar with accounting terminology is that depreciation reflects the asset's decline in market value. This concept of depreciation and amortization in an accounting context *does not necessarily match the change in the market value* of the asset. Thus, this concept differs from the layperson's usage in the statement that a new car "depreciates" when it is driven off the dealer's lot. In accounting, depreciation is a *cost allocation* concept, not a *valuation concept*. Accumulated Depreciation is the amount of the historical cost allocated to prior periods. It is a contra-asset account directly related to the Property and Equipment account.

Depreciation and amortization will be discussed in much greater detail in Chapter 8. To simplify matters until we reach that chapter, we assume that long-lived assets used in operations provide benefits to the company evenly over time. Therefore, the historical cost is depreciated or amortized in equal amounts each period. This is known as the *straight-line* method. Depreciation for each period is computed under the straight-line method using the following formula:

$$(\text{Cost} - \text{Residual value}) \div \text{Useful life} = \text{Depreciation or amortization expense for the period}$$

Residual value is the asset's estimated sales price or scrap value at the end of its useful life to the company. Intangible assets (such as patents and copyrights) do not usually have a residual value at the end of their useful lives. Plant and equipment often do, however. When the amount of depreciation is computed for a year (quarter or month), the useful life should be stated in the same time units (years, quarters, or months). The computation for the amount of depreciation in this illustration for January is as follows:

$$(\$235,300 - \$4,900) \div 96 \text{ months} = \$2,400 \text{ per month } (❸ \text{ in the example})$$

Accumulated Depreciation– Equipment (XA)			Depreciation Expense (E)		
	❶	107,650	❶	0	
	AJE ❸	**2,400**	AJE ❸ **2,400**		
	❷	110,050	❷	2,400	

Depreciation expense (E)   2,400
    Accumulated depreciation—equipment (XA)   2,400

The effect on the accounting equation is as follows:

Assets	=	Liabilities	+	Stockholders' Equity
Accumulated Depreciation – 2,400				Depreciation Expense – 2,400

Adjusting Accrual Accounts

Now we will adjust accruals, those revenues and expenses that are not yet recorded. From the trial balance, we identified investment income on marketable securities, amounts due from franchisees, interest expense on borrowed funds, and several accrued expenses (rent due to mall owners, wages due to employees, and amounts due for utilities not yet billed to Sbarro). Since we have identified potential accruals, we will use the adjustment process described earlier in the chapter to determine the proper adjusting entry in each case. Income Taxes Payable is determined after all other adjustments are made.

> **Adjustment (d)** Sbarro invested in marketable debt securities that pay interest revenue. We assume that these investments, which have a principal balance of $10,000 listed in the trial balance, pay 6 percent annual interest, but no cash for interest earned was received in January. Therefore, interest revenue needs to be accrued for January.

Interest is computed using the following formula:

Principal (P) × Annual interest rate (I) × Time period (part of year) (T) = Interest for the period
$10,000 × .06 × 1/12 = $50 for the month

Interest receivable (A)	50	
Interest revenue (R)		50

The effect on the accounting equation is as follows:

Assets	=	Liabilities	+	Stockholders' Equity	
Interest Receivable	+50			Interest Revenue	+50

> **Adjustment (e)** The franchisees reported that they owed Sbarro $130 in additional revenue for their sales in the fourth week of January. They will pay Sbarro in February.

The amount to be accrued is given as $130 in Franchise Related Income.

Receivables (A)	130	
Franchise related income (R)		130

The effect on the accounting equation is as follows:

Assets	=	Liabilities	+	Stockholders' Equity	
Receivables	+130			Franchise Related Income	+130

> **Adjustment (f)** The January rental fee for Sbarro's leased headquarters building is $90, which will be paid in February.

The amount for unrecorded rent expense for use of the headquarters building in January is given as $90. Such expenses are categorized as *general and administrative.*

Rent expense—general and administrative (E) 90

Accrued expenses payable (L) 90

The effect on the accounting equation is as follows:

Assets	=	Liabilities	+	Stockholders' Equity	
		Accrued Expenses Payable	+90	Rent Expense	–90

Adjustment (g) Sbarro received a utility bill on February 4 that included $65 for eight days of electric and gas usage at company-owned restaurants during January.

Most companies cannot adjust and issue financial statements on the last day of the accounting period because they need more time for analysis of necessary adjustments, preparation of financial statements, and completion of an audit. Therefore, it is possible to receive bills early in the next period relating to the prior period and make appropriate adjustments. If such a bill is not available, Sbarro estimates the amount owed.

The amount to be accrued as Utilities Expense is given as $65.

Utilities expense—occupancy and other (E) 65

Accrued expenses payable (L) 65

The effect on the accounting equation is as follows:

Assets	=	Liabilities	+	Stockholders' Equity	
		Accrued Expenses Payable	+65	Utilities Expense	–65

SELF-STUDY QUIZ

Now complete the next two accruals following the steps in the adjustment process just illustrated.

Adjustment (h) Employees in company-owned restaurants are paid every two weeks on Fridays. The last payday was January 23. Employees earned an additional $600 between January 23 and

_____ .... _____

Accrued expenses payable (L) .... _____

The effect on the accounting equation is as follows:

Assets	=	Liabilities	+	Stockholders' Equity	
		Accrued Expenses Payable	+600	Wages Expense	–600

Adjustment (i) Sbarro owes interest expense on the $1,200 note. Both principal and interest will be paid together when the note is due. Therefore, interest must be accrued over time until paid. The annual interest rate on the note is 10 percent.

Interest is accrued for January (one month).

The formula is _____ × _____ × _____ = _____

The amount is _____ × _____ × _____ = $10

Interest expense (E) 10

_____ 10

The effect on the accounting equation is as follows:

Assets	=	Liabilities	+	Stockholders' Equity
		Interest Payable +10		Interest Expense −10

You can check your answers with the solution in the footnote at the bottom of this page.*

Adjustment (j) The final adjusting journal entry is to record the accrual of state, federal, and foreign government income taxes due (an unrecorded expense). We will use a 39 percent income tax rate.

To compute the income taxes, we need to determine pretax income as follows:

All revenues	$26,480	$25,800 + 500 + 50 + 130
− All expenses	−18,325	$ 2,720 + 6,600 + 255 + 50 + 10 + 2,400 + 6,290
Income before taxes	$ 8,155	
× 39% tax rate	× 0.39	
Income tax expense	$ 3,180	

Income tax expense (E) 3,180

Income taxes payable (L) 3,180

The effect on the accounting equation is as follows:

Assets	=	Liabilities	+	Stockholders' Equity
		Income Taxes Payable +3,180		Income Tax Expense −3,180

Exhibit 4.3 now shows the adjusted trial balance, which was constructed by adding all of the adjustments made in Adjustments (*a*) through (*j*) to the appropriate account balances in the unadjusted trial balance in Exhibit 4.2. This is effectively similar to creating several T-accounts and determining ending balances. Any new accounts created during the adjustment process are included. From this group of adjusted balances, we can prepare a complete set of accrual-based financial statements at the end of the accounting period (February 2).

End-of-Period Adjustments and Auditing

Since end-of-period adjustments are the most complex portion of the annual recordkeeping process, they are prone to error. As noted in Chapter 1, external auditors (independent CPAs) examine the company's records on a test, or sample, basis. To maximize the chance of detecting any errors significant

---

* Adjustment (*h*)   The amount of the accrual is given as $600. The adjusting journal entry is

        Wages expense (E) 600

           Accrued expenses payable (L) 600

Adjustment (*i*)   The formula to compute interest is

Principal (P)	×	Annual interest rate (I)	×	Time period (part of year) (T)	=	Interest for the period
$1,200	×	.10	×	1/12	=	$10 for January

    The adjusting journal entry follows:

        Interest expense (E) 10

          Interest payable (L) 10

EXHIBIT 4.3
Adjusted Trial Balance for Sbarro, Inc.

	Unadjusted		Adjustments		Adjusted	
SBARRO, INC. AND SUBSIDIARIES Trial Balance At February 2, 1996						
	Debit	Credit	Debit	Credit	Debit	Credit
Cash	89,680				89,680	
Marketable securities	10,000				10,000	
Receivables (from franchisees and others)	3,100		(e) 130		3,230	
Interest receivable	0		(d) 50		50	
Inventory (supplies of food and paper products)	3,290			(a) 620	2,670	
Prepaid expenses	20,900			(b) 6,200	14,700	
Property and equipment	235,300				235,300	
Accumulated depreciation—equipment		107,650		(c) 2,400		110,050
Other assets	5,300				5,300	
Notes payable		1,200				1,200
Accounts payable		9,930				9,930
Accrued expenses payable (rent, payroll, and other)		27,000		(f) 90 (g) 65 (h) 600		27,755
Interest payable		0		(i) 10		10
Dividends payable		5,900				5,900
Income taxes payable		0		(j) 3,180		3,180
Unearned revenue		30				30
Deferred income taxes		14,100				14,100
Contributed capital		30,700				30,700
Retained earnings		153,100				153,100
Restaurant sales revenue		25,800				25,800
Franchise related income		500		(e) 130		630
Interest revenue		0		(d) 50		50
Cost of food and paper products	2,100		(a) 620		2,720	
Wages expense	6,000		(h) 600		6,600	
Rent expense (occupancy and other)	0		(b) 6,200		6,200	
Utilities expense (occupancy and other)	190		(g) 65		255	
Repairs expense (occupancy and other)	50				50	
Depreciation expense	0		(c) 2,400		2,400	
Rent expense (general and administrative)	0		(f) 90		90	
Interest expense	0		(i) 10		10	
Income tax expense	0		(j) 3,180		3,180	
Totals	375,910	375,910	13,345	13,345	382,435	382,435

enough to affect users' decisions, CPAs allocate more of their testing to transactions most likely to be in error. A number of accounting research studies have documented the most error-prone transactions for medium-sized manufacturing companies.* End-of-period accrual errors such as "failure to provide adequate product warranty liability," "failure to include items that should be accrued," and "end-of-period transactions recorded in the wrong period" (called *cut-off errors*) are in the top category and thus receive a great deal of attention from the auditors.

* J. R. Coakley and J. K. Loebbecke, "The Expectation of Accounting Errors in Medium-Sized Manufacturing Firms," *Advances in Accounting,* vol. 2 (1985), pp. 199–245.

Financial Statement Preparation

The next step of the accounting cycle is to prepare a complete set of financial statements:

- Income statement.
- Statement of stockholders' equity.[2]
- Balance sheet.
- Statement of cash flows.

LEARNING OBJECTIVE 3
Present a complete set of financial statements: income statement, statement of stockholders' equity, balance sheet, and statement of cash flows.

First, we will illustrate the relationships between the statements, that is, how the numbers in one statement flow into the next statement.

The transaction analysis model developed in Chapter 3 is reprinted in Exhibit 4.4. It illustrates how information flows from the income statement to the statement of stockholders' equity to the balance sheet. The portions of the model that relate to these three statements are indicated by overlapping circles.

Circle 1 highlights the information used on the income statement that can be represented by the income statement equation:

$$\text{Net income} = (\text{Revenues} + \text{Gains}) - (\text{Expenses} + \text{Losses})$$

Circle 2 highlights the components of the statement of stockholders' equity. Net income and dividends affect retained earnings, a component of stockholders' equity. These changes can be represented by the retained earnings equation:

$$\text{Ending retained earnings} = \text{Beginning retained earnings} + \text{Net income} - \text{Dividends}$$

EXHIBIT 4.4
Transaction Analysis Model

---

[2] Other complex transactions such as stock dividends, which also are reported on this statement, are discussed in Chapter 11.

Notice that net income from the first equation is included in the second equation. Stock issuances and repurchases (discussed in more detail in Chapter 11) can be represented by a similar equation:

$$\text{Ending contributed capital} = \text{Beginning contributed capital} + \text{Stock issuances} - \text{Stock repurchases}$$

The changes in retained earnings and contributed capital during the period are normally represented as separate columns on the statement of stockholders' equity. Then the ending balances in retained earnings, contributed capital, and total stockholders' equity are included in the balance sheet (Circle 3). These relationships are represented in the balance sheet equation:

$$\text{Assets} = \text{Liabilities} + \text{Stockholders' Equity}$$

The fourth and final statement of cash flows explains the difference between the ending and beginning balances in the Cash account on the balance sheet during the accounting period. Put simply, the cash flow statement is a categorized list of all transactions of the period that affected the Cash account. The three categories are operating, investing, and financing activities. Therefore, the equation for this statement becomes:

$$\text{Change in cash for the period} = \text{Cash from operations} \pm \text{Cash from investing activities} \pm \text{Cash from financing activities}$$

Now we can create a complete set of financial statements for Sbarro, Inc., for the month ended February 2, 1996, based on the account balances presented in the adjusted trial balance in Exhibit 4.3 and the preceding equations. We will follow the flow of information indicated in Exhibit 4.4.

Income Statement

Each income statement account (revenue, expense, gain, and loss) should be properly categorized on the income statement. Note that rent, utilities, and repairs expense are combined as occupancy and other expenses on the statement. In addition, rent expense is also classified as a general and administrative expense.

This statement based on adjusted balances more closely resembles the actual Sbarro annual income statement presented at the beginning of Chapter 3 in Exhibit 3.2 except for two items: (1) the amounts are for one month only and (2) Sbarro does not have any interest expense since it does not have any notes payable. Actual income statements prepared for external parties, as you may recall, are normally prepared quarterly and annually (presenting three years of data), although we have simplified this requirement in this chapter.

Earnings per share (EPS) also is reported on the income statement or in the notes to the statements. For companies such as Sbarro, Inc., which have simple capital structures (no other debt or equity securities that could potentially increase the number of shares of stock outstanding), earnings per share is computed as follows:

$$\text{EPS} = \frac{\text{Net income}}{\text{Weighted-average number of shares of stock outstanding during the period}}$$

REAL WORLD EXCERPT

SBARRO, INC.
Annual Report

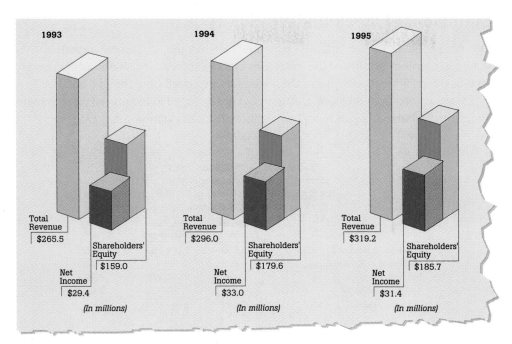

Sbarro also uses graphs to communicate key financial data.

The calculation of the denominator is complex and is presented in other accounting courses. Based on the actual Sbarro annual report for 1995, the weighted-average number of shares of stock outstanding was approximately 20,337,000. For simplicity, we can use this same denominator in the computations of the earnings per share shown on the income statement.

$$\$8,155,000 \div 20,337,000 = \$.40 \text{ per share (rounded)}$$

Additional EPS disclosures will be discussed in Chapter 5.

SBARRO, INC., AND SUBSIDIARIES
Income Statement
For the Month Ended February 2, 1996
(in thousands of dollars)

Revenues		
Restaurant sales		$25,800
Franchise related income		630
Interest revenue		50
Total revenues		$26,480
Costs and expenses		
Cost of food and paper products		2,720
Restaurant operating expenses:		
Payroll and other employee benefits (wages)	$6,600	
Occupancy and other expenses (rent, utilities, and repairs)	6,505	13,105
Depreciation expense		2,400
General and administrative expense (rent)		90
Total costs and expenses		$18,315
Income before interest and income taxes		8,165
Interest expense		10
Income after interest and before income taxes		$ 8,155
Income taxes		3,180
Net income		$ 4,975
Earnings per share		$ .40

Statement of Stockholders' Equity

The final total from the income statement, net income, is carried forward to the Retained Earnings portion of the statement of stockholders' (or shareholders') equity. To this, the additional elements of the statement are added from the trial balance.

Transactions from previous chapters also are included in the preceding statement: dividends declared (Chapter 3) and an additional stock issuance (Chapter 2).

SBARRO, INC. AND SUBSIDIARIES
Statement of Shareholders' Equity
For the Month Ended February 2, 1996
(in thousands of dollars)

	Contributed Capital	Retained Earnings	Total
Balance at December 31, 1995	$30,500	$155,100	$185,600
Additional stock issuance	200		200
Net income		4,975	4,975
Dividends declared		(2,000)	(2,000)
Balance at February 2, 1996	$30,700	$158,075	$188,775

Balance Sheet

The ending balances in the shareholders' equity accounts are then carried to the balance sheet with the remaining assets and liabilities taken from the trial balance.

SBARRO, INC. AND SUBSIDIARIES
Balance Sheets
At February 2, 1996 and December 31, 1995
(in thousands of dollars)

	February 2, 1996	December 31, 1995
ASSETS		
Cash	$ 89,680	$ 93,500
Marketable securities	10,000	10,000
Receivables (franchise fees, interest, and other)	3,280	2,600
Inventory	2,670	2,800
Prepaid expenses	14,700	1,700
Equipment (net of accumulated depreciation of $110,050 on February 2, 1996, and $107,650 on December 31, 1995)	125,250	126,800
Other assets	5,300	5,300
Total assets	**$250,880**	**$242,700**
LIABILITIES		
Notes payable	$ 1,200	$ 0
Accounts payable	9,930	7,400
Accrued expenses payable (rent, payroll, and other)	27,755	27,000
Interest payable	10	0
Dividends payable	5,900	3,900
Income taxes payable	3,180	4,700
Unearned revenue	30	0
Deferred income taxes	14,100	14,100
Total liabilities	$ 62,105	$ 57,100
STOCKHOLDERS' EQUITY		
Contributed capital	$ 30,700	$ 30,500
Retained earnings	158,075	155,100
Total stockholders' equity	188,775	185,600
Total liabilities and stockholders' equity	**$250,880**	**$242,700**

The balances for contributed capital and retained earnings from the statement of shareholders' equity flow into the balance sheet. You will notice that the contra-asset account, Accumulated Depreciation, has been subtracted from the Equipment account to reflect net book value (or carrying value) at month-end for balance sheet purposes. Detailed information on the cost of the equipment and the balance in the Accumulated Depreciation account could be provided in footnotes to the statements. You also will notice that three accounts (Marketable Securities, Other Assets, and Deferred Income Taxes) did not change during the month. No transactions affected these accounts.

Statement of Cash Flows

We stated earlier that the statement of cash flows describes the changes in cash for the period and categorizes the changes as to operating, investing, and financing activities. In Chapters 2 and 3, we analyzed and grouped the cash transactions into one of the three categories. Since no adjustments made in this chapter affected cash, we can combine the information from the previous chapters into a statement of cash flows for the month.

Recall that *operating activities* are those involving the sale of services or goods (products) to customers, including the payment of interest on debt and income taxes. *Investing activities* are those involving the purchase and sale of long-term investments, loans to others (e.g., employees, subsidiaries, franchisees), and the purchase and sale of long-term assets (such as equipment, land, and patents). *Financing activities* are those involving issuing or borrowing and repaying debt, issuing and repurchasing stock, and paying dividends.

SBARRO, INC. AND SUBSIDIARIES
Statement of Cash Flows
For the Month Ended February 2, 1996
(in thousands of dollars)

OPERATING ACTIVITIES		
Cash inflows		
From customers	$25,830	
From franchisees	0	
From investments	0	$25,830
Cash outflows		
To suppliers	$19,660	
To employees	6,000	
For income taxes	4,700	
For interest	0	30,360
Net cash provided by operating activities		$ (4,530)
INVESTING ACTIVITIES		
Cash inflows		
Repayment of loan by employee	$ 40	40
Cash outflows		
Purchase of equipment	190	
Loan to employee	40	230
Net cash used in investing activities		$ (190)
FINANCING ACTIVITIES		
Cash inflows		
Proceeds from bank borrowing	$ 1,000	
Additional stock issuance	200	1,200
Cash outflows		
Repayment of bank note	$ 300	
Payment of dividends	0	300
Net cash provided by financing activities		$ 900
Decrease in cash		$ (3,820)
Cash at the beginning of the month		93,500
Cash at the end of the month		$89,680

You can see that the statement ties to the balance sheet. The beginning cash balance for the month ($93,500) and the ending cash balance for the month ($89,680) on the balance sheet are the same as those reported on the statement of cash flows. Information is provided on how Sbarro acquired and spent cash during the month.

The format we have shown for operating activities is known as the *direct method,* although most companies use the *indirect method.* We will provide an example of this form in the statement of cash flows for Callaway Golf, Inc., in Chapter 5. In addition, we provide a more detailed look at constructing and using the statement of cash flows in Chapter 13.

FOCUS ON CASH FLOWS

A misconception is that positive net income is equivalent to an increase in cash. Because net income is calculated on the accrual basis, however, revenues may be recognized although the cash has not yet been received, and cash may have been paid before expenses are recognized. The Sbarro illustration in this chapter is a clear example of this. The net income for the month was determined to be a positive $4,975,000, yet we see in the statement of cash flows that cash actually declined for the period by $3,820,000 and cash flows from operations resulted in a negative $4,530,000.

We must be careful in drawing any conclusions from this observation because the time period is only one month. Over the long run, however, companies must have positive cash flows from operations to remain viable. In fact, Sbarro has generated approximately $54,000,000 in positive cash flows from operations each year since 1994.

Cash Flow from Operations, Net Income, and Financial Analysis

Many standard financial analysis texts warn analysts to be on the lookout for unusual deferrals and accruals when they attempt to predict future periods' earnings. They often suggest that wide disparities between net income and cash flow from operations is a useful warning sign. For example, Bernstein suggests that

> **Analysts prefer to relate CFO [cash flow from operations] to reported net income as a check on the quality of that income. Some analysts believe that the higher the ratio of CFO to net income, the higher the quality of that income. Put another way, a company with a high level of net income and a low cash flow may be using income recognition or expense accrual criteria that are suspect.***

** L. Bernstein, *Financial Statement Analysis* (Burr Ridge, IL: Richard D. Irwin, 1993), p. 461.*

QUESTION OF ETHICS

Incentives, Accruals, and Ethics

We noted in Chapter 1 that owners and managers of companies are most directly affected by the information presented in financial statements. If the financial performance and condition of the company appear strong, the company's stock price rises. Shareholders usually receive dividends and increase their investment value. Managers often receive bonuses based on the strength of a company's financial performance, and many in top management are compensated with options to buy their company's stock at prices below market. The higher the market value, the more compensation they earn. When actual performance lags behind expectations, managers and owners may be tempted to manipulate accruals and deferrals to make up part of the difference. For

example, managers may record cash received in advance of being earned as revenue in the current period or may fail to accrue certain expenses at year-end.

Evidence from studies of large samples of companies indicates that some do engage in such behavior. This research is borne out by enforcement actions of the Securities and Exchange Commission against companies and sometimes against their auditors. These SEC enforcement actions most often relate to accrual of revenue and receivables that should be deferred to future periods.* In many of these cases, the firms involved, their managers, and their auditors are penalized for such actions. Further, owners suffer because the company's stock price is affected negatively by news of an SEC investigation.

*E. H. Feroz, K. Park, and V. S. Pastena, "The Financial and Market Effects of the SEC's Accounting and Auditing Enforcement Releases," *Journal of Accounting Research* (Supplement 1991), pp. 107–142.

The Closing Process

You will notice in Exhibit 4.4 that a dashed line separates income statement accounts (revenues, expenses, gains, and losses) and dividends from the balance sheet accounts (assets, liabilities, and stockholders' equity). The balance sheet accounts are updated continuously throughout the accounting period, and the ending balance for the current period becomes the beginning account balance for the next. These accounts are *not* closed (cleared to a zero balance) periodically; therefore, they are often called **permanent** or **real accounts**. To illustrate, the ending cash balance of one accounting period must be the beginning cash balance of the next accounting period. The only time a permanent account has a zero balance is when the item represented is no longer owned or owed.

In contrast, revenue, expense, gain, and loss accounts are often called **temporary,** or **nominal accounts** because they are used to accumulate data for the current *accounting period only*. At the end of each period, their balances are transferred, or closed, to the Retained Earnings account. This periodic clearing of the balances of the income statement accounts into Retained Earnings is done by using closing entries.

The process of recording **closing entries** to transfer the balances of all temporary accounts to Retained Earnings is only a clerical phase. Closing entries have two purposes: (1) to transfer net income or loss to Retained Earnings and (2) to establish a zero balance in each of the temporary accounts to start the accumulation in the next accounting period. Accounts with credit balances are closed by debiting the total amount; accounts with debit balances are closed by crediting the total amount. The other half of the entry is closed directly to Retained Earnings (although companies may close income statement accounts to a special temporary summary account, called **Income Summary,** which is then closed to Retained Earnings). In this way, the income statement accounts are again ready for their temporary accumulation function for the next period.

Referring to Exhibit 4.4, the process involves closing the lowest level of accounts in the model to the permanent account (Retained Earnings):

1. Close all revenues and gains (income statement accounts with a credit balance) to Retained Earnings.
2. Close all expenses and losses (income statement accounts with a debit balance) to Retained Earnings.

Closing entries are dated the last day of the accounting period, entered in the usual debits-equal-credits format (in the journal), and immediately posted to the ledger (or

LEARNING OBJECTIVE 4
Explain the closing process.

Permanent (real) accounts are the balance sheet accounts that carry their ending balances into the next accounting period.

Temporary (nominal) accounts are income statement (and sometimes dividends declared) accounts that are closed at the end of the accounting period.

Closing entries are made at the end of the accounting period to transfer balances in temporary accounts to retained earnings and to establish a zero balance in each of the temporary accounts.

Income Summary is a temporary account used only during the closing process to facilitate closing revenues and expenses.

T-accounts). We illustrate the closing process by preparing and posting the closing entries for Sbarro, Inc., at February 2, 1996, although most companies close their records only at the end of the fiscal year. The amounts are taken from the adjusted trial balance in Exhibit 4.3. The T-accounts following the entries reflect the flow of the amounts into the permanent account, Retained Earnings. Closing entries are referenced with CE. For illustrative purposes, only summary T-accounts for revenues, expenses, gains, and losses are shown. Normally, each account is closed.

1. Close revenues and gains to Retained Earnings:

Restaurant sales revenue	25,800	
Franchise related income	630	
Interest revenue	50	
Retained earnings		26,480

2. Close expenses and losses to Retained Earnings:

Retained earnings	21,505	
Cost of food and paper products		2,720
Wages expense		6,600
Rent expense (occupancy and other)		6,200
Utilities expense (occupancy and other)		255
Repairs expense (occupancy and other)		50
Depreciation expense		2,400
Rent expense (general and administrative)		90
Interest expense		10
Income tax expense		3,180

Retained Earnings

			153,100
CE2	21,505	CE1	26,480
		Ending Balance	158,075

All Expenses and Losses			**All Revenues and Gains**		
21,505					26,480
	CE2	21,505	CE1	26,480	
0					0

After the closing process is complete, all of the income accounts have a zero balance. These accounts are then ready for recording revenues and expenses in the new accounting period. The ending balance in Retained Earnings now is up-to-date (matches the amount on the balance sheet) and is carried forward as the beginning balance for the next period. As the last step of the accounting information processing cycle, a **post-closing trial balance** should be prepared as a check that debits equal credits and that all temporary accounts have been closed.

A **post-closing trial balance** should be prepared as the last step of the accounting cycle to check that debits equal credits and all temporary accounts have been closed.

The Accounting Cycle and Communication Process

Although the preparation of statements and the closing of books represents the final stage of the formal recordkeeping process, it represents only the beginning of the formal process of communicating financial statement information to external users. In the next chapter we take a closer look at the preparation of financial statements and related disclosures that appear in a company's annual report, quarterly reports, and, for public companies, additional reports filed with the Securities and Exchange Commission. We also examine the process by which this and related information is disseminated to professional analysts, investors, and the public.

Demonstration Case

We take our final look at the accounting activities of Terrific Lawn Maintenance Corporation by illustrating the activities at the end of the accounting cycle: the adjustment process, financial statement preparation, and the closing process. Chapter 2 presented investing and financing activities, and Chapter 3 presented operating activities. No adjustments had been made to the accounts to reflect all revenues earned and expenses incurred in April, however. The trial balance for Terrific on April 30, 1998, based on the unadjusted balances in Chapter 3 is as follows:

TERRIFIC LAWN MAINTENANCE CORPORATION
Unadjusted Trial Balance
At April 30, 1998

	DEBIT	CREDIT
Cash	1,460	
Accounts receivable	1,700	
Prepaid expenses	300	
Lawn equipment	4,600	
Land	3,750	
Accounts payable		320
Dividends payable		300
Unearned revenue		1,600
Contributed capital		9,000
Retained earnings	300	
Mowing service revenue		5,200
Fuel expense	410	
Wages expense	3,900	
Totals	16,420	16,420

In reviewing the trial balance, three deferral accounts (Unearned Revenue, Prepaid Expenses, and Equipment) may need to be adjusted and additional accruals may be necessary. The following information is determined at the end of the accounting cycle:

DEFERRALS

(a) Unearned revenue received from the city at the beginning of April has been partially earned by the end of April.

(b) Prepaid expense for insurance has been partially used in April.

(c) Mowers and edgers (equipment) have been used and need to be depreciated. Mowers and edgers have a total cost of $4,000 and an estimated useful life of 10 years; rakes and hand tools have a total cost of $600 and an estimated useful life of 5 years. No residual value is expected.

ACCRUALS

(d) Wages have been paid through April 28. Wages earned in April by the employees but not yet paid accrue at $130 per day.

(e) An extra telephone line was installed in April. The telephone bill for $37 including hookup and usage charges was received on May 4.

(f) The estimated income tax rate for Terrific is 35 percent for state and federal income taxes.

Required:

1. *a.*   Set up T-accounts and their balances for Prepaid Expenses, Accumulated Depreciation, Unearned Revenue, Accrued Expenses Payable, Income Taxes Payable, Retained Earnings, Mowing Service Revenue, Insurance Expense, Depreciation Expense, Fuel Expense, Wages Expense, Utilities Expense, and Income Tax Expense. Insert the unadjusted balances from the trial balance just presented.

   b.   Analyze each deferral and each accrual using the process outlined in this chapter. Post the effects to the T-accounts. Compute ending balances.

   c.   Prepare an adjusted trial balance for April 30, 1998.

2.   Use the amounts on the adjusted trial balance from requirement (1) to prepare an income statement, statement of stockholders' equity, balance sheet, and statement of cash flows for the month ended April 30, 1998. For the statement of cash flows, review all cash transactions in Chapters 2 and 3, categorizing them as operating, investing, or financing cash flows.

3.   Prepare closing entries for April 30, 1998. Post these to the T-accounts in requirement (1).

Now you can check your answers with the following solution to these requirements.

Suggested Solution

1. *a.*   Create T-accounts.

   T-accounts used to facilitate the analysis are located together after the following analysis of deferrals and accruals.

   b.   Analysis of deferrals and accruals, adjusting entries, and T-accounts:

DEFERRALS

(a)

> The city paid $1,600 for mowing service for four months, April through July. One-fourth of the deferred amount has been earned by the end of April. This is a deferral for which the original entry was to Unearned Revenue (L). The balance in the liability account should be $1,200 (three months' mowing service due) with $400 shown as revenue earned in April.

Unearned revenue (L)	400	
Mowing service revenue (R)		400

(b)

> The $300 paid in April for six months of insurance coverage was originally recorded as a deferral in the Prepaid Expenses account. One-sixth ($50) of the insurance has now been used and $250 remains prepaid.

Insurance expense (E)	50	
Prepaid expenses (A)		50

(c)

> Long-lived assets have been used in the generation of revenues; therefore, a portion of the historical cost needs to be expensed. The straight-line formula to calculate periodic depreciation follows:

(Cost – Residual value) ÷ Useful life = Depreciation expense for the period
Mowers: ($4,000 – 0) ÷ 120 months = $33 per month
Tools: ($600 – 0) ÷   60 months = $10 per month.

| Depreciation expense (E) .... | 43 | |
| Accumulated depreciation (XA) .... | | 43 |

ACCRUALS

(d)

> The employees have earned two additional days of wages at $130 per day. $130 ×
> 2 days = $260 is the amount of wages expense and accrued expenses payable.

| Wages expense (E) .... | 260 | |
| Accrued expenses payable (L) .... | | 260 |

(e)

> An adjustment is necessary to record the telephone expenses for April that were not
> known until early May. The amount of $37 is given.

| Utilities expense (E) .... | 37 | |
| Accrued expenses payable (L) .... | | 37 |

(f)

> Income taxes are estimated to be 35 percent of net income on the accrual basis (see
> ending balances in the following T-accounts).

	Total revenues	$5,600	
−	Total expenses	− 4,700	($410 + 4,160 + 37 + 50 + 43)
	Income before taxes	900	
×	35%	× .35	
	Tax expense	$ 315	

| Income tax expense (E) .... | 315 | |
| Income tax payable (L) .... | | 315 |

T-Accounts Affected by Adjusting and Closing Entries

BALANCE SHEET (PERMANENT) ACCOUNTS

Prepaid Expenses (A)				Accumulated Depreciation (XA)				Unearned Revenue (L)		
Unadj. bal.	300				Unadj. bal.	0			Unadj. bal.	1,600
		AJE(b)	50		AJE(c)	43	AJE(a)	400		
End. bal.	250				End. bal.	43			End. bal.	1,200

Accrued Expenses Payable (L)				Income Tax Payable (L)				Retained Earnings (SE)		
		Unadj. bal.	0		Unadj. bal.	0	Unadj. bal.	300		0
		AJE(d)	260		AJE(f)	315	CE(2)	5,015	CE(1)	5,600
		AJE(e)	37		End. bal.	315			End. bal.	285
		End. bal.	297							

CE(2) = 410 + 4,160 + 43 + 50 + 37 + 315

TEMPORARY ACCOUNTS

Mowing Service Revenue (R)				Fuel Expense (E)				Wages Expense (E)		
		Unadj. bal.	5,200	Unadj. bal.	410			Unadj. bal.	3,900	
		AJE(a)	400					AJE(d)	260	
		End. bal	5,600	End. bal.	410			End. bal.	4,160	
CE(1)	5,600					CE(2)	410			CE(2)	4,160
		Closed bal.	0	Closed bal.	0			Closed bal.	0	

Depreciation Expense (E)			
Unadj. bal	0		
AJE(*c*)	43		
End. bal.	43		
		CE(2)	43
Closed bal.	0		

Insurance Expense (E)			
Unadj. bal.	0		
AJE(*b*)	50		
End. bal.	50		
		CE(2)	50
Closed bal.	0		

Utilities Expense (E)			
Unadj. bal.	0		
AJE(*e*)	37		
End. bal.	37		
		CE(2)	37
Closed bal.	0		

Income Tax Expense (E)			
Unadj. bal.	0		
AJE(*f*)	315		
End. bal.	315		
		CE(2)	315
Closed bal.	0		

1. *c.* Adjusted trial balance:

TERRIFIC LAWN MAINTENANCE CORPORATION
Pre-Closing Adjusted Trial Balance
At April 30, 1998

	Debit	Credit
Cash	1,460	
Accounts receivable	1,700	
Prepaid expenses	250	
Lawn equipment	4,600	
Accumulated depreciation		43
Land	3,750	
Accounts payable		320
Accrued expenses payable		297
Dividends payable		300
Unearned revenue		1,200
Income taxes payable		315
Contributed capital		9,000
Retained earnings	300	
Mowing service revenue		5,600
Fuel expense	410	
Wages expense	4,160	
Utilities expense	37	
Insurance expense	50	
Depreciation expense	43	
Income tax expense	315	
Totals	17,075	17,075

2. Financial statements

TERRIFIC LAWN MAINTENANCE CORPORATION
Income Statement
For the Period Ended April 30, 1998

Revenues	
Mowing service revenue	$5,600
Expenses	
Wages expense	4,160
Fuel expense	410
Insurance expense	50
Utilities expense	37
Depreciation expense	43
Total expenses	4,700
Income before income taxes	900
Income tax expense	315
Net income	$ 585
Earnings per share	$ .39

As indicated in Chapter 2, a total of 1,500 shares of stock was originally issued to the three owners. EPS is calculated as follows:

$$\$585 \text{ net income} \div 1,500 \text{ shares} = \$.39 \text{ per share}$$

TERRIFIC LAWN MAINTENANCE CORPORATION
Statement of Shareholders' Equity
For the Period Ended April 30, 1998

	Contributed Capital	Retained Earnings	Total
Beginning balances, April 1, 1998	$ 0	$ 0	$ 0
Stock issuance	9,000		9,000
Net income		585	585
Dividends declared		(300)	(300)
Ending balances, April 30, 1998	$9,000	$285	$9,285

The amount for net income ($585) flows from the income statement into the statement of shareholders' equity as an increase in retained earnings.

TERRIFIC LAWN MAINTENANCE CORPORATION
Balance Sheet
At April 30, 1998

Assets			Liabilities	
Cash		$ 1,460	Accounts payable	$ 320
Accounts receivable		1,700	Dividends payable	300
Prepaid expenses		250	Unearned revenue	1,200
Lawn equipment	$4,600		Accrued expenses payable	297
Accumulated depreciation	(43)	4,557	Income taxes payable	315
Land		3,750	Total Liabilities	$ 2,432
			Stockholders' Equity	
			Contributed capital	$ 9,000
			Retained earnings	285
			Total stockholders' equity	9,285
			Total Liabilities	
Total Assets		**$11,717**	**and Stockholders' Equity**	**$11,717**

TERRIFIC LAWN MAINTENANCE CORPORATION
Statement of Cash Flows
For the Month Ended April 30, 1998

Operating activities		
Cash inflows		
From customers		$5,100
Cash outflows		
To suppliers	$(4,790)	
To employees	(3,900)	(8,690)
Net cash used in operating activities		(3,590)
Investing activities		
Cash inflows		
Sale of land to city		1,250
Cash outflows		
Purchase of equipment	(200)	
Purchase of land	(5,000)	(5,200)
Net cash used in investing activities		(3,950)
Financing activities		
Cash inflows		
Issuance of stock		9,000
Net cash provided by financing activities		9,000
Net increase in cash		1,460
Beginning cash balance, 4/1/98		0
Ending cash balance, 4/30/98		$1,460

The ending cash balance on the statement of cash flows agrees with the ending cash balance on the balance sheet. The statement of cash flows reconciles the changes in cash for the month. You will notice that Terrific Lawn Maintenance Corporation did not have positive cash from operations. This is quite typical of new companies that often must undertake substantial financing and investing activities early in their start-up. In the long run, though, companies need to be able to realize positive cash flows from operations to remain in business.

3. Closing entries

    a. The closing entries follow:

        (1) Close revenues and gains to Retained Earnings:

Mowing service revenue (R)	5,600	
Retained earnings (SE)		5,600

        (2) Close expenses and losses to Retained Earnings:

Retained earnings (SE)	5,015	
Wages expense (E)		4,160
Fuel expense (E)		410
Insurance expense (E)		50
Utilities expense (E)		37
Depreciation expense (E)		43
Income tax expense (E)		315

    b. These entries were posted to the T-accounts in requirement (1). All temporary accounts now have zero balances to begin accumulating amounts for May activities.

Summary

An accounting system is designed to collect, process, and report financial information. During each period, an accounting information processing cycle starts with collecting data and ends with preparing the required financial statements and closing the temporary accounts. The phases of the cycle were summarized in Exhibit 4.1.

The accounting model that was described in Chapters 2 and 3 provides the basic framework for transaction analysis. The dual effect of each transaction can be stated in terms of its impact on assets, liabilities, and shareholders' equity. These effects are first recorded in the journal and then posted to a ledger (T-accounts), which includes a separate account for each type of asset, liability, shareholders' equity, revenue, and expense. At the end of the accounting period, accrual and deferral accounts must be updated to reflect that revenues have been earned and properly matched with their related expenses in the current period according to accrual accounting principles and that the balance sheet amounts are appropriate. Adjusting entries are prepared and posted to the ledger (T-accounts) to record the effects of these events. Either at this point or more likely after the adjustments are known, the financial statements are prepared.

The statements relate to each other. Net income from the income statement is included on the statement of shareholders' equity, which lists activities for the period in retained earnings and contributed capital. Then the ending balances on the statement of shareholders' equity are included on the balance sheet (stockholders' equity section). Finally, the Cash account on the balance sheet is analyzed on the statement of cash flows. The activities that generated or used cash during the period are categorized by type of activity: operating, investing, and financing.

Revenue and expense accounts reflect activities for only a single accounting period. At the beginning of each new period, their balances must be zero. Therefore, these temporary accounts are closed at the end of each period to return the balances of all revenue and expense accounts to zero and to transfer their balances to Retained Earnings. The balance sheet accounts are permanent accounts and are never closed. A post-closing trial balance should be prepared as a check for recording accuracy as the last step of the accounting information processing cycle.

This chapter discussed the important portions of the accounting process that take place at the end of the year. These include the adjustment process, the preparation of the four basic financial statements, and the closing process, which prepares the records for the next accounting period. This end to the internal portions of the accounting process, however, is just the beginning of the process of communicating accounting information to external users. In Chapter 5 we discuss the important players in this communication process, the many statement format choices available, the additional note disclosures that are required for both private and public companies, and the process, manner, and timing of the transmission of this information to users. At the same time, we discuss common uses of the information in investment analysis, debt contracts, and management compensation decisions. These discussions will help you consolidate much of what you have learned about the financial reporting process from previous chapters. It will also preview many of the important issues we will address later in the book.

Key Ratios

Earnings per share is a computation that measures an investor's return on investment in terms of the number of shares outstanding. It is required to be reported by companies, usually on the income statement. It is computed as follows (p. 190):

$$\text{EPS} = \frac{\text{Net income}}{\text{Weighted-average number of shares of stock outstanding during the period}}$$

Key Terms

Accruals Revenues that have been earned and expenses that have been incurred by the end of the current accounting period but that will not be collected or paid until a future accounting period. *172*

Adjusting Entries End-of-period entries necessary to measure income properly, correct errors, and provide for adequate valuation of balance sheet accounts. *176*

Book Value (Net Book Value, Carrying Value) The difference between an asset's acquisition cost and accumulated depreciation, its related contra account. *174*

Closing Entries Made at the end of the accounting period to transfer balances in temporary accounts to retained earnings and to establish a zero balance in each of the temporary accounts. *195*

Contra-Account An account that is an offset to, or reduction of, the primary account. *174*

Deferrals Previously recorded assets, liabilities, revenues, or expenses that need to be adjusted at the end of the period to reflect earned revenues or incurred expenses. *172*

Income Summary A temporary account used only during the closing process to facilitate the closing of revenues and expenses; closed to Retained Earnings. *195*

Permanent (Real) Accounts The balance sheet accounts that carry their ending balances into the next accounting period; not closed at the end of the period. *195*

Post-Closing Trial Balance Should be prepared as the last step in the accounting cycle to check that debits equal credits and all temporary accounts have been closed. *196*

Temporary (Nominal) Accounts Income statement (and sometimes dividends declared) accounts that are closed at the end of the accounting period. *195*

Trial Balance A list of all accounts with their balances to provide a check on the equality of the debits and credits. The unadjusted trial balance does not include the effects of the adjusting entries. *173*

Questions

1. Explain the accounting information processing cycle.
2. Identify, in sequence, the phases of the accounting information processing cycle.
3. What is a trial balance? What is its purpose?
4. Briefly explain adjusting entries. List the two types of adjusting entries, and give examples of each type.
5. XYZ Company collected $900 rent for the period December 1, 19A, to March 1, 19B. The $900 was credited to Rent Revenue Collected in Advance on December 1, 19A. Give the adjusting entry required on December 31, 19A (end of the accounting period).
6. On December 31, 19B, Company J recorded the following adjusting entry:

Rent revenue receivable	600	
Rent revenue		600

   Explain the situation that caused this entry and give the subsequent related entry.
7. On July 1, 19A, R Company paid a two-year insurance premium of $300 and debited Prepaid Insurance for that amount. Assuming that the accounting period ends in December, give the adjusting entries that should be made at the end of 19A, 19B, and 19C.
8. Explain estimated residual value. Why is it important in measuring depreciation expense?
9. What is a contra-asset? Give an example of one.
10. Explain why adjusting entries are entered in the journal on the last day of the accounting period and then are posted to the ledger.
11. Explain how the financial statements relate to each other.
12. What is the equation for each of the following statements: (a) income statement, (b) balance sheet, (c) statement of cash flows, and (d) statement of stockholders' equity?
13. How is earnings per share computed?
14. Baker Company reported net income of $1,142,400 for the year. There were 420,000 shares of stock outstanding all year. Calculate earnings per share for the year.
15. Contrast an unadjusted trial balance with an adjusted trial balance. What is the purpose of each?
16. What is the purpose of closing entries? Why are they recorded in the journal and posted to the ledger?
17. Differentiate among (a) permanent, (b) temporary, (c) real, and (d) nominal accounts.
18. Why are the income statement accounts closed but the balance sheet accounts are not?
19. What is a post-closing trial balance? Is it a useful part of the accounting information processing cycle? Explain.

Exercises

E4–1 Matching Definitions with Terms

Below are terms related to adjusting entries. Match each definition with its related term. There are two answers for each term.

TERMS   DEFINITIONS

1. Accrued expense   A. A revenue not yet earned; collected in advance.
2. Deferred expense   B. Office supplies on hand; used next accounting period
3. Accrued revenue   C. Rent revenue collected; not yet earned.
4. Deferred revenue   D. Rent not yet collected; already earned.
   E. An expense incurred; not yet paid or recorded. (AP)
   F. A revenue earned; not yet collected. (AR)
   G. An expense not yet incurred; paid in advance.
   H. Property taxes incurred; not yet paid.

E4–2 Matching Transactions with Terms

Match each transaction with its related term.

TERMS   TRANSACTIONS

_____ 1. Deferred revenue   (a) At the end of the year, wages payable of $3,600 had not been recorded or paid.
_____ 2. Accrued revenue
_____ 3. Deferred expense   (b) Supplies for office use were purchased during the year for $500, and $100 of the office supplies remained on hand (unused) at year-end.
_____ 4. Accrued expense
   (c) Interest of $250 on a note receivable was earned at year-end, although collection of the interest is not due until the following year.
   (d) At the end of the year, service revenue of $2,000 was collected in cash but was not yet earned.

E4–3 Making Two Simple Adjusting Entries

Evans Company completed its first year of operations on December 31, 19A. All of the 19A entries have been recorded, except for the following:

(a) At year-end, employees earned wages of $6,000, which will be paid on the next payroll date, January 6, 19B.
(b) At year-end, the company had earned interest revenue of $3,000. The cash will be collected March 1, 19B.

Required:
1. What is the annual reporting period for this company?
2. Give the required adjusting entry for transactions (a) and (b). Give appropriate dates and write a brief explanation of each entry.
3. Why are these adjustments made?

E4–4 Identifying Adjusting Entries from Unadjusted Trial Balance

Procter & Gamble

As stated in its annual report, "Procter & Gamble markets a broad range of laundry, cleaning, paper, beauty care, health care, food and beverage products in more than 140 countries around the world, with leading brands including Tide, Ariel, Crest, Crisco, Vicks and Max Factor." P&G employs 96,500 people worldwide. Following is a trial balance listing accounts that P&G uses. Assume that the balances are unadjusted at the end of a recent fiscal year ended June 30.

PROCTER & GAMBLE COMPANY AND SUBSIDIARIES
Unadjusted Trial Balance
At June 30, 19A
(millions of dollars)

	Debit	Credit
Cash	2,373	
Marketable securities	283	
Accounts receivable	3,115	
Inventories	2,877	
Prepaid expenses	624	
Property, plant, and equipment	15,896	
Accumulated depreciation		5,872
Goodwill and other intangible assets	4,510	
Accumulated amortization*		756
Other assets	2,485	
Accounts payable		3,264
Accrued liabilities		2,961
Taxes payable		0
Long-term debt		6,355
Other liabilities		3,683
Contributed capital		3,186
Retained earnings		2,740
Sales		30,296
Cost of products sold	17,355	
Marketing, administrative, and other operating expenses	9,361	
Interest expense	482	
Other income		248
Income tax expense	0	
	59,361	59,361

*Accumulated amortization is similar to accumulated depreciation. It is a contra-asset that represents the portion of the intangible assets' cost that has been used in past operations.

Required:

1. Based on the information in the unadjusted trial balance, list the balance sheet deferral accounts that may need to be adjusted at June 30 and the related account for each (no computations are necessary).

2. Based on the information in the unadjusted trial balance, list the balance sheet accrual accounts that may need to be recorded at June 30 and the related account for each (no computations are necessary).

E4–5 Preparing a Trial Balance

Latta Marketing Consultants, Inc., provides marketing research for clients in the retail industry. The company had the following unadjusted balances at September 30, 19A:

Accumulated Depreciation		Accrued Expenses Payable	
	18,100		25,650

Cash		General and Administative Expense		Supplies Inventory	
173,000		320,050		12,200	

Wages and Benefits Expense		Prepaid Expenses		Interest Expense	
1,590,000		10,200		17,200	

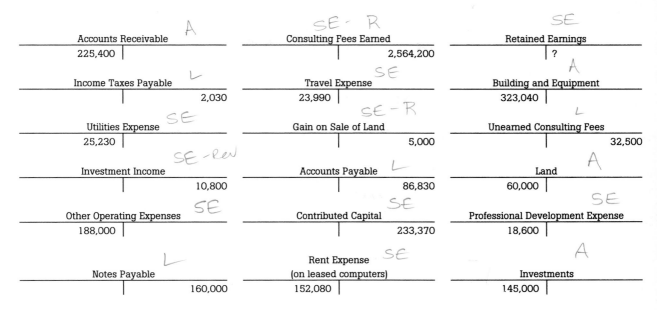

A Accounts Receivable		*SE - R* Consulting Fees Earned		*SE* Retained Earnings	
225,400			2,564,200		?

L Income Taxes Payable		*SE* Travel Expense		*A* Building and Equipment	
	2,030	23,990		323,040	

SE Utilities Expense		*SE - R* Gain on Sale of Land		*L* Unearned Consulting Fees	
25,230			5,000		32,500

SE - Rev Investment Income		*L* Accounts Payable		*A* Land	
	10,800		86,830	60,000	

SE Other Operating Expenses		*SE* Contributed Capital		*SE* Professional Development Expense	
188,000			233,370	18,600	

L Notes Payable		*SE* Rent Expense (on leased computers)		*A* Investments	
	160,000	152,080		145,000	

Required:

Prepare in good form an unadjusted trial balance for Latta Marketing Consultants, Inc., at September 30, 19A.

E4–6 Effects of Three Adjusting Entries on the Income Statement and Balance Sheet

Oklahoma Company started operations on January 1, 19A. It is now December 31, 19A, end of the annual accounting period. The part-time bookkeeper needs your help to analyze the following three transactions:

(a) On January 1, 19A, the company purchased a special machine for a cash cost of $12,000 (debited to the machine account). The machine has an estimated useful life of 10 years and no residual value.

(b) During 19A, the company purchased office supplies that cost $1,400. At the end of 19A, office supplies of $400 remained on hand.

(c) On July 1, 19A, the company paid cash of $400 for a two-year premium on an insurance policy on the machine that begins coverage on July 1, 19A.

Required:

Complete the following schedule of the amounts that should be reported for 19A:

Selected Balance Sheet Amounts at December 31, 19A	Amount to Be Reported
Assets	
Equipment	$_____
Accumulated depreciation	_____
Carrying value of equipment	_____
Office supplies inventory	_____
Prepaid insurance	_____
Selected Income Statement Amounts for the Year Ended December 31, 19A	
Expenses	
Depreciation expense	$_____
Office supplies expense	_____
Insurance expense	_____

E4–7 Recording Seven Typical Adjusting Entries

Crawford's Department Store is completing the accounting process for the year just ended, December 31, 19B. The transactions during 19B have been journalized and posted. The following data with respect to adjusting entries are available:

(a) Office supplies inventory at January 1, 19B, was $250. Office supplies purchased and debited to Office Supplies Inventory during the year amounted to $600. The year-end inventory showed $300 of supplies on hand.

(b) Wages earned during December 19B, unpaid and unrecorded at December 31, 19B, amounted to $2,700. The last payroll was December 28; the next payroll will be January 6, 19C.

(c) Three-fourths of the basement of the store is rented for $1,100 per month to another merchant, M. Riesman. Riesman sells compatible, but not competitive, merchandise. On November 1, 19B, the store collected six months' rent in the amount of $6,600 in advance from Riesman; it was credited in full to Unearned Rent Revenue when collected.

(d) The remaining basement space is rented to Rita's Specialty Shop for $520 per month, payable monthly. On December 31, 19B, the rent for November and December 19B was not collected or recorded. Collection is expected January 10, 19C.

(e) The store used delivery equipment that cost $30,000. The equipment was estimated to have a useful life of four years and a residual value of $6,000 at the end of the four years. Assume depreciation for a full year for 19B. The asset will be depreciated evenly over its useful life.

(f) On July 1, 19B, a two-year insurance premium amounting to $3,000 was paid in cash and debited in full to Prepaid Insurance. Coverage began on July 1, 19B.

(g) Crawford's operates an alteration shop to meet its own needs. The shop also does alterations for M. Riesman. At the end of December 31, 19B, Riesman had not paid for alterations completed amounting to $750. This amount has not yet been recorded as Alteration Shop Revenue. Collection is expected during January 19C.

Required:

1. Identify each of these transactions as either creating a deferral account during the year to be adjusted at the end of the year or creating an accrual account at the end of the year.

2. Give the adjusting entry for each situation that should be recorded for Crawford's Department Store at December 31, 19B.

E4–8 Effects of Adjustments for Interest on Two Notes

Note A: On April 1, 19B, Samrick Corporation received a $10,000, 10 percent note from a customer in settlement of a $10,000 open account receivable. According to the terms, the principal of the note, plus interest, is payable at the end of 12 months. The annual accounting period for Samrick ends on December 31, 19B.

Note B: On August 1, 19B, to meet a cash shortage, Samrick Corporation obtained a $20,000, 12 percent loan from a local bank. The principal of the note plus interest expense is payable at the end of 12 months.

Required:

Using the following headings, indicate the effect (amount and direction) of the transactions indicated in the following items. A sample is provided. Use + for increase, – for decrease, and NE for no effect. (*Reminder:* Assets = Liabilities + Stockholders' Equity; Revenues –

Expenses = Net Income; and Net Income accounts are closed to Retained Earnings, a part of Stockholders' Equity.)

Sample: The company made a $1,000 sale on account on March 1.

	Assets	Liabilities	Stockholders' Equity	Revenues	Expenses	Net Income
Sample	+ 1,000	NE	+ 1,000	+ 1,000	NE	+ 1,000

1. For Note A, what are the effects of the receipt of Note A on April 1, 19B, by Samrick?
2. For Note A, what are the effects of the adjustment required on December 31, 19B?
3. For Note A, what are the effects of collection of the principal and interest on the date of collection, March 31, 19C?
4. For Note B, what are the effects on the date of the borrowing, August 1, 19B?
5. For Note B, what are the effects of the adjustment required on December 31, 19B?
6. For Note B, what are the effects of payment of principal and interest on July 31, 19C?

E4–9 Adjusting Prepaid Insurance

Jenson Company is making adjusting entries for the year ended December 31, 19B. In developing information for the adjusting entries, the accountant learned that on September 1, 19B, a two-year insurance premium of $7,200 was paid for coverage beginning on that date.

Required:
1. What amount should be reported on the 19B income statement for insurance expense?
2. What amount should be reported on the December 31, 19B, balance sheet for prepaid insurance?
3. Give the adjusting entry at December 31, 19B, assuming that the premium was paid on September 1, 19B, and the bookkeeper debited the full amount to Prepaid Insurance.

E4–10 Focus on Cash Flows: Analysis of Adjustments for Unearned Subscriptions

You are the regional sales manager for Weld News Company. Weld is making adjusting entries for the year ended March 31, 19C. On September 1, 19B, $18,000 cash was received from customers in your region for three-year magazine subscriptions beginning on that date. The magazines are published and mailed to customers monthly. These were the only subscription sales in your region during the year.

Required:
1. What amount should be reported as cash from operations on the statement of cash flows?
2. What amount should be reported on the 19C income statement for subscription revenue?
3. What amount should be reported on the March 31, 19C, balance sheet for unearned subscription revenue?
4. Give the adjusting entry at March 31, 19C, assuming that the subscriptions received on September 1, 19B, were recorded for the full amount in Unearned Subscriptions Revenue.
5. The company expects your region's annual revenue target to be $4,000.
   a. Evaluate your region's performance assuming that the revenue target is based on cash sales.
   b. Evaluate your region's performance assuming that the revenue target is based on accrual accounting.

E4-11 Adjusting Entry for Supplies Inventory

Collens Company uses a large amount of shipping supplies that are purchased in large volume, stored, and used as needed. At December 31, 19B, the following data relating to shipping supplies were obtained from the records and supporting documents:

Shipping supplies on hand, January 1, 19B	$15,000
Purchases of shipping supplies during 19B	72,000
Shipping supplies on hand, per inventory December 31, 19B	11,000

Required:

1. What amount should be reported on the 19B income statement for Shipping Supplies Expense?
2. What amount should be reported on the December 31, 19B, balance sheet for Shipping Supplies Inventory?
3. Give the adjusting entry at December 31, 19B, assuming that the purchases of shipping supplies were debited in full to Shipping Supplies Inventory ($72,000).

Deere & Company

E4-12 Identifying Transactions

Deere & Company is the world's leading producer of agricultural equipment; a leading supplier of a broad range of industrial equipment for construction, forestry, and public works; a producer and marketer of a broad line of lawn and grounds care equipment; and a provider of credit, managed health care plans, and insurance products for businesses and the general public. The following information was from a recent annual report (in millions of dollars):

Income Taxes Payable			Dividends Payable			Interest Payable		
	Beg. bal.	71		Beg. bal.	43		Beg. bal.	45
(a)	? (b)	332	(c)	? (d)	176	(e)	297 (f)	?
	End. bal.	80		End. bal.	48		End. bal.	51

Required:

1. Identify the nature of each of the transactions (a)–(f). Specifically, what activities caused the accounts to increase and decrease?
2. For transactions (a), (c), and (f), compute the amount.

E4-13 Analyzing the Effects of Errors on Financial Statement Items

Campbell and Long, Inc., publishers of movie and song trivia books, made the following errors in adjusting the accounts at year-end (December 31):

a. Did not record depreciation on the equipment costing $130,000 ($30,000 residual value, 10-year useful life).
b. Failed to adjust the Unearned Revenue account to reflect that $3,000 was earned by the end of the year.
c. Recorded a full year of accrued interest expense on a $15,000, 12 percent note payable that has been outstanding only since November 1.
d. Failed to adjust Insurance Expense to reflect that $400 related to future insurance coverage.
e. Did not accrue $750 owed to the company by another company renting part of the building as a storage facility.

Required:

1. For each error, prepare the adjusting journal entry that was made, if any, or should have been made at year-end.

2. Using the following headings, indicate the effect of each error and the amount of the effect. Use O if the effect overstates the item, U if the effect understates the item, and NE if there is no effect. A sample is provided. (*Reminder:* Assets = Liabilities + Stockholders' Equity; Revenues – Expenses = Net Income; and Net Income accounts are closed to Retained Earnings, a part of Stockholders' Equity.)

Sample: Failed to adjust Supplies Inventory to reflect that supplies costing $560 were used during the period.

Analysis: The error caused Supplies Inventory to be too high and Supplies Expense to be too low.

Error	Assets	Liabilities	Stockholders' Equity	Revenues	Expenses	Net Income
Sample	O 560	NE	O 560	NE	U 560	O 560

E4–14 Correcting Income Statement and Balance Sheet Amounts for the Effects of Adjusting Entries

On December 31, 19B, Cohen and Company prepared an income statement and balance sheet and failed to take into account four adjusting entries. The income statement, prepared on this incorrect basis, reflected income of $30,000 before income taxes. The balance sheet (before the effect of income taxes) reflected total assets, $90,000; total liabilities, $40,000; and stockholders' equity, $50,000. The data for the four adjusting entries follow:

a. Depreciation for the year on equipment that cost $85,000 was not recorded; estimated useful life, 10 years; residual value, $5,000.

b. Wages amounting to $17,000 for the last three days of December 19B were not paid and not recorded (the next payroll will be on January 10, 19C).

c. Rent revenue of $4,800 was collected on December 1, 19B, for office space for the period December 1, 19B, to February 28, 19C. The $4,800 was credited in full to Unearned Rent Revenue when collected.

d. Income taxes were not recorded. The income tax rate for the company is 30 percent.

Required:
Complete the following tabulation to correct the financial statements for the effects of the four errors (indicate deductions with parentheses):

Items	Net Income	Total Assets	Total Liabilities	Stockholders' Equity
Balances reported	$30,000	$90,000	$40,000	$50,000
Effects of depreciation				
Effects of wages				
Effects of rent revenue				
Adjusted balances				
Effect of income taxes				
Correct balances				

E4–15 Preparing a Correct Income Statement and Earnings per Share to Include the Effects of Adjusting Entries

Barton, Inc., completed its first year of operations on December 31, 19A. Because this is the end of the annual accounting period, the company bookkeeper prepared the following tentative income statement:

Income Statement, 19A

Rental revenue		$114,000
Expenses	*28810*	
Salaries and wages expense	$28,500	
Maintenance expense	12,000 *11,000*	
Rent expense (on location)	9,000	
Utilities expense	4,000 *4,400*	
Gas and oil expense	3,000	
Miscellaneous expenses (items not listed elsewhere)	1,000	
Total expenses		57,500
Income		$ 56,500

An independent CPA reviewed the income statement and developed additional data as follows:

a. Wages for the last three days of December amounting to $310 were not recorded or paid (disregard payroll taxes).

b. The $400 telephone bill for December 19A has not been recorded or paid.

c. Depreciation on rental autos, amounting to $23,000 for 19A, was not recorded.

d. Interest on a $20,000, one-year, 10 percent note payable dated October 1, 19A, was not recorded. The 10 percent interest is payable on the maturity date of the note.

e. The Unearned Rental Revenue account includes $4,000 rental revenue for the month of January 19B.

f. Maintenance expense includes $1,000, which is the cost of maintenance supplies still on hand (per inventory) at December 31, 19A. These supplies will be used in 19B.

g. The income tax expense is $7,000. Payment of income tax will be made in 19B.

Required:

1. Give the adjusting entry at December 31, 19A, for each of the additional data items. If none is required, explain why.

2. Prepare a correct income statement for 19A, including earnings per share, assuming that 7,000 shares of stock are outstanding. Show computations.

E4–16 Recasting the Income Statement and Balance Sheet after Analyzing the Effects of Adjusting Entries

On December 31, 19C, the bookkeeper for Mesley Company prepared the following income statement and balance sheet summarized here but neglected to consider three adjusting entries.

	As Prepared	Effects of Adjusting Entries	Corrected Amounts
INCOME STATEMENT			
Revenues	$98,000		
Expenses	(72,000)		
Income tax expense			
Net income	$26,000		
BALANCE SHEET			
Assets			
Cash	$20,000		
Accounts receivable	22,000		
Rent receivable			
Equipment*	50,000		
Accumulated depreciation	(10,000)		
	$82,000		

	As Prepared	Effects of Adjusting Entries	Corrected Amounts
Liabilities			
Accounts payable	$10,000	_____	_____
Income taxes payable		_____	_____
Stockholders' Equity		_____	_____
Contributed capital	40,000	_____	_____
Retained earnings	32,000	_____	_____
	$82,000		

Data on the three adjusting entries follow:

a. Depreciation on the equipment for 19C was not recorded.

b. Rent revenue earned of $2,000 for December 19C was neither collected nor recorded.

c. Income tax expense for 19C was neither paid nor recorded; the amount was $6,900.

Required:

1. Prepare the three adjusting entries that were omitted. Use the account titles shown in the income statement and balance sheet data.

2. Complete the two columns to the right in the preceding tabulation to show the correct amounts on the income statement and balance sheet.

E4–17 Preparing Four Adjusting Entries

Cayuga Company prepared the following trial balance at the end of the accounting year, December 31, 19A. To simplify the case, the amounts given are in thousands of dollars.

Account Titles	Unadjusted TB Debit	Unadjusted TB Credit	Adjustments Debit	Adjustments Credit	Adjusted TB Debit	Adjusted TB Credit
Cash	38					
Accounts receivable	9					
Prepaid insurance	6			(a) 5		
Machinery (20–year life, no residual value)	80					
Accumulated depreciation		8		(b) 4		
Accounts payable		9				
Wages payable				(c) 7		
Income taxes payable				(d) 9		
Contributed capital (4,000 shares)		68				
Retained earnings	4					
Revenues (not detailed)		84				
Expenses (not detailed)	32		(a) 5 (b) 4			
Totals	169	169	(c) 7 (d) 9			

Other data not yet recorded at December 31, 19A:

a. Insurance expired during 19A, $5. D

b. Depreciation expense for 19A, $4. D

c. Wages payable, $7. A

d. Income tax expense, $9. A

Required:

1. Prepare the adjusting entries for 19A.

2. Complete the trial balance Adjustments and Adjusted columns.

E4–18 Prepare Financial Statements

Using the adjusted balances in E4–17, complete the following income statement, statement of stockholders' equity, and balance sheet for 19A.

Income Statement
For the Year Ended December 31, 19A

Revenues (not detailed)	$_____
Expenses (not detailed)	_____
Pretax income	_____
Income tax expense	_____
Net income	$_____
EPS	$_____

Statement of Stockholders' Equity
For the Year Ended December 31, 19A

	Contributed Capital	Retained Earnings	Total Stockholders' Equity
Beginning balances, 1/1/19A	$_____	$_____	$_____
Stock issuance	_____	_____	_____
Net income	_____	_____	_____
Dividends declared	_____	_____	_____
Ending balances, 12/31/19A	$_____	$_____	$_____

Balance Sheet
December 31, 19A

Assets		Liabilities	
Cash	$_____	Accounts payable	$_____
Accounts receivable	_____	Wages payable	_____
Prepaid insurance	_____	Income taxes payable	_____
Machinery	_____	Total liabilities	$_____
Accumulated depreciation	_____		
		Stockholders' Equity	
		Contributed capital	$_____
		Retained earnings	_____
		Total liabilities and	
Total assets	$_____	stockholders' equity	$_____

E4–19 Preparing Closing Entries

Using the adjusted balances in E4–17, give the closing entries for 19A. What is the purpose of "closing the books" at the end of the accounting period?

E4–20 Recording Transactions Including Adjustments

For each of the following 10 independent situations, give the journal entry by entering the appropriate code(s) and amount(s).

Codes	Accounts	Codes	Accounts
A	Cash	J	Contributed capital
B	Office supplies inventory	K	Retained earnings
C	Revenue receivable	L	Service revenue
D	Office equipment	M	Interest revenue
E	Accumulated depreciation	N	Wage expense
F	Note payable	O	Depreciation expense
G	Wages payable	P	Interest expense
H	Interest payable	Q	Supplies expense
I	Service revenue collected in advance	R	None of the above

	Independent Situations	Debit Code	Debit Amount	Credit Code	Credit Amount
a.	Accrued wages, unrecorded and unpaid at year-end, $400 (example).	N	400	G	400
b.	Service revenue collected in advance, $800.				
c.	Dividends declared and paid during year, $900.				
d.	Depreciation expense for year, $1,000.				
e.	Service revenue earned but not yet collected at year-end, $600.				
f.	Office Supplies Inventory account at beginning of the year, $400; inventory of supplies on hand at year-end, $150.				
g.	At year-end, interest on note payable not yet recorded or paid, $220.				
h.	Balance at year-end in Service Revenue account, $62,000. Give the closing entry at year-end.				
i.	Balance at year-end in Interest Expense account, $420. Give the closing entry at year-end.				

Problems

P4–1 Analyzing Four Simple Adjusting Entries

McGraw Company's annual accounting year ends on December 31. It is December 31, 19X, and all of the 19X entries except the following adjusting entries have been made:

(a) On September 1, 19X, McGraw collected six months' rent of $4,800 on storage space. At that date, McGraw debited Cash and credited Unearned Rent Revenue for $4,800.

(b) The company earned service revenue of $3,000 on a special job that was completed December 29, 19X. Collection will be made during January 19Y; no entry has been recorded.

(c) On November 1, 19X, McGraw paid a one-year premium for property insurance, $4,200, for coverage starting on that date. Cash was credited and Prepaid Insurance was debited for this amount.

(d) At December 31, 19X, wages earned by employees not yet paid, $1,100. The employees will be paid on the next payroll date, January 15, 19Y.

Required:

Give the adjusting entry required for each transaction.

P4–2 Analyzing Four Types of Adjusting Entries

Boynton Company started operations on September 1, 19A. It is now August 31, 19C, the end of its second year of operations. All entries for the annual accounting period have been journalized and posted to the ledger accounts. The following end-of-year entries are to be recorded:

(a) Service revenue collected in advance, $2,200. On August 15, 19C, the company debited Cash and credited Unearned Service Revenue for this amount. The services will be performed during September 19C.

(b) Revenue earned but not yet collected or recorded, $6,000. The company completed a large service job, which passed inspection on August 31, 19C. Collection is expected on September 6, 19C.

(c) Expense paid in advance, $2,500. The company purchased service supplies on August 1, 19C, at which time Supplies Inventory was debited and Cash credited for this amount. At August 31, 19C, one-half of these supplies was on hand (will be used later on other jobs).

(d) Expense incurred but not yet paid or recorded. The company used the consulting services of an engineer during the last two weeks of August 19C. The services have been performed, and the company expects to pay the $800 bill on September 15, 19C.

Required:

1. What is the accounting (i.e., reporting) year for this company? What accounting assumption supports your answer?

2. Prepare the required adjusting entry for each situation, including a brief explanation of each entry.

3. Explain the effect on net income if these entries are not made on August 31, 19C (disregard income tax).

P4–3 Analyzing Six Adjusting Entries and Related Balance Sheet Classifications

You own a small business and follow accrual accounting principles. In preparing the adjusting entries for the year ended December 31, 19B, the bookkeeper for your company assembled the following data:

a. On December 31, 19B, salaries earned by employees but not yet paid or recorded totaled $4,000.

b. Depreciation must be recognized on a service truck that cost $12,000 on July 1, 19B (estimated useful life is six years with no residual value).

c. Cash of $1,500 was collected on November 1, 19B, for services to be rendered evenly over the next year beginning on November 1 (Unearned Service Revenue was credited).

d. On December 27, 19B, the company received a tax bill of $300 from the city for 19B property taxes on land that is payable during January 19C.

e. On July 1, 19B, the company paid $900 cash for a two-year insurance policy on the service truck in (b). Prepaid Insurance was debited.

f. On October 1, 19B, the company borrowed $10,000 from a local bank and signed a 12 percent note for that amount. The principal and interest are payable on maturity date, September 30, 19C.

Required:

1. The bookkeeper has asked you to assist in analyzing the adjusting entries at December 31, 19B. For each preceding situation, give the adjusting entry and a brief explanation. If none is required, explain why.

2. Based on your entries given in requirement (1), complete the following schedule to reflect the amounts and balance sheet classifications:

			Check the Appropriate Balance Sheet Classification		
		19B			Stockholders'
Item	Accounts	Amount	Assets	Liabilities	Equity
a.	Salaries payable	$_____	_____	_____	_____
b.	Accumulated depreciation	_____	_____	_____	_____
c.	Unearned service revenue	_____	_____	_____	_____
d.	Property taxes payable	_____	_____	_____	_____
e.	Prepaid insurance	_____	_____	_____	_____
f.	Interest payable	_____	_____	_____	_____

P4–4 Analyzing the Effects of Eight Adjusting Entries

Handy Haulers Company is at the end of its accounting year, December 31, 19B. The following data that must be considered were developed from the company's records and related documents:

(a) On July 1, 19B, a three-year insurance premium on equipment in the amount of $1,200 was paid and debited in full to Prepaid Insurance on that date. Coverage began on July 1.

(b) During 19B, office supplies amounting to $800 were purchased for cash and debited in full to Supplies Inventory. At the end of 19A, the inventory count of supplies remaining on hand (unused) showed $200. The inventory of supplies on hand at December 31, 19B, showed $300.

(c) On December 31, 19B, Bert's Garage completed repairs on one of the company's trucks at a cost of $800; the amount is not yet recorded and by agreement will be paid during January 19C.

(d) In December 19B, a tax bill for $1,600 on land owned during 19B was received from the city. The taxes, which have not been recorded, are due and will be paid on February 15, 19C.

(e) On December 31, 19B, the company completed a contract for an out-of-state company. The bill was for $8,000 payable within 30 days. No cash has been collected, and no journal entry has been made for this transaction.

(f) On July 1, 19B, the company purchased a new hauling van at a cash cost of $23,600. The estimated useful life of the van was 10 years, with an estimated residual value of $1,600. No depreciation has been recorded for 19B (compute depreciation for six months in 19B).

(g) On October 1, 19B, the company borrowed $10,000 from the local bank on a one-year, 12 percent note payable. The principal plus interest is payable at the end of 12 months.

(h) The income before any of the adjustments or income taxes was $30,000. The company's federal income tax rate is 30 percent. Compute adjusted income based on (a) through (g) to determine income tax expense.

Required:

Using the headings on the following page, indicate the effect (amount and direction) of the preceding transactions. A sample is provided. Use + for increase, – for decrease, and NE for no effect. (*Reminder:* Assets = Liabilities + Stockholders' Equity; Revenues – Expenses = Net Income; and Net Income accounts are closed to Retained Earnings, a part of Stockholders' Equity.)

Sample: The company made a $16,000 sale on account on March 1.

	Assets	Liabilities	Stockholders' Equity	Revenues	Expenses	Net Income
Sample	+16,000	NE	+16,000	+16,000	NE	+16,000

P4–5 Computing Income Statement Amounts and Identifying Adjusting Entries

The following information was provided by the records of South Hill Apartments (a corporation) at the end of the annual fiscal period, December 31, 19B:

REVENUE

a. Rent revenue collected in cash during 19B for occupancy in 19B

(credited to Rent Revenue)

$512,000

b. Rent revenue earned for occupancy in December 19B; will not be collected until 19C   16,000

c. In December 19B, collected rent revenue in advance for January 19C
(credited to Rent Revenue)   12,000

SALARY EXPENSE

d. Cash payment made in January 19B for employee salaries earned in December 19A   4,000

e. Salaries incurred and paid during 19B (debited to Salary Expense)   62,000

f. Salaries earned by employees during December 19B; will not be paid until January 19C   3,000

g. Cash advance to employees in December 19B for salaries that will be earned in
January 19C (debited to Receivable from Employees)   1,500

SUPPLIES USED

h. Maintenance supplies inventory on January 1, 19B (balance on hand)   3,000

i. Maintenance supplies purchased for cash during 19B (debited to Maintenance
Supplies Inventory when purchased)   8,000

j. Maintenance supplies inventory on December 31, 19B   1,700

Required:

1. In conformity with the revenue and matching principles, compute the amounts that should be reported on South Hill's 19B income statement for
   a. Rent revenue
   b. Salary expense
   c. Maintenance supplies expense
   Reminder: T-accounts are useful tools for accumulating balances.)
   Show computations.

2. Check the items that need an adjusting entry at the end of 19B and indicate whether the checked item is an accrual or deferral:

	Need Adjusting Entry? Yes/No	If So, Accrual or Deferral?		Need Adjusting Entry? Yes/No	If So, Accrual or Deferral?
a.			f.		
b.			g.		
c.			h.		
d.			i.		
e.			j.		

P4–6 Analyzing the Effect of Five Adjusting Entries on the Income Statement

Alabama Air Company has completed its annual financial statements for the year ended December 31, 19C. The income statement follows. The company is a partnership; therefore, it does not pay income taxes. A CPA's audit of the records and financial statements revealed that the following items were not considered:

a. Service revenue of $850 earned but not collected on December 31, 19C, was not included in the $98,200 on the income statement.

b.   The $2,800 of service supplies used included $400 of service supplies still on hand in the supplies storeroom on December 31, 19C.

c.   Rent revenue of $100 that was collected in advance but not yet earned by December 31, 19C, was included in the $4,000 on the income statement.

d.   A property tax bill of $600 for 19C was received during December 19C but will be paid during January 19D (not included in the amounts on the income statement).

e.   A two-year insurance premium of $800 was paid on July 1, 19B; no premiums were paid in 19C.

Required:

1.   Use the following format to recast the income statement to include, exclude, or omit each of the items identified by the CPA. The income statement as reported reflected the following:

	Amounts as Reported	Corrections	Amounts That Should Be Reported
Revenues			
Service revenue	$ 98,200		
Rental revenue (office space)	4,000		
Total revenues	102,200		
Expenses			
Salaries and wages expense	46,000		
Service supplies used	2,800		
Depreciation expense	3,000		
Maintenance of equipment	2,050		
Rent expense (service building)	6,800		
Oil and gas for equipment	2,200		
Insurance expense	400		
Utilities expense	800		
Other expenses	7,700		
Total expenses	71,750		
Net income	$ 30,450		

2.   The owner of the company asked you to explain the following:

a.   The insurance premium was paid in 19B; therefore, why was insurance expense reported in 19C?

b.   Although the company paid no cash for depreciation expense, $3,000 was included in 19C as expense. Why was this so?

P4–7 Analyzing the Effects of Six Entries on the Income Statement and Balance Sheet

It is December 31, 19B, the end of the annual accounting period for Gore Company. The following are six independent transactions (summarized) that affected the company during 19B.

Required:

Analyze the transactions as to their effects on the balance sheet and income statement for 19B as indicated.

(a) On January 1, 19A, the company purchased a machine that cost $30,000 cash (estimated useful life six years and no residual value).

1.   Show how the machine should be reported on the 19B balance sheet.

2.   Show how the 19B income statement should report the effects of the machine usage.

(b) On September 1, 19B, the company signed a $9,000, one-year, 12 percent note payable. The principal plus interest is payable on the maturity date.

1.   Show how the liability should be reported on the 19B balance sheet.

    2.   Show how the effects of the note should be reported on the 19B income statement.

(c) During 19B, service revenues of $80,000 were collected, of which $20,000 was collected in advance.

    1.   Show how the $20,000 should be reported on the 19B balance sheet.

    2.   Show how the 19B income statement should report the effects of the transaction.

(d) In 19B, expenses paid in cash amounted to $50,000, of which $5,000 was paid for expenses yet to be incurred (prepaid).

    1.   Show how the 19B balance sheet should report the $5,000.

    2.   Show how the income statement should report this situation.

(e) In 19B, $95,000 cash revenues were collected; in addition, revenues of $10,000 were on credit.

    1.   Show how the $10,000 should be reported on the 19B balance sheet.

    2.   Show how the 19B income statement should report the revenues.

(f) In 19B, expenses amounting to $70,000 were paid in cash; in addition, expenses of $6,000 were on credit.

    1.   Show how the $6,000 should be reported on the 19B balance sheet.

    2.   Show how the expenses should be reported on the 19B income statement.

P4–8 Comparing Two Sets of Account Balances to Infer Year-End Adjustments and Computing Earnings per Share

Willenborg Company is completing the information processing cycle at the end of its fiscal year, December 31, 19B. Following are the correct balances at December 31, 19B, for the accounts both before and after the adjusting entries for 19B.

| | | ACCOUNT BALANCE, DECEMBER 31, 19B | | | | | | |
| | Items | Before Adjusting Entries | | Adjustments | | After Adjusting Entries | |
		Debit	Credit	Debit	Credit	Debit	Credit
a.	Cash	$ 9,000				$ 9,000	
b.	Service revenue receivable					400	
c.	Prepaid insurance	600				400	
d.	Operational assets	120,200				120,200	
e.	Accumulated depreciation, equipment		$31,500				$40,000
f.	Income taxes payable						4,700
g.	Contributed capital		80,000				80,000
h.	Retained earnings, January 1, 19B		14,000				14,000
i.	Service revenue		46,000				46,400
j.	Salary expense	41,700				41,700	
k.	Depreciation expense					8,500	
l.	Insurance expense					200	
m.	Income tax expense					4,700	
		$171,500	$171,500			$185,100	$185,100

Required:

1. Compare the amounts in the columns before and after the adjusting entries to reconstruct the adjusting entries that were made in 19B. Provide an explanation of each.

2. Compute the amount of income assuming that (a) it is based on the amounts before adjusting entries and (b) it is based on the amounts after adjusting entries. Which income amount is correct? Explain why.

3. Compute earnings per share assuming that 3,000 shares of stock are outstanding.

P4–9 **Computing the Effects of Adjustments on Balance Sheets, Income Statements, and Statements of Cash Flows in Two Consecutive Years**

On January 1, 19A, four persons organized Atlantic Company. The company has been operating for two years, 19A and 19B. The following are data relating to six selected transactions that affect both years. The annual accounting period ends December 31.

(a) On January 1, 19A, the company purchased a computer for use in the business at a cash cost of $22,500. The computer has an estimated useful life of five years and no residual value. It will be depreciated on a straight-line basis.

(b) On July 1, 19A, the company borrowed $15,000 cash from City Bank and signed a one-year, 10 percent interest-bearing note. The interest and principal are payable on June 30, 19B.

(c) The company owns its office building. On October 1, 19A, it leased some of its office space to A. B. Jones for $7,200 per year. Jones paid this amount in full on October 1, 19A, and expects to use the space for one year only. The company increased (debited) Cash for $7,200 and increased (credited) Unearned Rent Revenue for $7,200 on October 1, 19A.

(d) Office supplies were purchased for use in the business. Cash was decreased (credited), and Office Supplies Inventory was increased (debited). The unused supplies at each year-end are determined by inventory count. The amounts were

Year	Purchased	Year-End Inventory
19A	$600	$200
19B	400	100

(e) The company pays wages at the end of each two weeks. The last payroll date in December usually is four days before December 31. Therefore, at each year-end, unpaid wages exist that are paid in cash on the first payroll date in the next year. The wages paid in cash and the wages incurred but not yet paid or recorded at each year-end follow:

Year	Wages Paid in Cash during the Year	Wages Unpaid and Unrecorded at Dec. 31
19A	$35,000	$ 400
19B	41,000	4,000

(f) On July 1, 19A, the company paid a two-year insurance premium on the computer of $360. At that date, the company increased (debited) an asset account, Prepaid Insurance, and decreased (credited) Cash, $360.

Required:
Complete the following schedule for 19A and 19B by entering the amounts that should be reported on the financial statements of Atlantic Company. Show computations.

	19A	19B
BALANCE SHEET		
Assets		
Computer	$	$
Less: Accumulated depreciation		
Carrying value		
Office supplies inventory		
Prepaid insurance		

	19A	19B
BALANCE SHEET		
Liabilities		
Note payable, City Bank	$	$
Interest payable		
Unearned rent revenue		
Wages payable		
INCOME STATEMENT		
Rent revenue	$	$
Depreciation expense		
Interest expense		
Office supplies expense		
Wage expense		
Insurance expense		
STATEMENT OF CASH FLOWS		
Operating activities	$	$
Collections from leased space		
Payments to employees		
Payments to suppliers—supplies		
—insurance		
Payment of interest on debt		
Investing activities		
Purchase of computer		
Financing activities		
Borrowing from bank		
Repayment of note		

P4–10 Analyzing the Effects of Adjustments and Preparing a Balance Sheet and an Income Statement Including Earnings per Share from an Unadjusted Trial Balance

Crabbe and Sons, Inc., a small service company, keeps its records without the help of an accountant. After much effort, an outside accountant prepared the following unadjusted trial balance as of the end of the annual accounting period, December 31, 19D:

Account Titles	Debit	Credit
Cash	60,000	
Accounts receivable	13,000	
Service supplies inventory	800	
Prepaid insurance	1,000	−500
Service trucks (5-year life, no residual value)	20,000	
Accumulated depreciation, service trucks		12,000
Other assets	11,200	
Accounts payable		3,000
Wages payable		
Income taxes payable		
Note payable (3 years; 10% each December 31)		20,000
Contributed capital (5,000 shares outstanding)		28,200
Retained earnings		7,500
Service revenue		77,000
Remaining expenses (not detailed)*	41,700	
Income tax expense		
Totals	147,700	147,700

*Excludes income tax expense.

Data not yet recorded at December 31, 19D:

(a) The supplies inventory count on December 31, 19D, reflected $300 remaining on hand; to be used in 19E.

(b) Insurance expired during 19D, $500.

(c) Depreciation expense for 19D, $4,000.

(d) Wages earned by employees not yet paid on December 31, 19D, $900.

(e) Income tax expense was $7,350.

Required:

1. Give the 19D adjusting entries.

2. Complete the following financial statements (show computations) for 19D to include the effects of the preceding five transactions.

3. Give the 19D closing entries.

Income Statement
For the Year Ended December 31, 19D

Service revenue		$ 77,000
Supplies expense	$ 500	
Insurance expense	500	
Depreciation expense	4,000	
Wages expense	900	
Remaining expenses (not detailed)	41,700	
Total expenses		47,600
Pretax income		77,000
Income tax expense		7,350
Net income		$ 22,050
EPS		$ 4.41

(handwritten at right: 22,050 / 5,000)

Balance Sheet
At December 31, 19D

Assets		Liabilities	
Cash	$ 60,000	Accounts payable	$
Accounts receivable		Wages payable	
Service supplies inventory		Income taxes payable	
Prepaid insurance	500	Note payable, long-term	
Service trucks	20,000	Total liabilities	31,250
Accumulated depreciation		**Stockholders' Equity** – aka common stock	
Other assets (not detailed)		Contributed capital	
		Retained earnings	
		Total stockholders' equity	
Total assets	$ 89,000	Total liabilities and stockholders' equity	$ 37,750

P4–11 Analyzing T-Account Balances to Explain the Adjustments and Prepare the Closing Entries

The T-accounts of Longhorn Company at the end of the third year of operations, December 31, 19C (prior to the closing entries), follow. The 19C adjusting entries are identified by letters.

Cash			Note Payable 8%			Contributed Capital (8,000 shares)	
Bal.	20,000			1/1/19B	10,000	Bal.	56,000

Inventory, Maintenance Supplies			Interest Payable			Retained Earnings	
Bal.	500	(a) 300		(b)	800	Bal.	9,000

Service Equipment			Income Taxes Payable			Service Revenue	
1/1/19A	90,000			(f)	13,020	(c) 6,000	Bal. 220,000

Accumulated Depreciation, Service Equipment		Wages Payable		Expenses	
	Bal. 18,000	(e) 500	Bal. 160,000		
	(d) 9,000		(a) 300		
			(b) 800		
			(d) 9,000		
			(e) 500		
			(f) 13,020		

Remaining Assets		Revenue Collected in Advance	
Bal. 42,500		(c) 6,000	

Required:

1. Develop three 19C trial balances of Longhorn Company using the following format:

Account	Unadjusted Trial Balance		Adjusted Trial Balance		Post-Closing Trial Balance	
	Debit	Credit	Debit	Credit	Debit	Credit

2. Write an explanation for each adjusting entry for 19C.
3. Give the closing journal entries.
4. What was the apparent useful life of the service equipment? What assumptions must you make to answer this question?
5. What was the average income tax rate for 19C?
6. What was the average issue (sale) price per share of the capital stock?

P4–12 Comprehensive Review Problem: From Analyzing Transactions to Preparing Financial Statements Including Earnings per Share and Cash Flows (see Chapters 2, 3, and 4)

Herman's Service Company (a corporation) began operations on January 1, 19A. The annual reporting period ends December 31. The trial balance on January 1, 19B, was as follows (the amounts are rounded to thousands of dollars to simplify):

Account No.	Account Titles	Debit	Credit
01	Cash	3	
02	Accounts receivable	5	
03	Service supplies inventory	12	
04	Land		
05	Equipment	60	
06	Accumulated depreciation (equipment)		6
07	Remaining assets (not detailed to simplify)	4	
11	Accounts payable		5
12	Notes payable		
13	Wages payable		
14	Interest payable		
15	Income taxes payable		
21	Contributed capital (65,000 shares)		65
31	Retained earnings		8
35	Service revenue		
40	Depreciation expense		
41	Income tax expense		
42	Interest expense		
43	Remaining expenses (not detailed to simplify)		
	Totals	84	84

Transactions during 19B (summarized in thousands of dollars) follow:

(a) Borrowed $10 cash on a 12 percent note payable, dated March 1, 19B.
(b) Purchased land for future building site, paid cash, $9.
(c) Earned revenues for 19B, $160, including $40 on credit.
(d) Sold 3,000 additional shares of capital stock for $1 cash per share.
(e) Recognized remaining expenses for 19B, $85, including $15 on credit.
(f) Collected accounts receivable, $24.
(g) Purchased additional assets, $10 cash (debit Remaining Assets).
(h) Paid accounts payable, $13.
(i) Purchased on account service supplies for future use, $18 (debit to Account No. 3).
(j) Signed a $25 service contract to start February 1, 19C.
(k) Declared and paid cash dividend, $17.

Data for adjusting entries:

(l) Service supplies inventory counted on December 31, 19B, $14 (debit Remaining Expenses).
(m) Equipment, useful life 10 years (no residual or scrap value).
(n) Accrued interest on notes payable (to be computed).
(o) Wages earned since the December 24 payroll; not yet paid, $12.
(p) Income tax expense was $8, payable in 19C.

Required:
1. Analyze and journalize each of the first 11 transactions.
2. Set up the 19 T-accounts and post the entries.
3. Journalize and post the adjusting entries.
4. Prepare an income statement (including earnings per share), statement of stockholders' equity, balance sheet, and statement of cash flows.
5. Journalize and post the closing entries.
6. Prepare a post-closing trial balance.

P4–13 Comprehensive Problem: Preparing Six Adjusting Entries and Recasting the Income Statement and Balance Sheet

Meadville Corporation has been in operation since January 1, 19A. It is now December 31, 19A, the end of the annual accounting period. The company has not done well financially during the first year, although revenue has been fairly good. The three stockholders manage the company, but they have not given much attention to recordkeeping. In view of a serious cash shortage, they asked a local bank for a $20,000 loan. The bank requested a complete set of financial statements. The following 19A annual financial statements were prepared by a clerk and then were given to the bank.

MEADVILLE CORPORATION
Income Statement
For the period ended December 31, 19A

Transportation revenue	$85,000
Expenses	
Salaries expense	17,000
Maintenance expense	12,000
Other expenses	18,000
Total expenses	$47,000
Net income	$38,000

MEADVILLE CORPORATION
Balance Sheet
December 31, 19A

Assets

Cash	$ 2,000
Receivables	3,000
Inventory of maintenance supplies	6,000
Equipment	40,000
Prepaid insurance	4,000
Remaining assets	27,000
Total assets	$82,000

Liabilities

Accounts payable	$ 9,000

Stockholders' Equity

Contributed capital (10,000 shares outstanding)	35,000
Retained earnings	38,000
Total liabilities and stockholders' equity	$82,000

After briefly reviewing the statements and "looking into the situation," the bank requested that the statements be redone (with some expert help) to "incorporate depreciation, accruals, inventory counts, income taxes, and so on." As a result of a review of the records and supporting documents, the following additional information was developed:

a. The inventory of maintenance supplies of $6,000 shown on the balance sheet has not been adjusted for supplies used during 19A. An inventory count of the maintenance supplies on hand (unused) on December 31, 19A, showed $1,800. Supplies used were debited to Maintenance Expense.

b. The insurance premium paid in 19A was for years 19A and 19B; therefore, the prepaid insurance at December 31, 19A, amounted to $2,000. The total insurance premium was debited in full to Prepaid Insurance when paid in 19A.

c. The equipment cost $40,000 when purchased January 1, 19A. It had an estimated useful life of five years (no residual value). No depreciation has been recorded for 19A.

d. Unpaid (and unrecorded) salaries at December 31, 19A, amounted to $2,200.

e. At December 31, 19A, hauling revenue collected in advance amounted to $7,000. This amount was credited in full to Transportation Revenue when the cash was collected earlier during 19A.

f. Income tax expense was $3,650 (the tax rate is 25 percent).

Required:
1. Give the six adjusting entries required on December 31, 19A, based on the preceding additional information.
2. Recast the preceding statements after taking into account the adjusting entries. You do not need to use classifications on the statements. Suggested form for the solution:

			CHANGES		
Items		**Amounts Reported**	**Plus**	**Minus**	**Correct Amounts**
(List here each item from the two statements)					

3. Omission of the adjusting entries caused:
   a. Net income to be overstated or understated (select one) by $ _____ .
   b. Total assets on the balance sheet to be overstated or understated (select one) by $ _____ .

4. For both of the unadjusted and adjusted balances, calculate these ratios for the company: (a) debt-to-equity, (b) return on investment, and (c) earnings per share.
5. Write a brief, nontechnical report to the bank explaining the causes of these differences and the impact of these changes on financial analysis.

Cases and Projects

C4–1 Analyzing Four Transactions of a Real Estate Company That Involve Adjustments

Seneca Land Company, a closely held corporation, invests in commercial rental properties. Seneca's annual accounting period ends on December 31. At the end of each year, numerous adjusting entries must be made because many transactions completed during current and prior years have economic effects on the financial statements of the current and future years. This case concerns four transactions that have been selected for your analysis. Assume that the current year is 19D.

TRANSACTION (a)

On July 1, 19A, the company purchased office equipment costing $14,000 for use in the business. The company estimates that the equipment will have a useful life of 10 years and no residual value.

a. Over how many accounting periods will this transaction directly affect Seneca's financial statements? Explain.
b. Assuming straight-line depreciation, how much depreciation expense should be reported on the 19A and 19B income statements?
c. How should the office equipment be reported on the 19C balance sheet?
d. Would Seneca make an adjusting entry at the end of each year during the life of the equipment? Explain your answer.

TRANSACTION (b)

On September 1, 19D, Seneca collected $24,000 rent on office space. This amount represented the monthly rent in advance for the six-month period, September 1, 19D, through February 28, 19E. Unearned Rent Revenue was increased (credited), and Cash was increased (debited) for $24,000.

a. Over how many accounting periods will this transaction affect Seneca's financial statements? Explain.
b. How much rent revenue on this office space should Seneca report on the 19D income statement? Explain.
c. Did this transaction create a liability for Seneca as of the end of 19D? Explain. If yes, how much?
d. Should Seneca make an adjusting entry on December 31, 19D? Explain why. If your answer is yes, give the adjusting entry.

TRANSACTION (c)

On December 31, 19D, Seneca owed employees unpaid and unrecorded wages of $7,500 because the payroll was paid on December 27 and between this day and year-end, employees worked three more days in December 19D. The next payroll date is January 5, 19E.

a. Over how many accounting periods does this transaction affect Seneca's financial statements? Explain.
b. How would this $7,500 affect Seneca's 19D income statement and balance sheet?
c. Should Seneca make an adjusting entry on December 31, 19D? Explain why. If your answer is yes, give the adjusting entry.

(continued on next page)

TRANSACTION (d)

On January 1, 19D, Seneca agreed to supervise the planning and subdivision of a large tract of land for a customer, J. Ray. This service job that Seneca will perform involves four separate phases. By December 31, 19D, three phases had been completed to Ray's satisfaction. The remaining phase will be done during 19E. The total price for the four phases (agreed on in advance by both parties) was $60,000. Each phase involves about the same amount of services. On December 31, 19D, Seneca had collected no cash for the services already performed.

   a.   Should Seneca record any service revenue on this job for 19D? Explain why. If yes, how much?

   b.   If your answer to (*a*) is yes, should Seneca make an adjusting entry on December 31, 19D? If yes, give the entry. Explain.

   c.   What entry will Seneca make when it completes the last phase, assuming that the full contract price is collected on completion date, February 15, 19E?

C4–2 Analyzing How Alternative Ways of Recording a Transaction Affect Adjusting Entries

General situation: On December 1, 19A, Aniello Massa collected $6,000 cash for office space rented to an outsider. The rent was collected for the period December 1, 19A, through March 31, 19B. The annual accounting period ends on December 31.

Required:

   1.   How much of the $6,000 should Massa report as revenue on the 19A annual income statement? How much of it should be reported as revenue on the 19B income statement?

   2.   What is the amount of rent revenue collected in advance as of December 31, 19A? How should Massa report this amount on the 19A financial statements?

   3.   On December 1, 19A, Massa could have recorded the $6,000 collection in one of three different ways as follows:

Approach A

Cash	6,000	
Rent revenue		6,000

Approach B

Cash	6,000	
Rent revenue collected in advance		6,000

Approach C

Cash	6,000	
Rent revenue		1,500
Rent revenue collected in advance		4,500

For each approach, give the appropriate adjusting entry (in journal form) at December 31, 19A. If no adjusting entry is required, explain why.

   4.   Do you believe that one of these approaches is better than the other two? Which one? Explain.

C4–3 Identifying and Correcting Several Accounting Errors

Austin Company's bookkeeper prepared the following trial balance at December 31, 19B:

Account Titles	Debit	Credit
Notes receivable	6,000	
Supplies inventory		300
Accounts payable	600	
Land	14,000	
Contributed capital		22,000
Cash	5,045	
Interest revenue	300	
Note payable		4,000
Operating expenses	21,000	
Interest expense		600
Other assets	9,583	
Service revenue		29,583
Totals	56,483	56,483

An independent CPA (auditor) casually inspected the trial balance and saw that it had several errors.

Required:

Draft a correct trial balance and explain any errors that you discover. All of the dollar amounts except those for Other Assets are correct.

C4–4 A Complex Situation Requiring Technical Analysis of an Income Statement: Challenging

Cathy Webking, a local attorney, decided to sell her practice and retire. She has had discussions with an attorney from another state who wants to relocate. The discussions are at the complex stage of agreeing on a price. Among the important factors have been the financial statements of Webking's practice. Webking's secretary, under her direction, maintained the records. Each year they developed a statement of profits on a cash basis from the incomplete records maintained; no balance sheet was prepared. Upon request, Webking provided the other attorney with the following statements for 19F prepared by her secretary:

C. WEBKING
Statement of Profits
19F

Legal fees collected		$115,000
Expenses paid		
Rent for office space	$13,000	
Utilities expense	360	
Telephone expense	2,200	
Office salaries expense	22,000	
Office supplies expense	900	
Miscellaneous expenses	2,400	
Total expenses		40,860
Profit for the year		$ 74,140

Upon agreement of the parties, you have been asked to examine the financial figures for 19F. The other attorney said, "I question the figures because, among other things, they appear to be on a 100 percent cash basis." Your investigations revealed the following additional data at December 31, 19F:

a. Of the $115,000 legal fees collected in 19F, $32,000 was for services performed prior to 19F.

b. At the end of 19F, legal fees of $9,000 for services performed during the year were uncollected.

c. Office equipment owned and used by Webking cost $5,000 and had an estimated useful life of 10 years.

d. An inventory of office supplies at December 31, 19F, reflected $200 worth of items purchased during the year that were still on hand. Also, the records for 19E indicate that the supplies on hand at the end of that year were about $125.

e. At the end of 19F, a secretary whose salary is $18,000 per year had not been paid for December because of a long trip that extended to January 15, 19G.

f. The $1,400 phone bill for December 19F was not paid until January 11, 19G.

g. The $13,000 office rent paid was for 13 months (it included the rent for January 19G).

Required:

1. On the basis of this information, prepare a correct income statement for 19F. Show your computations for any amounts changed from those in the statement prepared by Webking's secretary. (Suggested solution format with four-column headings: Items; Cash Basis per Webking Statement, $; Explanation of Changes; and Corrected Basis, $.)

2. Write a comment to support your schedule prepared in requirement (1). The purpose should be to explain the reasons for your changes and to suggest other important items that should be considered in the pricing decision.

Scott Paper Company

C4–5 Analyzing the Fiscal Year for an Actual Company

An annual report for Scott Paper Company, the world's largest manufacturer and marketer of sanitary tissue products including Scott facial tissues, Baby Fresh wipes, and Scott towels, included the following note:

> **1. Accounting Policies**
> **Fiscal Year End**
> The Company's fiscal year ends on the last Saturday in December, which results in a 52- or 53-week year. Fiscal year 1994 consisted of 53 weeks while fiscal years 1993 and 1992 consisted of 52 weeks. To facilitate prompt reporting of Scott's financial results, the financial statements of most of the international subsidiaries and affiliates are based on the twelve months ending November 30.

Required:

1. Why would a company want to use a fiscal year of variable length?

2. As an analyst, would Scott Paper Company's fiscal year policy have any impact on your work?

C4–6 Analytical—Preparing Adjusting and Closing Entries by Analyzing Unadjusted and Adjusted Trial Balances; Answering 10 Analytical Questions

Rowland Company was organized on January 1, 19A. At the end of the first year of operations, December 31, 19A, the bookkeeper prepared the following trial balances (amounts in thousands of dollars):

Account No.	Account Titles	Unadjusted Trial Balance Debit	Unadjusted Trial Balance Credit	Adjustments		Adjusted Trial Balance Debit	Adjusted Trial Balance Credit
11	Cash	40				40	
12	Accounts receivable	17				17	
13	Prepaid insurance	2				1	
14	Rent receivable					2	
15	Operational assets	46				46	
16	Accumulated depreciation, operational assets						11
17	Other assets	6				6	
18	Accounts payable		27				27
19	Wages payable						3
20	Income taxes payable						5
21	Rent revenue collected in advance						4
22	Note payable (10%; dated January 1, 19A)		20				20
23	Contributed capital (1,000 shares)		30				30
24	Retained earnings	3				3	
25	Revenues (total)		105				103
26	Expenses (total including interest)	68				83	
27	Income tax expense					5	
	Totals	182	182			203	203

Required:

1. Based on inspection of the two trial balances, give the 19A adjusting entries developed by the bookkeeper (provide brief explanations).
2. Based on these data, give the 19A closing entries with brief explanations.
3. Answer the following questions (show computations):
    a. How many shares of stock were outstanding at year-end?
    b. What was the estimated useful life of the operational assets assuming a $2,000 residual value and a purchase date of January 1, 19A?
    c. What was the amount of interest expense included in the total expenses?
    d. What was the balance of Retained Earnings on December 31, 19A?
    e. What was the average income tax rate?
    f. How would the two accounts Rent Receivable and Rent Revenue Collected in Advance be reported on the balance sheet?
    g. Explain why cash increased by $40,000 during the year even though net income was comparatively very low.
    h. What was the amount of EPS for 19A?
    i. What was the average selling price of the shares?
    j. When was the insurance premium paid and over what period of time did the coverage extend?

C4–7 Analyzing The Matching Concept for an Actual Company

A recent annual report for Hershey Foods Corporation contained the following information:

Hershey Foods Corporation

SUPPLEMENTAL INCOME STATEMENT INFORMATION

Supplemental income statement information is provided in the table below. These costs are expensed in the year incurred.

For the Years Ended December 31 (in thousands of dollars)	Current Year	Previous Year
Promotion	$256,237	$230,187
Advertising	121,182	99,082
Maintenance and repairs	58,842	54,377
Depreciation expense	54,543	43,721
Rent expense	20,033	17,618
Research and development	16,094	15,695

Required:

1. What types of costs are included in the following categories: promotion, advertising, maintenance and repairs, and research and development?
2. In your judgment, should any of these costs have been recorded as an asset and allocated over several accounting periods?

Toys "R" Us

C4–8 Financial Statement Analysis

Refer to the financial statements of Toys "R" Us given in Appendix B at the end of this book.

Required:

1. Give examples of business documents that the company's accountants analyzed to record sales transactions.
2. How should the company record the payment of $500 on account by one of its credit customers?
3. How should the company record the purchase of $8,000 of inventory on credit from one of its suppliers?
4. Does the collection of an account receivable by the company affect its total assets? Does it affect cash flows from operating activities on the statement of cash flows?
5. When does the company's fiscal year end?
6. What company accounts would not appear on a post-closing trial balance?
7. Give the closing entry for Prepaid Expenses.
8. What are the company's earnings per share, return on investment, and debt-to-equity ratios for the more recent year?

C4–9 Project: Comparing Accrual and Deferral Accounts within Industries

Acquire the balance sheets from the annual reports or 10-Ks of three companies within an industry. (Library files, the SEC EDGAR service at www.sec.gov, Compustat CD, or the companies themselves are good sources.) Identify the accounts that result from accruals and those that are deferrals. Write a short report indicating any similarities and differences, if any, in the accounts used by the three.

C4–10 Project: Comparing Accrual and Deferral Accounts between Industries

Acquire the balance sheets from the annual reports or 10-Ks of three companies from different industries. (Library files, the SEC EDGAR service at www.sec.gov, Compustat CD, or the companies themselves are good sources.) Identify the accounts that result from accruals and those that are deferrals. Write a short report indicating any similarities and differences, if any, in the accounts used by the three.

C4–11 Project: Analyzing Differences in Earnings per Share among Competitors

Sbarro's competitors in the restaurant business include Outback Steakhouse, Boston Chicken, Cheesecake Factory, Au Bon Pain, and Uno's Pizzeria. Obtain the recent balance sheet and income statement for Sbarro and two of its competitors. (Library files, the SEC EDGAR service at www.sec.gov, Compustat CD, or the companies themselves are good sources. All of these companies are included under the SIC [Standard Industrial Classification] code 5812 for retail eating places.) Write a short memo comparing the companies' earnings per share ratios. Indicate what differences in their businesses might account for any differences in the ratio.

C4–12 Project: Focus on Cash Flows

Acquire the three most recent years' statements of cash flows for a single company. (Library files, the SEC EDGAR service at www.sec.gov, Compustat CD, or the company itself are good sources.) Compute the percentage of cash from operating activities to net income for each year. Write a short memo comparing the three percentages and discuss your perceptions about this company's quality of net income.

C4–13 Project: Financial Analysis Update

Acquire the most recent year's annual report and Form 10-K for Sbarro. (Library files, the SEC EDGAR service at www.sec.gov, Compustat CD, or the company itself are good sources.) Write a short memo comparing the company's earnings per share to Sbarro's EPS presented in the chapter. Indicate what might account for any difference in the ratio.

C4–14 Ethics Project: Analyzing Management's Incentives to Manipulate Financial Information

Obtain a recent news story concerning a corporate financial fraud that discusses management's motivation for its fraudulent acts. (Library files, the SEC EDGAR service at www.sec.gov, Compustat CD, or other news retrieval services are good sources.) Write a short memo outlining the nature of the fraud, what management's motivation was, and who was hurt or helped by the fraudulent financial information.

C4–15 Team Project: Analysis of Accruals, Earnings per Share, and Cash Flows

As a team, select an industry to analyze. Each team member should acquire the annual report or 10-K for one publicly traded company in the industry, with each member selecting a different company. (Library files, the SEC EDGAR service at www.sec.gov, Compustat CD, or the companies themselves are good sources.) On an individual basis, each team member should then write a short report listing the following:

1. The company's earnings per share for each year.
2. The percentage of cash flows from operating activities to net income for each year and your perceptions about the company's quality of earnings based on this ratio.
3. The amount of accrued expenses (a liability) on the balance sheet and the ratio of accrued expenses to total liabilities.
4. Summaries of any notes to the financial statements that describe accrued expenses in detail.

Then, as a team, write a short report comparing and contrasting your companies using these attributes. Discuss any patterns across the companies that you as a team observe. Provide potential explanations for any differences discovered.

CHAPTER FIVE

The Communication of Accounting Information

Callaway Golf

CLEAR COMMUNICATION WITH CUSTOMERS AND FINANCIAL
STATEMENT USERS IS A HALLMARK OF CALLAWAY'S SUCCESS

In just 13 years, Ely [pronounced EE-lee] Callaway took a small manufac-

turer of specialty golf clubs with $500,000 in annual sales and built it into an

industry leader with sales of more than $675 million. Callaway attributes this

success to the innovative Big Bertha oversized clubs, created by a team of

aerospace and metallurgical engineers, that make the game easier to learn

and play. Both touring pros and average golfers including Bill Clinton and

George Bush carry a Big Bertha driver in their golf bags. But industry insiders

attribute an equal portion of Ely Callaway's success to his marketing skills. He

spends hours each day talking to the pros who use his clubs at televised

events and the dealers who sell his clubs. He even writes much of the com-

pany's ad copy.

He and then chief financial officer (CFO) Carol Kerley applied that same personal marketing touch to the financial side of the business when they persuaded managers of the General Electric Pension Fund to invest $10 million in the company to provide the capital that fueled its initial growth in 1989. The same enthusiasm and clear approach to communication were apparent in the company's initial public offering (first stock issuance to the public, or IPO) in 1992. The CFO and her accounting staff worked tirelessly with the company's outside auditors, Price Waterhouse, and its investment bankers, Merrill Lynch, to prepare the detailed financial information necessary for the IPO. Callaway had prepared audited statements in the past. Now as a publicly traded company, it is required to provide even more information in regular filings with the Securities and Exchange Commission.

Clear communication with Callaway's four customer groups— professional endorsers, dealers, golfing consumers, and investors and other users of financial statements—continues to be a hallmark of its business strategy. This approach has met with success in each case. Callaway drivers are now the most popular on the Senior and Ladies PGA tours and second in the regular PGA tour, and Callaway is the fastest growing golfing equipment company in the world. The stock market has rewarded Callaway's operating successes and its financial communication strategy with a *quintupling* of its stock price over the first two years following the IPO. Marketing the company can be as important as marketing quality products.

Business Background

Callaway Golf Company designs, manufactures, and markets high-quality innovative golf clubs that sell at premium prices. Its Big Bertha oversized stainless steel and titanium woods and irons account for most of its sales. Many judge these clubs to be the "friendliest" in the game because they are less sensitive to off-center hits. The company manufactures its metal woods and irons in its new Carlsbad, California, factories using clubheads, shafts, and grips supplied by independent vendors such as Cast Alloys, Coastcast Corporation, Aldila, True Temper, Unifiber, and others. The clubs are sold primarily at high-end pro shops. Callaway invests considerable amounts in research and development and is known for introducing new innovative products long before the end of its existing products' life cycles. Although it *manufactures* golf clubs, Callaway also sells other golf-related equipment, including balls, bags, and head-covers, that others manufacture. Thus, it is a *merchandiser* for this other equipment.

Successful companies such as Callaway learn to match their financial reporting strategies to their business strategies. Marketing and communication are fundamental to both strategies. Although Callaway has a company policy of never publicly predicting future sales or financial results, it values integrity in the communication of financial results as much as it does in its relationships with suppliers, customers, and employees. It deals honestly and candidly with the financial press, financial analysts, and the investing public. Also, to its credit, the financial statements and related disclosures provided in its annual report are a model of clarity. Callaway's management believes that such an approach eases the company's access to capital from lenders and investors. This approach lowers the costs of borrowing (interest rates) and lowers investors' perceptions of the riskiness of Callaway's stock. These policies, the fact that the company has recently changed from private to public financing, and its astonishing business success make Callaway Golf an excellent example through which we can complete our discussion of the accounting communication process.

Chapters 2 through 4 focused on the mechanics of preparing the income statement, balance sheet, statement of stockholders' equity, and cash flow statement. In this chapter, we discuss the principles guiding the exact statement formats and additional disclosures provided in annual reports and related reports. We also focus on the sequential process that conveys accounting information to statement users during a typical year, as well as the people involved in that process.

Players in the Accounting Communication Process

Exhibit 5.1 summarizes the accounting communication process in terms of the people involved, their roles in the process, and the guidance they receive from legal and professional standards.

LEARNING OBJECTIVE 1

Recognize the people involved in the accounting communication process (managers, auditors, information intermediaries, government regulators, and users), their roles in the process, and the guidance they receive from legal and professional standards.

EXHIBIT 5.1
The Accounting Communication Process

"The Players"

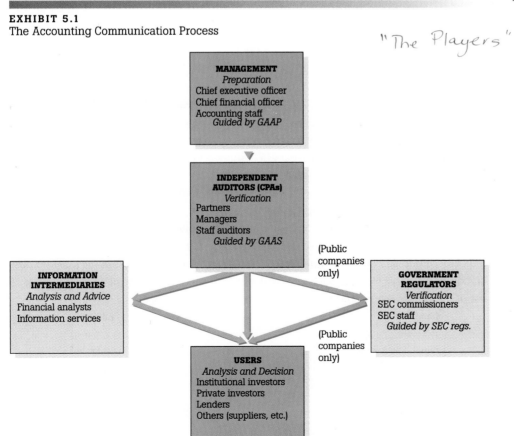

Managers (CEO, CFO, and Accounting Staff)

As noted in Chapter 1, the primary responsibility for the information in Callaway's financial statements and related disclosures lies with management as represented by the highest officer in the company, often called the *chairman and chief executive officer* (CEO) and the highest officer associated with the financial and accounting side of the business, often called the *chief financial officer* (CFO). These two officers normally sign the statement of management responsibility (as also discussed in Chapter 1) if one is included in the annual report. For public companies, the same officers sign the principal reports filed with the Securities and Exchange Commission (SEC). At Callaway, Ely Callaway, chairman and CEO, and Carol Kerley, then the CFO, had that responsibility at the time of Callaway's initial public offering (IPO). They were responsible for the conformance of the statements and related disclosures with GAAP (generally accepted accounting principles). Although their legal responsibility is smaller, the members of the *accounting staff* who actually prepare the details of the reports also have professional responsibility for the accuracy of this information. Their professional success in the future depends heavily on their reputations for honesty and competence.

Auditors

Even before Callaway Golf first issued stock to the public, the company submitted its statements for verification by a team of independent auditors, or CPAs, who conduct their examinations in conformance with generally accepted auditing standards (GAAS). The SEC requires publicly traded companies to have their statements audited by CPAs; many privately owned companies also have their statements audited. As we discussed in Chapter 1, by signing an **unqualified,** or **clean audit opinion,** the CPA firm assumes financial responsibility for the fairness of the financial statements and related presentations. This opinion adds credibility to the statements and often is required by agreements with lenders and private investors who are not actively involved in management of the companies. Callaway Golf was initially financed through investments by Mr. Callaway and some of his close friends and loans from financial institutions (e.g., banks and commercial finance companies). By subjecting the company's statements to independent verification, Callaway reduced the risk to the private investors and financial institutions that the company's condition was not as represented in the statements. As a consequence, rational investors and lenders should lower the rate of return (interest) they charge for providing capital.

> An **unqualified (clean) audit opinion** states that the financial statements are fair presentations in all material respects in conformity with GAAP.

Price Waterhouse (which along with KPMG Peat Marwick, Arthur Andersen, Ernst & Young, Deloitte & Touche, and Coopers & Lybrand* make up what are referred to as the "Big 6" CPA firms) is currently Callaway Golf's auditor. Each of these firms employs thousands of CPAs in offices scattered throughout the world. They audit the great majority of publicly traded companies and many privately held companies. Some public companies and most private companies are audited by CPA firms of smaller size. A list of a few well-known companies and their auditors follows.

Company	Industry	Auditor
The Boeing Company	Aircraft	Deloitte & Touche
Hilton Hotels Corporation	Hotels	Arthur Andersen
Honda Motor Co. Ltd. (Japan)	Automobiles	KPMG Peat Marwick
Singapore Airlines (Singapore)	Airline	Ernst & Young
Wendy's	Fast food	Coopers & Lybrand

Much of the evidence that the auditors gather to support their opinion is collected throughout the year. The busiest time for most auditors, however, is the end of the

---

*As we go to press, Price Waterhouse and Coopers & Lybrand have tentatively agreed to merge their practices.

reporting period when they apply final tests to the records and examine the final statements and other disclosures. Financial reporting standards set by the SEC and the Financial Accounting Standards Board (FASB), combined with the independent examination provided by CPAs and the legal liability that they assume, add significant credibility to a company's financial statements and related disclosures.

Carol Kerley, Callaway's CFO at the time of the initial public offering, and David A. Rane, current CFO, were senior managers with Price Waterhouse before moving to Callaway Golf. Companies often hire financial managers from their CPA firms because of their broad financial experience as well as their specific company knowledge gained during prior years' audits.

Information Intermediaries: Analysts and Information Services

The Role of Financial Analysts

Students often view the communication process between companies and financial statement users as involving a simple process of mailing the report to individual shareholders who read the reports and then make investment decisions based on what they have learned. This simple picture is far from today's reality. Now sophisticated *financial analysts* use modern information technology to gather and analyze information. They receive accounting reports and other information about the company from electronic information services (discussed later). They also gather information through personal phone conversations with company executives and visits to company facilities. They then combine the results of these analyses with information about competitors, the overall economy, and even population trends to make predictions of future earnings and stock price. These predictions form the basis of their buy, hold, or sell recommendations for a company's stock.

Analysts often work in the research departments of brokerage and investment banking houses such as Merrill Lynch, mutual fund companies such as Fidelity Investments,[1] and investment advisory services such as Value Line that sell their advice to others. Individual analysts often specialize in particular industries (such as sporting goods or energy companies) and in particular companies. For example, Hayley Kissel at Merrill Lynch and John W. Weiss of Montgomery Securities (both brokerage and investment banking companies) are among those who follow Callaway Golf. With other analysts at their firms, they write reports that analyze the company's future prospects.

Analysts' reports normally include their estimate or forecast of future quarterly and annual earnings per share for the company.[2] In making these **earnings forecasts,** the analysts rely heavily on their knowledge of the way the accounting system translates business events into the numbers on a company's financial statements.[3] This knowledge includes an understanding of the alternative accounting methods available to companies to account for different transactions and specialized industry practices that may be applied to a particular industry. We discuss both of these issues later in this chapter. Analysts' employers either use the reports directly or sell them to other investors. As a consequence, the analyst is transferring his or her knowledge of

Earnings forecasts are predictions of earnings for future accounting periods.

---

[1] Individuals buy shares in mutual fund companies, which invest that money in the stocks and bonds of various companies.

[2] For further discussion of analysts' forecasts, see K. Schipper, "Analysts' Forecasts," *Accounting Horizons,* December 1991, pp. 105–121.

[3] See G. J. Previts, R. J. Bricker, T. R. Robinson, and S. J. Young, "A Content Analysis of Sell-Side Financial Analyst Reports," *Accounting Horizons,* June 1994, pp. 55–70.

accounting, the company, and the industry to others who lack this expertise. Many believe that decisions made based on analysts' advice cause stock market prices to react quickly to accounting information announcements. A quick, unbiased reaction to information is called *market efficiency* in finance.

It is highly unlikely that unsophisticated investors can glean more information from financial statements than the sophisticated analysts have already learned. Careful analysis does not lead all analysts to the same conclusions, however. These differences of opinion are reflected in the earnings forecasts and stock recommendations for Callaway by three of the groups of analysts listed on the *Bloomberg Business News* service at the time this chapter was written.

REAL WORLD EXCERPT

Bloomberg Business News

COMPANY: CALLAWAY GOLF			
Firm	Stock Recommendation	Earnings Forecast for 12/97	Earnings Forecast for 12/98
ABN/Chicago Corp.	Buy	2.00	2.35
Hambrecht & Quist	Buy	2.08	2.46
Ladenberg Thalmann	Buy	2.00	2.37

The information services discussed in the next section allow investors to monitor the recommendations of a variety of analysts.

QUESTION OF ETHICS

It Pays to Be a Wary Investor

Recent events on Wall Street suggest that savvy investors should apply a healthy dose of skepticism along with their accounting knowledge when reading or listening to investment advice. Alleged ethical lapses, questionable business practices, and illegal activity by representatives of some of the largest, most highly respected brokerage and investment banking houses have recently made the news. These activities include the rigging of prices in securities auctions, excess trading of customers' accounts to generate higher commissions, insider trading, the sale of securities without full disclosure of their risks, and executing trades for some customers at more advantageous prices than others. Most analysts, brokers, and investment bankers act in an honest and ethical fashion; however, they earn profits by charging commissions on securities transactions. When brokers let their need to earn commissions cloud their investment advice, it can lead to unethical behavior.

Information Services

Financial analysts obtain much of the information they use from the wide variety of electronic information services available today. These services are normally either available on-line (via modem, computer networks, or satellite dish) or on CD-ROM (compact disk, read-only memory). Some of the services provide specialized information. For example, I/B/E/S, Inc., provides consensus (average) and analyst-by-analyst earnings forecasts for more than 17,000 domestic and foreign companies. More than 800 research analysts contribute earnings forecasts to the service. First Call provides a similar service. Samples of the consensus forecasts can be accessed on their World Wide Web sites:

WWW.IBES.COM
WWW.FIRSTCALL.COM

Some services provide broader access to financial statement and related news information. The Lexis-Nexis service is a major source of financial statement information. It provides full-text versions of annual reports and SEC filings, which we describe later, and other information via modem or network connection. It also allows users to search the database by key words, including various terms in financial statements. Companies such as Compustat (a unit of Standard & Poor's, which is a division of The McGraw-Hill Companies, which also owns the publisher of this book) and Disclosure provide a wide variety of historical financial statement data available on CD-ROM and other computer-readable media, as well as on-line services. Their websites describe their services in more detail:

WWW.LEXIS-NEXIS.COM
WWW.COMPUSTAT.COM
WWW.DISCLOSURE.COM/DGA_DEMO/

Companies actually can file SEC forms electronically with EDGAR (Electronic Data Gathering and Retrieval Service), sponsored by the SEC. Then this information is available to users through EDGAR within 24 hours of filing with the Commission, long before it is available through the mail in hard-copy form. EDGAR is currently a free service available on the World Wide Web at

WWW.SEC.GOV/CGI-BIN/SRCH-EDGAR

To look at EDGAR, just type the address on your Web browser. Then, at the search prompt, enter "Callaway Golf" and you will be led to Callaway's latest filings. The 10-K and 10-Q forms (described later) include the financial statements and notes. Many of the financial statement examples used in this book were downloaded (electronically copied) from different services.

More general information services include the Dow Jones News Retrieval Service and Bloomberg Financial Markets and Commodities News. Dow Jones provides access via modem or network to news stories about companies taken from publications and news wires owned by Dow Jones (e.g., *The Wall Street Journal*) and to current and historical stock price information (among other information). Many company press releases, including the initial announcements of annual and quarterly financial results, are available from this service. This information also is available electronically through the information service long before shareholders and others receive the hard-copy reports. The Bloomberg service provides an even wider spectrum of information including stock prices, news stories, press releases, financial statement information, earnings forecasts, general economic news, and much more. It also provides the ability to combine these sources of information in sophisticated analyses. The graph presented in Exhibit 5.2 plots Callaway's quarterly price per share and earnings per share over 10 quarters (2½ years). The graph was printed directly from a Bloomberg terminal. Preceding the graph are other financial statement and price statistics that can be directly plotted on the Bloomberg terminal. Their websites describe their services in more detail:

WWW.DOWJONES.COM
WWW.BLOOMBERG.COM

Many services provide their product(s) in multiple forms (e.g., CD-ROM, proprietary network, and World Wide Web). At the time that this book is being written, the general trend is toward providing services over the Web. Many companies provide direct access to their financial statements and other information over the Web. You can contact Callaway at

WWW.CALLAWAYGOLF.COM

EXHIBIT 5.2
Price and Earnings per Share Graph from Bloomberg Terminal

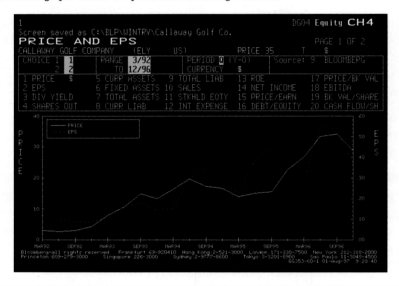

Information Services: Uses in Marketing, Classwork, and Job Search

Information services have become the primary tools used not only by sophisticated analysts but also by marketing strategists to analyze competing firms. Sales representatives also use the services to analyze potential customers. These analyses allow the sales representative to determine which customers have growing needs for their products and which have the financial strength necessary to qualify for credit. Such companies are the most profitable targets for the sales representative's efforts.

The information services are an important source of information to students for their term papers and even their job searches. Potential employers expect top job applicants to be knowledgeable about their company before an interview. We suggest that you contact the business or reference librarian at your college or university library or visit a local brokerage house to learn more about these modern electronic information services and the usage fees they charge.

Government Regulators

The *Securities and Exchange Commission* sets additional reporting standards for firms with publicly traded debt or equity securities. We discuss these requirements later in the chapter and throughout the text when relevant. The SEC staff reviews these reports for compliance with their standards, investigates irregularities, and punishes violators of their regulations. Research indicates that during a recent seven-year period, the SEC brought enforcement actions against 188 firms for accounting-related violations.[4] In 72 percent of the cases, target companies fired or forced the resignation of top managers, and in 81 percent of the cases, the shareholders subsequently sued the companies. The companies' auditors were also penalized in 42 percent of the cases.

---

[4] These statistics are reported in E. H. Feroz, K. Parke, and V. S. Pastena, "The Financial and Market Effects of the SEC's Accounting and Auditing Enforcement Releases," *Journal of Accounting Research,* Supplement 1991, pp. 107–142.

Users: Institutional and Private Investors, Creditors, and Others

Institutional investors include the managers of private pension funds (associated with unions and employees of specific companies); public pension funds (for state and municipal employees); mutual funds; and endowment, charitable foundation, and trust funds (such as the endowment of your college or university). These institutional stockholders usually employ their own analysts and use the information intermediaries just discussed. Institutional shareholders such as these control the majority of publicly traded shares of U.S. companies. For example, at the time this book was written, the following three institutional investors, along with the eight others owning between 1 and 2 million shares each, together owned more than 29 percent of Callaway's outstanding stock:

Institution	Approximate Ownership
Fidelity Management & Research	5.5 million shares
Nicholas–Applegate Capital Management	2.7 million shares
AIM Capital Management	2.2 million shares

An additional 63 other institutional investors such as Mellon Bank, Bankers Trust, and the New York State Common Retirement Fund owned between 100,000 and 1 million shares each. Most small investors own stock in companies such as Callaway Golf *indirectly* through mutual and pension funds such as these.

Private investors include large individual investors such as Ely Callaway and his friends who invested directly in Callaway Golf before it became a public company and small retail investors who, like most individuals, buy a small number of shares of publicly traded companies through brokers such as Merrill Lynch and E*TRADE. Retail investors normally lack the expertise to understand financial statements and the resources to gather other important data efficiently. As a consequence, they often rely on the advice of information intermediaries or turn their money over to the management of mutual and pension funds (institutional investors).

Lenders, or **creditors,** include suppliers, banks, commercial credit companies, and other financial institutions that lend money to companies. Lending officers and financial analysts in these organizations use these same public sources of information in their analyses. In addition, when companies borrow money from financial institutions, they often agree to provide additional financial information (e.g., monthly statements) as part of the lending contract. Lenders are often the primary external user group for financial statements of private companies. Individuals and mutual funds also become creditors when they buy publicly traded bonds and debentures issued by a company.[5]

> **Institutional investors** are managers of pension, mutual, endowment, and other funds that invest on the behalf of others.

> **Private investors** include individuals who purchase shares in companies.

> **Lenders (creditors)** include suppliers and financial institutions that lend money to companies.

Conflicting Interests of Managers, Stockholders, and Creditors

The economic interests of managers, stockholders, and creditors often differ. For example, paying dividends to stockholders benefits the stockholders but leaves less money available to pay creditors; refurnishing the offices occupied by managers benefits the managers but leaves less money to pay dividends. Expectations of ethical conduct and mutual trust play a major role in keeping these differing interests in check.

QUESTION OF ETHICS

---

[5] Debentures are debt securities not secured with specific collateral (no specific assets are pledged as security for the debt). Bonds normally are secured by specific collateral such as investments in stock of other companies.

> **Accounting and financial statements also play a major role in enforcing these relationships of trust. Later in the chapter we discuss how compliance with agreements between managers and stockholders and between stockholders and creditors are monitored with financial statement data.* When the U.S. negotiates arms treaties with other countries, "trust but verify" is a common rule that is followed. Applying the same rule in business practice is prudent.**
>
> *Research that examines the use of accounting in contracting is called *agency theory.*

As noted in Chapter 1, these same financial statements play an important role in the relationships between customers and suppliers. Customers evaluate the financial health of suppliers to determine whether they will be able to provide a reliable, up-to-date source of supply. Suppliers evaluate their customers to estimate their future needs and ability to pay their debts to the suppliers. Competitors also attempt to learn useful information about a company from its statements. The potential loss of competitive advantage is one of the costs to the preparer of public financial disclosures. Other uses of financial statement information in labor–management relations and in government regulation were discussed in Chapter 1.

Guiding Principles for Communicating Useful Information: The Remaining Parts of the Conceptual Framework

LEARNING OBJECTIVE 2
Understand the principles and constraints that guide management and the FASB in deciding what financial information should be reported.

Now that we know who the players are in communicating accounting information to users external to the company, we need to complete our understanding of the conceptual framework by examining the concepts that guide the quality of the information being reported. The portions of the framework that we discuss here are highlighted in Exhibit 5.3 in bold, white print.

Qualitative Characteristics of Financial Information

External decision makers expect financial information in reports to be *useful* to them in making their resource allocation decisions. To satisfy this primary objective of financial

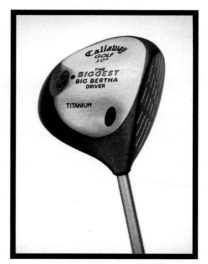

Why is new product development an important component in evaluating Callaway's stock?

EXHIBIT 5.3
Financial Accounting and Reporting Conceptual Framework

PRIMARY OBJECTIVE OF EXTERNAL FINANCIAL REPORTING
To provide useful economic information to external users for decision making (for assessing future cash flows) [Ch.2]

QUALITATIVE CHARACTERISTICS OF INFORMATION
[Ch. 5]
Primary
Relevance   Information influences decisions; it is timely and has predictive and feedback value.
Reliability   Information is accurate, unbiased, and verifiable.
Secondary
Comparability   Information can be compared to that of other businesses.
Consistency   Information can be compared across time.

ELEMENTS OF FINANCIAL STATEMENTS
Assets   Probable future economic benefits owned by the entity from past transactions. [Ch. 2]
Liabilities   Probable debts or obligations from past transactions to be paid with assets or services. [Ch. 2]
Stockholders' Equity   Financing provided by owners and operations. [Ch. 2]
Revenues   Increases in assets or settlements of liabilities from ongoing operations. [Ch. 3]
Expenses   Decreases in assets or increases in liabilities from ongoing operations. [Ch. 3]
Gains   Increases in assets or decreases in liabilities from peripheral transactions. [Ch. 3]
Losses   Decreases in assets or increases in liabilities from peripheral transactions. [Ch. 3]

ASSUMPTIONS
1. **Separate-entity** Transactions of the business are separate from transactions of the owners. [Ch.2]
2. **Unit-of-measure** Accounting measurements will be in the national monetary unit. [Ch. 2]
3. **Continuity** The entity will not go out of business in the near future. [Ch.2]
4. **Time-period** The long life of a company can be reported over a series of shorter time periods. [Ch. 3]

PRINCIPLES
1. **Cost** Historical cash-equivalent cost given up is the basis for initial recording of elements. [Ch. 2 and 3]
2. **Revenue** Record revenues when earned and measurable (an exchange has taken place, the earnings process is nearly complete, and collection is probable). [Ch. 3]
3. **Matching** Record expenses when incurred in earning revenue. [Ch. 3]
4. Full-disclosure   Disclose relevant economic information. [Ch. 5]

CONSTRAINTS
[Ch. 5]
1. Materiality   Relatively small amounts not likely to influence decisions are to be recorded in the most cost-beneficial way.
2. Cost-benefit   Benefits of recording and reporting information should outweigh costs.
3. Conservatism   Exercise care not to overstate assets and revenues or understate liabilities and expenses.
4. **Industry peculiarities** Differences in accounting and reporting for certain items are permitted if there is a clear precedent in the industry.

reporting, the FASB determined that several characteristics should guide it and management in deciding what financial information should be reported.

The two *primary qualitative characteristics* that useful information should possess are *relevance* and *reliability*. **Relevant information** is capable of influencing decisions. If the information is provided in a timely fashion and allows users to assess past activities (feedback value) and/or predict future activities (predictive value), it is relevant.

[handwritten margin note: having a connection w/ the matter @ hand]

Relevant information can influence a decision; it is timely and has predictive and/or feedback value.

[handwritten annotations: errorless, w/out prejudice, ability to prove the truth]

Reliable information is accurate, unbiased, and verifiable.

Reliable information must be accurate, unbiased, and verifiable (independent parties can agree on the nature of the transaction and amount).

If the information is relevant and reliable, accounting information should also possess the *secondary qualitative characteristics* of comparability and consistency. **Comparable information** means that users can compare financial information across businesses. This normally requires that similar accounting methods be applied. **Consistent information** means that within a company, information can be compared over time. This normally requires that similar accounting methods be applied over time. These secondary qualitative characteristics are of less importance than relevance and reliability; however, information that possesses each of these four qualitative characteristics is useful to decision makers.

Comparable information can be compared across businesses.

Consistent information can be compared over time.

Full-Disclosure Principle

The **full-disclosure principle** requires disclosure of all relevant economic information of the business.

The periodic financial statements of a business must clearly report all required relevant information about the economic affairs of a business. This is the **full-disclosure principle,** and it requires (1) a complete set of financial statements and (2) notes to the financial statements to explain accounting policy choices, elaborate on the "numbers," and provide information on other items with financial implications, such as pending lawsuits.

[handwritten annotation: the state of being confined or restricted within prescribed bounds]

Constraints of Accounting Measurement

Constraints of accounting measurement provide practical guidelines to reduce the *volume* and *cost* of reporting accounting information without reducing its value to decision makers. The constraints are *materiality, cost-benefit, conservatism,* and *industry practices.*

Materiality Constraint

Although items and amounts that are of low significance must be accounted for, they do not have to conform precisely to specified accounting guidelines or be separately reported if they would not influence reasonable decisions. Accountants usually designate such items and amounts as immaterial. Determining **material amounts** is often very subjective.

Material amounts are amounts that are large enough to influence a user's decision.

Cost-Benefit Constraint

The **cost-benefit constraint** suggests that the benefits of accounting for and reporting information should outweigh the costs.

The benefits that decision makers gain from accounting information should be greater than the cost of providing that information. This **cost-benefit constraint** recognizes that it is costly to produce and report accounting information. These costs include the costs of preparation *and* the loss of competitive advantage through disclosure of what had been secret information. Disclosure of information, the benefits of which do not outweigh the costs, clearly is uneconomical; however, measurement of benefits is difficult.

As an example of the application of both the materiality and cost-benefit constraints, consider the purchase of a few electric pencil sharpeners. They could be accounted for as equipment since they will benefit the company over several years; however, equipment is depreciated over time as it is used in operations. The effort of keeping track of the cost and depreciation for the minor purchase for years into the future exceeds the usefulness of the information and is too costly. In this case, the pencil sharpeners can be expensed immediately instead of being recorded as a long-lived asset and depreciated. The amounts also are immaterial (that is, they will not affect a user's decision).

Conservatism Constraint

The **conservatism constraint** requires that special care be taken to avoid (1) overstating assets and revenues and (2) understating liabilities and expenses. This guideline attempts to offset managers' natural optimism about their business operations, which sometimes creeps into the financial reports that they prepare. This constraint produces more conservative income statement and balance sheet amounts. When companies have choices in accounting methods and one choice does not dominate the others, the conservative approach is to choose the alternative with the least positive effect on net income. We will learn more about accounting method alternatives later in this chapter and throughout the rest of the text.

Conservatism suggests that care should be taken not to overstate assets and revenues or understate liabilities and expenses.

Industry Peculiarities

The final guideline relates to differences due to long-standing and accepted accounting and reporting practices in various industries. For example, public utilities (an industry regulated by government) often present balance sheet information in what appears to be upside-down order. That is, property, plant, and equipment are listed first, followed by the more liquid assets (cash, accounts receivable, and supplies). In like manner, the long-term debt that often is issued to finance the building of the property, plant, and equipment is listed first in the liabilities section, followed by the shorter-term liabilities. The reason for this presentation is that regulatory commissions in many states require public utilities to use this format. Property, plant, and equipment and its related long-term debt are the most significant items on the balance sheet of a public utility and are the primary items of interest to regulatory commissions that approve rates charged by the utilities to customers.

SELF-STUDY QUIZ

Match the players involved in the accounting communication process with their roles or the guiding principles for communicating information with their definitions.

1. Relevant information
2. CEO and CFO
3. Financial analyst
4. Auditor
5. Cost-benefit constraint
6. Conservatism

a. Management primarily responsible for accounting information.
b. An independent party who verifies financial statements.
c. Information that influences users' decisions.
d. Only information that provides benefits in excess of costs should be reported.
e. The avoidance of overstating assets and revenues and understating expenses and liabilities.
f. An individual who analyzes financial information and provides advice.

After you have completed the quiz, check your answers with those presented in the footnote at the bottom of this page.*

---

* 1c, 2a, 3f, 4b, 5d, 6e.

A Closer Look at Financial Statement Formats

We already know that the financial data contained in accounting reports are important factors in decisions made by investors, creditors, and analysts. To make financial statements more useful to decision makers, specific *classifications* of information are included on the statements.

A variety of classifications is used in practice. You should not be confused when you notice different formats used by different companies. You will find that each format is consistent with the principles discussed in this text. The following is a discussion of these classified financial statements.

A Classified Balance Sheet

The December 31, 1996, balance sheet for Callaway Golf is presented in Exhibit 5.4. First, notice the title of the statement, consolidated balance sheet. *Consolidated* means that the accounts of Callaway and the accounts of its wholly owned subsidiary, Callaway Golf (U.K.) Limited, have been added together through a consolidation process that results in a single number being reported for each item. (We discuss the consolidation process further in Chapter 12.) In addition, some companies choose to call the balance sheet the *statement of financial position* or *statement of financial condition.*

Callaway's balance sheet is shown in the report format (assets listed first and then liabilities and shareholders' equity accounts underneath in one column). Another common way to display the balance sheet data is in account format (assets on the left side and liabilities and shareholders' equity on the right).

Callaway's balance sheet also is classified. That is, assets and liabilities are listed in a particular order and are separated into current and noncurrent classifications. **Current assets** are defined as those that will be turned into cash or expire (be used up) within one year or by the end of the operating cycle, whichever is longer. In Chapter 3, we noted that the operating, or cash-to-cash, cycle varies by company and may be longer than one year. **Current liabilities** are defined as those obligations that will be paid with current assets, normally within one year. Typically a balance sheet is classified as follows:

Current assets are assets that will be turned into cash or expire (be used up) within the longer of one year or the operating cycle.
Current liabilities are obligations to be paid with current assets, normally within one year.

A. Assets (by order of liquidity)
   1. Current assets (short term)
      a. Cash and cash equivalents
      b. Short-term investments (marketable securities)
      c. Accounts receivable
      d. Inventory
      e. Prepaid expenses (i.e., expenses paid in advance of use)
      f. Other current assets
   2. Noncurrent assets
      a. Long-term investments
      b. Operational assets (property, plant, and equipment)—at cost less accumulated depreciation
      c. Intangible assets
      d. Deferred charges (long-term prepayments)
      e. Other (miscellaneous) assets
        Total assets

EXHIBIT 5.4
Balance Sheet of Callaway Golf*

Consolidated Balance Sheet

(in thousands, except share and per share data)	DECEMBER 31,	
	1996	**1995**
ASSETS		
Current assets:		
Cash and cash equivalents	$ 108,457	$ 59,157
Accounts receivable, net	74,477	73,906
Inventories, net	98,333	51,584
Deferred taxes	25,948	22,688
Other current assets	4,298	2,370
Total current assets	311,513	209,705
Property, plant and equipment, net	91,346	69,034
Other assets	25,569	11,236
	$ 428,428	$ 289,975
LIABILITIES AND SHAREHOLDERS' EQUITY		
Current liabilities:		
Accounts payable and accrued expenses	$ 14,996	$ 26,894
Accrued compensation and benefits	16,195	10,680
Accrued warranty	27,303	23,769
Income taxes payable	2,558	1,491
Total current liabilities	61,052	62,834
Long-term liabilities (Note 6)	5,109	2,207
Commitments (Note 7)		
Shareholders' equity:		
Preferred Stock, $.01 par value, 3,000,000 shares authorized, none issued and outstanding at December 31, 1996 and 1995		
Common Stock, $.01 par value, 240,000,000 shares authorized, 72,855,222 and 70,912,129 issued and outstanding at December 31, 1996 and 1995 (Note 4)	729	709
Paid-in capital	123,189	92,513
Retained earnings	238,349	131,712
Total shareholders' equity	362,267	224,934
	$ 428,428	$ 289,975

See accompanying notes to consolidated financial statements.

*To simplify, we have subtracted amounts for unearned compensation and grantor stock trust from the paid-in capital amounts. These amounts relate to the issuance of employee stock options, a topic beyond the scope of this text, and do not affect the interpretation of the balance sheet.

B. Liabilities (by order of time to maturity)
 1. Current liabilities (short-term)
  a. Accounts payable
  b. Accrued expenses payable
  c. Other short-term liabilities
 2. Long-term liabilities
  a. Notes and mortgages payable
  b. Lease obligations
  c. Bonds payable
   Total liabilities
C. Stockholders' equity (by source)
 1. Contributed capital (by owners)

2. Retained earnings (accumulated earnings minus accumulated dividends declared)
   Total stockholders' equity
   Total liabilities and stockholders' equity

It should be emphasized again that each financial statement item is a combination of a number of accounts used in the company's accounting system. Under Current Assets, Callaway does not separately report any short-term investments or prepaid expenses. Any such amounts are included and combined in Other Current Assets. The company does include Deferred Taxes in the Current Asset section, however. Deferred taxes, depending on the circumstances, can be listed in any of four places on the balance sheet: as a current asset, current liability, noncurrent asset, or noncurrent liability. The Deferred Taxes account represents the amount of income taxes that will most likely be paid or saved in the future based on differences in the application of tax laws and GAAP for recognizing revenues and expenses in the current period. If the amount is an asset (either current or noncurrent), future tax benefits (reductions) are expected. If the amount is a current or noncurrent liability, future tax payments are expected.

After the Current Asset section, *long-term investments* are reported. They include assets that are not used in operating the business. Examples include investments in real estate and stocks and bonds of other companies. This classification may include cash set aside in special funds (such as savings accounts) for use for a specified long-term purpose. Callaway does not separately report any long-term investments.

Operational assets are often called *fixed assets* or *property, plant, and equipment.* This group includes tangible assets that were acquired for use in operating the business rather than for resale as inventory items or held as investments. The assets included are buildings; land on which the buildings sit; and equipment, tools, furniture, and fixtures used in operating the business. Operational assets, with the exception of land, are depreciated as they are used. Their initial cost is apportioned to expense over their estimated useful lives. As we discussed in Chapter 4, this apportionment of cost is called *depreciation.* Land is not depreciated because it does not wear out like machinery, buildings, and equipment do. The amount of depreciation computed for each period is reported on the income statement as depreciation expense. The accumulated amount of depreciation expense for all past periods is deducted from the initial cost of the asset to derive the *book,* or *carrying, value* reported on the balance sheet (cost – accumulated depreciation). To illustrate, assume that Callaway purchased a new computer system for $22,000. It had an estimated useful life of five years. Depreciation expense is computed as $22,000 ÷ 5 years = $4,400 per year. The balance sheets developed during the five-year period would report the following, probably in a footnote to the financial statements:

	19A	19B	19C	19D	19E
Computer system (at cost)	$22,000	$22,000	$22,000	$22,000	$22,000
Less: Accumulated depreciation	4,400	8,800	13,200	17,600	22,000
Book, or carrying, value	$17,600	$13,200	$ 8,800	$ 4,400	$ 0

Intangible assets have no physical existence and have a long life. Their value is derived from the *legal rights* and *privileges* that accompany ownership. Examples are patents, trademarks, copyrights, franchises, and goodwill from purchasing other companies. Intangible assets usually are not acquired for resale but are directly related to the operations of the business. Although no intangible assets are separately reported in its financial statements, Callaway has at least 26 trademarks for its products and advertising slogans and numerous patents. As we discussed in Chapter 2, internally developed intangible assets often are not reflected on the balance sheets of companies because they relate to no identifiable transaction; only those that are material and purchased from others are included. Yet the value of these unrecorded internally developed intangible assets is significant.

Deferred charges are long-term prepayments for goods and services that are expected to help generate revenue in the future. They are often included in the classification Other Assets. Prepaid expenses and deferred charges are similar. The term *prepaid expense* typically is used for items classified as *current* assets; *deferred charges* is used for items classified as *noncurrent* assets.

Current liabilities are expected to be paid out of the current assets listed on the same balance sheet normally within the coming year. Current liabilities include accounts payable, short-term notes payable, wages payable, income taxes payable, and other expenses incurred (used) but not yet paid. Callaway combines Accounts Payable and Accrued Expenses Payable and lists Accrued Compensation and Benefits, Accrued Warranty, and Income Taxes Payable. As discussed in Chapters 3 and 4, accrued liabilities are obligations arising from expenses incurred in the current period that will be billed and paid for in the future.

Long-term liabilities are a company's debts that are not classified as current liabilities. Long-term liabilities have maturities that extend beyond one year from the balance sheet date. Examples include long-term bank loans, bond liabilities, mortgages, pension liabilities, and lease obligations. In 1996, Callaway's balance sheet showed long-term liabilities made up of pension and other post-retirement liabilities.

Stockholders' equity represents the residual claim of the owners (i.e., A − L = SE). This claim results from the initial contributions of the stockholders (contributed capital) plus retained earnings, which is the accumulated earnings of the company less the accumulated dividends declared. Retained earnings represents the amount of earnings that has been left in the company for growth. Typically, long-time successful companies have grown more from resources generated by operating activities than from additional contributions by investors for capital stock.

Until this chapter, we have identified the financing by investors as contributed capital. In practice, however, this account often is shown as two accounts: Common Stock and Contributed Capital in Excess of Par. Each share of common stock usually has a

Callaway's substantial investment in its diverse group of employees is not directly recognized as an asset on the balance sheet.

Par value is a legal amount per share established by the board of directors; it establishes the minimum amount a stockholder must contribute and has no relationship to the market price of the stock.

nominal (low) **par value** printed on the face of the certificate. Par value is a legal amount per share established by the board of directors; it has no relationship to the market price of the stock. Its significance is that it establishes the minimum amount that a stockholder must contribute. Callaway's common stock has a par value of $.01 per share, but the 1,039,000 shares were sold in its 1992 initial public offering at a market price of $15.84 per share (net of issuance costs).[6] When a corporation issues capital stock at net market value, the amount is recorded in part as Common Stock (number of shares × par value per share) and the excess as Capital in Excess of Par (also called *Additional Paid-in Capital, Contributed Capital in Excess of Par,* or *Paid-in Capital,* which Callaway uses). The journal entry to record Callaway's 1992 initial public offering follows:

Cash (A) ($15.84 × 1,039,000 shares)	16,457,760	
Common stock (SE)		
($.01 per share × 1,039,000 shares)		10,390
Paid-in capital (SE) $16,457,760 − 10,390)		16,447,370

The face of Callaway's balance sheet (as is common for most companies) discloses information on the number of shares that the company is authorized to issue (240 million), the number of shares "issued and outstanding" (72,855,222 at the end of 1996, issued to investors and not repurchased by the company). Callaway also has a second class of ownership called *preferred stock.* None of this type of stock has ever been issued, however. Additional discussion of accounting and reporting issues for owners' equity is presented in Chapter 11.

 *Financial*
ANALYSIS

Liquidity, Current Ratio, and Debt Contracts

Liquidity refers to a company's ability to meet its current maturing debts. Tests of liquidity focus on the relationship between current assets and current liabilities:

> **Working capital = Current assets − Current liabilities**

$$\text{Current ratio} = \frac{\text{Current assets}}{\text{Current liabilities}}$$

They measure the cushion of working capital that is maintained to allow for the unevenness in the flow of funds through the working capital accounts. For example, a current ratio of 2 means that the company has $2 of current assets for every $1 of current liabilities. Even if for a short period the current assets turn into cash half as quickly as the current liabilities come due, the company should have sufficient cash to pay its debts. At the end of 1996, Callaway's current ratio was 5.1 ($311,513 ÷ $61,052), indicating a high degree of liquidity.

When firms borrow money, they agree to make specific payments of interest and principal in the future. To provide protection for the creditors, they also often agree to other restrictions on their activities. For example, Callaway has a $50 million line of credit with its bank. This line of credit is not secured by specific assets of the company as collateral; however, as part of the agreement with the bank, Callaway agrees to maintain a minimum specified current ratio (and debt-to-equity ratio). Maintaining this level of the ratio assures the bank that the company has sufficient liquid assets, after the payment of other current liabilities, to pay its debt.

---

[6] These numbers are rounded.

Classified Income Statements

Callaway Golf's 1996 consolidated statement of income is reprinted for you in Exhibit 5.5. Other common titles include *statement of earnings* and *statement of operations*. Income statements have up to five major sections:

1. Continuing operations.
2. Discontinued operations.
3. Extraordinary items.
4. Cumulative effect of changes in accounting methods.
   Net income (sum of 1, 2, 3, and 4)
5. Earnings per share.

All companies' income statements have sections 1 (continuing operations) and 5 (earnings per share). These are the two sections in Callaway's income statement. Depending on their particular circumstances, one or more of sections 2, 3, and 4 will be reported. The amounts for section 1 and any of 2, 3, or 4 that are reported are summed to equal bottom line *Net Income*. We first focus on the most common and important section, *Continuing Operations*.

Continuing Operations

This first section of an income statement presents the results of continuing operations. Companies such as Callaway that do not have any discontinued operations (discussed later) do not title this section separately. This section can be presented, however, using one of three common formats:

1. Single step.
2. Multiple step with operating costs and expenses deducted from sales to show operating income as a subtotal.

EXHIBIT 5.5
Income Statement of Callaway Golf

Consolidated Statement of Income

(in thousands, except per share data)	Year ended December 31,					
	1996		1995		1994	
Net sales	$678,512	100%	$553,287	100%	$448,729	100%
Cost of goods sold	317,353	47%	270,125	49%	208,906	47%
Gross profit	361,159	53%	283,162	51%	239,823	53%
Selling expenses	80,701	12%	64,310	12%	59,065	13%
General and administrative expenses	74,476	11%	55,891	10%	47,848	11%
Research and development costs	16,154	2%	8,577	2%	6,380	1%
Income from operations	189,828	28%	154,384	28%	126,530	28%
Interest and other income, net	5,767		4,017		2,875	
Income before income taxes	195,595	29%	158,401	29%	129,405	29%
Provision for income taxes	73,258		60,665		51,383	
Net income	$122,337	18%	$ 97,736	18%	$ 78,022	17%
Earnings per common share	$1.73		$1.40		$1.07	
Common equivalent shares	70,661		69,855		73,104	

3. Multiple step with cost of goods sold deducted from sales to show gross margin (or gross profit) as a subtotal and then other operating expenses deducted to show operating income as a second subtotal.

Callaway's income statement follows the third format with a subtotal for gross profit and a subtotal for income from operations before adding or subtracting other income, gains, expenses, and losses. In previous chapters, however, we illustrated a simplified format known as the *single-step* format in which all revenue, income, and gains were listed first, and then all costs, expenses, and losses were subtracted. About one-third of the companies in a recent survey used the single-step approach.[7] In Exhibit 5.6, we reorder the accounts in Callaway's income statement to show you how the same 1996 data would be displayed using the single-step format. We also present the same information using the second approach (*multiple step, one subtotal*) in which only one subtotal for operating income is presented followed by other income, gains, expenses, and losses, and the third approach (*multiple step, two subtotals*).

No difference exists in the individual revenue, expense, gain, and loss items reported using the three formats. The differences relate only to the use of categories and subtotals, which are highlighted by shading in Exhibit 5.6. The primary difference between the single-step and two multiple-step approaches is the subtotal *Income from Operations* separating items relating to normal operations from those relating to peripheral activities of the company, such as earning interest on investments and incurring losses on sales of fixed assets. The primary difference between the two multiple-step approaches is the significance placed on relating sales to the cost of goods sold to report the subtotal *Gross Profit* before reporting the remaining operating items. Note that, regardless of format, nearly all companies separate income tax expense (provision for income taxes) and report a subtotal Income before Income Taxes.

We now describe the various accounts and subtotals on an income statement constructed using the *multiple-step, two-subtotal format*. *Net sales* are gross sales minus any discounts, returns, and allowances during the period. These latter items are discussed in Chapter 6.

Cost of goods sold is the cost of inventory sold by a merchandiser (a company that buys products from manufacturers for resale) or a manufacturer (a company that pro-

EXHIBIT 5.6
Alternative Income Statement Formats for Continuing Operations

Single Step	
Net sales	$678,512
Interest income and other income, net	5,767
Total revenues	684,279
Cost of goods sold	317,353
Selling expenses	80,701
General and administrative expenses	74,476
Research and development costs	16,154
Total expenses	488,684
Income before income taxes	195,595
Provision for income taxes	73,258
Net Income	$122,337

Multiple Step (one subtotal)	
Net sales	$678,512
Cost of goods sold	317,353
Selling expenses	80,701
General and administrative expenses	74,476
Research and development costs	16,154
Income from operations	189,828
Interest income and other income, net	5,767
Income before income taxes	195,595
Provision for income taxes	73,258
Net Income	$122,337

Multiple Step (two subtotals)	
Net sales	$678,512
Cost of goods sold	317,353
Gross profit	361,159
Selling expenses	80,701
General and administrative expenses	74,476
Research and development costs	16,154
Income from operations	189,828
Interest income and other income, net	5,767
Income before income taxes	195,595
Provision for income taxes	73,258
Net Income	$122,337

---

[7] American Institute of Certified Public Accountants, *Accounting Trends & Techniques* (New York: AICPA, 1996).

duces goods for sale to wholesalers or retail merchandisers). For example, assume that Callaway sold golf club inventory costing $90,000 to Sumitomo Corporation (which exports and sells Callaway's golf clubs in Japan) for $200,000 on account. The journal entries are as follows:

Accounts receivable (A)	200,000	
Sales revenue (R)		200,000
To reflect the earning of revenue in exchange for a		
promise to pay from the customer.		
Cost of goods sold (E)	90,000	
Inventory (A)		90,000
To reflect the use of inventory to generate revenues		
*in the period.**		

*This example illustrates a perpetual inventory system. Alternative systems are illustrated in Chapter 7.

Any inventory that is purchased or produced but not sold during the period is included in the inventory on the balance sheet. We presented a similar illustration in Chapter 4 when we discussed the amount of food, beverage, and paper products that Sbarro, Inc., had on hand at the end of the accounting period that was included on the balance sheet. Anything purchased for the period that was not on hand at the end was accounted for as the cost of food and paper products on the income statement. We will present additional discussion of accounting for sales and cost of goods sold for merchandising and manufacturing companies in Chapters 6 and 7.

Gross margin, or **gross profit**, is a subtotal, not an account. It is the difference between *Net Sales* and *Cost of Goods Sold*. You may hear of gross profit being discussed in terms of a percentage. The formula for calculating the gross profit (to sales) percentage is

Gross margin (gross profit) is net sales less cost of goods sold.

$$\text{Gross profit percentage} = \frac{\text{Gross profit}}{\text{Net sales}}$$

Notice in Exhibit 5.5 that Callaway also reports income statement line items as a percentage of net sales, including the gross profit percentage of 53 percent in 1996. Most companies do not report these percentages, which are often called *common-sized income statements*. Many analysts compute these common-sized statements as a first step in analysis, however, because they ease year-to-year comparisons. For example, in Callaway's income statement in Exhibit 5.5, you can easily see that gross profit percentages improved between 1995 and 1996 (that is, they increased from 51 percent in 1995 to 53 percent in 1996). This resulted from increases in sales of higher margin products.

Operating expenses are the usual expenses incurred in operating a business during an accounting period. Often they are classified between selling expense and general and administrative expense. *Selling Expense* includes all amounts incurred during the period in performing sales activities, such as salaries of salespeople. *General and Administrative Expense* includes the overall business expenses, such as the salary of the president. Callaway also adds a line for research and development expenses that represent about 2 percent of all operating expenses. Differences in the specific expense and revenue categories reported are common, depending on the nature of each company and industry. Another subtotal—**Income from Operations** (also called **Operating Income**)—is computed after subtracting operating expenses from gross profit.

Income from operations (operating income) equals net sales less cost of goods sold and other operating expenses.

Nonoperating (other) items are income, expenses, gains, and losses that are not considered as resulting from the central operations of the business but are not unusual

Income before income taxes (pretax earnings) is revenues minus all expenses except income tax expense.

or infrequent in nature. Examples are interest income, interest expense, and gains and losses on the sale of fixed assets. Interest expense on debt is sometimes combined (netted) with interest revenue so that only a single amount is reported. These nonoperating items are added to or subtracted from income from operations to obtain **Income before Income Taxes,** which is also called **Pretax Earnings.**

Accounting-Based Executive Bonuses

Callaway Golf believes in tying executives' compensation to the performance of the company as measured by accounting numbers. In addition to other compensation, Callaway pays its five executive officers bonuses up to 75 percent of base salary if pretax earnings growth (computed here) meets target amounts. Smaller growth statistics result in smaller bonuses. The current year target for maximum bonus was as follows:

	Target for Maximum Bonus
Pretax earnings growth % = (Current year pretax earnings – Last year pretax earnings) ÷ Last year pretax earnings	30%

Meeting this maximum goal in the current year will result in bonuses ranging from $300,000 to $525,000 for each of the five executive officers.

SELF-STUDY QUIZ

Callaway executives receive maximum bonuses if pretax earnings growth meets or exceeds the target of 30 percent. Use Exhibit 5.5 to see whether Callaway executives earned their maximum bonuses in the most recent year.

COMPUTATIONS

_____

_____

Discuss why Callaway might choose to pay executives based on performance and why they use the same accounting numbers used in reports to shareholders to measure the executives' performance.

_____

_____

Now check your answers to those in the footnote at the bottom of the page.*

Discontinued Operations

Any company that plans to dispose of a major segment of its business or customer line needs to present separate information on the income statement accompanied by disposal details written in a footnote. **Discontinued operations** can result from abandon-

Discontinued operations result from the disposal of a major segment of the business and are reported net of income tax effects.

---

*Pretax earnings growth % = (195,595 – 158,401) ÷ 158,401 = 23.5% versus 30% target.
They did not earn their maximum bonuses. (In reality, they received 64.2 percent of their maximum bonuses.) The company believes that higher pretax earnings growth will result in higher prices for Callaway stock. Paying Callaway executives a bonus for increasing earnings growth thus helps align the interests of the executives with those of the shareholders. In addition, companies often pay shareholders bonuses based on the numbers in the annual report because they have been independently verified by the auditors.

ing or selling the major segment. Any operating income generated by the discontinued segment is disclosed separately from any gain or loss on the disposal (the difference between the cost of the net assets being disposed of and the sale price or the abandonment costs). The disclosure of each can be in a footnote or on the face of the income statement. Each line is to be reported net of the income tax effects. Separate reporting informs users that these results of discontinued operations are less useful as predictors of the company's future.

An example of a partial income statement that includes discontinued operations is presented in Exhibit 5.7 for Tenneco Inc., a global manufacturer of automotive parts and packaging. The footnote accompanying the income statement reported that during 1996 Tenneco formed separate companies for its energy and shipbuilding segments and distributed the shares in the new companies to its existing shareholders (called a *spinoff*). The results of the energy and shipbuilding operations, net of tax, are listed as discontinued operations.

Extraordinary Items

Extraordinary items are gains or losses incurred by the company that are considered both unusual in nature and infrequent in occurrence. Examples include losses suffered from natural disasters such as floods and hurricanes in geographic areas where such disasters rarely occur. These items must be reported separately on the income statement net of income tax effects. Separate reporting informs decision makers that the items are not likely to recur and for that reason are less relevant to predicting the company's future. Footnote disclosure is needed to explain the nature of the extraordinary item. In 1996 and 1994, Tenneco Inc. also reported extraordinary losses due to the early retirement of long-term debt (Exhibit 5.7). Accounting for early retirement of debt is discussed in Chapter 10.

Extraordinary items are gains and losses that are both unusual in nature and infrequent in occurrence; they are reported net of tax on the income statement.

Cumulative Effects of Changes in Accounting Methods

The fourth section of the income statement reflects the income statement effects of any adjustment made to balance sheet accounts because of changing to a different acceptable accounting method. These amounts are called **cumulative effects of changes in accounting methods**. The goal is to determine what the balance sheet amount should be as if the new accounting method had always been applied, net of any tax effects. Often these changes are required by new FASB pronouncements. At other times, corporate management determines that a change to an alternative accounting method is necessary because of changes in business activities. Changing accounting principles, however, violates the qualitative characteristic of information related to consistent application of methods over time. Therefore, footnote disclosure to explain the nature and effects of the change is necessary.

Cumulative effects of changes in accounting methods are the amounts reflected on the income statement for adjustments made to balance sheet accounts when applying different accounting principles.

EXHIBIT 5.7
Partial Income Statements for Tenneco Inc.

REAL WORLD EXCERPT

TENNECO INC.
Annual Report

Tenneco Inc. and Consolidated Subsidiaries Statements of Income

(Millions Except Share Amounts)	Years Ended December 31,		
	1996	1995	1994
Income from continuing operations	218	258	238
Income from discontinued operations, net of income tax	428	477	214
Income before extraordinary loss	646	735	452
Extraordinary loss, net of income tax	(236)	—	(5)
Income before cumulative effect of change in accounting principle	410	735	447
Cumulative effect of change in accounting principle, net of income tax	—	—	(39)
Net income	410	735	408

We can see in Exhibit 5.7 that Tenneco Inc. also reported the cumulative effect of a change in accounting principles in 1994. It adopted new FASB rules relating to accounting for benefits to retired employees. The effect of this rule change is shown net of the income tax effect and disclosed in footnotes. The effects of accounting method changes are separated because they are normally not directly relevant to predicting the company's future.

Finally, we come to "the bottom line," Net Income. An income statement is not complete, however, without including earnings per share information for corporations.

Earnings Per Share

As we discussed in Chapter 4, simple computations for earnings per share (EPS) are as follows:

$$EPS = \frac{\text{Net income available to common shareholders}}{\text{Weighted average number of shares outstanding during the reporting period}}$$

Callaway discloses this amount as illustrated in Exhibit 5.5 (called *basic EPS*[8]). Any company that has a complex capital structure (that is, debt or equity securities convertible into common stock) must also compute the effect of these items as if they had been converted at the beginning of the period, or when initially issued if during the current reporting period (called *diluted EPS*). The computation of these amounts is beyond the scope of this text and is usually presented in advanced coursework for accounting majors. Any company that discloses discontinued operations, extraordinary items, or cumulative effect of changes in accounting methods also must display these effects on a per share basis. At the time this chapter is being written, the FASB is reviewing the exact nature of these disclosures.

A Note on Taxes

One of the features of the first four sections of the income statement is that each section shows the amount of income tax expense related to that section. This is known as *intraperiod income tax allocation*. Items presented after continuing operations are reported net of the tax effect. For example, a $1,000 extraordinary loss is reported as $600 ($1,000 – 400 tax effect).

Before income from continuing operations is computed, the *provision (expense) for income taxes* is calculated and subtracted. For Callaway Golf, income tax expense is approximately 37 percent of pretax income from operations. Income tax expense is incurred by a corporation but not by a sole proprietorship or partnership. Income taxes are payable each year (part in advance in quarterly estimates).

Comprehensive Income

For financial statements for fiscal years beginning after December 15, 1997, companies are also required to disclose *comprehensive income*. Comprehensive income is net income plus or minus three additional types of gains or losses not included in the computation of net income. These are unrealized gain or loss on securities, minimum pension liability adjustment, and foreign currency translation adjustment. The first item, unrealized gain or loss on securities, will be discussed in Chapter 12. The latter two items are discussed in intermediate accounting and advanced accounting courses, respectively. The computation can be disclosed as part of the income statement, the

---

[8] Before 1997, this was called *primary EPS. Diluted EPS* was formerly called *fully diluted EPS*. The titles and computations were changed by the issuance of *Statement of Financial Accounting Standards No. 128*.

statement of changes in stockholders' equity, or on a separate statement. At the time this chapter is being written, it is expected that most companies will use the separate statement format. Callaway Golf did not have any of the three items in 1996. If this state of affairs continues, it will not prepare the statement.

Statement of Cash Flows Classifications

We have introduced the statement of cash flow classifications in prior chapters. They are the following:

■ Cash flows from operating activities. This section reports cash flows associated with earning income.
■ Cash flows from investing activities. Cash flows in this section are associated with buying and selling productive assets (other than inventory) and investments in other companies.
■ Cash flows from financing activities. These cash flows are related to financing the business through debt and equity issuances and payments or repurchases.

Callaway's 1996 consolidated statement of cash flows is presented in Exhibit 5.8. It follows the sections indicated in the preceding list. The first section (cash from operations) can be illustrated using either the *direct* or *indirect* method. For Callaway, the first section (Cash Flows from Operating Activities) is reported using the indirect method as a reconciliation of net income on an accrual basis to cash flows from operations. This more common format is different from the presentation made in the statement prepared for Sbarro at the end of Chapter 4 that was constructed using the direct method.

The indirect method's Operating Activities section of the statement of cash flows helps the analyst understand the causes of differences between net income and the cash flows of a business. The income of a company and its cash flows from operating activities can be quite different. Remember that the income statement is prepared under the accrual concept. Revenues are recorded when earned without regard to when the related cash flows occur. Expenses are matched with revenues and recorded in the same period as the revenues without regard to when the related cash flows occur.

The statement of cash flows starts with the income number computed under the accrual concept and converts it to a cash basis. For example, since no cash is paid during the current period for Callaway's depreciation expense reported on the income statement, this amount is added back in the conversion process. Similarly, increases and decreases in current assets and liabilities also account for some of the difference between net income and cash flow from operations. Note that the cash paid to increase inventories of newly designed products accounted for the largest portion of the difference between Callaway's net income and cash flow from operations during 1996. As we cover different portions of the income statement and balance sheet in more detail in Chapters 6 through 12, we will also discuss the relevant sections of the cash flow statement. Then the complete cash flow statement will be discussed in detail in Chapter 13.

FOCUS ON CASH FLOWS

Notes to Financial Statements

The numbers reported on the various financial statements provide important information to decision makers, but most users require additional details to facilitate their

EXHIBIT 5.8
Cash Flow Statement of Callaway Golf

Consolidated Statement of Cash Flows

(in thousands)	Year ended December 31,		
	1996	1995	1994
Cash flows from operating activities:			
Net income	$122,337	$97,736	$78,022
Adjustments to reconcile net income to net cash provided by operating activities:			
Depreciation and amortization	12,691	10,778	6,184
Non-cash compensation	4,194	2,027	2,070
Increase (decrease) in cash resulting from changes in:			
Accounts receivable, net	3,510	(43,923)	(12,400)
Inventories, net	(44,383)	22,516	(45,045)
Deferred taxes	(4,420)	4,978	(11,737)
Other assets	(12,889)	(6,573)	(4,531)
Accounts payable and accrued expenses	(15,395)	9,227	5,569
Accrued employee compensation and benefits	2,031	1,322	3,247
Accrued warranty expense	3,534	5,587	8,451
Income taxes payable	626	(9,845)	11,372
Other liabilities	2,902	1,597	610
Net cash provided by operating activities	74,738	95,427	41,812
Cash flows from investing activities:			
Capital expenditures	(35,352)	(29,510)	(26,137)
Sale of fixed assets	72	55	
Acquisition of a business, net of cash acquired	(610)		
Net cash used in investing activities	(35,890)	(29,455)	(26,137)
Cash flows from financing activities:			
Issuance of Common Stock	12,258	7,991	5,050
Retirement of Common Stock		(67,022)	(14,942)
Tax benefit from exercise of stock options	14,244	11,236	6,410
Dividends paid, net	(16,025)	(13,350)	(6,850)
Net cash provided by (used in) financing activities	10,477	(61,145)	(10,332)
Effect of exchange rate changes on cash	(25)	(26)	17
Net increase in cash and cash equivalents	49,300	4,801	5,360
Cash and cash equivalents at beginning of year	59,157	54,356	48,996
Cash and cash equivalents at end of year	$108,457	$59,157	$54,356

analysis. All financial reports include additional information in notes that follow the statements. Callaway's 1996 footnotes are categorized in the following discussion by type of footnote (key accounting policies, additional detail supporting reported numbers, and relevant financial information not disclosed on the statements). Examples are provided.

Descriptions of Accounting Rules Applied in the Company's Statements

The first note typically is a summary of significant accounting policies. As you will see in your study of subsequent chapters, generally accepted accounting principles (GAAP) permit companies to select alternative methods for measuring the effects of transactions. The summary of significant accounting policies tells the user which accounting methods the company has adopted. It is impossible to analyze a company's financial results effectively without first understanding the various accounting methods that have been used. The policy for accounting for property, plant, and equipment is as follows:

Note 1
The Company and Significant Accounting Policies
PROPERTY, PLANT AND EQUIPMENT
Property, plant and equipment are stated at cost less accumulated depreciation. Depreciation is computed using the straight-line method over estimated useful lives of three to fifteen years. Repairs and maintenance costs are charged to expense as incurred.

REAL WORLD EXCERPT
CALLAWAY GOLF
Annual Report

Alternative Accounting Methods and GAAP

Financial
ANALYSIS

Many people have a misimpression concerning the nature of the rules that make up generally accepted accounting principles (GAAP): that GAAP permit only one accounting method to be used to compute each value on the financial statements (e.g., inventory). Actually, GAAP often allow selection of an accounting method from a menu of acceptable methods. This permits a company to choose the methods that most closely reflect its particular economic circumstances (economic reality). This adds an additional complexity to the financial statement users' task, however—they also must understand how the company's choice of accounting methods affects its financial statement presentations. As Gabrielle Napolitano and Abby Joseph Cohen of the investment banking firm of Goldman, Sachs & Co. note in their recent research report,

> There are numerous legitimate ways in which company accounts can be made obscure. Further, investors must be wary of the means by which reported earnings can be manipulated or smoothed. Users of financial statements (e.g., shareholders, creditors, and others) are often forced to wrestle with dramatic differences in reporting practices between firms.*

REAL WORLD EXCERPT
GOLDMAN, SACHS & CO.
Analysts' Report

For example, before analyzing two companies' statements prepared using different accounting methods, one company's statements must be converted to the other's methods to make them comparable. Otherwise, the reader is in a situation analogous to comparing distances in kilometers and miles without conversion to a common scale. In later chapters, we will focus on developing the ability to make these conversions.

*Gabrielle Napolitano and Abby Joseph Cohen, "The Quality of Reported Earnings Has Improved, But . . . Pointers on What to Look for in Company Reports," *U.S. Research* (New York: Goldman, Sachs & Co., January 2, 1997).

Additional Detail Supporting Reported Numbers

Note 2   Selected Financial Statement Information
Note 4   Common and Preferred Stock
Note 6   Employee Benefit Plans
Note 8   Income Taxes
Note 9   Sales Information
Note 10   Supplemental Statement of Cash Flows Information

The second category of notes provides supplemental information concerning the data shown on the financial statements. Among other information, these notes may show revenues broken out by geographic region or line of business, descriptions of unusual transactions, and expanded detail concerning a specific classification. For example, Callaway provides detail in Note 2 on cash; accounts receivable; inventory; property, plant, and equipment; accounts payable and accrued expenses; and accrued compensation and benefits. Note 9, which follows, shows sales information by geographic region:

Note 9
SALES INFORMATION
The Company is engaged in domestic and international sales through distributors located within the following geographic areas:

(in thousands)	Year Ended December 31,		
	1996	**1995**	**1994**
United States	$460,611	$367,359	$331,493
Japan	58,156	60,971	45,944
All others—individually less than 5% of net sales	159,745	124,957	71,292
	$678,512	$553,287	$448,729

Callaway provides a more detailed discussion of its international sales strategy in its form 10-K discussed later in the chapter.

Relevant Financial Information Not Disclosed on the Statements

Note 3	Bank Line of Credit
Note 5	Stock Options and Rights
Note 7	Commitments and Contingencies
Note 11	Subsequent Event

The final category includes information that impacts the company financially but is not specifically indicated on the statements. Examples include information on stock option plans, legal matters, and any material event that occurs subsequent to year-end but before the financial statements are published. Note 3 is as follows:

Note 3
BANK LINE OF CREDIT
The Company has a $50,000,000 bank line of credit with an interest rate equal to the bank's prime rate. The interest rate at December 31, 1996 was 8.25%. The line of credit has been primarily utilized to support the issuance of letters of credit of which there were $3,921,000 outstanding at December 31, 1996, reducing the amount available under the Company's line of credit to $46,079,000.

The line of credit is unsecured and is subject to renewal on December 15, 1997. The line requires the Company to maintain certain financial ratios, including current and debt to equity ratios. The Company is also subject to other restrictive covenants under the terms of the credit agreement.

Voluntary Disclosures

GAAP and SEC regulations set only a minimum level of required financial disclosures. Many companies, including Callaway, provide important disclosures beyond those required. Recall that Callaway provided required geographic area sales information in Note 9 (described earlier) using only three geographic regions. As part of its voluntary disclosures explaining its international growth strategy, it provides more detail in its 1996 annual report by breaking this information into nine regions. Similarly, in its recent earnings press release (discussed next; see Exhibit 5.9), Callaway discloses sales by major product line. To our knowledge, it is the only major golf club company to provide such detailed sales information. As part of the disclosure process, Callaway also makes other voluntary disclosures on an irregular basis to keep the market better informed about its prospects.

EXHIBIT 5.9
Earnings Press Release for Callaway Golf Company

CALLAWAY GOLF REPORTS RECORD SECOND QUARTER SALES AND EARNINGS

7/17/96

CARLSBAD, Calif., July 17—Callaway Golf Company (NYSE: ELY) today reported net sales of $210.0 million for the second quarter ended June 30, 1996, an increase of 35 percent over net sales of $155.7 million reported in the second quarter of 1995, according to Ely Callaway, Chairman, and Donald H. Dye, President and CEO. Net income increased 42 percent to $38.9 million in the second quarter of 1996 from $27.3 million in the comparable quarter of 1995, and fully diluted earnings per share gained 41 percent to $0.55 in 1996 from $0.39 in the second quarter of 1995.

For the six months ended June 30, 1996, net sales increased 26 percent to $345.1 million from $274.7 million for the same 262period in 1995. Net income increased 32 percent to $58.4 million ($0.83 per share fully diluted) from $44.2 million ($0.62 per share fully diluted) for the six months ended June 30, 1996 and 1995, respectively.

Net sales of $210.0 million for the second quarter were comprised of: $84.7 million of Great Big Bertha® Ruger Titanium Metal Woods, $62.7 million of stainless steel Big Bertha® War Bird® Metal Woods, $54.6 million of Big Bertha® Irons and $8.0 million of other sales.

Net sales of $345.1 million for the six months ended June 30, 1996, were comprised of: $128.5 million of Great Big Bertha® Ruger Titanium Metal Woods, $113.6 million of stainless steel Big Bertha® War Bird® Metal Woods, $89.5 million of Big Bertha® Irons and $13.5 million of other sales.

Mr. Dye said, "We are very pleased with the results of the second quarter. These results reflect the type of success one can obtain by bringing to market new and innovative designs at premium price points. These results also reflect the foresight of our management team in acquiring the capacity necessary to meet the strong worldwide demand for our products."

It was also announced that the Board of Directors has approved a quarterly dividend of $.06 per share payable August 20, 1996, to shareholders of record as of July 30, 1996.

2285 Rutherford Road • Carlsbad, CA 92008-8815
Telephone: (619) 931-1771 • Outside California (800) 228-2767
FAX: (619) 931-9539

The Disclosure Process

As noted in our discussion of information services and information intermediaries, the accounting communication process includes more steps and participants than one would envision in a world in which annual and quarterly reports were simply mailed to shareholders.

Press Releases

Callaway and most public companies announce quarterly and annual earnings through a **press release** as soon as the verified figures (audited for annual and reviewed for quarterly earnings) are available to provide timely information to external users and limit the possibility of selective leakage of information. Callaway normally issues its earnings press releases within four weeks of the end of the accounting period. The announcements are sent via fax to the major print and electronic news services includ-

LEARNING OBJECTIVE 4
Identify the steps in the accounting communication process, including the issuance of press releases, annual reports, quarterly reports, and SEC filings as well as the role of electronic information services in this process.

A **press release** is a written public news announcement normally distributed to major news services.

ing Dow Jones, the PR Newswire, and *Bloomberg Business News,* which make them immediately available to subscribers. The first page of a typical quarterly press release for Callaway is reprinted in Exhibit 5.9. It includes key financial figures and management's discussion of the results. Attached to the release are condensed income statements and balance sheets (unaudited) that will be included in the formal quarterly report to shareholders, mailed after the press release.

For actively traded stocks such as those of Callaway Golf, most of the stock market reaction (stock price increases and decreases from investor trading) to the news in the press release usually occurs quickly. Recall that a number of analysts follow Callaway and regularly predict the company's earnings. When the actual earnings are published, the market reacts *not* to the amount of earnings but to the difference between expectations of earnings and actual earnings. This amount is called *unexpected earnings.* For example, the Bloomberg News Service recently reported the following:

7/18 U.S. EQUITY PREVIEW

Callaway Golf Co. (ELY): The maker of golf clubs said its second-quarter earnings rose to 55 cents a share from 39 cents in the year-ago quarter, more than the average estimate of 50 cents from 10 analysts polled by Zacks Investment Research. Callaway shares rose 3 to 33 ½.

Compared to the average estimate, unexpected earnings were plus 5 cents per share, and the share price rose $3. The following excerpt from a recent article in *Fortune* magazine points out the growing importance of meeting or beating the average or consensus analysts' estimate:

LEARN TO PLAY THE EARNINGS GAME
(AND WALL STREET WILL *LOVE YOU*)

The simplest, most visible, most merciless measure of corporate success in the 1990s has become this one: Did you make your earnings last quarter?

This is new . . . it's only in the past decade with the rise to prominence of the consensus earnings estimates compiled first in the early 1970s by I/B/E/S . . . and now also by competitors Zacks, First Call, and Nelson's, that those expectations have become so explicit. . . .

Source: *Fortune,* March 31, 1997, p. 77.

Callaway is one of those companies that regularly meets or beats the consensus estimate.

Companies such as Callaway issue press releases concerning other important events including new product announcements, new appointments of officers and members of the board of directors, and new endorsement contracts with professional golfers. News services also gather information about Callaway from other sources. The stock market often appears to react to some of these important announcements. For example, a few years ago, Bloomberg reported the following:

CALLAWAY SHARES RISE AFTER SPOKESMAN WINS PRO-AM

New York, Feb. 7 (Bloomberg)—The shares of golf-club maker Callaway Golf Co. rose 6.6% today after Callaway's celebrity spokesman Johnny Miller won a California golf tournament yesterday . . . marking the 46-year-old golfer's first win in seven years.

This was the first tournament in which Miller had used Callaway's new Big Bertha irons. Presumably, the stock market inferred that this would provide an impetus for future sales of the new product.

Callaway's annual report also discusses the activities of its charitable foundation, which focuses on youth and health issues.

Press releases related to annual earnings and quarterly earnings often precede the issuance of the quarterly or annual report by 15 to 45 days. This time is necessary to prepare the additional detail and to print and distribute those reports.

Annual Reports

For privately held companies, *annual reports* are relatively simple documents photocopied on white bond paper. They normally include only the following:

1. Four basic financial statements: income statement, stockholders' equity or retained earnings statement, cash flow statement, and balance sheet.
2. Related footnotes or notes as described earlier.
3. Report of independent accountants (auditor's opinion).

The annual reports of public companies are significantly more elaborate, both because of additional SEC reporting requirements imposed on these companies and the fact that many companies use their annual reports as public relations tools to communicate nonaccounting information to shareholders, customers, the press, and others.

The annual reports of public companies are normally split into two sections: The first, "nonfinancial," section usually includes a letter to stockholders from the chairman and CEO, descriptions of the company's management philosophy, products, its successes (and occasionally its failures), and exciting prospects and challenges for the future. Beautiful photographs of products, facilities, and personnel often are included. Callaway took the unusual approach in 1996 of eliminating most color photos and instead repeating the letter to stockholders in German, French, Spanish, Chinese, and Japanese to better communicate with its international customer and investor base. The second, "financial," section, which is often printed on a different color of paper to make it easy to find, includes the core of the report. The SEC sets minimum disclosure standards for the financial section of the annual reports of public companies. The principal components of the financial section include these:

1. Summarized financial data for a 5- or 10-year period.
2. Management's Discussion and Analysis of Financial Condition and Results of Operations.
3. The four basic financial statements.

4. Footnotes (notes).
5. Report of Independent Accountants (Auditor's Opinion) and sometimes the Report of Management Responsibility.
6. Recent stock price information.
7. Summaries of the unaudited quarterly financial data (described later).
8. Lists of directors and officers of the company and relevant addresses.

The order of these components varies.

Most of these elements except for Management's Discussion and Analysis have been discussed earlier in the chapter. This element includes management's discussion and explanation of key figures on the financial statements and future risks the company faces. For example, in a recent annual report, Callaway explained a 23 percent increase in sales over the previous year as being "attributable to increased sales of Great Big Bertha Metal Drivers, and Great Big Bertha Fairway Woods which were introduced in January 1996, combined with increased sales of Big Bertha Irons. These sales increases were offset by a decrease in net sales of Big Bertha War Bird Metal Woods." This consistent introduction of new and improved products has been critical to Callaway's continued growth.

Future risks faced by the company are also discussed. For example, the report notes the following:

The Company is dependent on a limited number of suppliers for its club heads and shafts. In addition, some of the Company's products require specifically developed techniques and processes which make it difficult to identify and utilize alternative suppliers quickly. Consequently, if any significant delay or disruption in the supply of these component parts occurs, it may have a material adverse effect on the Company's business. . . .

A complete annual report from Toys "R" Us, which includes all of these sections, is reprinted in Appendix B at the end of this book.

Quarterly Reports

Quarterly reports normally begin with a short letter to shareholders. This is followed by a condensed income statement for the quarter, which often shows less detail than the annual income statement, and a condensed balance sheet dated at the end of the quarter (e.g., March 31 for the first quarter). These condensed financial statements are not audited and so are marked *unaudited*. Also, the cash flow statement, statement of stockholders' equity (or retained earnings statement), and notes to the financial statements often are not included. Private companies also normally prepare quarterly reports for lenders. These reports are usually similar to the ones prepared by public companies. Callaway's quarterly reports are issued about five weeks after the end of each quarter.

SEC Reports—10-K, 10-Q, 8-K

Public companies also must file periodic reports with the SEC. They include the annual report on Form 10-K, quarterly reports on Form 10-Q, and current event reports on Form 8-K. These reports are normally referred to by number (for example, the "10-K"). The SEC requires that the 10-K be filed within 90 days of the fiscal year-end and the 10-Q be filed within 45 days of the end of quarter. In general, the 10-K and 10-Q present all the information in the annual and quarterly reports, respectively, along with additional management discussion and several required schedules.

Form 10-K Annual Report

In the **Form 10-K,** companies provide a more detailed description of the business including items such as their products, product development, sales and marketing, manufacturing, and competitors. For example, Callaway states the following:

> The market in which the Company does business is highly competitive, and is served by a number of well-established and well-financed companies with recognized brand names. Several companies introduced new products in 1996 (e.g.: Ping "ISI" Irons, Taylor Made "Burner Bubble Shaft" Irons, Cobra "Ti" Titanium Metal Woods, "King Cobra II" Irons and Armour "Ti 100" Irons) that have generated increased market competition. . . .

It also lists properties owned and leased, any legal proceedings it is involved in, and significant contracts that the company has signed. This last point is particularly important given that, as we emphasized in Chapter 2, many important contracts between the company and other parties such as key employees, distributors, and others represent important economic assets and/or liabilities to the company. They are not included on the balance sheet, however. That is, they have no *book value.* For example, Callaway's 10-K lists employment contracts between Callaway Golf and Richard Helmstetter, the genius behind Callaway's research and product development group. This "human asset" is of tremendous economic value to the company but is not listed as an asset on its balance sheet.

 The 10-K also provides more detailed schedules concerning various figures on the income statement and balance sheet including bad debts, warranties, inventories, and advertising. We will discuss these disclosures in more detail in later chapters starting with the Chapter 6 discussion of bad debts.

The **Form 10-K** is the annual report that publicly traded companies must file with the SEC.

REAL WORLD EXCERPT
CALLAWAY GOLF
Form 10-K

Judging International Sales Strategy from the Form 10-K

International PERSPECTIVE

In its form 10-K, discussed above, Callaway disclosed a change in its international sales strategy:

> **SALES FOR DISTRIBUTION OUTSIDE OF THE UNITED STATES**
> Approximately 32%, 34% and 26% of the Company's net sales were derived from sales for distribution outside of the United States in 1996, 1995 and 1994, respectively. The majority of the Company's international sales are made through distributors specializing in the sale and promotion of golf clubs in specific countries or regions around the world. The Company currently has 21 distribution arrangements covering sales of the Company's products in over 40 foreign countries, including Japan, Canada, Singapore, Korea, Hong Kong, Australia, France, Spain, Argentina and South Africa. . . .
> During 1995, the Company began to evaluate growth opportunities in and outside of the golf equipment industry. One of the opportunities identified by the Company relates to the Company's acquisition of selected foreign distributors. The Company's management believes that controlling the distribution of its products throughout the world will be a key element in the future growth and success of the Company.
> The Company directly markets its products in the United Kingdom and Sweden through its wholly-owned British subsidiary, Callaway Golf (UK) Limited. In July 1996, the Company acquired a majority interest in its distributor in Germany, Golf Trading GmbH, which sells and promotes the Company's products in Germany, Austria, the Netherlands and Switzerland. . . .

REAL WORLD EXCERPT
CALLAWAY GOLF
Form 10-K

 The statistics disclosed suggest that, as a result of Callaway's change in distribution strategy, sales outside of the United States are growing at a faster rate than are domestic sales. A continuation of this strategy can lead to further gains for Callaway.

Form 10-Q Quarterly Report

Form 10-Q is the quarterly report that publicly traded companies must file with the SEC.

The **Form 10-Q** report includes all the information included in the quarterly report to shareholders, along with a statement of shareholders' equity and a cash flow statement for the quarter, a variety of footnotes, and a management discussion. The amount of information disclosed in the 10-Q is very close to that included in the annual report to shareholders but less than that required by the Form 10-K. Like the quarterly report to shareholders, the information in the 10-Q is unaudited.

Form 8-K Current Report

Form 8-K is used by publicly traded companies to disclose any material event not previously reported that is important to investors.

The **Form 8-K** Current Report is used to report any material event important to investors that has not been previously reported in the 10-Q or 10-K. It normally must be filed within 15 days of any event specified in the form. An example of an event requiring submission of a Form 8-K is a change of auditors.

Epilogue

As noted earlier, Callaway is well known for introducing innovative new products long before the end of existing products' life cycles. The year 1996 was no exception with five new product introductions. In its boldest move of the year, Callaway launched the Callaway Golf Ball Company, which plans to introduce product in 1999. In the past, some analysts have questioned whether Callaway could successfully penetrate a highly competitive market with a new product. Callaway has always responded, however, by making an additional voluntary disclosure to put any rumors to rest. Such disclosures are not required by generally accepted accounting principles but are consistent with Callaway's clear and forthright approach to communicating with users of financial statements.

Demonstration Case

Microsoft Corporation

Complete the following requirements before proceeding to the suggested solution. Microsoft Corporation, developer of a broad line of computer software including the Windows operating systems and Word (word processing) and Excel (spreadsheet) programs, is now the largest computer-related company in the world. Following is a list of the financial statement items and amounts adapted from a recent Microsoft income statement and balance sheet. These items have normal debit and credit balances and are reported in millions of dollars. For that year 303 million (weighted average) shares of stock were outstanding. The company closes its books on June 30.

Accounts payable	$ 239	Net revenues	$3,753
Accounts receivable	338	Other current assets	95
Accrued compensation	86	Other current liabilities	111
Cash and short-term investments	2,290	Other revenues and	
Common stock and paid-in capital	1,086	expenses (debit balance)	7
Cost of goods sold	633	Other noncurrent assets	88
General and administrative	119	Property, plant, and equipment (net)	867
Income taxes payable	127	Provision for income taxes	448
Interest income (net)	82	Research and development	470
Inventories	127	Retained earnings	2,156
		Sales and marketing	1,205

Required:

1. Prepare in good form a multiple-step income statement (showing both gross profit and operating income) and a classified balance sheet for the year.
2. Compute the current ratio and gross margin percentage. Briefly explain their meanings.

Suggested Solution

1.

MICROSOFT CORPORATION
Income Statement
For the period ended June 30, 19A
(in millions)

Net revenues	$3,753
Cost of goods sold	633
Gross profit	3,120
Operating expenses:	
Research and development	470
Sales and marketing	1,205
General and administrative	119
Total operating expenses	1,794
Operating income	**1,326**
Nonoperating income and expenses:	
Interest income (net)	82
Other revenues and expenses	(7)
Income before income taxes	1,401
Provision for income taxes	448
Net income	$ 953
Earnings per share	**$ 3.15**

MICROSOFT CORPORATION
Balance Sheet
June 30, 19A
(in millions)

Assets	
Current assets	
Cash and short-term investments	$2,290
Accounts receivable	338
Inventories	127
Other current assets	95
Total current assets	2,850
Noncurrent assets	
Property, plant, and equipment (net)	867
Other noncurrent assets	88
Total assets	$3,805
Liabilities	
Current liabilities	
Accounts payable	$ 239
Accrued compensation	86
Income taxes payable	127
Other current liabilities	111
Total current liabilities	563
Noncurrent liabilities	0
Stockholders' equity	
Common stock and paid-in-capital	1,086
Retained earnings	2,156
Total stockholders' equity	3,242
Total liabilities and stockholders' equity	$3,805

2. Current ratio as reported:

$$\$2{,}850 \div \$563 = 5.06$$

Gross margin ratio as reported:

$$\$3{,}120 \div \$3{,}763 = 0.83$$

The high current ratio indicates that Microsoft had more than $5 of current assets for every $1 of current liabilities. This indicates that even if current assets turn into cash one-fifth as quickly as current liabilities come due, Microsoft will have enough cash to pay its debts. The extraordinarily high gross margin percentage indicates that the actual production costs of computer software (the CD-ROM and manual) are quite low. Microsoft's major costs are marketing and research and development. It also indicates Microsoft's dominance of the computer software business, which allows it to charge premium prices for its products.

Summary

Company managers, auditors, government regulators, and information intermediaries including analysts and information services are the key players in the communication of accounting information. Management of the reporting company must decide on the appropriate format (categories) and level of detail to present in its financial statements. Management also must provide extensive additional disclosures in the notes to financial statements. The conceptual framework of accounting, in particular the qualitative characteristics of financial statements and constraints, provides guidance in this process. Financial statement announcements from public companies usually are first transmitted to users through electronic information services. These include earnings press releases, annual and quarterly reports, and the more detailed reports required by the SEC. Analysts play a major role in making this and other information available to average investors through their stock recommendations and earnings forecasts. These analysts consider the company's selection from the alternative measurement rules available under GAAP in making their assessments. A major focus of future chapters, which analyze each element of the financial statements, will be the financial statement effects of these alternative methods.

In Chapter 6, we begin our in-depth discussion of financial statements. We will begin with two of the most liquid assets, cash and accounts receivable, and transactions that involve revenue, adjustments to revenues, and certain selling expenses that relate to recording cash and accounts receivable. Many analysts and the SEC believe accuracy in revenue recognition and the related recognition of cost of goods sold (discussed in the next chapter) to be the most important determinants of the accuracy—and, thus, the usefulness—of financial statement presentations. We will also introduce concepts related to the management and control of cash and receivables, which is a critical business function. A detailed understanding of these topics is crucial to future managers, accountants, and financial analysts.

Key Ratios

Current ratio measures a company's ability to meet its currently maturing debts. It is computed as follows (p. 252):

$$\text{Current ratio} = \frac{\text{Current assets}}{\text{Current liabilities}}$$

Gross profit percentage measures the excess of sales prices over cost of goods sold as a percentage. It is computed as follows (p. 255):

$$\text{Gross profit percentage} = \frac{\text{Gross profit}}{\text{Net sales}}$$

Key Terms

Comparable Information Information that can be compared across businesses. *246*

Conservatism Care should be taken not to overstate assets and revenues or understate liabilities and expenses. *247*

Consistent Information Information that can be compared over time. *246*

Cost-Benefit Constraint The benefits of accounting for and reporting information should outweigh the costs. *246*

Cumulative Effects of Changes in Accounting Methods Amount reflected on the income statement for adjustments made to balance sheet accounts when applying different accounting principles. *257*

Current Assets Assets that will be turned into cash or expire (be used up) within the longer of one year or the operating cycle. *248*

Current Liabilities Obligations to be paid with current assets, normally within one year. *248*

 below bottom line

✗ **Discontinued Operations** Results from the disposal of a major segment of the business; reported net of income tax effects. *256*

Earnings Forecasts Predictions of earnings for future accounting periods. *239*

Extraordinary Items Gains and losses that are both unusual in nature and infrequent in occurrence; they are reported net of tax on the income statement. *257*

Form 8-K The report used by publicly traded companies to disclose any material event not previously reported that is important to investors. *268*

Form 10-K The annual report that publicly traded companies must file with the SEC. *267*

Form 10-Q The quarterly report that publicly traded companies must file with the SEC. *268*

Full-Disclosure Principle The requirement to disclose all relevant economic information of the business. *246*

Gross Margin (gross profit) Net sales less cost of goods sold. *255* (Before operating expenses)

Income before Income Taxes (Pretax Earnings) Revenues less all expenses except income tax expense. *256*

Income from Operations (Operating Income) Net sales less cost of goods sold and other operating expenses. *255*

Institutional Investors Managers of pension, mutual, endowment, and other funds that invest on the behalf of others. *243*

Lenders (Creditors) Suppliers and financial institutions that lend money to companies. *243*

Material Amounts Amounts that are large enough to influence a user's decision. *246*

Par Value A legal amount per share established by the board of directors; it establishes the minimum amount a stock-holder must contribute and has no relation-ship to the market price of the stock. *252*

Press Release A written public news announcement that is normally distributed to major news services. *263*

Private Investors Individuals who purchase shares in companies. *243*

Relevant Information Information that can influence a decision; it is timely and has predictive and/or feedback value. *245*

Reliable Information Information that is accurate, unbiased, and verifiable. *246*

Unqualified (Clean) Audit Opinion Auditors' statement that the financial state-ments are fair presentations in all material respects in conformity with GAAP. *238*

Questions

1. Describe the roles and responsibilities of management and independent auditors in the financial reporting process.
2. Define the following three users of financial accounting disclosures and the relation-ships among them: *financial analysts, private investors,* and *institutional investors.*
3. Briefly describe the role of information services in the communication of financial information.
4. Briefly explain why a conceptual framework of accounting is important.
5. Explain why information must be relevant and reliable to be useful.
6. Briefly explain the cost–benefit constraint.
7. The two secondary characteristics of accounting information involve what two comparisons?
8. What are the two primary characteristics of accounting information? Briefly explain each.
9. List the six categories that constitute the conceptual framework of accounting. Briefly explain each.
10. List and briefly explain the four accounting constraints.
11. Explain the basic difference between accrual basis accounting and cash basis accounting.
12. What basis of accounting do GAAP require on the (a) income statement, (b) balance sheet, and (c) statement of cash flows?
13. What is the primary purpose of the classifications of the information presented on financial statements?
14. What are the five major classifications on the income statement?
15. Define *extraordinary items.* Why should they be reported separately on the income statement?
16. List the six major classifications reported on a balance sheet.
17. Briefly define (a) *current assets,* (b) *current liabilities,* (c) *working capital,* and (d) *current ratio.*
18. For operational assets, as reported on the balance sheet, explain (a) cost, (b) accumu-lated depreciation, (c) book value, and (d) carrying value.
19. Briefly explain the major classifications of stockholders' equity for a corporation.
20. What are the three major classifications on a statement of cash flows?
21. List the four elements reported on the income statement. Explain the primary differ-ence between (a) revenues and gains and (b) expenses and losses.
22. What are the three major categories of notes or footnotes presented in annual reports? Cite an example of each.
23. Briefly explain the normal sequence and form of financial reports produced by private companies in a typical year.
24. Briefly explain the normal sequence and form of financial reports produced by public companies in a typical year.

Exercises

E5–1 Matching Players in the Accounting Communication Process with Their Definitions

Match each player with the related definition by entering the appropriate letter in the space provided.

Players	Definitions
_____ (1) SEC	A. Adviser who analyzes financial and other economic information to form forecasts and stock recommendations.
_____ (2) Independent auditor	
_____ (3) Institutional investor	B. Financial institution or supplier that lends money to the company.
_____ (4) CEO and CFO	
_____ (5) Creditor	C. Chief executive officer and chief financial officer who have primary responsibility for the information presented in financial statements.
_____ (6) Financial analyst	
_____ (7) Private investor	
_____ (8) Information service	D. Independent CPA who examines financial statements and attests to their fairness.
	E. Securities and Exchange Commission, which regulates financial disclosure requirements.
	F. A company that gathers, combines, and transmits (paper and electronic) financial and related information from various sources.
	G. Individual who purchases shares in companies.
	H. Manager of pension, mutual, and endowment funds that invests on the behalf of others.

E5–2 Matching Definitions with Terms from the Conceptual Framework

Match each definition with its related term by entering the appropriate letter in the space provided.

Terms	Definitions
_____ (1) User	A. Consistency with prior periods and comparability with other entities.
_____ (2) Cost-benefit constraint	
_____ (3) Secondary quality	B. Provides economic information useful to external decision makers.
_____ (4) Objective of financial reporting	
_____ (5) Immaterial amount	C. Decision maker who needs financial information.
_____ (6) Primary quality	D. Relevance to decisions and reliability.
	E. Amount not large enough to influence important decisions.
	F. Cost of developing and reporting should be less than the use value to decision makers.

E5–3 Matching Definitions with Terms from the Conceptual Framework

Match each definition with its related term by entering the appropriate letter in the space provided.

Terms	Definitions
_____ (1) Primary users of financial statements	A. To prepare the income tax return of the business.
_____ (2) Broad objective of financial reporting	B. Separate entity, continuity, time period, and unit of measure.
_____ (3) Qualitative characteristics of financial statements	C. Guidelines to apply the assumptions and principles. (GAAP)
_____ (4) Implementation assumptions	D. To provide economic information that is useful in making decisions.
_____ (5) Elements of financial statements	E. Relevance and reliability.
_____ (6) Implementation principle	F. Investor, creditor, and others who advise and represent them (decision maker).
_____ (7) Exceptions to implementation principles	G. Materiality, cost-benefit, conservatism, industry peculiarities.
_____ (8) Detailed accounting practices and procedures	H. Asset, liability, owners' equity, revenue, expense, gain, and loss.
_____ (9) None of the above	I. Revenue, cost, matching, full disclosure.

E5–4 Matching Financial Statements with the Elements of Financial Statements

Match each financial statement with the items presented on it by entering the appropriate letter in the space provided.

Elements of Financial Statements		Financial Statements
_____	(1) Liabilities	A. Income statement
_____	(2) Cash from operating activities	B. Balance sheet
_____	(3) Losses	C. Cash flow statement
_____	(4) Assets	D. None of the above
_____	(5) Revenues	
_____	(6) Cash from financing activities	
_____	(7) Gains	
_____	(8) Owners' equity	
_____	(9) Expenses	
_____	(10) Assets owned by a stockholder	

E5–5 Matching Definitions with Elements of Financial Statements

Match each element to its related definition by entering the appropriate letter in the space provided.

Elements	Definitions
INCOME STATEMENT	A. Cash received during the accounting period.
___F___ (1) Revenues	B. Debts or obligations from past transactions to be paid with assets or services.
___D___ (2) Expenses	C. Increase in net assets from peripheral transactions.
___C___ (3) Gains	D. Outflow of net assets from ongoing operations.
___I___ (4) Losses	E. Financing provided by owners and operations.
BALANCE SHEET	F. Inflow of net assets from major ongoing operations.
___H___ (5) Assets	G. Cash paid out during the period.
___B___ (6) Liabilities	H. Probable future economic benefits; owned by the entity from past transactions.
___E___ (7) Owners' equity	I. Decrease in net assets from peripheral transactions.

E5–6 Matching Definitions with Income Statement-Related Terms

Following are terms related to the income statement. Match each definition with its related term by entering the appropriate letter in the space provided.

Terms	Definitions
_____ (1) Cost of goods sold	A. Sales revenue – Cost of goods sold.
_____ (2) Interest expense	B. Item that is both unusual and infrequent.
_____ (3) Extraordinary item	C. Sales of services for cash or on credit.
_____ (4) Service revenue	D. Revenues + Gains – Expenses – Losses including effects of discontinued operations, extraordinary items, and cumulative effects of accounting changes (if any).
_____ (5) Income tax expense on operations	
_____ (6) Income before extraordinary items	E. Amount of resources used to purchase or produce the goods that were sold during the reporting period.
_____ (7) Net income	
_____ (8) Gross margin on sales	F. Income tax on revenues – Operating expenses.
_____ (9) EPS	G. Cost of money (borrowing) over time.
_____ (10) Operating expenses	H. Net income divided by average shares outstanding.
_____ (11) Pretax income from operations	I. Income before unusual and infrequent items and the related income tax.
	J. Total expenses directly related to operations.
	K. Income before all income tax and before discontinued operations, extraordinary items, and cumulative effects of accounting changes (if any).
	L. None of the above.

E5–7 Ordering the Classifications on a Typical Balance Sheet

Following is a list of classifications on the balance sheet. Number them in the order in which they normally appear on a balance sheet.

No.	Title
7	Current liabilities
8	Long-term liabilities
2	Long-term investments
4	Intangible assets
3	Operational assets (property, plant, and equipment)
1	Current assets
10	Retained earnings
9	Contributed capital
6	Other noncurrent assets
5	Deferred charges — income taxes (not in normal operations)

E5–8 Matching Definitions with Information Releases Made by Public Companies

Following are the titles of various information releases. Match each definition with the related release by entering the appropriate letter in the space provided.

Information Release	Definition
_____ (1) Annual report	A. Written public news announcement that is normally distributed to major news services.
_____ (2) Form 8-K	B. Report containing the four basic statements for the year, related notes, and often statements by management and auditors.
_____ (3) Press release	
_____ (4) Form 10-Q	C. Brief unaudited report for quarter normally containing summary income statement and balance sheet (unaudited).
_____ (5) Quarterly report	
_____ (6) Form 10-K	D. Annual report filed by public companies with the SEC that contains additional detailed financial information.
	E. Quarterly report filed by public companies with the SEC that contains additional unaudited financial information.
	F. Report of special events (e.g., auditor changes, mergers) filed by public companies with the SEC.

E5–9 Matching Information Items to Financial Reports

Following are information items included in various financial reports. Match each information item with the report(s) where it would most likely be found by entering the appropriate letter(s) in the space provided.

Information Item	Report
_____ (1) Summarized financial data for 5- or 10-year period.	A. Annual report
_____ (2) Initial announcement of quarterly earnings.	B. Form 8-K
_____ (3) Announcement of a change in auditors.	C. Press release
_____ (4) Complete quarterly income statement, balance sheet, and cash flow statement.	D. Form 10-Q quart – SEC
_____ (5) The four basic financial statements for the year.	E. Quarterly report
_____ (6) Summarized income statement information for the quarter.	F. Form 10-K Annual
_____ (7) Detailed discussion of the company's competition.	G. None of the above
_____ (8) Notes to financial statements.	
_____ (9) A description of those responsible for the financial statements.	
_____ (10) Initial announcement of hiring of new vice president for sales.	

E5–10 Reporting Operational Assets on the Balance Sheet

On January 1, 19B, Laura Anne's Bakery purchased a new oven for $6,800. It was expected that the oven would be used for four years and then would be sold for $2,000 on January 1, 19F. Prepare a schedule showing the amounts that would be reported on the balance sheets prepared at the end of 19B, 19C, 19D, and 19E for the oven (at cost), accumulated depreciation, and net book value.

E5–11 Recording Stock Issuances with Par Value and Reporting Stockholders' Equity

On February 17, 19A, Cayuga Kennels was organized to provide temporary care for dogs and cats of vacationing owners. The two founders contributed a total of $30,000 in exchange for 10,000 shares of $.01 par value stock. During 19A, Cayuga Kennels earned net income of $18,000 and paid no dividends.

Required:
1. Prepare the journal entry required to record the stock issuance on February 17, 19A. Write a brief explanation of the entry.
2. Prepare the stockholders' equity section of Cayuga Kennels' balance sheet at December 31, 19A.

Ben & Jerry's

E5–12 Recording Stock Issuances with Par Value

In a recent year, Ben & Jerry's Homemade, Inc., maker of Ben & Jerry's ice cream and frozen yogurt, issued 12,000 shares of its $.033 par value stock for $96,000 (these numbers are rounded). These additional shares were issued under a stock purchase plan available to current shareholders that allows them to purchase additional newly issued shares directly from Ben & Jerry's without paying a brokerage commission. Prepare the journal entry required to record the stock issuance.

PolyGram Group

E5–13 Recording Stock Issuances with Par Value

PolyGram Group, a Dutch company, is one of the three largest recorded music companies in the world. Its popular artists include Bryan Adams, Sting, U2, The Scorpions, Def Leppard, and many others. Its financial statements are denominated in Netherlands guilders (symbol NLG). To help finance its recent purchase of the legendary Motown recording label (Temptations, Boyz II Men), PolyGram issued 10 million additional shares (par value per share NLG 0.50) for NLG 599 million. Prepare the journal entry required to record the stock issuance.

Callaway Golf

E5–14 Interpreting Changes in Stockholders' Equity

Callaway Golf recently reported the following December 31 balances in its stockholders' equity accounts (in thousands):

	Current Year	Prior Year
Common stock	$ 169	$ 140
Paid-in capital	57,807	31,948
Retained earnings	58,601	17,662
Total shareholders' equity	$116,577	$49,750

During the current year, Callaway reported net income of $42,862. Assume that the only other transactions that affected stockholders' equity during the current year were a single stock issuance and a single cash dividend that was declared and paid during the current year.

Required:
Recreate the two journal entries reflecting the stock issuance and dividend.

Compaq Computer

E5–15 Understanding a Classified Balance Sheet and the Current Ratio with Discussion

Compaq Computer Corporation began as the first manufacturer of portable computers compatible with the MS-DOS operating system. These sewing machine–sized computers found

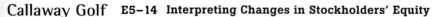

their most important market niche with independent CPAs for whom portability was a must. Today, Compaq is the leading manufacturer of computers compatible with the MS-DOS and Windows operating systems. Compaq sells a wide variety of desktop, portable, and home computers, as well as powerful servers that run business networks. Presented here are the items listed on its recent balance sheet (in millions) presented in alphabetical order:

Accounts payable	$ 637
Accounts receivable, net	1,377
Cash and cash equivalents	627
Common stock and capital in excess of par value	586
Deferred income taxes (noncurrent)	186 credit
Income taxes payable	69
Inventories	1,123
Other current liabilities	538
Other noncurrent assets	14
Prepaid expenses	164
Property, plant, and equipment, less accumulated depreciation	779
Retained earnings	2,068

Required:

1. Prepare a classified consolidated balance sheet for Compaq for the current year (ended December 31, 19A) using the categories presented in the chapter.
2. Compute the current ratio and briefly explain its meaning to Compaq's short-term creditors.

[handwritten: 3291 ÷ 1204 2.65 ample resources to meet it's short term obligations]

E5–16 Preparing and Interpreting a Classified Balance Sheet with Discussion of Terminology (Challenging)

Marvel Entertainment Group

Marvel Entertainment Group is a leading entertainment company aimed at the youth market. Its products include Marvel Comics (X-Men, Captain America, Spider Man, Fantastic Four) and Fleer sports picture trading cards (baseball, basketball, hockey, football). At the time the statements were prepared, Marvel was 80 percent owned by billionaire Ronald O. Perelman; the remaining 20 percent of the stock was publicly traded on the New York Stock Exchange under the symbol MRV. Presented here are the items listed on its recent balance sheet (in millions) presented in alphabetical order:

Accounts payable	$ 19.9
Accounts receivable, net	77.9
Accrued expenses and other	44.5
Additional paid-in capital	47.0
Cash	17.0
Common stock, $ .01 par value; 250,000,000 shares authorized, 97,642,992 shares issued and outstanding at December 31, 19A	1.0
Current portion of long-term debt	45.1
Deferred charges and other (noncurrent)	13.9
Deferred income taxes (current)	8.3 debit
Due to former stockholders of Fleer (long term)	0.1
Goodwill, net	274.6
Inventories	23.2
Investment in and advances to Toy Biz	14.2
Long-term debt	205.1
Other long-term liabilities	10.0
Prepaid expenses and other	6.1
Property, plant, and equipment, net	12.4
Retained earnings (including cumulative translation adjustment)	99.3
Trademarks and other intangibles, net	24.4

Required:

1. Prepare a classified consolidated balance sheet for Marvel Entertainment for the current year (ended December 31, 19A) using the categories presented in the chapter.
2. Four of the items end in the term *net.* Explain what this term means in each case.

Fruit of the Loom

E5–17 Analyzing the Effects of Transactions on Balance Sheet Categories, Working Capital, and the Current Ratio

Fruit of the Loom, Inc., is one of the largest domestic producers of underwear and activewear, selling products under the FRUIT OF THE LOOM®, BVD®, MUNSINGWEAR®, WILSON®, and other brand names. Presented here are selected items listed on its recent balance sheet dated December 31, 19A (in millions).

Current assets	$ 842.1
Total assets	2,547.0
Current liabilities	326.7
Total liabilities	1,481.7

Listed here are selected aggregate transactions from the first quarter of 19B (in millions). Complete the following tabulation, indicating the sign of the effect (+ for increase, – for decrease, and NE for no effect) of each additional transaction. Consider each item independently.

(a) Recorded sales on account of $501.0 and related cost of goods sold of $360.4.
(b) Borrowed $306.5 on line of credit with a bank with principal payable within one year.

Transaction	Current Assets	Working Capital	Current Ratio
(a)			
(b)			

Rowe Furniture

E5–18 Analyzing the Effects of Transactions on Balance Sheet Categories, Working Capital, and the Current Ratio

Rowe Furniture Corporation is a Virginia-based manufacturer of furniture. Presented here are selected items listed on its recent balance sheet dated December 31, 19A (in millions).

Current assets	$32.7
Total assets	58.0
Current liabilities	17.8
Total liabilities	22.4

The following are selected aggregate transactions from the first quarter of 19B (in millions) taken from the cash flow statement. Complete the following tabulation, indicating the sign of the effect (+ for increase, – for decrease, and NE for no effect) of each additional transaction. Consider each item independently.

(a) Recorded collections of cash from customers owed on open account of $32.2.
(b) Repaid $2.1 in principal on line of credit with a bank with principal payable within one year.

Transaction	Current Assets	Working Capital	Current Ratio
(a)			
(b)			

E5–19 Analyzing Income Statement Relationships

Supply the missing dollar amounts for the 19B income statement of Ultimate Style Company for each of the following independent cases:

	Case A	Case B	Case C	Case D	Case E
Sales revenue	$900	$700	$410	$ 118?	$1150?
Selling expense	50?	150	80	400	250
Cost of goods sold	500?	380	200?	500	310
→ Income tax expense	30?	30	20	40	30
Gross margin	400	320?	210 ?	490?	440
Pretax income	200	90	70?	190	110 ?
Administrative expense	150	80 ?	60	100	80
Net income	170	40 ?	50	? 150	80

E5–20 Preparing a Multiple-Step Income Statement Using the Gross Profit Percentage

The following data were taken from the records of Village Corporation at December 31, 19B:

Gross margin (35% ratio)	$24,500
Selling (distribution) expense	8,000
Administrative expense	?
Pretax income	12,000
Income tax rate	30%
Shares of stock outstanding	3,000

Required:

Prepare a complete multiple-step income statement for the company (showing both gross profit and income from operations). Show all computations. (*Hint:* Set up the side captions starting with sales revenue and ending with earnings per share; rely on the percentages given.)

E5–21 Preparing Single- and Multiple-Step Income Statements Using the Gross Profit Percentage

The following data were taken from the records of Kimberly Appliances, Incorporated, at December 31, 19D:

Sales revenue	$120,000
Administrative expense	10,000
Selling (distribution) expense	18,000
Income tax rate	25%
Gross profit ratio	40%
Shares of stock outstanding	2,000

Required:

1. Prepare a complete single-step income statement for the company. Show all computations. (*Hint:* Set up side captions starting with sales revenue and ending with earnings per share; rely on the percentages given.)
2. Prepare a complete multiple-step income statement for the company (showing both gross profit and income from operations).

E5–22 Analyzing the Effects of Transactions on Income Statement Categories and the Gross Profit Percentage

Apple Computer

Apple Computer popularized both the personal computer and the easy-to-use graphic inter-face. Today it is fighting for its life, however, against a bevy of companies that rely on Intel microprocessors and the Windows operating system. Presented here is its recent income statement (in millions).

Net sales	$ 9,833
Costs and expenses	
Cost of sales	8,865
Research and development	604
Selling, general and administrative	1,568
Restructuring costs	179
	11,216
Operating income (loss)	(1,383)
Interest and other income (expenses), net	88
Income (loss) before provision (benefit) for income taxes	(1,295)
Provision (benefit) for income taxes	(479)
Net income (loss)	$ (816)

Listed here are hypothetical *additional* transactions. Assuming that they had *also* occurred during the fiscal year, complete the following tabulation, indicating the sign of the effect of each *additional* transaction (+ for increase, – for decrease, and NE for no effect). Consider each item independently.

(a) Recorded sales on account of $500 and related cost of goods sold of $475.

(b) Incurred additional research and development expense of $100, which was paid in cash.

Transaction	Gross Profit	Gross Profit Percentage	Operating Income (Loss)
(a)			
(b)			

Callaway Golf E5–23 Understanding *The Wall Street Journal* Earnings Digest

For many public companies, *The Wall Street Journal* prints summary information from quarterly earnings announcements in its "Digest of Earnings Reports" on the day after the announcement. The following is the information reported in *The Wall Street Journal* "Digest" for Callaway Golf's recent fourth quarter.

CALLAWAY GOLF CO. (N)

	Quarter Ended December 31	
	1994	**1993**
Sales	$115,180,000	$68,248,000
Net income	19,526,000	10,334,000
Avg shares	36,530,000	a35,802,000
Shr earns (primary)		
Net income	.53	a.29
Year:		
Sales	448,729,000	254,645,000
Income	78,022,000	41,204,000
Acctg adj	. . . .	b1,658,000
Net income	78,022,000	42,862,000
Avg shares	36,552,000	a34,482,000
Shr earns (primary):		
Income	2.13	a1.19
Net income	2.13	a1.24
Shr earns (fully diluted):		
Income	2.13	a1.17
Net Income	2.13	a1.22

a—Adjusted for a 2-for-1 stock split paid in March 1994.

b—Cumulative effect on prior periods of an accounting change.

Required:

Using this information and the Callaway financial statements presented in the chapter, answer the following questions.

1. Match the common abbreviations used in the digest with the five major sections of the income statement presented in the chapter by placing the appropriate letter in front of each abbreviation.

Abbreviation	Income Statement Section
_____ (1) Acctg adj	A. Continuing operations
_____ (2) Extrd chg	B. Discontinued operations
_____ (3) Inco dis op	C. Extraordinary items
_____ (4) Inco cnt op	D. Cumulative effect of changes in accounting methods
_____ (5) Shr earns	E. Earnings per share
_____ (6) Extrd credit	

2. What accounts for the difference between the two earnings per share (primary) numbers reported for 1993?

E5–24 Focus on Cash Flows: Preparing a Simple Statement of Cash Flows

At the end of the annual reporting period, December 31, 19B, the records of Pluto Company showed the following:

a. Cash account: beginning balance, $40,000; ending balance, $27,000. — ⟨13,000⟩ *change*

b. From the income statement:

(1) Cash revenues $190,000 + 0

(2) Cash expenses   144,000 − 0

c. From the balance sheet:

(1) Additional capital stock sold: common stock, par $10; sold 3,000 shares at $12 per share.   36,000 F

(2) Borrowed cash on a long-term note, $20,000. + F

(3) Purchased equipment for use in the business: paid cash, $80,000. - I

(4) Paid a long-term note, $12,000. − F

(5) Declared and paid a cash dividend, $15,000. − F

(6) Purchased land for employee parking lot, $8,000. — I

Required:

Prepare the 19B statement of cash flows for Pluto Company using the direct method as discussed in Chapter 4.

Problems

P5–1 Matching Definitions with Balance Sheet-Related Terms

Following are terms related to the balance sheet. Match each definition with its related term by entering the appropriate letter in the space provided.

Terms	Definitions
_____ (1) Retained earnings	A. A miscellaneous category of assets.
_____ (2) Current liabilities	B. Current assets minus current liabilities.
_____ (3) Liquidity	C. Total assets minus total liabilities.
_____ (4) Contra-asset account	D. Nearness of assets to cash (in time).
_____ (5) Accumulated depreciation	E. Assets expected to be collected in cash within one year or
_____ (6) Intangible assets	operating cycle, if longer.
_____ (7) Other assets	F. Same as carrying value; cost less accumulated depreciation
_____ (8) Shares outstanding	to date. (continued)

Terms	Definitions
_____ (9) Normal operating cycle	G. Accumulated earnings minus accumulated dividends.
_____ (10) Book value	H. Asset offset account (subtracted from asset).
_____ (11) Working capital	I. Balance of the Common Stock account divided by the par value per share.
_____ (12) Liabilities	
_____ (13) Operational assets	J. Assets that do not have physical substance.
_____ (14) Shareholders' equity	K. Probable future economic benefits owned by the entity from past transactions.
_____ (15) Current assets	
_____ (16) Assets	L. Liabilities expected to be paid out of current assets normally within the next year.
_____ (17) Long-term liabilities	
	M. The average cash-to-cash time involved in the operations of the business.
	N. Sum of the annual depreciation expense on an asset from its acquisition to the current date.
	O. All liabilities not classified as current liabilities.
	P. Property, plant, and equipment.
	Q. Debts or obligations from past transactions to be paid with assets or services.
	R. None of the above.

P5–2 Matching Transactions with Concepts

Following are the concepts of accounting. Match each transaction with its related concept by entering the appropriate letter in the space provided. Use one letter for each blank.

Concepts

_____ (1) Users of financial statements
_____ (2) Objective of financial statements

Qualitative Characteristics

_____ (3) Relevance
_____ (4) Reliability

Implementation Assumptions

_____ (5) Separate entity
_____ (6) Continuity
_____ (7) Unit of measure
_____ (8) Time period

Elements of Financial Statements

_____ (9) Revenues
_____ (10) Expenses
_____ (11) Gains
_____ (12) Losses
_____ (13) Assets
_____ (14) Liabilities
_____ (15) Stockholders' equity

Implementation Principles

_____ (16) Cost
_____ (17) Revenue
_____ (18) Matching
_____ (19) Full disclosure

Constraints of Accounting

_____ (20) Materiality threshold
_____ (21) Cost-benefit constraint
_____ (22) Conservatism constraint
_____ (23) Industry peculiarities

Transactions

(a) Recorded a $1,000 sale of merchandise on credit.
(b) Counted (inventoried) the unsold items at the end of the period and valued them in dollars.
(c) Acquired a vehicle for use in operating the business.
(d) Reported the amount of depreciation expense because it likely will affect important decisions of statement users.
(e) Identified as the investors, creditors, and others interested in the business.
(f) Used special accounting approaches because of the uniqueness of the industry.
(g) Sold and issued bonds payable of $1 million.
(h) Paid a contractor for an addition to the building with $10,000 cash and $20,000 market value of the stock of the company ($30,000 was deemed to be the cash equivalent price).
(i) Engaged an outside independent CPA to audit the financial statements.
(j) Sold merchandise and services for cash and on credit during the year; then determined the cost of those goods sold and the cost of rendering those services.
(k) Established an accounting policy that sales revenue shall be recognized only when ownership to the goods sold passes to the customer.
(l) To design and prepare the financial statements to assist the users in making decisions.
(m) Established a policy not to include in the financial statements the personal financial affairs of the owners of the business.
(n) Sold an asset at a loss that was a peripheral or incidental transaction.
(o) The user value of a special financial report exceeds the cost of preparing it.
(p) Valued an asset, such as inventory, at less than its purchase cost because the replacement cost is less.
(q) Dated the income statement "For the Year Ended December 31, 19B."
(r) Used services from outsiders—paid cash for some and the remainder on credit.
(s) Acquired an asset (a pencil sharpener that will have a useful life of five years) and recorded it as an expense when purchased for $1.99.
(t) Disclosed in the financial statements all relevant financial information about the business; necessitated the use of notes to the financial statements.
(u) Sold an asset at a gain that was a peripheral or incidental transaction.
(v) Assets of $500,000 − Liabilities of $300,000 = Stockholders' Equity of $200,000.
(w) Accounting and reporting assume a "going concern."

P5–3 Preparing a Balance Sheet and Analyzing Some of Its Parts

King Jewelers is developing its annual financial statements for 19C. The following amounts were correct at December 31, 19C: cash, $42,000; accounts receivable, $51,300; merchandise inventory, $110,000; prepaid insurance, $800; investment in stock of Z corporation (long-term), $26,000; store equipment, $48,000; used store equipment held for disposal, $7,000; accumulated depreciation, store equipment, $9,600; accounts payable, $42,000; long-term note payable, $30,000; income taxes payable, $7,000; retained earnings, $86,500; and common stock, 100,000 shares outstanding, par $1 per share (originally sold and issued at $1.10 per share).

Required:

1. Based on these data, prepare a 19C balance sheet. Use the following major captions (list the individual items under these captions):
   - a. Assets: Current Assets, Long-Term Investments, Operational Assets, and Other Assets.
   - b. Liabilities: Current Liabilities and Long-Term Liabilities.
   - c. Stockholders' Equity: Contributed Capital and Retained Earnings.
2. What is the book or carrying value of the
   - a. Inventory?
   - b. Accounts receivable?
   - c. Store equipment?
   - d. Note payable (long-term)?

   Explain what these values mean.
3. What is the amount of working capital?

P5–4 Reporting Building, Land, and Depreciation Expense

Stewart Company is preparing its balance sheet at December 31, 19X. The following assets are to be reported:
- a. Building, purchased 15 years ago (counting 19X): original cost, $450,000; estimated useful life, 25 years from date of purchase; and no residual value.
- b. Land, purchased 15 years ago (counting 19X): original cost, $70,000.

Required:

1. Show how the two assets should be reported on the balance sheet. What is the total book value of these operational assets?
2. What amount of depreciation expense should be reported on the 19X income statement? Show computations.

P5–5 Preparing the Stockholders' Equity Section of a Balance Sheet

At the end of the 19A annual reporting period, Mesa Corporation's balance sheet showed the following:

MESA CORPORATION
Balance Sheet
At December 31, 19A

Stockholders' Equity	
Contributed capital	
Common stock (par $10, 7,000 shares)	$ 70,000
Contributed capital in excess of par	10,000
Total contributed capital	$ 80,000
Retained earnings	
Ending balance	50,000
Total stockholders' equity	$130,000

During 19B, the following selected transactions (summarized) were completed:

(a) Sold and issued 1,000 shares of common stock at $15 cash per share (at year-end).
(b) Determined net income, $40,000.
(c) Declared and paid a cash dividend of $3 per share on the beginning shares out-standing.

Required:

1. Prepare the stockholders' equity section of the balance sheet at December 31, 19B.
2. Give the journal entry to record the sale and issuance of the 1,000 shares of common stock.

Adolph Coors Company

P5–6 Preparing a Multiple-Step Income Statement with Discontinued Operations and Cumulative Effects of Accounting Changes (Challenging)

Adolph Coors Company, established in 1873, is the third-largest brewer of beer in the United States. Its products include Coors, Coors Light, ZIMA, and many other malt beverages. Recently, Coors discontinued its ceramics, aluminum, packaging, and technology-based developmental businesses. In the same year, it reported two changes in accounting methods mandated by the FASB. The items reported on its income statement for that year (ended December 26, 19A) are presented here (in thousands) in alphabetical order:

Cost of goods sold	$1,035,544
Cumulative effect of change in accounting for income taxes	30,500
Cumulative effect of change in accounting for post-retirement benefits (net of tax)	(38,800)
Income tax expense	22,900
Interest expense	16,014
Interest income	255
Marketing, general and administrative	429,573
Miscellaneous income—net	1,087
Net loss from discontinued operations	29,415
Net sales	1,550,788
Research and project development	12,370

Required:

1. Using appropriate headings and subtotals, prepare a multiple-step consolidated income statement (showing both gross profit and operating income).
2. What information does the multiple-step format emphasize that the single-step income statement does not?

P5–7 Preparing Both an Income Statement and Balance Sheet from a Trial Balance

Thomas Real Estate Company (organized as a corporation on April 1, 19A) has completed the accounting cycle for the second year, ended March 31, 19C. Thomas also has completed a correct trial balance as follows:

THOMAS REAL ESTATE COMPANY
Trial Balance
At March 31, 19C

Account Titles	Debit	Credit
Cash	53,000	
Accounts receivable	44,800	
Office supplies inventory	300	
Automobiles (company cars)	30,000	
Accumulated depreciation, automobiles		10,000
Office equipment	3,000	
Accumulated depreciation, office equipment		1,000
Accounts payable		20,250

Account Titles	Debit	Credit
Income taxes payable		0
Salaries and commissions payable		1,500
Note payable, long–term		30,000
Capital stock (par $1; 30,000 shares)		30,000
Contributed capital in excess of par		5,000
Retained earnings (on April 1, 19B)		7,350
Dividends declared and paid during the current year	8,000	
Sales commissions earned		77,000
Management fees earned		13,000
Operating expenses (detail omitted to conserve your time)	48,000	
Depreciation expense		
(on autos and including $500 on office equipment)	5,500	
Interest expense	2,500	
Income tax expense (not yet computed)		
Totals	195,100	195,100

Required:

1. Complete the financial statements, as follows:

    a. Income statement for the reporting year ended March 31, 19C. Include income tax expense, assuming a 30 percent tax rate. Use the following major captions: Revenues, Expenses, Pretax Income, Income Tax, Net Income, and EPS (list each item under these captions).

    b. Balance sheet at the end of the reporting year, March 31, 19C. Include (1) income taxes for the current year in income taxes payable and (2) dividends in retained earnings. Use the following captions (list each item under these captions).

    Assets

    Current assets
    Operational assets

    Liabilities

    Current liabilities
    Long-term liabilities

    Stockholders' Equity

    Contributed capital
    Retained earnings

2. Give the journal entry to record income taxes for the year (not yet paid).

P5–8 Focus on Cash Flows: Preparing a Simple Statement of Cash Flows

Blackwell Corporation is preparing its annual financial statements at December 31, 19A. The following cash flow data have been determined to be correct for 19A:

a. Sales and service revenues, $270,000, including $32,000 on credit and not yet collected.

b. Expenses, $247,000, including $15,000 noncash items.

c. Borrowed cash, $25,000, on a three-year note payable (10 percent interest payable each year-end). The note was dated December 31, 19A.

d. Purchased a new delivery truck for $12,000 cash.

e. Issued stock for $22,000 cash.

f. Purchased a tract of land for a future building site that cost $36,000; paid cash.

g. Cash account: balance, January 1, 19A, $36,000; and balance, December 31, 19A, $41,000.

Required:

Prepare the 19A statement of cash flows for Blackwell Corporation. The section reporting cash flows from operations should indicate revenues received in cash and expenses paid in cash (the direct method discussed in Chapter 4).

P5–9 Analyzing the Amounts on an Income Statement (Challenging)

Following is a partially completed income statement of Reginold Corporation for the year ended December 31, 19B.

Items	Other Data	Amounts
Net sales revenue		$260,000
Cost of goods sold		
Gross margin on sales	Gross margin as percent of sales, 35%	
Expenses		
Selling expense		
General and administrative expense		$28,000
Interest expense		4,000
Total expenses		
Pretax income		
Income tax on operations		
Income before extraordinary items		
Extraordinary gain		12,000
Income tax effect		
Net extraordinary gain		
Net income		
EPS (on common stock):		
Income before extraordinary gain		1.20
Extraordinary gain		
Net income		

Required:

Based on these data and assuming (1) a 20 percent income tax rate on all items and (2) 25,000 common shares outstanding, complete the income statement. Show all computations.

Cases and Projects

C5–1 Analyzing Financial Statements

The following amounts were selected from the annual financial statements for Genesis Corporation at December 31, 19C (end of the third year of operations):

From the 19C income statement	
Sales revenue	$ 275,000
Cost of goods sold	(170,000)
All other expenses (including income tax)	(95,000)
Net income	10,000
From the December 31, 19C, balance sheet	0
Current assets	90,000
All other assets	212,000
Total assets	302,000
Current liabilities	40,000
Long-term liabilities	66,000
Capital stock (par $10)	100,000
Contributed capital in excess of par	16,000
Retained earnings	80,000
Total liabilities and stockholders' equity	302,000

Required:

Analyze the data on the 19C financial statements of Genesis by answering the questions that follow. Show computations.

1. What was the gross margin on sales?
2. What was the amount of EPS?
3. What was the amount of working capital?
4. If the income tax rate was 25 percent, what was the amount of pretax income?
5. What was the average sales price per share of the capital stock?
6. Assuming that no dividends were declared or paid during 19C, what was the beginning balance (January 1, 19C) of retained earnings?

C5-2 Analyzing Some Simple Errors to Determine the Effects of Each on Income, Assets, and Liabilities

Megan Company (not a corporation) was careless about its financial records during its first year of operations, 19A. It is December 31, 19A, the end of the annual accounting period. An outside CPA examined the records and discovered numerous errors. All of those errors are described here. Assume that each error is independent of the others.

Required:

Analyze each error and indicate its effect on 19A and 19B income, assets, and liabilities if not corrected. Do not assume any other errors. Use these codes to indicate the effect of each dollar amount: O = overstated, U = understated, and N = no effect. Write an explanation of your analysis of each transaction to support your response.

	Independent Errors	Net Income 19A	Net Income 19B	Assets 19A	Assets 19B	Liabilities 19A	Liabilities 19B
		Effect On					
a.	Depreciation expense for 19A, not recorded in 19A, $950.	O $950	N	O $950	O $950	N	N
b.	Wages earned by employees during 19A not recorded or paid in 19A but will be paid in 19B, $500.						
c.	Revenue earned during 19A but not collected or recorded until 19B, $600.						
d.	Amount paid in 19A and recorded as expense in 19A but not an expense until 19B, $200.						
e.	Revenue collected in 19A and recorded as revenue in 19A but not earned until 19B, $900.						
f.	Sale of services and cash collected in 19A. Recorded as a debit to Cash and as a credit to Accounts Receivable, $300.						
g.	On December 31, 19A, bought land on credit for $8,000, not recorded until payment was made on February 1, 19B.						

Following is a sample explanation of analysis of errors if not corrected, using the first error as an example:

a. Failure to record depreciation in 19A caused depreciation expense to be too low; therefore, income was overstated by $950. Accumulated depreciation also is too low by $950, which causes assets to be overstated by $950 until the error is corrected.

Grand Metropolitan

C5–3 An International Perspective: A Challenging Case

As the economy becomes more international in scope, users of financial statements may be expected to analyze companies that are not incorporated in the United States. Grand Metropolitan is a major world corporation located in London. It owns many familiar U.S. businesses such as the Pillsbury Company, Burger King, and Häagen-Dazs ice cream.

Required:

Based on the concepts presented in this book, explain the meaning of the various account classifications shown on the portion of the Grand Metropolitan annual report presented here. (*Note:* There are five reserve accounts. The middle three relate to topics that are discussed in advanced accounting courses.)

GRAND METROPOLITAN
Consolidated Balance Sheet
At 30th September, 19B and 19A

	Notes	19B £m	19B £m	19A £m	19A £m
Fixed assets					
Intangible assets	11		2,652		588
Tangible assets	12		3,839		3,280
Investments	13		144		206
			6,635		4,074
Current assets					
Stocks	14	1,269		761	
Debtors	15	1,451		873	
Cash at bank and in hand		215		138	
		2,935		1,772	
Creditors—due within one year					
Borrowings	17	(362)		(187)	
Other creditors	19	(2,316)		(1,301)	
		(2,678)		(1,488)	
Net current assets	15		257		284
Total assets less current liabilities			6,892		4,358
Creditors—due after more than one year					
Borrowings	17	(3,494)		(702)	
Other creditors	20	(231)		(163)	
			(3,725)		(865)
Provisions for liabilities and charges	21		(325)		(55)
			2,842		3,438
Capital and reserves					
Called-up share capital	22		506		443
Reserves	23				
Share premium account		436		7	
Revaluation reserve		(944)		649	
Special reserve		—		282	
Related companies' reserves		10		16	
Profit and loss account		2,802		2,010	
			2,304		2,964
			2,810		3,407
Minority interests			32		31
			2,842		3,438

C5–4 An International Perspective

Grand Metropolitan is a major international company located in London. A recent annual report contained the following information concerning its accounting policies.

Grand Metropolitan

ACCOUNTING CONVENTION:

The financial statements of the group are prepared under the historical cost convention. They have been drawn up to comply in all material respects with U.K. statements of standard accounting practice in force at the relevant time.

Required:

Discuss how this accounting convention compares with accounting conventions in this country.

C5–5 Determining Income Statement–Based Executive Bonuses

Callaway Golf

As noted in the chapter, Callaway Golf believes in tying executives' compensation to the company's performance as measured by accounting numbers. In a recent year, Callaway had agreed to pay its five executive officers bonuses of up to 200 percent of base salary if sales growth and pretax earnings as a percentage of sales (computed here) met or exceeded target amounts. Callaway's income statements for the relevant years are presented below.

(in thousands, except per share data)	Year Ended December 31,			
	1993		1992	
Net sales	$254,645	100%	$132,058	100%
Cost of goods sold	115,458	45%	62,970	48%
Gross profit	139,187	55%	69,088	52%
Selling expenses	38,485	15%	19,810	15%
General and administrative expenses	28,633	11%	14,990	11%
Research and development costs	3,653	1%	1,585	1%
Income from operations	68,416	27%	32,703	25%
Other income (expense)				
Interest income (expense), net	1,024		403	
Other income, net	160		69	
Income before income taxes and cumulative effect of accounting change	69,600	27%	33,175	25%
Provision for income taxes	28,396		13,895	
Income before cumulative effect of accounting change	41,204	16%	19,280	15%
Cumulative effect of accounting change	1,658			
Net income	$ 42,862	17%	$ 19,280	15%

Callaway executives will receive bonuses if *sales growth* and *pretax earnings as a percent of sales* meet or exceed target amounts (35.l percent and 21.1 percent, respectively). Meeting these goals in the current year would result in bonuses ranging from $400,000 to $700,000 for each of the five executive officers.

1. Use the preceding information to determine whether Callaway executives earned their bonuses in the most recent year presented.
2. Sales increased in 1996 by 22.6 percent to $678,512. What might explain the slower growth rate in 1996 compared to 1993?

C5–6 Ethics Case: Management Incentives and Fraudulent Financial Statements

Mercury Finance

Mercury Finance Co. was a fast-growing auto-finance and insurance company. In January of 1997, however, the auditors discovered that recently announced 1996 earnings had been grossly overstated and prior years' earnings had been overstated to a lesser extent. The estimated size of the earnings overstatement for 1996 is described in the following excerpt:

BUSINESS BRIEF—MERCURY FINANCE CO.

Estimates for 1996 Revised Again, Now to a Big Loss

04/24/97 p. A8

The Wall Street Journal

Mercury Finance Co., which previously warned that it had grossly overstated earlier years' earnings, said it now expects to report up to a $55 million loss for 1996. In January, the Lake Forest, Ill., auto-finance company initially reported earnings of $120.7 million for 1996. Soon afterward, however, Mercury disclosed the accounting "irregularities" and estimated that last year's earnings probably would be about $56.7 million. Yesterday, Mercury said in an "update" that 1996 results will include an additional $125 million in loss provisions, as well as a $25 million reserve to cover the planned sale of its Lyndon insurance unit. As a result, the company anticipates a 1996 net loss of between $48 million and $55 million. In New York Stock Exchange composite trading, Mercury closed down 25 cents, or 13%, at $1.75.

Using more recent new reports (Wall Street Journal Index, Dow Jones News/Retrieval, and *Bloomberg Business News* are good sources), answer the following questions.

1. Whom did the courts and regulatory authorities hold responsible for the misstated financial statements?
2. What were Mercury's closing stock prices on the day before (January 28, 1997) and the day after (January 30, 1997) the announcement of the misstatement?
3. How might executive compensation plans that tied bonuses to accounting earnings motivate unethical conduct in this case?

Toys "R" Us

C5–7 Financial Statement Analysis

Refer to the financial statements of Toys "R" Us given in Appendix B at the end of this book. The full-disclosure principle requires companies to present all relevant economic information. The following questions illustrate the types of information that you can find in the financial statements. (*Hint:* Use the notes.)

Required:
1. What was the highest stock price for the company during 1996?
2. How much land did the company own at the end of the current year?
3. What was rent expense for the current year?
4. How much of the company's sales were earned in foreign locations during the current year?
5. In what season does the company generate the most sales activity?

Toys "R" Us

C5–8 Financial Statement Analysis

Refer to the financial statements of Toys "R" Us given in Appendix B at the end of this book.

Required:
1. Compute working capital and the current ratio for the current year and prior year. Has liquidity increased or decreased during the current year?
2. Compute the gross profit percentage for the current year and prior year. Has it improved during the current year? Does management provide any explanation for the change?

C5–9 Project: Examining Library and Computer Resources

Contact your school reference librarian and/or computer help desk. Determine what information resources are available at your school for (1) business-related news reports and announcements, (2) company annual reports, (3) SEC reports, and (4) analyst forecasts.

Prepare a brief memo outlining the information available from one resource for each type of information. Also indicate its format (hard copy, website, CD-ROM, etc.).

C5–10 Project: Contacting Information Intermediaries on the World Wide Web

Using your web-browser, contact one of the information intermediaries at its website (listed in the text). Determine what information that intermediary provides concerning (1) business-related news reports and announcements, (2) company annual reports, (3) SEC reports, and (4) analyst forecasts. Prepare a brief memo outlining the information available from that resource for each of the four types of information. Also indicate its format (hard copy, website, CD-ROM, etc.).

C5–11 Project: Understanding the Disclosure Process through the Microsoft Website   Microsoft

Using your web-browser, contact Microsoft at its website (http://www.microsoft.com/msft/). Examine the most recent quarterly earnings press release and the related Form 10-Q, and the most recent Form 10-K. Based on the information provided on the site, answer the following questions.

1. What were the release dates of the quarterly earnings press release and the Form 10-Q?
2. What additional information was provided in the Form 10-Q that was not reported in the earnings press release?
3. How do the statements and footnotes in the Form 10-K differ from those reported in the Form 10-Q?

C5–12 Project: Information Provided on Company Websites: Microsoft   Microsoft

Using your web-browser, contact Microsoft at its website (http://www.microsoft.com/msft/). Based on the information provided on the site, answer the following questions.

1. Which document(s) provided the most recent information on quarterly earnings?
2. For the most recent quarter, what was the change in the gross margin percentage compared to the same quarter one year earlier? What was management's explanation for the change (if any)?
3. In what formats is the latest income statement from the annual report provided?
4. What was the annual earnings per share, stock price per share, and price-earnings ratio (see Chapter 1) on the day of the most recent fourth quarter earnings press release?

C5–13 Project: Financial Analysis Update Using the Callaway Website   Callaway Golf

Using your web-browser, contact Callaway Golf at its website (http://www.callawaygolf.com). Find the latest Callaway annual report. (*Note:* The necessary information also can be accessed from its Form 10-K through EDGAR.)

Required:
1. What was Callaway's gross profit percentage in the most recent year and how did it compare to the latest figures provided in the text? What was management's explanation for the change (if any)?
2. What was Callaway's current ratio at the end of the most recent year and how did it compare to the latest figures provided in the text? What balance sheet items caused the bulk of the change?

C5–14 Project: Performing Comparative Analysis of Gross Profit Percentages   Microsoft
Compaq Computer

Using your web-browser, contact the websites of Microsoft, the leading computer *software* company (http://www.microsoft.com/msft/), and Compaq Computer, the leading manufacturer of personal computer *hardware* (http:// www.compaq.com). On the basis of information provided in their latest annual reports, determine their gross profit percentages. Write a short memo comparing the companies' ratios. Indicate what differences in their businesses might account for any difference in the ratios.

C5–15 **Project: Understanding Formats of Financial Statements and Earnings Announcements**

Using local library resources and company-provided information, your task is to understand the formats used for financial statements and notes in an annual report and to track the stock-price reaction to the most recent annual earnings announcement for a public company. Your instructor may assign a particular company for you to analyze, or you may choose one of the focus companies in this text, a competitor company in the same industry, or a company in which you have career-related interests.

Required:
1. Contact the website or investor relations department of the company and obtain a copy of the most recent annual report. Alternatively, if your instructor so assigns, look in *The Wall Street Journal* stock price listings and select one company marked with the "♣" symbol. Call *The Wall Street Journal* Annual Reports Service at 1-800-654-2582 (check a recent issue to determine whether the number has been changed) and request a copy of the most recent annual report for the selected company. (At publication time, this service was free.)
   a. Describe the formats used to present the balance sheet and the income statement.
   b. Describe the information contained in one footnote that describes an accounting rule applied in the company's statements, one footnote that presents additional detail about a reported financial statement number, and one footnote that reports financial statement information not listed in the statements.
2. Using the company's website, The Wall Street Journal Index, or Dow Jones News Retrieval Service (or an instructor-assigned resource), find one article reporting the company's annual earnings announcement. Using *The Wall Street Journal* or another newspaper, locate the stock price listing for the company.
   a. Prepare a graph of the closing stock price for your company for the date of the earnings announcement and the five days preceding and following the announcement.
   b. Describe the apparent effect of the announcement on the company's stock price.
   c. Describe any explanations for the reported earnings or the stock price changes provided in the press article. Discuss whether you find the explanations convincing.

C5–16 **Project: Analyzing News Announcements and Financial Reporting (Extended)**

Using local library resources and company-provided information, your task is to track the information announcement process for a public company for a three-month period following its most recent year-end. Your instructor may assign a particular company for you to analyze, or you may choose one of the focus companies in this text, a competitor in the same industry, or a company in which you have career-related interests.

Required:
1. Gathering the necessary information
   a. Contact the investor relations department of the company and obtain copies of the most recent annual report, Form 10-K, and a recent earnings press release.
   b. Using The Wall Street Journal Index or Dow Jones News Retrieval Service (or instructor-assigned resource), find one article reporting a nonearnings-related

significant event (new product introduction, merger, etc.) that took place during the last year.

    c. Using *The Wall Street Journal* or another source, prepare two separate graphs: (1) the closing stock price for your company for the day of the earnings press release and the five days preceding and following the earnings press release and (2) the closing stock price for the week of the news article selected in part (*b*) and the five days preceding and following the news event.

2. Analyzing the information announcements

    a. Based on the annual report and Form 10-K, determine the company's principal lines of business, CEO, CFO, auditors, and major competitors.

    b. Determine the format the company used to prepare its income statements and balance sheets in the annual report.

    c. Find one financial statement-related schedule that is included in the Form 10-K but not in the annual report.

    d. Compare the earnings per share, gross margin percentage, current ratio, debt-to-equity ratio, and return on investment for the chosen year to the preceding year.

3. Presenting the results of your analysis. Prepare a written report including the following components:

    a. A brief description of the company and its operations, major players, and competitors.

    b. The formats used in the income statement and balance sheet and an example of additional information provided in the Form 10-K.

    c. The earnings press release and selected important news announcement, the apparent effect on the company's stock price, and any explanations for the reported events or the stock price changes provided in the press.

    d. A summary of your comparative analysis of the company's performance, debt and equity position, and liquidity based on the company's earnings per share, gross margin percentage, and return on investment, debt-to-equity ratio, and current ratio.

C5–17 Ethics Project: Analyzing Irregularities and Management Compensation

Obtain a recent news story outlining an accounting irregularity (misstatement) in which the reporter linked the motive for the misstatement to management compensation based on reported accounting earnings. (Library files, Wall Street Journal Index, Dow Jones News/Retrieval, and *Bloomberg Business News* are good sources. Search for the terms *accounting irregularities* and *bonus*.) Write a short memo outlining the nature of the irregularity, the size of the necessary correction of previously reported earnings, the impact of the announcement of the irregularity on the company's stock price, the impact of the irregularity on management compensation, and any fines or civil penalties against the company and its officers.

C5–18 Team Project: Analyzing the Accounting Communication Process

As a group, select an industry to analyze. Each group member should acquire the annual report or 10-K for one publicly traded company in the industry, with each member selecting a different company. (Library files, the SEC EDGAR service at www.sec.gov, Compustat CD, or the company itself are good sources.) On an individual basis, each group member should write a short report answering the following questions about their selected company.

1. What formats are used to present the balance sheet and income statement?
2. Find one footnote that describes an accounting rule applied in the company's statements, one footnote that presents additional detail about a reported financial

statement number, and one footnote that reports financial statement information not listed in the statements. What information is provided in each?

3. If an appropriate source is available at your school, using the company's website, The Wall Street Journal Index, or Dow Jones News Retrieval Service (or an instructor assigned resource), find one article reporting the company's annual earnings announcement. How does the date of the announcement compare with the date on the annual report or 10-K?

4. Compute working capital and the current ratio for the current year and prior year. Has liquidity increased or decreased during the current year?

5. Compute the gross margin percentage for the current year and prior year. Has the gross margin percentage improved during the current year? Does management provide any explanation for the change?

Discuss any patterns across the three companies that you as a group observe. Then, as a group, write a short report comparing and contrasting your companies using these attributes. Provide potential explanations for any differences discovered.

CHAPTER SIX

Reporting and Interpreting Sales Revenue, Receivables, and Cash

The Timberland Company

TIMBERLAND FOOTWEAR—"VIRTUALLY WATERPROOF, BUNION-PROOF, AND WEAROUT-PROOF"

Initially aimed at outdoorsmen including hunters and hikers, Timberland's premium boots, casual shoes, boat shoes, and sandals are now as popular on the streets of New York City as they are on the 1,000-mile Iditarod Sled Dog Race in Alaska. Its footwear and apparel are sold through quality department, retail, and specialty stores in more than 60 countries and through company-owned specialty and outlet stores in the United States and abroad.

An emphasis on handsewn, high-quality construction, classic styling, and protection from the elements led to dramatic gains in revenues and profits for Timberland through the early 1990s, along with dramatic changes in its stock price.

Though it is a publicly traded company with sales of over $600 million, Timberland is also a family operation. Sidney Swartz (son of the company

founder) and his son Jeffrey are the top two officers of the company, and their family interests own about two-thirds of the company's stock. In the past, a key to Timberland's success had been maintaining higher prices and higher gross margin on sales than many of its competitors, such as Wolverine World Wide and Rocky Shoes and Boots. In 1994 and early 1995, however, Timberland management changed marketing strategies, lowering prices and increasing advertising in an attempt to boost sales volume.

For this strategy to be successful, the resulting increase in sales volume must be sufficient to offset the decrease in gross margin (sales less cost of goods sold) on each sale and related increases in selling expenses. Timberland must also ensure that, in its search for new customers, it extends credit only to those with the ability to pay their debts. Accounts receivable have value to the company only if they can be collected. The big question is whether expanding the company's exposure and providing better customer value will lead to increased success for Timberland.

■ ■ ■

Business Background

Planning an effective growth strategy requires careful coordination of marketing, production, and financing activities. Customer demand and changes in tastes must be accurately estimated, production must be adjusted, and financing must be arranged for the increased inventory and accounts receivable that Timberland must carry to support the growth in sales. The success of Timberland's new strategy can be evaluated based on information presented in the comparative statements of operations (income) presented in Exhibit 6.1. Following the multiple-step format for the income statement (with two subtotals as discussed in Chapter 5), Revenues (Sales Revenues) are reported first, and Cost of Goods Sold (an expense) is set out separately from the remaining expenses. Similar account titles sometimes used are Cost of Sales and Cost of Products Sold. Notice that the income statement then shows *gross profit* (*gross margin, gross profit margin*), which is net sales revenue minus cost of goods sold.

The effect of Timberland's change in business strategy on the gross profit on each sale can be determined by computing the gross profit percentage for each year.

	Gross Profit	÷	Net Sales	=	Gross Profit Percentage
1995	$203,397	÷	$655,138	=	31.0%
1994	$209,395	÷	$638,097	=	32.8%
1993	$153,851	÷	$420,062	=	36.6%

As planned, over the two years, sales increased by 56.0 percent [($655,138 − $420,062) ÷ $420,062], and the gross profit on each dollar of sales fell from $.366 to $.31. The large increase in total gross profit indicates that the increase in sales volume was more than sufficient to offset the decrease in gross profit on each sale. The income statement (Exhibit 6.1) indicates, however, that this increase in total gross profit was more than consumed by related increases in selling expenses and interest on debt necessary to carry the increase in receivables and inventory evident on the balance sheet. As a consequence, earnings declined in 1994 and, in 1995, Timberland reported its first net loss since going public in 1987.

EXHIBIT 6.1
Statements of Income*

CONSOLIDATED STATEMENTS OF OPERATIONS

For the Years Ended December 31, 1995, 1994 and 1993

(Amounts in Thousands Except Per Share Data)	1995	1994	1993
Revenues	$655,138	$638,097	$420,062
Cost of goods sold	451,741	428,702	266,211
Gross profit	203,397	209,395	153,851
Operating expenses			
Selling	145,924	124,386	82,585
General and administrative	46,721	40,213	28,956
Amortization of goodwill	1,685	1,180	774
Restructuring charge	16,000	–	–
Total operating expenses	210,330	165,779	112,315
Operating income (loss)	(6,933)	43,616	41,536
Other expense (income)			
Interest expense	22,861	15,052	6,252
Other, net	(11,028)	452	1,161
Total other expense	11,833	15,504	7,413
Income (loss) before income taxes	(18,766)	28,112	34,123
Provision (benefit) for income taxes	(7,131)	10,402	11,602
Net income (loss)	$(11,635)	$ 17,710	$ 22,521
Earnings (loss) per share	$ (1.04)	$ 1.58	$ 2.01
Weighted average shares outstanding			
and share equivalents	11,171	11,209	11,206

The accompanying notes are an integral part of these consolidated financial statements.

*Note that all of the account titles, formats, and amounts are taken directly from Timberland's annual report to shareholders.

A detailed understanding of this change of fortune requires further knowledge of how net sales and cost of goods sold are determined. In this chapter, we focus on the transactions that affect *net sales revenues* (and certain selling expenses) on the income statement and *cash* and *accounts receivable* on the balance sheet. In the next chapter, we will discuss transactions related to cost of goods sold on the income statement and inventories on the balance sheet.

Cash, accounts receivable, and inventories are important from the standpoint of cash management and the prevention of fraud. As we discuss later in this chapter and in Chapter 7, the primary source of operating cash for most organizations is the collection of accounts receivable, and a primary use is payments for inventories. As a consequence, careful management of receivables and inventory can be the key to avoiding a business failure driven by cash shortages. Cash also is a tempting target for fraud and embezzlement, so accounting systems commonly include controls to prevent and detect these misdeeds.

Lenders, shareholders, and analysts also carefully monitor these accounts because of their importance as predictors of the future success of companies. Their importance is supported by the fact that the majority of shareholder lawsuits and SEC enforcement actions against companies for misleading financial statements relate to these accounts. We discuss an actual example of misleading statements later in the chapter.

than it would if it provided credit directly to consumers. It can deposit credit card receipts directly to its bank account.

The credit card company charges a fee for the service it provides. For example, when Timberland deposits its credit card receipts in the bank, it might receive credit for an amount equal only to 98 percent of the sales price. The credit card company is charging a 2 percent fee (the **credit card discount**) for its service. If credit card sales were $3,000 at the same store for January 2, Timberland records the following entry.

> A **credit card discount** is the fee charged by the credit card company for services.

Jan. 2	Cash (A)	2,940	
	Credit card discounts (XR or E)	60	
	Sales revenue (R)		3,000

Credit Card Discounts may be reported as (1) a *contra revenue account* and thus a deduction in the computation of *net sales* or (2) an addition to *selling expenses*. In either case, it reduces net income by the same amount. Recall from Chapter 4 that a *contra account* is an account, related to a primary account, that is an offset (or reduction) to the primary account. Thus, a contra revenue account reduces the related revenue. Credit Card Discounts treated as a contra revenue account is a deduction from Sales Revenue in the computation of Net Sales reported on the income statement.

Credit Sales

Most of Timberland's sales to businesses are credit sales on open account; that is, there is no formal written promissory note indicating the amount owed to Timberland by the customer. In the case of a sale of $1,000 worth of footwear to a retailer, the following journal entry is made:

Jan. 2	Accounts receivable (A)	1,000	
	Sales revenue (R)		1,000

Credit Sales and Sales Discounts

When Timberland sells footwear to retailers on credit, credit terms are printed on each sales document and invoice (bill) sent to the customer. Often credit terms are abbreviated using symbols. For example, if the full price is due within 30 days of the invoice date, the credit terms would be noted as *n/30*. Here, the *n* means the sales amount *net* of or less any sales returns. The terms *10, EOM,* mean the full price is due not later than 10 days after the end of the month (EOM) in which the sale was made.

> A **sales** (or **cash**) **discount** is a cash discount offered to encourage prompt payment of an account receivable.

In other cases, a **sales discount** (often called a **cash discount**) is granted to the purchaser to encourage early payment. For example, let's assume that Timberland offers standard credit terms of 2/10, n/30, which means that the customer may deduct 2 percent from the invoice price if cash payment is made within 10 days from the date of sale. If cash payment is not made within the 10-day discount period, however, the full sales price (less any returns) is due within a maximum of 30 days from date of sale.

Timberland offers this sales discount to give its customers an incentive for fast payment of the accounts receivable. This benefits Timberland because prompt receipt of cash from customers reduces the necessity to borrow money from Morgan Guaranty Trust (and its other banks) to meet operating needs. Also, if a customer pays Timberland's bills earlier than the bills from other suppliers, it *decreases* the chances that the customer will run out of funds before Timberland's bill is paid.

Usually customers pay within the discount period because the savings are substantial. With terms 2/10, n/30, 2 percent is saved by paying 20 days early (the 10th day instead of the 30th), which is approximately 37 percent annual interest. This annual interest rate is obtained by first computing the interest rate for the discount period. When the 2 percent discount is taken, the customer pays only 98 percent of the gross sales price. Thus, the interest rate for the 20 day discount period is

$$(\text{Amount saved} \div \text{Amount paid}) = \text{Interest rate for 20 days}$$
$$(2\% \text{ of the bill} \div 98\% \text{ of the bill}) = 2.04\% \text{ for 20 days}$$

The annual interest rate is then computed in the following manner:

$$\text{Interest rate for 20 days} \times (365 \text{ days} \div 20 \text{ days}) = \text{Annual interest rate}$$
$$2.04\% \times (365 \text{ days} \div 20 \text{ days}) = 37.23\% \text{ Annual interest}$$

Credit customers would save a great deal even if they had to borrow cash from a bank at 15 percent to take advantage of cash discounts. Normally, the bank's interest rate is less than the high interest rate associated with failing to take cash discounts.

Companies commonly record sales discounts using the gross method by which sales revenue is recorded without deducting the sales discount.[2] The following journal entry is made for a $1,000 sale with terms 2/10, n/30:

Jan. 18	Accounts receivable (A)	1,000	
	Sales revenue (R)		1,000

The entry at collection depends on whether the payment is made within the discount period. If payment is made *within* the discount period (the usual case) with terms 2/10, n/30 ($1,000 \times 0.98 = \$980$), the following entry is made:

Jan. 27	Cash (A)	980	
	Sales discounts (XR or E)	20	
	Accounts receivable (A)		1,000

Alternatively, if payment is made *after* the discount period (the unusual case), the following entry is made:

Feb. 17	Cash (A)	1,000	
	Accounts receivable (A)		1,000

The Sales Discounts account may be reported as (1) a *contra revenue account* and thus a deduction in the computation of *net sales* or (2) a component of *selling expenses*. Note that both the purpose of sales discounts and the accounting for sales discounts are very similar to the purpose of and the accounting for credit card discounts. Both sales discounts and credit card discounts provide an attractive service to customers while promoting faster receipt of cash, reducing recordkeeping costs, and minimizing bad debts. Both are reported as either contra revenues or expenses on the income statement.

It is important not to confuse a cash discount with a trade discount. Vendors sometimes use a **trade discount** for quoting sales prices; the list or printed catalog price *less* the trade discount is the sales price. For example, an item may be quoted at $10 per unit subject to a 20 percent trade discount on orders of 100 units or more; thus, the price for the large order is $8 per unit. Similarly, the price on a slow-moving product

A trade discount is a discount deducted from list price to derive the actual sales price.

[handwritten margin notes: 25% vs Chain disc — 10-10-5 not an accting disc; not an accting discount]

---

[2] We use this method in all examples in this text. Some companies use the alternative net method, which records sales revenue after deducting the amount of the cash discount. Since the choice of method has little effect on the financial statements, discussion of this method is left for an advanced course.

line can be lowered simply by increasing the trade discount. Sales revenue should always be recorded net of trade discounts.

Stretching Out the Payables

Hoffa Shoes has been incurring significant interest charges (12 percent) on short-term borrowing from its bank.* Hoffa normally purchased shoes from suppliers on terms 1/10, n/30. The annual rate of interest earned by taking the discount was 18.43 percent computed as follows:

(Amount saved ÷ Amount paid)	=	Interest rate for 20 days
(1% ÷ 99%)	=	1.01% for 20 days,
Interest rate for 20 days × (365 days ÷ 20 days)	=	Annual interest rate
1.01% × (365 days ÷ 20 days)	=	18.43% annual interest

Hoffa's policy had been to take all purchase discounts even if it had to borrow at 12 percent to make the early payment. They reasoned that they earned 6.43 percent more than they paid in interest (18.43 percent – 12 percent).

A new employee suggested a new plan. Records indicated that, even though the terms of Hoffa's agreement with its suppliers (1/10, n/30) required payment of the full amount within a maximum of 30 days, the suppliers would not complain as long as payment was made within 55 days of the purchase, since they normally did not send out a second bill until 60 days after the purchase. She reasoned that Hoffa would be better off forgoing the discount and paying on the 55th day after the purchase. She argued that since Hoffa would now be paying in 55 days instead of 10 days of the purchase, not taking the discount would be borrowing for 45 days, not the 20 days used in the former analysis. The analysis supporting the proposal is as follows:

(Amount saved ÷ Amount paid)	=	Interest rate for 45 days
(1% ÷ 99%)	=	1.01% for 45 days
Interest rate for 45 days × (365 days ÷ 45 days)	=	Annual interest rate
1.01% × (365 days ÷ 45 days)	=	8.19% annual interest

In effect, her plan allows Hoffa to borrow from suppliers at 8.19 percent instead of the bank's rate of 12 percent, saving 3.81 percent. When she presented this plan to the management for discussion, the purchasing manager agreed with the arithmetic presented but objected nonetheless. Since the plan violated its agreement with suppliers, the purchasing manager thought it was unethical. Many ethical dilemmas in business involve trade-offs between monetary benefits and potential violations of moral values.

*Hoffa Shoes is a fictitious company, but this dilemma is faced by most companies.

Sales Returns and Allowances

For Timberland, prompt delivery of exactly what the customer ordered is a key to maintaining good relations with the retailers to whom they sell. Delivery of incorrect or damaged merchandise may cost the retailer sales and can destroy these relationships. When this occurs, the customers have a right to return unsatisfactory or damaged merchandise and receive a refund or an adjustment to their bill.

Although the Sales account could be debited (reduced) to record these reductions in sales, a separate account called **Sales Returns and Allowances** is often used. This account has an important purpose because it informs Timberland's management of the

Sales Returns and Allowances is a contra revenue account used to record return of or allowances for unsatisfactory goods.

How does allowing the use of credit cards benefit Timberland?

volume of returns and allowances and thus provides a measure of the quality of service provided to customers. The Sales Returns and Allowances account is a *contra revenue account*; therefore, it is a deduction from gross sales revenue. Assume that Fontana Shoes of Ithaca, New York, bought 40 pairs of hiking boots from Timberland for $2,000 on account. On the date of sale, Timberland makes the following journal entry:

Aug. 31	Accounts receivable (A)	2,000	
	Sales revenue (R)		2,000

Before paying for the boots, Fontana discovered that 10 pairs of boots were not the color ordered and returned them to Timberland. On that date Timberland records:

Sept. 10	Sales returns and allowances (XR)	500	
	Accounts receivable (A)*		500

*If payment had already been made, cash would be credited if a check were sent to Fontana Shoes.

Reporting Net Sales

On the company's books, credit card discounts, sales discounts, and sales returns and allowances are accounted for separately to allow monitoring of the costs of the related activities (returns of incorrect or damaged merchandise, offering sales discounts, allowing use of credit cards, respectively). The amount of net sales reported on the income statement is computed in the following manner:

Sales revenue	
Less:	Credit card discounts (if treated as a contra revenue)
	Sales discounts (if treated as a contra revenue)
	Sales returns and allowances
Net sales (reported on the income statement)	

As illustrated later, however, it often is difficult even for the well-educated external user to determine the effects of these items since the determinants of net sales are rarely disclosed in the annual report.

Financial ANALYSIS

Contra Revenues and Evaluating Gross Profit

The computation of net sales is rarely reported on the financial statements. Note that if sales discounts and credit card discounts are recorded as contra revenues, net sales is reduced, and thus both gross profit (and the gross profit percentage) and operating income are reduced. If they are treated as selling expenses, however, operating income is reduced, but gross profit is unaffected. Comparisons of gross profit percentages between firms using the alternative treatments can be distorted by this difference. For example, a comparison of the gross profit percentage of Kimberly-Clark, the manufacturer of Kleenex tissues and other paper products, and of its largest competitor, Scott Paper, based on numbers reported in their 1994 income statements yields the following results:

	Kimberly-Clark	Scott Paper
Gross Profit Percentage	33.4%	29.9%

When Kimberly-Clark acquired Scott in 1995, it disclosed that it had treated a variety of customer discounts as selling expenses while Scott had treated those same items as contra revenues. Converting Scott's statements to Kimberly-Clark's accounting treatment revealed quite a different gross profit picture:

	Kimberly-Clark	Scott Paper
Gross Profit Percentage	33.4%	41.0%

Astute financial analysts should quiz company officials about the possible effects of such differences in accounting treatments before making comparisons between companies.

REAL WORLD EXCERPT

THE TIMBERLAND COMPANY
Annual Report

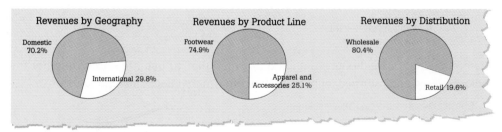

Graphics are often used to highlight key figures in the management discussion and analysis section of the annual report.

SELF-STUDY QUIZ

1. Assume that Timberland sold $2,000 worth of footwear to Mast Shoe Stores of Ann Arbor, Michigan, with terms 1/10, n/30 and recorded the transaction using the gross method. Ten days after the delivery of the footwear, Mast paid the $1,980 amount (purchase price less the discount). What journal entry does Timberland record for the collection of Mast's receivable?

---

2. Assume that Fast Shoes of Tuscaloosa, Alabama, returns $500 of footwear that it had purchased on account but had not paid for. What journal entry does Timberland record for the sales return?

After you have completed your answers, check them with the solutions presented in the footnote at the bottom of this page.*

Measuring and Reporting Receivables

Receivables Defined

Receivables are claims against other companies or persons for cash, goods, or services. Receivables may be classified in three common ways. First, the receivable may be either an account receivable or a note receivable. An **account receivable** is created when a credit sale on an open account occurs. For example, an account receivable is created if you use your Sears credit card to buy a new television. A **note receivable** is a promise in writing (i.e., a formal document) to pay (1) a specified sum of money on demand or at a definite future date known as the *maturity date* and (2) specified interest at one or more future dates. A note often involves two distinctly different amounts: (1) *principal,* which is the amount that the interest rate is based on, and (2) *interest,* which is the specified amount charged for use of the principal. The notes also require periodic recording of interest revenue. We discuss the computation of interest when we discuss notes payable in a later chapter.

Second, receivables may be classified as trade or nontrade receivables. A *trade receivable* is created in the normal course of business when a sale of merchandise or services on credit occurs. A *nontrade receivable* arises from transactions other than the normal sale of merchandise or services. For example, if Timberland loaned money to a new vice president for international operations to help finance a home at the new job location, the loan would be classified as a nontrade receivable. Third, in a classified balance sheet, receivables also are classified as either *current* or *noncurrent* (short term or long term), depending on when the cash is expected to be collected.

Like many companies, Timberland reports only one type of receivable account, Accounts Receivable from customers (trade receivables), and classifies the asset as a current asset (short term) because the accounts receivable are all due to be paid within one year. Companies also keep separate records (subsidiary records) for each customer to provide a basis for billing. Recall that Timberland was willing to pay a credit card discount fee to allow customers at the factory outlet stores to use credit cards because it would draw more customers to the stores. Similarly, Timberland allows its business customers (the retail stores that buy and then resell its footwear) to purchase goods on open account because they believe that providing this service will result in more sales to this type of customer.

As in the case of the credit card fee, providing this service to business customers also has a cost. Timberland must pay to maintain a billing system, and it must realize that not all customers will pay their debts. Further, from the financial statement user's perspective, inadequate accounting for bad debts can lead to highly misleading financial statements. From the reporting corporation's view, such misleading statements can lead to legal actions. For example, *The Wall Street Journal* reported the following:

Accounts receivable (trade receivables, receivables) are open accounts owed to the business by trade customers. **Notes receivable** are written promises that require another party to pay the business under specified conditions (amount, time, interest).

---

* 1. Dr. Cash (A) 1,980; Dr. Sales Discount (XR or E) 20; Cr. Accounts Receivable (A) 2,000.
  2. Dr. Sales Returns and Allowances (XR) 500; Cr. Accounts Receivable (A) 500.

REAL WORLD EXCERPT
The Wall Street Journal

T 2 MEDICAL DISCLOSES SEC INVESTIGATION RELATING TO TWO EARNINGS RESTATEMENTS

ALPHARETTA, GA.—T2 Medical Inc. disclosed that the Securities and Exchange Commission is investigating events surrounding the company's restatement of two quarterly earnings announcements. . . .

Last August, T2 Medical (pronounced T-squared) restated its earnings sharply downward for the first and second quarters of its 1993 fiscal year after the company said it discovered "accounting irregularities and errors." The original disclosure of accounting problems was accompanied by the resignation of T2 Medical's chief executive officer. . . .

The earnings restatements stemmed largely from inadequate provisions for "doubtful accounts. . . ."

SOURCE: *The Wall Street Journal*, January 7, 1994, p. A2.

The company, now part of Coram, paid $25 million to settle related shareholder lawsuits. Four former executives paid $456,000 to settle the above mentioned SEC charges.

ANALYSIS

Evaluating the Efficiency of Credit Granting and Collection Activities

The receivables turnover ratio measures the effectiveness of credit granting and collection activities. It is computed as follows:

$$\text{Receivables turnover} = \frac{\text{Net credit sales}}{\text{Average net trade accounts receivable}}$$

[Use the net sales amount if net credit sales is not available. The average net trade accounts receivable is normally computed as the beginning balance plus ending balance divided by 2.]

It reflects how many times average trade receivables were recorded, collected, and then recorded again during the period. Granting credit with later payment deadlines and using ineffective collection methods cause this ratio to be low. A sudden decline in this ratio may mean that a company is extending payment deadlines in an attempt to prop up lagging sales or even is recording sales that later will be returned by customers. Since differences across industries in the manner in which customer purchases are financed cause dramatic differences in the ratio, a particular firm's ratio should be compared only with its prior years' figures or with other firms in the same industry. Timberland's receivables turnover ratios for 1993, 1994, and 1995 were 5.70, 5.75, and 5.84, respectively (based on net sales). This indicates that Timberland has continued to strengthen credit and cash collection procedures. Dun & Bradstreet Information Services reports that the median men's footwear manufacturer's receivables turnover in 1995 was 5.79, nearly identical to that of Timberland.

Accounting for Bad Debts

LEARNING OBJECTIVE 3

Estimate, report, and evaluate the effects of uncollectible accounts receivable (bad debts) on financial statements.

Businesses that extend credit know that a certain amount of bad debts on credit sales occur. In fact, an extremely low rate of bad debts may not be good because it may indicate a too tight credit policy. If the credit policy is too restrictive, many good credit customers may be turned away, causing a loss of sales volume. The decision to loosen credit policies should be determined based on the *trade-off* between profits on additional sales and any additional bad debts. Bad debts can be thought of as a necessary expense associated with generating credit sales. Steps firms can take to limit bad debts are discussed at the end of this section.

Bad debt expense (doubtful accounts expense, uncollectible accounts expense, provision for uncollectible accounts) is the expense associated with estimated uncollectible accounts receivable. In conformity with the matching principle, bad debt expense should be recorded (matched) in the *same* accounting period in which the sales related to the uncollectible account were made rather than in the year that the seller learns that the customer is unable to pay. A well-managed company such as Timberland sells only to customers it believes will pay their bills, based on the information available at the time of sale. It is inevitable, however, that some customers will prove unable to pay their debts. Further, Timberland may not learn that any particular customers will not pay until the *next* accounting period.

Timberland resolves this problem and satisfies the matching principle by using the **allowance method** to measure bad debt expense. There is no way to know in advance which individual customers will not pay. Therefore, the allowance method is based on *estimates* of the expected amount of bad debts. Two primary steps in employing the allowance method are (1) the adjusting entry to record bad debt expense estimates and (2) writing off specific accounts determined to be uncollectible during the period.

Bad debt expense (doubtful accounts expense, uncollectible accounts expense, provision for uncollectible accounts) is the expense associated with estimated uncollectible accounts receivable.

The allowance method bases bad debt expense on an estimate of uncollectible accounts.

Recording Bad Debt Expense Estimates

The bad debt estimate is recorded by an *adjusting journal entry at the end of the accounting period*. For the year ended December 31, 1995, Timberland estimated bad debt expense to be $3,697,000 and made the following adjusting entry on December 31:

Bad debt expense (E)	3,697,000	
Allowance for doubtful accounts (XA)		3,697,000

Bad Debt Expense of $3,697,000 is reported on the current year's income statement. It is normally included in the category Selling on Timberland's income statement (see Exhibit 6.1). It is matched with the related sales revenue for the current year, the year in which the credit was granted. The Bad Debt Expense account is closed at the end of each accounting period along with the other expense accounts. The credit in the preceding journal entry was made to a *contra asset account* called **Allowance for Doubtful Accounts** (also called **Allowance for Bad Debts** or **Allowance for Uncollectible Accounts**). Accounts Receivable cannot be credited because there is no way to know which account receivable is involved. As a contra asset, the balance in Allowance for Doubtful Accounts is *always* subtracted from the balance of Accounts Receivable. Thus, it is treated exactly like Accumulated Depreciation, the first contra asset we discussed in Chapter 4. The balance in an account with the contra account subtracted is normally reported on the balance sheet with the term *net* following the account title.

Allowance for Doubtful Accounts (Allowance for Bad Debts, Allowance for Uncollectible Accounts) is a contra asset account containing the estimated uncollectible accounts receivable.

Allowance for Doubtful Accounts has a cumulative credit balance. It is not closed at the end of the accounting period because it is a balance sheet account. The balance of the allowance account is an approximation of the total amount of the accounts receivable that is estimated to be uncollectible. The balance of Accounts Receivable less the allowance account measures the *estimated net realizable value* (or how much Timberland expects to collect) of accounts receivable. As we noted in earlier chapters, the balance in a balance sheet account less the balance in the related contra account is called the *net book value* or *book value*, in this case, of accounts receivable.

Writing Off Specific Accounts Determined to Be Uncollectible

When a specific customer's account receivable is determined to be uncollectible (e.g., due to bankruptcy), the amount should be removed from the Accounts Receivable account with an offsetting reduction of the contra account Allowance for Doubtful

Accounts. Write-offs of individual bad debts are recorded as soon as it is determined that the customer will not pay its debts. Thus, bad debt write-offs are recorded through *a series of journal entries made throughout the year*. Timberland wrote off a total of $3,743,000 during 1995. The entries for these *write-offs during the year* are summarized in the following journal entry:

(debit) Allowance for doubtful accounts (XA) 3,743,000
(credit) Accounts receivable (A)   3,743,000

  Notice that this journal entry *did not affect any income statement accounts*. It did not record a bad debt expense because the estimated expense was recorded with an adjusting entry in the period of sale and the related allowance account was established. Also, the entry *did not change the net realizable value* (book value) of Accounts Receivable since the decrease in the asset account (Accounts Receivable) was offset by the decrease in the contra asset account (Allowance for Doubtful Accounts).

  When a customer makes a payment after an account has been written off, the journal entry to write off the account is reversed for the amount to be collected and the collection of cash recorded.

Actual Write-Offs Compared with Estimates

The amount of uncollectible accounts actually written off seldom equals the estimated amount previously recorded. This situation is resolved when the next adjusting entry is made at the end of the accounting period (a higher or lower amount is recorded to make up for the previous period's error in estimate). When estimates are found to be incorrect, financial statement values for *prior* annual accounting periods are *not* corrected.

Summary of the Accounting Process

Timberland's complete 1995 accounting process for bad debts can now be summarized in terms of the changes in Accounts Receivable and the Allowance for Doubtful Accounts:*

Accounts Receivable (A)			
Beginning balance	131,139,000	Collections on account	555,683,000
Sales on account	526,731,000	Write-offs	3,743,000
Ending balance	98,444,000		

Allowance for Doubtful Accounts (XA)		
Write-offs	3,743,000	Beginning balance	2,704,000
		Bad debt expense adjustment	3,697,000
		Ending balance	2,658,000

*This assumes that all sales to businesses (wholesale sales) are on account.

 *International* PERSPECTIVE

Foreign Currency Receivables

Export sales to non–U.S. businesses are an increasing aspect of the U.S. economy. For example, such exports amounted to 6.1 percent of Timberland's revenues in 1995. As is the case with domestic sales to other businesses, most of these export sales are on credit. When the buyer has agreed to pay Timberland in its local currency instead of U.S. dollars, these accounts receivable, which are denominated in foreign currency, cannot be added directly to Timberland's U.S. dollar accounts receivable. They must be converted first using the end-of-period exchange rate between the two currencies. For example, if a French department store owed Timberland FF20,000 (French francs) on December 31, 1995, and each franc was worth US$.20 on that date, it would add US$4,000 to its accounts receivable on the balance sheet.

Does this advertisement appeal to a broad market?

Reporting Accounts Receivable and Bad Debts

In Exhibit 6.2, Timberland reports accounts receivable, net of allowance for doubtful accounts, of $95,786 and $128,435. It also reports the amount of the allowance for each year.

The amounts of bad debt expense included in selling expenses on the income statement and accounts receivable written off for the period are normally not disclosed in the annual report. These amounts are reported on a schedule that publicly traded companies include in their Annual Report Form 10-K filed with the SEC (discussed in Chapter 5). Exhibit 6.3 presents this schedule from Timberland's 1995 filing. Write-offs

EXHIBIT 6.2
Accounts Receivable on the Balance Sheet

REAL WORLD EXCERPT

THE TIMBERLAND COMPANY
Annual Report

CONSOLIDATED BALANCE SHEETS
As of December 31, 1995 and 1994

(Dollars in Thousands, Except Per Share Data)	1995	1994
Assets		
Current assets		
Cash and equivalents	$ 38,389	$ 6,381
Accounts receivable, net of allowance for doubtful accounts of $2,658 in 1995 and $2,704 in 1994	95,786	128,435
Inventories	180,636	218,219
Prepaid expenses	12,752	13,504
Deferred and refundable income taxes	10,267	7,112
Total current assets	337,830	373,651

EXHIBIT 6.3
Accounts Receivable Valuation Schedule (Form 10–K)

THE TIMBERLAND COMPANY

VALUATION AND QUALIFYING ACCOUNTS
(In Thousands)

Description	Balance at Beginning of Period	Additions Charged to Costs and Expenses	Additions Charged to Other Accounts	Deductions Net of Write-Offs	Balance at End of Period
Allowance for doubtful accounts:					
Year ended					
December 31, 1995	$2,704	$3,697	—	$3,743	$2,658
December 31, 1994	1,014	1,938	—	248	2,704
December 31, 1993	1,821	1,131	—	1,938	1,014

are reported on Timberland's 10-K net of (less) reinstatements of previously written-off accounts.

It is important to remember that accounting for bad debts is a two-stage process:

1. *Bad Debt Expense* is recorded and the Allowance for Doubtful Accounts is increased in an *adjusting entry* (the bad debt adjustment) at the end of the accounting period. This stage affects both the income statement through the increase in Bad Debt Expense as well as the balance sheet where the increase in the Allowance for Doubtful Accounts decreases the net book value of accounts receivable.

2. *Write-offs* are recorded, however, by decreasing both Accounts Receivable and the Allowance for Doubtful Accounts *throughout the period* as specific customer accounts are determined to be uncollectible. This stage does *not* affect the income statement, since no expense is recorded. It also does not affect the balance sheet, since the decrease in the Allowance for Doubtful Accounts combined with the decrease in Accounts Receivable does not change the net book value of accounts receivable.

Accounts receivable, net of allowance for doubtful accounts, called the *net realizable value*, is reported on Timberland's balance sheet.

Methods for Estimating Bad Debts

The bad debt expense amount recorded in the end-of-period adjusting entry often is estimated in each accounting period based on either (1) the total credit sales for the period or (2) an aging of accounts receivable.

Percentage of Credit Sales

Percentage of credit sales method bases bad debt expense on the historical percentage of credit sales that result in bad debts.

Many companies make their estimates using the **percentage of credit sales method,** which bases bad debt expense on the historical percentage of credit sales that result in bad debts. This method is also called the *income statement method* because it involves the direct computation of the income statement number *bad debt expense* based on the income statement number *credit sales.*

The average percentage of credit sales that result in bad debts can be computed by dividing total bad debt losses by total *credit* sales. A company that has been operating for some years has sufficient experience to project probable future bad debt losses. For example, assume that Rogers and Lambert (a hypothetical company) had experienced the following in three recent years:

Year	Bad Debt Losses	Credit Sales
19A	$ 900	$190,000
19B	1,200	220,000
19C	1,400	290,000
Total	$3,500	$700,000

$3,500 ÷ $700,000 = 0.5% average loss rate for the three-year period 19A–19C.

If net credit sales in the current year were approximately $268,000 and the company used this method, the amount

$$\text{Credit sales} \times \text{Bad debt loss rate} = \text{Bad debt expense}$$
$$\$268,000 \times .5\% = \$1,340$$

is directly recorded as Bad Debt Expense (and Allowance for Doubtful Accounts) in the current year. New companies often rely on the experience of similar companies that have been operating for a number of years. A company usually adjusts the historical average loss rate to reflect future expectations. For example, if retail sales were rising, the company might decrease its rate to 0.4 percent, reasoning that fewer of its business customers (retailers) will become bankrupt.

Financial ANALYSIS

Judging the Accuracy of Bad Debt Estimates

Without access to detailed information concerning any changes in customer mix and credit terms, an outside financial analyst would have little basis for judging the accuracy of the current period's bad debt estimates. For example, in the case of T2 Medical discussed in *The Wall Street Journal* article reprinted earlier in the chapter, the company had increased its recognized bad debt expense from 5.4 percent of sales in the prior year to 6.5 percent of sales in recognition of an increase in the risk of bad debts. After the accounting irregularities were investigated, however, the accurate bad debt rate was determined to be 11 percent of sales. Although the financial community expected an increase in the bad debt rate, a doubling of the rate surprised most analysts because they were not aware of the dramatic changes in the company's credit sales policies.

Aging of Accounts Receivable

As an alternative to the percentage of credit sales method, many companies use the age that accounts receivable have been outstanding to estimate bad debt expense. This is called the **aging of accounts receivable method.** Older accounts receivable usually are less likely to be collectible. For example, a receivable due in 30 days that has not been paid after 60 days is more likely to be collected, on average, than a similar receivable that still remains unpaid after 120 days. Based on its prior experience, the company could estimate what portion of receivables of different ages will not be paid.

> **Aging of accounts receivable method** estimates uncollectible accounts based on the age of each account receivable.

This method is also called the *balance sheet method* because it involves the direct computation of the balance sheet number *allowance for doubtful accounts* based on the balance sheet number *accounts receivable*. Suppose that Rogers and Lambert split its receivables into five age categories, as presented in Exhibit 6.4. Management of the company might then *estimate* the following probable bad debt loss rates: not yet due,

EXHIBIT 6.4
Aging Schedule

ROGERS AND LAMBERT **Aging Anaysis of Accounts Receivable,** **December 31, 19A**						
Customer	**Not Yet Due**	**1–30 Days Past Due**	**31–60 Days Past Due**	**61–90 Days Past Due**	**Over 90 Days Past Due**	**Total**
Adams, Inc.	$600					$600
Baker Stores	300	$900	$100			1,300
Cox Co.			400	$900	$100	1,400
Zoe Stores	2,000		1,000			3,000
Total	$17,200	$12,000	$8,000	$1,200	$1,600	$40,000
Estimated % uncollectible	1%	3%	6%	10%	25%	
Estimated uncollectible accounts	$ 172	$ 360	$ 480	$ 120	$ 400	$ 1,532

1 percent; 1 to 30 days past due, 3 percent; 31 to 60 days, 6 percent; 61 to 90 days, 10 percent; over 90 days, 25 percent. The total of the amounts estimated to be uncollectible under the aging method is the balance that *should be* in the allowance for doubtful accounts at the end of the period. This is called the *estimated balance.*

The approach to recording bad debt expense using the aging method is different from that for the percentage of credit sales method. Recall that using the percentage of credit sales, we *directly computed* the amount to be recorded as bad debt expense on the income statement for the period in the adjusting journal entry. Alternatively, when using the aging method, we are computing the *final ending balance* we would like to have in the allowance for doubtful accounts on the balance sheet after we make the necessary entry. Thus, the *difference* between the actual balance in the account and the estimated balance is recorded as the adjusting entry for bad debt expense for the period.

The amount of bad debt expense for the period is the difference between the estimated uncollectible accounts (just calculated) and the balance of the allowance for doubtful accounts at the end of the period *before the adjusting entry* has been made.

COMPUTATION

Estimated balance (from aging schedule)	$1,532
Current balance (preadjustment balance from ledger account)	188
Bad debt expense adjustment to be recorded for the current year (solve)	$1,344

This computation also can be illustrated in T-account form. The current credit balance in the allowance, before the end-of-period adjustment, is $188. We insert the new ending balance from the aging schedule and then solve for the current amount of bad debt expense.

Allowance for Doubtful Accounts (XA)	
Unadjusted balance	188
Bad debt expense adjustment (solve)	1,344
Estimated balance (from aging)	1,532

The end-of-period adjusting entry to Bad Debt Expense and Allowance for Doubtful Accounts is made on December 31 for $1,344.

The percentage of credit sales method focuses on an income statement valuation (bad debt expense matched to the period's sales); the aging method focuses on a balance sheet valuation (estimated net realizable value of accounts receivable). Both methods are acceptable under GAAP and are widely used in practice.

Sales versus Collections—The Marketing/Financial Management Conflict

Inc. Magazine[*] reports that many managers of sales- and marketing-oriented companies fall into the trap of saying "get the sales now; work on collecting the receivables later." The article points out that these companies that emphasize sales without monitoring the collection of credit sales will soon find much of their current assets tied up in accounts receivable. Accounts receivable are good only if they can be collected in a short time. Bad debt expense as a percentage of sales ratio measures the amount of each dollar of sales the company expects to fail to collect because of bad debts; it is a measure of the restrictiveness of the company's credit policy. It is computed as follows:

$$\text{Bad debt expense as a percentage of sales ratio} = \frac{\text{Bad debt expense}}{\text{Net sales}}$$

The sharp rise in Timberland's *bad debt expense as a percentage of sales* from .27 percent to .56 percent between 1993 and 1995 suggests that it fell into this very trap as it tried to increase sales. In response, it has instituted an organizational change, separating the credit and collections unit from the sales department to avoid these problems in the future. *Inc. Magazine* recommends that companies minimize bad debts by following two procedures that involve a joint effort by the marketing and finance departments:

1. Establish customers' credit history before allowing them to charge their purchases. The savings from checking potential clients' credit history can be measured as the amount saved from fewer bad debts less the cost of the credit searches on potential customers.

2. Age accounts receivable periodically. Customers with overdue payments can then be contacted to encourage payment, and future sales can be made to them only on a cash basis.

* Jill Andersky Fraser, Inc. Magazine, June 1990, pp. 58–60.

Receivables and Cash Flows

The change in accounts receivable can be a major determinant of a company's cash flow from operations. As presented in Exhibit 6.5, Timberland's change in accounts receivable played a major role in turning the 1993 and 1994 profits into net cash used by operating activities and the 1995 loss into net cash provided by operating activities.

As do most public companies, Timberland uses the indirect method of preparing the cash flow statement, which reconciles (explains the difference between) net income and cash flow from operations for the period. The income statement reflects the revenues of the period, whereas the cash flow statement reflects the cash collections from customers for the same period. As we indicate later, the change in accounts receivable from the beginning to the end of the period is the difference between the two.

When the accounts receivable balance increases during the period, as was the case at Timberland in 1993 and 1994, the company recorded more net sales than it

FOCUS ON CASH FLOWS

EXHIBIT 6.5
Accounts Receivable on the Cash Flow Statement

CONSOLIDATED STATEMENTS OF CASH FLOWS

For the years ended December 31, 1995, 1994 and 1993

(Dollars in Thousands)	1995	1994	1993
Cash flows from operating activities:			
Net income (loss)	$(11,635)	$ 17,710	$ 22,521
Adjustments to reconcile net income (loss) to net			
cash provided (used) by operating activities:			
Deferred income taxes	(2,560)	2,383	2,339
Depreciation and amortization	19,138	15,348	10,279
Gain on distributorship transaction	(12,107)	–	–
Restructuring charge	9,914	–	–
Increase (decrease) in cash from changes			
in working capital items, net of effects of			
business acquisition and dispositions:			
Accounts receivable	29,186	(36,614)	(39,484)
Inventories	31,834	(101,009)	(41,560)
Prepaid expenses	884	(4,995)	(3,170)
Accounts payable	(11,967)	4,270	18,497
Accrued expenses	4,427	8,762	5,084
Income taxes	(8,999)	5,381	(1,184)
Net cash provided (used) by operating activities	48,115	(88,764)	(26,678)

collected in cash from customers during the period. Thus, the increase is subtracted in the computation of Timberland's cash flow from operations. Alternatively, when the accounts receivable balance decreases during the period, as was the case in 1995, the company collected more in cash from customers than it recorded as net sales during the period. Thus, the decrease is added in the computation of Timberland's cash flow from operations.[3]

SELF-STUDY QUIZ

1. In an earlier year, Timberland's Form 10-K reported beginning and ending balances in the Allowance for Doubtful Accounts of $723 and $904, respectively. It also reported that write-offs of bad debts amounted to $648 (all numbers in thousands). Assuming that no previously written-off accounts had been collected (there were no reinstatements), what amount did Timberland record as bad debt expense for the period? (*Solution approach:* Use the Allowance for Doubtful Accounts T-account to solve for the missing value.)

Allowance for Doubtful Accounts (XA)

---

[3] For companies with receivables in foreign currency or business acquisitions/dispositions, the amount of the change reported on the cash flow statement will not equal the change in the accounts receivable reported on the balance sheet. This is true in the case of Timberland.

2. In an earlier year, Timberland reported an increase of $6,098,000 in accounts receivable for the period. Was that amount added or subtracted on the (indirect method) cash flow statement in the computation of cash flow from operations? Explain your answer.

_____

_____

After you complete your answer, check it with the solution presented in the footnote at the bottom of this page.*

Reporting and Safeguarding Cash

Cash and Cash Equivalents Defined

Cash is defined as money or any instrument that banks will accept for deposit and immediate credit to the depositor's account, such as a check, money order, or bank draft. Cash excludes such items as notes receivable, IOUs, and postage stamps (a prepaid expense). Cash usually is divided into three categories: cash on hand, cash deposited in banks, and other instruments that meet the definition of cash.

FASB Statement 95 defines **cash equivalents** as investments with original maturities of three months or less that are readily convertible to cash and whose value is unlikely to change (that is, are not sensitive to interest rate changes). Typical instruments included as cash equivalents are bank certificates of deposit and treasury bills that the U.S. government issues to finance its activities.

All cash accounts and cash equivalents are usually combined as one amount for financial reporting purposes, even though a company may have several bank accounts and several types of cash equivalents. Timberland reports a single account, Cash and Equivalents. It also reports that the book values of cash equivalents on the balance sheet equal their fair market value, which we should expect given the nature of the instruments included as cash equivalents (investments whose value is unlikely to change).

Many businesses receive a large amount of cash, checks, and credit card receipts from their customers each day. Anyone can spend cash, so management must develop procedures to safeguard the cash that is used in the business. Effective cash management involves more than protecting cash from theft, fraud, or loss through carelessness. Other cash management responsibilities include these:

1. Accurate accounting so that reports of cash flows and balances may be prepared.
2. Controls to ensure that enough cash is on hand to meet (a) current operating needs, (b) maturing liabilities, and (c) unexpected emergencies.

LEARNING OBJECTIVE 4
Report, control, and safeguard cash.

Cash is money or any instrument that banks will accept for deposit and immediate credit to the depositor's account, such as a check, money order, or bank draft.

Cash equivalents are short-term investments with original maturities of three months or less that are readily convertible to cash and whose value is unlikely to change.

---

* 1.

Allowance for Doubtful Accounts (XA)

		Beginning balance	723
Write-offs	648	Bad debt expense (solve)	829
		Ending balance	904

Beginning + Bad debt expense – Write-offs = Ending; $723 + X – 648 = $904; X = $849

2. The amount is subtracted because an increase in the Accounts Receivable account indicates that sales revenue was in excess of cash collected from customers for the period.

3. Prevention of the accumulation of excess amounts of idle cash. Idle cash earns no revenue; therefore, it is often invested in securities to earn a revenue (return) pending future need for the cash.

Internal Control of Cash

Internal controls are policies and procedures designed to safeguard the assets of the business and ensure the accuracy of its financial records.

The term **internal controls** refers to policies and procedures that are designed to properly account for and safeguard all of the assets of the enterprise and to ensure the accuracy of financial records. Internal control procedures should extend to all assets: cash, receivables, investments, operational assets, and so on. Controls that ensure the accuracy of the financial records are designed to prevent inadvertent errors and fraud like that described in the Maxidrive example discussed in Chapter 1.

Because cash is the asset most vulnerable to theft and fraud, a significant number of internal control procedures should focus on cash. You have already observed internal control procedures for cash, although you may not have known it at the time. At most movie theaters, one employee sells tickets and another employee collects them. It would be less expensive to have one employee do both jobs, but it would also be easier for that single employee to steal cash and admit a patron without issuing a ticket. If different employees perform the tasks, a successful theft requires participation of both.

Effective internal control of cash should include the following:

1. Separation of duties.
    a. Complete separation of the jobs of receiving cash and disbursing cash.
    b. Complete separation of the procedures of accounting for cash receipts and cash disbursements.
    c. Complete separation of the physical handling of cash and all phases of the accounting function.
2. Responsibilities assigned to individuals.
    a. Require that all cash receipts be deposited in a bank daily. Keep any cash on hand under strict control.
    b. Require separate approval of the purchases and other expenditures and separate approval of the actual cash payments. Prenumbered checks should be used. Special care must be taken with payments by electronic funds transfers since the bank processes no controlled documents (checks).

c.   Assign the cash payment approval and the actual check signing or electronic funds transfer transmittal responsibilities to different individuals.

d.   Require monthly reconciliation of bank accounts with the cash accounts on the company's books (discussed in detail in the next section).

The separation of individual responsibilities and the use of prescribed policies and procedures are important phases in the control of cash. Separation of duties deters theft because the collusion of two or more persons is needed to steal cash and then conceal the theft in the accounting records. Prescribed procedures are designed so that the work done by one individual is checked by the results reported by other individuals. For example, the amount of cash collected at the cash register by the sales clerk can be compared with the amount of cash deposited at the bank by another employee. Reconciliation of the cash accounts to the bank statements provides a further control on deposits.

All cash disbursements should be made with prenumbered checks. If prenumbered checks are not used, an employee could easily write a check to a friend and not record it. Cash payments should involve separate responsibilities for (1) payment approvals, (2) check preparation, and (3) check signing. When procedures similar to these are followed, concealing a fraudulent cash disbursement is difficult without the collusion of two or more persons. Again, the bank reconciliation provides an additional control on disbursements. The level of internal control, which is reviewed by the outside independent auditor, increases the reliability of the financial statements of the business.

Reconciliation of the Cash Accounts and the Bank Statements

Bank Statements to Depositors

Proper use of the bank accounts of a business can be an important internal control procedure for cash. Each month, the bank provides the depositor (the company) with a **bank statement** that lists (1) each deposit recorded by the bank during the period, (2) each check cleared by the bank during the period, and (3) the balance in the depositor's account. The bank statement also shows the bank charges or deductions (such as service charges) made directly to the depositor's account by the bank. The bank statement may include copies of the deposit slips and all checks that cleared through the bank during the period covered by the statement, although this practice is declining because it increases the bank's processing costs. A typical bank statement (excluding the deposit slips and canceled checks) is shown in Exhibit 6.6.

Exhibit 6.6 lists three items that need explanation. Notice that on June 20, listed under Checks and Debits, there is a deduction for $18 coded *NC*.[4] A check for $18 was received from a customer, R. Smith, and deposited by J. Doe Company with its bank, the Texas Commerce Bank. The bank processed the check through banking channels to Smith's bank. Smith's account did not have sufficient funds to cover it; therefore, Smith's bank returned it to the Texas Commerce Bank, which then charged it back to J. Doe Company. This type of check often is called an *NSF check* (not sufficient funds). The NSF check is now a receivable; consequently, J. Doe Company must make an entry to debit Receivables (R. Smith) and credit Cash for the $18.

Notice the $6 listed on June 30 under Checks and Debits and coded *SC*. This is the code for bank service charges. The bank statement included a memo by the bank

A **bank statement** is a monthly report from a bank that shows deposits recorded, checks cleared, other debits and credits, and a running bank balance.

---

[4] These codes vary among banks.

EXHIBIT 6.6
Example of a Bank Statement

Texas Commerce Bank	7TH & LAVACA AUSTIN, TEXAS 78789 PHONE: 512/476-6611

Austin
NATIONAL ASSOCIATION

ACCOUNT NUMBER	STATEMENT DATE	PAGE NO.
877-95861	6-30-96	1

J. Doe Company
1000 Blank Road
Austin, Texas 78703

STATEMENT OF ACCOUNT
Please examine statement and checks promptly. If no error is reported within ten days, the account will be considered correct. Please report change of address.
For questions or problems call TCB-Austin's Hotline—476-6100

ON THIS DATE	YOUR BALANCE WAS	DEPOSITS ADDED		CHECKS AND DEBITS SUBTRACTED		SERVICE COST	RESULTING BALANCE
		NO.	AMOUNT	NO.	AMOUNT		
6-1-96	7 762 40	5	4 050 00	23	3 490 20	6 00	8 322 20

CHECKS AND DEBITS			DEPOSITS	DATE	DAILY BALANCE
			3 000 00	6-1-96	7 762 40
500 00				6-2-96	10 762 40
55 00	5 00	40 00		6-4-96	10 262 40
100 00			500 00	6-5-96	10 162 40
8 20	16 50	160 00		6-8-96	10 562 40
2 150 00	10 00		*100 00CM	6-10-96	10 377 70
7 50	15 30			6-12-96	8 317 70
35 00	1 50		150 00	6-16-96	8 294 90
40 20	15 00	6 00		6-17-96	8 408 40
*18 00NC				6-18-96	8 347 20
125 50	80 00	2 00		6-20-96	8 329 20
18 90			300 00	6-21-96	8 121 70
7 52	19 60			6-24-96	8 402 80
15 00	32 48			6-27-96	8 375 68
*6 00SC				6-28-96	8 328 20
				6-30-96	8 322 20

Code:
    CM–Credit Memo—Customer note collected
    NC–Not sufficient funds
    SC–Service charge

MEMBER F.D.I.C.   IMPORTANT: SEE REVERSE SIDE OF STATEMENT

explaining this service charge (which was not documented by a check). J. Doe Company must make an entry to reflect this $6 decrease in the bank balance as a debit to a relevant expense account, such as Bank Service Expense, and a credit to Cash.

Notice the $100 listed on June 12 under Deposits and the code *CM* for credit memo. The bank collected a note receivable owned by Doe and increased the depositor account of J. Doe Company. The bank service charge (SC) included the collection service cost. J. Doe Company must record the collection by making an entry to debit Cash and credit Note Receivable for the $100 (assume that interest on the note had been recorded).

A **bank reconciliation** is the process of comparing (reconciling) the ending cash balance in the company's records and the ending cash balance reported by the bank on the monthly bank statement. A bank reconciliation should be completed for each separate checking account (i.e., for each bank statement received from each bank) at the end of each month.

Usually, the ending cash balance as shown on the bank statement does not agree with the ending cash balance shown by the related Cash ledger account on the books of the depositor. For example, the Cash ledger account of J. Doe Company showed the following at the end of June (Doe has only one checking account):

> A **bank reconciliation** is the process of verifying the accuracy of both the bank statement and the cash accounts of a business.

Cash			
June 1 balance	7,010.00	June checks written	3,800.00
June deposits	5,750.00		
Ending balance	8,960.00		

The $8,322.20 ending cash balance shown on the bank statement (Exhibit 6.6) is different from the $8,960.00 ending book balance of cash shown on the books of the J. Doe Company. This difference exists because (1) some transactions affecting cash were recorded in the books of depositor Doe but were not shown on the bank statement and (2) some transactions were shown on the bank statement but had not been recorded in books of the depositor, Doe. The general format for the bank reconciliation follows:

Ending cash balance per books	$ xxx	Ending cash balance per bank statement	$ xxx
+ Collections by bank	xx	+ Deposits in transit	xx
– NSF Checks/Service charges	xx	– Outstanding checks	xx
± Depositor errors	xx	± Bank errors	xx
Ending correct cash balances	$ xxx	Ending correct cash balance	$ xxx

The most common causes of differences between the ending bank balance and the ending book balance of cash are as follows:

1. *Outstanding checks.* Checks written by the depositor and recorded in the depositor's ledger as credits to the Cash account. These checks have not cleared the bank (they are not shown on the bank statement as a deduction from the bank balance). The outstanding checks are identified by comparing the canceled checks that the bank returned with the record of checks (such as check stubs or a journal) maintained by the depositor.
2. *Deposits in transit.* Deposits sent to the bank by the depositor and recorded in the depositor's ledger as debits to the Cash account. The bank has not recorded these deposits (they are not shown on the bank statement as an increase in the bank balance). Deposits in transit usually happen when deposits are made one or two days before the close of the period covered by the bank statement. Deposits in transit are determined by comparing the deposits listed on the bank statement with the copies of the deposit slips retained by the depositor or other company records.

Think about how Timberland could effectively use internal control of cash at this site.

3. *Bank service charges.* An expense for bank services listed on the bank statement. This expense must be recorded in the depositor's ledger by making a debit to a relevant expense account, such as Bank Service Expense, and a credit to Cash.

4. *NSF checks.* A "bad check" that was deposited but must be deducted from the depositor's account. The depositor must make a journal entry to debit Accounts Receivable and credit Cash.

5. *Credit memo.* A note receivable collected by the bank for the depositor. It is recorded by making a debit to Cash and a credit to Notes Receivable.

6. *Errors.* Both the bank and the depositor may make errors, especially when the volume of cash transactions is large.

Bank Reconciliation Illustrated

The depositor should make a bank reconciliation immediately after receiving each bank statement. A bank reconciliation is an important element of internal control and is needed for accounting purposes. The bank reconciliation for the month of June prepared by J. Doe Company to reconcile the ending bank balance (Exhibit 6.6, $8,322.20) with the ending book balance ($8,960) is shown in Exhibit 6.7. On the completed reconciliation, Exhibit 6.7, the correct cash balance is $9,045. This balance is different from both the reported bank and book balances before the reconciliation with the bank statement. Space is provided for additions to and subtractions from each balance so that the last line shows the same correct cash balance (for the bank and the books). This correct balance is the amount that should be shown in the Cash account after the reconciliation. In this example, it is also the correct amount of cash that should be reported on the balance sheet (J. Doe Company has only one checking account and no cash on hand). J. Doe Company followed these steps in preparing the bank reconciliation:

1. *Identify the outstanding checks.* A comparison of the canceled checks returned by the bank with the company's records of all checks drawn showed the following checks still outstanding (not cleared) at the end of June:

Check No.	Amount
101	$ 145.00
123	815.00
131	117.20
Total	$1,077.20

This total was entered on the reconciliation as a deduction from the bank account. These checks will be deducted by the bank when they clear the bank.

2. *Identify the deposits in transit.* A comparison of the deposit slips on hand with those listed on the bank statement revealed that a deposit of $1,800 made on June 30 was not listed on the bank statement. This amount was entered on the reconciliation as an addition to the bank account. It will be added by the bank when it records the deposit.

3. *Record bank charges and credits:*
   a. Proceeds of note collected, $100—entered on the bank reconciliation as an addition to the book balance; it already has been included in the bank balance. A journal entry is needed to debit Cash and credit Note Receivable.
   b. NSF check of R. Smith, $18—entered on the bank reconciliation as a deduction from the book balance; it has been deducted from the bank statement

EXHIBIT 6.7
Bank Reconciliation Illustrated

J. DOE COMPANY
Bank Reconciliation
For the Month Ending June 30, 1996

Depositor's Books		Bank Statement	
Ending cash balance per books	$8,960.00	Ending cash balance per bank statement	$8,322.20
Additions		Additions	
Proceeds of customer note collected by bank	100.00	Deposit in transit	1,800.00
Error in recording check No. 137	9.00		
	9,069.00		10,122.20
Deductions		Deductions	
NSF check of R. Smith	$ 18.00	Outstanding checks	1,077.20
Bank service charges	6.00		
Ending correct cash balance	$9,045.00	Ending correct cash balance	$9,045.00

balance. A journal entry is needed to credit Cash and to debit Accounts Receivable.

c. Bank service charges, $6—entered on the bank reconciliation as a deduction from the book balance; it has been deducted from the bank balance. A journal entry is needed to credit Cash and to debit an expense account, Bank Service Expense.

4. *Determine the impact of errors.* At this point, J. Doe Company found that the reconciliation did not balance by $9. Because this amount is divisible by 9, a transposition was suspected. (A transposition, such as writing 27 for 72, always will cause an error that is exactly divisible by 9.) Upon checking the journal entries made during the month, a check written for $56 to pay an account payable was found. The check was recorded in the company's accounts as $65. The incorrect entry made was a debit to Accounts Payable and a credit to Cash for $65 (instead of $56). Therefore, $9 (i.e., $65 – $56) must be added to the book cash balance on the reconciliation; the bank cleared the check for the correct amount, $56. The following correcting entry must be made in the accounts: Cash, debit $9; Accounts Payable, credit $9.

Note that in Exhibit 6.7 the Depositor's Books and the Bank Statement sections of the bank reconciliation now agree at a correct cash balance of $9,045. This amount will be reported as cash on a balance sheet prepared at the end of the period. If the company had cash on hand for making change, it would be added to the $9,045, and the total would be reported on the balance sheet.

A bank reconciliation as shown in Exhibit 6.7 accomplishes two major objectives:

1. Checks the accuracy of the bank balance and the company cash records, which involves developing the correct cash balance. The correct cash balance (plus cash on hand, if any) is the amount of cash that is reported on the balance sheet.
2. Identifies any previously unrecorded transactions or changes that are necessary to cause the company's Cash account(s) to show the correct cash balance. These transactions or changes need journal entries. The preceding explanations of the development of the bank reconciliation of J. Doe Company cite such transactions and changes. Therefore, the following journal entries based on the Depositor's Books side of the bank reconciliation (Exhibit 6.7), must be entered into the company's records.

Accounts of J. Doe Company

(a)   Cash (A) 100
           Note receivable (A)   100
       To record note collected by bank.

(b)   Accounts receivable (A) 18
           Cash (A)   18
       To record NSF check.

(c)   Bank service expense (E)   6
           Cash (A)   6
       To record service fees charged by bank.

(d)   Cash (A)   9
           Accounts payable (L)   9
       To correct error made in recording a check payable to a creditor.

Cash Account of J. Doe Company

The Cash account prior to reconciliation was given earlier in this chapter. After the preceding journal entries are posted, the Cash account is as follows:

Cash (after Recording Results of Bank Reconciliation)				
June 1	Balance	7,010.00	June	Checks written	3,800.00
June	Deposits	5,750.00	June 30	NSF check*	18.00
June 30	Note collected*	100.00	June 30	Bank service charge*	6.00
June 30	Correcting entry*	9.00			
	Correct cash balance	$9,045.00			

*Based on the bank reconciliation.

Notice that all of the additions and deductions on the Depositor's Books side of the reconciliation need journal entries to update the Cash account. The additions and deductions on the Bank Statement side do not need journal entries because they will work out automatically when they clear the bank. The cash amount reported on the balance sheet and reflected in the Cash account will be the correct cash balance only if the proper journal entries are made after the bank reconciliation is completed.

SELF-STUDY QUIZ

Indicate which of the following items discovered while preparing a company's bank reconciliation will result in adjustment of the cash balance on the balance sheet.

1. Outstanding checks.
2. Deposits in transit.
3. Bank service charges.
4. NSF checks that were deposited.

After you complete your answer, check it with the solution presented in the footnote at the bottom of this page.*

---

*3. Bank service charges are deducted from the company's account; thus, cash must be reduced and an expense must be recorded. 4. NSF checks that were deposited were recorded on the books as increases in the Cash account; thus cash must be decreased and the related account receivable increased if payment is still expected.

Epilogue

During 1995, Timberland recognized that to turn its growth into profits, it had to (1) focus more attention on inventory management to ensure that the right products were available at the right times, (2) become a leaner manufacturer, taking advantage of lower cost production locations, and (3) continually refresh its product lines by introducing new technologies, new styles, and new product categories. It also recognized that, like its competitors, it could strengthen its brand identity through appropriate licensing agreements with other companies. Each of these efforts is aimed at increasing net sales and/or decreasing cost of goods sold, thereby increasing gross profit. It began these processes during the second half of 1995, but their success will not be evident until 1996.

The 1996 fiscal year results reveal the achievements of the plan. In February 1997, Timberland announced record sales revenues for 1996 combined with the second highest net earnings in its history. The results of the strategy can best be seen in the gross profit percentage, which returned to near 1993 levels of 36.5 percent ($251,909 ÷ $689,973) compared to 31.0 percent in 1995.

Demonstration Case A

(Complete the requirements before proceeding to the suggested solutions.)

Wholesale Warehouse Stores sold $950,000 in merchandise during 19C, $400,000 of which was on credit with terms 2/10, n/30. On December 31, 19C, the Accounts Receivable balance was $80,000 and the Allowance for Doubtful Accounts was $3,000 (credit balance).

Required:

1. Assume that during 19C, payment on a credit sale of $2,000 was received on the ninth day after the sale. Record the receipt of payment for this sale. (Wholesale uses the gross method of accounting for sales discounts.)
2. Assume that Wholesale uses the percentage of sales method for estimating bad debt expense and that it estimates that 2 percent of credit sales will produce bad debts. Record bad debt expense for 19C.
3. Assume that Wholesale uses the aging of accounts receivable method and that it estimates that $10,000 worth of current accounts are uncollectible. Record bad debt expense for 19C.

Suggested Solution

1. Using the gross method, any sales (cash) discounts taken by customers are recorded as sales discounts that may be treated as a *contra revenue* or an *expense* on the income statement.

Cash (A)	1,960	
Sales discounts (E or XR)	40	
Accounts receivable (A)		2,000

2. The percentage estimate of bad debts should be applied to credit sales. Cash sales never produce bad debts.

Bad debt expense (E) (2% × $400,000)	8,000	
Allowance for doubtful accounts (XA)		8,000

✳ 3. The entry made when using the aging of accounts receivable method is the estimated balance minus the unadjusted balance.

Bad debt expense (E) ($10,000 − $3,000)	7,000	
Allowance for doubtful accounts (XA)		7,000

Demonstration Case B

(Complete the requirements before proceeding to the suggested solution that follows.)

Heather Ann Long, a freshman at a large state university, has just received her first checking account statement. This was her first chance to attempt a bank reconciliation. She had the following information to work with:

Bank balance, September 1	$1,150
Deposits during September	650
Checks cleared during September	900
Bank service charge	25
Bank balance, October 1	875

Heather was surprised that the deposit of $50 she made on September 29 had not been posted to her account and was pleased that her rent check of $200 had not cleared her account. Her checkbook balance was $750.

Required:

1. Complete Heather's bank reconciliation.
2. Why is it important for individuals such as Heather and businesses to do a bank reconciliation each month?

Suggested Solution

1. Heather's bank reconciliation:

Heather's Books		Bank Statement	
October 1 cash balance	$750	October 1 cash balance	$875
Additions		Additions	
None		Deposit in transit	50
Deductions		Deductions	
Bank service charge	(25)	Outstanding check	(200)
Correct cash balance	$725	Correct cash balance	$725

2. Bank statements, whether personal or business, should be reconciled each month. This process helps ensure that a correct balance is reflected in the customer's books. Failure to reconcile a bank statement increases the chance that an error will not be discovered and may result in bad checks being written. Businesses must reconcile their bank statements for an additional reason: The correct balance that is calculated during reconciliation is recorded on the balance sheet.

Summary

This chapter discussed measuring, recording, and reporting revenues, cash, and receivables on the financial statements. Revenue recognition policies are widely recognized as one of the most important determinants of the fair presentation of financial statements. For most merchandisers and manufacturers, the required revenue recognition point is the time of shipment or delivery of goods. For service companies, it is the time that services are provided. Important issues facing these companies are the proper recording of credit card and sales discounts, sales returns and allowances, and bad debt expense.

Cash is the most liquid of all assets, flowing continually into and out of a business. As a result, cash presents some of the most critical control problems facing the managers. Also, management of cash may be critically important to decision makers who must have cash available to meet current needs yet must avoid excess amounts of idle cash that produces no revenue.

Closely related to recording revenue is recording the cost of what was sold. Chapter 7 will focus on transactions related to inventory and cost of goods sold. This topic is important because cost of goods sold has a major impact on a company's gross profit and net income, which are watched closely by investors, analysts, and other users of financial statements. Increasing emphasis on quality, productivity, and costs have further focused production managers' attention on cost of goods sold and inventory. Since inventory cost figures play a major role in product introduction and pricing decisions, they also are important to marketing and general managers. Finally, since inventory accounting has a major effect on many companies' tax liabilities, this is an important place to introduce the effect of taxation on management decision making and financial reporting.

Chapter Supplement A

APPLYING THE REVENUE PRINCIPLE IN SPECIAL CIRCUMSTANCES

The revenue principle was introduced in Chapter 3. As noted earlier, application of this principle in the case of Timberland and similar companies was fairly straightforward. Such companies record revenue when goods or services are shipped or delivered. We now expand our discussion of the revenue principle and see how it is applied in business practice by companies other than typical manufacturers, wholesalers, and retailers.

Delayed Revenue Recognition: Installment Method

Recall that to record revenue (1) an exchange must take place, (2) the earnings process must be nearly complete, and (3) collection must be probable. Failure to meet the third revenue recognition criterion (collection must be probable) requires that revenue recognition be delayed until after an initial exchange. When a great deal of uncertainty concerning the collectibility of the sales price exists, revenue recognition is postponed until *cash is collected from the customer*. This revenue recognition method, called the **installment method,** is considered to be a very conservative method since it postpones revenue recognition, sometimes long after goods are delivered. The most common application is in certain types of *real estate transactions* in which payment is made over a multiyear period, and a large proportion of customers stop making payments long before the final payment is due. Certain types of expensive equipment, such as supercomputers, are sometimes sold under contracts calling for payment to be made over a multiyear period and giving the customers the right to return

The **installment method** recognizes revenue on the basis of cash collection after the delivery of goods.

the equipment and cease making payments if they are dissatisfied. The installment method also is required here. Application of this specialized revenue recognition method is discussed in intermediate accounting courses.

Exceptions to the Revenue Recognition Criteria: Long-Term Construction Contracts

An important exception to the usual criteria exists for companies involved in long-term construction projects such as building an office complex for a large corporation. These projects may take a number of years to complete. As a result, if the company recorded no revenue or expenses directly related to the project during the years that it worked on the project and then recorded a massive amount of revenue in the year that it delivered the product to the customer, the financial statements would not accurately represent the company's economic activities. This method of accounting is often referred to as the *completed contract method*.

The **percentage of completion method** records revenue based on the percentage of work completed during the accounting period.

The **completed contract method** records revenue when the completed product is delivered to the customer.

To deal with this unique problem for long-term construction projects, many companies use the **percentage of completion method,** which records revenue based on the percentage of work completed during the accounting period, instead of the **completed contract method,** which records revenue when the completed product is delivered to the customer.

Under the percentage of completion method, revenues are based on the amount of work done each year. Typically, the amount of work accomplished each year is measured by the *percentage of total cost* that was incurred during the year. For example, assume that the total contract price was $50 million and the total cost for construction was $40 million. In 19A, the construction company spent $10 million, which was 25 percent of the contract cost ($10 million ÷ $40 million).[5] This percentage of completion is then multiplied by the total contract revenue to determine the amount of revenue to be reported in 19A (25% × $50,000,000 = $12,500,000).

The amount of expense reported each year is the actual cost incurred ($10,000,000 in 19A), and the amount of income is simply the difference between revenue and expense ($12,500,000 − $10,000,000 = $2,500,000 in 19A). It is important to note that the total revenue, expenses, and income for the two methods over the life of the contract are exactly the same. The methods differ only in terms of the accounting periods in which the various revenues and expenses are reported (their timing). Percentage of completion recognizes income throughout the contract period; completed contract recognizes income only in the year of completion.

Notice that the percentage of completion method does not completely satisfy the second revenue recognition criterion because revenue is reported before the earnings process is complete. It is the preferred method, however, in cases such as this because the completed contract method makes it appear that the contractor was not able to generate any profits for the initial years of the contract and then it became very profitable in the final year. In reality, the company was active in all years. Thus, the percentage of completion method better represents this type of underlying economic activity.

Companies may use the percentage of completion method when progress toward completion and costs to complete the contract can be reasonably estimated and they have a firm contract that guarantees payment to satisfy the cash collectibility revenue recognition criterion. In a recent survey of 600 companies,[6] 112 of them were involved in long-term construction contracts. Only 4 used the completed contract method. The remaining firms used the percentage of completion or a closely related method.

---

[5] Cost overruns (underruns), which did not occur in this simple example, create additional accounting problems.
[6] *Accounting Trends & Techniques* (New York: AICPA, 1996).

Exceptions to the Revenue Recognition Criteria: Service Contracts

Companies that provide services over more than one accounting period often follow revenue recognition policies similar to those followed for long-term construction contracts. They may record revenue after all services have been provided (after the contract is completed) or may recognize revenue from the completed portion of the services. Since the individual size of the contracts involved often is small (compared to construction contracts) and companies often are engaged in many service contracts with different beginning and ending dates, the distortion caused by the completed contract method is usually smaller than that of long-term construction contracts. Yet many service companies, such as Federal Express, which provides air delivery service, employ the percentage of completion revenue recognition policy as indicated in the following note:

FEDERAL EXPRESS CORPORATION AND SUBSIDIARIES

Notes to Consolidated Financial Statements
NOTE 1. SUMMARY OF SIGNIFICANT ACCOUNTING POLICIES
   Revenue recognition. Revenue is generally recognized upon delivery of shipments.
For shipments in transit, revenue is recorded based on the percentage of service completed.

REAL WORLD EXCERPT
FEDERAL EXPRESS
Annual Report

For the services in progress at the end of the accounting period, Federal Express uses the percentage of completion method for revenue recognition, recognizing only a percentage of the revenues and related costs of providing the services based on the degree of completion of the service. This method is also called the *proportional performance* method. This form of revenue recognition is very similar to Time Warner's accounting for its magazine subscription contracts and McDermott's accounting for its construction contracts. Each company recognizes revenues and expenses related to the *completed portion* of its contract with the customer. The major difference is that Time Warner is paid for the magazine subscriptions in advance, McDermott receives progress payments throughout the contract period, and Federal Express receives payment from its business customers after it completes provision of the service.

Revenue Recognition and Financial Statement Analysis

Financial analysts cannot evaluate the income earned by a company if they do not understand how it applied the revenue recognition criteria. As a result, all companies disclose any special revenue recognition issues in the notes to their financial statements. For example, General Motors' annual report states the following:

Certain sales under long-term contracts, primarily in the defense business, are recorded using the percentage-of-completion (cost-to-cost) method of accounting. Under this method, sales are recorded equivalent to costs incurred plus a portion of the profit expected to be realized on the contract, determined based on the ratio of costs incurred to estimated total costs at completion.

REAL WORLD EXCERPT
GENERAL MOTORS
Annual Report

This succinct explanation of the percentage of completion method is an adequate explanation for someone who has read this chapter, but it is doubtful that someone who has not studied accounting would understand its meaning. This is an excellent example of the importance of careful study of accounting even if you do not major in accounting.

Demonstration Case C

(Complete the requirements before proceeding to the suggested solution that follows.)

Assume that (1) Federal Express had shipments in transit involving fees totaling $20 million on December 31 of the current year, (2) none of the fees had been collected, and (3) on average, the shipments in transit were 60 percent completed.

Required:

1. Determine what amount related to the shipments in transit is recognized as revenue in the current year using the revenue recognition rule indicated in its footnote included in the prior section.
2. Indicate what asset(s) are affected by recording revenue from the shipments in transit (accounts and amounts).

Suggested Solution

1. Delivery revenue is recorded for $12,000,000.
2. Accounts Receivable increases by $12,000,000.

Key Ratios

Receivables turnover ratio measures the effectiveness of credit-granting and collection activities. It is computed as follows (p. 308):

$$\text{Receivables turnover} = \frac{\text{Net credit sales}}{\text{Average net trade accounts receivable}}$$

Bad debt expense as a percentage of sales ratio measures the amount of each dollar of sales the company expects to fail to collect because of bad debts; it is a measure of the restrictiveness of the company's credit policy. It is computed as follows (p. 315):

$$\text{Bad debt expense as a percentage of sales ratio} = \frac{\text{Bad debt expense}}{\text{Net sales}}$$

Key Terms

Accounts Receivable (Trade Receivables or Receivables) Open accounts owed to the business by trade customers. *307*

Aging of Accounts Receivable Method Estimates uncollectible accounts based on the age of each account receivable. *313*

Allowance for Doubtful Accounts (Allowance for Bad Debts or **Allowance for Uncollectible Accounts)** Contra asset account containing the estimated uncollectible accounts receivable. *309*

on test *Terms prior to completion of sales*

Allowance Method Bases bad debt expense on an estimate of uncollectible accounts. *309*

Bad Debt Expense (Doubtful Accounts Expense, Uncollectible Accounts Expense, or Provision for Uncollectible Accounts) Expense associated with estimated uncollectible accounts receivable. *309*

Bank Reconciliation Process of verifying the accuracy of both the bank statement and the cash accounts of the business. *320*

Bank Statement Monthly report from a bank that shows deposits recorded, checks cleared, other debits and credits, and a running bank balance. *319*

Cash Money and any instrument that banks will accept for deposit and immediate credit to the depositor's account, such as a check, money order, or bank draft. *317*

Cash Equivalents Short-term investments with original maturities of three months or less that are readily convertible to cash and whose value is unlikely to change. *317*

Completed Contract Method Records revenue when the completed product is delivered to the customer. *328*

Credit Card Discount Fee charged by the credit card company for its services. *302*

Installment Method Recognizes revenue on the basis of cash collection after the delivery of goods. *327*

Internal Controls Policies and procedures designed to safeguard the assets of the business and ensure the accuracy of financial records. *318*

Note Receivable A written promise that requires another party to pay the business under specified conditions (amount, time, interest). *307*

Percentage of Completion Method Records revenue based on the percentage of work completed during the accounting period. *328*

Percentage of Credit Sales Method Bases bad debt expense on the historical percentage of credit sales that result in bad debts. *312*

Sales (or Cash) Discount Cash discount offered to encourage prompt payment of an account receivable. *302*

Sales Returns and Allowances A contra revenue account used to record return of or allowances for unsatisfactory goods. *304*

Trade Discount A discount that is deducted from list price to derive the actual sales price. *303*

Questions

1. Explain the difference between sales revenue and net sales.
2. What is gross profit or gross margin on sales? How is the gross profit ratio computed? In your explanation, assume that net sales revenue was $100,000 and cost of goods sold was $60,000.
3. What is a credit card discount? How does it affect amounts reported on the income statement?
4. What is a sales discount? Use 1/10, n/30 in your explanation.
5. When merchandise invoiced at $2,000 is sold on terms 2/10, n/30, the seller must make the following entry:

   >   Accounts receivable
   >   Sales revenue

   What amounts should be used in this entry under the gross method of recording sales discounts? If the buyer pays within the discount period, how will amounts on the income statement be affected?

6. A sale is made for $700; terms are 2/10, n/30. At what amount should the sale be recorded under the gross method of recording sales discounts? Give the required entry with an explanation. Also give the collection entry, assuming that it is during the discount period.

7. What is the distinction between *sales allowances* and *sales discounts?*

8. Differentiate accounts receivable from notes receivable.

9. Which basic accounting principle is the allowance method of accounting for bad debts designed to satisfy?

10. Using the allowance method, is bad debt expense recognized in (a) the period in which sales related to the uncollectible were made or (b) the period in which the seller learns that the customer is unable to pay?

11. What is the effect of the write-off of bad debts (using the allowance method) on (a) net income and (b) accounts receivable, net?

12. Why are the revenue recognition criteria important?

13. What are the three revenue recognition criteria?

14. Define *cash* and *cash equivalents* in the context of accounting. Indicate the types of items that should be included and excluded.

15. Summarize the primary characteristics of an effective internal control system for cash.

16. Why should cash-handling and cash-recording activities be separated? How is this separation accomplished?

17. What are the purposes of a bank reconciliation? What balances are reconciled?

18. Briefly explain how the total amount of cash reported on the balance sheet is computed.

19. (Based on Supplement A) When is it acceptable to use the percentage of completion method?

20. (Based on Supplement A) How is the percentage that is complete determined under the percentage of completion method?

21. (Based on Supplement A) If an airline sells tickets months before a passenger flies and collects cash at the point of sale, when should it record revenue?

22. (Based on Supplement A) If a company defers revenue to a subsequent accounting period because it has not yet earned the revenue, how should it account for the expenses that are related to earning the revenue?

Exercises

E6–1 Analyzing Gross Profit Percentage on the Basis of a Multiple-Step Income Statement

The following summarized data were provided by the records of Slate, Incorporated, for the year ended December 31, 19B:

Sales of merchandise for cash	$220,000
Sales of merchandise on credit	32,000
Cost of goods sold	147,000
Selling expense	40,200
Administrative expense	19,000
Sales returns and allowances	7,000
Items not included in above amounts	
Estimated bad debt loss, 2.5% of credit sales	
Average income tax rate, 30%	
Number of shares of common stock outstanding, 5,000	

(handwritten annotations: "to be less", "has", "cash already", "you have", "41,000", "Bad Debt Expense 800", "credit")

Required:

1. Based on these data, prepare a multiple-step income statement (showing both gross profit and income from operations). Include a Percentage Analysis column.
2. What was the amount of gross profit margin? What was the gross profit percentage ratio? Explain what these two amounts mean.

E6–2 Analyzing Gross Profit Percentage on the Basis of a Multiple-Step Income Statement and Within-Industry Comparison

Wolverine World Wide

Wolverine World Wide Inc. prides itself as being the "world's leading marketer of U.S. branded non-athletic footwear." It competes in many markets with Timberland, often offering products at a lower price point. The following data were taken from its recent annual report (in thousands):

Sales of merchandise	$413,957
Income taxes	10,047
Cash dividends declared	2,347
Selling and administrative expense	85,993
Cost of products sold	290,469
Interest expense	3,678
Other income	297
Items not included in above amounts	
Number of shares of common stock outstanding, 17,114	

Required:

1. Based on these data, prepare a multiple-step income statement (showing both gross profit and income from operations). There were no extraordinary items. Include a Percentage Analysis column.
2. How much was the gross profit margin? What was the gross profit percentage ratio? Explain what these two amounts mean. Compare the gross profit percentage with that of Timberland. What do you believe accounts for the difference?

E6–3 Analyzing Financial Statement Effects of Credit Sales, Sales Discounts, Credit Card Sales, and Sales Returns and Allowances

Rockland Shoe Company records sales returns and allowances as contra revenues and sales discounts and credit card discounts as selling expenses. Complete the following tabulation, indicating the amount and effect (+ for increase, – for decrease, and NE for no effect) of each transaction. Do not record related cost of goods sold.

July	12	Sold merchandise to customer at factory store who charged the $300 purchase on her American Express card. American Express charges a 1 percent credit card fee.
July	15	Sold merchandise to Customer T at an invoice price of $5,000; terms 3/10, n/30.
July	20	Collected cash due from Customer T.
July	21	Before paying for the order, a customer returned shoes with an invoice price of $1,000.

Transaction	Net Sales	Gross Margin	Income From Operations
July 12			
July 15			
July 20			
July 21			

E6–4   Recording Credit Sales and Sales Discounts

During the months of January and February, Bronze Corporation sold goods to three cus-tomers. The sequence of events was as follows:

Jan.	6	Sold goods for $1,000 to S. Green and billed that amount subject to terms 2/10, n/30.
	6	Sold goods to M. Munoz for $800 and billed that amount subject to terms 2/10, n/30.
	14	Collected cash due from S. Green.
Feb	2	Collected cash due from M. Munoz.
	28	Sold goods for $500 to R. Reynolds and billed that amount subject to terms 2/10, n/45.

Required:
1.   Give the appropriate journal entry for each date. Do not record cost of goods sold.
2.   Assuming that Sales Discounts is treated as a contra revenue, compute net sales for the two months ended February 28.

E6–5   Recording Credit Sales, Sales Discounts, and Credit Card Sales

The following transactions were selected from the records of Evergreen Company:

July	12	Sold merchandise to Customer R who charged the $1,000 purchase on his Visa credit card. Visa charges Evergreen a 2 percent credit card fee.
	15	Sold merchandise to Customer S at an invoice price of $5,000; terms 3/10, n/30.
	20	Sold merchandise to Customer T at an invoice price of $3,000; terms 3/10, n/30.
	23	Collected payment from Customer S from July 15 sale.
Aug.	25	Collected payment from Customer T from July 20 sale.

Required:
Give the appropriate journal entry for each of these transactions. Do not record cost of goods sold.

E6–6   Recording Credit Sales, Sales Discounts, Sales Returns, and Credit Card Sales

The following transactions were selected from among those completed by Hailey Retailers in 19B:

Nov.	20	Sold two items of merchandise to Customer B who charged the $400 sales price on her Visa credit card. Visa charges Hailey a 2 percent credit card fee.
	25	Sold 20 items of merchandise to Customer C at an invoice price of $4,000 (total); terms 3/10, n/30.
	28	Sold 10 items of merchandise to Customer D at an invoice price of $6,000 (total); terms 3/10, n/30.
	30	Customer D returned one of the items purchased on the 28th; the item was defective, and credit was given to the customer.
Dec.	6	Customer D paid the account balance in full.
	30	Customer C paid in full for the invoice of November 25, 19B.

Required:

1. Give the appropriate journal entry for each of these transactions, assuming that the company records sales revenue under the gross method. Do not record cost of goods sold.
2. Assume that sales discounts and credit card discounts are treated as contra revenues; compute net sales for the two months ended December 31, 19B.

E6–7 Determining the Annual Interest Rate Implicit in a Sales Discount with Discussion of Management Choice of Financing Strategy

Laura's Landscaping bills customers subject to terms 3/10, n/60.

Required:

1. Compute the annual interest rate implicit in the sales discount.
2. If his bank charges 15 percent interest, should the customer borrow from the bank so that he can take advantage of the discount? Explain your recommendation.

E6–8 Analyzing Financial Statement Effects of Accounting for Bad Debts

During 19A, Gonzales Electronics, Incorporated, recorded credit sales of $720,000. Based on prior experience, it estimates a .5 percent bad debt rate on credit sales. Complete the following tabulation, indicating the amount and effect (+ for increase, – for decrease, and NE for no effect) of each transaction.

a. The appropriate bad debt expense adjustment was recorded for the year 19A.
b. On December 31, 19A, an account receivable for $300 from a prior year was determined to be uncollectible and was written off. *debit allowance...* *credit*

Transaction	Current Assets	Gross Margin	Income From Operations
(a)			
(b)			

E6–9 Interpreting Bad Debt Disclosures

Daimler-Benz

Daimler-Benz AG is the largest industrial group in Germany. Best known as the manufacturer of Mercedes-Benz cars and trucks, it also manufactures products in the fields of rail systems, aerospace, propulsion, defense, and information technology. In its recent filings pursuant to its listing on the New York Stock Exchange, it disclosed the following information concerning its allowance for doubtful accounts (in millions of German marks denoted DM):

Balance at Beginning of Period	Charged to Costs and Expenses	Amounts Written Off	Balance at End of Period
1,933	92	(52)	1,973

Required:

1. Record summary journal entries related to bad debts for the current year.
2. If Daimler-Benz had written off an additional DM10 million of accounts receivable during the period, how would receivables, net, and net income have been affected? Explain why.

E6–10 Drawing Financial Statement Inferences: Credit Sales and Bad Debts

Microsoft

Microsoft develops, produces, and markets a wide range of computer software including the Windows operating system. On a recent balance sheet, Microsoft reported the following information about net sales revenue and accounts receivable.

	19B	19A
Accounts receivable, net of allowances of $76 and $57	$ 338	$ 270
Net revenues	3,753	2,759

According to its Form 10-K, Microsoft recorded bad debt expense of $47 and did not reinstate any previously written-off accounts during 19B.

Required:
1. What amount of bad debts was written off during 19B? 28
2. Assuming that all of Microsoft's sales during the period were on open account, solve for cash collected from customers for 19B.

Sears   **E6–11 Analyzing the Impact of Uncollectible Accounts on Income and Working Capital**

A recent annual report for Sears contained the following information at the end of its fiscal year:

	Year 1	Year 2
Accounts receivable	$7,022,075,000	$7,336,308,000
Allowance for doubtful accounts	(86,605,000)	(96,989,000)
	$6,935,470,000	$7,239,319,000

A footnote to the financial statements disclosed that uncollectible accounts amounting to $55,000,000 were written off as bad during year 1 and $69,000,000 during year 2. Assume that the tax rate for Sears was 30 percent.

Required:
1. Determine the bad debt expense for year 2 based on the preceding facts.
2. *Working capital* is defined as current assets minus current liabilities. How was Sears's working capital affected by the write-off of $69,000,000 in uncollectible accounts during year 2? What impact did the recording of bad debt expense have on working capital in year 2?
3. How was net income affected by the $69,000,000 write-off during year 2? What impact did recording bad debt expense have on net income for year 2?

E6–12 Analyzing the Effects of Bad Debts on Receivables Turnover Ratio

During 19A, Leung Enterprises Corporation recorded credit sales of $650,000. Based on prior experience, it estimates a 1 percent bad debt rate on credit sales. At the beginning of the year, the balance in Net Trade Accounts Receivable was $50,000. At the end of the year, but *before* the bad debt expense adjustment was recorded and *before* any bad debts had been written off, the balance in Net Trade Accounts Receivable was $55,500.

Required:
1. Assume that on December 31, 19A, the appropriate bad debt expense adjustment was recorded for the year 19A and accounts receivable totaling $6,000 for the year were determined to be uncollectible and written off. What was the receivables turnover ratio for 19A?
2. Assume instead that on December 31, 19A, the appropriate bad debt expense adjustment was recorded for the year 19A and accounts receivable of $7,000 were determined to be uncollectible and written off. What was the receivables turnover ratio for 19A?
3. Explain why the answers to requirements (1) and (2) differ or do not differ.

E6–13 Analyzing and Evaluating a Bad Debt Estimate with Discussion

Connor Company started business on January 1, 19A. During the year 19A, the company's records indicated the following:

Sales on cash basis	$400,000
Sales on credit basis	150,000
Collections on accounts receivable	100,000

The company's manager is concerned about accounting for the bad debts. At December 31, 19A, although no accounts were considered bad, several customers were considerably overdue in paying their accounts. A friend of the manager suggested a 1 percent bad debt rate on sales, which the manager decided to use at the start.

Required:

1. You have been employed on a part-time basis to assist with the company's record-keeping. The manager told you to set up bad debt expense of $5,500. Give the required entry.
2. You are concerned about how the $5,500 was determined. The manager told you it was from another manager "who knew his business" and used 1 percent of sales. Do you agree with the estimate of bad debts? If you disagree, give the correct entry and explain the basis for your choice.
3. Show how the various accounts related to credit sales should be shown on the December 31, 19A, income statement and balance sheet.

E6–14 Analyzing and Evaluating a Bad Debt Estimate with Discussion

During 19G, Martin's Camera Shop had sales revenue of $170,000, of which $85,000 was on credit. At the start of 19G, Accounts Receivable showed a $10,000 debit balance, and the Allowance for Doubtful Accounts showed an $800 credit balance. Collections of accounts receivable during 19G amounted to $68,000.

Data during 19G:

a. On December 31, 19G, an Account Receivable (J. Doe) of $1,500 from a prior year was determined to be uncollectible; therefore, it was written off immediately as a bad debt.
b. On December 31, 19G, on the basis of experience, a decision was made to continue the accounting policy of basing estimated bad debt losses on 2 percent of credit sales for the year.

Required:

1. Give the required journal entries for the two items on December 31, 19G (end of the accounting period).
2. Show how the amounts related to Accounts Receivable and Bad Debt Expense would be reported on the income statement and balance sheet for 19G. Disregard income tax considerations. 25,500 24,500(net receivables)
3. On the basis of the data available, does the 2 percent rate appear to be reasonable? yes Explain.

E6–15 Interpreting Bad Debt Disclosures and the Bad Debt Expense as a Percentage of Sales Ratio   **Federal Express**

A recent annual report for Federal Express contained the following data:

	(in thousands)	
	Current Year	Previous Year
Accounts receivable	$1,034,608	$805,495
Less: Allowance for doubtful accounts	36,800	38,225
Net accounts receivable	$ 997,808	$767,270
Bad debt expense	55,147	31,388

Required:

1. Determine the amount of accounts receivable that was actually written off during the current year.
2. How was the bad debt expense as a percentage of sales ratio affected by the write-off during the current year?

Stride Rite

E6–16 Focus on Cash Flows: Analyzing Sales Declines, Changes in Receivables, and Cash Flow from Operations with Discussion

Stride Rite Corporation manufactures and markets shoes under the brand names Stride Rite®, Keds®, and Sperry Top-Sider®. Three recent years produced a combination of declining sales revenue and net income culminating in a net loss of $8,430,000. Each year, however, Stride Rite was able to report positive cash flows from operations. Contributing to that positive cash flow was the change in accounts receivable. The current and prior year balance sheets reported the following:

	(in thousands)	
	Current Year	Previous Year
Accounts and notes receivable, less allowances	$48,066	$63,403

Required:

1. On the current year cash flow statement (indirect method), how would the change in accounts receivable affect cash flow from operations? Explain why it would have this effect.
2. Explain how declining sales revenue often leads to (a) declining accounts receivable and (b) cash collections from customers being higher than sales revenue.

Nike

E6–17 Focus on Cash Flows: Analyzing Sales Growth, Changes in Receivables, and Cash Flow from Operations with Discussion

Nike, Inc., is the best known sports apparel and equipment company in the world. Three recent years produced a combination of dramatic increases in sales revenue and net income. Cash flows from operations declined during the period, however. Contributing to that declining cash flow was the change in accounts receivable. The current and prior year balance sheets reported the following:

	(in thousands)	
	Current Year	Previous Year
Accounts receivable, less allowance for doubtful accounts	$1,346,125	$1,053,237

Required:

1. On the current year cash flow statement (indirect method), how would the change in accounts receivable affect cash flow from operations? Explain why it would have this effect.
2. Explain how increasing sales revenue often leads to (a) increasing accounts receivable and thus (b) cash collections from customers being lower than sales revenue.

E6–18 Reporting Cash and Cash Equivalents When There Are Several Bank Accounts

Strake Corporation has manufacturing facilities in several cities and has cash on hand at several locations as well as in several bank accounts. The general ledger at the end of 19A showed the following accounts: Cash on Hand—Home Office, $700; City Bank—Home Office, $58,600; Cash Held for Making Change, $300 (included in the regular Cash account balance); Cash on Hand—Location A, $100; National Bank—Location A, $3,350; Cash on Hand—Location B, $200; Southwest Bank—Location B, $785; Cash on Hand—Location C, $200; State Bank—Location C, $965; Metropolitan Bank—3-month Certificate of Deposit, $5,800; and Southwest Bank—6-month Certificate of Deposit, $850.

The bank balances given represent the current cash balances as reflected on the bank reconciliations.

Required:
What cash and cash equivalents amount should be reported on the company's 19A balance sheet? Explain the basis for your decisions on any questionable items.

E6–19 Bank Reconciliation, Entries, and Reporting

Jones Company has the June 30, 19B, bank statement and the June ledger accounts for cash, which are summarized below:

Bank Statement

	Checks	Deposits	Balance
Balance, June 1, 19B			$ 7,200
Deposits during June		$17,000	24,200
Checks cleared through June	$18,100		6,100
Bank service charges	50		6,050
Balance, June 30, 19B			6,050

Cash

June 1	Balance	6,800	June	Checks written	18,400
June	Deposits	19,000			

Petty Cash

June 30 Balance	300

Required:
1. Reconcile the bank account. A comparison of the checks written with the checks that have cleared the bank shows outstanding checks of $700. Some of the checks that cleared in June were written prior to June. No deposits in transit were carried over from May, but a deposit is in transit at the end of June.
2. Give any journal entries that should be made as a result of the bank reconciliation.
3. What is the balance in the Cash account after the reconciliation entries?
4. What is the total amount of cash that should be reported on the balance sheet at June 30?

E6–20 Bank Reconciliation, Entries, and Reporting

The September 30, 19D, bank statement for Russell Company and the September ledger accounts for cash are summarized here:

Bank Statement

	Checks	Deposits	Balance
Balance, September 1, 19D			$ 6,300
Deposits recorded during September		$27,000	33,300
Checks cleared during September	$28,500		4,800
NSF checks—Betty Brown	150		4,650
Bank service charges	50		4,600
Balance, September 30, 19D			4,600

Cash

Sept 1	Balance	6,300	Sept.	Checks written	28,600
Sept.	Deposits	28,000			

Petty Cash

Sept 30	Balance	400

No outstanding checks and no deposits in transit were carried over from August; however, there are deposits in transit and checks outstanding at the end of September.

Required:

1. Reconcile the bank account.
2. Give any journal entries that should be made as the result of the bank reconciliation.
3. What should the balance in the Cash account be after the reconciliation entries? 5500
4. What total amount of cash should the company report on the September 30 balance sheet? 5900

E6–21 Bank Reconciliation

The March 31, 19C, bank statement for State Company and the March ledger accounts for cash are summarized as follows:

Bank Statement

	Checks	Deposits	Balance
Balance, March 1, 19C			$10,650
Deposits during March		$29,000	39,650
Notes collected for depositor			
(including $100 interest)		980	40,630
Checks cleared during March	$32,200		8,430
Bank service charges	25		8,405
Balance, March 31, 19C			8,405

Cash

Mar. 1	Balance	10,100	Mar.	Checks written	32,500
Mar. 1	Deposits	31,000			

Petty Cash

Mar. 30	Balance	200

A comparison of March deposits recorded on the company's books with deposits on the bank statement showed deposits in transit of $2,000. Outstanding checks at the end of March were determined to be $850.

Required:

1. Prepare a bank reconciliation for March. The bank figures have been verified as being correct.
2. Give any journal entries that the company should make based on the reconciliation.

3. What amount should be shown as the ending balance in the Cash account after the reconciliation entries? What total amount of cash should be reported on the company's balance sheet at the end of March?

E6–22 (Supplement A) Determining Income Using the Percentage of Completion Method

Jackson Construction Company entered into a long-term construction contract with the federal government to build a special landing strip at an Air Force base in Rapid City, South Dakota. The project took three years and cost the government $12 million. Jackson spent the following amounts each year: 19A, $2 million; 19B, $5 million; 19C, $3 million. The company uses the percentage of completion method. Cost estimates equaled actual costs.

Required:
Determine the amount of net income that Jackson can report each year for this project.

E6–23 (Supplement A) Determining Income Using the Percentage of Completion Method

Marine Division of General Construction signed a contract with the U.S. Navy to build a large aircraft carrier with several complex computer control systems. Marine Division spent the following amounts each year: 19A, $10 million; 19B, $5 million; 19C, $20 million; 19D, $5 million. The division expected to make $10 million on this contract. The division uses the percentage of completion method. Cost estimates equaled actual costs.

Required:
Determine the amount of revenue, expenses, and net income that Marine Division reports each year for this project.

E6–24 (Supplement A) Applying the Revenue Principle

At what point should revenue be recognized in each of the following independent cases?

Case A. For Christmas presents, a McDonald's restaurant sells coupon books for $10. Each of the $1 coupons may be used in the restaurant any time during the following 12 months. The customer must pay cash when purchasing the coupon book.

Case B. Howard Land Development Corporation sold a lot to Quality Builders to construct a new home. The price of the lot was $50,000. Quality made a down payment of $100 and agreed to pay the balance in six months. After making the sale, Howard learned that Quality Builders often entered into these agreements but refused to pay the balance if it did not find a customer who wanted a house built on the lot.

Case C. In 19A, Smilor Construction Company started a long-term construction project to build a large office complex. The project was completed in 19C. At the end of 19C, Smilor had not yet sold the project because it was asking top dollar for the office space. Smilor was very confident that they could sell the building for the asking price because there was a serious shortage of office space in the area.

Case D. Chrysler Corporation has always recorded revenue at the point of sale. Recently, it has extended its warranties to cover all repairs for a period of seven years. One young accountant with the company now questions whether Chrysler has completed its earning process when it sells the cars. She suggests that the warranty obligation for seven years means that a significant amount of additional work must be performed in the future.

Problems

P6–1 Understanding the Income Statement

The following data were taken from the year-end records of Nomura Export Company. You are to fill in all of the missing amounts. Show computations.

Income Statement Items	Independent Cases	
	Case A	Case B
Gross sales revenue	$160,000	$232,000
Sales returns and allowances	?	18,000
Net sales revenue	?	?
Cost of goods sold	(68%)?	?
Gross margin on sales	?	(30%)?
Operating expenses	18,500	?
Pretax income	?	20,000
Income tax expense (20%)	?	?
Income before extraordinary items	?	?
Extraordinary items	10,000 (gain)	2,000 (loss)
Less: Income tax (20%)	?	?
Net income	?	?
EPS (10,000 shares)	3.00	?

P6–2 Preparing a Multiple-Step Income Statement

Builders Company, Inc., sells heavy construction equipment. There are 10,000 shares of capital stock outstanding. The annual fiscal period ends on December 31. The following condensed trial balance was taken from the general ledger on December 31, 19D:

Account Titles	Debit	Credit
Cash	$ 42,000	
Accounts receivable	18,000	
Inventory, ending	65,000	
Operational assets	50,000	
Accumulated depreciation		$ 21,000
Liabilities		30,000
Capital stock		90,000
Retained earnings, January 1, 19D		11,600
Sales revenue		182,000
Sales returns and allowances	7,000	
Cost of goods sold	98,000	
Selling expense	17,000	
Administrative expense	18,000	
Interest expense	2,000	
Extraordinary loss, unusual and infrequent		
storm damage	8,000	
Income tax expense*	9,600	
Totals	$334,600	$334,600

*Assume a 30% average tax rate on both operations and the extraordinary loss.

Required:

Prepare a multiple-step income statement (showing both gross profit and income from operations).

P6–3 Preparing and Analyzing a Multiple-Step Income Statement

Big Tommy Corporation is a local grocery store organized seven years ago as a corporation. At that time, common stock totaling 6,000 shares was issued to the three organizers. The store is in an excellent location, and sales have increased each year. At the end of 19G, the bookkeeper prepared the following statement (assume that all amounts are correct; note the incorrect terminology and format):

BIG TOMMY CORPORATION
Profit and Loss
December 31, 19G

	Debit	Credit
Sales		$420,000
Cost of goods sold	$279,000	
Sales returns and allowances	10,000	
Selling expense	58,000	
Administrative and general expense	16,000	
Interest expense	1,000	
Extraordinary loss	6,000	
Income tax expense (on operations,		
less $1,800 saved on the extraordinary loss)	15,000	
Net profit	35,000	
Totals	$420,000	$420,000

Required:

Prepare a multiple-step income statement (showing both gross profit and income from operations). Assume an average 30 percent income tax rate.

P6–4 Recording Sales, Returns, and Bad Debts

The following data were selected from the records of May Company for the year ended December 31, 19C.

Balances January 1, 19C:	
Accounts receivable (various customers)	$102,000
Allowance for doubtful accounts	6,000

In the following order, except for cash sales, sold merchandise and made collections on credit terms 2/10, n/30 (assume a unit sales price of $500 in all transactions and use the gross method to record sales revenue).

Transactions during 19C:

(a) Sold merchandise for cash, $228,000.
(b) Sold merchandise to R. Jones; invoice price, $12,000.
(c) Sold merchandise to K. Black; invoice price, $26,000.
(d) Two days after purchase date, R. Jones returned one of the units purchased in (b) and received account credit.
(e) Sold merchandise to B. Sears; invoice price, $24,000.
(f) R. Jones paid his account in full within the discount period.
(g) Collected $98,000 cash from customer sales on credit in prior year, all within the discount periods.
(h) K. Black paid the invoice in (c) within the discount period.
(i) Sold merchandise to R. Roy; invoice price, $17,000.
(j) Three days after paying the account in full, K. Black returned seven defective units and received a cash refund.

(k) After the discount period, collected $7,000 cash on an account receivable on sales in a prior year.

(l) The company wrote off a 19A account of $2,900 after deciding that the amount would never be collected.

(m) The estimated bad debt rate used by the company was 1 percent of credit sales net of returns.

Required:

1. Give the journal entries for these transactions, including the write-off of the uncollectible account and the adjusting entry for estimated bad debts. Do not record cost of goods sold. Show computations for each entry.

2. Show how the accounts related to the preceding sale and collection activities should be reported on the 19C income statement. (Treat sales discounts as a contra revenue.)

Kimberly-Clark P6-5 Interpreting Disclosure of Allowance for Doubtful Accounts

Kimberly-Clark manufactures and markets a variety of paper and synthetic fiber products, the best known of which is Kleenex tissues. It recently disclosed the following information concerning the allowance for doubtful accounts on its Form 10-K Annual Report submitted to the Securities and Exchange Commission.

SCHEDULE VIII
Valuation and Qualifying Accounts
For the Years Ended December 31, 19C, 19B, AND 19A
(millions of dollars)

Description: Allowances for Doubtful Accounts	Balance at Beginning of Period	Charged to Costs and Expenses	Charged to Other Accounts[a]	Write-Offs	Balance at End of Period
December 31, 19C	$8.2	$4.5	$.2	$2.7	$10.2
December 31, 19B	7.1	4.8	—	(?)	8.2
December 31, 19A	6.4	(?)	.2	3.3	7.1

[a]Primarily bad debt recoveries.

Required:

1. Record summary journal entries related to bad debts for 19C.
2. Supply the missing dollar amounts noted by (?) for 19A and 19B.

P6-6 Determining Bad Debt Expense Based on Aging Analysis

Green Pastures Equipment Company uses the aging approach to estimate bad debt expense at the end of each accounting year. Credit sales occur frequently on terms n/60. The balance of each account receivable is aged on the basis of three time periods as follows: (1) not yet due, (2) up to one year past due, and (3) more than one year past due. Experience has shown that for each age group the average loss rate on the amount of the receivable at year-end due to uncollectability is (a) 1%, (b) 5%, and (c) 30%.

At December 31, 19F (end of the current accounting year), the Accounts Receivable balance was $41,000, and the Allowance for Doubtful Accounts balance was $1,020 (credit). To simplify, only five customer accounts are used; the details of each on December 31, 19F, follow:

B. Brown—Account Receivable

Date	Explanation	Debit	Credit	Balance
3/11/19E	Sale	14,000		14,000
6/30/19E	Collection		5,000	9,000
1/31/19F	Collection		4,000	5,000

Date	Explanation	Debit	Credit	Balance
D. Donalds—Account Receivable				
2/28/19F	Sale	22,000		22,000
4/15/19F	Collection		10,000	12,000
11/30/19F	Collection		8,000	4,000
N. Napier—Account Receivable				
11/30/19F	Sale	9,000		9,000
12/15/19F	Collection		2,000	7,000
S. Strothers—Account Receivable				
3/2/19D	Sale	5,000		5,000
4/15/19D	Collection		5,000	–0–
9/1/19E	Sale	10,000		10,000
10/15/19E	Collection		8,000	2,000
2/1/19F	Sale	19,000		21,000
3/1/19F	Collection		5,000	16,000
12/31/19F	Sale	3,000		19,000
T. Thomas—Account Receivable				
12/30/19F	Sale	6,000		6,000

Required:
1. Set up an aging analysis schedule and complete it.
2. Compute the estimated uncollectible amount for each age category and in total.
3. Give the adjusting entry for bad debt expense at December 31, 19F.
4. Show how the amounts related to accounts receivable should be presented on the 19F income statement and balance sheet.

P6–7 Analyzing Internal Control

Cripple Creek Company has one trusted employee who, as the owner said, "handles all of the bookkeeping and paperwork for the company." This employee is responsible for counting, verifying, and recording cash receipts and payments, making the weekly bank deposit, preparing checks for major expenditures (signed by the owner), making small expenditures from the cash register for daily expenses, and collecting accounts receivable. The owners asked the local bank for a $20,000 loan. The bank asked that an audit be performed covering the year just ended. The independent auditor (a local CPA), in a private conference with the owner, presented some evidence of the following activities of the trusted employee during the past year:

(a) Cash sales sometimes were not entered in the cash register, and the trusted employee pocketed approximately $50 per month.
(b) Cash taken from the cash register (and pocketed by the trusted employee) was replaced with expense memos with fictitious signatures (approximately $12 per day).
(c) A $300 collection on an account receivable of a valued out-of-town customer was pocketed by the trusted employee and was covered by making a $300 entry as a debit to Sales Returns and a credit to Accounts Receivable.
(d) An $800 collection on an account receivable from a local customer was pocketed by the trusted employee and was covered by making an $800 entry as a debit to Allowance for Doubtful Accounts and a credit to Accounts Receivable.

Required:
1. What was the approximate amount stolen during the past year?
2. What would be your recommendations to the owner?

P6–8 **Preparing a Bank Reconciliation and Related Journal Entries**

The bookkeeper at Hopkins Company has not reconciled the bank statement with the Cash account, saying, "I don't have time." You have been asked to prepare a reconciliation and review the procedures with the bookkeeper.

The April 30, 19D, bank statement and the April ledger accounts for cash showed the following (summarized):

Bank Statement

	Checks	Deposits	Balance
Balance, April 1, 19D			$25,850
Deposits during April		$36,000	61,850
Notes collected for depositor			
(including $70 interest)		1,070	62,920
Checks cleared during April	$44,200		18,720
NSF check—A. B. Wright	140		18,580
Bank service charges	50		18,530
Balance, April 30, 19D			18,530

Cash

Apr. 1	Balance	23,250	Apr.	Checks written	43,800
Apr.	Deposits	42,000			

Petty Cash

Apr. 30	Balance	100

A comparison of checks written before and during April with the checks cleared through the bank showed outstanding checks at the end of April of $2,200. No deposits in transit were carried over from March, but a deposit was in transit at the end of April.

Required:

1. Prepare a detailed bank reconciliation for April.
2. Give any required journal entries as a result of the reconciliation. Why are they necessary?
3. What were the balances in the cash accounts in the ledger on May 1, 19D?
4. What total amount of cash should be reported on the balance sheet at the end of April?

P6–9 **Computing Outstanding Checks and Deposits in Transit and Preparing a Bank Reconciliation and Journal Entries**

The August 19B bank statement for Martha Company and the August 19B ledger accounts for cash follow:

Bank Statement

Date		Checks	Deposits	Balance
Aug.	1			$17,470
	2	$300		17,170
	3		$12,000	29,170
	4	400		28,770
	5	250		28,520
	9	900		27,620
	10	300		27,320
	15		4,000	31,320
	21	400		30,920
	24	21,000		9,920
	25		7,000	16,920
	30	800		16,120
	30		2,180*	18,300
	31	100†		18,200

*$2,000 note collected plus interest.
†Bank service charge.

Cash

Aug. 1 Balance	16,520	Checks written	
Deposits		Aug. 2	300
Aug. 2	12,000	4	900
12	4,000	15	290
24	7,000	17	550
31	5,000	18	800
		18	400
		23	21,000

Petty Cash

Aug. 31 Balance	200	

Outstanding checks at the end of July were for $250, $400, and $300. No deposits were in transit at the end of July.

Required:

1. Compute the deposits in transit at the end of August.
2. Compute the outstanding checks at the end of August.
3. Prepare a bank reconciliation for August.
4. Give any journal entries that the company should make as a result of the bank reconciliation. Why are they necessary?
5. After the reconciliation journal entries are posted, what balances would be reflected in the cash accounts in the ledger?
6. What total amount of cash should be reported on the August 31, 19B, balance sheet?

P6–10 Computing Outstanding Checks and Deposits in Transit and Preparing a Bank Reconciliation

The December 31, 19B, bank statement for Packer Company and the December 19B ledger accounts for cash follow.

Bank Statement

Date		Checks	Deposits	Balance
Dec.	1			$48,000
	2	$400; 300	$17,000	64,300
	4	7,000; 90		57,210
	6	120; 180; 1,600		55,310
	11	500; 1,200; 70	28,000	81,540
	13	480; 700; 1,900		78,460
	17	12,000; 8,000		58,460
	23	60; 23,500	36,000	70,900
	26	900; 2,650		67,350
	28	2,200; 5,200		59,950
	30	17,000; 1,890; 300*	19,000	59,760
	31	1,650; 1,350; 150†	5,250‡	61,860

*NSF check, J. Left, a customer.
†Bank service charge.
‡Note collected, principal, $5,000 plus interest.

Cash

Dec. 1 Balance	64,100	Checks written during December:		
Deposits		60	5,000	2,650
Dec. 11	28,000	17,000	5,200	1,650
23	36,000	700	1,890	2,200
30	19,000	3,300	1,600	7,000
31	13,000	1,350	120	300
		180	90	480
		12,000	23,500	8,000
		70	500	1,900
		900	1,200	

Petty Cash			
Dec. 31	Balance	300	

The November 19B bank reconciliation showed the following: correct cash balance at November 30, $62,300; deposits in transit on November 30, $17,000; and outstanding checks on November 30, $400 + $500 = $900.

Required:

1. Compute the deposits in transit December 31, 19B.
2. Compute the outstanding checks at December 31, 19B.
3. Prepare a bank reconciliation at December 31, 19B.
4. Give any journal entries that should be made as a result of the bank reconciliation made by the company. Why are they necessary?
5. After the reconciliation journal entries, what balances would be reflected in the cash accounts in the ledger?
6. What total amount of cash should be reported on the December 31, 19B, balance sheet?

Cases and Projects

C6–1 Analyzing and Evaluating Internal Controls

Lane Manufacturing Company is a relatively small local business that specializes in the repair and renovation of antique furniture. The owner is an expert craftsperson. Although a number of skilled workers are employed, there is always a large backlog of work to be done. A long-time employee, who serves as clerk-bookkeeper, handles cash receipts, keeps the records, and writes checks for disbursements. The owner signs the checks. The clerk-bookkeeper pays small amounts in cash, subject to a month-end review by the owner. Approximately 80 regular customers are extended credit that typically amounts to less than $1,000. Although credit losses are small, in recent years the bookkeeper had established an allowance for doubtful accounts, and all write-offs were made at year-end. During January 19E (the current year), the owner decided to start construction as soon as possible of a building for the business that would provide many advantages over the presently rented space and would have space usable for expansion of facilities. As a part of the considerations in financing, the financing institution asked for 19D audited financial statements. The company statements never had been audited. Early in the audit, the independent CPA found numerous errors and one combination of amounts, in particular, that caused concern.

There was some evidence that a $2,500 job completed by Lane had been recorded as a receivable (from a new customer) on July 15, 19D. The receivable was credited for a $2,500 cash collection a few days later. The new account never was active again. The auditor also observed that shortly thereafter three write-offs of Accounts Receivable balances had been made to Allowance for Doubtful Accounts as follows: Jones, $800; Blake, $750; and Sellers, $950—all of whom were known as regular customers. These write-offs drew the attention of the auditor.

Required:

1. What caused the CPA to be concerned? Explain. Should the CPA report the suspicions to the owner?
2. What recommendations would you make with respect to internal control procedures for this company?

C6–2 Alternative Recognition Points and Financial Statement Analysis

UPS, Federal Express, and Airborne are three of the major players in the highly competitive package delivery industry. Comparability is a key qualitative characteristic of accounting numbers that allows analysts to compare similar companies. The revenue recognition footnotes of the three competitors reveal three different revenue recognition points for package delivery revenue: package delivery, percentage of service completed, and package pickup. These points correspond to the end, continuous recognition, and the beginning of the earnings process.

UNITED PARCEL SERVICE OF AMERICA, INC.

Revenue is recognized upon delivery of a package.

FEDERAL EXPRESS CORPORATION

Revenue is generally recognized upon delivery of shipments. For shipments in transit, revenue is recorded based on the percentage of service completed.

AIRBORNE FREIGHT CORP.

Domestic revenues and most domestic operating expenses are recognized when shipments are picked up from the customer. . . .

The Airborne footnote goes on to say, however: "The net revenue resulting from existing recognition policies does not materially differ from that which would be recognized on a delivery date basis."

Required:

1. Do you believe that the difference between Airborne's and UPS's revenue recognition policies materially affects their reported earnings? Why or why not?
2. Assume that all three companies pick up packages from customers and receive payment of $1 million for services each day of the year and that each package is delivered the next day. What would each company's service revenue be for a year given their stated revenue recognition policy?
3. Given your answers to requirement (2), under what conditions would that answer change?
4. Which revenue recognition rule do you prefer? Why?

C6–3 Financial Statement Analysis and Bad Debt Disclosure

Foster's Brewing controls more than 50 percent of the beer market in Australia and owns 40 percent of Molson Breweries of Canada and 100 percent of Courage Limited of the United Kingdom. As an Australian company, it follows Australian GAAP and uses Australian accounting terminology. In the footnotes to its recent annual report, it discloses the information on receivables presented on the next page (all numbers are reported in thousands of Australian dollars).

Required:

1. The account titles used by Foster's are different from those normally used by U.S. companies. What account titles does it use in place of Allowance for Doubtful Accounts and Bad Debts Expense?
2. Sales on account for 19B were $9,978,875. Compute the accounts receivable—trade debtors turnover ratio for 19B (ignore uncollectible accounts).
3. Compute Provision for Doubtful Debts as a percentage of current receivables separately for receivables from trade debtors and receivables from others. Explain why these percentages might be different.
4. What was the total amount of receivables written off in 19B?

Note 3: Receivables	19B	19A
CURRENT		
Trade debtors	792,193	999,159
Provision for doubtful debts	(121,449)	(238,110)
Other debtors	192,330	130,288
Provision for doubtful debts	(384)	(2,464)
NON-CURRENT		
Trade debtors	164,808	200,893
Other debtors	15,094	16,068
Provision for doubtful debts	(7,920)	(7,400)

Note 15: Operation Profit	19B	19A
Amounts set aside to provisions for		
Doubtful debts—trade debtors	(21,143)	(53,492)
Doubtful debts—other debtors	(228)	(2,570)

Platinum Software

C6–4 Ethics Case: Management Incentives, Revenue Recognition, and Sales with the Right of Return

Platinum Software was a fast-growing maker of accounting software. According to the federal charges, when business slowed and they were unable to meet the stock market's expectation for continued growth, the former chairman and CEO (the company's founder), former CFO, and former controller responded by improperly recording revenue and allowances for returns resulting in overstatement of net income by $18 million. The three recently settled both federal charges brought by the SEC and a shareholder suit by paying nearly $2.8 million in restitution and fines and being suspended from practice for differing periods. The exact nature of the fraud is described in the following excerpt:

Three Ex-Officers of O.C. Software Firm Sanctioned; SEC:
Platinum founder Gerald Blackie agrees to 10-year ban as officer of public company to settle suit over falsifying books. Two other former executives are fined.
JOHN O'DELL TIMES STAFF WRITER
Los Angeles Times Orange County Edition 5/10/96

. . . .

The SEC suit charged that Blackie, Tague and Erickson began falsifying sales records in 1993 and early 1994 in order to pump up Platinum's quarterly sales figures and make the company's financial situation appear stronger than it was.

For a period of at least nine months, ending early in 1994, the men backdated sales orders and reported as actual revenue fees that had not yet been received and were subject to secret cancellation agreements that the customers often exercised, the suit said.

In one case in 1993, the suit alleges, Blackie personally closed a $1.5-million software licensing deal with the Wackenhut Corp. on the day the fiscal year ended. He also executed a separate letter giving Wackenhut a 60-day right to cancel. Blackie then instructed Erickson to enter the $1.5 million as revenue in the just-completed fiscal year, even though the money had not been received.

Wackenhut later canceled the contract, the suit says, but Platinum did not disclose the cancellation or adjust for it when it later filed its annual report with the SEC.

In August 1993, with the company's stock price rising on the strength of the falsified financial reports, Blackie, Tague and Erickson all sold large amounts of stock. Blackie profited again with a stock sale in November 1993, the SEC suit says. After the company revealed the accounting irregularities and announced Blackie's resignation in April 1994, the stock price plummeted 64 percent.

The suit also says Blackie received $128,125 in performance bonuses for the nine-month period in which he was falsifying financial reports; Erickson got $50,000 and Tague received $6,000. "If they had been any lower in the company they would never have gotten away with this for as long as they did," said SEC attorney Nathan.

Required:

1. What facts, if any, presented in the article suggest that Platinum violated the revenue principle?
2. Assuming that Platinum did recognize revenue when contracts were signed, how could it have properly accounted for the fact that customers had a right to cancel the contracts (make an analogy with accounting for bad debts)?
3. What do you think may have motivated management to falsify the statements? Why was management concerned with reporting continued growth in net income?
4. Explain who was hurt by management's unethical conduct.
5. Assume that you are the auditor for other software licensing firms. After reading about the fraud, what types of transactions would you pay special attention to in the audit of your clients in this industry?

C6–5 Financial Statement Analysis

Toys "R" Us

Refer to the financial statements of Toys "R" Us given in Appendix B at the end of this book.

Required:

1. How much cash and cash equivalents does the company hold at the end of the current year?
2. The company does not report bad debt expense on the income statement. Explain why.
3. Compare the company's accounts and other receivables as a percentage of total assets to that of Timberland (see Exhibit 6.2), which has total assets of $421,408,000. Explain the differences in these percentages.

C6–6 Financial Statement Analysis

Toys "R" Us

Refer to the financial statements of Toys "R" Us given in Appendix B at the end of this book.

Required:

1. What does the company disclose about the market value of its cash and cash equivalents? Would you expect this statement to be true given the securities included in cash equivalents?
2. The company does not report allowance for doubtful accounts on the balance sheet or in the footnotes. Explain why.
3. Compare the company's gross profit percentage to that of Timberland (see Exhibit 6.1). What might cause the difference?

C6–7 Project: Comparing Revenue Recognition Policies within Industries

Acquire the revenue recognition note from the annual reports or 10-Ks of three companies within an industry. (Library files, the SEC EDGAR service at www.sec.gov, Compustat CD, or the companies themselves are good sources.) Write a short report indicating any differences, if any, among the accounting policies and their effect on timing of revenue recognition.

C6–8 Project: Comparing Revenue Recognition Policies between Industries

Acquire the revenue recognition note from the annual reports or 10-Ks of three companies from different industries. (Library files, the SEC EDGAR service at www.sec.gov, Compustat, or the companies themselves are good sources.) Write a short report indicating any differences among the accounting policies. Consider whether the differences in policy lead to earlier or later or no difference in timing of recognition of revenue and what differences in their lines of business may lead to the policy differences.

C6–9 **Project: Competitive Analysis of Differences in Bad Debt Expense as a Percentage of Sales Ratio**

Timberland's competitors in the shoe industry include Wolverine World Wide, Brown Group, Reebok, Nike, Stride Rite, and others. Obtain the income statement, balance sheet, and uncollectible accounts schedule (from the 10-K) for Timberland and two of its competitors. (Library files, the SEC EDGAR service at www.sec.gov, Compustat, or the companies themselves are good sources.) Write a short memo comparing the companies' bad debt expense as a percentage of sales ratio. Indicate what differences in their businesses might account for any differences in the ratio.

C6–10 **Project: Analysis of Changes in the Receivables Turnover Ratio**

Acquire the three most recent years' income statements and balance sheets for a single company. (Library files, the SEC EDGAR service at www.sec.gov, Compustat, or the company itself are good sources.) Write a short memo comparing the company's receivables turnover ratio over the three years. Indicate what differences in its operations might account for any differences in the ratio.

C6–11 **Project: Focus on Cash Flows**

Acquire the three most recent years' cash flow statements for a single company. (Library files, the SEC EDGAR service at www.sec.gov, Compustat, or the company itself are good sources.) Write a short memo describing the effect of the change in accounts receivable on the difference between net income and cash flow from operations for each year.

C6–12 **Project: Financial Analysis Update**

Acquire the most recent years' annual report and Form 10-K for Timberland. (Library files, the SEC EDGAR service at www.sec.gov, Compustat, or the company itself are good sources.) Write a short memo comparing the company's receivables turnover ratio and bad debt expense as a percentage of sales ratio to the 1995 figures presented in the chapter. Indicate what differences in its operations might account for any differences in the ratios.

C6–13 **Ethics Project: Analysis of Irregularities in Revenue Recognition**

Obtain a recent news story outlining an accounting irregularity related to revenue recognition. (Library files, Wall Street Journal Index, Dow Jones News/Retrieval, and *Bloomberg Business News* are good sources. Search for the term "accounting irregularities.") Write a short memo outlining the nature of the irregularity, how it specifically violated the revenue principle, the size of the necessary correction of previously reported earnings, the impact of the announcement of the irregularity on the company's stock price, and any fines or civil penalties against the company and its officers.

C6–14 **Team Project: Analyzing Revenues and Receivables**

As a group, select an industry to analyze. Each group member should acquire the annual report or 10-K for one publicly traded company in the industry, with each member selecting a different company. (Library files, the SEC EDGAR service at www.sec.gov, Compustat CD, or the company itself are good sources.) On an individual basis, each group member should then write a short report answering the following questions about their selected company.

1. What specific revenue recognition rule does the company follow?
2. What is the receivables turnover ratio?
3. If the 10-K is available, determine what additional disclosures are available concerning the allowance for doubtful accounts. If the necessary information is provided, what is the bad debt as a percentage of sales ratio?

4. What was the effect of the change in accounts receivable on cash flows from operations? Explain your answer.

Discuss any patterns across the companies that you as a group observe. Then, as a group, write a short report comparing and contrasting your companies using these attributes. Provide potential explanations for any differences discovered.

CHAPTER SEVEN

Reporting and Interpreting Cost of Goods Sold and Inventory

Harley-Davidson, Inc.

FROM TURMOIL TO TRIUMPH AS A WORLD-CLASS MANUFACTURER

Written off in the early 1980s as unable to compete with its

more reliable Japanese rivals, Harley-Davidson now controls nearly two-

thirds of the U.S. market for superheavyweight motorcycles. The Milwaukee-

based company has more than doubled motorcycle production in the last

decade, has dramatically expanded its riding and fashion apparel sales, and

even sells 30 percent of its bikes overseas. The Harley-Davidson eagle trade-

mark was once known best as a popular request in tattoo parlors. Now more

than $1 million worth of neckties emblazoned with its trademarks are sold

each year. The stunning popularity of its products across the tattoo and neck-

tie sets is the net result of involved employees working in teams to make

Harley-Davidson a world-class manufacturer of motorcycles in terms of

inventory quality and costs. While significant investments continue to be

LEARNING OBJECTIVES

After studying this chapter, you should be able to:

1. Apply the cost principle to identify the amounts that should be included in inventory and the matching principle to determine cost of goods sold for typical retailers, wholesalers, and manufacturers. 358

2. Measure the effects of inventory errors on financial statements. 364

3. Use the four inventory costing methods to determine the appropriate amounts to report as inventory and cost of goods sold. 365

4. Decide when the use of different inventory costing methods is beneficial to a company. 371

5. Analyze financial statements prepared using different inventory costing methods. 373

6. Apply the lower-of-cost-or-market (LCM) rule. 376

7. Keep track of inventory quantities and amounts in different circumstances. 378

made in new plant, the company also focuses on empowering, educating, and training both salaried and unionized employees to achieve personal growth, improvements in inventory quality, and reductions in the components of inventory cost: raw materials, labor, and overhead. Although Harley-Davidson does not manufacture the apparel it sells, it does work closely with apparel suppliers to maximize quality and minimize inventory costs. The provision of accurate and timely inventory accounting information is a key to many of these efforts. Furthermore, in a typical year, selection of appropriate accounting methods for inventory saves Harley-Davidson more than $700,000 in income taxes.

Competition in the motorcycle industry remains fierce, however, and consumer apparel tastes can change rapidly. Harley-Davidson's major competitors, Honda and Yamaha, have more financial and marketing resources available. Continuous improvement in manufacturing and inventory management will be necessary for the Harley-Davidson eagle to continue its rise.

■ ■ ■

Business Background

Concerns about the cost and quality of inventory face all modern manufacturers and merchandisers and turn our attention to *cost of goods sold (cost of sales, cost of products sold)* on the income statement and *inventory* on the balance sheet. Exhibit 7.1 presents the relevant excerpts from Harley-Davidson's financial statements that present these accounts. Cost of goods sold is subtracted from net sales to produce gross profit on its multiple-step income statement. (The multiple-step format is discussed in Chapter 5.) Inventory is a current asset on the balance sheet; it is reported below cash and accounts receivable because it is less liquid than those two current assets.

Harley-Davidson's successful management of production, cost of goods sold, and inventory requires a joint effort by human resource managers, engineers and production managers, marketing managers, and accounting and financial managers. It is truly a multidisciplinary task. The primary goals of inventory management are to have sufficient quantities of high-quality inventory available to serve customers' needs while minimizing the costs of carrying inventory (production, storage, obsolescence, financing, etc.). For example, purchasing or producing too *few* units of a hot-selling item causes stock-outs that mean lost sales revenue and decreases in customer satisfaction. Purchasing too *many* units of a slow-selling apparel item increases the storage costs and interest costs on short-term borrowings to finance the inventory purchases and may even lead to losses if the merchandise cannot be sold at normal prices.

To meet these inventory management goals, marketing, financial, and production managers must work together to forecast customer demand for different motorcycle models or apparel items and provide feedback so that production or purchasing adjustments can be made. Production, human resource, and purchasing managers also must work to control the cost of goods sold to improve gross profit margin. Toward the end of the chapter, we discuss the way that faulty inventory purchasing decisions can even affect Harley's income tax liability. As a consequence, managers, investors, and financial analysts emphasize cost of goods sold and inventory because they are such important determinants of a company's success.

EXHIBIT 7.1
Balance Sheet and Income Statement Excerpts

REAL WORLD EXCERPT

HARLEY-DAVIDSON, INC.
Annual Report

HARLEY-DAVIDSON, INC.
CONSOLIDATED STATEMENTS OF OPERATIONS

(In thousands, except per share amounts)

Years ended December 31,	1995	1994	1993
Net sales	$1,350,466	$1,158,887	$933,262
Cost of goods sold	939,067	800,548	641,248
Gross profit	411,399	358,339	292,014

HARLEY-DAVIDSON, INC.
CONSOLIDATED BALANCE SHEETS

(In thousands, except share amounts)

December 31,	1995	1994
ASSETS		
Current assets:		
Cash and cash equivalents	$ 31,462	$ 57,884
Accounts receivable, net	134,210	116,261
Inventories	84,427	89,880

The accounting system plays three roles in the inventory management process. First, the system must provide accurate information necessary for preparation of periodic financial statements and reports to tax authorities.[1] Second, it must provide up-to-date information on inventory quantities and costs to facilitate ordering and manufacturing decisions. Third, since inventories are subject to theft and other forms of misuse, the system also must provide the information necessary to help protect these important assets. First we discuss the important choices management must make in the financial and tax reporting process. Then we will briefly discuss how accounting systems are organized to keep track of inventory quantities and costs for decision making and control. This topic will be the principal subject matter of your managerial accounting course.

Harley's successful production and inventory management strategy and its mix of product lines make it a particularly good example for this chapter. The organization of Harley-Davidson's Motorcycle Division is illustrated in Exhibit 7.2. Although best known as a *manufacturer* of motorcycles, Harley also purchases and resells completed products such as its popular line of Motorclothes™ apparel. In the second case, it acts as a *wholesaler*. Both the motorcycle and Motorclothes™ product lines are sold to the public through a network of independent dealers who are the *retailers* for the products. From an accounting standpoint, these independent dealers are Harley-Davidson's customers. The inventory accounting problems faced by wholesalers and retailers (both often called *merchandisers*) are similar and are covered by discussing the Motorclothes™ line. The additional complexities that manufacturers face are discussed in the context of the motorcycle product line. We also will illustrate the application of these same inventory accounting principles to other companies that face different economic circumstances.

---

[1] As we discuss later, tax reports often differ from the statements prepared for other external users.

EXHIBIT 7.2
Harley–Davidson Motorcycle Division Product Lines

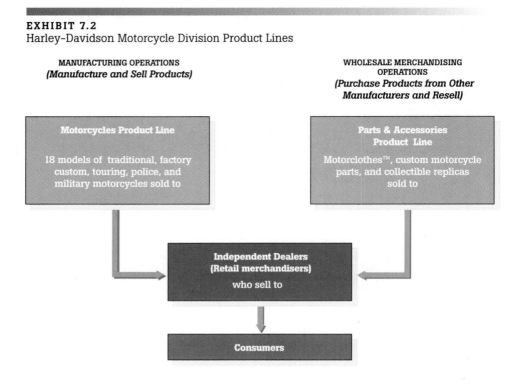

Nature of Inventory and Cost of Goods Sold

Items Included in Inventory

LEARNING OBJECTIVE 1
Apply the cost principle to identify the amounts that should be included in inventory and the matching principle to determine cost of goods sold for typical retailers, wholesalers, and manufacturers.

Inventory is tangible property held for sale in the normal course of business or used in producing goods or services for sale.
Merchandise inventory includes goods held for resale in the ordinary course of business.

Raw materials inventory includes items acquired for the purpose of processing into finished goods.

Work in process inventory includes goods in the process of being manufactured.

Inventory is tangible property that (1) is held for sale in the normal course of business or (2) is used to produce goods or services for sale. Inventory is reported on the balance sheet as a current asset because it usually is used or converted into cash within one year or within the next operating cycle of the business, whichever is longer. The types of inventory normally held depend on the characteristics of the business. Merchandisers (wholesale or retail businesses) hold the following:

Merchandise inventory   Goods (or merchandise) held for resale in the normal course of business. The goods usually are acquired in a finished condition and are ready for sale without further processing.

For Harley–Davidson, merchandise inventory includes the Motorclothes™ line and the other parts and accessories it purchases for sale to its independent dealers.
Manufacturing businesses hold the following:

Raw materials inventory   Items acquired by purchase, growth (such as food products), or extraction (natural resources) for processing into finished goods. Such items are included in raw materials inventory until used, at which point they become part of work in process inventory.

Work in process inventory   Goods in the process of being manufactured but not yet completed. When completed, work in process inventory becomes finished goods inventory.

In which ways does inventory accounting differ for merchandise (Motorclothes™) versus manufactured goods (motorcycles)?

Finished goods inventory   Goods manufactured by the business, completed and ready for sale.

Inventories related to Harley-Davidson's motorcycle manufacturing operations are recorded in these accounts.

Finished goods inventory includes manufactured goods that are completed and ready for sale.

Inventory Cost

Goods in inventory are recorded in conformity with the *cost principle.* The primary basis of accounting for inventory is cash equivalent cost, which is the price paid or consideration given to acquire an asset. Inventory cost includes, in principle, the sum of the applicable expenditures and charges directly or indirectly incurred in bringing an article to usable or salable condition and location.

When Harley-Davidson purchases raw materials for the motorcycle line and merchandise inventory for the Motorclothes™ line, it follows similar accounting practices. Theoretically, the amount recorded for purchase of raw materials or merchandise should include the invoice price and indirect expenditures related to the purchase, such as freight charges to deliver the items to its warehouses (freight-in) and inspection and preparation costs. In general, the company should cease accumulating costs of purchases when the raw materials are *ready for use* or when the merchandise inventory is in a condition and location *ready for shipment* to the dealers. Any additional costs related to selling the merchandise inventory to the dealers, such as marketing department salaries and dealer training sessions, should be included in Selling, General, and Administrative Expenses of the period of sale to the dealers since they are incurred after the inventory is ready for use in the normal course of business.

Applying the Materiality Constraint in Practice

Incidental costs such as inspection and preparation costs often are not material in amount (see the discussion of the materiality constraint in the Chapter 5 discussion of the Conceptual Framework of Accounting) and do not have to be assigned to the inventory cost. Thus, for practical reasons, many companies use the invoice price, less returns and discounts, to assign a unit cost to raw materials or merchandise and record other indirect expenditures as a separate cost that is reported as an expense. Invoice price may or may not include transportation charges (freight-in) for shipment to the warehouse.

Inventory Flows

The flow of inventory costs for merchandisers, both wholesalers and retailers, is relatively simple, as shown in Exhibit 7.3A. When merchandise is purchased, the merchandise inventory is increased. When the goods are sold, cost of goods sold is increased and the merchandise inventory is decreased.

The flow of inventory costs in a manufacturing environment is diagrammed in Exhibit 7.3B. For Harley-Davidson's motorcycle manufacturing operations, the flow of inventory costs is more complex. First raw materials must be purchased. These raw materials include steel and aluminum castings, forgings, sheet, and bars as well as

EXHIBIT 7.3
Flow of Inventory costs

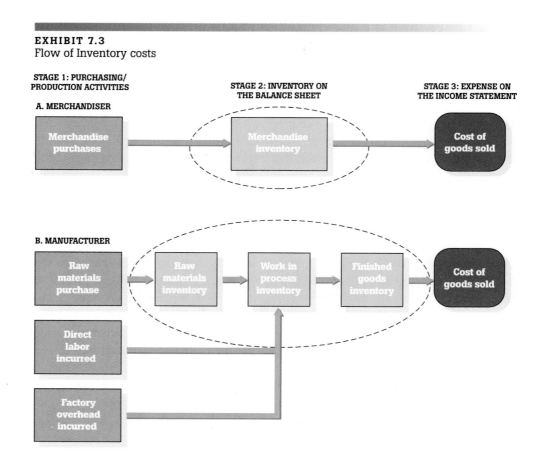

certain motorcycle component parts including carburetors, batteries, and tires, which are produced by its small network of suppliers. When used, the cost of each material is removed from the raw materials inventory and added to the work in process inventory, along with two other components of manufacturing costs.

Direct labor and factory overhead costs also are added to the work in process inventory when incurred in the manufacturing process. **Direct labor** cost represents the earnings of employees who work directly on the products being manufactured. **Factory overhead** costs include all manufacturing costs that are not raw material or direct labor costs. For example, the salary of the factory supervisor and the cost of heat, light, and power to operate the factory are included in factory overhead. When the motorcycles are completed and ready for sale, the related amounts in work in process inventory are transferred to finished goods inventory. When the finished goods are sold, cost of goods sold is increased and the finished goods inventory is decreased.

Note in Exhibit 7.3 that for *both* merchandisers and manufacturers, there are three stages to inventory cost flows. The first involves purchasing and/or production activities. In the second, these activities result in additions to inventory accounts on the balance sheet. At the third stage, the time of sale, these inventory amounts become cost of goods sold expense on the income statement.

Harley-Davidson's recent inventory footnote reports the following:

Direct labor refers to the earnings of employees who work directly on the products being manufactured.
Factory overhead costs are manufacturing costs that are not raw material or direct labor costs.

REAL WORLD EXCERPT
HARLEY-DAVIDSON, INC.
Annual Report

HARLEY-DAVIDSON, INC. NOTES TO CONSOLIDATED FINANCIAL STATEMENTS	
2. ADDITIONAL CASH FLOW AND BALANCE SHEET INFORMATION (In thousands)	
Raw materials and work in process	$32,284
Finished goods	19,290
Parts and accessories	52,182*

*These do not add up to the balance reported in Exhibit 7.1 because they do not include the LIFO adjustment discussed later.

Harley-Davidson combines the raw materials and work in process. Other companies separate these two components. The parts and accessories category includes purchased parts and Motorclothes™ and other accessories that make up merchandise inventory.

Modern Manufacturing Techniques and Inventory Costs

The flows of inventory costs diagrammed in Exhibit 7.3 represent the keys to manufacturing cost and quality control. Since the company must pay to finance and store raw materials and purchased parts, minimizing these inventories in keeping with projected manufacturing demand is the first key to the process. This requires that Harley-Davidson work closely with its suppliers in design, production, and delivery of manufactured parts and in planning raw materials deliveries; the related techniques often are called *just-in-time inventory*. Review and redesign of manufacturing operations and worker training and involvement programs are the keys to minimizing direct labor and factory overhead costs. New product designs often attempt to reduce manufacturing complexity, which leads to higher product quality and reduced scrap and rework costs. For example, at its Sportster assembly line in York, Pennsylvania, three-person teams are responsible for assembly of a complete vehicle, a process that has resulted in both cost and quality improvements.

Harley-Davidson's management accounting system is designed to monitor the success of these changes and provide information to allow continuous improvements in these manufacturing efforts. Issues faced in the design of such systems are the subject matter of management accounting and cost accounting courses.

Nature of Cost of Goods Sold

Cost of goods sold (CGS) is a major expense item for most nonservice businesses and is directly related to sales revenue. The amount of sales revenue during an accounting period is the number of units sold multiplied by the sales price. Cost of goods sold is the same number of units multiplied by their unit costs; it includes the cost of all merchandise and finished goods sold during the period. The measurement of cost of goods sold is an excellent example of the application of the matching principle.

The flow of inventory costs from merchandise inventory to cost of goods sold for the merchandiser and from finished goods inventory to cost of goods sold for the manufacturer involves similar processes. We focus on merchandise inventory to simplify the discussion.

Harley-Davidson starts each accounting period with a stock of inventory on hand called (BI) for sale to dealers. The merchandise and finished goods on hand at the end of an accounting period are called *ending inventory* (EI). The ending inventory for one accounting period automatically becomes the beginning inventory for the next period.

During the accounting period, the beginning inventory is increased by the purchase of more merchandise. The sum of the beginning inventory and the *purchases* of merchandise during the period (P) represents the **goods available for sale** during that period. The portion of goods available for sale that is sold becomes cost of goods sold on the income statement. Typically, not all of the goods available for sale are sold, so what remains becomes ending inventory on the balance sheet for the period. These relationships are represented visually in Exhibit 7.4

From these relationships, we can compute cost of goods sold as follows:

Goods available for sale refers to the sum of beginning inventory and purchases (or transfers to finished goods) for the period.

EXHIBIT 7.4
Nature of Cost of Goods Sold for Merchandise Inventory

*Last period's ending inventory.

Beginning inventory	+	Purchases of the period	−	Ending inventory	=	Cost of goods sold
Goods available for sale				*Goods left over*		*Goods sold*

Later in the chapter, this **cost of goods sold equation** serves as a basic tool for analyzing the effects of inventory errors and different accounting methods on the financial statements. To illustrate the relationships represented by the equation for merchandise inventory, assume that for the Motorclothes™ line, Harley-Davidson reported cost of goods sold of $60,000, which was computed as follows:

Cost of goods sold equation:

$$BI + P - EI = CGS$$

Beginning inventory (January 1, 19F)	$40,000
Add: Purchases of merchandise during 19F	+ 55,000
Goods available for sale	$95,000
Deduct: Ending inventory (December 31, 19F)	− 35,000
Cost of goods sold	$60,000

These same relationships can be represented in the merchandise inventory T-account as follows:

Merchandise Inventory (A)			
Beginning inventory	$40,000		
Add: Purchases	55,000	Deduct: Cost of goods sold	60,000
Ending inventory	$35,000		

The process works similarly for finished goods inventory.

Gross Profit Comparisons

Financial ANALYSIS

Analysts often calculate an amount called *gross profit* or *gross margin on sales,* which is the difference between net sales and cost of goods sold. This amount is reported on the multiple-step format of the income statement (see Exhibit 7.1). Gross profit reflects the total amount of markup on all goods sold during the period. It can be expressed as a dollar amount or as a ratio called the *gross profit percentage.* The gross profit percentage is calculated as gross profit ÷ net sales. Harley-Davidson's gross profit for the current year was $411,399,000; its ratio was 30.5 percent ($411,399,000 ÷ $1,350,466,000).

Analysts use the gross margin percentage to compare similar companies and to compare the operations of the same company over time. Using similar companies for comparison is important because companies in different industries often have highly different gross margins. For example, until mid-1995, Harley-Davidson produced both motorcycles and motorhomes. Although they are related industries, in a recent year the gross profit percentage was 30.4 percent on motorcycle sales but only 16.4 percent on motorhome sales. In part because of the low margins, Harley-Davidson sold the motorhome division in 1995, which accounts for the current overall gross profit percentage of 30.5 percent. The importance of gross profit percentage to analysts is indicated by the fact that Harley's stock price rose from 26⅞ to 31½ the morning of the sale.

If Harley-Davidson's gross profit percentage changed or a major competitor reported a much different gross profit percentage, analysts would attempt to determine the cause of the difference. For example, Harley-Davidson recently opened new production facilities that will increase production volume and decrease costs in the future. Start-up costs at these new facilities reduced the gross profit percentage on motorcycles in the short run, however. This suggests that even a short-term decline in gross profit percentage is not always bad news. This example illustrates how analysts can use accounting information to gain additional insight into the operations and competitiveness of a company.

Errors in Measuring Ending Inventory

LEARNING OBJECTIVE 2

Measure the effects of inventory errors on financial statements.

As the cost of goods sold equation indicates, a direct relationship exists between ending inventory and cost of goods sold because items not in the ending inventory are assumed to have been sold. Thus, the measurement of ending inventory affects both the balance sheet (assets) and the income statement (cost of goods sold, gross profit, and net income). The measurement of ending inventory affects not only the net income for that period but also the net income for the *next accounting period*. This two-period effect occurs because the ending inventory for one period is the beginning inventory for the next accounting period.

The Wall Street Journal recently reported that greeting card maker Gibson Greetings had overstated its current year profits by 20 percent because one division had overstated ending inventory for the year.[2] You can compute the effects of the error on both the current year's and next year's pretax profits using the cost of goods sold equation. Assume that ending inventory is overstated by $10,000 due to a clerical error that is not discovered the next year. It would have the following effects:

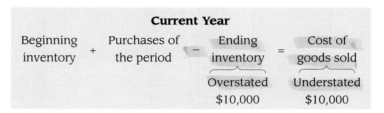

Current Year

$$\underset{\text{inventory}}{\text{Beginning}} + \underset{\text{the period}}{\text{Purchases of}} - \underset{\substack{\text{inventory} \\ \underbrace{}_{} \\ \text{Overstated} \\ \$10,000}}{\text{Ending}} = \underset{\substack{\text{goods sold} \\ \underbrace{}_{} \\ \text{Understated} \\ \$10,000}}{\text{Cost of}}$$

Thus, income before taxes would be *overstated* by $10,000 in the *current year*. Since the current year's ending inventory becomes the next year's beginning inventory, it would have the following effects next year:

Next Year

$$\underset{\substack{\text{inventory} \\ \underbrace{}_{} \\ \text{Overstated} \\ \$10,000}}{\text{Beginning}} + \underset{\text{the period}}{\text{Purchases of}} - \underset{\text{inventory}}{\text{Ending}} = \underset{\substack{\text{goods sold} \\ \underbrace{}_{} \\ \text{Overstated} \\ \$10,000}}{\text{Cost of}}$$

Income before taxes would be *understated* by the same amount in the *next year*. Each of these errors would flow into retained earnings so that at the end of the current year, retained earnings would be overstated by $10,000 (less the related income tax expense). This error would be offset in the next year, and retained earnings and inventory at the end of next year would be correct.

In this example, we assumed that the overstatement of ending inventory was inadvertent, the result of a clerical error. As we noted in Chapter 6, however, inventory fraud is one of the two most common forms of financial statement fraud. It occurred in the Maxidrive case discussed in Chapter 1 as well as in the real MiniScribe fraud. The problem is sufficiently severe that *The Wall Street Journal* recently reported the following:

---

[2] *The Wall Street Journal*, July 5, 1994, p. A4.

REAL WORLD EXCERPT
The Wall Street Journal

CONVENIENT FICTION

Inventory Chicanery Tempts More Firms, Fools More Auditors

A Quick Way to Pad Profits, It Is Often Revealed Only When Concern Collapses

* * * * *

When companies are desperate to stay afloat, inventory fraud is the easiest way to produce instant profits and dress up the balance sheet. . . .

Even auditors at the top accounting firms are often fooled.

SOURCE: *The Wall Street Journal,* December 14, 1992, p. A1.

SELF-STUDY QUIZ

Assume the following facts for Harley-Davidson's Motorclothes™ leather baseball jacket product line for the year 19F:

> Beginning inventory 500 units at unit cost of $75.
> Ending inventory 600 units at unit cost of $75.
> Sales 1,100 units at a sales price of $100 (cost per unit $75).

1. Using the cost of goods sold equation, compute the dollar amount of purchases of leather baseball jackets for the period.

Beginning inventory	+	Purchases of the period	−	Ending inventory	=	Cost of goods sold

2. Prepare the first three lines of a multiple-step income statement (showing gross profit) for the leather baseball jacket line for the year 19F.

After you have completed your answers, check them with the solutions presented in the footnote at the bottom of this page.*

Inventory Costing Methods

In the Motorclothes™ example presented in the self-study quiz, the cost of all units of the leather baseball jackets was the same—$75. If inventory costs normally do not change, this would be the end of our discussion of inventory costs. We are all aware, however, that the prices of most goods often change. The costs of many manufactured items such as automobiles and motorcycles have risen in recent years, but only at a

LEARNING OBJECTIVE 3
Use the four inventory costing methods to determine the appropriate amounts to report as inventory and cost of goods sold.

---

* 1.   BI   + P − EI   = CGS
       37,500 + P − 45,000 = 82,500
                      P   = 90,000

  2. Net sales $110,000
      Cost of goods sold   82,500
      Gross profit $ 27,500

moderate rate. In other industries, such as computers, however, costs of production (and retail prices) have dropped dramatically.

When inventory costs have changed, the determination of which inventory items to treat as sold and which as still remaining in ending inventory can turn profits into losses (and vice versa) and cause companies to pay or save hundreds of millions of dollars in taxes. Before we examine these complexities, we will use a simple example to discuss the mechanics of each accepted method for determining which goods to treat as sold. We will then look at which methods Harley-Davidson and other companies use and discuss the bases for their choices. Do not let the simplicity of our example mislead you. As you will see, the results of this example generalize broadly to actual company practices. The example is based on the following data.

New Company began operations on January 1, 19A. The following events took place during 19A:

Jan.	15	Purchased 1 unit of product A at $1
April	2	Purchased 1 unit of product A at $3
June	27	Purchased 1 unit of product A at $5
Nov.	5	Sold 2 units for $7 each.

Note that inventory costs are rising rapidly! On November 5, two units are sold for $7 each; revenues of $14 are recorded. What amount is recorded as cost of goods sold? The answer depends on which specific goods are assumed sold. Four generally accepted inventory costing methods are available for doing so:

1. First-in, first-out (FIFO).
2. Last-in, first-out (LIFO).
3. Weighted average.
4. Specific identification.

The four inventory costing methods are *alternative allocation methods* for assigning the total dollar amount of goods available for sale (beginning inventory and purchases) between (1) ending inventory (reported as an asset at the end of the period) and (2) cost of goods sold (reported as an expense of the period). It is important to note at this point that the choice among the four inventory costing methods is *not based on the physical flow* of goods on and off the shelves. For example, the actual physical flow of goods at a supermarket is first-in, first-out (FIFO). A supermarket can use LIFO or any of the inventory costing methods, however, to report cost of goods sold and inventory in its financial statements. Generally accepted accounting principles (GAAP) require only that the inventory costing method used be rational and systematic. Since the inventory costing methods need not follow the actual physical flow of inventory, they are often called *cost flow assumptions.*

A useful visual learning tool for representing inventory cost flows is a bin, or container. The different inventory costing methods then can be visualized as flows of inventory in and out of the various bins. We use this concept to illustrate inventory flow throughout the following sections.

First-In, First-Out Inventory Costing Method

The first-in, first-out method (FIFO) assumes that the oldest units (the first costs in) are the first units sold.

The **first-in, first-out method,** frequently called **FIFO,** assumes that the oldest units (the first costs in) are the first units sold (the first costs out) and the newest units are left in ending inventory. Under FIFO, cost of goods sold and ending inventory are computed as if the flows in and out of the FIFO inventory bin in Exhibit 7.5 had taken place. First, each purchase is treated as if it were deposited in the bin from the top in sequence (one unit each at $1, $3, and $5). Each good sold is then removed from the *bottom* in sequence (one unit at $1 and one at $3); *first in is first out*. These goods totaling $4 become cost of goods sold (CGS). The remaining unit ($5) becomes ending inventory. These financial statement effects are summarized in Exhibit 7.5. If any goods were in beginning inventory, they would be treated as if they were sold first. Then the units from the first purchase are sold next, and so on until the units left in the ending inventory all come from the most recent purchases. FIFO allocates the *oldest* unit costs to *cost of goods sold* and the *most recent* unit costs to the *ending inventory*.

Last-In, First-Out Inventory Costing Method

The **last-in, first-out method,** often called **LIFO,** assumes that the most recently acquired goods are sold first and the oldest units are left in ending inventory. This method can be visualized as involving a LIFO inventory bin such as that presented in Exhibit 7.5. As in the case of the FIFO bin, each purchase is treated as if it were deposited in the bin from the top in sequence ($1, $3, $5). Unlike the FIFO case, however, each good sold is then removed from the top in sequence ($5, $3). These goods totaling $8 become cost of goods sold (CGS). The remaining unit ($1) becomes ending inventory.

The **last-in, first-out method (LIFO)** assumes that the most recently acquired units are sold first.

EXHIBIT 7.5
FIFO and LIFO Inventory Flows—New Company, Year 1

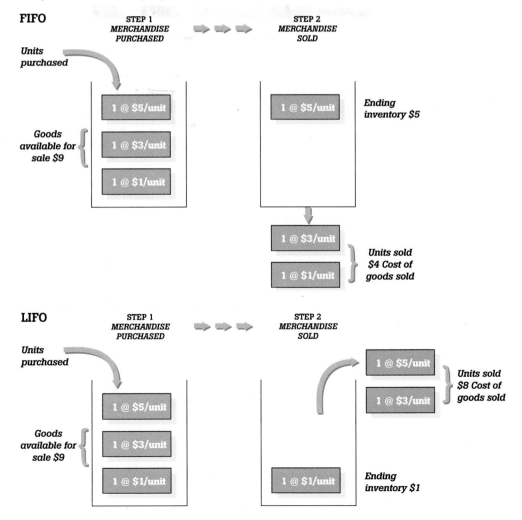

Harley-Davidson uses LIFO; are these goods really the most recently produced?

If any goods were in beginning inventory, they would be treated as if they were sold last. The units from the last purchase are always sold first, and so on until the units left in the ending inventory all come from the oldest purchases. Therefore, the unit costs of the beginning inventory and the earlier purchases remain in the ending inventory. LIFO allocates the *most recent* unit costs to *cost of goods sold* and the *oldest* unit costs to the *ending inventory*. The LIFO flow assumption is the exact opposite of the FIFO flow assumption. These relationships are summarized here:

	FIFO	LIFO
Cost of goods sold on income statement	Oldest unit costs	Most recent unit costs
Inventory on balance sheet	Most recent unit costs	Oldest unit costs

Weighted Average Inventory Costing Method

The **weighted average method** uses the weighted average unit cost of the goods available for sale for both cost of goods sold and ending inventory.

The **weighted average method** requires computation of the weighted average unit cost of the goods available for sale.[3] The computed unit cost is multiplied by the number of units in inventory to derive the total cost of ending inventory. Cost of goods sold is determined by subtracting the ending inventory amount from the amount of goods available for sale. For the New Company data, the weighted average cost is computed as follows:

Number of units	×	Unit cost	=	Total cost
1		$1		$1
1		$3		3
1		$5		5
3				$9

$$\text{Average cost} = \frac{\text{Cost of goods available for sale}}{\text{Number of units available for sale}}$$

$$\text{Average cost} = \frac{\$9}{3 \text{ units}} = \$3 \text{ per unit}$$

In these circumstances, cost of goods sold and ending inventory are assigned the same weighted average cost per unit of $3. Cost of goods sold is $6 for two units sold, and

---

[3] A weighted average unit cost rather than a simple average of the unit costs must be used. In most cases a simple average is incorrect because it does not consider the number of units at each unit cost. For example, if one unit were purchased at $1, one unit at $3, and two units at $5, the average cost is $3.50 ([$1 + $3 + $5 + $5] ÷ 4 units).

ending inventory is $3 for one unit. These financial statement effects are summarized in Exhibit 7.6.

Specific Identification Inventory Costing Method

When the **specific identification method** is used, the cost of each item sold is individually identified and recorded as cost of goods sold. This method requires keeping track of the purchase cost of each item. This is done by either (1) coding the purchase cost on each unit before placing it in stock or (2) keeping a separate record of the unit and identifying it with a serial number. In the New Company example, any two of the three items could have been sold, and the cost of those two items would become cost of goods sold. The cost of the remaining item would be ending inventory.

The **specific identification method** identifies the cost of the specific item that was sold.

Given the way in which some inventory accounting systems are organized (discussed later in this chapter), the specific identification method is impractical when large numbers of different items are stocked. On the other hand, when dealing with expensive items such as automobiles or fine jewelry, this method is appropriate because each item tends to differ from the other items. The method may be manipulated when the units are *identical* because one can affect the cost of goods sold and the ending inventory accounts by picking and choosing from among the several available unit costs, even though the goods are identical in other respects.

Different Methods for Different Types of Inventory

International
PERSPECTIVE

Asahi Chemical Industry Co., Ltd., is a major Japanese manufacturer of chemicals, plastics, fibers and textiles, and housing and construction materials. Most of its inventories are accounted for using average cost, which is very common in Japan. In addition, its housing and construction materials division constructs and sells homes. It accounts for both residential lots and dwellings under construction, which are expensive, distinguishable items, by using specific identification.

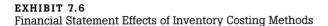

EXHIBIT 7.6
Financial Statement Effects of Inventory Costing Methods

	FIFO	LIFO	Weighted Average
COST OF GOODS SOLD CALCULATION			
Beginning inventory	$ 0	$ 0	$ 0
Add: Purchases	9	9	9
Goods available for sale	9	9	9
Deduct: Ending inventory (to balance sheet)	5	1	3
Cost of goods sold (to income statement)	$ 4	$ 8	$ 6
EFFECT ON THE INCOME STATEMENT			
Sales	$14	$14	$14
Cost of goods sold	4	8	6
Gross profit	$10	$ 6	$ 8
EFFECT ON THE BALANCE SHEET			
Inventory	$ 5	$ 1	$ 3

Comparison of the Inventory Costing Methods

Each of the four alternative inventory costing methods is in conformity with GAAP and the tax law. Each method may produce significantly different income and asset (ending inventory) amounts, however. To illustrate this difference, the comparative results for New Company using FIFO, LIFO, and weighted average are presented in Exhibit 7.6. Notice that the difference in the *gross margin* among each of the methods is the same as the difference in the *ending inventory* amounts. The method that gives the highest ending inventory amount also gives the highest gross margin and income amounts and vice versa. The weighted average cost method gives income and inventory amounts that are between the FIFO and LIFO extremes.

Note that in the comparison in Exhibit 7.6, unit costs were increasing. When unit costs are *rising, LIFO* produces *lower income* and a *lower inventory valuation* than FIFO. Even though we may be experiencing general inflation, some companies' costs decline. When unit costs are *declining, LIFO* produces *higher income* and *higher inventory* valuation than FIFO. These effects, *which hold as long as inventory quantities are constant or rising,*[4] are summarized in the following table:

NORMAL FINANCIAL STATEMENT EFFECTS OF RISING COSTS

	FIFO	LIFO
Cost of goods sold on income statement	Lower	Higher
Net income	Higher	Lower
Inventory on balance sheet	Higher	Lower

NORMAL FINANCIAL STATEMENT EFFECTS OF DECLINING COSTS

	FIFO	LIFO
Cost of goods sold on income statement	Higher	Lower
Net income	Lower	Higher
Inventory on balance sheet	Lower	Higher

These effects occur because LIFO causes the new unit costs to be reflected in cost of goods sold on the income statement, which is a realistic measurement of the current cost of items that were sold; FIFO causes the older unit costs to be reflected in cost of goods sold on the income statement. In contrast, on the balance sheet, the ending inventory amount under LIFO is based on the oldest unit costs, which may be an unrealistic valuation, whereas FIFO ending inventory is a realistic measurement of their current cost.

Which allocation method should be used in which circumstances? Our current system allows selection among the alternative methods for financial statements and a second selection for tax purposes. As we discuss later, a particular company's choice depends on management's incentives, the tax law, and the reporting company's particular economic circumstances. Because of the potential effects on reported performance and tax payments, an understanding of these choices is important to all managers and financial statement users.

Again, it is important to remember that regardless of the physical flow of goods, a company can use any of the inventory costing methods. Furthermore, a company is not required to use the same inventory costing method for all inventory items, and no particular justification is needed for the selection of one or more of the acceptable methods. Harley-Davidson, Asahi Chemical (discussed earlier), and most large companies use different inventory methods for different inventory items.

To enhance comparability, accounting rules require companies to apply their accounting methods on a consistent basis. A company is not permitted to use LIFO one period, FIFO the next, and then go back to LIFO. A change in method is allowed only if

---

[4] The impact of a decline in inventory quantity on LIFO amounts is discussed in Supplement A to this chapter.

the change will improve the measurement of financial results and financial position. Changing from one inventory costing method to another is a significant event. Such a change requires full disclosure about the reason for the change and the accounting effects.

Alternative Inventory Costing Methods in Practice

Choosing Inventory Costing Methods

Accounting Trends and Techniques reported that although 347 (58 percent) of the 600 companies surveyed reported using LIFO for some portion of inventories, only 14 (2 percent) use LIFO for all inventories.[5] This raises an important question: What motivates companies to choose different inventory costing methods? Our discussion in Chapter 5 suggests that management should choose the method allowed by GAAP that most closely reflects its economic circumstances for its external financial statements (book purposes). Management must also make a second choice of accounting method to use on its tax return (tax purposes). The choice from among the acceptable methods for use on the company's tax return should be the one that allows payment of the least amount of taxes as late as possible—the "least-latest rule."

LEARNING OBJECTIVE 4
Decide when the use of different inventory costing methods is beneficial to a company.

A business typically may use one set of accounting procedures for external financial statements and a different set of procedures for preparing its tax return. The choice of inventory costing methods is a special case, however, because of what is called the *LIFO conformity rule*. If LIFO is used on the income tax return, it must also be used to calculate inventory and cost of goods sold for the financial statements.[6] Since LIFO often minimizes taxes, the LIFO conformity rule leads many companies to adopt LIFO for *both* tax and financial reporting purposes. For most companies facing rising costs of inventory, LIFO is used for U.S. inventories. For inventory located in countries that do not allow LIFO for tax purposes or that do not have a LIFO conformity rule, FIFO or weighted average is mostly used. Similarly, when costs are falling, FIFO or weighted average is most often used. Since most companies in the same industry face similar cost structures, clusters of companies in the same industries often choose the same accounting method.

LIFO and International Comparisons

The methods of accounting for inventories discussed in this chapter are used in most major industrialized countries. In several countries, however, the LIFO method is not generally used. In England, for example, LIFO is not acceptable for tax purposes, nor is it widely used in financial reporting. LIFO is also not used in Australia and Hong Kong but may be used in Singapore only if the difference between LIFO and FIFO is reported. These differences can create comparability problems when one attempts to compare companies across international borders. For example, General Motors, Chrysler, and Ford use LIFO to value U.S. inventories and Honda (of Japan) and Daimler-Benz (maker of Mercedes-Benz of Germany) use FIFO.

---

[5] *Accounting Trends & Techniques* (New York: AICPA, 1996).
[6] Note that LIFO can be used for financial statement purposes along with FIFO or weighted average for tax purposes. However, this is rarely done.

The income tax effects associated with LIFO and FIFO for companies facing rising costs can be illustrated by continuing our simple New Company example. Using the data from Exhibit 7.6 and assuming that expenses other than cost of goods sold were $2 and the tax rate was 25 percent, the following differences in taxes result.

Inventory Costing Method

	FIFO	LIFO
Sales revenue	$14	$14
Cost of goods sold	4	8
Gross margin	$10	$ 6
Other expenses	2	2
Pretax income	$ 8	$ 4
Income tax expense (.25 × Pretax income)	2	1
Net income	$ 6	$ 3

In this situation, cost of goods sold and pretax income differed by $4, which was caused by the differences between the FIFO and LIFO methods. Costs were rising, and a significant difference existed between the old and new unit costs. When multiplied by the 25 percent income tax rate, the $4 difference in pretax income generates cash tax savings of $1. It is important to remember that this choice is independent of the actual physical flow of goods. This example illustrates the primary motivations for the choice of LIFO. In an inflationary world, most companies face cost increases. In the United States, the tax benefit in such circumstances plus the LIFO conformity rule explain the widespread use of the method.

This simple example illustrates the computations necessary to determine the tax savings but may not indicate the magnitude of the effect often faced in practice. Harley-Davidson is a fairly typical "mixed" LIFO company. The $84 million in inventory reported in Exhibit 7.1 included U.S. motorcycle inventories of $68 million at LIFO. As we will compute in the next section, Harley saved $719,000 in taxes in 1995 alone. It has saved a total of approximately $9 million in taxes from the date it adopted the LIFO method through 1995. This is a significant benefit to Harley. It does not use LIFO for its non–U.S. motorcycle inventory either because LIFO is not acceptable for tax purposes or no LIFO conformity rule exists in those countries.

LIFO and Conflicts between Managers' and Owners' Interests

As discussed earlier in this chapter, the selection of an inventory method can have significant effects on financial statements. Company managers may have incentives to select a particular method that may not be consistent with the objectives of the owners. For example, the use of LIFO during a period of rising prices may be in the best interests of the owners because LIFO often reduces the company's tax liability. On the other hand, managers may prefer FIFO because it typically results in higher profits, and the compensation of most managers is affected by reported profits.

A well-designed compensation plan should reward managers for acting in the best interests of the owners, but unfortunately this is not always the case. Clearly, a manager who selects an accounting method that is not optimal for the company, solely to increase his or her compensation, has engaged in questionable ethical behavior.

In theory, LIFO cannot provide permanent tax savings because (1) when inventory levels drop or (2) costs drop, the income effect reverses and the income taxes deferred must be paid. The economic advantage of deferring income taxes in such situations is due to the fact that interest can be earned on the money that otherwise would be paid as taxes for the current year. Much of this amount is postponed for a very long period, however, and some is never paid because of accumulated losses preceding the end of the company's life.

Alternatively, many high-technology companies are facing declining costs. In such circumstances, the FIFO method, in which the oldest, most expensive goods become cost of goods sold, produces the largest cost of goods sold, the lowest gross profit, and thus the lowest income tax liability. For example, Apple Computer, Compaq Computer, and Microsoft all account for inventories at FIFO.

Alternative Inventory Costing Methods and Financial Statement Analysis

Critics of GAAP charge that the existence of alternative accounting methods is inconsistent with the *comparability* characteristic of useful information. This quality is needed so that analysts can compare information for a company with that of other companies for the same time period. These types of comparisons are more difficult if companies use different accounting methods, since one company's statements must be converted to a comparable basis *before* meaningful comparisons can be made. However, careful readers of this text will be able to make many of the necessary adjustments.

Converting cost of goods sold and income before taxes from one inventory costing method to another is eased by the requirement that public companies using LIFO also report beginning and ending inventory on a FIFO, average cost, or related method basis in the notes if the LIFO and FIFO values are materially different. We can use this information along with the cost of goods sold equation to convert cost of goods sold and income before taxes to the FIFO basis. This process is similar to the manner in which we corrected errors in inventory earlier in this chapter. Recall the cost of goods sold equation:

$$\text{Beginning inventory} + \text{Purchases of the period} - \text{Ending inventory} = \text{Cost of goods sold}$$

Recall also that the choice of a cost flow assumption affects how goods available for sale are allocated to ending inventory and cost of goods sold. It does not affect the recording of purchases. Since last year's ending inventory is this year's beginning inventory, beginning inventory is also affected by the choice of a cost flow assumption. As a consequence, we can compute the effects of the *difference* in cost flow assumptions on cost of goods sold in the following manner:

$$\text{Difference in beginning inventory} - \text{Difference in ending inventory} = \text{Difference in cost of goods sold}$$

| Difference in beginning inventory (LIFO to FIFO) |
| Less: Difference in ending inventory (LIFO to FIFO) |
| Difference in cost of goods sold (LIFO to FIFO) |

Harley-Davidson provides a typical disclosure of the differences between LIFO and FIFO values for beginning and ending inventory. The difference between its inventory valued using FIFO and LIFO is labeled "Excess of FIFO over LIFO inventory" and is often referred to as the **LIFO Reserve**. As a consequence, the preceding computation can be thought of as

LEARNING OBJECTIVE 5
Analyze financial statements prepared using different inventory costing methods.

LIFO Reserve is a contra-asset for the excess of FIFO over LIFO inventory.

Beginning LIFO Reserve	
Less: Ending LIFO Reserve	
Difference in cost of goods sold (LIFO to FIFO)	

Companies that use a LIFO reserve keep their inventory account during the accounting period using FIFO (or possibly average cost). At the end of the year, they convert the balances in inventory and cost of goods sold to LIFO through an adjusting entry to the LIFO Reserve, which is a contra-asset to the Inventory account. The approach taken is very similar to that used when adjusting the Allowance for Doubtful Accounts employing the aging method (discussed in Chapter 6).

REAL WORLD EXCERPT

HARLEY-DAVIDSON, INC.
Annual Report

HARLEY-DAVIDSON, INC.
NOTES TO CONSOLIDATED FINANCIAL STATEMENTS
2. ADDITIONAL CASH FLOW AND BALANCE SHEET INFORMATION
(In thousands)

Inventories:	1995	1994	
Components at . . . FIFO	$103,756	$107,266	Inventory at FIFO
Excess of FIFO over LIFO inventories	19,329	17,386	LIFO Reserve
	$ 84,427	$ 89,880	Inventory at LIFO on Balance Sheet

The LIFO Reserve provides the needed information for the conversion. Using our formula, we can compute the difference in cost of goods sold for the current year when we convert from LIFO to FIFO (a *decrease* of $1,943).

Beginning LIFO Reserve	$17,386
Less: Ending LIFO Reserve	19,329
Difference in cost of goods sold (LIFO to FIFO)	($ 1,943)

Since cost of goods sold decreases pretax income, the conversion's effect on pretax income is the opposite—an *increase* of $1,943. To compute the tax savings (postponement) from using LIFO instead of FIFO for the current year, multiply this increase by Harley's 37 percent total income tax rate, which yields approximately $719.

Difference in pretax income (LIFO to FIFO)	$1,943
Tax rate	× .37
Difference in taxes (LIFO to FIFO)	$ 719

It is important to note that, even for companies facing rising costs, LIFO does not lead to a reduction in pretax income and taxes in every year. When ending inventory quantities are lower than beginning inventory quantities (that is, the company sells more than it buys or produces), LIFO actually boosts pretax income and taxes. This situation, called a *LIFO liquidation*, is discussed in more detail in Chapter Supplement A.

Because no inventory costing method can be considered best, the accounting profession has been unwilling to require all companies to follow a single method. As a result, users of financial statements must be knowledgeable about alternative accounting methods and how they affect statements. Users must be certain that their decisions are based on real differences, not artificial differences created by alternative accounting methods. Remember that the choice of inventory costing method does not affect the physical attributes or economic value of the inventory.

LIFO and Financial Statement Analysis

Analysts often use the inventory turnover ratio to measure the liquidity (nearness to cash) of the inventory. The computation is as follows:

$$\text{Inventory turnover} = \frac{\text{Cost of goods sold}}{\text{Average inventory [(Beginning + Ending)} \div 2]}$$

It reflects the relationship of the inventory to the volume of goods sold during the period. Higher inventory turnover indicates that inventory is turned into cash more quickly. It is also considered to be a measure of the efficiency of using inventory because it relates the cost of goods sold to the average amount of inventory kept on hand to generate those sales (higher ratio means greater efficiency). However, for many LIFO companies this measure can be deceptive. Consider Deere & Co., manufacturer of John Deere farm, lawn, and construction equipment. Its inventory footnote lists the following values:

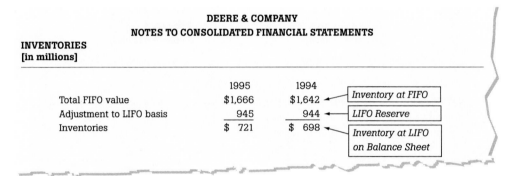

REAL WORLD EXCERPT

DEERE & COMPANY
Annual Report

DEERE & COMPANY
NOTES TO CONSOLIDATED FINANCIAL STATEMENTS

INVENTORIES
[in millions]

	1995	1994	
Total FIFO value	$1,666	$1,642	Inventory at FIFO
Adjustment to LIFO basis	945	944	LIFO Reserve
Inventories	$ 721	$ 698	Inventory at LIFO on Balance Sheet

John Deere's cost of goods sold for 1995 was $6,922.1 million. If the ratio were computed using the reported LIFO inventory values for the ratio, it would be

$$\text{Inventory turnover} = \frac{\$6,922.1}{(\$721 + \$698) \div 2} = 9.8$$

Converting cost of goods sold in the numerator to a FIFO basis and using the more current FIFO inventory values in the denominator, it would be:

$$\text{Inventory turnover} = \frac{\$6,922.1 - 1}{(\$1,666 + \$1,642) \div 2} = 4.2$$

Note that the major difference is in the denominator; FIFO inventory values are nearly 2½ times the LIFO values; the ratio is about 2/5 the amount. The LIFO beginning and ending inventory numbers are artificially small because they reflect old lower costs. Thus, the numerator in the first calculation does not relate in a meaningful way to the denominator.[7]

---

[7] Since the LIFO values for cost of goods sold on the income statement and the FIFO inventory numbers on the balance sheet are closer to current prices, they are often thought to be the most appropriate numerator and denominator, respectively, for use in this ratio.

Caterpillar Inc.

SELF-STUDY QUIZ

1. Caterpillar Inc., a major competitor of John Deere, reported pretax earnings of $1,615 million in 1995. Its inventory footnote indicated that "if the FIFO (first-in, first-out) method had been in use, inventories would have been $2,103, $2,035, and $1,818 higher than reported at December 31, 1995, 1994, and 1993, respectively." (The amounts noted are for the LIFO Reserve.) Convert pretax earnings for 1995 from a LIFO to a FIFO basis.

Beginning LIFO Reserve   _____
Less: Ending LIFO Reserve   _____
Difference in cost of goods sold (LIFO to FIFO)   _____

Pretax income (LIFO)   _____
Difference in pretax income (LIFO to FIFO)   _____
Pretax income (FIFO)   _____

2. Assume that OLD Company has employed the LIFO method for the past 20 years. Its beginning inventory and purchases for 19B included:

Beginning inventory	10 units @ $ 6 each
Purchases January	5 units @ $10 each
Purchases November	5 units @ $12 each

During 19B, 15 units were sold for $20 each; other operating expenses totaled $100.

    a. Compute cost of goods sold and pretax income for 19B.
    b. Assume that OLD Company was able to purchase an additional 5 units at $12 each on December 31. Compute cost of goods sold and pretax income for 19B.
    c. Explain how LIFO causes this difference in your answers to parts (a) and (b).

_____
_____
_____
_____
_____

After you have completed your answers, check them with the solutions presented in the footnote at the bottom of this page.*

Valuation at Lower of Cost or Market

LEARNING OBJECTIVE 6
Apply the lower-of-cost-or-market (LCM) rule.

Inventories should be measured at their purchase cost in conformity with the cost principle. When the goods remaining in ending inventory can be replaced with identical goods at a lower cost, however, the lower cost should be used as the inventory valuation. Damaged, obsolete, and deteriorated items in inventory should be assigned a unit cost that represents their current estimated net realizable value if that is below cost. This rule is known as measuring inventories at the **lower of cost or market (LCM)**.

Lower of cost or market (LCM) is a valuation method departing from the cost principle; it serves to recognize a loss when replacement cost or net realizable value drops below cost.

* 1.
Beginning LIFO Reserve	$2,035	Pretax income (LIFO) $1,615
Less: Ending LIFO Reserve	2,103	Difference in pretax income 68
Difference in cost of goods sold	($ 68)	Pretax income (FIFO) $1,683

2. *a.*   BI + P − EI = CGS   Sales − CGS − Operating exp. = Pretax income
     $60 + $110 − $30 = $140 $300 − $140 − $100 = $60

   b. $60 + $170 − $60 = $170 $300 − $170 − $100 = $30

   c.   Under LIFO, inventory most recently purchased is assumed sold. In part (*a*), lower-cost units from beginning inventory were assumed sold. In part (*b*), purchases were sufficient such that no items from beginning inventory were sold.

It is a departure from the cost principle because of the conservatism constraint (see Chapter 5) that requires special care to avoid overstating assets and income. It is particularly important for two types of companies: (1) high-technology companies such as Compaq Computer and Apple Computer that manufacture goods for which the cost of production and the selling price are declining and (2) companies such as The GAP or The Limited that sell seasonal goods such as clothing, the value of which drops dramatically at the end of each selling season (fall or spring).

For companies such as Compaq Computer, under LCM, a "holding" loss is recognized in the period in which the **replacement cost** of an item dropped rather than in the period in which the item is sold. The holding loss is the difference between purchase cost and the subsequent lower replacement cost and is added to the cost of goods sold of the period. To illustrate, assume that Compaq Computer has 1,000 Pentium microprocessor chips in the 19B ending inventory. It bought the chips for $250 each. At the end of the year, it can purchase the same chips for $200. The 1,000 chips should be recorded in the ending inventory at the lower of cost ($250) or current market ($200). Under LCM, the ending inventory should be reduced to $200 per unit. Compaq makes the following journal entry to record the write-down:

Replacement cost is the current purchase price for identical goods.

Cost of Goods Sold (E)	50,000	
Inventory* (A)		50,000

*Some companies credit a contra-asset to inventory called a *reserve,* which is adjusted at the end of each accounting period.

Several effects are caused by using a replacement cost of $200 instead of the original purchase cost of $250. By recording the chips in ending inventory at $50 per unit below their purchase cost, 19B pretax income will be $50,000 less (1,000 × $50) than had they been recorded in the inventory at $250 per unit. This $50,000 loss in the value of the inventory (the holding loss) is due to a decline in the replacement cost. Pretax income is reduced by $50,000 in the period in which the replacement cost dropped (19B) rather than in the next period (19C) when the chips will be used in the production of computers and sold. As a consequence, LCM transfers the added expense from the period of sale (19C) back to the current period (19B). Since the cost of goods sold for period 19B *increases* by $50,000 and the cost of goods sold for 19C *decreases* by $50,000, the total cost of goods sold expense (and net income before taxes) for the two periods (19B and 19C) combined does not change. On the balance sheet, the $50,000 loss in 19B reduces the amount of inventory that is reported on December 31, 19B.

In contrast, if the replacement cost had increased to $300 each, the company would have experienced an economic holding gain. Recognition of holding gains is not permitted by GAAP (except for certain marketable securities discussed in Chapter 12) because revenue and gains are normally recognized only at the date of sale.

In the case of seasonal goods such as clothing, obsolete goods, or damaged goods, if the sales price less selling costs (or **net realizable value**) drops below cost, this difference is subtracted from ending inventory and added to cost of goods sold of the period. This has the same effects on current and future periods' financial statements as the write-down to replacement cost.

Net realizable value is the expected sales price less selling costs (e.g., repair and disposal costs).

Under Generally Accepted Accounting Principles in the United States, the lower-of-cost-or-market rule can be applied to inventories the cost of which is determined using any of the four acceptable inventory costing methods. Note that in the two footnote examples that follow, both Harley-Davidson, which is a mixed LIFO company, and Compaq Computer, which is a FIFO company, report the use of lower of cost or market for financial statement purposes. For tax purposes, the lower-of-cost-or-market calculations may be applied with all inventory costing methods except LIFO.

HARLEY-DAVIDSON, INC.

NOTES TO CONSOLIDATED FINANCIAL STATEMENTS
1. SUMMARY OF SIGNIFICANT ACCOUNTING POLICIES
Inventories—Inventories are valued at lower of cost or market. Inventories located in the United States are valued using the last-in, first-out (LIFO) method. Other inventories, . . . , are valued at the lower of cost or market using the first-in, first-out (FIFO) method.

COMPAQ COMPUTER

NOTES TO CONSOLIDATED FINANCIAL STATEMENTS
NOTE 1—DESCRIPTION OF BUSINESS AND SIGNIFICANT ACCOUNTING POLICIES:
Inventories—Inventories are stated at the lower of cost or market, cost being determined on a first-in, first-out basis.

Inventories and Cash Flows

FOCUS ON CASH FLOWS

As with the change in accounts receivable, the change in inventories can be a major determinant of a company's cash flow from operations. As most public companies do, Harley-Davidson uses the indirect method of preparing the cash flow statement that reconciles (explains the difference between) net income and cash flow from operations for the period. The income statement reflects the cost of goods sold during the period whereas the cash flow statement should reflect the cash payments to suppliers for the same period. Cost of goods sold may be more or less than the amount of cash paid to suppliers during the period.

Since most inventory is purchased on open credit (the borrowing from a supplier is normally called *accounts payable*), reconciling cost of goods sold with cash paid to suppliers requires consideration of the changes in both the Inventory and Accounts Payable accounts. The simplest way to think about the effects of changes in inventory is that buying (increasing) inventory eventually decreases cash and selling (decreasing) inventory eventually increases cash. Similarly, borrowing from suppliers, which increases accounts payable, increases cash; paying suppliers, which decreases accounts payable, decreases cash. Thus, an increase in inventory or a decrease in accounts payable must be subtracted in the computation of cash flow from operations. Conversely, a decrease in inventory or an increase in accounts payable must be added. As shown in Exhibit 7.7, for 1995, Harley Davidson's inventory decreased by $5,453 and its accounts payable increased by $53,735. Both of these amounts must be added to net income in the computation of net cash flow from operations.

Keeping Track of Inventory Quantities and Costs

LEARNING OBJECTIVE 7
Keep track of inventory quantities and amounts in different circumstances.

To compute cost of goods sold, three amounts must be known: (1) beginning inventory, (2) purchases of merchandise (or transfers to finished goods) during the period, and (3) ending inventory. To simplify the discussion of how accounting systems keep track of these amounts, we will focus this discussion on the Motorclothes™ line for which Harley-Davidson is a wholesaler. Although the same general principles apply, the more complex details of manufacturing accounting systems are discussed in management accounting and cost accounting courses.

As noted earlier, the beginning inventory of one accounting period is the ending inventory of the previous period. The amount of purchases for the period is always

EXHIBIT 7.7
Inventories and Accounts Payable on the Cash Flow Statement

HARLEY-DAVIDSON, INC.
Consolidated Statements of Cash Flows

Years Ended December 31, 1995
(in thousands)

Cash flows from operating activities:	
Net income (loss)	$112,480
Adjustments to reconcile net income (loss) provided by operating activities:	
Depreciation and amortization	42,329

Net charges in other current assets and current liabilities	
Accounts receivable	(38,428)
Inventories	5,453
Prepaid expenses	(2,287)
Accounts payable	53,735
Total adjustments	56,592
Net cash provided by operating activities	168,072

accumulated in the accounting system. The amount of the ending inventory can be determined by using one of two different inventory systems: the periodic or perpetual inventory systems.

Periodic Inventory System

Under the **periodic inventory system,** no up-to-date record of inventory is maintained during the year. An actual physical count of the goods remaining on hand is required at the *end of each period.* The number of units of each type of merchandise on hand is multiplied by their unit cost to compute the dollar amount of the ending inventory. Cost of goods sold is calculated using the cost of goods sold equation as follows:

In a **periodic inventory system,** ending inventory and cost of goods sold are determined at the end of the accounting period based on a physical count.

$$\begin{array}{ccccccc} \text{Beginning} \\ \text{inventory} \end{array} + \begin{array}{c} \text{Purchases of} \\ \text{the period} \end{array} - \begin{array}{c} \text{Ending} \\ \text{inventory} \end{array} = \begin{array}{c} \text{Cost of} \\ \text{goods sold} \end{array}$$

Thus, the amount of inventory is not known until the end of the period, when the inventory count is taken. The amount of cost of goods sold cannot be determined reliably until the inventory count is completed. Companies using a periodic system must estimate the amount of inventory on hand.[8]

In the past, the primary reason for using the periodic inventory system was its low cost. Before affordable computers and bar code readers were available, the expense and difficulty associated with attempting to keep track of the number of units sold and the cost of each purchase and sale for thousands of items were very high. For example, in many retail stores, no record was made at the cash register of the cost and quantity of each item sold. As a consequence, only the total sales price was entered at the time of sale (for example, at an old-style cash register still used in some small retail businesses). The primary disadvantage of a periodic inventory system is the lack of inventory information. Managers are not provided with any information concerning low stock or overstocked situations. Most modern companies could not survive without this information. As noted at the beginning of the chapter, cost and quality pressures brought on by increasing competition, combined with dramatic declines in the cost of

---

[8] Methods for estimating inventory and cost of goods sold are discussed in intermediate accounting texts and courses.

computers, have made sophisticated perpetual inventory systems a minimum requirement at all but the smallest companies.

Perpetual Inventory System

In a **perpetual inventory system**, a detailed inventory record is maintained, recording each purchase and sale during the accounting period.

A **perpetual inventory system** involves the maintenance of up-to-date inventory records in the accounting system during the period. For each type of merchandise stocked, a detailed record is maintained that shows (1) units and cost of the beginning inventory, (2) units and cost of each purchase, (3) units and cost of the goods for each sale, and (4) the units and cost of the goods on hand at any point in time. This up-to-date record is maintained on a transaction-by-transaction basis throughout the period. In a complete perpetual inventory system, the inventory record gives both the amount of ending inventory and the cost of goods sold amount at any point in time. Under this system, a physical count must be performed from time to time to ensure that records are accurate in case errors or theft of inventory occur.

This system typically involves a computer system. Whether the accounting system is manual or computerized, the data that are recorded and reported are the same. The maintenance of a separate inventory record for each type of good stocked on a transaction-by-transaction basis usually is necessary for purchasing, manufacturing, and distribution decisions. A company such as Harley-Davidson relies heavily on this system and even shares some of this information electronically with its suppliers.

In a perpetual inventory system, purchase transactions are directly recorded in Inventory instead of a Purchases account. In addition, when each sale is recorded, a companion cost of goods sold entry is made. As a result, information on cost of goods sold and ending inventory is available on a continuous (perpetual) basis.

Comparison of Periodic and Perpetual Systems

The differences between the periodic and perpetual inventory systems can be summarized using the basic inventory equation:

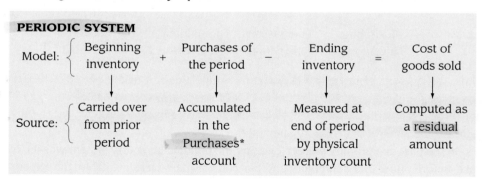

PERIODIC SYSTEM

Model:	Beginning inventory	+ Purchases of the period	− Ending inventory	= Cost of goods sold
Source:	Carried over from prior period	Accumulated in the Purchases* account	Measured at end of period by physical inventory count	Computed as a residual amount

*Purchases is a temporary account (T) which is closed to cost of goods sold at the end of the period.

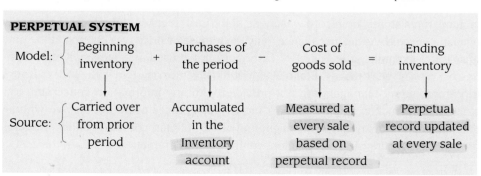

PERPETUAL SYSTEM

Model:	Beginning inventory	+ Purchases of the period	− Cost of goods sold	= Ending inventory
Source:	Carried over from prior period	Accumulated in the Inventory account	Measured at every sale based on perpetual record	Perpetual record updated at every sale

Assume, for this illustration only, that Harley-Davidson stocks and sells only one item, its Eagle Harness Boots, and that only the following events occur in 19F:

Jan.	1	Beginning inventory: 800 units, at unit cost of $50.
April	14	Purchased: 1,100 additional units, at unit cost of $50.
Nov.	30	Sold: 1,300 units, at unit sales price of $83.
Dec.	29	Return sale: 100 units (returned to stock and refunded sales price).

In the two types of inventory systems, the following sequential steps would take place as follows:

Periodic Records	Perpetual Records

1. Record all purchases in an account called *Purchases*.
 	
April 14, 19F:
 	
Purchases (T) (1,100 units at $50)............... 55,000
    Accounts payable (L) (or Cash) 55,000
	1. Record all purchases in the *Inventory* account and in a detailed perpetual inventory record.
	
	April 14, 19F:
	
	Inventory (A) (1,100 units at $50)* 55,000
	    Accounts payable (L) (or Cash) 55,000
	
	*Also entered in the detailed perpetual inventory record as 1,100 harness boots at $50 each.

2. Record all sales in a Sales Revenue account.
 	
November 30, 19F:
 	
Accounts receivable (A) (or Cash) 107,900
    Sales revenue (R) (1,300 units at $83) .. 107,900
	2. Record all sales in the Sales Revenue account and record the cost of goods sold.
	
	November 30, 19F:
	
	Accounts receivable (A) (or Cash) 107,900
	    Sales revenue (R) (1,300 units at $83) .. 107,900
	Cost of goods sold (E)..................................... 65,000
	    Inventory (A) (1,300 units at $50)* 65,000
	
	*Also entered in the perpetual inventory record as a reduction of 1,300 units at $50 each.

3. Record all sales returns.
 	
December 29, 19F:
 	
Sales returns and allowances (XR)
   (100 units at $83)....................................... 8,300
    Accounts receivable (A) (or Cash)........... 8,300
	3. Record all sales returns and related inventory.
	
	December 29, 19F:
	
	Sales returns and allowances (XR)
	   (100 units at $83) 8,300
	    Accounts receivable (A) (or Cash) 8,300
	Inventory (A) (100 units at $50) 5,000*
	    Cost of goods sold (E)............................. 5,000
	
	*This amount is also restored to the perpetual inventory record.

4. At end of period:
   a. Count the number of units on hand.
   b. Compute the dollar valuation of the ending inventory.
   c. Compute and record the cost of goods sold.
 	
Beginning inventory (last period's ending) $40,000
Add purchases (balance in the Purchases account)   55,000
                                      $95,000
Deduct ending inventory
   (physical count—700 units at $50)   35,000
Cost of goods sold $60,000
 	
December 31, 19F:
 	
Transfer beginning inventory and purchases (GAS) to cost of goods sold:
 	
Cost of goods sold (E)..................................... 95,000
    Inventory (A) (beginning)......................... 40,000
    Purchases (T) 55,000
 	
Subtract the ending inventory amount from the cost of goods sold to complete its computation and establish the ending inventory balance:
 	
Inventory (A) (ending) 35,000
    Cost of goods sold (E) 35,000
	4. Use cost of goods sold and inventory amounts. At the end of the accounting period, the balance in the Cost of Goods Sold account is the amount of that expense reported on the income statement. It is not necessary to compute cost of goods sold because under the perpetual inventory system, the Cost of Goods Sold account is up-to-date. Also, the Inventory account shows the ending inventory amount reported on the balance sheet. The sum of all the inventory balances in the various perpetual inventory records should equal the balance in the Inventory account in the ledger at any point in time. A physical inventory count is still necessary to assess the accuracy of the perpetual records and assess theft and other forms of misuse (called *shrinkage*).
	
	No entry

Perpetual Inventory Records in Practice

The decision to use a perpetual versus a periodic inventory system is based primarily on management's need for timely information for use in operating decisions and on the cost of the perpetual system. Further, the specific manner in which the perpetual system is designed will also be determined with these trade-offs in mind. Many inventory-ordering and production decisions require only exact information on inventory quantities, not costs. For example, at Harley-Davidson's Sportster™ assembly line in York, Pennsylvania, a bar code reader is used to keep track of each bike, which provides the needed information to schedule more purchases, production, and delivery of raw materials. This same information is necessary to provide up-to-date information for estimating delivery dates for finished motorcycles. If during testing of the completed motorcycles, problems are identified with a part such as a carburetor, the system provides the information necessary to track those problems back to the specific lot of purchased carburetors. Harley-Davidson can replace the defective carburetors before the motorcycles are delivered to customers and then work with the supplier to correct the problem. Note that the information necessary for efficient management of inventory, providing delivery information to dealers, and quality control did *not* require exact cost information.

Systems that do keep track of the costs of individual items or lots normally do so on a FIFO, estimated average (or standard) cost basis, or for distinguishable high-value items using specific identification. Perpetual records are rarely kept on a LIFO basis for two reasons: (1) it is more complex and costly to do so, and (2) doing so often causes LIFO liquidations, which can increase tax payments. The conversion to LIFO is made as an adjusting entry.

Methods for Estimating Inventory

When a periodic inventory system is used and detailed perpetual inventory records are not kept, cost of goods sold and the amount of ending inventory can be directly computed only when a physical inventory count is taken. Because taking a physical inventory is expensive, it is normally done only once each year. In these circumstances, managers who wish to prepare monthly or quarterly financial statements for internal use often estimate the cost of goods sold and ending inventory using the *gross margin method*. The gross margin method uses the historical gross profit percentage (introduced in Chapters 5 and 6) to estimate cost of goods sold.

For example, we noted that Harley-Davidson's historical gross profit percentage on motorcycles was approximately 30.5 percent. If it sold $100,000,000 of motorcycles in January, it would estimate cost of goods sold to be $69,500,000 ($100,000,000 × [100% − 30.5%]) for the month. If Harley keeps track of purchases and other additions to inventory, it could then use the cost of goods sold equation to solve for an estimate of ending inventory. Retailers often take their physical inventory counts based on the retail price instead of cost and then use a similar method (called the *retail method*) to estimate cost.

Additional Issues in Measuring Purchases

Purchase Returns and Allowances

Goods purchased may be returned to the vendor if they do not meet specifications, arrive in damaged condition, or otherwise are unsatisfactory. When the goods are returned or when the vendor makes an allowance because of the circumstances, the effect on the cost of purchases must be measured. The purchaser normally receives a cash refund or a reduction in the liability to the vendor for a return. Assume that Harley-Davidson returned unsatisfactory harness boots that cost $1,000 to a supplier. The return would be recorded by Harley-Davidson as follows:

Accounts payable (L) (or Cash) 1,000
    Purchase returns and allowances* (T) 1,000

*Inventory is credited when the perpetual inventory system is used.

Purchase returns and allowances are accounted for as a deduction from the cost of purchases.

Purchase returns and allowances is a deduction from the cost of purchases associated with unsatisfactory goods.

Purchase Discounts

Cash discounts must be accounted for by both the seller and the buyer (accounting by the seller was discussed in Chapter 6). When merchandise is bought on credit, terms such as 2/10, n/30, are sometimes specified. This means that if payment is made within 10 days from date of purchase, a 2 percent cash discount known as the **purchase discount** is granted. If payment is not made within the discount period, the full invoice cost is due 30 days after purchase. Assume that on January 17, Harley-Davidson bought goods that had a $1,000 invoice price with terms 2/10, n/30. Assuming that it uses the gross method discussed in Chapter 6, the purchase should be recorded as follows:

A **purchase discount** is a cash discount received for prompt payment of an account payable.

Date of purchase:

Jan. 17   Purchases* (T) 1,000
        Accounts payable (L) 1,000

*Inventory is debited when a perpetual inventory system is used.

Date of payment, within the discount period:

Jan. 26   Accounts payable (L) 1,000
        Purchase discounts (T) 20
        Cash (A) 980

If for any reason Harley-Davidson did not pay within the 10-day discount period, the following entry would be needed:

Feb. 1   Accounts payable (L) 1,000
        Cash (A) 1,000

Purchase Discounts should be reported as a deduction from the cost of purchases in the calculation of cost of goods sold.

Demonstration Case A

(Complete the requirements before proceeding to the suggested solution that follows.)

    Metal Products, Incorporated, has been operating for three years as a distributor of a line of metal products. It is now the end of 19C, and for the first time, the company will undergo an audit by an independent CPA. The company uses a *periodic* inventory system. The annual income statements (note which column is the current year) prepared by the company are as follows:

	FOR THE YEAR ENDED DECEMBER 31			
	19B		19C	
Sales revenue		$750,000		$800,000
Cost of goods sold				
Beginning inventory	45,000		40,000	
Add purchases	460,000		484,000	
Goods available for sale	505,000		524,000	
Less ending inventory	40,000		60,000	
Cost of goods sold		465,000		464,000
Gross margin on sales		285,000		336,000
Operating expenses		275,000		306,000
Pretax income		10,000		30,000
Income tax expense (20%)		2,000		6,000
Net income		$ 8,000		$ 24,000

During the early stages of the audit, the independent CPA discovered that the ending inventory for 19B was understated by $15,000.

Required:

1. Based on the preceding income statement amounts, compute the gross margin ratio on sales for each year. Do the results suggest an inventory error? Explain.
2. Correct and reconstruct the two income statements.
3. Answer the following questions:
    a. What are the correct gross margin ratios?
    b. What effect did the $15,000 understatement of the ending inventory have on 19B pretax income? Explain.
    c. What effect did the inventory error have on the 19C pretax income? Explain.
    d. How did the inventory error affect income tax expense?

Suggested Solution

1. Gross margin ratios as reported:

    19B: $285,000 ÷ $750,000 = 0.38
    19C: $336,000 ÷ $800,000 = 0.42

    The change in the gross margin ratio from 0.38 to 0.42 suggests the possibility of an inventory error in the absence of any other explanation.
2. Income statements corrected:

	FOR THE YEAR ENDED DECEMBER 31			
	19B		19C	
Sales revenue		$750,000		$800,000
Cost of goods sold				
Beginning inventory	45,000		55,000*	
Add purchases	460,000		484,000	
Goods available for sale	505,000		539,000	
Less ending inventory	55,000*		60,000	
Cost of goods sold		450,000		479,000
Gross margin on sales		300,000		321,000
Operating expenses		275,000		306,000
Pretax income		25,000		15,000
Income tax expense (20%)		5,000		3,000
Net income		$ 20,000		$ 12,000

*Increased by $15,000.

3. *a.* Correct gross margin ratios:

> 19B: $300,000 ÷ $750,000 = 0.400
> 19C: $321,000 ÷ $800,000 = 0.401

The inventory error of $15,000 was responsible for the difference in the gross margin ratios reflected in requirement 1. The error in the 19B ending inventory affected gross margin for both 19B and 19C—in the opposite direction but by the same amount, $15,000.

  b. Effect on pretax income in 19B: Ending inventory *understatement* ($15,000) caused an *understatement* of pretax income by the same amount.

  c. Effect on pretax income in 19C: Beginning inventory *understatement* (by the same $15,000 since the inventory amount is carried over from the prior period) caused an *overstatement* of pretax income by the same amount.

  d. Total income tax expense for 19B and 19C combined was the same ($8,000) regardless of the error. However, there was a shift of $3,000 ($15,000 × 20%) income tax expense from 19B to 19C.

OBSERVATION An ending inventory error in one year affects pretax income by the amount of the error and in the next year affects pretax income again by the same amount but in the opposite direction.

Demonstration Case B

(Complete the requirements before proceeding to the suggested solution that follows.)

This case reviews a periodic inventory system assuming that the LIFO inventory costing method is applied.

Balent Appliances distributes a number of high-cost household appliances. One product, microwave ovens, has been selected for case purposes. Assume that the following summarized transactions were completed during the accounting period in the order given (assume that all transactions are cash):

		Units	Unit Cost
a.	Beginning inventory	11	$200
b.	Purchases	9	220
c.	Purchase returns (damaged in shipment)	1	220
d.	Sales (selling price, $420)	8	?
e.	Sales returns (can be resold as new)	1	220

Required:

1. Compute the following amounts, assuming the application of the LIFO inventory costing method:

ENDING INVENTORY		COST OF GOODS SOLD	
Units	Dollars	Units	Dollars

  LIFO (costed at end of period)

2. Give the indicated journal entries for transactions (*b*) through (*e*).

Suggested Solution

1.

	ENDING INVENTORY		COST OF GOODS SOLD	
	Units	Dollars	Units	Dollars
LIFO (costed at end of period)	12	$2,420	7	$1,540

Computations:

Goods available for sale $=$ Beginning inventory $+$ (Purchases – Purchase returns)

$=$ (11 units × $200 = $2,200) $+$ (8 units × $220 = $1,760)

$=$ $3,960

LIFO inventory (costed at end of period):

Ending inventory: (11 units × $200 = $2,200) + (1 unit × $220 = $220) = $2,420.

Cost of goods sold: (Goods available, $3,960) – (Ending inventory, $2,420) = $1,540.

2. Journal Entries:

b. Purchases:

Purchases (T)	1,980	
Cash (A) (9 × $220)		1,980

c. Purchase returns:

Cash (A)	220	
Purchase returns (T)		220

d. Sales:

Cash (A) (8 × $420)	3,360	
Sales revenue (R)		3,360

e. Sales returns:

Sales returns (XR)	420	
Cash (A) (1 × $420)		420

Summary

Costs flow into inventory when goods are purchased or manufactured and flow out (as an expense) when the goods are sold or disposed of otherwise. In conformity with the matching principle, the total cost of the goods sold during the period must be matched with the sales revenue earned during the period. Cost of goods sold measures the cost of inventory that was sold; sales revenue measures the selling price of the same inventory. When cost of goods sold is deducted from sales revenue for the period, the difference is called *gross profit* or *gross margin on sales.* From this amount, the remaining expenses must be deducted to derive income.

This chapter focused on the problem of measuring cost of goods sold and ending inventory when unit costs change during the period. Inventory should include all the items held for resale that the entity owns. When different unit cost amounts occur, a rational and systematic method must be used to allocate costs to the units remaining in inventory and to the units sold. The chapter discussed four different inventory costing methods and their applications in different economic circumstances. The methods discussed were FIFO, LIFO, weighted average cost, and specific identification. Each of the inventory costing methods is in conformity with GAAP. The selection of a method of inventory costing is important because it will affect reported income, income tax expense (and, hence, cash flow), and the inventory valuation reported on the balance sheet. In a period of rising prices, FIFO normally results in a higher income than does LIFO; in a period of falling prices, the opposite result occurs. Public companies using LIFO provide footnote disclosures that allow conversion of inventory and cost of goods sold to FIFO amounts.

Ending inventory should be measured on the basis of the lower of actual cost or replacement cost (LCM basis), which can have a major effect on the statements of companies facing declining costs. Damaged, obsolete, and deteriorated items in inventory also should be assigned a unit cost that represents their current estimated net realizable value if that is below cost.

Two inventory systems were discussed for keeping track of the ending inventory and cost of goods sold for the period: (1) the perpetual inventory system, which is based on the maintenance of detailed and continuous inventory records for each kind of inventory stocked; and (2) the periodic inventory system, which is based on a physical inventory count of ending inventory and the costing of those goods to determine the proper amounts for cost of goods sold and ending inventory.

In the current and previous chapters, we discussed the current assets of a business. These assets are critical for the operations of a business, but many of them do not directly produce value. A business could not survive without cash, but cash does not produce goods or services that can be sold to customers. In Chapter 8, we will discuss noncurrent assets that are sometimes called *productive assets.* Many of the noncurrent assets produce value, such as a factory that manufactures cars. These assets present some interesting accounting problems because they benefit a number of accounting periods.

Chapter Supplement A

LIFO LIQUIDATIONS

When a LIFO company sells more inventory than it purchases or manufactures, items from beginning inventory become part of cost of goods sold. This is called a **LIFO liquidation.** For companies facing rising inventory costs, these items in beginning inventory have lower costs, which produce a higher gross margin when they are sold. (People often call items purchased at the same price *LIFO layers.*) We illustrate this process by continuing our simple New Company example into its second year.

In its first year of operation, units were purchased for $1, $3, and $5 in sequence, and the $5 and $3 units were sold under LIFO, leaving the $1 unit in ending inventory. These events were represented using a LIFO inventory bin in Exhibit 7.5. We continue this illustration in Exhibit 7.8. The ending inventory from year 1 becomes the beginning inventory for year 2. In part A of the exhibit, we assume that in year 2, New Company purchased a total of

A **LIFO liquidation** is a sale of a lower-cost inventory item from beginning LIFO inventory.

EXHIBIT 7.8
Inventory Flows—New Company, Year 2

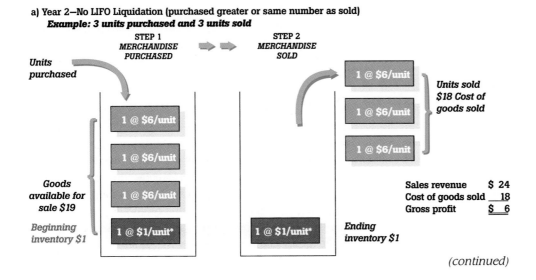

a) Year 2—No LIFO Liquidation (purchased greater or same number as sold)
Example: 3 units purchased and 3 units sold

(continued)

EXHIBIT 7.8
Concluded

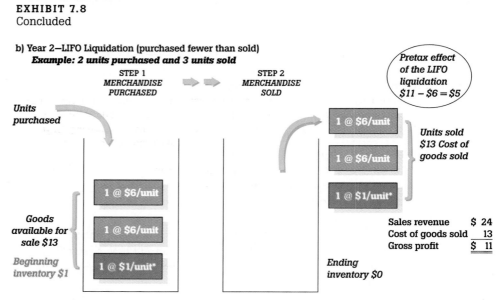

b) Year 2—LIFO Liquidation (purchased fewer than sold)
  Example: 2 units purchased and 3 units sold

*Beginning inventory = Ending inventory from year 1.

three inventory units at the current $6 price before year-end, the sales price has been raised to $8, and three units are sold. Using LIFO, the three recently purchased $6 inventory items become part of cost of goods sold of $18, and the old $1 item from beginning inventory becomes ending inventory. Given that revenue is $8 per unit, the gross margin on the three newly purchased units is 3 units × $2 = $6.

Now assume instead, as we do in part B of Exhibit 7.8, that New Company purchased only *two* additional units at $6 each. Using LIFO, these two new $6 units and the old $1 unit would become cost of goods sold. Given that revenue is $8 per unit, the gross margin on the newly purchased units is 2 units × $2 = $4. Since the cost of the old unit is only $1, the gross margin on this one unit is $7 ($8 – $1) instead of $2, raising total gross profit to $11. This calculation is presented in Exhibit 7.8.

Compared to part A, cost of goods sold decreases by $5 to $13, and gross profit and income before taxes increase by $5. This $5 change is the *pretax effect of the LIFO liquidation,* which took place in part B. Given the assumed tax rate of 25 percent, taxes paid are $1.25 (.25 × $5) higher in this second situation.

In part A, the LIFO liquidation and extra tax payment are avoided even if the third purchase takes place *after* the sale of the third item because the tax law allows LIFO to be applied *as if* all purchases during an accounting period take place before any sales and cost of goods sold are recorded. Because of this feature, temporary LIFO liquidations can be eliminated by purchasing additional inventory before year-end. Most companies apply LIFO in this manner.

LIFO Liquidations and Financial Statement Analysis

During the decade prior to 1993, Deere & Company and other companies in its industry faced declining demand and increasing competition in most major segments of their business. This reduced the inventory quantities necessary to meet customers' needs. Deere had also instituted modern manufacturing techniques that further decreased inventory levels. Deere, a long-time LIFO user, experienced continuing LIFO liquidations over this period. Companies must disclose the effects of LIFO liquidations in the footnotes when they are material, as Deere did in the note that follows. The second paragraph of the note explains the effect. The last sentence lists the pretax (after-tax) effects of the liquidations.

DEERE & COMPANY
NOTES TO CONSOLIDATED FINANCIAL STATEMENTS

INVENTORIES

Substantially all inventories owned by Deere & Company and its United States equipment subsidiaries are valued at cost on the "last-in, first-out" (LIFO) method. . . .

Under the LIFO inventory method, cost of goods sold ordinarily reflects current production costs thus providing a matching of current costs and current revenues in the income statement. However when LIFO–valued inventories decline, as they did in 1993 and 1992, lower costs that prevailed in prior years are matched against current year revenues, resulting in higher reported net income. Benefits from the reduction of LIFO inventories totaled $51 million ($33 million or $ .43 per share after income taxes) in 1993, $65 million ($43 million or $0.56 per share after income taxes) in 1992 and $128 million ($84 million or $1.11 per share after income taxes) in 1991.

Over the past three years, LIFO liquidations have increased Deere's reported income before taxes by a total of $244 million ($51 + $65 + $128). (These numbers are the equivalent of the $5 effect of the liquidation computed in the New Company example.) To compute pre-tax income as if the liquidations had not taken place (as if current year's production were large enough so that no items from beginning inventory were sold), simply subtract the LIFO liquidation effect from pretax income.

Pretax income on LIFO for 3 years (reported on the income statements)	$290
Less: Pretax effect of LIFO liquidations (from footnote)	244
Pretax income on LIFO for 3 years basis as if no liquidations	$ 46

Fully 84 percent ($244 ÷ $290) of Deere's reported pretax profit over the three years is the result of LIFO liquidations. Since the $46 million pretax profit figure reflects Deere's current costs of production, educated analysts use this figure when comparing Deere's performance to that of other LIFO companies. It is important to emphasize that these numbers still are on a *LIFO* basis but are prepared *as if no liquidation took place.*

Inventory Management and LIFO Liquidations

Several research studies have documented the year-end inventory purchasing decisions of firms that use LIFO.[9] Many firms avoid LIFO liquidations and the accompanying increase in tax expense by purchasing sufficient quantities of inventory at year-end to ensure that ending inventory quantities are greater than or equal to beginning inventory quantities. While this practice increases the costs of carrying inventory (storage, financing, etc.), for these firms, the taxes saved exceed these amounts.

As noted earlier in the chapter, Harley-Davidson and many other firms have moved to more efficient just-in-time inventory techniques that greatly reduce the amount of inventory manufacturers keep on hand. When managers compare the savings in carrying costs against the costs of implementing the new system (new computers, training, etc.), they must also consider the added taxes they may pay if they account for the inventory using the LIFO method. When the company switches to the new just-in-time system, ending inventory quantity will normally decline below beginning inventory quantity, causing a LIFO liquidation and a one-time increase in taxes. This cost should be considered when deciding whether to adopt the new system. In this case the tax law provides an incentive for U.S. companies not to become more efficient.

[9] M. Frankel and R. Trezevant, "The Year-End LIFO Inventory Purchasing Decision: An Empirical Test," *The Accounting Review* (April 1994), pp. 382–98.

Key Ratios

Inventory turnover ratio measures the liquidity (nearness to cash) of inventory. It is computed as follows (p. 375):

$$\text{Inventory turnover} = \frac{\text{Cost of goods sold}}{\text{Average inventory [(Beginning + Ending)} \div 2]}$$

Key Terms

Cost of Goods Sold Equation BI + P – EI = CGS *363*

Direct Labor The earnings of employees who work directly on the products being manufactured. *361*

Factory Overhead Manufacturing costs that are not raw material or direct labor costs. *361*

Finished Goods Inventory Manufactured goods that are completed and ready for sale. *359*

First-In, First-Out Method (FIFO) Inventory costing method that assumes that the oldest units are the first units sold. *366*

Goods Available for Sale The sum of beginning inventory and purchases (or transfers to finished goods) for the period. *362*

Inventory Tangible property that is held for sale in the normal course of business or will be used in producing goods or services for sale. *358*

Last-In, First-Out Method (LIFO) Inventory costing method that assumes that the most recently acquired units are sold first. *367*

LIFO Liquidation A sale of a lower-cost inventory item from beginning LIFO inventory. *387*

LIFO Reserve A contra-asset for the excess of FIFO over LIFO inventory. *373*

Lower of Cost or Market (LCM) Valuation method departing from cost principle that recognizes a loss when replacement cost or net realizable value drops below cost. *376*

Merchandise Inventory Goods held for resale in the ordinary course of business. *358*

Net Realizable Value The expected sales price less selling costs (e.g., repair and disposal costs). *377*

Periodic Inventory System Ending inventory and cost of goods sold are determined at the end of the accounting period based on a physical inventory count. *379*

Perpetual Inventory System A detailed inventory record is maintained recording each purchase and sale during the accounting period. *380*

Purchase Discount Cash discount received for prompt payment of an account payable. *383*

Purchase Returns and Allowances A deduction from the cost of purchases associated with unsatisfactory goods. *383*

Raw Materials Inventory Items acquired for the purpose of processing into finished goods. *358*

Replacement Cost The current purchase price for identical goods. *377*

Specific Identification Method Inventory costing method that identifies the cost of the specific item that was sold. *369*

Weighted Average Method Inventory costing method that uses the weighted average unit cost of the goods available for sale for both cost of goods sold and ending inventory. *368*

Work in Process Inventory Goods in the process of being manufactured. *358*

Questions

1. Match the type of inventory with the type of business in the following matrix:

	Type of Business	
Type of Inventory	Merchandising	Manufacturing
Merchandise		
Finished goods		
Work in process		
Raw materials		

2. Why is inventory an important item to both internal (management) and external users of financial statements?
3. What are the general guidelines for deciding which items should be included in inventory?
4. Define *goods available for sale.* How does it differ from cost of goods sold?
5. Define *beginning inventory* and *ending inventory.*
6. In measuring cost of goods sold and inventory, why is passage of ownership an important issue? When does ownership of goods usually pass? Explain.
7. Explain the application of the cost principle to an item in the ending inventory.
8. Assume the 19A ending inventory was understated by $100,000. Explain how this error would affect the 19A and 19B pretax income amounts. What would be the effects if the 19A ending inventory were overstated by $100,000 instead of understated?
9. The chapter discussed four inventory costing methods. List the four methods and briefly explain each.
10. Explain how income can be manipulated when the specific identification inventory costing method is used.
11. Contrast the effects of LIFO versus FIFO on reported assets (i.e., the ending inventory) when (a) prices are rising and (b) prices are falling.
12. Contrast the income statement effect of LIFO versus FIFO (i.e., on pretax income) when (a) prices are rising and (b) prices are falling.
13. Contrast the effects of LIFO versus FIFO on cash outflow and inflow.
14. Explain briefly the application of the LCM concept to the ending inventory and its effect on the income statement and balance sheet when market is lower than cost.
15. When should net realizable value be used in costing an item in the ending inventory?
16. Briefly explain the comparability quality. How might it relate to the inventory costing methods?
17. When a perpetual inventory system is used, unit costs of the items sold are known at the date of each sale. In contrast, when a periodic inventory system is used, unit costs are known only at the end of the accounting period. Why are these statements correct?
18. The periodic inventory calculation is BI + P − EI = CGS. The perpetual inventory calculation is BI + P − CGS = EI. Explain the significance of the difference between these two calculations.

Exercises

E7–1 Analyzing Income Statement Relationships

Supply the missing dollar amounts for the 19B income statement of Lewis Retailers for each of the following independent cases:

R - CGS=GM-E =

Cases	Sales Revenue	Beginning Inventory	Purchases	Total Available	Ending Inventory	Cost of Goods Sold	Gross Margin	Expenses	Pretax Income or (Loss)
A	$ 650	$100	$700	$800?	$500	$30?	$350?	$200	$150 ?
B	900	200	800	1000?	?	?	150 ?	150	0
C	?	150	?	?	300	200	400	100	?
D	800	?	600	?	250	?	?	250	100
E	1,000	?	900	1,100	?	?	500	?	(50)

E7–2 Finding Missing Amounts Based on Income Statement Relationships

Supply the missing dollar amounts for the 19D income statement of Travis Company for each of the following independent cases:

	Case A	Case B	Case C
Sales revenue	$ 8,000	$ 6,000	$?
Sales returns and allowances	150	?	275
Net sales revenue	?	?	5,920
Beginning inventory	11,000	6,500	4,000 +
Purchases	5,000	?	9,420 +
Transportation-in	100?	120	170
Purchase returns	350	600	?
Goods available for sale	15750?	14,790	13,370
Ending inventory	10,000	10,740	?
Cost of goods sold	?	?	5,400
Gross margin	?	1,450	?
Expenses	1,300	?	520
Pretax income	800	(500)	–0–

15750
15630
100

E7–3 Correcting Costs Included in the Cost of Purchases for a Merchandiser

Elite Apparel purchased 80 new shirts and recorded a total cost of $3,140 determined as follows:

Invoice cost	$2,600
Less: Cash discount 3% taken	
Shipping charges *freight—in*	165
Import taxes and duties	115
Interest paid in advance (10%) on $2,600 borrowed to finance the purchase *(finance cost)*	260
	$3,140

Required:
Make the needed corrections in this calculation. Give the journal entry(ies) to record this purchase in the correct amount assuming a periodic inventory system. Show computations.

E7–4 Costs Included in the Cost of Inventories for a Manufacturer

Operating costs incurred by a manufacturing company become either (a) part of the cost of inventory to be expensed as cost of goods sold at the time the finished goods are sold or (b) expenses at the time they are incurred. Indicate whether each of the following costs belongs in category (a) or (b).

	(a) Part of Inventory	(b) Expense as Incurred
1. Wages of factory workers		
2. Sales salaries		
3. Costs of raw materials purchased		
4. Heat, light, and power for the factory building		
5. Heat, light, and power for the headquarters office building		

E7-5 Using the Cost of Goods Sold Equation to Estimate Purchases

J. C. Penney Company, Inc., is a major retailer with department stores in all 50 states. The dominant portion of the company's business consists of providing merchandise and services to consumers through department stores that include catalog departments. In a recent annual report, J. C. Penney reported cost of goods sold was $10,969 million, ending inventory for the current year was $3,062 million, and ending inventory for the previous year was $2,969 million.

Required:

Is it possible to develop a reasonable estimate of the merchandise purchases for the year? If yes, prepare the estimate; if not, explain why.

J. C. Penney

E7-6 Analyzing Merchandise Purchases

The Gap, Inc., is a specialty retailer that operates stores selling clothes under the trade names Gap, GapKids, BabyGap, and Banana Republic. Assume that you are employed as a stock analyst and your boss has just completed a review of the new Gap annual report. She provided you with her notes, but they are missing some information that you need. Her notes show that the ending inventory for Gap in the current year was $243,482,000 and in the previous year was $193,268,000. Net sales for the current year were $1,586,596,000. Gross margin was $540,360,000; net income was $97,628,000. For your analysis, you determine that you need to know the amount of purchases for the year and cost of goods sold.

The Gap, Inc.

Required:

Do you need to ask your boss for her copy of the annual report, or can you develop the information from her notes? Explain and show calculations.

E7-7 Analyzing the Impact of an Inventory Error

Dallas Corporation prepared the following two income statements (simplified for illustrative purposes):

	First Quarter 19B		Second Quarter 19B	
Sales revenue		$15,000		$18,000
Cost of goods sold				
Beginning inventory	$ 3,000		$ 4,000 *4400*	
Purchases	7,000		12,000	
Goods available for sale	10,000		16,000 *16400*	
Ending inventory	4,000 *4400*		9,000	
Cost of goods sold		6,000 *5600*		7,000 *7400*
Gross margin		9,000 *9400*		11,000 *10600*
Expenses		5,000		6,000
Pretax income		$ 4,000 *4400*		$ 5,000 *4600* 9000

(handwritten: 9000)

During the third quarter it was discovered that the ending inventory for the first quarter should have been $4,400.

Required:

1. What effect did this error have on the combined pretax income of the two quarters? Explain.
2. Did this error affect the EPS amounts for each quarter? (See Chapter 5 discussion of EPS.) Explain.
3. Prepare corrected income statements for each quarter.
4. Set up a schedule that reflects the comparative effects of the correct and incorrect amounts.

E7–8 Analyzing the Effects of an Error in Recording Purchases

Garraway Ski Company had mistakenly recorded purchases of inventory on account received during the last week of December 19A as purchases during January of 19B (this is called a *purchases cutoff error*). Garraway uses a periodic inventory system, and ending inventory was correctly counted and reported each year. Assuming that no correction was made in 19A or 19B, indicate whether each of the following financial statement amounts will be understated, overstated, or correct.

1. Net Income for 19A.
2. Net Income for 19B.
3. Retained Earnings for December 31, 19A.
4. Retained Earnings for December 31, 19B.

Lafayette Radio Electronics

E7–9 Analyzing the Effect of an Inventory Error Disclosed in an Actual Note to a Financial Statement

Several years ago, the financial statements of Lafayette Radio Electronics Corporation contained the following footnote:

> Subsequent to the issuance of its financial statements the company discovered a computational error in the amount of $1,046,000 in the calculation of its year-end inventory which resulted in an overstatement of ending inventory.

Assume that Lafayette reported an incorrect net income amount of $3,101,000 for the year in which the error occurred and that the income tax rate is 40 percent.

Required:
1. Compute the amount of net income that Lafayette should report after correcting the inventory error. Show computations.
2. Assume that the inventory error was not discovered. Identify the financial statement accounts that would have been incorrect for the year the error occurred and for the subsequent year. State whether each account was understated or overstated.

E7–10 Choosing between LIFO and FIFO with Discussion of Management Motivation

Lunar Company uses a periodic inventory system. At the end of the annual accounting period, December 31, 19B, the accounting records provided the following information for Product 2:

Transactions	Units	Unit Cost
1. Inventory, December 31, 19A	3,000	$12
For the year 19B:		
2. Purchase, April 11	9,000	$10
3. Purchase, June 1	⊤ 8,000	$13
4. Sale, May 1 ($40 each)	5,000 ⟩ sold	
5. Sale, July 3 ($40 each)	– 6,000	
6. Operating expenses (excluding income tax expense), $195,000.	9,000 unsold	

Required:
1. Prepare a separate income statement through pretax income that details cost of goods sold for
   a. Case A: FIFO.
   b. Case B: LIFO.
   For each case, show the computation of the ending inventory. (*Hint:* Set up adjacent columns for each case.)

2. Compare the pretax income and the ending inventory amounts between the two cases. Explain the similarities and differences.
3. Which inventory costing method may be preferred for income tax purposes? Explain.

E7–11 **Choosing between LIFO and FIFO with Declining Costs with Discussion of Management Motivation**

The records at the end of January 19B for All Star Company showed the following for a particular type of merchandise:

Transactions	Units	Unit Cost	Total Cost
Inventory, December 31, 19A	19	$16	$304
Purchase, January 9, 19B	25	15	375
Purchase, January 20, 19B	50	14	700
Sale, January 11, 19B (at $38 per unit)	40	1520	94 units $1379
Sale, January 27, 19B (at $39 per unit)	28	1092	

68   26 EI

Assume cash transactions and a periodic inventory system.

Required:

1. Compute (*a*) goods available for sale, (*b*) cost of goods sold, and (*c*) ending inventory for Case A, FIFO, and Case B, LIFO.
2. In parallel columns, give the journal entries for each purchase and sale transaction, assuming that a periodic inventory system is used for each case. Set up headings as follows:

	FIFO		LIFO	
Accounts	Debit	Credit	Debit	Credit

3. Prepare an income statement through gross margin and explain why the FIFO and LIFO ending inventory, cost of goods sold, and gross margin amounts are different.
4. Which inventory costing method may be preferred for income tax purposes? Explain.

E7–12 **Choosing between LIFO and FIFO Based on Cash Flow and Income Effects**

During January 19B, Camry Company reported sales revenue of $370,000 for the one item stocked. The inventory for December 31, 19A, showed 9,000 units on hand with a cost of $21 $189,000. During January 19B, two purchases of the item were made: the first was for 6,000 units at $22 per unit, and the second was for 4,850 units at $23 each. The periodic inventory count reflected 10,600 units remaining on hand on January 31, 19B. Total operating expense for the month was $97,000.

19850
194,500

Sold   9250
EI   10600

Required:

1. On the basis of this information, complete the 19B summary income statements under FIFO and LIFO. Use a single list of side captions, including computation of cost of goods sold. Set up three separate column headings as follows: Units, FIFO, and LIFO. Show your computations of the ending inventory.
2. Which method gives the higher pretax income? Why? AFO
3. Which method gives the more favorable cash flow effects? By how much, assuming a 30 percent tax rate?

200 - 137
32 - 19
25 - 10
25 - 22
282

E7–13 **Analyzing the Effects of the LIFO/FIFO Choice on Inventory Turnover Ratio**

The records at the end of January 19B for All Star Company showed the following for a particular kind of merchandise:

Inventory, December 31, 19A at FIFO 19 Units @ $14 = 266
Inventory, December 31, 19A at LIFO 19 Units @ $10 = 190

Transactions	Units	Unit Cost	Total Cost
Purchase, January 9, 19B	25	15	375
Purchase, January 20, 19B	50	16	800
Sale, January 11, 19B (at $38 per unit)	40		
Sale, January 27, 19B (at $39 per unit)	28		

Required:

Assuming the use of a periodic inventory system, compute the inventory turnover ratio under the FIFO and LIFO inventory costing methods (show computations and round to the nearest dollar). Explain which you believe is the more accurate indicator of the liquidity of inventory.

E7–14 Choosing among Three Alternative Inventory Methods Based on Cash Flow and Income Effects

Courtney Company uses a periodic inventory system. Data for 19B: beginning merchandise inventory (December 31, 19A), 2,000 units at $35; purchases, 8,000 units at $38; expenses (excluding income taxes), $142,000; ending inventory per physical count at December 31, 19B, 1,800 units; sales price per unit, $70; and average income tax rate, 30 percent.

Required:

1. Prepare income statements under the FIFO, LIFO, and weighted average costing methods. Use a format similar to the following:

			INVENTORY COSTING METHOD	
Income Statement	Units	FIFO	LIFO	Weighted Average
Sales revenue	____	$____	$____	$____
Cost of goods sold	____	____	____	____
Beginning inventory	____	____	____	____
Purchases	____	____	____	____
Goods available for sale	____	____	____	____
Ending inventory	____	____	____	____
Cost of goods sold	____	____	____	____
Gross margin		____	____	____
Expenses		____	____	____
Pretax income		____	____	____
Income tax expense		____	____	____
Net income		____	____	____

2. Between FIFO and LIFO, which method is preferable in terms of (*a*) net income and (*b*) cash flow? Explain.
3. What would your answer to requirement 2 be assuming that prices were falling? Explain.

E7–15 Analyzing Cash Flow Effects of Alternative Inventory Methods

Following is partial information for the income statement of Timber Company under three different inventory costing methods assuming the use of a periodic inventory system:

	FIFO	LIFO	Weighted Average
Unit sales price, $50			
Cost of goods sold			
Beginning inventory (330 units)	$11,220	$11,220	$11,220
Purchases (475 units)	17,100	17,100	17,100
Goods available for sale			
Ending inventory (510 units)			
Cost of goods sold			
Expenses, $1,600			

Required:

1. Compute cost of goods sold under the FIFO, LIFO, and weighted average inventory costing methods.
2. Prepare an income statement through pretax income for each method.
3. Rank the three methods in order of favorable cash flow and explain the basis for your ranking.

E7–16 Analyzing Footnotes to Adjust Inventory from LIFO to FIFO

Ford Motor Company

The following note was contained in a recent Ford Motor Company annual report:

> **Inventory Valuation—Automotive.** Inventories are stated at the lower of cost or market. The cost of most US inventories is determined by the last-in, first-out ("LIFO") method. The cost of the remaining inventories is determined substantially by the first-in, first-out ("FIFO") method.
>
> If FIFO were the only method of inventory accounting used by the company, inventories would have been $1,235 million higher than reported this year and $1,246 million higher than reported last year.

The major classes of inventory for the company's Automotive business segment at December 31 were as follows:

	INVENTORY (IN $ MILLIONS)	
	Current Year	Previous Year
Finished products	$3,413.8	$3,226.7
Raw material and work in process	2,983.9	2,981.6
Supplies	419.1	429.9
Total	$6,816.8	$6,638.2

Required:

1. Determine the ending inventory that would have been reported in the current year if Ford had used only FIFO.
2. The cost of goods sold reported by Ford for the current year was $74,315 million. Determine the cost of goods sold that would have been reported if Ford had used only FIFO for both years.

E7–17 Analyzing Footnotes to Adjust Inventory from LIFO to FIFO with Discussion of Management Motivation

Chrysler Corporation

The following note was contained in a recent Chrysler Corporation annual report:

Inventories

Inventories are valued at the lower of cost or market. The cost of approximately 44 percent and 50 percent of inventories for the current and previous years, respectively, is determined on a Last-In, First-Out (LIFO) basis. The balance of inventory cost is determined on a First-In, First-Out (FIFO) basis.

Inventories and Cost of Sales

Inventories are summarized by major classification as follows (in $ millions):

	Current Year	Previous Year
Finished products, including service parts	$1,145	$ 972
Raw materials, finished production		
parts and supplies	985	1,165
Vehicles held for short-term lease	760	336
Total	$2,890	$2,473

Inventories valued on the LIFO basis would have been $160 million and $123 million higher than reported had they been valued on the FIFO basis at December 31 of the current year and previous year, respectively.

Total automotive manufacturing cost of sales aggregated $27.2 billion and $26.3 billion for the current year and previous year, respectively.

Required:

1. Determine the ending inventory that would have been reported in the current year if Chrysler had used only FIFO.
2. Determine the cost of goods sold that would have been reported if Chrysler had used only FIFO for both years.
3. Explain why Chrysler management chose to use LIFO for certain of its inventories.

E7–18 Alternative Applications of Lower of Cost or Market

Peterson Company is preparing the annual financial statements dated December 31, 19B. Ending inventory information about the five major items stocked for regular sale follows:

	ENDING INVENTORY, 19B		
Item	Quantity on Hand	Unit Cost When Acquired (FIFO)	Replacement Cost (Market) at Year-End
A	50	$15	$13
B	75	40	40
C	10	50	52
D	30	30	30
E	400	8	6

Required:

1. Compute the valuation that should be used for the 19B ending inventory using the LCM rule applied on an item-by-item basis. (*Hint:* Set up columns for Item, Quantity, Total Cost, Total Market, and LCM Valuation.)
2. Compute the valuation of ending inventory using the LCM rule applied to total cost and total market value of the inventory.
3. Which method, 1 or 2, is preferable? Why?

First Team Sports, Inc.

E7–19 Focus on Cash Flows: Interpreting the Effect of Changes in Inventories and Accounts Payable on Cash Flow from Operations

First Team Sports, Inc. is engaged in the manufacture (through independent contractors) and distribution of in-line roller skates, ice skates, street hockey equipment, and related accessory products. Its recent annual report included the following on its balance sheet:

CONSOLIDATED BALANCE SHEETS
February 29, 19B and February 28, 19A

	19B	19A
. . . .		
Inventory (Note 3)	22,813,850	20,838,171
. . . .	. . .	. . .
Trade accounts payable	9,462,883	9,015,376

Required:

Explain the effects of the changes in inventory and trade accounts payable in 19B on Cash Flow from Operating Activities for 19B.

E7–20 Recording Sales and Purchases with Cash Discounts

The Cycle Shop sells merchandise on credit terms of 2/10, n/30. A sale invoiced at $800 was made to Missy Clemons on February 1, 19B. The company uses the gross method of recording sales discounts.

Required:

1. Give the journal entry to record the credit sale. Assume use of the periodic inventory system.
2. Give the journal entry assuming that the account was collected in full on February 9, 19B.
3. Give the journal entry assuming, instead, that the account was collected in full on March 2, 19B.

On March 4, 19B, the company purchased bicycles and accessories from a supplier on credit, invoiced at $8,000; the terms were 1/15, n/30. The company uses the gross method to record purchases.

Required:

4. Give the journal entry to record the purchase on credit. Assume the use of the periodic inventory system.
5. Give the journal entry assuming that the account was paid in full on March 12, 19B.
6. Give the journal entry assuming, instead, that the account was paid in full on March 28, 19B.

E7–21 (Supplement A) Analyzing the Effects of a Reduction in the Amount of LIFO Inventory

Standard Oil

An annual report of Standard Oil Company (Indiana) contained the following footnote:

During this year and last year, the company reduced certain inventory quantities that were valued at lower LIFO costs prevailing in prior years. The effect of these reductions was to increase aftertax earnings this year by $71 million, or $0.24 per share, and $74 million, or a $0.25 per share last year.

Required:

1. Explain why the reduction in inventory quantity increased after-tax earnings (net income) for Standard Oil.
2. If Standard Oil had used FIFO, would the reductions in inventory quantity during the two years have increased after-tax earnings? Explain.

Problems

P7–1 Analyzing Possible Inventory Errors

Reggie Company has just completed a physical inventory count at year-end, December 31, 19B. Only the items on the shelves, in storage, and in the receiving area were counted and costed on a FIFO basis. The inventory amounted to $70,000. During the audit, the independent CPA developed the following additional information:

a. Goods costing $500 were being used by a customer on a trial basis and were excluded from the inventory count at December 31, 19B.

b. Goods in transit on December 31, 19B, from a supplier, with terms FOB destination, cost $600. Because these goods had not arrived, they were excluded from the physical inventory count.

c. On December 31, 19B, goods in transit to customers, with terms FOB shipping point, amounted to $1,000 (expected delivery date January 10, 19C). Because the goods had been shipped, they were excluded from the physical inventory count.

d. On December 28, 19B, a customer purchased goods for cash amounting to $2,000 and left them "for pickup on January 3, 19C." Reggie Company had paid $1,200 for the goods and because they were on hand, included the latter amount in the physical inventory count.

e. On the date of the inventory, the company received notice from a supplier that goods ordered earlier, at a cost of $2,200, had been delivered to the transportation company on December 27, 19B; the terms were FOB shipping point. Because the shipment had not arrived by December 31, 19B, it was excluded from the physical inventory.

f. On December 31, 19B, the company shipped $950 worth of goods to a customer, FOB destination. The goods are expected to arrive at their destination no earlier than January 8, 19C. Because the goods were not on hand, they were not included in the physical inventory count.

g. One of the items sold by the company has such a low volume that the management planned to drop it last year. To induce Reggie Company to continue carrying the item, the manufacturer-supplier provided the item on a consignment basis. At the end of each month, Reggie Company (the consignee) renders a report to the manufacturer on the number sold and remits cash for the cost. At the end of December 19B, Reggie Company had five of these items on hand; therefore, they were included in the physical inventory count at $1,000 each.

Required:

Note that the point where title (ownership) changes hands is determined by the shipping terms in the sales contract. When goods are shipped "F.O.B. shipping point," title changes hands at shipment and the buyer normally pays for shipping. When they are shipped "F.O.B. destination," title changes hands on delivery and the seller normally pays for shipping. Begin with the $70,000 inventory amount and compute the correct amount for the ending inventory. Explain the basis for your treatment of each of the preceding items. (*Hint:* Set up three columns: Item, Amount, and Explanation.)

P7–2 Analyzing Inventory Errors

The income statements for four consecutive years for Clement Company reflected the following summarized amounts:

	19A	19B	19C	19D
Sales revenue	$50,000	$51,000	$62,000	$58,000
Cost of goods sold	32,500	35,000	43,000	37,000
Gross margin	17,500	16,000	19,000	21,000
Expenses	10,000	12,000	14,000	12,000
Pretax income	$ 7,500	$ 4,000	$ 5,000	$ 9,000

Subsequent to development of these amounts, it has been determined that the physical inventory taken on December 31, 19B, was understated by $3,000.

Required:

1. Recast the income statements to reflect the correct amounts, taking into consideration the inventory error.
2. Compute the gross margin ratio for each year (a) before the correction and (b) after the correction. Do the results lend confidence to your corrected amounts? Explain.
3. What effect would the error have had on the income tax expense assuming a 30 percent average rate?

P7–3 Analyzing and Correcting an Error in Ending Inventory

The income statement for Sherwood Company summarized for a four-year period shows the following:

	19A	19B	19C	19D
Sales revenue	$2,000,000	$2,400,000	$2,500,000	$3,000,000
Cost of goods sold	1,400,000	1,630,000	1,780,000	2,100,000
Gross margin	600,000	770,000	720,000	900,000
Expenses	450,000	500,000	520,000	550,000
Pretax income	150,000	270,000	200,000	350,000
Income tax expense (30%)	45,000	81,000	60,000	105,000
	$ 105,000	$ 189,000	$ 140,000	$ 245,000

An audit revealed that in determining these amounts, the ending inventory for 19B was overstated by $20,000. The company uses a periodic inventory system.

Required:

1. Recast these income statements on a correct basis.
2. Did the error affect cumulative net income for the four-year period? Explain.
3. Did the error affect cash inflows or outflows? Explain.

P7–4 Choosing among Four Alternative Inventory Methods Based on Income and Cash Flow

Allsigns Company uses a periodic inventory system. At the end of the annual accounting period, December 31, 19E, the accounting records for the most popular item in inventory showed the following:

Transactions	Units	Unit Cost
Beginning inventory, January 1, 19E	400	$30
Transactions during 19E:		
1. Purchase, February 20	600	32
2. Sale, April 1 ($46 each)	(700)	
3. Purchase, June 30	500	36
4. Sale, August 1 ($46 each)	(100)	
5. Sales return, August 5 (related to transaction 4)	20	

Required:

Compute the amount of (*a*) goods available for sale, (*b*) ending inventory, and (*c*) cost of goods sold at December 31, 19E, under each of the following inventory costing methods (show computations and round to the nearest dollar):

1. Weighted average cost.
2. First-in, first-out.
3. Last-in, first-out.
4. Specific identification, assuming that the April 1, 19E, sale was selected one-fifth from the beginning inventory and four-fifths from the purchase of February 20, 19E. Assume that the sale of August 1, 19E, was selected from the purchase of June 30, 19E.

P7–5 Analyzing and Using Four Alternative Inventory Methods

At the end of January 19B, the records of Atlanta Company showed the following for a particular item that sold at $18 per unit:

Transactions	Units		Amount
Inventory, January 1, 19B	500	@ 5	$2,500
Sale, January 10	(400)		
Purchase, January 12	600	@ 6	3,600
Sale, January 17	(300)		
Purchase, January 26	160 150	@ 8	1,280
Purchase return, January 28	(10)		Out of Jan. 26 purchase

Required:

1. Assuming the use of a periodic inventory system, prepare a summarized income statement through gross margin on sales under each method of inventory: (*a*) weighted average cost, (*b*) FIFO, (*c*) LIFO, and (*d*) specific identification. For specific identification, assume that the first sale was out of the beginning inventory and the second sale was out of the January 12 purchase. Show the inventory computations in detail.
2. Between FIFO and LIFO, which method would result in the higher pretax income? Which would result in the higher EPS?
3. Between FIFO and LIFO, which method would result in the lower income tax expense? Explain, assuming a 30 percent average tax rate.
4. Between FIFO and LIFO, which method would produce the more favorable cash flow? Explain.

P7–6 Manipulating Income under the LIFO Inventory Method

Pacific Company sells electronic test equipment that it acquires from a foreign source. During the year 19W, the inventory records reflected the following:

	Units	Unit Cost	Total Cost
Beginning inventory	15	$12,000	$180,000
Purchases	40	10,000	400,000
Sales (45 units at $25,000 each)			

The company uses the LIFO inventory costing method. On December 28, 19W, the unit cost of the test equipment was decreased to $8,000. The cost will be decreased again during the first quarter of the next year.

Required:

1. Complete the following income statement summary using the LIFO method and the periodic inventory system (show computations):

Sales revenue	$ _____
Cost of goods sold	_____
Gross margin	_____
Expenses	300,000
Pretax income	$ _____
Ending inventory	$ _____

2. The management, for various reasons, is considering buying 20 additional units before December 31, 19W, at $8,000 each. Restate the income statement (and ending inventory), assuming that this purchase is made on December 31, 19W.

3. How much did pretax income change because of the decision on December 31, 19W? Is there any evidence of income manipulation? Explain.

P7–7 Changing Inventory Method from FIFO to LIFO with Discussion of Stockholder Evaluation

Allendale Corporation reported the following summarized annual data at the end of 19X:

	(Millions)
Sales revenue	$850
Cost of goods sold*	400
Gross margin	450
Expenses	310
Pretax income	$140

*Based on ending FIFO inventory of $120 million. On a LIFO basis, this ending inventory would have been $75 million.

Before issuing the preceding statement, the company decided to change from FIFO to LIFO for 19X because "it better reflects our operating results." The company has always used FIFO.

Required:

1. Restate the summary income statement on a LIFO basis.

2. How much did pretax income change due to the LIFO decision for 19X? What caused the change in pretax income?

3. If you were a stockholder, what would be your reaction to this change? Explain.

P7–8 Choosing between LIFO and FIFO When Costs Are Rising and Falling

Income is to be evaluated under four different situations as follows:

a. Prices are rising:
   1. Situation A: FIFO is used.
   2. Situation B: LIFO is used.
b. Prices are falling:
   1. Situation C: FIFO is used.
   2. Situation D: LIFO is used.

The basic data common to all four situations are sales, 500 units for $12,500; beginning inventory, 300 units; purchases, 400 units; ending inventory, 200 units; and operating expenses, $4,000. The following tabulated income statements for each situation have been set up for analytical purposes:

| | PRICES RISING | | PRICES FALLING | |
	Situation A FIFO	Situation B LIFO	Situation C FIFO	Situation D LIFO
Sales revenue	$12,500	$12,500	$12,500	$12,500
Cost of goods sold				
Beginning inventory	3,600	?	?	?
Purchases	5,200	?	?	?
Goods available for sale	8,800	?	?	?
Ending inventory	2,600	?	?	?
Cost of goods sold	6,200	?	?	?
Gross margin	6,300	?	?	?
Expenses	4,000	4,000	4,000	4,000
Pretax income	2,300	?	?	?
Income tax expense (30%)	690	?	?	?
Net income	$ 1,610			

700 avail

sold 500

200 remaining

Required:

1. Complete the preceding tabulation for each situation. In Situations A and B (prices rising), assume the following: beginning inventory, 300 units at $12 = $3,600; purchases, 400 units at $13 = $5,200. In Situations C and D (prices falling), assume the opposite; that is, beginning inventory, 300 units at $13 = $3,900; purchases, 400 units at $12 = $4,800. Use periodic inventory procedures.
2. Analyze the relative effects on pretax income and on net income as demonstrated by requirement (1) when prices are rising and when prices are falling.
3. Analyze the relative effects on the cash position for each situation.
4. Would you recommend FIFO or LIFO? Explain.

General Motors

P7–9 Analyzing Footnotes to Adjust Inventory and Taxes Paid from LIFO to FIFO

An annual report for General Motors Corporation included the following footnote:

> Inventories are stated generally at cost, which is not in excess of market. The cost of substantially all domestic inventories was determined by the last-in, first-out (LIFO) method. If the first-in, first-out (FIFO) method of inventory valuation had been used by the Corporation for U.S. inventories, it is estimated that they would be $2,077.1 million higher at the end of this year, compared with $1,784.5 million higher at the end of last year.

For the year, GM reported net income (after taxes) of $320.5 million. At year-end, the balance of the GM retained earnings account was $15,340 million.

Required:

1. Determine the amount of net income that GM would have reported for the year if it had used the FIFO method (assume a 30 percent tax rate).
2. Determine the amount of retained earnings that GM would have reported at year-end if it always had used the FIFO method (assume a 30 percent tax rate).
3. Use of the LIFO method reduced the amount of taxes that GM had to pay for the year compared with the amount that would have been paid if it had used FIFO. Calculate the amount of this reduction (assume a 30 percent tax rate).

P7–10 Evaluating the Income Statement and Cash Flow Effects of Lower of Cost or Market

Smart Company prepared its annual financial statements dated December 31, 19B. The company uses a periodic inventory system and applies the FIFO inventory costing method; however, the company neglected to apply LCM to the ending inventory. The preliminary 19B income statement follows:

Sales revenue		$280,000
Cost of goods sold		
Beginning inventory	$ 30,000	
Purchases	182,000	
Goods available for sale	212,000	
Ending inventory (FIFO cost)	44,000	
Cost of goods sold		168,000
Gross margin		112,000
Operating expenses		61,000
Pretax income		51,000
Income tax expense (30%)		15,300
Net income		$ 35,700

Assume that you have been asked to restate the 19B financial statements to incorporate LCM. You have developed the following data relating to the 19B ending inventory:

		ACQUISITION COST		CURRENT REPLACEMENT UNIT COST
Item	Quantity	Unit	Total	(Market)
A	3,000	$3	$ 9,000	$4
B	1,500	4	6,000	2
C	7,000	2	14,000	4
D	3,000	5	15,000	3
			$44,000	

Required:
1. Restate this income statement to reflect LCM valuation of the 19B ending inventory. Apply LCM on an item-by-item basis and show computations.
2. Compare and explain the LCM effect on each amount that was changed in requirement (1).
3. What is the conceptual basis for applying LCM to merchandise inventories?
4. Thought question: What effect did LCM have on the 19B cash flow? What will be the long-term effect on cash flow?

P7–11 Accounting for Cash Discounts by the Vendor and the Purchaser

Assume the following summarized transactions between Company V, the vendor, and Company P, the purchaser. Assume that each company uses a periodic inventory system and each uses the gross method to record sales revenue and purchases.
(vs net)
(a) Company V sold Company P merchandise for $7,000; terms 3/10, n/30.
(b) Prior to payment, Company P returned $700 (one-tenth) of the merchandise for credit because it did not meet P's specifications.

Required:
Using the numbers to the left as the date notations, give the following journal entries in parallel columns for each party:
1. The sale/purchase transaction.
2. The return transaction.
3. Payment in full, assuming that it was made within the discount period.
4. Payment in full assuming, instead that it was made after the discount period. Use a form similar to the following:

		CO. V—VENDOR		CO. P—PURCHASER	
Date	Accounts	Debit	Credit	Debit	Credit

P7–12 Reporting Sales and Purchases with Cash Discounts

Campus Stop, Incorporated, is a student co-op. On January 1, 19X, the beginning inventory was $150,000, the Accounts Receivable balance was $4,000, and the Allowance for Doubtful Accounts had a credit balance of $800. It uses a periodic inventory system and records purchases using the gross method. Ending inventory was $95,000.

The following transactions (summarized) have been selected from 19X for case purposes:

(a)	Merchandise sales for cash	$275,000
(b)	Merchandise returned by customers as unsatisfactory, for cash refund	1,600
	Merchandise purchased from vendors on credit; terms 3/10, n/30	
(c)	August Supply Company invoice price before deduction of cash discount	5,000
(d)	Other vendors, invoice price, before deduction of cash discount	122,000
(e)	Purchased equipment for use in store; paid cash	2,200
(f)	Purchased office supplies for future use in the store; paid cash	700
(g)	Freight on merchandise purchased; paid cash	
	(set up a separate account for this item)	400

Accounts payable paid in full during the period as follows:

(h)	August Supply Company, paid after the discount period	5,000
(i)	Other vendors, paid within the 3% discount period	116,400

Required:

1. Prepare journal entries for each of the preceding transactions.
2. Prepare a partial income statement through gross margin on sales.

P7–13 Reporting Sales and Purchases with Cash Discounts and Returns on the Financial Statements

The following transactions were selected from those occurring during the month of January 19D for Dan's Store, Incorporated. A wide line of goods is offered for sale. Credit sales are extended to a few select customers; the usual credit terms are n/EOM.

(a)	Sales to customers:	
	Cash	$228,000
	On credit	72,000
(b)	Unsatisfactory merchandise returned by customers:	
	Cash	3,000
	Credit	2,000

Merchandise purchased from vendors on credit; terms 2/10, n/30:

(c)	XYZ Supply Company, amount billed, before deduction of cash discount	4,000
(d)	From other vendors, amount billed, before deduction of cash discount	68,000
(e)	Freight paid on merchandise purchased; paid cash	
	(set up a separate account for this item)	1,500
(f)	Collections on accounts receivable	36,000

The accounts payable were paid in full during the period as follows:

(g)	XYZ Supply Company, paid after the discount period	4,000
(h)	Other vendors, paid within the discount period	66,640
(i)	Purchased two new typewriters for the office; paid cash	1,000

Required:

Prepare journal entries for these transactions, assuming that a periodic inventory system is in use. Record purchases using the gross method.

P7–14 **(Supplement A) Analyzing LIFO and FIFO When Inventory Quantities Decline Based on an Actual Note**

General Electric

In a recent annual report, General Electric reported the following in their inventory footnote:

December 31 (In millions)	19B	19A
Raw materials and work in progress	$5,603	$5,515
Finished goods	2,863	2,546
Unbilled shipments	246	280
	8,712	8,341
Less revaluation to LIFO	(2,226)	(2,076)
LIFO value of inventories	$6,486	$6,265

They also reported a $23 million change in cost of goods sold due to "lower inventory levels."

Required:

1. Compute the increase or decrease in the pretax operating profit (loss) that would have been reported for the current year had GE employed FIFO accounting for all inventory for both years.
2. Compute the increase or decrease in pretax operating profit that would have been reported had GE employed LIFO but not reduced inventory quantities during the current year.

Cases and Projects

C7–1 **An International Perspective**

Grand Metropolitan

As the economy becomes more international in scope, users of financial statements may be expected to analyze companies that are not incorporated in the United States. Grand Metropolitan is a major world corporation located in London. It owns many U.S. businesses such as The Pillsbury Company, Burger King, and Häagen-Dazs ice cream.

Required:

Based on the concepts presented in this book, explain the meaning of the various account classifications shown on the portion of the Grand Metropolitan annual report presented here. (*Note:* "Share of profits of related companies" and "minority interests and preference dividends" pertain to topics introduced in subsequent chapters.)

GRAND METROPOLITAN
Consolidated Profit and Loss Account
For the Year Ended 30th September 19B

	Notes	19B £m	19A £m
Turnover	1	9,298	6,029
Operating costs	2	(8,349)	(5,387)
		949	642
Share of profits of related companies	3	18	12
Trading profit		967	654
Profit on sale of property		80	39
Reorganisation costs		(35)	(25)
Interest	4	(280)	(93)
Profit on ordinary activities before taxation		732	575
Taxation on profit on ordinary activities		(216)	(155)
Profit on ordinary activities after taxation		516	420
Minority interests and preference dividends	5	(8)	(8)

(continued on next page)

GRAND METROPOLITAN
Consolidated Profit and Loss Account
Continued

	Notes	19B £m	19A £m
Profit attributable to ordinary shareholders		508	412
Extraordinary items	6	560	290
Profit for the financial year		1,068	702
Ordinary dividends	7	(167)	(129)
Transferred to reserves		901	573
Earnings per share	8	55.6p	46.9p

Dana Corporation

C7–2 Effect of a Change in Accounting for Production-Related Costs

Dana Corporation designs and manufactures component parts for the vehicular, industrial, and mobile off-highway original equipment markets. In a recent annual report, Dana's inventory footnote indicated the following:

> Dana changed its method of accounting for inventories effective January 1 . . . to include in inventory certain production-related costs previously charged to expense. This change in accounting principle resulted in a better matching of costs against related revenues. The effect of this change in accounting increased inventories by $23.0 and net income by $12.9.

Required:

1. Under Dana's previous accounting method, certain production costs were recognized as expenses on the income statement in the period they were incurred. When will they be recognized under the new accounting method?
2. Explain how including these costs in inventory increased both inventories and net income for the year.

Micro Warehouse

C7–3 Ethics Case: Earnings, Inventory Purchases, and Management Bonuses

Micro Warehouse is a computer software and hardware catalogue sales company. A recent *Wall Street Journal* article disclosed that:

> **MICRO WAREHOUSE IS REORGANIZING TOP MANAGEMENT**
> Micro Warehouse Inc. announced a "significant reorganization" of its management, including the resignation of three senior executives.
> The move comes just a few weeks after the Norwalk, Conn., computer catalogue sales company said it overstated earnings by $28 million since 1992 as a result of accounting irregularities. That previous disclosure prompted a flurry of shareholder lawsuits against the company. In addition, Micro Warehouse said it is cooperating with an "informal inquiry" by the Securities and Exchange Commission.

SOURCE: Stephan E. Frank, *The Wall Street Journal*, November 21, 1996, p. B2.

Its Form 10-Q quarterly report filed with the Securities and Exchange Commission two days before indicated that inaccuracies involving understatement of purchases and accounts payable in current and prior periods amounted to $47.3 million. It also indicated that, as a result, $2.2 million of executive bonuses for 1995 would be rescinded. Micro Warehouse's total tax rate is approximately 40.4 percent. Both cost of goods sold and executive bonuses are fully deductible for tax purposes.

Required:

As a new staff member at Micro Warehouse's auditing firm, you are assigned to write a memo outlining the effects of the understatement of purchases and the rescinding of the bonuses. In your report, be sure to include the following:

1. The total effect on pretax and after-tax earnings of the understatement of purchases.
2. The total effect on pretax and after-tax earnings of the rescinding of the bonuses.
3. An estimate of the percent of after-tax earnings management is receiving in bonuses.
4. A discussion of why Micro Warehouse's board of directors may have decided to tie managers' compensation to reported earnings and the possible relation between this type of bonus scheme and the accounting errors.

C7–4 Analyzing the Effects of the LIFO/FIFO Choice on Inventory Turnover   Caterpillar

In a recent annual report, Caterpillar, Inc., a major manufacturer of farm and construction equipment, reported the following information concerning its inventories:

> The cost of inventories is determined principally by the LIFO (last-in, first-out) method of inventory valuation. This method was first adopted for the major portion of inventories in 1950. The value of inventories on the LIFO basis represented approximately 90% of total inventories at current cost value on December 31, 1995, 1994, and 1993. If the FIFO (first-in, first-out) method had been in use, inventories would have been $2,103, $2,035, and $1,818 higher than reported at December 31, 1995, 1994, and 1993, respectively.

On its balance sheet, it reported:

	1995	1994	1993
Inventories	$1,921	$1,835	$1,525

On its income statement, it reported:

	1995	1994	1993
Cost of goods sold	$12,000	$10,834	$9,075

Required:

As a recently hired financial analyst, you have been asked to analyze the efficiency with which Caterpillar has been managing its inventory. Specifically, you have been asked to compute inventory turnover for 1995 and compare it with two standards: (1) Caterpillar for the prior year 1994 and (2) its chief competitor, John Deere (discussed in the chapter), for 1995. In your report, include

1. The appropriate ratios computed based on FIFO and LIFO.
2. An explanation for the differences in the ratios across the FIFO and LIFO methods.
3. An explanation of whether the FIFO or LIFO ratios provide a more accurate representation of the companies' efficiency in use of inventory.

C7–5 Analysis of the Effect of a Change to LIFO–Based Operating Results   Quaker Oats

A recent annual report for Quaker Oats included the following information:

> The company adopted the LIFO cost flow assumption for valuing the majority of remaining U.S. Grocery Products inventories. The Company believes that the use of the LIFO method better matches current costs with current revenues. The cumulative effect of this change on retained earnings at the beginning of the year is not determinable, nor are the pro forma effects of retroactive application of LIFO to prior years. The effect of this change on the current year was to decrease net income by $16.0 million, or $0.20 per share.

Required:
1. In addition to the reason that was cited, why did management adopt LIFO?
2. As an analyst, how would you react to the $0.20 per share decrease in income caused by the adoption of LIFO?

General Motors

C7–6 (Supplement A) Analysis of the Effects of LIFO Liquidations

Several years ago, General Motors reported the following in their inventory note:

> The cost of substantially all domestic inventories was determined by the last-in, first-out (LIFO) method. If the first-in, first-out (FIFO) method of inventory valuation had been used by the Corporation for U.S. inventories, it is estimated they would be $1,886.0 million higher at December 31, [current year] compared with $2,077.1 million at December 31, [prior year]. As a result of decreases in unit sales and actions taken to reduce inventories, certain LIFO inventory quantities carried at lower costs prevailing in prior years, as compared with the costs of current purchases, were liquidated. . . . These inventory adjustments favorably affected income (loss) before income taxes by approximately $305.0 million [current year].

In the current year, GM recorded a small pretax operating profit of $22.8 million.

Required:
1. Compute the amount of pretax operating profit (loss) that GM would have reported had it not reduced inventory quantities during the current year.
2. Compute the amount of pretax operating profit (loss) for the current year that GM would have reported had it employed FIFO accounting in both years.
3. What is the normal relationship between pretax operating profit computed using LIFO and FIFO when costs are rising? Why is this relationship not in evidence in this case?

Toys "R" Us

C7–7 Financial Statement Analysis

Refer to the financial statements of Toys "R" Us given in Appendix B at the end of this book.

1. Estimate the amount of merchandise that the company purchased during the current year.
2. At what point does the company recognize revenue?
3. Sales revenue increased in the current year. Is this increase attributable to an increase in the number of stores or an increase in sales volume at existing stores?

Toys "R" Us

C7–8 Financial Statement Analysis

Refer to the financial statements of Toys "R" Us given in Appendix B at the end of this book.

1. What method does the company use to determine the cost of its inventory?
2. If the inventories had all been valued at FIFO, inventories would show no change at year-end. How do you explain that different accounting methods would produce the same results?
3. If the company switched to the average cost method, would you expect the reported inventory to increase or decrease by a significant amount?

C7–9 Project: Comparing Inventory Accounting Policies within Industries

Acquire the inventory accounting note from the annual reports or 10-Ks of three companies within an industry. (Library files, the SEC EDGAR service at www.sec.gov, Compustat CD, or the companies themselves are good sources.) Write a short report indicating any similarities or differences among the accounting policies. Consider what characteristics of the companies and their inventories may have led to the choices of methods. If the company used LIFO, indicate whether it paid higher or lower taxes as a result in the current year.

C7–10 Project: Comparing Inventory Accounting Policies among Industries

Acquire the inventory accounting note from the annual reports or 10-Ks of three companies from different industries. (Library files, the SEC EDGAR service at www.sec.gov, Compustat, or the companies themselves are good sources.) Write a short report indicating any similarities or differences among the accounting policies. Consider what characteristics of the companies and their inventories may have led to the choices of methods. If the company used LIFO, indicate whether it paid higher or lower taxes as a result in the current year.

C7–11 Project: Competitive Analysis of Differences in Inventory Turnover Ratio

Timberland's competitors in the shoe industry include Brown Group, Reebok, Nike, Stride Rite, and others. Obtain the income statement, balance sheet, and inventory footnote for Timberland and two of its competitors. (Library files, the SEC EDGAR service at www.sec.gov, Compustat, or the companies themselves are good sources.) Write a short memo comparing the companies' inventory turnover ratios. Indicate what differences in their businesses might account for any differences. Consider the possible effect of the use of LIFO on your analysis.

C7–12 Project: Analysis of Changes in the Inventory Turnover Ratio

Acquire the three most recent years' income statements, balance sheets, and inventory footnotes for a single company. (Library files, the SEC EDGAR service at www.sec.gov, Compustat, or the company itself are good sources.) Write a short memo comparing the company's inventory turnover ratio over the three years. Indicate what differences in its operations might account for any differences in the ratio. Consider the possible effect of the use of LIFO on your analysis.

C7–13 Project: Focus on Cash Flows

Acquire the three most recent years' cash flow statements for a single company. (Library files, the SEC EDGAR service at www.sec.gov, Compustat, or the company itself are good sources.) Write a short memo describing the effect of the change in inventory and accounts payable on the difference between Net Income and Cash Flow from Operations for each year.

C7–14 Project: Financial Analysis Update

Acquire the most recent year's annual report and Form 10-K for Harley-Davidson. (Library files, the SEC EDGAR service at www.sec.gov, Compustat, or the company itself are good sources.) Write a short memo comparing the company's inventory turnover ratio to the 1995 figures presented in the chapter. Indicate what differences in its operations might account for any differences in the ratios.

C7–15 Ethics Project: Analysis of Irregularities in Inventory

Obtain a recent news story outlining an accounting irregularity related to inventory. (Library files, Wall Street Journal Index, Dow Jones News/Retrieval, and *Bloomberg Business News* are good sources. Search for the term *accounting irregularities*.) Write a short memo outlining the nature of the irregularity, the size of the necessary correction of previously reported earnings, the impact of the announcement of the irregularity on the company's stock price, and any fines or civil penalties against the company and its officers.

C7–16 Team Project: Analyzing Inventories

As a group, select an industry to analyze. Each group member should acquire the annual report or 10-K for one publicly traded company in the industry, with each member selecting a different company. (Library files, the SEC EDGAR service at www.sec.gov, Compustat CD, or the company itself are good sources.) On an individual basis, each group member should then write a short report answering the following questions about his or her selected company.

1. What inventory costing method is applied to U.S. inventories? What do you think motivated this choice?
2. If the company used LIFO, how much higher or lower would net income before taxes be if it had used FIFO or a similar method instead?
3. What is the inventory turnover ratio?
4. What was the effect of the change in inventories on cash flow from operations? Explain your answer.

Discuss any patterns across the companies that you as a group observe. Then, as a group, write a short report comparing and contrasting your companies using these attributes. Provide potential explanations for any differences discovered.

Reporting and Interpreting Property, Plant, and Equipment; Natural Resources; and Intangibles

Delta Air Lines
MANAGING PROFITS THROUGH CONTROL OF PRODUCTIVE CAPACITY

Delta Air Lines is a major air carrier providing service to 153 domestic cities in 43 states and 44 international cities in 25 foreign countries. Delta is a capital-intensive company with more than $6,795,000,000 in property, plant, and equipment reported on its balance sheet. In one recent year alone, Delta took delivery of 29 new aircraft and spent $2,053,211,000 on flight equipment. Demand for air travel is seasonal, with peak demand occurring during the summer months because of vacation time. Demand is very sensitive to general economic conditions. As a result, planning for optimal productive capacity in the airline industry is very difficult.

On March 20, 1997, Delta Air Lines signed a major long-term agreement with Boeing Co., the world's largest manufacturer of aircraft, to buy planes

LEARNING OBJECTIVES
After studying this chapter, you should be able to:

1. Define, classify, and explain the nature of noncurrent productive assets. 418
2. Apply the cost principle to measure the acquisition of property, plant, and equipment. 418
3. Understand the financial statement impact of management's decisions regarding ordinary and extraordinary repairs, various cost allocation methods, and changes in estimates as assets are held and used over time. 422
4. Explain the impact of cost allocation methods on cash flows. 437
5. Analyze the disposal of property, plant, and equipment. 438
6. Understand the measurement and reporting of natural resources and intangible assets. 439
7. Explain the effect of asset impairment on the financial statements. 444

exclusively from Boeing Co. over the next 20 years. The contract included an initial firm order to purchase 106 jets with list prices totaling $6.7 billion and a flexible agreement (options) "to buy as many as 644 planes from Boeing during the next two decades at pre-arranged discount prices."*

The exclusive deal signals a dramatic shift from traditional purchasing practices—a deal that effectively shuts out other competitors. Delta hopes that a more modern fleet will attract additional passengers and reduce operating costs. Buying from a single supplier also should dramatically simplify maintenance of aircraft and employee training. Improved management of productive capacity will be a key to Delta's success in the 21st century.

■ ■ ■

* J. Cole,and M. Brannigan, "Delta's Pact to Buy Only Boeing Jets Draws Sharp Rebuke from Rival Airbus," *The Wall Street Journal*, March 21, 1997, p. A3.

Business Background

One of the major challenges facing managers of most businesses is forecasting the level of productive capacity needed in the long term. If managers underestimate the need, the company will not be able to produce goods or services that are in demand and will miss the opportunity to earn revenue. On the other hand, if needed productive capacity is overestimated, the company will incur excessive costs that will reduce profitability.

The airline industry provides an outstanding example of the difficulty associated with planning for and analyzing productive capacity. If an airplane takes off from Kansas City, Missouri, en route to New York City with empty seats, the economic value associated with those seats is lost forever. There is obviously no way to sell the seat to a customer after the airplane has left the gate. Unlike a manufacturer, an airline cannot "inventory" seats for the future.

Likewise, if a large number of people want to board a flight, the airline must turn away customers if seats are not available. You might be willing to buy a television set from Sears even if you are told that it is out of stock and there will be a one-week delay in delivery. You probably wouldn't fly home for Thanksgiving on an airline that told you that you would have to wait one week because no seats were available on its flights. You would simply pick another airline or use a different mode of transportation.

The asset section of the balance sheet from Delta's annual report for the fiscal year ended June 30, 1996, is shown in Exhibit 8.1. Additional information about property, plant, and equipment is contained in Delta's 10–K report. The 10–K report shows the amount of new investment in equipment for the year, the amount of equipment that was sold or retired, and the specific number of each type of aircraft that Delta owns. We discuss some of these data in this chapter.

Delta has a number of large competitors with familiar names such as American, U·S Airways, United, and Southwest. The notes to the Delta annual report mention that "all domestic routes served by Delta are subject to competition from new and existing carriers, and service over virtually all of Delta's domestic routes is highly competitive. Service over most of Delta's international routes is highly competitive."

Much of the battle for passengers in the airline industry is fought in terms of property, plant, and equipment. Passengers want convenient schedules (which require a large number of aircraft) and to fly with new, modern equipment.

EXHIBIT 8.1
Delta Air Lines Asset Section of the Balance Sheet

REAL WORLD EXCERPT

DELTA AIR LINES
Annual Report

CONSOLIDATED *balance sheets*
June 30, 1996 and 1995

ASSETS	1996	1995
	(In Millions)	
Current Assets:		
Cash and cash equivalents.	$ 1,145	$ 1,233
Short-term investments	507	529
Accounts receivable, net of allowance for		
uncollectible accounts of $44 at June 30,		
1996, and $29 at June 30, 1995.	968	755
Maintenance and operating supplies, at average cost.	73	68
Deferred income taxes.	352	234
Prepaid expenses and other.	237	195
Total current assets.	3,282	3,014
Property and Equipment:		
Flight equipment	8,202	9,288
Less: Accumulated depreciation	3,235	4,209
	4,967	5,079
Flight equipment under capital leases.	515	537
Less: Accumulated amortization	127	99
	388	438
Ground property and equipment	2,697	2,442
Less: Accumulated depreciation	1,532	1,354
	1,165	1,088
Advance payments for equipment	275	331
	6,795	6,936
Other Assets:		
Marketable equity securities	473	398
Deferred income taxes.	415	506
Investments in associated companies.	266	265
Cost in excess of net assets acquired, net of		
accumulated amortization of $84 at		
June 30, 1996, and $75 at June 30, 1995	265	274
Leasehold and operating rights, net of accumulated		
amortization of $183 at June 30, 1996,		
and $165 at June 30, 1995	140	177
Other.	590	573
	2,149	2,193
	$12,226	$12,143

Because airlines have such a large investment in equipment with no opportunity to inventory unused seats, they work very hard to fill aircraft to capacity for each flight. The frequent fare wars that you read about in newspaper advertisements are caused by airlines trying to build customer demand to use their large investments in productive capacity. A note to the Delta annual report that appears at the top of page 418 addresses this issue.

As you can see from this discussion, issues surrounding property, plant, and equipment have a pervasive impact on a company in terms of strategy, pricing decisions, and profitability. Managers devote considerable time planning optimal levels

Delta expects that low-fare competition is likely to continue in domestic and international markets. If price reductions are not offset by increases in traffic or changes in the mix of traffic that improve the passenger mile yield, Delta's operating results will be adversely affected.

of productive capacity, and financial analysts closely review statements to determine the impact of management decisions.

Classification of Operational Assets

LEARNING OBJECTIVE 1

Define, classify, and explain the nature of noncurrent productive assets.

Operational assets (or long-lived assets) are tangible and intangible assets owned by a business and used in its operations.

Tangible assets are operational assets (or fixed assets) that have physical substance.

The assets that determine productive capacity are often called **operational assets** (or **long-lived assets**). They have different characteristics, depending on the nature of the business. These assets are listed as noncurrent on the balance sheet and have the following characteristics:

1. **Tangible assets** are operational assets that have physical substance; that is, they are tangible. This classification usually is called *property, plant, and equipment* (or *fixed assets*). The three kinds of tangible assets are
    a. *Land* (held for use in operations; not subject to depreciation). As is the case with Delta, land often is not shown as a separate item on the balance sheet.
    b. *Buildings, fixtures, and equipment* (held for use in operations; subject to depreciation). For Delta, this category includes aircraft, ground equipment to service aircraft, and office space.
    c. *Natural resources* (held for use in operations; subject to depletion). Delta does not report any natural resources on its balance sheet.

Intangible assets are operational assets that have special rights but not physical substance.

2. **Intangible assets** are operational assets without physical substance that the business holds because of the use rights they confer on the owner. Examples are patents, copyrights, franchises, licenses, and trademarks. Leasehold and operating rights shown on the Delta balance sheet are intangible assets.

Following the natural life cycle of operational assets, we first discuss the measuring and reporting issues related to the acquisition of land, buildings, and equipment. Then we examine the variety of issues related to holding and using these assets over time. We also discuss the disposal of land, buildings, and equipment, and then focus on measuring and reporting natural resources and intangible assets.

Measuring and Recording Acquisition Cost

LEARNING OBJECTIVE 2

Apply the cost principle to measure the acquisition of property, plant, and equipment.

For the sake of illustration, let's assume that Delta received the first new 737 aircraft from Boeing under the new agreement on July 1, 1997 (the beginning of Delta's fiscal year). The list price was $63 million (the average price in the new contract). Under the cost principle, all reasonable and necessary costs incurred in acquiring an operational asset, placing it in its operational setting, and preparing it for use should be recorded in a designated asset account (that is, should be capitalized). These costs, including any sales taxes, legal fees, transportation costs, and installation costs, are added to the purchase price of the aircraft. Any special discounts or financing charges associated with the purchase should not, however, be included in the cost of the asset. Financing charges should be reported as interest expense.

Although details of the discounts negotiated by Boeing and Delta are not publicly available, we can make assumptions for illustration purposes. Let's assume that

How does depreciation impact the net book value of these airplanes on Delta's balance sheet?

Boeing offered Delta a discount of $4 million for signing the exclusive agreement. That means the price to Delta is $59 million. Let's also assume that Delta paid for transportation charges of $200,000 and preparation costs of $800,000 for the new plane to make it ready for use. The amount recorded for the purchase is called the **acquisition cost,** which is the net cash equivalent amount paid or to be paid for the asset.

The **acquisition cost** is the net cash equivalent amount paid or to be paid for the asset.

Delta calculates the acquisition cost of the new aircraft as follows:

Invoice price of the aircraft	$63,000,000
Less: Special discount for the agreement	4,000,000
Net cash invoice price	$59,000,000
Add: Transportation charges paid by Delta	200,000
Installation (prepration) costs paid by Delta	800,000
Cost—amount added to the asset account	$60,000,000

In addition to purchasing buildings and equipment, a company may acquire undeveloped land, typically with the intent to build a new factory or office building. When land is purchased, all of the incidental costs paid by the purchaser, such as title fees, sales commissions, legal fees, title insurance, delinquent taxes, and surveying fees, should be included in the cost of the land. Because land is not subject to depreciation, it must be recorded as a separate operational asset.

Sometimes an old building or used machinery is purchased for operational use in the business. Renovation and repair costs incurred by the purchaser prior to use should be included in the asset account as a part of the cost of the asset.

Various Acquisition Methods

For Cash

Assuming that Delta paid cash for the aircraft, it records the following journal entry:

Flight equipment (A)	60,000,000	
Cash (A)		60,000,000

For Debt

It might seem unusual for Delta to pay cash to purchase new assets that cost $60 million, but this is often the case. When it acquires operational assets, a company may pay with cash that was generated from operations or cash that was recently borrowed. It also is possible for the seller to finance the purchase on credit.

Now let's assume that Delta signed a note payable for the new aircraft and cash for the transportation and preparation costs. Delta records the following journal entry:

Flight equipment (A)	60,000,000	
Note payable (L)		59,000,000
Cash (A)		1,000,000

For Noncash Consideration (including Equity)

Noncash consideration might be part of the transaction, such as a company's common stock or a right given by the company to the seller to purchase the company's goods or services at a special price over a specified period of time. When noncash consideration is included in the purchase of an asset, the cash-equivalent cost is measured as any cash paid plus the current market value of the noncash consideration given. Alternatively, if the market value of the noncash consideration given cannot be determined, the current market value of the asset purchased is used for measurement purposes.

Now assume that Delta gave 400,000 shares of its common stock (par value of $3 per share) with a market value of $85 per share (the approximate stock price on the date of the transaction) and paid Boeing the balance in cash including cash for the transportation and preparation. The journal entry follows:

Flight equipment (A)	60,000,000	
Cash (A)		26,000,000
Common stock ($3 par value × 400,000) (SE)		1,200,000
Additional paid-in capital ($82 × 400,000) (SE)		32,800,000

By Construction

Capitalized interest represents interest expenditures included in the cost of a self-constructed asset.

In some cases, a company may construct an asset for its own use instead of buying it from a manufacturer. When a company does this, the cost of the asset includes all necessary costs associated with construction, such as labor and materials. In most situations, these costs also include interest incurred during the construction period. The amount that is included in the cost of an asset is called **capitalized interest.** Interest on self-constructed assets should be capitalized even when it did not borrow funds directly to support the construction. The amount of interest capitalized is based on the amount of funds that actually are invested in the construction project.

Delta Air Lines includes a note on capitalized interest in a recent annual report:

**NOTES TO CONSOLIDATED
FINANCIAL STATEMENTS**

1. Summary of Significant Accounting Policies:

   . . .

   Interest Capitalized. Interest attributable to funds used to finance the acquisition of new aircraft and construction of major ground facilities is capitalized as an additional cost of the related asset. Interest is capitalized at the Company's weighted average interest rate on long-term debt or, where applicable, the interest rate of specific borrowings. Capitalization of interest ceases when the property or equipment is placed in service.

As a Basket Purchase of Assets

Basket purchase is an acquisition of two or more assets in a single transaction for a single lump sum.

When several operational assets, such as land, building, and equipment, are acquired in a single transaction and for a single lump sum, known as a **basket purchase,** the cost of each asset must be measured and recorded separately. This is true because land is not depreciated, but buildings and equipment are, although at different rates. The purchase price must be apportioned between the land, the building, and the equipment on a rational basis.

Relative market value of the several assets on the date of acquisition is the most logical basis on which to allocate the single lump sum. Appraisals or tax assessments often must be used to indicate the market values. Assume that Delta Air Lines paid $300,000 cash to purchase a building and the land on which the building is located. The separate, true market values of the building and land were not known; therefore, a professional appraisal was obtained. This appraisal, totaling $315,000, showed the following estimated market values: $189,000 for the building and $126,000 for the land. The apportioned purchase price based on a percentage of the relative market value is computed as follows:

	Building			**Land**	
$\dfrac{\text{Market value}}{\text{Total market value}}$	$= \dfrac{\$189,000}{\$315,000}$	$= 60\%$	$\dfrac{\text{Market value}}{\text{Total market value}}$	$= \dfrac{\$126,000}{\$315,000}$	$= 40\%$
$60\% \times \$300,000$ total cost $= \underline{\$180,000}$			$40\% \times \$300,000$ total cost $= \underline{\$120,000}$		

The ratio of the market value of the land to the total market value ($126,000 ÷ $315,000 = 40 percent) is multiplied by the total cost to measure the cost of the land ($300,000 × 40 percent). Similarly, the ratio of the market value of the building to the total market value ($189,000 ÷ $315,000 = 60 percent) is multiplied by the total cost to measure the cost of the building ($300,000 × 60 percent). Assuming that Delta purchases the assets with cash, the entry is as follows:

Land (A)	120,000	
Building (A)	180,000	
Cash (A)		300,000

Perhaps the most common example of a basket purchase of assets occurs when one corporation buys another corporation. In this case, the basket includes all of the assets owned by the acquired corporation. We discuss corporate acquisitions in a subsequent chapter.

SELF-STUDY QUIZ

In 1995, McDonald's Corporation purchased property, plant, and equipment priced at $2 billion. Assume that the company paid $60 million for sales tax, $3 million for transportation costs, $700,000 for installation and preparation of the property, plant, and equipment before use, and $100,000 in maintenance contracts to cover repairs to the property, plant, and equipment during use.

McDonald's Corporation

1. Compute the acquisition cost for the buildings and equipment:

2. Under the various following assumptions, indicate the effects of this acquisition on the following financial statement categories. Use + for increase and – for decrease and indicate the accounts and amounts:

	Assets	**Liabilities**	**Stockholders' Equity**
1. Paid 30% in cash and the rest by signing a note payable.			
2. Issued 10 million shares of common stock ($.10 per share stated value) at a market price of $45 per share and the balance in cash.			

After you have completed your answers, check them with the solutions presented in the footnote at the bottom of this page.*

Using Property, Plant, and Equipment after Acquisition

Repairs, Maintenance, and Additions

LEARNING OBJECTIVE 3
Understand the financial statement impact of management's decisions regarding ordinary and extraordinary repairs, various cost allocation methods, and changes in estimates as assets are held and used over time.

Capital expenditures provide future benefits and are recorded as increases in asset accounts, not as expenses.

Revenue expenditures provide benefits during the current accounting period only and are recorded as expenses.

Most assets require substantial expenditures during their lives to maintain or enhance their productive capacity. One of the major reasons that Delta is switching to a single supplier for its aircraft is to reduce these costs. These expenditures include ordinary repairs and maintenance, major repairs, replacements, and additions. Some unsophisticated investors assume that the terms *expenditure* and *expense* are synonymous, but such is not the case. An expenditure is the payment of money to acquire goods or services. These goods and services may be recorded as either assets or expenses, depending on whether they benefit future periods or only the current period. Expenditures made after an asset is acquired are classified as follows:

1. **Capital expenditures**—expenditures that provide benefits for one or more accounting periods beyond the current period. Therefore, they are added to the appropriate *asset* accounts.

2. **Revenue expenditures**—expenditures that provide benefits during the current accounting period only. Therefore, they are added to the appropriate current *expense* accounts when incurred.

In many cases, no clear line distinguishes between capital expenditures (assets) and revenue expenditures (expenses). In these situations, managers must exercise professional judgment and make a subjective decision. Many managers prefer to classify an item as a capital expenditure for financial reporting because net income for the period is higher by not reporting the total amount as an expense in the current period. Of course, most managers prefer to classify the expenditure as a deductible expense on the income tax return to pay lower taxes in the current period. Because these decisions are subjective, auditors closely review the items reported as capital and revenue expenditures.

To avoid spending too much time on classifying capital and revenue expenditures, some companies develop simple policies that govern the accounting for these expenditures. For example, one large computer company expenses all individual items that

---

* 1.

Property, Plant, and Equipment (PPE)	
Acquisition cost	$2,000,000,000
Sales tax	60,000,000
Transportation	3,000,000
Installation	700,000
Total	$2,063,700,000

The maintenance contracts are not necessary for bringing the assets ready for use and are therefore not included in the acquisition cost.

2.

	Assets		Liabilities	Stockholders' Equity	
1. Cash	− 619,110,000		Notes payable + 1,444,590,000		
PPE	+ 2,063,700,000				
Net effect	+ 1,444,590,000				
2. Cash	− 1,613,700,000			Common stock +	1,000,000
PPE	+ 2,063,700,000			Paid-in capital +	449,000,000
Net effect	+ 450,000,000			Net effect +	450,000,000

cost less than $1,000. These policies are acceptable because of the *materiality constraint*. The following are various types of revenue and capital expenditures.

[handwritten: on test]

Ordinary Repairs and Maintenance

Ordinary repairs and maintenance expenditures are for normal maintenance and upkeep of operational assets and are necessary to keep the assets in their usual condition. These expenditures are recurring in nature, involve relatively small amounts at each occurrence, and do not directly lengthen the useful life of the asset. Cash outlays for ordinary repairs and maintenance are revenue expenditures. They are *recorded as an expense* in the accounting period in which incurred.

In the case of Delta Air Lines, examples of ordinary repairs would include changing oil in engines, replacing lights in the control panels, and fixing torn fabric in a passenger seat. Although each expenditure for ordinary repairs is relatively small, in the aggregate these expenditures can be substantial. In a recent year, Delta paid more than $376 million for aircraft repairs. This amount was reported as an expense on its income statement.

*[handwritten: * should last what we think it should last]*

> **Ordinary repairs and maintenance** expenditures are for normal operating upkeep of operational assets.
>
> *[handwritten: Rev expenditure]*

Extraordinary Repairs

Extraordinary repairs are classified as capital expenditures. The cost of an extraordinary repair is *added to the related asset account*. Extraordinary repairs occur infrequently, involve large amounts of money, and increase the economic usefulness of the asset in the future because of either increased efficiency or longer life. Examples are major overhauls, complete reconditioning, and major replacements and improvements. The complete replacement of an engine on an aircraft is an example of an extraordinary repair.

> **Extraordinary repairs** are expenditures for major, high-cost, long-term repairs that increase the economic usefulness of the asset.
>
> *[handwritten: Capital expenditure]*

Additions

Additions are extensions to, or enlargements of, existing assets, such as the addition of a wing to a building. These additions are capital expenditures. Therefore, the cost of additions should be added to the existing account for the asset.

> **Additions** are extensions to, or enlargements of, existing assets that increase the cost of the existing asset.
>
> *[handwritten: Capital expenditure]*

Depreciation

An operational asset that has a limited useful life (such as an airplane purchased by Delta Air Lines) represents the prepaid cost of a bundle of future services or benefits that will help earn future revenues. The matching principle requires that a portion of the cost of operational assets (other than land) be allocated as an expense in the periods in which revenue is earned as a result of using those assets. Thus, the cost of operational assets is matched in a systematic and rational manner with the revenues that are earned by using the asset. Delta Air Lines earns revenue by flying its aircraft and incurs an expense by using up part of the limited life of its aircraft.

The term used to identify the matching of the cost of buildings and equipment with revenues generated by the assets is depreciation. **Depreciation** is defined as

[handwritten: make sense]

> The systematic and rational *allocation of the acquisition cost* of tangible operational assets, other than land, to future periods in which the assets contribute services or benefits to help earn revenue.

[handwritten: step by step in order]

> **Depreciation** is the systematic and rational allocation of the cost of property, plant, and equipment (but not land) over their useful lives.

The amount of depreciation recorded during each period is reported on the income statement as an expense for the period. The amount of depreciation accumulated since the acquisition date is reported on the balance sheet as a contra-account, Accumulated Depreciation, and is deducted from the asset cost to which it pertains.

Students often are confused about the concept of depreciation as accountants use it. Depreciation in accounting is a process of *cost allocation.* It is not a process of determining the current market value of the asset. When an asset is depreciated, the remaining balance sheet amount *probably does not* represent the current market value of the asset. The balance sheet amounts are called *book,* or *carrying, values.* The **book (or carrying) value** of an operational asset is its acquisition cost, less the accumulated depreciation (accumulated allocated cost) from acquisition date to the date of the balance sheet.

Book (or carrying) value is the acquisition cost of an operational asset less accumulated depreciation, depletion, or amortization.

Under the cost principle, the cost of an operational asset is recorded at its current market value only on the acquisition date. At subsequent balance sheet dates, the undepreciated cost is not measured on a market value basis. Instead, the acquisition cost is reduced by the accumulated depreciation.

Financial ANALYSIS

Fixed Asset Turnover

One of the key ratios used by financial analysts is the *fixed asset turnover ratio.* This ratio measures how efficiently the company utilizes its investment in property, plant, and equipment over time. An increasing rate over time probably signals more efficient fixed asset use.

Analysts must interpret differences carefully, however. A lower or declining rate may instead indicate a company that is expanding in anticipation of higher sales in the future. On the other hand, an increasing ratio could signal a firm that has cut back on capital expenditures due to anticipation of a downturn in business. The ratio is computed as follows:

$$\text{Fixed asset turnover} = \frac{\text{Sales (or operational revenues)}}{\text{Average fixed assets (net)}}$$
$$\downarrow$$
$$\text{(Beginning balance + Ending balance)} \div 2$$

For Delta, the 1996 ratio is (amounts in millions)

$$1.81 = \frac{\$12,455 \text{ operating revenues}}{(\$6,936 + \$6,795) \div 2}$$

Delta's fixed asset turnover ratio has been increasing in recent years, suggesting improvements in asset efficiency. Delta also has written down flight equipment as part of its restructuring efforts, however, which in turn has had a positive impact on the ratio:

1993	1994	1995	1996
1.64	1.76	1.80	1.81

Another use of the fixed asset ratio is to compare companies across the same industry. The following is a sample of ratios for two other companies in the same industry:

U•S Airways	1.79
Singapore Airlines	.72

Unlike the domestic carriers, Singapore Airlines flies predominantly jumbo jets and has one of the youngest fleets in the industry. The lower turnover ratio reflects a higher net book value for the aircraft.

Depreciation Concepts

The purpose of depreciation is to allocate the cost of a tangible operational asset over its useful life. The need for depreciation can be illustrated with a simple example. If you were the president of Delta in a year when it acquired a new aircraft for $60 million in cash, you probably would object strongly if the accountant tried to charge the entire cost to expense in the year of acquisition. You would argue that the aircraft should produce revenue for several years, so the cost of the asset should be charged to expense over the period in which it will earn revenue. Failure to do so would understate income in the year of acquisition and overstate income in each year that the aircraft was used. This explains why accountants depreciate tangible operational assets and why depreciation is an important part of measuring the profitability of a company.

The calculation of depreciation expense requires three amounts for each asset:

1. Acquisition cost. *(Historical cost)*
2. *Estimated* useful life to the company. *— yrs, miles, hours, units of output*
3. *Estimated* residual (or salvage) value at end of the asset's useful life to the company.

Of these three amounts, two (useful life and residual value) are estimates. Therefore, *depreciation expense is an estimate*. To compute depreciation expense for the aircraft acquired by Delta Air Lines in our earlier illustration, we use the same estimates as described in a recent Delta annual report:

REAL WORLD EXCERPT

DELTA AIR LINES
Annual Report

NOTES TO CONSOLIDATED FINANCIAL STATEMENTS

1. Summary of Significant Accounting Policies:

. . .

Depreciation and Amortization. Flight equipment is depreciated on a straight-line basis to residual values (5% of cost) over a 20-year period from the dates placed in service (unless earlier retirement of the aircraft is planned).

. . .

Therefore, the annual depreciation expense is measured as follows:

Acquisition cost	$60,000,000
Less: Estimated residual value (5% of cost)	3,000,000
Amount to be depreciated over the useful life	$57,000,000

Estimated useful life is 20 years
Annual depreciation expense: Depreciable amount ÷ 20 years = **$ 2,850,000**

Adjusting entry

Depreciation expense ($57,000,000 ÷ 20 years) (E)	2,850,000	
Accumulated depreciation (XA)		2,850,000

If the aircraft had been purchased and used during the year, say on April 1, instead of at the beginning of the year, the depreciation expense would be computed for the part of the year in use. April 1 is three months before year-end. Therefore, depreciation expense is $712,500 ($2,850,000 annual expense × $^3/_{12}$ of a year).[1]

---

[1] Most of the examples that we discuss in this chapter assume that assets were acquired on the first day of the year and depreciated for the entire year. In practice, assets are purchased at various times during the year. Most companies adopt a policy to cover partial year depreciation, such as "to the nearest full month" or "half year in the year of acquisition."

This Delta hub is owned by the city of Atlanta; the right to operate is an intangible asset on the balance sheet.

ANALYSIS

Book Value as an Approximation of Remaining Life

Some analysts compare the book value of assets to their original cost as an approximation of their remaining life. If the book value of an asset is 100 percent of its cost, it is a new asset; if the book value is 25 percent of its cost, the asset has about 25 percent of its estimated life remaining. In Delta's case, the book value of its flight equipment is 61 percent of its original cost. This compares with 82 percent for Continental Airlines and 80 percent for Southwest Airlines. This comparison suggests that the flight equipment used by Delta has less of its estimated life remaining than that of some other major airlines. This comparison is only a rough approximation and is influenced by some of the accounting issues discussed in the next section.

Residual (or salvage) value is the estimated amount to be recovered, less disposal costs, at the end of the company's estimated useful life of an operational asset.

Residual (or salvage) value must be deducted from acquisition cost to compute depreciation expense. This value represents that part of the acquisition cost that is expected to be recovered by the user upon disposal of the asset at the end of its estimated useful life to the entity. The estimated net residual value is not necessarily the value of the asset as salvage or scrap. Rather, it may be the value to another user at the date on which the current owner intends to dispose of it. In the case of the aircraft owned by Delta Air Lines, it may be the amount it expects to receive when it sells the asset to a small regional airline that operates older equipment.

Residual value is the estimated amount to be recovered less any estimated costs of dismantling, disposal, and sale. In many cases, disposal costs may approximately equal the gross residual value. Therefore, many depreciable assets are assumed to have no residual value. In the case of Delta Air Lines, the notes to its financial statements indicate that it estimates residual value to be 5 percent of the cost of the asset.

Estimated useful life is the expected service life of an operational asset to the present owner.

Estimated useful life represents the useful *economic life* to the *present owner* rather than the total economic life to all potential users. In the Delta Air Lines example, the aircraft is able to fly for more than 20 years, but Delta wants to offer its customers a higher level of service by providing modern equipment. For accounting purposes, Delta uses a 20-year estimated useful life, and the subsequent owner (the regional airline) uses an estimated useful life based on its own policies.

The determination of estimated useful life of an operational asset must conform to the *continuity assumption*. This assumption holds that the business will continue indefinitely to pursue its commercial objectives and will not liquidate in the foreseeable future. A business should not estimate the life of an operational asset to be less than its potential life because of some conjecture that the business will liquidate in the near future.

Differences in Estimated Lives within a Single Industry

Notes to actual financial statements of companies in the airline industry reveal the following estimates for lives of aircraft:

Company	Estimated Life (in years)
Delta	20
TWA	16 to 25
U·S Airways	5 to 20
Singapore Airlines	5 to 10
Southwest	15 to 20

The differences in estimated lives may be attributable to a number of a factors such as type of aircraft used by each company, replacement plans, differences in operations, and degree of management conservatism. In addition, given the same type of aircraft, companies that plan to use the equipment over fewer years may estimate higher residual values than do companies that plan on a longer useful life. For example, Singapore Airlines uses a residual value of 20 percent over a relatively short useful life, as compared to 5 percent for Delta Air Lines over a 20-year useful life.

Differences in estimated lives and residual values of assets used by specific companies can have a large impact on the comparison of the profitability of the companies. Analysts must be certain that they identify the causes for the differences in depreciable lives.

Alternative Depreciation Methods

Accountants have not been able to agree on a single, best method of depreciation because of significant differences among companies and the assets that they own. As a result, several different depreciation methods are commonly used in financial statements. The different depreciation methods are based on the same concept; each method allocates a portion of the cost of a depreciable asset to each future period in a systematic and rational manner. Nevertheless, each method allocates to each period a different portion of the cost to be depreciated. We discuss the following most common depreciation methods:

1. Straight line.
2. Units of production.
3. Accelerated depreciation method: declining balance.

The common set of facts and notations shown in Exhibit 8.2 will be used to illustrate these methods. This example is based on the assumption that Delta Air Lines acquired a service vehicle (ground equipment) with an estimated life of three years.

Straight-Line Method

More companies, including Delta, use **straight-line (SL) depreciation** in their financial statements than all other methods combined. Under the straight-line method, an equal portion of the acquisition cost less the estimated residual value is allocated to each

Straight-line (SL) depreciation is the method that allocates the cost of an operational asset in equal periodic amounts over its useful life.

EXHIBIT 8.2
Illustrative Data for Computing Depreciation under Alternative Methods

Delta Air Lines

Acquisition cost of repair truck, purchased on July 1, 19A	$62,500
Estimated life (in years)	3
Estimated residual value	$ 2,500
Estimated life in units (miles driven)	100,000 miles
Actual miles driven in	
Year 19A 30,000 miles	
Year 19B 50,000 miles	
Year 19C 20,000 miles	

accounting period during the asset's estimated useful life. The formula to estimate annual depreciation expense follows:

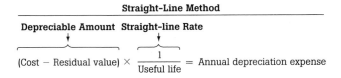

Straight-Line Method

Depreciable Amount   Straight-line Rate

$$(\text{Cost} - \text{Residual value}) \times \frac{1}{\text{Useful life}} = \text{Annual depreciation expense}$$

"Cost minus residual value" is the depreciable amount. "1 ÷ Useful life" is the straight-line rate. Using the data provided in Exhibit 8.2, the annual depreciation expense is measured as follows:

$$(\$62,500 - \$2,500) \times \tfrac{1}{3} = \$20,000 \text{ annual depreciation expense}$$

Depreciation expense for Delta using the straight-line method is $20,000 per year. A *depreciation schedule* for the entire useful life of the machine follows:

Year	Computations	Depreciation Expense (on the income statement)	Accumulated Depreciation (on the balance sheet at year-end)	Book Value (cost – accumulated depreciation at year-end)
At acquisition				$62,500
19A	($62,500 – $2,500) × 1/3	$20,000	$20,000	42,500
19B	($62,500 – $2,500) × 1/3	20,000	40,000	22,500
19C	($62,500 – $2,500) × 1/3	20,000	60,000	2,500

Notice that (1) depreciation expense is a constant amount for each year, (2) accumulated depreciation increases by an equal amount each year, and (3) book value decreases by the same amount each year. This is the reason for the designation of straight line. Also notice that, from this schedule, the adjusting entry can be prepared and the effect on the income statement and ending balance on the balance sheet are known. Delta Air Lines uses the straight-line method for all of its assets. Delta reported depreciation expense in the amount of $634,000,000 for 1996, which was 5.1 percent of the revenues earned for the year. Most companies in the airline industry use the straight-line method.

Units-of-Production Method

Units-of-production depreciation is the method that allocates the cost of an operational asset over its useful life based on its periodic output related to its total estimated output.

Units-of-production depreciation relates depreciable cost to the total estimated productive output. The formula to estimate annual depreciation expense under this method follows:

Units-of-Production Method

Depreciation Rate Per Unit

$$\frac{(\text{Cost} - \text{Residual value})}{\text{Estimated total production}} \times \text{Actual annual production} = \text{Annual depreciation expense}$$

As before, the "cost – residual value" is the depreciable amount. By dividing the depreciable amount by estimated total production, the depreciation rate per unit of production also can be computed and then multiplied by the actual annual production to determine depreciation expense. Using the information in Exhibit 8.2, the computation of the depreciation rate per unit follows:

$$\frac{\$62,500 - \$2,500}{100,000 \text{ miles}} = \$0.60 \text{ annual depreciation rate}$$

For every mile that the vehicle is driven, Delta records depreciation expense of $0.60. The depreciation schedule for Delta under the units-of-production method follows:

Year	Computations	Depreciation Expense (income statement)	Accumulated Depreciation (balance sheet at year-end)	Book Value (at year-end)
At acquisition				$62,500
19A	$0.60 × 30,000 miles	$18,000	$18,000	44,500
19B	$0.60 × 50,000 miles	30,000	48,000	14,500
19C	$0.60 × 20,000 miles	12,000	60,000	2,500

Notice that depreciation expense, accumulated depreciation, and book value vary from period to period directly with the units produced. When the units-of-production method is used, depreciation expense is said to be a *variable expense* because it varies directly with production or use.

Exxon Corporation is in the energy industry with the worldwide exploration, production, transportation, and sale of crude oil and natural gas. The company uses the units-of-production method:

1. Summary of Accounting Policies

Property, Plant and Equipment. Depreciation, depletion, and amortization, based on cost less estimated salvage value of the asset, are primarily determined under either the unit of production method or the straight-line method. Unit of production rates are based on oil, gas and other mineral reserves estimated to be recoverable from existing facilities. The straight-line method of depreciation is based on estimated asset service life taking obsolescence into consideration.

REAL WORLD EXCERPT
EXXON CORPORATION
Annual Report

The units-of-production method is based on an estimate of the total productive capacity of an asset. As you would expect, it is very difficult to estimate future output. This is another example of the degree of subjectivity that is inherent in accounting.

Accelerated Depreciation—Declining Balance Method

Accelerated depreciation means that in the early years of the useful life of an asset, depreciation expense amounts are higher, and in the later years the amounts are lower. Accelerated depreciation is used for the following reasons:

1. A depreciable asset produces more revenue in its early life because it is more efficient in earlier years than in later years.
2. Repair costs increase in later years; therefore, total use cost per period should include decreasing depreciation expense to offset the increasing repair expense each period.

Accelerated depreciation methods result in higher depreciation expense in the early years of an operational asset's life and lower expense in the later years.

How do extraordinary repairs differ from ordinary repairs with regard to asset life and its related depreciation?

The relationship between accelerated depreciation expense, repair expense, and total use expense can be illustrated as follows for Delta:

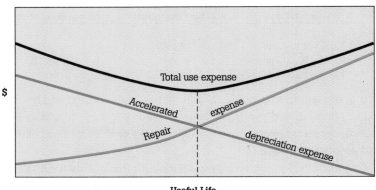

Accelerated methods are seldom used for financial reporting purposes. The accelerated method used more frequently than others is the declining-balance method, which is illustrated here. Another method, sum-of-the-years'-digits, is adopted less frequently and is described in higher level accounting textbooks.

Declining-balance (DB) depreciation is based on applying an acceleration rate to the straight-line (SL) rate. The declining-balance (DB) rate is found by (1) computing the SL rate, ignoring residual value, and then (2) multiplying that SL rate by a selected acceleration rate, which may not exceed 200 percent. For example, if the estimated useful life is 10 years, the straight-line rate is 10 percent (1 ÷ 10), and the declining-balance rate at 200 percent is 20 percent (2 × the straight-line rate of 10 percent). Typical acceleration rates are 150 percent, 175 percent, and 200 percent. The 200 percent rate, often termed the *double-declining-balance (DDB) rate,* is adopted most frequently by companies utilizing the accelerated method and will be used in our illustration.

To calculate depreciation expense under the double-declining-balance method, the net book value of the asset is multiplied by the DDB rate as follows:

> **Declining-balance (DB) depreciation** is the method that allocates the cost of an operational asset over its useful life based on a multiple of (often two times) the straight-line rate.

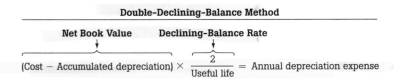

Double-Declining-Balance Method

Net Book Value   Declining-Balance Rate

$$(\text{Cost} - \text{Accumulated depreciation}) \times \frac{2}{\text{Useful life}} = \text{Annual depreciation expense}$$

Notice at this stage of the calculation, residual value is not used in computing depreciation expense (i.e., it is not subtracted from cost). An asset's book value cannot be depreciated below residual value, however. Therefore, if the annual computation creates an accumulated depreciation balance that is too high (and therefore a net book value that is below residual value), a lower amount of depreciation expense is recorded so that net book value equals residual value. Then no additional depreciation expense is computed in subsequent years. Computation of declining-balance depreciation expense is illustrated using the data given in Exhibit 8.2 and assuming an acceleration rate of 200 percent:

Year	Computations	Depreciation Expense (income statement)	Accumulated Depreciation (balance sheet at year-end)	Book Value (at year-end)
At acquisition				$62,500
19A	($62,500 – $0) × 2/3	$41,667	$41,667	20,833
19B	($62,500 – $41,667) × 2/3	13,889	55,556	6,944
19C	($62,500 – $55,556) × 2/3	4,629 is too high, so record only 4,444	60,000	2,500

Notice that the calculated depreciation expense for year 19C ($4,629) is not the same as the amount actually reported on the income statement ($4,444). An asset should never be depreciated below its residual value. The asset owned by Delta has an estimated residual value of $2,500. If depreciation expense were recorded in the amount of $4,629, the book value of the asset would be less than $2,500. The correct depreciation expense for year 19C is $4,444 ($6,944 – $2,500), which is the amount that will reduce the book value to exactly $2,500. As you can see, it is necessary to check each year to be certain that the calculated amount of depreciation expense does not reduce the book value of the asset below its estimated residual value. In most cases when this occurs, depreciation expense is limited to the amount that reduces book value to the exact amount of the estimated residual value.

Companies in industries that expect fairly rapid obsolescence of equipment and many Japanese companies use the declining-balance method. Sony is one of the companies that uses this method.

REAL WORLD EXCERPT
SONY
Annual Report

Summary of Significant Accounting Policies:
Note 1: Property, plant and equipment is stated at cost. Depreciation is computed on the declining balance method for the parent company and Japanese subsidiaries and on the straight line method for foreign subsidiaries at rates based on the estimated useful life of the assets.

As this note indicates, companies may use different depreciation methods for different classes of assets. Under the consistency principle, they are expected to apply the same methods over time.

The following summarizes the methods and computations and graphs the differences in depreciation expense over time between straight-line and declining-balance methods. The units-of-production method varies with the amount of actual production during the period; therefore, it is not on the graph:

Method	Computation
Straight line	$(\text{Cost} - \text{Residual value}) \times \dfrac{1}{\text{Useful life}}$
Units of production	$\dfrac{\text{Cost} - \text{Residual value}}{\text{Estimated total production}} \times \text{Actual production}$
Double-declining balance	$(\text{Cost} - \text{Accumulated depreciation}) \times \dfrac{2}{\text{Useful life}}$

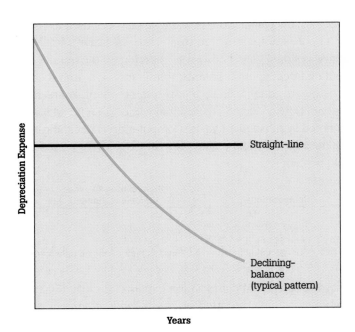

Impact of Alternative Depreciation Methods

Assume that you are analyzing two companies that are exactly the same except for the fact that one uses accelerated depreciation and the other uses the straight-line method. Which company would you expect to report higher net income? Actually, the question is a bit tricky. The answer is that you cannot say for certain.

The accelerated methods report higher depreciation during the early years of the life of an asset and therefore report lower net income. As the age of the asset increases, this effect reverses; therefore, companies that use accelerated depreciation report lower depreciation expense and higher net income during the later years of an asset's life. The preceding graph shows the pattern of depreciation over the life of an asset for the two methods discussed in this chapter. When the curve for the accelerated method falls below the curve for the straight-line method, the accelerated method causes higher net income to be reported compared to straight-line.

Users of financial statements must understand the impact of differences in the methods of account-ing for depreciation and the way that the passage of time affects those differences. Significant differ-ences in the reported net incomes of companies can be caused by differences in depreciation methods rather than by real economic differences.

SELF-STUDY QUIZ

Assume that Delta acquired new computer equipment at a cost of $240,000. The equipment has an estimated life of six years (and an estimated operating life of 50,000 hours) with an estimated residual value of $30,000. Determine depreciation expense for the first full year under each of the following methods:

1. Straight-line depreciation. _____.
2. 200 percent-declining-balance method. _____.
3. Units-of-production method (assuming the equipment ran for 8,000 hours in the first year). _____.

After you have completed your answers, check them with the solutions presented in the footnote at the bottom of this page.*

Managers' Selection among Accounting Alternatives

The 1996 edition of *Accounting Trends & Techniques* (published by the AICPA) reported the depreciation methods used by 600 companies:

Straight line	572
Declining balance	27
Sum-of-the-years' digits	12
Accelerated, but not specified	49
Units of production	38

Note that the number of methods exceeds the number of companies because some companies use more than one method for various asset categories.

The method used by more than 95 percent of the companies for some or all of their assets is the straight-line method. Corporate managers find this method to be easy to use and to explain. During the early years of an asset's life, the straight-line method also reports higher income than the accelerated methods do.

Depreciation and Federal Income Tax

Delta Air Lines, like most public companies, maintains two sets of accounting records. One set of records is prepared under GAAP and for reporting to stockholders. The other set of records is prepared to determine the company's tax obligation under the Internal Revenue Code. When they first learn that companies maintain two sets of books, some people question the ethics or the legality of the practice. In reality, it is both legal and ethical to maintain separate records for tax accounting and financial reporting.

The reason that it is legal to maintain two sets of books is simple: The objectives of GAAP and the Internal Revenue Code differ.

Financial Reporting (GAAP)	Tax Reporting (IRS)
Financial reporting rules following generally accepted accounting principles are designed to provide economic information about a business that is useful in projecting the future cash flows of the business.	The objective of the Internal Revenue Code is to raise sufficient revenues to pay for the expenditures of the federal government with many provisions designed to encourage certain behaviors that are thought to benefit our society (e.g., contributions to charities are tax deductible to encourage people to support worthy programs).

It is easy to understand why two sets of accounting records are permitted, but perhaps the more interesting aspect concerns the reason that managers elect to go to the extra cost of maintaining two sets of books. In some cases, differences between the Internal Revenue Code and GAAP leave the manager no choice but to have separate records. In other cases, the explanation is an economic one. It is often called the *least and the latest rule*. All taxpayers want to pay the lowest amount of tax that is legally permitted and they want to pay it at the latest possible date. If you had the choice of paying $100,000 to the federal government at the end of this year or the end of next year, you would choose the end of next year. By doing so, you would be able to invest the money for an extra year and earn a significant return on the investment.

---

* 1. ($240,000 – $30,000) × $\frac{1}{6}$ = $35,000

2. ($240,000 – 0) × $\frac{2}{6}$ = $80,000

3. [($240,000 – $30,000) ÷ 50,000] × 8,000 = $33,600

By maintaining two sets of books, corporations are able to defer (delay) paying taxes in the amount of millions and sometimes billions of dollars. The following companies are entities that have reported significant gross deferred tax obligations in a recent year by choosing accounting methods that delay tax payments. Much of the deferral is due to differences in asset cost allocation methods:

Company	Deferred Tax Liabilities	Percentage Due to Differences in Asset Cost Allocation Methods
Delta Air Lines	$1,343 million	81%
PepsiCo	2,649 million	80
AT&T Corp.	6,801 million	78
Kmart Corp.	749 million	49

Some of the depreciation methods discussed in the previous section are not acceptable for federal income tax reporting. Most corporations use the Modified Accelerated Cost Recovery System (MACRS) for calculating depreciation expense for their tax statement. MACRS is similar to the declining-balance method and is applied over relatively short asset lives, yielding high depreciation expense in the early years. It is not used for financial reporting purposes.

MACRS does not attempt to match the cost of an asset with the revenue it produces over its useful life in conformity with the matching principle. Instead, MACRS provides for rapid depreciation of an asset over a life that is usually much shorter than its estimated useful life. The intent of MACRS is to provide an incentive for corporations to invest in modern property, plant, and equipment to be competitive in world markets. The high depreciation expense reported under MACRS reduces a corporation's taxable income and therefore the amount it must pay in taxes.

Depreciation Methods in Other Countries

The various depreciation methods discussed in this chapter are widely used by corporations in most countries. Some methods used in other countries are not generally used in the United States. German companies may depreciate based on the hours that an asset is used, and British companies may use the annuity method, which results in lower depreciation during the early years of the life of an asset (contrasted with accelerated depreciation, which results in higher depreciation during the early years).

Many countries, including Australia, Brazil, England, Hong Kong, Mexico, and Singapore, also permit the revaluation of property, plant, and equipment to their current cost as of the balance sheet date. The primary argument in favor of such revaluation is that the historical cost of an asset purchased 15 or 20 years ago is not meaningful because of the impact of inflation. For example, most people would not compare the original price of a 1965 Ford to the original price of a 1995 Ford because the purchasing power of the dollar changed dramatically during the period. Revaluation to current cost is prohibited in the United States (under GAAP), Canada, Germany, and Japan. A primary argument against restatement is the lack of objectivity involved in estimating the current cost of an asset.

Changes in Depreciation Estimates

Depreciation is based on two estimates—useful life and residual value. These estimates are made at the time a depreciable asset is acquired. One or both of these initial estimates may have to be revised as experience with the asset accumulates. In addition, extraordinary repairs and additions may be added to the original acquisition cost at some time during the asset's usage. When it is clear that either estimate should be revised to a material degree or the asset's cost has been increased, the undepreciated asset balance less any residual value at that date should be apportioned, based on the new estimate, over the remaining estimated life. This is called a *change in estimate.*

For any of the depreciation methods described here, substitute the new cost for the original acquisition cost, the new residual value for the original amount, and estimated remaining life in place of the original estimated life. As an illustration, the computation using the straight-line method is as follows.

Assume the following for an aircraft owned by Delta:

Cost of aircraft when acquired	$60,000,000
Estimated useful life	20 years
Estimated residual value	$3,000,000
Accumulated depreciation through year 6 (assuming the SL method is used):	

$$(\$60,000,000 - \$3,000,000) \times {}^1\!/_{20} = \$2,850,000 \text{ per year}$$
$$\$2,850,000 \times 6 \text{ years} = \$17,100,000$$

Shortly after the start of year 7, Delta changed the initial estimated life to 16 years, and raised the estimated residual value to $900,000. At the end of year 7, the computation of the new amount for depreciation expense is as follows:

Acquisition cost	$60,000,000
Less: Accumulated depreciation, years 1–6	17,100,000
Undepreciated balance	$42,900,000
Less: New residual value	900,000
New depreciable amount	$42,000,000
Annual depreciation based on remaining life:	
$42,000,000 ÷ (16 years – 6 years)	$ 4,200,000

The adjusting entry at the end of year 7 (and future years) is as follows:

Depreciation expense (E)	4,200,000	
Accumulated depreciation (XA)		4,200,000

Companies also may make a change in depreciation methods (for example, from declining balance to straight line), although such change requires significantly more disclosure since the consistency principle is violated. Under GAAP, changes in accounting estimates and depreciation methods should be made only when the new estimate or accounting method "better measures" the periodic income of the business. The *consistency principle* requires that accounting information reported in the financial statements be comparable across accounting periods. This principle places a significant constraint on changing depreciation estimates and methods unless the effect is to improve the measurement of depreciation expense and net income.

The 1993 financial statement from Delta Air Lines contained the following note:

Prior to the current year, substantially all of the Company's flight equipment was being depreciated on a straight-line basis to residual values (10% of cost) over a 15-year period from the dates placed in service. As a result of a review of its fleet plan, effective this year, the Company increased the estimated useful lives of substantially all of its flight equipment. Flight equipment that was not already fully depreciated is being depreciated on a straight-line basis to residual values (5% of cost) over a 20-year period from the dates placed in service. The effect of this change was a $34.3 million decrease in depreciation expense.

REAL WORLD EXCERPT
DELTA AIR LINES
Annual Report

Notice that Delta changed both the estimated life of its flight equipment and its estimated residual value. Why would Delta's management revise the estimates of useful life and residual value? The most likely explanation is found in other notes to the Delta financial statements. Delta and its competitors in the airline industry were managing in the face of an economic downturn in the early 1990s, one that caused losses or lowered operating profits for many. To improve financial performance at that time, management announced a number of cost control initiatives including "a $5.4 billion reduction in planned aircraft capital expenditures." As the result of planning to acquire fewer new aircraft, Delta decided to realize longer service from its existing equipment. Because of longer service, the equipment has less residual value when it is eventually sold.

Increased Profitability due to an Accounting Adjustment? Reading the Footnotes

Financial analysts are particularly interested in changes in accounting estimates because they can have a large impact on a company's before-tax operating income. In Delta's case, the changes added $34.3 million because of reduced depreciation expense and add a similar amount each year over the remaining life of the aircraft. Analysts pay close attention to this number because it represents increased profitability due to an accounting adjustment.

As another example, in May 1996, "Japan Airlines, the country's largest carrier, reported its first operating profit since 1991. The company attributed the improvement in the 12 months to March to its extensive restructuring and strong demand in growing Asian markets. But a change in its method of accounting for depreciation also improved JAL's results."* The company changed from the declining-balance method (higher depreciation expense) to the straight-line method (lower depreciation expense), and reported an increase in recurring profit compared with last year of ¥10.9 billion. "Although the move suggested the company would have recorded a large recurring loss for the year under the old principles, JAL said the change was a fairer reflection of the costs and benefits of the big outlays on new airports and other facilities recently made by JAL."

*SOURCE: Gerard Baker, *Financial Times*, May 30, 1996.

SELF-STUDY QUIZ

Assume that Delta Air Lines owned a service truck that originally cost $100,000. When purchased, the truck had an estimated useful life of 10 years with no residual value. After operating the truck for five years, Delta determined that the remaining life was only two more years. Based on this change in estimate, what amount of depreciation should be recorded over the remaining life of the asset? Delta uses the straight-line method.

Check your answer with the footnote at the bottom of this page.*

---

* $50,000 (book value after 5 years) ÷ 2 years (remaining life) = $25,000 depreciation expense per year.

Depreciation and Cash Flows

Depreciation expense is commonly called a *noncash expense* because it does not directly affect cash flows. The cash outflow associated with depreciation occurred when the related asset was acquired. Each period when depreciation is recorded, no cash payment is made (i.e., there is not a credit to Cash related to recording depreciation expense). Most other expenses cause an immediate or subsequent outflow of cash. The recording of salary expense, for example, is associated with either the immediate payment of cash or a subsequent payment when salaries payable are paid.

Effect on Statement of Cash Flows

Exhibit 8.3 is a segment of Delta's statement of cash flows. In capital-intensive industries such as airlines, depreciation expense is a significant noncash expense. In the case of Delta, except for the nonrecurring charges, depreciation expense is the single largest adjustment to net income in determining cash flows from operations. It averages approximately 50 percent of operating cash flows.

Some analysts misinterpret the meaning of a noncash expense and often say that "cash is provided by depreciation." This may be caused by finding depreciation added in the operating section of the statement of cash flows. Depreciation is not a source of cash, however. Cash from operations can be provided only by selling goods and services. A company with a large amount of depreciation expense does not generate more cash compared with a company that reports a small amount of depreciation expense (assuming that they are exactly the same in every other respect). Depreciation expense reduces the amount of reported net income for a company, but it does not reduce the amount of cash generated by the company because it is a noncash expense. That is why, on the statement of cash flows, depreciation expense is added back to net income (accrual basis) to compute cash flows from operations.

Effect on Taxes

Although depreciation is a noncash expense, depreciation policy for tax purposes can affect a company's cash flows. Depreciation is a deductible expense for income tax purposes (i.e., taxes are based on income, or revenues minus expenses). The higher the amount of depreciation recorded by a company for tax purposes, the lower the

FOCUS ON CASH FLOWS

LEARNING OBJECTIVE 4
Explain the impact of cost allocation methods on cash flows.

EXHIBIT 8.3
Depreciation Expense on Delta's Statement of Cash Flows

DELTA AIR LINES, INC. Consolidated Statements of Cash Flows For the years ended June 30, 1996, 1995 and 1994 (In millions)			
	1996	1995	1994
CASH FLOWS FROM OPERATING ACTIVITIES			
Net income (loss)	$ 156	$ 408	$ (409)
Adjustments to reconcile net income (loss) to cash provided by operating activities			
Cumulative effect of accounting changes		(114)	
Restructuring and other nonrecurring charges	829		526
Depreciation and amortization	**634**	**622**	**678**
(total of various other adjustments listed)	(228)	198	529
Net cash provided by operating activities	$1,391	$1,114	$1,324

taxable income and the taxes that must be paid. Because taxes must be paid in cash, a reduction in the tax obligation of a company results in a reduction of cash outflows for the company.

Disposal of Operational Assets

LEARNING OBJECTIVE 5
Analyze the disposal of property, plant, and equipment.

In some cases, a business may *voluntarily* decide not to hold an operational asset for its entire life. The company may drop a product from its line and no longer need the equipment that was used to produce the product, or it may want to trade in a machine for a more efficient one. These disposals include sale, trade-in, or retirement. When it disposes of an old aircraft, Delta may sell it to a cargo airline or regional airline. A business may also dispose of an asset *involuntarily* as the result of a casualty, such as a storm, fire, or accident.

Disposals of operational assets seldom occur on the last day of the accounting period. Therefore, the depreciation must be updated to the date of disposal. The disposal of a depreciable operational asset usually requires two entries: (1) an adjusting entry to update the depreciation expense and accumulated depreciation accounts and (2) an entry to record the disposal. Then the cost of the asset and any accumulated depreciation (book value) at the date of disposal must be removed from the accounts. The difference between any resources received on disposal of an operational asset and the book, or carrying, value of the asset at the date of disposal is a gain or loss on disposal of operational assets. This gain (or loss) is reported on the income statement. It is not revenue (or expense), however, because it is from "peripheral or incidental" activities rather than from normal operations.

Assume that, at the end of year 17, Delta Air Lines sold an aircraft that was no longer needed because of the elimination of flight service to a small city. The aircraft was sold for $4,000,000 cash. The original cost of the flight equipment was $20 million and was depreciated using the straight-line method over 20 years with no residual value ($1,000,000 depreciation expense per year). The last accounting for depreciation was at the end of year 16; thus, depreciation expense must be recorded for year 17. The computations are as follows:

Cash received		$4,000,000
Original cost of flight equipment	$20,000,000	
Less: Accumulated depreciation ($1,000,000 × 17 years)	17,000,000	
Book value at date of sale		3,000,000
Gain on sale of flight equipment		$1,000,000

The entries on the date of the sale follow:

Depreciation expense (E)	1,000,000	
Accumulated depreciation (XA)		1,000,000
Cash (A)	4,000,000	
Accumulated depreciation (XA)	17,000,000	
Flight equipment (A)		20,000,000
Gain on sale of operational asset (R)		1,000,000

A gain or loss on disposal occurs because (1) depreciation expense is based on estimates that may differ from actual experience and (2) depreciation is based on original cost, not current market value. Because the gain or loss on disposal is not part of the continuing operating activities of a company, it usually is shown as a separate line item on the income statement. In the past, Delta Air Lines sold 18 DC–9 aircraft and reported a gain of $64,843,000 as a separate item on its income statement.

International
PERSPECTIVE

Taking a Different Strategy to Success

Singapore Airlines, formed in 1972, has recognized continued profitability as one of the world's largest operators of the most technologically advanced "jumbo jets," the Boeing 747–400. Unlike the rest of the airline industry with an average fleet age of more than 12 years, Singapore Airlines uses its aircraft for an average of just under six years. This strategy for managing the company's operational productivity has a dual effect. Depreciation expense is significantly higher due to the shorter estimated useful life, thus reducing net income. Singapore Airlines sells its used aircraft, however, an activity that has resulted in gains (entitled "Surplus on Sale of Aircraft and Spares") reported on the income statement. Both depreciation computations (through the use of estimates) and asset sales (through differences in the timing of the sales) provide management with the flexibility to manage earnings.

On October 28, 1996, *The Straits Times* (p. 48) reported that Singapore Airlines' six-month earnings were up 7.2 percent compared to the same period in the prior year. The surplus on sales of aircraft was up 734.7 percent, however. "Without the surplus in the six months ended Sept. 30, the national carrier's net earnings would have declined for the first time since 1994."

Natural Resources

You are probably most familiar with large companies that are involved in manufacturing goods (Ford, Black & Decker), distribution of goods (Sears, Home Depot), or performing a service (Federal Express, Holiday Inn). A number of large companies, some of which are less well known, develop raw materials and products from **natural resources,** which include mineral deposits (such as gold or iron ore), oil wells, and timber tracts. These resources are often called *wasting assets* because they are depleted (i.e., physically used). Companies involved with natural resources are critical to the economy because they produce such essential items as lumber for construction, fuel for heating and transportation, and food for consumption. Companies involved with natural resources also attract considerable attention because of the significant effect they can have on the environment. Concerned citizens often read financial statements from companies involved in exploration for oil, coal, and various ores to determine the amount of money spent to protect the environment.

LEARNING OBJECTIVE 6
Understand the measurement and reporting of natural resources and intangible assets.
Natural resources are assets that occur in nature, such as mineral deposits, timber tracts, oil, and gas.

Acquisition and Cost Allocation

When natural resources are acquired or developed, they are recorded in conformity with the *cost principle*. As a natural resource is used up, its acquisition cost, in conformity with the *matching principle*, must be apportioned among the various periods in which the resulting revenues are earned. The term *depletion* describes the process of periodic cost allocation over the economic life of a natural resource. The concept of depletion is exactly the same as depreciation; the only difference is the type of asset that is being accounted for.[2]

Depletion: The systematic and rational allocation of the acquisition cost of natural resources to future periods in which the use of those natural resources contributes to revenue.

Depletion is the systematic and rational allocation of the cost of a natural resource over the period of exploitation.

---

[2] Consistent with the procedure for recording depreciation, an Accumulated Depletion account may be used. In practice, most companies credit the asset account directly for the periodic depletion. This procedure is typically used for intangible assets, discussed in the next section.

Example: Depletion of the $530,000 cost of a timber tract over the estimated period of cutting based on a "cutting" rate of approximately 20 percent per year:

Adjusting entry

Depletion expense ($530,000 × 20%) (E)	106,000	
Timber tract (or Accumulated depletion) (A)		106,000

A *depletion rate* is computed by dividing the total acquisition and development cost (less any estimated residual value, which is rare) by the estimated units that can be withdrawn economically from the resource. The depletion rate is multiplied each period by the actual number of units withdrawn during the accounting period. This procedure is the same as the units-of-production method of calculating depreciation.

When buildings and similar improvements are acquired for the development and exploitation of a natural resource, they should be recorded in separate asset accounts and *depreciated*—not depleted. Their estimated useful lives cannot be longer than the time needed to exploit the natural resource unless they have a significant use after the source is depleted.

The following is a partial asset section of the 1996 balance sheet for International Paper and the related footnote describing the accounting policies for its natural resource, forestlands:

REAL WORLD EXCERPT

INTERNATIONAL PAPER
Annual Report

CONSOLIDATED BALANCE SHEET

In Millions at December 31	1996	1995
ASSETS		
. . .		
Plants, Properties and Equipment, Net	$13,217	$10,997
Forestlands	3,342	2,803
. . .		
TOTAL ASSETS	$28,252	$23,977

Forestlands

Forestlands are stated at cost, less accumulated depletion representing the cost of timber harvested. Forestlands include owned property as well as certain timber harvesting rights with terms of one or more years. Costs attributable to timber are charged against income as trees are cut. The depletion rate charged is determined annually based on the relationship of remaining costs to estimated recoverable volume.

Intangible Assets

An intangible asset, like any other asset, has value because of certain rights and privileges conferred by law on the owner of the asset. An intangible asset has no material or physical substance as do tangible assets such as land and buildings, however. Examples include patents, trademarks, and licenses. Most intangible assets, except for goodwill discussed later, usually are evidenced by a legal document.

Acquisition and Cost Allocation

Intangible assets are recorded in conformity with the *cost principle* only if they are purchased. If an intangible asset is developed internally, the cost of development normally is recorded as an expense. For example, Abbott Laboratories (a manufacturer of pharmaceutical and nutritional products) recently spent more than $1,072 million on research to discover new products. This amount was reported as an expense, not an asset. If Abbott Labs had spent an equivalent amount to purchase patents for new products from other drug companies, it would have recorded the expenditure as an asset.

In a process similar to depreciation and depletion, intangible assets are amortized on a straight-line basis over the shorter of their legal life, useful life, or 40 years (the maximum allowable allocation period under GAAP). Most companies do not estimate a residual value for their intangible assets. Amortization expense is included on the income statement each period; intangible assets are reported at cost less accumulated amortization on the balance sheet.

Amortization:	The systematic and rational allocation of the acquisition cost of intangible assets to future periods in which the benefits contribute to revenue.
Example:	Amortization of the $850,000 purchase cost of a patent over its estimated economic useful (and legal) life to the entity of 17 years:

> **Amortization** is the systematic and rational allocation of the acquisition cost of an intangible asset over its useful life.

Adjusting entry

```
Patent expense ($850,000 ÷ 17 years) (E) ...............    50,000
      Patents (or Accumulated amortization) (A) ..............          50,000
```

Examples of Intangible Assets

The AICPA's 1996 *Accounting Trends & Techniques* summarizes intangible assets most frequently disclosed by the 600 companies surveyed:

Goodwill recognized in a business combination	402
Patents, patent rights	72
Trademarks, brand names, copyrights	57
Licenses, franchises, memberships	24
Noncompete covenants	24
Customer lists	15
Technology	14
Other–described in the annual report	42

Goodwill

By far, the most frequently reported intangible asset is goodwill. Goodwill, as used by most business people, is the favorable reputation that a company has with its customers. Goodwill arises from such factors as customer confidence, reputation for good service or quality goods, and financial standing. From its first day of operations, a successful business continually builds goodwill. In this context, the goodwill is said to be *internally generated* and is not reported as an asset (i.e., it was not purchased).

The only way to report goodwill as an asset is to purchase another business. Often the purchase price of the business exceeds the fair market value of all of the assets minus liabilities owned or owed by the business. Why would a company pay more for a company as a whole than it would pay if it bought the assets individually? The answer is to obtain its goodwill. You could easily buy modern bottling equipment to produce and sell a new cola drink, but you would not make as much money as you would if you could acquire the goodwill associated with Coke or Pepsi.

For accounting purposes, **goodwill** (often reported as **cost in excess of net assets acquired**) is defined as the difference between the purchase price of a company as a whole and the fair market value of all of its assets minus the fair market value of its liabilities.

> For accounting purposes, **goodwill (cost in excess of net assets acquired)** is the excess of the purchase price of a business over the market value of the business's assets and liabilities.

Purchase price
− Fair market value of identifiable assets and liabilities
Goodwill to be reported

Both parties estimate an acceptable amount for the goodwill of the business and add it to the appraised fair value of the business's assets and liabilities. Then the sale price of the business is negotiated. In conformity with the *cost principle*, the resulting amount of goodwill is recorded as an intangible asset only when it actually is purchased at a measurable cost.

A number of years ago, Delta Air Lines acquired Western Air Lines, a regional carrier. Delta purchased the entire company as an entity and paid a price in excess of the fair market value of the tangible assets owned by Western. The balance sheet prepared by Delta (Exhibit 8.1) includes the individual assets from Western and an item valued at $265 million called Cost in Excess of Net Assets Acquired (which is another term for goodwill). The notes to the statements include the following:

COST IN EXCESS OF NET ASSETS ACQUIRED. The cost in excess of net assets acquired (goodwill), which is being amortized over 40 years, is related to the Company's acquisition of Western Air Lines, Inc. on December 18, 1986. The Company periodically reviews the value assigned to goodwill to determine whether there exists any impairment, as defined by SFAS 121. Management believes that goodwill is appropriately valued.

Like other intangible assets, goodwill must be amortized to expense over its estimated economic life, usually on a straight-line basis. Because it is particularly difficult to estimate the life of goodwill, GAAP (*APB Opinion 17*) requires goodwill to be amortized over a period not to exceed 40 years. Delta's income statement included amorti-

Delta owns only 15% of its partner airline SkyWest, thus SkyWest's assets are not included in Delta's property, plant, and equipment.

zation of cost in excess of net assets acquired (goodwill) of $9 million. When Delta records amortization of goodwill, it reduces the Goodwill account rather than the contra-account Accumulated Amortization. Most companies follow this practice.

Patents

A **patent** is an exclusive right granted by the federal government for a period of 17 years. It is typically granted to an inventor who invents a new product or discovers a new process. The patent enables the owner to use, manufacture, and sell the subject of the patent and the patent itself. Without the protection of a patent, inventors likely would be unwilling to search for new products. The patent prevents a competitor from simply copying a new invention or discovery until the inventor has had a period of time to earn an economic return on the new product.

A patent that is *purchased* is recorded at cost. An *internally developed* patent is recorded at only its registration and legal cost because GAAP requires the immediate expensing of research and development costs. In conformity with the *matching principle*, the cost of a patent must be amortized over the shorter of its economic life or its remaining legal life. Amortization usually is recorded with a debit to Amortization Expense and a credit directly to the asset account instead of a contra-account Accumulated Amortization.

> A **patent** is granted by the federal government for an invention; it is an exclusive right given to the owner to use, manufacture, and sell the subject of the patent.

Trademarks

A **trademark** is a special name, image, or slogan identified with a product or a company; it is protected by law. Trademarks are often some of the most valuable assets that a company can own. Most of us cannot imagine the Walt Disney Company without Mickey Mouse. You probably enjoy your favorite soft drink more because of the image that has been built up around its name. Many people can identify the shape of a corporate logo as quickly as they can recognize the shape of a stop sign. Trademarks are valuable assets, but they are rarely seen on balance sheets. The reason is simple; intangible assets are not recorded unless they are purchased. Companies often spend millions of dollars developing trademarks, but these expenditures usually are recorded as expenses and not capitalized.

> A **trademark** is an exclusive legal right to use a special name, image, or slogan.

Copyrights

A **copyright** gives the owner the exclusive right to publish, use, and sell a literary, musical, or artistic piece of work for a period not exceeding 50 years after the author's death. The book that you are reading has a copyright to protect the publisher and the authors. It would be against the law, for example, if an instructor copied several chapters from this book and handed them out in class. The same principles, guidelines, and procedures used in accounting for the cost of patents also are used for copyrights.

> A **copyright** is the exclusive right to publish, use, and sell a literary, musical, or artistic work.

Franchises

Franchises may be granted by either the government or other businesses for a specified period and purpose. A city may grant one company a franchise to distribute gas to homes for heating purposes, or a company may sell franchises, such as the right for a local outlet to operate a KFC restaurant. Franchise agreements are contracts that can have a variety of provisions. Franchises usually require an investment by the franchisee to acquire them; therefore, they should be accounted for as intangible assets. The life of the franchise agreement depends on the contract and may be for a single year or an indefinite period. Blockbuster Video is a popular company in the home video rental business. To expand rapidly, the company enters into franchise agreements with

> A **franchise** is a contractual right to sell certain products or services, use certain trademarks, or perform activities in a geographical region.

local operators. The franchise agreement requires the payment of a franchise fee and covers a period of 20 years. Blockbuster has more than 750 stores under franchise agreements.

Leaseholds

A **leasehold** is the right granted in a contract called a *lease* to use a specific asset. Leasing is a common type of business contract. For a consideration called *rent*, the owner (lessor) extends to another party (lessee) certain rights to use specified property. Leases may vary from simple arrangements, such as the month-to-month lease of an office or the daily rental of an automobile, to long-term leases having complex contractual arrangements.

The Delta balance sheet (Exhibit 8.1) shows an asset Leasehold and Operating Rights for $140 million. The leasehold rights are improvements to rented space at the airports where Delta provides services. The operating rights are authorized landing slots that are regulated by the government and are in limited supply at many airports. They are intangible assets that can be bought and sold by the airlines.

Lessees sometimes make significant improvements to a leased property when they enter into a long-term lease agreement. A company that agrees to lease office space on a 15-year lease may install new fixtures or move walls to make the space more useful. These improvements are called *leasehold improvements* and are recorded as an asset by the lessee despite the fact that the lessor usually owns the leasehold improvements at the end of the term of the lease. The cost of leasehold improvements should be amortized over the estimated useful life of the related improvements or the remaining life of the lease, whichever is shorter.

Impaired Assets

Under a recent FASB pronouncement, corporations must review long-lived assets and certain identifiable intangibles for impairment. Impairment occurs when events or changed circumstances cause the book value of these assets to be higher than estimates of future cash flows (future benefits). If the estimated future cash flows are less than the book value of the asset, an impairment loss should be recognized. We say the assets are *written down.* Delta Air Lines reported the following write-down in a recent annual report:

> The $829 million pretax charge for restructuring and other non-recurring charges recorded in fiscal 1996 includes a $452 million write-down of Delta's Lockheed L-1011 fleet and related assets. In connection with its decision to accelerate the replacement of its 55 L-1011 aircraft fleet, the Company performed an evaluation to determine, in accordance with SFAS 121 (see Note 1), whether future cash flows (undiscounted and without interest charges) expected to result from the use and the eventual disposition of the L-1011 fleet will be less than the aggregate carrying amount of the L-1011 aircraft and related assets. As a result of the evaluation, management determined that the estimated future cash flows expected to be generated by L-1011 assets will be less than their carrying amount, and therefore, the L-1011 assets are impaired as defined by SFAS 121. Consequently, the original cost basis of the L-1011 fleet was reduced to reflect the fair market value at the time of the evaluation, resulting in a $452 million non-recurring charge. In determining the fair market value of L-1011 assets, the Company considered recent transactions involving sales of L-1011 aircraft and market trends in aircraft dispositions.

Delta's L-1011 aircraft are among the oldest in its fleet. The planes will be retired and replaced with the flight equipment from the new Boeing order.

Leaseholds are rights granted to a lessee under a lease contract.

Amor

How they're classified

✗ know)

LEARNING OBJECTIVE 7
Explain the effect of asset impairment on the financial statements.

REAL WORLD EXCERPT

DELTA AIR LINES
Annual Report

QUESTION OF ETHICS

Fierce Pressure to Report Smooth, Ever Higher Earnings

Corporate executives have been under intense pressure over the past decade to keep earnings rising smoothly to meet the consensus expectations of analysts. As the expectations have become more explicit, so too have the mechanisms executives use to manage earnings and hit their targets. Long-lived assets can play a significant role in the ability of companies to meet or beat the estimates, as indicated in the financial press:

. . .

How the pros do it

Plan ahead: Time store openings or asset sales to keep earnings rising smoothly. In most cases, this is earnings management at its least controversial. The master of it is General Electric.

. . .

Capitalize it: Usually it's pretty clear which costs you capitalize and which you expense. But there are gray areas–software R & D is one–and you can get creative about the length of time an asset should be depreciated. America Online was, until it stopped in October, a noted aggressive capitalizer.

Write it off: Take a "big bath" and charge a few hundred million in restructuring costs, and meeting future earnings targets will be easier. Among the biggest restructurers in the 1990s: IBM.

. . .

REAL WORLD EXCERPT

"Learn to Play the Earnings Game (and Wall Street will love you)"

SOURCE: *Fortune,* March 31, 1997, pp. 77–80.

Epilogue

By the 1990s, the airline industry faced excess capacity. Simply too many aircraft were competing for a limited number of customers. After losing nearly $2 billion between 1991 and 1994, Delta announced a campaign (Leadership 7.5) to slash $2 billion in expenses by eliminating 15,000 jobs. The company has since been profitable.

Wall Street analysts have been impressed with Delta's success in achieving greater productivity from its operational assets. When the major deal was signed with Boeing, however, Delta's stock slipped 12.5 cents a share to $84.375 as the market reacted warily to the announced shift in managing operational assets. Given the long life of Delta's productive assets, we will be well into the next century before we can assess the success of Delta's plan.

Demonstration Case

(Resolve the requirements before proceeding to the suggested solution that follows.)

Diversified Industries has been operating for a number of years. It started as a residential construction company. In recent years, it expanded into heavy construction, ready-mix concrete, sand and gravel, construction supplies, and earth-moving services.

The following transactions were selected from those completed during 19D. They focus on the primary issues discussed in this chapter. Amounts have been simplified for case purposes.

19D

Jan. 1 The management decided to buy a building that was about 10 years old. The location was excellent, and there was adequate parking space. The company bought the building and the land on which it was situated for $305,000. They paid $100,000 in cash and signed a mortgage note payable for the rest. A reliable appraiser provided the following market values: land, $126,000; and building, $174,000.

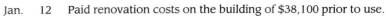

Jan.   12   Paid renovation costs on the building of $38,100 prior to use.

June   19   Bought a third location for a gravel pit (designated No. 3) for $50,000 cash. The location had been carefully surveyed. It was estimated that 100,000 cubic yards of gravel could be removed from the deposit.

July   10   Paid $1,200 for ordinary repairs on the building.

Aug.   1   Paid $10,000 for costs of preparing the new gravel pit for exploitation.

Dec.   31   Year-end adjustments:

   a.   The building will be depreciated on a straight-line basis over an estimated useful life of 30 years. The estimated residual value is $35,000.

   b.   During 19D, 12,000 cubic yards of gravel were removed from gravel pit No. 3 and sold.

   c.   The company owns a patent right that is used in operations. On January 1, 19D, the patent account had a balance of $3,300. The patent has an estimated remaining useful life of six years (including 19D).

   d.   At the beginning of the year, the company owned equipment with a cost of $650,000 and a book value of $500,000. The equipment is being depreciated using the double-declining-balance method, with a useful life of 20 years with no residual value.

   e.   At year-end, the company identified a piece of old excavation equipment with a cost of $156,000 and remaining book value of $120,000. Due to its smaller size and lack of safety features, the old equipment has limited use. The company reviewed the asset for possible impairment of value. The future cash flows are expected to be $40,000.

December 31, 19D, is the end of the annual accounting period.

Required:

1.   Indicate the accounts affected and the amount and direction (+ for increase and – for decrease) of the effect for each of the above events on the financial statement categories at year end. Using the following headings:

Date	Assets	Liabilities	Stockholders' Equity

2.   Record the adjusting journal entries based on the information for December 31 (*a* and *b* only).

3.   Show the December 31, 19D, balance sheet classifications and amount for each of the following items:

   Fixed assets—land, building, equipment, and gravel pit
   Intangible asset—patent

4.   Assuming that the company had sales of $1,000,000 for the year and a net book value of $500,000 for fixed assets at the beginning of the year, compute the fixed asset turnover ratio. Explain its meaning.

Suggested Solution

1.   Effects of events (with computations):

Date	Assets		Liabilities		Stockholders' Equity
Jan. 1	Cash	− 100,000	Note	+ 205,000	
(1)	Land	+ 128,100	payable		
	Building	+ 176,900			
Jan. 12	Cash	− 38,100			
	Building	+ 38,100			
June 19	Cash	− 50,000			
	Gravel pit	+ 50,000			

(continued on next page)

Date	Assets			Liabilities	Stockholders' Equity		
July 10	Cash	−	1,200		Repairs expense	−	1,200
August 1	Cash	−	10,000				
	Gravel pit	+	10,000				
Dec. 31 *a*	Accumulated				Depreciation expense	−	6,000
(2)	depreciation	−	6,000				
Dec. 31 *b*	Gravel pit	−	7,200		Depletion expense	−	7,200
(3)							
Dec. 31 *c*	Patent	−	550		Amortization expense	−	550
(4)							
Dec. 31*d*	Accumulated				Depreciation expense	− 50,000	
(5)	depreciation	−	50,000				
Dec. 31 *e*	Accumulated				Loss due to asset		
(6)	depreciation	−	80,000		impairment	− 80,000	

(1)

	Land		Building		Total
Market	$126,000	+	$174,000	=	$300,000
Percentage of total	42%	+	58%	=	100%
Cost	$128,100		$176,100	=	$315,000

(2) Cost of building

Initial payment	$176,900
Repairs prior to use	38,100
Acquisition cost	$215,000

Straight-line depreciation

($215,000 cost − $35,000 residual value) ×
1/30 years = $6,000 annual depreciation

(3) Cost of gravel pit

Initial payment	$50,000
Preparation costs	10,000
Acquisition cost	$60,000

Units-of-production depletion

($60,000 cost/100,000 estimated production) × 12,000 actual
production = $7,200 annual depletion

(4) Straight-line amortization

Unamortized cost of patent	$3,300
÷ Remaining useful life	÷ 6 years
Annual amortization	$ 550

(5) Double-declining-balance depreciation

($650,000 cost − $150,000 accumulated depreciation) × 2/20 = $50,000 annual depreciation

(6) Asset impairment

Book value of old equipment	$120,000
Expected future cash flows	40,000
Loss due to impairment	$ 80,000

2. Adjusting entries Dec. 31, 19D:

(a)	Depreciation expense, building (E)		6,000	
	Accumulated depreciation (XA)			6,000
(b)	Depletion expense (E)		7,200	
	Gravel pit (No. 3) (A)			7,200

3. Balance sheet, December 31, 19D:

Assets

Fixed assets		
Land		$128,100
Building	$215,000	
Less: Accumulated depreciation	6,000	209,000
Equipment	650,000	
Less: Accumulated depreciation		
($150,000 + 50,000 + 80,000)	280,000	370,000
Gravel pit		52,800
Total fixed assets		$759,900
Intangible asset		
Patent ($3,300 − $550)		$ 2,750

4. Fixed asset turnover ratio:

$$\frac{\text{Sales}}{(\text{Beginning net fixed asset balance} + \text{Ending net fixed asset balance}) \div 2} = \frac{\$1,000,000}{(\$500,000 + \$759,900) \div 2} = 1.59$$

This construction company is capital intensive. The fixed asset turnover ratio measures the company's efficiency at using its investment in property, plant, and equipment to generate sales.

Summary

This chapter discussed accounting for operational assets. These are the noncurrent assets that a business retains for long periods of time for use in the course of normal operations rather than for sale. They include tangible assets and intangible assets. At acquisition, an operational asset is recorded at cost. Cost includes the cash-equivalent purchase price plus all reasonable and necessary expenditures made to acquire and prepare the asset for its intended use.

Expenditures related to operational assets are classified as follows:

1. *Capital expenditures:* Those expenditures that provide benefits for one or more accounting periods beyond the current period. They are debited to appropriate asset accounts and depreciated, depleted, or amortized over their useful lives.
2. *Revenue expenditures:* Those expenditures that provide benefits during the current accounting period only. They are debited to appropriate current expense accounts when incurred.

Ordinary repairs and maintenance costs are revenue expenditures. Extraordinary repairs and asset additions are capital expenditures.

An operational asset represents a bundle of future services and benefits that have been paid for in advance. As an operational asset is used, this bundle of services gradually is used to earn revenue. Therefore, in conformity with the matching principle, cost (less any estimated residual value) is allocated to periodic expense over the periods benefited. In this way, the expense associated with the use of operational assets is matched with the revenues earned. This allocation process is called *depreciation* in the case of property, plant, and equipment; *depletion* in the case of natural resources; and *amortization* in the case of intangibles.

Three of the most widely used methods of depreciation are straight line, units of production, and declining balance.

Operational assets may be disposed of voluntarily by sale or retirement, or involuntarily through casualty, such as storm, fire, or accident. Upon disposal, such assets must be depreciated, depleted, or amortized up to the date of disposal. The disposal transaction is recorded by removing the cost of the old asset and the related accumulated depreciation, depletion, or amortization amount from the accounts. A gain or loss on disposal of an operational asset results when the disposal price is different from the book value of an old asset. When an asset's ability to provide benefits in the future is impaired, the asset is written down to the expected future cash flows and a loss due to impairment is recorded.

In the previous chapters, we discussed business and accounting issues related to the assets a company holds. In Chapters 9, 10, and 11, we shift our focus to the other side of the balance sheet to see how managers finance the operations of their business and the acquisition of productive assets. We discuss various types of liabilities in Chapters 9 and 10 and examine owners' equity in Chapter 11.

Key Ratios

Fixed asset turnover ratio measures how efficiently a company utilizes its investment in property, plant, and equipment over time. Its ratio can be compared to the ratio of its competitors. It is computed as follows (p. 424):

$$\text{Fixed asset turnover} = \frac{\text{Sales}}{(\text{Beginning net fixed asset balance} + \text{Ending net fixed asset balance}) \div 2}$$

Key Terms

Accelerated Depreciation Methods that result in higher depreciation expense in the early years of an operational asset's life and lower expense in the later years. *429*

Acquisition Cost Net cash equivalent amount paid or to be paid for the asset. *419*

Additions Extensions to, or enlargements of, existing assets that increase the cost of the existing asset; a capital expenditure. *423*

Amortization Systematic and rational allocation of the acquisition cost of an intangible asset over its useful life. *441*

Basket Purchase Acquisition of two or more assets in a single transaction for a single lump sum. *420*

Book (or Carrying) Value Acquisition cost of an operational asset less accumulated depreciation, depletion, or amortization. *424*

Capital Expenditures Expenditures that provide future benefits and are recorded as increases in asset accounts, not as expenses. *422*

Capitalized Interest Interest expenditures included in the cost of a self-constructed asset. *420*

Copyright Exclusive right to publish, use, and sell a literary, musical, or artistic work. *443*

Declining-Balance (DB) Depreciation The method that allocates the cost of an operational asset over its useful life based on a multiple of (often two times) the straight-line rate. *430*

Depletion Systematic and rational allocation of the cost of a natural resource over the period of exploitation. *439*

Depreciation Systematic and rational allocation of the cost of property, plant, and equipment (but not land) over their useful lives. *423*

Estimated Useful Life Expected service life of an operational asset to the present owner. *426*

Extraordinary Repairs Expenditures for major, high-cost, long-term repairs that increase the economic usefulness of the asset; increase an asset account (or decrease accumulated depreciation); a capital expenditure. *423*

Franchise A contractual right to sell certain products or services, use certain trademarks, or perform activities in a geographical region. *443*

Goodwill (Cost in Excess of Net Assets Acquired) For accounting purposes, the excess of the purchase price of a business over the market value of the business's assets and liabilities. *441*

Intangible Assets Operational assets that have special rights but not physical substance. *418*

Leaseholds Rights granted to a lessee under a lease contract. *444*

Natural Resources Assets occurring in nature, such as mineral deposits, timber tracts, oil, and gas. *439*

Operational Assets (Long-Lived Assets) Tangible and intangible assets owned by a business and used in its operations. *418*

Ordinary Repairs and Maintenance Expenditures for the normal operating upkeep of operational assets; increase an expense for ordinary repairs. *423*

Patent An exclusive right granted by the federal government for an invention; gives the owner the right to use, manufacture, and sell the subject of the patent. *443*

Residual (or Salvage) Value Estimated amount to be recovered, less disposal costs, at the end of the company's estimated useful life of an operational asset. *426*

Revenue Expenditures Expenditures that provide benefits during the current account-ing period only and are recorded as expenses. *422*

Straight-Line (SL) Depreciation Method that allocates the cost of an operational asset in equal periodic amounts over its useful life. *427*

Tangible Assets Operational assets (or fixed assets) that have physical substance. *418*

Trademark An exclusive legal right to use a special name, image, or slogan. *443*

Units-of-Production Depreciation Method that allocates the cost of an operational asset over its useful life based on its peri-odic output related to its total estimated output. *428*

Questions

1. Define *operational assets*. Why are they considered a "bundle of future services"?
2. What are the classifications of operational assets? Explain each.
3. Relate the cost principle to accounting for operational assets.
4. Describe the relationship between the matching principle and accounting for opera-tional assets.
5. Define and calculate the book value of a three-year-old operational asset that cost $21,500, has an estimated residual value of $1,500, and has an estimated useful life of five years. Relate book value to carrying value and market value.
6. Under the cost principle, what amounts usually should be included in the acquisition cost of an operational asset?
7. What is a basket purchase? What measurement problem does it pose?
8. Distinguish between depreciation, depletion, and amortization.
9. In computing depreciation, three values must be known or estimated; identify and explain the nature of each.
10. Estimated useful life and residual value of an operational asset relate to the current owner or user rather than all potential users. Explain this statement.
11. What type of depreciation-expense pattern is provided under the straight-line method? When is its use appropriate?
12. What type of depreciation-expense pattern emerges under the units-of-production method? When is its use appropriate?
13. What are the arguments in favor of accelerated depreciation?
14. Distinguish between capital expenditures and revenue expenditures.
15. Distinguish between ordinary and extraordinary repairs. How is each accounted for?
16. Over what period should an addition to an existing operational asset be depreciated? Explain.
17. Define *intangible asset*.
18. What period should be used to amortize an intangible asset?
19. Define *goodwill*. When is it appropriate to record goodwill as an intangible asset?

20. Distinguish between a leasehold and a leasehold improvement.
21. Over what period should a leasehold improvement be amortized? Explain.
22. How is the fixed asset turnover ratio computed? Explain its meaning.

Exercises

E8–1 Identifying the Nature of Long-Lived Assets

For each of the following long-lived assets, indicate its nature and related cost allocation concept. Use the following symbols:

Nature		Cost Allocation Concept	
L	Land	DR	Depreciation
B	Building	DP	Depletion
E	Equipment	A	Amortization
NR	Natural resource	NO	No cost allocation
I	Intangible	O	Other
O	Other		

	Asset	Nature	Cost Allocation			Asset	Nature	Cost Allocation
a.	Copyright				f.	Operating license		
b.	Land held for use	O (investment)			g.	Land held for sale		
c.	Warehouse				h.	Delivery vans		
d.	Oil well				i.	Timber tract		
e.	New engine for old machine				j.	Production plant		

E8–2 Analyzing a Basket Purchase of Assets and Straight-Line Depreciation

Lion Company bought a building and the land on which it is located for a total cash price of $178,000. The company paid transfer *title* costs of $2,000. Renovation costs on the building were $21,200. An independent appraiser provided market values for the building, $158,384; and land, $50,016.

add this to build. cost

Required:

1. Apportion the cost of the property on the basis of the appraised values. Show computations.
2. Give the journal entry to record the purchase of the property, including all expenditures. Assume that all transactions were for cash and that all purchases occurred at the start of the year.
3. Compute straight-line depreciation at the end of one year assuming an estimated 12-year useful life and a $14,000 estimated residual value.
4. What would be the book value of the property at the end of year 2?

E8–3 Applying the Cost Principle and Straight-Line Depreciation

Cooper Company purchased a machine on March 1, 19A, at an invoice price of $20,000. On date of delivery, March 2, 19A, the company paid $8,000 on the machine, and the balance was on credit at 12 percent interest. On March 3, 19A, it paid $250 for freight on the machine. On March 5, Cooper paid installation costs relating to the machine amounting to $1,200. On October 1, 19A, the company paid the balance due on the machine plus the interest. On December 31, 19A (the end of the accounting period), Cooper recorded depreciation on the machine using the straight-line method with an estimated useful life of 10 years and an estimated residual value of $3,450.

Required (round all amounts to the nearest dollar):

1. Compute the acquisition cost of the machine.
2. Compute the depreciation expense to be reported for 19A.
3. What is the impact on the cost of the machine of the interest paid on the 12 percent note? Under what circumstances can interest expense be included in acquisition cost?
4. What would be the book value of the machine at the end of 19B?

Hilton Hotels **E8–4 Reporting Interest on Self-Constructed Assets**

The financial statements for Hilton Hotels include the following note:

> **Summary of Significant Accounting Policies**
> *Property, Equipment and Depreciation*
> Property and equipment are stated at cost. Interest incurred during construction of facilities is capitalized and amortized over the life of the asset.

Required:

1. Why is it appropriate to capitalize interest on self-constructed assets?
2. What is the impact of this policy on Hilton's financial statements?

E8–5 Computing Depreciation for Four Years Using Alternative Depreciation Methods

Wendy Kay Corporation bought a machine at the beginning of the year at a cost of $6,400. The estimated useful life was four years, and the residual value was $800. Assume that the estimated productive life of the machine is 80,000 units. Yearly production was year 1, 28,000 units; year 2, 22,000 units; year 3, 18,000 units; and year 4, 12,000 units.

Required:

1. Determine the amount for each cell in the following schedule. Show your computations, and round to the nearest dollar.

	Depreciation Expense		
Year	**Straight-Line**	**Units of Production**	**200% Declining Balance**
1			
2			
3			
4			
Totals			

2. Assuming that the machine was used directly in the production of one of the products that the company manufactures and sells, what factors might be considered in selecting a preferable depreciation method in conformity with the matching principle?

E8–6 Focus on Cash Flows: Computing Depreciation and Book Value for Two Years Using Alternative Depreciation Methods and the Impact on Cash Flows

Heald Company bought a machine for $65,000. The estimated useful life was five years, and the estimated residual value was $5,000. Assume that the estimated useful life in productive units is 150,000. Units actually produced were 40,000 in year 1 and 45,000 in year 2.

Required:

1. Determine the appropriate amounts to complete the following schedule. Show computations, and round to the nearest dollar.

Method of Depreciation	Depreciation Expense		Book Value at End of	
	Year 1	Year 2	Year 1	Year 2
Straight line				
Units of production				
Double-declining balance				

2. Which method would result in the lowest EPS for year 1? For year 2?
3. Which method would result in the highest amount of cash outflows in year 1? Why?

E8–7 Computing and Interpreting the Effect of a Change in Useful Life and Residual Value on Financial Statements and Cash Flows

Moore Company owns the office building occupied by its administrative office. The office building was reflected in the accounts at the end of last year as follows:

Cost when acquired	$450,000
Accumulated depreciation (based on straight-line depreciation, an estimated life of 30 years, and a $30,000 residual value)	196,000

During January of this year, on the basis of a careful study, management decided that the total estimated useful life should be changed to 25 years (instead of 30) and the residual value reduced to $23,000 (from $30,000). The depreciation method will not change.

Required:
1. Compute the annual depreciation expense prior to the change in estimates.
2. Compute the annual depreciation expense after the change in estimates.
3. What will be the net effect on the balance sheet, net income, and cash flows of changing estimates?

E8–8 Identifying Capital and Revenue Expenditures

For each of the following items, enter the correct number to the left to show the type of expenditure. Use the following:

TYPE OF EXPENDITURE

A   Capital expenditure

B   Revenue expenditure *– period exp*

C   Neither

TRANSACTIONS

_____ (1) Paid $400 for ordinary repairs.

_____ (2) Paid $6,000 for extraordinary repairs.

_____ (3) Paid cash, $20,000, for addition to old building;

_____ (4) Paid for routine maintenance, $200, on credit.

__A__ (5) Purchased a machine, $7,000; gave long-term note.

__A__ (6) Paid $2,000 for organization costs. *intangible – set-up*

__A__ (7) Paid three-year insurance premium, $900.

_____ (8) Purchased a patent, $4,300 cash.

__B__ (9) Paid $10,000 for monthly salaries.

_____ (10) Paid cash dividends, $20,000. *– not an exp – it's a distribution of earnings*

E8–9 Recording Depreciation, Repairs, and Amortization

Donnelly Company operates a small manufacturing facility as a supplement to its regular service activities. At the beginning of 19L, an operational asset account for the company showed the following balances:

Manufacturing equipment	$80,000
Accumulated depreciation through 19K	55,000

During 19L, the following expenditures were incurred for repairs and maintenance:

Routine maintenance and repairs on the equipment	$ 850
Major overhaul of the equipment	10,500

The equipment is being depreciated on a straight-line basis over an estimated life of 15 years with a $5,000 estimated residual value. The annual accounting period ends on December 31.

Required:

1. Give the adjusting entry for depreciation on the manufacturing equipment that was made at the end of 19K. Starting with 19L, what is the remaining estimated life?
2. Give the journal entries to record the two expenditures for repairs and maintenance during 19L.
3. Give the adjusting entry that should be made at the end of 19L for depreciation of the manufacturing equipment, assuming no change in the estimated life or residual value. Show computations.

E8–10 Recording Depreciation, Extraordinary Repairs, and Changes in Estimated Useful Life and Residual Value

At the end of the annual accounting period, December 31, 19C, Nina Company's records reflected the following:

Machine A	
Cost when acquired	$28,000
Accumulated depreciation	10,000

During January 19D, the machine was renovated, including several major improvements, at a cost of $11,000. As a result, the estimated life increased from five years to eight years, and the residual value increased from $3,000 to $5,000. The company uses straight-line depreciation.

Required:

1. Give the journal entry to record the renovation. How old was the machine at the end of 19C?
2. Give the adjusting entry at the end of 19D to record straight-line depreciation for the year.
3. Explain the rationale for your entries in requirements (1) and (2).

Eastman Kodak

E8–11 Analyzing Depreciation Policy

The annual report for Eastman Kodak contained the following note:

Significant Accounting Policies

Depreciation. Depreciation expense is provided based on historical cost and the estimated useful lives of the assets. The Company generally uses the straight–line method for calculating the provision for depreciation. For assets in the United States acquired prior to January 1, 1992, the provision for depreciation is generally calculated using accelerated methods.

Required:

1. Explain the term *historical cost*. What is the meaning of "provision for depreciation"?
2. Why do you think the company changed its depreciation method for assets acquired in 1992 and subsequent years? What impact did the change have on net income?

E8–12 Comparing Depreciation for Tax and Financial Reporting

Federal Express

The annual report for Federal Express Corporation includes the following information:

> For financial reporting purposes, depreciation and amortization of property and equipment is provided on a straight-line basis over the asset's service life. For income tax purposes, depreciation is generally computed using accelerated methods.

Required:

Explain why Federal Express uses different methods of depreciation for financial reporting and tax purposes.

E8–13 Computing and Interpreting the Fixed Asset Turnover Ratio

Apple Computer, Inc.

The following data were included in a recent Apple Computer annual report:

In millions	1996	1995	1994	1993	1992	1991	1990	1989	1988	1987
Net sales	$9,833	$11,062	$9,180	$7,977	$7,086	$6,309	$5,558	$5,284	$4,071	$2,661
Net property, plant, and equipment	598	711	667	660	462	448	398	334	207	130

Required:

1. Compute Apple's fixed asset turnover ratio for 1988, 1990, 1992, 1994, and 1996 (the even years).
2. How might an analyst interpret the results?

E8–14 Analyzing the Effects of a Depreciation Error on Key Ratios

REX Stores Corporation

REX Stores Corporation, headquartered in Dayton, Ohio, is one of the nation's leading consumer electronics retailers operating 222 stores in 35 states. The following is a note from a recent annual report:

(1) SUMMARY OF SIGNIFICANT ACCOUNTING POLICIES—

(e) Property and Equipment—Property and equipment is recorded at cost. Depreciation is computed using the straight-line method. Estimated useful lives are 30 to 40 years for buildings and improvements, and 3 to 12 years for fixtures and equipment. Leasehold improvements are depreciated over 10–12 years. The components of cost at January 31, 1997 and 1996 are as follows:

	1997	1996
	(In thousands)	
Land	$23,530	$18,452
Buildings and improvements	53,890	40,492
Fixtures and equipment	14,386	12,294
Leasehold improvements	9,409	7,740
	101,215	78,978
Less: Accumulated depreciation	(11,577)	(8,671)
	$89,638	$70,307

Required:

1. Assuming that REX Stores did not sell any property, plant, and equipment in 1997, what was the amount of depreciation expense recorded in 1997?
2. Assume that REX Stores failed to record depreciation in 1997. Indicate the effect of the error on the following ratios:
   a. Earnings per share.

b. Fixed asset turnover.

c. Current ratio.

d. Return on investment.

Federal Express

E8–15 **Recording the Disposal of an Asset at Three Different Assumed Sale Prices**

Federal Express has developed a worldwide network that delivers more than 1.7 million packages every working night. In addition to the world's largest fleet of all-cargo aircraft, the company has more than 28,000 ground vehicles that are used to pick up and deliver packages. Assume that Federal Express sold a small delivery truck that had been used in the business for three years. The records of the company reflected the following:

Delivery truck	$18,000
Accumulated depreciation	13,000

Required:

1. Give the journal entry for the disposal of the truck, assuming that the sales price was $5,000.

2. Give the journal entry for the disposal of the truck, assuming that the sales price was $5,600.

3. Give the journal entry for the disposal of the truck, assuming that the sales price was $4,600.

4. Summarize the effects of the disposal of the asset under the preceding three different situations.

Fisher-Price

E8–16 **Focus on Cash Flows: Analyzing the Disposal of an Operational Asset and the Effects on Financial Statements**

Fisher-Price manufactures and markets high-quality preschool and infant toys. The company's revenues exceed $600 million. In the toy business, it is very difficult to determine the life expectancy of a product. Products that kids love one year may sit on the shelf the following year. As a result, companies in the toy business often sell productive assets that are no longer needed. Assume that on December 31, 19D (after adjusting entries), Fisher-Price's records showed the following data about a machine that was no longer needed to make a toy that was popular last year:

Machine, original cost	$52,000
Accumulated depreciation	27,500*

*Based on an eight-year estimated useful life, an $8,000 residual value, and straight-line depreciation.

On April 1, 19E, the machine was sold for $26,000 cash. The accounting period ends on December 31.

Required:

1. How old was the machine on January 1, 19E? Show computations.

2. Compute the effect of the sale of the machine on April 1, 19E, on total assets, net income, and cash flows.

E8–17 **Recording Accident and Insurance Indemnity on an Operational Asset**

On January 1, 19C, the records of Barken Corporation showed the following:

Truck (estimated residual value, $2,000)	$12,000
Accumulated depreciation (straight line, two years)	4,000

On September 30, 19C, the delivery truck was a total loss as the result of an accident. The truck was insured; therefore, the company collected $5,600 cash from the insurance company on October 5, 19C.

Required:

1. Based on the data given, compute the estimated useful life of the truck.
2. Give all journal entries with respect to the truck from January 1 through October 5, 19C. Show computations.

E8–18 Computing the Acquisition and Depletion of a Natural Resource

Freeport–McMoran is a natural resources company involved in the business of exploration, development, and extraction of natural resources. Annual revenues exceed $1 billion. Assume that in February 19A, Freeport-McMoran paid $700,000 for a mineral deposit in Wyoming. During March, it spent $65,000 in preparing the deposit for exploitation. It was estimated that 900,000 total cubic yards could be extracted economically. During 19A, 60,000 cubic yards were extracted. During January 19B, the company spent another $6,000 for additional developmental work. After conclusion of the latest work, the estimated remaining recovery was increased to 1,200,000 cubic yards over the remaining life. During 19B, 50,000 cubic yards were extracted.

Freeport–McMoran

Required:

1. Compute the acquisition cost of the deposit in 19A.
2. Compute depletion for 19A.
3. Compute the acquisition cost of the deposit after payment of the January 19B developmental costs.
4. Compute annual depletion for 19B.

E8–19 Analyzing the Acquisition, Amortization, and Reporting of Three Different Intangible Assets

Wyatt Company had three intangible operational assets at the end of 19F (end of the accounting year):

a. A patent purchased from R. Jay on January 1, 19H, for a cash cost of $5,640. Jay had registered the patent with the U.S. Patent Office seven years earlier on January 1, 19A. Amortize over the remaining legal life.

b. A franchise acquired from the local community to provide certain services for five years starting on January 1, 19H. The franchise cost $25,000 cash.

c. A lease on some property for a five-year term beginning January 1, 19H. The company immediately spent $7,800 cash for long-term improvements (estimated useful life, eight years; no residual value). At the termination of the lease, there will be no recovery of these improvements.

Required:

1. Compute the acquisition cost of each intangible asset.
2. Compute the amortization of each intangible at December 31, 19H. The company does not use contra-accounts.
3. Show how these assets and any related expenses should be reported on the balance sheet and income statement for 19H.

E8–20 Analyzing the Financial Statement Effects of the Acquisition and Amortization of Three Intangibles

Flagg Company, with a fiscal year ending December 31, acquired three intangible operational assets during 19F. For each of the following transactions, indicate the accounts and amounts affected and the direction of the effect (+ for increase, – for decrease, and NE for no effect). Use the following headings:

Event	Assets	Liabilities	Stockholders' Equity

a. On January 1, 19F, the company purchased a patent from M. Masters for $6,000 cash. Masters had developed the patent and registered it with the Patent Office on January 1, 19A.

b. On December 31, 19F, amortize the patent over the remaining legal life.

c. On January 1, 19F, the company purchased a copyright for a total cash cost of $14,000, and the remaining legal life was 25 years. The company executives estimated that the copyright would have no value by the end of 20 years.

d. On December 31, 19F, amortize the copyright.

e. The company purchased another company in January 19F at a cash cost of $120,000. Included in the purchase price was $30,000 for goodwill; the balance was for plant, equipment, and fixtures (no liabilities were assumed).

f. On December 31, 19F, amortize the goodwill over the maximum period permitted.

Starbucks Coffee Company

E8–21 Recording and Amortizing Rent Paid in Advance, Leasehold Improvements, and Periodic Rent

Starbucks Coffee Company is a rapidly expanding retailer of specialty coffee. It has more than 250 stores in 10 markets. Assume that Starbucks planned to open a new store on Commonwealth Avenue near Boston University and obtained a 15-year lease, starting January 1, 19D. Although a serviceable building was on the property, the company had to build an additional structure for storage. The 15-year lease required a $12,000 cash advance payment, plus cash payments of $4,000 per month during occupancy. During January 19D, the company spent $60,000 cash building the structure. The new structure has an estimated life of 18 years with no residual value (straight-line depreciation).

needs to be amoritized
15
800

Required:

1. Give the journal entries for the company to record the payment of the $12,000 advance on January 1, 19D, and the first monthly rental.
2. Give the journal entry to record the construction of the new structure.
3. Give any adjusting entries required at the end of the annual accounting period on December 31, 19D, with respect to (a) the advance payment and (b) the new structure. Show computations.
4. Compute the total amount of expense resulting from the lease for 19D.

Problems

P8–1 Applying the Cost Principle to Determine the Cost of an Operational Asset

On January 1, 19A, O'Neil-Hughes Company bought a machine for use in operations. The machine has an estimated useful life of eight years and an estimated residual value of $1,500. The company provided the following expenditures:

a. Invoice price of the machine, $70,000.
b. Less: Cash discount of 2 percent on all cash paid by January 10.
c. Freight paid by the vendor per sales agreement, $800.
d. Installation costs, $2,000.
e. Payment of the $70,000 was made on January 15, 19A, as follows:
   (1) O'Neil-Hughes Company common stock, par $1; 2,000 shares (market value, $3 per share).
   (2) Note payable, $40,000, 12 percent due April 16, 19A (principal plus interest).
   (3) Balance of the invoice price settled with cash.

Required:

Compute the cost of the machine that the company should record. Explain the basis you used for any questionable items.

P8–2 Computing the Basket Purchase Allocation and Recording Depreciation under Three Alternative Methods

At the beginning of the year, BSJ Company bought three used machines from Manor, Inc., for a total cash price of $58,000. Transportation costs on the machines were $2,000. The machines immediately were overhauled, installed, and started operating. The machines were different; therefore, each had to be recorded separately in the accounts. An appraiser was employed to estimate their market value at date of purchase (prior to the overhaul and installation). The book values shown on Manor's books also are available. The book values, appraisal results, installation costs, and renovation expenditures follow:

	Machine A	Machine B	Machine C
Book value—Manor	$8,000	$12,000	$6,000
Appraisal value	9,500	32,000	8,500
Installation costs	300	500	200
Renovation costs prior to use	2,000	400	600

By the end of the first year, each machine had been operating 8,000 hours.

Required:

1. Compute the cost of each machine by making a supportable allocation. Explain the rationale for the allocation basis used.
2. Give the entry to record depreciation expense at the end of year 1, assuming the following:

Machine	ESTIMATES Life	Residual Value	Depreciation Method
A	5	$1,500	Straight line
B	40,000 hours	900	Units of production
C	4	2,000	200% declining balance

P8–3 Computing and Recording Depreciation Using Three Methods, and Explaining Effect of Depreciation on Cash Flows and EPS

Southwestern Bell

Southwestern Bell provides telecommunication services to customers in Arkansas, Kansas, Missouri, Oklahoma, and Texas. The company's assets exceed $22 billion. As a result, depreciation is a significant item on Southwestern Bell's income statement. Assume that you are a financial analyst for Southwestern Bell and have been asked to determine the impact of alternative depreciation methods. For your analysis, you have been asked to compare methods based on a machine that cost $68,225. The estimated useful life is 10 years, and the estimated residual value is $2,225. The machine has an estimated useful life in productive output of 88,000 units. Actual output was 10,000 in year 1 and 8,000 in year 2.

Required:

1. Determine the appropriate amounts for the following table. Show your computations.

		DEPRECIATION EXPENSE		BOOK VALUE AT END OF	
Method of Depreciation		Year 1	Year 2	Year 1	Year 2
Straight line					
Units of production					
200% declining balance					

2. Give the adjusting entries for years 1 and 2 under each method.
3. In selecting a depreciation method, some companies assess the comparative effect on cash flow and EPS. Briefly comment on the depreciation methods in terms of effects on cash flow and EPS.

Reader's Digest

P8–4 Analyzing and Recording Entries Related to a Change in Estimated Life and Residual Value

Reader's Digest is a global publisher of magazines, books, and music and video collections, and one of the world's leading direct mail marketers. Many direct mail marketers use high-speed Didde press equipment to print their advertisements. These presses can cost more than $1 million. Assume that Reader's Digest owns a Didde press acquired at an original cost of $400,000. It is being depreciated on a straight-line basis over a 20-year estimated useful life and has a $50,000 estimated residual value. At the end of 19H, the press had been depreciated for a full eight years. In January 19I, a decision was made, on the basis of improved maintenance procedures, that a total estimated useful life of 25 years and a residual value of $73,000 would be more realistic. The accounting period ends December 31.

Required:
1. Compute (a) the amount of depreciation expense recorded in 19H and (b) the book value of the printing press at the end of 19H.
2. Compute the amount of depreciation that should be recorded in 19I. Show computations.
3. Give the adjusting entry for depreciation at December 31, 19I.

Singapore Airlines

P8–5 Inferring Activities Affecting Fixed Assets from Notes to the Financial Statements

Singapore Airlines reported the following information in the notes to a recent annual report (in Singapore dollars):

SINGAPORE AIRLINES
Notes to the Accounts (31 March 1996)
13. **Fixed Assets** (in $ Million)
   The Company

	1 April 1995	Additions	Disposals/ Transfers	31 March 1996
Cost				
Aircraft	10,293.1	954.4	296.4	10,951.1
Other fixed assets (summarized)	3,580.9	1,499.1	1,156.7	3,923.3
	13,874.0	2,453.5	1,453.1	14,874.4
Accumulated depreciation				
Aircraft	4,024.8	683.7	290.1	4,418.4
Other fixed assets (summarized)	1,433.4	158.5	73.8	1,518.1
	5,458.2	842.2	363.9	5,936.5

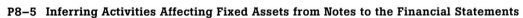

Singapore Airlines also reported the following cash flow details:

13. Cash Flow from Operating Activities (in $ Million)

	The Company	
	1995-96	**1994-95**
OPERATING PROFIT	755.9	816.5
Adjustments for:		
Depreciation of fixed assets	842.2	837.5
Loss/(surplus) on sale of fixed assets	(1.3)	(0.3)
Other adjustments (summarized)	82.3	39.4
NET CASH PROVIDED BY OPERATING ACTIVITIES	1,679.1	1,693.1

Required:
1. Give the journal entry to record the acquisitions of fixed assets in 1996.
2. Give the journal entry to record the depreciation of fixed assets for 1996.
3. What was the amount of cash the company received for disposals and transfers? Show computations.

P8–6 Focus on Cash Flows: Analyzing the Effects of Repairs, an Addition, and Depreciation

Federal Express

A recent annual report for Federal Express included the following note:

Property and equipment

Expenditures for major additions, improvements, flight equipment modifications and overhaul costs are capitalized. Maintenance and repairs are charged to expense as incurred.

Assume that Federal Express made extensive repairs on an existing building and added a new wing. The building is a garage and repair facility for delivery trucks that serve the Denver area. The existing building originally cost $420,000, and by the end of 19J (10 years), it was half depreciated on the basis of a 20-year estimated useful life and no residual value. Assume straight-line depreciation computed to the nearest month. During 19K, the following expenditures related to the building were made:

a. Ordinary repairs and maintenance expenditures for the year, $7,000 cash.
b. Extensive and major repairs to the roof of the building, $22,000 cash. These repairs were completed on June 30, 19K.
c. The new wing was completed on June 30, 19K, at a cash cost of $130,000. The wing had an estimated useful life of 10 years and no residual value.

Required:
1. Applying the policies of Federal Express, complete the following, indicating the effects for the preceding expenditures. If there is no effect on an account, write NE on the line:

	Building	Accumulated Depreciation	Depreciation Expense	Repairs Expense	Cash
Balance January 1, 19K	$420,000				
Depreciation through June 30					
Balance prior to expenditures	$420,000				
Expenditure *a*					
Expenditure *b*					
Expenditure *c*					
Depreciation July–Dec. 31:					
Existing building					
Repairs and addition					
Balance December 31, 19K					

2. What was the book value of the building on December 31, 19K?
3. Explain the effect of depreciation on cash flows.

P8–7 Recording the Disposal of Three Operational Assets

During 19K, Baldwin Company disposed of three different assets. On January 1, 19K, prior to their disposal, the accounts reflected the following:

Assets	Original Cost	Residual Value	Estimated Life	Accumulated Depreciation (straight line)
Machine A	$20,000	$3,000	8 years	$12,750 (6 years)
Machine B	42,600	4,000	10 years	30,880 (8 years)
Machine C	76,200	4,200	15 years	57,600 (12 years)

The machines were disposed of in the following ways:

a. Machine A: Sold on January 1, 19K, for $8,200 cash.

b. Machine B: Sold on April 1, 19K, for $10,000; received cash, $3,000, and a $7,000 interest-bearing (12%) note receivable due at the end of 12 months.

c. Machine C: On July 2, 19K, this machine suffered irreparable damage from an accident. On July 10, 19K, a salvage company removed the machine immediately at no cost. The machine was insured, and $18,500 cash was collected from the insurance company.

Required:

Give all journal entries related to the disposal of each machine. Explain the accounting rationale for the way that you recorded each disposal.

P8–8 Analyzing Five Transactions to Give Original Entry and Any Related Depreciation and Amortization Adjusting Entries

During the 19E annual accounting period, Boyd Company completed the following transactions:

(*a*) On January 10, 19E, paid $7,000 for a complete reconditioning of each of the following machines acquired on January 1, 19A (total cost, $14,000):

    (1) Machine A: Original cost, $26,000; accumulated depreciation (straight line) to December 31, 19D, $18,400 ($3,000 residual value).

    (2) Machine B: Original cost, $32,000; accumulated depreciation (straight line) $13,000 ($6,000 residual value).

(*b*) On July 1, 19E, purchased a patent for $19,600 cash (estimated useful life, seven years).

(*c*) On January 1, 19E, purchased another business for cash $60,000, including $16,000 for goodwill. The company assumed no liabilities.

(*d*) On September 1, 19E, constructed a storage shed on land leased from A. Katz. The cost was $10,800; the estimated useful life was five years with no residual value. The company uses straight-line depreciation. The lease will expire in three years.

(*e*) Total expenditures during 19E for ordinary repairs and maintenance were $4,800.

(*f*) On July 1, 19E, sold Machine A for $6,000 cash.

Required:

1. For each of these transactions, give the entry (or entries) that should be made during 19E.

2. For each of these transactions, give any adjusting entry that should be made at December 31, 19E (compute depreciation and amortization to the nearest month).

P8–9 Computing Adjusting Entries and Book Value Related to Five Different Intangible Assets

Distance Company has five different intangible assets to be accounted for and reported on the financial statements. The management is concerned about the amortization of the cost of each of these intangibles. Facts about each intangible follow:

a. *Patent.* The company purchased a patent at a cash cost of $54,600 on January 1, 19E. The patent had a legal life of 17 years from date of registration with the U.S. Patent Office, which was January 1, 19A. Amortize it over its remaining legal life.

b. *Copyright.* On January 1, 19E, the company purchased a copyright for $22,500 cash. The legal life remaining from that date is 30 years. It is estimated that the copyrighted item will have no value by the end of 25 years.

c. *Franchise.* The company obtained a franchise from X Company to make and distribute a special item. It obtained the franchise on January 1, 19E, at a cash cost of $14,400 for a 12-year period.

d. *License.* On January 1, 19D, the company secured a license from the city to operate a special service for a period of five years. Total cash expended to obtain the license was $14,000.

e. *Goodwill.* The company started business in January 19C by purchasing another business for a cash lump sum of $400,000. Included in the purchase price was "Goodwill, $60,000." Company executives stated that "the goodwill is an important long-term asset to us." Amortize it over the maximum period permitted.

Required:

1. Compute the amount of amortization that should be recorded for each intangible asset at the end of the annual accounting period, December 31, 19E.
2. Give the book value of each intangible asset on January 1, 19G.

P8–10 Recording Purchase of a Business, Including Goodwill, Depreciation of Assets Acquired, and Amortization of Goodwill

Reebok

Reebok International is a leading worldwide designer, marketer, and distributor of sport, fitness, and lifestyle products, including footwear and apparel. The notes to a recent annual report from Reebok included the following:

Business Acquisitions

During the current year, the Company acquired the assets of Perfection Sport Fashions, Inc., a designer and marketer of performance apparel and accessories marketed under the *Tinley* brand name.

Assume that Reebok acquired Perfection Sport Fashions on January 5, 19A. Reebok acquired the name of the company and all of its assets, except cash, for $400,000 cash. Reebok did not assume the liabilities. The transaction was closed on January 5, 19A, at which time the balance sheet of Perfection Sport Fashions reflected the following book values:

PERFECTION SPORT FASHIONS
January 5, 19A

	Book Value	Market Value*
Accounts receivable (net)	$ 45,000	$ 45,000
Inventory	220,000	210,000
Operational assets (net)	32,000	60,000
Other assets	3,000	10,000
Total assets	$300,000	
Liabilities	$ 60,000	
Owners' equity	240,000	
Total liabilities and owners' equity	$300,000	

*These values for the assets purchased were provided to Reebok by an independent appraiser.

Required:

1. Compute the amount of goodwill resulting from the purchase. (*Hint:* Assets are purchased at market value in conformity with the cost principle.)
2. Compute the adjustments that Reebok would make at the end of the annual accounting period, December 31, 19A, for
   a. Depreciation of the operational assets (straight line), assuming an estimated remaining useful life of 20 years and no residual value.
   b. Amortization of goodwill, assuming that the maximum amortization period is used.

Cases and Projects

Black & Decker

C8–1 Analyzing the Age of Assets

A note to a recent annual report for Black & Decker contained the following information (in thousands of dollars):

	Current Year	Previous Year
Land and improvements	$ 69,091	$ 20,963
Buildings	298,450	160,570
Machinery and equipment	928,151	626,453
	1,295,692	807,986
Less accumulated depreciation	468,511	404,591
	$ 827,181	$403,395

Depreciation expense (in thousands of dollars) charged to operations was $99,234 in the current year and $81,459 in the previous year. Depreciation generally is computed using the straight-line method for financial reporting purposes.

Required:

1. What is your best estimate of the average expected life for Black & Decker's depreciable assets?
2. What is your best estimate of the average age of Black & Decker's depreciable assets?

Amerada Hess Corporation

C8–2 Determining the Impact of the Capitalization of Interest on an Accounting Ratio

The capitalization of interest associated with self-constructed assets was discussed in this chapter. A recent annual report for Amerada Hess Corporation disclosed the following information concerning capitalization of interest:

Interest costs related to certain long-term construction projects are capitalized to comply with FAS No. 34, "Capitalization of Interest Cost." Capitalized interest in the current year amounted to $34,897,000.

The income statement for that year disclosed that interest expense was $224,200,000. A popular accounting ratio used by some analysts is the interest coverage ratio (income ÷ interest expense). Explain why an analyst would calculate this ratio. Did Amerada Hess include the $34,897,000 in the reported interest expense of $224,200,000? If not, should an analyst include it when calculating the interest coverage ratio? Explain.

C8–3 Analyzing a Note Concerning Depreciation

The Coca-Cola Company

A recent annual report for The Coca-Cola Company contained the following note:

Property, plant, and equipment is stated at cost, less allowance for depreciation. Depreciation expense is determined principally by the straight-line method. The annual rates of depreciation are 2 percent to 10 percent for buildings and improvements and 7 percent to 34 percent for machinery, equipment, and containers.

Required:
1. What is the range of expected lives for buildings and improvements?
2. Explain why Coca-Cola depreciates the cost of its containers instead of including the total in cost of goods sold in the year the product is sold.

C8–4 Analyzing an Accounting Change

Ford Motor Company

A recent annual report for Ford Motor Company included the following information:

Note 6. Net Property, Depreciation and Amortization—Automotive
Assets placed in service before January 1, 1993, are depreciated using an accelerated method. Assets placed in service beginning in 1993 will be depreciated using the straight-line method of depreciation. This change in accounting principle is being made to reflect improvements in the design and flexibility of manufacturing machinery and equipment and improvements in maintenance practices. These improvements have resulted in more uniform productive capacities and maintenance costs over the useful life of an asset. Straight-line is preferable in these circumstances. The change is expected to improve 1993 after-tax results by $80 to $100 million.

Required:
1. Prepare any journal entries that are required to reflect this accounting change.
2. What impact does this change have on cash flows for Ford?
3. Explain why "straight-line is preferable in these circumstances."
4. What other factors do you think management considered when it decided to make this accounting change?
5. As an investor, how would you react to the fact that Ford's net income will increase by $80 to $100 million as the result of this change?

C8–5 Analyzing Financial Statements Including Fixed Asset Turnover Ratio and Cash Flows

The Seagram Company Ltd.

The Seagram Company Ltd., with headquarters in Montreal, Quebec, Canada, operates in both the beverages and entertainment industries. Seagram produces well-known spirits and wines and Tropicana and Dole beverages. In June 1995, Seagram purchased an 80 percent interest in MCA, Inc., which produces and distributes motion picture, television, and home video products and recorded music; publishes books; and operates theme parks (Universal

Studios) and retail stores. The purchase resulted in $2.7 billion in goodwill, which is being amortized over 40 years. The company also wrote down $120 million in assets due to impairment. Selected data from the annual report are as follows (amounts are in millions of U.S. dollars):

PROPERTY, PLANT, EQUIPMENT, AND INTANGIBLES FROM THE CONSOLIDATED BALANCE SHEET	1996	1995
Film costs, net of amortization	$ 790	—
Artists' contracts, advances, and other entertainment assets	712	—
Property, plant, and equipment, net	2,806	$1,267
Excess of cost over fair value of assets acquired	4,298	1,547
FROM THE CONSOLIDATED STATEMENT OF INCOME		
Total revenues	$9,747	$6,399
FROM THE CONSOLIDATED STATEMENT OF CASH FLOWS		
Income from continuing operations	$ 174	$ 194
Adjustments		
Amortization of film costs	642	—
Depreciation and amortization of assets	255	138
Amortization of excess of cost over fair value of assets acquired	113	46
Other adjustments (summarized)	(159)	141
Net cash provided by continuing operations	$1,025	$ 519
FROM THE NOTES TO THE FINANCIAL STATEMENTS		
Accumulated depreciation on property, plant, and equipment	$1,056	$ 858

Required:

1. What was the approximate age of the property, plant, and equipment at the end of 1996?
2. Compute the fixed asset turnover ratio for 1996. Explain your results.
3. Compute the book value of the property, plant, and equipment, assuming that the assets were not impaired. Explain your answer.
4. What is Excess of Cost over Fair Value of Assets Acquired? Compute an estimate of the amount to be amortized in the next year.
5. On the consolidated statement of cash flows, why are the amortization and depreciation amounts added to income from continuing operations?

Eastman Kodak

C8–6 Analyzing the Sale of Assets

A recent annual report for Eastman Kodak reported that the balance of property, plant, and equipment at the end of the current year was $16,774 million. At the end of the previous year, it had been $15,667 million. During the current year, the company bought $2,118 million worth of new equipment. The balance of accumulated depreciation at the end of the current year was $8,146 million and at the end of the previous year was $7,654 million. Depreciation expense for the current year was $1,181 million. The annual report does not disclose any gain or loss on the disposition of property, plant, and equipment, so you may assume that the amount was zero. What amount of proceeds did Eastman Kodak receive when it sold property, plant, and equipment during the current year? (*Hint:* Set up T-accounts.)

Grand Metropolitan

C8–7 Comparing Depreciation Methods in Different Countries

Grand Metropolitan is a major international company located in London. A recent annual report contained the following information concerning its accounting policies.

Fixed assets and depreciation

Fixed assets are stated at cost or at professional valuation. Cost includes interest, net of any tax relief, on capital employed in major developments.

No depreciation is provided on freehold land. Other leaseholds are depreciated over the unexpired period of the lease. All other buildings, plant, equipment, and vehicles are depreciated to residual values over their estimated useful lives within the following ranges:

Industrial buildings	25 to 100 years
Plant and machinery	3 to 25 years
Fixtures and fittings	3 to 17 years

Required:

Compare accounting for fixed assets and depreciation in England with procedures used in this country.

C8–8 Financial Statement Analysis

Toys "R" Us

Refer to the financial statements of Toys "R" Us given in Appendix B at the end of this book.

Required:

1. What method of depreciation does the company use?
2. What is the amount of accumulated depreciation and amortization at the end of the current year?
3. For depreciation purposes, what is the estimated useful life of furniture and equipment?
4. What was the original cost of buildings owned by the company at the end of the current year?
5. What amount of depreciation and amortization was reported as expense for the current year?
6. What is the fixed asset turnover ratio? What does it suggest?

C8–9 Project: Comparing Balance Sheets within Industries

Acquire the annual reports or 10-Ks of three companies within an industry. (Library files, the SEC EDGAR service at www.sec.gov, Compustat CD, or the companies themselves are good sources.) Write a short report indicating any differences, if any, in the long-lived asset accounts used by the three companies (including intangible assets), in the cost allocation methods and estimates used, in the approximate average life of the assets, and in the percentage of property, plant, and equipment to total assets.

C8–10 Project: Comparing Balance Sheets among Industries

Acquire the annual reports or 10-Ks of three companies from different industries. (Library files, the SEC EDGAR service at www.sec.gov, Compustat CD, or the companies themselves are good sources.) Write a short report indicating any differences in the long-lived asset accounts used by the three companies (including intangible assets), in cost allocation methods and estimates used, in the approximate average life of the assets, and in the percentage of property, plant, and equipment to total assets.

C8–11 Project: Analyzing Differences in Fixed Asset Turnover Ratios among Competitors

Obtain the recent annual reports or 10-Ks of three competitors in the same industry. (Library files, the SEC EDGAR service at www.sec.gov, Compustat CD, or the companies themselves are good sources). Write a short memo comparing the companies' fixed asset turnover ratios. Indicate what differences in their businesses might account for any differences in the ratios.

C8–12 Project: Analyzing Changes in Fixed Asset Turnover Ratios

Acquire the three most recent years' annual reports or 10-Ks for a single company. (Library files, the SEC EDGAR service at www.sec.gov, Compustat CD, or the company itself are good sources.) Write a short memo comparing the company's fixed asset turnover ratio over the three years. Indicate what differences in activities or strategies might account for any difference in the ratio.

C8–13 Project: Focus on Cash Flows

Acquire the three most recent years' annual reports or 10-Ks for a single company. (Library files, the SEC EDGAR service at www.sec.gov, Compustat CD, or the company itself are good sources.) Write a short memo describing each of the noncash revenues and expenses related to long-lived assets for each year presented.

C8–14 Project: Financial Analysis Update

Acquire the most recent year's annual report and Form 10-K for Delta Air Lines. (Library files, the SEC EDGAR service at www.sec.gov, Compustat CD, or the company itself are good sources.) Write a short memo comparing the company's fixed asset ratio to the Delta Air Lines ratio presented in the chapter. Indicate what differences in activities might account for any difference in the ratio.

C8–15 Ethics Project: Managing Earnings through Long-Lived Assets

Obtain a recent news story concerning a company managing earnings through strategies or changes in estimates or methods related to long-lived assets. (Library files, the SEC EDGAR service at www.sec.gov, Compustat CD, or the company itself are good sources.) Write a short memo outlining the nature of the earnings management strategy, the reasons given by management for the strategy or change, and what other reasons may be driving management's choices.

C8–16 Team Project: Analysis of Long-Lived Assets

As a group, select an industry to analyze. Each group member should then acquire the annual report or 10-K for one publicly traded company in the industry, with each member selecting a different company. (Library files, the SEC EDGAR service at www.sec.gov, Compustat CD, or the company itself are good sources.)

Required:
1. On an individual basis, each team member should then write a short report listing the following:
   a. The accounts and amounts of the company's long-lived assets (property, plant, and equipment; intangible assets; and natural resources).
   b. The cost allocation method(s) and estimates used for each type of long-lived asset.
   c. The approximate average life of the assets.
   d. The fixed asset turnover ratio.
2. Discuss any patterns that you as a team observe. Then, as a group, write a short report comparing and contrasting your companies according to the preceding attributes.

CHAPTER NINE

Reporting and Interpreting Liabilities

General Mills
MANAGING CAPITAL STRUCTURE

Throughout the 1980s and 1990s, General Mills has been known as a

leader in the food industry. The company sells a full line of familiar breakfast

cereals, numerous snack foods, and the popular Betty Crocker products. Until

1995, General Mills operated Red Lobster and Olive Garden restaurants. In 1995,

the restaurant operations were spun off into a new independent company.

General Mills management has established aggressive goals for the

company to meet by the year 2000. As you would expect, many of these goals

involve increasing sales volume and improving operating efficiencies. We

have abstracted one of its financial goals from its annual report:

General Mills' financial goal for the 1990s is to achieve performance that places us in the top 10 percent of major American companies, ranked by the combination of growth in earnings per share and return on capital over a five-year period. Our major financial targets for top-decile performance include:

******

• Maintaining a Balance Sheet with a Strong "A" Bond Rating which will allow access to financing at reasonable costs.

each year. A few years ago, IBM managers offered employees an incentive to take vacation before the end of the fiscal year in an effort to reduce the amount of the accrued vacation liability reported on the balance sheet.

General Mills does not separately disclose the amount of accrued vacation liability. Instead, it shows on the balance sheet as part of accrued payroll. Apparently, in management's opinion, the amount of accrued vacation liability is not a material factor in the analysis of General Mills. Most analysts would probably agree.

Deferred Revenues and Service Obligations

In most business transactions, cash is paid after the product or service has been delivered. In some cases, cash is paid before delivery. You have probably paid for several magazines that you will receive at some time in the future. The publisher collects money for your subscription in advance of publishing the magazine. When a company collects cash before the related revenue has been earned, this cash is called **deferred revenues** (or *unearned revenues* or *revenues collected in advance*). Under the revenue principle, revenue cannot be recorded until it has been earned.

Deferred revenues are revenues that have been collected but not earned; they are liabilities until the goods or services are provided.

Deferred revenues are reported as a liability because cash has been collected but the related revenue has not been earned by the end of the accounting period. The obligation to provide the services or goods in the future exists. Accounting for deferred revenues was discussed in Chapter 6.

Another example of a liability associated with the obligation to provide a service in the future is the frequent flyer programs offered by most major airlines. Under these programs, customers earn free tickets by flying a certain number of miles or trip segments. Each year, these airlines must make an adjusting entry to record the estimated expense and related liability associated with awarding free tickets. The following note from a recent Southwest Airlines annual report illustrates this policy:

REAL WORLD EXCERPT

SOUTHWEST AIRLINES
Annual Report

Frequent flyer awards. The Company accrues the estimated incremental cost of providing free travel awards under its Rapid Rewards frequent flyer program.

Notice that the amount of the liability is the incremental cost of providing free travel, not the actual selling price of an airline ticket. Some analysts believe that the true cost of a frequent flyer program is the lost revenue associated with giving a ticket to a customer instead of selling it. These analysts believe that the liabilities reported for frequent flyer programs are severely understated. Currently, GAAP permit recording these liabilities based on incremental cost because no accurate method estimates the number of travelers who would have bought tickets if they had not earned a free award.

Many companies offer warranties on the products they sell. This is another form of future service obligation. The cost of providing repair work must be estimated and recorded as a liability (and expense) in the period in which the product is sold. General Mills, like most companies, quickly refunds money for any defective products that it sells. The company does not report a liability for this type of obligation because it estimates this amount to be immaterial.

Another type of obligation a company may face is related to the impact that its operations may have on the environment. Some companies incur significant obligations associated with the environmental impact of their operations. Freeport-McMoRan is a leading company in the production and sale of phosphate fertilizers used to grow grains. The process of extracting natural resources from the land has a major impact on the environment. Under state and federal laws, Freeport-McMoRan is obligated to

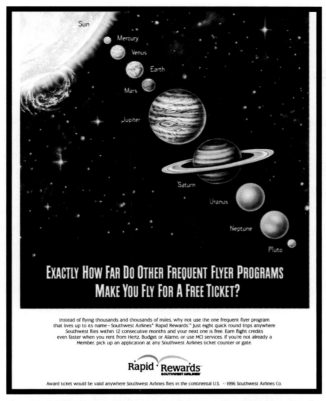

How would Southwest Airlines record the service obligation that is associated with its frequent flyer program?

restore the land once it has completed removing natural resources. The balance sheet for the company reports a $129 million liability for reclamation of land, and the notes included the following statement.

REAL WORLD EXCERPT
FREEPORT-MCMORAN
Annual Report

Environmental Remediation and Compliance. Estimated future expenditures to restore properties and related facilities to a state required to comply with environmental and other regulations are accrued over the life of the properties. The future expenditures are estimated based on current costs, laws and regulation.

Liabilities associated with future service obligations often are based on estimates that are very difficult to develop accurately. The cost of cleaning up pollution in the future depends on a number of factors including changing technology and federal standards. Many companies have faced bankruptcy because they underestimated the cost of environmental regulations. Managers and analysts must be very cautious in evaluating potential costs associated with activities that impact on our environment.

Notes Payable

Most companies need to borrow money to finance their operations. Creditors are willing to lend cash because they will earn interest to compensate them for giving up the use of their money for a period of time. This simple concept is called the **time value of money.** The word *time* is significant because the longer borrowed money is held, the larger is the total dollar amount of interest expense. Interest for a two-year loan, at a given interest rate, is more than for a one-year loan. To the *borrower*, interest is an expense; to the *creditor*, interest is a revenue.

The **time value of money** is interest that is associated with the use of money over time.

To calculate interest, three variables must be considered: (1) the principal (i.e., the cash that was borrowed), (2) the annual interest rate, and (3) the time period for the loan. The interest formula is

$$\text{Interest} = \text{Principal} \times \text{Interest rate} \times \text{Time}$$

The basic accounting for a note is the same whether it is long term or short term. Assume that on November 1, 19A, General Mills borrowed $100,000 cash on a one-year, 12 percent note payable. The interest is payable on December 31 and June 30. The principal is payable at the maturity date of the note, October 31, 19B. The note is recorded in the accounts as follows:

Nov. 1, 19A	Cash (A)	100,000	
	Note payable, short-term (L)		100,000

Interest is an expense of the period when the money is used. Under the matching concept, interest expense is recorded when it is incurred rather than when the cash actually is paid. When does General Mills incur interest cost associated with the note that was recorded in the previous journal entry? Because the company uses the money for two months during 19A, it records interest expense in 19A for two months. During 19B, the company uses the money for 10 months; therefore, it should record interest expense for 10 months in 19B.

The computation of interest expense follows:

Interest	=	Principal	×	Interest rate	×	Time
$2,000	=	$100,000	×	12%	×	$2/12$

The entry to record interest expense is

Dec. 31, 19A	Interest expense (E)	2,000	
	Cash (A)		2,000

Current Portion of Long-Term Debt

The distinction between current and long-term debt is important for both managers and analysts because current debt must be paid within the next year. The company must have sufficient cash to repay currently maturing debt. To provide accurate information concerning current liabilities, a company must reclassify long-term debt within a year of its maturity date as a current liability. Assume that General Mills signed a note payable of $5 million on January 1, 19A. Repayment is in two installments as follows: December 31, 19D, $2.5 million and December 31, 19E, $2.5 million. The December 31, 19B, 19C, and 19D, balance sheets report the following:

DECEMBER 31, 19B	
Long-term liabilities	
Note payable	$5,000,000

DECEMBER 31, 19C	
Current liabilities	
Current portion of long-term note	2,500,000
Long-term liabilities	
Long-term note	2,500,000

DECEMBER 31, 19D	
Current liabilities:	
Current portion of long-term note	2,500,000

An example of this type of disclosure can be seen in Exhibit 9.1. Notice that General Mills reported $75.4 million as the current portion of long-term debt in 1996 that will be paid in full during the following accounting period.

Refinanced Debt: Current or Noncurrent?

Financial ANALYSIS

Many companies refinance their debt when it matures. Instead of repaying the debt from current cash that is available, the company either signs a new loan agreement with a new maturity date or borrows money from a new creditor and repays the original creditor. An interesting accounting question arises if a company intends to refinance debt and has the ability to do so: Should currently maturing debt that will be refinanced be classified as a current or long-term liability? Remember that analysts are interested in a company's current liabilities because these liabilities will generate cash outflows in the next accounting period. If the liability will not generate a cash outflow in the next accounting period, GAAP require that it not be classified as current. This rule can be illustrated with a note from the General Mills annual report.

We have a revolving credit agreement expiring in 1999 that provides us with the ability to refinance short-term borrowing on a long-term basis, and therefore we have reclassified a portion of our notes payable to long-term debt.

REAL WORLD EXCERPT
GENERAL MILLS
Annual Report

Working Capital Management

Remember that the dollar difference between current assets and current liabilities is called *working capital.* Management of working capital is an important activity that can have a dramatic impact on a company's profitability. All businesses maintain inventory to meet the needs of customers. The purchase of inventory generates accounts payable. Suppliers expect to be paid on a timely basis, but a when a business sells inventory, it generates an accounts receivable that it will not collect for a period of time. If a company has too much inventory that doesn't sell or has customers who pay slowly, it may not be able to meet its obligations to its suppliers. At best, this strains relations; at worst, it may force a company into bankruptcy.

Many companies use sophisticated management techniques and state-of-the-art computer systems to manage working capital. They do not want to have cash invested in unproductive assets (such as excess inventory) but they do want to meet their obligations to creditors on a timely basis.

The annual report for General Mills states that "continuing operations generated less cash in 1996 than in the previous year primarily due to an increase in working capital." To understand the meaning of this statement, you should reflect back on our previous discussions of the Statement of Cash Flows. Remember that an increase in many current liabilities represents a cost that was incurred but not paid in cash. An increase in an accounts payable occurs when an item is acquired for inventory but not paid for. Cash is spent when the accounts payable is paid.

The Statement of Cash Flows for General Mills included the table at the top of the following page. Notice that the cash flows for the year were increased by $93.2 (million) because of the increase in accounts payable. General Mills was able to acquire goods from suppliers but did not have to pay for them during the current accounting period.

FOCUS ON CASH FLOWS

In Millions	Fiscal Year Ended		
	May 26, 1996	May 28, 1995	May 29, 1994
Cash Flows – Operating Activities:			
Earnings from continuing operations	$ 476.4	$ 259.7	$ 336.5
Adjustments to reconcile earnings to cash flow:			
Depreciation and amortization	186.7	191.4	173.8
Deferred income taxes	42.4	59.0	(34.0)
Change in current assets and liabilities, net of effects from business acquired	(25.9)	(227.8)	(79.1)
Unusual expenses	–	183.2	146.9
Other, net	(3.2)	(8.1)	17.2
Cash provided by continuing operations	676.4	457.4	561.3
Cash provided (used) by discontinued operations	(16.6)	210.1	259.3
Net Cash Provided by Operating Activities	659.8	667.5	820.6
Cash Flows – Investment Activities:			
Purchases of land, buildings and equipment	(128.8)	(156.5)	(212.5)
Investments in businesses, intangibles and affiliates, net of dividends	(40.0)	(48.8)	(140.7)
Purchases of marketable securities	(21.6)	(21.7)	(83.8)
Proceeds from sale of marketable securities	22.5	49.1	33.7
Proceeds from disposal of land, buildings and equipment	6.2	1.2	3.3
Proceeds from disposition of businesses	–	188.3	–
Other, net	(11.3)	(27.5)	(45.9)
Discontinued operations investment activities, net	–	(357.5)	(336.3)
Net Cash Used by Investment Activities	(173.0)	(373.4)	(782.2)
Cash Flows – Financing Activities:			
Increase (decrease) in notes payable	(42.4)	(330.4)	93.2
Issuance of long-term debt	42.3	135.0	273.6
Payment of long-term debt	(164.7)	(117.2)	(79.1)
Common stock issued	38.0	24.3	13.3
Purchases of common stock for treasury	(35.6)	(57.7)	(145.7)
Dividends paid	(303.6)	(297.2)	(299.4)
Other, net	(13.2)	(13.6)	(4.2)
Discontinued operations financing activities	–	347.9	–
Net Cash Used by Financing Activities	(479.2)	(308.9)	(148.3)
Increase (Decrease) in Cash and Cash Equivalents	7.6	(14.8)	(109.9)
Cash and Cash Equivalents – Beginning of Year	13.0	27.8	137.7
Cash and Cash Equivalents – End of Year	$ 20.6	$ 13.0	$ 27.8
Cash Flow from Changes in Current Assets and Liabilities:			
Receivables	$ (59.5)	$ (11.9)	$ (11.5)
Inventories	(23.7)	(52.7)	(76.1)
Prepaid expenses and other current assets	(6.3)	(11.9)	(22.2)
Accounts payable	93.2	(18.1)	(5.7)
Other current liabilities	(29.6)	(133.2)	36.4
Change in Current Assets and Liabilities	$ (25.9)	$(227.8)	$ (79.1)

SELF-STUDY QUIZ

Earlier in this chapter, we defined the current ratio and working capital. For this quiz, assume that the current ratio for General Mills is 2.0. For each of the following events, tell whether the current ratio and working capital will increase or decrease:

1. General Mills incurs an account payable of $250,000, with no change in current assets.
2. The company borrows $1,000,000 in long-term debt.
3. The company pays taxes payable in the amount of $750,000.
4. General Mills finances a new building with long-term debt.

After you have completed your answers, check them with the solutions in the footnote at the bottom of this page.*

---

* **CURRENT RATIO**   **WORKING CAPITAL**
1. Decrease   Decrease
2. Increase   Increase
3. Increase   No change
4. No change   No change

Long-Term Liabilities

Many companies use long-term liabilities to generate funds to purchase operational assets. Indeed, many financial analysts like to see companies maintain a reasonable balance between the expected life of an asset and the term of the financing that was used to acquire the asset. To illustrate the analysts' concern, consider what would happen if General Mills purchased equipment that had an expected life of 10 years during which time it was expected to provide a 12 percent return on investment. The company would create additional risk if it financed the purchase with a one-year bank loan that it intended to renew each year during the life of the asset. In the first year, interest rates might be 8 percent, which would provide a net return on the equipment of 4 percent (12 percent − 8 percent). If interest rates increased in subsequent years, General Mills might experience losses on the operation of the equipment. If interest rates were 14 percent when the loan was renewed, the company would have a net negative return of 2 percent (12 percent − 14 percent). General Mills could lessen this type of risk by using long-term debt to finance the acquisition of long-lived assets.

Long-term liabilities include long-term notes payable and bonds payable, which are contracts that specify the terms of the borrowing agreement (e.g., interest rate and repayment schedule). **Long-term liabilities** include all of the entity's obligations that are not classified as current liabilities.

> **Long-term liabilities** are all of the entity's obligations not classified as current liabilities.

To reduce risk for creditors who are willing to lend money for a long period (which, in turn, reduces the interest rate that must be paid), some companies pledge specific assets as security for the liability. A liability supported by this type of pledge (typically a mortgage) is called *secured debt*. An *unsecured debt* is one for which the creditor relies primarily on the borrower's integrity and general earning power.

Long-term liabilities are reported on the balance sheet immediately following current liabilities. Notice the example for General Mills in Exhibit 9.1. The accounts Long-Term Debt, Deferred Income Taxes, Deferred Income Taxes—Tax Leases, and Other Liabilities are all long-term liabilities despite the fact that no separate caption identifies them as such.

Long-Term Debt

Companies can raise long-term debt capital directly from a number of financial service organizations including banks, insurance companies, and pension plans. Raising debt from one of these organizations is known as *private placement*. This type of debt often is called a *note payable*, which is a written promise to pay a stated sum at one or more specified future dates called the *maturity dates*.

In many cases, a company's need for debt capital exceeds the financial ability of any single creditor. In these situations, the company may issue publicly traded debt called *bonds*. The bonds can be traded in established markets that provide bondholders with liquidity. They can sell their bonds to other investors prior to maturity if they have an immediate need for cash. Notes and bonds are very similar because they are both written promises to pay a debt. Bonds will be discussed in detail in the next chapter.

PERSPECTIVE

Borrowing in Foreign Currencies

Over the past years, business operations have become more global. Successful corporations market their products in many countries and locate manufacturing facilities around the world based on cost and productivity considerations. The financing of corporations also has become international, even in cases when the company does not have international operations.

Many corporations with foreign operations elect to finance those operations with foreign debt to lessen the exchange rate risk. This type of risk exists because the relative value of each nation's currency varies virtually on a daily basis because of various economic factors. As this book is being written, the British pound is worth approximately $1.50. A year earlier, it was worth $1.60. A U.S. company that owed debt denominated in pounds would gain from this decline in the value of the pound.

A U.S. corporation that conducts business operations in England might decide to borrow pounds to finance its operations. The profits from the business will be in pounds, which can be used to pay off the debt, which is in pounds. If the business earned profits in pounds but paid off debt in dollars, it would be exposed to exchange rate risk because the relative value of the dollar and the pound fluctuates.

Foreign corporations face this same problem. A note to a recent annual report from Toyota (a Japanese company) stated:

REAL WORLD EXCERPT

TOYOTA
Annual Report

Earnings declined in the current year ended, as the appreciation of the yen aggravated the adverse effects of sluggish demand. . . . The movement in exchange rates reduced operating income of the company. Losses on currency exchange thus offset most of the cost savings we achieved.

Toyota has borrowed a large amount of money in the United States to lessen the exchange rate risk that it faces. The company also owns and operates many factories in this country.

Even if a company does not have international operations, it may elect to borrow in foreign markets. When a country is experiencing a recession, interest rates often are low. These situations give corporations the opportunity to borrow money at a lower cost.

Accountants must convert, or translate, foreign debt into U.S. dollars for reporting purposes. Conversion rates for all major currencies are published in most newspapers. To illustrate foreign currency translation, assume that General Mills borrowed 1 million pounds (£). For the General Mills annual report, the accountant must use the conversion rate for the balance sheet date, which we assume was £1.00 to $1.60. The dollar equivalent of the debt is $1,600,000 (£1,000,000 × 1.60 = $1,600,000). As you can see, the dollar equivalent of foreign debt may change if the conversion rate changes even when no additional borrowings or repayments occur.

The notes to the balance sheet for General Mills indicate that the company has borrowed money primarily in the United States and Canada. In contrast, consider the following note from Toys "R" Us (in millions):

REAL WORLD EXCERPT

TOYS "R" US
Annual Report

	1996	1995
British pound sterling 11% bonds due in 2017	$198.4	$206.6
Japanese yen loans payable in varying amounts through 2012	178.3	192.9
8¼% sinking fund debentures, due 2017	88.3	88.2
Mortgage notes payable at annual interest rates from 6% to 11%	19.2	13.0

Toys "R" Us is an international company with more than 25 percent of its sales and assets located outside the United States. The company borrows heavily in international markets to minimize the risk associated with variations in exchange rates. This is typical for most large corporations and is further justification for business executives to develop an understanding of international markets.

General Mills has a joint venture with PepsiCo to compete in European markets.

SELF-STUDY QUIZ

In an earlier example, we assumed that the $100,000 note payable for General Mills required payment of interest on December 31 and June 30 of each year. Review that example and now assume that the note required the payment of interest on January 31 and July 31 of each year.

1. What adjusting entry should General Mills make at the end of its fiscal year on December 31, 19A?
2. What entry should the company make on January 31, 19B?
3. What entry should the company make on July 31, 19B?

After you have completed your answers, check them with the solutions in the footnote at the bottom of this page.*

Other Topics

Two areas of business operations may result in the creation of either an asset or a liability. These areas involve accounting for income taxes and employee retirement benefits. On most financial statements, you will see these items as liabilities, so we will discuss them along with other liabilities.

---

*1.	Interest expense	2,000	
	Interest payable		2,000
2.	Interest expense	1,000	
	Interest payable	2,000	
	Cash		3,000
3.	Interest expense	6,000	
	Cash		6,000

Deferred Taxes

In previous chapters, we made simplifying assumptions concerning tax expense. We often told you the amount of tax expense (e.g., $100,000) and had you make a journal entry similar to the following:

Tax expense (E)	100,000	
Taxes payable (L)		100,000

Because separate rules govern the preparation of financial statements (GAAP) and tax returns (Internal Revenue Code), the amount of income before taxes reported on the income statement is normally different from the amount of taxable income computed on the tax return. This difference creates an interesting accounting problem: Should tax expense on the income statement be based on the income that is reported on the income statement or income reported on the tax return? Accountants have resolved this issue by applying the matching concept. They determine tax expense based on the amount of income reported on the income statement because tax expense is a necessary cost associated with earning income and therefore should be recorded in the same period as the related income. This means that the amount of *tax expense* and the amount of *taxes payable* normally are different. To have our journal entry balance, we need a new account. This new account is called *Deferred Taxes*. In practice, deferred taxes can be either assets or liabilities. Notice in Exhibit 9.1 that General Mills has deferred tax amounts reported as both assets and liabilities.

Deferred tax items exist because of timing differences in reporting revenues and expenses on a company's income statement and tax return. These **temporary differences** are caused by differences in GAAP that govern financial statement preparation and the Internal Revenue Code that governs the preparation of tax returns. General Mills uses straight-line depreciation for its financial statements and accelerated depreciation for its tax return. As a result, it reports lower income on its tax return than on its income statement. Assume that General Mills computed taxes payable of $80,000 based on the numbers reported on the tax return and tax expense of $100,000 based on the income statement. The company records its tax obligation as follows:

Tax expense (E)	100,000	
Deferred taxes (L)		20,000
Taxes payable (L)		80,000

The deferred tax amount is paid in the future when depreciation expense "reverses." By this, we mean that at some point in the future, the accelerated depreciation recorded on the tax return will be less than the straight-line depreciation reported on the income statement (remember from Chapter 8 that accelerated depreciation causes higher depreciation expense compared to straight-line in the early years of an asset's life and lower depreciation in the later years). When a temporary difference reverses, the deferred tax amount is reduced.

The notes to the General Mills annual report contain the information on the following page concerning the causes of its deferred taxes.

The computation of deferred taxes involves some complexities that are discussed in advanced accounting courses. At this point, we want you to understand that deferred tax assets and liabilities are caused by temporary differences between the income statement and the tax return. Each temporary difference has an impact on the income statement in one accounting period and the tax return in another.

The tax effects of temporary differences that give rise to deferred tax assets and liabilities are as follows:

In Millions	May 26, 1996	May 28, 1995
Accrued liabilities	$ 84.6	$ 80.6
Unusual charge for oats matter	3.1	9.5
Unusual charge for restructuring	9.4	42.5
Compensation and employee benefits	53.3	55.2
Disposition liabilities	15.4	29.1
Foreign tax loss carryforward	12.4	19.4
Other	9.0	11.2
Gross deferred tax assets	187.2	247.5
Depreciation	130.5	139.4
Prepaid pension asset	138.1	125.1
Intangible assets	11.3	12.8
Other	37.5	53.8
Gross deferred tax liabilities	317.4	331.1
Valuation allowance	11.2	11.2
Net deferred tax liability	$141.4	$ 94.8

Accrued Retirement Benefits

Most employers provide retirement programs for their employees. In a *defined contribution* program, the employer makes cash payments to a fund that invests the money and earns income. When employees retire, they are entitled to a portion of the fund. If the investment strategy of the fund is successful, the retirement income for the employees will be larger. If the strategy is not successful, it will be lower. The employer's only obligation is to make the required annual payments to the fund, which are recorded as pension expense.

As an alternative, some employers offer *defined benefit* programs. Under these programs, an employee's retirement benefits are based on a percentage of his or her pay at retirement or a certain number of dollars for each year of employment. The employer must record pension expense each year. Basically, the amount of pension expense that must be accrued each year is the change in the current cash value of the employee's retirement package. The current cash value changes each year for a variety of reasons. For example, the current cash value changes (1) as the employee is closer to receiving benefits, (2) as the retirement benefits increase as the result of higher pay or longer service, or (3) if the employee's life expectancy changes. The company must report a pension liability based on any portion of the current cash value of the retirement program that has not actually been funded. For example, if the company transferred $8 million to the pension fund manager but the current cash value of the pension program was $10 million, the company reports a $2 million pension liability on its balance sheet.

The financial obligation associated with defined benefit retirement programs can be very large for many corporations, especially those with unionized work forces. A recent financial statement for Ford Motor Company disclosed the following information:

LEARNING OBJECTIVE 5
Explain liabilities for retirement benefits.

NOTE 2
EMPLOYEE RETIREMENT BENEFITS
(in millions)
Accumulated Postretirement Benefit Obligation

Retirees	$ 7,035.0
Active employees eligible to retire	2,269.6
Other active employees	5,090.6
Total accumulated obligation	$14,395.2

To put the size of this obligation in perspective, it represents an amount nearly equal to the company's total stockholders' equity. The retirement benefit expense for the year was $1.3 billion, which exceeded the income that Ford earned for the previous three years.

General Mills does not have a pension liability on its balance sheet because it has made cash payments to the retirement fund that are higher than the current value of the pension benefits. The notes report the following:

NOTE SIX
BALANCE SHEET INFORMATION
(in millions)

	1996	1995
Other assets:		
Prepaid pension	$351.9	$320.7

This information is important to analysts who are forecasting a company's future cash flows. Ford has a much larger obligation to transfer cash to its retirement fund than does General Mills.

In recent years, employer-provided health care benefits have been the subject of a great deal of discussion. Many large companies pay for a portion of their employees' health insurance costs. The payments are recorded as an expense in the current accounting period. Some employers agree to continue to pay for health care costs after employees retire. The cost of these future benefits must be estimated and recorded as an expense in the periods when the employees perform services. The recording of future health care costs for retired employees is an excellent example of the use of estimates in accounting. Imagine the difficulty of estimating future health care costs when you do not know how long employees will live, how healthy they will be during their lives, and how much doctors and hospitals will charge for their services in the future.

Accounting for retirement benefits is a complex topic that is discussed in detail in subsequent accounting courses. This topic is introduced at this point as another example of the application of the matching concept, which requires that expenses be recorded in the year in which the benefit is received. It also illustrates how accounting avoids the creation of improper incentives for managers. If the future cost of retirement benefits were not included in the period in which work was performed, managers might have the incentive to offer employees increases in their retirement benefits instead of increases in their salaries. In this manner, managers could understate the true cost of employee services and make their companies appear more profitable. Many economists argue that the local, state, and federal governments have fallen into this trap. Government officials can give large pensions to current workers without the cost being recognized until the employee retires. By doing this, governments can appear to be very efficient when in reality they are simply deferring costs to the future.

Contingent Liabilities

[handwritten: depends upon something else happened]

Each of the liabilities that we have discussed is reported on the balance sheet with a specific dollar amount. Each of these liabilities involves the *probable* future sacrifice of economic benefits. Some transactions or events create a *potential* (but not probable) future sacrifice of economic benefits. These situations create **contingent liabilities,** which are potential liabilities that have arisen as a result of a past event. The conversion of a contingent liability to a recorded liability depends on one or more future events. A situation that causes a contingent liability also causes a contingent loss.

Whether a situation causes a recorded or a contingent liability depends on the probability of the future economic sacrifice and the ability of management to estimate the amount of the liability. The following chart illustrates the various possibilities:

	Probable	Reasonably Possible	Remote
Subject to estimate	Record as liability	Disclose in note	Disclosure not required
Not subject to estimate	Disclose in note	Disclose in note	Disclosure not required

[handwritten: Part of disclosure]

The probabilities of occurrence are defined in the following manner:

1. Probable—the chance that the future event or events will occur is high. *[handwritten: (can measure)]*
2. Reasonably possible—the chance that the future event or events will occur is more than remote but less than likely.
3. Remote—the chance that the future event or events will occur is slight.

When recording liabilities, a company must determine whether the amount of any liability can be reasonably estimated. The general accounting guidelines are (1) a liability that is *both* probable and can be reasonably estimated must be recorded and reported on the balance sheet, (2) a liability that is reasonably possible (whether it can be estimated or not) must be disclosed in a note in the financial statements, and (3) remote contingencies are not disclosed.

The notes to General Mills' annual report include the following:

> We are contingently liable under guarantees and comfort letters for $96.4 million. The guarantees and comfort letters are issued to support borrowing arrangements primarily for our joint ventures.

The company did not have to record a liability on the balance sheet because the chance of having a loss from these guarantees was not probable. Harley-Davidson disclosed another contingency that is common:

> **NOTE 7**
> **COMMITMENTS AND CONTINGENCIES**
> A state court jury in California found the Company liable for compensatory and punitive damages of $7.2 million, including interest, in a lawsuit brought by a supplier of aftermarket exhaust systems. The Company immediately appealed the verdict.

In this case, the existence of a liability was a reasonable possibility. As a result, GAAP required Harley-Davidson to disclose the lawsuit. The company subsequently reached an out-of-court settlement for $5 million. At that point, the loss was probable, which required recording the loss and the related liability.

LEARNING OBJECTIVE 6
Report contingent liabilities.

A **contingent liability** is a potential liability that has arisen as the result of a past event; not an effective liability until some future event occurs.

REAL WORLD EXCERPT
GENERAL MILLS
Annual Report

REAL WORLD EXCERPT
HARLEY-DAVIDSON
Annual Report

Other Obligations

As we have just seen with contingencies, not all financial obligations result in the recording of all liabilities on the balance sheet. Another example involves situations in which an agreement is made to have an exchange in the future. Many businesses enter into labor contracts with senior executives under which they agree to pay a certain salary for a specified period of time. This financial obligation is not recorded as a liability because it involves making a payment in the future for a service that is performed in the future. Once the executive performs the service, a liability is created.

A similar situation exists when a company leases an asset. A lease contract permits a company to pay in the future for an asset that it will use in the future. As a result, many lease contracts do not create an immediate liability. Known as *operating leases,* these leases require the recording of lease expense and lease payable with the passage of time.

An underlying accounting concept requires that transactions be recorded in terms of their substance, not their form. Many corporations enter into long-term lease contracts that permit them to use an asset for its entire life. In essence, this represents the purchase and financing of an asset even though it is legally a lease agreement; such a lease is called a *capital lease.* A lease that covers at least 75 percent of the life of an asset must be recorded as a capital lease (additional criteria are discussed in subsequent accounting courses). These leases are accounted for as if an asset had been purchased (an asset and a liability are recorded). The recorded value is the current cash equivalent of the lease payments. In the next section on present value concepts, we show you how this amount is actually computed.

Epilogue

In the year after the restructuring, General Mills was successful in focusing its attention on its core business. The company announced a record year in terms of profitability. Strong cash flow permitted General Mills to reduce debt by nearly $200 million.

Present and Future Value Concepts

LEARNING OBJECTIVE 7

Apply the concepts of the future and present values of a single amount.

We have discussed the account classifications that you will encounter on most of the balance sheets that you will study. Before we leave the topic of liabilities, we want to introduce you to an important concept underlying most liabilities.

In our earlier discussion of notes payable, we looked at a very basic situation. To properly analyze more complex liabilities, you will use some relatively simple mathematics called *present* and *future value concepts.* These concepts represent an important part of our discussion of bond liabilities in the next chapter.

The concepts of future value (FV) and present value (PV) focus on the time value of money. Money received today is worth more than money received one year from today (or at any other future date) because it can be used to earn interest. If you invest $1,000 today at 10 percent, you will have $1,100 in one year. In contrast, if the $1,000 is to be received one year from today, you lose the opportunity to earn the $100 interest revenue for the year. The difference between the $1,000 and $1,100 is interest that can be earned during the year.

In some business situations, you will know the dollar amount of a cash flow that occurs in the future and will need to determine its value now. This is known as a **present value** problem. The opposite situation occurs when you know the dollar amount of a cash flow that occurs today and need to determine its value at some point in the future. This is called a **future value** problem. The value of money changes over time because money can earn interest (in other words, a dollar today is worth more than a dollar received in the future). The following illustrates the basic difference between present value and future value problems:

	Now	Future
Present value	?	$1,000
Future value	$1,000	?

In addition to the two types of business situations that you will encounter (the need to determine either a present value or a future value), there are two types of cash flows: *single payment* situations that involve one payment and *annuities* that involve a series of cash payments. This means that four different types of situations are related to the time value of money; they are identified in Exhibit 9.2. Each type of problem is based on the interest formula that was discussed earlier in this chapter:

$$\text{Interest} = \text{Principal} \times \text{Interest rate} \times \text{Time}$$

Many inexpensive hand-held calculators can do the detailed arithmetic computations required in computing future value and present value problems. In subsequent courses and in all business situations, you will probably use a calculator to solve these problems. At this stage, we encourage you to solve problems using the tables (Tables A–1 through A–4 in Appendix A at the end of this book) that give values for each of the four types of problems for different periods of time *(n)* and at different rates of interest *(i)*. We believe that use of the tables will give you a better understanding of how and why present and future value concepts apply to business problems.

The values given in the tables are based on payments of $1. If a problem involves payments other than $1, it is necessary to multiply the value from the table by the amount of the payment.[1] We now examine each of the four types of present value and future value problems.

Future and Present Values of a Single Amount

Future Value of a Single Amount (f)

In future value of a single amount problems, you will be asked to calculate how much money you will have in the future as the result of investing a certain amount in the

> **Present value** is the current value of an amount to be received in the future; a future amount discounted for compound interest. **Future value** is the sum to which an amount will increase as the result of compound interest.

EXHIBIT 9.2
Four Types of Future and Present Value Problems

	SYMBOL	
Payment or Receipt	**Future Value**	**Present Value**
Single amount	f	p
Annuity (equal payments or receipts for a series of equal time periods)	F	P

[1] Present value and future value problems involve cash flows. The basic concepts are the same for cash inflows (receipts) and cash outflows (payments). No fundamental differences exist between present value and future value calculations for cash payments versus cash receipts.

present. If you received a gift of $10,000, you might decide to put it in a savings account and use the money as a down payment on a house when you graduate from college. The future value computation will tell you how much money will be available when you graduate.

To solve a future value problem, you need to know three items: (1) the amount to be invested, (2) the interest rate (i) that the amount will earn, and (3) the number of periods (n) in which the amount will earn interest.

The future value concept is based on compound interest. Therefore, the amount of interest for each period is calculated by multiplying the principal plus any interest that accrued in prior interest periods (but was not paid out) by the interest rate.

To illustrate, assume that on January 1, 19A, you deposit $1,000 in a savings account at 10 percent annual interest, compounded annually. At the end of three years, the $1,000 originally deposited has increased to $1,331 as follows:

Year	Amount at Start of Year	+	Interest during the Year	=	Amount at End of Year
1	$1,000	+	$1,000 × 10% = $100	=	$1,100
2	1,100	+	1,100 × 10% = $110	=	1,210
3	1,210	+	1,210 × 10% = $121	=	1,331

We can avoid the detailed arithmetic by referring to Table A–1, Appendix A, Future Value of $1, f. For i = 10%, n = 3, we find the value 1.331. We can compute the balance at the end of year 3 as $1,000 × 1.331 = $1,331. The increase of $331 is due to the time value of money. It is interest revenue to the owner of the savings account and interest expense to the savings institution. A convenient format to display the computations for this problem is $1,000 × $f_{i = 10\%, n = 3}$ (Table A–1, Appendix A, 1.3310) = $1,331. Exhibit 9.3 summarizes this future value concept.

Present Value of a Single Amount (p)

The present value of a single amount is what it is worth to you today to be able to receive that amount at some date in the future. You might be offered the opportunity to invest in a debt instrument that would pay you $10,000 in 10 years. You would want to determine the present value of the instrument before you decided whether to invest.

To compute the present value of an amount to be received in the future, the amount is subjected to discounting (which is the opposite of compounding) at i interest rate for n periods. In discounting, the interest is subtracted rather than added (as is the case with compounding).

To illustrate, assume that today is January 1, 19A, and you have the opportunity to receive $1,000 cash on December 31, 19C (i.e., three years from now). With an interest rate of 10 percent per year, how much is the $1,000 worth to you on January 1, 19A? You could set up a discounting computation, year by year, that would be the inverse to the tabulation shown for the future value.[2] To facilitate the computation, however, we can refer to Table A–2, Appendix A, Present Value of $1, p. For i = 10%, n = 3, we find that the present value of $1 is 0.7513. The $1,000 to be received at the end of three years has a present value (today) of $1,000 × 0.7513 = $751.30. The difference (i.e., the discount) of $248.70 is interest. A convenient format to display the computations for

---

[2] The detailed discounting is as follows:

Periods	Interest for the Year	Present Value[*]
1	$1,000 − ($1,000 × 1/1.10) = $90.91	$1,000 − $90.91 = $909.09
2	$909.09 − ($909.09 × 1/1.10) = $82.65	$909.09 − $82.65 = 826.44
3	$826.44 − ($826.44 × 1/1.10) = $75.14†	$826.44 − $75.14 = 751.30

*Verifiable in Table A–2.

†Adjusted for rounding.

EXHIBIT 9.3
Overview of Future and Present Value Determinations

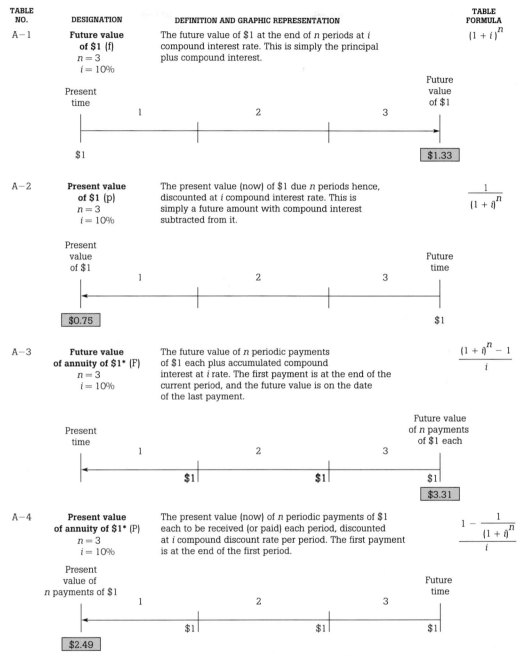

TABLE NO.	DESIGNATION	DEFINITION AND GRAPHIC REPRESENTATION	TABLE FORMULA
A–1	**Future value of \$1** (f) $n = 3$ $i = 10\%$	The future value of \$1 at the end of n periods at i compound interest rate. This is simply the principal plus compound interest.	$(1 + i)^n$
A–2	**Present value of \$1** (p) $n = 3$ $i = 10\%$	The present value (now) of \$1 due n periods hence, discounted at i compound interest rate. This is simply a future amount with compound interest subtracted from it.	$\dfrac{1}{(1 + i)^n}$
A–3	**Future value of annuity of \$1*** (F) $n = 3$ $i = 10\%$	The future value of n periodic payments of \$1 each plus accumulated compound interest at i rate. The first payment is at the end of the current period, and the future value is on the date of the last payment.	$\dfrac{(1 + i)^n - 1}{i}$
A–4	**Present value of annuity of \$1*** (P) $n = 3$ $i = 10\%$	The present value (now) of n periodic payments of \$1 each to be received (or paid) each period, discounted at i compound discount rate per period. The first payment is at the end of the first period.	$\dfrac{1 - \dfrac{1}{(1 + i)^n}}{i}$

*Notice that these are ordinary annuities; that is, they are often called end-of-period annuities. Thus, the table values for F, the future amount, are on the date of the last payment; and for P, the present value, are at the beginning of the period of the first payment. Annuities due assume the opposite; that is, they are "beginning-of-period" annuities. Ordinary annuity values can be converted to annuities due simply by multiplication of $(1 + i)$.

this problem is $\$1,000 \times p_{i = 10\%,\ n = 3}$ (Table A–2, Appendix A, 0.7513) = \$751.30. The concept of the present value of \$1 is summarized in Exhibit 9.3.

It is not difficult to learn how to compute a present value amount, but it is more important that you understand what it means. The \$751.30 is the amount that you would pay to have the right to receive \$1,000 at the end of three years, assuming an interest rate of 10 percent. Conceptually, you would be indifferent about having

$751.30 today and having $1,000 in three years. You are indifferent because you can use financial institutions to convert dollars from the present to the future and vice versa. If you had $751.30 today but preferred $1,000 in three years, you could simply deposit the money in a savings account and it would grow to $1,000 in three years. Alternatively, if you had a contract that promised you $1,000 in three years, you could sell it to an investor for $751.30 cash today because it would permit the investor to earn 10 percent on her money.

SELF-STUDY QUIZ

1. If the interest rate in a present value problem increases from 8 percent to 10 percent, will the present value increase or decrease?
2. What is the present value of $10,000 to be received 10 years from now if the interest rate is 5 percent compounded annually?

Check your answers in the footnote at the bottom of this page.*

Future and Present Values of an Annuity

An annuity is a series of periodic cash receipts or payments that are equal in amount each interest period.

Many business problems involve multiple cash payments over a number of periods instead of a single payment. An **annuity** is a series of consecutive payments characterized by

1. An equal dollar amount each interest period.
2. Interest periods of equal length (year, semiannual, quarter, or month).
3. An equal interest rate each interest period.

Examples of annuities include monthly payments on an automobile or a home, yearly contributions to a savings account, and monthly retirement benefits received from a pension fund.

Future Value of an Annuity (F)

If you are saving money for some purpose, such as a new car or a trip to Europe, you might decide to deposit a fixed amount of money in a savings account each month. The future value of an annuity computation will tell you how much money will be in your savings account at some point in the future.

The future value of an annuity includes *compound interest* on each payment from the date of payment to the end of the term of the annuity. Each payment accumulates less interest than the prior payments did only because the number of periods remaining to accumulate interest decreases.

Assume that you deposit $1,000 cash in a savings account each year for three years at 10 percent interest per year (i.e., a total principal of $3,000). The first $1,000 deposit is made on December 31, 19A, the second one on December 31, 19B, and the third and last one on December 31, 19C. The first $1,000 deposit earns compound interest for two years (for a total principal and interest of $1,210); the second deposit

---

* 1. The present value will be less.
   2. $10,000 × 0.6139 = $6,139

earns interest for one year (for a total principal and interest of $1,100); and the third deposit earns no interest because it was made on the day that the balance is computed. Thus, the total amount in the savings account at the end of three years is $3,310 ($1,210 + $1,100 + $1,000).

We could compute the interest on each deposit to derive the future value of this annuity. We can refer to Table A–3, Appendix A, Future Value of Annuity of $1 (F) for $i =$ 10%, $n = 3$, however, to find the value 3.3100. The total of your three deposits of $1,000 each increased to $1,000 × 3.31, or $3,310, by December 31, 19C. The increase of $310 was due to interest. A convenient format for this problem is $1,000 × $F_{i = 10\%, \, n = 3}$ (Table A–3, Appendix A, 3.3100) = $3,310. This concept is summarized in Exhibit 9.3.

Present Value of an Annuity (P)

The present value of an annuity is the value now of a series of equal amounts to be received each period for some specified number of periods in the future. It involves discounting each of the equal periodic amounts. A good example of this type of problem is a retirement program that offers the retiree a monthly income for a period of time.

To illustrate, assume that it is now January 1, 19A, and you are to receive $1,000 cash on each December 31, 19A, 19B, and 19C. How much would the sum of these three $1,000 future amounts be worth now, on January 1, 19A, assuming an interest rate of 10 percent per year? We could use Table A–2, Appendix A values to calculate the present value as follows:

Year	Amount		Value from Table A–2, Appendix A, $i = 10\%$		Present Value
1	$1,000	×	0.9091 $(n = 1)$	=	$ 909.10
2	$1,000	×	0.8264 $(n = 2)$	=	826.40
3	$1,000	×	0.7513 $(n = 3)$	=	751.30
			Total present value	=	$2,486.80

The present value of this annuity can be more easily computed, however, by using one present value amount from Table A–4, Appendix A as follows:

$1,000 × $P_{i=10\%, \, n=3}$ (Table A–4, Appendix A, 2.4869) = $2,487 (rounded)

This concept is summarized in Exhibit 9.3.

Interest Rates and Interest Periods

Notice that the preceding illustrations assumed annual periods for compounding and discounting. Although interest rates almost always are quoted on an annual basis, most interest compounding periods encountered in business are less than one year (such as semiannually or quarterly). When interest periods are less than a year, the values of n and i must be restated to be consistent with the length of the interest period.

To illustrate, 12 percent interest compounded annually for five years requires use of $n = 5$ and $i = 12\%$. If compounding is quarterly, the interest period is one quarter of a year (i.e., four periods per year), and the quarterly interest rate is one quarter of the annual rate (i.e., 3 percent per quarter); therefore, 12 percent interest compounded quarterly for five years requires use of $n = 20$ and $i = 3\%$.

Truth in Advertising

A number of advertisements in newspapers, magazines, and on television easily can be misinterpreted if the consumer does not understand present value concepts. We discuss two examples.

Most car companies offer seasonal promotions with special financing incentives. A car dealer may advertise 4 percent interest on car loans when banks are charging 10 percent. Typically, the lower interest rate is not a special incentive because the dealer simply charges a higher price for cars that the dealership finances. It may be better to borrow from the bank and "pay cash" at the dealership to negotiate a lower price. Customers should use the present value concepts illustrated in this chapter to compare financing alternatives.

Another misleading advertisement is seen every January and promises a chance to become an instant millionaire. The fine print discloses that the winner will receive $25,000 for 40 years, which is $1,000,000 (40 × $25,000), but the present value of this annuity at 8 percent is only $298,000. Most winners are happy to get the money, but they are not really millionaires.

Some consumer advocates criticize businesses that use these types of advertisements. They argue that consumers should not have to study present value concepts to understand advertisements. Some of these criticisms may be valid, but the quality of information contained in advertisements that include interest rates has improved during the past few years.

Accounting Applications of Future and Present Values

LEARNING OBJECTIVE 8

Apply present value concepts to liabilities.

Many business transactions require the use of future and present value concepts. We illustrate two such cases so that you can test your understanding of these concepts:

CASE A   On January 1, 19A, General Mills bought some new delivery trucks. The company signed a note and agreed to pay $200,000 for the trucks on December 31, 19B. The market interest rate for this note was 12 percent. The $200,000 represents the cash equivalent price of the trucks and the interest that will be earned for two years.

1.   How should the accountant record the purchase?

Answer: This case requires application of the present value of a single amount. In conformity with the cost principle, the cost of the trucks is their current cash equivalent price, which is the present value of the future payment. The present value of the $200,000 is computed as follows:

$$\$200,000 \times p_{i=12\%,\,n=2} \text{ (Table A–2, Appendix A, 0.7972)} = \$159,440$$

Therefore, the journal entry is as follows:

Jan. 1, 19A	Delivery trucks (A)	159,440	
	Note payable (L)		159,440

Some companies prefer to record the following journal entry:

Jan. 1, 19A	Delivery trucks (A)	159,440	
	Discount on notes payable (XL)	40,560	
	Note payable (L)		200,000

The discount account is a contra liability account that represents the interest that will be earned on the note over its life. This account will be used extensively in the next chapter during our discussion of bonds.

Think about how this photograph reflects a response to customer preferences.

2. What journal entry should be made at the end of the first and second years for interest expense?

Answer: Each year's interest expense on the amount in the Note Payable account is recorded in an adjusting entry as follows:

Dec. 31, 19A	Interest expense (E)	19,133*	
	Note payable (L)		19,133
	(or Discount on note payable)		

*$159,440 × 12% = $19,133.

Dec. 31, 19B	Interest expense (E)	21,429*	
	Note payable (L)		21,429
	(or Discount on note payable)		

*($159,440 + $19,133) × 12% = 21,429.

3. What journal entry should be made on December 31, 19B, to record the payment of the debt?

Answer: At this date the amount to be paid is the balance of Note Payable, which is the same as the maturity amount on the due date. The journal entry to record full payment of the debt follows:

Dec. 31, 19B	Note payable (L)	200,000	
	Cash (A)		200,000

CASE B On January 1, 19A, General Mills bought new printing equipment. The company elected to finance the purchase with a note payable to be paid off in three equal annual installments of $163,686. Each installment includes principal plus interest on the unpaid balance at 11 percent per year. The equal annual installments are due on December 31, 19A, 19B, and 19C.

1. What is the amount of the note?

Answer: The note is the present value of each installment payment, $i = 11\%$ and $n = 3$. This is an annuity because payment is made in three equal installments. The amount of the note is computed as follows:

$$\$163,686 \times P_{i=11\%, n=3} \text{ (Table A–4, Appendix A, 2.4437)} = \$400,000$$

The acquisition is recorded as follows:

| Jan. 1, 19A | Printing equipment (A) .... | 400,000 | |
| | Note payable (L) .... | | 400,000 |

2.   What was the total amount of interest expense in dollars?

Answer:

$$\$163,686 \times 3 = \$491,058 - \$400,000 = \$91,058$$

3.   What journal entry should be made at the end of each year to record the payment on this $400,000 note payable?

Answer:

Dec. 31, 19A	Note payable (L)	119,686	
	Interest expense (E) ($400,000 × 11%)	44,000	
	Cash (A)		163,686
	To record the first installment payment on the note.		

Dec. 31, 19B	Note payable (L)	132,851	
	Interest expense (E) [($400,000 – $119,686) × 11%]	30,835	
	Cash (A)		163,686
	To record the second installment payment on the note.		

Dec. 31, 19C	Note payable (L)	147,462	
	Interest expense (E)	16,224*	
	Cash (A)		163,686
	To record final installment payment on the note.		

*Interest: ($400,000 − $119,686 − $132,851) × 11% = $16,224 (rounded to accommodate rounding errors).

4.   Prepare a debt payment schedule that shows the entry for each payment and the effect on interest expense and the unpaid amount of principal each period.

Answer:

DEBT PAYMENT SCHEDULE

Date	Cash Payment (Credit)	Interest Expense (Prior Balance × 11%) (Debit)	Principal Decrease (Debit)	Unpaid Principal
1/1/A				$400,000
12/31/A	$163,686	$400,000 × 11% = $44,000	$119,686[a]	280,314[b]
12/31/B	163,686	280,314 × 11% = $30,834*	132,852	147,462
12/31/C	163,686	147,462 × 11% = $16,224*	147,462	0
Total	$491,058		$91,058*	$400,000

*To accommodate rounding error.
Computations:
[a] $163,686 – $44,000 = $119,686, etc.
[b] $400,000 – $119,686 = $280,314, etc.

Notice in the debt payment schedule that for each successive payment, an increasing amount is payment on principal and a decreasing amount is interest expense. This effect occurs because the interest each period is based on a lower amount of unpaid principal. When an annuity is involved, schedules such as this one often are a useful analytical tool.

In the next chapter, we will use the present value techniques that you have just learned. As you will see, present value concepts are needed to understand how bonds function in our economy.

Summary

Liabilities are obligations of either a known or estimated amount. Detailed information about an entity's liabilities is important to many decision makers, whether internal or external to the enterprise, because liabilities represent claims against the entity's resources. The existence and amount of liabilities sometimes are easy to conceal from outsiders. Use of the accounting model and the verification by an independent CPA are the best assurances that all liabilities are disclosed.

Current liabilities are short-term obligations that will be paid within the coming year or the normal operating cycle of the business, whichever is longer. All other liabilities (except contingent liabilities) are reported as long-term liabilities. A contingent liability is a potential claim that results from some event or transaction that has happened, but its materialization as an effective liability is not certain because it depends on some future event or transaction. At the end of the accounting period, a contingent liability must be recorded (as a debit to a loss account and a credit to a liability account) if (1) it is probable that a loss will occur and (2) if the amount of the loss can be estimated reasonably. Contingent liabilities that are reasonably possible must be disclosed in the notes to the financial statements.

Future and present value concepts often must be applied in accounting for liabilities. These concepts focus on the time value of money (i.e., interest). *Future value* is the amount that a principal amount will increase to in the future as the result of compound interest. *Present value* is the amount that a future principal amount is worth today. It is computed by discounting future cash flows. Future and present values are related to (1) a single amount or (2) a series of equal periodic amounts (called *annuities*). Typical applications of future and present values are to create a fund, determine the cost of an asset, account for notes payable, and account for installment debts and receivables.

In this chapter, we discussed many types of liabilities commonly found on most balance sheets. For many companies, the largest liability classification is bonds payable. In Chapter 10, we examine the business purpose and accounting treatment of bonds in considerable depth. You will use the present value concepts that were introduced in this chapter to determine the current value of bonds. We will also discuss bond investments in Chapter 10.

Chapter Supplement A

FEDERAL INCOME TAX CONCEPTS

A business may be organized as a sole proprietorship, partnership, or corporation. Sole proprietorships and partnerships are not required to pay federal income taxes, but their owners must report and pay taxes on their personal tax returns. Corporations, as separate legal entities, are required to pay income taxes.

Corporations must prepare a U.S. Corporate Tax Return (Form 1120), which lists revenue and expenses for the year. The amount of the tax payable is based on the taxable income reported on the tax return. Taxable income is usually different from the income reported on the income statement because the income statement is prepared in conformity with GAAP and the tax return is prepared in conformity with the Internal Revenue Code.

Calculation of Taxes Payable

In most cases, a large corporation's tax obligation is determined by multiplying its taxable income by 35 percent. Rates are graduated, however, so that very small corporations pay lower rates than large corporations do. Exhibit 9.4 illustrates the calculation of taxes payable at various income levels.

Notice in Case C that a portion of the income is taxed at a rate that is actually higher than the maximum of 35 percent. The purpose of the 39 percent rate is to phase out the benefits of the lower rates that were intended to benefit only smaller corporations. The $136,000 taxes payable on taxable income of $400,000 is an effective tax rate of exactly 34 percent.

The 35 percent tax rate applies to taxable incomes higher than $10 million. A provision phases out the 34 percent tax rate for very large corporations. The tax rate from $15,000,000 to $18,333,333 is 38 percent. At higher incomes, the rate reverts to 35 percent. This results in an effective tax rate of 35 percent once a corporation earns more than $18,333,333.

Revenue and Expense Recognition for Income Tax Purposes

Several differences between GAAP and the rules that govern the preparation of the federal income tax return exist. The following are common examples:

1. Interest revenue on state and municipal bonds is generally excluded from taxable income, although it is included in accounting income.
2. Revenue collected in advance (e.g., rent revenue) is included in taxable income when it is collected but it is included in accounting income when it is earned.
3. Proceeds from life insurance policies (e.g., key executive insurance) is excluded from taxable income but is included in accounting income.
4. Corporations that own less than 20 percent of another corporation's stock may exclude 70 percent of the dividends received from taxable income, although all the dividends

EXHIBIT 9.4
Calculation of Taxes Payable

CASE A: TAXABLE INCOME	$ 90,000
Computation	
15% of first $50,000	$ 7,500
25% of next $25,000	6,250
34% of $15,000	5,100
Taxes payable	$ 18,850
CASE B: TAXABLE INCOME	**$ 150,000**
Computation	
15% of first $50,000	$ 7,500
25% of next $25,000	6,250
34% of next $25,000	8,500
39% of $50,000 ($150,000 − $100,000)	19,500
Taxes payable	$ 41,750
CASE C: TAXABLE INCOME	**$ 400,000**
Computation	
15% of first $50,000	$ 7,500
25% of next $25,000	6,250
34% of next $25,000	8,500
39% of next $235,000	91,650
34% of $65,000 ($400,000 − $335,000)	22,100
Taxes payable	$ 136,000

are included in accounting income. The exclusion is 80 percent if the corporation owns more than 20 percent of the other corporation's stock.

5. Depreciation expense for tax purposes is generally based on the Accelerated Cost Recovery System (ACRS) if the assets were placed in service after 1980 but before 1987, or the Modified Accelerated Cost Recovery System (MACRS) if the assets were placed in service after 1986. These methods were discussed in Chapter 8.

Tax Minimization versus Tax Evasion

Most large corporations spend considerable time and money developing strategies that *minimize* the amount of federal income taxes that must be paid. Nothing is wrong with this approach because courts have stated that there is no legal obligation to pay more taxes than the law demands. Even if you do not major in accounting, you will probably want to take a course in federal income taxation because knowledge of the Internal Revenue Code is important for most executives. This knowledge offers opportunities to save significant amounts of money.

In contrast, tax evasion involves illegal means to avoid paying taxes that are due. Use of accelerated depreciation is an example of *tax minimization*; failure to report revenue that was collected in cash is an example of *tax evasion*. Efforts at tax minimization represent good business practice, but tax evasion is morally and legally wrong. Individuals who evade taxes run the risk of severe financial penalties and the possibility of being sent to jail.

Key Ratios

Current ratio measures the ability of a company to pay its current obligations. It is computed as follows (p. 474):

$$\text{Current ratio} = \frac{\text{Current assets}}{\text{Current liabilities}}$$

Payable turnover is a measure of how quickly a company pays its creditors. It is computed as follows (p. 475):

$$\text{Payable turnover} = \frac{\text{Costs of goods sold}}{\text{Accounts payable}}$$

Key Terms

Accrued Liabilities   Expenses that have been incurred but have not been paid at the end of the accounting period. *475*

Annuity   A series of periodic cash receipts or payments that are equal in amount each interest period. *494*

Contingent Liability   Potential liability that has arisen as the result of a past event; not an effective liability until some future event occurs. *489*

Current Liabilities   Short-term obligations that will be paid within the current operating cycle or one year, whichever is longer. *474*

Deferred Revenues   Revenues that have been collected but not earned; liabilities until the goods or services are provided. *478*

Deferred Tax Items   Difference between income tax expense and income tax liability; caused by temporary differences; may be a liability or an asset. *486*

Future Value   The sum to which an amount will increase as the result of compound interest. *491*

Liabilities   Probable future sacrifices of economic benefits that arise from past transactions. *473*

Long-Term Liabilities   All of the entity's obligations that are not classified as current liabilities. *483*

Present Value   The current value of an amount to be received in the future; a future amount discounted for compound interest. *491*

Temporary Differences   Timing differences that cause deferred income taxes and will reverse, or turn around, in the future. *486*

Time Value of Money   Interest that is associated with the use of money over time. *479*

Working Capital   The dollar difference between total current assets and total current liabilities. *474*

Questions

1. Define *liability*. Differentiate between a current liability and a long-term liability.
2. How can external parties be informed about the liabilities of a business?
3. Liabilities are measured and reported at their current cash equivalent amount. Explain.
4. A *liability* is a known obligation of either a definite or estimated amount. Explain.
5. Define *working capital*. How is it computed?
6. What is the current ratio? How is the current ratio related to the classification of liabilities?
7. Define *accrued liability*. What type of entry usually reflects an accrued liability?
8. Define *deferred revenue*. Why is it a liability?
9. Define *note payable*. Differentiate between a secured and an unsecured note.
10. Non-interest-bearing notes do not include an explicit interest rate. Differentiate between an interest-bearing note and a non-interest-bearing note.
11. Define *deferred income tax*. Explain why deferred income tax "reverses, or turns around," in subsequent periods.
12. What is a contingent liability? How is a contingent liability reported?
13. Compute 19A interest expense for the following note: face, $4,000; 12 percent interest; date of note, April 1, 19A.
14. Explain the time value of money.
15. Explain the basic difference between future value and present value.
16. If you deposited $10,000 in a savings account that earns 10 percent, how much would you have at the end of 10 years? Use a convenient format to display your computations.
17. If you hold a valid contract that will pay you $8,000 cash 10 years hence and the going rate of interest is 10 percent, what is its present value? Use a convenient format to display your computations.
18. What is an annuity?
19. Complete the following schedule:

		TABLE VALUES		
Concept	Symbol	$n = 4, i = 5\%$	$n = 7, i = 10\%$	$n = 10, i = 14\%$
FV of $1				
PV of $1				
FV of annuity of $1				
PV of annuity of $1				

20. If you deposit $1,000 for each of 10 interest periods (ordinary annuity) that earns 8 percent interest, how much would you have at the end of period 10? Use a convenient format to display your computations.

21. You purchased an XIT auto for $18,000 by making a $3,000 cash payment and six semiannual installment payments for the balance at 12 percent interest. Use a convenient format to display computation of the amount of each payment.

Exercises

E9-1 Computing Owners' Equity and Working Capital; Discussion of the Current Ratio and Working Capital

Flair Corporation is preparing its 19B balance sheet. The company records show the following related amounts at the end of the accounting period, December 31, 19B:

CA – CL

Total current assets	$170,100
Total all remaining assets	525,000
Liabilities:	
Notes payable (8%, due in 5 years)	18,000
Accounts payable	60,000
Income taxes payable	12,000
Liability for withholding taxes	3,000
Rent revenue collected in advance	4,000
Bonds payable (due in 15 years)	100,000
Wages payable	7,800
Property taxes payable	2,000
Note payable (10%; due in 6 months)	10,000
Interest payable	400

Required:
1. Compute total owners' equity.
2. Compute (a) working capital and (b) the current ratio (show computations). Why is working capital important to management? How do financial analysts use the current ratio?
3. Compute the amount of interest expense for 19B on the long-term note. Assume that it was dated October 1, 19B. *I = P r t*
4. Give any adjusting entry required for the long-term note payable on December 31, 19B.

E9-2 Accounting for and Reporting Accrued Liabilities and Deferred Revenue, with Discussion

During 19B, Riverside Company completed the following two transactions. The annual accounting period ends December 31.
a. Wages paid and recorded during 19B were $130,000; however, at the end of December 19B, three days' wages are unpaid and unrecorded because the weekly payroll will not be paid until January 6, 19C. Wages for the three days are $3,600.
b. On December 10, 19B, the company collected rent revenue of $2,400 on office space that it rented to another party. The rent collected was for 30 days from December 10, 19B, to January 10, 19C, and was credited in full to Rent Revenue.

Required:
1. Give (a) the adjusting entry required on December 31, 19B, and (b) the January 6, 19C, journal entry for payment of any unpaid wages from December 19B.
2. Give (a) the journal entry for the collection of rent on December 10, 19B, and (b) the adjusting entry on December 31, 19B.
3. Show how any liabilities related to these transactions should be reported on the company's balance sheet at December 31, 19B.
4. Explain why the accrual method of accounting provides more relevant information to financial analysts than the cash method.

Dayton Hudson

E9–3   Accounting for a Note Payable through Its Time to Maturity with Discussion of Management Strategy

Many businesses borrow money during periods of increased business activity to finance inventory and accounts receivable. Dayton Hudson is one of America's largest general merchandise retailers. Each Christmas, Dayton Hudson builds up its inventory to meet the needs of Christmas shoppers. A large portion of Christmas sales are on credit. As a result, Dayton Hudson often collects cash from the sales several months after Christmas. Assume that on November 1, 19A, Dayton Hudson borrowed $4.5 million cash from Metropolitan Bank for working capital purposes and signed an interest-bearing note due in six months. The interest rate was 10 percent per annum payable at maturity. The accounting period ends December 31.

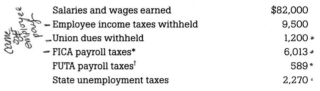

Required:

1. Give the journal entry to record the note on November 1.
2. Give any adjusting entry required at the end of the annual accounting period.
3. Give the journal entry to record payment of the note and interest on the maturity date, April 30, 19B.
4. If Dayton Hudson needs extra cash during every Christmas season, should management borrow money on a long-term basis to avoid the necessity of negotiating a new short-term loan each year?

E9–4   Recording a Payroll, Including Deductions; Discussion of Labor Costs

Town Lake Company has completed the payroll for January 19B, reflecting the following data:

Salaries and wages earned	$82,000
Employee income taxes withheld	9,500
Union dues withheld	1,200
FICA payroll taxes*	6,013
FUTA payroll taxes†	589
State unemployment taxes	2,270

*Assessed on both employer and employee (i.e., $6,013 each).
†Unemployment taxes.

Required:

1. Give the journal entry to record payment of the payroll and employee deductions.
2. Give the journal entry to record employer payroll taxes.
3. What amount of additional labor expense to the company was due to tax laws? What was the amount of the employees' take-home pay?
4. List the liabilities and their amounts that are reported on the company's January 31, 19B, balance sheet.
5. Would employers react differently to a 10 percent increase in the employer's share of FICA than to a 10 percent increase in the basic level of salaries? Would financial analysts react differently?

E9–5   Accounting for Accounts Payable and a Note Payable; Discussion of Cash Flows

Bryant Company sells a wide range of goods through two retail stores that are operated in adjoining cities. Most purchases of goods for resale are on invoices. Occasionally, a short-term note payable is used to obtain cash for current use. The following transactions were selected from those occurring during 19B:

(a) On January 10, 19B, purchased merchandise on credit, $18,000; the company uses a periodic inventory system.

(b) On March 1, 19B, borrowed $40,000 cash from City Bank and gave an interest-bearing note payable: face amount, $40,000, due at the end of six months, with an annual interest rate of 8 percent payable at maturity.

Required:
1. Give the journal entry for each of these transactions.
2. Give the journal entry for the payment of the note payable plus interest on its maturity date.
3. Discuss the impact of each transaction on Bryant's cash flows.

E9–6   **Identifying a Liability with Discussion**

The annual report for Ford Motor Company contained the following information:

Ford Motor Company

POSTRETIREMENT HEALTH CARE AND LIFE INSURANCE BENEFITS
The company and certain of its subsidiaries sponsor unfunded plans to provide selected health care and life insurance benefits for retired employees. The company's employees may become eligible for those benefits if they retire while working for the company. However, benefits and eligibility rules may be modified from time to time.

Required:
Should Ford report a liability for these benefits on its balance sheet? Explain.

E9–7   **Deferred Income Tax: One Temporary Difference, with Discussion**

The comparative income statements of Martin Corporation at December 31, 19B, showed the following summarized pretax data:

	Year 19A	Year 19B
Sales revenue	$65,000	$72,000
Expenses (excluding income tax)	50,000	54,000
Pretax income	$ 15,000	$ 18,000

Included in the 19B data is a $2,800 expense that was deductible only in the 19A income tax return (rather than in 19B). The average income tax rate was 30 percent. Taxable income from the income tax returns was 19A, $14,000, and 19B, $17,400.

Required:
1. For each year compute (a) income taxes payable and (b) deferred income tax. Is the deferred income tax a liability or an asset? Explain.
2. Give the journal entry for each year to record income taxes payable, deferred income tax, and income tax expense.
3. Show what amounts related to income taxes should be reported each year on the income statement and balance sheet. Assume that income tax is paid on April 15 of the next year.
4. Explain why tax expense is not simply the amount of cash paid during the year.

E9–8   **Deferred Income Tax: One Temporary Difference;**
Discussion of Management Strategy

The comparative income statement for Chung Corporation at the end of December 31, 19B, provided the following summarized pretax data:

	Year 19A	Year 19B
Revenues	$80,000	$88,000
Expenses (excluding income tax)	65,000	69,000
Pretax income	$ 15,000	$ 19,000

Included in the data is a $5,000 revenue that was taxable only in the 19A income tax return. The average income tax rate was 32 percent. Taxable income shown in the tax returns was 19A, $13,000, and 19B, $18,500.

Required:

1. For each year compute (a) income taxes payable and (b) deferred income tax. Is the deferred income tax a liability or an asset? Explain.
2. Give the journal entry for each year to record income taxes payable, deferred income tax, and income tax expense.
3. Show what amounts related to income taxes should be reported each year on the income statement and balance sheet. Assume that income tax is paid on April 15 of the next year.
4. Why would management want to incur the cost of maintaining separate tax and financial accounting records to defer the payment of taxes?

E9–9   Deferred Income Tax: Depreciation

Amber Corporation reported the following summarized pretax data at the end of each year:

Income Statement at December 31	19A	19B	19C
Revenues	$170,000	$182,000	$195,000
Expenses (including depreciation)*	122,000	126,000	130,000
Pretax income	$ 48,000	$ 56,000	$ 65,000

*Depreciation expense on the income statement on a machine purchased January 1, 19A, for $75,000 was straight line. The machine has a three-year estimated life and no residual value. The company used accelerated depreciation on the income tax return as follows: 19A, $37,500, 19B, $25,000, and 19C, $12,500. The average income tax rate is 28 percent for the three years.

Taxable income from the income tax return was as follows: 19A, $32,000, 19B, $56,000, and 19C, $85,000.

Required:

1. For each year compute (a) income taxes payable and (b) deferred income tax. Is the deferred income tax a liability or an asset? Explain.
2. Give the journal entry for each year to record income taxes payable, deferred income tax, and income tax expense.
3. Show what amounts related to income taxes should be reported each year on the income statement and balance sheet.

Colgate–Palmolive

E9–10   Deferred Tax Accounting

The annual report for Colgate-Palmolive contains the following information (in millions):

INCOME TAXES

Differences between accounting for financial statement purposes and accounting for tax purposes result in taxes currently payable (lower) higher than the total provision for income taxes as follows:

	1992	1991	1990
Excess tax over book depreciation	$(18.0)	$(19.8)	$(18.9)
Other	$(31.4)	$76.6	$(25.5)
Total	$(49.4)	$56.8	$(44.4)

Required:

1. Determine whether tax expense is higher or lower than taxes payable for each year.
2. Explain the most likely reason for tax depreciation to be higher than book depreciation.
3. Is the deferred tax liability reported on the 1992 balance sheet $49.4 million? Explain.

E9–11 Applying the Four Kinds of Present and Future Values

On January 1, 19A, Wesley Company completed the following transactions (assume an 11 percent annual interest rate):

(*a*) Deposited $12,000 in Fund A.

(*b*) Established Fund B by agreeing to make six annual deposits of $2,000 each. Deposits are made each December 31.

(*c*) Established Fund C by depositing a single amount that will increase to $40,000 by the end of year 7.

(*d*) Decided to deposit a single sum in Fund D that will provide 10 equal annual year-end payments of $15,000 to a retired employee (payments starting December 31, 19A).

Required (show computations and round to the nearest dollar):

1. What will be the balance of Fund A at the end of year 9?
2. What will be the balance of Fund B at the end of year 6?
3. What single amount must be deposited in Fund C on January 1, 19A?
4. What single sum must be deposited in Fund D on January 1, 19A?

E9–12 Accounting for a Savings Account: A Single Amount

On January 1, 19A, you deposited $6,000 in a savings account. The account will earn 10 percent annual compound interest, which will be added to the fund balance at the end of each year.

Required (round to the nearest dollar):

1. What will be the balance in the savings account at the end of 10 years?
2. What is the interest for the 10 years?
3. How much interest revenue did the fund earn in 19A? 19B?
4. Give the journal entry to record interest revenue at the end of 19A and 19B.

E9–13 Computing Deposit Required and Accounting for a Single-Sum Savings Account

On January 1, 19A, Alan King decided to deposit an amount in a savings account that will provide $80,000 four years later to send his son to college. The savings account will earn 8 percent, which will be added to the fund each year-end.

Required (show computations and round to the nearest dollar):

1. How much must Alan deposit on January 1, 19A?
2. Give the journal entry that Alan should make on January 1, 19A.
3. What is the interest for the four years?
4. Give the journal entry that Alan should make on (a) December 31, 19A, and (b) December 31, 19B.

E9–14 Accounting for a Savings Account with Equal Periodic Payments

On each December 31, you plan to deposit $2,000 in a savings account. The account will earn 9 percent annual interest, which will be added to the fund balance at year-end. The first deposit will be made December 31, 19A (end of period).

Required (show computations and round to the nearest dollar):

1. Give the required journal entry on December 31, 19A.
2. What will be the balance in the savings account at the end of the 10th year (i.e., 10 deposits)?
3. What is the interest earned on the 10 deposits?

4. How much interest revenue did the fund earn in 19B? 19C?

5. Give all required journal entries at the end of 19B and 19C.

E9–15 Accounting for a Savings Fund with Periodic Deposits

On January 1, 19A, you plan to take a trip around the world upon graduation four years from now. Your grandmother wants to deposit sufficient funds for this trip in a savings account for you. On the basis of a budget, you estimate that the trip currently would cost $15,000. To be generous, your grandmother decided to deposit $3,500 in the fund at the end of each of the next four years, starting on December 31, 19A. The savings account will earn 6 percent annual interest, which will be added to the savings account at each year-end.

Required (show computations and round to the nearest dollar):
1. What journal entry should your grandmother make on December 31, 19A, to record the first deposit?
2. How much money will you have for the trip at the end of year 4 (i.e., after four deposits)?
3. What is the interest for the four years?
4. How much interest revenue did the fund earn in 19A, 19B, 19C, and 19D?
5. Give the journal entries at the end of 19B, 19C, and 19D. Yes, you left on January 1, 19E.

E9–16 Valuing an Asset Based on Present Value

You have the chance to purchase the royalty interest in an oil well. Your best estimate is that the net royalty income will average $25,000 per year for five years. There will be no residual value at that time. Assume that the cash inflow is at each year-end and that considering the uncertainty in your estimates, you expect to earn 15 percent per year on the investment.

Required (show computations and round to the nearest dollar):
1. What should you be willing to pay for this investment on January 1, 19A?
2. Give the required journal entry (cash paid in full for the royalty interest) on January 1, 19A.
3. Give the required journal entries on December 31, 19A, assuming that the net cash received was equal to your estimate. Assume that the cost of royalty interest is depleted on a straight-line basis.

Carnival Cruise Lines

E9–17 Determination of a Liability

Carnival Cruise Lines provides exotic vacations on board luxurious passenger ships. In 1989, the company moved its offices and included the following note in its current annual report:

LEASES
On March 27, 1989, the Company entered into a ten-year lease for 230,000 square feet of office space located in Miami, Florida. The Company moved its operation to this location in October 1989. The total rent payable over the ten-year term of the lease is approximately $24 million.

Required:
Based on these facts, do you think the company should report this obligation on its balance sheet? Explain. If the obligation should be reported as a liability, how should the amount be measured?

Problems

P9–1 Recording and Reporting Five Current Liabilities with Discussion of Cash Flow Effects

Curb Company completed the following transactions during 19B. The annual accounting period ends December 31, 19B.

Jan.	8	Purchased merchandise for resale at an invoice cost of $13,580; assume a periodic inventory system.
	17	Paid January 8 invoice.
Apr.	1	Borrowed $40,000 from National Bank for general use; executed a 12-month, 12 percent interest-bearing note payable.
June	3	Purchased merchandise for resale at an invoice cost of $17,820.
July	5	Paid June 3 invoice.
Aug.	1	Rented a small office in a building owned by the company and collected six months' rent in advance amounting to $5,100. (Record the collection in a way that will not require an adjusting entry at year-end.)
Dec.	20	Received a $100 deposit from a customer as a guarantee to return a large trailer "borrowed" for 30 days.
	31	Determined wages of $6,500 earned but not yet paid on December 31 (disregard payroll taxes).

Required:
1. Prepare journal entries for each of these transactions.
2. Prepare all adjusting entries required on December 31, 19B.
3. Show how all of the liabilities arising from these transactions are reported on the balance sheet at December 31, 19B.
4. For each transaction, state whether cash flow from operating activities is increased, decreased, or there is no effect.

P9–2 Accounting for a Note Payable, with Adjusting Entries

Carlyle Golf, Inc., is a small company that designs and markets high-quality golf shirts sold in pro shops at exclusive country clubs. Many golf professionals on the PGA tour wear Carlyle shirts. Assume that the company purchased a computer-aided design system to permit it to shorten the design time for new golf shirts. Carlyle bought the equipment for $180,000 on April 1, 19A, with a cash down payment of $50,000, and gave a $130,000 interest-bearing note (including a mortgage on the equipment) for the balance. The note specified 8 percent annual interest. Two payments of $65,000 each on principal, plus interest on the unpaid balance on March 31, 19B, and March 31, 19C, are required—these will be unequal cash payments. The accounting period ends December 31.

Carlyle Golf, Inc.

Required:
1. Give all of the related journal entries for the terms of this note.
2. Show how the liabilities should be reported on the company's 19A and 19B balance sheets.

P9–3 Analysis of Note Describing Retirement Plan

A recent annual report for Chrysler contained the following note:

Chrysler Corporation

EMPLOYEE RETIREMENT PLANS

Noncontributory benefits are based on a fixed rate per year of service. Annual contributions to the pension trust fund are in compliance with federal law. All income accruing to the fund is used solely to pay pension benefits. Chrysler made pension fund contributions totaling $816 million in 1992, $327 million in 1991 and $776 million in 1990.

The components of periodic pension cost are as follows:

in millions of dollars	1992	1991	1990
Service costs—benefits earned during the year	$ 171	$ 125	$ 120
Interest costs on future benefits	742	737	651
Return on plan's assets	(945)	(883)	88
Other	836	805	(338)
Net pension expense	$804	$784	$ 521

This note introduces many terms that were not discussed in the chapter. Based on the general discussion in the chapter and your knowledge of pension programs, explain how the yearly cost of Chrysler's pension program is determined.

P9–4 Deferred Income Tax: Two Temporary Differences, with Discussion of Financial Analysis

The records of Calib Corporation provided the following summarized data for 19D and 19E:

	YEAR-END DECEMBER 31	
	19D	19E
Income statement		
Revenues	$210,000	$218,000
Expenses (excluding income tax)	130,000	133,000
Pretax income	$ 80,000	$ 85,000

a. Income tax rate, 32 percent. Assume that income taxes payable are paid 80 percent in the current year and 20 percent on April 15 of the next year.

b. Temporary differences:

   (1) The 19E expenses include an $8,000 expense that must be deducted only in the 19D tax return.

   (2) 19E revenues include a $6,000 revenue that was taxable only in 19F.

c. Taxable income shown in the tax returns was 19D, $82,000, and 19E, $85,000.

Required:

1. For each year compute (a) income taxes payable and (b) deferred income tax. Is each deferred income tax a liability or an asset? Explain.

2. Give the journal entry for each year to record income taxes payable, deferred income tax, and income tax expense.

3. Show what amounts related to income taxes should be reported each year on the income statement and balance sheet.

4. As a financial analyst, would you evaluate differently a deferred tax liability compared with taxes currently payable?

P9–5 Deferred Income Tax: Depreciation

At December 31, 19A, the records of Pearson Corporation provided the following information:

Income statement	
Revenues	$160,000 *
Depreciation expense (straight line)	(11,000)[†]
Remaining expenses (excluding income tax)	(90,000)
Pretax income	$ 59,000

*These revenues include $20,000 interest on tax-free municipal bonds.

[†]Equipment depreciated—acquired January 1, 19A, cost $44,000; estimated useful life, four years and no residual value. Accelerated depreciation is used on the tax return as follows: 19A, $17,600; 19B, $13,200; 19C, $8,800; and 19D, $4,400.

a. Income tax rate, 30 percent. Assume that 85 percent is paid in the year incurred.

b. Taxable income from the 19A income tax return, $80,000.

Required:

1. Compute income taxes payable and deferred income tax for 19A. Is the deferred income tax a liability or an asset? Explain.
2. Give the journal entry to record income taxes for 19A.
3. Show what amounts related to 19A income taxes should be reported on the income statement and balance sheet.

P9–6 Accounting for Payroll Costs with Discussion

McLoyd Company completed the salary and wage payroll for March 19A. The payroll provided the following details:

Salaries and wages earned	$230,000
Employee income taxes withheld	46,000
Union dues withheld	3,000
Insurance premiums withheld	1,200
FICA taxes*	16,445
FUTA taxes†	1,610
State unemployment taxes	6,210

*$16,445 each for employer and employees.
† Federal unemployment taxes.

Required:

1. Give the journal entry to record the payroll for March, including employee deductions.
2. Give the journal entry to record the employer's payroll taxes.
3. Give a combined journal entry to show the payment of amounts owed to governmental agencies and other organizations.
4. What was the total labor cost for the company? Explain. What percent of the payroll was take-home pay? From the employers' perspective does an economic difference between the cost of salaries and the cost of fringe benefits exist? From the employee's perspective, does a difference exist?

P9–7 Looking at Various Liabilities   Polaroid

Polaroid designs, manufactures, and markets products primarily in instant image recording. Its annual report contained the following note:

PRODUCT WARRANTY:
Estimated product warranty costs are accrued at the time products are sold.

1. Assume that estimated warranty costs for 19A were $2 million and that the warranty work was performed during 19B. Prepare the necessary journal entries based on Polaroid's policy.

Reader's Digest Association is a publisher of magazines, books, and music collections. The following note is from its annual report: **Reader's Digest Association**

REVENUES
Sales of subscriptions to magazines are recorded as unearned revenue at the time the order is received. Proportional shares of the subscription price are recognized as revenues when the subscription is fulfilled.

2. Assume that Reader's Digest collected $10 million in 19A for magazines that will be delivered in future years. During 19B, the company delivered $8 million worth of magazines on those subscriptions. Prepare any necessary journal entries based on Reader's Digest's policy.

Brunswick Corporation

Brunswick Corporation is a multinational company that manufactures and sells marine and recreational products. Its annual report contained the following information:

> **LITIGATION**
> The Company is subject to certain legal proceedings and claims which have arisen in the ordinary course of its business and have not been finally adjudicated. In 1992, 1991, 1990, the Company recorded pretax provisions of $4.8 million, $38.0 million and $12.1 million respectively for litigation matters.

3. Prepare any journal entries required to record the results of litigation in 1992. What impact, if any, does litigation have on Brunswick's financial statements?

The Coca-Cola Company

4. A recent annual report for The Coca-Cola Company reported current assets of $4,247,677 and current liabilities of $5,303,222. Based on the current ratio, do you think that Coca-Cola is experiencing financial difficulty?

Alcoa

Alcoa is involved in the mining and manufacturing of aluminum. Its products can become an advanced alloy for the wing of a Boeing 777 or a common recyclable Coca–Cola can. The annual report for Alcoa stated the following:

> **ENVIRONMENTAL EXPENDITURES**
> Liabilities are recorded when remedial efforts are probable and the costs can be reasonably estimated.

5. In your own words, explain the Alcoa accounting policy for environmental expenditures. What is the justification for this policy?

P9–8 Applying Four PV and FV Concepts

On January 1, 19A, Plymouth Company completed the following transactions (use an 8 percent annual interest rate for all transactions):

(a) Deposited $50,000 in a debt retirement fund. Interest will be computed at six-month intervals and added to the fund at those times (i.e., semiannual compounding). (*Hint*: Think carefully about *n* and *i*.)   L   PV → FV

FV → PV L
(b) Established a plant addition fund of $400,000 to be available at the end of year 5. A single sum will be deposited on January 1, 19A, that will grow to $400,000.

(c) Established a pension retirement fund of $500,000 to be available by the end of year 6

FV — PV A by making six equal annual deposits each at year-end, starting on December 31, 19A.

(d) Purchased a $180,000 machine on January 1, 19A, and paid cash, $60,000. A four-year

PV — FV A note *payable* is signed for the balance. The note will be paid in four equal year-end payments starting on December 31, 19A.

Required (show computations and round to the nearest dollar):

1. In transaction (a), what will be the balance in the fund at the end of year 4? What is the total amount of interest revenue that will be earned?

2. In transaction (b), what single sum amount must the company deposit on January 1, 19A? What is the total amount of interest revenue that will be earned?

3. In transaction (c), what is the required amount of each of the six equal annual deposits? What is the total amount of interest revenue that will be earned?
4. In transaction (d), what is the amount of each of the equal annual payments that will be paid on the note? What is the total amount of interest expense that will be incurred?

P9–9 Accounting for a Fund: Fund Accumulation Schedule and Entries

On January 1, 19A, Jalopy Company decided to accumulate a fund to build an addition to its plant. The company will deposit $320,000 in the fund at each year-end, starting on December 31, 19A. The fund will earn 9 percent interest, which will be added to the fund at each year-end. The accounting period ends December 31.

Required:
1. What will be the balance in the fund immediately after the December 31, 19C, deposit?
2. Complete the following fund accumulation schedule:

Date	Cash Payment	Interest Revenue	Fund Increase	Fund Balance
12/31/19A				
12/31/19B				
12/31/19C				
Total				

3. Give journal entries on December 31, 19A, 19B, and 19C.
4. The plant addition was completed on January 1, 19D for a total cost of $1,060,000. Give the entry, assuming that this amount is paid in full to the contractor.

P9–10 Accounting for a Plant Fund: A Single Amount

Texas Company will build another plant during 19C estimated to cost $800,000. At the present time, January 1, 19A, the company has excess cash, some of which will be set aside in a savings account to cover the plant cost. The savings account will earn 8 percent annual interest, which will be added to the savings account each year-end.

Required (show computations and round to the nearest dollar):
1. What single amount must be deposited in the savings account on January 1, 19A, to create the desired amount by the end of 19C?
2. What amount of interest will be earned by the end of 19C?
3. How much interest revenue will be earned each year (19A through 19C)?
4. Give the following journal entries:
   a. Establishment of the fund.
   b. Interest earned at each year-end.
   c. Use of the fund and other cash needed to pay for the plant (completed December 31, 19C, at a cost of $825,000).

P9–11 Accounting for a Debt Retirement Fund: A Single Amount

On January 1, 19A, Athletic Company set aside a fund to provide cash to pay off the principal amount of a $100,000 long-term debt that will be due at the end of six years. The single deposit will be made with an independent trustee. The fund will earn 10 percent annual interest, which will be added to the fund balance at each year-end.

Required (show computations and round to the nearest dollar):
1. How much must be deposited as a single sum on January 1, 19A, to pay off the debt?
2. What amount of interest will be earned during the six years?

3. How much interest revenue will the fund earn in 19A? 19B?
4. Give the journal entries for the company to record
    a. The deposit on January 1, 19A.
    b. The interest revenue for 19A and 19B (separately).
    c. Payment of the maturing liability at the end of the sixth year.
5. Show how the effects of the fund will be reported on the 19B income statement and balance sheet.

P9–12 Accounting for a Debt Fund: Equal Periodic Deposits

On December 31, 19A, Post Company set aside in a fund the cash to pay the principal amount of a $140,000 debt due on December 31, 19D. The company will make four equal annual deposits on each December 31, 19A, 19B, 19C, and 19D. The fund will earn 7 percent annual interest, which will be added to the balance of the fund at each year-end. The fund trustee will pay the loan principal (to the creditor) upon receipt of the last fund deposit. The company's accounting period ends December 31.

Required (show computations and round to the nearest dollar):
1. How much must be deposited each December 31?
2. What amount of interest will be earned?
3. How much interest revenue will the fund earn in 19A, 19B, 19C, and 19D?
4. Give journal entries for the company on the following dates:
    a. For the first deposit on December 31, 19A.
    b. For all amounts at the ends of 19B and 19C.
    c. For payment of the debt on December 31, 19D.
5. Show how the effect of the fund will be reported on the December 31, 19B, income statement and balance sheet.

P9–13 Paying Debt in Equal Installments: Debt Payment Schedule and Entries

On January 1, 19A, Idaho Company sold a new machine to U.S. Company for $80,000. U.S. Company made a cash down payment of $30,000 and signed a $50,000, 8 percent note for the balance due. The note is to be paid off in three equal installments due on December 31, 19A, 19B, and 19C. Each payment is to include principal plus interest on the unpaid balance. U.S. recorded the purchase as follows:

Jan. 1, 19A	Machine	80,000	
	Cash		30,000
	Note payable		50,000

Required (show computations and round to the nearest dollar):
1. What is the amount of the equal annual payments that U.S. Company must make?
2. What is the interest on the note?
3. Complete the following debt payment schedule:

Date	Cash Payment	Interest Expense	Principal Decrease	Unpaid Principal
1/1/19A				
12/31/19A				
12/31/19B				
12/31/19C				
Total				

4. Give the journal entries for each of the three payments.
5. Explain why interest expense decreased in amount each year.

P9–14 **Paying for Auto in Equal Periodic Installments: Debt Payment Schedule and Entries**

On January 1, 19A, you bought a new ZS238 automobile for $22,000. You made a $5,000 cash down payment and signed a $17,000 note, payable in four equal installments on each December 31, the first payment to be made on December 31, 19A. The interest rate is 12 percent per year on the unpaid balance. Each payment will include payment on principal plus the interest.

Required:
1. Compute the amount of the equal payments that you must make.
2. What is the interest on the installment debt during the four years?
3. Complete a schedule using the following format:

DEBT PAYMENT SCHEDULE

Date	Cash Payment	Interest Expense	Reduction of Principal	Unpaid Principal
1/1/A				
12/31/A				
12/31/B				
12/31/C				
12/31/D				
Totals				

4. Explain why the amount of interest expense decreases each year.
5. Give the journal entries on December 31, 19A, and 19B.

Cases and Projects

C9–1 **Accounting for Warranty Expense and Warranty Liability: A Challenging Case**

Dayton Hudson

Dayton Hudson operates a number of general merchandise stores under a variety of names including Target, Mervyn's, and Marshall Field's, as well as Dayton Hudson. This case relates to CD players sold by a single electronics department in a Target store. During 19A, the department sold CD players for $220,000 cash; the related cost of goods sold was $100,000. Each CD player is guaranteed for one year for defective parts. In case of a defective part, the part is replaced and the labor cost of replacing it involves no cost to the customer. Experience by the manufacturer shows that the average cost to make good on the warranty is approximately 5 percent of cost of goods sold. Assume that Target uses a perpetual inventory system and the accounting period ends December 31.

Actual expenditures for warranties (i.e., replacement parts and labor) during 19A were $3,400. During 19A, this amount was debited to the account Warranty Expense and credited to Cash. CD player sales were much higher during December than in any other prior month.

Required:
1. Give the two summary journal entries for the company to record the sales of CD players during 19A.
2. Explain why the company debited the actual 19A warranty expenditures to Warranty Expense.
3. Explain the nature of any liability that the company should record at the end of 19A related to the warranties.
4. Compute the estimated amount of any warranty liability that exists at December 31, 19A.
5. Give any entry needed based on your answer to requirement (4).
6. Show how warranty expense and any warranty liability should be reported in the 19A income statement and balance sheet.

C9–2 Hidden Interest in a Real Estate Deal: Present Value

Many advertisements contain offers that seem too good to be true. Often these offers are not what they seem to be. A few years ago, an actual newspaper ad offered "a $150,000 house with a zero interest rate mortgage" for sale. If the purchaser made monthly payments of $3,125 for four years ($150,000 ÷ 48 months), there would be no additional charge for interest. When the offer was made, mortgage interest rates were 12 percent. Present value for $n = 48$, and $i = 1\%$ is 37.9740.

Required:
1. Did the builder actually provide a mortgage at zero interest?
2. Estimate the true price of the home that was advertised. Assume that the monthly payment was based on an implicit interest rate of 12 percent.

Southwest Airlines

C9–3 Accrued Liability for a Frequent Flyer Program

Most major airlines have frequent flyer programs that permit passengers to earn free tickets based on the number of miles they have flown. A recent Southwest Airlines annual report contained the following note:

> **FREQUENT FLYER AWARDS**
> The Company accrues the estimated incremental cost to provide transportation for travel awards when earned under its Company Club frequent flyer program.

The phrase *incremental cost* means the additional expense associated with an extra passenger taking the flight (e.g., the cost of a soft drink and a snack).

Required:
1. What cost measures other than incremental cost could Southwest use?
2. What account should Southwest debit when it accrues this liability?

H. J. Heinz Company

C9–4 Liability for Retirement Benefits

Many companies provide health care benefits for employees who have retired. A recent H. J. Heinz Company annual report contained the following note:

> In addition to providing pension benefits, the company and certain of its subsidiaries provide health care and life insurance benefits for retired employees. Substantially all of the company's U.S. and Canadian employees may become eligible for these benefits. The cost of retiree health care and life insurance benefits is expensed as incurred. These costs were $4.9 million for the current year and $4.2 million for the previous year.

Since this annual report was issued, the Financial Accounting Standards Board issued a new rule, which stated that the cost of future health care for retirees should be estimated and recorded as a current expense while employees were working rather than when they received the benefits.

Required:
1. How would the FASB justify the new rule?
2. What problems would you anticipate in implementing the new rule?

PepsiCo, Inc.

C9–5 Classification of Short-Term Borrowings

PepsiCo, Inc., engages in a number of activities that are part of our daily lives. Its businesses include Pepsi-Cola, Frito-Lay, KFC, and Pizza Hut. A recent PepsiCo annual report contained the following information:

At the end of the current year, $3.6 billion of short-term borrowings were classified as long-term, reflecting PepsiCo's intent and ability to refinance these borrowings on a long-term basis, through either long-term debt issuances or rollover of existing short-term borrowings. The significant amount of short-term borrowings classified as long-term, as compared to the end of the previous year when no such amounts were reclassified, primarily reflects the large commercial paper issuances in the current year, but also resulted from a refined analysis of amounts expected to be refinanced beyond one year.

Required:

As an analyst, comment on the company's classification of short-term borrowings as long-term liabilities. What conditions should exist to permit a company to make this type of classification?

C9–6 **Present Value of Lease Obligations**   Delta Air Lines

A recent annual report for Delta Air Lines included the following note:

At June 30, 1990, the Company's minimum rental commitments under capital leases and non-cancelable operating leases with initial or remaining terms of more than one year were as follows:

Years Ending June 30	Operating Leases (in thousands)
1991	$ 533,891
1992	533,106
1993	523,391
1994	515,457
1995	512,897
After 1995	$6,984,779
Total minimum lease payments	$9,603,521

You are a lending officer for a large commercial bank and for comparative purposes want to compute the present values of these leases.

Required:

Determine the present value of the minimum lease payments shown as of June 30, 1990. You may assume an interest rate of 10 percent. Identify other assumptions that you must make.

C9–7 **Comparing Accounting for Deferred Taxes in Different Countries**   Grand
                                                                                  Metropolitan
Grand Metropolitan is a major international company located in London. A recent annual report contained the following information concerning its accounting policies.

TAXATION
The charge for taxation is based on the profit for the year and takes into account taxation deferred because of timing differences between the treatment of certain items for taxation and accounting purposes. However, no provision is made for taxation deferred, principally by accelerated taxation allowances on capital expenditure, if there is reasonable evidence that such deferred taxation will not be payable or recoverable in the foreseeable future.

Compare and contrast accounting for deferred taxes in England with procedures used in this country.

Toys "R" Us

C9–8   Financial Statement Analysis

Refer to the financial statements of Toys "R" Us given in Appendix B at the end of this book.

Required:

1. How much money does the company owe its suppliers at the end of the current year?
2. How much interest was capitalized during the current year?
3. What is the amount of federal income tax expense for the current year?
4. How much of the tax expense for the current year was deferred?
5. Compute and evaluate the current ratio.

C9–9   Project: Ratio Analysis

Find financial statements for two companies in the same industry and compute the current ratio for at least three years. Compare the set of ratios for the two companies and write a brief memo explaining any insights that you have obtained as the result of this analysis.

C9–10   Project: Financial Analysis and Cash Flows

As a young analyst at a large mutual fund, you have found two companies that meet the basic investment criteria of the fund. One company has a very high current ratio but a relatively low amount of cash flow from operating activity reported on the Statement of Cash Flows. The other company has a very low current ratio but very significant cash flows from operating activities. Which company would you tend to prefer?

C9–11   Ethics Project: Managing Reported Results

The president of a regional wholesale distribution company planned to borrow a significant amount of money from a local bank at the beginning of the next fiscal year. He knew that the bank placed a heavy emphasis on the liquidity of potential borrowers. To improve the company's current ratio, the president told his employees to stop shipping new merchandise to customers and to stop accepting merchandise from suppliers for the last three weeks of the fiscal year. Is this behavior ethical? Would your answer be different if the president had been concerned about reported profits and asked all of the employees to work overtime to ship out merchandise that had been ordered at the end of the year?

C9–12   Ethics Project: Fair Disclosure

Find an advertisement that includes the time value of money (for example, an ad about a bank loan, a lease on a new car, or a lottery payoff). Write a memo evaluating the fairness of the information that is disclosed. Does the average reader have enough information to make an informed decision?

C9–13   Project: Interpreting a Complex Note

Find a financial statement that includes disclosure of a retirement program. We briefly introduced you to this topic in this chapter. This is a complex issue that will be discussed in greater depth in subsequent courses. Based on your understanding at this time, write a memo to a retired person covered by the plan explaining the information contained in the note. Write a separate memo to your instructor asking specific questions about information from the note that you cannot understand.

C9–14   Project: Analyzing Contingent Liabilities

Locate an annual report that includes information about a contingent liability. Write a brief memo explaining why the liability should be reported as contingent, not as a liability that is reported on the balance sheet.

C9–15   Project: Ethics and the Environment

Many companies have a significant impact on our environment (for example, oil exploration and timber companies). Look up the annual report for a company that you think has an impact on our environment. Write a memo analyzing the quality of the company's reporting on this sensitive issue. Consider this question from the perspectives of both financial analysts and the average citizen concerned about the world in which we live.

C9–16   Project: Assessing Contingent Liabilities

If a liability is both probable and subject to estimate, it must be recorded as a liability on the balance sheet. The Financial Accounting Standards Board defined *probable* as "the future event or events are likely to occur." Working in a small group, decide on a specific probability that is appropriate for this standard (for example, is an 80 percent chance of occurrence probable?). Be prepared to justify your determination.

C9–17   Focus on Cash Flows: Changes in Current Liabilities

Review the Statement of Cash Flows for a large company. Write a brief memo explaining how changes in the current liability accounts affected cash flows from operating activities.

C9–18   Team Project: Examining an Annual Report

As a group, select an industry to analyze. Each group member should acquire the annual report or 10-K for one publicly traded company in the industry, with each member selecting a different company. (Library files, the SEC EDGAR service at www.sec.gov, Compustat CD, or the company itself are good sources.) On an individual basis, each group member should then write a short report answering the following questions about his or her selected company.

1. Review the liabilities for your company. What strategy has the company followed with respect to borrowed funds?
2. Compare the individual liability accounts over several years. How have they changed?
3. Does the company have any contingent liabilities? If so, evaluate the risk associated with the contingency.
4. Compare the company's liabilities to its assets, income, and cash flows. Do you have any concerns?

Discuss any patterns across the companies that you as a group observe. Then, as a group, write a short report comparing and contrasting your companies using these attributes. Provide potential explanations for any differences discovered.

CHAPTER TEN

Reporting and Interpreting Bonds

Showboat, Inc.

FINANCING GROWTH WITH BONDS PAYABLE

A few years ago, Showboat, Inc., issued bonds in the amount of $275 million. This money was needed because the company is actively pursuing expansion opportunities in emerging gaming (gambling) markets in the United States and internationally. Gaming has become big business. Showboat currently owns gambling casinos in Atlantic City and Nevada. The Atlantic City Showboat is a 24-story casino hotel featuring a 60,000 square foot gambling area with 2,138 slot machines and 69 table games. The parking facilities include a 14-bus depot and space for 2,500 cars.

The gaming industry has become more competitive in recent years. As a result, gaming operators have been forced to expand and modernize their operations. The Atlantic City Showboat was completed in 1987, and the company has already started a $53.5 million expansion project for the hotel and casino.

LEARNING OBJECTIVES

After studying this chapter, you should be able to:

1. Explain corporations' use of bonds payable. 522
2. Classify bonds payable. 524
3. Report bonds payable and interest expense. 527
4. Analyze bonds sold at a discount. 529
5. Analyze bonds sold at a premium. 532
6. Use the effective-interest method of amortization. 535
7. Report the early retirement of bonds. 538
8. Explain the use of bond sinking funds. 540
9. Report bond investments held to maturity. 541

Because of the company's strategy of expanding into new markets and the need to modernize existing facilities, Showboat, Inc., has had to raise large amounts of new capital in addition to retaining a large amount of its income. Why did management decide to raise this money through the issuance of bonds? We will answer the question in this chapter.

■   ■   ■

Business Background

LEARNING OBJECTIVE 1
Explain corporations' use of bonds payable.

security – state of being secure – freedom from danger.

In Chapter 9, we introduced the term *capital structure,* which is the mixture of debt and equity that is used to finance a company's operations. Almost all companies employ some debt in their capital structure. Indeed, large corporations need to borrow billions of dollars, which makes borrowing money from individual creditors impractical for them. Instead, these corporations can issue bonds to raise debt capital.

Bonds are securities that corporations and governmental units issue when they borrow large amounts of money. After bonds are issued, they can be traded on established exchanges such as the New York Bond Exchange. The ability to sell a bond on the bond exchange is a significant advantage for creditors because it provides them with *liquidity,* or the ability to convert their investment into cash. If you lend money directly to a corporation for 20 years, you must wait that long to have your cash investment repaid. If you lend money by purchasing a bond, you can sell it to another creditor if you need cash before the bond matures.

The liquidity that is available with publicly traded bonds offers an important advantage to corporations. Because most creditors are reluctant to lend money for long periods of time with no opportunity to receive cash prior to the maturity date of the debt, they demand a higher interest rate to compensate them for long-term loans. The liquidity associated with bonds permits corporations to reduce the cost of borrowing money for long periods of time.

The use of bonds to raise long-term capital offers other significant advantages to corporations such as Showboat:

1. Ownership and control of the company are not diluted. In contrast to stockholders, bondholders do not participate in the management (by voting) and accumulated earnings of the company.
2. Cash payments to the bondholders are limited to the specified interest payments and the principal of the debt.
3. Interest expense is a tax-deductible expense, but dividends paid to stockholders are not. The tax deductibility of interest expense reduces the net cost of borrowing. For example, if a corporation paid $100,000 interest during the year, its taxable income is $100,000 lower. If the tax rate is 35 percent, the corporation pays $35,000 less in taxes (35% × $100,000) because of the lower taxable income. Thus, the **net interest cost** is $65,000 ($100,000 – $35,000). If the corporation paid $100,000 in dividends, the net cost is $100,000 because dividends are not tax deductible.
4. It is often possible to borrow funds at a low interest rate and invest them at a higher rate, which is called positive **financial leverage.** To illustrate financial leverage, assume that Home Video, Inc., owns a video rental store. The company has stockholders' equity of $100,000 invested in the store and no debt. The com-

Net interest cost is interest cost less any income tax savings associated with interest expense.
Financial leverage is the use of borrowed funds to increase the rate of return on owners' equity; it occurs when the interest rate on debt is lower than the earnings rate on total assets.

pany earns net income of $20,000 per year on the store (which is a 20 percent return on the stockholders' investment). Management plans to open a new store which will also cost $100,000 and will earn $20,000 per year. If the stockholders provide the new funds, they will still earn 20 percent on their investment ($40,000 ÷ $200,000), but if the company borrows $100,000 for the new store at a net after-tax interest cost of 8 percent, the stockholders' rate of return will actually increase. They will earn $20,000 on the first store and $12,000 on the second store ($20,000 – $8,000 interest) for a total return of $32,000. Because the company borrowed money, stockholders' equity remains at $100,000 with a rate of return of 32 percent ($32,000 ÷ $100,000).

Unfortunately, the issuance of bonds has some disadvantages. The primary disadvantages are (1) the required interest payments must be made each interest period and (2) the large principal amount must be paid at the maturity date. Interest payments to bondholders are fixed charges, which increase the risk of business. Interest payments legally must be paid each period, whether the corporation earns income or incurs a loss. In contrast, dividends usually are paid to stockholders only if earnings are satisfactory. Each year, some companies go bankrupt because of their inability to make their required interest payments to creditors. Sound business practice requires maintaining an appropriate balance between debt and equity capital.

Evaluating the Risk Associated with Debt

Because of the importance of the balance between debt and equity, most analysts use the *debt-to-equity ratio,* which—as the name implies—is computed by dividing total debt by total equity:

$$\text{Debt-to-equity ratio} = \frac{\text{Total liabilities}}{\text{Owners' equity}}$$

This ratio shows how much debt a company has for each dollar of its stockholders' equity. A company with a large debt-to-equity ratio is called a *highly leveraged company*. These companies normally are considered to be riskier than less highly leveraged companies. Companies that are highly leveraged have a large amount of debt and, consequently, a large amount of debt payments. If they experience a difficult financial period, they may not be able to meet their obligatory payments and could face bankruptcy.

In addition to the debt-to-equity ratio, many analysts also compute an interest coverage ratio called *times interest earned*:

$$\text{Times interest earned} = \frac{\text{Net income} + \text{Interest expense} + \text{Income tax expense}}{\text{Interest expense}}$$

The ratio measures how well a company has its interest obligations covered with income from current operations. A company with a high interest coverage ratio is generating a large amount of income compared to its obligatory payments to creditors. This suggests a lower level of risk of defaulting on required interest payments.

Corporate bonds also have risk which must be evaluated.

Characteristics of Bonds Payable

LEARNING OBJECTIVE 2
Classify bonds payable.

not seen often because most people want some security/ collateral

A **debenture** is an unsecured bond; no assets are specifically pledged to guarantee repayment.

The **bond principal** is the amount (a) payable at the maturity of the bond and (b) on which the periodic cash interest payments are computed.

Par value is another name for bond principal, or the maturity amount of a bond.

Face amount is another name for principal, or the principal amount of the bond.

The **stated rate** is the rate of cash interest per period specified in the bond contract.

An **indenture** is a bond contract that specifies the legal provisions of a bond issue.

Different types of bonds have different characteristics. Exhibit 10.1 summarizes many of the most common features of corporate bonds. At first, it may seem perplexing to see so many different types of bonds, but there is a solid economic reason for them. Different types of creditors have different types of risk and return preferences. A retired person, for example, may be willing to receive a lower interest rate in return for having more security. This type of creditor might want a mortgage bond that pledges a specific asset as security if the company is unable to repay the bond (called a *secured bond*). Another creditor might be willing to accept a low interest rate and an unsecured status if the company provides the opportunity to convert the bond into common stock at some point in the future if the company does very well. A bond that is not secured with the pledge of a specific asset is called a **debenture.** Companies try to design bond features that are attractive to different groups of creditors just as automobile manufacturers try to design cars that appeal to different groups of consumers.

A bond usually requires the payment of interest over its life with the repayment of principal on the maturity date. The **bond principal** is the amount (1) payable at the maturity date and (2) on which the periodic cash interest payments are computed. It does not change. The principal also is called the **par value, face amount,** and *maturity value*. All bonds have a par value, which is the amount that will be paid when the bond matures. For most bonds, the par value is $1,000, but it can be any amount.

A bond always specifies a **stated rate** of interest and when periodic cash interest payments must be paid—usually annually or semiannually. Each periodic interest payment is computed as principal times the stated interest rate. The selling price of a bond does not affect the periodic cash payment of interest. For example, a $1,000, 8 percent bond always pays cash interest of (1) $80 on an annual basis or (2) $40 on a semiannual basis.

When Showboat, Inc., decided to issue new bonds, it prepared a bond **indenture** (bond contract) that specified the legal provisions of the bonds. These provisions include the maturity date, rate of interest to be paid, date of each interest payment, and

EXHIBIT 10.1
Bond Characteristics and Classifications of Bonds

Bond Classification	Bond Characteristic
1. On the basis of collateral (assets)	
a. Unsecured bonds (often called *debentures*).	*a.* Bonds that do not include a mortgage or pledge of specific assets as a guarantee of repayment at maturity.
b. Secured bonds (often designated on the basis of the type of asset pledged, such as a real estate mortgage).	*b.* Bonds that include the pledge of specific assets as a guarantee of repayment at maturity.
2. On the basis of repayment of principal	
a. Ordinary or single-payment bonds.	*a.* The principal that is payable in full at a single specified maturity date in the future.
b. Serial bonds.	*b.* The principal that is payable in installments on a series of specified maturity dates in the future.
3. On the basis of early retirement	
a. Callable bonds.	*a.* Bonds that may be called for early retirement at the option of the issuer.
b. Redeemable bonds.	*b.* Bonds that may be turned in for early retirement at the option of the bondholder.
c. Convertible bonds.	*c.* Bonds that may be converted to other securities of the issuer (usually common stock) at the option of the bondholder.

any conversion privileges (explained later). The indenture also contains covenants designed to protect the creditors. The Showboat indenture included limitations on new debt and on the amount of dividends that could be paid. Because they may limit future action, covenants that are least restrictive are preferred by management. Creditors, however, prefer more restrictive covenants, which lessen the risk of the investment. As in any business transaction, the final result is achieved through a process of negotiation. Bond covenants are typically reported in the notes to the financial statements.

6. LONG-TERM DEBT

The Bond Indenture places significant restrictions on the incurrence of additional debt by Showboat and its subsidiaries, the creation of additional liens on the collateral securing the Bonds, transactions with affiliates and payment of certain restricted payments including dividends.

As we will see later in the chapter, one of the covenants included in the indenture prevented Showboat management from taking advantage of a new business opportunity. We will see what management did to overcome the restrictions in the covenant.

Showboat also prepared a *prospectus*, which is a legal document given to potential buyers of the bonds. The prospectus describes the company, the bonds, and how the proceeds of the bonds will be used. Most companies work with an underwriter who either buys the entire issue of bonds and then resells them to individual creditors (called a *firm commitment underwriter*) or simply sells the bonds without any obligation to purchase them (called a *best efforts underwriter*). Showboat used two underwriters (on a firm commitment basis), Donaldson, Lufkin & Jenrette, and Lehman Brothers. The underwriting commission paid to these firms was $6,531,250 on a bond issue of $275 million.

When a bond is issued to the investor, the person receives a **bond certificate.** All of the bond certificates for a single bond issue are identical. The face of each certificate shows the same maturity date, interest rate, interest dates, and other provisions.

A **bond certificate** is the bond document that each bondholder receives.

This certificate contains important information about the bond.

Gaming casinos must have dramatic facades to attract customers, just as bonds must have dramatic features to attract investors.

A **trustee** is an independent party appointed to represent the bondholders.

A third, independent party, called the **trustee,** usually is appointed to represent the bondholders. A trustee's duties are to ascertain whether the issuing company fulfills all of the provisions of the bond indenture. Showboat, Inc., appointed IBJ Schroder Bank & Trust Company to act as trustee.

As mentioned earlier, each bond issue has characteristics that are specified in the bond indenture. The issuing company often adds special characteristics to a bond to make it more attractive to investors who normally have a large number of investment alternatives from which to select.

Bonds sometimes offer different features with respect to early retirement:

Callable bonds may be called for early retirement at the option of the issuer.
Redeemable bonds may be turned in for early retirement at the option of the bondholder.
Convertible bonds may be converted to other securities of the issuer (usually common stock).

Callable bonds may be called for early retirement at the option of the issuer.
Redeemable bonds may be turned in for early retirement at the option of the bondholder.
Convertible bonds may be converted to other securities of the issuer (usually common stock) at the option of the bondholder. *(Cost more to get this option)*

Bonds also differ in terms of their status in relationship to other debt:

Senior debt receives preference over other creditors in the event of bankruptcy or default.
Subordinated debt is paid off after some other group of creditors. Obviously, subordinated debt is riskier than senior debt.

Each year, corporations introduce new features that are included with their bonds. For example, The Walt Disney Company recently issued the first bond with a 100-year maturity. Despite an increase in unusual features, the basics that we discuss in this chapter permit you to deal with most types of bonds.

Because of the complexities associated with bonds, several agencies exist to evaluate the probability that a bond issuer will not be able to meet the requirements specified in the indenture. This risk is called *default risk*. Moody's and Standard and Poor's use letter ratings to specify the quality of a bond. Ratings above Baa/BBB are investment grade; ratings below that level are speculative and are often called *junk bonds*. Many banks, mutual funds, and trusts are permitted to invest only in bonds that are of investment grade quality.

— lower the rating the higher the risk

Measuring Bonds Payable and Interest Expense

When Showboat issued its bonds, it specified two types of cash payments in the bond contract:

1. *Principal.* This is usually a single payment made when the bond matures. It is also called the *par,* or *face, value.*
2. *Cash interest payments.* These payments represent an annuity and are computed by multiplying the principal amount times the interest rate, called the *contract, stated,* or **coupon rate** of interest stated in the bond contract. The bond contract specifies whether these payments are made quarterly, semiannually, or annually.

Neither Showboat nor the underwriter determines the price at which the bonds sell. Instead, the market determines the price using the present value concepts that were introduced in the previous chapter. To determine the present value of the bond, you compute the present value of the principal (a single payment) and the present value of the interest payments (an annuity) and add the two amounts together.

Creditors demand a certain rate of interest to compensate them for the risks related to bonds. The interest rate demanded by these creditors is the **market interest rate** (also called the **yield,** or **effective-interest rate**). The market rate is the interest rate on a debt when incurred; it should be used in computing the present value of the bond.

The present value of a bond may be the same as par, above par (**bond premium**), or below par (**bond discount**). If the stated and the market interest rates are the same, a bond sells at par; if the market rate is higher than the stated rate, a bond sells at a discount; and if the market rate is lower than the stated rate, the bond sells at a premium. These relationships can be understood in commonsense terms. If a bond pays an interest rate that is less than creditors demand, they will not buy it unless its price is reduced (i.e., a discount must be provided). If a bond pays more than creditors demand, they will be willing to pay a premium to buy it.

When a bond is issued at par, the issuer receives cash equal to its par value. When a bond is issued at a discount, the issuer receives less cash than its par value. When a bond is issued at a premium, the issuer receives more cash than the par value.

Basically, corporations and creditors do not care whether a bond is issued at par, a discount, or a premium because bonds are always priced to provide the market rate of interest. To illustrate, consider a corporation that issues three separate bonds on the same day. The bonds are exactly the same except one has a stated interest of 8 percent, another 10 percent, and a third 11 percent. If the market rate of interest was 10 percent, the first would be issued at a discount, the second at par, and the third at a premium, but a creditor who bought any one of the bonds would earn the market interest rate of 10 percent. Later in this chapter, we will use present value concepts to illustrate this point.

LEARNING OBJECTIVE 3
Report bonds payable and interest expense.

The **coupon rate** is the stated rate of interest on bonds.

Market interest rate is the current rate of interest on a debt when incurred; also called the **yield,** or **effective-interest rate.**

Bond premium is the difference between the selling price and par when the bond is sold for more than par.

Bond discount is the difference between the selling price and par when the bond is sold for less than par.

Bond Information from the Business Press

As mentioned earlier, bonds are widely used because they offer creditors liquidity. A creditor who needs immediate cash can sell a bond to another creditor instead of waiting until its maturity date. These transactions are between individual creditors and do not affect the financial statements of the company that issued the bonds.

Bond prices are reported each day in the business press based on transactions that occurred on the bond exchange. The following is typical of the information that you will find:

Bond	Yield	Volume	Close	Change
Safeway 9.6 04	9.6	58	100	$-\frac{1}{4}$
Sears 9½ 99	9.1	25	104¼	$-\frac{3}{8}$
Showboat 9¼ 08	11.3	580	82⅛	$-\frac{7}{8}$

This listing means that the Showboat bond has a coupon interest rate of $9\frac{1}{4}$ percent and will mature in the year 2008. The bond currently provides a cash yield of 11.3 percent with a selling price that is $82\frac{1}{8}$ percent of par or $821.25. On this particular date, 580 bonds were sold and the price fell $\frac{7}{8}$ point from the previous trading date. A point is 1 percent.

Although analysts may study the daily price changes of bonds, remember that these changes do not affect the company's financial statements. For financial reporting purposes, the company uses the interest rates that existed when the bonds were first sold to the public. Subsequent changes do not affect the company's accounting for the bonds.

SELF-STUDY QUIZ

Your study of bonds will be easier if you understand the new terminology that has been introduced in this chapter. Let's review some of those terms. Define the following:

1. Market interest rate.
2. Synonyms for market interest rate.
3. Coupon interest rate.
4. Synonyms for coupon interest rate.
5. Bond discount.
6. Bond premium.

Check your answers in the footnote at the bottom of this page.*

Analyzing Bond Transactions

In this section of the chapter, we illustrate three different cases of accounting for bonds payable: (1) bonds issued at par, (2) bonds issued at a discount, and (3) bonds issued at a premium. We use Showboat, Inc., for our illustration, but for the sake of simplification, we assume that the company issued bonds with a maturity value of $400,000.

Bonds Issued at Par

Bonds sell at their par value when buyers are willing to invest in them at the interest rate stated on the bond. To illustrate, let's assume that on January 1, 19A, Showboat, Inc., issued 10 percent bonds with a par value of $400,000 and received $400,000 in cash (which means that the bonds sold at par). The bonds were dated to start interest

---

*1. The market rate is the interest rate demanded by creditors. It is the rate used in the present value computations to discount future cash flows.
2. Market interest rate is also called *yield* or *effective-interest rate*.
3. Coupon interest rate is the stated rate on the bonds.
4. Coupon rate is also called *stated rate* and *contract rate*.
5. A bond that sells for less than par is sold at a discount. This occurs when the coupon rate is lower than the market rate.
6. A bond that sells for more than par is sold at a premium. This occurs when the coupon rate is higher than the market rate.

on January 1, 19A, and will pay interest each June 30 and December 31. The bonds mature in 10 years on December 31, 19J. On the date of issuance, Showboat records the receipt of $400,000 cash and the creation of a liability for the same amount.

The creditors who bought the bonds did so with the expectation that they would earn interest over the life of the bond. Showboat will pay interest at 5 percent (i.e., 10 percent per year) on the par value of the bonds each June 30 and December 31 until the bond's maturity date. The amount of interest each period will be $20,000 (5% × $400,000). The entry to record the interest payments follows:

June 30, 19A	Bond interest expense (E)	20,000	
	Cash (A)		20,000

Bond interest payment dates rarely coincide with the last day of a company's fiscal year. Under the matching concept, interest expense that has been incurred but not paid must be accrued with an adjusting entry. If the Showboat fiscal year ended on May 31, the company would accrue interest for five months and record interest expense and interest payable.

Notice in the preceding journal entry that interest expense and cash interest paid are the same amount. This is the case when the effective interest rate and the stated rate are the same. When bonds are sold at a discount or a premium, this is not the case. We illustrate these cases later in the chapter.

The $400,000 cash that Showboat received when the bonds were sold is the present value of the future cash flows associated with the bonds. This is computed using the present value tables contained in Appendix A:

	Present Value
a. Principal: $400,000 × $P_{n=20,\ i=5\%}$ (0.3769)	$150,760
b. Interest: $20,000 × $P_{n=20,\ i=5\%}$ (12.4622)	249,240*
Issue price of Showboat bonds	$400,000
*Rounded.	

When the effective rate of interest equals the stated rate of interest, the present value of the future cash flows associated with a bond *always* equals the bond's par amount. It is important to remember that a bond's selling price is determined by the present value of its future cash flows, not the par value. Bond liabilities also are initially recorded at the present value of future cash flows on date of issue, not par value.

Bonds Issued at a Discount

Bonds sell at a discount when the buyers are willing to invest in them only if the buyers receive the market rate of interest, which is *higher* than the stated interest rate on them. Let's now assume that the market rate of interest was 12 percent when Showboat sold its bonds (which have a par value of $400,000). The bonds have a stated rate of 10 percent, payable semiannually, which is less than the rate demanded by the market. Therefore, the bonds sold at a discount. To compute the cash issue price of the bonds requires computation of the present value, at the *market rate of interest,* of the future cash flows specified on the bond: (1) the principal ($n = 20, i = 6\%$) and (2) the cash interest paid each semiannual interest period ($n = 20, i = 6\%$). Thus, the cash issue price of the Showboat bonds is computed as follows:

LEARNING OBJECTIVE 4
Analyze bonds sold at a discount.

	Present Value
a. Principal: $400,000 × $P_{n=20,\ i=6\%}$ (0.3118)	$124,720
b. Interest: $20,000 × $P_{n=20,\ i=6\%}$ (11.4699)	229,398
Issue (sale) price of Showboat bonds	$354,118*
*Discount: $400,000 – $354,118 = $45,882.	

The cash price of the bonds issued by Showboat is $354,118. Some people refer to this price as 88.5, which means that the bonds were sold at 88.5 percent of their par value ($354,118/$400,000).

When a bond is sold at a discount, the Bonds Payable account is credited for the par amount, and the discount is recorded as a debit to Discount on Bonds Payable. The issuance of the Showboat bonds at a discount is recorded as follows:

Jan. 1, 19A	Cash (A)	354,118	
	Discount on bonds payable (XL)	45,882	
	Bonds payable (L)		400,000

This journal entry shows the discount in a separate contra liability account (Discount on Bonds Payable) as a debit. The balance sheet reports the bonds payable at their book value, which is their maturity amount less any unamortized discount.

Remember that Showboat actually issued bonds with a maturity value of $275 million. The company's annual report shows the bonds at their maturity value less unamortized discount.

REAL WORLD EXCERPT

SHOWBOAT, INC.
Annual Report

	December 31,	
	1995	1994
	(In Thousands)	
9¼% First Mortgage Bonds due 2008 net of unamortized discount of $4,632,000 and $5,008,000 at December 31, 1995 and 1994, respectively	$270,368	$269,992

Notice that the book value of the bonds increased from 1994 to 1995 and the amount of unamortized discount decreased. In the next section, we see how this change occurs.

Measuring and Recording Interest on Bonds Issued at a Discount

During the 10-year term of the bonds, Showboat must make 20 semiannual cash interest payments of $20,000 (i.e., $400,000 × 5%) and at maturity pay back the $400,000 cash principal. Therefore, in addition to the cash interest, Showboat must repay more money than it received when it sold the bonds (i.e., it borrowed $354,118 but must repay $400,000). This extra cash that it must pay is an adjustment of interest expense that ensures that creditors earn the market rate of interest on the bonds. To adjust interest expense, the bond discount must be apportioned (*amortized*) to each semiannual interest period as an increase in interest expense. Therefore, the amortization of bond discount results in an increase in bond interest expense.

The bond discount can be allocated using two amortization methods: (1) straight line and (2) effective interest. Straight-line amortization is easy to compute. The effective-interest method is discussed later in this chapter.

Straight-line amortization of a bond discount or premium is a simplified method that allocates an equal dollar amount to each interest period.

STRAIGHT-LINE AMORTIZATION   To amortize the $45,882 bond discount over the life of the Showboat bonds on a straight-line basis, an equal dollar amount is allocated to each interest period. The Showboat bonds have 20 six-month interest periods. Therefore, the computation is $45,882 ÷ 20 periods = $2,294 amortization on each semiannual interest date. This amount is added to the cash payment of interest ($20,000) to compute interest expense for the period ($22,294). The interest payments on the Showboat bonds each period are as follows:

June 30, 19A	Bond interest expense (E)	22,294	
	Discount on bonds payable (XL)		2,294
	Cash (A)		20,000

Bonds payable should be reported on the balance sheet at their *book value*; that is, the maturity amount less any unamortized bond discount (or plus any unamortized bond premium). Therefore, on June 30, 19A, the book value of the Showboat bonds is $356,412 ($354,118 + $2,294).

In each succeeding interest period, the unamortized discount decreases by $2,294; therefore, the book value of the bonds increases by $2,294 each interest period. At the maturity date of the bonds, the unamortized discount (i.e., the balance in the Discount on Bonds Payable account) is *zero*. At that time, the maturity amount of the bonds and the book value are the same (i.e., $400,000).

A note from the annual report for Ames Department Stores effectively summarizes our discussion of this point:

Debt:

Debt obligations that carried face interest rates significantly less than market were discounted to their present values using estimated market rates. The discount amount will be amortized to interest expense over the term of the related obligation. The determination of appropriate interest rates was based upon evaluation of Ames' credit standing, the nature of the collateral, if any, and other terms pertaining to the debt, and the prevailing rates for similar instruments or issues with similar credit rating.

REAL WORLD EXCERPT

AMES DEPARTMENT STORES
Annual Report

Bonds are recorded at the present value of their future cash flows using an interest rate determined by the market on the date the bonds were sold. The accounting for the bonds is not affected by subsequent changes in the market rate of interest. This interest rate is based on the terms of the debt issue and the risk characteristics of the debt.

Zero Coupon Bonds

Some bonds do not pay periodic cash interest. These bonds are often called *zero coupon bonds* because the coupon interest rate is zero. Why would an investor buy a bond that did not pay interest? Our discussion of bond discounts has probably given you a pretty good idea of the right answer. The coupon interest rate on a bond can be virtually any amount and the price of the bond will be adjusted so that investors earn the market rate of interest. A bond with a zero coupon interest rate is simply a *deep discount bond* that will sell for substantially less than its maturity value.

Let's use the $400,000 Showboat bond to illustrate a zero coupon. Assume that instead of paying 10 percent cash interest, the bond paid *no* cash interest. The selling price of the bond is the present value of the maturity amount because no other cash payments are made over the life of the bond:

	Present Value
a. Principal: $400,000 \times p_{n=20,\ i=6\%}$ (0.3118)	$124,720

This zero coupon bond is recorded as follows:

Cash (A)	124,720	
Discount on bond payable (XL)	275,280	
Bonds payable (L)		400,000

As you can see, the accounting for the zero coupon bond is no different than any bond sold at a discount. The only difference is that the amount of the discount is much larger. The annual report for General Mills contained the following information concerning zero coupon bonds:

9 Long-term Debt

In Millions	May 26, 1996	May 28, 1995
Medium-term notes, 5.2% to 9.1%, due 1996 to 2033	$ 978.1	$1,094.4
Zero coupon notes, yield 11.1%, $284.0 due August 15, 2013	44.5	43.1

The note from the General Mills annual report illustrates two important points concerning zero coupon bonds. Notice that the book value of the bonds increased between 1995 and 1996. This increase occurred because of the amortization of the bond discount. Also notice that despite the fact that these bonds do not pay cash interest, they have been priced to provide the investor with effective interest of 11.1 percent.

Bonds Issued at a Premium

Bonds sell at a bond premium when the market rate of interest is *lower* than the stated interest rate on the bonds. For example, let's assume that the market rate of interest was 8½ percent while the Showboat bonds paid cash interest of 10 percent. In this case, the bonds sell at a premium. The cash issue price for the Showboat bonds when the market rate of interest was 8½ percent is computed as follows:

	Present Value
a. Principal: $400,000 × $p_{n=20, \, i=4^1/_4\%}$ (0.4350)	$174,000
b. Interest: $20,000 × $P_{n=20, \, i=4^1/_4\%}$ (13.2944)	265,888
Issue (sale) price of Showboat bonds	$439,888

When a bond is sold at a premium, the Bonds Payable account is credited for the par amount, and the premium is recorded as a credit to Premium on Bonds Payable. The issuance of the bonds of Showboat at a premium is recorded as follows:

Jan. 1, 19A	Cash (A)	439,888	
	Premium on bonds payable (L)		39,888
	Bonds payable (L)		400,000

The book value of the bond is the sum of the two accounts, Premium on Bonds Payable and Bonds Payable, or $439,888.

Measuring and Recording Interest Expense on Bonds Issued at a Premium

The premium of $39,888 recorded by Showboat must be apportioned to each of the 20 interest periods. Using the straight-line method, the amortization of premium each semiannual interest period is $39,888 ÷ 20 periods = $1,994. This amount is subtracted from the cash interest payment ($20,000) to calculate interest expense ($18,006). Therefore, amortization of the bond premium decreases interest expense. The payment of interest on the bonds is recorded as follows:

June 30, 19A	Bond interest expense (E)	18,006	
	Premium on bonds payable (L)	1,994	
	Cash (A)		20,000

Bonds are traded in public markets where prices can change on a minute-by-minute basis.

Notice that the $20,000 cash paid each period includes $18,006 interest expense and $1,994 premium amortization. Thus, the cash payment to the investors includes the current interest they have earned plus a return of part of the premium they paid when they bought the bonds.

The book value of the bonds is the amount in the Bonds Payable account plus any unamortized premium. On June 30, 19A, the book value of the bonds is $437,894 ($400,000 + $39,888 − $1,994).

At maturity date, after the last interest payment, the $39,888 bond premium is fully amortized, and the maturity amount of the bonds and the book value of the bonds is the same (i.e., $400,000). At maturity, December 31, 19J, the bonds are paid off in full, resulting in the same entry whether the bond was originally sold at par, a discount, or a premium.

The effect of the amortization of bond discount and bond premium on a $1,000 bond is illustrated in Exhibit 10.2.

EXHIBIT 10.2
Amortization of Bond Discount and Premium Compared

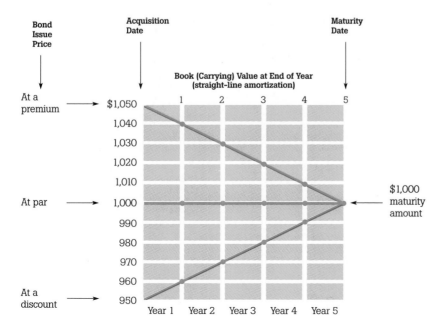

Assume that Showboat issued $100,000 bonds that will mature in 10 years. The bonds pay interest twice each year at an annual rate of 9 percent. They were sold when the market rate was 8 percent. Determine the bonds' selling price.

Check your answer with the footnote at the bottom of this page.*

FOCUS ON CASH FLOWS

The Statement of Cash Flows (SCF) reports cash flows from three types of activities: operating activities, financing activities, and investing activities. As you have seen in this chapter, Showboat raised a large amount of cash required for expansion by issuing bonds. The sale of these bonds is reported on the SCF as a financing activity. Exhibit 10.3 shows the financing activities section of Showboat's SCF.

Notice that interest payments on the bonds are not listed in this section of the SCF. Interest payments are directly related to earning income and are therefore reported in the operating activities section of the SCF.

Bonds Issued at a Variable Interest Rate

We have discussed a number of risks associated with bonds and need to consider one more. You already have observed the impact of inflation on our economy. You may have saved up for a major purchase only to find that the item's price had increased by

EXHIBIT 10.3
Financing Activities on the SCF

SHOWBOAT, INC. AND SUBSIDIARIES
CONSOLIDATED STATEMENTS OF CASH FLOWS
Years ended December 31, 1995, 1994 and 1993
(continued)

	1995	1994	1993
	(In thousands)		
Cash flows from financing activities:			
Principal payments of long-term debt	$ (20)	$ (3,575)	$ (3,914)
Proceeds from issuance of long-term debt	–	120,000	275,000
Early extinguishment of debt	–	–	(208,085)
Debt issuance costs	(542)	(4,474)	(7,593)
Payment of dividends	(1,543)	(1,509)	(1,400)
Distribution to bond holders	–	(5,195)	–
Issuance of common stock	4,604	530	2,510

* $ 4,500 × 13.5903 = $ 61,156
  100,000 × 0.4564 =   45,640
                        $106,796

the time you were ready to buy it. *Inflation,* which is defined as a general rise in prices in an economy, has a powerful impact on long-term borrowing arrangements. If you lend money during a period of inflation, you will get back dollars that have less purchasing power. When people lend money, they want to be compensated both for giving up the use of their money and for any decline in the purchasing power of the dollar caused by inflation. Interest on debt has to compensate creditors for both factors. Unfortunately, it is impossible to estimate future inflation accurately. Most bonds are issued with a fixed interest rate for the life of the bond. If unexpected inflation occurs, creditors will not be adequately compensated for the declining purchasing power of the money they lent to borrowers. To compensate creditors for the effect of unexpected inflation, some debt is issued with a variable interest rate. The indenture for debt with a variable interest rate specifies an agreed upon index, such as the prime rate. When the prime rate changes, the interest rate on the debt changes. If interest rates increase, a borrower pays higher interest each period and reports higher interest expense. When rates fall, the borrower pays lower interest and reports lower expense.

International Financial Markets

International PERSPECTIVE

In Chapter 9, we saw that some companies borrow money in international markets, an act that may expose them to exchange rate risk. Because of the importance of international markets, U.S. institutions no longer dominate borrowing arrangements. Consider the following note from the Showboat annual report:

LONG-TERM DEBT
On August 4, 1995, the Company obtained a two year term loan for general working capital purposes totaling $25.0 million. Interest is payable monthly at LIBOR plus 2.5%.

REAL WORLD EXCERPT
SHOWBOAT, INC.
Annual Report

Notice that this is a variable rate debt. Although the borrowing arrangement involved two domestic institutions, the agreement specifies an international index for determining future interest rate changes. LIBOR is an abbreviation for the London Interbank Offer Rate, which is the interest rate that international banks charge each other for overnight loans. It has become a widely accepted benchmark for determining adjustable interest rates for both corporate and government borrowers.

Additional Topics in Accounting for Bonds Payable

In the following sections, we discuss four topics commonly encountered in accounting for bonds payable: (1) effective-interest amortization of bond discounts and premiums, (2) bonds sold between interest dates, (3) early retirement of debt, and (4) bond sinking funds.

LEARNING OBJECTIVE 6
Use the effective-interest method of amortization.

Effective-Interest Amortization of Bond Discounts and Premiums

We introduced you to the straight-line method for amortizing a bond discount or premium earlier in this chapter. The only advantage of the straight-line method is the simplicity of its calculation. Under GAAP, the straight-line method may be used only if the reported results are not materially different from the effective-interest method. The **effective-interest method** is a conceptually superior method to amortize a bond discount or premium. We believe it provides a better basis for understanding why the amortization of a bond discount or premium is an adjustment to interest expense.

The **effective-interest method** amortizes a bond discount or premium on the basis of the effective-interest rate; theoretically preferred method.

Interest expense is the cost of borrowing money and is correctly measured by multiplying the *true* interest rate times the amount of money that was actually borrowed. The true interest rate is the rate that the market used to determine the present value of the bond. The actual amount borrowed is the cash that was received when the bond was sold, not the maturity value of the bond.

Under the effective-interest method, interest expense for a bond is computed by multiplying the current unpaid balance (i.e., the amount that was actually borrowed) times the market rate of interest that existed on the date the bonds were sold. The periodic amortization of a bond premium or discount is then calculated as the difference between interest expense and the amount of cash paid or accrued.

Earlier in this chapter, we illustrated accounting for bonds issued at a discount. Let's expand that example to see how the discount is amortized under the effective-interest method. The previous example involved 10 percent Showboat bonds with a par value of $400,000 that were issued when the market rate was 12 percent. The issue price of the bonds was $354,118, and the bond discount was $45,882.

The first interest payment on the Showboat bonds is on June 30, 19A. The journal entry to record interest expense is basically the same as the one shown earlier in this chapter under the straight-line method. The only difference is the amount. The interest expense at the end of the first six months is calculated by multiplying the amount that was actually borrowed by the market rate of interest for six months ($354,118 \times 12\% \times 6/12 = \$21,247$). The amount of cash that is paid is calculated by multiplying the principal by the stated rate of interest for six months ($400,000 \times 10\% \times 6/12 = \$20,000$). The difference between the interest expense and the cash paid (or accrued) is the amount of discount that has been amortized ($21,247 - \$20,000 = \$1,247$).

The amortization of the bond discount reduces the balance of the Discount on Bonds Payable account. A reduction of a contra liability account increases the book value of the liability, as shown:

	January 1, 19A	June 30, 19A
Bonds payable	$400,000	$400,000
Discount on bonds payable	45,882	44,635*
Book value	$354,118	$355,365

*$45,882 – $1,247 = $44,635.

Each period, the amortization of the bond discount increases the bond's book value (or unpaid balance). The $1,247 amortization of bond discount can be thought of as interest that was earned by the bondholders but not paid to them. During the first six months of 19A, the bondholders earned interest of $21,247 but received only $20,000 in cash. The additional $1,247 was added to the principal of the bond and will be paid when the bond matures.

Interest expense for the second six months of 19A must reflect the change in the unpaid balance of bonds payable that occurred with the amortization of the bond discount. The interest expense for the second half of 19A is calculated by multiplying the unpaid balance on June 30, 19A, by the market rate of interest for six months ($355,365 × 12% × $^6/_{12}$ = $21,322). The amortization of the bond discount in the second period is $1,322.

Notice that interest expense for the second half of 19A is more than the amount for the first six months of 19A. This is logical because Showboat effectively borrowed more money during the second half of the year (i.e., the $1,247 unpaid interest). Interest expense will increase each year during the life of the bond because of the amortization of the bond discount.

An example that demonstrates both a bond premium and an adjusting entry to record accrued interest under the effective-interest amortization method is provided in the demonstration case at the end of this chapter.

Some companies use a bond amortization schedule to assist them with the detailed computations required under the effective-interest amortization method. A typical schedule follows:

Date	(a) Cash Interest	(b) Interest Expense	(c) Amortization	(d) Unpaid Balance
1/1/19A				$354,118
6/30/19A	$20,000	$21,247	$1,247	355,365
12/31/19A	20,000	21,322	1,322	356,687

Interest expense (column b) is computed by multiplying the market rate of interest by the unpaid balance at the beginning of the period (column d). Amortization is computed by subtracting cash interest (column a) from interest expense (column b). The unpaid balance (column d) is computed by adding amortization (column c) to the unpaid balance at the beginning of the period.

Understanding Alternative Amortization Methods

Financial ANALYSIS

Although the effective-interest method is preferred conceptually, some companies use the straight-line method because of the materiality constraint. Accounting for various transactions should conform with generally accepted accounting principles (GAAP) unless the amounts involved are immaterial and will not affect the decisions made by users of the statements. The straight-line method is permitted when the difference in periodic amortization between the two methods is not material in amount. Because differences are immaterial, most financial statements do not disclose which method the company uses. An exception is Showboat, which indicates the following in its notes:

Summary of Significant Accounting Policies
Original issue discount is amortized over the life of the related indebtedness using the effective interest method.

REAL WORLD EXCERPT
SHOWBOAT, INC.
Annual Report

Compare the note for Showboat to one from Kansas City Southern Industries:

Note 5: Debt

Debt was issued at a discount of $1.6 million which will be amortized over the respective debt maturities on a straight line basis which is not materially different from the interest method.

Notice that in both cases, the analysts cannot quantify the impact of using one method versus the other. As a result, most analysts are not concerned about which method a company chooses.

Bonds Sold between Interest Dates

For the sake of illustration, we have assumed that bonds were sold on the first day of an interest period. In practice, bonds are sold at a variety of dates during the interest period. Bonds that are sold between interest dates sell for their market value *plus* any interest that has accrued on them since the last interest payment.

From our previous example, if Showboat sold $400,000 worth of 10 percent bonds at par on April 1 instead of January 1, the investor must pay accrued interest (remember the bonds paid interest on June 30 and December 31). The amount of interest is computed as follows:

Accrued Interest	=	Face Value	×	Coupon Rate	×	Time
$10,000	=	$400,000	×	10%	×	3/12

To record the issuance of the bonds, Showboat records the following:

Cash (A)	410,000	
Bonds payable (L)		400,000
Interest payable (L)		10,000

When the interest is paid on June 30, 19A, Showboat makes the following entry:

Interest expense (E)	10,000	
Interest payable (L)	10,000	
Cash (A)		20,000

By accounting for interest in this way, the interest expense is properly measured (i.e., Showboat records interest expense for only the three months that it actually borrowed money). This method also avoids the complication of preparing numerous different interest checks for different investors if the bonds had been sold to multiple investors at different times.

Early Retirement of Debt

LEARNING OBJECTIVE 7
Report the early retirement of bonds.

Bonds are normally issued for long periods of time, such as 20 or 30 years. As mentioned earlier in the chapter, bondholders who need cash prior to the maturity date can simply sell the bonds to another investor. This transaction does not affect the books of the company that issued the bonds.

In several situations, a corporation decides to retire a bond before its maturity date. A bond with a *call feature* may be called in for early retirement at the issuer's option. Typically, the bond indenture includes a call premium if the bonds are retired before the maturity date. This call premium often is stated as a percentage of the par value of the bonds. The prospectus for Showboat's bonds included the following:

The bonds will be subject to redemption at the option of the Company, in whole or in part . . . at the redemption prices set forth below plus accrued and unpaid interest thereon:

Year	Percentage
2000	102.775%
2001	101.850%
2002	100.925%
2003 and thereafter	100.000%

REAL WORLD EXCERPT

SHOWBOAT, INC.
Bond Prospectus

Assume that in 1994, Showboat issued 10 percent bonds in the amount of $1 million and that the bonds sold at par. If the bonds were called in 2001 with 90 days of accrued interest, Showboat makes the following journal entry:

Bonds payable (L)	1,000,000	
Interest expense (E)	25,000*	
Loss on bond call (Loss)	18,500	
Cash (A)		1,043,500

*$1,000,000 × 10% × 90/360 = $25,000

The loss on bond call is the amount over par that must be paid according to the bond indenture. This amount is 1.850 percent (101.850% − 100.000%), which is multiplied by the par value of the bond to derive the expense of $18,500 (1.850% × $1,000,000). The loss on bond call is reported on the income statement as an extraordinary item.

Southwestern Bell recently engaged in a transaction similar to the one just illustrated; it included the following description in the notes to its statements:

The Telephone Company reflected an extraordinary loss on the early extinguishment of debt as the result of refinancing $732,000,000 of long-term bonds. Expense associated with the refinancing, including a call premium of $67,500,000, totaled $129,300,000.

REAL WORLD EXCERPT

SOUTHWESTERN BELL
Annual Report

In other cases, a company may elect to retire debt early by purchasing it in the open market, just as an investor would. This approach is necessary if the bond did not have a call feature. It might also be an attractive approach if the price of the bonds fell after the date of issue.

What factors could cause the price of a bond to fall? The most common cause is a rise in interest rates. As you may have noticed during our discussion of present value concepts earlier in this chapter, bond prices move in the opposite direction of interest rates. If interest rates go up, bond prices fall, and vice versa. When interest rates have gone up, a company that wants to retire a bond before maturity may find that it is less expensive to buy the bond in the market than to pay a call premium.

Showboat, Inc., engaged in this type of transaction as described in the notes to its statement:

In the current and previous years, the Company purchased $12,096,000 and $18,460,000 face value, respectively, of the 11⅜% Mortgage-Backed Bonds Due 2002 for $11,696,000 and $12,258,000, respectively. Accordingly, the Company realized an extraordinary gain in the current year of $273,000 before income taxes of $93,000, resulting in an after-tax gain of $180,000 or $.02 per share. In the previous year, the Company realized an extraordinary gain of $6,015,000 before income taxes of $2,045,000, resulting in an after-tax gain of $3,970,000 or $.35 per share.

REAL WORLD EXCERPT

SHOWBOAT, INC.
Annual Report

The note illustrates three important issues. The gain or loss on the early retirement of debt is always reported separately on the income statement as an extraordinary item. The gain from this transaction is taxable, which is an important cost for managers to consider. The amount of the gain from the early retirement of debt can be substantial. The $.35 per share gain mentioned in the Showboat note was more than 60 percent of the income reported in that year. Analysts must use caution when evaluating gains from debt retirement because these gains do not represent profits from the company's ongoing business activities.

Bond Sinking Funds

To reduce risk for bondholders, many bond indentures include the requirement that the company establish a **bond sinking fund,** which is a special cash fund to be used to meet the principal payment when the bond matures. This fund assures creditors that cash will be available for retirement of the bonds at their maturity date. Managers, on the other hand, prefer not to have a sinking fund requirement because it forces them to put cash in a special fund instead of investing it in productive assets related to the operations of the business.

Normally, cash contributions are made to the fund each year. The cash often is deposited with an independent trustee (a designated third party such as a bank or another financial institution). The trustee invests the cash and adds the earnings to the fund balance each year. Interest earned on a sinking fund is recorded as an increase in the fund balance (a debit) and as interest revenue (a credit). Thus, a bond sinking fund has the characteristics of a savings account. At the maturity date, the balance of the fund is used to pay the bondholders. Any excess cash is returned to the issuing corporation, or, in the case of a deficit, the issuer makes it up.

The purpose of a sinking fund is to reduce the risk that the issuer will not be able to meet the principal payment when bonds mature. As a result, many bond indentures permit the issuing corporation to meet sinking fund requirements either by making cash payments to a fund or by redeeming outstanding bonds. A note to a recent annual report for Harrow Industries illustrates a typical disclosure concerning sinking funds:

REAL WORLD EXCERPT
HARROW INDUSTRIES
Annual Report

> The debentures require annual sinking fund payments of $6,500,000 beginning April 15, 1995. Sinking fund payments may be deferred to the extent that debentures purchased on the open market are tendered for cancellation. The Company has repurchased debentures totalling $26,970,000 which are available for such purpose.

By repurchasing debentures, Harrow Industries is able to satisfy sinking fund requirements for nearly four years. As a result, it will not have to make deposits of $6.5 million for each of those years. This type of information is important to analysts who wish to project the future cash flows of a business.

A bond sinking fund normally is reported on the balance sheet as a noncurrent asset. This is done because the cash in the fund is not available for ongoing business activities or to pay current liabilities. It would be misleading for financial analysts to conclude that a bond sinking fund was part of a company's working capital.

Financial ANALYSIS

Understanding Notes to Financial Statements

As mentioned earlier, features are included in bond indentures to make the bond issue more attractive to potential creditors. The wide variety of features available can make some bond contracts quite complex. Fortunately, most of the features are based on the concepts that have been discussed in this chapter. As a result, you should be able to analyze most bonds issued by corporations. To illustrate, consider the following note from the Eastman Kodak annual report:

REAL WORLD EXCERPT

EASTMAN KODAK
Annual Report

Bond liabilities:

The zero coupon convertible subordinated debentures due in 2011 ($3,680 million face value, 6.75% yield to maturity) are convertible at the option of the holder at any time prior to maturity for the Company's common stock at a conversion rate of 5.622 shares per debenture. At the option of the holder, the debenture must be purchased by the Company at October 15, 2001 and 2006 at a price equal to the issue price plus amortized discount.

This note would be impossible to understand if you had not studied the chapter, but, as you can see, it includes many of the issues that we have discussed.

SELF-STUDY QUIZ

Which company has the higher level of risk associated with debt—a company that has a high debt-equity ratio and a high interest coverage ratio or a company with a low debt-equity ratio and a low interest coverage ratio?

Check your answer with the footnote at the bottom of this page.*

Long-Term Investments in Bonds

To this point, we have discussed bonds from the issuer's perspective. Let's change that perspective and consider bonds from the point of view of a corporation that purchases bonds from another corporation. The only reason to invest in bonds is to earn a return on funds because bonds do not permit the holder to exert influence over another company, as is the case with an investment in common stock. Corporate bonds are riskier than government securities and savings accounts. As a result, an investment in the bonds of another corporation permits an investing corporation to earn a higher rate of return.

LEARNING OBJECTIVE 9
Report bond investments held to maturity.

Bonds may be held for either short-term or long-term purposes. Short-term investments in bonds will be discussed with short-term investments in common stock in Chapter 11. In this chapter, we discuss accounting for long-term investments in bonds.

As was discussed earlier in this chapter, bonds have a fixed maturity date. This fixed maturity date offers important advantages to corporations that invest in bonds. Why would managers of a corporation invest in bonds of another corporation? A key responsibility for senior executives is cash flow management, both short term and long term. Just as a corporation must have cash on hand to meet its current obligations, it must plan to have cash available to meet its long-term needs, such as the maturity of debt or the replacement of productive assets. Bonds permit management of the investing corporation to plan future cash flows with a minimum of risk. Management that

---

* A company can be forced into bankruptcy if it does not meet its interest obligations to creditors. Many successful companies borrow very large amounts of money without creating unreasonable risk because they generate sufficient funds from normal operations to meet their obligations. Even a small amount of debt can be a problem if a company cannot generate funds to meet current interest obligations. Usually, the company with a high debt-to-equity ratio and a high interest coverage ratio is viewed as being less risky.

needs cash in five years can purchase bonds that mature in five years. Bonds will pay their face value on their maturity date, which permits the creditor to budget future cash flows effectively. Prior to maturity, a bond may sell for more or less than its face value, depending on interest rates in the market. If a bond must be sold prior to maturity, the amount of cash that will be available is uncertain. By holding bonds to maturity, a corporation can eliminate this uncertainty.

When management plans to hold a bond until its maturity, it is reported in an account appropriately called **Held-to-Maturity Investment.** Bonds should be listed as held-to-maturity securities if management has the intent and the ability to hold them until maturity. These bonds are listed at cost (adjusted for the amortization of any bond discount or premium), not at their fair market value. Cost is considered to be a more reasonable measure of value because, by definition, the bonds will be held to maturity, at which time they will be worth face value. Unrealized gains and losses on bonds will disappear as the bonds approach their maturity date. Therefore, it is misleading to record these gains and losses during the life of the bonds.

Showboat does not show any bond investments on its balance sheet. This probably is not surprising given the growth strategy the company adopted. Management currently wants to invest all available cash in new facilities instead of the bonds of other corporations.

Halliburton Corporation includes held-to-maturity securities on its balance sheet. Its notes to the statements indicate the following:

> A **held-to-maturity investment** is a long-term investment in bonds that management has the ability and intent to hold until maturity.

REAL WORLD EXCERPT

HALLIBURTON
CORPORATION
Annual Report

Note 1: Significant accounting policies.
Investments classified as held-to-maturity are measured at amortized cost. This classification is based on the company's intent and ability to hold these securities to full maturity.

The annual report for American Brands shows investments in stock and bonds of other corporations in excess of $5.8 billion. Its largest investment is the held-to-maturity classification (which includes only bonds). This portfolio is valued in excess of $4.5 billion or 78 percent of its total investments. Why does the American Brands investment strategy rely so heavily on bonds? The answer is related to the nature of its business. It owns an insurance subsidiary, Franklin Life. Actuaries can predict with great accuracy the life expectancy of various groups in our society. As a result, Franklin Life can forecast when it will have to pay life insurance benefits for its policyholders. Franklin would assume a large amount of risk if it invested all of its cash in the stock market. It might have difficulty in paying benefits if stock prices were severely depressed, as was the case with the stock market crash of 1987. By investing in bonds, Franklin Life can match the maturity date of bonds with the actuarially determined date that it must pay benefits. Through this matching process, Franklin substantially reduces the market risk of its investments.

Reporting Bond Investments Held to Maturity

At the date of purchase, a bond investment that management intends to hold to maturity is recorded in conformity with the *cost principle*. The purchase cost, including all incidental acquisition costs (such as transfer fees and broker commissions), is debited to the Held-to-Maturity account. This amount may be the same as the maturity amount (if acquired at par), less than the maturity amount (if acquired at a discount), or more than the maturity amount (if acquired at a premium). Usually the premium or discount on a bond investment is not recorded in a separate account as is done for bonds payable. The investment account shows the current book value.

When discussing a bond, many analysts refer to its price as a percentage of par. *The Wall Street Journal* might report, for example, that an Exxon bond with a par value of $1,000 is selling at 82.97, which means that it would cost $829.70 (82.97 percent of $1,000) to buy the bond. Bond prices traditionally are quoted as a percentage of par, but the determination of the price is based on the present value techniques discussed earlier in this chapter. The concepts underlying accounting for bond investments are the same as accounting for bond liabilities.

Bonds Purchased at Par

To illustrate accounting for bond investments, assume that on July 1, 19F, Showboat invested $100,000 in 10-year, 8 percent bonds purchased in the open market. The bonds were issued originally on July 1, 19A, and mature on June 30, 19K. The 8 percent interest is paid each June 30 and December 31. Showboat management plans to hold the bonds until maturity.

When bond investors accept a rate of interest on a bond investment that is the same as the stated rate of interest on the bonds, the bonds will sell at par (i.e., at 100). The journal entry to record the purchase of the bond follows:

Held-to-maturity investment (A)	100,000	
Cash (A)		100,000

If a bond investment was acquired at par, the book value remains constant over the life of the investment because no premium or discount must be amortized. In this situation, revenue earned from the investment each period is measured as the amount of cash interest collected (or accrued). The following journal entry records the receipt of interest on December 31:

Cash (A) ($100,000 × 8% × $6/12$)	4,000	
Interest revenue (R)		4,000

Bonds Purchased at a Discount

If bond investors demand a rate of interest that is higher than the stated rate, bonds sell at a *bond discount*. When a bond is purchased at a discount, the investor receives the periodic interest payments stated in the bond contract plus the maturity value, which is an amount higher than the initial cash invested. As a result, the investor earns a return that is higher than the stated rate.

To illustrate accounting for a bond issued at a discount, assume that on July 1, 19F, Showboat bought 8 percent bonds with a maturity value of $250,000 and paid $240,000 cash (the bonds sold at a discount). The bonds will mature in five years (in 19K); interest is paid each June 30 and December 31. Showboat management intends to hold the bonds until maturity.

The purchase of the bonds is recorded as follows:

Held-to-maturity investment (A)	240,000	
Cash (A)		240,000

Notice that the purchase cost is recorded in the investment account. It is not necessary to record the investment at par and establish a separate bond discount account; however, it is necessary to keep track of the bond discount and amortize it over the life of the bond.

The interest earned on the bonds purchased by Showboat will total more than the annual interest payments (8% × $250,000 × 5 years = $100,000). This is true because Showboat will receive $250,000 when the bonds mature but paid only $240,000 when it purchased them. This extra $10,000 is additional interest revenue.

Interest revenue is recorded on December 31 as follows:

Cash (A) ($250,000 × 8% × $^6/_{12}$)	10,000	
Held-to-maturity investment (A)	1,000	
Interest revenue (R)		11,000

The debit to the Held-to-Maturity Investment account represents amortization of the bond discount. The discount is amortized over the life of the bond; most companies use the straight-line amortization method for bond investments. The life of the bonds purchased by Showboat is five years or 10 interest periods because the bonds pay interest every six months. The bond discount is allocated with an equal amount to each period, $10,000 ÷ 10 periods, or $1,000. Interest revenue for the period is cash received (or accrued) plus the amortization of the bond discount. Some companies may use the effective-interest amortization method. The procedures are similar to the ones illustrated earlier in this chapter for bond liabilities.

When a bond is held to maturity, a portion of the bond discount is amortized each period. Through amortization of the discount, the balance of the investment account is increased each period so that the book value will be the same as the par amount on the maturity date. In the case of a bond premium, amortization reduces the balance of the investment account so that the book value will be the same as the par value on the maturity date.

In our example, the bonds purchased by Showboat mature on June 30, 19K. At that point, the bond discount will be fully amortized and Showboat will receive their maturity value. The following journal entry records the cash received upon maturity:

Cash (A)	250,000	
Held-to-maturity investment (A)		250,000

Accounting for bond investments when bonds are purchased at a premium is based on the same concepts as accounting for bonds purchased at a discount.

Epilogue

Showboat successfully sold $275 million of its 9¼ percent first mortgage bonds and continued its expansion efforts. Within a year, the company had new expansion opportunities and returned to the debt market to raise additional funds. Unfortunately, a restrictive debt covenant in the indenture for the 9¼ percent bonds discussed in this chapter made it difficult to sell new bonds. Showboat management had to contact all of the owners of the 9¼ percent bonds to ask them to agree to modify their bond indenture. The documents sent to the bondholders included the following incentive:

As compensation, Showboat will pay holders who consent to the proposed amendments a cash fee equal to .50% of the outstanding principal amount of the bonds held by each holder.

The bondholders agreed to modify the indenture, and Showboat was able to sell a new issue of bonds. The funds were used to develop a new gaming property in Sydney, Australia.

Demonstration Case

(Try to resolve the requirements before proceeding to the suggested solution that follows.)

To raise funds to build a new plant, Reed Company management issued bonds. The board of directors approved a bond indenture. Some provisions in the bond indenture specified on the bond certificates follow:

Par value of the bonds ($1,000 bonds) $600,000.

Date of bond issue—February 1, 19A; due in 10 years on January 31, 19K.

Interest—10 percent per annum, payable 5 percent on each July 31 and January 31.

All of the bonds were sold on February 1, 19A, at 102½. The annual accounting period for Reed Company ends on December 31.

Required:

1. How much cash did Reed Company receive from the sale of the bonds payable on February 1, 19A? Show computations.
2. What was the amount of premium on the bonds payable? Over how many months should it be amortized?
3. Compute the amount of amortization of premium per month and for each six-month interest period; use straight-line amortization. Round to the nearest dollar.
4. Give the journal entry on February 1, 19A, to record the sale and issuance of the bonds payable.
5. Give the journal entry for payment of interest and amortization of premium for the first interest payment on July 31, 19A.
6. Give the adjusting entry required on December 31, 19A, at the end of the accounting period.
7. Give the journal entry to record the second interest payment and the amortization of premium on January 31, 19B.
8. Show how bond interest expense and bonds payable are reported on the financial statements at December 31, 19A.

Suggested Solution

1. Sale price of the bonds: $600,000 × 102.5% = $615,000.
2. Premium on the bonds payable: $600,000 × 2.5% = $15,000.
   Months amortized: From date of sale, February 1, 19A, to maturity date, January 31, 19K = 120 months.
3. Premium amortization: $15,000 ÷ 120 months = $125 per month, or $750 each six-month interest period (straight line).
4. February 1, 19A (issuance date):

Cash (A)	615,000	
Premium on bonds payable (L)		15,000
Bonds payable (L)		600,000
To record sale of bonds payable at 102½.		

5. July 31, 19A (first interest payment date):

Bond interest expense (E) ($30,000 – $750)	29,250	
Premium on bonds payable (L)	750	
Cash (A) ($600,000 × 5%)		30,000
To record payment of semiannual interest.		

6. December 31, 19A (end of the accounting period):

Bond interest expense (E)	24,375	
Premium on bonds payable (L) ($125 × 5 months)	625	
Bond interest payable (L) ($600,000 × 10% × $^5/_{12}$)		25,000
Adjusting entry for five months' interest accrued plus		
amortization of premium, August 1 to December 31, 19A.		

7. January 31, 19B (second interest date):

Bond interest payable (L)	25,000	
Premium on bonds payable (L)	125	
Bond interest expense (E)	4,875	
Cash (A)		30,000
To record payment of semiannual interest.		

8. Interest expense reported on the 19A income statement should be for the period outstanding during the year (i.e., for 11 months, February 1 through December 31). Interest expense, per these entries, is $29,250 + $24,375 = $53,625; alternatively, ($600,000 × 10% × $^{11}/_{12}$ = $55,000) − ($125 × 11 months = $1,375) = $53,625.

Income statement for 19A:

Interest expense	$ 53,625
Balance sheet, December 31, 19A:	
Long-term liabilities:	
Bonds payable, 10% (due January 31, 19K)	600,000
Add unamortized premium*	13,625
	$613,625

*$15,000 − ($750 + $625) = $13,625.

Summary

This chapter discussed bonds payable that represent a primary way to obtain funds to acquire long-term assets and to expand a business. An important advantage of bonds payable is that the cost of borrowing the funds—interest expense—is deductible for income tax purposes, which reduces the interest cost to the business.

Bonds may be sold at their par amount, at a premium, or at a discount, depending on the stated interest rate on the bonds compared with the market rate of interest. In each case, bonds are recorded at the present value of their future cash flows. The price of a bond varies based on the relationship between the market rates and stated rates of interest. If the market rate is higher than the stated rate on the bond, the bonds will sell at a discount. Conversely, if the market rate is lower than the stated rate on the bond, the bonds will sell at a premium.

Discounts and premiums on bonds payable are adjustments to interest expense for the issuing company during the term of the bonds. Therefore, a discount or premium on bonds payable is amortized over the period outstanding from issue date to maturity date.

To ensure that funds are available to retire bonds payable at maturity, a company may set aside cash in advance by means of periodic contributions to a bond sinking fund. Such a fund is like a savings account. The bond sinking fund usually is administered by an independent trustee. Interest earned on the fund balance is added to the fund each period. At the bonds' maturity date, the fund is used to pay the bondholders. The fund is reported on the balance sheet under the caption Investments and Funds. Interest earned on the fund is reported on the income statement as Interest Revenue.

In this chapter and Chapter 9, we discussed accounting and business issues related to funds provided by creditors. In Chapter 11, we examine issues pertaining to funds provided by the owners of a business. We focus primarily on the corporate form, the most prominent type of business in this country.

Key Ratios

Debt-to-equity ratio measures the balance between debt and equity. Debt funds are viewed as being riskier than equity funds. The ratio is computed as follows (p. 523):

$$\text{Debt-to-equity} = \frac{\text{Total liabilities}}{\text{Owners' equity}}$$

Times interest earned ratio measures a company's ability to generate resources from current operations to meet its interest obligations. The computation of this ratio follows (p. 523):

$$\text{Times interest earned} = \frac{\text{Net income} + \text{Interest expense} + \text{Income tax expense}}{\text{Interest expense}}$$

Key Terms

Bond Certificate The bond document that each bondholder receives. *525*

Bond Discount The difference between selling price and par when a bond is sold for less than par. *527*

Bond Premium The difference between selling price and par when a bond is sold for more than par. *527*

Bond Principal The amount (a) payable at the maturity of the bond and (b) on which the periodic cash interest payments are computed. *524*

Bond Sinking Fund A cash fund accumulated for payment of a bond at maturity. *540*

Callable Bonds Bonds that may be called for early retirement at the option of the issuer. *526*

Convertible Bonds Bonds that may be converted to other securities of the issuer (usually common stock). *526*

Coupon Rate The stated rate of interest on bonds. *527*

Debenture An unsecured bond; no assets are specifically pledged to guarantee repayment. *524*

Effective-Interest Method Amortizes a bond discount or premium on the basis of the effective-interest rate; theoretically preferred method. *536*

Effective-Interest Rate Another name for the market rate of interest on a bond. *527*

Face Amount Another name for principal or the principal amount of a bond. *524*

Financial Leverage Use of borrowed funds to increase the rate of return on owners' equity; occurs when the interest rate on debt is lower than the earnings rate on total assets. *522*

Held-to-Maturity Investment A long-term investment in bonds that management has the ability and intent to hold until maturity. *542*

Indenture A bond contract that specifies the legal provisions of a bond issue. *524*

Market Interest Rate Current rate of interest on a debt when incurred; also called *yield* or *effective-interest rate.* *527*

Net Interest Cost Interest cost less any income tax savings associated with interest expense. *522*

Par Value Another name for bond principal or the maturity amount of a bond. *524*

Redeemable Bonds Bonds that may be turned in for early retirement at the option of the bondholder. *526*

Stated Rate The rate of cash interest per period specified in the bond contract. *524*

Straight-Line Amortization Simplified method of amortizing a bond discount or premium that allocates an equal dollar amount to each interest period. *530*

Trustee An independent party appointed to represent the bondholders. *526*

Yield Another name for the market rate of interest on a bond. *527*

Questions

1. What are the primary characteristics of a bond? For what purposes are bonds usually issued?
2. What is the difference between a bond indenture and a bond certificate?
3. Differentiate secured bonds from unsecured bonds.
4. Differentiate among callable, redeemable, and convertible bonds.
5. From the perspective of the issuer, what are some advantages of issuing bonds instead of issuing capital stock?
6. As the tax rate increases, the net cost of borrowing money decreases. Explain.
7. Explain financial leverage. Can it be negative?
8. At the date of issuance, bonds are recorded at their current cash equivalent amount. Explain.
9. What is the nature of the discount and premium on bonds payable? Explain.
10. What is the difference between the stated interest rate and the effective-interest rate on a bond?
11. Differentiate between the stated and effective rates of interest on a bond (a) sold at par, (b) sold at a discount, and (c) sold at a premium.
12. Why are bond discounts and premiums amortized over the outstanding life of the related bonds payable rather than the period from the date of the bonds to their maturity date?
13. What is the book value of a bond payable?
14. Why is the lender (i.e., the purchaser of a bond) charged for the accrued interest from the last interest date to the date of purchase of the bonds?
15. If a 10-year bond dated January 1, 19A, is sold on April 1, 19B, how many months are used as the period outstanding for amortizing any bond premium or discount?
16. What is a bond sinking fund? How should it be reported in the financial statements?
17. Explain the basic difference between straight-line amortization and effective-interest methods of amortizing bond discount or premium. Explain when each method should or may be used.
18. If management plans (and has the ability) to hold a common stock investment for the long term, should it be reported in the Held-to-Maturity account? Explain.

Exercises

E10–1 **Computing Issue Prices of Bonds for Three Cases and Recording Bond Issuances**

Thompson Corporation is planning to issue $100,000, five-year, 8 percent bonds. Interest is payable _semiannually_ each June 30 and December 31. All of the bonds will be sold on January 1, 19A; they mature on December 31, 19E.

Required:
1. Compute the issue (sale) price on January 1, 19A, for each of the following independent cases (show computations):
    a. **Case A:** Market (yield) rate, 8 percent.
    b. **Case B:** Market (yield) rate, 6 percent.
    c. **Case C:** Market (yield) rate, 10 percent.
2. Give the journal entry to record the issuance for each case.

E10–2 **Recording Bond Issue and First Interest Payment, with Discount, and Verifying Issue Price**

On January 1, 19A, Seton Corporation sold a $200,000, 8 percent bond issue (9 percent market rate). The bonds were dated January 1, 19A, pay interest each December 31, and mature 10 years from January 1, 19A.

Required:
1. Give the journal entry to record the issuance of the bonds.
2. Give the journal entry to record the interest payment on December 31, 19A. Assume straight-line amortization.
3. Show how the bond interest expense and the bonds payable should be reported on the December 31, 19A, annual financial statements.

E10–3 **Recording Bond Issue and First Interest Payment, with Premium, Showing Reporting, and Verifying the Issue Price**

Grocery Corporation sold a $250,000, 11 percent bond issue on January 1, 19A, at a market rate of 8 percent. The bonds were dated January 1, 19A, with interest to be paid each December 31; they mature 10 years from January 1, 19A.

Required:
1. Give the journal entry to record the issuance of the bonds.
2. Give the journal entry for the interest payment on December 31, 19A. Assume straight-line amortization.
3. Show how the bond interest expense and the bonds payable should be reported on the December 31, 19A, annual financial statements.

E10–4 **Analyzing Bond Issue Price and Stated Interest Rate: Entries for Issuance and Interest**

Northland Corporation had $400,000, 10-year coupon bonds outstanding on December 31, 19A (end of the accounting period). Interest is payable each December 31. The bonds were issued (sold) on January 1, 19A. The 19A annual financial statements showed the following:

Income statement	
Bond interest expense (straight-line amortization)	$ 33,200
Balance sheet	
Bonds payable (net liability)	389,200

Required (show computations):
1. What was the issue price of the bonds? Give the issuance entry.
2. What was the coupon rate on the bonds? Give the entry to record 19A interest.

E10–5 **Effective-Interest Amortization of a Bond Discount**

Eagle Corporation issued $10,000, 10 percent bonds dated April 1, 19A. The market rate of interest was 12 percent with interest paid each March 31. The bonds mature in three years on March 31, 19D. Eagle's accounting period ends each December 31.

S 10 < M 12
DISC

Required:
1. Give the journal entry to record the bond issuance on April 1, 19A.
2. Give the adjusting entry required on December 31, 19A. Use the effective-interest method of amortization.
3. Show how the bonds should be reported on the balance sheet at December 31, 19A.
4. Give the journal entry to record the first interest payment on March 31, 19B.

E10–6 Analyzing a Bond Amortization Schedule: Reporting Bonds Payable

Stein Corporation issued a $1,000 bond on January 1, 19A. The bond specified an interest rate of 9 percent payable at the end of each year. The bond matures at the end of 19C. It was sold at a market rate of 11 percent per year. The following schedule was completed:

	Cash	Interest	Amortization	Balance
January 1, 19A (issuance)				$ 951
End of year 19A	$90	$105	$15	966
End of year 19B	90	106	16	982
End of year 19C	90	108	18	1,000

Required:

1. What was the bond's issue price?
2. Did the bond sell at a discount or a premium? How much was the premium or discount?
3. What amount of cash was paid each year for bond interest?
4. What amount of interest expense should be shown each year on the income statement?
5. What amount(s) should be shown on the balance sheet for bonds payable at each year-end? (For year 19C, show the balance just before retirement of the bond.)
6. What method of amortization was used?
7. Show how the following amounts were computed for year 19B: (1) $90, (2) $106, (3) $16, and (4) $982.
8. Is the method of amortization that was used preferable? Explain why.

E10–7 Preparing a Debt Payment Schedule with Effective-Interest Method of Amortization: Entries

Shuttle Company issued a $10,000, three-year, 10 percent bond on January 1, 19A. The bond interest is paid each December 31. The bond was sold to yield 9 percent.

Required:

1. Complete a bond payment schedule. Use the effective-interest method.
2. Give the interest and amortization entries at the end of 19A, 19B, and 19C.

Apple Computer

E10–8 Understanding Why Debt Is Sold at a Discount

The annual report of Apple Computer, Inc., contained the following note:

Long-Term Debt

On February 10, 1994, the Company issued $300 million aggregate principal amount of its 6.5% unsecured notes. The notes were sold at 99.925% of par, for an effective yield of 6.51%. The notes pay interest semiannually and mature on February 15, 2004.

After reading this note, one student asked why Apple didn't simply sell the notes for an effective yield of 6.5 percent and avoid having to account for a very small discount over the next 10 years. How would you respond to the question?

Carnival Cruise Lines

E10–9 Explaining Bond Terminology

The balance sheet for Carnival Cruise Lines includes "zero coupon convertible subordinated notes." In your own words, explain the features of this debt. The balance sheet does not report a premium or a discount associated with this debt. Do you think it is recorded at par?

C10–3 Bonds and Present Value Concept

Times Company issued a $100,000 bond with a stated interest rate of 8 percent. When the bond was issued, the market rate was 6 percent. The bond matures in 10 years and pays interest on December 31 each year. The bond was issued on January 1, 19A.

Required:
1. Record the issuance of the bond on January 1, 19A.
2. Compute the present value of the difference between the interest paid each year ($8,000) and the interest demanded by the market ($100,000 × 6% = $6,000). Use the market rate of interest and the 10-year life of the bond in your present value computation. Compare this amount to the bond premium recorded in requirement (1). Explain.
3. Record the payment of interest during 19A, 19B, and 19C using the effective-interest method. Why does interest expense change each year?
4. What is the book value of the bond at the end of 19C?
5. Compute the present value of the Times Company bonds, assuming that they had a 7-year instead of 10-year life. Compare this amount to the book value computed in requirement (4). Explain.

C10–4 Financial Statement Analysis

Toys "R" Us

Refer to the financial statement of Toys "R" Us given in Appendix B at the end of this book.

Required:
1. What is the fair market value of the company's debt on February 1, 1997?
2. What is the current portion of long-term debt reported in the current year?
3. What amount of long-term debt matures in 1998?
4. The company reports debt denominated in Japanese yen and British pounds sterling. In your opinion, why didn't management borrow all the needed funds in dollars?

C10–5 Project: Analyzing Leverage

Find financial information on two companies. One company should be highly leveraged and the other should have a low amount of leverage. Write a brief memo to explain the following: (1) why you believe that one company is highly leveraged and the other is not and (2) why you believe that management of each company selected the degree of leverage that it did.

C10–6 Project: Analyzing a Bond Issue

Using library resources, identify a company that has issued a new bond during the previous year. Determine the reason that the company needed to raise additional funds. Based on available information, why do you think management elected to raise the fund by issuing a bond instead of borrowing money with a short-term bank loan or the issuance of new common stock?

C10–7 Project: Analyzing Risk and Return

As explained in the chapter, the use of financial leverage offers shareholders the opportunity to earn higher returns, but it also creates higher risk. Different individuals have different preferences for risk and return, so determining the optimal balance of risk and return is not an easy matter. To illustrate the problem, conduct the following exercise in a small group.

You are offered the opportunity to participate in one of the following lotteries that require an investment of $10,000:

1. There is a 100 percent probability that you will get back $10,500 at the end of one year.
2. There is a 50 percent probability that you will get back $10,000 at the end of one year and a 50 percent probability that you will get $12,000.

3. There is a 50 percent probability that you will get back $8,000 at the end of one year and a 50 percent probability that you will get $16,000.

Determine which of the three lotteries you prefer and then attempt to reach a group consensus as to which lottery the group will accept.

C10–8 Project: Analyzing Bond Price Changes

When this book was written, the 9¼ percent Showboat bonds discussed in this chapter were selling for 95. Explain what it means for a bond to sell at 95. Determine the current market price for these bonds. If it is different than 95, explain why. If the price is exactly 95, explain why the price has not changed.

C10–9 Focus on Cash Flows: Financing Activities

Look up Showboat's current financial statement and review the financing activities section of the Statement of Cash Flows. Write a brief explanation concerning each of the items reported in this section. What insights can you gain by reviewing this information?

C10–10 Project: International Financing

Find the financial statements for a company that has borrowed money in a currency other than the dollar. (*Hint:* look for companies with international operations.) Write a brief memo explaining why the company borrowed money in a foreign currency.

C10–11 Ethics Project

Many retired people invest a significant portion of their money in bonds of corporations because of their relatively low level of risk. During the 1980s, significant inflation caused some interest rates to rise to as high as 15 percent. Retired people who bought bonds that paid only 6 percent continued to earn at the lower rate. During the 1990s, inflation subsided and interest rates declined. Many corporations took advantage of call options on bonds and refinanced high interest rate debt with low interest rate debt. In your judgment, is it ethical for corporations to continue paying low interest rates when rates increase but to call bonds when rates decrease?

C10–12 Ethics Project

Assume that you are a portfolio manager for a large insurance company. The majority of the money you manage is from retired school teachers who depend on the income you earn on their investments. You have invested a significant amount of money in the bonds of a large corporation and have just received a call from the company's president explaining that it is unable to meet its current interest obligations because of deteriorating business operations related to increased international competition. The president has a recovery plan that will take at least two years. During that time, the company will not be able to pay interest on the bonds and the president admits that if the plan does not work, bondholders will probably lose more than half of their money. As a creditor, you can force the company into immediate bankruptcy and probably get back at least 90 percent of the bondholders' money. You also know that your decision will cause at least 10,000 people to lose their jobs if the company ceases operations. Given only these two options, what should you do?

C10–13 Team Project: Examining an Annual Report

As a group, select an industry to analyze. Each group member should acquire the annual report or 10-K for one publicly traded company in the industry, with each member selecting a different company. (Library files, the SEC EDGAR service at www.sec.gov, Compustat CD, or the company itself are good sources.) On an individual basis, each group member should then write a short report answering the following questions about his or her selected company.

1. Review the types of bonds issued by the company. Do you observe any unusual features?
2. Compute and analyze the debt equity and times interest earned ratios.
3. Review the Statement of Cash Flows. Has the company either issued or repaid money associated with a bond? If so, can you determine the reason?
4. Has the company issued bonds denominated in a foreign currency? Can you determine why?
5. Does the company hold any bond investments?
6. Were bonds issued at either a premium or a discount? If so, does the company use the straight-line or effective-interest amortization method?

Discuss any patterns across the companies that you as a group observe. Then, as a group, write a short report comparing and contrasting your companies using these attributes. Provide potential explanations for any differences discovered.

CHAPTER ELEVEN

Reporting and Interpreting Owners' Equity

Wal-Mart
FINANCING CORPORATE GROWTH BY SELLING STOCK

Wal-Mart is a real American success story. Today it operates more than 2,200 discount department stores, 255 Supercenters, 470 Sam's Clubs, and four hypermarkets. The company sells more than $96 billion worth of merchandise each year (which requires more than 850,000 truck trailers to ship) and employs more than 675,000 people. To put this size in perspective, each year Wal-Mart sells 2,550,000 bicycles, 227,592,400 clothes pins, and 1,851,000,000 coffee filters. Every two seconds, it sells a Barbie Doll.

The home office controls substantially all merchandise purchases. Approximately 77 percent of each Wal-Mart store's merchandise is shipped from one of the company's 22 distribution centers. Centralized buying is a key component of the company's strategy. The large volume of merchandise purchased by Wal-Mart permits it to negotiate aggressively with its vendors.

These cost savings permit the company to achieve its advertising slogan of "Everyday Low Price," which is critical to its large market share, rapid growth, and overall success.

Shares of Wal-Mart stock were first sold to the public in 1970 at a cost of $16.50 per share. If you had purchased one thousand shares of Wal-Mart stock in 1970 for $16,500, your investment would be worth $2,355,200 today!

Stock, like bonds, can provide many different features. Managers must identify the best mixture of features to attract investors.

■ ■ ■

Business Background

To some people, the words *corporation* and *business* are almost synonymous terms. You've probably heard friends refer to business careers as "the corporate world." Equating business and corporations is understandable because corporations are the dominant form of business organization in terms of volume of operations. If you were to write the names of 50 familiar companies on a piece of paper, all probably would be corporations.

The popularity of the corporate form can be attributed to a critical advantage that a corporation has over the sole proprietorship and the partnership: it is easy for individuals to participate in the ownership of corporations. This ease is related to three important factors. First, it is simple for people to become part owners by purchasing shares of stock in small amounts. You could buy a single share of Wal-Mart stock for about $35 and become one of the owners of this very successful company. Second, the corporate form facilitates the transfer of separate ownership interests because stock can be transferred easily to others by selling it on established markets such as the New York Stock Exchange. Third, corporations provide the stockholder with limited liability.[1]

The corporation is the only business form that the law recognizes as a separate entity. As a distinct entity, the corporation enjoys a continuous existence separate and apart from its owners. It may own assets, incur liabilities, expand and contract in size, sue others, be sued, and enter into contracts independently of the stockholder owners.

Many Americans own stock, either directly or indirectly through a mutual fund or pension program. Stock ownership offers the opportunity to earn higher returns than are available through deposits to bank accounts or investments in corporate bonds. Unfortunately, stock ownership also involves higher risk. The proper balance between risk and expected returns depends on the preferences of each individual.

Exhibit 11.1 includes consolidated statements of shareholders' equity for Wal-Mart as well as consolidated balance sheets. We use this exhibit to illustrate our discussion of stockholders' equity.

---

[1] In case of a corporation's insolvency, the creditors have recourse for their claims only to the corporation's assets. Thus, the stockholders stand to lose, as a maximum, only their equity in the corporation. In the case of a partnership or sole proprietorship, creditors have recourse to the owners' personal assets if the assets of the business are insufficient to meet its outstanding debts.

EXHIBIT 11.1
Consolidated Balance Sheets and Statements of Shareholders' Equity

REAL WORLD EXCERPT

WALL-MART STORES, INC.
Annual Report

CONSOLIDATED BALANCE SHEETS

(Amounts in millions) January 31,	1996	1995
Assets		
Current Assets:		
Cash and cash equivalents	$ 83	$ 45
Receivables	853	900
Inventories:		
At replacement cost	16,300	14,415
Less LIFO reserve	311	351
Inventories at LIFO cost	15,989	14,064
Prepaid expenses and other	406	329
Total Current Assets	17,331	15,338
Property, Plant, and Equipment, at Cost:		
Land	3,559	3,036
Buildings and improvements	11,290	8,973
Fixtures and equipment	5,665	4,768
Transportation equipment	336	313
	20,850	17,090
Less accumulated depreciation	3,752	2,782
Net property, plant, and equipment	17,098	14,308
Property under capital leases	2,476	2,147
Less accumulated amortization	680	581
Net property under capital leases	1,796	1,566
Other Assets and Deferred Charges	1,316	1,607
Total Assets	$37,541	$32,819
Liabilities and Shareholders' Equity		
Current Liabilities:		
Commercial paper	$ 2,458	$ 1,795
Accounts payable	6,442	5,907
Accrued liabilities	2,091	1,819
Accrued federal and state income taxes	123	365
Long-term debt due within one year	271	23
Obligations under capital leases due within one year	69	64
Total Current Liabilities	11,454	9,973
Long-Term Debt	8,508	7,871
Long-Term Obligations Under Capital Leases	2,092	1,838
Deferred Income Taxes and Other	731	411
Shareholders' Equity:		
Preferred stock ($.10 par value; 100 shares authorized, none issued)		
Common stock ($.10 par value; 5,500 shares authorized, 2,293 and 2,297 issued		
and outstanding in 1996 and 1995, respectively)	229	230
Capital in excess of par value	545	539
Retained earnings	14,394	12,213
Foreign currency translation adjustment	(412)	(256)
Total Shareholders' Equity	14,756	12,726
Total Liabilities and Shareholders' Equity	$37,541	$32,819

See accompanying notes.

(continued)

Ownership of a Corporation

When you invest in a corporation, you are known as a *stockholder* or *shareholder*. As a stockholder, you receive shares of capital stock (a stock certificate) that you can subsequently sell on established stock exchanges without affecting the corporation. The stock certificate states the name of the stockholder, date of purchase, type of stock, number of shares represented, and the characteristics of the stock. The back of the certificate has instructions and a form to be completed when the shares are sold or transferred to another party.

As an owner of common stock, you receive the following rights:

LEARNING OBJECTIVE 1

Describe the basic nature of a corporation.

EXHIBIT 11.1
Concluded

CONSOLIDATED STATEMENTS OF SHAREHOLDERS' EQUITY

(Amounts in millions except per share data)	Number of shares	Common stock	Capital in excess of par value	Retained earnings	Foreign currency translation adjustment	Total
Balance — January 31, 1993	2,300	$230	$527	$ 8,003	$ —	$ 8,760
Net income				2,333		2,333
Cash dividends ($.13 per share)				(299)		(299)
Other	(1)		9	(50)		(41)
Balance — January 31, 1994	2,299	230	536	9,987	—	10,753
Net income				2,681		2,681
Cash dividends ($.17 per share)				(391)		(391)
Foreign currency translation adjustment					(256)	(256)
Other	(2)		3	(64)		(61)
Balance — January 31, 1995	2,297	230	539	12,213	(256)	12,726
Net income				2,740		2,740
Cash dividends ($.20 per share)				(458)		(458)
Foreign currency translation adjustment					(156)	(156)
Other	(4)	(1)	6	(101)		(96)
Balance — January 31, 1996	2,293	$229	$545	$14,394	$(412)	$14,756

1. You may vote in the stockholders' meeting (or by proxy) on major issues concerning management of the corporation.[2]
2. You may participate proportionately with other stockholders in the distribution of the corporation's profits.
3. You may share proportionately with other stockholders in the distribution of corporate assets upon liquidation.

Owners, unlike creditors, are able to vote at the annual stockholders' meeting. The following Notice of Annual Meeting of Shareholders was recently sent to all owners of Wal-Mart stock:

Notice is hereby given that the annual meeting of shareholders of Wal-Mart Stores, Inc., a Delaware corporation, will be held May 27 at 10:00 A.M., in Fisher Theater in Detroit Michigan, for the following purposes:

(1) To elect directors.

(2) To consider and act upon a proposal to ratify the adoption by the Board of Directors of the Directors Deferred Compensation Plan.

(3) To transact other business as may properly come before the meeting or any adjournment thereof.

Only shareholders of record at the close of business on April 2, are entitled to notice of and to vote at the meeting.

The notice of the annual meeting contained several pages of information concerning deferred compensation plans and the people who were nominated to be members of the board of directors. Most owners do not actually attend the annual meeting. To

---

[2] A voting proxy is written authority given by a stockholder that gives another party the right to vote the stockholder's shares in the annual meeting of the stockholders. Typically, proxies are solicited by, and given to, the president of the corporation.

permit those people to vote, the notice included a proxy card, which is similar to an absentee ballot. Each owner may complete the proxy and mail it to the company. It will then be included in the votes at the annual meeting.

To protect everyone's rights, the creation and governance of corporations are tightly regulated by law. Corporations are created by making application to a specific state government (not the federal government). Each state has different laws that govern the organization of corporations created within their boundaries. Wal-Mart has its headquarters in Arkansas, but it elected to be incorporated in the state of Delaware. You will find that an unusually large number of corporations are incorporated in Delaware. The reason is simple: The state has some of the most favorable laws for establishing corporations.

To create a corporation, an application for a charter must be submitted to the appropriate state official. The application must specify the name of the corporation, the purpose (type of business), the types and amounts of capital stock authorized, and a minimum amount of capital that the owners must invest at the date of organization. Most states require a minimum of three stockholders when the corporation is formed. Upon approval of the application, the state issues a *charter,* sometimes called the *articles of incorporation*. The governing body of a corporation is the board of directors, which the stockholders elect.

Most corporations adopt organization structures similar to the one shown in Exhibit 11.2. The actual structure depends on the nature of the company's business. Wal-Mart has seven executive vice-presidents. One is responsible for each of the following areas: information systems, real estate and construction, finance and

EXHIBIT 11.2
Typical Organizational Structure of a Corporation

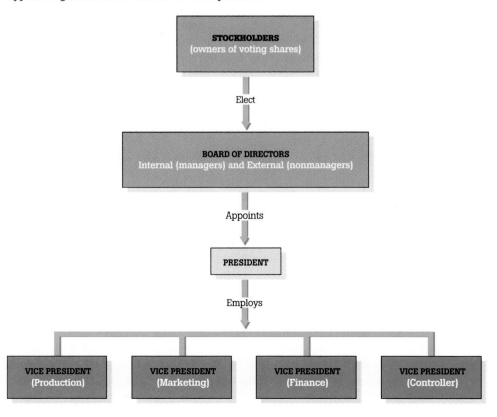

accounting, and each of the four operating divisions. This structure is unique to Wal-Mart because of the nature of its business. It might seem unusual to assign one of the most senior executives to real estate and construction, but this area is critical for Wal-Mart's strategy. Last year, for example, it opened more than 34.5 million square feet of new retail space.

Dividend Yield

One of the most important rights associated with the ownership of common stock is the right to receive dividends. Financial analysts normally compute two ratios when they compare dividends paid by different corporations.

The *dividend yield ratio* compares the dividends paid to the current price of the company's stock:

$$\text{Dividend yield ratio} = \frac{\text{Dividend per share}}{\text{Market price per share}}$$

Dividend yields for most stock are quite low, often in the range of 1–2 percent. The yield for Wal-Mart is actually less than 1 percent. You may wonder why someone would invest in a stock that pays less than 1 percent when bonds and other investments offer much higher yields. Remember that dividends are only part of the return available to stockholders. The other component of return is price appreciation. Most investors purchase common stock with the expectation that stock price will appreciate.

A second ratio used by analysts is called the *dividend payout ratio;* it measures the percentage of earnings paid as dividends:

$$\text{Dividend payout ratio} = \frac{\text{Dividends}}{\text{Earnings}}$$

The dividend payout ratio for Wal-Mart is about 16 percent of earnings. Companies that are growing rapidly pay a relatively small percent of their income, often less than 10 percent and, in some cases, zero. Compaq Computers, for example, pays no dividends and reinvests 100 percent of its earnings back into its operations. Companies in stable industries with little growth potential pay a much higher percentage, often more than 50 percent. Last year, American Brands paid 69 percent of its earnings in dividends to stockholders.

Authorized, Issued, and Outstanding Capital Stock

The authorized number of shares is the maximum number of shares of capital stock of a corporation that can be issued as specified in the charter.

Issued shares are the total number of shares of stock that have been issued.

Outstanding shares refer to the total number of shares of stock that are owned by stockholders on any particular date.

Unissued shares are authorized shares of a corporation's stock that never have been issued.

When a corporation is created, the corporate charter must specify the maximum number of shares of capital stock that it can sell to the public. This maximum is called the **authorized number of shares.** In the case of Wal-Mart, the number of authorized shares of common stock is 5,500,000,000 as shown in Exhibit 11.1. Typically, the corporate charter authorizes a larger number of shares than the corporation expects to issue initially. This strategy provides future flexibility for the issuance of additional shares without the need to amend the charter.

The number of **issued shares** and the number of **outstanding shares** are determined by the corporation's stock transactions. Authorized shares of stock that never have been sold to the public are called **unissued shares.** For Wal-Mart, the number of issued shares and of outstanding shares are the same; in 1996, this number was

2,293,000,000. The number of issued shares may differ from the number of outstanding shares if the company has bought back some of its shares from the owners. As you can see, Wal-Mart can issue more than 3,200,000,000 additional shares without exceeding the maximum authorized in its charter.

If a corporation needs to sell more shares than its charter authorizes, it must seek permission from the current stockholders to modify the charter. A few years ago, Greyhound Lines Inc. faced possible bankruptcy. The company worked out an agreement with creditors by which it would trade debt for stock, but the company did not have a sufficient number of unissued shares to complete the agreement. Management was forced to ask the stockholders to approve an increase in the number of shares authorized. As *Bloomberg Business News* reported, the vote was close:

> Greyhound President Craig Lentzsch said 9.9 million of the company's 14 million outstanding shares voted in favor of the plan. Greyhound needed 9.7 million for the plan to be approved. A total of 10 million shares were voted.

REAL WORLD EXCERPT
Bloomberg Business News

Exhibit 11.3 defines and illustrates the terms usually used in respect to corporate shares.

Types of Capital Stock

When people refer to *corporate stock*, they usually have in mind common stock, which all corporations must issue. Some corporations also issue preferred stock, which grants preferences that the common stock does not have. Notice in Exhibit 11.1 that Wal-Mart has authorized the issuance of preferred stock but has not issued any.

LEARNING OBJECTIVE 2
Compare and contrast the various types of capital stock.

EXHIBIT 11.3
Authorized, Issued, and Outstanding Shares

Definitions	Illustrations	
Authorized number of shares:		
The maximum number of shares that can be issued as specified in the charter of the corporation.	Charter specifies "authorized capital stock, 100,000 shares, par value $1 per share."	
Issued number of shares:		
The total cumulative number of shares that the corporation has issued to date.	To date, XYZ Corporation has sold and issued 30,000 shares of its capital stock.	
Unissued number of shares:		
The number of authorized shares that have never been issued to date.	Authorized shares	100,000
	Issued shares	30,000
	Unissued shares	70,000
Treasury stock:*		
Shares that have been issued to investors and then reacquired by the issuing corporation.	To date, XYZ Corporation has repurchased 1,000 shares of previously issued stock.	
Outstanding number of shares:		
The number of shares currently owned by stockholders; that is, the number of shares authorized minus the total number of unissued shares and minus the number of treasury shares.	Authorized shares	100,000
	Treasury stock	(1,000)
	Unissued shares	(70,000)
	Outstanding shares	29,000

*Treasury stock will be discussed later. Notice that when treasury stock is held, the number of shares issued and the number outstanding differ by the number of shares of treasury stock held (treasury stock is included in "issued" but not in "outstanding").

In Chapter 10, we mentioned that corporations issue many different types of bonds to appeal to the risk and return preferences of individual creditors. The same is true of stock. In this chapter, we introduce you to many features that are used to encourage investors to buy stock.

Common Stock

Common stock is the basic voting stock issued by a corporation. It is often called the *residual equity* because it ranks after the preferred stock for dividends and assets distributed upon liquidation of the corporation. The dividend rate for common stock is determined by the board of directors based on the company's profitability, unlike the dividend rate on preferred stock, which is fixed by contract. In the jargon of Wall Street, common stock has more "upside potential" than preferred stock and more "downside risk." This means that if the company is profitable, common stock dividends may grow to be more than preferred dividends and in fact, may increase each year (upside potential). When the company is not profitable, the board may cut or eliminate common stock dividends, but in most cases it cannot reduce preferred dividends. As a result, common stock dividends may be less than preferred stock dividends during troubled times (downside risk).

> **Common stock** is the basic, normal, voting stock issued by a corporation; called *residual equity* because it ranks after preferred stock for dividend and liquidation distributions.

The fact that common stock dividends may increase with increases in the company's profitability helps explain why investors can make money in the stock market. Basically, you can think of the price of a share of stock as the present value of all of its future dividends. If a company's profitability improves so that it can pay out higher dividends, the present value of its common stock increases. In this situation, you would not expect the value of the preferred stock to change significantly because preferred dividends are fixed.

Par Value and No-Par Value Stock

Par value is a nominal value per share established in the charter of the corporation. It has no relationship to the market value of the stock. Notice in Exhibit 11.1 that Wal-Mart common stock lists a par value of $0.10; the market value of the stock is several hundred times higher than its par value. Stock that is sold by the corporation to investors above par value is said to sell at a premium, whereas stock sold below par is said to sell at a discount. The initial sale of stock by the corporation to investors cannot be below par value.[3]

> **Par value** is the nominal value per share of capital stock specified in the charter; serves as the basis for legal capital.

Most states require stock to have a par value. This was originally to protect the creditors of a company, but the restriction has little importance today to financial analysts. The concept of par value was to protect creditors by specifying a permanent amount of capital that the owners could not withdraw as long as the corporation existed. Thus, owners could not withdraw all of their capital in anticipation of business failure and bankruptcy and leave creditors with an empty corporate shell. This permanent amount of capital is called **legal capital.**

> **Legal capital** is the permanent amount of capital, defined by state law, that must remain invested in the business; serves as a cushion for creditors.
>
> **No-par value stock** is capital stock that has no par value specified in the corporate charter.

Many states permit the issuance of **no-par value stock,** which does not have an amount per share specified in the charter. It may be issued at any price without a discount or premium. When a corporation issues no-par stock, the legal, or stated, capital is as defined by the state law.

---

[3] Our discussions concerning the sale of capital stock refer to the initial sale of the stock by the corporation rather than to later sales between investors. Because the sale of stock by a corporation at a discount no longer is legal in many states, no further discussion of it is included. The sale of stock among individuals is not recorded in the corporation's accounts.

Par Value and Legal Capital

Legal capital, which usually cannot be used as the basis for dividends, represents the amount of capital that must remain invested in the corporation until it is liquidated. The definition of legal capital varies among states, but it usually is viewed as the par value of the stock outstanding. In the case of no-par stock, legal capital is viewed as either the stated value set by the company or the amount for which the stock was sold originally.

In most situations, financial analysts do not include par value and legal capital in their review of a company. Although these concepts have important legal implications, they are usually of no analytical significance.

Preferred Stock

In addition to common stock, some corporations issue **preferred stock,** which is stock with certain special rights. Some investors have risk and return preferences that can best be met by combining some of the features of bonds with some of the features of common stock. Preferred stock is sometimes the right choice for these investors; it does not appeal to investors who want some control over the operations of the corporation because preferred stock usually does not convey voting rights. Indeed, this is one of the main reasons that some corporations issue preferred stock to raise equity capital. Preferred stock permits them to raise funds without diluting the common stockholders' control of the company.

Preferred stock is stock that has specified rights over common stock. *(more like debt — what is stated on certificate)*

Preferred stock may be no-par value, although typically it has a par value. Most preferred stock has a fixed dividend rate. For example, "6 percent preferred stock, par value $10 per share" pays an annual dividend of 6 percent of par, or $0.60 per share. If the preferred stock is no-par value, the preferred dividend is specified as $0.60 per share.

Generally, preferred stock is less risky than common stock because of the priority it receives on dividend payments and asset distributions. We will compare common stock dividends and preferred stock dividends later in this chapter.

The priority on distribution of assets for the preferred stock occurs if the corporation goes out of business. Preferred stock usually has a specified amount per share that must be paid to the preferred stockholders upon dissolution before any assets can be distributed to the common stockholders.

Special Features of Preferred Stock

Some corporations issue **convertible preferred stock,** which provides preferred stockholders the option to exchange their preferred shares for shares of common stock of the corporation. The terms of the conversion specify dates and a conversion ratio. The notes to the annual report for Chrysler contain typical information concerning convertible preferred stock:

Convertible preferred stock is preferred stock that is convertible to common stock at the option of the holder.

The annual dividend on convertible preferred stock is $46.25 per share. The convertible preferred stock is convertible at a rate of 27.78 shares of common stock for each share of convertible preferred, which is equivalent to a conversion price of $18.00 per share of common stock.

REAL WORLD EXCERPT
CHRYSLER CORPORATION
Annual Report

Some preferred stock is *callable.* At the option of the issuing corporation, holders of callable preferred stock can be required to return the shares to it for a specified amount of cash. The call price usually is higher than the par value. Creative Learning Products described its call feature in the following note to its annual report:

REAL WORLD EXCERPT

CREATIVE LEARNING
PRODUCTS
Annual Report

> The Company may, at its option, call all or a part of the preferred stock for redemption at $1.50 per share, plus all accrued but unpaid dividends.

Accounting for Capital Stock

LEARNING OBJECTIVE 3
Analyze transactions affecting capital stock.

Notice the stockholders' equity section of the balance sheet for Wal-Mart shown in Exhibit 11.1. Four different stockholder equity accounts are reported on the Wal-Mart balance sheet. These accounts represent the two primary sources of stockholders' equity:

1. *Contributed capital* from the sale of stock, which is the amount invested by stockholders through the purchase of shares of stock from the corporation. Contributed capital has two distinct components: (a) par or stated value derived from the sale of capital stock and (b) additional contributed capital in excess of par or stated value. This often is called *additional paid-in capital.* The contributed capital accounts for Wal-Mart are preferred stock, common stock, and capital in excess of par value.

2. *Retained earnings* generated by the profit-making activities of the company. This is the *cumulative* amount of net income earned since the organization of the corporation less the cumulative amount of dividends paid by the corporation since organization.

Most companies generate a significant part of their stockholders' equity from retained earnings rather than from capital raised through the sale of stock. In the case of Wal-Mart, retained earnings generated more than 90 percent of the total stockholders' equity.

Sale and Issuance of Capital Stock

Two names are applied to transactions involving the initial sale of a company's stock to the public. An *initial public offering,* or *IPO,* involves the very first sale of a company's stock to the public (i.e., when the company first "goes public"). A *seasoned new issue* is the subsequent sale of new stock to the public. As was the case with bonds (discussed in Chapter 10), most companies use an underwriter to assist in the sale of stock. The underwriter is usually an investment bank that acts as an intermediary between the corporation and the investors. The underwriter advises the corporation on matters concerning the sale and is directly involved in the sale of shares to the public.

Most sales of stock to the public are cash transactions. To illustrate accounting for an initial sale of stock, assume that Wal-Mart sold 100,000 shares of its $0.10 par value stock for $22 per share. The company records the following journal entry:

Cash (A) (100,000 × $22)	2,200,000	
Common stock (SE) (100,000 × $0.10)		10,000
Capital in excess of par value (SE)		2,190,000

The sale of common stock is reported on the balance sheet in the format shown in Exhibit 11.1.

Some corporations do not specify a par value for their stock. In these cases, depending on state law, common stock is recorded under one of the following two approaches:

1. The corporation must specify in its bylaws a stated value per share as legal capital. This stated value is used as a substitute for par value, and the sale of common stock is recorded in a manner similar to the previous journal entry.
2. The corporation must record the total proceeds received from each sale of no-par stock as legal capital. In this case, the total proceeds are recorded in the Common Stock account and there is no account called Capital in Excess of Par.

Secondary Markets

When a company sells stock to the public, the transaction is between the issuing corporation and the buyer. As a result, the company records the sale on its books in the manner shown earlier.

Subsequent transactions affecting the stock are between two investors and do not directly affect the corporation's accounting records. For example, if investor Jon Drago sold 1,000 shares of Wal-Mart stock to Jennifer Lea, Wal-Mart does not record a journal entry on its books. Mr. Drago received cash for the shares he sold, and Ms. Lea received stock for the cash she paid. Wal-Mart itself did not receive or pay anything because of the transaction.

Each business day, *The Wall Street Journal* reports the results of thousands of transactions between investors in the secondary markets. These markets include the New York Stock Exchange (NYSE), the American Stock Exchange (AMEX), and the over-the-counter (OTC) market.

Managers of corporations follow very closely the movements in the price of their company's stock. Stockholders expect to earn money on their investment because of dividends and increases in the price of the stock. In many instances, senior management has been replaced because of poor performance of the stock in the secondary markets. Although managers watch the stock price on a daily basis, it is important to remember that the transactions between investors do not directly affect the company's books (i.e., journal entries are not prepared to record the transactions).

Going Public

As noted, an initial public offering (IPO) is the first sale of stock to the public. Prior to that sale, the company was a private company. A company might want to go public for two common reasons. For it to grow and meet consumer demand, it must expand its productive capacity. The need for new capital may be beyond the capability of the private owners. By going public, the company can raise the funds needed to expand.

In some cases, the company may not need significant funds, but the current owners may want to create a market for its shares. Often selling shares of stock is difficult if the company is not listed on a major stock exchange. By going public, a company can increase the liquidity of its shares.

Initial public offerings often create a great deal of interest among investors. Some good opportunities are available to earn excellent returns by investing in growing companies. Substantial risk also is associated with many IPOs.

From private company to public company—Wal-Mart then and now.

Capital Stock Sold and Issued for Noncash Assets and/or Services   *(like trading)*

Small companies are playing an increasingly important role in the U.S. economy. They created a large percentage of the new jobs that have been created in the past decade. Many of today's corporate giants were small start-up companies just a few years ago. Companies such as Dell Computers, Microsoft, and Apple Computer began literally as basement operations in the homes of their founders.

One feature common to all start-up companies is a shortage of cash. Because these companies often cannot afford to pay cash for needed assets and services, they sometimes issue stock to people who can supply these assets and services. Indeed, many executives will join start-up companies for very low salaries because they also earn shares of stock. An executive who was given Netscape stock during its early days would be very wealthy today.

When a company issues stock to acquire assets or services, the acquired items are recorded at the *market value* of the stock issued at the date of the transaction in accordance with the *cost principle.* If the market value of the stock issued cannot be determined, the market value of the consideration received should be used.

To illustrate, assume that during its early years of operations, Wal-Mart was unable to pay cash for needed legal services. The company issued 10,000 shares of stock to the Rose law firm when the stock was selling for $15 per share. At that time, the company recorded the following journal entry:

Legal fees (E)	150,000	
Common stock (SE) (10,000 × $0.10)		1,000
Capital in excess of par value (SE)		149,000

Notice that the value of the legal services received is assumed to be the same as the value of the stock that was issued. This assumption is reasonable because two independent parties usually keep negotiating a deal until the value of what is given up equals the value of what is received.

Stock Options

One of the advantages of the corporate form is the possibility to separate management and ownership. This separation also can be a disadvantage, because some managers may not act in the owners' best interests. This problem can be overcome in a number of ways. Compensation packages can be developed to reward managers for meeting goals that are important to stockholders. Another strategy is to offer managers *stock options,* which permit them to buy stock at a fixed price. The holder of a stock option has an interest in a company's performance in the same manner as an owner.

The Wal-Mart annual report contains the following note:

REAL WORLD EXCERPT
WAL-MART STORES, INC.
Annual Report

> **Note 6 Stock Option Plans**
> At January 31, 1996, 75 million shares of common stock were reserved for issuance under stock option plans. The options granted under the stock option plans expire 10 years from the date of grant. Options may be exercised in seven annual installments.

The options issued by Wal-Mart specified that stock could be bought at the stock's current market price. Granting a stock option is a form of compensation even if the grant price and the current stock price are the same. If someone gives you a stock option, you could think of it as a risk-free investment. If you hold a stock option when the stock price declines, you have lost nothing. If the price of the stock increases, you can exercise your option for the low price and sell the stock for the high price.

Stock options are a widely used form of executive compensation. Most companies offer them with a grant price equal to the current market price of the stock (as is the case with Wal-Mart). Compensation expense is reported based on the fair value of the options at the date of grant. Fair value is determined by using a complex mathematical formula called an *option pricing model* that will be discussed in advanced accounting courses.

Treasury Stock

A corporation may want to purchase its own stock from existing stockholders for a number of strategic reasons. A common reason is the existence of an employee bonus plan that provides workers with shares of the company's stock as part of their compensation. Because of Securities and Exchange Commission regulations concerning newly issued shares, most companies find that it is less costly to give their employees shares of stock that were purchased from stockholders than to issue new shares.

Stock that was issued to stockholders and then subsequently *reacquired* and held by that corporation is called **treasury stock.** While this stock is held by the issuing corporation, it has no voting, dividend, or other stockholder rights.

Two alternative approaches generally are used to account for treasury stock—the cost method and the par value method. We limit our discussions to the cost method because it is more widely used. The par value method is discussed in most accounting texts at the intermediate level. The recording of the purchase of treasury stock is based on the cost of the shares that were purchased. Assume that Wal-Mart bought 100,000 shares of its stock in the open market when it was selling for $22 per share. Using the cost method, the company records the following journal entry:

Treasury stock (XSE) (100,000 × $22) 2,200,000
Cash (A) 2,200,000

LEARNING OBJECTIVE 4
Define and account for treasury stock.

Treasury stock is a corporation's own stock that had been issued but was subsequently reacquired and is still being held by that corporation.

Intuitively, many students expect the Treasury Stock account to be reported as an asset. Such is not the case because a company cannot create an asset by investing in itself. The Treasury Stock account is actually a *contra equity account*, which means that it is reported as a subtraction from the total stockholders' equity. This makes sense because treasury stock is stock that is no longer outstanding and, therefore, should not be included as part of stockholders' equity.

As the information in Exhibit 11.1 indicates, Wal-Mart does not report any treasury stock on its balance sheet. The company actually purchased treasury stock, but it uses a fairly unusual accounting alternative that treats the purchase of its own stock as a retirement of the stock. Under this alternative, the common stock account and paid-in capital accounts are reduced. If Wal-Mart had used the cost method, its stockholders' equity section would appear as follows (numbers in thousands, based on the previous example):

Wal-Mart Stores, Inc.
Shareholders' Equity (Summarized)

Common stock	$ 229,964,000	
Capital in excess of par	526,647,000	
Retained earnings	8,002,569,000	
Less: Treasury stock	(2,200,000)	
Total stockholders' equity		$8,756,980,000

If Wal-Mart eventually sells its treasury stock, it will not report an accounting profit or loss on the transaction even if it sells the stock for more or less than it paid. GAAP do not permit a corporation to report income or losses from investments in its own stock because transactions with the owners are not considered to be normal profit-making activities. Based on the previous example, assume that Wal-Mart sold 10,000 shares of treasury stock for $30 per share. Remember that the company had purchased the stock for $22 per share. Wal-Mart records the following entry:

Cash (A) (10,000 × $30)	300,000	
Treasury stock (XSE) (10,000 × $22)		220,000
Contributed capital from treasury stock transactions (SE)		80,000

If treasury stock were sold at a price below its purchase price (i.e., an economic loss), the Contributed Capital from Treasury Stock Transactions account would be debited for the amount of the loss. Retained Earnings would be debited for some or all of the amount of the economic losses only if there were an insufficient credit balance in the Contributed Capital account.

Neither the purchase nor sale of treasury stock affects the number of shares of stock that are issued or unissued. Treasury stock affects only the number of shares of outstanding stock. The basic difference between treasury stock and unissued stock is that treasury stock has been sold at least once.

SELF-STUDY QUIZ

1. Assume that Applied Technology Corporation issued 10,000 shares of its common stock, par value $2, for $150,000 cash. Prepare the journal entry to record this transaction.
2. Assume that Applied Technology purchased 5,000 shares of its stock in the open market for treasury stock when the stock was selling for $12 per share. Record this transaction using the cost method.

Check your answer with the one provided in the footnote at the bottom of this page.*

---

*1. Cash	150,000	
Common stock		20,000
Contributed capital in excess of par		130,000
2. Treasury stock	60,000	
Cash		60,000

Accounting for Cash Dividends

Dividends Defined

Investors buy common stock because they expect a return on their investment. This return can come in two forms: stock price appreciation and dividends to owners. Some investors prefer to buy stocks that pay little or no dividends. Companies that reinvest the majority of their earnings tend to increase their future earnings potential. By increasing their future earnings potential, these companies often experience increases in their stock price. Wealthy investors in high tax brackets prefer to receive their return on stock investments in the form of higher stock prices because capital gains may be taxed at a lower rate than dividend income.

LEARNING OBJECTIVE 5
Account for dividends on common and preferred stock.

Other investors, such as retired people, prefer to receive their return on an investment in the form of dividends because they need a steady income. These people often seek stock that will pay very high dividends. Many retired people hold utility stocks because they are usually conservative investments that pay high dividends.

The board of directors must approve (i.e., declare) dividends before they can be paid. A corporation does not have a legal obligation to pay dividends. Creditors can force a company into bankruptcy if it does not meet required interest payments on debt, but stockholders do not have a similar right if a corporation is unable to pay dividends.

Without a qualifier, the term *dividend* means a cash dividend. Dividends also can be paid in assets other than cash. Some corporations issue stock dividends, which are dividend distributions of the corporation's own stock. The most common type of dividend is a cash dividend.

Although a corporation does not have a legal obligation to pay a dividend, it creates a liability once the board formally declares one. An actual press release announcing a dividend declaration for Wal-Mart contained the following information:

> **DATELINE: BENTONVILLE, ARK., DECEMBER 6, 1996**
> The Board of Directors of Wal-Mart Stores, Inc. today declared a quarterly cash dividend on common stock of five-and-one-quarter cents ($0.0525) a share, payable January 17, 1997 to shareholders of record December 13, 1996.

REAL WORLD EXCERPT

WAL-MART STORES, INC.
Dividend Declaration

This declaration creates a liability. Immediately on December 6, Wal-Mart records the following journal entry to reflect the declaration of a cash dividend based on 2,293,000,000 shares outstanding ($0.0525 × 2,293,000,000 = $120,382,500):

December 6, 1996:	Retained earnings (SE) (or Dividends declared, which is closed to Retained earnings)	120,382,500	
	Dividends payable (L)		120,382,500

The subsequent payment of the liability on January 17, 1997, is recorded as follows:

January 17, 1997:	Dividends payable (L)	120,382,500	
	Cash (A)		120,382,500

Notice that the declaration and payment of a cash dividend have two impacts: they reduce assets (cash) and stockholders' equity (retained earnings) by the same amount. This observation helps us understand the two fundamental requirements for the payment of a cash dividend:

1. *Sufficient retained earnings.* The corporation must have accumulated a sufficient amount of retained earnings to cover the amount of the dividend. State incorporation laws usually place restrictions on cash dividends. For example, the state laws often limit cash dividends to the balance in the Retained Earnings account.

2. *Sufficient cash.* The corporation must have access to sufficient cash to pay the dividend and to meet the continuing operating needs of the business. The mere fact that the Retained Earnings account has a large credit does not mean that the board of directors can declare and pay a cash dividend. The cash generated in the past by earnings represented in the Retained Earnings account may have been expended to acquire inventory, buy operational assets, and pay liabilities. Consequently, no necessary relationship exists between the balance of retained earnings and the balance of cash on any particular date (simply, retained earnings is not cash).

Dividend Dates

Refer back to the earlier example of a dividend declaration by Wal-Mart. Notice that the declaration includes three important dates:

> The **declaration date** is the date on which the board of directors officially approves a dividend.
>
> The **record date** is the date on which the corporation prepares the list of current stockholders as shown on its records; dividends can be paid only to the stockholders who own stock on that date.
>
> The **payment date** is the date on which a cash dividend is paid to the stockholders of record.

1. **Declaration date—December 6, 1996.** This is the date on which the board of directors officially approved the dividend. As soon as it makes the declaration, it creates a dividend liability.

2. **Date of record—December 13, 1996.** This date follows the declaration date. It is the date on which the corporation prepares the list of current stockholders based on its stockholder records. The dividend is payable only to those names listed on the record date. No journal entry is made on this date.

3. **Date of payment—January 17, 1997.** This is the date on which the cash is disbursed to pay the dividend liability. It follows the date of record as specified in the dividend announcement.

For instructional purposes, the time lag between the date of declaration and the date of payment may be ignored because it does not pose any substantive issues. When all three dates fall in the same accounting period, a single entry on the date of payment may be made in practice for purely practical reasons.

Impact of Dividends on Stock Price

An additional date is important in understanding dividends but it has no accounting implications. The date two business days before the date of record is known as the *ex-dividend date*. This date is established by the stock exchanges to make certain that dividend checks are sent to the right people. If you buy stock before the ex-dividend date, you receive the dividend. If you buy the stock on the ex-dividend date or later, the previous owner receives the dividend.

If you follow the prices of some stock, you will notice that a stock's price often falls on the ex-dividend date. The reason is simple. On that date the stock is worth less because it no longer includes the right to receive the next dividend.

Dividends on Preferred Stock

Investors who purchase preferred stock give up certain advantages that are available to investors in common stock. Generally, preferred stockholders do not have the right to vote at the annual meeting, nor do they share in increased earnings if the company becomes more profitable. To compensate these investors, preferred stock offers some advantages not available to common stockholders. Perhaps the most important advantage is dividend preference. You will frequently encounter the following dividend preferences:

1. Current dividend preference.
2. Cumulative dividend preference.

Current Dividend Preference on Preferred Stock

Preferred stock always carries a **current dividend preference**. It requires that the current preferred dividend be paid before any dividends are paid on the common stock. When the current dividend preference has been met and no other preference is operative, dividends can be paid to the common stockholders.

Declared dividends must be allocated between the preferred and common stock. First, the preferences of the preferred stock must be met, and then the remainder of the total dividend can be allocated to the common stock. Exhibit 11.4, Case A, illustrates the allocation of the current dividend preference under three different assumptions concerning the total amount of dividends to be paid.

Cumulative Dividend Preference on Preferred Stock

Cumulative preferred stock has a **cumulative dividend preference** that states if all or a part of the specified current dividend is not paid in full, the unpaid amount becomes **dividends in arrears**. The amount of any cumulative preferred dividends in arrears must be paid before any common dividends can be paid. Of course, if the preferred stock is noncumulative, dividends never can be in arrears. Therefore, any dividends passed (i.e., not declared) are lost permanently by the preferred stockholders. Because preferred stockholders are not willing to accept this unfavorable feature, preferred stock is usually cumulative.

Dividends are never an actual liability until the board of directors declares them. Dividends in arrears are not reported on the balance sheet but are disclosed in the notes to the statements.

The allocation of dividends between cumulative preferred stock and common stock is illustrated in Exhibit 11.4, Case B, under four different assumptions concerning the total amount of dividends to be paid. Observe that the dividends in arrears are paid first, then the current dividend preference is paid, and, finally, the remainder is paid to the common stockholders.

Current dividend preference is the feature of preferred stock that grants priority on preferred dividends over common dividends.

— not a legal liab unless a cash dividend declared:

Cumulative dividend preference is the preferred stock feature that requires specified current dividends not paid in full to accumulate for every year in which they are not paid. These cumulative preferred dividends must be paid before any common dividends can be paid.

Dividends in arrears are dividends on cumulative preferred stock that have not been declared in prior years.

EXHIBIT 11.4
Dividends on Preferred Stock

Case A—Current dividend preference only
Preferred stock outstanding, 6%, par $20; 2,000 shares = $40,000 par.
Common stock outstanding, par $10; 5,000 shares = $50,000 par.
Allocation of dividends between preferred and common stock assuming current dividend preference only:

Assumptions	Total Dividends Paid	6% Preferred Stock (2,000 shares at $20 par = $40,000)*	Common Stock (5,000 shares at $10 Par = $50,000)
No. 1	$ 2,000	$2,000	0
No. 2	3,000	2,400	$ 600
No. 3	18,000	2,400	15,600

*Preferred dividend preference, $40,000 × 6% = $2,400, or 2,000 shares × $1.20.

(continued)

EXHIBIT 11.4
Concluded

Case B—Cumulative dividend preference

Preferred and common stock outstanding—same as in Case A. Dividends in arrears for the two preceding years.

Allocation of dividends between preferred and common stock assuming cumulative preference:

Assumptions (dividends in arrears, 2 years)	Total Dividends Paid	6% Preferred Stock (2,000 shares at $20 par = $40,000)*	Common Stock (5,000 shares at $10 Par = $50,000)
No. 1	$ 2,400	$2,400	0
No. 2	7,200	7,200	0
No. 3	8,000	7,200	$ 800
No. 4	30,000	7,200	22,800

*Current dividend preference, $40,000 × 6% = $2,400; dividends in arrears preference, $2,400 × 2 years = $4,800; and current dividend preference plus dividends in arrears = $7,200.

Impact of Dividends in Arrears

The existence of dividends in arrears is important information for analysts. This situation limits a company's ability to pay dividends to its common stockholders and has implications for the company's future cash flows. The following note from Lone Star Industries is typical if a company has dividends in arrears:

REAL WORLD EXCERPT

LONE STAR INDUSTRIES
Annual Report

The total of dividends in arrears on the $13.50 preferred stock at the end of the year was $11,670,000. The aggregate amount of such dividend must be paid before any dividends are paid on common stock.

Remember that various issues of preferred stock can offer different features. Most preferred stock has the cumulative dividend preference to provide stockholders with extra security. Companies can offer additional features to provide even more security. Many companies offer the feature described in the following note from Bally Manufacturing:

REAL WORLD EXCERPT

BALLY MANUFACTURING
Annual Report

The holders of preferred stock do not have voting rights except that the holders would have the right to elect two additional directors of Bally if dividends on the preferred stock are in arrears in an amount equal to at least six quarterly dividends.

By electing two members of the board of directors, preferred stockholders have specific individuals to represent their interests. Bally included this feature with their preferred stock to make it more attractive to potential stockholders.

Wal-Mart generates a very large amount of its cash flow from operating activities. In 1996, the amount of cash generated was more than $2.3 billion and in 1995, it was nearly $3 billion. With this ability to generate cash flow, Wal-Mart has not needed to issue new stock to finance its growth. Its Statement of Cash Flows (SCF) includes a section called *Cash Flows from Financing Activities* which reports on how the company has financed its operations. This section of the SCF for Wal-Mart follows:

FOCUS ON CASH FLOWS

Wal-Mart operates Sam's Club. Think about how the success of this division depends on new capital from stockholders.

Cash flows from financing activities:			
Increase (decrease) in commercial paper	660	220	(14)
Proceeds from issuance of long-term debt	1,004	1,250	3,108
Dividends paid	(458)	(391)	(299)
Payment of long-term debt	(126)	(37)	(19)
Payment of capital lease obligations	(81)	(70)	(437)
Other financing activities	(12)	(61)	(40)
Net cash provided by financing activities	987	911	2,299

REAL WORLD EXCERPT

WAL-MART STORES, INC.
Annual Report

As you can see, the primary financing activities involve debt, both commercial paper and long-term debt. Notice that dividends paid ($458 million) are shown as a financing activity. Dividends are classified in this manner because they represent payments to the suppliers of long-term capital. When owners purchase stock from a company, the cash payment is reported as an inflow in the financing activities section of the SCF. When the company pays dividends to these owners, it is reported as a cash outflow in the same section of the SCF.

SELF-STUDY QUIZ

Answer the following questions concerning dividends:

1. On which dividend date is a liability created?
2. A cash outflow occurs on which dividend date?
3. When are dividends in arrears reported on the balance sheet as a liability?
4. What are the two fundamental requirements for the payment of a dividend?

Check your response with the answers contained in the footnote at the bottom of the page.*

---

*1. Declaration date.
2. Date of payment.
3. Dividends are reported as a liability only after the date of declaration.
4. Dividends can be paid only if sufficient retained earnings and sufficient cash are both available.

Accounting for Stock Dividends and Stock Splits

Stock Dividends

Each year, hundreds of corporations issue stock dividends. A **stock dividend** is a distribution of additional shares of a corporation's own capital stock on a pro rata basis to its stockholders at no cost. Stock dividends usually consist of common stock issued to the holders of common stock. *Pro rata basis* means that each stockholder receives additional shares equal to the percentage of shares already held. A stockholder with 10 percent of the outstanding shares receives 10 percent of any additional shares issued as a stock dividend.

You should be careful as you read annual reports and the business press. The term *stock dividend* is sometimes ambiguous. A recent *Wall Street Journal* headline announced that a particular company had just declared a "stock dividend." A close reading of the article revealed that the company had declared a cash dividend on the stock. Just remember that a dividend paid in stock is a stock dividend and one paid in cash is a cash dividend.

The value of a stock dividend is the subject of much debate. In reality, a stock dividend has no economic value, as such. All stockholders receive a pro rata distribution of shares, which means that each owns exactly the same portion of the company both before and after the stock dividend. The value of an investment is determined by the percentage of the company that is owned, not the number of shares that are held. If you get change for a dollar, you do not have more wealth because you hold *four* quarters instead of only *one* dollar. Similarly, if you own 10 percent of a company, you do not have more wealth simply because the company declares a stock dividend and gives you (and all other stockholders) more shares of stock. At this point, you may still wonder why having extra shares of stock does not make an investor wealthier. The reason is simple: The stock market reacts immediately when a stock dividend is issued, and the stock price falls proportionally. If the stock price was $60 before a stock dividend, normally (in the absence of events affecting the company) the price falls to $30 if the number of shares is doubled. Thus, an investor could own 100 shares worth $6,000 before the stock dividend (100 × $60) and 200 shares worth $6,000 after the stock dividend (200 × $30).

In reality, the price of a stock does not fall exactly in proportion to the number of new shares that are issued. In some cases, the stock dividend makes the stock more attractive to new investors. Many investors prefer to buy stock in *round lots,* which are multiples of 100 shares. An investor with $10,000 might not buy a stock selling for $150 because she cannot afford to buy 100 shares. She might buy the stock, however, if the price is less than $100 as the result of a stock dividend. In other cases, stock dividends are associated with increases in cash dividends, which would be attractive to some investors. A recent press release announcing a stock dividend for Alcoa contained both of these elements:

The Board of Directors of Alcoa today declared a 100% stock dividend. The additional shares are being issued to encourage wider distribution of Alcoa stock.

The Board also approved an increase in the company's base quarterly dividend from 40 cents per share to 45 cents per share.

Stock dividends are very common for companies that grow rapidly. Wal-Mart has issued 10 stock dividends since it went public. Its last stock dividend was in January 1992, when the business press reported the following story:

> Wal-Mart Stores, Inc., the largest retailer in the United States, said yesterday that its board of directors had declared a stock dividend, its first since July 1990. The company will issue a 100 percent stock dividend February 25 to shareholders of record on February 2. Wal-Mart has 1,149,819,000 shares outstanding. The stock was the seventh-most-active stock on the New York Stock Exchange, with volume of nearly four million shares.

REAL WORLD EXCERPT
WAL-MART STORES, INC.

In Exhibit 11.1, notice that the statement of shareholders' equity does not mention the stock dividend. Financial analysts would have to consult statements that included the year 1992 to learn more about the stock dividend. The note from the 1992 annual report follows. In the note, Wal-Mart uses the term "two-for-one stock split." The Securities and Exchange Commission requires this terminology when a stock dividend is 25 percent or more of the outstanding shares.

> On January 22, 1992, The Company announced a two-for-one stock split which has been accounted for as a 100% stock dividend.

REAL WORLD EXCERPT
WAL-MART STORES, INC.
Annual Report

Stock dividends are classified as either large or small. A *large* stock dividend involves the distribution of additional shares that are more than 20–25 percent of the currently outstanding shares. A *small* stock dividend involves additional shares that are less than 20–25 percent of the outstanding shares. Because the Wal-Mart stock dividend was equal to 100 percent of the outstanding shares, it should be classified as a large dividend. The company makes the following entry to record a large stock dividend:

Retained earnings (SE) ($0.10 × 1,149,819,000)	114,981,900	
Common stock (SE)		114,981,900

Notice that this journal entry moves an amount from Retained Earnings to the company's permanent contributed capital. The stock dividend did *not* change total stockholders' equity—it changed only the balances of some of the accounts that constitute stockholders' equity. This process of transferring an amount from Retained Earnings to Contributed Capital often is called *capitalizing earnings* because it reduces ⟵ the amount of retained earnings available for future dividends.

important

The amount transferred from Retained Earnings to Contributed Capital was based on the par value of the shares issued as a stock dividend. Par value is used when the stock dividend is classified as large. In those cases when a stock dividend is small (i.e., less than 20–25 percent), the amount transferred should be the total market value of the shares issued.

Stock Splits

Stock splits are *not* dividends. They are similar to a stock dividend but are quite different in terms of their impact on the stockholders' equity accounts. In a **stock split,** the *total* number of authorized shares is increased by a specified amount, such as a 2-for-1 split. In this instance, each share held is called in, and two new shares are issued in its place. Typically, a stock split is accomplished by reducing the par or stated value per share of all authorized shares so that the total par value of all authorized shares is unchanged. If Wal-Mart executes a 2-for-1 stock split, it reduces the par value of its stock from $0.10 to $0.05 and it doubles the number of shares outstanding. In contrast to a stock dividend, a stock split does *not* result in a transfer of retained earnings to contributed capital. No transfer is needed because the reduction in the par value per share compensates for the increase in the number of shares.

A **stock split** is an increase in the total number of authorized shares by a specified ratio; does not decrease retained earnings.

In both a stock dividend and a stock split, the stockholder receives more shares of stock but does not disburse any additional assets to acquire the additional shares. A stock dividend requires a journal entry; a stock split does not require one. A stock split is disclosed in the notes to the financial statements.

The comparative effects of a stock dividend versus a stock split may be summarized as follows:

	Stockholders' Equity		
	Before	After a	
		100% Stock Dividend	Two-for-One Stock Split
Contributed capital			
Number of shares outstanding	30,000	60,000	60,000
Par value per share	$ 10	$ 10	$ 5
Total par value outstanding	300,000	600,000	300,000
Retained earnings	650,000	350,000	650,000
Total stockholders' equity	950,000	950,000	950,000

SELF-STUDY QUIZ

Barton Corporation issued 100,000 new shares of common stock (par value $10) in a stock dividend when the market value was $30 per share.

1.   Record this transaction assuming that it was a small stock dividend.
2.   Record this transaction assuming that it was a large stock dividend.
3.   What journal entry is required if the transaction is a stock split?

Check your response with the answer contained in the footnote at the bottom of this page.*

Retained Earnings

LEARNING OBJECTIVE 7
Measure and report retained earnings.

Retained earnings represents income that has been earned less dividends that have been paid out since the first day of operations for the company. In Exhibit 11.1, you can see the changes in the Wal-Mart retained earnings that took place during 1996 (amounts in thousands):

Balance—January 31, 1995	$12,213,000
Net income	2,740,000
Cash dividends	(458,000)
Other	(101,000)
Balance—January 31, 1996	$14,394,000

This represents a fairly typical statement of changes in retained earnings. Under rare circumstances, you may see a statement that includes an adjustment to the beginning balance of retained earnings. This adjustment is called a **prior period adjustment,**

A **prior period adjustment** is an amount debited or credited directly to retained earnings to correct an accounting error of a prior period.

---

*1. Retained earnings   3,000,000
          Common stock   1,000,000
          Contributed capital in excess of par   2,000,000
   2. Retained earnings   1,000,000
          Common stock   1,000,000
   3. No journal entry is required in the case of a stock split.

which is a correction of an accounting error that occurred in the financial statements of a prior period.

If an accounting error from a previous period is corrected by making an adjustment to the current income statement, net income for the current period is improperly measured. To avoid this problem, prior period adjustments are reported as an adjustment of the beginning balance of Retained Earnings because the incorrect amount of net income from the earlier year was closed to Retained Earnings in the year the error was made. Prior period adjustments are not reported on the current income statement.

An example of an accounting error that could result in a prior period adjustment was discussed in Chapter 7. Several years ago, the financial statements of Lafayette Radio Electronics Corporation contained the following note:

Subsequent to the issuance of its financial statements the company discovered a computational error in the amount of $1,046,000 in the calculation of its year-end inventory which resulted in an overstatement of ending inventory.

REAL WORLD EXCERPT
LAFAYETTE RADIO
ELECTRONICS CORPORATION
Annual Report

Lafayette Radio's overstatement of inventory resulted in an overstatement of pretax income by $1,046,000. If the company corrected the error in the year it was discovered, pretax income would have been understated by $1,046,000. The incorrect measurement of income for each year could mislead some users of financial statements.

Restrictions on Retained Earnings

As the result of several types of business transactions, restrictions may be placed on retained earnings to limit a company's ability to pay dividends to its owners. The most typical example occurs when a business borrows money from a bank. For additional security, some banks include a loan covenant that limits the amount of dividends that a corporation can pay by placing a restriction on its retained earnings.

The *full-disclosure principle* requires restrictions on retained earnings be reported in the financial statements or in a separate note to the financial statements. Analysts are particularly interested in information concerning these restrictions because of the impact they have on the company's dividend policy.

Most companies report restrictions on retained earnings in the notes to the statements. An example of such a note from the annual report of May Department Store follows:

Under the most restrictive covenants of long-term debt agreements, $1.2 billion of retained earnings was restricted as to the payment of dividends and/or common share repurchase.

REAL WORLD EXCERPT
MAY DEPARTMENT STORE
Annual Report

This type of note describes other restrictions that were imposed as the result of debt covenants. These restrictions often include a limit on borrowing and required minimum balances of cash or working capital. If debt covenants are violated, the creditor can demand immediate repayment of the debt. For this reason, analysts want to review these restrictions to be sure that companies are not close to violating loan agreements.

Accounting and Reporting for Unincorporated Businesses

LEARNING OBJECTIVE 8
Discuss the differences among corporations, proprietorships, and partnerships.

The three forms of business organizations are corporations, sole proprietorships (one owner), and partnerships (two or more owners). The fundamentals of accounting and reporting for unincorporated businesses are the same as for a corporation except for owners' equity. Typical account structures for the three forms of business organizations are outlined in Exhibit 11.5.

Accounting for sole proprietorships and partnerships is discussed in Chapter Supplement A.

Epilogue

In early 1995, Wal-Mart issued the following press release:

REAL WORLD EXCERPT

WAL-MART STORES, INC.
Press Release

> Wal-Mart Stores, Inc., the nation's largest retailer, said Wednesday that it will repurchase up to $100 million of its common stock from time to time on the open market. "We believe that the stock is an excellent long-term value," said David Glass, President and Chief Executive.

During the 18 months preceding this announcement, Wal-Mart stock had fallen in value by more than one-third. Clearly, investments in common stock offer the opportunity to earn significant returns. Unfortunately, losing large amounts of money is also possible when stock prices fall. In these situations, management often reacts quickly to attempt to create shareholder value. By late 1997, Wal-Mart's stock price increased by nearly 50 percent.

Demonstration Case

(Try to resolve the requirements before proceeding to the suggested solution that follows.)

This case focuses on the organization and operations for the first year of Shelly Corporation, which was organized on January 1, 19A. The laws of the state specify that the

EXHIBIT 11.5
Comparative Account Structures among Types of Business Entities

Typical Account Structure		
Corporation (Stockholders' Equity)	**Sole Proprietorship (Owner's Equity)**	**Partnership (Partners' Equity)**
Capital Stock Contributed Capital in Excess of Par	Doe, Capital	Able, Capital Baker, Capital
Retained Earnings	Not used	Not used
Dividends Paid	Doe, Drawings	Able, Drawings Baker, Drawings
Revenues, expenses, gains, and losses	Same	Same
Assets and liabilities	Same	Same

legal capital for no-par stock is the full sale amount. The corporation was organized by 10 local entrepreneurs for the purpose of operating a business to sell various supplies to hotels. The charter authorized the following capital stock:

Common stock, no-par value, 20,000 shares.

Preferred stock, 5 percent, $100 par value, 5,000 shares (cumulative, nonconvertible, and nonvoting; liquidation value, $110).

The following summarized transactions, selected from 19A, were completed on the dates indicated:

(a) Jan. Sold a total of 7,500 shares of no-par common stock to the 10 entrepreneurs for cash at $52 per share. Credit the No-par Common Stock account for the total issue amount.

(b) Feb. Sold 1,890 shares of preferred stock at $102 per share; cash collected in full.

(c) Mar. Purchased land for a store site and made full payment by issuing 100 shares of preferred stock. Early construction of the store is planned. Debit Land (store site). The preferred stock is selling at $102 per share.

(d) Apr. Paid $1,980 cash for organization costs. Debit the intangible asset account Organization Cost.

(e) May Issued 10 shares of preferred stock to A. B. Cain in full payment of legal services rendered in connection with organization of the corporation. Assume that the preferred stock is selling regularly at $102 per share. Debit Organization Cost.

(f) June Sold 500 shares of no-par common stock for cash to C. B. Abel at $54 per share.

(g) July Purchased 100 shares of preferred stock that had been sold and issued earlier. The stockholder was moving to another state and needed the money. Shelly Corporation paid the stockholder $104 per share.

(h) Aug. Sold 20 shares of the preferred treasury stock at $105 per share.

(i) Dec. 31 Purchased equipment for $600,000; paid cash. No depreciation expense should be recorded in 19A.

(j) Dec. 31 Borrowed $20,000 cash from the City Bank on a one-year, interest-bearing note. Interest is payable at a 12 percent rate at maturity.

(k) Dec. 31 Calculated the following for the year: gross revenues, $129,300; expenses, including corporation income tax but excluding amortization of organization costs, $98,000. Assume that these summarized revenue and expense transactions involved cash. Because the equipment and the bank loan transactions were on December 31, no related adjusting entries at the end of 19A are needed.

(l) Dec. 31 Decided that a reasonable amortization period for organization costs, starting as of January 1, 19A, is 10 years. This intangible asset must be amortized to expense. Give the required adjusting entry for 19A.

Required:

1. Give appropriate journal entries, with a brief explanation for each of these transactions.
2. Give appropriate closing entries at December 31, 19A.
3. Prepare a balance sheet for Shelly Corporation at December 31, 19A. Emphasize full disclosure of stockholders' equity.

Suggested Solution

1.   Journal entries:

(a) Jan. 19A	Cash	390,000	
	No-par common stock (7,500 shares)		390,000
	Sale of no-par common stock ($52 × 7,500 shares = $390,000).		
(b) Feb. 19A	Cash	192,780	
	Preferred stock, 5% (par $100, 1,890 shares)		189,000
	Contributed capital in excess of par, preferred		
	stock [1,890 shares × ($102 − $100)]		3,780
	Sale of preferred stock ($102 × 1,890 shares = $192,780).		
(c) March 19A	Land (store site)	10,200	
	Preferred stock, 5% (par $100, 100 shares)		10,000
	Contributed capital in excess of par, preferred stock		200
	Purchased land for future store site; paid in full by issuance		
	of 100 shares of preferred stock.		
	The market value is $102 × 100 shares = $10,200.		
(d) Apr. 19A	Organization cost	1,980	
	Cash		1,980
	Paid organization cost.		
(e) May 19A	Organization cost	1,020	
	Preferred stock 5% (par $100, 10 shares)		1,000
	Contributed capital in excess of par, preferred stock		20
	Organization cost (legal services) paid by issuance of		
	10 shares of preferred stock. The implied market value is		
	$102 × 10 shares = $1,020.		
(f) June 19A	Cash	27,000	
	No-par common stock (500 shares)		27,000
	Sold 500 shares of the no-par common stock		
	($54 × 500 shares = $27,000).		
(g) July 19A	Treasury stock, preferred (100 shares at $104)	10,400	
	Cash		10,400
	Purchased 100 shares of preferred treasury stock		
	($104 × 100 shares = $10,400).		
(h) Aug. 19A	Cash (20 shares at $105)	2,100	
	Treasury stock, preferred (20 shares at $104)		2,080
	Contributed capital from treasury stock transactions		20
	Sold 20 shares of the preferred treasury stock at $105.		
(i) Dec. 31, 19A	Equipment	600,000	
	Cash		600,000
	Purchased equipment.		
(j) Dec. 31, 19A	Cash	20,000	
	Note payable		20,000
	Borrowed on one-year, 12 percent interest-bearing note.		
(k) Dec. 31, 19A	Cash	129,300	
	Revenues		129,300
	Expenses	98,000	
	Cash		98,000
	To record summarized revenues and expenses.		
(l) Dec. 31, 19A	Expenses	300	
	Organization cost		300
	Adjusting entry to amortize organization cost		
	for one year [($1,980 + $1,020) ÷ 10 years = $300].		

2. Closing entries:

(m) Dec. 31, 19A Revenues 129,300

           Income summary 129,300

         Income summary 98,300

           Expenses ($98,000 + $300) 98,300

         Income summary 31,000

           Retained earnings ($129,300 − $98,300 = $31,000) 31,000

3. Balance Sheet

SHELLY CORPORATION
Balance Sheet
At December 31, 19A

Assets

Current assets		
Cash		$ 50,800
Tangible assets		
Land	$ 10,200	
Equipment (no depreciation assumed in the problem)	600,000	610,200
Intangible assets		
Organization cost (cost, $3,000 less		
amortization, $300)		2,700
Total assets		$663,700

Liabilities

Current liabilities		
Note payable, 12%		$ 20,000

Stockholders' Equity

Contributed capital		
Preferred stock, 5% (par value $100; authorized 5,000 shares, issued 2,000 shares of which 80 shares are held as treasury stock)	$200,000	
Common stock (no-par value; authorized 20,000 shares, issued and outstanding 8,000 shares)	417,000	
Contributed capital in excess of par, preferred stock	4,000	
Contributed capital from treasury stock transactions	20	
Total contributed capital	$621,020	
Retained earnings	31,000	
Total contributed capital and retained earnings	$652,020	
Less cost of preferred treasury stock held (80 shares)	(8,320)	
Total stockholders' equity		643,700
Total liabilities and stockholders' equity		$663,700

Summary

This chapter discussed accounting for owners' equity in corporations. Sole proprietorships and partnerships are discussed in Chapter Supplement A. Except for owners' equity, accounting basically is unaffected by the type of business organization. Separate accounts are kept for the two basic sources of owners' equity for a corporation, contributed capital and retained earnings. Separate accounts are kept for each type of common and preferred stock that has been issued.

Frequently a corporation purchases its own stock in the marketplace. Stock previously issued by the corporation and subsequently reacquired is known as *treasury stock* as long as the issuing corporation holds it. The purchase of treasury stock is to reduce the amount of corporate capital; the subsequent resale of the treasury stock increases corporate capital.

A corporation's earnings that are not retained in the business for growth and expansion are distributed to the stockholders by means of dividends. Dividends are paid only when formally declared by the corporation's board of directors. A cash dividend results in a decrease in assets (cash) and a commensurate decrease in stockholders' equity (retained earnings). In contrast, a stock dividend does not change assets, liabilities, or total stockholder's equity. A stock dividend results in a transfer of retained earnings to the permanent or contributed capital of the corporation by the amount of the stock dividend. Therefore, a stock dividend affects only certain account balances within stockholders' equity. A stock split affects only the par value of the stock and the number of shares outstanding; the individual equity account balances are not changed.

Corporations invest in the securities of other corporations for a variety of reasons. Often the investment is for a short term to earn a return on idle funds. Other investments are for the long term; this may be designed to provide the investing corporation with significant influence or control over the other corporation. In Chapter 12, we will discuss different methods of accounting for these different types of investments.

Chapter Supplement A

ACCOUNTING FOR OWNERS' EQUITY FOR SOLE PROPRIETORSHIPS AND PARTNERSHIPS

Owner's Equity for a Sole Proprietorship

A sole proprietorship is an unincorporated business owned by one person. The only owner's equity accounts needed are (1) a capital account for the proprietor (J. Doe, Capital) and (2) a drawing (or withdrawal) account for the proprietor (J. Doe, Drawings). The capital account of a sole proprietorship is used for two purposes: to record investments by the owner and to accumulate the periodic income or loss. Thus, the Income Summary account is closed to the capital account at the end of each accounting period. The drawing account is used to record the owner's withdrawals of cash or other assets from the business. The drawing account is closed to the capital account at the end of each accounting period. The capital account reflects the cumulative total of all investments by the owner plus all earnings of the entity less all withdrawals of resources from the entity by the owner. In most respects, the accounting for a sole proprietorship is the same as for a corporation.

Exhibit 11.6 presents the recording of selected transactions and the owner's equity section of the balance sheet of Doe Retail Store to illustrate the accounting for owner's equity for a sole proprietorship.

A sole proprietorship does not pay income taxes. Therefore, its financial statements do not reflect income tax expense or income taxes payable. The net income of a sole proprietorship is taxed when it is included on the owner's *personal* income tax return. Because an employer/employee contractual relationship cannot exist with only one party involved, a "salary" to the owner is not recognized as an expense of a sole proprietorship. The owner's salary is accounted for as a distribution of profits (i.e., a withdrawal).

Owners' Equity for a Partnership

The Uniform Partnership Act, which most states have adopted, defines *partnership* as "an association of two or more persons to carry on as co-owners of a business for profit." Small businesses and professionals such as accountants, doctors, and lawyers use the partnership form of business. It is formed by two or more persons reaching mutual agreement about the

EXHIBIT 11.6
Accounting for Owner's Equity for a Sole Proprietorship

Selected Entries during 19A

JANUARY 1, 19A

J. Doe started a retail store by investing $150,000 of personal savings. The journal entry for the business is as follows:

Cash	150,000	
J. Doe, capital		150,000
Investment by owner.		

DURING 19A

Each month during the year, Doe withdrew $1,000 cash from the business for personal living costs. Accordingly, each month the following journal entry was made:

J. Doe, drawings	1,000	
Cash		1,000
Withdrawal of cash by owner for personal use.		

NOTE At December 31, 19A, after the last withdrawal, the drawings account will reflect a debit balance of $12,000.

DECEMBER 31, 19A

Usual journal entries for the year, including adjusting and closing entries for the revenue and expense accounts, resulted in an $18,000 credit balance in the Income Summary account (i.e., $18,000 net income). The next closing entry follows:

Income summary	18,000	
J. Doe, capital		18,000
Closing entry to transfer net income for the year to the owner's equity account.		

DECEMBER 31, 19A:

The journal entry required on this date to close the drawings account follows:

J. Doe, capital	12,000	
J. Doe, drawings		12,000
Closing entry to transfer drawings for the year to the capital account.		

BALANCE SHEET DECEMBER 31, 19A (PARTIAL)

Owner's equity		
J. Doe, capital, January 1, 19A	$150,000	
Add: Net income for 19A	18,000	
Total	168,000	
Less: Withdrawals for 19A	(12,000)	
J. Doe, capital, December 31, 19A		$156,000

terms of the partnership. The law does not require an application for a charter as it does in the case of a corporation. The agreement between the partners constitutes a partnership contract that should be in writing. The agreement should specify matters such as division of periodic income, management responsibilities, transfer or sale of partnership interests, disposition of assets upon liquidation, and procedures to be followed in case of the death of a partner. If the partnership agreement does not specify these matters, the laws of the resident state are binding. The primary advantages of a partnership are (1) ease of formation, (2) complete control by the partners, and (3) lack of income taxes on the business itself. The primary disadvantage is the unlimited liability of each partner for the partnership's liabilities. As a result of unlimited liability, creditors of the partnership can take the partners' personal assets if the partnership does not have sufficient assets to satisfy outstanding debt.

As with a sole proprietorship, accounting for a partnership follows the same underlying fundamentals of accounting as any other form of business organization except for those entries that directly affect owners' equity. Accounting for partners' equity follows the same pattern as illustrated earlier for a sole proprietorship except that separate partner capital and drawings accounts must be established for each partner. Investments by each partner are credited to the partner's capital account. Withdrawals from the partnership by each partner are debited to the respective drawings account. The net income for a partnership is divided between the partners in the profit ratio specified in the partnership agreement. The Income Summary account is closed to the respective partner capital accounts. The respective drawings accounts also are closed to the partner capital accounts. Therefore, after the closing process, each partner's capital account reflects the cumulative total of all investments of that individual partner plus the partner's share of all partnership earnings less all withdrawals by the partner.

Exhibit 11.7 presents selected journal entries and partial financial statements for AB Partnership to illustrate the accounting for the distribution of income and partners' equity.

The financial statements of a partnership follow the same format as those for a corporation except that (1) the income statement includes an additional section entitled Distribution of Net Income, (2) the partners' equity section of the balance sheet is detailed for each partner in conformity with the full-disclosure principle, (3) they have no income tax expense because partnerships do not pay income tax (each partner must report his or her share of the partnership profits on his or her individual tax return), and (4) salaries paid to partners are not recorded as expense but are treated as a distribution of earnings (withdrawals).

EXHIBIT 11.7
Accounting for Partners' Equity

Selected Entries during 19A

JANUARY 1, 19A

A. Able and B. Baker organized AB Partnership on this date. Able contributed $60,000 and Baker $40,000 cash in the partnership and agreed to divide net income (and net loss) 60% and 40%, respectively. The journal entry for the business to record the investment follows:

Cash	100,000	
A. Able, capital		60,000
B. Baker, capital		40,000
Investment to initiate a partnership.		

DURING 19A

The partners agreed that Able would withdraw $1,000 and Baker $650 per month in cash. Accordingly, each month the following journal entry for the withdrawals was made:

A. Able, drawings	1,000	
B. Baker, drawings	650	
Cash		1,650
Withdrawal of cash by partners for personal use.		

DECEMBER 31, 19A

Assume that the normal closing entries for the revenue and expense accounts resulted in a $30,000 credit balance in the Income Summary account (i.e., $30,000 net income). The next closing entry is as follows:

Income summary	30,000	
A. Able, capital		18,000
B. Baker, capital		12,000
Closing entry to transfer net income to the respective capital accounts.		

(continued on the next page)

EXHIBIT 11.7
Concluded

Net income is divided as follows:

A. Able, $30,000 × 60%	$18,000	
B. Baker, $30,000 × 40%	12,000	
Total	$30,000	

DECEMBER 31, 19A

The journal entry required to close the drawings accounts follows:

A. Able, capital	12,000	
B. Baker, capital	7,800	
A. Able, drawings		12,000
B. Baker, drawings		7,800
Closing entry to transfer drawings for the year to the respective capital accounts.		

After the closing entries, the partners' accounts reflect the following balances:

Income summary	0
A. Able, drawings	0
B. Baker, drawings	0
A. Able, capital	$66,000
B. Baker, capital	44,200

Reporting partners' distribution of net income and partners' equity:

Income statement for the year ended December 31, 19A

Net income		$30,000
Distribution of net income		
A. Able (60%)	$18,000	
B. Baker (40%)	12,000	
	$30,000	

BALANCE SHEET DECEMBER 31, 19A

Partners' equity		
A. Able, capital	$66,000	
B. Baker, capital	44,200	
Total partners' equity		$110,200

A separate statement of partners' capital similar to the following customarily is prepared to supplement the balance sheet:

AB PARTNERSHIP
Statement of Partners' Capital
For the Year Ended December 31, 19A

	A. Able	B. Baker	Total
Investment, January 1, 19A	$60,000	$40,000	$100,000
Add: Additional investments during the year	0	0	0
Net income for the year	18,000	12,000	30,000
Totals	78,000	52,000	130,000
Less: Drawings during the year	(12,000)	(7,800)	(19,800)
Partners' equity, December 31, 19A	$66,000	$44,200	$110,200

Key Ratios

Dividend yield ratio measures the dividend return on the current price of the stock. The ratio is computed as follows (p. 568):

$$\text{Dividend yield ratio} = \frac{\text{Dividend per share}}{\text{Market price per share}}$$

Dividend payout ratio measures the portion of net income that is paid to common stockholders in the form of dividends. The ratio is computed as follows (p. 568):

$$\text{Dividend payout ratio} = \frac{\text{Dividends}}{\text{Earnings}}$$

Key Terms

Authorized Number of Shares Maximum number of shares of capital stock of a corporation that can be issued as specified in the charter. *568*

Common Stock The basic, normal, voting stock issued by a corporation; called *residual equity* because it ranks after preferred stock for dividend and liquidation distributions. *570*

Convertible Preferred Stock Preferred stock that is convertible to common stock at the option of the holder. *571*

Cumulative Dividend Preference Preferred stock feature that requires specified current dividends not paid in full to accumulate for every year in which they are not paid. These cumulative preferred dividends must be paid before any common dividends can be paid. *579*

Current Dividend Preference The feature of preferred stock that grants a priority on preferred dividends over common dividends. *579*

Dividend Dates

Declaration Date Date on which the board of directors officially approves a dividend. *578*

Payment Date Date on which a cash dividend is paid to the stockholders of record. *578*

Record Date Date on which the corporation prepares the list of current stockholders as shown on its records; dividends can be paid only to the stockholders who own stock on that date. *578*

Dividends in Arrears Dividends on cumulative preferred stock that have not been declared in prior years. *579*

Issued Shares Total number of shares of stock that have been issued; shares outstanding plus treasury shares held. *568*

Legal Capital The permanent amount of capital defined by state law that must remain invested in the business; provides a "cushion" for creditors. *570*

No-Par Value Stock Shares of capital stock that have no par value specified in the corporate charter. *570*

Outstanding Shares Total shares of stock that are owned by stockholders on any particular date. *568*

Par Value Nominal value per share of capital stock specified in the charter; serves as the basis for legal capital. *570*

Preferred Stock Shares of stock that have specified rights over common stock. *571*

Prior Period Adjustment Amount debited or credited directly to retained earnings to correct an accounting error of a prior period. *584*

Stock Dividend Distribution of additional shares of a corporation's own capital stock to current stockholders on a pro rata basis at no cost; decreases retained earnings. *582*

Stock Split An increase in the total number of authorized shares by a specified ratio; does not decrease retained earnings. *583*

Treasury Stock A corporation's own stock that it had issued but subsequently reacquired and that it still holds. *575*

Unissued Shares Authorized shares of a corporation's stock that never have been issued. *568*

Questions

1. Define *corporation* and identify its primary advantages.
2. What is the charter of a corporation?
3. Explain each of the following terms: (a) *authorized capital stock,* (b) *issued capital stock,* (c) *unissued capital stock,* and (d) *outstanding capital stock.*
4. Differentiate between common stock and preferred stock.
5. Explain the distinction between par value stock and no-par value capital stock.
6. What are the usual characteristics of preferred stock?
7. What are the two basic sources of stockholders' equity? Explain each.
8. Owners' equity is accounted for by source. What does *source* mean?
9. Define *treasury stock.* Why do corporations acquire treasury stock?
10. How is treasury stock reported on the balance sheet? How is the "gain or loss" on treasury stock that has been sold reported on the financial statements?
11. What are the two basic requirements to support a cash dividend? What are the effects of a cash dividend on assets and stockholders' equity?
12. Differentiate between cumulative and noncumulative preferred stock.
13. Define *stock dividend.* How does it differ from a cash dividend?
14. What are the primary purposes of issuing a stock dividend?
15. Identify and explain the three important dates with respect to dividends.
16. Define *retained earnings.* What are the primary components of retained earnings at the end of each period?
17. Define *prior period adjustments.* How are they reported?
18. What does *restrictions on retained earnings* mean?

Exercises

E11–1 Reporting Stockholders' Equity and Determining Dividend Policy

Sampson Corporation was organized in 19A to operate a financial consulting business. The charter authorized the following capital stock: common stock, par value $8 per share, 12,000 shares. During the first year, the following selected transactions were completed:

(a) Sold and issued 6,000 shares of common stock for cash at $20 per share.
(b) Issued 600 shares of common stock for a piece of land that will be used for a facilities site; construction began immediately. Assume that the stock was selling at $22 per share at the date of issuance. Debit Land.
(c) Sold and issued 2,000 shares of common stock for cash at $23 per share.
(d) At year-end, the accounts reflected a $7,000 loss. Because a loss was incurred, no income tax expense was recorded.

Required:

1. Give the journal entry required for each of these transactions.
2. Prepare the stockholders' equity section as it should be reported on the year-end balance sheet.
3. Can Sampson pay dividends at this time? Explain.

E11–2 Analyzing the Impact of Dividend Policy

McDonald and Associates is a small manufacturer of electronic connections for local area networks. Consider three independent situations.

> **Case 1:** McDonald increases its cash dividends by 50 percent, but no other changes occur in the company's operations.
> **Case 2:** The company's income and cash flows increase by 50 percent but this does not change its dividends.
> **Case 3:** McDonald issues a 50 percent stock dividend, but no other changes occur.

Required:

1. Determine the impact of each case on the company's stock price.
2. If the company changed its accounting policies and reported higher net income, would the change have an impact on the stock price?

E11–3 Analyzing Transactions Affecting Stockholders' Equity and Evaluating Dividend Policy

Shelby Corporation was organized in January 19A by 10 stockholders to operate an air conditioning sales and service business. The charter issued by the state authorized the following capital stock:

> Common stock, $1 par value, 200,000 shares.
> Preferred stock, $10 par value, 6 percent, 50,000 shares.

During January and February 19A, the following stock transactions were completed:

(*a*) Collected $40,000 cash from each of the 10 organizers and issued 2,000 shares of common stock to each of them.
(*b*) Sold 15,000 shares of preferred stock at $25 per share; collected the cash and immediately issued the stock.

Required:

1. Give the journal entries to record these stock transactions.
2. Net income for 19A was $40,000; cash dividends declared and paid at year-end were $10,000. Prepare the stockholders' equity section of the balance sheet at December 31, 19A.

E11–4 Comparing the Issuance of Common and Preferred Stock

Kelly, Incorporated, was issued a charter on January 15, 19A, that authorized the following capital stock:

> Common stock, no-par, 100,000 shares.
> Preferred stock, 7 percent, par value $10 per share, 5,000 shares.

The board of directors established a stated value on the no-par common stock of $6 per share. During 19A, the following selected transactions were completed in the order given:

(a)   Sold and issued 20,000 shares of the no-par common stock at $18 cash per share.

(b)   Sold and issued 3,000 shares of preferred stock at $22 cash per share.

(c)   At the end of 19A, the accounts showed net income of $38,000.

Required:

1.   Give the journal entry indicated for each of these transactions.

2.   Prepare the stockholders' equity section of the balance sheet at December 31, 19A.

3.   Assume that you are a common stockholder. If Kelly needed additional capital, would you prefer to have it issue additional common stock or additional preferred stock? Explain.

E11–5   Stockholders' Equity Transactions, Including Noncash Consideration: Write a Brief Memo

Teacher Corporation obtained a charter at the start of 19A that authorized 50,000 shares of no-par common stock and 20,000 shares of preferred stock, par value $10. The corporation was organized by four individuals who "reserved" 51 percent of the common stock shares for themselves. The remaining shares were to be sold to other individuals at $40 per share on a cash basis. During 19A, the following selected transactions occurred:

(a)   Collected $15 per share cash from three of the organizers and received two adjoining lots of land from the fourth organizer. Issued 4,000 shares of common stock to each of the four organizers and received title to the land.

(b)   Sold and issued 6,000 shares of common stock to an outsider at $40 cash per share.

(c)   Sold and issued 8,000 shares of preferred stock at $20 cash per share.

(d)   At the end of 19A, the accounts reflected after-tax income of $36,000.

Required:

1.   Give the journal entries indicated for each of these transactions.

2.   Write a brief memo to explain the basis that you used to determine the cost of the land.

E11–6   Finding Amounts Missing from the Stockholders' Equity Section

The stockholders' equity section on the December 31, 19D, balance sheet of Chemfast Corporation follows:

Stockholders' Equity

Contributed capital	
Preferred stock (par $20; authorized 10,000 shares,	
? issued, of which 500 shares are held as treasury stock)	$104,000
Common stock (no-par; authorized 20,000 shares,	
issued and outstanding 8,000 shares)	600,000
Contributed capital in excess of par, preferred	14,300
Contributed capital, treasury stock transactions	1,500
Retained earnings	30,000
Cost of treasury stock, preferred	9,500

Required:

Complete the following statements and show your computations.

1.   The number of shares of preferred stock issued was _____.

2.   The number of shares of preferred stock outstanding was _____.

3.   The average sale price of the preferred stock when issued was $_____ per share.

4.   Have the treasury stock transactions (a) increased corporate resources _____ or (b) decreased resources _____? By how much? _____ .

5. The treasury stock transactions increased (decreased) stockholders' equity by

   _____.
6. How much did the treasury stock held cost per share? $_____.
7. Total stockholders' equity is $_____.
8. The average issue price of the common stock was $_____.
9. Assuming that one-fourth of the treasury stock is sold at $35 per share, the remaining balance in the Treasury Stock account is $_____.

PepsiCo, Inc.

E11–7 Finding Information Missing from an Annual Report

The annual report for PepsiCo, Inc., contained the following information:

(a) Retained earnings at the end of 1992 totaled $5,439.7 million.
(b) Treasury stock amounted to $667 million at the end of 1992 and $913.2 million at the end of 1993.
(c) Net income for 1993 was $1,587.9 million.
(d) Par value of the stock is $1\frac{2}{3}$ cents per share.
(e) Cash dividends declared in 1993 were 61 cents per share.
(f) The Common Stock, Par Value account was $14.4 million at the end of both 1992 and 1993.

Required: (Assume that no other information concerning stockholders' equity is relevant.)
1. Estimate the number of shares outstanding during 1993.
2. Estimate the amount of retained earnings at the end of 1993.
3. Did the number of shares outstanding change during 1993?

E11–8 Accounting for Treasury Stock Transactions and Analyzing Their Impact

During 19C, the following selected transactions affecting stockholders' equity occurred for Italy Corporation:

(a) Feb 1   Purchased in the open market 200 shares of the company's own common stock at $22 cash per share.
(b) Jul 15   Sold 100 of the shares purchased on February 1, 19C, for $24 cash per share.
(c) Sept 1   Sold 60 more of the shares purchased on February 1, 19C, for $20 cash per share.
(d) Dec 15   Sold an additional 20 of the treasury shares for $15 per share.

Required:
1. Give the indicated journal entries for each of the four transactions.
2. What impact does the purchase of treasury stock have on dividends paid?
3. What impact does the sale of treasury stock for an amount higher than the purchase price have on net income and the Statement of Cash Flows?

Philip Morris Companies, Inc.

E11–9 Computing Shares Outstanding

The 1993 annual report for Philip Morris Companies, Inc., disclosed that 4 billion shares of common stock have been authorized. At the end of 1992, 935,320,439 shares had been issued and the number of shares in treasury stock was 42,563,254. During 1993, no additional shares were issued, but 17,278,900 additional shares were purchased for treasury stock and 1,612,405 were sold from treasury stock. Determine the number of shares outstanding at the end of 1993.

E11–10 Evaluating Various Types of Preferred Stock

The records of Hoffman Company reflected the following balances in the stockholders' equity accounts at December 31, 19H:

> Common stock, par $12 per share, 40,000 shares outstanding.
> Preferred stock, 8 percent, par $10 per share, 6,000 shares outstanding.
> Retained earnings, $220,000.

On September 1, 19H, the board of directors was considering the distribution of a $62,000 cash dividend. No dividends were paid during 19F and 19G. You have been asked to determine the total and per share amounts that would be paid to the common stockholders and to the preferred stockholders under two independent assumptions (show computations):

a. The preferred stock is noncumulative.
b. The preferred stock is cumulative.

Required:
1. Give the journal entry to record dividends separately for preferred and common stock under each assumption.
2. Write a brief memo to explain why the dividends per share of common stock were less for the second assumption.
3. What factor would cause a more favorable per share result to the common stockholders?

E11–11 Analyzing Dividends in Arrears   TWA

The annual report for TWA contained the following note:

> Dividends were suspended in 1991 and at December 31, 1992, $29,700,000 of cumulative dividends were in arrears on the $2.25 preferred stock.

not a legal liab but must be disclosed

A student who read the note suggested that the TWA preferred stock would be a good investment because of the large amount of dividend income that would be earned when TWA started paying dividends again: "As the owner of the stock, I'll get dividends for the period I hold the stock plus some previous periods when I didn't even own the stock." Do you agree? Explain.

E11–12 Recording Dividends

Average Corporation has the following capital stock outstanding at the end of 19B:

> Preferred stock, 6 percent, par $15, outstanding shares, 8,000.
> Common stock, par $8, outstanding shares, 30,000.

On October 1, 19B, the board of directors declared dividends as follows:

> Preferred stock: Full cash preference amount, payable December 20, 19B.
> Common stock: 10 percent common stock dividend (i.e., one additional share for each 10 held), issuable December 20, 19B.

On December 20, 19B, the market prices were preferred stock, $40, and common stock, $32.

Required:
1. Give any required journal entry(ies) to record the declaration and subsequent payment of the dividend on the preferred stock.

2. Give any required journal entry(ies) to record the declaration and issuance of the stock dividend on the common stock.

3. Explain the overall effect of each of the dividends on the assets, liabilities, and stockholders' equity of the company.

Sears, Roebuck and Co.

E11–13 Recording the Payment of Dividends

A recent annual report for Sears, Roebuck and Co. disclosed that the company paid preferred dividends in the amount of $119.9 million. The company declared and paid dividends on common stock in the amount of $2 per share. During the year, Sears had 1,000,000,000 shares of common authorized; 387,514,300 shares had been issued; 41,670,000 shares were in treasury stock. Assume that the transaction occurred on July 15.

Required:

Prepare a journal entry to record the declaration and payment of dividends.

E11–14 Analyzing Stock Dividends

On December 31, 19E, the stockholders' equity section of the balance sheet of R & B Corporation reflected the following:

Common stock (par $10; authorized 60,000 shares, outstanding 25,000 shares)	$250,000
Contributed capital in excess of par	12,000
Retained earnings	75,000

On February 1, 19F, the board of directors declared a 12 percent stock dividend to be issued April 30, 19F. The market value of the stock on February 1, 19F, was $18 per share. The market value will be capitalized.

Required:

1. Give any required journal entry(ies) to record the declaration and issuance of the stock dividend.
2. For comparative purposes, prepare the stockholders' equity section of the balance sheet (a) immediately before the stock dividend and (b) immediately after the stock dividend. (*Hint:* Use two amount columns for this requirement.)
3. Explain the effects of this stock dividend on the assets, liabilities, and stockholders' equity.

Apple Computer

E11–15 Analyzing the Repurchase of Stock

A recent annual report for Apple Computer contained the following note:

STOCK REPURCHASE PROGRAMS

In November 1992, the Board of Directors authorized the purchase of up to 10 million shares of the Company's common stock in the open market. No shares were repurchased in the current year, while 3.4 million shares were repurchased in 1993.

Required:

1. Prepare the journal entry, if any is required, to record the authorization to purchase the 10 million shares.
2. Prepare the journal entry, if any is required, to record the purchase of the 3.4 million shares. Apple stock had no par value, and it was selling for $38 per share when the stock was repurchased.
3. What impact will this purchase have on Apple's future dividend obligations?

E11–16 Preparing a Statement of Retained Earnings and Evaluating Dividend Policy

The following account balances were selected from the records of Blake Corporation at December 31, 19E, after all adjusting entries were completed:

Common stock (par $15; authorized 100,000 shares, issued 35,000 shares, of which 1,000 shares are held as treasury stock)	$525,000
Contributed capital in excess of par	180,000
Bond sinking fund	90,000
Dividends declared and paid in 19E	18,000
Retained earnings, January 1, 19E	76,000
Correction of prior period accounting error (a debit, net of income tax)	8,000
Treasury stock at cost (1,000 shares)	20,000
Income summary for 19E (credit balance)	28,000

Restriction on retained earnings equal to the cost of treasury stock held is required by law in this state.

Required:

1. Prepare the statement of retained earnings for 19E.
2. Prepare the stockholders' equity section of the balance sheet at December 31, 19E.
3. Compute and evaluate the dividend yield ratio. Determine the number of shares of stock which received dividends.

E11–17 Declaring and Paying Dividends

The annual report for Carnival Cruise Lines contained the following note:

NOTE 6—SHAREHOLDERS' EQUITY

On January 15, 1993, the Company declared a cash dividend of $.14 per share payable on March 15, 1993, to shareholders of record on March 1, 1993.

At this time, Carnival had 399,500,000 shares authorized and 113,590,000 issued and outstanding. The par value for Carnival stock is $.01 per share.

Required:

Prepare journal entries as appropriate for each date mentioned in the note.

Carnival Cruise Lines

E11–18 Comparing Stock Dividends and Splits

On July 1, 19B, Jones Corporation had the following capital structure:

Common stock (par $1, authorized shares)	$200,000
Common stock (par $1, unissued shares)	50,000
Contributed capital in excess of par	88,000
Retained earnings	72,000
Treasury stock, none.	

Required:

1. The number of issued shares is _____.
2. The number of outstanding shares is _____.
3. Total stockholders' equity is _____.
4. Assume that the board of directors declared and issued a 10 percent stock dividend when the stock was selling at $4 per share. Give any required journal entry(ies). If none is required, explain why.
5. Disregard the stock dividend in requirement (4). Assume that the board of directors voted a 6-to-5 stock split (i.e., a 20 percent increase in the number of shares).

The market price prior to the split was $4 per share. Give any required journal entry(ies). If none is required, explain why.

6. Complete the following comparative tabulation followed by comments on the comparative effects:

Items	Before Dividend and Split	After Stock Dividend	After Stock Split
Common stock account	$	$	$
Par per share	$1	$	$
Shares outstanding	#	#	#
Contributed capital in excess of par	$88,000	$	$
Retained earnings	72,000		
Total stockholders' equity	$	$	$

Sizzler

E11-19 Paying Cash Dividends

Sizzler is a chain of popular family restaurants. As its annual report noted, "Closing the books on fiscal 1993 marks the end of a challenging year." In 1993, Sizzler lost $9,482,000. Nevertheless, the company declared and paid dividends in the amount of $4,666,000.

Required:

1. Prepare the journal entry to record Sizzler's payment of dividends, recognizing that the company experienced a loss.
2. Explain why Sizzler can pay dividends despite its loss in 1993.
3. What factors did the board of directors consider when it declared the dividends?

Problems

P11-1 Preparing the Stockholders' Equity Section of the Balance Sheet

Skyhawk Corporation received its charter during January 19A. The charter authorized the following capital stock:

Preferred stock: 8 percent, par $10, authorized 20,000 shares.
Common stock: par $8, authorized 50,000 shares.

During 19A, the following transactions occurred in the order given:

(a) Issued a total of 40,000 shares of the common stock to the four organizers at $11 per share. The company collected cash in full from three of the organizers and received legal services from the other organizer in full payment for the shares. The stock was issued immediately.
(b) Sold 5,000 shares of the preferred stock at $18 per share. Collected the cash and issued the stock immediately.
(c) Sold 3,000 shares of the common stock at $14 per share and 1,000 shares of the preferred stock at $28. Collected the cash and issued the stock immediately.
(d) Total revenues for 19A were $310,000 and total expenses (including income tax) were $262,000.

Required:

1. Give all the journal entries required for these transactions, including closing entries.
2. Prepare the stockholders' equity section of the balance sheet at December 31, 19A.
3. What was the average issue price of the common stock?
4. Write a brief memo explaining the basis you used to value the legal services in the first journal entry.

P11–2 Analyzing Dividend Policy

Dana and David, two young financial analysts, were discussing the 1995 annual report for Compaq, one of the world's largest manufacturers of personal computers. Dana noted that the company did not report any dividends in the financing activity section of the Statement of Cash Flows and said, "*Forbes* magazine recently named Compaq as one of the 12 best performing companies. If it's so good, I wonder why it isn't paying any dividends." David wasn't convinced that Dana was looking in the right place for dividends but didn't say anything.

Dana continued the discussion by noting, "Compaq's sales doubled over the past two years just as they doubled over the previous two years. Its income was only $789 million this year compared with $867 million last year, but cash flow from operating activities was $943 million this year compared to an outflow of $101 million last year."

At that point, David noted that the SCF reported that Compaq had invested $703 million in new property this year compared with $408 million last year. He also was surprised to see that inventory and accounts receivable had increased by $1 billion this year and nearly $2 billion last year. "No wonder it can't pay dividends; it generated less than $1 billion from operating activities and had to put it all back in accounts receivable and inventory."

Required:
1. Correct any misstatements that either Dana or David made. Explain.
2. Which of the factors presented in the case help you understand Compaq's dividend policy?

P11–3 Analyzing Transactions Affecting Stockholders' Equity

Kerr Corporation began operations in January 19A. The charter authorized the following capital stock:

> Preferred stock: 9 percent, $10 par, authorized 40,000 shares.
> Common stock: No-par, authorized 80,000 shares. The corporation, in conformity with state laws, established a stated value per share of $5 for the no-par common stock.

During 19A, the following transactions occurred in the order given:

(*a*) Issued 20,000 shares of the no-par common stock to each of the three organizers. Collected $9 cash per share from two of the organizers and received a plot of land with a small building on it in full payment for the shares of the third organizer and issued the stock immediately. Assume that 30 percent of the noncash payment received applies to the building.

(*b*) Sold 6,000 shares of the preferred stock at $18 per share. Collected the cash and issued the stock immediately.

(*c*) Sold 500 shares of the preferred stock at $20 and 1,000 shares of the no-par common stock at $12 per share. Collected the cash and issued the stock immediately.

(*d*) Operating results at the end of 19A were as follows:

Revenue accounts	$220,000
Expense accounts, including income taxes	160,000

Required:
1. Give the journal entries indicated (including closing entries) for each of these transactions.
2. Write a brief memo explaining what you used to determine the cost of the land and the building in the first journal entry.

P11–4 Comparing Par and No-Par Stock

McNally Company was issued a charter in January 19A, which authorized 100,000 shares of common stock. During 19A, the following selected transactions occurred in the order given:

(a) Sold 9,000 shares of the stock for cash at $60 per share. Collected the cash and issued the stock immediately.

(b) Acquired land to be used as a future plant site; made payment in full by issuing 600 shares of stock. Assume a market value per share of $66.

(c) At the end of 19A, the Income Summary account reflected a credit balance of $48,000.

Three independent cases are assumed as follows for comparative study purposes:

> **Case A:** Assume that the common stock was $25 par value per share. The state law specifies that par value is legal capital.
>
> **Case B:** Assume that the common stock was no-par and that the total sale price is credited to the Common Stock, No-par, account because the state law specifies this amount as legal capital.
>
> **Case C:** Assume that the common stock is no-par with a stated value, specified by the board of directors, of $15 per share.

Required:

1. Give the journal entries for each of the three transactions.
2. Should total stockholders' equity be the same amount among the three independent cases? Explain.
3. Should the noncash asset (land) be recorded at the same cost under each of the three independent cases? Explain.
4. Should a stockholder care whether a company issues par, no-par, or stated value stock? Explain.

P11–5 Analyzing Stockholders' Equity Transactions

Worldwide Company obtained a charter from the state in January 19A, which authorized 200,000 shares of common stock, $10 par value. The stockholders were 30 local citizens. During the first year, the following selected transactions occurred in the order given:

(a) Sold 60,000 shares of the common stock to the 30 stockholders at $12 per share. Collected the cash and issued the stock.

(b) Purchased 2,000 shares at $15 cash per share from one of the 30 stockholders who needed cash and wanted to sell the stock back to the company.

(c) Resold 1,000 of the shares of the treasury stock purchased in (b) two months later to another individual at $18 cash per share.

(d) Sold an additional 500 shares of the treasury stock at $14 cash per share.

(e) Determined on December 31, 19A, the end of the first year of business, that the accounts reflected income of $38,200.

Required:

1. Give the indicated journal entry for each of these transactions.
2. Prepare the stockholders' equity section of the balance sheet at December 31, 19A.
3. What dollar effect did the treasury stock transactions have on the assets, liabilities, and stockholders' equity of the company? Explain.

P11–6 Analyzing Stockholder Transactions, Including Noncash Consideration

Arnold Company was granted a charter that authorized the following capital stock:

Common stock: No-par, 100,000 shares. Assume that the no-par stock is not assigned a stated value per share.

Preferred stock: 8 percent, par $5, 20,000 shares.

During the first year, 19A, the following selected transactions occurred in the order given:

(a) Sold 30,000 shares of the no-par common stock at $40 cash per share and 5,000 shares of the preferred stock at $26 cash per share. Collected cash and issued the stock immediately. For the no-par stock, credit the full selling price to the common stock account.

(b) Issued 2,000 shares of preferred stock as full payment for a plot of land to be used as a future plant site. Assume the stock was selling at $26.

(c) Purchased 3,000 shares of the no-par common stock sold earlier; paid cash, $38 per share.

(d) Sold all of the treasury stock (common) purchased in requirement (c). The sale price was $39 per share.

(e) Purchased 1,000 shares of the company's own preferred stock at $28 cash per share.

(f) At December 31, 19A, the accounts reflected income of $33,500.

Required:

1. Give the journal entries indicated for each of these transactions.
2. Explain the economic difference between acquiring an asset for cash compared with acquiring it by issuing stock. Is it "better" to acquire a new asset without having to give up another asset?

P11-7 Comparing Stock and Cash Dividends

Water Tower Company had the following stock outstanding and retained earnings at December 31, 19E:

Common stock (par $8; outstanding, 30,000 shares)	$240,000
Preferred stock, 7% (par $10; outstanding, 6,000 shares)	60,000
Retained earnings	280,000

The board of directors is considering the distribution of a cash dividend to the two groups of stockholders. No dividends were declared during 19C or 19D. Three independent cases are assumed:

Case A: The preferred stock is noncumulative; the total amount of dividends is $30,000.

Case B: The preferred stock is cumulative; the total amount of dividends is $12,600.

Case C: Same as Case B, except the amount is $66,000.

Required:

1. Compute the amount of dividends, in total and per share, that would be payable to each class of stockholders for each case. Show computations.
2. Give the journal entry to record the cash dividends declared and paid in 19E for Case C only. Assume that the declaration and payment occurred simultaneously on December 31, 19E.
3. Give the required journal entry assuming, instead of a cash dividend, the declaration and issuance of a 10 percent common stock dividend on the outstanding common stock. Assume that the market value per share of common stock was $24.
4. Complete the following comparative schedule including explanation of the comparative differences.

	AMOUNT OF DOLLAR INCREASE (DECREASE)	
Item	Cash Dividend—Case C	Stock Dividend
Assets	$	$
Liabilities	$	$
Stockholders' equity	$	$

Capital Cities/ ABC, Inc.

P11–8 Dividend Policy

Capital Cities/ABC, Inc., is a diversified communications company that owns television and radio stations, newspapers, publishing companies, and ABC and ESPN networks. The company's annual report contains the following information:

> **COMMON STOCK AND STOCKHOLDER INFORMATION**
>
> As of February 26, 1993, the approximate number of holders of common stock was 9,150. Dividends of $.05 per share have been paid for each quarter of 1992 and 1991. The common stock is traded on the New York and Pacific Stock Exchanges. The high price of the stock during the previous year was $521 and the low price was $410.

At the time this report was issued, Capital Cities stock was the second most expensive stock traded on the New York Stock Exchange. If you were an adviser to the board of directors, would you recommend that it consider announcing a stock split or stock dividend? Justify your position.

P11–9 Recording Dividends

Lynn Company has outstanding 60,000 shares of $10 par value common stock and 25,000 shares of $20 par value preferred stock (8 percent). On December 1, 19B, the board of directors voted an 8 percent cash dividend on the preferred stock and a 10 percent common stock dividend on the common stock. At the date of declaration, the common stock was selling at $35 and the preferred at $20 per share. The dividends are to be paid, or issued, on February 15, 19C. The annual accounting period ends December 31.

Required:
1. Give any journal entry(ies) required to record the declaration and payment of the cash dividend.
2. Give any journal entry(ies) required to record the declaration and issuance of the stock dividend.
3. Explain the comparative effects of the two dividends on the assets, liabilities, and stockholders' equity (a) through December 31, 19B, (b) on February 15, 19C, and (c) the overall effects from December 1, 19B, through February 15, 19C. A schedule similar to the following might be helpful:

	COMPARATIVE EFFECTS EXPLAINED	
Item	Cash Dividend on Preferred	Stock Dividend on Common
1. Through December 31, 19B:		
Assets, etc.		

P11–10 Analyzing Stockholders' Equity Transactions, Including Treasury Stock

1. Compare a stock dividend with a cash dividend.
2. Compare a large stock dividend with a small stock dividend.
3. Describe the impact of the sale of treasury stock for more than cost on the income statement and the statement of cash flows.
4. Explain why a company might purchase treasury stock.

P11–11 **Preparing the Stockholders' Equity Section of the Balance Sheet**

Fulbright Company is completing its year-end accounting, including the preparation of the annual financial statements, at December 31, 19E. The stockholders' equity accounts reflected the following balances at the end of the year, 19E:

Common stock (par $20; shares outstanding, 40,000)	$800,000
Contributed capital in excess of par	70,000
Retained earnings, January 1, 19E (credit)	175,000
Cash dividends declared and paid during 19E (debit)	50,000
Income summary account for 19E (credit balance; after tax)	48,000

The following selected transactions occurred near the end of 19E; they are not included in the above amounts:

(a) Recognized that it would lose the $30,000 lawsuit brought against it during 19D. Therefore, in 19D, the company should have debited a loss and credited a liability for this amount. This journal entry was not made, and the accounting error was found in 19E. (*Hint:* credit Liability for Damages.) Disregard any income tax effects.

(b) Declared a voluntary restriction of $125,000 on retained earnings voted by the board of directors. It is to be designated "earnings appropriated for plant expansion" effective for the 19E financial statements.

Required:

1. Give the appropriate journal entries for these transactions. If no entry is given, explain.
2. Prepare a statement of retained earnings for 19E and the stockholders' equity section of the balance sheet at December 31, 19E.

P11–12 **Recording Dividends**

The business press reported the following story about a well-known stock brokerage firm:

Charles Schwab Corp.

January 17, 1995

Charles Schwab Corp. said today that it raised its quarterly dividend to $0.09 a share from $0.07 a share and declared a 50 percent stock dividend. It said the cash dividend is payable February 15, 1995, to holders of record on February 1, 1995. The 50 percent stock dividend is payable March 1, 1995, to shareholders of record February 1, 1995.

Required:

1. Prepare any journal entries that Schwab should make as the result of information in the preceding report. Assume that the company has 2 million shares outstanding, the par value is $0.10 per share, and the market value is $40 per share.
2. What do you think happened to the company's stock price after the January 17 announcement?
3. What factors did the board of directors consider in making this decision?

P11–13 **Recording Stockholders' Equity Transactions**

Kmart

The annual report for Kmart described the following transactions that affected stockholders' equity:

(a) Declared cash dividends of $0.92 per share; total dividends were $374 million.
(b) Sold series B convertible preferred stock (no-par) in the amount of $157 million.
(c) Sold treasury stock for $10 million; original cost was $8 million.
(d) Issued a 100 percent stock dividend on common stock; its par value was $206 million, and the market value was $784 million.

Required:

Prepare journal entries to record each of these transactions.

P11–14 Chapter Supplement A: Comparing Stockholders' Equity Sections for Alternative Forms of Organization

Assume for each of the following independent cases that the annual accounting period ends on December 31, 19W, and that the Income Summary account at that date reflected a debit balance (loss) of $20,000.

Case A: Assume that the company is a *sole proprietorship* owned by Proprietor A. Prior to the closing entries, the capital account reflected a credit balance of $50,000 and the drawings account a balance of $8,000.

Case B: Assume that the company is a *partnership* owned by Partner A and Partner B. Prior to the closing entries, the owners' equity accounts reflected the following balances: A, Capital, $40,000; B, Capital, $38,000; A, Drawings, $5,000; and B, Drawings, $9,000. Profits and losses are divided equally.

Case C: Assume that the company is a *corporation*. Prior to the closing entries, the stockholders' equity accounts showed the following: Capital Stock, par $10, authorized 30,000 shares, outstanding 15,000 shares; Contributed Capital in Excess of Par, $5,000; Retained Earnings, $65,000.

Required:

1. Give all the closing entries indicated at December 31, 19W, for each of the separate cases.
2. Show how the owners' equity section of the balance sheet would appear at December 31, 19W, for each case.

Cases and Projects

C11–1 Finding Missing Amounts

At December 31, 19E, the records of Nortech Corporation provided the following selected and incomplete data:

Common stock (par $10; no changes during 19E)
  Shares authorized, 200,000.
  Shares issued, ____?___; issue price $17 per share; cash collected in full, $2,125,000.
  Shares held as treasury stock, 3,000 shares, cost $20 per share.
Net income for 19E, $118,000.
Dividends declared and paid during 19E, $73,200.
Bond sinking fund balance, $40,000.
Prior period adjustment, correction of 19B accounting error, $9,000 (a credit, net of income tax).
Retained earnings balance, January 1, 19E, $155,000.
State law places a restriction on retained earnings equal to the cost of treasury stock held.
The treasury stock was acquired after the split was issued. Extraordinary gain (net of income tax), $12,000.

Required:

1. Complete the following tabulation:
   Shares authorized _____.
   Shares issued _____.
   Shares outstanding _____.

2. The balance in the Contributed Capital in Excess of Par account appears to be $_____.

3. EPS on net income is $_____.

4. Dividend paid per share of common stock is $_____.

5. The bond sinking fund should be reported on the balance sheet under the classification _____.

6. Net income before extraordinary items was $_____.

7. The prior period adjustment should be reported on the _____ as an addition of _____ or a deduction of _____.

8. Treasury stock should be reported on the balance sheet under the major caption _____ in the amount of $_____.

9. The amount of retained earnings available for dividends on January 1, 19E, was $_____.

10. Assume that the board of directors voted a 100 percent stock split (the number of shares will double). After the stock split, the par value per share will be $_____, and the number of outstanding shares will be _____.

11. Assuming the stock split given in requirement (10), give any journal entry that should be made. If none, explain why.

12. Disregard the stock split (assumed in requirements [10] and [11]). Assume instead that a 10 percent stock dividend was declared and issued when the market price of the common stock was $21. Give any journal entry that should be made.

C11–2 Computing Dividends for an Actual Company

Halliburton

A recent annual report for Halliburton Company contained the following information (in $ millions):

Stockholders' Equity	Current Year	Previous Year
Common stock, par value $2.50, authorized 2,000 shares	$ 298.3	$ 298.4
Paid–in capital in excess of par	130.5	129.9
Retained earnings	2,080.8	2,052.3
Less 12.8 and 13.0 treasury stock, at cost	382.2	384.7

In the current year, Halliburton declared and paid cash dividends of $1 per share. What would be the total amount of dividends declared and paid if they had been based on the amount of stock outstanding at the end of the year?

C11–3 Financial Statement Analysis

Toys "R" Us

Refer to the financial statements of Toys "R" Us given in Appendix B at the end of this book.

Required:
1. What is the par value of the company's stock?
2. What was the average price paid per share for treasury stock at the end of the current year?
3. What amount of dividends was paid in 1996?
4. How many stockholders have invested in this company?
5. What was the amount of earnings per share for the current year?

C11–4 Project: Evaluating Dividend Policy

Review several financial statements and find one company with a relatively high dividend payout ratio and another with a relatively low ratio. Study both statements to determine reasons that help you understand why the companies have different dividend policies. Write a brief memo explaining your understanding of the reasons that the policies differ.

C11-5   Project: Financial Analysis

Assume that you are a stockbroker with two clients. One is a recent college graduate and the other is a retired couple. Review several financial statements and find one company with a low dividend yield and another with a high dividend yield. Write a memo to each of your clients and recommend one of the two companies that you have found. Explain why the company meets the client's investment objectives.

C11-6   Project: Analyzing Capital Structures

Review several financial statements and find two companies with different financial structures (i.e., one company that uses a large amount of debt and one that uses very little debt). Analyze the two companies to determine reasons that the two companies decided to employ different capital structures. Write a brief memo to report your findings.

C11-7   Project: Analysis of Dividend Changes

Review several business publications and locate a company that has recently announced a change in its dividend policy. Determine the stated reasons for the change and conduct your own analysis. Do you agree with the stated reasons for the change? Could there be any unstated reasons for the change? What impact did the change have?

C11-8   Project: Analyzing Dividend Policy Over Time

For a single company, compute the dividend yield and dividend payout ratios for a 10-year period. (*Hint:* Some financial statements include a 10-year summary that reports the necessary data. As an alternative, you may want to use an electronic data source.) Write a brief memo explaining what you learn by comparing these numbers over a long period of time.

C11-9   Focus on Cash Flows: New Stock Issue

Review the Statement of Cash Flows for a company that has recently issued new stock. Analyze the investing and financing activities for three or four years before the sale of stock. Write a brief memo identifying factors that you think may have caused management to decide to issue new stock.

C11-10   Focus on Cash Flows: Transaction Affecting Cash Flows

Find financial statements for a company or companies that include each of the following: (a) interest expense, (b) stock dividend, and (c) dividends on common stock. Review the Statement of Cash Flows and write a brief memo explaining how each one affected it.

C11-11   Team Project: Stock Compensation

Break into two groups. One group should play the role of labor union representatives and the other the role of senior management. The labor union wants all of its employees to receive an additional 10 percent of their compensation in the form of company stock. Management believes that this proposal is too expensive and that the board of directors would probably fire the management team if it ever approved the proposal. Write an outline of the points that can support your position and enter a negotiation to resolve the conflict. As a group, write a final recommendation to present to the board.

C11-12   Ethics Project: Performance Based Compensation

Michael Eisner, CEO of Disney, made headlines a few years ago when it was announced that his compensation package included stock options worth $750 million. His compensation agreement included a bonus (paid in stock options). Eisner earned a percentage of Disney's income once the company earned an agreed upon rate of return. Write a brief memo identifying any ethical issues you see in this type of agreement.

C11–13 Ethics Project: Treasury Stock Transactions

You are on the board of directors of a medium-sized manufacturing company traded on the New York Stock Exchange. The president of the company has recommended that the company buy back 5 percent of its outstanding shares within the next 10 days. The buyback is being recommended because the company has a large amount of cash that it does not need in the business. Earlier in the day, you learned that within a month, the company will announce a new product improvement that will have a substantial impact on company profitability and stock price. You are concerned about the suggestion that the company should purchase large amounts of stock before an announcement is made about the new product. The president has assured the board that there is no problem because the company cannot report profits on treasury stock transactions and if there is an economic gain, it will benefit all of the stockholders. Write a brief memo to the board recommending the action that you believe is appropriate.

C11–14 Team Project: Examining an Annual Report

As a group, select an industry to analyze. Each team member should acquire the annual report or 10-K for one publicly traded company in the industry, with each member selecting a different company. (Library files, the SEC EDGAR service at www.sec.gov, Compustat CD, or the company itself are good sources.) On an individual basis, each team member should then write a short report answering the following questions about his or her selected company.

1. Has the company issued both common and preferred stock?
2. Does the company pay dividends? If so, compute the dividend payout ratio.
3. Has the company issued a stock dividend or had a stock split?
4. Does the company report treasury stock? If so, has it recently purchased or sold treasury stock?
5. What is the current market value of the stock? Has it been increasing or decreasing in value during the past few years?

Discuss any patterns across the companies that you as a group observe. Then, as a group, write a short report comparing and contrasting your companies using these attributes. Provide potential explanations for any differences discovered.

CHAPTER TWELVE

Reporting and Interpreting Investments in Other Corporations

General Electric Company
DIVERSIFICATION AS A BUSINESS STRATEGY

General Electric, a household name, manufactures and markets many familiar products. Despite our familiarity with General Electric, few people know that GE has business operations in all of the following areas: aircraft engines, appliances, capital services (including insurance), lighting, medical systems, network television, plastics, power systems, information systems, electrical distribution, and transportation systems. You may be wondering about the rationale for a company to be involved in selling an inexpensive lightbulb, broadcasting a popular television show, and manufacturing a jet engine for the new Boeing 777. GE management believes that globalization, changes in technology, and the need for large amounts of capital have created opportunities for a new kind of company, "one that has, and uses, all the strengths of a big company while moving with the speed, hunger and urgency of a small company."

General Electric has achieved diversification by investing in the stock of other companies (for example, GE now owns NBC Television). GE's annual report acknowledges that some people are questioning its business strategy:

> The hottest trend in business—and the one that hits closest to home—was the rush toward breaking up multi-business companies and "spinning-off" their components, under the theory that their size and diversity inhibited their competitiveness. We are a Company intent on getting bigger—a Company whose only answer to the trendy question—"What do you intend to spin off?"—is "cash—and lots of it."

When most people think of a company following a growth strategy, they think in terms of direct investments in new productive assets. If Ford Motor Company wanted to produce and sell more cars, it might invest in a new factory. As the General Electric annual report suggests, some companies seek growth by investing in the stock of existing companies. In the following section, we discuss some reasons that motivate business managers to invest in securities instead of productive assets.

◼ ◼ ◼

Business Background

Many strategic reasons motivate managers to invest in securities. It is easier to understand the business purpose of an investment if you first classify it in one of three categories:

1. *Short-term investment.* These investments are made to earn a high rate of return on funds that may be needed for operating purposes in the future. Instead of leaving cash in a checking account that does not earn interest, many companies buy securities that provide a higher return. Some companies can be very aggressive with these investments and actively trade the securities on established exchanges in an effort to maximize return. Most companies, however, invest in very low-risk securities; these investments typically include stocks, bonds, Treasury bills (short-term debt issued by the federal government), and commercial paper (short-term debt issued by corporations).

2. *Long-term investments made with no intent of exerting influence over another corporation.* The purpose of these investments is similar to the purpose of short-term investments. In this case, management invests funds that are not needed for operating purposes but may be needed for some long-term purpose. During the 1980s, a depression in the oil industry significantly slowed business activity. McDermott Corporation manufactures oil well equipment. Because of the business slowdown during that period, McDermott placed nearly $1 billion in long-term investments with the intent of using the funds to buy new equipment when oil drilling activity resumed. Long-term investments include stocks, bonds, and Treasury notes.

3. *Long-term investments made with the intent of influencing another corporation.* By being active in the management of another corporation, an investor may be able to earn a higher return on the investment. In some cases, it may be possible to

achieve synergy between two or more companies when the combined effectiveness of their operations is more than the sum of their individual activities. In other cases, the investing corporation may intend to exert an absolute minimum of influence. These investments can achieve diversification so that a company does not depend on the economic fortunes of a single area of business. General Electric acquired a controlling influence in NBC Television to obtain both diversification and the opportunity to more effectively exploit technology developments.

In Chapter 10, we discussed investments in bonds. In this chapter, we focus on investments in stock. When one corporation acquires common stock of another corporation, it usually purchases outstanding shares from other stockholders for cash or exchanges some of its own stock for outstanding stock of the other corporation. A transaction between the acquiring corporation and the stockholders of the acquired corporation affects only the acquiring corporation's accounting records. The transaction has no effect on the accounting records of the acquired corporation. The following diagram illustrates a typical transaction.

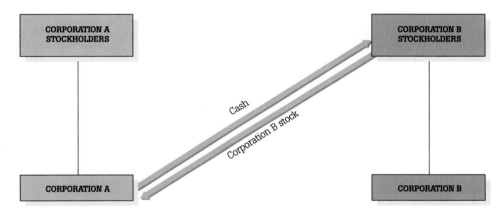

Accounting for Investments in Securities

The accounting methods used to record investments are directly related to the purpose of the investment. A critical feature that determines the appropriate accounting method is the nature of the relationship between the investor corporation and the investee. This relationship can be characterized based on the degree of influence and control the investor corporation can exert over the investee. Significant influence and control are defined as follows:

1. **Significant influence.** The ability of the investing company to have an *important impact* on the operating and financing policies of another company in which it owns shares of voting stock. Significant influence may be indicated by (1) membership on the board of directors of the other company, (2) participation in the policy-making processes, (3) material transactions between the two companies, (4) interchange of management personnel, or (5) technological dependency. In the absence of a clear-cut distinction based on these factors, significant influence is presumed if the investing company owns at least 20 percent but not more than 50 percent of the outstanding voting shares of the other company.

2. **Control.** The ability of the investing company to *determine* the operating and financing policies of another company in which it owns shares of the voting stock. For all practical purposes, control is presumed when the investing

Significant influence is the ability of an investing company to have an important impact on the operating and financing policies of another company.

Control is the ability of the investing company to determine the operating and financing policies of another company in which it owns shares of the voting stock.

company owns more than 50 percent of the outstanding voting stock of the other company.

Once you have determined the purpose of the investment in terms of significant influence or control, it is easy to determine the appropriate accounting method to use for the investment. The three basic approaches are

LEVEL OF OWNERSHIP	MEASURING AND REPORTING METHOD
1. Neither significant influence nor control	Market value method
2. Significant influence but not control	Equity method
3. Control	Consolidated statement method

Each of these approaches is outlined in Exhibit 12.1. The following note from a recent Chiquita Brands annual report is a good example of the way that many companies describe their use of the market value and equity methods:

REAL WORLD EXCERPT

CHIQUITA BRANDS
Annual Report

Investments representing minority interests are accounted for by the equity method when Chiquita has the ability to exercise significant influence in the investees' operations; otherwise, they are accounted for by the market value method.

EXHIBIT 12.1
Measuring and Reporting Long-Term Investments in Voting Stock of Another Company

Status of Ownership	Method	Measurement at Date of Acquisition	Investment	Revenue
1. **Investor can exercise no significant influence or control.** Presumed if investor owns less than 20% of the outstanding voting stock of the investee company.	Market value method	Investor records the investment at cost. *Cost* is the total outlay made to acquire the shares.	Investor reports the investment on the balance sheet at market value.	Investor recognizes revenue each period when the investee company declares dividends. An unrealized gain or loss is recorded each accounting period.
2. **Investor can exercise significant influence, but not control,** over the operating and financing policies of the investee company. Presumed if the investor owns at least 20%, but not more than 50%, of the outstanding voting shares of the investee company.	Equity method	Same as above	Investor measures and reports the investment at cost plus the investor's share of the earnings (or less the losses) and minus the dividends received from (i.e., declared by) the other company. (Dividends received are not considered revenue. To recognize dividends as revenue, rather than as a reduction in the investment, involves double counting.)	Investor recognizes as revenue each period the investor's proportionate share of the earnings (or losses) reported each period by the investee company. A realized gain or loss is recognized when the investment is sold.
3. **Investor can exercise control over the operating and financing policies of the investee company.** Control is presumed if the investor owns more than 50% of the outstanding voting stock of the investee company.	Consolidated financial statement method	Same as above	Consolidated financial statements required each period .	

Market Value Method

The **market value method** of accounting reports securities at their current market value. It must be used when the number of shares of stock held does not give the investing corporation the ability to exercise significant influence or control. An investment in stock with voting rights is accounted for under the market value method if less than 20 percent of the outstanding stock is held. All nonvoting stock is accounted for under the market value method without regard to the level of ownership.

Investments in stock accounted for under the market value method are classified in one of the following two categories:

1. **Trading securities** are all investments in stocks or bonds held primarily for the purpose of selling them in the near future. The trading securities portfolio is managed with the objective of generating profits on short-term differences in the price of the securities. The management philosophy for this portfolio is similar to the approach taken by many mutual funds. The portfolio manager actively seeks opportunities to buy and sell securities.

2. **Available-for-sale securities** are all investments other than trading securities that are accounted for under the market value method. This portfolio is not as actively traded as the trading securities portfolio; its purpose is to earn a return on funds that may be required for operating purposes in the future.

The trading securities portfolio is always reported on the balance sheet as a current asset. The available-for-sale securities portfolio may be reported as either a current asset or a noncurrent asset, depending on the intent of management. If management intends to sell securities within the next year, they should be classified as current. Otherwise, the securities should be classified as noncurrent.

The notes to General Electric's annual report contain the following information concerning its investment portfolios:

> **INVESTMENT SECURITIES**
>
> The Company has designated its investments in debt securities and marketable equity securities as available-for-sale. Those securities are reported at fair value, with net unrealized gains and losses included in equity, net of applicable taxes. Unrealized losses that are other than temporary are recognized in earnings.

In the following sections, we examine the accounting procedures described in this note.

Recording Investments at Market Value

Accounting for investments under the market value method represents an important departure from the *cost principle* that governs the reporting of all other assets. Under the cost principle, assets are reported on the balance sheet based on their cost, not on their current fair market value. An exception is made for investments held in the trading securities portfolio and the available-for-sale portfolio. These securities are reported on the balance sheet in terms of their current market value as of the date of the balance sheet.

LEARNING OBJECTIVE 2
Compare the available-for-sale and trading securities portfolios.
Market value method reports securities at their current market value.

Trading securities are all investments in stocks or bonds held primarily for the purpose of selling them in the near future.

Available-for-sale securities are all investments other than trading securities that are accounted for under the market value method.

REAL WORLD EXCERPT
GENERAL ELECTRIC
COMPANY
Annual Report

LEARNING OBJECTIVE 3
Use the market value method.

Before we discuss the specific accounting for investments, we should consider an important question: Why are investments accounted for under the market value method the only assets that are reported at fair market value on the balance sheet? Two primary factors are involved in the answer to this question:

1. *Relevance.* Analysts who study financial statements often attempt to forecast a company's future cash flows. They want to know how a company can generate cash for purposes such as expansion of the business, payment of dividends, or survival during a prolonged economic downturn. One source of cash is the sale of stock from the trading securities portfolio or the available-for-sale portfolio. The best estimate of the cash that could be generated by the sale of these securities is their current market value. Notice that these investments are different from most assets the company holds. In the normal course of business, a company uses but does not sell productive assets such as manufacturing equipment or office buildings. Investments do not serve that same purpose. They cannot produce goods or services; their only value comes from an ability to convert them into cash.

2. *Measurability.* Accountants can record only items that can be measured in dollar terms with a high degree of reliability (an unbiased and verifiable measurement). Determining the fair market value of most assets is very difficult because they are not actively traded. The John Hancock building is an important part of the Boston skyline. John Hancock's balance sheet reports the building in terms of its original cost in part because of the difficulty in determining an objective value for it. Contrast the difficulty of determining the value of a building with the ease of determining the value of securities that John Hancock may own. It is relatively easy to use *The Wall Street Journal* to determine the current price of IBM or Exxon stock because these securities are traded each day on established stock exchanges.

Holding Gains and Losses

At this point in our discussion, you may have anticipated another important issue concerning investments. Under the double-entry method of accounting, every journal entry affects at least two accounts. If accountants adjust the value of an investment account to reflect changes in fair market value, what other account is impacted when the asset account is increased or decreased? The answer is that **unrealized holding gains and losses** (which are amounts associated with price changes of securities that are currently held) are recorded whenever the fair market value of investments changes. If the value of the investments increased by $100,000 during the year, a journal entry records the increase in the asset account and an unrealized holding gain for $100,000. If the value of the investments decreased by $75,000 during the year, a journal entry records the decrease in the asset and an unrealized holding loss.

Recording an unrealized holding gain is a departure from the revenue principle that states that revenues and gains should be recorded when the company has completed the earnings process that generated them. Recording revenues and gains normally takes place at the point of sale. The word *unrealized* in the name unrealized holding gain (or loss) is intended to emphasize that the gain (or loss) did not occur as the result of a sale but instead was recorded as part of an adjusting entry to reflect a change in the fair market value of the investments in securities account.

The accounting impact of unrealized holding gains or losses depends on the classification of the investment:

1. *Trading securities portfolio.* Unrealized holding gains and losses are included on the income statement and are included in the computation of net income. In

Unrealized holding gains and losses are amounts associated with price changes of securities that are currently held.

other words, holding gains increase net income, and holding losses decrease net income.

2. *Available-for-sale portfolio.* Unrealized holding gains and losses are reported as a separate component of stockholders' equity. They are not reported on the income statement and do not affect net income. These gains and losses are reflected in a required supplemental disclosure called *comprehensive income,* which is net income adjusted for certain unrealized gains and losses.

Based on our discussion of accounting for investments, let's examine the financial reporting over the life of an investment. Assume that General Electric purchased 10,000 shares of Lucas Films, Inc., stock at a price of $25 per share on February 1, 19A. Management intends to hold these securities for a long period of time as a cushion against a future business downturn. This investment is recorded in the available-for-sale portfolio.

If management had purchased these securities as part of its portfolio of trading securities, the cost would have been recorded in the trading securities portfolio. The initial recording of the investment is the same for either portfolio. It is very unusual for a company to have only a single security as an investment. It is much less risky to own a portfolio of securities. We illustrate our discussion with a single security because we have found that it is easier for you to see the impact of the accounting procedures without the burden of additional details. Just remember that the procedures apply to the total value of the portfolio without regard to the number of securities in the portfolio.

Investments in securities earn a return from two sources: price appreciation and dividend income. Dividend income is reported as Revenue from investments, shown on the income statement, and included in the computation of net income for the period. This account is the same for dividend income received for shares in both the trading securities and available-for-sale portfolios.

At the end of each accounting period, the value of the investment portfolios must be determined, and any unrealized holding gain or loss must be computed. The unrealized holding gain or loss can be determined by comparing the market value of the portfolio at the end of the period with the market value at the beginning, adjusted for the purchase or sale of securities during the year. To illustrate, assume that the value of the Lucas Films, Inc., stock purchased by General Electric was $275,000 on December 31, 19A. The stock was purchased during 19A at a cost of $250,000. Therefore, General Electric records an unrealized holding gain for the available-for-sale portfolio:

| Dec. 31, 19A | Allowance to adjust to market (A) .... | 25,000 | |
| | Unrealized holding gain (SE) .... | | 25,000 |

The debit in this journal entry is made to a special asset adjustment account instead of directly to the asset account. This account is reported on the balance sheet as an adjustment in the carrying value of the investment, which means that the available-for-sale securities are reported at $275,000 (cost plus the allowance). The use of this account facilitates accounting for the investment. In subsequent years, the cost of the securities in the portfolio can be compared to their market value, and this difference then can be compared to the balance in the Allowance to Adjust to Market account. The unrealized holding gain or loss is simply the amount needed to change the balance in the allowance account to the amount of the difference between the total cost and the total market.

To illustrate, assume that by the end of 19B the market value of Lucas Films, Inc., stock had fallen to $200,000. What is the amount of the holding loss? Some people might be tempted to say that the loss was $50,000 (General Electric paid $250,000 for stock that is now worth $200,000, for a loss of $50,000). This answer is wrong. The unrealized loss is $75,000, which is the difference between the value of the portfolio at the beginning of the year ($275,000) and the value at the end of the year ($200,000). This answer makes good economic sense because management could have sold the Lucas Films, Inc., stock for $275,000 in cash at the end of 19A. Instead, it held the stock for an extra year and now can sell it for only $200,000. Clearly, an economic loss of $75,000 has occurred.

Notice how the use of the allowance account facilitates computation of the unrealized holding loss:

Available-for-Sale Securities			
Beginning balance	250,000		
Ending balance	250,000		

Allowance to Adjust to Market			
Beginning balance	25,000		
		Adjustment	75,000
		Ending balance	50,000

At the beginning of 19B, the account had a debit balance (that increased the carrying value of the portfolio). At the end of 19B, it should have a credit balance of $50,000 to reduce the $250,000 cost to a $200,000 carrying value. Accordingly, a $75,000 credit should be made to the allowance account, which is the amount of the holding loss. General Electric makes the following journal entry to record the holding loss:

| Dec. 31, 19B | Unrealized holding loss (SE) .... | 75,000 | |
| | Allowance to adjust to market (A) .... | | 75,000 |

The Allowance to Adjust to Market account (with a $50,000 credit balance) is subtracted from the investment account that is reported on the balance sheet. The net result is a carrying value of $200,000, which is the current market value of the securities.

The recording of holding gains and losses is essentially the same for both the trading securities and available-for-sale portfolios. The primary difference is the impact of the recorded unrealized holding gain or loss. In the case of trading securities, the gain or loss is reported on the income statement. In the case of available-for-sale securities, the gain or loss is a component of stockholders' equity.

The actual unrealized holding gains on investment securities for General Electric are shown in Exhibit 12.2. This information is very important to financial analysts. As you can see, the note to the statement (Exhibit 12.3) shows financial statement users the fair market value of the investment portfolio, which is the amount of cash available to General Electric if it sells the securities in the portfolio.

The asset section of the General Electric balance sheet reports more than $58 million in the investment portfolio, which represents nearly 20 percent of the company's total assets. This amount is much larger than most companies would report. Why do you suppose that General Electric has invested so much of its assets in debt and equity securities? If you are thinking about the various types of businesses owned by General Electric, you are thinking along the right line. GE owns an insurance subsidiary. Companies in the insurance business collect policy premiums (cash) from customers and pay out cash in the future when some event occurs, such as a fire or a car accident. Insurance companies are able to earn substantial profits by investing this cash before it must be paid out to meet the claims of policyholders. These companies have found that they can maximize their return by investing in debt and equity securities. Balance sheets for all insurance companies show a large amount in investments.

EXHIBIT 12.2
Unrealized Holding Gain on General Electric Balance Sheet

Liabilities and equity		
Short-term borrowings (note 19)	$ 80,200	$ 64,463
Accounts payable, principally trade accounts	10,205	9,061
Progress collections and price adjustments accrued	2,161	1,812
Dividends payable	855	767
All other GE current costs and expenses accrued (note 18)	7,086	5,898
Long-term borrowings (note 19)	49,246	51,027
Insurance liabilities, reserves and annuity benefits (note 20)	61,327	39,699
All other liabilities (note 21)	18,917	15,033
Deferred income taxes (note 22)	8,273	7,710
Total liabilities	238,270	195,470
Minority interest in equity of consolidated affiliates (note 23)	3,007	2,956
Common stock (1,857,013,000 shares issued)	594	594
Unrealized gains on investment securities — net	671	1,000
Other capital	2,498	1,663
Retained earnings	38,670	34,528
Less common stock held in treasury	(11,308)	(8,176)
Total share owners' equity (notes 25 and 26)	31,125	29,609
Total liabilities and equity	**$272,402**	**$228,035**

EXHIBIT 12.3
Note to General Electric Financial Statements

10 GECS Investment Securities

(In millions)	Amortized cost	Gross unrealized gains	Gross unrealized losses	Estimated fair value
December 31, 1996				
Debt securities				
U.S. corporate	$22,080	$ 308	$(641)	$21,747
State and municipal	10,232	399	(34)	10,597
Mortgage-backed	11,072	297	(108)	11,261
Corporate — non-U.S.	5,587	142	(13)	5,716
Government — non-U.S.	3,347	99	(2)	3,444
U.S. government and federal agency	2,340	34	(7)	2,367
Equity securities	4,117	677	(54)	4,740
	$58,775	$1,956	$(859)	$59,872
December 31, 1995				
Debt securities				
U.S. corporate	$12,313	$ 463	$ (63)	$12,713
State and municipal	9,460	570	(11)	10,019
Mortgage-backed	5,991	255	(65)	6,181
Corporate — non-U.S.	3,764	98	(34)	3,828
Government — non-U.S.	3,123	115	(3)	3,235
U.S. government and federal agency	1,817	77	(3)	1,891
Equity securities	2,843	412	(59)	3,196
	$39,311	$1,990	$(238)	$41,063

Sale of an Investment

LEARNING OBJECTIVE 4
Report the sale of investments.

Because accounting methods for each investment portfolio differ, accountants use different procedures to record the sale of securities from the different portfolios. In the following section, we discuss the various methods. We do not discuss the sale of securities accounted for under the equity method; these sales are fairly rare because of the strategic purpose of this type of investment (i.e., to achieve influence over another corporation).

Securities Sold from the Trading Portfolio

To illustrate accounting for the sale of stock from the trading portfolio, assume that General Electric sold stock on January 15, 19C, for $509,000. It had purchased the stock during 19B at a cost of $500,000. On December 31, 19B, the fair market value of the stock was $505,000. On that date, an unrealized holding gain of $5,000 was recorded. General Electric recorded the following entry on the date of sale:

Jan. 15, 19C	Cash (A)	509,000	
	Trading securities (A)		500,000
	Gain on sale of trading securities (G)		9,000

Notice that the gain is not affected by the previous recording of unrealized gains. At this point, an obvious double counting of a portion of the gain occurs (once when the adjusting entry was recorded and a second time when the securities were sold). This double counting is corrected at the end of the accounting period when the trading security portfolio is reviewed. Remember that at the end of each accounting period, the market value of the portfolio is compared to its cost and the allowance account is adjusted to reflect this difference. Because General Electric sold the stock during 19C, no difference between cost and market for the securities exists at year-end. General Electric's records still show a $5,000 balance in the Allowance to Adjust to Market entry related to the entry made at the end of 19B to record an unrealized holding gain.

Trading Securities			
Beginning balance	500,000		
		Sale of securities	500,000
Ending balance	0		

Allowance to Adjust to Market			
Beginning balance	5,000		
		Year-end adjustment	5,000
Ending balance	0		

As a result, General Electric must make the following adjusting entry at the end of 19C:

| Dec. 31, 19C | Adjustment for unrealized gain (SE) .... | 5,000 | |
| | Allowance to adjust to market (A) .... | | 5,000 |

The adjustment for the unrealized gain is reported on the income statement as a deduction from the gain associated with the sale on January 15, 19C. This adjustment avoids double counting part of the gain. In most cases, many securities would be in the portfolio at year-end. The adjusting entry normally causes an unrealized gain or loss to be recorded (rather than an adjustment for unrealized gain that General Electric recorded because it sold the last security in the portfolio).

Securities Sold from the Available-for-Sale Portfolio

To illustrate the sale of stock from the available-for-sale portfolio, let's use the same assumptions as for our previous example of a sale from the trading portfolio. Assume that General Electric sold stock on January 15, 19C, for $509,000. It had purchased the stock during 19B at a cost of $500,000. On December 31, 19B, the stock's fair market value was $505,000. On that date, GE recorded an unrealized holding gain of $5,000. To record the sale, General Electric makes the following entries:

Jan. 15, 19C	Cash (A)	509,000	
	Available-for-sale securities (A)		500,000
	Gain on sale of investment (G)		9,000
Dec. 31, 19C	Unrealized gains on investment (SE)	5,000	
	Allowance to adjust to market (A)		5,000

The Unrealized Gains on Investment account is a stockholders' equity account. Its balance represents previously recorded unrealized gains. The debit is made to this account to eliminate the balance because the security related to the gain is being sold. This debit does not affect the income statement. The amount of the Gain on Sale of Investment is the difference between the selling price ($509,000) and the purchase price ($500,000). The full amount of the gain is reported in the year of sale because the previously recorded unrealized gains were reflected in a stockholders' equity account and were not reported on the income statement.

SELF-STUDY QUIZ

Answer the following questions:

1. What is the name of the portfolio of securities held primarily for the purpose of selling them in the near future?
2. Which portfolio of securities can be reported on the balance sheet as either a current asset or a noncurrent asset, depending on management's intent?
3. What impact does the recording of an unrealized holding gain have on cash flows?
4. After the recording of an unrealized holding loss, the Allowance to Adjust to Market has a credit balance. How is this reported on the financial statements?

Check your response with the answer provided in the footnote at the bottom of this page.*

Equity Method

When General Electric invests cash in various securities reported on its balance sheet, it is a passive investor. It seeks to earn a high rate of return on these investments, but it does not become involved in exerting influence over the financing and operating

LEARNING OBJECTIVE 5
Use the equity method.

---

*1. Trading securities
 2. Available-for-sale securities
 3. There are no cash flow effects.
 4. This account is subtracted from the investment account reported on the balance sheet.

activities of the companies in which it invests. Accountants presume that investors are passive when they purchase less than 20 percent of the outstanding stock of another company, that is, when the market value method is used.

In many other situations, an investor may want to be able to exert influence without becoming the majority owner (i.e., an investment in 20 percent to 50 percent of the outstanding stock). A company may want to exert influence over another company for a variety of strategic reasons. For example, a retailer may want to influence a manufacturer to be sure that it can get certain products designed to its specifications; a manufacturer may want to influence a computer consulting firm to ensure that it can incorporate cutting-edge technology in its manufacturing processes; a furniture manufacturer may recognize that a service company lacks experienced management and could prosper with additional managerial support. As shown in Exhibit 12.1, the **equity method** is used when an investor can exert significant influence over an investee. This method permits the investor to report its share of the investee's income.

Equity method permits recording of investor's share of investee's income.

Under the equity method, the investment is presumed to have been made for a long-term strategic purpose. *In contrast,* the market value method is based on the presumption that the investment was made to earn a return on cash that is not currently needed for operating purposes. Earlier in the chapter, we discussed the fact that investments under the market value method are reported at their fair market value because the intent is to convert them to cash at some future time. Investments under the equity method are *not* reported at fair market value because they are made for long-term strategic purposes.

The equity method recognizes that the investing company has the ability to exert influence over the investee company and may, therefore, be involved in the investee's operations. As a result, the investing corporation reports income on the investment based on the income earned by the investee company instead of the dividends paid by the investee company.

To illustrate the equity method, assume that General Electric bought 3,000 shares of Davis Corporation stock at $120 per share on January 15, 19A. This represents 30 percent of Davis's outstanding stock. The initial recording of an investment in stock is similar under the market value method and the equity method. General Electric records the investment under the equity method as follows:

| Jan. 15, 19A | Long-term investment (A) .... | 360,000 | |
| | Cash (A) ($120 × 3,000 shares) .... | | 360,000 |

Subsequent to the initial recording of an investment, significant differences between the market value method and the equity method exist. When dividends are paid on stock accounted for under the equity method, the dividend is treated as a return of part of the investment. Therefore, under the equity method, dividends reduce the carrying value of the investment. Assume that Davis Corporation declared and paid a $1 per share dividend on June 14, 19A. General Electric records the dividend as follows:

| June 14, 19A | Cash (A) ($1 × 3,000 shares) .... | 3,000 | |
| | Long-term investment (A) .... | | 3,000 |

Notice that the dividend does not affect the income reported by General Electric (as it would if the market value method were used). The reason for this accounting treatment is important. Because General Electric can exert significant influence over Davis, it is able to affect the dividend policy of Davis. If investment income were based on the amount of dividends paid, it would be possible for the investor to manipulate its income when significant influence existed.

With equity investments, the investor often is actively involved in significant operating and financing decisions affecting the investee company. Because the investor participates in the process of earning income for the investee company, it is appropriate to base the investment income on the earnings of the investee company instead of the dividends it paid. To illustrate, assume, on December 31, 19A, Davis Corporation reported net income of $40,000. General Electric owns 30 percent of Davis; therefore its proportionate share of income is $12,000 ($40,000 × 30%). General Electric makes the following entry to record its share of the income reported by Davis:[1]

| Dec. 31, 19A | Long-term investment (A) .... | 12,000 | |
| | Revenue from investments* (R) .... | | 12,000 |

*Sometimes called Equity in earnings of affiliated company.

Based on these last two journal entries, you can see that the Long-Term Investment account reported on the balance sheet does not reflect either cost or market. The investment account is increased for the cost of shares that were purchased and the proportionate share of the investee company's income. The account is reduced by the amount of dividends received from the investee company. At the end of the accounting period, accountants do not adjust the investment account to reflect changes of the fair market value of the securities that are held.

Under the equity method, an investor also must report its share of any loss incurred by the investee corporation. The proportionate share of the loss is recorded with a debit to the Loss on Investment account and a credit to Long-Term Investment.

Managers' Selection of Accounting Alternatives

Financial
ANALYSIS

The market value and equity methods are two alternative methods used to account for investments. The selection of a specific method is determined by the facts surrounding the investment, not by management discretion. Managers can freely choose between LIFO and FIFO or accelerated depreciation and straight-line depreciation. In the case of investments, managers may not simply choose either the market value or equity methods. Investments of less than 20 percent of the outstanding stock of a company are accounted for under the market value method, and investments of 20 percent to 50 percent are recorded under the equity method.

In some cases, managers may be able to structure the acquisition of stock in a manner that permits them to use the accounting method that they prefer. For example, a company that wants to use the market value method could purchase only 19.9 percent of the outstanding stock of another company. Why would managers want to be able to avoid using the market value method or the equity method? A typical explanation has to do with earnings volatility. Most managers prefer to minimize variations in reported earnings. If a company were going to buy stock in a firm that reported large earnings in some years and large losses in others, it might want to use the market value method. In this way, the investor would not have to report its share of the investee firm's earnings and losses. Likewise, an investor may want to use the equity method if the investee firm had relatively stable earnings but more significant variations in its stock price. By using the equity method, the investor does not have to report unrealized gains and losses on the investment.

Analysts who compare several companies must understand the way that differences in the market value and equity methods can affect earnings associated with similar investments. Analysts also should examine how management may affect reported earnings through the level of ownership that is acquired.

---

[1] In this example, we assume that the investment was purchased at book value. More complex situations are discussed in advanced accounting courses.

Consolidation. The consolidated financial statements represent the adding together of all affiliates—companies that General Electric directly or indirectly controls, either through majority ownership or otherwise. The effects of transactions between separate companies are eliminated.

As the GE note indicates, eliminating any *intercompany* items is necessary when consolidated statements are prepared. Remember that consolidated statements make it appear as if a single company exists when in fact two or more separate legal entities exist. Intercompany items would not exist for only a single corporation. For example, a debt owed by GE (the parent) to one of its subsidiaries is not reported on a consolidated statement because a company cannot owe itself money.

Before we discuss the specific process of consolidation, let's examine different methods that one company can use to acquire a controlling influence in another company.

Methods of Acquiring a Controlling Interest

From an accounting perspective, two methods are used to acquire a controlling interest. In some cases, the stock of one company, such as Gallaher Tobacco (the subsidiary), is acquired by exchanging shares for shares of another company, such as American Tobacco (the parent). Before the merger, the owners of Gallaher Tobacco held shares in that company. After the merger, they hold shares in American Tobacco. If certain additional criteria are met, this type of acquisition is called a **pooling of interests.** To be accounted for as a pooling of interests, a transaction must meet a rigid list of criteria (discussed in advanced accounting courses). Basically, a pooling occurs when a stock-for-stock swap occurs. Under the pooling method, the assets of all of the affiliated companies are added together based on their *book value.* The assets are not revalued because a pooling is viewed as a rearrangement of ownership interest, not a purchase.

A **pooling of interests** is an acquisition that is completed by exchanging parent company stock for subsidiary voting capital stock.

The operations of this subsidiary company will be combined in consolidated financial statements.

As an alternative, American Tobacco could offer cash to the owners of Gallaher Tobacco. In that case, after the merger the former owners of Gallaher Tobacco hold cash and no stock in either company. This type of acquisition is known as a combination by **purchase.**

In this chapter, we focus on the purchase method of consolidation because it is used most often in practice. We have found that discussions of consolidation procedure can become complex. To make the discussion a little easier, we use simplified data for two hypothetical companies; information for Company P (the parent) and Company S (the acquired subsidiary) is shown in Exhibit 12.4.

> A **purchase** is an acquisition that is completed by purchasing subsidiary company voting capital stock for cash.

Purchase Method

Under the purchase method, the stockholders of the acquired company receive cash for the shares of stock they sell and are no longer owners of either the parent or the subsidiary. Accountants view this as a *purchase/sale transaction.* As you learned in earlier chapters, assets that are purchased should be recorded in terms of their cost. Thus, there is no conceptual difference between the direct purchase of a building worth $500,000 and the purchase of a company that has a single asset, a building worth $500,000. On the acquisition date, the investment account reflects the *market value* of the acquired shares.

> **LEARNING OBJECTIVE 7**
> Apply the purchase method and prepare elimination entries.

Company P paid $165,000 cash to buy all the stock of Company S, although the total *book value* of the stockholders' equity of Company S was only $150,000. Thus, Company P paid $15,000 more than book value. Why would Company P pay more than book value for the investment? Actually, the answer is simple: Remember that the book value of an asset is not the same as its fair market value. Company P had to pay fair market value to acquire Company S. The former owners would not have been willing to sell their stock for only book value. An analysis of Company B's assets revealed the following facts: (1) the plant and equipment owned by Company S had a market value of $50,000 at the acquisition date (compared with the book value of $45,000 reported by Company S) and (2) Company S had developed a good reputation with its customers,

EXHIBIT 12.4
Illustrative Data for Consolidation

COMPANY P AND COMPANY S
Separate Balance Sheets
January 1, 19A, Immediately after Acquisition

ASSETS	Company P	Company S
Cash	$ 40,000	$ 35,000
Inventories	170,000	70,000
Investment in Company S	165,000	
Plant and equipment (net)*	100,000	45,000
Total assets	$475,000	$150,000
LIABILITIES AND STOCKHOLDERS' EQUITY		
Stockholders' equity		
Common stock	300,000	100,000
Retained earnings	175,000	50,000
Total liabilities and stockholders' equity	$475,000	$150,000

* Plant and equipment, less accumulated depreciation. The net amounts are used to simplify the example. The end results are the same as they would have been had the separate control accounts been used.

which increased the overall value of Company S. For these reasons, Company P was willing to pay $15,000 more than book value to acquire Company S's stock.

In consolidation, the separate financial statements are combined into a single consolidated statement. The investment account must be eliminated to avoid double counting the subsidiary's assets and the parent company's investment in those assets. The investment account balance of $165,000 on Company P's books represents market value at the date of acquisition. It must be eliminated against the stockholders' equity of Company S, which is at *book value* because the stock is no longer outstanding from a consolidated perspective. Remember that Company P paid $15,000 more than book value to acquire Company S for two reasons: (1) Company S's plant and equipment had a market value of $50,000 at acquisition (compared with its book value of $45,000) and (2) Company S had developed a good reputation with its customers, which increased its overall value. The difference between the purchase cost and the book value of the investment may be analyzed as follows:

Purchase price for 100% interest in Company S	$165,000
Net assets purchased, valued at market	
Book value, $150,000, plus market value increment	
of plant and equipment, $5,000	
Total market value purchased	(155,000)
Goodwill purchased	$ 10,000

Goodwill is the amount that was paid for the good reputation and customer appeal of an acquired company.

Accountants define **goodwill** as the difference between the purchase price of a company and the fair market value of the net assets (assets minus liabilities) that were acquired. The following note from the Lands' End annual report provides a good definition of goodwill:

REAL WORLD EXCERPT

LANDS' END
Annual Report

Intangible assets consist primarily of goodwill which is the excess cost over the fair market value of net assets of businesses purchased.

Goodwill is created by a number of factors such as a good reputation, customer appeal, and general acceptance of the business. All successful companies have some amount of goodwill, but it can be reported on the balance sheet only if it is acquired in a purchase transaction. Goodwill is never recorded in a pooling of interests. General Electric's balance sheet includes goodwill in Intangible Assets. Some companies identify goodwill separately on the balance sheet.

To eliminate the Company P investment account and the owners' equity accounts of Company S, the following five steps must be completed:

1. Increase the plant and equipment of Company S from the book value of $45,000 to market value of $50,000; the increase is $5,000.
2. Recognize the $10,000 goodwill purchased as an asset.
3. Eliminate the investment account balance of $165,000.
4. Eliminate the Company S common stock balance of $100,000.
5. Eliminate the Company S retained earnings balance of $50,000.

When the purchase method is used, the balance of the Retained Earnings account for the subsidiary at acquisition is eliminated. This elimination is made with the purchase method because the retained earnings of the subsidiary were, in effect, paid to Company S's former stockholders when they were bought out for cash.

These five steps are implemented with the following adjustments:

Think of the different ways that GE could record goodwill in the annual report.

Common stock Company S (decrease)	100,000
Retained earnings Company S (decrease)	50,000
Plant and equipment (increase)	5,000
Goodwill (increase)	10,000
Investment (decrease)	165,000

These adjustments and eliminations are normally entered on a consolidation worksheet (which will be discussed in subsequent accounting courses). Due to the simplicity of this example, you can do the mental math to make these adjustments to the individual account balances shown in Exhibit 12.4 and then add together the amounts for each company. When these procedures are accomplished, the financial statement shown in Exhibit 12.5 is produced.

Ratio Analysis to Relate Earnings to Investment

Many financial analysts use the return on investment (ROI) ratio to evaluate management's effectiveness. This ratio relates the earnings of a company to the total investment that was used to earn the return. The ratio is computed in several different ways. One popular method is as follows:

$$\text{Return on investment} = \frac{\text{Net income + Interest expense (net of tax)}}{\text{Total assets}}$$

Analysts who use this ratio to compare companies need to understand the purchase method of consolidation. Remember that assets shown on the balance sheet are reported at historical cost. After an acquisition accounted for under the purchase method, the subsidiary's assets are reported at fair market value as of the date of purchase. This "revaluation" of assets often has a large impact on ROI because the denominator (total assets) increases. A company with significant acquisitions accounted for under the purchase method may have a lower ROI compared with that for other companies. Analysts need to understand that the differences may be the result of consolidation procedures, not underlying economic differences.

EXHIBIT 12.5
Consolidated Balance Sheet

COMPANY P AND S
Consolidated Balance Sheet
January 1, 19A

ASSETS

Cash	$ 75,000
Inventories	240,000
Plant and equipment (net)	150,000
Goodwill	10,000
Total assets	$475,000

LIABILITIES AND STOCKHOLDERS' EQUITY

Stockholders' equity

Common stock	$300,000
Retained earnings	175,000
Total liabilities and stockholders' equity	$475,000

NIKE

Goodwill is being amortized on a straight-line basis primarily over 25 to 40 years.

The period over which goodwill is amortized is an important factor for analysts to consider. Goodwill can be a large portion of some companies' assets. The decision to amortize goodwill over 40 years instead of 20 years can have a significant impact on reported earnings. Because the amortization of goodwill is a noncash expense, decisions concerning amortization periods have no impact on cash flows.

SELF-STUDY QUIZ

Lexis Corporation owns 100 percent of Nexis Company and reports on a consolidated basis. An intercompany account payable/receivable of $150,000 exists.

1. Prepare the elimination entry for the intercompany accounts, assuming the use of the purchase method.
2. Do you expect that cash reported on the consolidated balance sheet to be more, less, or the same as the sum of the individual cash balances for Lexis and Nexis?
3. What amount of ownership generally is necessary to prepare consolidated statements?

Check your responses with the answers in the footnote at the bottom of this page.*

**FOCUS ON CASH
FLOWS**

Investments and Cash Flows

A number of topics discussed in this chapter have an impact on a company's reported cash flows. Under the market value method, unrealized holding gains or losses in the trading securities portfolio affect net income but not cash flows. These gains (and losses) are subtracted from (added to) net income to compute cash flows from operating activities on the Statement of Cash Flows. Cash flows are affected when the securities are bought or sold, not when unrealized gains or losses are recorded.

Despite the fact that unrealized gains and losses do not affect current cash flows, analysts are interested in these items because they may be useful in predicting future cash flows. A company that has large unrealized gains will have more cash when it sells securities than will a company with large unrealized losses, assuming the same initial investment.

As noted under the equity method, revenue from investments is recorded based on the investing company's proportionate share of the investee company's net income. If you review the journal entry for this transaction earlier in this chapter, you will note that the Cash account is not affected. As a result, this is a noncash item that must be subtracted from net income to compute cash flow from operating activities on the Statement of Cash Flows.

We also discussed the recording and amortization of goodwill, which often is recognized when one company purchases another. The amortization of goodwill is a noncash item (like depreciation) that must be added to net income when computing cash flow from operating activities.

---

* 1. Account payable 150,000
    Account receivable 150,000
2. The same
3. Generally, more than 50 percent of the outstanding common stock with voting rights must be acquired.

Demonstration Case

(Try to resolve the requirements before proceeding to the suggested solution that follows.)

Case A: Howell Equipment Corporation sells and services a major line of farm equipment. Both sales and service operations have been profitable. The following transactions affected the company during 19S:

(a) Jan.　1　Purchased 2,000 shares of common stock of Dear Company at $40 per share. This was 1 percent of the shares outstanding. Management intends to actively trade these shares.

(b) Dec.　28　Received $4,000 cash dividend on the Dear Company stock.

(c) Dec.　31　Learned the current market price of the Dear stock, $39.

Required:
Give the journal entry for each of these transactions.

Suggested Solution

(a) Jan. 1, 19S:	Trading securities	80,000	
	Cash		80,000
	Purchased 2,000 shares Dear Company		
	common stock at $40 per share.		
(b) Dec. 28, 19S:	Cash	4,000	
	Revenue from investments		4,000
	Received dividend on Dear Company stock.		
(c) Dec. 31, 19S:	Unrealized loss on trading securities	2,000	
	Allowance to adjust to market		2,000
	To record unrealized loss on Dear stock:		
	2,000 shares × $1 ($40 − $39) = $2,000.		

Case B: On January 1, 19A, Connaught Company purchased 100 percent of the outstanding voting shares of London Company in the open market for $85,000 cash. On the date of acquisition, the market value of London Company's operational assets was $79,000.

Required:
1. Was this combination by pooling of interests or by purchase? Explain.
2. Give the journal entry that Connaught Company should make at date of acquisition. If none is required, explain why.
3. Give the journal entry that London Company should make at date of acquisition. If none is required, explain why.
4. Analyze the acquisition to determine the amount of goodwill purchased.
5. Should London Company's assets be included on the consolidated balance sheet at book value or market value? Explain.

Suggested Solution

1. The purchase method should be used because the subsidiary's stock was acquired for cash.

2. Jan. 1, 19A:　Investment in subsidiary 85,000

　　　　　　　　　Cash 85,000

3. London Company does not record a journal entry related to the purchase of stock by Connaught Company: the transaction was between Connaught and the stockholders of London Company. The transaction did not directly involve London Company.

4.	Purchase price for London Company	$85,000
	Market value of net assets purchased	79,000
	Goodwill	$ 6,000

5. Under the purchase method, London Company's assets should be included on the consolidated balance sheet at their market values as of the date of acquisition. The cost principle applies because a purchase/sale transaction is assumed when the combination is accounted for as a purchase. When the pooling of interests method is used, the subsidiary's assets are reported on the consolidated balance sheet at their book value.

Summary

Reporting and interpreting long-term investments in the capital stock of another company are determined by the percentage of shares owned in relation to the total number of shares outstanding. If the ownership level of *voting* shares is less than 20 percent, or if the ownership is of nonvoting stock, the market value method must be used. Under this method, the investment amount for common stock reported by the investor is based on the current market value of the stock.

Investments in equity securities accounted for under the market value method are reported on the balance sheet in either the trading securities portfolio or the available-for-sale portfolio. Unrealized holding gains and losses are recorded on investments held in both the trading securities and the available-for-sale portfolios. Unrealized gains and losses on securities in the trading portfolio are reported on the income statement, and unrealized gains and losses on securities in the available-for-sale portfolio are reported as a component of stockholders' equity and in a supplemental disclosure called comprehensive income.

If the ownership is at least 20 percent but not more than 50 percent, the equity method must be used. Under this method, the investor records the investment at cost at the date of acquisition. Each period thereafter, the investment amount is increased (or decreased) by the proportionate interest in the income (or loss) reported by the investee corporation and decreased by the proportionate share of the dividends declared by the investee corporation. Each period the investor recognizes as revenue its proportionate share of the income (or loss) reported by the investee company.

Consolidated financial statements are required in most situations when one corporation owns more than 50 percent of the outstanding voting stock of another corporation. The concept of consolidation is based on the view that a parent company and its subsidiaries constitute one economic entity. Therefore, the separate income statements, balance sheets, and statements of cash flows should be combined each period on an item-by-item basis as a single set of consolidated financial statements.

Ownership of a controlling interest of another corporation may be accounted for as either a pooling of interests or a combination by purchase. The measurement of amounts reported on the consolidated financial statements is influenced by these two different accounting methods.

The pooling of interests method usually is used when the parent company exchanges shares of its own voting stock for a controlling interest in the voting shares of the subsidiary. Under the purchase method, the parent company usually pays cash and/or incurs debt to acquire the voting shares of the subsidiary. In these circumstances, a purchase/sale transaction has been completed, and the acquisition is accounted for in conformity with the cost principle. Therefore, the subsidiary's assets must be measured at their acquisition market values when combined with the the the parent company's statements.

Each year, many companies report healthy profits but file for bankruptcy. Some investors consider this situation to be a paradox, but sophisticated analysts understand how this situation can occur. These analysts recognize that the income statement is prepared under the accrual concept (revenue is reported when earned and the related expense is matched with the revenue). The income statement does not report cash collections and cash payments. Troubled companies usually file for bankruptcy because they cannot meet their cash obligations (for example, they cannot pay their suppliers or meet their required interest payments). The income statement does not help analysts assess the cash flows of a company. The statement of cash flows discussed in Chapter 13 is designed to help statement users evaluate a company's cash inflows and outflows.

Key Ratios

The **return on investment ratio** compares the income earned and the assets that were employed to earn that return. The ratio is computed as follows (p. 631):

$$\text{Return on investment} = \frac{\text{Net income} + \text{Interest expense (net of tax)}}{\text{Total assets}}$$

Key Terms

Available-for-Sale Securities All investments other than trading securities that are accounted for under the market value method. *617*

Consolidated Financial Statements The financial statements of two or more companies that have been combined into a single set of financial statements. *627*

Control The ability of the investing company to determine the operating and financing policies of another company in which it owns shares of the voting stock; presumed to exist when more than 50 percent of the voting stock of an entity is owned by one investor. *615*

Equity Method Method used by investor if 20 percent to 50 percent of the voting stock of the investee company is owned by the investor. It permits recording of investor's share of investee's income. *624*

Goodwill The amount that was paid for the good reputation and customer appeal of an acquired company. *630*

Market Value Method Method used by the investor if less than 20 percent of the voting stock of the investee company is owned by the investor; unrealized gains and losses

are reported based on changes in the prices of securities that are held. *617*

Parent The company that has a significant investment in a subsidiary company. *627*

Pooling of Interests An acquisition that is completed by exchanging parent company stock for subsidiary voting capital stock. *628*

Purchase An acquisition that is completed by purchasing subsidiary company voting capital stock for cash. *629*

Significant Influence The ability of an investing company to have an important impact on the operating and financing policies of another company (the investee). *615*

Subsidiary The company that is owned by a parent company as evidenced by more than 50 percent of the voting capital stock. *627*

Trading Securities All investments in stocks or bonds that are held primarily for the purpose of selling them in the near future; accounted for under the market value method. *617*

Unrealized Holding Gains and Losses Amounts recorded when the price of securities that are currently held changes. *618*

Questions

1. Explain the difference between a short-term investment and a long-term investment.
2. Match the following:

   MEASUREMENT METHOD
   _____ Market value method
   _____ Equity method
   _____ Consolidation

   LEVEL OF OWNERSHIP OF THE VOTING CAPITAL STOCK
   a. More than 50 percent ownership.
   b. Less than 20 percent ownership.
   c. At least 20 percent but not more than 50 percent ownership.

3. Explain the application of the cost principle to the purchase of capital stock in another company.
4. Under the market value method, when and how does the investor company measure revenue?
5. Under the equity method, why does the investor company measure revenue on a pro- portionate basis when income is reported by the investee company rather than when dividends are declared?
6. Under the equity method, dividends received from the investee company are not recorded as revenue. To record dividends as revenue involves double counting. Explain.
7. Match the following items that relate to the long-term investment amount reported on the balance sheet of the investor company:

   MEASUREMENT METHOD
   _____ Market value method
   _____ Equity method

   EXPLANATION OF BALANCE IN THE INVESTMENT ACCOUNT
   a. Market value.
   b. Original cost plus proportionate part of the income of the investee, less proportion- ate part of the dividends declared by investee.

8. What is a parent–subsidiary relationship?
9. Explain the basic concept underlying consolidated statements.
10. What is the basic element that must be present before consolidated statements are appropriate?
11. What is pooling of interests?
12. What is a combination by purchase?
13. What are intercompany eliminations?
14. Explain why the investment account must be eliminated against stockholders' equity when consolidated statements are prepared.
15. Explain why additional depreciation expense usually must be recognized on consolida- tion when the combination was by purchase.
16. What is goodwill?

Exercises

E12–1 Comparing Primary Characteristics of Market Value and Equity Methods

Company A purchased a certain number of Company B's outstanding voting shares at $18 per share as a long-term investment. Company B had outstanding 20,000 shares of $10 par value stock. On a separate sheet, complete the following matrix relating to the measurement and reporting by Company A after acquisition of the shares of Company B stock.

Questions	Market Value Method	Equity Method
a. What is the applicable level of ownership by Company A of Company B to apply the method?	Percent	Percent
For (b), (e), (f), and (g), assume the following:		
Number of shares acquired of Company B stock	1,500	5,000
Net income reported by Company B in the first year	$60,000	$60,000
Dividends declared by Company B in the first year	$15,000	$15,000
Market price at end of first year, Company B stock, $15		
b. At acquisition, the investment account on the books of Company A should be debited at what amount?	$	$
c. On what basis should Company A recognize revenue earned on the stock of Company B? Explanation required.		
d. After acquisition date, on what basis should Company A change the balance of the investment account in respect to the stock of Company B owned (other than for disposal of the investment)? Explanation required.		
e. What is the balance in the investment account on the books of Company A at the end of the first year?	$	$
f. What amount of revenue from the investment in Company B should Company A report at the end of the first year?	$	$
g. What amount of unrealized loss should Company A report at the end of the first year?	$	$

E12–2 Reporting Long-Term Investment in Equity Securities

During 19B, Princeton Company acquired some of the 50,000 outstanding shares of the common stock, par $10, of Cox Corporation as a long-term investment. The accounting period for both companies ends December 31. The following transactions occurred during 19B:

July 2 Purchased 8,000 shares of Cox common stock at $28 per share.

Dec. 31 Received the 19B annual financial statement of Cox Corporation that reported net income of $52,000.

31 Cox Corporation declared and paid a cash dividend of $2 per share.

31 Learned the current market price of Cox stock, $25 per share.

Required:

1. What accounting method should the company use? Why?
2. Give the journal entries for each of these transactions. If no entry is required, explain why.
3. Show how the long-term investment and the related revenue should be reported on the 19B financial statements of the company.

E12–3 Recording and Reporting a Long-Term Investment in an Equity Security

Felicia Company acquired some of the 60,000 shares of outstanding common stock (no-par) of Nueces Corporation during 19E as a long-term investment. The annual accounting period for both companies ends December 31. The following transactions occurred during 19E:

Jan. 10 Purchased 21,000 shares of Nueces common stock at $12 per share.

Dec. 31 Received the 19E financial statement of Nueces Corporation, which reported net income of $90,000.

| Dec. | 31 | Nueces Corporation declared and paid a cash dividend of $0.60 per share. |
| | 31 | Determined market price of Nueces stock to be $11 per share. |

Required:

1. What accounting method should the company use? Why?
2. Give the journal entries for each of these transactions. If no entry is required, explain why.
3. Show how the long-term investment and the related revenue should be reported on the 19E financial statements of the company.

E12–4 Analyzing a Long-Term Investment in an Equity Security

During 19H, Russell Company purchased some of the 90,000 shares of common stock, par $8, of Sea Tuna, Inc., as a long-term investment. The annual accounting period for each company ends December 31. The following transactions occurred during 19H:

Jan.	7	Purchased 9,000 shares of Sea Tuna common stock at $32 per share.
Dec.	31	Received the 19H financial statement of Sea Tuna, which reported net income of $200,000.
	31	Sea Tuna declared and paid a cash dividend of $3 per share.
	31	Learned the current market price of Sea Tuna stock, $40 per share.

Required:

1. What accounting method should the company use? Why?
2. Give the journal entries for each of these transactions. If no entry is required, explain why.
3. Show how the long-term investment and the related revenue should be reported on the 19H financial statements of the company.

E12–5 Accounting for a Long-Term Investment in an Equity Security

Use the same situation for Russell Company and the data given in Exercise 12–4, except for the January 7, 19H, transaction. Assume that it was as follows:

| Jan. | 7 | Purchased 40,500 shares of Sea Tuna stock at $32 per share. |

(The data for December 31 are unchanged.)

Required:

1. What accounting method should the company use? Why?
2. Give the journal entries for each transaction (refer also to transactions given in Exercise 12–4). If no entry is required, explain why.
3. Show how the long-term investment and the related revenue should be reported on the 19H financial statements of the company.

E12–6 Reporting Gains and Losses in the Trading Security Portfolio

On June 30, 19A, MetroMedia, Inc., purchased 10,000 shares of Mitek stock for $20 per share. Management purchased the stock for speculative purposes and recorded the stock in the trading security portfolio. The following information pertains to the price per share of Mitek stock:

	Price
12/31/19A	$24
12/31/19B	31
12/31/19C	25

MetroMedia sold all of the Mitek stock on February 14, 19D, at a price of $23 per share. Prepare any journal entries that are required by the facts presented in this case.

E12–7 Reporting Gains and Losses in the Available-for-Sale Portfolio

Using the data in the previous exercise, assume that MetroMedia management purchased the Mitek stock for the available-for-sale portfolio instead of the trading securities portfolio. Prepare any journal entries that are required by the facts presented in the case.

E12–8 Reporting Gains and Losses in the Trading Security Portfolio

On March 10, 19B, General Solutions, Inc., purchased 5,000 shares of MicroTech stock for $50 per share. Management purchased the stock for speculative purposes and recorded it in the trading security portfolio. The following information pertains to the price per share of MicroTech stock:

	Price
12/31/19B	$55
12/31/19C	40
12/31/19D	42

General Solutions sold all of the MicroTech stock on September 12, 19E, at a price of $39 per share. Prepare any journal entries that are required by the facts presented in this case.

E12–9 Reporting Gains and Losses in the Available-for-Sale Portfolio

Using the data in the previous exercise, assume that General Solutions management purchased the MicroTech stock for the available-for-sale portfolio instead of the trading securities portfolio. Prepare any journal entries that are required by the facts presented in the case.

E12–10 Financial Reporting Using the Consolidation Method

On January 1, 19A, Company P purchased 100 percent of the outstanding voting shares of Company S in the open market for $80,000 cash. On that date (prior to the acquisition), the separate balance sheets (summarized) of the two companies reported the following book values:

	PRIOR TO ACQUISITION	
	Company P	**Company S**
Cash	$ 92,000	$14,000
Receivable from Company P		4,000
Operational assets (net)	48,000	42,000
Total assets	$140,000	$60,000
Liabilities	$ 36,000	$ 9,000
Payable to Company S	4,000	
Common stock:		
Company P (no-par)	90,000	
Company S (par $10)		40,000
Retained earnings	10,000	11,000
Total liabilities and stockholders' equity	$140,000	$60,000

It was determined on the date of acquisition that the market value of the operational assets of Company S was $56,000.

Required:

1. Was this a combination by pooling of interests or by purchase? Explain why.
2. Give the journal entry that Company P should make at date of acquisition. If none is required, explain why.
3. Give the journal entry that Company S should make at date of acquisition. If none is required, explain why.
4. Analyze the acquisition to determine the amount of goodwill purchased.
5. Should Company S assets be included on the consolidated balance sheet at book value or market value? Explain.
6. Prepare a consolidated balance sheet immediately after acquisition.

E12–11 Reporting Consolidated Operations after Acquisition

On January 4, 19A, Company P acquired all of the outstanding stock of Company S for $12 cash per share. At the date of acquisition, the balance sheet of Company S reflected the following:

Common stock (par $5)	$40,000
Retained earnings	36,000

Immediately after the acquisition, the balance sheets reflected the following:

	BALANCES, JAN. 4, 19A, IMMEDIATELY AFTER ACQUISITION	
	Company P	Company S
Cash	$ 22,000	$14,000
Receivable from Company P		9,000
Investment in Company S (100%), at cost	96,000	
Operational assets (net)	132,000	65,000*
Total assets	$250,000	$88,000
Liabilities	$ 18,000	$12,000
Payable to Company S	9,000	
Common stock (par $5)	120,000	40,000
Retained earnings	103,000	36,000
Total liabilities and stockholders' equity	$250,000	$88,000

*Determined by Company P to have a market value of $72,000 at date of acquisition.

Required:

1. Was this a combination by pooling of interests or by purchase? Explain why.
2. Give the journal entry that Company P should make to record the acquisition.
3. Analyze the acquisition to determine the amount of goodwill purchased.
4. Should Company S's assets be included on the consolidated balance sheet at book value or market value? Explain.
5. Prepare a consolidated balance sheet immediately after acquisition.

Chrysler Corporation

E12–12 Explaining Consolidation Policy

The annual report for Chrysler includes the statement that "intercompany accounts and transactions have been eliminated in consolidation." In your own words, explain the meaning of this statement. Why is it necessary to eliminate all intercompany accounts and transactions in consolidation?

Maytag

E12–13 Explaining Consolidation Policy

The annual report for Maytag includes the following note:

Principles of Consolidation: The consolidated financial statements include the accounts and transactions of the Company and its wholly owned subsidiaries. Subsidiaries located outside the United States are consolidated as of one month earlier than subsidiaries in the United States.

Although this issue was not discussed directly in the chapter, why do you suppose foreign affiliates are consolidated as of one month earlier than U.S. affiliates?

E12–14 Interpreting Accounting Policy

Martin Marietta Corporation is involved in the manufacture of leading edge technologies. The company's annual report states "costs in excess of net assets acquired are amortized ratably over appropriate periods ranging from 20 to 40 years." Based on the discussion in this chapter, express this policy in your own words.

E12–15 Analyzing an Acquisition

The notes to the financial statements of Colgate-Palmolive contained the following information:

2. Acquisitions
In March 1992, the Company acquired the Menner Company for an aggregate price of $670 million paid with 11.6 million shares of the Company's common stock and $127 million in cash.

Should Colgate-Palmolive account for this transaction as a purchase or a pooling? Explain.

E12–16 Analysis of Goodwill

Capital Cities, Inc., owns television and radio stations, newspapers, and television networks, including ABC and ESPN. Capital Cities' balance sheet reports goodwill in the amount of $2,047,191, which is more than 30 percent of the company's total assets. This percentage is very large compared to that of most companies. Explain why you think Capital Cities has such a large amount of goodwill reported on its balance sheet.

Martin Marietta Corporation

Colgate-Palmolive

Capital Cities, Inc.

Problems

P12–1 Reporting Investments

On August 4, 19A, Coffman Corporation purchased 1,000 shares of Wefald Company for $45,000. The following information applies to the stock price of Wefald Company:

	Price
12/31/19A	$52
12/31/19B	47
12/31/19C	38

Wefald Company declares and pays cash dividends of $2 per share on June 1 of each year.

Required:
1. Prepare journal entries to record the facts in the case, assuming that Coffman purchased the shares for the trading portfolio.
2. Prepare journal entries to record the facts in the case, assuming that Coffman purchased the shares for the available-for-sale portfolio.

3. Prepare journal entries to record the facts in the case, assuming that Coffman used the equity method to account for the investment. Coffman owns 30 percent of Wefald and Wefald reported $50,000 in income each year.

P12–2 Reporting Investments

On March 1, 19A, HiTech Industries purchased 10,000 shares of Integrated Services Company for $20 per share. The following information applies to the stock price of Integrated Services:

	Price
12/31/19A	$18
12/31/19B	24
12/31/19C	30

Required:

1. Prepare journal entries to record the facts in the case, assuming that HiTech purchased the shares for the trading portfolio.
2. Prepare journal entries to record the facts in the case, assuming that HiTech purchased the shares for the available-for-sale portfolio.

P12–3 Reporting Investments

On September 15, 19A, James Media Corporation purchased 5,000 shares of Community Broadcasting Company for $30 per share. The following information applies to the stock price of Community Broadcasting:

	Price
12/31/19A	$32
12/31/19B	24
12/31/19C	20

Required:

1. Prepare journal entries to record the facts in the case, assuming that James Media purchased the shares for the trading portfolio.
2. Prepare journal entries to record the facts in the case, assuming that James Media purchased the shares for the available-for-sale portfolio.

P12–4 Reporting Using the Proper Method to Account for an Equity Investment

During January 19A, Hexagon Company purchased 12,000 shares of the 200,000 outstanding common shares (no-par value) of Seven Corporation at $30 per share. This block of stock was purchased as a long-term investment. Assume that the accounting period for each company ends December 31.

Subsequent to acquisition, the following data were available:

	19A	19B
Income reported by Seven Corporation at December 31	$40,000	$60,000
Cash dividends declared and paid by Seven Corporation during the year	60,000	80,000
Market price per share of Seven common stock on December 31	28	29

Required:

1. What accounting method should the company use? Why?
2. Give the journal entries for the company for each year (use parallel columns) for the following (if none, explain why):
   a. Acquisition of Seven Corporation stock.
   b. Net income reported by Seven Corporation.
   c. Dividends received from Seven Corporation.
   d. Market value effects at year-end.

3. Show how the following amounts should be reported on the financial statements for each year:
   a. Long-term investment.
   b. Stockholders' equity—unrealized loss.
   c. Revenues.

P12–5 Reporting Using the Proper Method to Account for Two Different Equity Investments

During January 19A, Crystal Company purchased the following shares as a long-term investment:

Stock	Number of Shares Outstanding	Purchase	Cost per Share
Q Corporation Common (no-par)	90,000	12,600	$ 5
R Corporation Preferred, nonvoting (par $10)	20,000	12,000	30

Subsequent to acquisition, the following data were available:

	19A	19B
Net income reported at December 31:		
Q Corporation	$30,000	$36,000
R Corporation	40,000	48,000
Dividends declared and paid per share during the year		
Q Corporation common stock	$0.80	$0.85
R Corporation preferred stock	0.90	0.90
Market value per share at December 31		
Q Corporation common stock	4.00	4.00
R Corporation preferred stock	29.00	30.00

Required:
1. What accounting method should be used for the investment in Q common stock? R preferred stock? Why?
2. Give the journal entries for the company for each year in parallel columns (if none, explain why) for each of the following:
   a. Purchase of the investments.
   b. Income reported by Q and R Corporations.
   c. Dividends received from Q and R Corporations.
   d. Market value effects at year-end.
3. For each year, show how the following amounts should be reported on the financial statements for 19A:
   a. Long-term investment.
   b. Stockholders' equity—unrealized loss.
   c. Revenues.

P12–6 Comparing Methods to Account for Various Levels of Ownership of Voting Stock

Company C had outstanding 30,000 shares of common stock, par value $10 per share. On January 1, 19B, Company D purchased some of these shares at $25 per share. At the end of 19B, Company C reported the following: income, $50,000, and cash dividends declared and paid during the year, $25,500. The market value of Company C stock at the end of 19B was $22 per share.

Required:

1. For each of the following cases (in the tabulation), identify the method of accounting that Company D should use. Explain why.
2. Give the journal entries for Company D at the dates indicated for each of the two independent cases. If no entry is required, explain why. Use the following format:

Tabulation of Items	Case A 3,600 Shares Purchased	Case B 10,500 Shares Purchased
a. Entry to record the acquisition at January 1, 19B.		
b. Entry to recognize the income reported by Company C for 19B.		
c. Entry to recognize the dividends declared and paid by Company C.		
d. Entry to recognize market value effect at end of 19B.		

3. Complete the following schedule to show the separate amounts that should be reported on the 19B financial statements of Company D:

	DOLLAR AMOUNTS	
	Case A	Case B
Balance sheet		
Investments and funds		
Stockholders' equity		
Income statement		
Revenue from investments		

4. Explain why assets, stockholders' equity, and revenues for the two cases are different.

P12–7 Comparing the Market Value and Equity Methods

Packer Company purchased, as a long-term investment, some of the 200,000 shares of the outstanding common stock of Boston Corporation. The annual accounting period for each company ends December 31. The following transactions occurred during 19E:

Jan. 10 Purchased shares of common stock of Boston at $15 per share as follows:

Case A—30,000 shares.
Case B—80,000 shares.

Dec. 31 Received the 19E financial statements of Boston Corporation; the reported net income was $90,000.

31 Received a cash dividend of $0.60 per share from Boston Corporation.

31 Learned the current market price of Boston stock, $9 per share.

Required:

1. For each case, identify the accounting method that the company should use. Explain why.
2. Give the journal entries for each case for these transactions. If no entry is required, explain why. (*Hint:* Use parallel columns for Case A and Case B.)
3. Give the amounts for each case that should be reported on the 19E financial statements. Use the following format:

	Case A	Case B
Balance sheet (partial)		
Investments and funds:		
Investments in common stock, Boston Corporation		
Stockholders' equity		
Unrealized loss		
Income statement (partial)		
Revenue from investments		

P12–8 Comparing the Market Value and Equity Methods

Ship Corporation had outstanding 100,000 shares of no-par common stock. On January 10, 19B, Shore Company purchased a block of these shares in the open market at $20 per share. At the end of 19B, Ship reported net income of $300,000 and cash dividends of $.60 per share. At December 31, 19B, Ship stock was selling at $18 per share. This problem involves two separate cases:

> **Case A** Purchase of 10,000 shares of Ship common stock.
> **Case B** Purchase of 40,000 shares of Ship common stock.

Required:

1. For each case, identify the accounting method that the company should use. Explain why.
2. For each case, in parallel columns, give the journal entries for each of the following (if no entry is required, explain why):
   a. Acquisition.
   b. Revenue recognition.
   c. Dividends received.
   d. Market value effects.
3. For each case, show how the following should be reported on the 19B financial statements:
   a. Long-term investments.
   b. Market effects.
   c. Revenues.
4. Explain why the amounts reported in requirement (3) are different for the two cases.

P12–9 Comparing Accounting for Equity Securities with Accounting for Debt Securities

(*Hint:* You may want to review material in Chapter 10.)

On January 1, 19B, Duplex Company purchased $80,000, 12 percent bonds of Quatro Company as a long-term investment at 100 (plus any accrued interest). Interest is payable annually on December 31. The bonds have six years to maturity from December 31, 19A. The company's annual accounting period ends December 31. In addition, on January 2, 19B, the company purchased in the market 10 percent of the 20,000 shares of outstanding common stock of Quatro Company at $50 per share.

Required:

1. Give the journal entry to record the purchase of the bonds on January 1, 19B. The company intends to hold the bonds until maturity.
2. Give the journal entry to record the purchase of the common stock on January 2, 19B.
3. Give the journal entry, assuming a cash dividend of $3 per share was declared and received on the Quatro stock on December 28, 19B.
4. Give the required journal entries for December 31, 19B.
5. Show how the long-term investments and the related revenues should be reported on the 19B annual financial statements. Market price of Quatro stock was $55 at the end of 19B.

P12–10 Analyzing Goodwill and Preparing a Consolidated Balance Sheet

On January 5, 19A, Company P purchased all the outstanding stock of Company S for $80,000 cash. Immediately after the acquisition, the separate balance sheets of the two companies showed the following:

	JAN. 5, 19A, IMMEDIATELY AFTER ACQUISITION	
	Company P	Company S
Cash	$ 18,000	$ 7,000
Accounts receivable (net)	12,000	5,000
Receivable from Company S	3,000	
Inventory	40,000	22,000
Investment in Company S (at cost)	80,000	
Operational assets (net)	128,000	54,000
Other assets	10,000	2,000
Total assets	$291,000	$90,000
Accounts payable	$ 15,000	$23,000
Payable to Company P		3,000
Bonds payable	70,000	
Common stock (par $10)	160,000	50,000
Contributed capital in excess of par	16,000	
Retained earnings	30,000	14,000
Total liabilities and stockholders' equity	$291,000	$90,000

Company S's operational assets were estimated to have a market value of $62,000 at date of acquisition.

Required:
1. Was this a combination by pooling of interests or by purchase? Explain why.
2. Give the journal entry that Company P should make at the date of acquisition.
3. Analyze the acquisition to determine the amount of goodwill purchased.
4. Should Company S's assets be included on the consolidated balance sheet at book value or market value? Explain.
5. Prepare a consolidated balance sheet immediately after acquisition.

Cases and Projects

C12–1 Analyzing the Financial Effects of the Market Value and Equity Methods

On January 1, 19B, Woodrow Company purchased 30 percent of the outstanding common stock of Trevor Corporation at a total cost of $560,000. Management intends to hold the stock for the long term. On the December 31, 19B, balance sheet, the investment in Trevor Corporation was $720,000, but no additional Trevor stock was purchased. The company received $80,000 in cash dividends from Trevor. The dividends were declared and paid during 19B. The company used the equity method to account for its investment in Trevor. The market price of Trevor stock increased during 19B to a total value of $600,000.

Required:
1. Explain why the investment account balance increased from $560,000 to $720,000 during 19B.
2. What amount of revenue from the investment was reported during 19B?
3. If Woodrow used the market value method, what amount of revenue from the investment should have been reported in 19B?
4. If the market value method were used, what amount should be reported as the investment in Trevor Corporation on the December 31, 19B, balance sheet?

C12–2 An International Perspective

Grand Metropolitan is a major international company located in London. A recent annual report contained the following information concerning its accounting policies.

Grand Metropolitan

> **Acquisitions**   On the acquisition of a business, including an interest in a related company, fair values are attributed to the group's share of net tangible assets and significant owned brands acquired. Where the cost of acquisition exceeds the values attributable to such net assets, the difference is treated as goodwill and is written off directly to reserves in the year of acquisition.
>
> **Intangible assets**   Significant owned brands, acquired after 1st January 1985, the value of which is not expected to diminish in the foreseeable future, are recorded in the balance sheet as fixed intangible assets. No amortisation is provided on these assets but their value is reviewed annually by the directors and the cost written down as an exceptional item where permanent diminution in value has occurred.

Grand Metropolitan used the word *reserves* to mean *retained earnings*. Discuss how this accounting treatment compares with procedures used in this country.

C12–3 Financial Statement Analysis

Refer to the financial statement of Toys "R" Us given in Appendix B at the end of this book.

Required:

The notes indicate that the company eliminates all intercompany balances and transactions during consolidation. Explain.

C12–4 Project: Analysis of Acquisition Strategy

Review several business publications or electronic databases to identify a company that has recently announced the acquisition of another company. Analyze financial statements for both companies. Write a brief report identifying the strategic reasons for the acquisition and your evaluation of that strategy.

C12–5 Project: Analysis of an Investment Strategy

Review financial statements or electronic data sources to identify a company with significant investment in securities reported on its balance sheet (approximately 10 percent or more of total assets). Determine why the company has invested in securities rather than investing in productive assets or paying higher dividends to owners.

C12–6 Project: Explanation of Consolidated Statements

Assume that you are a stockbroker who has just received a letter from a new client who is a first-time investor. The client has just received the annual report for General Electric and noticed that the statements are "consolidated." The customer has asked you to explain what that means and what impact it has on his evaluation of the company. Write a brief letter to answer the investor's questions.

C12–7 Focus on Cash Flows: Cash Flows from Investments

The chapter mentions that Revenue from Investments is a noncash item because it is not associated with an inflow of cash. Write a brief memo explaining when the investing company reports cash from investments accounted for under the equity method.

C12–8 Project: Financial Analysis

Assume that you are a financial analyst for a large investment banking firm. You are responsible for analyzing companies in the retail sales industry. You have just learned that a large West Coast retailer has acquired a large East Coast retail chain. You have reviewed the separate financial statements for the two companies before the acquisition was announced. You have been asked to write a brief report explaining what will happen when the financial results of the companies are consolidated under the purchase method, including the impact on the return on investment ratio.

C12–9 **Project: Financial Analysis**

Assume that you are an analyst for a large mutual fund. The mutual fund manager has asked you to review a company that has a very aggressive acquisition policy and has purchased new companies each year for the past 12 years. The company has reported significant increases in sales revenue and net income each year and has been viewed as a growth company. Your review has determined that the growth in revenue and income each year is attributable to the acquisition of each new company. Write a brief memo analyzing this company's growth strategy.

C12–10 **Project: Ethics**

Assume that you are on the board of directors of a company that has decided to buy 80 percent of the outstanding stock of another company within the next three or four months. The discussions have convinced you that this company is an excellent investment opportunity, so you decide to buy $10,000 worth of the company's stock. Is there an ethical problem with your decision? Would your answer be different if you planned to invest $500,000? Are there different ethical considerations if you don't buy the stock but recommend that your brother do so?

C12–11 **Project: Financial Update**

Obtain the most recent annual report for General Electric and recent articles about GE reported in business publications. Prepare an analysis of the company's diversification strategy. Consider the success of GE's individual business lines and the company's ability to manage broadly diversified businesses.

C12–12 **Team Project: Examining an Annual Report**

As a group, select an industry to analyze. Each team member should acquire the annual report or 10-K for one publicly traded company in the industry, with each member selecting a different company. (Library files, the SEC EDGAR service at www.sec.gov, Compustat CD, or the company itself are good sources.) On an individual basis, each group member should then write a short report answering the following questions about his or her selected company.

1. Determine if the company prepared consolidated financial statements. If so, did it use the purchase or pooling method?
2. Does the company use the equity method for any of its investments?
3. Does the company hold any investments in securities? If so, what is their market value? Does the company have any unrealized gains or losses?
4. Identify the company's lines of business. Why does management want to engage in these business activities?

Discuss any patterns across the companies that you as a group observe. Then, as a group, write a short report comparing and contrasting your companies using these attributes. Provide potential explanations for any differences discovered.

CHAPTER THIRTEEN

Statement of Cash Flows

Boston Beer Company
MANAGING PRODUCTION AND CASH FLOWS IN A GROWTH STRATEGY

I t was no accident when 36-year-old Jim Koch, founder of Boston Beer

Company, named his products for Samuel Adams, the American revolutionary

who led the Boston Tea Party. When Koch delivered the first 25 cases of

Samuel Adams Boston Lager to a Boston bar in 1985, he fired the first shot in a

revolution that stunned the brewing industry. At that point, mega-brewers

like Anheuser-Busch and Miller dominated beer brewing; and annual sales by

small "craft" brewers were just over 100,000 barrels. In just ten years, craft

brewers' annual sales grew to nearly 4,000,000 barrels. Boston Beer is the

clear leader among craft brewers with a 25 percent market share and 1995

net income of more than $12 million.

Although it may seem puzzling, growing profitable operations like

those of Boston Beer do not always ensure positive cash flow. Also, seasonal

fluctuations in sales and purchases of inventory and advertising may cause

high *profits* and net cash *outflows* in some quarters and *losses* and net cash *inflows* in others. As we emphasized in earlier chapters, this results because revenues and expenses are not equal to cash inflows and outflows. As a consequence, Boston Beer must carefully manage cash flows as well as profits. For the same reasons, financial analysts must consider the information provided in its cash flow statement as well as the income statement and balance sheet.

■　■　■

Business Background

Clearly, net income is an important number, but cash flow is also critical. Cash flow permits a company to expand its operations, replace needed assets, take advantage of market opportunities, and pay dividends to its owners. Some Wall Street analysts go as far as saying "cash flow is king." Both managers and analysts need to understand the various sources and uses of cash that are associated with business activity.

The cash flow statement focuses attention on a firm's ability to generate cash internally, its management of current assets and current liabilities, and the details of its investments in productive assets and external financing. It is designed to help both managers and analysts answer important cash-related questions such as these:

- Will the company have enough cash to pay its short-term debts to suppliers and others without additional borrowing?
- Is the company adequately managing its accounts receivable, inventory, and so on?
- Has the company made necessary investments in new productive capacity?
- Did the company generate enough cash flow internally to finance necessary investments, or did it rely on external financing?
- Is the company changing the makeup of its external financing?

Three main categories of activities generate and use cash: activity related to operating the business, activity related to investments in productive assets, and activity related to financing the business. The statement of cash flows is designed to provide managers and analysts with information concerning these important activities. Boston Beer is a particularly good example to illustrate the importance of the cash flow statement for two reasons. First, like all companies in its industry, Boston Beer's inventory purchases and sales vary with the seasons. This seasonal variation has surprising effects on cash flows and net income. Second, an important element of its business strategy is the outsourcing of much of its product manufacturing (called *contract brewing*). This dramatically affects its investments in plant and equipment and the need for external financing to support growth. The statement of cash flows taken from a recent quarterly report for The Boston Beer Company is shown in Exhibit 13.1. We will now discuss the information that this required statement provides.

LEARNING OBJECTIVE 1

Classify cash flow statement items as part of net cash flows from operating, investing, and financing activities.

A **cash equivalent** is a short-term, highly liquid investment with an original maturity of less than three months.

Classifications on the Statement of Cash Flows

Basically, the statement of cash flows explains how the cash balance at the beginning of the period became the cash balance at the end of the period. For purposes of this statement, the definition of *cash* includes cash and cash equivalents. **Cash equivalents** are short-term, highly liquid investments that are both

EXHIBIT 13.1
Consolidated Statement of Cash Flows

THE BOSTON BEER COMPANY, INC.
CONSOLIDATED STATEMENT OF CASH FLOWS
(in thousands)

	Quarter ended March 30, 1996
Cash flows from operating activities:	
Net Income	$2,640
Adjustments to reconcile net income to net cash provided by operating activities:	
Depreciation and amortization	539
Stock option compensation expense	78
Changes in assets & liabilities:	
Accounts receivable	(8,383)
Inventory	(3,428)
Prepaid expenses	58
Other current assets	1,393
Other assets	1,262
Accounts payable	5,394
Accrued expenses	(939)
Total adjustments	(4,026)
Net cash provided by (used for) operating activities	(1,386)
Cash flows from investing activities:	
Additions to fixed assets	(2,845)
Purchases of restricted investments	(614)
Maturities of restricted investments	597
Net cash used in investing activities	(2,862)
Cash flows from financing activities:	
Net borrowings under line of credit	240
Net cash provided by financing activities	240
Net decrease in cash and cash equivalents	(4,008)
Cash and cash equivalents at beginning of period	36,607
Cash and cash equivalents at end of period	$32,599

The accompanying notes are an integral part of the financial statements.

1. Readily convertible to known amounts of cash.
2. So near their maturity that they present insignificant risk of changes in value because of changes in interest rates.

Generally, only investments with original maturities of less than three months qualify as a cash equivalent under this definition.[1] Examples of cash equivalents are Treasury bills (a form of short-term U.S. government debt), money market funds, and commercial paper (short-term notes payable issued by large corporations).

As you can see in Exhibit 13.1, the statement of cash flows reports cash inflows and outflows based on three broad categories: (1) operating activities, (2) investing activities, and (3) financing activities. To improve comparability, *FASB Statement 95* defines each category included in the required statement. These definitions (with explanations) are presented in the following sections.

---

[1] *Original maturity* means original maturity to the entity holding the investment. For example, both a three-month Treasury bill and a three-year Treasury note purchased three months from maturity qualify as cash equivalents. A Treasury note purchased three years ago, however, does not become a cash equivalent when its remaining maturity is three months.

Cash Flows from Operating Activities

Cash flows from operating activities (cash flows from operations) are the cash inflows and cash outflows that directly relate to income from normal operations reported on the income statement. As we illustrated in Chapters 4 and 5, two alternative approaches for presenting the operating activities section of the statement are available:

1. The **direct method** reports the components of cash flows from operating activities listed as gross receipts and gross payments:

Inflows	Outflows
Cash received from	*Cash paid for*
Customers	Purchase of goods for resale and services
Dividends and interest on investments	(electricity, etc.)
	Salaries and wages
	Income taxes
	Interest on liabilities

This method starts with cash receipts and cash expenditures to compute net cash inflow (outflow) from operating activities. The difference between the preceding inflows and outflows is called the *net cash inflow (outflow) from operating activities*. For Boston Beer, this amount was an outflow of $1,386,000 for the first quarter of 1996. The FASB recommends the direct method, but it is rarely seen in practice. Many financial executives have reported that they do not use it because it is more expensive to implement than the indirect method. This method will be illustrated briefly later in this chapter.

2. The **indirect method** adjusts net income by eliminating noncash items to compute net cash inflow (outflow) from operating activities. Boston Beer (Exhibit 13.1) and most other companies use this method. Notice in Exhibit 13.1 that in the first quarter of 1996, Boston Beer reported *positive* net income of $2,640,000 but generated *negative* cash flows from operating activities of $1,386,000. Recall why the income of a company and its cash flows from operating activities should be so different. Remember that the income statement is prepared under the accrual concept. Revenues are recorded when earned without regard to when the related cash flows occur. Expenses are matched with revenues and recorded in the same period as the revenues without regard to when the related cash flows occur.

The statement of cash flows prepared under the indirect method starts with the income number computed under the accrual concept and adjusts it to a cash basis. The adjustments are discussed in detail later in this chapter. By reviewing the operating activities section of the statement prepared under the indirect method, you can determine the specific reasons that cash flows from operating activities were negative in the first quarter of 1996, even though net income for the same period was positive.

According to *Accounting Trends & Techniques*,[2] 97.5 percent of the surveyed companies use the indirect method. Because of the extensive use of this method in actual financial reporting, we emphasize it in our discussions. For now, the most important thing to remember about the two methods is that they are simply alternative ways to compute the same number. The total amount of cash flows from operating activities is *always the same* (an outflow of $1,386,000 in Boston Beer's case) regardless of whether it is computed using the direct or indirect method.

---

[2] *Accounting Trends & Techniques* (New York: American Institute of CPAs, 1996), p. 461.

Cash Flows from Investing Activities

Cash flows from investing activities are cash inflows and outflows related to the purchase and disposal of productive facilities used by the company and investments in the securities of other companies. Under this classification, the cash outflows represent the entity's "investments" of cash to acquire these assets. The cash inflows occur only when cash is received from disposal (sale or collection) of the prior investments. Typical cash flows from investing activities follow:

Inflows	Outflows
Cash received from	*Cash paid for*
Sale or disposal of property, plant, and equipment	Purchase of property, plant, and equipment
Sale or maturity of investments in securities	Purchase of investments in securities

The difference between these cash inflows and outflows is called *net cash inflow (outflow) from investing activities*.

For Boston Beer, this amount was an outflow of $2,862,000 for the first quarter of 1996. The Investing Activities section of the statement shows Boston Beer's long-term investment strategy. The Management Discussion and Analysis (MD&A) section of the report indicated that the company was continuing to invest in improved packaging and brewing equipment (listed as "Additions to fixed assets"). It is also reinvesting the proceeds of maturing investments.

Cash Flows from Financing Activities

Cash flows from financing activities include both cash inflows and outflows that relate to the way that cash was obtained from external sources (owners and creditors) to finance the enterprise and its operations. Under this classification, the cash inflows represent the financing activities that obtain cash from owners and creditors. The cash outflows occur only when cash is paid back to the owners and creditors for their previous cash-providing activities. Usual cash flows from financing activities include these:

Inflows	Outflows
Cash received from	*Cash paid for*
Borrowing on notes, mortgages, bonds, etc. from creditors	Repayment of principal to creditors (excluding interest, which is an operating activity)
Issuing equity securities to owners	Repurchasing equity securities from owners
	Dividends to owners

The difference between these cash inflows and outflows is called *net cash inflow (outflow) from financing activities*. For Boston Beer, this amount was an inflow of $240,000 for the first quarter of 1996.

The financing activities section of the statement shows that Boston Beer has generated none of its financial resources from owners during the period and only a small amount, $240,000, from creditors. This results from the strong cash flows that Boston Beer generates from operating activities in other quarters and its successful initial public offering of stock in 1995 that we will discuss later.

To give you a better understanding of the statement of cash flows, we now discuss in more detail Boston Beer's statement and the way that it relates to the income statement and balance sheet. As we go through the statement, we emphasize the way that each section of the statement describes a set of important decisions that Boston Beer management made. We then discuss the way that financial analysts use each section to evaluate the company.

Pete's Brewing Company

SELF-STUDY QUIZ

Pete's Brewing Company, brewer of Pete's Wicked Ale, is the second largest craft brewer in the United States. The items included in its recent first-quarter statement of cash flows follow. Indicate whether each item is disclosed in the operating activities (O), investing activities (I), or financing activities (F) section of the statement. (Refer to Exhibit 13.1 as a guide.)

_I_a. Purchase of available-for-sale securities   _O_f. Change in inventories
_O_b. Net income   _I_g. Sale of other (fixed) assets
_O_c. Change in trade accounts receivable   _O_h. Depreciation and amortization
_I_d. Additions to property and equipment   _F_i. Issuance of common shares
_O_e. Change in prepaid expenses and other   _O_j. Change in trade accounts payable
     current assets   and accrued liabilities

After you have completed your answers, check them with the solutions presented in the footnote at the bottom of this page.*

Relationships to the Balance Sheet and Income Statement

Both preparing and interpreting the cash flow statement require analyzing the balance sheet and income statement accounts that relate to the three sections of the statement. As we discussed in previous chapters, companies record transactions as journal entries that are posted to T-accounts, which are used to prepare the income statement and the balance sheet. Companies cannot prepare the statement of cash flows by using amounts recorded in T-accounts because these amounts are based on accrual accounting. Instead, they must analyze numbers recorded under the accrual method and adjust them to a cash basis. To prepare the statement of cash flows, they need the following data:

1. Comparative balance sheets used in preparing the cash flows from all activities (operating, investing, and financing). To ease the preparation process, it is useful to compute the change from the beginning to the end of the period for each balance sheet item.
2. A complete income statement used primarily in preparing cash flows from operating activities.
3. Additional details concerning selected accounts that reflect several different types of transactions and events. Analysis of individual accounts is necessary because often the total change amount in an account balance during the year does not reveal the underlying nature of the cash flows.

The first two items of information for Boston Beer are shown in Exhibit 13.2. Note that Boston Beer reports financial statement numbers in thousands. We follow that policy in the remainder of the chapter.

The approach that we take to prepare and understand the cash flow statement focuses on the changes in the balance sheet accounts. It relies on a simple algebraic manipulation of the balance sheet equation. Since

---

* a. I, b. O, c. O, d. I, e. O, f. O, g. I, h. O, i. F, j. O.

$$\text{Assets} = \text{Liabilities} + \text{Stockholders' Equity}$$

the changes (Δ) between the beginning and end of the period in these amounts must also be equal:

$$\Delta \text{ Assets} = \Delta \text{ Liabilities} + \Delta \text{ Stockholders' Equity}$$

Assets can be split further into cash and noncash assets:

$$\Delta \text{ Cash} + \Delta \text{ Noncash Assets} = \Delta \text{ Liabilities} + \Delta \text{ Stockholders' Equity}$$

If we move the noncash assets to the right side of the equation, then

$$\Delta \text{ Cash} = \Delta \text{ Liabilities} + \Delta \text{ Stockholders' Equity} - \Delta \text{ Noncash Assets}$$

Thus, the change in cash can be explained by the changes in the other balance sheet items. As you can see in Exhibit 13.2, each of these other balance sheet changes can

---

EXHIBIT 13.2
The Boston Beer Company: Current Income Statement and Comparative Balance Sheet (in thousands)

THE BOSTON BEER COMPANY, INC.
CONSOLIDATED BALANCE SHEETS

REAL WORLD EXCERPT
BOSTON BEER COMPANY
Quarterly Report

CASH FLOW SECTION	(Unaudited) (in thousands) ASSETS	March 30, 1996	December 31, 1995	CHANGE
	Current Assets:			
ΔCash	Cash & cash equivalents	$32,599	$36,607	−4,008
O	Accounts receivable, net	24,473	16,090	+8,383
O	Inventories	12,708	9,280	+3,428
O	Prepaid expenses	379	437	−58
O	Deferred income taxes	1,011	1,011	0
O	Other current assets	465	1,858	−1,393
	Total current assets	71,635	65,283	
I	Restricted investments	619	602	+17
I*	Equipment and leasehold improvements, net	8,465	6,159	+2,306
O	Deferred income taxes	1,777	1,777	0
I or O	Other assets (long-term receivables)	1,607	2,869	−1,262
	Total assets	$84,103	$76,690	
	LIABILITIES AND STOCKHOLDERS EQUITY			
	Current Liabilities:			
O	Accounts payable	$13,998	$ 8,604	+5,394
F	Notes payable Bank	240		+240
O	Accrued expenses	10,399	11,338	−939
F	Current maturities of long-term debt	75	75	0
	Total current liabilities	24,712	20,017	
F	Long-term debt, less current maturities	1,875	1,875	0
	Stockholders Equity:			
F**	Class A Common Stock, $.01 par value; 20,300,000 shares authorized; 15,643,664 issued and outstanding	156	156	0
F**	Class B Common Stock, $.01 par value; 4,200,000 shares authorized; 4,107,355 issued and outstanding	41	41	0
F**	Additional paid-in capital	53,051	52,973	+78
O and F	Retained earnings	4,268	1,628	+2,640
	Total stockholders equity	57,516	54,798	
	Total liabilities and stockholders equity	$84,103	$76,690	

*The accumulated depreciation account is also related to operations because it relates to depreciation.
**If stock is issued as payment to employees or suppliers, the change can be related to operating activities.

(continued)

EXHIBIT 13.2
Concluded

THE BOSTON BEER COMPANY, INC.
CONSOLIDATED STATEMENT OF INCOME
(Unaudited)
(In thousands, except per share data)

	Quarter ended March 30, 1996
Sales	$48,276
Less excise taxes	5,147
Net sales	43,129
Cost of sales	21,865
Gross profit	21,264
Operating expenses:	
Advertising, promotional and selling expenses	13,845
General and administrative expenses	3,167
Total operating expenses	17,012
Operating income	4,252
Other income:	
Interest income	498
Interest expense	(57)
Other, net	(7)
Total other income	434
Income before taxes	4,686
Income taxes	2,046
Net income	$2,640

be classified as relating to operating (O), investing (I), or financing (F) activities. Each section of the cash flow statement focuses on how the changes in the balance sheet accounts related to that type of activity explain the change in cash.

Reporting and Interpreting Cash Flows from Operating Activities

LEARNING OBJECTIVE 2

Report and interpret differences between net income and cash flows from operating activities.

The operating activities section of the cash flow statement focuses attention on the firm's ability to generate cash internally through operations and its management of current assets and current liabilities (also called *working capital*). Most analysts believe that this is the most important section of the statement because, in the long run, operations are the only source of cash. That is, investors will not invest in a company if they do not believe that it will be able to pay them dividends or make reinvestments with cash generated from operations. Similarly, creditors will not lend money if they do not believe that cash generated from operations will be available to pay back the loan.

A recent issue of *Worth* magazine[3] notes that a common rule of thumb followed by financial and credit analysts is to stay away from firms with rising net income but falling cash flow from operations. A situation where rapidly rising inventories and receivables are the cause often predicts a future slump in profits and the need for external financing. In the first quarter of 1996, Boston Beer exhibited just such a

---

[3] C. Willis, "How to Stay Cool in a Hot Market: Studying the Financials Can Reveal a Stock About to Stumble," *Worth,* June 1996, pp. 122–124.

pattern. Is this a sign of troubled waters ahead for the leader of the craft beer industry? Why also, as indicated in the following chart, did net income decline in the second quarter, but cash flow from operations rebound to all-time highs?

	Net Income		Cash Flows from Operations
1st quarter	$2,640	>	($1,386)
2nd quarter	$2,361	<	$4,071

To answer these questions, we must carefully analyze how its operating activities are reported in the cash flow statement. At the same time, we also must learn more about the brewing industry to properly interpret this information.

Preparing the operating section requires analyzing changes in the balance sheet accounts related to earning income. Normally, the relevant balance sheet accounts include all *current assets other than cash and short-term investments* and all *current liabilities other than notes payable to financial institutions* (often called *short-term debt*) *and current maturities of long-term debt.*[4] In Exhibit 13.2, we noted the changes related to the operating section with an O. The retained earnings change also is related to both the operating and financing sections; it increases by the amount of net income, which is the starting point for the operating section (O), and it decreases by the dividends declared and paid, which is a financing outflow (noted by an F). In addition, the accumulated depreciation account (part of Equipment and Leasehold Improvement, Net) is relevant to operations because it relates to depreciation expense. As we discuss later in the chapter, assets or liabilities related to advance payment or deferral of taxes also are relevant to the cash flow from operations calculation. The following relationships are the ones most frequently encountered:

Income Statement Amounts or Balance Sheet Changes	Impact on the Statement of Cash Flows
Net Income	Starting point for computation
Depreciation expense and other "noncash expenses" and losses	Added
"Noncash revenues" and gains	Subtracted
Decreases in current assets	Added
Increases in current liabilities	Added
Increases in current assets	Subtracted
Decreases in current liabilities	Subtracted

[handwritten: ↓A + ↓L −]
[handwritten: ↑A − ↑L +]
[handwritten: Depre + Noncash Rev −]

As noted earlier, under the indirect method, we begin the operating activities section with net income of $2,640 reported on Boston Beer's income statement (see Exhibit 13.2). We then go through a two-step process to adjust net income to cash flow from operations. These steps involve adjusting for the following:

1. "Noncash" expenses (and revenues) such as depreciation expense, which do not eventually involve a debit or credit to cash (or other current assets or current liabilities).

2. Changes in each of the individual current assets (other than cash and short-term investments) and current liabilities (other than notes payable to financial institutions and current maturities of long-term debt, which relate to financing), which reflect differences in the timing of accrual basis net income and cash flows.

To keep track of all the adjustments made to convert net income to cash flows from operations, it is useful to set up a schedule to record the computations. An example for Boston Beer is shown in Exhibit 13.3.

---

[4] Current maturities of long-term debt are amounts of debt with an original term of more than one year that are due within one year of the statement date.

EXHIBIT 13.3
Boston Beer Company: Schedule for Net Cash Flow from Operating Activities,
Indirect Method (in thousands)

Conversion of net income to net cash flow from operating activities:

Items	Amount	Explanation Column
Net income, accrual basis	$2,640	From income statement.
Add (subtract) to convert to cash basis:		
Depreciation expense	+ 539	Add because depreciation expense is a noncash expense.
Stock option compensation expense	+ 78	Add because the expense is a noncash expense (paid with stock).
Accounts receivable increase	−8,383	Subtract because cash received from sales transactions is less than accrual basis revenues.
Inventory increase	−3,428	Subtract because more inventories were purchased than sold.
Prepaid expense decrease	+ 58	Add because cash payments for expenses are less than accrual basis expenses.
Other current assets decrease	+1,393	Add because cash payments for expenses are less than accrual basis expenses.
Other assets (long-term receivables) decrease	+1,262	Add because cash received is more than accrual basis revenues.
Accounts payable increase	+5,394	Add because cash payments to suppliers are less than amounts purchased on account (borrowed from suppliers).
Accrued expenses decrease	− 939	Subtract because cash payments for expenses are more than the accrual basis expenses.
Net cash outflow from operating activities	($1,386)	Reported on the statement of cash flows.

Noncash Expenses

Noncash expenses, such as depreciation, are reported on most income statements. Recording noncash expenses does not involve either a credit or debit to Cash or any other current asset or current liability. Since noncash expenses have been subtracted from revenue to determine net income, we always add them to income in the process of converting net income to cash flow from operations. In the case of Boston Beer, we need to add depreciation expense of $539 and compensation expense paid in a form of stock (called *options*) of $78 to net income to convert it to a cash basis (see Exhibit 13.3). Some companies report noncash revenues, which, by the same logic, are subtracted. We discuss gains and losses in Chapter Supplement A.

Changes in Current Assets and Current Liabilities

Each change in the current assets (other than cash and short-term investments) and current liabilities (other than notes payable to financial institutions and current maturities of long-term debt, which relate to financing) causes a difference between net income and cash flow from operations. In Exhibit 13.2, these items are noted by an O.

Change in Accounts Receivable

The first such item is accounts receivable. Accrual basis sales revenue often includes sales that did not generate cash. These *noncash* amounts cause changes in the balance of accounts receivable. When sales are recorded, accounts receivable increases, and when cash is collected, accounts receivable decreases. Given this, we can generalize the rule:

When a net *decrease in accounts receivable* for the period occurs, cash collected from customers is always more than accrual revenue; thus, the decrease must be *added* in computing cash flows from operations.

When a net *increase in accounts receivable* occurs, cash collected from customers is always less than accrual revenue; thus, the increase must be *subtracted* in computing cash flows from operations.

Since the balance sheet for Boston Beer Company (Exhibit 13.2) indicates an *increase* in accounts receivable of $8,383 for the period, cash collected is less than reported sales revenue.

SECTION	BALANCE SHEET	March 30, 1996	December 31, 1995	CHANGE
O	Accounts receivable, net	24,473	16,090	+ 8,383

Thus, to reflect the smaller cash inflow, the amount of the increase must be *subtracted* from net income to convert income to cash flow from operating activities in Exhibit 13.3. A decrease would be added.

Financial
ANALYSIS

Income Growth and Declining Cash Flows: A Warning Sign?

Managers sometimes attempt to boost declining sales by extending credit terms (for example, 30 to 60 days) or lowering credit standards (lending to riskier customers). The resulting increase in accounts receivable can cause net income to outpace cash flow from operations. As a consequence, many analysts view this pattern as a warning sign. In the first quarter of 1996, Boston Beer's net income was $2,640 (in thousands), yet it reported a cash *outflow* from operations of $1,386, caused mainly by an $8,383 increase in receivables. Does this suggest that Boston Beer may be facing more difficult times?

Analysts who cover the beverage industry know that this is a result of normal seasonal fluctuations in beer sales to distributors. First, they know that virtually all of Boston Beer's sales to distributors are on account and that it normally collects cash the month *after* sales revenue is recorded. Second, they recognize that beer sales to distributors are *low* in the last month of the fourth quarter, *December*, because of the onset of winter. Similarly, they are *high* at the end of the first quarter, *March*, in anticipation of spring.

Because of the lower sales in December, receivables decline and cash receipts from customers for the month outstrip sales revenue. The higher March sales have the opposite effect, however, causing growth in accounts receivable and cash receipts from customers to lag behind sales revenue. (Note that collections based on those higher March sales go up the next month.) This normal seasonal fluctuation in sales then causes a large increase in accounts receivable between the end of the fourth quarter (December 31) and the end of the first quarter (March 30). The following chart presents a simplified representation of this pattern of seasonal sales and a one-month lag in cash collections.

BEER SALES AND CASH COLLECTIONS

Sales revenue

Cash collected from customers

Dec.   Mar.

Beer sales, like the harvesting of hops, are seasonal.

On the cash flow statement, this results in a negative effect on cash flow from operations for the first quarter. This is clearly *not* a sign of problems, however, for Boston Beer.

Change in Inventory

Cost of goods sold represents the cost of merchandise sold during the accounting period. It may be more or less than the amount of cash paid to suppliers during the period. Both the change in inventory and the change in accounts payable (borrowing from suppliers) determine the magnitude of this difference. It is easiest to think about the change in inventory in terms of the simple case in which the company pays cash to suppliers of inventory. We address the added complexity involved when purchases are made on account when we discuss the adjustment for the change in accounts payable.

In the case of Boston Beer Company, inventory increased during the quarter. This means that the company bought or produced more inventory than it sold to its customers (became cost of goods sold). Given this, we can generalize another rule:

> When a net *decrease in inventory* for the period occurs, purchases of inventory are always less than the cost of goods sold expense; thus, the decrease must be *added* in computing cash flows from operations.

> When a net *increase in inventory* for the period occurs, purchases of inventory are always more than the cost of goods sold expense; thus, the increase must be *subtracted*.

Boston Beer's balance sheet indicates inventory *increased* by $3,428.

SECTION	BALANCE SHEET	March 30, 1996	December 31, 1995	CHANGE
O	Inventories	12,708	9,280	+ 3,428

This means that more inventory was purchased or produced than was sold during the quarter. Thus, to reflect the higher cash outflow (independent of the change in accounts payable, which we deal with later), the change must be *subtracted* from net income to convert to cash flow from operations in Exhibit 13.3.

Change in Prepaid Expenses

Under accrual accounting, the total amount of an expense may be different from the cash outflow associated with that activity. Some expenses are paid for before they are recognized as expenses (e.g., prepaid rent). In this case, when payments are made, the balance in the asset prepaid expenses increases; when expenses are recorded, prepaid expenses decreases. Given this, we can generalize another rule:

> When a net *decrease in a prepaid expense* or other operating asset for the period occurs, cash prepayments for the expense are always less than the expense (expirations of the prepayments); thus, the decrease must be *added* in computing cash flows from operations.
>
> When an *increase in a prepaid expense* or other operating asset occurs, cash prepaid for the expense is always more than the expense; thus, the increase must be *subtracted*.

Since the Boston Beer balance sheet (Exhibit 13.2) indicates a $58 decrease in prepaid expenses, cash payments are less than reported expenses.

SECTION	BALANCE SHEET	March 30, 1996	December 31, 1995	CHANGE
O	Prepaid expenses	379	437	− 58

Thus, to reflect the smaller outflow, this amount must be *added* to net income to convert income to cash flow from operating activities in Exhibit 13.3.

Analyzing Inventory Changes and Cash Flows from Operations

An unexpected increase in inventory can be another cause for net income to outpace cash flow from operations. Such inventory growth can be a sign that planned sales growth did not materialize. Boston Beer's increase in inventory of $3,428 (in thousands) was a major contributor to its negative cash flows from operations in the first quarter. Should analysts be troubled?

This is a second case for which industry knowledge quickly eases any concerns. The largest component of Boston Beer's inventory is the raw material hops. This plant is harvested once a year in the fall and delivered to Boston Beer during the first quarter. It is then used in the brewing process for the rest of the year. This normal seasonal fluctuation in purchases is no cause for alarm. The obvious importance of detailed industry knowledge to accurate financial statement analysis causes most analysts to become specialists in only a few industries. For example, David Goldman follows Boston Beer for The Robinson-Humphrey Company. He specializes in companies in the beverages and foods industries.

Changes in Other Current Assets and Other Assets

Other current assets usually include operating items such as interest receivable. Other assets (noncurrent) may or may not include operating items such as long-term customer receivables. When they do, as is Boston Beer's case, they must also be

How do seasonal beer sales to this distributor impact the financial statements of Boston Beer?

considered in the calculation of cash flow from operations. As with the example of accounts receivable, when these accounts for the period reflect a net increase, cash collected is always less than accrual revenue; when there is a decrease, cash collected is always more than accrual revenue.

The Boston Beer balance sheet shows a *decrease* in both other current assets and other assets, which indicates that more money was collected than earned in both cases.

SECTION	BALANCE SHEET	March 30, 1996	December 31, 1995	CHANGE
O	Other current assets	465	1,858	− 1,393
O	Other assets (long-term receivables)	1,607	2,869	− 1,262

Thus, the decrease of $1,393 in other current assets and $1,262 in other assets must be *added* to net income to convert to cash flow from operations in Exhibit 13.3. Had other assets included nonoperating assets such as equipment to be disposed of, its change would not be considered in the operating section. It would affect the investing section. *Most other noncurrent assets affect the investing section.*

Change in Accounts Payable

As we noted in our discussion of changes in inventory, most inventory is purchased on account. Thus, the difference between cost of goods sold expense and cash paid to suppliers is captured in the change both in inventory and in accounts payable. When purchases are recorded, accounts payable increases, and when cash is paid to suppliers, accounts payable decreases. Accounts payable then can be thought of as amounts that we have borrowed from our suppliers for the purchase of goods. Given this, we can generalize the rule:

> When a net *increase in accounts payable* for the period occurs, cash paid to suppliers is always less than purchases on account; thus, the increase must be *added* in computing cash flows from operations.
>
> When a net *decrease in accounts payable* for the period occurs, cash paid to suppliers is always more than purchases on account; thus, the decrease must be *subtracted* in computing cash flows from operations.

Accounts payable *increased* by $5,394, which indicates that more money was borrowed from suppliers than was paid back.

SECTION	BALANCE SHEET	March 30, 1996	December 31,1995	CHANGE
O	Accounts payable	$13,998	$8,604	+ 5,394

To reflect the smaller cash outflow, this amount must be *added* to net income in Exhibit 13.3.

Change in Accrued Expenses

We should analyze another expense item for Boston Beer that results when some expenses are paid for after they are recognized (e.g., accrued wage expense). In this case, when expenses are recorded, the balance in the liability accrued expenses increases; when payments are made, accrued expenses decrease. Given this, we can generalize another rule:

When a net *increase in an accrued expense payable* for the period occurs, cash paid for the expense is always less than the recorded expense; thus, the increase must be *added* in computing cash flows from operations.

When a *decrease in an accrued expense payable* occurs, cash paid for the expense is always more than the recorded expense; thus, the decrease must be *subtracted* in computing cash flows from operations.

Since Boston Beer's accrued expenses on the balance sheet (Exhibit 13.2) *decreased* by $939 for the period, cash payments are more than the reported expense.

SECTION	BALANCE SHEET	March 30, 1996	December 31, 1995	CHANGE
O	Accrued expenses	10,399	11,338	– 939

Thus, to reflect the larger cash outflow, the amount must be *subtracted* from net income to convert income to cash flow from operating activities in Exhibit 13.3.

Summary

We can summarize the typical adjustments that are required to reconcile net income with cash flow from operating activities as follows:

Item	Plus and Minus Adjustments to Net Income	
	When Item Increases	When Item Decreases
Depreciation, depletion, and amortization	+	
Accounts receivable (trade)	–	+
Prepaid expense assets	–	+
Inventory	–	+
Other current assets	–	+
Accounts payable (trade)	+	–
Accrued expense liabilities	+	–

Notice in this table that adjustments that involve an *increase in an asset or a decrease in a liability* are always *subtracted* to reconcile net income to a cash basis. Adjustments that involve a *decrease in an asset or an increase in a liability* are always *added* to reconcile net income to a cash basis. The cash flow statement for Boston Beer (Exhibit 13.1) shows the same adjustments to net income to convert it to a cash basis described in Exhibit 13.3.

Net Income versus Cash Flow From Operations

As our earlier discussions suggest, analysts focus a great deal of attention on the reconciliation of net income to cash flow from operations. They often first compute the quality of income ratio.[*]

$$\text{Quality of Income Ratio} = \frac{\text{Cash Flow From Operations}}{\text{Net Income}}$$

This tells us what portion of income was generated in cash that can then be used for new investing activities or repayments of financing. When this ratio does not equal 1, analysts ask a number of questions to determine the significance of the findings:[†]

1. What are the sources of the difference?
2. Is the ratio changing over time and what are the causes of any change?
3. Are the changes in receivables, inventories, and payables normal and are there adequate explanations for the changes?

As we noted earlier, the difference between net income and cash flow from operations in the case of Boston Beer was not a cause for alarm. It was due to normal seasonal changes in sales and inventory purchases. In other cases, however, it also can indicate obsolescent inventory, slowing sales, or failed expansion plans.

[*] C. A. Carslaw and J. R. Mills, "Developing Ratios for Effective Cash Flow Statement Analysis," *Journal of Accountancy*, November 1991, pp. 63–69.
[†] K. G. Palepu, V. L. Bernard, and P. M. Healy, *Business Analysis and Valuation Using Financial Statements*. Cincinnati, OH: South-Western, 1996.

Additional Issues in Interpreting Cash Flows from Operations

The reconciliation of net income to cash flow from operations may contain other adjusting items, most of which relate to topics covered in an intermediate accounting course. We describe these items briefly here.

1. *Gain or loss on sale of property, plant, and equipment.* As discussed in the next section, the total cash proceeds from the sale of property, plant, and equipment should be included in the investing section of the statement. Since the gain or loss already is included in net income, to avoid counting the effect of the gain or loss twice, it must be eliminated from the operating section by *subtracting the gain* or *adding the loss*. Chapter Supplement A discusses this issue in more detail.
2. *Deferred income taxes.* Deferred taxes result from timing differences that exist between GAAP used for financial reporting and U.S. tax law that governs preparation of tax returns. An increase in a deferred tax liability is associated with an expense in the current period even though it will not cause a cash outflow until some future accounting period. Because an *increase* in a deferred tax liability does not cause a cash outflow in the current period, it is *added* to net income on the statement of cash flows. Deferred taxes always reverse at some point in the future and cause a cash outflow. When they do, the *decrease* in the liability must be *subtracted* from net income on the statement of cash flows.
3. *Equity in income or losses of unconsolidated affiliates.* When the equity method is used to account for an intercorporate investment, the investor must record its share of any profits or losses generated by the affiliate. This share of profit or loss does not affect cash flows. Therefore, equity *profits* must be *subtracted* from net

income because there is no cash inflow, and equity *losses* must be *added* back because there is no cash outflow.

Two additional complicating factors should be noted. Consolidated statements may include one or more subsidiaries whose statements are denominated in a currency other than the U.S. dollar (for example, French francs). The process of translating those statements into dollars may cause the changes in the current assets and liabilities on the balance sheet not to match the changes reported on the cash flow statement.[5] Acquisitions of new subsidiaries during the period can have a similar effect.

Errors and Irregularities and Cash Flow from Operations

The cash flow statement often gives outsiders the first hint that financial statements may contain errors and irregularities. The importance of this indicator as a predictor is receiving more attention in new auditing standards as *Business Week* reports.

> The new standard will require auditors to look for a lengthy list of "risk factors" found in previous cases of chicanery. Is management being hyperaggressive in pursuit of overly ambitious financial targets? Does a sharp mismatch exist between reported earnings and cash flow?

As noted in earlier chapters, unethical managers sometimes attempt to reach earnings targets by manipulating accruals and deferrals of revenues and expenses to inflate income. Since these adjusting entries do not affect the cash account, they have no effect on the cash flow statement. As a consequence, a growing difference between net income and cash flow from operations can be a sign of such manipulations. This early warning sign has been evident before some famous bankruptcies, such as that of W. T. Grant. This company had inflated income by failing to make adequate accruals of expenses for uncollectible accounts receivable and obsolete inventory. The growing difference between net income and cash flow from operations that resulted was noted by the more astute analysts who recommended selling the stock long before the bankruptcy.

SOURCE: *Business Week,* December 9, 1996, p. 68.

QUESTION OF ETHICS

REAL WORLD EXCERPT
BUSINESS WEEK

SELF-STUDY QUIZ

Indicate which of the following items taken from Pete's Brewing Company's cash flow statement would be added (+), subtracted (−), or not included (0) in the reconciliation of net income to cash flow from operations.

Pete's Brewing Company

___ a. Increase in inventories.
___ b. Net borrowings from revolving credit agreement with bank.
___ c. Depreciation and amortization.
___ d. Decrease in trade accounts receivable.
___ e. Increase in trade accounts payable and accrued expenses.
___ f. Increase in prepaid expenses and other current assets.

After you have completed your answers, check them with the solutions presented in the footnote at the bottom of this page.*

---

[5] P. R. Bahnson, P. B. W. Miller, and B. P. Budge, "Nonarticulation in Cash Flow Statements and Implications for Education, Research and Practice," *Accounting Horizons,* December 1996, pp. 1–15.
* a. −, b. 0, c. +, d. +, e. +, f. −.

A Comparison of the Direct and Indirect Methods

The indirect method of reporting cash flows from operating activities starts with net income and makes adjustments to compute net cash inflow or outflow. In contrast, the direct method accumulates into categories all of the operating transactions that result in either a debit or credit to cash. It is important to note again that the net cash inflow or outflow is the *same* regardless of whether the direct or indirect method of presentation is used. The two methods differ only in terms of the details reported on the statement.

Exhibit 13.4 presents a comparison of these two reporting alternatives. Like most companies using the indirect method of reporting, Boston Beer does not report sufficient information to prepare the direct method presentation. Therefore, we made a number of simplifying assumptions in our computations, and the numbers do not exactly reflect Boston Beer's actual direct method cash flows.

The most important fact about Exhibit 13.4 to note is that the amount reported as net cash outflow from operating activities is the *same* for both the direct and indirect methods of presentation. They differ only in the method of computation. The FASB prefers but does not require the direct method because it provides to users additional information that cannot be derived from the indirect method and other statements. As noted earlier, however, because of the perceived additional costs involved, few companies use the direct method. Those that do are required to present the indirect method as an additional disclosure.

Australian Practices

Foster's Brewing is the first name in Australian beer and a major player in world beverage markets. Besides developing large markets in the United States and elsewhere for imported Foster's beer, Foster's China brews Foster's beer as well as special local brands in Shanghai and elsewhere. Foster's also owns 40 percent of Molson Breweries, the largest brewer in Canada. Following Australian GAAP, which require use of the direct method of presentation, Foster's cash flow from operations is presented:

REAL WORLD EXCERPT

FOSTER'S BREWING
Annual Report

STATEMENT OF CASH FLOWS FOR THE YEAR ENDED 30 JUNE 1996 ($M)

Operating Activities	
Receipts from customers	3,638.0
Payments to suppliers, employees, principals	(3,345.0)
Dividends received	1.4
Interest received	20.9
Interest paid	(132.7)
Income tax paid	(24.1)
Funds withdrawn from Molson Breweries Partnership	62.9
Net cash flows from operating activities	221.4

Note that Foster's combines payments to suppliers, employees, and principals (officers), but other companies report these items separately. The amount Funds withdrawn from Molson Breweries Partnership includes Foster's 40 percent share of the cash Molson distributed to owners for the reporting period. Like U.S. companies that choose the direct method, Foster's reports the indirect presentation in a note to the financial statements.

EXHIBIT 13.4
Comparison of Indirect and Direct Methods

BOSTON BEER COMPANY
Statement of Cash Flows
(in thousands)

OPERATING ACTIVITIES SECTION OF THE STATEMENT OF CASH FLOWS UNDER THE INDIRECT AND DIRECT METHOD

Indirect Method		Direct Method (estimated)	
Cash flows from operating activities:		Cash flows from operating activities:	
Net income	$2,640	Cash collected from customers	$36,008
Adjustments to reconcile net income to		Cash payments to suppliers	(19,899)
net cash flow		Cash payments for administrative and	
Depreciation expense	539	selling expense	(17,276)
Stock option compensation expense	78	Cash collected for interest on investments	1,827
Accounts receivable increase	(8,383)	Cash payments for income taxes	(2,046)
Inventory increase	(3,428)	Net cash outflow from operating activities	($ 1,386)
Prepaid expense decrease	58		
Other current assets decrease	1,393		
Other assets (long-term rec.) decrease	1,262		
Accounts payable increase	5,394		
Accrued expenses decrease	(939)		
Net cash outflow from operating activities	($1,386)		

Reporting and Interpreting Cash Flows from Investing Activities

This section requires analyzing the accounts related to the purchase and disposal of productive facilities used by the company, investments in the securities of other companies, and lending to other than customers. Normally, the relevant balance sheet accounts include short-term investments and long-term asset accounts such as long-term investments and property, plant, and equipment. The following relationships are the ones that you will encounter most frequently:

LEARNING OBJECTIVE 3
Report and interpret cash flows from investing activities.

Related Balance Sheet Account(s)	Investing Activity	Cash Flow Effect
Property, Plant, and Equipment	Purchase of property, plant, and equipment for cash	Outflow
	Sale of property, plant, and equipment for cash	Inflow
Short- or Long-Term Investments	Purchase of investment securities for cash	Outflow
	Sale (maturity) of investment securities for cash	Inflow

Typical investing activities include these:

1. Cash expenditures that include the acquisition of tangible productive assets such as buildings and equipment or intangible assets such as trademarks and patents. Only purchases paid for with cash or cash equivalents are included. Purchases made using debt issued to the seller, for example, are excluded.
2. Cash proceeds from the sale of productive assets such as buildings and equipment or intangible assets such as trademarks and patents. This is the amount of cash that was received from the sale of assets, regardless of whether the assets were sold at a gain or loss.
3. Purchase of short- or long-term investments for cash. These investments can include stocks or bonds issued by other companies, bank certificates of deposit, or government securities with maturities of more than three months. (Remember that those with maturities of three months or less are cash equivalents.)

4. Cash proceeds from the sale or maturity of short- or long-term investments. Again, this is the amount of cash that was received from the sale, regardless of whether the assets were sold at a gain or loss.

In the case of Boston Beer Company, the analysis of changes in the balance sheet (shown in Exhibit 13.2) finds two noncurrent assets that have changed during the period (noted with an *I*). This indicates investing activities involving these two assets: buildings and equipment (fixed assets) and investments (restricted investments). Company records would then be searched to determine the causes of changes in these assets.

The company purchased new buildings and equipment for cash in the amount of $2,846, which is a cash outflow. It did not sell any other buildings and equipment for cash. Such sales would have resulted in a cash inflow. This item less the amount of depreciation expense added back in the operations section, $539, explains the increase in Equipment and Leasehold Improvements, Net of $2,306 (with rounding).

SECTION	BALANCE SHEET	March 30, 1996	December 31, 1995	CHANGE
I and O	Equipment and leasehold improvements, net	8,465	6,159	+ 2,306

Cash purchases and sales of plant and equipment are listed separately on the statement of cash flows.

Boston Beer also collected $597 in principal when certain investments[6] in debt securities reached maturity; this is a cash inflow. These investments consisted of U.S. treasury notes (a form of U.S. government debt) that mature within one year. The company also purchased additional U.S. treasury notes for $614, which is a cash outflow. Each of these items should be listed in Boston Beer's schedule shown in Exhibit 13.5. Together, they explain the $17 increase in restricted investments reported on the balance sheet.

The net cash flow from investing activities that results is a $2,862 outflow.

SECTION	BALANCE SHEET	March 30, 1996	December 31, 1995	CHANGE
I	Restricted investments	619	602	+ 17

EXHIBIT 13.5
Boston Beer Company: Schedule for Net Cash Flow from Investing Activities (in thousands)

Items from Balance Sheet and Account Analysis	Cash Inflow (Outflows)	Explanation
Purchase of fixed assets	($2,846)	Payment in cash for buildings and equipment.
Purchase of investments	(614)	Payment in full for new investments.
Maturities (sale) of investments	597	Total cash received from maturity (sale) of investment.
Net cash inflow (outflow) from investing activities	($2,862)	Reported on the statement of cash flows.

---

[6] These investments are "restricted" in the following sense. As part of a loan agreement, Boston Beer agreed to spend the proceeds of the loan to develop its Boston brewery. Any unexpended amounts were to be invested in government securities until the cash was needed for further development of the brewery.

Manufacturing Strategy, Outsourcing, and Cash Investments

Financial
ANALYSIS

The investing activities section of the statement of cash flows reveals important information about a company's strategy. To many, the tangible nature of plant and equipment may suggest that it is a low-risk investment. When companies in an industry build more productive capacity than is necessary to meet customer demand, however, the costs of maintaining and financing idle plant can drive a company to ruin. The brewing industry currently has significant excess capacity. Boston Beer minimizes the risks of its plant and equipment investments by outsourcing a significant portion of its production to other brewers. This practice, called *contract brewing*, gives Boston Beer advantages through lower borrowing and depreciation costs and through lower costs of transportation compared to companies using a single large brewery. It also avoids the risk of excess capacity.

Alternatively, Minnesota Brewing follows a strategy of building all new plant and equipment. The effects of the alternative strategies are made evident on the financial statements. Whereas Boston Beer had invested only $.04 in net plant and equipment to generate $1 of 1995 sales revenue, Minnesota Brewing had invested $.12. As a result of this risky strategy, Minnesota Brewing's unused capacity costs drove the company to a $471 loss for the first quarter of 1996 compared to Boston Beer's large profit.

Analysts often compute the capital acquisitions ratio to assess ability to finance purchases of plant and equipment from operations.

$$\text{Capital Acquisitions Ratio} = \frac{\text{Cash Flow From Operations}}{\text{Cash Paid for Plant and Equipment}}$$

For the period 1993 through 1995, Boston Beer's ratio was 2.74 ($21,339 ÷ $7,782), a very high value indicating more than sufficient cash for expansion, marketing, and distributions to owners. Minnesota Brewing's ratio for the same period was −1.42 (−$2,731 ÷ 1,919), a very low value indicating heavy reliance on external financing.

Reporting and Interpreting Cash Flows from Financing Activities

LEARNING OBJECTIVE 4
Report and interpret cash flows from financing activities.

This section reflects changes in two current liabilities, *notes payable to financial institutions* (often called *short-term debt*), *current maturities of long-term debt,* as well as changes in *long-term liabilities and stockholders' equity accounts.* These balance sheet accounts relate to the issuance and retirement of debt and stock and the payment of dividends. The following relationships are the ones that you will encounter most frequently:

Related Balance Sheet Account(s)	Financing Activity	Cash Flow Effect
Notes Payable—Bank	Issuance of bank note for cash	Inflow
	Repayment of principal on bank note	Outflow
Long-Term Debt	Issuance of bonds for cash	Inflow
	Repayment of principal on bonds	Outflow
Common Stock and	Issuance of stock for cash	Inflow
Additional Paid-In Capital	Repurchase (retirement) of stock with cash	Outflow
Retained Earnings	Payment of cash dividends	Outflow

Financing activities are associated with generating capital from creditors and owners. Typical financing activities include the following:

Think about the benefits associated with contract brewing.

1. *Proceeds from issuance of short- and long-term debt.* This represents cash received from borrowing from banks and other financial institutions and issuance of bonds to the public. If the debt is issued for other than cash (for example, issued directly to a supplier of equipment to pay for a purchase), it is not included.

2. *Principal payments on short- and long-term debt.* Cash outflows associated with debt include the periodic repayment of principal as well as the early retirement of debt. As you saw in previous chapters, most debt requires periodic payments of both principal and interest. The portion of the cash payment associated with principal is listed as a cash flow from financing activities. The portion that is associated with interest is a cash flow from operating activities.

3. *Proceeds from the issuance of common stock.* This represents cash received from the sale of common stock to investors. If the stock is issued for other than cash (for example, issued directly to an employee as part of salary), it is not included.

4. *Purchase of treasury stock or retirement of stock.* This cash outflow includes cash payments for repurchase of the company's own stock from shareholders.

5. *Cash portion of dividends.* This is the amount of cash dividends paid to owners during the year. Some students wonder why cash payments made to creditors (interest) are shown as an operating activity but cash payments to owners (dividends) are shown as a financing activity. Remember that interest is reported on the income statement and is, therefore, directly associated with earning income (it is an operating activity). Dividend payments are not reported on the income statement because they represent a distribution of income. Dividends are more appropriately shown as a financing activity.

To compute cash flows from financing activities, you should review changes in debt and stockholders' equity accounts. In the case of Boston Beer Company, the analysis of changes in the balance sheet (shown in Exhibit 13.2) finds that only notes payable and additional paid-in-capital changed during the period (noted with an F). The change in paid-in-capital did not involve cash; as noted, it was paid as compensation to employees. As a result, it does not result in a cash flow from financing. Company records indicate that the change in notes payable resulted from borrowing $240 from its bank. This item should be listed in Exhibit 13.6. This accounts for the $240 increase in Notes Payable—Bank.

SECTION	BALANCE SHEET	March 30, 1996	December 31, 1995	CHANGE
F	Notes payable—Bank	240	0	+240

Since only one transaction affected cash flows from financing activities, the net cash inflow from financing activities that results is $240.

EXHIBIT 13.6

Boston Beer Company: Schedule for Net Cash Flow from Financing Activities (in thousands)

Items from Balance Sheet and Account Analysis	Cash Inflows (Outflows)	Explanation
Borrowing under line of credit	$240	Proceeds from borrowing from bank on long-term note payable
Net cash inflow (outflow) from financing activities	$240	Reported on the statement of cash flows

No other financing was necessary during the quarter since Boston Beer had just completed its initial public offering (issuance) of stock collecting $49,691 cash in 1995. That amount was reported as an inflow from financing in the 1995 cash flow statement. When Boston Beer pays back the bank debt (principal only) or retires some of its own stock, it will report them as cash outflows in the financing section for that period. Should Boston Beer ever decide to pay dividends, it would also list them as financing cash outflows.

Financing Growth

The long-term growth of a company is normally financed from three sources: internally generated funds (cash from operating activities), the issuance of stock, and money borrowed on a long-term basis. As we discussed in Chapter 10, companies can adopt a number of different capital structures (the balance of debt and equity). The financing sources that management uses to fund growth will have an important impact on the firm's risk and return characteristics. The statement of cash flows shows how management has elected to fund its growth. This information is used by analysts who wish to evaluate the capital structure and growth potential of a business.

SELF-STUDY QUIZ

Indicate which of the following items taken from Pete's Brewing Company's cash flow statement would be reported in the investing section (I) or financing section (F) and whether the amount would be an inflow (+) or an outflow (−).

Pete's Brewing Company

____ a. Net payments on revolving credit agreement with bank.
____ b. Additions to property and equipment (for cash).
____ c. Additions to other (intangible) assets.
____ d. Proceeds from sale (issuance) of common shares.

After you have completed your answers, check them with the solutions presented in the footnote at the bottom of this page.*

Presentation of the Statement of Cash Flows

The formal statement of cash flows for Boston Beer Company is shown in Exhibit 13.1. As you can see, it is a simple matter to construct the statement after the detailed analysis of the accounts and transactions has been completed (shown in Exhibits 13.3, 13.5, and 13.6). As you would expect, the preparation of the statement for a larger, more complex company is more difficult than was the case for Boston Beer. Despite the added complexity, the preparation of the statement for all companies is based on the same analytical approach that we have just discussed. Companies also must provide two other disclosures related to the cash flow statement.

---

* a. F−, b. I−, c. I−, d. F+.

Noncash Investing and Financing Activities

Certain transactions are important investing and financing activities but have no cash flow effects. These are called **noncash investing and financing activities.** For example, the purchase of a $100,000 building with a $100,000 mortgage given by the former owner does not cause either the inflow or the outflow of cash. As a result, they are not listed in the three main sections of the cash flow statement. *FASB Statement 95* requires supplemental disclosure of these transactions in either narrative or schedule form. Boston Beer's statement of cash flows does not list any noncash investing and financing activities. The following schedule from the annual report of U·S Airways illustrates the significance and diversity of these noncash transactions.

REAL WORLD EXCERPT

U·S AIRWAYS
Annual Report

	(in thousands)		
	1995	**1994**	**1993**
Noncash investing and financing activities			
Issuance of debt for aircraft acquisitions, net	$169,725	$224,614	$343,188
Issuance of debt for additions to other property	—	—	669
Reduction of debt—aircraft purchase deposits	70,837	—	—
Reduction of debt—aircraft related	—	—	47,685

Supplemental Cash Flow Information

Companies such as Boston Beer that use the indirect method of presenting cash flows from operations also must provide two other figures: cash paid for interest and cash paid for income taxes. These are normally listed at the bottom of the statement or, more frequently, in the notes.

Epilogue

Our more detailed analysis of Boston Beer's first quarter cash flow indicates that positive net income and negative cash flows in the first quarter were not a cause for alarm. In fact, they were normal consequences of seasonal variations in sales, purchases of raw materials, and advertising expenditures. On the income statement, lower sales in the first quarter are usually more than offset by the decline in advertising in the same period, resulting in strong earnings. The upsurge in sales in March, however, causes receivables to rise and first quarter purchases of hops adds to inventory, resulting in negative cash flow from operations. Collections of these receivables in the second quarter account for much of the upsurge in cash flows from operations in that quarter. Our further analysis of Boston Beer's investing and financing indicates that the cash needs of a continuation of its investment strategy will be more than met by operations.

In fact, the year ended December 28, 1996, was one of record cash flow from operations for Boston Beer, $15,763. In his most recent report on Boston Beer, David Goldman of Robinson-Humphrey[7] does not see any problems related to cash flow. He sees a more competitive environment caused by many new start-ups, however, leading to tougher times for the whole craft beer segment in 1997. In the longer term, though, he believes that Boston Beer will be among the growth leaders in the segment. Successful competition for retail shelf space and new product introductions at home

---

[7] D. Goldman, Robinson-Humphrey Company Inc. Research Note, December 3, 1996, p. 1.

along with brewing agreements with San Miguel Brewery (Hong Kong), Whitbread PLC of the United Kingdom, and other international brewers will be keys to Boston Beer's future growth.

Demonstration Case

(Try to resolve the requirements before proceeding to the suggested solution that follows.)

During a recent year (ended December 31, 19A), Redhook Ale Brewery, a Seattle-based craft brewer, reported net income of $3,182 (all numbers in thousands) and cash and cash equivalents at the beginning of the year of $472. It also engaged in the following activities:

Redhook Ale Brewery

(a) Paid $18,752 in principal on debt.
(b) Received $46,202 in cash from initial public offering of common stock.
(c) Other noncash operating expenses were $857.
(d) Paid $18,193 in cash for purchase of fixed assets.
(e) Accounts receivable increased by $881.
(f) Borrowed $16,789 from various lenders.
(g) Refundable deposits payable increased by $457.
(h) Inventories increased by $574.
(i) Made cash deposits on equipment of $5,830.
(j) Income tax refund receivable decreased by $326.
(k) Sold (issued) stock to employees for $13 in cash.
(l) Accounts payable decreased by $391.
(m) Received $4 from other investing activities.
(n) Accrued expenses increased by $241.
(o) Prepaid expenses increased by $565.
(p) Recorded depreciation of $1,324
(q) Paid $5 cash in other financing activities.

Required:
Based on this information, prepare the cash flow statement using the indirect method.

Suggested Solution

REDHOOK ALE BREWERY
Statement of Cash Flows
For the Year Ended December 31, 19A
(in thousands)

Operating activities	
Net income	$ 3,182
Adjustments	
Depreciation	1,324
Other noncash expenses	857
Change in accounts receivable	(881)
Change in inventories	(574)
Change in income taxes receivable	326
Change in prepaid expenses	(565)
Change in accounts payable	(391)
Change in accrued expenses	241
Change in refundable deposits payable	457
Net cash flow from operating activities	3,976

Investing activities	
Expenditures for fixed assets	(18,193)
Deposits on equipment	(5,830)
Other	4
Net cash flow from investing activities	(24,019)
Financing activities	
Proceeds from debt	16,789
Repayment of debt	(18,752)
Proceeds from sale of stock (IPO)	46,202
Proceeds from sale of stock (options)	13
Other	(5)
Net cash flow from financing activities	44,247
Increase in cash and cash equivalents	24,204
Cash and cash equivalents:	
Beginning of year	472
End of year	$24,676

Summary

The statement of cash flows is one of the required financial statements. Its primary purpose is to provide cash flow information in a manner that maximizes its usefulness to investors, creditors, and others in projecting future cash flows related to the enterprise.

The statement has three main sections: cash flows from operating activities, which are related to earning income from normal operations; cash flows from investing activities, which are related to the acquisition and sale of productive assets; and cash flows from financing activities, which are related to financing the enterprise. The net cash inflow or out-flow for the year is the same amount as the increase or decrease in cash and cash equiva-lents for the year on the balance sheet. Cash equivalents are highly liquid investments with original maturities of less than three months.

Two different methods for reporting cash flows from operating activities—called the *direct* and *indirect methods*—are permitted. Investing and financing activities are reported in exactly the same way under both methods. The direct method reports the cash flows from the main classifications of revenues and expenses. In contrast, the indirect method reports operating activities by showing a reconciliation of net income with net cash flow from oper-ating activities. The amount of net cash flow from operations reported is the same.

Throughout the preceding chapters, we emphasized the conceptual basis of accounting. An understanding of the rationale underlying accounting is important for both preparers and users of financial statements. In Chapter 14, we introduce the major users of financial statements and explain how they analyze and use them. We discuss and illustrate many widely used analytical techniques. As you study Chapter 14, you will see that an under-standing of accounting rules and concepts is essential for effective analysis of financial statements.

Chapter Supplement A

ADJUSTMENT FOR GAINS AND LOSSES

As noted earlier, the operating activities section of the statement may include an adjustment for gains and losses reported on the income statement. The transactions that cause gains and losses should be classified on the cash flow statement as operating, investing, or financing activities, depending on their dominant characteristics. For example, if the sale of a productive asset (e.g., a delivery truck) produced a gain, it would be classified as an investing activity.

An adjustment must be made in the operating activities section to avoid double counting the gain or loss. To illustrate, consider the following entry for Boston Beer to record the disposal of a delivery truck:

Cash (A)	8,000	
Accumulated depreciation (XA)	4,000	
Operational assets (A)		10,000
Gain on disposal (R)		2,000

The inflow of cash was $8,000, but only the reported gain of $2,000 was shown on the income statement. This transaction should be reported on the statement of cash flows as an investing activity with a cash inflow of $8,000. Because the gain was included in the computation of income, it is necessary to remove the $2,000 gain from the operating activities section of the statement to avoid double counting. If we avoid the double counting by reporting only $6,000 cash inflow from investing activities, we misstate the actual effects of the transaction.

When a loss is reported on the income statement, it also must be removed when preparing the cash flow statement. Consider the following entry to record the sale of assets:

Cash (A)	41,000	
Accumulated depreciation (XA)	15,000	
Loss (E)	12,000	
Operational assets (A)		68,000

On the cash flow statement, the loss of $12,000 must be removed from operating activities, and the total cash collected of $41,000 must be shown in the investing activities section of the statement.

Chapter Supplement B

SPREADSHEET APPROACH—STATEMENT OF CASH FLOWS: INDIRECT METHOD

As situations become more complex, the analytical approach that we used to prepare the statement of cash flows for Boston Beer Company becomes cumbersome and inefficient. In actual practice, most companies use a spreadsheet approach to prepare the statement of cash flows. The spreadsheet is based on the same logic that we used in our previous illustration. The spreadsheet's primary advantage is that it offers a more systematic way to keep track of data. You may find it useful even in simple situations because it minimizes the possibility of errors.

Exhibit 13.7 shows Boston Beer Company's spreadsheet, which is organized as follows:

1. Four columns to record dollar amounts are established. The first column is for the beginning balances for items reported on the balance sheet; the next two columns reflect debit and credit changes to those balances; the final column contains the ending balances for the balance sheet accounts.
2. On the far left of the top half of the spreadsheet, each account name from the balance sheet is entered.
3. On the far left of the bottom half of the spreadsheet, the name of each item that will be reported on the statement of cash flows is entered.

EXHIBIT 13.7
Spreadsheet to Prepare Statement of Cash Flows, Indirect Method

BOSTON BEER COMPANY
Quarter ended March 30, 1996
(in thousands)

	Beginning Balances, 12/31/1995	ANALYSIS OF CHANGES		Ending Balances 3/30/1996
		Debit	Credit	
ITEMS FROM BALANCE SHEET				
Cash and cash equivalents	36,607		(o) 4,008	32,599
Accounts receivable, net	16,090	(d) 8,383		24,473
Inventories	9,280	(e) 3,428		12,708
Prepaid expenses	437		(f) 58	379
Deferred income taxes	1,011			1,011
Other current assets	1,858		(g) 1,393	465
Restricted investments	602	(l) 614	(m) 597	619
Equipment and leasehold improvements	9,690	(k) 2,845		12,535
Accumulated depreciation	(3,531)		(b) 539	(4,070)
Deferred income taxes	1,777			1,777
Other assets	2,869		(h) 1,262	1,607
Accounts payable	8,604		(i) 5,394	13,998
Notes payable–Bank	—		(n) 240	240
Accrued expenses	11,338	(j) 939		10,399
Current maturities of long-term debt	75			75
Long-term debt, less current maturities	1,875			1,875
Common stock A	156			156
Common Stock B	41			41
Additional paid-in capital	52,973		(c) 78	53,051
Retained earnings	1,628		(a) 2,640	4,268

		Inflows	Outflows	Subtotals
STATEMENT OF CASH FLOWS				
Cash flows from operating activities				
Net income	(a)	2,640		
Adjustments to reconcile net income to net cash provided by operating activities				
Depreciation and amortization	(b)	539		
Stock option compensation expense	(c)	78		
Changes in assets and liabilities				
Accounts receivable	(d)		8,383	
Inventory	(e)		3,428	
Prepaid expenses	(f)	58		
Other current assets	(g)	1,393		
Others assets	(h)	1,262		
Accounts payable	(i)	5,394		
Accrued expenses	(j)		939	
				(1,386)
Cash flows from investing activities				
Additions to fixed assets	(k)		2,845	
Purchases of restricted investments	(l)		614	
Maturities of restricted investments	(m)	597		
				(2,862)
Cash flows from financing activities				
Net borrowings under line of credit	(n)	240		
				240
Net decrease in cash and cash equivalents	(o)	4,008		
		32,418	32,418	(4,008)

Changes in the various balance sheet accounts are analyzed in terms of debits and credits in the top half of the spreadsheet with the offsetting debits and credits being recorded in the bottom half of the spreadsheet in terms of their impact on cash flows. Each change in the noncash balance sheet accounts explains part of the change in the Cash account. To illustrate, let's examine each of the entries on the spreadsheet for Boston Beer Company shown in Exhibit 13.7. You will note that they follow each of the items presented in the schedule to prepare the cash flow statement shown in Exhibits 13.3, 13.5, and 13.6.

(a) This entry is used to start the reconciliation; net income is shown as an inflow in the operating activities section to be reconciled by the noncash reconciling entries. The credit to Retained Earnings reflects the effects of the original closing entry. This is the starting point for the reconciliation.

(b) Depreciation expense is a noncash expense. It is added back to net income because this type of expense does not cause a cash outflow when it is recorded. The credit to Accumulated Depreciation reflects the effects of the original entry to record depreciation.

(c) Stock option compensation expense is a noncash expense (an expense paid with common stock). It is added back to net income because this type of expense does not cause a cash outflow when it is recorded. The credit to Additional Paid-In Capital (and Common Stock of an amount less than $1) reflects the original entry for the issuance of the stock.

(d) This entry reconciles the change in accounts receivable during the period with net income. It is subtracted from net income because cash collections from customers totaled less than sales revenue.

(e) This entry reconciles the purchases of inventory with cost of goods sold. It is subtracted from net income because more inventory was purchased than was sold.

(f) This entry reconciles the prepayment of expenses with their expiration. It is added to net income because cash payments for new prepayments are less than the amounts that expired and were recorded on the income statement during the period.

(g) This entry reconciles payments for purchases of other current assets and their expiration. It is added to net income because cash payments for new other current assets are less than the amounts that expired and were recorded on the income statement during the period.

(h) This entry reconciles cash received from long-term receivables and accrual basis revenues. It is added because more cash is received than revenues recorded.

(i) This entry reconciles cash paid to suppliers with purchases on account. It is added because less cash was paid than was borrowed during the period.

(j) This entry reconciles the accrual of expenses with payments for these expenses. It is subtracted because cash payments for expenses are higher than new accruals.

(k) This entry records the purchases of new plant and equipment (fixed assets) for cash.

(l) This entry records the purchases of investments for cash.

(m) This entry records the cash received from sale of existing investments.

(n) This entry records the cash received from new borrowing from the bank.

(o) This entry shows that the net increase or decrease reported on the statement of cash flows is the same as the change in the cash balance on the balance sheet during the period.

The preceding entries complete the spreadsheet analysis because all accounts are reconciled. The accuracy of the analysis can be checked by adding the two analysis columns to verify that Debits = Credits. The formal statement of cash flows can be prepared directly from the spreadsheet.

The preparation of a statement of cash flows is more difficult than preparing an income statement or a balance sheet. To develop the statement of cash flows, it is necessary to analyze changes in various accounts to determine the cash flow effects. The other statements can be prepared easily by taking the balances from various accounts in the ledger.

The analytical technique that you have learned for preparing the statement of cash flows will help you deal with other significant business problems. For example, this type of analysis is useful for developing cash budgets for a business. Many small businesses that experience rapid sales growth get into serious financial difficulties because they did not forecast the cash flow effects associated with credit sales and large increases in inventory.

Key Ratios

Quality of earnings ratio indicates what portion of income was generated in cash that then can be used for investing activities. It is computed as follows (p. 668):

$$\text{Quality of Income Ratio} = \frac{\text{Cash Flow From Operations}}{\text{Net Income}}$$

Capital acquisitions ratio measures the ability to finance purchases of plant and equipment from operations. It is computed as follows (p. 673):

$$\text{Capital Acquisitions Ratio} = \frac{\text{Cash Flow From Operations}}{\text{Cash Paid for Plant and Equipment}}$$

Key Terms

Cash Equivalent A short-term, highly liquid investment with original maturity of less than three months. Statement of cash flows reports changes in cash and cash equivalents. *654*

Cash Flows from Financing Activities Cash inflows and outflows related to the way that cash was obtained from external sources (owners and creditors) to finance the enterprise. *657*

Cash Flows from Investing Activities Cash inflows and outflows related to the acquisition or sale of productive facilities and investments in the securities of other companies. *657*

Cash Flows from Operating Activities (Cash Flows from Operations) Cash inflows and outflows directly related to earnings from normal operations. *656*

Direct Method Reports components of cash flows from operating activities as gross receipts and gross payments. *656*

Indirect Method The method of presenting the operating section of the statement of cash flows that adjusts net income to compute cash flows from operating activities. *656*

Noncash Expenses Expenses that do not cause an immediate cash outflow; for example, depreciation expense. *662*

Noncash Investing and Financing Activities Transactions that do not have direct cash flow effects; reported as a supplement to the statement of cash flows in narrative or schedule form. *676*

Questions

1. Compare the purposes of the income statement, the balance sheet, and the statement of cash flows.
2. What information does the statement of cash flows report that is not reported on the other required financial statements? How do investors and creditors use that information?
3. What are the major categories of business activities reported on the statement of cash flows? Define each of these activities.
4. What are the typical cash inflows from operating activities? What are the typical cash outflows from operating activities?
5. What are the typical cash inflows from investing activities? What are the typical cash outflows from investing activities?
6. What are the typical cash inflows from financing activities? What are the typical cash outflows from financing activities?
7. What are noncash investing and financing activities? Give two examples. How are they reported on the statement of cash flows?
8. What are cash equivalents? How are purchases and sales of cash equivalents reported on the statement of cash flows?
9. If a business purchases a Treasury bill that matures in six months, is the Treasury bill considered a cash equivalent? Will that Treasury bill be considered a cash equivalent when it has only three months remaining to maturity?
10. How is the sale of equipment reported on the statement of cash flows using the indirect method?
11. Compare the two methods of reporting cash flows from operating activities in the statement of cash flows.
12. Under the indirect method, depreciation expense is added to net income to report cash flows from operating activities. Does depreciation cause an inflow of cash?
13. How is depreciation expense handled on a statement of cash flows using the direct method? Using the indirect method? What other expenses are handled similarly to depreciation?
14. Assume that you are preparing a statement of cash flows and are trying to determine if there were any investing activities. Where would you find this information?
15. Assume that you are preparing a statement of cash flows and are trying to determine if there were any financing activities. Where would you find this information?
16. Explain why cash paid during the period for purchases and for salaries is not specifically reported on the statement of cash flows, indirect method, as cash outflows.
17. Explain why a $50,000 increase in inventory during the year must be included in developing cash flows for operating activities under both the direct and indirect methods.

Exercises

E13–1 Determining Cash Flow Statement Effects of Transactions

Stanley Furniture

Stanley Furniture Company is a Virginia-based furniture manufacturer. For each of the following first-quarter transactions, indicate whether *net cash inflows (outflows)* from operating activities (NCFO), investing activities (NCFI), or financing activities (NCFF) is affected and whether the effect is an inflow (+) or outflow (–), or (NE) if the transaction has no effect on cash. (*Hint*: Determine the journal entry recorded for the transaction. The transaction affects net cash flows if and only if the account Cash is affected.)

_____ 1. Paid cash to purchase new equipment.
_____ 2. Purchased raw materials inventory on account.
_____ 3. Collected payments on account from customers.
_____ 4. Recorded an adjusting entry to record an accrued salaries expense.
_____ 5. Recorded and paid interest on debt to creditors.
_____ 6. Repaid principal on revolving credit loan from bank.
_____ 7. Prepaid rent for the following period.
_____ 8. Sold used equipment for cash at book value.
_____ 9. Made payment to suppliers on account.
_____ 10. Declared and paid cash dividends to shareholders.

Compaq Computer

E13–2 Determining Cash Flow Statement Effects of Transactions

Compaq Computer Corporation is a leading manufacturer of personal computers and servers for the business and home markets. For each of the following recent transactions, indicate whether _net cash inflows (outflows)_ from operating activities (NCFO), investing activities (NCFI), or financing activities (NCFF) is affected and whether the effect is an inflow (+) or outflow (–), or (NE) if the transaction has no effect on cash. (_Hint:_ Determine the journal entry recorded for the transaction. The transaction affects net cash flows if and only if the account Cash is affected.)

_____ 1. Recorded and paid income taxes to the federal government.
_____ 2. Issued common stock for cash.
_____ 3. Prepaid rent for the following period.
_____ 4. Recorded an adjusting entry for expiration of a prepaid expense.
_____ 5. Paid cash to purchase new equipment.
_____ 6. Issued long-term debt for cash.
_____ 7. Collected payments on account from customers.
_____ 8. Purchased raw materials inventory on account.
_____ 9. Recorded and paid salaries to employees.
_____ 10. Purchased new equipment by signing a three-year note.

Adolph Coors

E13–3 Classifying Items Reported on the Cash Flow Statement (Indirect Method)

Adolph Coors Company, founded in 1873, is the third largest U.S. brewer. Its tie to the magical appeal of the Rocky Mountains is one of its most powerful trademarks. Some of the items included in its recent annual consolidated statement of cash flows presented using the _indirect method_ are listed here. Indicate whether each item is disclosed in the operating activities (O), investing activities (I), or financing activities (F) section of the statement or (NA) if the item does not appear on the statement. (_Note:_ This is the exact wording used on the actual statement.)

_____ 1. Proceeds from sale of properties.
_____ 2. Purchase of stock. (This involves repurchase of its own stock.)
_____ 3. Depreciation, depletion, and amortization.
_____ 4. Net income.
_____ 5. Inventories (decrease).
_____ 6. Principal payment on long-term debt.
_____ 7. Accounts payable (decrease).
_____ 8. Additions to properties.
_____ 9. Dividends paid.
_____ 10. Accounts and notes receivable (decrease).

E13–4 Classifying Items Reported on the Cash Flow Statement (Indirect Method)　　　Nike

Nike, Inc., is the best-known sports shoe, apparel, and equipment company in the world due to its association with sports legends such as Michael Jordan, teams such as the Michigan Wolverines, and events such as the Olympics. Some of the items included in its recent annual consolidated statement of cash flows presented using the *indirect method* are listed here. Indicate whether each item is disclosed in the operating activities (O), investing activities (I), or financing activities (F) section of the statement or (NA) if the item does not appear on the statement. (*Note:* This is the exact wording used on the actual statement.)

____ 1. Depreciation.
____ 2. Additions to property, plant, and equipment.
____ 3. Increase (decrease) in notes payable. (The amount is owed to financial institutions.)
____ 4. (Increase) decrease in other current assets.
____ 5. Disposal of property, plant, and equipment.
____ 6. Reductions in long-term debt including current portion.
____ 7. Repurchase of stock.
____ 8. (Increase) decrease in inventory.
____ 9. Net income.
____ 10. Additions to long-term debt.

E13–5 Analyzing Noncash Expenses from a Management Perspective

QuickServe, a chain of convenience stores, was experiencing some serious cash flow difficulties because of rapid growth. The company did not generate sufficient cash from operating activities to finance its new stores, and creditors were not willing to lend money because the company had not produced any income for the previous three years. The new controller for QuickServe proposed a reduction in the estimated life of store equipment to increase depreciation expense; thus, "we can improve cash flows from operating activities because depreciation expense is added back on the statement of cash flows." Other executives were not sure that this was a good idea because the increase in depreciation would make it more difficult to have positive earnings: "Without income, the bank will never lend us money."

Required:
What action would you recommend for QuickServe? Why?

E13–6 Comparing the Direct and Indirect Methods

To compare statement of cash flows reporting under the direct and indirect methods, enter check marks to indicate which items are used with each method.

Cash Flows (and Related Changes)	Direct	Indirect
1. Revenues from customers		
2. Accounts receivable increase or decrease		
3. Payments to suppliers		
4. Inventory increase or decrease		
5. Accounts payable increase or decrease		
6. Payments to employees		
7. Wages payable, increase or decrease		
8. Depreciation expense		
9. Net income		
10. Cash flows from operating activities		
11. Cash flows from investing activities		
12. Cash flows from financing activities		
13. Net increase or decrease in cash during the period		

E13–7 Reporting Cash Flows from Operating Activities, Indirect Method

The following information pertains to Day Company:

Sales		$80,000
Expenses		
Cost of goods sold	$50,000	
Depreciation expense	6,000	
Salaries expense	12,000	68,000
Net income		$12,000
Accounts receivable increase	$ 5,000	
Merchandise inventory decrease	8,000	
Salaries payable increase	500	

Required:

Present the operating activities section of the statement of cash flows for Day Company using the indirect method.

E13–8 Reporting and Interpreting Cash Flows from Operating Activities, Indirect Method, from an Analyst's Perspective

Kane Company completed its income statement and balance sheet for 19D and provided the following information:

Service revenue		$50,000
Expenses		
Salaries	$42,000	
Depreciation	7,000	
Amortization of copyrights	300	
Utilities	7,000	
Other expenses	1,700	58,000
Net loss		($ 8,000)
Decrease in accounts receivable	$12,000	
Bought a small service machine	5,000	
Increase in salaries payable	9,000	
Decrease in service revenue collected in advance	4,000	

Required:

1. Present the operating activities section of the statement of cash flows for Kane Company using the indirect method.
2. What were the major reasons that Kane was able to report a net loss but positive cash flow from operations? Why are the reasons for the difference between cash flow from operations and net income important to financial analysts?

Sizzler International, Inc.

E13–9 Reporting and Interpreting Cash Flows from Operating Activities, Indirect Method, from an Analyst's Perspective

Sizzler International, Inc., operates 700 family restaurants around the world. The company's annual report contained the following information (in thousands):

	1993
Net loss	(9,482)
Depreciation and amortization	33,305
Increase in receivables	170
Decrease in inventories	643
Increase in prepaid expenses	664
Decrease in accounts payable	2,282
Decrease in accrued liabilities	719
Increase in income taxes payable	1,861
Reduction of long-term debt	12,691
Additions to equipment	29,073

Required:

1. Based on this information, compute cash flow from operating activities using the indirect method.
2. What were the major reasons that Sizzler was able to report a net loss but positive cash flow from operations? Why are the reasons for the difference between cash flow from operations and net income important to financial analysts?

E13–10 **Analyzing the Difference between Net Income and Cash Flows from Operating Activities**

Colgate–Palmolive

The statement of cash flows for Colgate-Palmolive reported the following information (in millions):

Operating Activities	1992
Net income	$477.0
Depreciation	192.5
Cash effect of changes in	
Receivables	(38.0)
Inventories	28.4
Other current assets	10.6
Payables	(10.0)
Other	(117.8)
Net cash provided by operations	$542.7

Required:

Based on the information reported on the statement of cash flows for Colgate-Palmolive, determine whether the following accounts increased or decreased during 1992: Receivables, Inventories, Other Current Assets, and Payables.

E13–11 **Analyzing the Difference between Net Income and Cash Flows from Operating Activities**

Apple Computer, Inc.

The statement of cash flows for Apple Computer contained the following information (in thousands):

Operations	1994
Net income	$310,178
Depreciation	167,958
Changes in assets and liabilities	
Accounts receivable	(199,401)
Inventories	418,204
Other current assets	33,616
Accounts payable	139,095
Income taxes payable	50,045
Other current liabilities	39,991
Other adjustments	(222,691)
Cash generated by operations	$736,995

Required:

For each of the asset and liability accounts listed on the statement of cash flows, determine whether the account balances increased or decreased during 1994.

E13–12 **Analyzing Cash Flows from Operating Activities; Interpreting the Quality of Earnings Ratio**

PepsiCo

The annual report for PepsiCo contained the following information for 1993 (in millions):

Net income	$1,587.9
Depreciation and amortization	1,444.2
Increase in accounts receivable	161.0
Increase in inventory	89.5
Decrease in prepaid expense	3.3
Increase in accounts payable	143.2
Decrease in taxes payable	125.1
Decrease in other current liabilities	96.7
Cash dividends paid	461.6
Treasury stock purchased	463.5

Required:

1. Compute cash flows from operating activities for PepsiCo using the indirect method.
2. Compute the quality of earnings ratio.
3. What were the major reasons that Pepsi's quality of earnings ratio did not equal 1?

Rowe Furniture

E13-13 Reporting Cash Flows from Investing and Financing Activities

Rowe Furniture Corporation is a Virginia-based manufacturer of furniture. In a recent quarter, it reported the following activities:

Net income	$ 4,135
Purchase of property, plant, and equipment	871
Borrowings under line of credit (bank)	1,417
Proceeds from issuance of stock	11
Cash received from customers	29,164
Payments to reduce long-term debt	46
Sale of marketable securities	134
Proceeds from sale of property and equipment	6,594
Dividends paid	277
Interest paid	90
Purchase of treasury stock (stock repurchase)	1,583

Required:

Based on this information, present the cash flow from investing and financing activities sections of the cash flow statement.

Gibraltar Steel

E13-14 Reporting and Interpreting Cash Flows from Investing and Financing Activities with Discussion of Management Strategy

Gibraltar Steel Corporation is a Buffalo, New York–based manufacturer of high-value-added cold-rolled steel products. In a recent year, it reported the following activities:

Net income	$ 5,213
Purchase of property, plant, and equipment	10,468
Payments of notes payable (bank)	8,598
Net proceeds of initial public offering	26,061
Depreciation and amortization	3,399
Long-term debt reduction	17,832
Proceeds from sale of marketable securities	131
Proceeds from sale of property, plant, and equipment	1,817
Proceeds from long-term debt	10,242
Decrease in accounts receivable	1,137
Proceeds from notes payable (bank)	3,848

Required:

1. Based on this information, present the cash flow from investing and financing activities sections of the cash flow statement.

2. What do you think was Gibraltar management's plan for the use of the cash generated by the initial public offering of stock?

E13–15 Analyzing and Interpreting the Capital Acquisitions Ratio

Pete's Brewing

A recent annual report for Pete's Brewing Company contained the following data for the three most recent years:

	(In thousands)		
	19C	19B	19A
Cash flow from operation activities	$ 821	$ 1,460	$ 619
Cash flow from investing activities	(1,404)	(1,315)	(862)
Cash flow from financing activities	42,960	775	360

Assume that all investing activities involved acquisition of new plant and equipment.

Required:
1. Compute the capital acquisitions ratio for the three-year period in total.
2. What portion of Pete's investing activities was financed from external sources or pre-existing cash balances during the three-year period?
3. What do you think is the likely explanation for the dramatic increase in cash flow from financing activities during 19C?

E13–16 Reporting Noncash Transactions on the Statement of Cash Flows; Interpreting the Effect on the Capital Acquisitions Ratio

An analysis of Martin Corporation's operational asset accounts provided the following information:

a. Martin acquired a large machine that cost $26,000, paying for it by giving a $15,000, 12 percent interest-bearing note due at the end of two years and 500 shares of its common stock, with a par value of $10 per share and a market value of $22 per share.
b. Martin acquired a small machine that cost $8,700. Full payment was made by transferring a tract of land that had a book value of $8,700.

Required:
1. Show how this information should be reported on the statement of cash flows.
2. What would be the effect of these transactions on the capital acquisitions ratio? How might these transactions distort interpretation of the ratio?

E13–17 (Supplement A) Determining Cash Flows from the Sale of Property

AMC Entertainment

AMC Entertainment is the second-largest motion picture exhibitor in the United States. The following was abstracted from the company's statement of cash flows (in thousands):

	1993	1992	1991
Cash flows from operating activities:			
Gain on sale of property	(9,638)	(7,314)	—
Cash flows from investing activities:			
Proceeds from disposition of property	14,768	11,623	1,797

Required:
Determine the cash flow from the sale of property for each year for AMC.

E13–18 (Supplement A) Determining Cash Flows from the Sale of Equipment

During 19F, English Company sold some excess equipment at a loss. The following information was collected from the company's accounting records:

FROM THE INCOME STATEMENT:	
Depreciation expense	$ 700
Loss on sale of equipment	3,000
FROM THE BALANCE SHEET:	
Beginning equipment	12,500
Ending equipment	8,000
Beginning accumulated depreciation	2,000
Ending accumulated depreciation	2,400

No new equipment was bought during 19F.

Required:

For the equipment that was sold, determine its original cost, its accumulated depreciation, and the cash received from the sale.

E13–19 (Supplement B) Preparing a Statement of Cash Flows, Indirect Method: Complete Spreadsheet

Analysis of accounts: (1) purchased an operational asset, $20,000, issued capital stock in full payment; (2) purchased a long-term investment for cash, $15,000; (3) paid cash dividend, $12,000; (4) sold operational asset for $6,000 cash (cost, $21,000, accumulated depreciation, $19,000); and (5) sold capital stock, 500 shares at $12 per share cash.

Items from Financial Statements	Beginning Balances, 12/31/19A	ANALYSIS OF CHANGES		Ending Balances 12/31/19B
		Debit	Credit	
Income statement items				
Sales			$140,000	
Cost of goods sold		$59,000		
Depreciation		7,000		
Wage expense		28,000		
Income tax expense		9,000		
Interest expense		5,000		
Remaining expenses		15,800		
Gain on sale of operational asset			4,000	
Net income		20,200		
Balance sheet items				
Cash	$ 20,500			$ 19,200
Accounts receivable	22,000			22,000
Merchandise inventory	68,000			75,000
Investments, long-term				15,000
Operational assets	114,500			113,500
Total debits	$225,000			$244,700
Accumulated depreciation	$ 32,000			$ 20,000
Accounts payable	17,000			14,000
Wages payable	2,500			1,500
Income taxes payable	3,000			4,500
Bonds payable	54,000			54,000
Common stock, no par	100,000			126,000
Retained earnings	16,500			24,700
Total credits	$225,000			$244,700

	Inflows	Outflows
Statement of cash flows		
Cash flows from operating activities:		
Cash flows from investing activities:		
Cash flows from financing activities:		
Net increase (decrease) in cash		
Totals		

Required:

Complete the statement of cash flows, indirect method, spreadsheet.

Problems

P13–1 Using Schedule Approach to Prepare the Statement of Cash Flows, Indirect Method

The income statement of Frank Corporation follows.

FRANK CORPORATION
Income Statement
For the Year Ended December 31, 19B
Accrual Basis

Sales revenue (one-fourth on credit; accounts receivable year's end 19A, $12,000; 19B, $17,000)		$400,000
Cost of goods sold (one-third on credit; accounts payable year's end 19A, $10,000; 19B, $7,000; inventory at year's end—19A, $60,000; 19B, $52,000)		268,000
Expenses		
Salaries and wages (including accrued wages payable at year's end—19A, $1,000; 19B, $800)	$51,000	
Depreciation expense	9,200	
Rent expense (no accruals)	5,800	
Interest expense (no accruals)	12,200	
Income tax expense (income taxes payable at year's end—19A, $3,000; 19B, $5,000)	$11,800	
Total expenses		90,000
Net income		$ 42,000
Cash flow from operating activities		

Analysis of Selected 19B Account Balances and Transactions:

(a) Purchased investment securities for $5,000 cash.

(b) Borrowed $15,000 on a two-year, 8 percent interest-bearing note.

(c) During 19B, sold machinery for its net book value; received $11,000 in cash.

(d) Purchased machinery for $50,000; paid $9,000 in cash and signed a four-year note payable to the dealer for $41,000.

(e) At December 31, 19B, declared and paid a cash dividend of $10,000.

(f) Cash balance on December 31, 19A was $21,000.

Required:

Prepare a statement of cash flows, indirect method, using the schedule approach. Include any additional required note disclosures.

P13–2 Using Schedule Approach to Prepare the Statement of Cash Flows, Indirect Method

Stonewall Company was organized on January 1, 19A. During the year ended December 31, 19A, the company provided the following data:

INCOME STATEMENT	
Sales revenue	$ 80,000
Cost of goods sold	(35,000)
Depreciation expense	(4,000)
Remaining expenses	(32,000)
Net income	$ 9,000

BALANCE SHEET

Cash	$ 48,000
Accounts receivable	18,000
Merchandise inventory	15,000
Machinery (net)	25,000
Total assets	$106,000
Accounts payable	$ 10,000
Accrued expenses payable	21,000
Dividends payable	2,000
Note payable, short-term	15,000
Common stock	54,000
Retained earnings	4,000
Total liabilities and stockholders' equity	$106,000

Analysis of Selected Accounts and Transactions:

(a) Sold 3,000 shares of common stock, par $10, at $18 per share; collected cash.

(b) Borrowed $15,000 on a one-year, 8 percent interest-bearing note; the note was dated June 1, 19A.

(c) During 19A, purchased machinery; paid $29,000.

(d) Purchased merchandise for resale at a cost of $50,000 (debited Inventory because the perpetual system is used); paid $40,000 cash, balance credited to Accounts Payable.

(e) At December 31, 19A, declared a cash dividend of $5,000; paid $3,000 in December 19A; the balance will be paid March 1, 19B.

(f) Because this is the first year of operations, all account balances are zero at the beginning of the year; therefore, the changes in the account balances are equal to the ending balances.

Required:

Prepare a statement of cash flows, indirect method, using the schedule approach.

P13–3 Using Schedule Approach to Prepare the Statement of Cash Flows, Indirect Method

Rocky Mountain Chocolate Factory

Rocky Mountain Chocolate Factory manufactures an extensive line of premium chocolate candies for sale at its franchised and company-owned stores in malls throughout the United States. Its balance sheet for the first quarter of 1996 is presented along with an analysis of selected accounts and transactions:

ROCKY MOUNTAIN CHOCOLATE FACTORY, INC.
Balance Sheets

Assets	May 31, 1996 (Unaudited)	February 29, 1996
CURRENT ASSETS		
Cash and cash equivalents	$ 921,505	$ 528,787
Accounts and notes receivable—trade, less allowance for doubtful accounts of $43,196 at May 31 and $28,196 at February 29	1,602,582	1,463,901
Inventories	2,748,788	2,504,908
Deferred tax asset	59,219	59,219
Other	581,508	224,001
Total current assets	5,913,602	4,780,816

Assets (cont.)	May 31, 1996 (Unaudited)	February 29, 1996
Property and equipment—at cost	14,010,796	12,929,675
Less accumulated depreciation and amortization	−2,744,388	−2,468,084
	11,266,408	10,461,591
OTHER ASSETS		
Notes and accounts receivable due after one year	100,206	111,588
Goodwill, net of accumulated amortization of $259,641 at		
May 31 and $253,740 at Feb. 29	330,359	336,260
Other	574,130	624,185
	1,004,695	1,072,033
	$18,184,705	$16,314,440

Liabilities and Equity		
CURRENT LIABILITIES		
Short-term debt	0	$1,000,000
Current maturities of long-term debt	429,562	134,538
Accounts payable—trade	1,279,455	998,520
Accrued liabilities	714,473	550,386
Income taxes payable	11,198	54,229
Total current liabilities	2,434,688	2,737,673
Long-term debt, less current maturities	4,193,290	2,183,877
Deferred income taxes	275,508	275,508

Stockholders' Equity		
Common stock—authorized 7,250,000 shares, $.03 par value;		
issued 3,034,302 shares at May 31 and at Feb. 29	91,029	91,029
Additional paid-in capital	9,703,985	9,703,985
Retained earnings	2,502,104	2,338,267
	12,297,118	12,133,281
Less common stock held in treasury, at cost—		
129,153 shares at May 31 and at February 29	1,015,899	1,015,899
	11,281,219	11,117,382
	$18,184,705	$16,314,440

The accompanying notes are an integral part of these statements.

Analysis of Selected Accounts and Transactions:

(a) Net income was $163,837. Notes and accounts receivable due after one year relate to operations.

(b) Depreciation and amortization totaled $282,205.

(c) No "other" noncurrent assets (which relate to investing activities) were purchased this period.

(d) No property, plant, and equipment were sold during the period. No goodwill was acquired or sold.

(e) Proceeds from issuance of long-term debt were $4,659,466 and principal payments were $2,355,029. (Combine the current maturities with the long-term debt in your analysis.)

(f) No dividends were declared or paid.

Required:

Prepare a statement of cash flows, indirect method, using the schedule approach.

P13–4 Comparing Cash Flows from Operating Activities Using Direct and Indirect Methods

Beta Company's accountants just completed the income statement and balance sheet for the year and have provided the following information (in thousands):

Income Statement

Sales revenue		$20,600
Expenses		
Cost of goods sold	$9,000	
Depreciation expense	2,000	
Salaries expense	5,000	
Rent expense	2,500	
Insurance expense	800	
Utilities expense	700	
Interest expense on bonds	600	
Loss on sale of investments	400	21,000
Net loss		$ (400)

Selected Balance Sheet Accounts

	19A	19B
Merchandise inventory	$ 60	$ 82
Accounts receivable	450	380
Accounts payable	210	240
Salaries payable	20	29
Rent payable	6	2
Prepaid rent	7	2
Prepaid insurance	5	14

Other Data:

The company issued $20,000, 8 percent bonds payable during the year.

Required:

1. Prepare the cash flows from operating activities section of the statement of cash flows using the direct method.
2. Prepare the cash flows from operating activities section of the statement of cash flows using the indirect method.

P13–5 (Supplement B) Preparing Statement of Cash Flows Spreadsheet, Statement of Cash Flows, and Schedules Using Indirect Method

Hunter Company is developing its annual financial statements at December 31, 19B. The statements are complete except for the statement of cash flows. The completed comparative balance sheets and income statement are summarized:

	19A	19B
Balance sheet at December 31		
Cash	$ 18,000	$ 44,000
Accounts receivable	29,000	27,000
Merchandise inventory	36,000	30,000
Operational assets (net)	72,000	75,000
	$155,000	$176,000
Accounts payable	$ 22,000	$ 25,000
Wages payable	1,000	800
Note payable, long-term	48,000	38,000
Common stock, no par	60,000	80,000
Retained earnings	24,000	32,200
	$155,000	$176,000

	19A	19B
Income statement for 19B		
Sales		$100,000
Cost of goods sold		(61,000)
Expenses		(27,000)
Net income		$ 12,000

Additional Data:

(a) Bought operational assets for cash, $9,000.

(b) Paid $10,000 on the long-term note payable.

(c) Sold unissued common stock for $20,000 cash.

(d) Declared and paid a $3,800 cash dividend.

(e) Expenses included depreciation, $6,000; wages, $10,000; taxes, $3,000; other, $8,000.

Required:

1. Prepare a statement of cash flows spreadsheet using the indirect method to report cash flows from operating activities.
2. Prepare the statement of cash flows.
3. Prepare a schedule of noncash investing and financing activities if necessary.

P13–6 (Supplement B) Preparing Statement of Cash Flows Spreadsheet and Statement of Cash Flows Using Indirect Method: Includes Noncash Investing and Financing Activity and Sale of an Asset at Book Value

Ellington Company is developing its 19B annual report. The following information is provided:

	19A	19B
Cash	$21,000	$22,400
Accounts receivable	18,000	21,000
Inventory	35,000	32,000
Prepaid insurance	2,400	1,400
Investments, long-term	12,500	9,300
Operational assets (net)	31,100	59,600
Patent	2,000	1,500
Accounts payable	27,000	15,000
Wages payable	4,000	1,000
Income taxes payable	2,000	2,200
Note payable, long-term	20,000	10,000
Common stock ($10 par)	50,000	80,000
Contributed capital in excess of par	3,000	6,000
Retained earnings	16,000	33,000

Other Information:

(a) Sold long-term investment at book value, $3,200. Purchased operational assets by issuing 3,000 shares of common stock; market value of common stock, $11 per share.

(b) Revenues, $150,000.

(c) Expenses: depreciation, $4,500; patent amortization, $500; insurance, $2,000; wages, $48,500; income taxes, $7,000; and cost of goods sold, $62,000.

Required:

1. Prepare a statement of cash flows spreadsheet using the indirect method to report cash flows from operating activities.
2. Prepare the statement of cash flows.
3. Prepare a schedule of noncash investing and financing activities.

Cases and Projects

Carlyle Golf, Inc.

C13–1 Analyzing Cash Flow for a New Company

Carlyle Golf, Inc., was formed in September 1992. The company designs, contracts for the manufacture of, and markets a line of men's golf apparel. A portion of the statement of cash flows for Carlyle follows:

	1993
Cash flows from operating activities	
Net income	$(460,089)
Depreciation	3,554
Noncash compensation (stock)	254,464
Deposits with suppliers	(404,934)
Increase in prepaid assets	(42,260)
Increase in accounts payable	81,765
Increase in accrued liabilities	24,495
Net cash flows	$(543,005)

Management expects a solid increase in sales in the near future. To support the increase in sales, it plans to add $2.2 million to inventory. The company did not disclose a sales forecast. At the end of 1993, Carlyle had less than $1,000 in cash. It is not unusual for a new company to experience a loss and negative cash flows during its start-up phase. Evaluate the problems facing Carlyle.

Big Rock Brewery

C13–2 International Case: Analyzing a Canadian Cash Flow Statement

Big Rock Brewery Ltd. is the largest craft brewer in Canada. As do all Canadian companies, the Calgary-based company follows Canadian Generally Accepted Accounting Principles. Its cash flow statement prepared according to those principles follows:

BIG ROCK BREWERY LTD.
Statement of Changes in Financial Position
Years ended March 31

	1996 $	1995 $
	(Denominated in Canadian Dollars)	
OPERATING ACTIVITIES		
Net income for year	1,303,923	1,742,332
Items not affecting cash		
Amortization	681,025	405,451
(Gain) loss on disposal of capital assets	(22,554)	441,130
Deferred income taxes	532,400	522,000
Net change in non-cash working capital [note 14]	(442,811)	(1,333,187)
Cash provided by operating activities	2,051,983	1,777,726

	1996 $	1995 $
	(Denominated in Canadian Dollars)	
FINANCING ACTIVITIES		
Construction loan borrowings	8,751,246	—
Term loan repayments	(225,007)	(282,426)
Term loan borrowings	—	1,300,000
Advances (repayments) under demand operating loans, net	(365,754)	365,754
Share capital issued	41,502	40,000
Increase in construction costs payable	1,281,187	—
Cash provided by financing activities	9,483,174	1,413,328
INVESTING ACTIVITIES		
Additions to capital assets	(11,323,613)	(3,681,936)
Increase in deferred charges and other assets	(33,290)	(19,535)
Proceeds on disposal of capital assets	39,997	198,457
Cash used in investing activities	(11,316,906)	(3,503,014)
Net increase (decrease) in cash	218,251	(311,960)
Cash, beginning of year	—	311,960
Cash, end of year	218,251	—

Required:

1. Which of the two basic reporting approaches for the statement of cash flows did the company adopt?
2. Compare Big Rock's statement with that of Boston Beer presented in Exhibit 13.1. What differences do you see in the U.S. and Canadian versions of the statement?

C13-3   Financial Statement Analysis

Toys "R" Us

Refer to the financial statements of Toys "R" Us given in Appendix B at the end of this book.

Required:

1. Which of the two basic reporting approaches for the statement of cash flows did the company adopt?
2. What amount of tax payments did the company make during the current year?
3. Short-term borrowings are shown in the financing activity section. Does this amount include interest payments on this debt? Explain.
4. Cash from operating activities was higher than net income in the current year. Evaluate this difference.
5. The company has not paid cash dividends for a number of years. Use the statement of cash flows to explain why.

C13-4   Project: Comparing Direct and Indirect Cash Flow Statements within Industries

Acquire the cash flow statement from the annual reports or 10-Ks of Compaq Computer Company and one of its competitors (e.g., IBM, Apple, Hewlett-Packard). (Library files, the SEC EDGAR service at www.sec.gov, Compustat CD, or the companies themselves are good sources.) Write a short report indicating any differences, if any, between the information disclosed in Compaq's direct method presentation and its competitor's indirect presentation.

C13-5   Project: Comparing Cash Flow from Investing and Financing Activities within Industries

Acquire the cash flow statements from the annual reports or 10-Ks of two companies from the same industry. (Library files, the SEC EDGAR service at www.sec.gov, Compustat, or the companies themselves are good sources.) Write a short report indicating any differences in the investing and financing activities of the two companies over the last three years. Indicate what differences in business strategy the documents indicate.

C13–6 **Project: Competitive Analysis of Differences in Quality of Earnings Ratio**

Boston Beer's competitors in the craft brewing industry include Redhook, Pete's, Big Rock, Minnesota Brewing, and others. Obtain the cash flow statement for Boston Beer and two of its competitors. (Library files, the SEC EDGAR service at www.sec.gov, Compustat, or the companies themselves are good sources.) Write a short memo comparing the companies' quality of earnings ratios. Based on the reconciliation of net income to cash flow from operations, indicate what caused the differences in their ratios.

C13–7 **Project: Financial Analysis Update**

Acquire the most recent year's first quarter report for Boston Beer. (Library files, the SEC EDGAR service at www.sec.gov, Compustat, or the company itself are good sources.) Write a short memo comparing the quality of earnings ratio with that determined from the first quarter 1996 figures presented in the chapter. Indicate what differences in its operations might account for any differences in the ratios between the two periods.

C13–8 **Ethics Project: Analyzing Irregularities in Revenue Recognition**

Obtain a recent news story outlining an accounting irregularity related to accounts receivable or inventories. (Library files, Wall Street Journal Index, Dow Jones News/Retrieval, and *Bloomberg Business News* are good sources. Search for the term *accounting irregularities*.) Examine the company's cash flow statements for the three years prior to disclosure of the irregularity. Write a short memo outlining the nature of the irregularity and whether there were indications of the pending problem in the company's cash flow statements.

C13–9 **Team Project: Analyzing Cash Flows**

As a group, select an industry to analyze. Each group member should acquire the annual report or 10-K for one publicly traded company in the industry, with each member selecting a different company. (Library files, the SEC EDGAR service at www.sec.gov, Compustat CD, or the company itself are good sources.) On an individual basis, each group member should then write a short report answering the following questions about their selected company.

1. Which of the two basic reporting approaches for the statement of cash flows did the company adopt?
2. What is the quality of earnings ratio for the most current year? What were the major causes of differences between net income and cash flow from operations?
3. What is the capital acquisitions ratio for the three-year period presented in total? How is the company financing its capital acquisitions?
4. What portion of the cash from operations in the current year is being paid to stockholders in the form of dividends?

Discuss any patterns across the three companies that you as a group observe. Then, as a group, write a short report comparing and contrasting your companies using these attributes. Provide potential explanations for any differences discovered.

CHAPTER FOURTEEN

Analyzing Financial Statements

Home Depot

FINANCIAL ANALYSIS: BRINGING IT ALL TOGETHER

The history of Home Depot is an unusual success story. Founded in

1978 in Atlanta, Home Depot has grown to be America's largest home

improvement retailer and, according to *Fortune* magazine, ranks among the

nation's 30 largest retailers. Financial statements for Home Depot are pre-

sented in Exhibit 14.1.

As you can see, Home Depot is continuing its rapid growth. Sales rev-

enue for the year ended February 2, 1997, was 56 percent higher than in

1995, and the company's net earnings increased by more than 55 percent.

Despite this rapid growth, financial analysts offer a variety of recom-

mendations concerning Home Depot's stock. Merrill Lynch does not currently

recommend buying it, noting that the "stock has performed like a passbook

savings account. Over the past four years, the company has generated an

EXHIBIT 14.1
Home Depot Financial Statements

Consolidated Balance Sheets

THE HOME DEPOT, INC. AND SUBSIDIARIES
AMOUNTS IN THOUSANDS, EXCEPT SHARE DATA

	FEBRUARY 2, 1997	JANUARY 28, 1996
ASSETS		
Current Assets:		
Cash and Cash Equivalents	$ 146,006	$ 53,269
Short-Term Investments, including current maturities of long-term investments (note 7)	412,430	54,756
Receivables, Net	388,416	325,384
Merchandise Inventories	2,708,283	2,180,318
Other Current Assets	54,238	58,242
Total Current Assets	3,709,373	2,671,969
Property and Equipment, at cost:		
Land	1,855,251	1,510,619
Buildings	2,470,310	1,885,742
Furniture, Fixtures and Equipment	1,083,638	857,082
Leasehold Improvements	339,498	314,933
Construction in Progress	284,369	308,365
Capital Leases (notes 2 and 5)	116,750	92,154
	6,149,816	4,968,895
Less Accumulated Depreciation and Amortization	712,770	507,871
Net Property and Equipment	5,437,046	4,461,024
Long-Term Investments (note 7)	8,480	25,436
Notes Receivable	39,518	54,715
Cost in Excess of the Fair Value of Net Assets Acquired, net of accumulated amortization of $14,864 at February 2, 1997 and $10,536 at January 28, 1996	86,540	87,238
Other	60,753	53,651
	$9,341,710	$7,354,033
LIABILITIES AND STOCKHOLDERS' EQUITY		
Current Liabilities:		
Accounts Payable	$1,089,736	$ 824,808
Accrued Salaries and Related Expenses	249,356	198,208
Sales Taxes Payable	129,284	113,066
Other Accrued Expenses	322,503	242,859
Income Taxes Payable	48,728	35,214
Current Installments of Long-Term Debt (notes 2, 5 and 6)	2,519	2,327
Total Current Liabilities	1,842,126	1,416,482
Long-Term Debt, excluding current installments (notes 2, 5 and 6)	1,246,593	720,080
Other Long-Term Liabilities	134,034	115,917
Deferred Income Taxes (note 3)	66,020	37,225
Minority Interest (note 9)	97,751	76,563
STOCKHOLDERS' EQUITY (notes 2 and 4):		
Common Stock, par value $0.05. Authorized: 1,000,000,000 shares; issued and outstanding – 480,515,000 shares at February 2, 1997 and 477,106,000 shares at January 28, 1996	24,026	23,855
Paid-in Capital	2,523,093	2,407,815
Retained Earnings	3,406,592	2,579,059
Cumulative Translation Adjustments	2,173	(6,131)
Unrealized Loss on Investments, Net	(168)	(47)
	5,955,716	5,004,551
Less: Notes Receivable From ESOP (note 6)	–	16,539
Shares Held in Employee Benefit Trust (note 6)	530	246
Total Stockholders' Equity	5,955,186	4,987,766
Commitments and Contingencies (notes 5, 8 and 9)		
	$9,341,710	$7,354,033

(continued)

average annual return of just 2 percent. This lackluster performance has occurred despite strong earnings."

Another investment analyst, Smith Barney, recommends buying the stock, concluding that "Home Depot's lackluster stock performance represents an attractive buying opportunity. The company's operating profit margins are beginning to rise, which could lead to a higher stock price."

Given this conflicting advice, would you want to buy Home Depot stock? To make a rational decision, you would want to consider more factors than just the company's rapid growth in profitability and the

EXHIBIT 14.1
Continued

Consolidated Statements of Cash Flows

THE HOME DEPOT, INC. AND SUBSIDIARIES
AMOUNTS IN THOUSANDS

	FISCAL YEAR ENDED		
	FEBRUARY 2, 1997 (53 WEEKS)	JANUARY 28, 1996 (52 WEEKS)	JANUARY 29, 1995 (52 WEEKS)
CASH PROVIDED FROM OPERATIONS:			
Net Earnings	$ 937,739	$ 731,523	$ 604,501
Reconciliation of Net Earnings to Net Cash Provided by Operations:			
Depreciation and Amortization	232,340	181,205	129,609
Deferred Income Tax Expense (Benefit)	28,795	17,976	(2,468)
Increase in Receivables, Net	(57,937)	(69,907)	(69,023)
Increase in Merchandise Inventories	(525,154)	(429,270)	(405,197)
Increase in Accounts Payable and Accrued Expenses	434,259	215,633	280,056
Increase (Decrease) in Income Taxes Payable	24,584	36,159	(11,126)
Other	25,484	29,661	(10,870)
Net Cash Provided by Operations	1,100,110	712,980	515,482
CASH FLOWS FROM INVESTING ACTIVITIES:			
Capital Expenditures, net of $53,789, $30,271 and $31,183 of non-cash capital expenditures in fiscal 1996, 1995 and 1994, respectively	(1,194,422)	(1,278,104)	(1,100,654)
Acquisition of Canadian Partnership Interest	–	–	(161,548)
Proceeds from Sales of Property and Equipment	21,775	29,357	49,718
Proceeds from Sales of Investments	40,737	30,721	526,696
Purchases of Investments	(409,015)	(370,327)	(230,538)
Proceeds from Maturities of Investments	27,193	416,316	159,396
Repayments of Advances Secured by Real Estate, Net	6,128	(4,955)	2,650
Net Cash Used in Investing Activities	(1,507,604)	(1,176,992)	(754,280)
CASH FLOWS FROM FINANCING ACTIVITIES:			
(Repayments of) Issuance of Commercial Paper Obligations, Net	(620,000)	520,000	100,000
Proceeds from Long-Term Borrowings, Net	1,092,960	–	–
Repayments of Notes Receivable from ESOP	16,539	15,271	13,041
Principal Repayments of Long-Term Debt	(2,723)	(22,817)	(2,175)
Proceeds from Sale of Common Stock, Net	104,495	68,458	77,926
Cash Dividends Paid to Stockholders	(110,206)	(89,748)	(67,792)
Minority Interest Contributions to Partnership	19,012	24,577	19,031
Net Cash Provided by Financing Activities	500,077	515,741	140,031
Increase (Decrease) in Effect of Exchange Rate Changes on Cash	154	386	(76)
Increase (Decrease) in Cash and Cash Equivalents	92,737	52,115	(98,843)
Cash and Cash Equivalents at Beginning of Year	53,269	1,154	99,997
Cash and Cash Equivalents at End of Year	$ 146,006	$ 53,269	$ 1,154
SUPPLEMENTAL DISCLOSURE OF CASH PAYMENTS MADE FOR:			
Interest (net of interest capitalized)	$ 3,350	$ 21,685	$ 30,537
Income Taxes	$ 547,604	$ 407,643	$ 393,915

recommendation of a financial analyst. The information contained in Home Depot's financial statements and the analytical tools discussed in this chapter provide an important basis to help you decide whether to invest in Home Depot stock.

■ ■ ■

Business Background

In the United States, companies spend billions of dollars each year preparing, auditing, and publishing their financial statements. These statements are mailed to current and prospective investors. Each year Home Depot sends out more than 66,000 copies of its financial statements to current stockholders. Most companies also make financial information available on the Internet. Home Depot has a particularly interesting home

LEARNING OBJECTIVE 1
Identify the major users of financial statements and explain how they use statements.

EXHIBIT 14.1
Concluded

Consolidated Statements of Earnings

THE HOME DEPOT, INC. AND SUBSIDIARIES
AMOUNTS IN THOUSANDS, EXCEPT PER SHARE DATA

	FISCAL YEAR ENDED		
	FEBRUARY 2, 1997 (53 WEEKS)	JANUARY 28, 1996 (52 WEEKS)	JANUARY 29, 1995 (52 WEEKS)
NET SALES	$19,535,503	$15,470,358	$12,476,697
COST OF MERCHANDISE SOLD	14,101,423	11,184,772	8,991,204
GROSS PROFIT	5,434,080	4,285,586	3,485,493
OPERATING EXPENSES:			
Selling and Store Operating	3,521,429	2,783,956	2,216,921
Pre-Opening	54,709	52,342	51,307
General and Administrative	324,292	269,464	230,456
Total Operating Expenses	3,900,430	3,105,762	2,498,684
OPERATING INCOME	1,533,650	1,179,824	986,809
INTEREST INCOME (EXPENSE):			
Interest and Investment Income	25,577	19,597	28,510
Interest Expense (note 2)	(16,087)	(4,148)	(35,949)
Interest, Net	9,490	15,449	(7,439)
MINORITY INTEREST (note 9)	(8,371)	30	381
EARNINGS BEFORE INCOME TAXES	1,534,769	1,195,303	979,751
INCOME TAXES (note 3)	597,030	463,780	375,250
NET EARNINGS	$ 937,739	$ 731,523	$ 604,501
EARNINGS PER COMMON AND COMMON EQUIVALENT SHARE	$ 1.94	$ 1.54	$ 1.32
WEIGHTED AVERAGE NUMBER OF COMMON AND COMMON EQUIVALENT SHARES	487,752	477,977	475,947

page (http://www.homedepot.com) that contains current financial statements, recent news articles about the company, and a variety of relevant information.

The reason that Home Depot spends so much money to provide information to investors is simple: Financial statements help people make better economic decisions. Two broad groups of people use financial statements. One group is the management of the business; it relies on accounting data to make important operating decisions, such as the pricing of products or expansion of productive capacity. The second group is external decision makers. This group consists primarily of investors (both present and potential owners), investment analysts, creditors, governmental units, labor organizations, and the public.

Users of financial statements are interested in three types of information:

1. *Information about past performance.* Information concerning such items as income, sales volume, cash flows, and return earned on the investment helps assess the success of the business and the effectiveness of its management. Such information also helps the decision maker compare one company with others.

2. *Information about the present condition of a business.* This type of information helps answer questions such as these: What types of assets are owned? How much debt does the business owe, and when is it due? What is its cash position? What are its EPS, return on investment, and debt-to-equity ratios? What is the inventory position? Answers to these and similar questions help people assess the successes and failures of the past; more important, they provide information useful in assessing the cash flow and profit potentials of the business.

3. *Information about the future performance of the business.* Decision makers select from among several alternative courses of action. All decisions are future ori-

ented. As you know, financial statements report on the past and cannot predict the future. Nevertheless, reliable measurements of what has happened in the past are an important part of predicting what will happen in the future. For example, the recent sales and earnings trends of a business are good indicators of what might be expected in the future. In other words, you must know where you are to be able to plan where you are able to go.

The Investment Decision

Perhaps the single largest group of people who use financial statements is composed of investors including current owners, potential owners, and investment analysts (because they advise investors). Investors purchase stock with the expectation of earning a return on their investment. The return on a stock investment has two components: (1) dividend revenue during the investment period and (2) increases in the market value of the shares owned.

When considering a stock investment, the investor should evaluate the future income and growth potential of the business on the basis of three factors:

1. *Economywide factors.* Often the overall health of the economy has a direct impact on the performance of an individual business. Investors should consider such data as the gross national product, productivity, unemployment rate, general inflation rate, and changes in interest rates. For example, increases in interest rates often slow economic growth because consumers are less willing to buy merchandise on credit when interest rates are high.
2. *Industry factors.* Certain events have a major impact on each company within an industry but have only a minor impact on other companies. For example, a major drought may be devastating for food-related industries but have no effect on the electronics industry.
3. *Individual company factors.* To properly analyze a company, you should get to know as much as you can about it. Good analysts do not rely only on the information contained in the financial statements. They visit the company, buy its products, and read about it in the business press. If you evaluate McDonald's, it is equally important to assess the quality of its balance sheet and the quality of its Big Mac. The importance of nonquantitative information can be illustrated by a research report on Home Depot written by Salomon Brothers, a large investment banking firm:

We believe that the company's strong culture—which focuses on employee empowerment and customer service—is the key reason that it has become the nation's largest home center chain in only 12 years and that it will be able to dramatically expand its national market share over the next several years, as it expands its presence across the country and around the world.

Understanding a Company's Strategy

Financial statement analysis is more than just "crunching numbers." Before you start looking at numbers, you should know what you are looking for. The best place to start is with a solid understanding of the company's business strategy. To evaluate how a company is doing, you must know what it is trying to do. You can learn a great deal about a company's strategy by reading its complete annual report, especially the letter from the president. It also is useful to read articles about the company in the business press.

Home Depot's business strategy is described by Salomon Brothers as follows:

REAL WORLD EXCERPT

HOME DEPOT
Salomon Brothers
Research Report

> The Home Depot successful formula combines the low everyday prices of a large store, "category killer" retailer, with the service usually found only in a small, local hardware store. Few if any of its competitors are able to duplicate both of these customer driven strategies.

This strategy has several implications for our analysis of Home Depot:

1. Cost control is critical. Home Depot must be able to purchase merchandise at low prices to beat competitors.
2. Stores must be able to generate high volume to cover the cost of operating large stores.
3. Employee compensation and training costs are higher than competitors' costs to offer a high level of service. This puts pressure on Home Depot to control costs in other areas.

By understanding the company's strategy, the analyst is able to attach more meaning to the information contained in the financial statements.

Financial Statement Analysis

Financial statements include a large volume of quantitative data supplemented by disclosure notes. It is impossible to analyze financial data without a basis of comparison. For example, would you be impressed with a company that earned $1 million last year? You probably answered the question by thinking, "It depends." A $1 million profit might be very good for a company that lost money the year before but not good for a company that made $500 million during the previous year; it might be good for a small company but not good for a very large company; it might be good if all the other companies in the industry lost money but not good if they all earned much larger profits. As you can see from this simple example, financial results cannot be evaluated in isolation. You must develop appropriate comparisons to properly analyze the information reported in financial statements. Finding an appropriate benchmark requires judgment and is not always an easy task. For this reason, financial analysis is a sophisticated skill instead of a mechanical process.

The two types of benchmarks for making financial comparisons are as follows:

1. *Time series analysis.* In this type of analysis, information for a single company is compared over time. For example, a company may have a current ratio (current assets divided by current liabilities) of 1.2. Without additional information, this ratio does not tell us very much. Time series analysis might tell you that the ratio has declined each year for the past five years, from a high of 2. This time series information might cause you to do further study concerning the factors that caused a steady deterioration of this ratio in the recent past.
2. *Comparison with similar companies.* Financial results often are affected by industry and economywide factors. By comparing a company with another one in the same line of business, the analyst can get better insights concerning specific company performance. An analyst would be concerned if General Motors' sales

revenue fell by 2 percent in a given year. The analyst might be less concerned if for the same period Ford experienced a 10 percent decline and Chrysler had a 16 percent decline. This comparison would indicate that the entire automobile industry had a bad year but that General Motors had done well compared to its major domestic competitors.

Finding comparable companies often is very difficult. American Brands is a well-known company that sells tobacco, distilled spirits, life insurance, home improvement products, office products, and golf equipment. No other company sells exactly that group of products. Care must be exercised when selecting comparable companies from the same basic industry. Days Inn, La Quinta, Hilton, Four Seasons, Marriott, and Mirage Resorts are all in the hotel industry but not all could be considered comparable companies for purposes of financial analysis.

The federal government has established *standard industrial classification codes* that are used to report economic data. Analysts often use these four-digit codes to make industry comparisons for various companies. Financial information services, such as Robert Morris Associates, provide averages for many common accounting ratios for various industries as defined by the standard industrial classification codes. Because of the diversity of companies included in each industry classification, you should use these data with great care. Some analysts prefer to compare two companies that are very similar instead of using industrywide comparisons.

Ratio and Percentage Analyses

All financial analysts use **ratio analysis,** or **percentage analysis,** when they review companies. A ratio or percent expresses the proportionate relationship between two different amounts. A ratio or percent is computed by dividing one quantity by another quantity. For example, the fact that a company earned net income of $500,000 assumes greater significance when net income is compared with the stockholders' investment in the company. Assuming that stockholders' equity is $5 million, the relationship of earnings to stockholder investment is $500,000 ÷ $5,000,000 = 10 percent. This measure indicates a different level of performance than would be the case if stockholders' equity were $50 million. Ratio analysis helps decision makers identify significant relationships and compare companies more realistically than if only single amounts were analyzed.

Ratios may be computed using amounts within one statement, such as the income statement, or between different statements, such as the income statement and the balance sheet. The current ratio (current assets divided by current liabilities) is based on information from a single statement. Return on assets (net income divided by total assets) is based on information from the income statement and the balance sheet.

Financial statement analysis is a judgmental process. No single ratio can be identified as appropriate to all situations. Each analytical situation may require the calculation of several ratios. We will discuss several ratios that are appropriate to many situations.

Component Percentages

Component percentages are used to express each item on a particular statement as a percentage of a single *base amount*, the denominator of the ratio. To compute component percentages for the income statement, the base amount is net sales revenue.

LEARNING OBJECTIVE 2
Explain the objectives of ratio analysis.
Ratio (percentage) analysis is an analytical tool designed to identify significant relationships; it measures the proportional relationship between two financial statement amounts.

A **component percentage** expresses each item on a particular financial statement as a percentage of a single base amount.

Each expense is expressed as a percentage of net sales revenue. On the balance sheet, the base amount is total assets. The percentages are derived by dividing each balance sheet account by total assets.

Discerning important relationships and trends in the Home Depot income statement shown in Exhibit 14.1 is difficult without using component percentages. Income increased by more than 50 percent between 1995 and 1997, which is obviously very good, but it is difficult for an analyst to evaluate the operating efficiency of Home Depot based on the reported numbers on the income statement.

Exhibit 14.2 shows a component analysis for Home Depot's income statement (from Exhibit 14.1). If you simply reviewed the dollar amounts on the income statement, you might be concerned about several significant differences. For example, cost of goods sold increased by nearly $3 million between 1996 and 1997. Is this increase reasonable? Should you be concerned as an analyst? By reviewing the component analysis, you quickly see that cost of goods sold for each year is approximately 27.7 percent of sales revenue. In other words, cost of goods sold has increased primarily because of the increase in sales revenue. The component analysis helps highlight several additional issues:

1. The majority of the increase in net income can be attributed to an increase in sales revenue. Net income increased by more than $300 million between 1995 and 1997, but it remained at 4.8 percent of sales revenue.
2. Selling and store operating costs rose from 17.8 percent of sales to 18 percent between 1995 and 1996 and remained unchanged in 1997. This change may seem small, but remember that the percentage is based on total revenue. The small decrease in operating efficiency (from 17.8 percent to 18 percent) reduced 1997 earnings before taxes by nearly $31 million.
3. Cost of goods sold as a percentage of sales declined between 1995 and 1996 but increased in 1997. This may indicate that increased competition is forcing Home Depot to cut its selling prices. An analyst would want to gather more information concerning this important issue.

EXHIBIT 14.2
Component Percentages for Home Depot

| | COMPONENT PERCENTAGES | | |
Income Statement	1997	1996	1995
Net sales	100.0%	100.0%	100.0%
Cost of merchandise sold	72.2	72.3	72.1
Gross profit	27.8	27.7	27.9
Operating expenses			
Selling and store operating	18.0	18.0	17.8
Pre-opening	0.3	0.3	0.4
General and administrative	1.7	1.7	1.8
Total operating expenses	20.0	20.1	20.0
Operating income	7.9	7.6	7.9
Interest income	0.1	0.1	0.2
Interest expense	(0.0)	(0.0)	(0.3)
Interest, net	0.0	0.1	(0.1)
Earnings, before taxes	7.9	7.7	7.9
Income taxes	3.0	3.0	3.0
Net earnings	4.8	4.7	4.8

4. Significant stability in all of the income statement relationships indicates a well-run company. Notice that all of the individual income statement items changed by less than one percentage point over a three-year period.

5. Preopening costs increased significantly between 1995 and 1996 but declined as a percentage of sales.

Commonly Used Ratios

In addition to component percentages, analysts use a large number of ratios to compare related items from the financial statements. You have been introduced to many of these ratios earlier in this book. For example, the current ratio compares current assets and current liabilities. This comparison is widely used as a measure of liquidity, or the ability of a company to pay its short-term debt. The comparison makes sense because current liabilities may be paid with current assets.

Numerous ratios can be computed from a single set of financial statements, but only a selected number may be useful in a given situation. It is never useful to compare cost of goods sold to property, plant, and equipment because these items have no natural relationship. A common approach is to compute certain widely used ratios and then decide which additional ratios are relevant to the particular decision. For example, research and development costs as a percentage of sales is not a common ratio but it is useful in some special situations. You would want to look at that ratio if you were evaluating companies that depended on new products, such as manufacturers of drugs or computers.

When you compute ratios, it is important to remember a basic fact about financial statements. Balance sheet amounts relate to one instant in time, and income statement amounts relate to a period of time. Therefore, when an income statement account is compared with a balance sheet amount, a balance sheet *average amount* should be used to reflect changes in the balance sheet amounts. The selected balance sheet amount usually is computed as the average of the amounts shown on the beginning and ending balance sheets. In many cases, analysts simply use data from the ending balance sheet. This approach is appropriate only if no significant changes in balance sheet amounts have occurred. For consistency, we always use average amounts.

Commonly used financial ratios can be grouped into the five categories shown in Exhibit 14.3.

LEARNING OBJECTIVE 3
List five categories of accounting ratios.

Tests of Profitability

Profitability is a primary measure of the overall success of a company. Indeed, it is a necessary condition for survival. Investors and creditors prefer a single measure of profitability that is meaningful in all situations. Unfortunately, no single measure can be devised to meet this comprehensive need. Tests of profitability focus on measuring the adequacy of income by comparing it with one or more primary activities or factors that are measured in the financial statements. Several different tests of profitability are commonly used.

LEARNING OBJECTIVE 4
Identify and compute widely used accounting ratios.

EXHIBIT 14.3
Widely Used Accounting Ratios

Ratio	Basic Computation
TESTS OF PROFITABILITY	
1. Return on owners' investment (ROI_O)	$\dfrac{\text{Income}}{\text{Average owners' equity}}$
2. Return on total investment (ROI_t)	$\dfrac{\text{Income + Interest expense (net of tax)}}{\text{Average total assets}}$
3. Financial leverage $(ROI_O - ROI_t)$	Return on owners' investment $-$ Return on total investment
4. Earnings per share	$\dfrac{\text{Income}}{\text{Average number of shares of common stock outstanding}}$
5. Quality of income	$\dfrac{\text{Cash flow from operating activities}}{\text{Net income}}$
6. Profit margin	$\dfrac{\text{Income (before extraordinary items)}}{\text{Net sales revenue}}$
7. Fixed asset turnover ratio	$\dfrac{\text{Net sales revenue}}{\text{Net fixed assets}}$
TESTS OF LIQUIDITY	
8. Cash ratio	$\dfrac{\text{Cash + cash equivalents}}{\text{Current liabilities}}$
9. Current ratio	$\dfrac{\text{Current assets}}{\text{Current liabilities}}$
10. Quick ratio	$\dfrac{\text{Quick assets}}{\text{Current liabilities}}$
11. Receivable turnover	$\dfrac{\text{Net credit sales}}{\text{Average net trade receivables}}$
12. Inventory turnover	$\dfrac{\text{Cost of goods sold}}{\text{Average inventory}}$
TESTS OF SOLVENCY AND EQUITY POSITION	
13. Times interest earned	$\dfrac{\text{Net income + Interest + Income tax expense}}{\text{Interest expense}}$
14. Cash coverage	$\dfrac{\text{Cash flow from operating activities (before interest and tax expense)}}{\text{Interest paid}}$
15. Debt-to-equity ratio	$\dfrac{\text{Total liabilities}}{\text{Owners' equity}}$
MARKET TESTS	
16. Price/earnings ratio	$\dfrac{\text{Current market price per share}}{\text{Earnings per share}}$
17. Dividend yield ratio	$\dfrac{\text{Dividends per share}}{\text{Market price per share}}$
MISCELLANEOUS RATIO	
18. Book value per share	$\dfrac{\text{Common stock equity}}{\text{Number of shares of common stock outstanding}}$

1. Return on Owners' Investment (ROI_O)

Return on owners' investment is a fundamental test of profitability. It relates income to the investment that was made by the owners to earn income. It reflects the simple fact that investors expect to earn more money if they invest more money. Two investments that offer a return of $10,000 are not comparable if one requires a $100,000 investment and the other requires a $250,000 investment. The return on owners' investment ratio is computed as follows:[1]

$$\text{Return on owners' investment} = \frac{\text{Income*}}{\text{Average owners' equity}^\dagger}$$

$$\text{Home Depot 1997} = \frac{\$937,739}{\$5,471,476^\dagger} = 17.1\%$$

*Income **before** extraordinary items should be used.

$\dagger$Average owners' equity is preferable when available. For Home Depot, it is computed as ($5,955,186 + $4,987,766) ÷ 2 = $5,471,476.

Home Depot earned 17.1 percent, after income taxes, on the investment provided by the owners. Is this return good or bad? The question can be answered only by comparing its ROI with the ROI of similar companies. The return on owners' investment for three of Home Depot's competitors follows:

Lowe's	8.6%
Hechinger	(3.1)
Grossman's	2.2
Home Depot	17.1

Clearly, this comparison indicates that Home Depot is doing very well. Hechinger experienced a loss for the year, which resulted in a negative return.

2. Return on Total Investment (ROI_t)

Another view of the return on investment concept relates income to total assets (i.e., total investment) used to earn income. Many analysts consider the *return on total investment* ratio to be a better measure of management's ability to effectively utilize assets independent of how the assets were financed. The return on owners' investment could be very large for a company that was highly leveraged (i.e., employed a large amount of debt) even though management earned a low rate of return on total assets. Return on total investment is computed as follows:

$$\text{Return on owners' investment} = \frac{\text{Income* + Interest expense (net of tax)}}{\text{Average total assets}^\dagger}$$

$$\text{Home Depot 1997} = \frac{\$937,739 + (\$16,087 \times 66\%)}{\$8,347,872^\dagger} = 11.4\%$$

*Income before extraordinary items should be used. This illustration uses a corporate tax rate of 34 percent.

$\dagger$Average total assets should be used. For Home Depot that is ($9,341,710 + $7,354,033) ÷ 2 = $8,347,872.

Home Depot earned 11.4 percent on the total resources it used during the year. Under this ROI concept, investment is the amount of resources provided by both owners and creditors. Notice that the measure of return includes the return to both owners

---

[1] The figures for Home Depot used throughout the following ratio examples are taken from the financial statements in Exhibit 14.1.

Home Depot strives for profitability by meeting customer needs in-store.

and creditors. To compute return on total investment, interest expense (net of income tax) is added back to income because interest is the return on the creditors' investment. It must be added back because it was previously deducted to compute net income. The denominator represents total investment; therefore, the numerator (income) must include the total return that was available to the suppliers of funds. Interest expense is measured net of income tax because it represents the net cost to the corporation for the funds provided by creditors.

As you would expect, return on total investment usually is smaller than return on owners' investment. The return on total investment for Home Depot's competitors is shown here. Each of these ratios is less than the return on owners' investment ratio shown earlier.

Lowe's	4.3%
Hechinger	(1.1)
Grossman's	1.9
Home Depot	11.4

3. Financial Leverage

Financial leverage is the advantage, or disadvantage, that occurs as the result of earning a return on owners' investment that is different from the return earned on total investment (i.e., $ROI_O - ROI_t$). Most companies have positive leverage. Positive leverage occurs when the rate of return on a company's investments is higher than the average after-tax interest rate on borrowed funds. Basically, the company borrows at one rate and invests at a higher rate of return.

Financial leverage can be measured by comparing the two return on investment ratios as follows:

Financial leverage	=	Return on owners' investment	−	Return on total investment		(positive leverage)
Home Depot 1997	=	17.1%	−	11.4%	=	5.7%

When a company is able to borrow funds at an after-tax interest rate and invest those funds to earn a higher after-tax rate of return, the difference accrues to the benefit of the owners. The notes to Home Depot's annual report indicate that the company has borrowed money at rates ranging from 4.5 percent to 11.5 percent and invested this money in assets earning 11.4 percent. The difference between the money that the company earns and the amount that it pays out in interest to creditors is available for the owners of Home Depot. Financial leverage is the primary reason that most companies obtain a significant amount of resources from creditors rather than obtaining resources only from the sale of their capital stock.

4. Earnings per Share (EPS)

Some analysts are critical of the return on investment ratios because they are based on historical cost data. The amount of owners' investment represents their original investment plus retained earnings, not the current market value of that investment. The same concern applies to the return on total assets.

Earnings per share is based on the number of shares outstanding instead of dollar amounts reported on the balance sheet. Investors easily can interpret EPS in terms of their personal circumstances. An investor with 1,000 shares of stock can quickly compute the return on his or her investment using EPS. The investor would not be able to compute his or her return with only the information that the company had earned 17.1 percent on owners' equity. Basically, EPS is computed as follows:

$$\text{Earnings per share} = \frac{\text{Income}}{\text{Average number of shares of common stock outstanding}}$$

$$\text{Home Depot 1997} = \frac{\$937,739}{478,810^*} = \$1.96 \text{ per share}$$

*Average number of shares is (480,515 + 477,106) ÷ 2 = 478,810

Notice that our computation of EPS ($1.96) is different from the amount actually reported on the income statement for Home Depot shown in Exhibit 14.1 ($1.94). This difference is caused by some additional complexities in the computation of EPS that are discussed in advanced accounting courses.

Earnings per share is probably the single most widely watched ratio. Companies' announcement of their EPS each quarter during the fiscal year is normally reported in the business press. The following report concerning Home Depot appeared in Reuters News Service in mid-1997:

> Shares of Home Depot stock rose in heavy trading on the New York Stock Exchange after the company posted strong first quarter earnings. Shares rose 3/8 to 61 1/8 with the stock on the list of most active NYSE issues. The company posted quarterly earnings of 53 cents per share compared with 41 cents last year, ahead of estimates of 51 cents.

REAL WORLD EXCERPT

HOME DEPOT
EPS Announcement
in Reuters News Service

5. Quality of Income

As you saw in earlier chapters, some accounting procedures (e.g., accelerated depreciation, LIFO) are considered conservative because they tend to produce lower reported earnings compared to less conservative procedures. Financial analysts often talk about the *quality* of a company's earnings. These analysts are concerned with the issue of whether a company's earnings are generated by its operations or the aggressive use of liberal accounting policies. A measure of the *quality of income* is computed as follows:

$$\text{Quality of income} = \frac{\text{Cash flows from operating activities}}{\text{Net income}}$$

$$\text{Home Depot 1997} = \frac{\$1,100,110}{\$937,739} = 1.17$$

A ratio higher than 1 is considered to indicate higher-quality earnings because each dollar of income is supported by at least one dollar of cash flow. A ratio below 1 represents lower-quality earnings.

6. Profit Margin

The *profit margin* percentage is based on two income statement amounts. It is computed as follows:

$$\text{Profit margin} = \frac{\text{Income (before extraordinary items)}}{\text{Net sales revenue}}$$

$$\text{Home Depot 1997} = \frac{\$937,739}{\$19,535,503} = 5.0\%$$

This profitability measurement represents the percentage of each sales dollar, on the average, that is profit. For Home Depot, each dollar of sales generated 5.0 cents of profit. Care must be used in analyzing the profit margin because it does not consider the amount of resources employed (i.e., total investment) to earn income. For example, the hypothetical income statements of Home Depot and Hechinger might show the following:

		Home Depot	Hechinger
a.	Sales revenue	$100,000	$150,000
b.	Income	$ 5,000	$ 7,500
c.	Profit margin (b) ÷ (a)	5%	5%
d.	Total investment	$ 50,000	$125,000
e.	Return on total investment* (b) ÷ (d)	10%	6%

*Assuming no interest expense.

In this example, both companies reported the same profit margin (5 percent). Home Depot, however, appears to be performing much better because it is earning a 10 percent return on the total investment versus the 6 percent earned by Hechinger. The profit margin percentages do not reflect the effect of the $50,000 total investment in Home Depot compared to the $125,000 total investment in Hechinger. The effect of the different amounts of investment in each company is reflected in the return on investment (ROI) percentages. Thus, the profit margin omits one of the two important factors that should be used in evaluating return on the investment.

Comparing profit margins for companies in different industries is difficult. For example, profit margins in the food industry are low while profit margins in the jewelry business are large. Both types of businesses can be quite profitable because they differ in terms of the sales volume that can be generated from a given level of investment. Grocery stores have small margins but generate a large sales volume from relatively inexpensive stores and inventory. Jewelry stores earn more profit from each sales dollar but require a large investment in luxury stores and very expensive inventory. This relationship between profit margin and sales volume can be stated in very simple terms: would you prefer to have 5 percent of $1,000,000 or 10 percent of $100,000? As you can see, a larger percentage is not always better.

The operating strength of Home Depot comes more clearly into focus when you compare its profit margin with that of major competitors:

Lowe's	2.2%
Hechinger	(0.7)
Grossman's	1.0
Home Depot	5.0

7. Fixed Asset Turnover Ratio

A key measure of management effectiveness is its ability to effectively utilize available resources. The *fixed asset turnover ratio* measures management's ability to generate sales given an investment in fixed assets. The term *fixed assets* is synonymous with *property, plant, and equipment.* The ratio is computed as follows:

$$\text{Fixed asset turnover} = \frac{\text{Net sales revenue}}{\text{Net fixed assets}}$$

$$\text{Home Depot 1997} = \frac{\$19,535,503}{\$4,949,035^*} = 3.95$$

*Average total asset is ($5,437,046 + $4,461,024) ÷ 2 = $4,949,035

The fixed asset turnover ratio for Home Depot is exactly the same as that for Lowe's (3.95). Clearly, Home Depot does not have a competitive advantage over Lowe's in terms of its ability to effectively utilize its fixed assets to generate revenue.

The fixed asset turnover ratio is widely used to analyze capital-intensive companies such as airlines and electric utilities. Analysts often calculate a different turnover ratio for companies that have large amounts of inventory and accounts receivable. The asset turnover ratio is based on total assets:

$$\text{Asset turnover} = \frac{\text{Net sales revenue}}{\text{Total assets}}$$

$$\text{Home Depot 1997} = \frac{\$19,535,503}{\$8,347,872^*} = 2.34$$

*Average total asset is ($9,341,710 + $7,354,033) ÷ 2 = $8,347,872

This ratio shows the analyst that Home Depot was able to generate $2.34 in revenue for each dollar that was invested in the company's assets. This ratio compares to Lowe's ratio of $2.15. Remember that the fixed asset ratios for Lowe's and Home Depot were exactly the same but notice that the asset turnover ratio for Home Depot is better. This difference suggests that Home Depot is doing a better job of managing assets such as inventory and accounts receivable.

Clearly, one strategy to improve profitability is to generate more sales dollars from the company's assets. Home Depot has shown consistent improvement in its asset turnover ratio each year. Many analysts consider this type of improvement to be an important indication of the quality of its management.

Return on investment is directly related to a company's ability to generate sales with a given amount of assets and the profitability of those sales. Notice that if you multiply the asset turnover ratio by the profit margin ratio, net sales revenue cancels out, resulting in income divided by total assets (which is the return on investment ratio).

SELF-STUDY QUIZ

Show how to compute the following ratios:

1.   Return on owners' investment = _____
2.   Return on total investment = _____
3.   Profit margin = _____

Check your answers with the solution in the footnote at the bottom of this page.*

Tests of Liquidity

Tests of liquidity are ratios that measure a company's ability to meet its currently maturing obligations.

Liquidity refers to a company's ability to meet its currently maturing debts. **Tests of liquidity** focus on the relationship between current assets and current liabilities. A company's ability to pay its current liabilities is an important factor in evaluating its short-term financial strength. For example, a company that does not have cash available to pay for purchases on a timely basis will lose its cash discounts and run the risk of having its credit discontinued by vendors. Three ratios are used to measure liquidity: the cash ratio, the current ratio, and the quick ratio. Recall that *working capital* is the dollar difference between total current assets and total current liabilities.

8. Cash Ratio

Cash is the lifeblood of a business. Without cash, a company cannot pay its employees or meet obligations to its creditors. In other words, a business will fail without sufficient cash. A measure of the adequacy of available cash is called the *cash ratio*. It is computed as follows:

$$\text{Cash ratio} = \frac{\text{Cash + Cash equivalents}}{\text{Current liabilities}}$$

$$\text{Home Depot 1997} = \frac{\$146,006}{\$1,842,126} = 0.079 \text{ to } 1$$

Analysts often use this ratio to compare comparable companies. The cash ratio for Lowe's is only 0.03, which indicates that Home Depot has a larger cash reserve compared to its current liabilities. A company should be careful not to have a cash ratio that is too high, however. Holding excess cash usually is uneconomical.

Another appropriate use of this ratio is to compare it over time for a single company. The cash ratio for Home Depot has increased over recent years, showing a stronger cash position. Analysts become very concerned if this ratio deteriorates over a period of time because it often is an early indication of financial distress.

Some analysts do not use this ratio because it is very sensitive to small events. The collection of a large account receivable, for example, may have a significant impact on

---

*1. $\dfrac{\text{Income}}{\text{Average owners' equity}}$

2. $\dfrac{\text{Income + Interest expense (net of tax)}}{\text{Average total assets}}$

3. $\dfrac{\text{Income (before extraordinary items)}}{\text{Net sales}}$

the cash ratio. The current ratio and the quick ratio are much less sensitive to the timing of certain transactions.

9. Current Ratio

The *current ratio* measures the relationship between total current assets and total current liabilities at a specific date. It is computed as follows:

$$\text{Current ratio} = \frac{\text{Current assets}}{\text{Current liabilities}}$$

$$\text{Home Depot 1997} = \frac{\$3,709,373}{\$1,842,126} = 2.0 \text{ to } 1$$

At year-end, current assets for Home Depot were 2.0 times current liabilities or, for each $1 of current liabilities, there were $2 of current assets. The current ratio measures the cushion of working capital maintained to allow for the inevitable unevenness in the flow of funds through the working capital accounts. Because the current ratio measures the adequacy of working capital, it sometimes is called the *working capital ratio*.

Analysts consider a current ratio of 2 to be conservative. Indeed, most companies have current ratios that are less than 2. The optimal level for a current ratio depends on the business environment in which a company operates. If cash flows are predictable and stable (a utility company, for example), the current ratio can be just a little higher than 1. For a business with highly variable cash flows (such as an airline), a current ratio closer to 2 may be desirable.

It is possible to have a current ratio that is too high. It is normally considered to be inefficient to tie up too much money in inventory or accounts receivable. If a Home Depot store sells 100 hammers a month, there is no reason to have 1,000 in stock. A very high current ratio may indicate serious operating difficulties.

10. Quick Ratio (Acid Test)

The *quick ratio* is similar to the current ratio except that it is a more stringent test of short-term liquidity. It is computed as follows:

$$\text{Quick ratio} = \frac{\text{Quick assets}}{\text{Current liabilities}}$$

$$\text{Home Depot 1997} = \frac{\$946,852}{\$1,842,126} = .51 \text{ to } 1$$

Quick assets are readily convertible into cash at approximately their book values. Quick assets include cash, short-term investments, and accounts receivable (net of the allowance for doubtful accounts). Inventories usually are omitted from quick assets because of the uncertainty of when cash will be received from the sale of inventory in the future. Prepaid expenses also are excluded from quick assets. Thus, the quick, or acid test, ratio is a more severe test of liquidity than is the current ratio.

11. Receivable Turnover

Short-term liquidity and operating efficiency can be measured in terms of *turnover* of certain current assets. Two additional ratios that measure nearness to cash are receivable turnover and inventory turnover.

Receivable turnover is computed as follows:

$$\text{Receivable turnover} = \frac{\text{Net credit sales*}}{\text{Average net trade receivables}}$$

$$\text{Home Depot 1997} = \frac{\$19,535,503}{\$356,900^\dagger} = 54.7 \text{ times}$$

*When the amount of credit sales is not known, total sales may be used as a rough approximation.

†($388,416 + $325,384) ÷ 2 = $356,900

This ratio is called a *turnover* because it reflects how many times the trade receivables were recorded, collected, and then recorded again during the period (i.e., "turnover"). Receivable turnover expresses the relationship of the average balance in Accounts Receivable to the transactions (i.e., credit sales) that created those receivables. This ratio measures the effectiveness of the company's credit-granting and collection activities. A high receivable turnover ratio suggests effective collection activities. Granting credit to poor credit risks and making ineffective collection efforts will cause this ratio to be low. A very low ratio obviously is a problem, but a very high ratio also can be a problem. A very high ratio may indicate an overly stringent credit policy that could cause lost sales and profits.

The receivable turnover ratio often is converted to a time basis known as the *average age of receivables*. The computation is as follows:

$$\text{Average age of trade receivables} = \frac{\text{Days in year}}{\text{Receivable turnover}}$$

$$\text{Home Depot 1997} = \frac{365}{54.7} = 6.7 \text{ average days to collect}$$

The effectiveness of credit and collection activities sometimes is judged by the rule of thumb that the average days to collect should not exceed 1½ times the credit terms. For example, if the credit terms require payment in 30 days, the average days to collect should not exceed 45 days (i.e., not more than 15 days past due). Like all rules of thumb, this one has many exceptions.

When you evaluate financial statements, you should always think about the reasonableness of the numbers you compute. We computed the average age of receivables for Home Depot as 6.6 days. Is that number reasonable? Probably not. It is very unlikely that Home Depot collects cash from its credit customers on average in just 6.6 days. Remember that we do not know the amount of credit sales for Home Depot and had to use total sales as an approximation. In reality, Home Depot grants very little credit under its own name. Instead, it utilizes major credit cards such as Mastercard and Visa, which are recorded virtually the same as cash from the perspective of the seller. As a result, the accounts receivable turnover ratio is not meaningful for Home Depot.

12. Inventory Turnover

Inventory turnover measures the liquidity of the inventory. It reflects the relationship of the inventory to the volume of goods sold during the period. The computation is as follows:

$$\text{Inventory turnover} = \frac{\text{Cost of goods sold}}{\text{Average inventory}}$$

$$\text{Home Depot 1997} = \frac{\$14,101,423}{\$2,444,300^*} = 5.8 \text{ times}$$

*($2,708,283 + $2,180,318) ÷ 2 = $2,444,300

The inventory for Home Depot "turned over" 5.8 times during the year. Because profit normally is realized each time the inventory is sold (i.e., turned over), an increase in the ratio is usually favorable. If the ratio is too high, however, sales may be lost because of items that are out of stock.

The inventory turnover ratio is critical for companies that have adopted the Home Depot strategy. They want to be able to offer the customer the right product when it is needed at a price that beats the competition. If they do not effectively manage their inventory levels, they will incur extra costs that must be passed on to the customer. Let's compare the Home Depot inventory turnover to that of its major competitors:

Lowe's	5.0
Hechinger	3.2
Grossman's	6.1
Home Depot	5.8

As you can see, Home Depot does not have a competitive advantage over its competitors in terms of inventory turnover. Indeed, inventory turnover for the company has slowed in recent years, having reached a high of 6.3 as recently as 1992. Home Depot recently spent $9 million to upgrade computer systems in all of its stores and is now transmitting data via satellite. One of the announced goals of this investment is to increase inventory turnover. Management and analysts will watch closely to see whether inventory turnover improves.

The turnover ratio often is converted to a time-basis expression called *the average days' supply in inventory*. The computation is

$$\text{Average days' supply in inventory} = \frac{\text{Days in year}}{\text{Inventory turnover}}$$

$$\text{Home Depot 1997} = \frac{365}{5.8}$$

$$= 63 \text{ average days' supply in inventory}$$

What problems would arise if Home Depot's turnover ratios were very low and its inventory ratio were very high?

Turnover ratios vary significantly by industry classification. Companies in the food industry (grocery stores and restaurants) have high inventory turnover ratios because their inventory is subject to rapid deterioration in quality. Companies that sell expensive merchandise (automobile dealers and high-fashion clothes) have much lower ratios because sales of these items are infrequent but customers want to have a selection to choose from when they do buy.

SELF-STUDY QUIZ

Show how to compute the following ratios:

1. Quality of income = _____
2. Quick ratio = _____
3. Cash ratio = _____

Check your answers with the solution in the footnote at the bottom of this page.*

Tests of Solvency and Equity Position

Tests of solvency are ratios that measure a company's ability to meet its long-term obligations.

Solvency refers to the ability of a company to meet its long-term obligations on a continuing basis. **Tests of solvency** measure a company's ability to meet these obligations. Certain critical relationships can be identified by analyzing the way that a company has financed its assets and activities.

13. Times Interest Earned Ratio

Interest payments are a company's fixed obligation. Failure to make required interest payments may result in creditors forcing the company into bankruptcy. Because of the importance of interest payments, analysts often compute a ratio called *times interest earned:*

$$\text{Times interest earned} = \frac{\text{Net income} + \text{Interest expense} + \text{Income tax expense}}{\text{Interest expense}}$$

$$\text{Home Depot 1997} = \frac{\$937,739 + \$16,087 + \$597,030}{\$16,087} = 96.4 \text{ times}$$

This ratio compares the amount of income that has been generated in the current period to the interest obligation for the same period. It represents the margin of protection for the creditors. Home Depot generated more than $96 in income for each $1 of interest expense. This is a very high ratio and, therefore, a very secure position for creditors. Some analysts prefer to calculate this ratio including all contractually required payments. These include principal payments and rent obligations under lease contracts. Other analysts believe that this ratio is flawed because interest expense and other obligations are paid in cash, not with net income. They prefer to compute the cash coverage ratio.

---

*1. $\dfrac{\text{Cash flows from operating activities}}{\text{Net income}}$

2. $\dfrac{\text{Quick assets}}{\text{Current liabilities}}$

3. $\dfrac{\text{Cash} + \text{Cash equivalents}}{\text{Current liabilities}}$

14. Cash Coverage Ratio

Given the importance of cash flows and required interest payments, it is easy to understand why the *cash coverage ratio* is important. It is computed as follows:

$$\text{Cash coverage} = \frac{\text{Cash flows from operating activities before interest and taxes}}{\text{Interest paid (from SCF)}}$$

$$\text{Home Depot 1997} = \frac{\$1,100,110 + \$16,087 + \$597,030}{\$3,350} = 511.41$$

The cash coverage ratio for Home Depot shows that the company generated $511.41 in cash for every $1 of interest expense. This is very strong coverage. Notice that in the denominator of the ratio, we used interest payments reported on the statement of cash flows (SCF) instead of interest expense. The cash coverage ratio compares the cash generated with the cash obligations of the period. Remember that analysts are concerned about the ability of a company to make required interest payments. Accrued interest and interest payments normally are similar in amount each period, but not always. Consider a company that has a 20-year, zero coupon bond. The company reports accrued interest each period, but it does not have to make an interest payment until the bond matures in the 20th year. In this case, interest payments are a better measure of the company's current obligation than is accrued interest expense.

15. Debt-to-Equity Ratio

The *debt-to-equity ratio* expresses the proportion between debt and owners' equity.[2] It is computed as follows:

$$\text{Debt-to-equity ratio} = \frac{\text{Total liabilities (i.e., creditors' equity)}}{\text{Owners' equity}}$$

$$\text{Home Depot 1997} = \frac{\$3,386,524}{\$5,955,186} = 0.57 \text{ (or 57\%)}$$

This ratio means that for each $1 of owners' equity, there were 57 cents of liabilities. Debt is risky for a company because it imposes important contractual obligations. There are (1) specific maturity dates for the principal amounts and (2) specific interest payments that must be made. Debt obligations are enforceable by law and do not depend on the earnings of the company. In contrast, dividends for stockholders are always at the discretion of the company and are not legally enforceable until declared by the board of directors. Owners' equity is "permanent" capital that does not have a maturity date. Thus, equity capital usually is seen as much less risky than debt for a company.

---

[2]The relationship between debt and owners' equity alternatively may be calculated with the following two ratios:

$$\text{Owners' equity to total equities} = \frac{\text{Owners' equity}}{\text{Total equities}}$$

$$\text{Home Depot 1997} = \frac{\$5,955,186}{\$9,341,710} = 63.7\%$$

$$\text{Creditors' equity to total equities} = \frac{\text{Creditors' equity}}{\text{Total equities}}$$

$$\text{Home Depot 1997} = \frac{\$3,386,524}{\$9,341,710} = 36.3\%$$

Despite the risk associated with debt, most companies obtain significant amounts of resources from creditors because of the advantages of financial leverage discussed earlier in this chapter. In addition, interest expense is a deductible expense on the income tax return. When selecting a capital structure, a company must balance the higher returns that are available with leverage against the higher risk associated with debt. Because of the importance of this risk-and-return relationship, most analysts consider the debt-to-equity ratio to be a key part of any company evaluation.

Market Tests

Market tests are ratios that tend to measure the market worth of a share of stock.

Several ratios measure the "market worth" of a share of stock. These **market tests** relate the current market price of a share of stock to an indicator of the return that might accrue to the investor. The tests focus on the current market price of the stock because that is the amount the buyer would invest. Two market test ratios used by analysts and investors are the price/earnings ratio and the dividend yield ratio.

16. Price/Earnings (P/E) Ratio

The *price/earnings (P/E) ratio* measures the relationship between the current market price of the stock and its earnings per share. A recent price for Home Depot stock was $61 per share. The EPS for Home Depot calculated earlier was $1.96. The P/E ratio for the company is computed as follows:

$$\text{Price/earnings ratio} = \frac{\text{Current market price per share}}{\text{Earnings per share}}$$

$$\text{Home Depot 1997} = \frac{\$61}{\$1.96} = 31.1$$

Home Depot stock was selling at 31.1 times the EPS. The P/E ratio often is referred to as the *multiple*, as in price/earnings multiple. The P/E ratio is used as an indicator of the future performance of the stock. A high price/earnings multiple indicates that the market expects earnings to grow rapidly. The P/E ratio for Home Depot is high compared to its major competitors (because Hechinger reported a loss for the year, its P/E ratio is not meaningful):

Lowe's	18.3
Hechinger	NM
Grossman's	12.5
Home Depot	31.1

Although the P/E ratio for Home Depot is high compared to that of its competitors, the ratio has declined significantly over the past few years. As recently as 1992, the ratio was above 60. This decline in the P/E ratio explains why the Home Depot stock has not performed well despite a significant increase in earnings.

REAL WORLD EXCERPT

Merrill Lynch
Research Report

The lackluster performance has occurred despite strong earnings because of a declining price earnings multiple. We think the decline in the multiple during the past four years partly reflects a growing awareness about the Company's sensitivity to macroeconomic issues. The multiple could continue declining if the company's growth rate keeps on moderating. However, we think a large competitive shakeout will occur soon and the multiple could rally.

Sometimes the components of the P/E ratio are inverted, giving the *capitalization rate*. This is the rate at which the stock market apparently is capitalizing the current earnings. Computation of the capitalization rate on current earnings per share for Home Depot is $1.96 ÷ $61 = 3.2 percent.

17. Dividend Yield Ratio

When investors buy stock, they expect returns from two sources: price appreciation and dividend income. The *dividend yield ratio* measures the relationship between the dividends per share paid and the current market price of the stock. Home Depot paid dividends of 23 cents per share when the market price per share was $61. The dividend yield ratio for Home Depot is computed as follows:

$$\text{Dividend yield ratio} = \frac{\text{Dividend per share}}{\text{Market price per share}}$$

$$\text{Home Depot 1997} = \frac{\$0.23}{\$61} = 0.4\%$$

Dividend yields for most stocks are not very high compared to alternative investments. A regular savings account, for example, pays an investor much more than 0.4 percent. Investors are willing to accept low dividend yields when they expect that the price of the stock will increase while they own it. Stocks with low growth potential often offer much higher dividend yields than do stocks with high growth potential. These stocks often appeal to investors who are retired and need current income rather than future growth potential.

Miscellaneous Ratio

18. Book Value per Share

The *book value per share* of stock measures the owners' equity in terms of each share of common stock outstanding. In the case of a simple capital structure, with *only* common stock outstanding, the computation of book value per share is not difficult. The computation of book value per share is

$$\frac{\text{Book value per}}{\text{common share}} = \frac{\text{Total owners' equity}}{\text{Common shares outstanding}}$$

$$\text{Home Depot 1997} = \frac{\$5,955,186}{480,515 \text{ shares}} = \$12.39$$

Notice that book value per share has no relationship to market value. The book value of a share of Home Depot stock was $12.39 when the market value was $61. For most companies, book value per share is less than the market value. Some analysts compute a price/book value ratio that compares the current market value of the stock (i.e., selling price) with the book value. The price/book ratio for Home Depot is $61 ÷ $12.39 = 4.9. Over the past five years, this ratio has ranged from a low of 2.9 to a high of 12. A high ratio indicates a company with good growth potential.

SELF-STUDY QUIZ

Show how to compute the following ratios:

1. Current ratio = _____
2. Inventory turnover = _____
3. Price/earnings ratio = _____

Check your answers with the solution shown in the footnote at the bottom of this page.*

Other Analytical Considerations

The ratios that we have discussed so far are general-purpose ratios that are useful in most analytical considerations. Each company is different, and your evaluation of each company should be different.

To illustrate, let's look at some special factors that might affect our analysis of Home Depot.

1. *Rapid growth.* In some cases, a company that opens many new stores each year may obscure the fact that existing stores are not meeting customer needs and are experiencing declining sales. In other words, growth in total sales volume does not always indicate that a company is successful. The family pizza chain Chuck-E-Cheese reported rapid growth in total sales revenue for a number of years, but it was generated by opening new stores. New stores initially generated very large sales volumes because they were very popular with families with young children. Unfortunately, the novelty of the Chuck-E-Cheese stores proved to be short-lived fads, and same-store sales volume fell quickly. The company was forced to reorganize. In contrast, the annual report for Home Depot shows that the company has had same-store sales increases in each of the previous 10 years, which indicates that it is able to generate increases in sales volume from both new and existing stores.

2. *Uneconomical expansion.* Some growth-oriented companies open stores in less desirable locations once all the good locations have been taken. These poor locations can cause the stores' average productivity to decline. One measure of productivity in the retail industry is sales volume per square foot of selling space. For Home Depot, productivity results are mixed:

Year	Sales per Square Foot
1997	$398
1996	390
1995	404
1994	398
1993	387

The sales per square foot for Home Depot have stabilized in recent years after rapid growth in the early 90s when the figure increased by more than $100 per

*
1. Current assets
    Current liabilities
2. Cost of goods sold
    Average inventory
3. Current market price per share
    Earnings per share

square foot. Management explains that this has occurred as the direct result of its strategy:

> We continue our cannibalization strategy, whereby we take the pressure off a busy store by opening another one nearby. While some challenge this approach because it tends to lower sales productivity, this strategy results in better service and greater customer satisfaction, which ultimately translates into higher sales and profits.

REAL WORLD EXCERPT

HOME DEPOT
Annual Report

3. *Subjective factors.* It is important to remember that vital information about a company is not contained in the annual report. We discussed earlier that a strategy of Home Depot is to be a price leader. The best way to evaluate that strategy is to visit the stores of Home Depot and of several competitors. The analyst who studied Home Depot for Salomon Brothers did exactly that:

> On July 15, we surveyed the Boca Raton, Florida market. The Home Depot store is about two years old and was particularly impressive with respect to its in-stock position, customer service and total store presentation. We were able to compare Home Depot's pricing on 20 sample items. Our price analysis revealed that Home Depot is the price leader in the market by an average of 11 percent below the average total price of our 20-item market basket. Given the Home Depot's low cost structure, we believe that it will remain the price leader in this important market.

REAL WORLD EXCERPT

HOME DEPOT
Salomon Brothers
Research Report

As these examples illustrate, no single approach can be used to analyze all companies. Furthermore, effective analysis requires going beyond the information contained in an annual report.

Interpreting Ratios

The computation of any particular ratio is not standardized. Neither the accounting profession nor security analysts have prescribed the manner in which a ratio must be computed (except for earnings per share). Thus, users of financial statements should compute the various ratios in accordance with their decision objectives. Before using ratios computed by others, the analyst should determine the computational approach that was used.

LEARNING OBJECTIVE 5
Interpret accounting ratios.

Home Depot's successful expansion included the acquisition of Aikenhead's, a Canadian chain of home improvement stores.

To interpret a ratio, it should be compared with some standard that represents an optimal or desirable value. For example, the return on investment ratio may be compared with alternative investment opportunities. Some ratios, by their characteristics, are unfavorable if they are either too high or too low. For example, analysis may indicate that a current ratio of approximately 2:1 may be considered optimal for a company. In this situation, a ratio of 1:1 may indicate a danger of being unable to meet maturing debts. A ratio of 3:1 may indicate that excess funds are being left idle rather than being employed profitably. Furthermore, an optimal ratio for one company often is not the optimal ratio for another company. Comparisons of ratios for different companies are appropriate only if the companies are indeed comparable. Noteworthy differences in industry, nature of operations, size, and accounting policies can make the value of many comparisons questionable.

Most ratios represent averages. Therefore, they may obscure underlying factors that are of interest to the analyst. To illustrate, a current ratio of 2:1 may be considered optimal in a given industry. But even an optimal current ratio may obscure a short-term liquidity problem if the company has a very large amount of inventory and a minimal amount of cash with which to pay debts as they mature. Careful analysis can uncover this liquidity problem. In other cases, careful analysis cannot uncover obscured problems. For example, consolidated statements include financial information about the parent and its subsidiaries. The parent company may have a high current ratio and the subsidiary a low ratio. When the statements are consolidated, the current ratio (in effect, an average of the parent and the subsidiary) may be within an acceptable range. Obscured is the fact that the subsidiary may have a serious liquidity problem.

Despite limitations, ratio analysis is a useful analytical tool. Financial ratios are effective for predicting bankruptcy. Exhibit 14.4 gives the current and debt-to-equity ratios for Braniff International Corporation for each year before it filed for bankruptcy. Notice the deterioration of these ratios each year. Analysts who studied the financial ratios probably were not surprised by Braniff's bankruptcy. After selling many of its assets and undergoing a complete financial restructuring, Braniff was able to resume limited flight operations but was forced to file for bankruptcy for a second time after additional financial difficulty.

Impact of Accounting Alternatives on Ratio Analysis

LEARNING OBJECTIVE 6
Describe how accounting alternatives affect ratio analysis.

Financial statements provide information for the average investor. Users who understand basic accounting are able to more effectively analyze the information contained in financial statements. While studying this book, you have developed an understand-

EXHIBIT 14.4
Selected Financial Ratios for Braniff International

| | YEARS BEFORE BANKRUPTCY | | | | |
	5	4	3	2	1
Current ratio	1.20	0.91	0.74	0.60	0.49
Debt-to-equity ratio	2.03	2.45	4.88	15.67	N/A*

*In the year before bankruptcy, Braniff reported negative owners' equity as the result of a large net loss that produced a negative balance in retained earnings. Creditors' equity exceeded total equities.

ing of the accounting vocabulary. A knowledge of this vocabulary is necessary to understand financial statements.

Familiarity with the underlying accounting concepts also is essential for proper analysis of statements. Some unsophisticated users do not understand the cost principle and believe that assets are reported on the balance sheet at their fair market value. We have stressed accounting concepts throughout the book because it is impossible to interpret accounting numbers without an understanding of the concepts that were used to develop the numbers.

When comparing companies, you will find that they rarely use exactly the same accounting policies. If the comparisons are to be useful, the analyst must understand the impact of various accounting alternatives. One company may use conservative accounting alternatives such as accelerated depreciation and LIFO while another may use income-maximizing alternatives such as straight-line depreciation and FIFO. Users who do not understand the effects of accounting methods may misinterpret financial results. Perhaps the most important first step in analyzing financial statements is a review of the accounting policies that the company has selected. This information must be disclosed in a note to the statements. An example of this disclosure is shown in the annual report in Appendix B.

Insider Information

QUESTION OF ETHICS

Financial statements are an important source of information for investors. Announcement of an unexpected earnings increase or decrease can cause a substantial movement in the price of a company's stock.

Accountants for a company may become aware of important financial information before it is made available to the public. This type of data is called *insider information*. It might be tempting for some people to buy or sell stock based on insider information, but to do so is a serious criminal offense. The Securities and Exchange Commission has brought a number of cases against individuals who traded on insider information, which resulted in large fines and time in jail.

In some cases, it may be difficult to decide whether something is insider information. An individual may simply overhear a comment made in the company elevator by two executives. A well-respected Wall Street investment banker gave good advice: "If you are not sure if something is right or wrong, apply the newspaper headline test. Ask yourself how you would feel to have your family and friends read about what you had done in the newspaper." Interestingly, many people who spent time in jail and lost small fortunes in fines because of insider trading convictions say that the most difficult part of the process was telling their families.

To uphold the highest ethical standard, many public accounting firms have rules that prevent members of their professional staff from investing in companies that the firm audits. These rules are designed to ensure that the company's auditors cannot be tempted to engage in insider trading.

Information in an Efficient Market

Considerable research has been performed on how the stock markets react to new information. Much of this evidence supports the view that the markets react very quickly to new information in an unbiased manner (the market does not systematically overreact or underreact to new information). A market that reacts to information in this manner is called an **efficient market.** In an efficient market, the price of a security fully reflects all available information.

Efficient markets are securities markets in which prices fully reflect available information.

It is not surprising that the stock markets react quickly to new information. Many professional investors manage stock portfolios valued in the hundreds of millions of dollars. These investors have a large financial incentive to find new, relevant information about a company and to trade quickly based on that information.

The research on efficient markets has important implications for financial analysis. It probably is not beneficial to study old information (say an annual report that was released six months earlier) to identify a stock that has been undervalued by the market. In an efficient market, the price of the stock reflects all of the information contained in the report shortly after it was released.

In an efficient market, we expect that it is not possible for a company to manipulate the price of its stock by manipulating accounting policy. The market should be able to differentiate a company with increasing earnings due to improved productivity from one that has increased earnings by changing from conservative to liberal accounting policies.

Summary

Interpretation of amounts reported on financial statements may be enhanced by expressing certain relationships as ratios or percentages. Although many ratios can be calculated, only a few are useful for a given decision. Having selected the relevant ratios, the analyst has the problem of evaluating the results. This evaluation involves the task of selecting one or more realistic standards with which to compare the results. Four types of standards are used: (1) historical standards, (2) external standards, (3) experience, and (4) planned standards. The interpretation of ratios may suggest strengths and weaknesses in the operations and/or the financial position of the company that should be accorded in-depth investigation and evaluation.

Key Terms

Component Percentage Expresses each item on a particular financial statement as a percentage of a single base amount. *707*

Efficient Markets Securities markets in which prices fully reflect available information. *727*

Market Tests Ratios that tend to measure the market worth of a share of stock. *722*

Ratio (Percentage) Analysis An analytical tool designed to identify significant relation-

ships; measures the proportional relationship between two financial statement amounts. *707*

Tests of Liquidity Ratios that measure a company's ability to meet its currently maturing obligations. *716*

Tests of Solvency Ratios that measure a company's ability to meet its long-term obligations. *720*

Questions

1. What are three fundamental uses of external financial statements by decision makers?
2. What are some of the primary items on financial statements about which creditors usually are concerned?
3. Explain why the notes to the financial statements are important to decision makers.
4. What is the primary purpose of comparative financial statements?

5. Why are statement users interested in financial summaries covering several years? What is the primary limitation of long-term summaries?
6. What is ratio analysis? Why is ratio analysis useful?
7. What are component percentages? Why are component percentages useful?
8. Explain the two concepts of return on investment.
9. What is *financial leverage?* How is it measured?
10. Is profit margin a useful measure of profitability? Explain.
11. Compare and contrast the current ratio and the quick ratio.
12. What does the debt-to-equity ratio reflect?
13. What are market tests?
14. Identify two factors that limit the effectiveness of ratio analysis.

Exercises

E14–1 Analyzing Comparative Financial Statements Using Percentages

The comparative financial statements prepared at December 31, 19B, for Goldfish Company showed the following summarized data:

	19B	19A
INCOME STATEMENT		
Sales revenue	$180,000*	$165,000*
Cost of goods sold	110,000	100,000
Gross margin	70,000	65,000
Operating expenses and interest expense	56,000	53,000
Pretax income	14,000	12,000
Income tax	4,000	3,000
Net income	$ 10,000	$ 9,000
BALANCE SHEET		
Cash	$ 4,000	$ 8,000
Accounts receivable (net)	14,000	18,000
Inventory	40,000	35,000
Operational assets (net)	45,000	38,000
	$103,000	$ 99,000
Current liabilities (no interest)	$ 16,000	$ 19,000
Long-term liabilities (10% interest)	45,000	45,000
Common stock (par $5)	30,000	30,000
Retained earnings†	12,000	5,000
	$103,000	$ 99,000

*One-third were credit sales.
†During 19B, cash dividends amounting to $9,000 were declared and paid.

Required:
1. Complete the following columns for each item in the preceding comparative financial statements:

	INCREASE (DECREASE) 19B OVER 19A	
	Amount	Percent

2. Answer the following questions:
    a. Compute the percentage increase in sales revenue, net income, cash, inventory, liabilities, and owners' equity.
    b. By what amount did working capital change?
    c. What was the percentage change in the average income tax rate?

  d. What was the amount of cash inflow from revenues for 19B?

  e. By what percent did the average markup realized on goods sold change?

  f. How much did the book value per share change?

E14–2 Analyzing a Financial Statement Using Component Percentages and Selected Ratios

Use the data given in Exercise 14–1 for Goldfish Company.

Required:

1. Present component percentages for 19B only.
2. Answer the following questions for 19B:

  a. What was the average percentage markup on sales?

  b. What was the average income tax rate?

  c. Compute the profit margin. Was it a good or poor indicator of performance? Explain.

  d. What percentage of total resources was invested in operational assets?

  e. Compute the debt-to-equity ratio. Does it look good or bad? Explain.

  f. What was the return on owners' investment?

  g. What was the return on total investment?

  h. Compute the financial leverage percentage. Was it positive or negative? Explain.

  i. What was the book value per share of common stock?

E14–3 Analyzing a Financial Statement Using the Ratios Discussed in the Chapter

Use the data in Exercise 14–1 for Goldfish Company. Assume a common stock price of $28 per share. Compute appropriate ratios and explain the meaning of each.

E14–4 Matching Each Ratio with Its Computational Definition

Match each computation with its related ratio or percentage by entering the appropriate letters in the blanks.

RATIOS OR PERCENTAGES	DEFINITIONS
_____ (1) Profit margin	A. Income (before extraordinary items) ÷ Net sales.
_____ (2) Inventory turnover ratio	B. Days in year ÷ Receivable turnover.
_____ (3) Average collection period	C. Income ÷ Average owners' equity.
_____ (4) Creditors' equity to total equities	D. Income ÷ Average number of shares of common stock outstanding.
_____ (5) Dividend yield ratio	E. Return on owners' investment – Return on total investment.
_____ (6) Return on owners' investment	F. Quick assets ÷ Current liabilities.
_____ (7) Current ratio	G. Current assets ÷ Current liabilities.
_____ (8) Debt-to-equity ratio	H. Cost of goods sold ÷ Average inventory.
_____ (9) Price/earnings ratio	I. Net credit sales ÷ Average net trade receivables.
_____ (10) Financial leverage	J. Creditors' equity (debt) ÷ Total equities.
_____ (11) Receivable turnover ratio	K. Days in year ÷ Inventory turnover.
_____ (12) Average days' supply of inventory	L. Total liabilities ÷ Owners' equity.
_____ (13) Owners' equity to total equities	M. Dividends per share ÷ Market price per share.
_____ (14) Earnings per share	N. Owners' equity ÷ Total equities.
_____ (15) Return on total investment	O. Current market price per share ÷ Earnings per share.
_____ (16) Quick ratio	P. Owners' equity ÷ Shares outstanding.
_____ (17) Book value per share	Q. Income + Interest expense (net of tax) ÷ Total assets.
_____ (18) Times interest earned	R. Cash from operating activities (before interest and taxes) ÷ Interest paid.
_____ (19) Cash coverage ratio	S. Net sales revenue ÷ Net fixed assets.
_____ (20) Fixed asset turnover	T. (Net income + interest expense + income tax expense) ÷ Interest expense.

E14–5 Analyzing the Impact of Selected Transactions on the Current Ratio

Current assets totaled $54,000, and the current ratio was 1.8. Assume that the following transactions were completed: (1) purchased merchandise for $6,000 on short-term credit and (2) purchased a delivery truck for $10,000, paid $1,000 cash, and signed a two-year interest-bearing note for the balance.

Required:
Compute the cumulative current ratio after each transaction.

E14–6 Analyzing the Impact of Selected Transactions on Accounts Receivable and Inventory Turnover

Sales for the year were $400,000, of which one-half was on credit. The average gross margin rate was 30 percent on sales. Account balances follow:

	Beginning	Ending
Accounts receivable (net)	$25,000	$15,000
Inventory	24,000	18,000

Required:
Compute the turnover for the accounts receivable and inventory, the average age of receivables, and the average days' supply of inventory.

E14–7 Analyzing the Impact of Selected Transactions on Financial Leverage

The financial statements reported the following at year-end:

Total assets	$150,000
Total debt (10% interest)	80,000
Net income (average tax rate 30%)	25,000

Required:
Compute the financial leverage. Was it positive or negative?

E14–8 Analyzing the Impact of Selected Transactions on the Current Ratio

Current assets totaled $100,000, and the current ratio was 1.5. Assume that the following transactions were completed: (1) paid $6,000 for merchandise purchased on short-term credit, (2) purchased a delivery truck for $10,000 cash, (3) wrote off a bad account receivable for $2,000, and (4) paid previously declared dividends in the amount of $25,000.

Required:
Compute the cumulative current ratio after each transaction.

E14–9 Analyzing the Impact of Selected Transactions on Accounts Receivable and Inventory Turnover

Sales for the year were $600,000, of which one-half was on credit. The average gross margin rate was 40 percent on sales. Account balances follow:

	Beginning	Ending
Accounts receivable (net)	$40,000	$60,000
Inventory	70,000	30,000

Required:
Compute the turnover for the accounts receivable and inventory, the average age of receivables, and the average days' supply of inventory.

E14–10 Analyzing the Impact of Selected Transactions on the Current Ratio

Current assets totaled $500,000, the current ratio was 2.0, and the company uses the periodic inventory method. Assume that the following transactions were completed: (1) sold $12,000 in merchandise on short-term credit, (2) declared but did not pay dividends of $50,000, (3) paid prepaid rent in the amount of $12,000, (4) paid previously declared dividends in the amount of $50,000, (5) collected an account receivable in the amount of $12,000, and (6) reclassified $40,000 of long-term debt as a short-term liability.

Required:
Compute the cumulative current ratio after each transaction.

E14–11 Analyzing a Financial Statement Using Ratios and Percentage Changes

Taber Company has just prepared the following comparative annual financial statements for 19B:

TABER COMPANY
Comparative Income Statement
For the Years Ended December 31, 19B, and 19A

		FOR THE YEAR ENDED		
		19B		19A
Sales revenue (one–half on credit)		$110,000		$99,000
Cost of goods sold		52,000		48,000
Gross margin		$ 58,000		$51,000
Expenses (including $4,000 interest expense each year)		40,000		37,000
Pretax income		$ 18,000		$14,000
Income tax on operations (30%)		5,400		4,200
Income before extraordinary items		$ 12,600		$ 9,800
Extraordinary loss	$2,000			
Less income tax saved	600	1,400		
Extraordinary gain			$3,000	
Applicable income tax			900	2,100
Net income		$ 11,200		$11,900

TABER COMPANY
Comparative Balance Sheet
At December 31, 19B, and 19A

ASSETS	19B	19A
Cash	$ 49,500	$ 18,000
Accounts receivable (net; terms 1/10, n/30)	37,000	32,000
Inventory	25,000	38,000
Operational assets (net)	95,000	105,000
Total assets	$206,500	$193,000
LIABILITIES		
Accounts payable	$ 42,000	$ 35,000
Income taxes payable	1,000	500
Note payable, long-term	40,000	40,000
STOCKHOLDERS' EQUITY		
Capital stock (par $10)	90,000	90,000
Retained earnings	33,500	27,500
Total liabilities and stockholders' equity	$206,500	$193,000

Required (round percents and ratios to two decimal places):

1. For 19B, compute the tests of (*a*) profitability, (*b*) liquidity, (*c*) solvency, and (*d*) market. Assume that the quoted price of the stock was $23 for 19B. Dividends declared and paid during 19B were $6,750.

2. Respond to the following for 19B:

   a. Compute the percentage changes in sales, income before extraordinary items, net income, cash, inventory, and debt.

   b. What appears to be the pretax interest rate on the note payable?

3. Identify at least two problems facing the company that are suggested by your responses to requirements (*a*) and (*b*).

E14–12 Using Financial Information to Identify Mystery Companies

The following selected financial data pertain to four unidentified companies:

	COMPANIES			
	1	2	3	4
BALANCE SHEET DATA				
(component percentage)				
Cash	3.5	4.7	8.2	11.7
Accounts receivable	16.9	28.9	16.8	51.9
Inventory	46.8	35.6	57.3	4.8
Property and equipment	18.3	21.7	7.6	18.7
INCOME STATEMENT DATA				
(component percentage)				
Gross profit	22.0	22.5	44.8	N/A*
Profit before taxes	2.1	0.7	1.2	3.2
SELECTED RATIOS				
Current ratio	1.3	1.5	1.6	1.2
Inventory turnover	3.6	9.8	1.5	N/A
Debt-to-equity	2.6	2.6	3.2	3.2

*N/A = Not applicable

This financial information pertains to the following companies:

a. Retail fur store

b. Advertising agency

c. Wholesale candy company

d. Car manufacturer

Required:

Match each company with its financial information.

E14–13 Using Financial Information to Identify Mystery Companies

The following selected financial data pertain to four unidentified companies:

	COMPANIES			
	1	2	3	4
BALANCE SHEET DATA				
(component percentage)				
Cash	7.3	21.6	6.1	11.3
Accounts receivable	28.2	39.7	3.2	22.9
Inventory	21.6	0.6	1.8	27.5
Property and equipment	32.1	18.0	74.6	25.1

	COMPANIES			
	1	2	3	4
INCOME STATEMENT DATA				
(component percentage)				
Gross profit	15.3	N/A*	N/A	43.4
Profit before taxes	1.7	3.2	2.4	6.9
SELECTED RATIOS				
Current ratio	1.5	1.2	0.6	1.9
Inventory turnover	27.4	N/A	N/A	3.3
Debt-to-equity	1.7	2.2	5.7	1.3

*N/A = Not applicable

This financial information pertains to the following companies:
- a. Travel agency
- b. Hotel
- c. Meat packer
- d. Drug company

Required:
Match each company with its financial information.

E14–14 Using Financial Information to Identify Mystery Companies

The following selected financial data pertain to four unidentified companies:

	COMPANIES			
	1	2	3	4
BALANCE SHEET DATA				
(component percentage)				
Cash	5.1	8.8	6.3	10.4
Accounts receivable	13.1	41.5	13.8	4.9
Inventory	4.6	3.6	65.1	35.8
Property and equipment	53.1	23.0	8.8	35.7
INCOME STATEMENT DATA				
(component percentage)				
Gross profit	N/A*	N/A	45.2	22.5
Profit before taxes	0.3	16.0	3.9	1.5
SELECTED RATIOS				
Current ratio	0.7	2.2	1.9	1.4
Inventory turnover	N/A	N/A	1.4	15.5
Debt-to-equity	2.5	0.9	1.7	2.3

*N/A = Not applicable

This financial information pertains to the following companies:
- a. Cable TV company
- b. Grocery store
- c. Accounting firm
- d. Retail jewelry store

Required:
Match each company with its financial information.

E14–15 Using Financial Information to Identify Mystery Companies

The following selected financial data pertain to four unidentified companies:

	COMPANIES			
	1	2	3	4
BALANCE SHEET DATA				
(component percentage)				
Cash	11.6	6.6	5.4	7.1
Accounts receivable	4.6	18.9	8.8	35.6
Inventory	7.0	45.8	65.7	26.0
Property and equipment	56.0	20.3	10.1	21.9
INCOME STATEMENT DATA				
(component percentage)				
Gross profit	56.7	36.4	14.1	15.8
Profit before taxes	2.7	1.4	1.1	0.9
SELECTED RATIOS				
Current ratio	0.7	2.1	1.2	1.3
Inventory turnover	30.0	3.5	5.6	16.7
Debt-to-equity	3.3	1.8	3.8	3.1

This financial information pertains to the following companies:

a. Full-line department store

b. Wholesale fish company

c. Automobile dealer (both new and used cars)

d. Restaurant

Required:

Match each of the companies with its financial information.

Problems

P14–1 Analyzing a Financial Statement Using Several Ratios

Summer Corporation has just completed its comparative statements for the year ended December 31, 19B. At this point, certain analytical and interpretive procedures are to be undertaken. The completed statements (summarized) are as follows:

	19B	19A
INCOME STATEMENT		
Sales revenue	$450,000*	$420,000*
Cost of goods sold	250,000	230,000
Gross margin	200,000	190,000
Operating expenses (including interest on bonds)	167,000	168,000
Pretax income	33,000	22,000
Income tax	10,000	6,000
Net income	$ 23,000	$ 16,000
BALANCE SHEET		
Cash	$ 6,800	$ 3,900
Accounts receivable (net)	42,000	28,000
Merchandise inventory	25,000	20,000
Prepaid expenses	200	100
Operational assets (net)	130,000	120,000
	$204,000	$172,000

*Credit sales totaled 40 percent.

	19B	19A
Accounts payable	$ 17,000	$ 18,000
Income taxes payable	1,000	2,000
Bonds payable (10% interest rate)	70,000	50,000
Common stock (par $5)	100,000†	100,000
Retained earnings	16,000‡	2,000
	$204,000	$172,000

†The market price of the stock at the end of 19B was $18 per share.
‡During 19B, the company declared and paid a cash dividend of $40,000.

Required:

1. Compute appropriate ratios and explain the meaning of each.
2. Answer the following questions for 19B:
   a. Evaluate the financial leverage. Explain its meaning using the computed amount(s).
   b. Evaluate the profit margin amount and explain how a stockholder might use it.
   c. Explain to a stockholder why the current ratio and the quick ratio are different. Do you observe any liquidity problems? Explain.
   d. Assuming that credit terms are 1/10, n/30, do you perceive an unfavorable situation for the company related to credit sales? Explain.

P14–2 Using Ratios to Analyze Several Years of Financial Data, Identify Favorable and Unfavorable Factors, and Give Recommendations to Improve Operations

The following information was contained in the annual financial statements of Pine Company, which started business January 1, 19A (assume account balances only in Cash and Capital Stock on this date; all amounts are in thousands of dollars).

	19A	19B	19C	19D
Accounts receivable (net; terms n/30)	$11	$12	$18	$ 24
Merchandise inventory	12	14	20	30
Net sales (3/4 on credit)	44	66	80	100
Cost of goods sold	28	40	55	62
Net income (loss)	(8)	5	12	11

Required (show computations and round to two decimal places):

1. Complete the following tabulation.

	Items	19A	19B	19C	19D
a.	Profit margin—percentage				
b.	Gross margin—ratio				
c.	Expenses as percentage of sales, excluding cost of goods sold				
d.	Inventory turnover				
e.	Days' supply in inventory				
f.	Receivable turnover				
g.	Average days to collect				

2. Evaluate the results of the related ratios a, b, and c to identify the favorable or unfavorable factors. Give your recommendations to improve the company's operations.
3. Evaluate the results of the last four ratios (d, e, f, and g) and identify any favorable or unfavorable factors. Give your recommendations to improve the company's operations.

P14–3 Comparing Alternative Investment Opportunities Using Ratios

Discussed in the Chapter: Prepare Investment Recommendations

The 19B financial statements for Armstrong and Blair companies are summarized here:

	Armstrong Company	Blair Company
BALANCE SHEET		
Cash	$ 35,000	$ 22,000
Accounts receivable (net)	40,000	30,000
Inventory	100,000	40,000
Operational assets (net)	140,000	400,000
Other assets	85,000	308,000
Total assets	$400,000	$800,000
Current liabilities	$100,000	$ 50,000
Long-term debt (10%)	60,000	70,000
Capital stock (par $10)	150,000	500,000
Contributed capital in excess of par	30,000	110,000
Retained earnings	60,000	70,000
Total liabilities and stockholders' equity	$400,000	$800,000
INCOME STATEMENT		
Sales revenue (1/3 on credit)	$450,000	$810,000
Cost of goods sold	(245,000)	(405,000)
Expenses (including interest and income tax)	(160,000)	(315,000)
Net income	$ 45,000	$ 90,000
SELECTED DATA FROM THE 19A STATEMENTS		
Accounts receivable (net)	$ 20,000	$ 38,000
Inventory	92,000	45,000
Long-term debt	60,000	70,000
OTHER DATA		
Per share price at end of 19B (offering price)	$ 18	$ 15
Average income tax rate	30%	30%
Dividends declared and paid in 19B	$ 36,000	$150,000

The companies are in the same line of business and are direct competitors in a large metropolitan area. Both have been in business approximately 10 years, and each has had steady growth. The management of each has a different viewpoint in many respects. Blair is more conservative, and as its president said, "We avoid what we consider to be undue risk." Neither company is publicly held. Armstrong Company has an annual audit by a CPA but Blair Company does not.

Required:

1. Complete a schedule that reflects a ratio analysis of each company. Compute the ratios discussed in the chapter.
2. A client of yours has the opportunity to buy 10 percent of the shares in one or the other company at the per share prices given and has decided to invest in one of the companies. Based on the data given, prepare a comparative evaluation of the ratio analyses (and any other available information) and give your recommended choice with the supporting explanation.

P14–4 Comparing Loan Requests from Two Companies Using Several Ratios

The 19B financial statements for Rand and Tand companies are summarized here:

	Rand Company	Tand Company
BALANCE SHEET		
Cash	$ 25,000	$ 45,000
Accounts receivable (net)	55,000	5,000
Inventory	110,000	25,000
Operational assets (net)	550,000	160,000
Other assets	140,000	57,000
Total assets	$880,000	$292,000
Current liabilities	$120,000	$ 15,000
Long-term debt (12%)	190,000	55,000
Capital stock (par $20)	480,000	210,000
Contributed capital in excess of par	50,000	4,000
Retained earnings	40,000	8,000
Total liabilities and stockholders' equity	$880,000	$292,000
INCOME STATEMENT		
Sales revenue (on credit)	(1/2) $800,000	(1/4) $280,000
Cost of goods sold	(480,000)	(150,000)
Expenses (including interest and income tax)	(240,000)	(95,000)
Net income	$ 80,000	$ 35,000
SELECTED DATA FROM THE 19A STATEMENTS		
Accounts receivable, net	$ 47,000	$ 11,000
Long-term debt (12%)	190,000	55,000
Inventory	95,000	38,000
OTHER DATA		
Per share price at end of 19B	$ 14.00	$ 11.00
Average income tax rate	30%	30%
Dividends declared and paid in 19B	$ 20,000	$ 9,000

These two companies are in the same line of business and in the same state but in different cities. Each company has been in operation for about 10 years. Rand Company is audited by one of the national accounting firms; Tand Company is audited by a local accounting firm. Both companies received an unqualified opinion (i.e., the independent auditors found nothing wrong) on the financial statements. Rand Company wants to borrow $75,000 cash, and Tand Company needs $30,000. The loans will be for a two-year period and are needed for "working capital purposes."

Required:
1. Complete a schedule that reflects a ratio analysis of each company. Compute the ratios discussed in the chapter.
2. Assume that you work in the loan department of a local bank. You have been asked to analyze the situation and recommend which loan is preferable. Based on the data given, your analysis prepared in requirement (1), and any other information, give your choice and the supporting explanation.

P14–5 Assessing the Solvency of an Actual Company Using Selected Ratios

The following information was contained in the actual financial statements of a large manufacturing company that currently is listed on The New York Stock Exchange.

Balance Sheet
December 31
(millions of dollars)

	19B	19A
ASSETS		
Current assets		
Cash	$ 188.2	$ 123.2
Time deposits	120.8	248.8
Marketable securities	165.3	150.8
Accounts receivable (less allowance for doubtful accounts:		
19B—$34.9 million; 19A—$16.7 million)	610.3	848.0
Inventories—at the lower of cost		
(substantially FIFO) or market	1,873.8	1,980.8
Prepaid insurance, taxes, and other expenses	162.3	210.2
Total current assets	$3,120.7	$3,561.8
Total investments and other assets	1,183.5	1,396.5
Property, plant, and equipment		
Land, buildings, machinery, and equipment	3,733.1	3,391.3
Less accumulated depreciation	2,097.1	1,963.9
	1,636.0	1,427.4
Special tools	712.9	595.5
Net property, plant, and equipment	$2,348.9	$2,022.9
Total assets	$6,653.1	$6,981.2
LIABILITIES AND STOCKHOLDERS' INVESTMENT		
Current liabilities		
Accounts payable	$1,530.4	$1,725.0
Accrued expenses	807.9	698.0
Short-term debt	600.9	49.2
Payment due within one year on long-term debt	275.6	12.4
Taxes on income	16.8	1.2
Total current liabilities	3,231.6	2,485.8
Total long-term debt and other liabilities	1,559.1	1,564.1
Minority interest in consolidated subsidiaries	38.3	4.8
Preferred stock—no-par value	218.7	217.0
Common stock—par value $6.25 per share	416.9	397.7
Additional paid-in capital	692.2	683.1
Net earnings retained	496.3	1,628.7
Total liabilities and stockholders' investment	$6,653.1	$6,981.2

Income Statement
For the Year Ending December 31
(millions of dollars)

	19B	19A
Net sales	$12,004.3	$13,669.8
Cost of goods sold	11,631.5	12,640.1
Depreciation of plant and equipment	180.6	154.0
Amortization of special tools	220.0	198.2
Selling and administrative expenses	598.5	572.1
Pension plans	260.6	262.3
Interest expense	215.4	128.9
	13,106.6	$13,955.6
Loss before taxes on income	(1,102.3)	(285.8)
Taxes on income (credit)	(5.0)	(81.2)
Net loss	$ (1,097.3)	$ (204.6)

Required:
1. Calculate the following ratios:
    a. Return on owners' investment.
    b. Return on total investment. (For purposes of this case, assume that the interest expense reported on the income statement is net of income taxes.)
    c. Financial leverage.
    d. Earnings per share.
    e. Current ratio.
    f. Quick ratio.
    g. Inventory turnover.
    h. Debt-to-equity ratio.
2. Based on your analysis of the ratios that you calculated in requirement (1), do you think that this company will be able to continue in existence? Explain. Would you be willing to invest in this company? Explain.

P14–6 Analyzing the Impact of Alternative Inventory Methods on Selected Ratios

Company A uses the FIFO method to cost inventory, and Company B uses the LIFO method. The two companies are exactly alike except for the difference in inventory costing methods. Costs of inventory items for both companies have been rising steadily in recent years, and each company has increased its inventory each year. Each company has paid its tax liability in full for the current year (and all previous years), and each company uses the same accounting methods for both financial reporting and income tax reporting.

Required:

Identify which company will report the higher amount for each of the following ratios. If it is not possible, explain why.

1. Current ratio.
2. Quick ratio.
3. Debt-to-equity ratio.
4. Return on owners' investment.
5. Earnings per share.

Cases and Projects

C14–1 Analyzing the Impact of Alternative Depreciation Methods on Ratio Analysis

Speedy Company uses the sum-of-years'-digits method to depreciate its property, plant, and equipment, and Turtle Company uses the straight-line method. Both companies use 175 per-cent declining-balance depreciation for income tax purposes. The two companies are exactly alike except for the difference in depreciation methods.

Required:
1. Identify the financial ratios discussed in this chapter that are likely to be affected by the difference in depreciation methods.
2. Which company will report the higher amount for each ratio that you have identified? If you cannot be certain, explain why.

C14–2 Determining the Impact of Selected Transactions on Measures of Liquidity

Three commonly used measures of liquidity are the current ratio, the quick ratio, and working capital. For each of the following transactions, determine whether the measure will increase, decrease, or not change. You should assume that both ratios are higher than 1 and that working capital is positive.

(a) The company purchased $100,000 of inventory on credit.

(b) Merchandise, which cost $35,000, was sold on credit for $50,000. The company uses the periodic inventory method.

(c) Previously declared dividends are paid in cash.

(d) Depreciation expense is recorded.

(e) A customer pays money on his account receivable.

C14–3 Analyzing an Investment by Comparing Selected Ratios

You have the opportunity to invest $10,000 in one of two companies from a single industry. The only information you have follows. The word *high* refers to the top third of the industry; *average* is the middle third; *low* is the bottom third. Which company would you select? Write a brief paper justifying your recommendation.

Ratio	Company A	Company B
Current	High	Average
Quick	Low	Average
Debt-to-equity	High	Average
Inventory turnover	Low	Average
Price/earnings	Low	Average
Dividend yield	High	Average

C14–4 Analyzing an Investment by Comparing Selected Ratios

You have the opportunity to invest $10,000 in one of two companies from a single industry. The only information you have is shown here. The word *high* refers to the top third of the industry; *average* is the middle third; *low* is the bottom third. Which company would you select? Write a brief paper justifying your recommendation.

Ratio	Company A	Company B
Current	Low	Average
Quick	Average	Average
Debt-to-equity	Low	Average
Inventory turnover	High	Average
Price/earnings	High	Average
Dividend yield	Low	Average

C14–5 Analyzing an Investment by Comparing Selected Ratios

You have the opportunity to invest $10,000 in one of two companies from a single industry. The only information you have is shown here. The word *high* refers to the top third of the industry; *average* is the middle third; *low* is the bottom third. Which company would you select? Write a brief paper justifying your recommendation.

Ratio	Company A	Company B
EPS	High	Low
ROI (total)	Low	High
Debt-to-equity	High	Average
Current	Low	Average
Price/earnings	Low	High
Dividend yield	High	Average

C14–6 Analyzing an Investment by Comparing Selected Ratios

You have the opportunity to invest $10,000 in one of two companies from a single industry. The only information you have is shown here. The word *high* refers to the top third of the industry; *average* is the middle third; *low* is the bottom third. Which company would you select? Write a brief paper justifying your recommendation.

Ratio	Company A	Company B
ROI (total)	High	Average
Profit margin	High	Low
Leverage	High	Low
Current	Low	High
Price/earnings	High	Average
Debt-to-equity	High	Low

C14-7 Analyzing the Impact of Business Transactions on Ratio Analysis

Almost Short Company requested a sizable loan from First Federal Bank to acquire a large tract of land for future expansion. Almost Short reported current assets of $1,900,000 ($430,000 in cash) and current liabilities of $1,075,000. First Federal denied the loan request for a number of reasons, including the fact that the current ratio was below 2:1. When Almost Short was informed of the loan denial, the comptroller of the company immediately paid $420,000 that was owed to several trade creditors. The comptroller then asked First Federal to reconsider the loan application. Based on these abbreviated facts, would you recommend that First Federal approve the loan request? Why?

Toys "R" Us

C14-8 Analyzing a Financial Statement

Refer to the financial statement of Toys "R" Us given in Appendix B at the end of this book.

Required:

Compute each of the accounting ratios (for 1997) discussed in this chapter. Assume that the tax rate is 35 percent and that the current market price per share of common stock is $40.

C14-9 Project: Developing an Investment Recommendation

You have recently been hired as a stockbroker with a major national firm. Your first client is a retired school teacher who is 72 years old. He lives on a small pension and has less than $100,000 available to invest. He wants to invest $25,000 of this money in a single stock. Using library resources, identify a stock that you think would be appropriate for him. Write a brief report justifying your recommendation.

C14-10 Project: Developing an Investment Recommendation

You have recently been hired as a stockbroker with a major national firm. Your first client is a young couple saving for their first house, which they hope to buy within five years. They both work and have a combined income of $55,000. They received almost $15,000 in cash for wedding gifts and want to invest this money in a single stock. Using library resources, identify a stock that you think would be appropriate for your client. Write a brief report justifying your recommendation.

C14-11 Project: Developing an Investment Recommendation

You have recently been hired as a stockbroker with a major national firm. Your first client is a single woman, age 37. She is currently saving a large portion of her income with the goal of retiring at the earliest possible time. She has indicated that she will retire as soon as she has an investment portfolio worth at least $1 million. Your client wants to invest $50,000 of this money in a single stock and has indicated that if you do well, she will let you manage her entire portfolio. Using library resources, identify a stock that you think would be appropriate for your client. Write a brief report justifying your recommendation.

C14-12 Project: Updating Financial Analysis

Acquire the most recent financial statements for Home Depot. The text describes recent investment performance as "lackluster" and notes that investment analysts have mixed recommendations for the stock. Write a brief report comparing the company's current performance to the results described in this chapter. Your report should include a specific recommendation concerning whether this stock should be bought at this time.

C14–13 Project: Determining Quality of Earnings

Using library resources, identify one company with a low quality of income and another with a high quality of income. Review the financial statements for both companies to determine reasons that help explain the difference in their quality of income (e.g., different accounting methods). Write a brief report explaining why the quality of earnings for the two is different.

C14–14 Project: Predicting Bankruptcy

Using library resources, identify a company that filed for bankruptcy. Locate financial information for the company for at least four or five years prior to the announced bankruptcy. Compute the ratios discussed in this chapter to determine whether any provided an early warning of impending bankruptcy. Write a brief report to identify the ratios that you believe are useful in predicting bankruptcy and justify your conclusion.

C14–15 Team Project: Examining an Annual Report

As a group, select an industry to analyze. Each group member should acquire the annual report or 10-K for one publicly traded company in the industry, with each member selecting a different company. (Library files, the SEC EDGAR service at www.sec.gov, Compustat CD, or the company itself are good sources.) On an individual basis, each group member should write a brief report analyzing his or her company using the techniques discussed in this chapter.

Discuss any patterns across the companies that you as a group observe. Then, as a group, write a short report comparing and contrasting your companies. Provide potential explanations for any differences discovered.

Appendix A

TABLE A.1 ~~lump sum~~
Future Value of \$1, $F = (1 + i)^n$

Periods	2%	3%	3.75%	4%	4.25%	5%	6%	7%	8%
0	1.	1.	1.	1.	1.	1.	1.	1.	1.
1	1.02	1.03	1.0375	1.04	1.0425	1.05	1.06	1.07	1.08
2	1.0404	1.0609	1.0764	1.0816	1.0868	1.1025	1.1236	1.1449	1.1664
3	1.0612	1.0927	1.1168	1.1249	1.1330	1.1576	1.1910	1.2250	1.2597
4	1.0824	1.1255	1.1587	1.1699	1.1811	1.2155	1.2625	1.3108	1.3605
5	1.1041	1.1593	1.2021	1.2167	1.2313	1.2763	1.3382	1.4026	1.4693
6	1.1262	1.1941	1.2472	1.2653	1.2837	1.3401	1.4185	1.5007	1.5869
7	1.1487	1.2299	1.2939	1.3159	1.3382	1.4071	1.5036	1.6058	1.7138
8	1.1717	1.2668	1.3425	1.3686	1.3951	1.4775	1.5938	1.7182	1.8509
9	1.1951	1.3048	1.3928	1.4233	1.4544	1.5513	1.6895	1.8385	1.9990
10	1.2190	1.3439	1.4450	1.4802	1.5162	1.6289	1.7908	1.9672	2.1589
20	1.4859	1.8061	2.0882	2.1911	2.2989	2.6533	3.2071	3.8697	4.6610

Periods	9%	10%	11%	12%	13%	14%	15%	20%	25%
0	1.	1.	1.	1.	1.	1.	1.	1.	1.
1	1.09	1.10	1.11	1.12	1.13	1.14	1.15	1.20	1.25
2	1.1881	1.2100	1.2321	1.2544	1.2769	1.2996	1.3225	1.4400	1.5625
3	1.2950	1.3310	1.3676	1.4049	1.4429	1.4815	1.5209	1.7280	1.9531
4	1.4116	1.4641	1.5181	1.5735	1.6305	1.6890	1.7490	2.0736	2.4414
5	1.5386	1.6105	1.6851	1.7623	1.8424	1.9254	2.0114	2.4883	3.0518
6	1.6771	1.7716	1.8704	1.9738	2.0820	2.1950	2.3131	2.9860	3.8147
7	1.8280	1.9487	2.0762	2.2107	2.3526	2.5023	2.6600	3.5832	4.7684
8	1.9926	2.1436	2.3045	2.4760	2.6584	2.8526	3.0590	4.2998	5.9605
9	2.1719	2.3579	2.5580	2.7731	3.0040	3.2519	3.5179	5.1598	7.4506
10	2.3674	2.5937	2.8394	3.1058	3.3946	3.7072	4.0456	6.1917	9.3132
20	5.6044	6.7275	8.0623	9.6463	11.5231	13.7435	16.3665	38.3376	86.7362

TABLE A.2 ~~lump sum~~
Present Value of \$1, $p = 1/(1 + i)^n$

Periods	2%	3%	3.75%	4%	4.25%	5%	6%	7%	8%
1	0.9804	0.9703	0.9639	0.9615	0.9592	0.9524	0.9434	0.9346	0.9259
2	0.9612	0.9426	0.9290	0.9246	0.9201	0.9070	0.8900	0.8734	0.8573
3	0.9423	0.9151	0.8954	0.8890	0.8826	0.8638	0.8396	0.8163	0.7938
4	0.9238	0.8885	0.8631	0.8548	0.8466	0.8227	0.7921	0.7629	0.7350
5	0.9057	0.8626	0.8319	0.8219	0.8121	0.7835	0.7473	0.7130	0.6806
6	0.8880	0.8375	0.8018	0.7903	0.7790	0.7462	0.7050	0.6663	0.6302
7	0.8706	0.8131	0.7728	0.7599	0.7473	0.7107	0.6651	0.6227	0.5835
8	0.8535	0.7894	0.7449	0.7307	0.7168	0.6768	0.6274	0.5820	0.5403
9	0.8368	0.7664	0.7180	0.7026	0.6876	0.6446	0.5919	0.5439	0.5002
10	0.8203	0.7441	0.6920	0.6756	0.6595	0.6139	0.5584	0.5083	0.4632
20	0.6730	0.5534	0.4789	0.4564	0.4350	0.3769	0.3118	0.2584	0.2145

Periods	9%	10%	11%	12%	13%	14%	15%	20%	25%
1	0.9174	0.9091	0.9009	0.8929	0.8850	0.8772	0.8696	0.8333	0.8000
2	0.8417	0.8264	0.8116	0.7972	0.7831	0.7695	0.7561	0.6944	0.6400
3	0.7722	0.7513	0.7312	0.7118	0.6931	0.6750	0.6575	0.5787	0.5120
4	0.7084	0.6830	0.6587	0.6355	0.6133	0.5921	0.5718	0.4823	0.4096
5	0.6499	0.6209	0.5935	0.5674	0.5428	0.5194	0.4972	0.4019	0.3277
6	0.5963	0.5645	0.5346	0.5066	0.4803	0.4556	0.4323	0.3349	0.2621
7	0.5470	0.5132	0.4817	0.4523	0.4251	0.3996	0.3759	0.2791	0.2097
8	0.5019	0.4665	0.4339	0.4039	0.3762	0.3506	0.3269	0.2326	0.1678
9	0.4604	0.4241	0.3909	0.3606	0.3329	0.3075	0.2843	0.1938	0.1342
10	0.4224	0.3855	0.3522	0.3220	0.2946	0.2697	0.2472	0.1615	0.1074
20	0.1784	0.1486	0.1240	0.1037	0.0868	0.0728	0.0611	0.0261	0.0115

TABLE A.3
Future Value of Annuity of $1 (ordinary), $F = (1 + i)^n - 1/i$

stream of equal payment

Periods*	2%	3%	3.75%	4%	4.25%	5%	6%	7%	8%
1	1.	1.	1.	1.	1.	1.	1.	1.	1.
2	2.02	2.03	2.0375	2.04	2.0425	2.05	2.06	2.07	2.08
3	3.0604	3.0909	3.1139	3.1216	3.1293	3.1525	3.1836	3.2149	3.2464
4	4.1216	4.1836	4.2307	4.2465	4.2623	4.3101	4.3746	4.4399	4.5061
5	5.2040	5.3091	5.3893	5.4163	5.4434	5.5256	5.6371	5.7507	5.8666
6	6.3081	6.4684	6.5914	6.6330	6.6748	6.8019	6.9753	7.1533	7.3359
7	7.4343	7.6625	7.8386	7.8983	7.9585	8.1420	8.3938	8.6540	8.9228
8	8.5830	8.8923	9.1326	9.2142	9.2967	9.5491	9.8975	10.2598	10.6366
9	9.7546	10.1591	10.4750	10.5828	10.6918	11.0266	11.4913	11.9780	12.4876
10	10.9497	11.4639	11.8678	12.0061	12.1462	12.5779	13.1808	13.8164	14.4866
20	24.2974	26.8704	29.0174	29.7781	30.5625	33.0660	36.7856	40.9955	45.7620

Periods*	9%	10%	11%	12%	13%	14%	15%	20%	25%
1	1.	1.	1.	1.	1.	1.	1.	1.	1.
2	2.09	2.10	2.11	2.12	2.13	2.14	2.15	2.20	2.25
3	3.2781	3.3100	3.3421	3.3744	3.4069	3.4396	3.4725	3.6400	3.8125
4	4.5731	4.6410	4.7097	4.7793	4.8498	4.9211	4.9934	5.3680	5.7656
5	5.9847	6.1051	6.2278	6.3528	6.4803	6.6101	6.7424	7.4416	8.2070
6	7.5233	7.7156	7.9129	8.1152	8.3227	8.5355	8.7537	9.9299	11.2588
7	9.2004	9.4872	9.7833	10.0890	10.4047	10.7305	11.0668	12.9159	15.0735
8	11.0285	11.4359	11.8594	12.2997	12.7573	13.2328	13.7268	16.4991	19.8419
9	13.0210	13.5975	14.1640	14.7757	15.4157	16.0853	16.7858	20.7989	25.8023
10	15.1929	15.9374	16.7220	17.5487	18.4197	19.3373	20.3037	25.9587	33.2529
20	51.1601	57.2750	64.2028	72.0524	80.9468	91.0249	102.4436	186.6880	342.9447

*There is one payment each period.

TABLE A.4
Present Value of Annuity of $1, $P = 1 - 1/(1 + i)^n/i$

Periods*	2%	3%	3.75%	4%	4.25%	5%	6%	7%	8%
1	0.9804	0.9709	0.9639	0.9615	0.9592	0.9524	0.9434	0.9346	0.9259
2	1.9416	1.9135	1.8929	1.8861	1.8794	1.8594	1.8334	1.8080	1.7833
3	2.8839	2.8286	2.7883	2.7751	2.7620	2.7232	2.6730	2.6243	2.5771
4	3.8077	3.7171	3.6514	3.6299	3.6086	3.5460	3.4651	3.3872	3.3121
5	4.7135	4.5797	4.4833	4.4518	4.4207	4.3295	4.2124	4.1002	3.9927
6	5.6014	5.4172	5.2851	5.2421	5.1997	5.0757	4.9173	4.7665	4.6229
7	6.4720	6.2303	6.0579	6.0021	5.9470	5.7864	5.5824	5.3893	5.2064
8	7.3255	7.0197	6.8028	6.7327	6.6638	6.4632	6.2098	5.9713	5.7466
9	8.1622	7.7861	7.5208	7.4353	7.3513	7.1078	6.8017	6.5152	6.2469
10	8.9826	8.5302	8.2128	8.1109	8.0109	7.7217	7.3601	7.0236	6.7101
20	16.3514	14.8775	13.8962	13.5903	13.2944	12.4622	11.4699	10.5940	9.8181

Periods*	9%	10%	11%	12%	13%	14%	15%	20%	25%
1	0.9174	0.9091	0.9009	0.8929	0.8850	0.8772	0.8696	0.8333	0.8000
2	1.7591	1.7355	1.7125	1.6901	1.6681	1.6467	1.6257	1.5278	1.4400
3	2.5313	2.4869	2.4437	2.4018	2.3612	2.3216	2.2832	2.1065	1.9520
4	3.2397	3.1699	3.1024	3.0373	2.9745	2.9137	2.8550	2.5887	2.3616
5	3.8897	3.7908	3.6959	3.6048	3.5172	3.4331	3.3522	2.9906	2.6893
6	4.4859	4.3553	4.2305	4.1114	3.9975	3.8887	3.7845	3.3255	2.9514
7	5.0330	4.8684	4.7122	4.5638	4.4226	4.2883	4.1604	3.6046	3.1611
8	5.5348	5.3349	5.1461	4.9676	4.7988	4.6389	4.4873	3.8372	3.3289
9	5.9952	5.7590	5.5370	5.3282	5.1317	4.9464	4.7716	4.0310	3.4631
10	6.4177	6.1446	5.8892	5.6502	5.4262	5.2161	5.0188	4.1925	3.5705
20	9.1285	8.5136	7.9633	7.4694	7.0248	6.6231	6.2593	4.8696	3.9539

*There is one payment each period.

Appendix B

1978

A New **Generation**

1996

TOYS"R"US ANNUAL REPORT

YEAR ENDED FEBRUARY 1, 1997

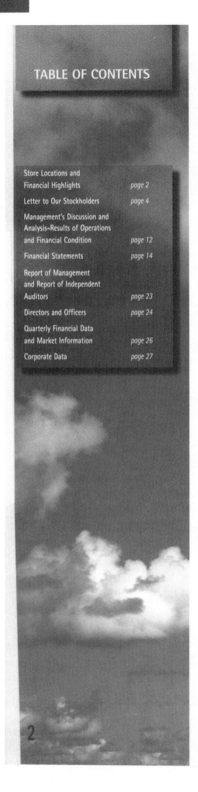

STORE LOCATIONS

TOYS"R"US UNITED STATES - 682 LOCATIONS

Alabama - 7	Indiana - 12	Nebraska - 3	South Carolina-8
Alaska - 1	Iowa - 8	Nevada - 4	South Dakota - 2
Arizona - 11	Kansas - 4	New Hampshire - 5	Tennessee - 14
Arkansas - 4	Kentucky - 8	New Jersey - 24*	Texas - 51
California - 84	Louisiana - 11	New Mexico - 4	Utah - 5
Colorado - 11	Maine - 2	New York - 45	Virginia - 22*
Connecticut - 11	Maryland - 19	North Carolina - 16	Vermont - 1
Delaware - 2	Massachusetts - 19	North Dakota - 1	Washington - 14
Florida - 44	Michigan - 25	Ohio - 31	West Virginia - 4
Georgia - 18	Minnesota - 12	Oklahoma - 5	Wisconsin - 11
Hawaii - 1	Mississippi - 5	Oregon - 8	
Idaho - 2	Missouri - 12	Pennsylvania - 31	Puerto Rico - 4
Illinois - 34	Montana - 1	Rhode Island - 1	

* Includes a KidsWorld location.

TOYS"R"US INTERNATIONAL - 396 LOCATIONS

Australia - 22	Hong Kong - 4 (a)	Netherlands - 9 (a)	Switzerland - 4
Austria - 8	Indonesia - 2 (a)	Portugal - 3	Taiwan - 6 (a)
Belgium - 3	Israel - 3 (a)	Saudi Arabia - 1 (a)	Turkey - 1 (a)
Canada - 61	Italy - 5 (a)	Singapore - 4	United Arab Emirates - 3 (a)
Denmark - 9 (a)	Japan - 51 (b)	South Africa - 6 (a)	
France - 41	Luxembourg - 1	Spain - 28	United Kingdom - 56
Germany - 58	Malaysia - 4 (a)	Sweden - 3 (a)	

(a) Franchise or joint venture.
(b) 80 % owned.

KIDS"R"US UNITED STATES - 212 LOCATIONS

Alabama - 1	Iowa - 1	Missouri - 5	Pennsylvania - 14
California - 24	Kansas - 1	Nebraska - 1	Rhode Island - 1
Connecticut - 6	Maine - 1	New Hampshire - 2	Tennessee - 2
Delaware - 1	Maryland - 9	New Jersey - 18	Texas - 9
Florida - 10	Massachusetts - 6	New York - 22	Utah - 3
Georgia - 4	Michigan - 13	North Carolina - 1	Virginia - 7
Illinois - 20	Minnesota - 2	Ohio - 18	Wisconsin - 3
Indiana - 7			

BABIES"R"US UNITED STATES - 82 LOCATIONS

Alabama - 2	Indiana - 2	Minnesota - 1	Oklahoma - 1
Arizona - 1	Kansas - 1	Missouri - 2	Pennsylvania - 2
California - 2	Kentucky - 1	New Jersey - 3	South Carolina - 3
Colorado - 2	Louisiana - 1	New York - 1	Tennessee - 4
Florida - 10	Maryland - 3	North Carolina - 5	Texas - 12
Georgia - 7	Michigan - 1	Ohio - 5	Virginia - 6
Illinois - 4			

2

FINANCIAL HIGHLIGHTS

TOYS"R"US, INC. AND SUBSIDIARIES

(Dollars in millions except per share data)   Fiscal Year Ended

	Feb. 1, 1997*	Feb. 3, 1996*	Jan. 28, 1995	Jan. 29, 1994	Jan. 30, 1993	Feb. 1, 1992	Feb. 2, 1991	Jan. 28, 1990	Jan. 29, 1989	Jan. 31, 1988
OPERATIONS:										
Net Sales	$ 9,932	$ 9,427	$ 8,746	$ 7,946	$ 7,169	$ 6,124	$ 5,510	$ 4,788	$ 4,000	$ 3,137
Net Earnings	427	148	532	483	438	340	326	321	268	204
Earnings Per Share	1.54	.53	1.85	1.63	1.47	1.15	1.11	1.09	.91	.69
FINANCIAL POSITION AT YEAR END:										
Working Capital	619	326	484	633	797	328	177	238	255	225
Real Estate-Net	2,411	2,336	2,271	2,036	1,877	1,751	1,433	1,142	952	762
Total Assets	8,023	6,738	6,571	6,150	5,323	4,583	3,582	3,075	2,555	2,027
Long-Term Obligations	909	827	785	724	671	391	195	173	174	177
Stockholders' Equity	4,191	3,432	3,429	3,148	2,889	2,426	2,046	1,705	1,424	1,135
NUMBER OF STORES AT YEAR END:										
Toys"R"Us - United States	680	653	618	581	540	497	451	404	358	313
Toys"R"Us - International	396	337	293	234	167	126	97	74	52	37
Kids"R"Us - United States	212	213	204	217	211	189	164	137	112	74
Babies"R"Us - United States	82	–	–	–	–	–	–	–	–	–
KidsWorld - United States	2	–	–	–	–	–	–	–	–	–

* After other charges as described in the Notes to the Consolidated Financial Statements.

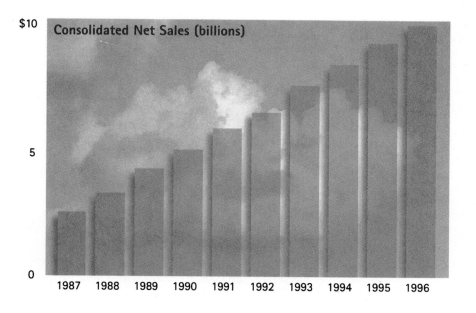

3

TO OUR STOCKHOLDERS

Introduction

In our annual report for the year ended February 3, 1980, our 85 toy stores in the United States reported net sales approaching $500 million. In our letter to our stockholders that year, we stated, "Much of this annual report is devoted to financial information. The true heart of our business, however, is our customer." During the next seventeen years, we grew our business to 1,372 stores in 27 countries, with sales approaching $10 billion. Delivering the best selection at great prices, we became the biggest toy store in town.

In 1997, just as in 1980, the heart of our business is the customer. In last year's annual report, we said that one of the major reasons we undertook our restructuring program was in response to our customers' feedback. In this letter, we will describe the many initiatives we have completed and are undertaking to improve our customers' shopping experience. By continuing to service the customer first and foremost, we will continue to grow profitably for you, our stockholders. We are confident that our ever-increasing emphasis on customer service will enhance our reputation as the finest retailer of children's products in the world.

1996 Financial Highlights

Our 1996 sales grew to $9.9 billion, a 5% percent increase over the $9.4 billion reported in the prior year. This is our 18th consecutive year of record sales since Toys"R"Us became a public company. In 1996, operating earnings more than doubled from the prior year and net earnings increased to $427.4 million versus $148.1 million in 1995. Earnings per share increased to $1.54 as compared to $.53 a year ago. Our results for both the 1996 and 1995 years were impacted by special charges. In 1996, a $37.8 million after tax charge was recorded for a judgement rendered against the Company related to a dispute involving a 1982 franchise agreement for toy store operations in the Middle East. In 1995, the Company underwent a strategic restructuring program and, as a result, incurred a $269.1 million after tax charge. Excluding the impact of these non-recurring charges, our 1996 net earnings increased 12% to $465.2 million from $417.2 million and earnings per share increased to $1.68 from $1.51 in the prior year.

1996 saw the successful implementation of our worldwide restructuring program. The most important initiative, our strategic inventory repositioning, has been completed. We have significantly streamlined our assortment and reduced the number of items we carry in our stores by more than 20%. This inventory repositioning program was initiated because the breadth of our assortment sometimes made our stores difficult to shop. Listening to our customers enabled us to enhance our selection advantage with larger facings and more dramatic presentations of desired items.

The other significant elements of our restructuring program, including store closings and the consolidation of certain distribution centers and administrative facilities, are substantially complete. Reducing our cost structure allows us to bring the right product to our stores more efficiently. Finally, the restructuring has had a positive financial impact. Our balance sheet is in excellent condition, as demonstrated by the significant decrease in debt, net of investments, and by our improved working capital and strong cash flow.

We are pleased to report that all of our divisions: Toys"R"Us - USA, International and Kids"R"Us, experienced comparable store sales increases and improved operating earnings for 1996.

Left: Michael Goldstein,
Vice Chairman and Chief Executive Officer
Right: Robert C. Nakasone,
President and Chief Operating Officer

While the 1996 holiday selling season fell short of our expectations – due primarily to a shortage of hot selling products like Tickle Me Elmo and Nintendo 64, as well as a limited selection of new video game software titles – we are pleased to report that even at this early stage in 1997, the demand for new products is very strong, and toy and video game manufacturers are geared up to meet that need. We fully expect that as a result of our traditional strength as <u>the</u> place to go for the best selection, in stock position and price, we will be able to meet the customers' expectations and generate increased sales and earnings for you, our stockholders.

Our Customer Focus

Last year, we told you that we would unveil a revolutionary new toy store design in 1996 with the goal of creating a shopping experience like no other. We completed 13 of our "Concept 2000" stores in 1996 with outstanding results, both in terms of sales and customer satisfaction. The shopping environment we have created is completely different from the Toys"R"Us of yesterday. At the grand opening of our first "Concept 2000" store in Raritan, New Jersey, we overheard one of our customers say "people are going to shop for hours in this store." As a retailer, this is mighty praise indeed! In 1997, the "Concept 2000" format will be expanded as we will remodel 57 stores and all new toy stores in the United States will be built using this format.

In 1996, Toys"R"Us entered the superstore arena with the launch of Toys"R"Us KidsWorld, our 90,000 square foot prototype encompassing all of our formats – Toys"R"Us, Kids"R"Us and Babies"R"Us – under one roof. We know our customers are excited by this concept. Our two day grand opening in Elizabeth, New Jersey drew such enormous crowds that car traffic backed up the New Jersey Turnpike for miles. In our proud history, we have had many outstanding grand opening events, but the customer reaction to KidsWorld has been extraordinary. We are especially pleased with our licensed

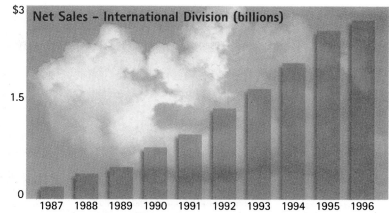

Net Sales – International Division (billions)

$3

1.5

0

1987　1988　1989　1990　1991　1992　1993　1994　1995　1996

Consolidated Total Assets (billions)

$10

5

0

1987　1988　1989　1990　1991　1992　1993　1994　1995　1996

shops which provide our customers with food, fun, footwear and photographs. Our market research indicates the average customer stays in our KidsWorld store for well over an hour. Our goal of creating a new type of destination store for kids has been achieved.

Our customer focus has been extended to the existing base of our toy stores as well. In 1996, we rolled out 200 customer information centers, with more to follow. These provide a fixed single location in the center of the store where help can be received and questions can be answered. Due to the wide selection of merchandise we carry, as well as the shortage of hot product we have experienced, our customer information center is essential in improving our overall customer service. Through the

use of our automated store inventory system, our customer information center enables us to communicate with our customer as never before.

And what better way to communicate with our customers than have them communicate with each other! While our Baby Registry has been available all year, we made registering even easier in 1996. We successfully tested in-store radio frequency technology and hand-held scanners and we'll use them to a greater extent in 1997. With this technology, our customers can now simply scan their desired selections for automatic registration into our computers. We complemented our Baby Registry this year by testing a Gift Registry where children can create a wish list for their

5

families and friends, no matter where they live in the United States. This Gift Registry was tested in three of our markets this year and will be rolled out to the entire country beginning in 1997. Not only do our Registry programs make shopping easier, but they eliminate the time consuming process of returning or exchanging duplicate items and unwanted gifts.

Our revolving feature shop area continues to be a strong customer draw. While we are proud of our 1996 Toy Story, Barbie, Nerf and Hunchback of Notre Dame shops, we were thrilled by our customers' response to our Video Test Drive Shop last summer. We were able to provide first-hand playing experience on the new hardware platforms so that our customers could make educated decisions before making this significant purchase. We believe there is no retailer in the world as committed to the video game business as Toys"R"Us. In order to provide our customers with better in stock levels of high demand video game products, as well as computer software and VHS tapes, we will open our state-of-the-art centralized "piece pick" operation in 1997. Centralized piece pick will allow us to distribute new titles across our chain faster than ever before. In addition, we can provide quicker inventory replenishment for these important categories.

Improving our in-stock levels at Toys"R"Us is an important element in our desire to improve our customer service. In 1996, one third of our chain installed a new sales floor replenishment tool which we call the Sales Improvement System. With the use of hand-held radio frequency technology, our associates can pinpoint the exact location of merchandise, not only on the sales floor, but also in our stockrooms. This will enable us to quickly identify out of stock or low stock positions and allow us to bring hot product to the sales floor quicker than ever.

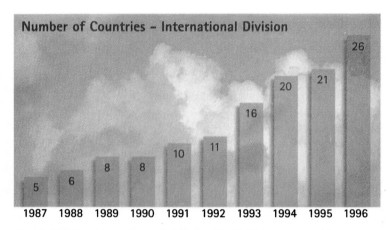

Number of Countries – International Division

1987	1988	1989	1990	1991	1992	1993	1994	1995	1996
5	6	8	8	10	11	16	20	21	26

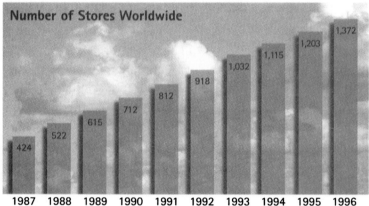

Number of Stores Worldwide

1987	1988	1989	1990	1991	1992	1993	1994	1995	1996
424	522	615	712	812	918	1,032	1,115	1,203	1,372

Babies"R"Us

In 1996, our newest division, Babies"R"Us, was born. We opened 6 Babies"R"Us stores, utilizing many elements from our "Concept 2000" store design and capitalizing on our Toys"R"Us and Kids"R"Us systems and infrastructure. Our merger with Baby Superstore on February 3, 1997 immediately makes Toys"R"Us a stronger player in the juvenile marketplace by adding 76 existing stores to the Babies"R"Us family. We have long admired the competitive spirit of the Baby Superstore associates and we recognize the value that they bring to Toys"R"Us in terms of their ability to provide outstanding customer service. Combining the successful Baby Superstore company with the financial resources, sophisticated distribution network and operational "know-how" of Toys"R"Us makes us the premier retailer of juvenile products in the United States.

Outlook

In 1996, we added 104 stores: 30 toy stores in the United States, 59 international toy stores, of which 27 were franchise stores, including our first franchise stores in Indonesia, Italy, Saudi Arabia, South Africa and Turkey, as well as 7 Kids"R"Us stores, 6 Babies"R"Us stores and 2 KidsWorld stores. In 1997, we intend to add approximately 105 stores: 25 USA toy stores in addition to the 57 Concept 2000 remodels, 40 international toy stores including 15 franchise stores, 5 Kids"R"Us stores and 20 Babies"R"Us stores in addition to converting the 76 Baby Superstore locations.

In terms of product, 1997 promises to be an exciting year for Toys"R"Us. The video game business remains strong and the introduction of Nintendo 64 into Europe should continue the excitement in another part of the world. In addition, the recent price reductions for Nintendo 64 and Sony Playstation should fuel the video game momentum not only in video hardware but software as well.

Licensed toy product related to movie releases has historically been successful for Toys"R"Us. Typically, a great movie license generates sales for us in many categories such as action figures, dolls, plush, party goods, and board and video games to name a few. This year there will be more children-oriented movies with related toy product than at any other point in our history. These movies include the Star Wars Trilogy and Little Mermaid re-releases, The Lost World: Jurassic Park, Batman and Robin, Hercules and Anastasia. We will be ready to supply our customers with exciting products related to all of these movies.

Corporate Citizenship

Toys"R"Us maintains a company-wide giving program focused on improving the health care needs of children by supporting many national and regional children's health care organizations.

The Counsel on Economic Priority recently awarded Toys"R"Us the Pioneer Award in Global Ethics. This award was the direct result of the implementation of our Code of Conduct for suppliers which outlines the Company's position against child labor and unsafe working conditions. In order for a vendor's product to be sold in any of our stores, they must comply with our Code of Conduct.

If you would like to receive more information on Toys"R"Us' corporate citizenship please write to Roger Gaston at the address noted on the back inside cover.

HUMAN RESOURCES

All of these initiatives are made possible by the excellent management team we have assembled here at Toys"R"Us. To prepare ourselves for 1997 and beyond, we have made the following important executive announcements:

ADDITIONS:

Roger C. Gaston
Senior Vice President - Human Resources
Mitchell Loukota
Vice President - Divisional Merchandise Manager
Toys "R" Us
Gregg Treadway
General Manager
Toys"R"Us
Antonio Urcelay
Managing Director - Toys"R"Us Iberia
David S. Walker
Vice President - Advertising
Kids"R"Us

PROMOTIONS:

Corporate & Toys"R"Us, USA
Robert J. Weinberg
Senior Vice President -
General Merchandise Manager
David Brewi
Vice President - Divisional Merchandise Manager
Thomas DeLuca
Vice President - Imports, Product Development and Safety Assurance
Truvillus Hall
General Manager
Charlene Mady
Vice President - Area Merchandise Planning
Gerald S. Parker
Vice President - Regional Operations
Timothy J. Slade
Vice President - Transportation and Traffic
William A. Stephenson
Vice President -
Merchandise Planning and Allocation
Kevin VanderGriend
General Manager
Robert S. Zarra
Vice President -
Internal Audit

Toys"R"Us, International
Larry D. Gardner
Vice President - Toys"R"Us Asia
Larry S. Johnson
Vice President - Franchise Markets
Michael C. Taylor
Vice President - Logistics

Kids"R"Us & Babies"R"Us
William Farrell
Vice President - Physical Distribution,
Kids"R"Us
Christopher M. Scherm
Vice President -
Divisional Merchandise Manager, Kids"R"Us
David E. Schoenbeck
Vice President - Operations, Babies"R"Us

We would like to thank Milton Gould and Harold Wit, who have served on our Board of Directors since we became a public company in 1978, for their guidance, counsel and contributions, in helping make Toys"R"Us the world's premier retailer of children's products. We extend to them our heartfelt thanks and best wishes for continued success, health and prosperity as they retire from our Board of Directors.

SUMMARY

We hope you are excited about all of the customer initiatives we will implement in 1997. We recognize our need for change and we are well on our way to implementing our strategic plan. We thank our associates throughout the world who are advancing our mission to grow our business and service our customer.

Yesterday, today and, most importantly, tomorrow our customers will remain the true heart of our business. Listening to our customers over the last two decades has made us strong. Listening harder to each and every one of our customers will make us even stronger.

We look forward to impressing our customers with outstanding service and impressing you, our stockholders, with outstanding results – And along the way, making children all over the world want to visit our stores again and again.

Sincerely,

Michael Goldstein

Michael Goldstein
Vice Chairman and Chief Executive Officer

Robert C. Nakasone

Robert C. Nakasone
President and Chief Operating Officer

March 24, 1997

7

A NEW GENERATION

Toys"R"Us is the world's premier retailer of children's products bringing toys, apparel, baby needs and much more to children (and their parents, too!)

Building Our Business with Customer Service

Today's highly competitive retail environment constantly challenges us to find more ways to distinguish the Toys"R"Us shopping experience. For the savvy, value-conscious consumer of the '90's, well-stocked shelves, great prices and sales promotions are expected from every retail store. There has to be "something more..." In response to this, we have been placing more and more emphasis on customer service. Throughout 1996, a number of opportunities enabled us to show our customers that we understand their needs, and that we are working towards providing the best service possible everyday... at every Toys"R"Us store.

Toys"R"Us Becomes a Public Company

1978

First Kid"R"Us Store Opens

1983

Toys"R"Us Goes International

1984

8

Concept 2000:

AND THE ADVENT OF CUSTOMER-FRIENDLY STORE DESIGN

In 1996, we unveiled thirteen stores with the innovative store format we call Concept 2000 — combining the ultimate in shopping convenience and aesthetics. Wider aisles, color-coded merchandise displays, attractive signage, specialty areas for video games and popular toys, animated icons and other visually stimulating features were introduced to entertain and motivate children and parents as they shop. Within our Concept 2000 and regular Toys"R"Us stores,

we also enhanced service at our Customer Information Centers. Customers can now count on the assistance of trained employees who are able to access computer screens and identify product availability within our stores. In our Islands of Service program, we have sales assistants who are 'subject experts' in various categories to help customers answer product-specific questions and explain key product features.

We have successfully made our definition of Customer Service more expansive. Whether it is by giving our shoppers personalized attention and assistance, promoting key services that enhance the shopping experience, or simply by providing them with a pleasant environment in which to shop, we work to ensure customer satisfaction.

WHAT CUSTOMERS ARE SAYING ABOUT CONCEPT 2000:

"Walking into the new store, I was blown away by how much it has changed..."

"It was so much easier to find what I was looking for..."

"I was impressed by the merchandise displays and selection..."

"It was a pleasure to shop here because the store is so bright and colorful..."

"Wow!"

Toys"R"Us Opens First Store in Japan

Introduction of Baby Registry: A New Innovation in Customer Service

Toys"R"Us Announces Worldwide Restructuring to Position Itself for a New Generation

1991   1993   1996   9

Toys"R"Us:

SPECIAL PROGRAMS
AND NEW INITIATIVES

A welcome convenience for parents-to-be, the Toys"R"Us Baby Registry lets friends and family members find the right gifts for new parents with ease and confidence. After a simple registration process, parents-to-be can make their selection from any of the products in the store. With its focus on gift-giving for baby, this service shows our customers that we have thought of every shopping benefit!

Another new service coming soon is the Gift Registry. Kids simply sign up and create their own "wish list" with the toys they really want for birthdays, holidays and special occasions. Gift-givers will be able to choose the perfect gift every time! The Gift Registry will be rolled out to all stores beginning in 1997. We're exploring customer service opportunities on the Internet, too! Our new website (www.toysrus.com) provides fun for the kids , and gives parents direct access to store and product information instantly!

KidsWorld: TOTAL ONE-STOP SHOPPING

The two KidsWorld stores that opened in 1996 showcased the very best of one-stop shopping and customer service. Shoppers came for the full range of advantages from Toys"R"Us, Kids"R"Us and Babies"R"Us, plus other family-friendly "attractions" such as Kids Footlocker,

Focus Pocus (a photo studio), Cartoon Cuts (a hair salon), Jeepers Junior (a restaurant), Fuzziwig's Candy Factory, plus arcade games and rides. Coming to KidsWorld means more than just a shopping trip. It's a real family event!

First Babies"R"Us Store Opens and Toys"R"Us Merges with Baby Superstore

Toys"R"Us Redesigned for the 21st Century – "Concept 2000"

First KidsWorld Superstore Opens

1996

Babies"R"Us:

DELIVERING NEW OPPORTUNITIES FOR SUCCESS

There are great expectations for the newest arrival in the "R"Us family. In 1996, Babies"R"Us successfully opened six bright, spacious new stores (designed after the Concept 2000 model) that showcase total one-stop shopping and expert customer service. The recent merger with the Baby Superstore chain in February 1997 has quickly catapulted Babies"R"Us into the premier retailer of juvenile products in the country! Customers can expect advantages like an amazing product selection, everyday low prices, and the popular no-hassle returns policy. Other customer-friendly services include The Baby Registry that makes it easy for new parents to choose the gifts they want from friends and family, and the Special Orders desk where customers can order merchandise in specific styles or colors not currently available in the store. Our sales associates are expertly trained for customer interaction through classes, product seminars, videos and a regular product information newsletter. Expectant parents and gift-givers now have the ideal place to shop for everything for baby!

International:

HIGHLIGHTS FROM AROUND THE WORLD

Fifty-nine international Toys"R"Us stores opened in 1996, demonstrating our continuing growth as a global retailer. Franchise operations in Indonesia, Italy, Saudi Arabia, South Africa, and Turkey bring our current international presence to nearly 400 stores in 26 countries. Milestones for the year included the opening of our 50th store in Japan, and the celebration of our 10th year in Hong Kong. As the Toys"R"Us world gets bigger and better, new and exciting opportunities abound for strengthening relationships with all our customers!

M ANAGEMENT'S DISCUSSION AND ANALYSIS -
Results of Operations and Financial Condition

RESULTS OF OPERATIONS*

The Company posted its 18th consecutive record sales year in 1996, reporting sales of $9.9 billion. Sales increased by 5.4% in 1996, 7.8% in 1995 and 10.1% in 1994. The sales growth is primarily attributable to the Company's continued store expansion and the increase in comparable U.S.A. toy store sales of 2% in 1996. The Company opened 102 new U.S.A. toy stores, 163 international toy stores, including franchise and joint venture stores, 22 children's clothing stores, 6 baby specialty stores and 2 superstores during the three year period. Comparable U.S.A. toy store sales decreased 2% in 1995 and increased 2% in 1994.

Cost of sales as a percentage of sales decreased to 69.4% in 1996 from 69.9% in 1995 primarily due to an improved markup on basic toy products, partially offset by the strengthening of the lower margin video hardware business. Cost of sales as a percentage of sales increased in 1995 from 68.7% in 1994 primarily due to an intensively competitive retail environment, the Company's aggressive pricing strategy and an unfavorable shift in the merchandise mix.

Selling, advertising, general and administrative expenses as a percentage of sales were 20.3% in 1996, 20.1% in 1995 and 19.0% in 1994. The increases in 1996 and 1995 were primarily due to heavier advertising and promotional efforts, as well as the Company's increased emphasis on customer service.

The Company's 1996 results were impacted by a charge of $59.5 million ($37.8 million, net of tax benefits or $.14 cents per share) relating to an arbitration award rendered against the Company involving a dispute over a 1982 franchise agreement to operate stores in the Middle East. Although the arbitration award was recently confirmed in the District Courts, the Company has filed an appeal with the United States Court of Appeals for the Second Circuit.

The Company's 1995 results were impacted by charges of $396.6 million ($269.1 million, net of tax benefits or $.98 cents per share) to restructure its worldwide operations and to early adopt FAS No. 121, "Accounting for the Impairment of Long-Lived Assets and Long-Lived Assets to be Disposed Of." Elements of the restructuring plan are described below and in the notes to the consolidated financial statements and consisted of certain asset write offs and contractual obligations, primarily in the United States and Europe.

*References to 1996, 1995, and 1994 are for the 52 weeks ended February 1, 1997, 53 weeks ended February 3, 1996 and the 52 weeks ended January 28, 1995.

In 1996, the Company substantially completed its restructuring program action plan, including the closing of 3 Toys"R"Us and 7 Kids"R"Us stores in the United States, the consolidation of 3 distribution centers and various administrative facilities in the United States and Europe and, pending certain regulatory approvals, the franchising of 9 toy stores in the Netherlands. The Company also successfully completed the most important component of the restructuring program, its strategic inventory repositioning initiative designed to streamline the merchandise assortment in its toy stores and enhance its selection advantage. The Company has reduced the number of items carried in its toy stores by more than 20%.

At February 1, 1997, the Company had approximately $90 million of liabilities remaining for its restructuring program primarily relating to long-term lease obligations and other commitments. The Company believes these reserves are adequate to complete the restructuring program.

Interest expense decreased by 4.5% in 1996 as compared to 1995 primarily due to the Company's improved cash flow as a result of increased earnings, the benefits from its worldwide restructuring program and a $325.4 million medium term financing which replaced borrowings carrying higher interest rates. Interest expense increased in 1995 as compared to 1994 due to increased average borrowings and a change in the mix of borrowings and interest rates among countries.

The Company's effective tax rate was 36.5%, 44.2% and 37.0% in 1996, 1995 and 1994, respectively. The higher effective tax rate in 1995 was primarily due to the restructuring of its worldwide operations.

The Company believes that its risks attendant to foreign operations are minimal as the countries in which it owns assets and operates stores are politically stable. The Company's foreign exchange risk management objectives are to stabilize cash flow from the effect of foreign currency fluctuations. The Company will, whenever practical, offset local investments in foreign currencies with borrowings denominated in the same currency. The Company also enters into forward foreign exchange contracts or purchases options to eliminate specific transaction currency risk.

International sales were unfavorably impacted by the translation of local currency results into U.S. dollars by approximately $150 million in 1996 and was favorably impacted by approximately $140 million and $90 million in 1995 and 1994, respectively. Neither the translation of local currency results into U.S. dollars nor inflation had a material effect on the Company's operating results for the last three years.

LIQUIDITY AND CAPITAL RESOURCES **

The Company's impressive financial position is evidenced by the liquidity of its assets and its strong cash flow.

The Company's newest division, Babies"R"Us opened its first 6 stores in 1996. The Company accelerated the growth of this division with the acquisition of Baby Superstore, Inc. on February 3, 1997 for 13 million treasury shares of the Company's common stock valued at approximately $376.0 million. This acquisition has been accounted for as a purchase at February 1, 1997 and the excess of purchase price over net assets acquired in the amount of $365.0 million has been recorded as goodwill and will be amortized over 40 years.

Baby Superstore, with 76 stores primarily in the southeast and midwest United States, was a leading retailer of baby and young children's products. The Company plans to operate these stores under its Babies"R"Us format, utilizing its Toys"R"Us and Kids"R"Us infrastructure to leverage its combined financial and operational strengths.

The Company's cash and cash equivalents have increased to $760.9 million at February 1, 1997 from $202.7 million at February 3, 1996. This increase is primarily attributable to the following factors: increased net earnings, due in part to the benefits of the Company's worldwide restructuring program, $67.5 million of cash received with the acquisition of Baby Superstore and an increase in net cash provided by financing activities of $112.1 million.

The Company's working capital improved to $618.9 million at February 1, 1997, from $326.1 million at February 3, 1996 due in part to the closing of a medium term $325.4 million financing in 1996, the proceeds of which reduced short term debt.

The long-term debt, net of current maturities, to equity percentage was 21.7% at February 1, 1997 as compared to 24.1% at February 3, 1996.

In 1997, the Company plans to open approximately 25 toy stores in the United States utilizing the new "Concept 2000" store design and also plans to remodel 57 toy stores in the United States to this format. The Company plans to open approximately 40 new international toy stores, including 15 franchise stores. Our newest division, Babies"R"Us, will open approximately 20 stores in the United States. Finally, there are plans to open approximately 5 Kids"R"Us children's clothing stores. The Company opened 89 toy stores in 1996, 80 in 1995 and 96 in 1994, and 7 Kids"R"Us children's clothing stores in 1996, 9 in 1995 and 6 in 1994. The Company also added its first 2 KidsWorld stores, one of which is a retrofit of an existing Toys"R"Us and Kids"R"Us location, and the first 6 Babies"R"Us stores in 1996. In addition to the stores closed in 1996 that were part of the Company's worldwide restructuring program, the Company closed 1 store in the United Kingdom in 1995 and 19 Kids"R"Us clothing stores in 1994 which did not meet its expectations. These closures did not have a significant impact on the Company's financial position.

For 1997, capital requirements for real estate, store and warehouse fixtures and equipment, leasehold improvements and other additions to property and equipment are estimated at $630 million (including real estate and related costs of $375 million). The Company's policy is to purchase its real estate where appropriate and it plans to continue this policy.

The Company has an existing $1 billion share repurchase program. As of February 1, 1997, the Company has repurchased 21.3 million shares of its common stock for $693.9 million under this program since it was announced in January of 1994.

The seasonal nature of the business (approximately 47% of sales take place in the fourth quarter) typically causes cash to decline from the beginning of the year through October as inventory increases for the holiday selling season and funds are used for land purchases and construction of new stores, which usually open in the first ten months of the year. The Company has a $1 billion multi-currency unsecured committed revolving credit facility expiring in February 2000, from a syndicate of financial institutions. Cash requirements for operations, capital expenditures, lease commitments and the share repurchase program will be met primarily through operating activities, borrowings under the revolving credit facility, issuance of short-term commercial paper and other bank borrowings for foreign subsidiaries.

**The Company's consolidated balance sheet at February 1, 1997 includes the effects of the acquisition of Baby Superstore, Inc.

13

CONSOLIDATED STATEMENTS OF EARNINGS

TOYS"R"US, INC. AND SUBSIDIARIES

		Year Ended	
(In millions except per share data)	February 1, 1997	February 3, 1996	January 28, 1995
Net sales	$ 9,932.4	$ 9,426.9	$ 8,745.6
Costs and expenses:			
Cost of sales	6,892.5	6,592.3	6,008.0
Selling, advertising, general and administrative	2,019.7	1,894.8	1,664.2
Depreciation and amortization	206.4	191.7	161.4
Other charges	59.5	396.6	−
Interest expense	98.6	103.3	83.9
Interest and other income	(17.4)	(17.4)	(16.0)
	9,259.3	9,161.3	7,901.5
Earnings before taxes on income	673.1	265.6	844.1
Taxes on income	245.7	117.5	312.3
Net earnings	$ 427.4	$ 148.1	$ 531.8
Earnings per share	$ 1.54	$ .53	$ 1.85

See notes to consolidated financial statements.

14

CONSOLIDATED BALANCE SHEETS

TOYS"R"US, INC. AND SUBSIDIARIES

(In millions)	February 1, 1997	February 3, 1996
ASSETS		
Current Assets:		
Cash and cash equivalents	$ 760.9	$ 202.7
Accounts and other receivables	142.1	128.9
Merchandise inventories	2,214.6	1,999.5
Prepaid expenses and other current assets	42.0	87.8
Total Current Assets	3,159.6	2,418.9
Property and Equipment:		
Real estate, net	2,410.6	2,336.0
Other, net	1,636.8	1,522.2
Total Property and Equipment	4,047.4	3,858.2
Goodwill	365.0	–
Other Assets	451.2	460.4
	$ 8,023.2	$ 6,737.5
LIABILITIES AND STOCKHOLDERS' EQUITY		
Current Liabilities:		
Short-term borrowings	$ 303.5	$ 332.8
Accounts payable	1,346.5	1,182.0
Accrued expenses and other current liabilities	720.0	438.1
Income taxes payable	170.7	139.9
Total Current Liabilities	2,540.7	2,092.8
Long-Term Debt	908.5	826.8
Deferred Income Taxes	222.5	228.7
Other Liabilities	160.9	156.9
Stockholders' Equity:		
Common stock	30.0	30.0
Additional paid-in capital	488.8	542.8
Retained earnings	4,120.1	3,692.7
Foreign currency translation adjustments	(60.6)	12.9
Treasury shares, at cost	(387.7)	(846.1)
Total Stockholders' Equity	4,190.6	3,432.3
	$ 8,023.2	$ 6,737.5

See notes to consolidated financial statements.

15

CONSOLIDATED STATEMENTS OF CASH FLOWS

TOYS"R"US, INC. AND SUBSIDIARIES

(In millions)	February 1, 1997	February 3, 1996	January 28, 1995
CASH FLOWS FROM OPERATING ACTIVITIES			
Net earnings	**$ 427.4**	$ 148.1	$ 531.8
Adjustments to reconcile net earnings to net cash provided by operating activities:			
Other charges	–	396.6	–
Depreciation and amortization	**206.4**	191.7	161.4
Deferred income taxes	**23.4**	(66.7)	(14.5)
Changes in operating assets and liabilities:			
Accounts and other receivables	**(14.3)**	(10.8)	(17.4)
Merchandise inventories	**(194.6)**	(193.1)	(221.6)
Prepaid expenses and other operating assets	**(10.1)**	(15.7)	(31.7)
Accounts payable, accrued expenses and other liabilities	**261.4**	(150.5)	183.5
Income taxes payable	**43.8**	(49.3)	(2.0)
Net cash provided by operating activities	**743.4**	250.3	589.5
CASH FLOWS FROM INVESTING ACTIVITIES			
Cash received with the acquisition of Baby Superstore	**67.5**	–	–
Capital expenditures, net	**(415.4)**	(467.5)	(585.7)
Other assets	**(35.8)**	(67.4)	(44.6)
Net cash used in investing activities	**(383.7)**	(534.9)	(630.3)
CASH FLOWS FROM FINANCING ACTIVITIES			
Short-term borrowings, net	**(9.7)**	210.1	(117.2)
Long-term borrowings	**325.4**	82.2	34.6
Long-term debt repayments	**(133.1)**	(9.3)	(1.1)
Exercise of stock options	**28.5**	16.2	26.0
Share repurchase program	–	(200.2)	(469.7)
Sale of stock to Petrie Stores Corporation	–	–	161.6
Net cash provided by/(used in) financing activities	**211.1**	99.0	(365.8)
Effect of exchange rate changes on cash and cash equivalents	**(12.6)**	18.5	(15.5)
CASH AND CASH EQUIVALENTS			
Increase/(decrease) during year	**558.2**	(167.1)	(422.1)
Beginning of year	**202.7**	369.8	791.9
End of year	**$ 760.9**	$ 202.7	$ 369.8

SUPPLEMENTAL DISCLOSURES OF CASH FLOW INFORMATION

The Company considers its highly liquid investments purchased as part of its daily cash management activities to be cash equivalents. During 1996, 1995 and 1994, the Company made income tax payments of $177.2, $234.5 and $318.9 and interest payments (net of amounts capitalized) of $108.6, $118.4 and $123.6, respectively.

See notes to consolidated financial statements.

16

CONSOLIDATED STATEMENTS OF STOCKHOLDERS' EQUITY

TOYS"R"US, INC. AND SUBSIDIARIES

| (In millions) | Common Stock | | | | Additional paid-in capital | Retained earnings | Foreign currency translation adjustments |
| | Issued | | In Treasury | | | | |
	Shares	Amount	Shares	Amount			
Balance, January 29, 1994	297.9	$ 29.8	(8.4)	$ (292.4)	$ 454.0	$ 3,012.8	$ (56.0)
Net earnings for the year	–	–	–	–	–	531.8	–
Share repurchase program	–	–	(13.1)	(469.7)	–	–	–
Exercise of stock options, net of tax benefit	0.1	–	1.1	41.9	(15.8)	–	–
Exchange with and sale of stock to Petrie Stores Corporation	–	–	2.2	78.5	83.1	–	–
Foreign currency translation adjustments	–	–	–	–	–	–	30.9
Balance, January 28, 1995	298.0	29.8	(18.2)	(641.7)	521.3	3,544.6	(25.1)
Net earnings for the year	–	–	–	–	–	148.1	–
Share repurchase program	–	–	(7.6)	(200.2)	–	–	–
Exercise of stock options, net of tax benefit	–	–	.9	34.2	(16.7)	–	–
Corporate inversion	2.4	0.2	(2.4)	(38.4)	38.2	–	–
Foreign currency translation adjustments	–	–	–	–	–	–	38.0
Balance, February 3, 1996	300.4	30.0	(27.3)	(846.1)	542.8	3,692.7	12.9
Net earnings for the year	–	–	–	–	–	427.4	–
Acquisition of Baby Superstore, Inc.	–	–	13.0	400.2	(24.2)	–	–
Exercise of stock options, net of tax benefit	–	–	1.7	58.2	(29.8)	–	–
Foreign currency translation adjustments	–	–	–	–	–	–	(73.5)
Balance, February 1, 1997	**300.4**	**$ 30.0**	**(12.6)**	**$ (387.7)**	**$ 488.8**	**$ 4,120.1**	**$(60.6)**

See notes to consolidated financial statements.

NOTES TO CONSOLIDATED FINANCIAL STATEMENTS

(Amounts in millions except per share data)

SUMMARY OF SIGNIFICANT ACCOUNTING POLICIES

Fiscal Year

The Company's fiscal year ends on the Saturday nearest to January 31. Reference to 1996, 1995 and 1994 are for the 52 weeks ended February 1, 1997, 53 weeks ended February 3, 1996 and the 52 weeks ended January 28, 1995, respectively.

Principles of Consolidation

The consolidated financial statements include the accounts of the Company and its subsidiaries. The consolidated balance sheet and statement of cash flows also reflect the acquisition of Baby Superstore, Inc. at February 1, 1997. All material intercompany balances and transactions have been eliminated. Assets and liabilities of foreign operations are translated at current rates of exchange at the balance sheet date while results of operations are translated at average rates in effect for the period. Translation gains or losses are shown as a separate component of stockholders' equity.

Merchandise Inventories

Merchandise inventories for the U.S.A. toy store operations, which represent over 60% of total inventories, are stated at the lower of LIFO (last-in, first-out) cost or market, as determined by the retail inventory method. If inventories had been valued at the lower of FIFO (first-in, first-out) cost or market, inventories would show no change at February 1, 1997 or February 3, 1996. All other merchandise inventories are stated at the lower of FIFO cost or market as determined by the retail inventory method.

Property and Equipment

Property and equipment are recorded at cost. Depreciation and amortization are provided using the straight-line method over the estimated useful lives of the assets or, where applicable, the terms of the respective leases, whichever is shorter.

The Company's policy to recognize impairment losses relating to long-lived assets is based on several factors including, but not limited to, management's plans for future operations, recent operating results and projected cash flows.

Preopening Costs

Preopening costs, which consist primarily of advertising, occupancy and payroll expenses, are amortized over expected sales to the end of the fiscal year in which the store opens.

Capitalized Interest

Interest on borrowed funds is capitalized during construction of property and is amortized by charges to earnings over the depreciable lives of the related assets. Interest of $3.3, $6.1 and $6.9 was capitalized during 1996, 1995 and 1994, respectively.

18

Financial Instruments

The carrying amounts reported in the balance sheets for cash and cash equivalents and short-term borrowings approximate their fair market values.

Forward Foreign Exchange Contracts

The Company enters into forward foreign exchange contracts to eliminate the risk associated with currency movement relating to its short-term intercompany loan program with foreign subsidiaries and inventory purchases denominated in foreign currency. Gains and losses, which offset the movement in the underlying transactions, are recognized as part of such transactions. Gross deferred unrealized gains and losses on the forward contracts were not material at either February 1, 1997 or February 3, 1996. The related receivable, payable and deferred gain or loss are included on a net basis in the balance sheet. The Company had approximately $205.0 of short term outstanding forward contracts at both February 1, 1997 and February 3, 1996 maturing in 1997 and 1996, respectively, which are entered into with counterparties that have high credit ratings and with which the Company has the contractual right to net forward currency settlements. In addition, the Company had a $325.4 currency swap obligation outstanding at February 1, 1997 related to its £200 note payable due 2001.

Use of Estimates

The preparation of financial statements in conformity with generally accepted accounting principles requires management to make estimates and assumptions that affect the amounts reported in the consolidated financial statements and accompanying notes. Actual results could differ from those estimates.

ACQUISITION

On February 3, 1997, the Company acquired all of the outstanding common shares of Baby Superstore, Inc. ("Baby Superstore") for 13 million shares of its treasury stock valued at approximately $376.0. Each Baby Superstore shareholder received .8121 of a share of Company stock for each Baby Superstore share, except for the Chairman and Chief Executive Officer of Baby Superstore who received .5150 of a share.

Baby Superstore, a leading retailer of baby and young children's products, opened its first store in 1971 and has operated as a public company since November, 1994. Baby Superstore operated 76 stores in 23 states, primarily in the southeast and midwest. Products sold by Baby Superstore were directed toward newborns and children up to three years old. The Company plans to operate substantially all the acquired stores.

This acquisition has been accounted for as a purchase at February 1, 1997. The excess of purchase price over net assets acquired of $365.0 has been recorded as goodwill and will be amortized on a straight-line basis over 40 years.

Consolidated pro forma income and earnings per share, as if the acquisition had taken place as of the beginning of 1995, would not have been materially different from the reported amounts for 1996 and 1995.

OTHER CHARGES

On July 12, 1996, an arbitrator rendered an award against the Company in connection with a dispute involving rights under a 1982 license agreement for toy store operations in the Middle East. Accordingly, the Company has recorded a provision of $59.5, ($37.8 after tax or $.14 cents per share) representing all costs in connection with this matter. The Company has filed an appeal with the United States Court of Appeals for the second circuit.

On February 1, 1996, the Company recorded charges of $396.6 ($269.1 after tax or $.98 cents per share) to restructure its worldwide operations (the "restructuring") and to early adopt Financial Accounting Standards Board ("FAS No. 121"), "Accounting for the Impairment of Long-Lived Assets and Long-Lived Assets to be Disposed Of." The restructuring charge included $184.0 related to strategic inventory repositioning, $84.4 related to the closing or franchising of 25 stores, $71.6 for the consolidation of three distribution centers and seven administrative facilities and $32.4 of other costs. Total restructuring and other charges were comprised of $208.8 relating to operations in the United States and $187.8 for international operations. The charge to early adopt FAS No.121 was $24.2, primarily related to a write down of certain store assets to fair value, based on discounted cash flows. At February 1, 1997, the Company had approximately $90 million of liabilities remaining for its restructuring program primarily relating to long-term lease obligations and other commitments. The Company believes these reserves are adequate to complete the restructuring program.

PROPERTY AND EQUIPMENT

	Useful Life (in years)	February 1, 1997	February 3, 1996
Land		$ 821.2	$ 802.4
Buildings	45-50	1,834.3	1,745.3
Furniture and equipment	5-20	1,521.9	1,351.9
Leaseholds and leasehold improvements	121\2-50	1,060.1	959.0
Construction in progress		37.1	45.6
Leased property under capital leases		30.6	25.1
		5,305.2	4,929.3
Less accumulated depreciation and amortization		1,257.8	1,071.1
		$ 4,047.4	$ 3,858.2

SEASONAL FINANCING AND LONG-TERM DEBT

	February 1, 1997	February 3, 1996
5.61% £200 note payable, due 2001(a)	$ 325.4	$ -
8 3\4% debentures, due 2021, net of expenses	198.2	198.1
Japanese yen loans payable at annual interest rates from 3.45% to 6.47%, due in varying amounts through 2012	150.2	178.3
4 7\8 % convertible subordinated notes payable, due October 2000(b)	115.0	-
8 1\4% sinking fund debentures, due 2017, net of discounts	88.4	88.3
Industrial revenue bonds, net of expenses (c)	70.0	74.2
7% British pound sterling loan payable, due quarterly through 2001(d)	67.1	77.3
Mortgage notes payable at annual interest rates from 6% to 11% (e)	12.2	19.2
Obligations under capital leases	17.1	12.8
11% British pound sterling Stepped Coupon Guaranteed Bonds	-	198.4
	1,043.6	846.6
Less current portion (f)	135.1	19.8
	$ 908.5	$ 826.8

(a) Supported by a £200 bank letter of credit. This note has been converted by an interest rate and currency swap to a floating rate, US dollar obligation at 3 month LIBOR less approximately 110 basis points.

(b) Obligation of Baby Superstore. Convertible into shares of the Company's common stock at the conversion price of $66.34. These notes are subject to an offer to purchase at par, plus accrued interest, which will close on April 16, 1997. Accordingly, these notes have been classified as current obligations.

(c) Bank letters of credit of $52.7, expiring in 1998, support certain of these industrial revenue bonds. The Company expects that the bank letters of credit will be renewed. The bonds have fixed or variable interest rates with an average rate of 3.4% at February 1, 1997.

(d) Collateralized by property with a carrying value of $159.5 at February 1, 1997.

(e) Collateralized by property and equipment with an aggregate carrying value of $18.2 at February 1, 1997.

(f) Included in accrued expenses and other current liabilities on the consolidated balance sheets.

The fair market value of the Company's long-term debt at February 1, 1997 was approximately $1,007.0. The fair market value was estimated using quoted market rates for publicly traded debt and estimated interest rates for non-public debt.

The Company has a $1 billion unsecured committed revolving credit facility expiring in February 2000. This multi-currency facility permits the Company to borrow at the lower of LIBOR plus a fixed spread or a rate set by competitive auction. The facility is available to support domestic commercial paper borrowings and to meet worldwide cash requirements.

Additionally, the Company also has lines of credit with various banks to meet the short-term financing needs of its foreign subsidiaries. The weighted average interest rate on short-term borrowings outstanding at February 1, 1997 and February 3, 1996 was 3.1% and 4.0%, respectively.

19

The annual maturities of long-term debt at February 1, 1997 are as follows:

1997	$ 135.1
1998	25.7
1999	26.4
2000	26.0
2001	334.0
2002 and subsequent	496.4
	$ 1,043.6

LEASES

The Company leases a portion of the real estate used in its operations. Most leases require the Company to pay real estate taxes and other expenses; some require additional amounts based on percentages of sales.

Minimum rental commitments under noncancelable operating leases having a term of more than one year as of February 1, 1997 are as follows:

	Gross minimum rentals	Sublease income	Net minimum rentals
1997	$ 331.8	$ 17.4	$ 314.4
1998	328.3	16.9	311.4
1999	326.3	15.6	310.7
2000	322.1	12.9	309.2
2001	317.5	11.8	305.7
2002 and subsequent	3,303.3	65.2	3,238.1
	$ 4,929.3	$ 139.8	$ 4,789.5

Total rental expense was as follows:

			Year ended
	February 1, 1997	February 3, 1996	January 28, 1995
Minimum rentals	$ 295.3	$ 284.3	$ 226.4
Additional amounts computed as percentages of sales	5.5	5.6	6.3
	300.8	289.9	232.7
Less sublease income	18.8	17.0	10.3
	$ 282.0	$ 272.9	$ 222.4

STOCKHOLDERS' EQUITY

The common shares of the Company, par value $.10 per share, were as follows:

	February 1, 1997	February 3, 1996
Authorized shares	650.0	650.0
Issued shares	300.4	300.4
Treasury shares	12.6	27.3
Issued and outstanding shares	287.8	273.1

Earnings per share is computed by dividing net earnings by the weighted average number of common shares outstanding after reduction for treasury shares and assuming exercise of dilutive stock options computed by the treasury stock method using the average market price during the year. Weighted average number of common and common equivalent shares used in computing earnings per share were 277.5, 276.9 and 287.4 at February 1, 1997, February 3, 1996 and January 28, 1995, respectively.

Effective January 1, 1996, the Company formed a new parent company (the "Surviving Company") thus making the former parent company (the "Predecessor Company") a wholly-owned subsidiary of the Surviving Company. As a result of this corporate inversion, each share of common stock of the Predecessor Company was converted into one share of common stock of the Surviving Company.

In April 1994, the Company entered into an agreement with Petrie Stores Corporation ("Petrie"), the then holder of 14% of the Company's outstanding Common Stock. The Company consummated its transaction with Petrie on January 24, 1995, wherein 42.1 shares of the Company's common stock were issued from its treasury in exchange for 39.9 shares of the Company's common stock and $165.0 in cash.

TAXES ON INCOME

The provisions for income taxes consist of the following:

			Year ended
	February 1, 1997	February 3, 1996	January 28, 1995
Current:			
Federal	$ 135.9	$ 137.1	$ 251.6
Foreign	56.8	26.7	29.2
State	29.6	20.4	46.0
	222.3	184.2	326.8
Deferred:			
Federal	58.6	(21.8)	8.9
Foreign	(39.2)	(41.6)	(24.7)
State	4.0	(3.3)	1.3
	23.4	(66.7)	(14.5)
Total tax provision	$ 245.7	$ 117.5	$ 312.3

The tax effects of temporary differences and carryforwards that give rise to significant portions of deferred tax assets and liabilities consist of the following:

			Year ended
	February 1, 1997	February 3, 1996	January 28, 1995
Deferred tax assets:			
Net operating loss carryforwards	$154.8	$108.9	$ 94.0
Restructuring	53.1	122.1	0.0
Other	31.5	21.4	35.9
Gross deferred tax assets	239.4	252.4	129.9
Valuation allowance	(36.8)	(29.5)	(17.9)
	$202.6	$222.9	$112.0
Deferred tax liabilities:			
Property, plant and equipment	249.3	245.0	217.0
LIFO inventory	63.7	64.3	49.9
Other tax	3.8	4.4	4.0
Gross deferred liability	$316.8	$313.7	$270.9
Net deferred tax liability	$114.2	$ 90.8	$158.9

A reconciliation of the federal statutory tax rate with the effective tax rate follows:

	February 1, 1997	February 3, 1996	Year ended January 28, 1995
Statutory tax rate	**35.0%**	35.0%	35.0%
State income taxes, net of federal income tax benefit	**3.7**	3.4	3.7
Foreign	**(2.3)**	(1.3)	(0.4)
Restructuring and other charges	**–**	7.2	–
Other, net	**0.1**	(0.1)	(1.3)
Effective tax rate	**36.5%**	44.2%	37.0%

Deferred income taxes are not provided on unremitted earnings of foreign subsidiaries that are intended to be indefinitely invested. Unremitted earnings were approximately $361.0 at February 1, 1997, exclusive of amounts that if remitted would result in little or no tax under current U.S. tax laws. Net income taxes of approximately $114.0 would be due if these earnings were to be remitted.

PROFIT SHARING PLAN

The Company has a profit sharing plan with a 401(k) salary deferral feature for eligible domestic employees. The terms of the plan call for annual contributions by the Company as determined by the Board of Directors, subject to certain limitations. The profit sharing plan may be terminated at the Company's discretion. Provisions of $30.8, $32.3 and $31.4 have been charged to earnings in 1996, 1995, and 1994, respectively.

STOCK OPTIONS

The Company has Stock Option Plans (the "Plans") which provide for the granting of options to purchase the Company's common stock to substantially all employees and non-employee directors of the Company. The Plans provide for the issuance of non-qualified options, incentive stock options, performance share options, performance units, stock appreciation rights, restricted shares and unrestricted shares. The Plans provide for a variety of vesting dates with the majority of the options vesting approximately five years from the date of grant. The options granted to non-employee directors are exercisable 20% each year on a cumulative basis commencing one year from the date of grant.

In addition to the aforementioned plans, 3.4 stock options were granted to certain senior executives during the period from 1988 to 1996 pursuant to stockholder approved individual plans. Of this total, 2.9 options vest 20% each year on a cumulative basis commencing one year from the date of grant with the balance of the options vesting five years from the date of grant. The exercise price per share of all options granted has been the average of the high and low market price of the Company's common stock on the date of grant. Most options must be exercised within ten years from the date of grant.

At February 1, 1997, an aggregate of 36.2 shares of authorized common stock were reserved for all of the Plans noted above, of which 13.0 were available for future grants. All outstanding options expire at dates ranging from May 1997 to January 2007.

21

Stock option transactions are summarized as follows:

	Incentive	Non-Qualified	Weighted-Average Exercise Price
		Shares Under Option	
Outstanding February 3, 1996	.2	20.2	$ 24.08
Granted *	.4	6.3	34.59
Exercised	(.2)	(2.1)	17.67
Canceled	-	(1.6)	25.20
Outstanding February 1, 1997	.4	22.8	$25.82
Options exercisable at February 1, 1997	-	9.2	$24.15

*Includes options assumed with the acquisition of Baby Superstore.

The Company utilizes a restoration feature to encourage the early exercise of options and retention of shares, thereby promoting increased employee share ownership. This feature provides for the grant of new options when previously owned shares of Company stock are used to exercise existing options. Restoration option grants are non-dilutive as they do not increase the combined number of shares of Company stock and options held by an employee prior to exercise. The new options are granted at a price equal to the fair market value on the date of the new grant, become exercisable six months from the date of grant and generally expire on the same date as the original options that were exercised.

The Company has adopted the disclosure only provisions of Statement of Financial Accounting Standards (FAS) No. 123, "Accounting for Stock-Based Compensation", issued in October 1995. In accordance with the provisions of FAS No. 123, the Company applies APB Opinion 25 and related interpretations in accounting for its stock option plans and, accordingly, does not recognize compensation cost. If the Company had elected to recognize compensation cost based on the fair value of the options granted at grant date as prescribed by FAS No. 123, net income and earnings per share would have been reduced to the pro forma amounts indicated in the table below:

	1996	1995
Net income—as reported	$ 427.4	$ 148.1
Net income—pro forma	411.3	139.5
Earning per share—as reported	1.54	.53
Earnings per share—pro forma	1.48	.50

The weighted-average fair value at date of grant for options granted in 1996 and 1995 were $24.58 and $31.49, respectively. The fair value of each option grant is estimated on the date of grant using the Black-Scholes option pricing model. As there were a number of options granted throughout the 1995 and 1996 years, a range of assumptions are provided below:

Expected stock price volatility	.241 - .328
Risk-free interest rate	5.0% - 7.1%
Weighted average expected life of options	6 years

The effects of applying FAS 123 and the results obtained through the use of the Black-Scholes option pricing model are not necessarily indicative of future values.

FOREIGN OPERATIONS

Certain information relating to the Company's foreign operations is set forth below. Corporate assets include all cash and cash equivalents and other related assets.

	February 1, 1997	February 3, 1996	January 28, 1995
			Year ended
Sales			
Domestic	$ 7,151.2	$ 6,791.5	$ 6,644.8
Foreign	2,781.2	2,635.4	2,100.8
Total	$ 9,932.4	$ 9,426.9	$ 8,745.6
Operating Profit			
Domestic	$ 692.2	$ 432.8 [b]	$ 778.7
Foreign	131.3	(74.2)[c]	140.8
General corporate expenses	(69.2)[a]	(7.1)	(7.5)
Interest expense, net	(81.2)	(85.9)	(67.9)
Earnings before taxes on income	$ 673.1	$ 265.6	$ 844.1
Identifiable Assets			
Domestic	$ 4,877.9	$ 4,013.2	$ 3,950.5
Foreign	2,345.6	2,483.0	2,216.1
Corporate	799.7	241.3	404.6
Total	$ 8,023.2	$ 6,737.5	$ 6,571.2

(a) After an arbitration award charge of $59.5.
(b) After restructuring and other charges of $208.8.
(c) After restructuring and other charges of $187.8.

OTHER MATTERS

On May 22, 1996, the Staff of the Federal Trade Commission (the "FTC") filed an administrative complaint against the Company alleging that the Company is in violation of Section 5 of the Federal Trade Commission Act for its practices relating to warehouse clubs. The complaint alleges that the Company reached understandings with various suppliers that such suppliers not sell to the clubs the same items that they sell to the Company. The complaint also alleges that the Company "facilitated understandings" among the manufacturers that such manufacturers not sell to clubs. The complaint seeks an order that the Company cease and desist from this practice. Hearings on this complaint commenced on March 5, 1997.

Since the filing of the FTC complaint, several class action suits have been filed against the Company, alleging that the Company has violated certain state competition laws as a consequence of the behavior alleged in the FTC complaint. These class action suits seek damages in unspecified amounts and other relief under state law.

The Company believes that both its policy and its conduct in connection with the foregoing are within the law and plans to contest these actions vigorously. The Company also believes that these actions will not have a material adverse effect on its financial condition or results of operations.

22

REPORT OF MANAGEMENT

Responsibility for the integrity and objectivity of the financial information presented in this Annual Report rests with the management of Toys"R"Us. The accompanying financial statements have been prepared from accounting records which management believes fairly and accurately reflect the operations and financial position of the Company. Management has established a system of internal controls to provide reasonable assurance that assets are maintained and accounted for, in accordance with its policies and that transactions are recorded accurately on the Company's books and records.

The Company's comprehensive internal audit program provides for constant evaluation of the adequacy of the adherence to management's established policies and procedures. The Company has distributed to key employees its policies for conducting business affairs in a lawful and ethical manner.

The Audit Committee of the Board of Directors, which is comprised solely of outside directors, provides oversight to the financial reporting process through periodic meetings with our independent auditors, internal auditors and management.

The financial statements of the Company have been audited by Ernst & Young LLP, independent auditors, in accordance with generally accepted auditing standards, including a review of financial reporting matters and internal controls to the extent necessary to express an opinion on the consolidated financial statements.

Michael Goldstein
Vice Chairman and
Chief Executive Officer

Louis Lipschitz
Executive Vice President
and Chief Financial Officer

REPORT OF INDEPENDENT AUDITORS

The Board of Directors and Stockholders
Toys"R"Us, Inc.

We have audited the accompanying consolidated balance sheets of Toys"R"Us, Inc. and subsidiaries as of February 1, 1997 and February 3, 1996, and the related consolidated statements of earnings, stockholders' equity and cash flows for each of the three years in the period ended February 1, 1997. These financial statements are the responsibility of the Company's management. Our responsibility is to express an opinion on these financial statements based on our audits.

We conducted our audits in accordance with generally accepted auditing standards. Those standards require that we plan and perform the audit to obtain reasonable assurance about whether the financial statements are free of material misstatement. An audit includes examining, on a test basis, evidence supporting the amounts and disclosures in the financial statements. An audit also includes assessing the accounting principles used and significant estimates made by management, as well as evaluating the overall financial statement presentation. We believe that our audits provide a reasonable basis for our opinion.

In our opinion, the financial statements referred to above present fairly, in all material respects, the consolidated financial position of Toys"R"Us, Inc. and subsidiaries at February 1, 1997 and February 3, 1996, and the consolidated results of their operations and their cash flows for each of the three years in the period ended February 1, 1997, in conformity with generally accepted accounting principles.

Ernst & Young LLP

New York, New York
March 12, 1997

23

DIRECTORS AND OFFICERS

DIRECTORS

Charles Lazarus
Chairman of the Board of the Company

Robert A. Bernhard
Real Estate Developer

RoAnn Costin
President, Reservoir Capital
Management, Inc.

Michael Goldstein
Vice Chairman and
Chief Executive Officer of the Company

Milton S. Gould
Attorney-at-law; Of Counsel to
LeBoeuf, Lamb, Greene & MacRae

Shirley Strum Kenny
President, State University of
New York at Stony Brook

Norman S. Matthews
Former President, Federated Department
Stores, Inc; Consultant

Howard W. Moore
Former Executive Vice President -
General Merchandise Manager
of the Company; Consultant

Robert C. Nakasone
President and Chief Operating
Officer of the Company

Harold M. Wit
Managing Director, Allen & Company
Incorporated

OFFICERS - CORPORATE AND ADMINISTRATIVE

Michael Goldstein
Vice Chairman and
Chief Executive Officer

Robert C. Nakasone
President and
Chief Operating Officer

Louis Lipschitz
Executive Vice President
and Chief Financial Officer

Roger C. Gaston
Senior Vice President -
Human Resources

Michael P. Miller
Senior Vice President -
Real Estate

Thomas J. Reinebach
Senior Vice President and
Chief Information Officer

Gayle C. Aertker
Vice President -
Real Estate

Michael J. Corrigan
Vice President -
Compensation and Benefits

Eileen C. Gabriel
Vice President -
Information Systems

Jon W. Kimmins
Vice President -
Treasurer

Joseph J. Lombardi
Vice President -
Controller

Matthew J. Lombardi
Vice President -
Information Technology

Michael L. Tumolo
Vice President -
Counsel

Peter W. Weiss
Vice President -
Taxes

Robert S. Zarra
Vice President -
Internal Audit

Andre Weiss
Secretary -
Partner-Schulte Roth & Zabel, LLP

TOYS"R"US UNITED STATES - OFFICERS AND GENERAL MANAGERS

Michael J. Madden
President -
Store Operations

Robert J. Weinberg
Senior Vice President -
General Merchandise Manager

Van H. Butler
Senior Vice President -
Divisional Merchandise Manager

Ernest V. Speranza
Senior Vice President -
Advertising/Marketing

David Brewi
Vice President -
Divisional Merchandise Manager

Kristopher M. Brown
Vice President -
Distribution and Traffic

Richard N. Cudrin
Vice President -
Human Resources
and Corporate Employee Relations

John F. Cummo
Vice President -
Creative Services

Thomas DeLuca
Vice President - Imports, Product
Development and Safety Assurance

Harvey J. Finkel
Vice President -
Regional Operations

Martin E. Fogelman
Vice President -
Divisional Merchandise Manager

Michael A. Gerety
Vice President -
Store Planning

Debra M. Kachurak
Vice President -
Operations Development

Mitchell Loukota
Vice President -
Divisional Merchandise Manager

Charlene Mady
Vice President -
Area Merchandise Planning

Gerald S. Parker
Vice President -
Regional Operations

Lee Richardson
Vice President -
Advertising

Timothy J. Slade
Vice President -
Transportation and Traffic

John P. Sullivan
Vice President -
Divisional Merchandise Manager

William A. Stephenson
Vice President -
Merchandise Planning and Allocation

Dennis J. Williams
Vice President-
Regional Operations and
General Manager
New York/Northern New Jersey

GENERAL MANAGERS

Robert F. Price
Vice President-
Southern California/
Arizona/Nevada/Hawaii

Thomas A. Drugan
Illinois/Wisconsin/Minnesota

Cathy Filion
Michigan/N.W. Ohio

Mark H. Haag
Pacific Northwest/Alaska

Truvillus Hall
Northern California/Utah

Michael K. Heffner
Alabama/Georgia/South
Carolina/Tennessee

Daniel D. Hlavaty
Central Ohio/Indiana/Kentucky

Richard A. Moyer
S.Texas/Louisiana/Mississippi

John J. Prawlocki
Florida/Puerto Rico

Edward F. Siegler
Maryland/Virginia/North Carolina

Carl P. Spaulding
New England

Gregg Treadway
Colorado/Kansas/Missouri/
Iowa/Nebraska

Kevin VanderGriend
N.E. Ohio/W. Pennsylvania/
N. New York

TOYS"R"US INTERNATIONAL - OFFICERS AND COUNTRY MANAGEMENT

Gregory R. Staley
President

Lawrence H. Meyer
Vice President -
Chief Financial Officer

Joan W. Donovan
Vice President -
General Merchandise Manager

Joseph Giamelli
Vice President -
Information Systems

Jeff Handler
Vice President -
International Advertising

Larry S. Johnson
Vice President -
Franchise Markets

Adam F. Szopinski
Vice President -
Operations

Michael C. Taylor
Vice President -
Logistics

Pierre Buuron
President -
Toys"R"Us Central Europe

Jacques LeFoll
President -
Toys"R"Us France/Belgium

David Rurka
Managing Director -
Toys"R"Us United Kingdom

John Schryver
Managing Director -
Toys"R"Us Australia

Manabu Tazaki
President -
Toys"R"Us Japan

Antonio Urcelay
Managing Director -
Toys"R"Us Iberia

Keith Van Beek
President-
Toys"R"Us Canada

Larry D. Gardner
Vice President -
Toys"R"Us Asia

Scott Chen
General Manager -
Toys"R"Us Taiwan

Joe Tang
General Manager -
Toys"R"Us Hong Kong

Michael Yeo
General Manager -
Toys"R"Us Singapore

KIDS"R"US/BABIES"R"US - OFFICERS*

Richard L. Markee
President -
Kids"R"Us and Babies"R"Us

Gwen Manto
Senior Vice President -
General Merchandise Manager

James G. Parros
Senior Vice President -
Stores and
Distribution Center Operations

Jonathan M. Friedman
Vice President -
Chief Financial Officer -
Kids"R"Us and Babies"R"Us

James L. Easton
Vice President -
Divisional Merchandise Manager

William Farrell
Vice President -
Physical Distribution

Jerel G. Hollens
Vice President -
Merchandise Planning and
Management Information Systems

Debra G. Hyman
Vice President -
Divisional Merchandise Manager

Elizabeth S. Jordan
Vice President -
Human Resources

John C. Morrow
Vice President -
Management Information Systems

Christopher M. Scherm
Vice President -
Divisional Merchandise Manager

David E. Schoenbeck
Vice President -
Operations - Babies "R" Us

David S. Walker
Vice President-
Advertising

*Kids"R"Us Officer, unless
otherwise indicated.

QUARTERLY FINANCIAL DATA AND MARKET INFORMATION

QUARTERLY FINANCIAL DATA

(In millions except per share data)

The following table sets forth certain unaudited quarterly financial information.

Year Ended	First Quarter	Second Quarter	Third Quarter	Fourth Quarter*
February 1, 1997				
Net Sales	$ 1,645.5	$ 1,736.4	$ 1,883.0	$ 4,667.5
Cost of Sales	1,124.4	1,177.3	1,280.4	3,310.4
Other Charges	–	55.0	–	4.5
Net Earnings (Loss)	18.7	(7.5)	33.3	382.9
Earnings (Loss) per Share	$ .07	$ (.03)	$ .12	$ 1.37
February 3, 1996				
Net Sales	$ 1,493.0	$ 1,614.2	$ 1,714.5	$ 4,605.2
Cost of Sales	1,017.3	1,104.5	1,168.5	3,302.0
Other Charges	–	–	–	396.6
Net Earnings	18.4	15.8	20.9	93.0
Earnings per Share	$ .07	$ .06	$ .08	$ .34

*For the 13 weeks ended February 1, 1997 and the 14 weeks ended February 3, 1996

MARKET INFORMATION

The Company's common stock is listed on the New York Stock Exchange. The following table reflects the high and low prices (rounded to the nearest one-eighth) based on New York Stock Exchange trading since January 28, 1995.

The Company has not paid any cash dividends, however, the Board of Directors of the Company reviews this policy annually.

The Company had approximately 32,300 Stockholders of Record on March 11, 1997.

			High	Low
1995	1st	Quarter	30 7\8	23 3\4
	2nd	Quarter	29 1\2	24 1\4
	3rd	Quarter	28 3\4	21 5\8
	4th	Quarter	24 3\8	20 1\2
1996	1st	Quarter	29 7\8	21 7\8
	2nd	Quarter	30 7\8	23 3\4
	3rd	Quarter	34 1\16	25 7\8
	4th	Quarter	37 5\8	24 3\8

26

C ORPORATE DATA

Annual Meeting
The Annual Meeting of the Stockholders of Toys"R"Us
will be held at the Somerset Hills Hotel, 200 Liberty Corner Road,
at exit 33 off I-78, Warren, NJ 07059
on Wednesday, June 4, 1997 10:00 A.M.

The office of the Company is located at
461 From Road
Paramus, New Jersey 07652
Telephone: 201-262-7800

General Counsel
Schulte Roth & Zabel, LLP
900 Third Avenue
New York, New York 10022

Independent Auditors
Ernst & Young, LLP
787 Seventh Avenue
New York, New York 10019

Stockholder Information
The Company will supply to any owner of Common Stock, upon
written request to Mr. Louis Lipschitz of the Company at the above
address and without charge, a copy of the Annual Report on Form
10-K for the year ended February 1, 1997, which has been filed
with the Securities and Exchange Commission.

Stockholder information including quarterly earnings and other
corporate news releases, can be obtained by calling 800-785-TOYS.
Significant news releases are anticipated to be available as follows:

Call After... For the following...
May 19, 1997	1st Quarter Results
Aug. 18, 1997	2nd Quarter Results
Nov. 17, 1997	3rd Quarter Results
Jan. 8, 1998	Christmas Sales Results
Mar. 11, 1998	1997 Results

Common Stock Listed
New York Stock Exchange,
Symbol: TOY

Registrar and Transfer Agent
American Stock Transfer and Trust Company
40 Wall Street, New York, New York 10005
Telephone: 718-921-8200

Visit us on the Internet at www.toysrus.cc

27

Appendix C
The Formal
Recordkeeping System

For those interested in a deeper understanding of the formal records and processes used in the accounting system, the following discussion describes and illustrates the use of the General Journal and General Ledger during the accounting period, the construction of the worksheet at year-end, and the use of reversing entries at the beginning of the next accounting period.

General Journal

LEARNING OBJECTIVE 1
Utilize a formal General Journal and General Ledger format in preparing journal entries and accumulating account balances.

A journal is the record that lists chronologically the effects of transactions; the book of orginal entry.

After transaction analysis, the economic effects of each transaction are formally entered into the accounting system in a record known as the **journal** (or General Journal). The effects of each transaction are recorded in journal entries in chronological order (i.e., in order of date of occurrence). Typically, the effects of transaction analysis are recorded first in the journal. Thus, the General Journal is referred to as *the book of original entry.* The journal is the only place in the accounting system where the economic effects of each transaction are linked physically and recorded chronologically. In most businesses, the formal records have been computerized. For educational purposes, it is easier to understand the formal records if we illustrate them in a manual system.

You will recall from Chapter 2 that journal entries prepared as analytical tools include a date, the account(s) to be debited on the top, and the account(s) to be credited on the bottom and indented to the right. Formal journal entries also include an explanation of the transaction with sufficient detail for tracing the entry to the source documents (to provide an **audit trail** for future reference) and the account, or reference, number from the company's chart of accounts. Exhibit C.1 illustrates the first two transactions for Terrific Lawn Maintenance Corporation (from the Demonstration Case at the end of Chapters 2, 3, and 4).

An audit trail is the referencing system with sufficiently detailed explanations necessary for tracing an entry back to its source documents.

General Ledger

A ledger contains all of the individual accounts for revenues, expenses, assets, liabilities, and stockholders' equity; the book of final entry.

In Chapters 2 through 4, we illustrated the use of T-accounts as tools to reflect the effects of transactions for each account and to accumulate balances. Collectively, these individual T-accounts resemble pages from the second formal record known as the **ledger,** or General Ledger. The ledger may take on many forms. Handwritten accounting systems may use a loose-leaf ledger with one page for each account. With a

EXHIBIT C.1
Illustration of the Journal

	GENERAL JOURNAL			
			Page	1
Date	Account Titles and Explanation	Posted Ref.	Debit	Credit
4/1/98	Cash	101	9,000	
	Contributed capital	301		9,000
	Issued 1,500 shares of stock to investors (names).			
4/3/98	Equipment	110	600	
	Cash	101		200
	Accounts payable	201		400
	Purchased hand tools (supplier and invoice data			
	indicated), paying part in cash (check number			
	indicated) and part on account.			

computerized accounting system, the ledger is kept on electronic storage devices, but individual accounts are still maintained. Each account is identified by a descriptive name and an assigned number (e.g., Cash, 101; Accounts Payable, 201; and Sales Revenue, 401).

The ledger contains information that initially was recorded in the journal and then transferred to the appropriate accounts in the ledger. The transfer of information from the journal to the ledger is called *posting*. This transfer from the chronological arrangement in the journal to the account format in the ledger is important because the ledger reflects the data classified as assets, liabilities, owners' equity, revenues, and expenses. This reclassification of the data facilitates the subsequent preparation of financial statements.

The economic data concerning transactions end up in the ledger; therefore, it has been called the *book of final entry*. Exhibit C.2 shows a page from the ledger of Terrific Lawn Maintenance Corporation in columnar format. The T-account concept is maintained with a running balance added.

A business of the size of a doctor's office or local retail shop usually records its transactions in the journal each day and posts to the ledger less frequently, perhaps every few days. Of course, the timing of these activities varies with the data processing system used and the complexity of the entity. In many computerized systems, the transactions can be posted instantaneously to the ledger when recorded in the journal. Many affordable computerized accounting software packages are available for small businesses.

To post to the ledger, the debits and credits shown in the journal entries are transferred directly as debits and credits to the appropriate accounts in the ledger. Both the journal and the ledger have a Posted Reference column for cross-reference between these two records. When posting has occurred, the appropriate reference is indicated in each formal record. In the journal, the numbers in the Posted Reference column indicate the ledger account to which the dollar amounts were posted. In the ledger account, the numbers in the Posted Reference column indicate the journal page from which the dollar amounts were posted. Reference numbers are used in the posting phase (1) to indicate that posting has been done and (2) to provide an *audit trail*.

EXHIBIT C.2
Illustration of a Ledger Account in Columnar Format

GENERAL LEDGER					
Account Title _Cash_			Account Number _101_		
Date	Explanation	Posted Ref.	Debit	Credit	Balance
4/1/98	Investments by owners	1	9,000		9,000
4/3/98	Hand tools purchased	1		200	8,800
4/4/98	Land purchased	1		5,000	3,800
4/5/98	Fuel purchased	1		90	3,710
4/6/98	Revenue in advance	2	1,600		5,310
4/10/98	Collection from customers	2	3,500		8,810
4/11/98	Suppliers paid	2		700	8,110
4/14/98	Wages paid	3		1,950	6,160
4/21/98	Suppliers paid	3		3,700	2,460
4/26/98	Purchased insurance	3		300	2,160
4/28/98	Wages paid	4		1,950	210
4/29/98	Collection from city	4	1,250		1,460

Accounting Worksheets

LEARNING OBJECTIVE 2
Construct a year-end worksheet that
includes a trial balance, adjustments,
and amounts for the income statement and balance sheet.

At the end of the accounting period, an accounting worksheet may be prepared; if so, it is prepared before the adjusting and closing entries are recorded. The completed worksheet provides all the data needed to complete the remaining end-of-period steps by bringing together in one place, in an orderly way, (1) the unadjusted trial balance, (2) the amounts for adjusting entries, (3) the income statement, (4) the statement of retained earnings, and (5) the balance sheet. Closing entries also can be prepared from the information provided on the worksheet.

Illustration

A simplified case for High-Rise Apartments, Inc., illustrates the preparation of a worksheet at the end of the accounting period. To make the illustration easier, two exhibits are given:

Exhibit C.3   Worksheet format with the unadjusted trial balance and adjusting entry amounts.

Exhibit C.4   Completed worksheet with the income statement, statement of retained earnings, and balance sheet.

The sequential steps used to develop the worksheet are as follows:

Step 1.   Set up the worksheet format by entering the appropriate column headings. This step is shown in Exhibit C.3. The left column shows the account titles (taken directly from the ledger). There are six separate pairs of Debit-Credit money columns. Notice that the last three pairs of Debit-Credit columns show the data for the financial statements.

Step 2.   Enter the unadjusted trial balance as of the end of the accounting period directly from the ledger into the first pair of Debit-Credit columns. When all the current entries for the period, excluding the adjusting entries, have been recorded in the journal and posted to the ledger, the amounts for the Unadjusted Trial Balance columns are the balances of the respective ledger accounts. Before going to the next step, the equality of the debits and credits should be tested by totaling each column ($491,460). Adding a column is called *footing*. When a worksheet is used, developing a separate unadjusted trial balance is not necessary because it can be developed on the worksheet.

Step 3. The second pair of Debit-Credit columns, headed Adjusting Entries, is completed by developing and then entering the amounts of the adjusting entries directly on the worksheet. The adjustments for High-Rise Apartments shown in Exhibit C.3 were entered for illustration purposes. Review each entry to be sure that you can explain why it was recorded. To facilitate examination (for potential errors), the adjusting entries usually are coded on the worksheet as illustrated in Exhibit C.3. Some of the adjusting entries may need one or more account titles in addition to those of the original trial balance listing (see last five account titles in Exhibit C.3). After the adjusting entries are completed on the worksheet, the equality of debits and credits for those amounts is checked by totaling the two columns ($14,200 each).

The remaining steps to complete the worksheet are shown in the last six columns in Exhibit C.4. These steps are as follows:

Step 4. The pair of Debit-Credit columns headed Adjusted Trial Balance is completed. Although not essential, this pair of columns helps to ensure accuracy. The adjusted trial balance reflects the line-by-line combined amounts of the unadjusted trial balance, plus or minus the amounts entered as adjusting entries in the second pair of columns. For example, the Rent Revenue account shows a $128,463 credit balance under Unadjusted Trial Balance. To this amount is added the credit amount, $600, minus the debit amount, $500, for a combined amount of $128,563, which is entered as a credit under Adjusted Trial Balance. (Adding across such as this is called *cross-footing*.) For those accounts that were not affected by the adjusting entries, the unadjusted trial balance amount is carried directly across to the Adjusted Trial Balance column. After each line has been completed, the equality of the debits and credits under Adjusted Trial Balance is checked (column totals, $503,560).

Step 5. The amount on each line under Adjusted Trial Balance is extended horizontally across the worksheet and entered under the heading for the financial statement on which it must be reported (income statement, retained earnings, or balance sheet). Debit amounts are carried across as debits, and credit amounts are carried across as credits.

You can see that (1) each amount extended across was entered under only one of the six remaining columns and (2) debits remain debits and credits remain credits in the extending process.

Step 6. At this point, the two Income Statement columns are summed (subtotals). The difference between these two subtotals is the pretax income (or loss). Income tax expense then is computed by multiplying this difference by the tax rate. In Exhibit C.4, the computation was (revenues of $128,563 – pretax expenses of $92,263) × tax rate of 20 percent = $7,260. The adjusting entry for income tax then was entered at the

EXHIBIT C.3
Worksheet Format with Unadjusted Trial Balance and Adjusting Entry Amounts Already Entered

HIGH-RISE APARTMENTS, INC.
Worksheet for the Year Ended December 31, 19B

Account Titles	Unadjusted Trial Balance Debit	Unadjusted Trial Balance Credit	Adjusting Entries Debit	Adjusting Entries Credit	Adjusted Trial Balance Debit	Adjusted Trial Balance Credit	Income Statement Debit	Income Statement Credit	Retained Earnings Debit	Retained Earnings Credit	Balance Sheet Debit	Balance Sheet Credit
Cash	12,297											
Prepaid insurance	2,400			(c) 1,200								
Inventory of maintenance supplies	600			(e) 400								
Land	25,000											
Apartment building	360,000											
Accumulated depreciation, building		10,000		(d) 10,000								
Note payable, long-term		30,000										
Mortgage payable, long-term		238,037										
Contributed capital		55,000										
Retained earnings, Jan. 1, 19B		29,960										
Dividends declared and paid	12,000											
Rent revenue		128,463	(a) 500	(b) 600								
Advertising expense	500											
Maintenance expense	3,000		(e) 400									
Salary expense	17,400		(f) 900									
Interest expense	19,563		(g) 600									
Utilities expense	34,500											
Miscellaneous expenses	4,200											
Rent collected in advance				(a) 500								
Insurance expense			(c) 1,200									
Depreciation expense			(d) 10,000									
Salaries payable				(f) 900								
Interest payable				(g) 600								
Rent revenue receivable			(b) 600									
	491,460	491,460	14,200	14,200								

(a) $500 rent collected, not yet earned.
(b) Rent earned, not yet collected, $600.
(c) Used $1,200 of insurance.
(d) Annual depreciation of buildings, $10,000.
(e) Used $400 of maintenance supplies.
(f) Accrued wages, $900.
(g) Accrued $600 interest on note payable.

EXHIBIT C.4
Accounting Worksheet Completed

HIGH-RISE APARTMENTS, INC.
Worksheet for the Year Ended December 31, 19B

Account Titles	Unadjusted Trial Balance Debit	Unadjusted Trial Balance Credit	Adjusting Entries Debit	Adjusting Entries Credit	Adjusted Trial Balance Debit	Adjusted Trial Balance Credit	Income Statement Debit	Income Statement Credit	Retained Earnings Debit	Retained Earnings Credit	Balance Sheet Debit	Balance Sheet Credit
Cash	12,297				12,297						12,297	
Prepaid insurance	2,400			(c) 1,200	1,200						1,200	
Inventory of maintenance supplies	600			(e) 400	200						200	
Land	25,000				25,000						25,000	
Apartment building	360,000				360,000						360,000	
Accumulated depreciation, building		10,000		(d) 10,000		20,000						20,000
Note payable, long-term		30,000				30,000						30,000
Mortgage payable, long-term		238,037				238,037						238,037
Contributed capital		55,000				55,000						55,000
Retained earnings, Jan. 1, 19B		29,960				29,960				29,960		
Dividends declared and paid	12,000				12,000				12,000			
Rent revenue		128,463	(a) 500	(b) 600		128,563		128,563				
Advertising expense	500				500		500					
Maintenance expense	3,000		(e) 400		3,400		3,400					
Salary expense	17,400		(f) 900		18,300		18,300					
Interest expense	19,563		(g) 600		20,163		20,163					
Utilities expense	34,500				34,500		34,500					
Miscellaneous expenses	4,200				4,200		4,200					
Rent collected in advance				(a) 500		500						500
Insurance expense			(c) 1,200		1,200		1,200					
Depreciation expense			(d) 10,000		10,000		10,000					
Salaries payable				(f) 900		900						900
Interest payable				(g) 600		600						600
Rent revenue receivable			(b) 600		600						600	
	491,460	491,460	14,200	14,200	503,560	503,560	92,263	128,563				
Income tax expense			(h) 7,260		7,260		7,260					
Income tax payable				(h) 7,260		7,260						7,260
Net income							29,040			29,040		
							128,563	128,563	12,000	59,000		
									47,000	59,000		47,000
											399,297	399,297

(a) $500 rent collected, not yet earned.
(b) Rent earned, not yet collected, $600.
(c) Used $1,200 of insurance.
(d) Annual depreciation of buildings, $10,000.
(e) Used $400 of maintenance supplies.
(f) Accrued wages, $900.
(g) Accrued $600 interest on note payable.
(h) Income tax ($36,300 pretax income × 20% rate).

bottom of the worksheet. Income tax expense and income taxes payable now can be extended horizontally to the Income Statement and Balance Sheet columns. Net income is entered as a balancing debit amount in the Income Statement column and as a credit in the Retained Earnings column. This represents the entry in the closing process that results in a debit to all revenues and gains, a credit to all expenses and losses, and a credit to Retained Earnings. A net loss appears as a credit in the Income Statement column and as a debit in the Retained Earnings column.

Step 7. The two Retained Earnings columns are summed. The difference is the ending balance of retained earnings. This balance amount is entered as a balancing debit amount under Retained Earnings and as a balancing credit amount under Balance Sheet (i.e., an increase to owners' equity). At this point, the two Balance Sheet columns should sum to equal amounts. The continuous checking of the equality of debits and credits in each pair of Debit-Credit columns helps to ensure the correctness of the worksheet. The balancing feature alone does not ensure, however, that the worksheet has no errors. For example, if an expense amount (a debit) were extended to either the Retained Earnings Debit column or to the Balance Sheet Debit column, the worksheet would balance in all respects; however, at least two columns would have one or more errors. Therefore, special care must be used in selecting the appropriate Debit-Credit columns during the horizontal extension process. Financial statements for High-Rise Apartments can be prepared directly from the completed worksheet in Exhibit C.4.

Reversing Entries

LEARNING OBJECTIVE 3
Explain and prepare reversing entries.
Reversing entries are optional entries made at the start of the next accounting period to reverse the effects of certain adjusting entries; facilitates subsequent entries and simplifies the book-keeping function.

Some accountants add an optional phase to the accounting cycle by making **reversing entries.** Reversing entries are given this name because at the start of the next account-ing period they reverse the effects of certain adjusting entries made at the end of the previous period. They are used for the sole purpose of facilitating certain subsequent entries in the accounts. Due to the rather continuous nature of the operating cycle, cer-tain revenues and expenses are recorded routinely as such. When the end of the accounting period falls between the points for earning or incurring revenues or expenses and the cash receipt or payment dates, assets (such as Prepaid Rent Expense) and liabilities (such as Wages Payable) are created in the adjustment process. If revers-ing entries are not employed on the first day of the next accounting period, the routine entry causes an error in recognizing revenues and expenses properly in the next period. Let's look at an example.

Let's assume that Day Company, which has a fiscal year ending on December 31, records payroll every two weeks using the following entry:

Wages expense (E)	8,400	
Cash (A)		8,400

If the last payday was December 22, an adjustment is necessary to record an additional nine days of wages expense in the current period, although payment will be made in the following period.

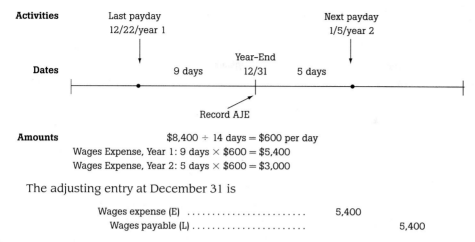

Activities	Last payday 12/22/year 1		Next payday 1/5/year 2

| Dates | 9 days | Year-End 12/31 | 5 days |

Record AJE

Amounts	$8,400 \div 14$ days $= 600 per day
	Wages Expense, Year 1: 9 days $\times$ $600 = $5,400$
	Wages Expense, Year 2: 5 days $\times$ $600 = $3,000$

The adjusting entry at December 31 is

Wages expense (E)	5,400	
Wages payable (L)		5,400

The adjusting entry is posted to the appropriate T-accounts. Then the records are closed for Year 1, resulting in the following balances (the unadjusted balance in wages expense is assumed to be $200,000):

Wages Expense (E)				Wages Payable (L)		
Unadj. bal.	200,000			Unadj. bal.		0
AJE	5,400			AJE		5,400
		CE	205,400			
Closed bal.	0			End. bal.		5,400

If no reversing entry is made at the beginning of the accounting period, on January 5 the payroll system records a routine journal entry for $8,400 as wages expense in Year 2 (credit to Cash). Only $3,000 was incurred by the company in Year 2, however. In addition, the Wages Payable account is not reduced, even though it was paid off on January 5. Both the expense and the liability are overstated in Year 2:

IN ERROR

Wages Expense (E)				Wages Payable (L)		
Year 1				Year 1		
Unadj. bal.	200,000			Unadj. bal.		0
AJE	5,400			AJE		5,400
		CE	205,400			
Closed bal.	0			End. bal.		5,400
Year 2				Year 2		
January 5	8,400					
End. bal.	8,400			End. bal.		5,400

If a reversing entry (RE) is made on January 1, the balances after the reversing entry reflect no liability and a negative amount in Wages Expense. Then, when the January payroll entry is made, the correct balance in Wages Expense for Year 2 results:

CORRECT

Wages Expense (E)				Wages Payable (L)		
Year 1				Year 1		
Unadj. bal.	200,000			Unadj. bal.		0
AJE	5,400			AJE		5,400
		CE	205,400			
Closed bal.	0			End. bal.		5,400
Year 2				Year 2		
		RE	5,400	RE	5,400	
January 5	8,400					
End. bal.	3,000			End. bal.		0

The reversing entry made on January 1 in this example follows:

Wages payable (L)	5,400	
Wages expense (E)		5,400

If reversing entries are not used, the only way to avoid the error is to monitor and manually record payroll on January 5 as follows:

Wages payable (L)	5,400	
Wages expense (E)	3,000	
Cash (A)		8,400

Therefore, either reversing entries are used or numerous transactions must be monitored throughout the next accounting period to make manual entries to avoid any overstatement errors. Most companies use the reversing-entry option whether the system is manual or computerized.

Not all adjusting entries should be reversed, however. The following can be reversed:

- All adjusting entries related to accruals.
- Only adjusting entries for deferrals that created (or increased) an asset or liability account as part of the adjusting process.

To illustrate reversing entries, let's assume the following December 31 year-end adjustments for an orthodontist's office:

(a) Earned $1,200 interest on investments that will be received next month. This is an accrual at year-end.

(b) Estimated $430 in utility usage for the current month, which will be paid next month. This is an accrual at year-end.

(c) Depreciated office equipment costing $130,000 with an estimated residual value of $20,000 and an estimated useful life of 10 years. This is a deferral, which was originally recorded in an asset account. Depreciation expense is $11,000 for the year [($130,000 cost − $20,000 residual value) ÷ 10 years].

(d) Paid $30,000 in insurance on August 1 for one year of coverage. The account Insurance Expense was debited on August 1. This is a deferral. By December 31, five months of coverage ($30,000 ÷ 12 = $2,500 per month × 5 months = $12,500 insurance expense) has been used. Insurance Expense is overstated by $17,500 ($30,000 − $12,500), and Prepaid Insurance representing seven months of future coverage is understated by the same amount.

(e) Received $24,000 cash on November 1 for annual rent from businesses leasing other floors of the office building. The Rent Revenue account was credited on November 1. This is a deferral. By December 31, only two months of rent revenue ($24,000 ÷ 12 months = $2,000 per month × 2 months = $4,000) has been earned. Rent Revenue is overstated by $20,000 ($24,000 − $4,000); Unearned Rent Revenue is understated by the same amount.

(f) Received $870 cash in advance of dental services on December 1. Half of the services were performed by December 31. The liability account Fees Collected in Advance was credited on December 1. This is a deferral. By December 31, $435 (half of $870) is earned and $435 remains a liability to be paid in services in the future. The liability account is overstated and the Fees Revenue account is understated by the same amount.

Adjusting Entry	Is a Reversing Entry Possible?

a. Interest receivable (A) 1,200
    Interest revenue (R) 1,200
	This is an accrual. Accruals can be reversed.
	    Interest revenue (R) 1,200
	        Interest receivable (A) 1,200
	When the cash is received, credit Interest Revenue.

b. Utilities expense (E) 430
    Accrued utilities payable (L) 430
	This is an accrual. Accruals can be reversed.
	    Accrued utilities payable (L) 430
	        Utilities expense (E) 430
	When the cash is paid, debit Utilities Expense.

c. Depreciation expense (E) .... 11,000 Accumulated depreciation (XA) 11,000	This is an adjustment of a deferral. The adjusting entry decreases an asset account. To reverse this would reflect that no depreciation has been recorded on the equipment. Do not reverse the adjusting entry.

d. Prepaid insurance (A) 17,500
    Insurance expense (E) 17,500
	This is an adjustment of a deferral. The adjusting entry created an asset account. To reverse this would reflect $17,500 in insurance expense for the next year and an elimination of the asset account. Since this is the desired effect, a reversing entry can be made.
	    Insurance expense (E) 17,500
	        Prepaid insurance (A) 17,500

e. Rent revenue (R) 20,000
    Unearned rent revenue (L) 20,000
	This is an adjustment of a deferral. The adjusting entry created a liability account. To reverse this would reflect $20,000 in rent revenue for the next year and an elimination of the liability account. Since this is the desired effect, a reversing entry can be made.
	    Unearned rent revenue (L) 20,000
	        Rent revenue (R) 20,000

f. Fees collected in advance (L) .... 435 Fees revenue (R) 435	This is an adjustment of a deferral. The adjusting entry decreases a liability account. To reverse this would reflect that service is due on all the fees collected in advance. Do not reverse the adjusting entry.

As indicated, the first two adjusting entries are accruals. They can be reversed since the cash receipt or payment is in the future. The last four adjusting entries adjust deferral accounts. Entries c and f were initially recorded as assets or liabilities. To reverse these would result in an error by increasing the amount of the asset and liability that has already been used up or earned. Entries d and e increased assets or liabilities. A reversal of the adjusting entry in the next period would (1) eliminate the asset or liability account as if it were earned or used up by the end of the next year and (2) reflect the appropriate amount of expense or revenue in the next period. These can be reversed.

Reversing entries allow routine recording of events during the next period so that special adjustments must be made only during the year-end process. Perhaps the most compelling reason for reversing entries is to increase the likelihood that the effects of certain adjusting entries will not be overlooked when recording the next related transaction in the following period.

Key Terms

Audit Trail The referencing system with sufficiently detailed explanations necessary for tracing an entry back to its source documents. *774*

Journal A record that lists chronologically the effects of transactions; the book of original entry. *774*

Ledger Contains all of the individual accounts for revenues, expenses, assets,

liabilities, and stockholders' equity; the book of final entry. *774*

Reversing Entries Optional entries made at the start of the next accounting period to reverse the effects of certain adjusting entries; facilitates subsequent entries and simplifies the bookkeeping function. *780*

Questions

1. What are (a) the book of original entry and (b) the book of final entry?
2. Define *journal*. What is its purpose?
3. Define *ledger*. What is its purpose?
4. What is an audit trail?
5. What is the basic purpose of the worksheet?
6. Why are adjusting entries entered on the worksheet?
7. Why are adjusting entries recorded in the journal and posted to the ledger even though they are entered on the worksheet?
8. What are reversing entries? When are reversing entries useful?
9. Give one example of (a) an adjusting entry that should be reversed and (b) one that should not be reversed.

Exercises

EC-1 Journalizing and Computing Account Balances

On January 1, 19A, Hamilton and Dyson organized Tennis Company, Inc. The completed transactions from January 1, 19A, through February 3, 19A, can be summarized as follows:

Jan.	1	Cash invested by the organizers: Hamilton, $40,000 (for 4,000 shares) and Dyson, $30,000 (for 3,000 shares).
	3	Paid monthly rent, $2,000.
	15	Purchased equipment that cost $28,000 for use in the business; paid $4,000 down and signed a 10% note payable for the balance. Monthly payments made up of part principal and part interest are to be paid on the note.
	30	Paid cash for operating expenses amounting to $25,000; in addition, operating expenses of $6,000 were incurred on credit.
	30	Service fees earned amounted to $60,000, of which $48,000 was collected and the balance was on credit.
Feb.	1	Collected $8,000 on account for services performed in January and originally recorded as an account receivable and service revenue.
	2	Paid $2,000 on the operating expenses incurred in January and originally recorded as an account payable and operating expenses.
	3	Paid the first installment of $750 on the equipment note, including $200 interest expense.

Required:

1. Analyze and journalize each of the preceding transactions in proper general journal format.
2. Create general ledger pages and post each entry to the ledger.
3. Compute the following:
   a. Cash balance at February 3, 19A.
   b. Pretax income for the period January 1, 19A, through February 3, 19A.

EC–2 Writing Journal Entries from T-Accounts

The following T-accounts for Seattle Service Company, Inc., show six different transactions (entries). Create a general journal and prepare a journal entry in good form for each transaction. Write a complete description of each one. (*Hint:* Notice that some transactions have two debits or two credits.)

	Cash		
(a)	60,000	(c)	10,000
(b)	30,000	(e)	2,000
(d)	3,000	(f)	7,000

	Accounts Receivable		
(b)	4,000	(d)	3,000

	Equipment
(f)	25,000

	Accounts Payable		
(e)	2,000	(c)	3,000

	Note Payable	
	(f)	18,000

Contributed Capital (6,000 shares)		
	(a)	60,000

	Service Revenue	
	(b)	34,000

	Operating Expenses
(c)	13,000

EC–3 Identifying Adjusting Entries by Comparing Unadjusted and Adjusted Trial Balances

Nally Company is in the process of completing the information processing cycle at the end of the accounting year, December 31, 19B. The worksheet and financial statements have been prepared. The next step is to journalize the adjusting entries. The following two trial balances were taken directly from the completed worksheet.

		December 31, 19B			
		Unadjusted Trial Balance		Adjusted Trial Balance	
Account Titles		Debit	Credit	Debit	Credit
a.	Cash	9,300		9,300	
b.	Accounts receivable			500	
c.	Prepaid insurance	2,000		1,350	
d.	Equipment	120,000		120,000	
e.	Accumulated depreciation		22,000		25,000
f.	Income taxes payable				4,100
g.	Contributed capital		50,000		50,000
h.	Retained earnings, January 1, 19B		26,300		26,300
i.	Service revenue		51,000		51,500
j.	Salary expense	18,000		18,000	
k.	Depreciation expense			3,000	
l.	Insurance expense			650	
m.	Income tax expense			4,100	
		149,300	149,300	156,900	156,900

Required:
By examining the amounts in each trial balance, reconstruct the adjusting entries that were made between the unadjusted trial balance and the adjusted trial balance. Give an explanation of each adjusting entry.

EC-4 Completing a Worksheet Starting with an Unadjusted Trial Balance

Fairbanks Company is completing its annual accounting information processing cycle at December 31, 19B. The following worksheet has been started (to simplify, amounts given are in thousands of dollars).

Unadjusted Trial Balance			
Account No.	Account Titles	Debit	Credit
101	Cash	28	
102	Accounts receivable	40	
103	Inventory	21	
104	Prepaid insurance	4	
110	Equipment (10-year life, no residual value)	80	
111	Accumulated depreciation, equipment		8
119	Accounts payable		12
120	Wages payable		
121	Income taxes payable		
122	Revenue collected in advance		
123	Note payable, long-term		
	(10% interest due each December 31)		25
130	Contributed capital		77
140	Retained earnings		12
145	Revenues		108
146	Expenses	69	
147	Income tax expense		
		$242	$242

Data not yet recorded for 19B:
  a. Insurance expense, $2.
  b. Depreciation expense, $8.
  c. Wages earned by employees; not yet paid, $1.
  d. Revenue collected by Fairbanks; not yet earned, $4.
  e. Income tax rate, 25 percent.
(*Note:* No accrued interest is recorded because interest is paid on each December 31. In addition, the company declared dividends of $10 during the year against Retained Earnings.)

Required:

Complete the worksheet in every respect (you may use account numbers instead of account titles). Set up additional column headings for Adjusting Entries, Adjusted Trial Balance, Income Statement, Retained Earnings, and Balance Sheet. Record all revenues and expenses except income tax in the two accounts given (145 and 146).

EC-5 Completing a Worksheet Starting with an Unadjusted Trial Balance

Ricci Corporation, a small company, is completing its annual accounting information processing cycle at December 31, 19B. The worksheet, prior to the adjusting entries, has been started as follows:

Account Titles	Unadjusted Trial Balance	
	Debit	Credit
Cash	16,000	
Accounts receivable	8,000	
Equipment	20,000	
Accumulated depreciation		5,000
Other assets	38,000	
Accounts payable		7,000
Note payable, long-term		8,000
Contributed capital		36,000
Retained earnings		10,000
Revenues		50,000
Expenses	34,000	
	116,000	116,000
Income tax expense		
Income taxes payable		
Net income		

Data not yet recorded for 19B:
a. Depreciation expense, $3,000.
b. Income tax rate, 30 percent.

Required:

Complete the worksheet in all respects, including a legend explaining the adjustments. Set up additional column headings for Adjusting Entries, Adjusted Trial Balance, Income Statement, Retained Earnings, and Balance Sheet.

EC–6 Determining When to Use a Reversing Entry

Canadian Company has completed its accounting information processing cycle for the year ended December 31, 19A. Reversing entries are under consideration on January 1, 19B, for two different adjusting entries made on December 31, 19A. For case purposes, the relevant data are given in T-accounts:

Prepaid Insurance

| 1/1/19A Balance | 400 | (a) 12/31/19A Adj. entry | 200 |

Insurance Expense

| (a) 12/31/19A Adj. entry | 200 | (c) 12/31/19A Closing entry | 200 |

Accrued Wages Payable

| | | (b) 12/31/19A Adj. entry | 2,000 |

Wages Expense

| Paid during 19A | 20,000 | (d) 12/31/19A Closing entry | 22,000 |
| (b) 12/31/19A Adj. entry | 2,000 | | |

Retained Earnings

12/31/19A Closing entries		1/1/19A Balance	300,000
(c)	200		
(d)	22,000		

Required:

Would a reversing entry on January 1, 19B, facilitate the next related entry for (*a*) Prepaid Insurance and (*b*) Accrued Wages Payable? Explain why.

Problems

PC–1 Completing the First Four Steps of the Accounting Information Processing Cycle

Four Seasons Company, Inc., was started on January 1, 19A. During the first year ended December 31, 19A (end of the accounting period), the following summarized entries were completed:

Date	Transaction
(*a*)	Issued 30,000 shares of its common stock for $80,000 cash.
(*b*)	Purchased equipment for use in operations that cost $50,000 cash. Estimated life, 10 years.
(*c*)	Borrowed $40,000 cash on a long-term note payable (10% interest).
(*d*)	Revenues earned, $102,000, of which $8,000 was on credit (not yet collected at year-end).
(*e*)	Expenses incurred (including interest on the note payable), $70,000, of which $8,000 was on credit (not yet paid at year-end).
(*f*)	Paid cash dividend, $7,000. (*Hint:* Debit Retained Earnings.)
(*g*)	Recorded depreciation expense. Assume no income tax.

Required:

Process these transactions through the accounting information processing cycle by steps as follows:

Step 1. Analyze: Write your analysis of each transaction in terms of Assets = Liabilities + Stockholders' Equity; Debits = Credits (as discussed in Chapters 2 and 3).

Step 2. Journalize each transaction: Start your general journal with page 1. Use the date letters to identify transactions.

Step 3. Post to the ledger: Set up the following ledger accounts and account numbers: Cash, 101; Accounts Receivable, 102; Equipment, 105; Accumulated Depreciation, 106; Accounts Payable, 201; Note Payable, Long-Term, 205; Contributed Capital, 301; Retained Earnings, 303; Revenues, 310; and Expenses, 315. Post the journal entries to the ledger accounts (as you complete each journal entry or after the last journal entry).

Step 4. Prepare a trial balance.

PC–2 Completing a Worksheet Starting with the Adjusted Trial Balance, Computing the Amounts for the Adjusting Entries, and Giving the Closing Entries

Anderson Corporation has partially completed the following worksheet for the year ended December 31, 19E:

Account Titles	Unadjusted Trial Balance		Adjusting Entries			
	Debit	Credit	Debit		Credit	
Cash	33,000					
Accounts receivable	22,000					
Supplies inventory	1,200				(a)	600
Interest receivable			(b)	300		
Long-term note receivable (10%; dated September 1, 19E)	9,000					
Equipment (8-year life, no residual value)	80,000					
Accumulated depreciation		35,000			(c)	10,000
Accounts payable		10,000				
Note payable, short-term (12%; dated July 1, 19E)		12,000				
Interest payable					(d)	720
Income taxes payable					(e)	3,620
Contributed capital		35,000				
Retained earnings		20,000				
Service revenue		72,000				
Interest revenue					(b)	300
Expenses (not detailed)	38,800		(a)	600		
Depreciation expense			(c)	10,000		
Interest expense			(d)	720		
Income tax expense			(e)	3,620		
Totals	184,000	184,000		15,240		15,240

Required:

1. Use additional columns for Adjusted Trial Balance, Income Statement, Retained Earnings, and Balance Sheet; and complete the worksheet.
2. Show how the following adjusting entry amounts were computed:
   (a) $600, (b) $300, (c) $10,000, (d) $720.
3. Give the closing entries.
4. Why are the adjusting and closing entries journalized and posted?

PC–3 Solving Comprehensive Worksheet Problem, Starting with an Unadjusted Trial Balance and Ending with the Closing Entries

Marine Pool Service & Repair, Inc., has been in operation for several years. Revenues have increased gradually from both the pool cleaning and repair services. The annual financial statements prepared in the past have not conformed to GAAP. The newly employed president decided that a balance sheet, income statement, and statement of retained earnings should be prepared in conformity with GAAP. The first step was to employ a full-time bookkeeper and engage a local CPA firm. It is now December 31, 19C, the end of the current accounting year. The bookkeeper has developed a trial balance from the ledger. A member of the staff of the CPA firm will advise and assist the bookkeeper in completing the accounting information processing cycle for the first time. The unadjusted trial balance at December 31, 19C, follows.

MARINE POOL SERVICE & REPAIR, INC.
Unadjusted Trial Balance
December 31, 19C

Debits		Credits	
Cash	27,500	Accumulated depreciation	24,000
Accounts receivable	2,080	Accounts payable	8,000
Office supplies inventory	170	Wages payable	
Prepaid insurance	800	Interest payable	
Land for future building site (not in use)	5,000	Revenue collected in advance	
Equipment	72,000	Income taxes payable	
Remaining assets (not detailed)	22,000	Note payable (12%)	20,000
Salary expense	60,000	Contributed capital (25,000 shares)	25,000
Advertising expense	2,000	Retained earnings	9,800*
Utilities expense	1,400	Repair revenue	72,000
Maintenance expense	3,200	Cleaning revenue	38,000
Miscellaneous expenses	650		
Insurance expense			
Wage expense			
Depreciation expense			
Interest expense			
Income tax expense			
	196,800		196,800

* The company declared and paid $3,000 in dividends during the year against Retained Earnings.

Examination of the records and related documents provided the following additional information that should be considered for adjusting entries:

a. A physical count of office supplies inventory at December 31, 19C, reflected $70 on hand. Office supplies used are a miscellaneous expense. Office supplies purchased during 19C were debited to this inventory account.

b. On July 1, 19C, a two-year insurance premium was paid amounting to $800; it was debited to Prepaid Insurance.

c. The equipment cost $72,000 when acquired. Annual depreciation expense is $12,000.

d. Unpaid and unrecorded wages earned by employees at December 31, 19C, amounted to $900.

e. The $20,000 note payable was signed on October 1, 19C, for a 12 percent bank loan; principal and interest are due at the end of 12 months from that date.

f. Cleaning revenue collected and recorded as earned before December 31, 19C, included $150 collected in advance from three customers for cleanings to be done in January, 19D. (*Hint:* Reduce Cleaning Revenue.)

g. Gasoline, oil, and fuel purchased for the vehicles and used during the last two weeks of December 19C amounting to $200 have not been paid for or recorded (this is considered maintenance expense).

h. The average income tax rate is 20 percent, which produces income tax expense of $5,720.

Required:

1. Enter the unadjusted trial balance on a worksheet; then, based on the preceding data, enter the adjusting entries. Complete the worksheet.

2. Using the worksheet, prepare an income statement (use two captions: Revenues and Expenses), statement of retained earnings, and balance sheet.

3. Using the worksheet, prepare the 19C adjusting entries in journal form.

4. Using the worksheet, prepare the 19C closing entries in journal form.

PC–4 Selecting Adjusting Entries That Often Are Reversed

Global Corporation has completed all information processing including the annual financial statements at December 31, 19D. The adjusting entries recorded at that date were as follows:

a.	Insurance expense	250	
	Prepaid insurance		250
b.	Interest receivable	400	
	Interest revenue		400
c.	Supplies expense	90	
	Supplies inventory		90
d.	Depreciation expense	3,000	
	Accumulated depreciation		3,000
e.	Wage expense	700	
	Wages payable		700
f.	Interest expense	600	
	Interest payable		600
g.	Income tax expense	5,500	
	Income taxes payable		5,500

Required:

Indicate whether each of these adjusting entries usually is reversed. Give the reversing entry in each instance (if none, so state) and explain the basis for your response.

Glossary

A

Accelerated Depreciation Methods that result in higher depreciation expense in the early years of an operational asset's life and lower expense in the later years. *429*

Account A standardized format that organizations use to accumulate the dollar effects of transactions on each financial statement item. *60*

Accounting A system that collects and processes (analyzes, measures, and records) financial information about an organization and reports that information to decision makers. *6*

Accounting Cycle The recordkeeping process used during and at the end of the accounting period that results in the preparation of financial statements. *124*

Accounting Entity The organization for which financial data are to be collected (separate and distinct from its owners). *8*

Accounting Period The time period covered by the financial statements. *13*

Accounts Receivable (Trade Receivables or Receivables) Open accounts owed to the business by trade customers. *307*

Accrual Basis Accounting Revenues are recorded when earned and expenses when incurred, regardless of when the related cash is received or paid. *117*

Accruals Revenues that have been earned and expenses that have been incurred by the end of the current accounting period but that will not be collected or paid until a future accounting period. *172*

Accrued Liabilities Expenses that have been incurred but have not been paid at the end of the accounting period. *475*

Acquisition Cost Net cash equivalent amount paid or to be paid for the asset. *419*

Additions Extensions to, or enlargements of, existing assets that increase the cost of the existing asset; a capital expenditure. *423*

Adjusting Entries End-of-period entries necessary to measure income properly, correct errors, and provide for adequate valuation of balance sheet accounts. *176*

Aging of Accounts Receivable Method Estimates uncollectible accounts based on the age of each account receivable. *313*

Allowance for Doubtful Accounts Contra-asset account containing the estimated uncollectible accounts receivable; also called *allowance for bad debts* or *allowance for uncollectible accounts*. *309*

Allowance Method Bases bad debt expense on an estimate of uncollectible accounts. *309*

Amortization Systematic and rational allocation of the acquisition cost of an intangible asset over its useful life. *441*

Annuity A series of periodic cash receipts or payments that are equal in amount each interest period. *494*

Assets Probable future economic benefits owned by the entity as a result of past transactions. *55*

Audit An examination of the financial reports to ensure that they represent what they claim and conform with generally accepted accounting principles. *27*

Audit Trail The referencing system with sufficiently detailed explanations necessary for tracing an entry back to its source documents. *774*

Authorized Number of Shares Maximum number of shares of capital stock of a corporation that can be issued as specified in the charter. *568*

Available-for-Sale Securities All investments other than trading securities that are accounted for under the market value method. *617*

B

Bad Debt Expense (Doubtful Accounts Expense, Uncollectible Accounts Expense, or **Provision for Uncollectible Accounts)** Expense associated with estimated uncollectible accounts receivable. *309*

Balance Sheet (Statement of Financial Position) A statement that reports the financial position (assets, liabilities, and stockholders' equity) of an accounting entity at a point in time. *8*

Bank Reconciliation Process of verifying the accuracy of both the bank statement and the cash accounts of the business. *320*

Bank Statement Monthly report from a bank that shows deposits recorded, checks cleared, other debits and credits, and a running bank balance. *319*

Basic Accounting Equation (Balance Sheet Equation) Assets = Liabilities + Stockholders' Equity. *10*

Basket Purchase Acquisition of two or more assets in a single transaction for a single lump sum. *420*

Bond Certificate The bond document that each bondholder receives. *525*

Bond Discount The difference between selling price and par when a bond is sold for less than par. *527*

Bond Premium The difference between selling price and par when a bond is sold for more than par. *527*

Bond Principal The amount (a) payable at the maturity of the bond and (b) on which the periodic cash interest payments are computed. *524*

Bond Sinking Fund A cash fund accumulated for payment of a bond at maturity. *540*

Book (or Carrying) Value Acquisition cost of an operational asset less accumulated depreciation, depletion, or amortization. *424*

Book Value (Net Book Value, Carrying Value) The difference between an asset's acquisition cost and accumulated depreciation, its related contra-account. *174*

C

Callable Bonds Bonds that may be called for early retirement at the option of the issuer. *526*

Capital Expenditures Expenditures that provide future benefits and are recorded as increases in asset accounts, not as expenses. *422*

Capitalized Interest Interest expenditures included in the cost of a self-constructed asset. *420*

Cash Money and any instrument that banks will accept for deposit and immediate credit to the depositor's account, such as a check, money order, or bank draft. *317*

Cash Basis Accounting Revenues are recorded when cash is received and expenses are recorded when cash is paid, regardless of when the revenues are earned or expenses are incurred. *117*

Cash Equivalent A short-term, highly liquid investment with original maturity of less than three months. Statement of cash flows reports changes in cash and cash equivalents. *654*

Cash Equivalents Short-term investments with original maturities of three months or less that are readily convertible to cash and whose value is unlikely to change. *317*

Cash Flows from Financing Activities Cash inflows and outflows related to the way that cash was obtained from external sources (owners and creditors) to finance the enterprise. *657*

Cash Flows from Investing Activities Cash inflows and outflows related to the acquisition or sale of productive facilities and investments in the securities of other companies. *657*

Cash Flows from Operating Activities (Cash Flows from Operations) Cash inflows and outflows directly related to earnings from normal operations. *656*

Closing Entries Made at the end of the accounting period to transfer balances in temporary accounts to retained earnings and to establish a zero balance in each of the temporary accounts. *195*

Common Stock The basic, normal, voting stock issued by a corporation; called *residual equity* because it ranks after preferred stock for dividend and liquidation distributions. *570*

Comparable Information Information that can be compared across businesses. *246*

Completed Contract Method Records revenue when the completed product is delivered to the customer. *328*

Component Percentage Expresses each item on a particular financial statement as a percentage of a single base amount. *707*

Conservatism Care should be taken not to overstate assets and revenues or understate liabilities and expenses. *247*

Consistent Information Information that can be compared over time. *246*

Consolidated Financial Statements The financial statements of two or more companies that have been combined into a single set of financial statements. *627*

Contingent Liability Potential liability that has arisen as the result of a past event; not an effective liability until some future event occurs. *489*

Continuity Assumption (Going-Concern) The belief that businesses are assumed to continue to operate into the foreseeable future. *55*

Contra-Account An account that is an offset to, or reduction of, the primary account. *174*

Contributed Capital Cash (and sometimes other assets) provided to the business by owners. *59*

Control The ability of the investing company to determine the operating and financing policies of another company in which it owns shares of the voting stock; presumed to exist when more than 50 percent of the voting stock of an entity is owned by one investor. *615*

Convertible Bonds Bonds that may be converted to other securities of the issuer (usually common stock). *526*

Convertible Preferred Stock Preferred stock that is convertible to common stock at the option of the holder. *571*

Copyright Exclusive right to publish, use, and sell a literary, musical, or artistic work. *443*

Cost-Benefit Constraint The benefits of accounting for and reporting information should outweigh the costs. *246*

Cost of Goods Sold Equation $BI + P - EI = CGS$ *363*

Cost Principle An accounting rule that requires assets to be recorded at the historical cash-equivalent cost, which on the date of the transaction is cash paid plus the current dollar value of all noncash considerations also given in the exchange. *59*

Coupon Rate The stated rate of interest on bonds. *527*

Credit Card Discount Fee charged by the credit card company for its services. *302*

Cumulative Dividend Preference Preferred stock feature that requires specified current dividends not paid in full to accumulate for every year in which they are not paid. These cumulative preferred dividends must be paid before any common dividends can be paid. *579*

Cumulative Effects of Changes in Accounting Methods Amount reflected on the income statement for adjustments made to balance sheet accounts when applying different accounting principles. *257*

Current Assets Assets that will be turned into cash or expire (be used up) within the longer of one year or the operating cycle. *248*

Current Dividend Preference The feature of preferred stock that grants a priority on preferred dividends over common dividends. *579*

Current Liabilities Obligations to be paid with current assets, normally within one year. *248*

D

Debenture An unsecured bond; no assets are specifically pledged to guarantee repayment. *524*

Debits and Credits *Debit* is the name for the left side of an account. Debits represent increases in assets and decreases in liabilities and stockholders' equity. *Credit* is the name for the right side of an account. Credits represent decreases in assets and increases in liabilities and stockholders' equity. *69*

Declining-Balance (DB) Depreciation The method that allocates the cost of an operational asset over its useful life based on a multiple of (often two times) the straight-line rate. *430*

Deferrals Previously recorded assets, liabilities, revenues, or expenses that need to be adjusted at the end of the period to reflect earned revenues or incurred expenses. *172*

Deferred Revenues Revenues that have been collected but not earned; liabilities until the goods or services are provided. *478*

Deferred Tax Items Difference between income tax expense and income tax liability; caused by temporary differences; may be a liability or an asset. *486*

Depletion Systematic and rational allocation of the cost of a natural resource over the period of exploitation. *439*

Depreciation Systematic and rational allocation of the cost of property, plant, and equipment (but not land) over their useful lives. *423*

Direct Method Reports components of cash flows from operating activities as gross receipts and gross payments. *656*

Direct Labor The earnings of employees who work directly on the products being manufactured. *361*

Discontinued Operations Results from the disposal of a major segment of the business; reported net of income tax effects. *256*

Dividend Dates

Declaration Date Date on which the board of directors officially approves a dividend. *578*

Payment Date Date on which a cash dividend is paid to the stockholders of record. *578*

Record Date Date on which the corporation prepares the list of current stockholders as shown on its records; dividends can be paid only to the stockholders who own stock on that date. *578*

Dividends in Arrears Dividends on cumulative preferred stock that have not been declared in prior years. *579*

E

Earnings Forecasts Predictions of earnings for future accounting periods. *239*

Effective-Interest Method Amortizes a bond discount or premium on the basis of the effective-interest rate; theoretically preferred method. *536*

Effective-Interest Rate Another name for the market rate of interest on a bond. *527*

Efficient Markets Securities markets in which prices fully reflect available information. *727*

Equity Method Method used by investor if 20 percent to 50 percent of the voting stock of the investee company is owned by the investor. It permits recording of investor's share of investee's income. *624*

Estimated Useful Life Expected service life of an operational asset to the present owner. *426*

Expenses Expenses are decreases in assets or increases in liabilities from ongoing operations. *113*

Extraordinary Items Gains and losses that are both unusual in nature and infrequent in occurrence; they are reported net of tax on the income statement. *257*

Extraordinary Repairs Expenditures for major, high-cost, long-term repairs that increase the economic usefulness of the asset; increase an asset account (or decrease accumulated depreciation); a capital expenditure. *423*

F

Face Amount Another name for principal or the principal amount of a bond. *524*

Factory Overhead Manufacturing costs that are not raw material or direct labor costs. *361*

Financial Accounting Standards Board (FASB) The private sector body given the primary responsibility to work out the detailed rules that become generally accepted accounting principles. *23*

Financial Leverage Use of borrowed funds to increase the rate of return on owners' equity; occurs when the interest rate on debt is lower than the earnings rate on total assets. *522*

Finished Goods Inventory Manufactured goods that are completed and ready for sale. *359*

First-In, First-Out Method (FIFO) Inventory costing method that assumes that the oldest units are the first units sold. *366*

Form 8-K The report used by publicly traded companies to disclose any material event not previously reported that is important to investors. *268*

Form 10-K The annual report that publicly traded companies must file with the SEC. *267*

Form 10-Q The quarterly report that publicly traded companies must file with the SEC. *268*

Franchise A contractual right to sell certain products or services, use certain trademarks, or perform activities in a geographical region. *443*

Full-Disclosure Principle The requirement to disclose all relevant economic information of the business. *246*

Future Value The sum to which an amount will increase as the result of compound interest. *491*

G

Gains Gains are increases in assets or decreases in liabilities from peripheral transactions. *114*

Generally Accepted Accounting Principles (GAAP) The measurement rules used to develop the information in financial statements. *23*

Goods Available for Sale The sum of beginning inventory and purchases (or transfers to finished goods) for the period. *362*

Goodwill The amount that was paid for the good reputation and customer appeal of an acquired company. *630*

Goodwill (Cost in Excess of Net Assets Acquired) For accounting purposes, the excess of the purchase price of a business over the market value of the business's assets and liabilities. *441*

Gross Margin (Gross Profit) Net sales less cost of goods sold. *255*

H

Held-to-Maturity Investment A long-term investment in bonds that management has the ability and intent to hold until maturity. *542*

I

Income before Income Taxes (Pretax Earnings) Revenues less all expenses except income tax expense. *256*

Income from Operations (Operating Income) Net sales less cost of goods sold and other operating expenses. *255*

Income Statement (Statement of Income, Statement of Earnings, or Statement of Operations) A statement that reports the revenues less the expenses of the accounting period. *13*

Income Summary A temporary account used only during the closing process to facilitate the closing of revenues and expenses; closed to Retained Earnings. *195*

Indenture A bond contract that specifies the legal provisions of a bond issue. *524*

Indirect Method The method of presenting the operating section of the statement of cash flows that adjusts net income to compute cash flows from operating activities. *656*

Installment Method Recognizes revenue on the basis of cash collection after the delivery of goods. *327*

Institutional Investors Managers of pension, mutual, endowment, and other funds that invest on the behalf of others. *243*

Intangible Assets Operational assets that have special rights but not physical substance. *418*

Internal Controls Policies and procedures designed to safeguard the assets of the business and ensure the accuracy of financial records. *318*

Inventory Tangible property that is held for sale in the normal course of business or will be used in producing goods or services for sale. *358*

Issued Shares Total number of shares of stock that have been issued; shares outstanding plus treasury shares held. *568*

J

Journal A record that lists chronologically the effects of transactions; the book of original entry. *774*

Journal Entry An accounting method for expressing the effects of a transaction on accounts in a debits-equal-credits format. *70*

L

Last-In, First-Out Method (LIFO) Inventory costing method that assumes that the most recently acquired units are sold first. *367*

Leaseholds Rights granted to a lessee under a lease contract. *444*

Ledger Contains all of the individual accounts for revenues, expenses, assets, liabilities, and stockholders' equity; the book of final entry. *774*

Legal Capital The permanent amount of capital, defined by state law, that must remain invested in the business; provides a "cushion" for creditors. *570*

Lenders (Creditors) Suppliers and financial institutions that lend money to companies. *243*

Liabilities Probable debts or obligations of the entity as a result of past transactions, which will be paid with assets or services. *58*

LIFO Liquidation A sale of a lower-cost inventory item from beginning LIFO inventory. *387*

LIFO Reserve A contra-asset for the excess of FIFO over LIFO inventory. *373*

Long-Term Liabilities All of the entity's obligations that are not classified as current liabilities. *483*

Losses Losses are decreases in assets or increases in liabilities from peripheral transactions. *114*

Lower of Cost or Market (LCM) Valuation method departing from cost principle that recognizes a loss when replacement cost or net realizable value drops below cost. *376*

M

Market Interest Rate Current rate of interest on a debt when incurred; also called *yield* or *effective-interest rate*. *527*

Market Tests Ratios that tend to measure the market worth of a share of stock. *722*

Market Value Method Method used by the investor if less than 20 percent of the voting stock of the investee company is owned by the investor; unrealized gains and losses are reported based on changes in the prices of securities that are held. *617*

Matching Principle Expenses are recognized (recorded) when incurred in earning revenue. *121*

Material Amounts Amounts that are large enough to influence a user's decision. *246*

Merchandise Inventory Goods held for resale in the ordinary course of business. *358*

N

Natural Resources Assets occurring in nature, such as mineral deposits, timber tracts, oil, and gas. *439*

Net Interest Cost Interest cost less any income tax savings associated with interest expense. *522*

Net Realizable Value The expected sales price less selling costs (e.g., repair and disposal costs). *377*

Noncash Expenses Expenses that do not cause an immediate cash outflow; for example, depreciation expense. *662*

Noncash Investing and Financing Activities Transactions that do not have direct cash flow effects; reported as a supplement to the statement of cash flows in narrative or schedule form. *676*

No-Par Value Stock Shares of capital stock that have no par value specified in the corporate charter. *570*

Note Receivable A written promise that requires another party to pay the business under specified conditions (amount, time, interest). *307*

Notes (Footnotes) Supplemental information about the financial condition of a company, without which the financial statements cannot be fully understood. *20*

O

Operating Cycle The time it takes for a company to purchase goods or services from suppliers, sell those goods or services to customers, and collect cash from customers. It is also known as the *cash-to-cash cycle* or the *earnings process.* *115*

Operational Assets (Long-Lived Assets) Tangible and intangible assets owned by a business and used in its operations. *418*

Ordinary Repairs and Maintenance Expenditures for the normal operating upkeep of operational assets; increase in expense for ordinary repairs. *423*

Outstanding Shares Total shares of stock that are owned by stockholders on any particular date. *568*

P

Parent The company that has a significant investment in a subsidiary company. *627*

Par Value A legal amount per share established by the board of directors; it establishes the minimum amount a stockholder must contribute and has no relationship to the market price of the stock. Also, par value is another name for bond principal or the maturity amount of a bond. *252*

Patent An exclusive right granted by the federal government for an invention; gives the owner the right to use, manufacture, and sell the subject of the patent. *443*

Percentage of Completion Method Records revenue based on the percentage of work completed during the accounting period. *328*

Percentage of Credit Sales Method Bases bad debt expense on the historical percentage of credit sales that result in bad debts. *312*

Periodic Inventory System Ending inventory and cost of goods sold are determined at the end of the accounting period based on a physical inventory count. *379*

Permanent (Real) Accounts The balance sheet accounts that carry their ending balances into the next accounting period; not closed at the end of the period. *195*

Perpetual Inventory System A detailed inventory record is maintained recording each purchase and sale during the accounting period. *380*

Pooling of Interests An acquisition that is completed by exchanging parent company stock for subsidiary voting capital stock. *628*

Post-Closing Trial Balance Should be prepared as the last step in the accounting cycle to check that debits equal credits and all temporary accounts have been closed. *196*

Preferred Stock Shares of stock that have specified rights over common stock. *571*

Present Value The current value of an amount to be received in the future; a future amount discounted for compound interest. *491*

Press Release A written public news announcement that is normally distributed to major news services. *263*

Primary Objective of External Financial Reporting Providing useful economic information about a business to help external parties make sound financial decisions. *55*

Prior Period Adjustment Amount debited or credited directly to retained earnings to correct an accounting error of a prior period. *584*

Private Investors Individuals who purchase shares in companies. *243*

Purchase An acquisition that is completed by purchasing subsidiary company voting capital stock for cash. *629*

Purchase Discount Cash discount received for prompt payment of an account payable. *383*

Purchase Returns and Allowances A deduction from the cost of purchases associated with unsatisfactory goods. *383*

R

Ratio (Percentage) Analysis An analytical tool designed to identify significant relationships; measures the proportional relationship between two financial statement amounts. *707*

Raw Materials Inventory Items acquired for the purpose of processing into finished goods. *358*

Redeemable Bonds Bonds that may be turned in for early retirement at the option of the bondholder. *526*

Relevant Information Information that can influence a decision; it is timely and has predictive and/or feedback value. *245*

Reliable Information Information that is accurate, unbiased, and verifiable. *246*

Replacement Cost The current purchase price for identical goods. *377*

Report and Account Forms Two common balance sheet preparation forms. The report form lists assets on the top and liabilities and stockholders' equity on the bottom. The account form lists assets on the left side and liabilities and stockholders' equity accounts on the right side. *81*

Report of Independent Accountants (Audit Report) A report that describes the auditors' opinion of the fairness of the financial statement presentations and the evidence gathered to support that opinion. *26*

Report of Management A report that indicates management's primary responsibility for financial statement information and the steps taken to ensure the accuracy of the company's records. *26*

Residual (or Salvage) Value Estimated amount to be recovered, less disposal costs, at the end of the company's estimated useful life of an operational asset. *426*

Retained Earnings Cumulative earnings of a company that are not distributed to the owners and are reinvested in the business. *59*

Revenue Expenditures Expenditures that provide benefits during the current accounting period only and are recorded as expenses. *422*

Revenue Principle Revenues are recognized (recorded) when the earnings process is complete or nearly complete, an exchange has taken place, and collection is probable. *118*

Revenues Revenues are increases in assets or settlements of liabilities from ongoing operations. *113*

Reversing Entries Optional entries made at the start of the next accounting period to reverse the effects of certain adjusting entries; facilitates subsequent entries and simplifies the bookkeeping function. *780*

S

Sales (or Cash) Discount Cash discount offered to encourage prompt payment of an account receivable. *302*

Sales Returns and Allowances A contra revenue account used to record return of or allowances for unsatisfactory goods. *304*

Securities and Exchange Commission (SEC) The U.S. government agency that determines the financial statements that public companies must provide to stockholders and the measurement rules that they must use in producing those statements. *23*

Separate-Entity Assumption The concept that business transactions are separate from the transactions of the owners. *55*

Significant Influence The ability of an investing company to have an important impact on the operating and financing policies of another company (the investee). *615*

Specific Identification Method Inventory costing method that identifies the cost of the specific item that was sold. *369*

Stated Rate The rate of cash interest per period specified in the bond contract. *524*

Statement of Cash Flows A statement that reports inflows and outflows of cash during the accounting period in the categories of operations, investing, and financing. *18*

Statement of Retained Earnings A statement that reports the way that net income and the distribution of dividends affected the financial position of the company during the accounting period. *16*

Stock Dividend Distribution of additional shares of a corporation's own capital stock to current stockholders on a pro rata basis at no cost; decreases retained earnings. *582*

Stock Split An increase in the total number of authorized shares by a specified ratio; does not decrease retained earnings. *583*

Stockholders' Equity (Owners' Equity or Shareholders' Equity) The financing provided by the owners and the operations of the business. *58*

Straight-Line Amortization Simplified method of amortizing a bond discount or premium that allocates an equal dollar amount to each interest period. *530*

Straight-Line (SL) Depreciation Method that allocates the cost of an operational asset in equal periodic amounts over its useful life. *427*

Subsidiary The company that is owned by a parent company as evidenced by more than 50 percent of the voting capital stock. *627*

T

T-accounts An analytical tool for summarizing transaction effects for each account, determining balances for financial statement preparation, and drawing inferences about a company's activities. *71*

Tangible Assets Operational assets (or fixed assets) that have physical substance. *418*

Temporary Differences Timing differences that cause deferred income taxes and will reverse, or turn around, in the future. *486*

Temporary (Nominal) Accounts Income statement (and sometimes dividends declared) accounts that are closed at the end of the accounting period. *195*

Tests of Liquidity Ratios that measure a company's ability to meet its currently maturing obligations. *716*

Tests of Solvency Ratios that measure a company's ability to meet its long-term obligations. *720*

Timeline A visual representation of a series of business activities, listing dates and amounts over time. *119*

Time Period Assumption The long life of a company can be reported in shorter time periods, usually months, quarters, and years. *112*

Time Value of Money Interest that is associated with the use of money over time. *479*

Trade Discount A discount that is deducted from list price to derive the actual sales price. *303*

Trademark An exclusive legal right to use a special name, image, or slogan. *443*

Trading Securities All investments in stocks or bonds that are held primarily for the purpose of selling them in the near future; accounted for under the market value method. *617*

Transaction (1) An exchange between a business and one or more external parties, such as borrowing money from a bank, or (2) a measurable event internal to a business, such as adjustments for the use of assets in operations. *60*

Transaction Analysis The process of studying a transaction to determine its economic effect on the business in terms of the accounting equation: Assets = Liabilities + Stockholders' Equity. *63*

Treasury Stock A corporation's own stock that it had issued but subsequently reacquired and that it still holds. *575*

Trial Balance A list of all accounts with their balances to provide a check on the equality of the debits and credits. The unadjusted trial balance does not include the effects of the adjusting entries. *173*

Trustee An independent party appointed to represent the bondholders. *526*

U

Unissued Shares Authorized shares of a corporation's stock that never have been issued. *568*

Unit-of-Measure Assumption Accounting information is measured and reported in the national monetary unit. *55*

Units-of-Production Depreciation Method that allocates the cost of an operational asset over its useful life based on its periodic output related to its total estimated output. *428*

Unqualified (Clean) Audit Opinion Auditors' statement that the financial statements are fair presentations in all material respects in conformity with GAAP. *238*

Unrealized Holding Gains and Losses Amounts recorded when the price of securities that are currently held changes. *618*

W

Weighted Average Method Inventory costing method that uses the weighted average unit cost of the goods available for sale for both cost of goods sold and ending inventory. *368*

Work in Process Inventory Goods in the process of being manufactured. *358*

Working Capital The dollar difference between total current assets and total current liabilities. *474*

Y

Yield Another name for the market rate of interest on a bond. *527*

Illustration Credits

Chapter 1

Photo 1-1, p. 2 Tony Stone Images; Photo 1–2, p. 9, Tony Stone Images; Photo 1-3, p. 17, Richard Hamilton Smith/Tony Stone Images/PNI; Photo 1-4, p. 25, Anthony James Dugal Photography.

Chapter 2

Photo 2-1, p. 52, James McGoon Photography; Photo 2-2, p. 57, Courtesy Sbarro, Inc.; Photo 2-3, p. 63, Courtesy Nations Restaurant News Magazine.

Chapter 3

Photo 3-1, p. 108, Courtesy Sbarro, Inc.; Photo 3-2, p. 114, Courtesy Sbarro, Inc.; Photo 3-3, p. 122, Courtesy Sbarro, Inc.

Chapter 4

Photo 4-1, p. 170, Courtesy Sbarro, Inc.; Photo 4-2, p. 181, Courtesy Sbarro, Inc.

Chapter 5

Photo 5-1, p. 234, Courtesy Callaway Golf; Photo 5-2, p. 244, Courtesy Callaway Golf; Photo 5-3, p. 251, Courtesy Callaway Golf; Photo 5-4, p. 265, Courtesy Callaway Golf; Exhibit 5-2, p. 242, © Bloomberg L.P. 1997 All Rights Reserved.

Chapter 6

Photo 6-1, p. 296, Courtesy The Timberland Company; Photo 6-2, p. 305, Courtesy The Timberland Company; Photo 6-3, p. 311, Courtesy The Timberland Company; Photo 6-4, p. 321, © Tom Crane Photography/Courtesy Bergmeyer Associates, Inc.

Chapter 7

Photo 7-1, p. 354, Blair Seitz Photography; Photo 7-2, p. 359, James Schnepf Photography; Photo 7-3, p. 368, James Schnepf Photography.

Chapter 8

Photo 8-1, p. 414, Brian Stablyk/Tony Stone Images; Photo 8-2, p. 419, Tony Stone Images; Photo 8-3, p. 426, David Gilkey Photography; Photo 8-4, p. 430, William Bake/Corbis; Photo 8-5, p. 442, Courtesy SkyWest Airlines.

Chapter 9

Photo 9-1, p. 470, Courtesy Parallel Productions, Inc.; Photo 9-2, p. 479, Courtesy Southwest Airlines; Photo 9-3, p. 485, Courtesy General Mills, Inc. and PepsiCo; Photo 9-4, p. 497, Robert Daemmrich/Tony Stone Images.

Chapter 10

Photo 10-1, p. 520, Courtesy Showboat, Inc.; Photo 10-2, p. 523, F. Stuart Westmorland/Tony Stone Images/PNI; Photo 10-3, p. 525, Courtesy Showboat, Inc.; Photo 10-4, p. 526, Courtesy Showboat, Inc.; Photo 10-5, p. 533, Roger Tully/Tony Stone Images.

Chapter 11

Photo 11-1, p. 562, Courtesy Wal-Mart, Inc. and Revolution; Photo 11-2a, p. 574, Courtesy Wal-Mart, Inc.; Photo 11-2b, p. 574, Courtesy Wal-Mart, Inc.; Photo 11-3, p. 581, Sygma.

Chapter 12

Photo 12-1a, p. 612, Tobey Sanford/Courtesy General Electric; Photo 12-1b, p. 612, © Brownie Harris/Courtesy General Electric, 1997; Photo 12-1c, p. 612, Tara Sosrowardoyo/Liaison International/Courtesy General Electric; Photo 12-1d, p. 612, Tobey Sanford/Courtesy General Electric; Photo 12-2, p. 628, Courtesy General Electric; Photo 12-3, p. 630, © Brownie Harris/Courtesy General Electric, 1997.

Chapter 13

Photo 13-1, p. 652, Rick Friedman/Black Star/PNI; Photo 13-2, p. 664, © Malyszko, 1997; Photo 13-3, p. 666, Richard Pasley/Stock Boston/PNI; Photo 13-4, p. 673, Buck Miller/Black Star/PNI.

Chapter 14

Photo 14-1, p. 700, Courtesy Home Depot; Photo 14-2, p. 712, Courtesy Home Depot; Photo 14-3, p. 719, Courtesy Home Depot; Photo 14-4, p. 725, Courtesy Home Depot.

General Index

Business Index